12th Edition

Select Material from

# Adolescence

John W. Santrock
University of Texas at Dallas



McGraw Hill Learning Solutions

Boston Burr Ridge, IL Dubuque, IA New York San Francisco St. Louis
Bangkok Bogotá Caracas Lisbon London Madrid
Mexico City Milan New Delhi Seoul Singapore Sydney Taipei Toronto

The McGraw·Hill Companies

Select Material from
Adolescence, Twelfth Edition





1 2 3 4 5 6 7 8 9 0 DIG DIG 12 11 10 09

ISBN-13: 978-0-07-742017-8
ISBN-10: 0-07-742017-9

*Learning Solutions Specialist: Melani Moorman*
*Production Editor: Jennifer Beecher*
*Cover Design: Stephanie Miller*
*Printer/Binder: Digital Impressions*

*To Tracy and Jennifer, who, as they have matured, have helped me appreciate the marvels of adolescent development.*

# ABOUT THE AUTHOR

## JOHN W. SANTROCK

Received his Ph.D. from the University of Minnesota in 1973. He taught at the University of Charleston and the University of Georgia before joining the psychology department at the University of Texas at Dallas. He has been a member of the editorial boards of *Developmental Psychology and Child Development.* His research on father custody is widely cited and used in expert witness testimony to promote flexibility and alternative considerations in custody disputes. John has also authored these exceptional McGraw-Hill texts: *Child Development,* Eleventh Edition; *Children,* Tenth Edition; *Life-Span Development,* Eleventh Edition; *Essentials of Life-Span Development,* First Edition. *A Topical Approach to Life-Span Development,* Fourth Edition; *Human Adjustment,* First Edition; and *Educational Psychology,* Third Edition.

For many years, John was involved in tennis as a player, teaching professional, and coach of professional tennis players. He has been married for more than 35 years to his wife, Mary Jo, who is a realtor. He has two daughters—Tracy, who is studying to become a financial planner at Duke University, and Jennifer, who is a medical sales specialist at Medtronic. He has one granddaughter, Jordan, age 16, and two grandsons, Alex age 3 and Luke, age 2. Tracy recently completed the New York Marathon, and Jennifer was in the top 100 ranked players on the Women's Professional Tennis Tour. In the last decade, John also has spent time painting expressionist art.

John Santrock, teaching an undergraduate class.

# BRIEF CONTENTS

# CONTENTS

## Chapter 2
# PUBERTY, HEALTH, AND BIOLOGICAL FOUNDATIONS 52

## Chapter 3
# THE BRAIN AND COGNITIVE DEVELOPMENT 90

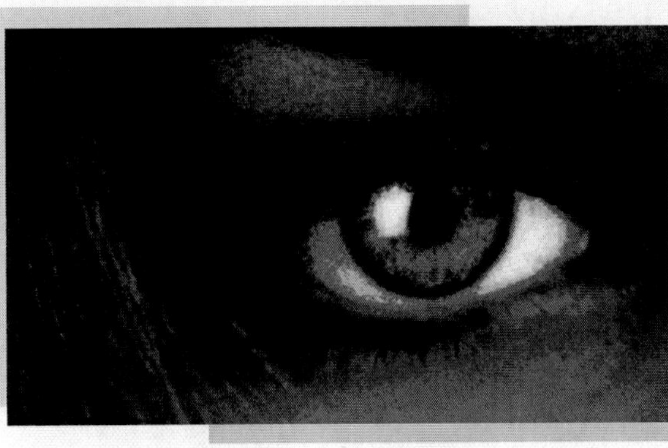

## Chapter 8
## FAMILIES 272

## Chapter 9
## PEER AND ROMANTIC RELATIONSHIPS 316

## Chapter 13
## PROBLEMS IN ADOLESCENCE AND EMERGING ADULTHOOD 462

# EXPERT CONSULTANTS

*Adolescent development has become an enormous, complex field, and no single author, or even several authors, can possibly keep up with all of the rapidly changing content in the many different areas of adolescent development. To solve this problem, author John Santrock sought the input of leading experts about content related to a number of topics. The experts provided detailed evaluations and recommendations for one or two chapters in their area(s) of expertise. The biographies and photographs of the experts, who literally represent a who's who in the field of adolescent development, follow.*

## SUSAN HARTER

**Susan Harter** is widely recognized as one of the world's leading experts on the development of the self. Dr. Harter is a professor of psychology and head of the Developmental Psychology Program (both graduate and postdoctoral components) at the University of Denver. She received her Ph.D. from Yale University, obtaining a joint degree in developmental and child-clinical psychology. After obtaining her Ph.D. from Yale, she became the first faculty woman in the Yale psychology department, accepting a joint faculty appointment in the psychology department and the Yale Child Study Center, where she served as chief psychologist. Her research—focusing on self-esteem, the construction of multiple selves, false-self behavior, classroom motivation, and emotional development—has been funded by NICHD and by the W. T. Grant Foundation. Her interests and research also include the study of gender issues across the life span. Most recently, she has turned her attention to school violence and the role of the self-system in provoking both depressive and violent ideation.

Dr. Harter's research has resulted in the creation of a number of assessments that are widely used around the world. She has published numerous scholarly articles and chapters as well as a leading book, *The Construction of the Self: A Developmental Perspective*. Dr. Harter has served on NIMH study sections, including chairing the Committee on Cognition, Emotion, and Personality. She is also a member of several editorial boards (*Developmental Psychology, Child Development, Psychological Review, Psychological Bulletin, Development and Psychopathology,* and *American Education Research Journal*). At the University of Denver, Dr. Harter has received two major faculty awards, the University Lecturer of the Year and the John Evans Professorship Award (the highest scholarly honor the university can bestow upon a faculty member).

## DANIEL KEATING

**Daniel Keating** is one of the world's leading experts on cognitive development and the development of the brain in adolescence. Dr. Keating is a Fellow of the Canadian Institute for Advanced Research, a member and former director of the Canadian Institute for Advanced Research Human Development Program, and a mentor in the Robert Wood Johnson Foundation Health and Society Scholars Program at the University of Michigan. His research focuses on integrating knowledge about biodevelopmental processes, population patterns in developmental health, and social factors affecting individual and population development. His recent and current work has been organized around three major topics: (1) basic processes in adolescent cognitive and brain development, including neurocognitive and neuroimaging studies of prefrontal development and their relation to health-related risk behavior; (2) analyses of longitudinal datasets to study population outcomes of development health with regard to how those patterns may be explained by underlying developmental mechanisms, some of which he has conducted collaboratively as a principal investigator on the NICHD Study of Early Child Care and Youth Development, and which will also be a focus of forthcoming research of the Michigan Alliance for the National Children's Study; and (3) a community-based longitudinal study on the factors that influence high school girls' engagement with and participation in mathematics and science in and beyond high school.

## RUTH CHAO

**Ruth Chao** is a leading expert on diversity, parenting, and adolescent development. She is a professor in the Department of Psychology at the University of California–Riverside. Dr. Chao obtained her undergraduate degree from the University of California–Irvine, and her Ph.D. from the University of California–Los Angeles. She formerly was a professor in the Department of Child and Families Studies at Syracuse University. Dr. Chao's research interests include sociocultural perspectives of parenting and the family, with an emphasis on Asian immigrants. She is currently conducting a five-year longitudinal study, funded by the National Institutes of Health, that examinies the influence of parental control, warmth, and involvement in school on adolescents' school performance and behavioral adjustment. Dr. Chao's research also includes studies of the language acculturation of Asian immigrant families across time and its link to adolescent's adjustment.

## JOHN SCHULENBERG

**John Schulenberg** is one of the world's leading experts on adolescence transitions and adolescent and emerging adult problems. He is a professor in the Department of Psychology, and research professor in the Institute for Social Research and Center for Human Growth and Development, at the University of Michigan. He has published widely on several topics concerning adolescent development and the transition to adulthood, focusing broadly on how developmental transitions and tasks relate to health risks and adjustment difficulties. His current research focuses on substance use and psychopathology, especially on continuities and discontinuities during adolescence and emerging adulthood. He is a lead researcher on the National Institute of Drug Abuse–funded national Monitoring the Future study of substance use among U.S. adolescents and emerging adults. Dr. Schulenberg has served on several advisory and review committees for the National Institutes of Health, the National Science Foundation, and the Society for Research on Adolescence. He is a Fellow of the American Psychological Association.

## L. MONIQUE WARD

**L. Monique Ward** is a leading expert on adolescent development with a special emphasis on gender, sexuality, and the media. She is a professor of psychology at the University of Michigan. Her research examines children's and adolescents' developing conceptions of gender and sexuality, and explores how these important aspects of development influence adolescents' social and sexual decision making. Dr. Ward is especially interested in the media's role in adolescent sexual socialization, publishing extensively on this topic in several academic journals, including *Developmental Review, Psychology of Women Quarterly,* and *Journal of Research on Adolescence.* She served as a member of APA's Task Force on the Sexualization of Girls, and also on the editorial board of both the *Journal of Adolescent Research* and *Media Psychology*. She also was an associate editor for the *Encyclopedia of Children, Adolescents, and the Media.*

## DIANE HALPERN

**Diane Halpern** is one of the world's leading experts on gender. She is a professor of psychology and director of the Berger Institute for Work, Family, and Children at Claremont McKenna College. Dr. Halpern was the 2004 president of the American Psychological Association and has published over 350 articles and a number of books, including *Thought and Knowledge: An Introduction to Critical Thinking* (4th ed.), and *Sex Differences in Cognitive Abilities* (3rd ed.) In addition, she has served as president of the Western Psychological Association, the Society for the Teaching of Psychology, and the Division of General Psychology of the American Psychological Association. Dr. Halpern is currently chairing an APA Taskforce that is planning a National Conference on Undergraduate Education in Psychology for 2008 and co-chairing an APS Taskforce on Life-Long Learning at Work and at Home. She also is working with Fanny Cheung from Chinese University on a cross-cultural book titled *Women at the Top: How Powerful Leaders Combine Work and Family,* which is based on more than 60 interviews with women with substantial family responsibilities in powerful leadership positions.

## ALLAN WIGFIELD

**Allan Wigfield** is professor and chair of the Department of Human Development and Distinguished Scholar-Teacher at the University of Maryland. He received his Ph.D. in educational psychology from the University of Illinois in 1982. His research focuses on how children's motivation develops across the school years in different areas, including reading. In the reading area, Dr. Wigfield has conducted research on the development of children's motivation for reading, and how different instructional practices influence children's reading motivation. His research has been supported by grants from NSF, NICHD, IERI, and the Spencer Foundation. He has authored more than 95 peer-reviewed journal articles and book chapters on children's motivation and other topics, including the chapter on the development of motivation in the recently published *Handbook of Child Psychology* (sixth edition). He has edited three books and four special issues of journals on the development of motivation, and the development of reading comprehension and motivation. Dr. Wigfield was associate editor of the *Journal of Educational Psychology* from 2000 to 2002 and associate editor of *Child Development* from 2001 to 2005. He currently edits the Teaching, Learning, and Human Development section of the *American Educational Research Journal*. He is a Fellow of Division 15 (educational psychology) of the American Psychological Association, and has won several awards for his research and teaching.

## LORAH DORN

**Lorah Dorn** is a leading expert on the biological foundations of adolescence. Dr. Dorn currently is Professor of Pediatrics in the University of Cincinnati College of Medicine and Director of Research in the Division of Adolescent Medicine at Cincinnati Children's Hospital and Medical Center. Her research focuses on the potential vulnerability of biological transitions in early adolescence. Specifically she focuses on the biological transition of puberty and the concomitant changes in stress and reproductive hormones and how they are associated with both physical and mental health outcomes.

## LAWRENCE WALKER

**Lawrence Walker** is one of the world's leading experts on the psychology of moral development. He earned his Ph.D. at the University of Toronto and currently is a professor of psychology at the University of British Columbia in Vancouver, Canada. Dr. Walker is also the director of the Graduate Program in Psychology at UBC and associate editor of the *Merrill-Palmer Quarterly*, as well as serving on the editorial boards of several other journals. He is past-president of the Association for Moral Education, the major international scholarly organization in the fields of moral psychology and moral education, and a Fellow of both the Canadian and American Psychological Associations. Dr. Walker has published extensively on the psychology of moral development and has received awards for excellence in research, university teaching, and contributions to the profession. His current research focuses on moral exemplarity and formative aspects of the moral personality and identity. Dr. Walker is also an avid ocean kayaker and cyclist.

## JENNIFER CONNOLLY

**Jennifer Connolly** is a leading expert on adolescent romantic and peer relations. She is a professor in clinical-developmental psychology at York University and is the director of the LaMarsh Centre for Research on Violence and Conflict Resolution. Her research examines social development in adolescence, especially romantic relationships. She studies developmental trajectories of romantic development in North America as well as cross-culturally, focusing on both the beginnings and endings of relationships. Her goals are to identify the attributes of successful relationships as well as those of conflictual or aggressive relationships.

# PREFACE

It is very gratifying that more undergraduate students in the world continue to learn about the field of adolescent development from this text than from any other. As with adolescent development, there have been major changes and transitions across these twelve editions. Most texts that are in their twelfth edition don't change that much. However, because research in the field of adolescent development has expanded so dramatically in recent years, I have made a number of significant changes in the twelfth edition. I have been writing various editions of this text since the late 1970s and seen the field transformed from one in which there were only a handful of scholars studying adolescent development to the thousands of researchers today who are making enormous strides in our understanding of development in adolescence and emerging adulthood. Over the course of the last three decades, I have seen not only a dramatic increase in the quantity of research studies on adolescence and emerging adulthood, but an equally impressive increase in the quality of research. For example, there are far more high-quality, published longitudinal studies that provide important information about developmental changes from childhood through emerging adulthood than even five years ago. As a result of the research growth in our field, the twelfth edition of *Adolescence* represents the most extensive changes and new research of any of the previous ten revisions.

## MAIN CHANGES IN THE TWELFTH EDITION

The main changes in the twelfth edition are (1) reduction in the number of chapters from 15 to 13, (2) substantial increase in material on emerging adulthood, (3) much expanded coverage of health and well-being, (4) movement of brain discussion from the chapter on puberty to the beginning of the chapter on cognitive development and increased coverage of brain development, and (5) extensive research updating.

### Reduction in Number of Chapters from 15 to 13

Instructors and reviewers indicated that a 13-chapter text is easier to complete during the course of a term than a 15-chapter text. To accomplish this reduction in chapters, Chapters 1 and 2 in the eleventh edition were combined into a single chapter (Chapter 1). Some of the content, such as Freud's theory, was reduced at the request of adopters and reviewers. Also, Chapter 15 in the previous edition ("Health, Stress, and Coping") was deleted in favor of integrating and expanding the discussion of health throughout the text.

### Substantial Increase in Material on Emerging Adulthood

There has been a dramatic increase in research on emerging adulthood (approximately 18 to 25 years of age), and every chapter in this edition of *Adolescence* devotes more space to the new research and thinking about emerging adulthood. Here is a brief description of some of the new coverage of emerging adulthood:

- Chapter 1: New coverage of Arnett's (2006) recent description of five main themes of emerging adulthood; new *Through the Eyes of Emerging Adults* insert on a 24-year-old's view of his life (Jayson, 2006); new material on changes in risk taking in emerging adulthood (Schulenberg & Zarrett, 2006); and new description of an emerging adult's life in the chapter-opening story
- Chapter 3: New discussion of Labouvie-Vief's (2006) view on how cognitive development changes in emerging adulthood
- Chapter 4: New coverage of self-esteem in emerging adulthood (Galambos, Barker, & Krahn, 2006); new description of James Cote's (2006) view on identity development in emerging adulthood; new section on identity development in emerging adulthood (Phinney, 2006), and new *Through the Eyes of Emerging Adults* insert on developing an identity before intimacy (Kroger, 2007)
- Chapter 6: Coverage of a recent study on college women's sexual experiences (Gilmartin, 2006); new *Through the Eyes of Emerging Adults* insert, Christine's Thoughts About Sexual Relationships; research on link between goal setting by college women and sexual decision making (Moore & Davidson, 2006); longitudinal research on early adolescent sexual activity and problems in emerging adulthood (Cornelius & others, 2006); new section, further Exploration of Heterosexual Attitudes and Behavior in Emerging Adults (Lefkowitz & Gillen, 2006); new research on adolescents' characteristics and their likelihood of having problems as adults (Oxford & others, 2006); inclusion of recent research on sexual harassment of college women (American Association of University Women, 2006)

- Chapter 7: New cross-cultural data on emerging adults' religious values (Lippman & Keith, 2006)
- Chapter 8: New section, Attachment in Emerging Adults (Mikulincer & Shaver, 2007); new section, Emerging Adults' Relationships with Their Parents (Aquilino, 2006); new discussion of strategies for emerging adults and their parents (Furman, 2005); new *Through the Eyes of Emerging Adults* insert, College Students Reflect on Growing Up in a Divorced Family (Clarke-Stewart & Brentano, 2006); and new coverage of the emerging adult outcomes of growing up in divorced and stepparent families (Hetherington, 2006)
- Chapter 9: New section, Friendship in Emerging Adulthood, including recent research (Collins & van Dulmen, 2006); new section, Emerging Adult Lifestyles; inclusion of recent data on the percentage of emerging adults who are single and married; new coverage of cohabitation in emerging adulthood (Kenney & McLanahan, 2006); and new material on divorced emerging adults
- Chapter 11: New section, College Advising and Your Major; recent data on the work profiles of U.S. college students (National Center for Education Statistics, 2006); and new section, Work in Emerging Adulthood, including recent research and analyses (Hamilton & Hamilton, 2006; Setterson & others, 2005)
- Chapter 12: New section, The Online Social Environment of Adolescents and Emerging Adults, including coverage of MySpace and Facebook
- Chapter 13: New coverage of coping strategies in emerging adulthood; new discussion of resilience in emerging adulthood (Masten & Obradović, 2007); new material on mental health in emerging adulthood (Schulenberg & Zarrett, 2006); updated and expanded description of drug use in emerging adulthood (Park & others, 2006); new discussion of connections between early/late onset of delinquency and problems in emerging adulthood (Schulenberg & Zarrett, 2006); and new discussion of depression in emerging adulthood (Schulenberg & Zarrett, 2006)

## Integrated and Expanded Coverage of Health and Well-Being

The topic of adolescent and emerging adult health and well-being has emerged as a major area of study in recent years. This has occurred because adolescence and emerging adulthood are increasingly recognized as critical junctures in development. At the request of adopters and reviewers, I changed the discussion of health and well-being in three ways: (1) deleted previous Chapter 15, "Health, Stress, and Coping"; (2) integrated coverage of health, stress, and coping throughout the book; and (3) expanded the material on health and well-being.

Content on health, stress, and coping that was previously in Chapter 15 is now mainly in Chapter 2 ("Puberty, Health, and Biological Foundations," which now includes the topics of health, exercise, nutrition, and sleep) and Chapter 13 ("Problems in Adolescence and Emerging Adulthood," which now includes the topics of stress and coping, as well as eating disorders). Adopters told us that in many cases they weren't able to get to the health, stress, and coping chapter (Chapter 15) and requested that the material be integrated into earlier chapters so they would be able to cover these important topics.

In the effort to expand coverage of health and well-being, a new feature that appears once in each chapter is *Health and Well-Being,* an interlude that focuses on some aspect of the health and well-being of adolescents and emerging adults related to the topic being discussed in the chapter. Among the *Health and Well-Being* interludes are:

- Chapter 1: Changes in Emerging Adulthood (Schulenberg & Zarrett, 2006)
- Chapter 3: The Personal Fable and Adolescent Adjustment (Aalsma, Lapsley, & Flannery, 2006)
- Chapter 6: Toward Effective Sex Education
- Chapter 8: Strategies for Emerging Adults and Their Parents (Furman, 2005)
- Chapter 9: Strategies for Reducing Loneliness
- Chapter 13: Coping Strategies in Adolescence and Emerging Adulthood

Other examples of the expanded discussion of health and well-being of adolescents and emerging adults are:

- Chapter 1: Expanded opening story of Michael Maddaus, who got his life together in emerging adulthood following a troubled childhood and adolescence, and a new section on resilience and emerging adulthood (Masten, Obradović, & Burt, 2006)
- Chapter 2: New section on body art (Suris & others, 2007); discussion of eight research studies from 2006 on body image and body dissatisfaction during adolescence; coverage of social capital and risk taking (Youngblade & others, 2006); description of exercise patterns of youth from the National Youth Risk Survey (MMWR, 2006); expanded coverage of sleep (Fuligni & Hardway, 2006); and research on the positive benefits of sports participation (Fredricks & Eccles, 2006)
- Chapter 3: New discussion of adolescent egocentrism and adjustment
- Chapter 4: Coverage of recent longitudinal study on self-esteem (Trzesniewski & others, 2006); and new research on parenting and identity development in college students (Luyckz & others, 2006)
- Chapter 5: New research on gender differences and stress (Uhart & others, 2006)
- Chapter 6: Coverage of recent research on college women's sexual experiences (Gilmartin, 2006); goal setting and responsible sexual decision making (Moore

& Davidson, 2006); two longitudinal studies on early sexual experience/characteristics of adolescents and problems in emerging adulthood (Cornelius & others, 2006; Oxford & others, 2006); expanded coverage of risk factors in adolescent sexual activity (Marin & others, 2006); friendship and condom use (Henry & others, 2007); early condom use (Shafi, Stovel, & Holmes, 2007); Centers for Disease Control and Prevention (2007) reccomendation for use of a vaccine to fight off HPV and cervical cancer; positive and negative aspects of adolescents with different sexual orientations (Busseri & others, 2006); and cross-cultural research review of sex education programs (Kirby, Laris, & Rolleri, 2007)

- Chapter 7: Expanded coverage of research on service learning (Nucci, 2006); character education programs (Berkowitz & others, 2006); and religious interest and problem behavior (Sinha, Cnaan, & Gelles, 2006)
- Chapter 8: Recent research on family functioning and academic achievement in African American boys (Mandara, 2006); sibling conflict and adjustment (Kim & others, 2007); outcomes for emerging adults from divorced and stepparent families (Hetherington, 2006); working parents and adolescent adjustment (Crouter, 2006); how ethnic minority families deal with stress (Kagitcibasi, 2007); coparenting conflict (Feinberg, Kan, & Hetherington, 2007); research on secure attachment and its outcomes (Allen & others, 2007)
- Chapter 9: New research on antisocial peer affiliation and links to other problems (Connell & Dishion, 2006); cohabitation (Manning, Longmore, & Giordano, 2007); premarital education (Stanley & others, 2006); and whether there is a best age to get married (Furstenberg, 2007)
- Chapter 10: New coverage of effectively managing classrooms (Evertson & Weinstein, 2006); new section on the benefits of extracurricular activities (Fredricks & Eccles, 2006); recent research on links between bullying and negative developmental outcomes (Brunstein & others, 2007); new description of Jonathan Kozol's (2005) recent book, *The Shame of the Nation*; and new research on the benefits of exercise for individuals with ADHD (Ferrando-Lucas, 2006)
- Chapter 11: Recent research on mentoring Latino youth (Buchanan & others, 2006); and new section on work in emerging adulthood (Hamilton & Hamilton, 2006)
- Chapter 12: Recent experimental study an effective poverty intervention (Huston & others, 2006); updating of material on acculturation and adolescent problems (Gonzales & others, 2007); and recent research on racial discrimination and adolescent problems (DeGarmo & Martinez, 2006)
- Chapter 13: New coverage of coping strategies; new section on resilience in adolescence and emerging adulthood (Masten & Obradović, 2007); new coverage of continuity and discontinuity in mental health problems in adolescence and emerging adulthood (Schulenberg & Zarrett, 2006); updated U.S. data on adolescent drug use (Johnston & others, 2007); cross-cultural comparisons of U.S. and European adolescents' drug use (Hibell & others, 2004); recent research on adolescent drug use (Dodge & others, 2006); recent research on juvenile delinquency (Nation & Heflinger, 2006); expanded coverage of developmental changes in depression in adolescence and emerging adulthood (Schulenberg & Zarrett, 2006); recent research on eating disorders (Bulik & others, 2007; Kirsch & others, 2007); new discussion of the role of after-school programs in obesity prevention (Story, Kaphingst, & French, 2006); updated coverage of Joy Dryfoos' analysis of successful programs to prevent/intervene in adolescent problems (Dryfoos & Barkin, 2006); and description of recent research involving the Fast Track intervention program (Dodge & the Conduct Problems Prevention Research Group, 2007)

## Movement of Brain Discussion to Chapter 3 and Expansion of This Topic

A number of adopters and reviewers recommended that we move the coverage of the brain to the chapter on cognitive development and expand the discussion of brain development. Thus, Chapter 3 is now titled "The Brain and Cognitive Development," with coverage of the brain now opening this chapter, resulting in more attention to this rapidly increasing area of interest in adolescent development. Also, we examine the intriguing topic of whether research on the brain can be used to decide whether an adolescent should be given the death penalty (Ash, 2006).

## Extensive Research Updating

As indicated earlier, research in the field of adolescent development is rapidly expanding. Here are the ways that I conveyed the improving research foundation of the field:

**Contemporary Research Citations** As an indication of the breadth of updating in the twelfth edition of this book, it includes more than 1,600 twenty-first-century citations, including more than 800 from 2006, 2007, and 2008. You will find substantial research updating in each of the 13 chapters of *Adolescence*, twelfth edition.

**Expert Consultants** Adolescence has become an enormous, complex field, and no single author can possibly be an expert in all areas of the field. To solve this problem, I have sought the input of some of the world's leading experts in different areas of adolescent development. The experts provided me with detailed recommendations on new research to include in every chapter. The expert consultants, whose photographs and biographies appear on pages xiv–xvi of the Preface, for the twelfth edition of *Adolescence* were:

| | |
|---|---|
| **Lorah Dorn,** ***University of Cincinnati*** | **Chapter 2: Puberty, Health, and Biological Foundations** |
| **Daniel Keating,** ***University of Toronto*** | **Chapter 3: The Brain and Cognitive Development** |
| **Susan Harter,** ***University of Denver*** | **Chapter 4: The Self, Identity, Emotions, and Personality** |
| **Diane Halpern,** ***Claremont McKenna College*** | **Chapter 5: Gender** |
| **L. Monique Ward,** ***University of Michigan*** | **Chapter 6: Sexuality** |
| **Lawrence Walker,** ***University of British Columbia*** | **Chapter 7: Moral Development, Values, and Religion** |
| **Ruth Chao,** ***University of California–Riverside*** | **Chapter 8: Families; Chapter 12: Culture** |
| **Jennifer Connolly,** ***York University*** | **Chapter 9: Peer and Romantic Relationships** |
| **Allan Wigfield,** ***University of Maryland*** | **Chapter 10: Schools; Chapter 11: Achievement, Work, and Careers** |
| **John Schulenberg,** ***University of Michigan*** | **Chapter 13: Problems in Adolescence and Emerging Adulthood** |

## CHAPTER-BY-CHAPTER CONTENT CHANGES

Substantial changes and updating of content occurred in every chapter of the book. Here are some of the main content changes in each chapter:

### Chapter 1 INTRODUCTION

- At the request of adopters of reviewers, material in Chapters 1 and 2 of the previous edition has been combined in this single chapter.
- Reduced coverage of some theories, including Freud's theory
- Expanded opening story to include Michael Maddaus, who got his life together in emerging adulthood following a troubled childhood and adolescence
- New coverage of changes in youth in the late twentieth and early twenty-first centuries, including technology and diversity issues
- Updated and expanded discussion of emerging adulthood, including Arnett's (2006) recent description of five main themes of emerging adulthood
- New section on resilience in emerging adulthood, including Ann Masten's recent research (Masten, Obradović, & Burt, 2006)
- New *Health and Well-Being* interlude, Changes in Emerging Adulthood (Schulenberg & Zarrett, 2006)
- New *Through the Eyes of Emerging Adults*, Chris Barnard, a 24-year-old emerging adult (Jayson, 2006)
- New recommendation of a recently published book on adolescent problems and strategies for preventing and intervening in them (Dryfoos & Barkin, 2006)

### Chapter 2 PUBERTY, HEALTH, AND BIOLOGICAL FOUNDATIONS

- At the request of adopters and reviewers, material on adolescence as a critical juncture in health, nutrition, exercise and sports, and sleep were moved to this chapter because many of them indicated that they wanted the health material integrated into chapters instead of in a final chapter, which they often did not get to in teaching their course
- Expanded and updated coverage of adrenarche and gonadarche (Dorn & others, 2006)
- Also at the request of adopters and reviewers, the material on the brain was moved to the beginning of Chapter 3 (now titled "The Brain and Cognitive Development") to more closely connect the development of the brain and cognition in adolescence
- New section on the determinants of puberty, Weight at Birth and in Infancy, including a description of recent research studies (Dunger, Ahmed, & Ong, 2006; Ibanez & de Zegher, 2006)
- New section on the determinants of puberty, Sociocultural and Environmental Influences, including links between pubertal timing and culture, socioeconomic status, father absence, and conflict (Bogaert, 2005)
- New section, Body Art, that describes the increased use of tattooing and body piercing by adolescents and college students (Armstrong, Caliendo, & Roberts, 2006; Deschesnes, Fines, & Demers, 2006; Suris & others, 2007)
- Coverage of eight recent research studies on body image and body dissatisfaction during adolescence that focus on ethnicity, appearance, developmental changes, mental health problems, health, and the best and worst aspects of being a boy or a girl (Bearman & others, 2006; Dyl, Kittler, & Hunt, 2006; Gillen, Lefkowitz, & Shearer, 2006; Grabe & Hyde, 2006; Neumark-Sztainer & others, 2006; Nishina & others, 2006; Schooler & others, 2004; Zittleman, 2006)
- Description of recent study on life events, hormones, and aggression in young adolescent girls (Graber, Brooks-Gunn, & Warren, 2006)
- Discussion of 39-year longitudinal study on links between early/late maturation in boys and success, as

well as problem behavior, in mid-life (Taga, Markey, & Friedman, 2006)
- New *Health and Well-Being* interlude, Health-Care Consultation for Early and Late Maturers
- Discussion of recent research on activities, resources, and relationships that are related to adolescents' health-enhancing behaviors (Youngblade & Curry, 2006)
- Coverage of recent research study on social capital and adolescent risk-taking behavior (Youngblade & others, 2006)
- Updated statistics on causes of death in U.S. adolescents (National Center for Health Statistics, 2005)
- Inclusion of recent data from the 2005 National Youth Risk Survey on high school students' decreased intake of fruits and vegetables (MMWR, 2006)
- Discussion of recent data from the 2005 National Youth Risk Survey on adolescents' exercise patterns, with a special focus on gender and ethnic variations (MMWR, 2006)
- Update on how little adolescents exercise during physical education classes (Cawley, Meyerhoefer, & Newhouse, 2006)
- Description of results from the recent National Sleep Foundation (2006) survey on adolescent sleep patterns
- Coverage of two recent research studies that linked sleep deprivation in adolescence to health-compromising behaviors (Chen, Wang, & Jeng, 2006; Fuligni & Hardway, 2006)
- Discussion of recent study finding a decline in physical activity from 12 to 17 years of age and a link between physical activity and having a physically active friend (Duncan & others, 2007)
- Updated research on the female athlete triad (Beals & Hill, 2006, 2007; Nichols & others, 2006)
- Description of three recent studies that confirmed the positive benefits of sports participation in adolescence (Fredricks & Eccles, 2006; Nelson & Gordon-Larsen, 2006; Simpkins & others, 2006)
- Reduction of material on evolutionary developmental psychology to keep the focus more on adolescent development
- Reduction of material on heredity
- Updated material on the specification of the number of genes that humans possess (21,774) (Ensembl Human, 2007)
- Coverage of recent study on how stress hormones can inflict DNA damage (Flint & others, 2007)

## Chapter 3
## THE BRAIN AND COGNITIVE DEVELOPMENT

- New title for chapter ("The Brain and Cognitive Development"), with the material from the brain moved from the physical development chapter to this chapter to more closely connect the development of the brain and the development of cognition, at the request of adopters and reviewers
- Extensive expansion, revision, and updating of brain development in adolescence with a new section: Brain Structure, Cognition, and Emotion
- New Figure 3.2, which vividly shows the brain's myelination and white matter
- New discussion of the implications of the recent research on brain development in adolescence for the legal system, including whether this research can be used to decide whether an adolescent should be given the death penalty (Ash, 2006)
- Update on brain development and education (Bransford & others, 2006)
- Updated and revised criticism of Piaget's view of formal operational thought (Kuhn & Franklin, 2006; Wigfield, Byrnes, & Eccles, 2006)
- Discussion of Gisela Labouvie-Vief's (2006) recent view of how cognitive development changes in emerging adulthood
- New coverage of Michael Pressley's research on how secondary schools spend inadequate time teaching strategies to students (Pressley & Harris, 2006; Pressley & others, 2004)
- New section, Domain-Specific Thinking Skills (Mayer & Wittrock, 2006)
- At the request of adopters and reviewers, considerable reduction in the material on the psychometric/intelligence view
- New *Health and Well-Being* interlude on the personal fable and adolescent adjustment (Aalsma, Lapsley, & Flannery, 2006).

## Chapter 4
## THE SELF, IDENTITY, EMOTIONS, AND PERSONALITY

- Discussion of recent study of emerging adults and self-esteem (Galambos, Barker, & Krahn, 2006)
- Description of longitudinal study linking low self-esteem with a number of problems in adulthood (Trzesniewski & others, 2006)
- New coverage of James Cote's (2006) view on identity development in emerging adulthood
- New section on self-understanding in emerging adulthood that highlights Labouvie-Vief's (2006) view and research
- New discussion of the recent interest in expanding Marcia's concepts of identity exploration and commitment to include more in-depth exploration and ongoing evaluation of one's commitment (Goossens, 2006; Luyckx, 2006)
- New coverage of the narrative approach to assessing identity changes and the role that life events and meaning-making play in the development of an identity (McAdams, Josselson, & Lieblich, 2006; McLean & Pratt, 2006; Pals, 2006)

- New description of recent research on parents' psychological control and identity development of college students (Luyckx & others, 2006)
- New section, Ethnic Identity in Emerging Adulthood, based on Jean Phinney's (2006) recent ideas
- New *Through the Eyes of Emerging Adults,* Developing an Identity Before Intimacy (Kroger, 2007)
- Discussion of recent research on ethnic identity in African Americans (Yip & others, 2006)
- Coverage of recent research on a link between identity and intimacy (Montgomery, 2005)
- Description of recent research revealing a link between conscientiousness and higher-quality friendship and peer relationships (Jensen-Campbell & Malcolm, 2007)

## Chapter 6
## SEXUALITY

- Coverage of recent national survey on trends in sexual activity in U.S. ninth- to twelfth-graders from 1991 to 2005 (MMWR, 2006)
- Description of recent research on patterns of TV viewing by high school students and links to their sexual stereotyping and sexual experience (Ward & Friedman, 2006)
- Discussion of a recent in-depth study of college women's sexual experiences (Gilmartin, 2006)
- New *Through the Eyes of Emerging Adults,* Christine's Thoughts About Sexual Relationships (Gilmartin, 2006)
- Discussion of a link between goal setting by college women and responsible sexual decision making (Moore & Davidson, 2006)
- New section, Oral Sex, that describes the dramatic increase in oral sex during adolescence, as well as recent research (Bersamin & others, 2006)
- Description of longitudinal study from 10 to 12 years of age to 25 years of age involving early sexual intercourse and problems in emerging adulthood (Cornelius & others, 2006)
- Expanded and updated coverage of risk factors in adolescent sexual activity, including recent studies on boys having a girlfriend by the seventh grade linked to an increased risk of being sexually active in the ninth grade (Marin & others, 2006), low levels of parental monitoring being related to sexual risk taking (Wight, Williamson, & Henderson, 2006), amount of time spent home alone and perception that peers have had sex being associated with early initiation of sex (Buhi & Goodson, 2007), and the role of weak self-regulation and risk proneness in risky sexual behavior (Crockett, Raffaelli, & Shen, 2006)
- New section, Further Exploration of Heterosexual Attitudes and Behavior in Emerging Adults (Lefkowitz & Gillen, 2006)
- Coverage of recent study on casual sex and depressive symptoms in emerging adult women and men (Grello, Welsh, & Harper, 2006)
- Inclusion of information about a recent large-scale study of the positive and negative aspects of adolescents with different sexual orientations (Busseri & others, 2006)
- Discussion of recent longitudinal study on adolescent contraceptive use (Anderson, Santelli, & Morrow, 2006)
- Inclusion of recent research on factors involved in inconsistent contraceptive use by African American female adolescents living in low-income circumstances (Davies & others, 2006)
- Updated description of the reduction in U.S. adolescent pregnancy rates (Child Trends, 2006)
- Discussion of recent research on the Baby Think It Over simulation doll with primarily ninth-grade Latinas (de Anda, 2006)
- New coverage of the dramatic increase in children and adolescents in sub-Saharan Africa who have become orphans because their parents died of AIDS (UNICEF, 2006)
- New mention of recommendation by the Centers for Disease Control and Prevention (2007) that all 11- and 12-year-old girls be given a vaccine that helps to fight off HPV and cervical cancer
- Description of longitudinal study of the characteristics of adolescents that were related to their likelihood of having problems as emerging adults (Oxford & others, 2006)
- Revised and updated discussion of sources of sexual information to include the Internet and concerns about the accuracy of information adolescents have access to
- Description of recent study linking friends' sexual intercourse without condoms to adolescents' subsequent engagement in sexual intercourse without condoms (Henry & others, 2007)
- Discussion of longitudinal study on links between condom use during first sexual intercourse and sexual activity later in adolescence (Shafii, Stovel, & Holmes, 2007)
- Coverage of recent research on communication between parents and adolescents/emerging adults about sex (Lefkowitz & Espinosa-Hernandez, 2006; Lefkowitz & Stoppa, 2006)
- New description of how politically charged abstinence-only and comprehensive sex education programs are in the United States
- Coverage of recent research on the sexual harassment of college women (American Association of University Women, 2006; Huerta & others, 2006)
- Inclusion of information about the low frequency of parent-adolescent communication about sex in China (Zhang & others, 2007)
- Description of a recent research review of 86 sex education programs around the world, with two-thirds of them being linked to lowering sexual risk-taking behavior in youth (Kirby, Laris, & Rolleri, 2007)
- Discussion of recent criticisms of abstinence-only sex education programs (Santelli & others, 2006)
- New *Health and Well-Being* interlude, Toward Effective Sex Education

## Chapter 8
## FAMILIES

- New description of recent research on parental management, including routine, and African American adolescents' achievement and competence in school (Taylor & Lopez, 2005)
- Discussion of recent study on discrepancies in non-Latino White and Chinese American adolescents' perceptions of an ideal parent and actual parents (Wu & Chao, 2005)
- New coverage of a recent research review on family functioning and the academic achievement of African American boys (Mandara, 2006)
- Discussion of longitudinal study on coparenting conflict and adolescent outcomes (Feinberg, Kan, & Hetherington, 2007)
- Description of recent research studies linking secure attachment in adolescence with positive outcomes (Allen & others, 2007; Mayseless & Scharf, 2007)
- New section, Attachment in Emerging Adults, including a recent research review and conceptualization by leading experts Mario Mikulincer and Phillip Shaver (2007)
- New section, Emerging Adults' Relationships with Their Parents (Aquilino, 2006)
- New coverage of recent longitudinal study on different leaving home patterns of emerging adults and psychological health of emerging adults (Seiffge-Krenge, 2006)
- New *Health and Well-Being* interlude, Strategies for Emerging Adults and Their Parents (Furman, 2005)
- New description of three main characteristics of sibling relationships in adolescence (Dunn, 2007)
- Coverage of recent research on siblings, including a longitudinal study of sibling conflict and adjustment (Kim & others, 2007; Shebloski, Conger, & Widaman, 2005)
- Discussion of recent study on what adolescent siblings talk about when they are together (Tucker & Winzeler, 2007)
- New discussion of sibling relationships in emerging adulthood
- New *Through the Eyes of Emerging Adults* insert, College Students Reflect on Growing Up in a Divorced Family (Clarke-Stewart & Brentano, 2006)
- New discussion of outcomes for emerging adults from divorced families (Hetherington & Kelly, 2002)
- Updated coverage of Hetherington's longitudinal study on adolescents in divorced families and description of another recent German longitudinal study on divorce and adolescent development (Walper & Beckh, 2006)
- Description of recent research on the onset of divorce and its link to the types of problems children and adolescents develop (Landsford & others, 2006)
- Extensively revised and updated coverage of working parents and adolescent development (Crouter, 2006)
- Discussion of Hetherington's (2006) recent analysis of the types of stepfamilies that are likely to show the least adjustment problems
- New Figure 8.6, which illustrates the dramatic increase in the number of gay male and lesbian adults who are rearing children and adolescents
- Expanded and updated discussion of how ethnic minority families deal with stress (Kagitcibasi, 2006)
- Updated *Resources for Improving the Lives of Adolescents* including recent books on many aspects of socialization (Grusec & Hastings, 2007) and divorce (Clarke-Stewart and Brentano, 2006)

## Chapter 9
## PEER AND ROMANTIC RELATIONSHIPS

- Expanded chapter title change from "Peers" to "Peer and Romantic Relationships," to indicate the increase in material related to romantic relationships and lives of emerging adults
- New description of research on characteristics of friends and initiation of sexual intercourse (Sieving & others, 2006)
- New *Through the Eyes of Adolescents* insert, We Defined Each Other with Adjectives
- New section, Friendship in Emerging Adulthood, including recent research (Collins & van Dulmen, 2006)
- New main section, Emerging Adult Lifestyles, as part of the increased coverage of emerging adulthood in this text
- Discussion of three recent studies linking affiliation with deviant, antisocial peers in adolescents drug use, delinquency, and depression (Connell & Dishion, 2006; Laird others, 2005; Nation & Heflinger, 2006)
- New main section, Loneliness
- New *Health and Well-Being* interlude, Strategies for Reducing Loneliness
- Description of recent study on having a boyfriend or a girlfriend (especially an older one) in middle school as a risk factor for early sexual activity (Marin & others, 2006)
- New coverage of dissolving a romantic relationship, including recent research on positive outcomes of relationship breakup in college students
- Description of recent data on the percentage of emerging adults who are single and married at 18 to 20 years of age and 21 to 24 years of age (Jekielek & Brown, 2005)
- Recent information about the dramatic increase in cohabitation, potential problems, and links to future marital satisfaction/divorce (Kenney & McLanahan, 2006; Popenoe & Whitehead, 2006)
- Coverage of recent study on adolescents' expectations to cohabit and to marry (Manning, Longmore, & Giordano, 2007)

- New section on married adults, including information about whether there is a best age to get married (Furstenberg, 2007)
- New section on marital education and its link with positive relationship outcomes in emerging adulthood and adulthood (Stanley & others, 2006)
- New material on divorced emerging adults
- New coverage of relationships in gay male and lesbian couples

## Chapter 13
## PROBLEMS IN ADOLESCENCE AND EMERGING ADULTHOOD

- Sections on stress and coping moved to this chapter from chapter on health in the previous edition of the book
- Section on eating disorders moved to this chapter from the chapter on health in the previous edition
- New *Health and Well-Being* interlude: Coping Strategies in Adolescence and Emerging Adulthood
- New coverage of resilience in emerging adulthood (Masten & Obradović; 2007; Masten, Obradović, & Burt, 2006)
- New discussion of continuity and discontinuity of well-being, mental health disorders, and problems from adolescence to emerging adulthood (Schulenberg & Zarrett, 2006)
- Updated description of U.S. drug use in adolescence from the Monitoring the Future Study (Johnston & others, 2007)
- New coverage of cross-country comparison of illicit drug use by U.S. and European adolescents, including new Figure 13.4 (Hibell & others, 2004).
- Updated and expanded coverage of drug use in emerging adulthood (Park & others, 2006)
- New cross-country comparison of drinking behavior by U.S. and European adolescents, including new Figure 13.5
- Description of the peaking of cigarette smoking in emerging adulthood (Park & others, 2006; Substance Abuse and Mental Health Services Administration, 2005)
- Coverage of the sequence of circumstances that predict whether an adolescent will use drugs by 12 years of age (Dodge & others, 2006)
- Inclusion of recent research on links between a school's social network and substance use in middle school students (Ennett & others, 2006)
- Description of recent study indicating that associating with antisocial peers and engaging in juvenile delinquency were linked with adolescent binge drinking and marijuana use (Nation & Heflinger, 2006)
- Inclusion of recent research on the role of early drinking in becoming alcohol dependent (Hingson, Heeren, & Winter, 2006)
- Description of a recent research review on the motives and personality traits that are linked to drinking in adolescence and emerging adulthood (Kuntsche & others, 2006)
- Coverage of longitudinal study of changing links between adolescent smoking and risk-taking behaviors in 1991 and 2003 (Camenga, Klein, & Roy, 2006)
- New discussion of early-onset and late-onset antisocial behavior and their links with outcomes in emerging adulthood (Roisman, Aguilar, & Egelund, 2004; Schulenberg & Zarrett, 2006)
- Updated description of the incidence of various aspects of school violence in a national study (Eaton & others, 2006)
- Updated and expanded coverage of early onset of depression in adolescence and developmental changes in depression during emerging adulthood (Schulenberg & Zarrett, 2006)
- Coverage of recent study linking adolescent depression to parent-adolescent conflict and low parental support (Sheeber & others, 2007)
- Updated description of suicide rates in adolescence and new information about the increase in suicide in emerging adulthood (Minino, Heron, & Smith, 2006; Park & others, 2006)
- New discussion of the Federal Drug Administration's (2004) review of a link between antidepressant use and an increase in suicidal thoughts in adolescents, and research showing no link (Valuck & others, 2004)
- Discussion of recent research review showing a link between adolescents' suicidal thoughts and whether they had experienced physical or sexual abuse (Evans, Hawton, & Rodham, 2005)
- Discussion of recent research review showing a link between adolescents' suicidal thoughts and whether they had experienced physical or sexual abuse (Evans, Hawton, & Rodham, 2005) and their alcohol use (Swahn & Bossarte, 2007)
- Coverage of recent research linking suicidal thoughts to eating disorders in adolescence (Whetstone, Morrissey, & Cummings, 2007)
- Inclusion of recent research indicating a link between frequently reading about dieting and weight loss with unhealthy weight-control behaviors (van den Berg & others, 2007)
- Discussion of a research study linking perception and importance of physical appearance to eating disorders in adolescence (Kirsch & others, 2007)
- Description of recent data on the increase in the percentage of adolescents who are overweight and new discussion of the percentage of emerging adults who are obese (Eaton & others, 2006; Park & others, 2006)
- Coverage of recent longitudinal data showing a strong link between being at risk for overweight at 3 years of age and being overweight at 12 years of age (Nader & others, 2006)
- Inclusion of research about how the family environment and adolescent behavior are linked to obesity in emerging adulthood (Crossman, Sullivan, & Benin, 2006)

- Discussion of recent research review of school-based obesity interventions in adolescence (Sharma, 2006)
- Description of recent information about including obesity prevention/intervention in after-school programs and healthier eating at school (Paxson & others, 2006; Story, Kaphingst, & French, 2006)
- Recent research on the increasing recognition of the importance of family functioning in anorexia nervosa and its treatment (Benninghoven & others, 2007; Bulik & others, 2007)
- Discussion of recent research on bulimia, body perception, depression, and self-esteem (Hrabosky & others, 2007)
- Updated coverage of Joy Dryfoos' view on at-risk youth and successful programs to prevent problems or intervene in them (Dryfoos & Barkin, 2006)
- Updated description of recent research involving the Fast Track intervention program (Dodge & the Conduct Problems Prevention Research Group, 2007)

## APPLICATIONS

It is important to not only present the scientific foundations of adolescent development to students, but also to provide applied examples of concepts, and to give students a sense that the field of adolescent development has personal meaning for them. Special attention throughout the text has been given to health and well-being, parenting, and educational applications.

Instructors and students have provided extremely positive feedback about the emphasis on careers in adolescent development in the text. The twelfth edition continues this emphasis. *Careers in Adolescent Development* profiles feature an individual whose career relates to the chapter's content. Most of these inserts have a photograph of the person at work.

In addition, a Careers in Adolescent Development Appendix follows Chapter 1. The Careers in Adolescent Development Appendix describes a number of careers in education/research, clinical/counseling/medical, and family/relationships categories. Numerous Web site links provide students opportunities to read about these careers in greater depth.

## DIVERSITY

Diversity is another key aspect of adolescent development. I made every effort to explore diversity issues in a sensitive manner in each chapter. The twelfth edition of *Adolescence* continues to have an entire chapter devoted to culture and diversity. I also have integrated culture and diversity into the discussion in the other 12 chapters of the text.

## ACCESSIBILITY AND INTEREST

The new edition of this text should be accessible to students because of the extensive rewriting, organization, and learning system.

### Writing and Organization

Every sentence, paragraph, section, and chapter of this book was carefully examined and when appropriate revised and rewritten. The result is a much clearer, better organized presentation of material in this new edition.

### The Learning System

I strongly believe that students should not only be challenged to study hard and think more deeply and productively about adolescent development, but should also be provided with an effective learning system. Instructors and students have commented about how student-friendly this book has become in recent editions.

Now more than ever, students struggle to find the main ideas in their courses, especially in courses like adolescent development, which include so much material. The learning system centers on learning goals that, together with the main text headings, keep the key ideas in front of the reader from the beginning to the end of the chapter. Each chapter has no more than five main headings and corresponding learning goals, which are presented side-by-side in the chapter-opening spread. At the end of each main section of a chapter, the learning goal is repeated in a feature called Review and Reflect, which prompts students to review the key topics in the section and poses a question to encourage them to think critically about what they have read. At the end of the chapter, under the heading Reach Your Learning Goals, the learning goals guide students through the chapter review, which is linked to the questions posed in each of the chapter's Review and Reflect sections.

In addition to the verbal tools just described, maps that link up with the learning goals are presented at the beginning of each major section in the chapter. At the end of each chapter, the section maps are reflected in the Reach Your Learning Goals summary. The complete learning system, including many additional features not mentioned here, is presented later in the Preface in a section titled Visual Tour for Students.

## ACKNOWLEDGMENTS

I very much appreciate the support and guidance provided to me by many people at McGraw-Hill. Beth Mejia, Publisher, has done a marvelous job of directing and monitoring the development and publication of this text. Mike Sugarman, Executive Editor, has brought a wealth of publishing knowledge and vision to bear on improving my texts. Maureen Spada has done an excellent job of handling the page-by-page changes to this new edition. Dawn Groundwater, Director of Development, has done a superb job of organizing and monitoring the many tasks necessary to move this book through the editorial process. Jillian Allison, Editorial Coordinator, has done a competent job of obtaining reviewers and handling many editorial chores. James Headley, Marketing Manager, has contributed in numerous positive ways to this book. Beatrice Sussman did a superb job as the book's copy editor. Marilyn Rothenberger did a terrific job in coordinating the book's production.

I also want to thank my wife, Mary Jo, our children, Tracy and Jennifer, and my granddaughter, Jordan, for their wonderful contributions to my life and for helping me to better understand the marvels and mysteries of adolescent development.

Special thanks go to the many reviewers of the twelfth edition of this text. Their extensive contributions have made this a far better book.

## PREREVISION REVIEWERS

**Ioakim Boutakidis,** *Fullerton*
**Mark Chapell,** *Rowan University*
**Jerome B. Dusek,** *Syracuse University*
**Lisa Diamond,** *University of Utah*
**Laura Duvall,** *Heartland Community College*
**Kimberly DuVall-Early,** *James Madison University*
**Kim Hyatt,** *Weber State*
**Michelle Kelley,** *Old Dominion University*
**Delores Vantrice Oates,** *Texas Southern University*
**Ian Payton,** *Bethune-Cookman College*
**Dr. Vicki Ritts,** *St. Louis Comm. College*
**Dr. Ken Springer,** *Southern Methodist University*
**Angela Vaughan Williamson,** *Wesley College*

## TWELFTH EDITION REVIEWERS

**Kristi Blankenship,** *University of Tennessee at Knoxville*
**Jane Brower,** *University of Tennessee at Chattanooga*
**Gypsy Denzine,** *Northern Arizona University*
**Rick Froman,** *John Brown University*
**Kim Hyatt,** *Weber State University*
**D. Rush McQueen, Ph.D.,** *Auburn University*
**Sean Meegan,** *Western Illinois University*
**Gayle Reed,** *University of Wisconsin at Madison*

## REVIEWERS OF FIRST ELEVEN EDITIONS

**Alice Alexander,** *Old Dominion University*
**Joseph Allen,** *University of Virginia*
**Sandy Arntz,** *Northern Illinois University*
**Frank Ascione,** *Utah State University*
**Carole Beale,** *University of Massachusetts*
**Peter Benson,** *Search Institute, Minneapolis*
**Luciane A. Berg,** *Southern Utah University*
**David K. Bernhardt,** *Carleton University*
**Fredda Blanchard-Fields,** *Louisiana State University*
**Kristi Blankenship,** *University of Tennessee*
**Belinda Blevins-Knabe,** *University of Arkansas*
**Robert Bornstein,** *Miami University*
**Geraldine Brookins,** *University of Minnesota*
**Deborah Brown,** *Friends University*
**Christy M. Buchanan,** *Wake Forest University*
**Duane Buhrmester,** *University of Texas at Dallas*
**Nancy Busch-Rossnagel,** *Fordham University*
**James I. Byrd,** *University of Wisconsin at Stout*
**James Byrnes,** *University of Maryland*
**Cheryl A. Camenzuli,** *Hofstra University*
**Elaine Cassel,** *Marymount University*
**Mark Chapell,** *Rowan University*
**P. Lindsey Chase-Lansdale,** *University of Chicago*
**Stephanie M. Clancy,** *Southern Illinois University at Carbondale*
**Catherine R. Cooper,** *University of California at Santa Cruz*
**Ronald K. Craig,** *Cincinnati State College*
**Gary Creasey,** *Illinois State University*
**Rita Curl,** *Minot State University*
**Peggy A. DeCooke,** *Northern Illinois University*
**Nancy Defates-Densch,** *Northern Illinois University*
**Imma Destefanis,** *Boston College*
**Lisa Diamond,** *University of Utah*
**R. Daniel DiSalvi,** *Kean College*
**Lorah Dorn,** *University of Cincinnati*
**James A. Doyle,** *Roane State Community College*
**Joy Dryfoos,** *Hastings-on-Hastings, New York*
**Mark W. Durm,** *Athens State University*
**Jerome Dusek,** *Syracuse University State University*
**Laura Duvall,** *Heartland Community College*
**Carol Dweck,** *Columbia University*
**Celina Echols,** *Southern Louisiana State University*
**Richard M. Ehlenz,** *Lakewood Community College*
**Glen Elder,** *University of North Carolina*
**Gene Elliot,** *Glassboro State University*
**Steve Ellyson,** *Youngstown State University*
**Robert Enright,** *University of Wisconsin at Madison*
**Jennifer Fager,** *Western Michigan University*
**Shirley Feldman,** *Stanford University*
**Douglas Fife,** *Plymouth State College*
**Urminda Firlan,** *Michigan State University*
**Leslie Fisher,** *Cleveland State University*
**Constance Flanagan,** *Pennsylvania State University*
**Martin E. Ford,** *Stanford University*
**Gregory T. Fouts,** *University of Calgary*
**Mary Fraser,** *San Jose State University*
**Charles Fry,** *University of Virginia*
**Wyndol Furman,** *University of Denver*
**Nancy L. Galambos,** *University of Alberta in Edmonton*
**Anne R. Gayles-Felton,** *Florida A&M University*
**Margaret J. Gill,** *Kutztown University*
**Sam Givham,** *Mississippi State University*
**Page Goodwin,** *Western Illinois University*
**William Gnagey,** *Illinois State University*
**Sandra Graham,** *UCLA*
**Nicole Graves,** *South Dakota State University*
**Harold Grovevant,** *University of Minnesota*
**B. Jo Hailey,** *University of Southern Mississippi*
**Dick E. Hammond,** *Southwest Texas State University*
**Frances Harnick,** *University of New Mexico, Indian Children's Program, and Lovelace-Bataan Pediatric Clinic*
**Algea Harrison,** *Oakland University*
**Susan Harter,** *University of Denver*
**Dan Houlihan,** *Minnesota State University*
**June V. Irving,** *Ball State University*
**Charles Irwin,** *University of California—San Francisco*
**Beverly Jennings,** *University of Colorado at Denver*
**Joline Jones,** *Worcester State College*
**Linda Juang,** *San Francisco State University*
**Alfred L. Karlson,** *University of Massachusetts at Amherst*
**Lynn F. Katz,** *University of Pittsburgh*

**Carolyn Kaufman,** *Columbus State Community College*
**Daniel P. Keating,** *University of Toronto*
**Marguerite D. Kermis,** *Canisius College*
**Roger Kobak,** *University of Delaware*
**Tara Kuther,** *Western Connecticut State University*
**Emmett C. Lampkin,** *Scott Community College*
**Royal Louis Lange,** *Ellsworth Community Center*
**Philip Langer,** *University of Colorado*
**Reed W. Larson,** *University of Illinois at Urbana-Champaign*
**Daniel Lapsley,** *Brandon University*
**Brett Laursen,** *Florida Atlantic University*
**Bonnie Leadbeater,** *University of Victoria*
**Nancy Leffert,** *Search Institute, Minneapolis*
**Heidi Legg-Burross,** *University of Arizona*
**Tanya Letourneau,** *Delaware County College*
**Neal E. Lipsitz,** *Boston College*
**Nancy Lobb,** *Alvin Community College*
**Daniel Lynch,** *University of Wisconsin at Oshkosh*
**Beth Manke,** *University of Houston*
**James Marcia,** *Simon Fraser University*
**Joseph G. Marrone,** *Siena College*
**Ann McCabe,** *University of Windsor*
**Susan McCammon,** *East Carolina University*
**Sherri McCarthy-Tucker,** *Northern Arizona University*
**E. L. McGarry,** *California State University at Fullerton*
**Jessica Miller,** *Mesa State College*
**John J. Mirich,** *Metropolitan State College*
**John J. Mitchell,** *University of Alberta*
**Suzanne F. Morrow,** *Old Dominion University*
**Lloyd D. Noppe,** *University of Wisconsin at Green Bay*
**Daniel Offer,** *University of Michigan*
**Shana Pack,** *Western Kentucky University*
**Michelle Paludi,** *Michelle Paludi & Associates*
**Joycelyn G. Parish,** *Kansas State University*
**Ian Payton,** *Bethune-Cookman College*
**Peggy G. Perkins,** *University of Nevada*
**Emilie Phillips Smith,** *Pennsylvania State University*
**Richard Pisacreta,** *Ferris State University*
**James D. Reid,** *Washington University*
**Anne Robertson,** *University of Wisconsin at Milwaukee*
**Tonie E. Santmire,** *University of Nebraska*
**Douglas Sawin,** *University of Texas*
**Mary Schumann,** *George Mason University*
**Jane Sheldon,** *University of Michigan at Dearborn*
**Kim Shifren,** *Towson University*
**Susan Shonk,** *State University of New York*
**Dale Shunk,** *Purdue University*
**Elizabeth J. Susman,** *Pennsylvania State University*
**Ruby Takanishi,** *Foundation for Child Development*
**Vern Tyler,** *Western Washington University*
**Rhoda Unger,** *Montclair State College*
**Angela Vaughn,** *Wesley College*
**Fred W. Vondracek,** *Pennsylvania State University*
**Elizabeth Vozzola,** *Saint Joseph's College*
**Barry Wagner,** *Catholic University of America*
**Lawrence Walker,** *University of British Columbia*
**Rob Weisskrich,** *California State University at Fullerton*
**Deborah Welsh,** *University of Tennessee*
**Kathryn Wentzel,** *University of Maryland, College Park*
**Allan Wigfield,** *University of Maryland, College Park*
**Wanda Willard,** *State University of New York at Oswego*
**Carolyn L. Williams,** *University of Minnesota*
**Shelli Wynants,** *California State University*
**Melanie Zimmer-Gembeck,** *Griffith University*

## SUPPLEMENTS

The supplements listed here may accompany *Adolescence,* twelfth edition. Please contact your McGraw-Hill representative for details concerning policies, prices, and availability.

### For The Instructor

The instructor side of the Online Learning Center at http://www.mhhe.com/santrocka12e contains the Instructor's Manual, Test Bank files, PowerPoint slides, Image Gallery, CPS Questions, and other valuable material to help you design and enhance your course. Ask your local McGraw-Hill representative for your password.

### Instructor's Manual

**by Jessica Herrick, Mesa State College**

Each chapter of the *Instructor's Manual* is introduced by a Total Teaching Package Outline. This fully integrated tool helps instructors more easily locate and choose among the many resources available for the course by linking each element of the Instructor's Manual to a particular teaching topic within the chapter. These elements include suggested lecture topics, classroom discussion prompts, in-class activities, critical thinking exercises, short scenarios, research articles, student research projects, essay questions, internet activities, and exercises to accompany the video clips posted on the Online Learning Center.

### Test Bank and Computerized Test Bank

**by Virginia Powers-Lagac, Westfield State College**

This comprehensive Test Bank includes more than 1,800 multiple-choice questions, of which approximately 25% are conceptual, approximately 25% are applied, and the remainder factual. In addition, each chapter offers five or more essay questions. Every question indicates the correct answer and is identified by type of question (conceptual, applied, or factual), refers to the chapter topic it addresses, and indicates the page number in the text where the corresponding material can be found. All test questions are compatible with EZ Test, McGraw-Hill's Computerized Test Bank program.

## Powerpoint Slides

**by Len Mendola, Adelphi University**

These presentations cover the key points of each chapter and include charts and graphs from the text. They can be used as is, or you may modify them to meet your specific needs.

## CPS Questions

**by Alisha Janowsky, University of Central Florida**

These questions, formatted for use with the interactive Classroom Performance System, are organized by chapter and designed to test factual, applied, and conceptual understanding. These test questions are also compatible with EZTest, McGraw-Hill's Computerized Test Bank program.

## McGraw-Hill's Visual Asset Database for Lifespan Development ("VAD")

McGraw-Hill's Visual Assets Database for Lifespan Development (VAD 2.0) (www.mhhe.com/vad) is an on-line database of videos for use in the developmental psychology classroom, created specifically for instructors. You can customize classroom presentations by downloading the videos to your computer and showing the videos on their own or insert them into your course cartridge or PowerPoint presentations. All of the videos are available with or without captions. Ask your McGraw-Hill representative for access information.

## Multimedia Courseware For Child Development

**Charlotte J. Patterson, University of Virginia**

This video-based set of two CD-ROMS covers classic and contemporary experiments in child development. Respected researcher Charlotte J. Patterson selected the content and wrote accompanying modules that can be assigned to students. These modules include suggestions for additional projects as well as a testing component. Multimedia Courseware can be packaged with the text at a discount.

## Annual Editions: Child Growth and Development 08/09

This reader is a collection of articles on topics related to the latest research and thinking in human development. Annual Editions are updated regularly and include useful features such as a topic guide, an annotated table of contents, unit overviews, and a topical index.

## Taking Sides: Clashing Views in Childhood and Society

Current controversial issues are presented in a debate-style format designed to stimulate student interest and develop critical thinking skills. Each issue is thoughtfully framed with an issue summary, an issue introduction, and a postscript.

## Cases in Child and Adolescent Development for Teachers

Containing more than 40 cases, *Case Studies in Child and Adolescent Development for Teachers* brings developmental issues to life. The reality-based cases address a variety of developmental issues, giving students an opportunity to think critically about the way development influences children everyday.

# FOR THE STUDENT:

## Online Learning Center (OLC)

This companion website, at www.mhhe.com/santrocka12e offers a wide variety of student resources. **Multiple Choice, True/False, and Matching Tests** for each chapter reinforce key principles, terms, and ideas, and cover all the major concepts discussed throughout the text. Entirely different from the test items in the Test Bank, the questions have been written to quiz students but also to help them learn. Key terms from the text are reproduced in a **Glossary of Key Terms** where they can be accessed in alphabetical order for easy reference and review. **Decision Making Scenarios** present students with the opportunity to apply the information in the chapter to realistic situations, and see what effects their decisions have. Streamable online **Videos** reinforce chapter content.

# VISUAL TOUR FOR STUDENTS

This book provides you with important study tools to help you more effectively learn about adolescent development. Especially important is the learning goals system that is integrated throughout each chapter. In the visual walk-through of features, pay special attention to how the learning goals system works.

## THE LEARNING GOALS SYSTEM

Using the learning goals system will help you to learn the material more easily. Key aspects of the learning goals system are the learning goals, chapter maps, Review and Reflect, and Reach Your Learning Goals sections, which are all linked together.

At the beginning of each chapter, you will see a page that includes both a chapter outline and three to six learning goals that preview the chapter's main themes and underscore the most important ideas in the chapter. Then, at the beginning of each major section of a chapter, you will see a mini–chapter map that provides you with a visual organization of the key topics you are about to read in the section. At the end of each section is Review and Reflect, in which the learning goal for the section is restated, a series of review questions related to the mini–chapter map are asked, and a question that encourages you to think critically about a topic related to the section appears. At the end of the chapter, you will come to a section titled Reach Your Learning Goals. This includes an overall integrated chapter map that visually organizes all of the main headings, a restatement of the chapter's learning goals, and a summary of the chapter's content that is directly linked to the chapter outline at the beginning of the chapter and the questions asked in the Review part of Review and Reflect within the chapter. The Reach Your Learning Goals section at the end of the chapter provides brief answers to the questions asked in the within-chapter Review sections.

## THE LEARNING GOALS SYSTEM

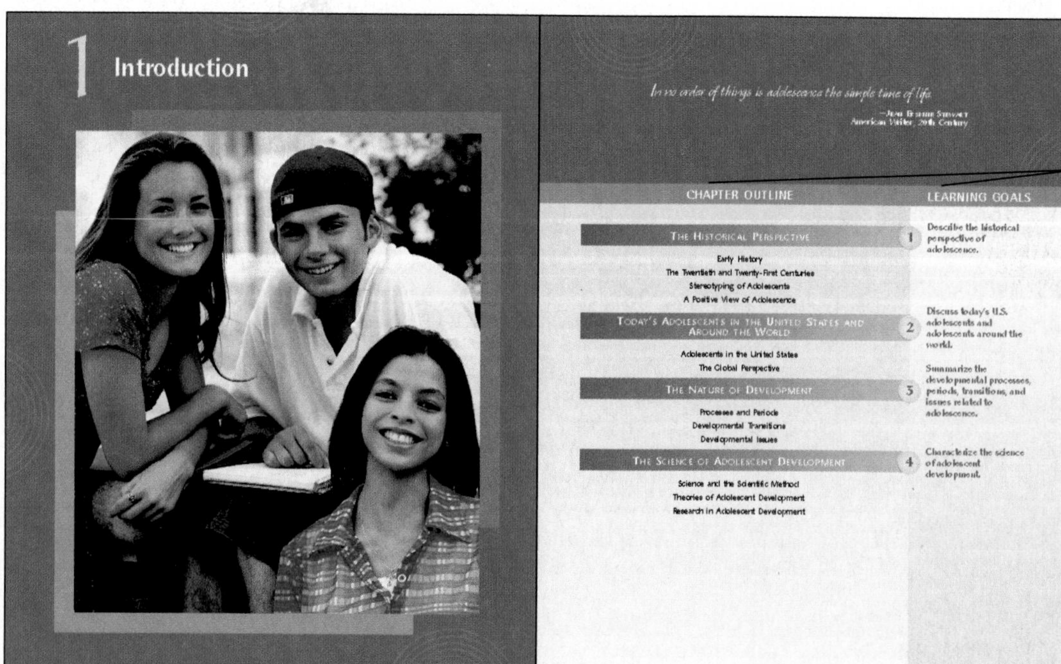

1 Introduction
In no order of things is adolescence the simple time of life.
CHAPTER OUTLINE
LEARNING GOALS
The Historical Perspective
Early History
The Twentieth and Twenty-First Centuries
Stereotyping of Adolescents
A Positive View of Adolescence
1 Describe the historical perspective of adolescence.
Today's Adolescents in the United States and Around the World
Adolescents in the United States
The Global Perspective
2 Discuss today's U.S. adolescents and adolescents around the world.
The Nature of Development
Processes and Periods
Developmental Transitions
Developmental Issues
3 Summarize the developmental processes, periods, transitions, and issues related to adolescence.
The Science of Adolescent Development
Science and the Scientific Method
Theories of Adolescent Development
Research in Adolescent Development
4 Characterize the science of adolescent development.


CHAPTER-OPENING OUTLINE AND LEARNING GOALS

## MINI-CHAPTER MAP

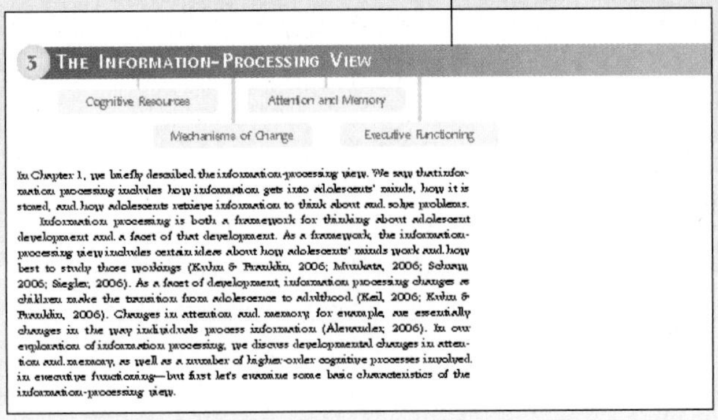

3 THE INFORMATION-PROCESSING VIEW

Cognitive Resources | Attention and Memory | Mechanisms of Change | Executive Functioning

In Chapter 1, we briefly described the information-processing view. We saw that information processing includes how information gets into adolescents' minds, how it is stored, and how adolescents retrieve information to think about and solve problems.

Information processing is both a framework for thinking about adolescent development and a facet of that development. As a framework, the information-processing view includes certain ideas about how adolescents' minds work and how best to study those workings (Kuhn & Franklin, 2006; Munakata, 2006; Schunn, 2006; Siegler, 2006). As a facet of development, information processing changes as children make the transition from adolescence to adulthood (Keil, 2006; Kuhn & Franklin, 2006). Changes in attention and memory, for example, are essentially changes in the way individuals process information (Alexander, 2006). In our exploration of information processing, we discuss developmental changes in attention and memory, as well as a number of higher-order cognitive processes involved in executive functioning—but first let's examine some basic characteristics of the information-processing view.

## REVIEW AND REFLECT

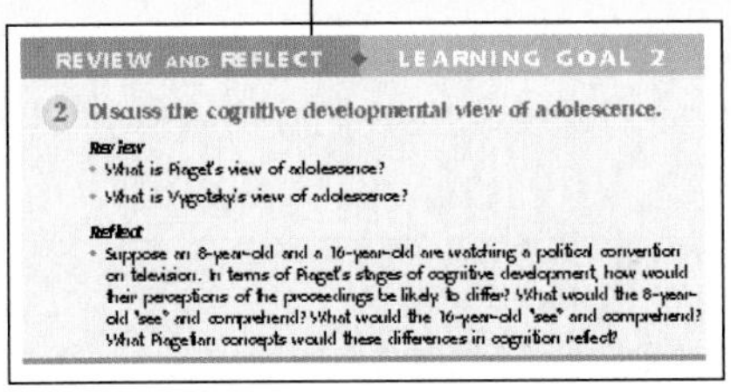

REVIEW AND REFLECT • LEARNING GOAL 2

2 Discuss the cognitive developmental view of adolescence.

**Review**
- What is Piaget's view of adolescence?
- What is Vygotsky's view of adolescence?

**Reflect**
- Suppose an 8-year-old and a 16-year-old are watching a political convention on television. In terms of Piaget's stages of cognitive development, how would their perceptions of the proceedings be likely to differ? What would the 8-year-old "see" and comprehend? What would the 16-year-old "see" and comprehend? What Piagetian concepts would these differences in cognition reflect?

## REACH YOUR LEARNING GOALS

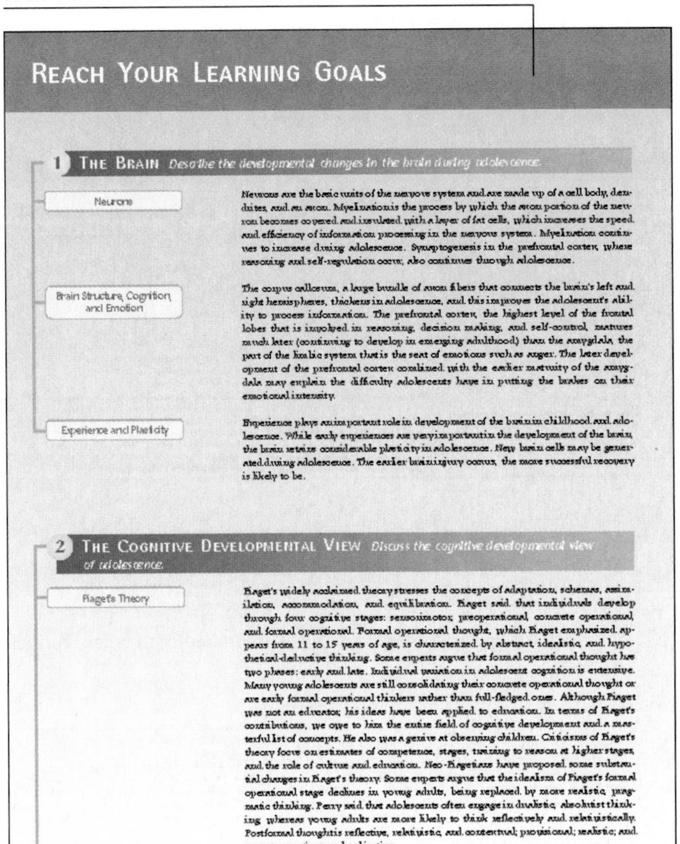

REACH YOUR LEARNING GOALS

1 THE BRAIN *Describe the developmental changes in the brain during adolescence.*

Neurons: Neurons are the basic units of the nervous system and are made up of a cell body, dendrites, and an axon. Myelination is the process by which the axon portion of the neuron becomes covered and insulated with a layer of fat cells, which increases the speed and efficiency of information processing in the nervous system. Myelination continues to increase during adolescence. Synaptogenesis in the prefrontal cortex, where reasoning and self-regulation occur, also continues through adolescence.

Brain Structure, Cognition, and Emotion: The corpus callosum, a large bundle of axon fibers that connects the brain's left and right hemispheres, thickens in adolescence, and this improves the adolescent's ability to process information. The prefrontal cortex, the highest level of the frontal lobes that is involved in reasoning, decision making, and self-control, matures much later (continuing to develop in emerging adulthood) than the amygdala, the part of the limbic system that is the seat of emotions such as anger. The later development of the prefrontal cortex combined with the earlier maturity of the amygdala may explain the difficulty adolescents have in putting the brakes on their emotional intensity.

Experience and Plasticity: Experience plays an important role in development of the brain in childhood and adolescence. While early experiences are very important in the development of the brain, the brain retains considerable plasticity in adolescence. New brain cells may be generated during adolescence. The earlier brain injury occurs, the more successful recovery is likely to be.

2 THE COGNITIVE DEVELOPMENTAL VIEW *Discuss the cognitive developmental view of adolescence.*

Piaget's Theory: Piaget's widely acclaimed theory stresses the concepts of adaptation, schemas, assimilation, accommodation, and equilibration. Piaget said that individuals develop through four cognitive stages: sensorimotor, preoperational, concrete operational, and formal operational. Formal operational thought, which Piaget emphasized, appears from 11 to 15 years of age, is characterized by abstract, idealistic, and hypothetical-deductive thinking. Some experts argue that formal operational thought has two phases: early and late. Individual variation in adolescent cognition is extensive. Many young adolescents are still consolidating their concrete operational thought or are early formal operational thinkers rather than full-fledged ones. Although Piaget was not an educator, his ideas have been applied to education. In terms of Piaget's contributions, we owe to him the entire field of cognitive development and a masterful list of concepts. He also was a genius at observing children. Criticisms of Piaget's theory focus on estimates of competence, stages, training to reason at higher stages, and the role of culture and education. Neo-Piagetians have proposed some substantial changes in Piaget's theory. Some experts argue that the idealism of Piaget's formal operational stage declines in young adults, being replaced by more realistic, pragmatic thinking. Perry said that adolescents often engage in dualistic, absolutist thinking, whereas young adults are more likely to think reflectively and relativistically. Postformal thought is reflective, relativistic, and contextual; provisional; realistic; and open to emotions and subjective.

# OTHER LEARNING SYSTEM FEATURES

## IMAGES OF ADOLESCENT DEVELOPMENT

Each chapter opens with a high-interest story that is linked to the chapter's content.

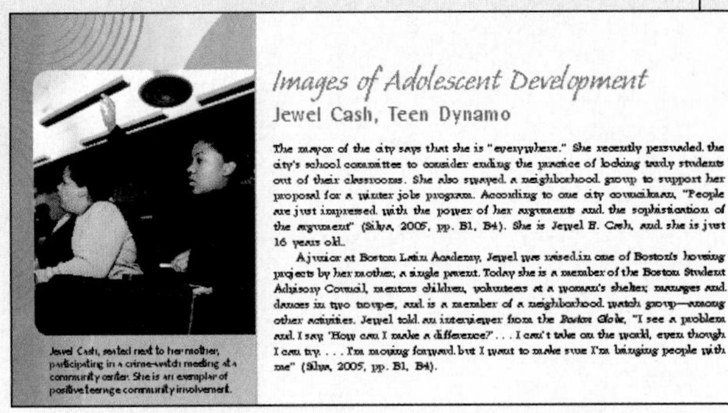

*Images of Adolescent Development*

Jewel Cash, Teen Dynamo

The mayor of the city says that she is "everywhere." She recently persuaded the city's school committee to consider ending the practice of locking tardy students out of their classrooms. She also swayed a neighborhood group to support her proposal for a winter jobs program. According to one city councilman, "People are just impressed with the power of her arguments and the sophistication of the argument" (Silva, 2005, pp. B1, B4). She is Jewel E. Cash, and she is just 16 years old.

A junior at Boston Latin Academy, Jewel was raised in one of Boston's housing projects by her mother, a single parent. Today she is a member of the Boston Student Advisory Council, mentors children, volunteers at a woman's shelter, manages and dances in two troupes, and is a member of a neighborhood watch group—among other activities. Jewel told an interviewer from the *Boston Globe*, "I see a problem and I say 'How can I make a difference?' . . . I can't take on the world, even though I can try. . . . I'm moving forward but I want to make sure I'm bringing people with me" (Silva, 2005, pp. B1, B4).

Jewel Cash, seated next to her mother, participating in a crime-watch meeting at a community center. She is an exemplar of positive teenage community involvement.

## THROUGH THE EYES OF ADOLESCENTS/ THROUGH THE EYES OF EMERGING ADULTS

At appropriate places throughout the book, adolescents and emerging adults describe their experiences and attitudes in their own words.

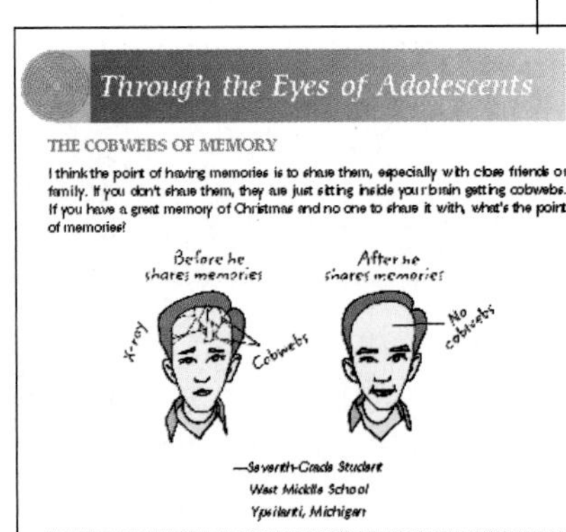

*Through the Eyes of Adolescents*

THE COBWEBS OF MEMORY

I think the point of having memories is to share them, especially with close friends or family. If you don't share them, they are just sitting inside your brain getting cobwebs. If you have a great memory of Christmas and no one to share it with, what's the point of memories!



—*Seventh-Grade Student*
*West Middle School*
*Ypsilanti, Michigan*

## CAREERS IN ADOLESCENT DEVELOPMENT APPENDIX

A Careers in Adolescent Development Appendix that describes a number of careers appears after Chapter 1.

### Careers in Adolescent Development

Some of you may be quite sure about what you plan to make your life's work. Others may not have decided on a major yet and are uncertain about which career path you want to follow. Each of us wants to find a rewarding career and enjoy the work we do. The field of adolescent development offers an amazing breadth of career options that can provide extremely satisfying work.

If you decide to pursue a career in adolescent development, what career options are available to you? There are many. College and university professors teach courses in adolescent development, education, family development, and medicine. Middle school and high school teachers impart knowledge, understanding, and skills to adolescents. Counselors, clinical psychologists, and physicians help adolescents to cope more effectively with the unique challenges of adolescence. And various professionals work with families of adolescents to improve the adolescent's development.

By choosing one of these career options, you can guide youth in improving their lives, help others to understand them better, or even advance the state of knowledge in the field. You can have an enjoyable time while you are doing these things. Although an advanced degree is not absolutely necessary in some areas of adolescent development, you usually can expand your opportunities (and income) considerably by obtaining a graduate degree. Many careers in adolescent development pay reasonably well. For example, psychologists earn well above the median salary in the United States.

If you are considering a career in adolescent development, as you go through this term, try to spend some time with adolescents of different ages. Observe their behavior; talk with them about their lives. Think about whether you would like to work with youth in your life's work.

Another worthwhile activity is to talk with people who work with adolescents. For example, if you have some interest in becoming a school counselor, call a school, ask to speak with a counselor, and set up an appointment to discuss the counselor's career path and work. Be prepared with a list of questions to ask, and take notes if you wish.

Working in one or more jobs related to your career interests while you are in college can also benefit you. Many colleges and universities offer internships or work experiences for students who major in fields such as development. In some instances, these opportunities are for course credit or pay; in others, they are strictly on a volunteer basis. Take advantage of these opportunities. They can provide you with valuable experiences to help you decide if this is the right career area for you, and they can help you get into graduate school, if you decide you want to go.

In the following sections, we profile careers in three areas: education/research; clinical/counseling/medical; and families/relationships. These are not the only career options in the field of adolescent development, but they should provide you with an idea of the range of opportunities available and information about some of the main career avenues you might pursue. In profiling these careers, we address the amount of education required, the nature of the training, and a description of the work.

EDUCATION/RESEARCH

Education and research offer a wide range of career opportunities to work with adolescents. These range from being a college professor to secondary school teacher to school psychologist.

College/University Professor Courses in adolescent development are taught in different programs and schools in college and universities, including psychology, education, child and family studies, social work, and medicine. They are taught at research universities that offer one or more master's or Ph.D. programs in development; at four-year colleges with no graduate programs; or at community colleges. The work college professors do includes teaching courses either at the undergraduate or graduate level (or both); conducting research in a specific area; advising students and/or directing their research; and serving on college or university committees. Some college instructors do not conduct research but instead focus mainly on teaching. Research is most likely to be part of the job description at universities with master's and Ph.D. programs.

A Ph.D. or master's degree almost always is required to teach in some area of adolescent development in a college or university. Obtaining a doctoral degree usually takes four to six years of graduate work. A master's degree requires approximately two years of graduate work. The training involves taking graduate courses, learning to conduct research, and attending and presenting papers at professional meetings. Many graduate students work as teaching or research assistants to professors, an apprenticeship relationship that helps them to develop their teaching and research skills.

If you are interested in becoming a college or university professor, you might want to make an appointment with your instructor to learn more about the profession and what his or her career/work is like.

Researcher In most instances, individuals who work in research positions will have either a master's degree or Ph.D. in some area of adolescent development. They might work at a university, perhaps in a research program; in government at agencies such as the National Institute of Mental Health; or in private industry. Those who have full-time research positions generate innovative research ideas, plan studies, and

48

## KEY TERMS AND GLOSSARY

Key terms appear in boldface. Their definitions appear in the margin near where they are introduced.

[...] adrenarche and gonadarche (Susman & Rogol, 2004). **Adrenarche** involves hormonal changes in the adrenal glands, located just above the kidneys. These changes occur surprisingly early, from about 6 to 9 years of age in girls and about one year later in boys, before what is generally considered the beginning of puberty (Dorn & others, 2006). During adrenarche and continuing through puberty, the adrenal glands secrete adrenal androgens, such as dehydroepiandrosterone (DHEA) (Blogowska, Rzepka-Gorska, & Krzyzanowska-Swiniarska, 2005). Adrenarche is still not well understood (Dorn & others, 2006).

**Gonadarche,** which follows adrenarche by about two years, is the period most people think of as puberty (Archibald, Graber, & Brooks-Gunn, 2003). Gonadarche involves the maturation of primary sexual characteristics (ovaries in females, testes in males) and secondary sexual characteristics (pubic hair, breast, and genital development) (Dorn & others, 2006). "The hallmark of gonadarche is reactivation of the hypothalamic-pituitary-gonadal axis (HPG). . . . The initial activation of the HPG axis was during the fetal and neonatal period" (Dorn & others, 2006, p. 35).

In the United States, the gonadarche period begins at approximately 9 to 10 years of age in non-Latino White girls, and 8 to 9 years in African American girls (Herman-Giddens, Kaplowitz, & Wasserman, 2004). In boys, gonadarche begins at about 10 to 11 years of age. **Menarche,** the first menstrual period, occurs in mid to late gonadarche in girls. In boys, **spermarche,** a boy's first ejaculation of semen, occurs in early to mid gonadarche. Robert, Angie, Ann, and Jim, the adolescents we described in *Images of Adolescent Development*, are each in various phases of adrenarche and gonadarche.

**adrenarche** Puberty phase involving hormonal changes in the adrenal glands, located just above the kidneys. These changes occur from about 6 to 9 years of age in girls and about one year later in boys, before what is generally considered the beginning of puberty.

**gonadarche** Puberty phase involving the maturation of primary sexual characteristics (ovaries in females, testes in males) and secondary sexual characteristics (pubic hair, breast, and genital development). This period follows adrenarche by about two years and is what most people think of as puberty.

**menarche** A girl's first menstrual period.

**spermarche** A boy's first ejaculation of semen.

Key terms also are listed and page-referenced at the end of each chapter.

KEY TERMS

| | | | |
|---|---|---|---|
| puberty 54 | adaptive behavior 77 | adoption study 81 | shared environmental experiences 82 |
| hormones 55 | evolutionary psychology 77 | passive genotype-environment correlations 81 | nonshared environmental experiences 82 |
| androgens 55 | chromosomes 78 | evocative genotype-environment correlations 81 | epigenetic view 83 |
| estrogens 55 | DNA 78 | active (niche-picking) genotype-environment correlations 82 | |
| adrenarche 57 | genes 78 | | |
| gonadarche 57 | genotype 80 | | |
| menarche 57 | phenotype 80 | | |
| spermarche 57 | behavior genetics 80 | | |
| secular trends 62 | twin study 81 | | |
| female athlete triad 75 | | | |

Key terms are alphabetically listed, defined, and page-referenced in a Glossary at the end of the book.

GLOSSARY

A

**accommodation** An adjustment to new information. 97

**acculturation** Cultural change that results from continuous, firsthand contact between two distinctive cultural groups. 434

**acculturative stress** The negative consequences that result from contact between two distinctive cultural groups. 470

[...] about one year later in boys, before what is generally considered the beginning of puberty. 57

**affectionate love** Also called companionate love, this love occurs when an individual desires to have another person near and has a deep, caring affection for that person. 343

**AIDS** Acquired immune deficiency syndrome, a sexually transmitted syndrome caused by the HIV virus, which destroys the [...]

[...] and little verbal exchange is allowed. This style is associated with adolescents' socially incompetent behavior. 282

**authoritative parenting** This style encourages adolescents to be independent but still places limits and controls on their actions. Extensive verbal give-and-take is allowed, and parents are warm and nurturant toward the adolescent. This style is associated with adolescents' socially competent behavior. 283

## CAREERS IN ADOLESCENT DEVELOPMENT

These profiles appear one or more times in each chapter and provide a description of an individual who works in the field of adolescent development.

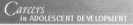

Careers in ADOLESCENT DEVELOPMENT

**Pam Reid**

**Educational and Developmental Psychologist**

When she was a child, Pam Reid liked to play with chemistry sets. Pam majored in chemistry during college and wanted to become a doctor. However, when some of her friends signed up for a psychology class as an elective, she also decided to take the course. She was intrigued by learning about how people think, behave, and develop—so much so that she changed her major to psychology. Pam went on to obtain her Ph.D. in psychology (American Psychological Association, 2003, p. 16).

For a number of years, Pam was professor of education and psychology at the University of Michigan, where she also was a research scientist at the Institute for Research on Women and Gender. Her main focus has been on how children and adolescents develop social skills, with a special interest in the development of African American girls (Reid & Zalk, 2001). In 2004, Pam became provost and executive vice president at Roosevelt University in Chicago.

Pam Reid (back row, center) with graduate students she mentored at the University of Michigan.

## QUOTATIONS

These appear occasionally in the margins to stimulate further thought about a topic.

*The interaction of heredity and environment is so extensive that to ask which is more important, nature or nurture, is like asking which is more important to a rectangle, height or width.*

—William Greenough
*Contemporary Psychologist, University of Illinois*

neighborhood in which gunshots and crime are everyday occurrences, and inadequate schooling. In which of these environments are the adolescent's genes likely to manufacture the biological underpinnings of criminality?

A controversy erupted when Judith Harris (1998) published *The Nurture Assumption*. In this provocative book, she argued that what parents do does not make a difference in their children's and adolescents' behavior. Yell at them. Hug them. Read to them. Ignore them. Harris says it won't influence how they turn out. She argues that genes and peers are far more important than parents in children's and adolescents' development.

Genes and peers do matter, but Harris' descriptions of peer influences do not take into account the complexity of peer contexts and developmental trajectories

## CRITICAL-THINKING AND CONTENT QUESTIONS IN PHOTOGRAPH CAPTIONS

Most photographs have a caption that ends with a critical-thinking or knowledge question in italics to stimulate further thought about a topic.

Jean Piaget, the famous Swiss developmental psychologist, changed the way we think about the development of children's minds. *What are some key ideas in Piaget's theory?*

## KEY PEOPLE

The most important theorists and researchers in chapter are listed and page-referenced at the end of each chapter.

### KEY PEOPLE

| | | | |
|---|---|---|---|
| G. Stanley Hall 6 | Marian Wright Edelman 12 | Sigmund Freud 26 | B. F. Skinner 32 |
| Margaret Mead 6 | Peter Benson 12 | Peter Blos 28 | Albert Bandura 32 |
| Leta Hollingworth 6 | Bernice Neugarten 13 | Anna Freud 28 | Urie Bronfenbrenner 33 |
| Kenneth and Mamie Clark 6 | Brad Brown and Reed Larson 14 | Erik Erikson 28 | Reed Larson and Maryse Richards 36 |
| George Sanchez 8 | Jeffrey Arnett 19 | Jean Piaget 29 | |
| Daniel Offer 9 | Ann Masten 22 | Lev Vygotsky 30 | |
| | | Robert Siegler 31 | |

## RESOURCES FOR IMPROVING THE LIVES OF ADOLESCENTS

At the end of each chapter, recommended readings, research journals, and organizations are provided.

### RESOURCES FOR IMPROVING THE LIVES OF ADOLESCENTS

**Adolescence: Growing Up in America**
by Joy Dryfoos and Carol Barkin (2006)
New York: Oxford University Press

A follow-up to Dryfoos' (1990) earlier landmark book on adolescent problems. In *Adolescence: Growing Up in America*, the authors examine the problems adolescents are having today and the prevention and intervention strategies that work.

**Children's Defense Fund** www.childrensdefense.org
The Children's Defense Fund, headed by Marian Wright Edelman, exists to provide a strong and effective voice for children and adolescents who cannot vote, lobby, or speak for themselves.

**The Search Institute** www.search-institute.org
The Search Institute has available a large number of resources for improving the lives of adolescents. The brochures and books available address school improvement, adolescent literacy, parent education, program planning, and adolescent health—and include resource lists. A free quarterly newsletter is available.

**Handbook of Adolescent Psychology**
edited by Richard Lerner and Laurence Steinberg (2004, 2nd ed.)
New York: John Wiley

An outstanding collection of articles by leading researchers in the field of adolescent development. Includes chapters on social policy, health, volunteering, parent-adolescent relationships, peers, delinquency, sex, puberty, and many other topics.

**Emerging Adults in America**
edited by Jeffrey Arnett and Jennifer Tanner (2006)
Mahwah, NJ: Erlbaum

An excellent set of chapters that provide a contemporary look at major themes and issues in emerging adulthood.

## E-LEARNING RESOURCES

This feature appears at the end of each chapter and consists of four parts: *Taking It to the Net* Internet problem-solving exercises, *Self-Assessment,* which consists of one or more self-evaluations, *Health and Well-Being, Parenting and Education* exercises, which provide an opportunity to practice decision-making skills, and *Video Clips,* which are available online. By going to the Online Learning Center for this book, where you will find many learning activities to improve your knowledge and understanding of the chapter, you can complete these valuable and enjoyable exercises for this book.

### E-LEARNING TOOLS

To help you master the material in this chapter, visit the Online Learning Center for *Adolescence,* twelfth edition (**www.mhhe.com/santrockal2**), where you will find these additional resources:

#### Taking It to the Net

1. About a century ago, G. S. Hall wrote that adolescence was an especially stressful period of time, a stereotype that continues today as evidenced in media representations of adolescence as well as in literary works. Adolescents often are portrayed as interested only in drugs, engaging in promiscuous and risky sex, and alcohol abusers. What is the evidence about the percentages of adolescents using drugs and alcohol and engaging in promiscuous sex?
2. As individuals delay finishing their education, beginning careers, achieving financial independence, and getting married, many people believe that, compared with other generations, youth today are not reaching adulthood until later in life. This transition period between adolescence and adulthood has been termed emergent adulthood. Do you think that emerging adulthood is a separate developmental period? Why or why not? Do you think this trend will continue or change? Why?
3. Child maltreatment (abuse and neglect) is a grave problem. It affects children and adolescents and has implications for how they will rear their own future children. Write an outline of how you might use Bronfenbrenner's theory to organize information about the factors underlying child maltreatment in a paper or class presentation.

#### Self-Assessment

The Online Learning Center includes the following self-assessments for further exploration:

- Do I Have the Characteristics of an Emerging Adult?
- Models and Mentors in My Life
- Evaluating My Interest in a Career in Adolescent Development

#### Health and Well-Being, Parenting, and Education

To practice your decision-making skills, complete the health and well-being, parenting, and education exercises on the Online Learning Center.

#### Video Clips

The Online Learning Center includes the following videos for this chapter:
Relational Aggression
Impact of Media on Children

# *Adolescence*

# 1 Introduction

*In no order of things is adolescence the simple time of life.*

—JEAN ERSKINE STEWART
American Writer, 20th Century

## CHAPTER OUTLINE

## LEARNING GOALS

### THE HISTORICAL PERSPECTIVE

Early History
The Twentieth and Twenty-First Centuries
Stereotyping of Adolescents
A Positive View of Adolescence

1 Describe the historical perspective of adolescence.

### TODAY'S ADOLESCENTS IN THE UNITED STATES AND AROUND THE WORLD

Adolescents in the United States
The Global Perspective

2 Discuss today's U.S. adolescents and adolescents around the world.

### THE NATURE OF DEVELOPMENT

Processes and Periods
Developmental Transitions
Developmental Issues

3 Summarize the developmental processes, periods, transitions, and issues related to adolescence.

### THE SCIENCE OF ADOLESCENT DEVELOPMENT

Science and the Scientific Method
Theories of Adolescent Development
Research in Adolescent Development

4 Characterize the science of adolescent development.

# *Images of Adolescent Development*

## The Youths of Jeffrey Dahmer, Alice Walker, and Michael Maddaus

Jeffrey Dahmer's senior portrait in high school.

Alice Walker

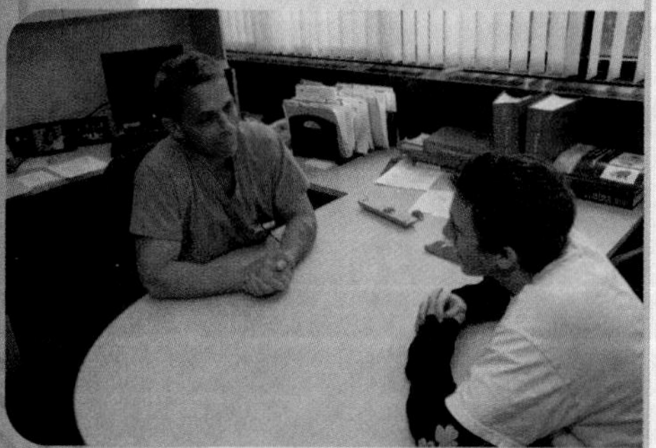

Dr. Michael Maddaus talking with troubled youth.

Jeffrey Dahmer had a troubled childhood and adolescence. His parents constantly bickered before they divorced. His mother had emotional problems and doted on his younger brother. Jeffrey felt that his father neglected him, and he had been sexually abused by another boy when he was 8 years old. But the vast majority of people who suffered through a painful childhood and adolescence do not become serial killers as Dahmer did. Dahmer murdered his first victim in 1978 with a barbell and went on to kill 16 other individuals before being caught and sentenced to 15 life terms in prison.

A decade before Dahmer's first murder, Alice Walker, who would later win a Pulitzer Prize for her book *The Color Purple,* spent her days battling racism in Mississippi. Born the eighth child of Georgia sharecroppers, Walker knew the brutal effects of poverty. Despite the counts against her, she went on to become an award-winning novelist. Walker writes about people who, as she puts it, "make it, who come out of nothing. People who triumph."

Consider also the changing life of Michael Maddaus (Broderick, 2003; Masten, Obradovic, & Burt, 2006). Growing up as a child and adolescent in Minneapolis, his mother drank heavily and his stepfather abused him. He coped by spending increasing time on the streets, being arrested more than 20 times for his delinquency, frequently being placed in detention centers, and rarely going to school. At 17, he joined the Navy and the experience helped him to gain self-discipline and hope. After his brief stint in the Navy, he completed a GED and began taking community college classes. However, he continued to have some setbacks with drugs and alcohol. A defining moment as an emerging adult came when he delivered furniture to a surgeon's home. The surgeon became interested in helping Michael, and his mentorship led to Michael volunteering at a rehabilitation center, then to a job with a neurosurgeon. Eventually, he obtained his undergraduate degree, went to medical school, got married, and started a family. Today, Michael Maddaus is a successful surgeon. One of his most gratifying volunteer activities is telling his story to troubled youth.

What leads one adolescent like Jeffrey Dahmer, so full of promise, to commit brutal acts of violence and another, like Alice Walker, to turn poverty and trauma into a rich literary harvest? How can we attempt to explain how one individual like Michael Maddaus can turn a childhood and adolescence shattered by abuse and delinquency into becoming a successful surgeon, whereas another one seems to come unhinged by life's minor hassles? Why is it that some adolescents are whirlwinds—successful in school, involved in a network of friends, and full of energy—while others hang out on the sidelines, mere spectators of life? If you have ever wondered what makes adolescents tick, you have asked yourself the central question we explore in this book.

PREVIEW

***Adolescence*, twelfth edition, is a window into the nature of adolescent development—your own and that of every other adolescent. In this first chapter, you will read about the history of the field, the characteristics of today's adolescents, both in the United States and the rest of the world, and the way in which adolescents develop.**

# 1 The Historical Perspective

- Early History
- The Twentieth and Twenty-First Centuries
- Stereotyping of Adolescents
- A Positive View of Adolescence

What have the portraits of adolescence been like at different points in history? When did the scientific study of adolescence begin?

## Early History

In early Greece, the philosophers Plato and Aristotle both commented about the nature of youth. According to Plato (fourth century B.C.), reasoning doesn't belong to childhood, but rather first appears in adolescence. Plato thought that children should spend their time in sports and music, whereas adolescents should study science and mathematics.

Aristotle (fourth century B.C.) argued that the most important aspect of adolescence is the ability to choose, and that self-determination is a hallmark of maturity. Aristotle's emphasis on the development of self-determination is not unlike some contemporary views that see independence, identity, and career choice as the key themes of adolescence. Aristotle also recognized adolescents' egocentrism, commenting once that adolescents think they know everything and are quite sure about it.

In the Middle Ages, children and adolescents were viewed as miniature adults and were subjected to harsh discipline. In the eighteenth century, French philosopher Jean-Jacques Rousseau offered a more enlightened view of adolescence, restoring the belief that being a child or an adolescent is not the same as being an adult. Like Plato, Rousseau thought that reasoning develops in adolescence. He said that curiosity should especially be encouraged in the education of 12- to 15-year-olds. From 15 to 20 years of age, Rousseau believed individuals mature emotionally, and their selfishness is replaced by an interest in others. Thus, Rousseau revived the belief that development has distinct phases. But his ideas were speculative; not until the beginning of the twentieth century did the scientific exploration of adolescence begin.

## The Twentieth and Twenty-First Centuries

The end of the nineteenth century and the early part of the twentieth century saw the invention of the concept we now call adolescence. Between 1890 and 1920, a number of psychologists, urban reformers, educators, youth workers, and counselors began to mold the concept. At this time, young people, especially boys, were increasingly seen as being passive and vulnerable—qualities previously associated only with the adolescent female. When G. Stanley Hall's book on adolescence was published in 1904 (see the next section), it played a major role in restructuring thinking about adolescence. Hall wrote that although many adolescents appear to be passive, they are experiencing considerable turmoil within.

When educators, counselors, and psychologists began to develop behavior norms for adolescents, Hall's view substantially influenced those norms. As a result, in the 1900 to 1920 period, adults tried to impose conformity and passivity on adolescents. Examples of this conformity included the encouragement of school spirit, loyalty, and hero worship on athletic teams. In the following sections, we explore Hall's view, as well as two other prominent viewpoints of the twentieth century.

G. Stanley Hall, father of the scientific study of adolescence.

### G. Stanley Hall's Storm-and-Stress View

Historians have described G. Stanley Hall (1844–1924) as the father of the scientific study of adolescence. In 1904, Hall published his ideas in a two-volume set: *Adolescence*. Hall was strongly influenced by Charles Darwin, the famous evolutionary theorist. Applying Darwin's view to the study of adolescent development, Hall proposed that all development is controlled by genetically determined physiological factors. The environment, he thought, plays a minimal role in development, especially during infancy and childhood. Hall did acknowledge that environment accounts for more developmental change in adolescence than in earlier periods, however. At least with regard to adolescence, then, Hall stressed—as we do today—that heredity interacts with environmental influences to determine an individual's development.

According to Hall (1904), adolescence is the period from 12 to 23 years of age, and it is characterized by considerable upheaval. The **storm-and-stress view** is Hall's concept that adolescence is a turbulent time charged with conflict and mood swings. Hall borrowed the label *storm and stress* from the *Sturm und Drang* descriptions of German writers, such as Goethe and Schiller, who wrote novels full of idealism, passion, and feeling. Hall sensed a parallel between the themes of the German authors and the psychological development of adolescents. In his view, adolescents' thoughts, feelings, and actions oscillate between conceit and humility, good intentions and temptation, happiness and sadness. An adolescent might be nasty to a peer one moment and kind the next moment; in need of privacy one moment but seconds later want companionship.

Hall was a giant in the field of adolescence. He began the theorizing, systematizing, and questioning that went beyond mere speculation and philosophizing. Indeed, we owe the beginnings of the scientific study of adolescence to Hall.

Anthropologist Margaret Mead (*left*) with a Samoan adolescent girl. Mead found that adolescence in Samoa was relatively stress-free, although recently her findings have been criticized. *How does Mead's view of adolescence contrast with Hall's view?*

### Margaret Mead's Sociocultural View of Adolescence

Anthropologist Margaret Mead (1928) studied adolescents on the South Sea island of Samoa. She concluded that the basic nature of adolescence is not biological, as Hall envisioned, but rather sociocultural. In cultures that provide a smooth, gradual transition from childhood to adulthood, which is the way adolescence is handled in Samoa, she found little storm and stress associated with the period. Mead's observations of Samoan adolescents revealed instead that their lives were relatively free of turmoil. Mead concluded that cultures that allow adolescents to observe sexual relations, see babies born, regard death as natural, do important work, engage in sex play, and know clearly what their adult roles will be tend to promote a relatively stress-free adolescence. However, in cultures like the United States, in which children are considered very different from adults, and adolescence is not characterized by the same experiences, the period is more likely to be stressful.

More than half a century after Mead's Samoan findings, her work was criticized as biased and error-prone (Freeman, 1983). Current criticism states that Samoan adolescence is more stressful than Mead suggested and that delinquency appears among Samoan adolescents just as it does among Western adolescents. Despite the controversy over Mead's findings, some researchers have defended Mead's work (Holmes,1987).

**storm-and-stress view** G. Stanley Hall's concept that adolescence is a turbulent time charged with conflict and mood swings.

**The Inventionist View** Although adolescence has a biological base, as G. Stanley Hall argued, it also has a sociocultural base, as Margaret Mead maintained. Indeed, sociohistorical conditions contributed to the emergence of the concept of adolescence. According to G. Stanley Hall, father of the scientific study of adolescence **inventionist view,** adolescence is a sociohistorical creation. Especially important in this view of adolescence are the sociohistorical circumstances at the beginning of the twentieth century, a time when legislation was enacted that ensured the dependency of youth and made their move into the economic sphere more manageable. These sociohistorical circumstances included a decline in apprenticeship; increased mechanization during the Industrial Revolution, which raised the level of skill required of laborers and necessitated a specialized division of labor; the separation of work and home; age-graded schools; urbanization; the appearance of youth groups such as the YMCA and the Boy Scouts; and the writings of G. Stanley Hall.

Schools, work, and economics are important dimensions of the inventionist view of adolescence (Elder, 1975; Fasick, 1994; Lapsley, Enright, & Serlin, 1985). Some scholars argue that the concept of adolescence was invented mainly as a by-product of the movement to create a system of compulsory public education. In this view, the function of secondary schools is to transmit intellectual skills to youth. However, other scholars argue that the primary purpose of secondary schools is to deploy youth within the economic sphere, and to serve as a cog in the authority structure (Lapsley, Enright, & Serlin, 1985). In this view, American society conferred the status of adolescence on youth through child-saving legislation. By developing special laws for youth, adults restricted their options, encouraged their dependency, and made their move into the world of work more manageable.

Historians now call the period between 1890 and 1920 the "age of adolescence." In this period, lawmakers enacted a great deal of compulsory legislation aimed at youth. In virtually every state, they passed laws that excluded youth from most employment and required them to attend secondary school. Much of this legislation included extensive enforcement provisions.

Two clear changes resulted from this legislation: decreased employment and increased school attendance among youth. From 1910 to 1930, the number of 10- to 15-year-olds who were gainfully employed dropped about 75 percent. In addition, between 1900 and 1930 the number of high school graduates increased substantially. Approximately 600 percent more individuals graduated from high school in 1930 than in 1900.

An analysis of the content of the oldest continuing journal in developmental psychology, the *Journal of Genetic Psychology* (formerly called the *Pedagogical Seminary*) provides further evidence of history's role in the creation of adolescence (Enright & others, 1987). Four historical periods—the depressions of the 1890s and 1930s and the two world wars—produced quite different appraisals of the capacities of youths. During the depression periods, scholars wrote about the psychological immaturity of youth and their educational needs. In contrast, during the world wars, scholars did not describe youths as immature, but rather underscored their importance as draftees and factory workers. Let's take a closer look at how popular conceptions of adolescence changed with the changing times of the twentieth century.

### Further Changes in the Twentieth Century and the Twenty-First Century

By 1950, the developmental period we refer to as adolescence had come of age. It possessed not only physical and social identities, but a legal identity as well, for every state had developed special laws for youth between the ages of 16 and 18 to 20. Getting a college degree—the key to a good job—was on the minds of many adolescents during the 1950s, as was getting married, having a family, and settling down to the life of luxury displayed in television commercials.

**inventionist view** The view that adolescence is a sociohistorical creation. Especially important in this view are the sociohistorical circumstances at the beginning of the twentieth century, a time when legislation was enacted that ensured the dependency of youth and made their move into the economic sphere more manageable.

Women have often been overlooked in the history of psychology. In the field of adolescence, one such overlooked individual is Leta Hollingworth (*above*). She was the first individual to use the term *gifted* to describe youth who scored exceptionally high on intelligence tests (Hollingworth, 1916). She also played an important role in criticizing theories of her time that promoted the idea that males were superior to females (Hollingworth, 1914). For example, she conducted a research study refuting the myth that phases of the menstrual cycle are associated with the decline in performance in females.

While adolescents' pursuit of higher education continued into the 1960s, many African American adolescents not only were denied a college education but received an inferior secondary education as well. Ethnic conflicts in the form of riots and sit-ins became pervasive, and college-age adolescents were among the most vocal participants.

Political protests reached a peak in the late 1960s and early 1970s, when millions of adolescents reacted violently to what they saw as the United States' immoral participation in the Vietnam War. By the mid-1970s, the radical protests of adolescents began to abate along with U.S. involvement in Vietnam. They were replaced by increased concern for upward mobility through achievement in high school, college, or vocational training. Material interests began to dominate adolescents' motives again, while ideological challenges to social institutions began to recede.

In the 1970s, the women's movement changed both the description and the study of adolescence. In earlier years, descriptions of adolescence had pertained more to males than to females. The dual family and career objectives that female adolescents have today were largely unknown to female adolescents of the 1890s and early 1900s. And for many years, barriers had prevented most females and ethnic minorities from entering the field of adolescent development. Those dedicated individuals who did obtain doctoral degrees had to overcome considerable bias. One pioneer was Leta Hollingworth, who conducted important research on adolescent development, mental retardation, and gifted children. Pioneering African American psychologists included Kenneth and Mamie Clark, who conducted research on the self-esteem of African American children (Clark & Clark, 1939). And in 1932, George Sanchez documented cultural bias in intelligence tests for children and adolescents.

Are there further changes that have characterized adolescents in the late twentieth century and the beginning of the twenty-first century? Clearly, one of the major changes involves the dramatic increase in the use of media and technology by adolescents. "Unlike their parents, they have never known anything but a world dominated by technology. Even their social lives revolve around the Web, iPods, and cellphones" (Jayson, 2006, p. 1D).

Another change in today's U.S. adolescents is their increased diversity (Kottak & Kozaitis, 2008). Many are more tolerant and open-minded than their counterparts in previous generations. One survey indicated that 60 percent of today's adolescents say their friends include someone from diverse ethnic groups (Teenage Research Unlimited, 2004). Another recent survey found that 60 percent of U.S. 18- to 29-year-olds had dated someone from a different ethnic group (Jones, 2005).

We have described the important sociohistorical circumstances surrounding the development of the concept of adolescence, and we have evaluated how society viewed adolescents at different points in history. Next we explore why we need to exercise caution in generalizing about the adolescents of any era.

## Stereotyping of Adolescents

A **stereotype** is a generalization that reflects our impressions and beliefs about a broad category of people. All stereotypes carry an image of what the typical member of a particular group is like. We live in a complex world. Stereotyping is one way we simplify this complexity. We simply assign a label to a group of people. For example, we say that youth are promiscuous. Then we have much less to consider when we think about this group of people. Once we assign a stereotype, it is difficult to abandon it, even in the face of contradictory evidence.

**stereotype** A generalization that reflects our impressions and beliefs about a broad group of people. All stereotypes refer to an image of what the typical member of a particular group is like.

Stereotypes of adolescents are plentiful: "They say they want a job, but when they get one, they don't want to work"; "They are all lazy"; "They are all sex fiends"; "They are all into drugs, every last one of them"; "Kids today don't have the moral fiber of my generation"; "The problem with adolescents today is that they all have it too easy"; "They are a bunch of egotistical smart alecks."

Indeed, during most of the twentieth century, adolescents have been portrayed as abnormal and deviant rather than normal and nondeviant. Consider Hall's image of storm and stress. Consider, too, media portrayals of adolescents as rebellious, conflicted, faddish, delinquent, and self-centered—*Rebel Without a Cause* in the late 1950s and *Easy Rider* in the 1960s. Consider the image of the stressed and disturbed adolescent—*Sixteen Candles* and *The Breakfast Club* in the 1980s, *Boyz N the Hood* in the 1990s. In one analysis of local television coverage, the most frequently reported topics involving youth were crime victimization, accidents, and violent juvenile crime, which accounted for nearly half (46 percent) of all coverage of youth (Gilliam & Bales, 2001). Especially distressing is that when given evidence of youths' positive accomplishments—that a majority of adolescents participate in community service, for example—many adults either deny the facts or say that they must be exceptions (Gilliam & Bales, 2001; Youniss & Ruth, 2002).

Stereotyping of adolescents is so widespread that adolescence researcher Joseph Adelson (1979) coined the term **adolescent generalization gap,** which refers to generalizations that are based on information about a limited, often highly visible group of adolescents. Some adolescents develop confidence in their abilities despite negative stereotypes about them. And some individuals (like Alice Walker and Michael Maddaus, discussed in the opening of this chapter) triumph over poverty, abuse, and other adversities.

*Have adolescents been stereotyped too negatively?* Explain.

## A Positive View of Adolescence

The negative stereotyping of adolescents is overdrawn (Benson & others, 2006; Collins & Steinberg, 2006). In a cross-cultural study, Daniel Offer and his colleagues (1988) found no support for such a negative view. The researchers assessed the self-images of adolescents around the world—in the United States, Australia, Bangladesh, Hungary, Israel, Italy, Japan, Taiwan, Turkey, and West Germany—and discovered that at least 73 percent of the adolescents had a positive self-image. The adolescents were self-confident and optimistic about their future. Although there were some exceptions, as a group, the adolescents were happy most of the time, enjoyed life, perceived themselves as capable of exercising self-control, valued work and school, expressed confidence in their sexuality, showed positive feelings toward their families, and felt they had the capacity to cope with life's stresses—not exactly a storm-and-stress portrayal of adolescence.

### Old Centuries and New Centuries

For much of the last century in the United States and other Western cultures, adolescence was perceived as a problematic period of the human life span akin to G. Stanley Hall's (1904) storm-and-stress portrayal. But as the research study just described indicates, a large majority of adolescents are not nearly as disturbed and troubled as the popular stereotype suggests.

The end of an old century and the beginning of the next has a way of stimulating reflection on what was, as well as visions of what could and should be. In the field of psychology in general, as in its subfield of adolescent development, psychologists have looked back at a century in which the discipline became too negative (Seligman & Csikszentmihalyi, 2000; Snyder & Lopez, 2006). Psychology had became an overly grim science in which people were too often characterized as being passive victims. Psychologists are now calling for a focus on the positive side of human experience and greater emphasis on hope, optimism, positive individual traits, creativity, and positive group and civic values, such as responsibility, nurturance, civility, and tolerance (Benson & others, 2006; Reinders & Youniss, 2006).

*In case you're worried about what's going to become of the younger generation, it's going to grow up and start worrying about the younger generation.*

–ROGER ALLEN
*Contemporary American Writer*

**adolescent generalization gap** Adelson's concept of generalizations about adolescents based on information about a limited, highly visible group of adolescents.

## Through the Eyes of Adolescents

### WANTING TO BE TREATED AS AN ASSET

Many times teenagers are thought of as a problem that no one really wants to deal with. People are sometimes intimidated and become hostile when teenagers are willing to challenge their authority. It is looked at as being disrespectful. Teenagers are, many times, not treated like an asset and as innovative thinkers who will be the leaders of tomorrow. Adults have the power to teach the younger generation about the world and allow them to feel they have a voice in it.

*–Zula, Age 16*
*Brooklyn, New York*

**Generational Perceptions and Misperceptions** Adults' perceptions of adolescents emerge from a combination of personal experience and media portrayals, neither of which produces an objective picture of how typical adolescents develop (Feldman & Elliott, 1990). Some of the readiness to assume the worst about adolescents likely involves the short memories of adults. Adults often portray today's adolescents as more troubled, less respectful, more self-centered, more assertive, and more adventurous than they were.

However, in matters of taste and manners, the youth of every generation have seemed radical, unnerving, and different from adults—different in how they look, how they behave, the music they enjoy, their hairstyles, and the clothing they choose. It is an enormous error to confuse adolescents' enthusiasm for trying on new identities and indulging in occasional episodes of outrageous behavior with hostility toward parental and societal standards. Acting out and boundary testing are time-honored ways in which adolescents move toward accepting, rather than rejecting, parental values.

### REVIEW AND REFLECT ◆ LEARNING GOAL 1

**1 Describe the historical perspective of adolescence.**

***Review***
- What was the early history of interest in adolescence?
- What characterized adolescence in the twentieth century, and how are adolescents changing in the twenty-first century?
- How extensively are adolescents stereotyped?
- Why is a more positive view of adolescence needed?

***Reflect***
- You likely experienced some instances of stereotyping as an adolescent. What are some examples of circumstances in which you think you were stereotyped as an adolescent?

# 2 Today's Adolescents in the United States and Around the World

- Adolescents in the United States
- The Global Perspective

You should now have a good sense of the historical aspects of adolescence. With this background in mind, what is the current status of adolescents in the United States?

## Adolescents in the United States

In many ways, today is both the best of times and the worst of times for adolescents in the United States. They possess longer life expectancies and luxuries inconceivable less than a century ago. Televisions, computers, cell phones, and air travel are often the norm, not the exception. However, the temptations and hazards of the adult world descend on them so early that too often they are not cognitively and emotionally ready to handle them effectively.

Every stable society transmits values from one generation to the next. Today, there is special concern about the values being communicated to American adolescents. Only half a century ago, two of three families in the United States consisted of a breadwinner father, a stay-at-home mother, and the children and adolescents they were raising. In many ways, today's adolescents inhabit an environment that is less stable than that of adolescents several decades ago. High divorce rates, high adolescent pregnancy rates, and increased geographic mobility of families contribute to this lack of stability. The rate of adolescent drug use in the United States is the highest in the industrialized world.

Growing up has never been easy. In many ways, the developmental tasks today's adolescents face are no different from those of adolescents 50 years ago. For a large majority of youth, adolescence is not a time of rebellion, crisis, pathology, and deviance. Rather it is a time of evaluation, decision making, commitment, and finding a place in the world.

Our discussion underscores an important point about adolescents: they are not a homogeneous group (Masten, Obradovic, & Burt, 2006; Wigfield & others, 2006). Most adolescents successfully negotiate the lengthy path to adult maturity, but a large minority do not (Dryfoos & Barkin, 2006). Socioeconomic, ethnic, cultural, gender, age, and lifestyle differences influence the developmental trajectory of every adolescent (Conger & Dogan, 2007; McLoyd, Aikens, & Burton, 2006).

**Social Contexts** Of special interest to researchers is how social contexts influence adolescent development (Bronfenbrenner & Morris, 2006; Schulenberg, 2006; Youngblade & Theokas, 2006). **Contexts** are the settings in which development occurs; they are influenced by historical, economic, social, and cultural factors. To understand how important contexts are in adolescent development, consider the task of a researcher who wants to discover whether today's adolescents are more racially tolerant than those of a decade or two ago. Without reference to the historical, economic, social, and cultural aspects of race relations, adolescents' racial tolerance cannot be fully evaluated. Each adolescent's development occurs against a cultural backdrop of contexts that includes family, peers, school, church, neighborhood, community, region, and nation, each with its cultural legacies (Berry, 2007; McLoyd, Aikens, & Burton, 2006; Rothbaum & Trommsdorff, 2007; Shiraev & Levy, 2007).

The cultural context for U.S. adolescents is changing with the dramatic increase in the number of adolescents immigrating from Latino and Asian countries (Berry, 2007; Berry & others, 2006; Phinney, 2006; Spring, 2007). Figure 1.1 shows the projected percentage increase for White non-Latino, Latino, African American, and Asian American adolescents through 2100. Notice that Asian Americans are expected to be the fastest-growing ethnic group of adolescents with a growth rate of more than 500 percent growth by 2100. Latino adolescents are projected to increase almost 400 percent by 2100. Figure 1.2 shows the actual numbers of adolescents in different ethnic groups in the year 2000, as well as the projected numbers projected through 2100. Notice that by 2100, Latino adolescents are expected to outnumber non-Latino White adolescents.

These changing social contexts receive special attention in this book. Chapters 8 to 12 are devoted to contexts, with separate emphasis on families, peers, schools, work, and culture. As we see next, some experts argue that the social policy of the United States should place stronger emphasis on improving the contexts in which adolescents live.

**Social Policy and Adolescents' Development** **Social policy** is the course of action designed by the national government to influence the welfare of its citizens.

**contexts** The settings in which development occurs. These settings are influenced by historical, economic, social, and cultural factors.

**social policy** A national government's course of action designed to influence the welfare of its citizens.

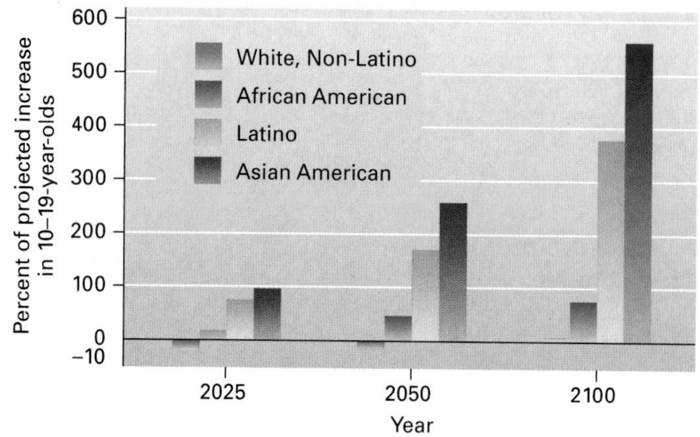


**FIGURE 1.1 Projected Percentage Increase in Adolescents Aged 10–19, 2025–2100** An actual decrease in the percentage of non-Latino White adolescents from 10 to 19 years of age is projected through 2050. By contrast, dramatic percentage increases are projected for Asian American (233% in 2050 and 530% in 2100) and Latino (175% in 2050 and 371% in 2100) adolescents.

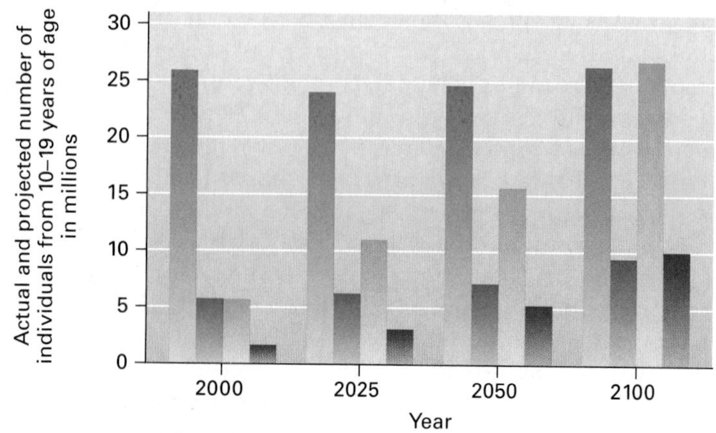


**FIGURE 1.2 Actual and Projected Number of U.S. Adolescents Aged 10–19, 2000–2100** In 2000, there were more than 25 million White, non-Latino adolescents aged 10–19 years of age in the United States, while the numbers for ethnic minority groups were substantially lower. However, projections for 2025 through 2100 reveal dramatic increases in the number of Latino and Asian American adolescents to the point at which in 2100 it is projected that there will be more Latino than White non-Latino adolescents in the United States and more Asian American than African American adolescents.

Currently, many researchers in adolescent development are attempting to design studies whose results will lead to wise and effective social policy decision making (Benson & others, 2006; Brown, 2007; Eccles, Brown, & Templeton, 2007; Petersen, 2006).

Marian Wright Edelman, president of the Children's Defense Fund, has been a tireless advocate for children's rights. Especially troublesome to Edelman (1997) are the indicators of social neglect that place the United States at or near the bottom of the list of industrialized nations in the treatment of children and adolescents. Edelman maintains that parenting and nurturing the next generation of children and youth is our society's most important function, and that we need to take it more seriously than we have in the past. She points out that while we hear a lot from politicians these days about "family values," when we examine our nation's policies for families, they do not reflect the politicians' words. We need a better health-care system for families, safer schools and neighborhoods, better parent education, and improved family support programs, Edelman says.

Peter Benson and his colleagues (2004, 2006) argue that the United States has a fragmented social policy for youth that too often has focused only on the negative developmental deficits of adolescents, especially health-compromising behaviors such as drug use and delinquency, and not enough on positive strength-based approaches. According to Benson and his colleagues (2004, p. 783), a strength-based approach to social policy for youth "adopts more of a wellness perspective, places particular emphasis on the existence of healthy conditions, and expands the concept of health to include the skills and competencies needed to succeed in employment, education, and life. It moves beyond the eradication of risk and deliberately argues for the promotion of well-being." In their view, what the United States needs is a *developmentally attentive youth policy*, which would emphasize "the family, neighborhood, school, youth organization, places of work, and congregations as policy intervention points. Transforming schools into more developmentally rich settings, building linkages across multiple socializing institutions, launching community-wide initiatives organized around a shared vision of strength building, and expanding funding for quality out-of-school programs" would reflect this policy (Benson & others, 2004, p. 798). To read about Peter Benson's career and work, see the *Careers in Adolescent Development* profile.

At the same time that U.S. adolescents have been suffering from governmental neglect, older generations have been benefiting from social policy. **Generational inequity,** in which older adults receive inequitably large allocations of resources, such as Social Security and Medicare benefits, at the expense of younger generations, raises questions about whether the young should have to pay for the old. Older adults enjoy publicly provided pensions, health care, food stamps, housing subsidies, tax breaks, and other benefits that younger groups do not. While the trend toward greater services for the elderly has been developing, the percentage of children and adolescents living in poverty has been rising. Adolescents have been especially underserved by the government.

Bernice Neugarten (1988) says the problem should not be viewed as one of generational inequity, but rather as a major shortcoming of our nation's economic and social policy. She stresses we should develop a spirit of support for people of all ages. It is important to keep in mind that children will one day become older adults and be supported by the efforts of their children. If there were no Social Security system, many adult children would have to support their aging parents, which would reduce resources available to their children (Schaie, 2000).

The well-being of adolescents should be one of America's foremost concerns (Benson & others, 2006; Petersen, 2006). The future of our youth is the future of our society. Adolescents who do not reach their full potential, who make fewer contributions to society than it needs, and who do not take their place in society as productive adults diminish our society's future.

## Careers in ADOLESCENT DEVELOPMENT

**Peter Benson**
**Director, Search Institute**

Peter Benson has been the Director of the Search Institute in Minneapolis since 1985. The Search Institute is an independent, nonprofit organization whose mission is to advance the well-being of adolescents. The Institute conducts applied scientific research, provides information about many aspects of improving adolescents' lives, gives support to communities, and trains people to work with youth.

Peter obtained his undergraduate degree in psychology from Augustana College, master's degree in the psychology of religion from Yale University, and Ph.D. in social psychology from the University of Denver. Peter directs a staff of 80 individuals at the Search Institute, lectures widely about youth, and consults with a number of communities and organizations on adolescent issues.

Under Peter's direction, the Search Institute has determined through research that a number of assets (such as family support and good schools) serve as a buffer to prevent adolescents from developing problems and increase the likelihood that adolescents will competently make the transition from adolescence to adulthood. We further discuss these assets in Chapter 13, "Problems in Adolescence and Emerging Adulthood."

Peter Benson talking with adolescents.

## The Global Perspective

The way we present adolescence in this text is based largely on the writing and research of scholars in the Western world, especially Europe and North America. In fact, some experts argue that adolescence is typically thought of in a "Eurocentric" way (Nsamenang, 2002). Others note that advances in transportation and telecommunication are spawning a global youth culture in which adolescents everywhere wear the same type of clothing and have similar hairstyles, listen to the same music, and use similar slang expressions (Schlegel, 2000). But cultural differences among adolescents have by no means disappeared (Berry, 2007; Larson & Wilson, 2004; Saraswathi, 2006). Consider some of the following variations of adolescence around the world (Brown & Larson, 2002):

- Two-thirds of Asian Indian adolescents accept their parents' choice of a marital partner for them (Verma & Saraswathi, 2002).
- In the Philippines, many female adolescents sacrifice their own futures by migrating to the city to earn money that they can send home to their families.
- Street youth in Kenya and other parts of the world learn to survive under highly stressful circumstances. In some cases abandoned by their parents, they may engage in delinquency or prostitution to provide for their economic needs.

**generational inequity** The unfair treatment of younger members of an aging society, in which older adults pile up advantages by receiving inequitably large allocations of resources, such as Social Security and Medicare.

Boys-only Muslim school in Middle East.

- In the Middle East, many adolescents are not allowed to interact with the other sex, even in school (Booth, 2002).
- Youth in Russia are marrying earlier to legitimize sexual activity (Stetsenko, 2002).

Thus, depending on the culture being observed, adolescence may involve many different experiences (Larson & Wilson, 2004; Saraswathi, 2006).

Rapid global change is altering the experience of adolescence, presenting new opportunities and challenges to young people's health and well-being. Around the world, adolescents' experiences may differ depending on their gender, families, schools, and peers (Brown & Larson, 2002; Larson & Wilson, 2004). However, some adolescent traditions remain the same in various cultures. Brad Brown and Reed Larson (2002) summarized some of these changes and traditions in the world's youth:

- *Health and well-being.* Adolescent health and well-being has improved in some areas but not in others. Overall, fewer adolescents around the world die from infectious diseases and malnutrition now than in the past (Call & others, 2002; World Health Organization, 2002). However, a number of adolescent health-compromising behaviors (especially illicit drug use and unprotected sex) are increasing in frequency (Blum & Nelson-Mmari, 2004). Extensive increases in the rates of HIV in adolescents have occurred in many sub-Saharan countries (World Health Organization, 2002).
- *Gender.* Around the world, the experiences of male and female adolescents continue to be quite different (Brown & Larson, 2002; Larson & Wilson, 2004). Except in a few areas, such as Japan, the Philippines, and Western countries, males have far greater access to educational opportunities than females do. In many countries, adolescent females have less freedom to pursue a variety of careers and engage in various leisure acts than males do. Gender differences in sexual expression are widespread, especially in India, Southeast Asia, Latin America, and Arab countries, where there are far more restrictions on the sexual activity of adolescent females than males. These gender differences do appear to be narrowing over time. In some countries, educational and career opportunities for women are expanding, and in some parts of the world, control over adolescent girls' romantic and sexual relationships is weakening.

Asian Indian adolescents in a marriage ceremony.

- *Family.* In some countries, adolescents grow up in closely knit families with extensive extended kin networks "that provide a web of connections and reinforce a traditional way of life" (Brown & Larson, 2002, p. 6). For example, in Arab countries, "adolescents are taught strict codes of conduct and loyalty" (p. 6). However, in Western countries such as the United States, adolescents are growing up in much larger numbers in divorced families and stepfamilies. Parenting in Western countries is less authoritarian than in the past.

  Other trends that are occurring in many countries around the world "include greater family mobility, migration to urban areas, family members working in distant cities or countries, smaller families, fewer extended-family households, and increases in mothers' employment" (Brown & Larson, 2002, p. 7). Unfortunately, many of these changes may reduce the ability of families to provide time and resources for adolescents.
- *School.* In general, the number of adolescents in school in developing countries is increasing. However, schools in many parts of the world—especially Africa, South Asia, and Latin America—still do not provide education to all adolescents. Indeed, there has been a decline in recent years in the percentage of Latin American adolescents who have access to secondary and higher education (Welti, 2002). Furthermore, many schools do not provide students with the skills they need to be successful in adult work.

Street youth in Rio De Janeiro.

- *Peers.* Some cultures give peers a stronger role in adolescence than others (Brown, 2004; Brown & Larson, 2002). In most Western nations, peers figure prominently in adolescents' lives, in some cases taking on responsibilities that are otherwise assumed by parents. Among street youth in South America, the peer network serves as a surrogate family that supports survival in dangerous and stressful settings. In other regions of the world, such as in Arab countries, peers have a very restrictive role, especially for girls (Booth, 2002).

In sum, adolescents' lives are characterized by a combination of change and tradition. Researchers have found both similarities and differences in the experiences of adolescents in different countries (Larson & Wilson, 2004). In Chapter 12, "Culture," we discuss these cross-cultural comparisons further.

**REVIEW AND REFLECT ◆ LEARNING GOAL 2**

**2 Discuss today's U.S. adolescents and adolescents around the world.**

***Review***
- What is the current status of today's adolescents? What is social policy? What are some important social policy issues concerning today's adolescents?
- How is adolescence changing for youth around the globe?

***Reflect***
- How are today's adolescents similar to, or different from, the adolescents of 20 to 30 years ago?

## 3 The Nature of Development

Processes and Periods | Developmental Transitions | Developmental Issues

In certain ways, each of us develops like all other individuals; in other ways, each of us is unique. Most of the time, our attention focuses on our individual uniqueness, but researchers who study development are drawn to our shared as well as our unique characteristics. As humans, we travel some common paths. Each of us—Leonardo da Vinci, Joan of Arc, George Washington, Martin Luther King, Jr., you, and I—walked at about the age of 1, talked at about the age of 2, engaged in fantasy play as a young child, and became more independent as a youth.

What do we mean when we speak of an individual's development? **Development** is the pattern of change that begins at conception and continues through the life span. Most development involves growth, although it also includes decay (as in death and dying). The pattern is complex because it is the product of several processes.

### Processes and Periods

Human development is determined by biological, cognitive, and socioemotional processes. It is often described in terms of periods.

**Biological, Cognitive, and Socioemotional Processes** **Biological processes** involve physical changes in an individual's body. Genes inherited from parents, the development of the brain, height and weight gains, advances in motor skills, and the hormonal changes of puberty all reflect biological processes. These biological processes are discussed extensively in Chapter 2.

**development** The pattern of change that begins at conception and continues through the life span. Most development involves growth, although it also includes decay (as in death and dying).

**biological processes** Physical changes in an individual's body.

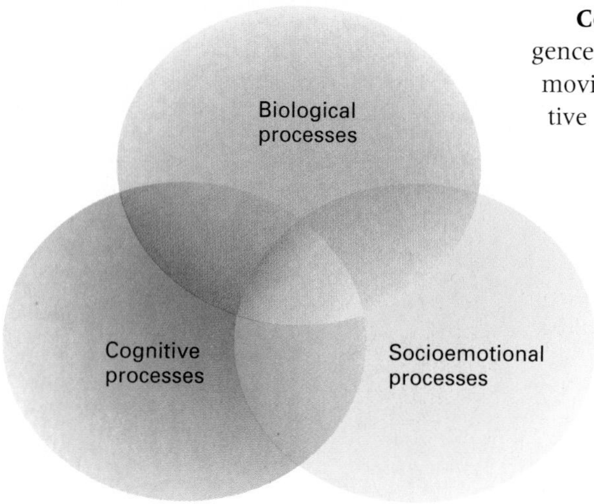


**FIGURE 1.3 Developmental Changes Are the Result of Biological, Cognitive, and Socioemotional Processes** These processes interact as individuals develop.

**Cognitive processes** involve changes in an individual's thinking and intelligence. Memorizing a poem, solving a math problem, and imagining what being a movie star would be like all reflect cognitive processes. Chapter 3 discusses cognitive processes in detail.

**Socioemotional processes** involve changes in an individual's emotions, personality, relationships with others, and social contexts. Talking back to parents, aggression toward peers, assertiveness, enjoyment of social events such as an adolescent's senior prom, and gender-role orientation all reflect the role of socioemotional processes. Chapters 4 through 12 focus on socioemotional processes in adolescent development.

Biological, cognitive, and socioemotional processes are intricately interwoven. Socioemotional processes shape cognitive processes; cognitive processes advance or restrict socioemotional processes; and biological processes influence cognitive processes. Although you read about these processes in separate chapters of the book, keep in mind that you are studying about the development of an integrated human being who has only one interdependent mind and body (see Figure 1.3).

**Periods of Development** Human development is commonly described in terms of periods. We consider developmental periods that occur in childhood, adolescence, and adulthood. Approximate age ranges are given for the periods to provide a general idea of when they begin and end.

**Childhood** Childhood includes the prenatal period, infancy, early childhood, and middle and late childhood.

The **prenatal period** is the time from conception to birth—approximately 9 months. It is a time of tremendous growth—from a single cell to an organism complete with a brain and behavioral capabilities.

**Infancy** is the developmental period that extends from birth to 18 or 24 months of age. Infancy is a time of extreme dependency on adults. Many psychological activities—for example, language, symbolic thought, sensorimotor coordination, social learning, and parent-child relationships—begin in this period.

**Early childhood** is the developmental period that extends from the end of infancy to about 5 or 6 years of age, sometimes called the preschool years. During this time, young children learn to become more self-sufficient and to care for themselves. They develop school readiness (following instructions, identifying letters) and spend many hours in play and with peers. First grade typically marks the end of early childhood.

**Middle and late childhood** is the developmental period that extends from the age of about 6 to 10 or 11 years of age. In this period, sometimes called the elementary school years, children master the fundamental skills of reading, writing, and arithmetic, and they are formally exposed to the larger world and its culture. Achievement becomes a central theme of the child's development, and self-control increases.

**Adolescence** As our developmental timetable suggests, considerable development and experience have occurred before an individual reaches adolescence. No girl or boy enters adolescence as a blank slate, with only a genetic code to determine thoughts, feelings, and behaviors. Rather, the combination of heredity, childhood experiences, and adolescent experiences determines the course of adolescent development. As you read through this book, keep in mind this continuity of development between childhood and adolescence.

A definition of adolescence requires a consideration not only of age but also of sociohistorical influences: recall our discussion of the inventionist view of adolescence. With the sociohistorical context in mind, we define **adolescence** as the period of transition between childhood and adulthood that involves biological, cognitive, and

**cognitive processes** Changes in an individual's thinking and intelligence.

**socioemotional processes** Changes in an individual's personality, emotions, relationships with other people, and social contexts.

**prenatal period** The time from conception to birth.

**infancy** The developmental period that extends from birth to 18 or 24 months of age.

**early childhood** The developmental period extending from the end of infancy to about 5 or 6 years of age; sometimes called the preschool years.

**middle and late childhood** The developmental period extending from about 6 to about 10 or 11 years of age; sometimes called the elementary school years.

**adolescence** The developmental period of transition from childhood to adulthood; it involves biological, cognitive, and socioemotional changes.

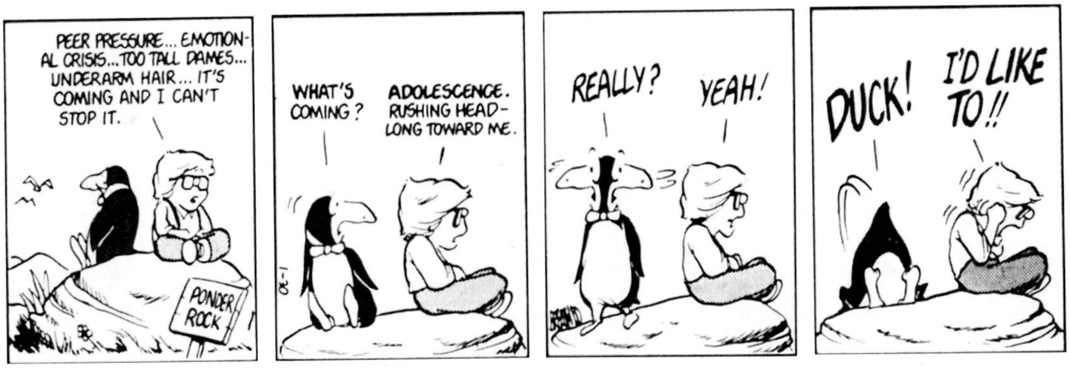




socioemotional changes. A key task of adolescence is preparation for adulthood. Indeed, the future of any culture hinges on how effective this preparation is.

Although the age range of adolescence can vary with cultural and historical circumstances, in the United States and most other cultures today, adolescence begins at approximately 10 to 13 years of age and ends between the ages of about 18 and 22. The biological, cognitive, and socioemotional changes of adolescence range from the development of sexual functions to abstract thinking processes to independence.

Increasingly, developmentalists describe adolescence in terms of early and late periods. **Early adolescence** corresponds roughly to the middle school or junior high school years and includes most pubertal change. **Late adolescence** refers approximately to the latter half of the second decade of life. Career interests, dating, and identity exploration are often more pronounced in late adolescence than in early adolescence. Researchers often specify whether their results generalize to all of adolescence or specifically to early or late adolescence.

The old view of adolescence was that it is a singular, uniform period of transition resulting in entry to the adult world. Current approaches emphasize a variety of transitions and events that define the period, as well as their timing and sequence (Wigfield, Byrnes, & Eccles, 2006). For instance, puberty and school events are seen as key transitions that signal entry into adolescence; completing school or taking one's first full-time job are key transitional events that signal an exit from adolescence and entry into adulthood.

Today, developmentalists do not believe that change ends with adolescence (Baltes, Lindenberger, & Staudinger, 2006; Schaie, 2007). Remember that development is defined as a lifelong process. Adolescence is part of the life course and as such is not an isolated period of development (Elder & Shanahan, 2006). Though it has some unique characteristics, what takes place during adolescence is connected with development and experiences in both childhood and adulthood (Collins & van Dulmen, 2006; Huston & others, 2006; Simpkins & others, 2006).

**Adulthood** Like childhood and adolescence, adulthood is not a homogeneous period of development. Developmentalists often describe three periods of adult development: early adulthood, middle adulthood, and late adulthood. **Early adulthood** usually begins in the late teens or early twenties and lasts through the thirties. It is a time of establishing personal and economic independence, and career development intensifies.

**Middle adulthood** begins at approximately 35 to 45 years of age and ends at some point between approximately 55 and 65 years of age. This period is especially important in the lives of adolescents whose parents are either in, or about to enter, this adult period. Middle adulthood is a time of increasing interest in transmitting values to the next generation, increased reflection about the meaning of life, and enhanced concern about one's body. In Chapter 8, we see how the maturation of both adolescents and parents contributes to the parent-adolescent relationship.

**early adolescence** The developmental period that corresponds roughly to the middle school or junior high school years and includes most pubertal change.

**late adolescence** Approximately the latter half of the second decade of life. Career interests, dating, and identity exploration are often more pronounced in late adolescence than in early adolescence.

**early adulthood** The developmental period beginning in the late teens or early twenties and lasting through the thirties.

**middle adulthood** The developmental period that is entered at about 35 to 45 years of age and exited at about 55 to 65 years of age.

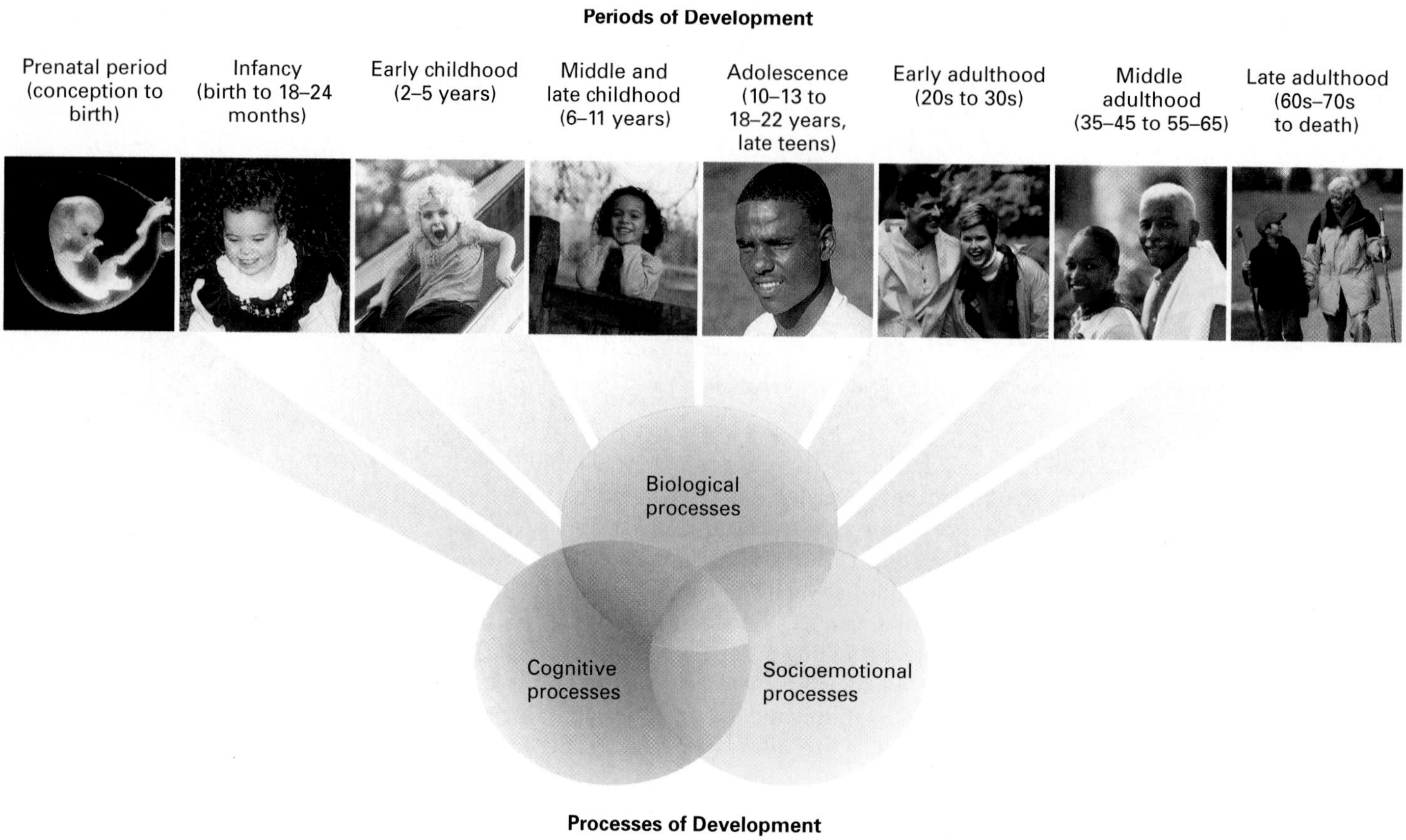


**FIGURE 1.4 Processes and Periods of Development** The unfolding of life's periods of development is influenced by the interaction of biological, cognitive, and socioemotional processes.

Eventually, the rhythm and meaning of the human life span wend their way to **late adulthood,** the developmental period that lasts from approximately 60 or 70 years of age until death. This is a time of adjustment to decreasing strength and health, and to retirement and reduced income. Reviewing one's life and adapting to changing social roles also characterize late adulthood, as do lessened responsibility and increased freedom. Figure 1.4 summarizes the developmental periods in the human life span and their approximate age ranges.

## Developmental Transitions

Developmental transitions are often important junctures in people's lives. Such transitions include moving from the prenatal period to birth and infancy, from infancy to early childhood, and from early childhood to middle and late childhood. For our purposes, two important transitions are from childhood to adolescence and from adolescence to adulthood. Let's explore these transitions.

### Childhood to Adolescence

The transition from childhood to adolescence involves a number of biological, cognitive, and socioemotional changes (Harold, Colarossi, & Mercier, 2007). Among the biological changes are the growth spurt, hormonal changes, and sexual maturation that come with puberty. In early adolescence, changes take place in the brain that allow for more advanced thinking. Also at this time, adolescents begin to stay up later and sleep later in the morning.

Among the cognitive changes that occur during the transition from childhood to adolescence are increases in abstract, idealistic, and logical thinking. As they make this transition, adolescents begin to think in more egocentric ways, often sensing that they are onstage, unique, and invulnerable. In response to these changes, parents place more responsibility for decision making on the young adolescents' shoulders.

Among the socioemotional changes adolescents undergo are a quest for independence, conflict with parents, and a desire to spend more time with peers. Con-

**late adulthood** The developmental period that lasts from about 60 to 70 years of age until death.

**emerging adulthood** The developmental period occurring from approximately 18 to 25 years of age; this transitional period between adolescence and adulthood is characterized by experimentation and exploration.

Developmental transitions from childhood to adolescence involve biological, cognitive, and socioemotional changes. *What are some of these changes?*

versations with friends become more intimate and include more self-disclosure. As children enter adolescence, they attend schools that are larger and more impersonal than their neighborhood grade schools. Achievement becomes more serious business, and academic challenges increase. Also at this time, increased sexual maturation produces a much greater interest in romantic relationships. Young adolescents also experience greater mood swings than they did when they were children.

In sum, the transition from childhood to adolescence is complex and multidimensional, involving change in many different aspects of an individual's life (Wigfield, Byrnes, & Eccles, 2006). Negotiating this transition successfully requires considerable adaptation and thoughtful, sensitive support from caring adults.

**Adolescence to Adulthood** Another important transition occurs from adolescence to adulthood (Arnett & Tanner, 2006). It has been said that adolescence begins in biology and ends in culture. That is, the transition from childhood to adolescence begins with the onset of pubertal maturation, whereas the transition from adolescence to adulthood is determined by cultural standards and experiences.

**Emerging Adulthood** Recently, the transition from adolescence to adulthood has been referred to as **emerging adulthood**, approximately 18 to 25 years of age (Arnett, 2000, 2004, 2006, 2007). Experimentation and exploration characterize the emerging adult. At this point in their development, many individuals are still exploring which career path they want to follow, what they want their identity to be, and which lifestyle they want to adopt (for example, single, cohabiting, or married).

**Key Features** Jeffrey Arnett (2006) recently concluded that five key features characterize emerging adulthood:

- *Identity exploration, especially in love and work.* Emerging adulthood is the time during which key changes in identity take place for many individuals (Kroger, 2007).
- *Instability.* Residential changes peak during early adulthood, a time during which there also is often instability in love, work, and education.

## *Through the Eyes of Emerging Adults*

### CHRIS BARNARD

Emerging adult Chris Barnard is a single 24-year-old. Two years ago he moved back in with his parents, worked as a temp, and thought about his next step in life. One of the temp jobs became permanent. He now works with a trade association in Washington, D.C. With the exception of technology, he says that his life is similar to what his parents' lives must have been like as they made the transition to adulthood. Chris' living arrangements reflect the "instability" characteristic of emerging adulthood. While in college, he changed dorms each year, then as a senior moved to an off-campus apartment. Following college, he moved back home, then moved to another apartment, and now is in yet another apartment. In Chris' words, "This is going to be the longest stay I've had since I went to college. . . . I've sort of settled in" (Jayson, 2006, p. 2D).

Chris Barnard, 24-year-old emerging adult, in the apartment he shares with two roommates.

- *Self-focused.* According to Arnett (2006, p. 10), emerging adults "are self-focused in the sense that they have little in the way of social obligations, little in the way of duties and commitments to others, which leaves them with a great deal of autonomy in running their own lives."
- *Feeling in-between.* Many emerging adults don't consider themselves adolescents or full-fledged adults.
- *The age of possibilities, a time when individuals have an opportunity to transform their lives.* Arnett (2006) describes two ways in which emerging adulthood is the age of possibilities: (1) many emerging adults are optimistic about their future, and (2) for emerging adults who have experienced difficult times while growing up, emerging adulthood presents an opportunity to direct their lives in a more positive direction (Masten, Obradovic, & Burt, 2006; Schulenberg & Zarrett, 2006).

Does life get better for individuals when they become emerging adults? To read about this question, see the *Health and Well-Being* interlude.

## Health and Well-Being

### CHANGES IN EMERGING ADULTHOOD

What is the health and well-being of individuals in emerging adulthood compared to adolescence? John Schulenberg and his colleagues (Johnston & others, 2004; Schulenberg & Zarrett, 2006) have examined this question. For the most part, life does get better for most emerging adults. For example, Figure 1.5 shows a steady increase in self-reported well-being from 18 years of age through 26 years of age. Figure 1.6 indicates that risk taking decreases during the same time frame.

Why does the health and well-being of emerging adults improve over their adolescent levels? One possibility is the increasing choices individuals have in their daily living and life decisions during emerging adulthood. This increase can lead to more opportunities for individuals to exercise self-control in their lives. Also, as we indicated earlier, emerging adulthood provides an opportunity for individuals who engaged in problem behavior during adolescence to get their lives together. However, the lack of structure and support that often characterizes emerging adulthood can produce a downturn in health and well-being for some individuals (Schulenberg & Zarrett, 2006).

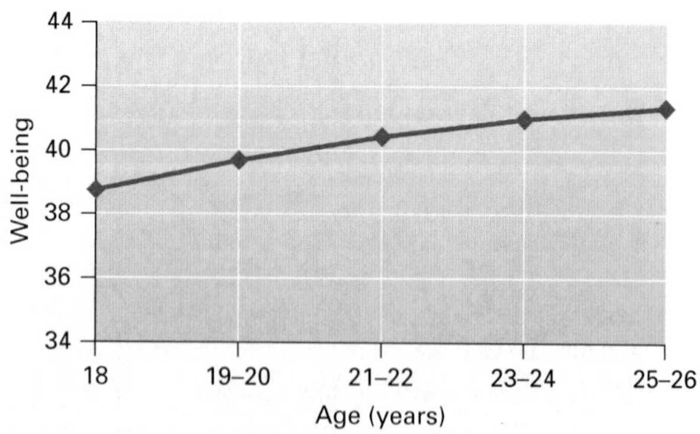


**FIGURE 1.5 Well-Being Through Emerging Adulthood**
*Note:* Scores based on a combination of self-esteem (8 items), self-efficacy (5 items), and social support (6 items); possible responses ranged from disagree (1) to agree (5).

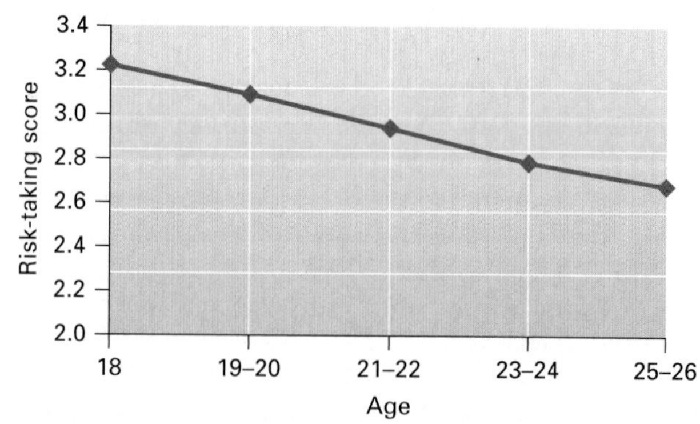


**FIGURE 1.6 Risk Taking Through Emerging Adulthood**
*Note:* The two Risk-Taking Scale items ranged from 1 (disagree) to 5 (agree). The risk-taking score was the average of the 2 items that assessed whether the emerging adult got a kick out of doing things that are a little dangerous and enjoyed doing something a little risky.

**Becoming an Adult** Determining just when an individual becomes an adult is difficult. The most widely recognized marker of entry into adulthood is when an individual takes a more or less permanent, full-time job, which usually happens when an individual finishes school—high school for some, college for others, graduate or professional school for still others. However, other criteria are far from clear. Economic independence is considered one marker of adult status, but developing it is often a long, drawn-out process. Increasingly, college graduates are returning to live with their parents as they seek to get their feet on the ground financially. About 40 percent of individuals in their late teens to early twenties move back into their parents' home at least once (Goldscheider & Goldscheider, 1999).

Self-responsibility and independent decision making are other possible markers of adulthood. Indeed, in one study, adolescents cited taking responsibility for themselves and making independent decisions as the markers of entry into adulthood (Scheer & Unger, 1994). In another study, more than 70 percent of college students said that being an adult means accepting responsibility for the consequences of one's actions; deciding on one's own beliefs and values; and establishing a relationship equal with parents (Arnett, 1995).

Is there a specific age at which individuals become an adult? One study examined emerging adults' perception of whether they were adults (Arnett, 2000). The majority of the 18- to 25-year-olds responded neither "yes" nor "no," but "in some respects yes, in some respects no" (see Figure 1.7). In this study, not until the late twenties and early thirties did a clear majority of respondents agree that they had reached adulthood. Thus, these emerging adults saw themselves as neither adolescents nor full-fledged adults, reflecting the characteristic of emerging adulthood we described earlier—feeling in-between. In another study, however, 21-year-olds said that they had reached adult status when they were 18 to 19 years old (Scheer, 1996). In this study, both social status factors (financial status and graduation/education) and cognitive factors (being responsible and making independent decisions) were cited as markers for reaching adulthood. Clearly, reaching adulthood involves more than just attaining a specific chronological age (Cohen & others, 2003).

At some point in the late teens through the early twenties, then, individuals reach adulthood. In becoming an adult, they accept responsibility for themselves, become capable of making independent decisions, and gain financial independence from their parents (Arnett, 2004, 2006).

What we have said so far about the determinants of adult status mainly addresses individuals in industrialized societies, especially the United States (Nelson, Badger, & Wu, 2004). In developing countries, marriage is often a more significant marker for entry into adulthood than in the United States, and it usually occurs much earlier than in the United States (Arnett, 2007; Davis & Davis, 1989). Thus, some developmentalists argue that the term emerging adulthood applies more to Western countries, such as the United States and European countries, and some Asian countries, such as Japan, but less to developing countries (Arnett, 2004, 2007).

Contextual variations in emerging adulthood also may occur in cultures within a country. For example, in the United States, "Mormons marry early and begin having children . . . so they have a briefer period of emerging adulthood before taking on adult roles" (Arnett, 2004, p. 22). Further, in some countries such as China and India, emerging adulthood is more likely to occur in urban areas but less so in rural areas because young people in the urban areas of these countries "marry later, have children later,

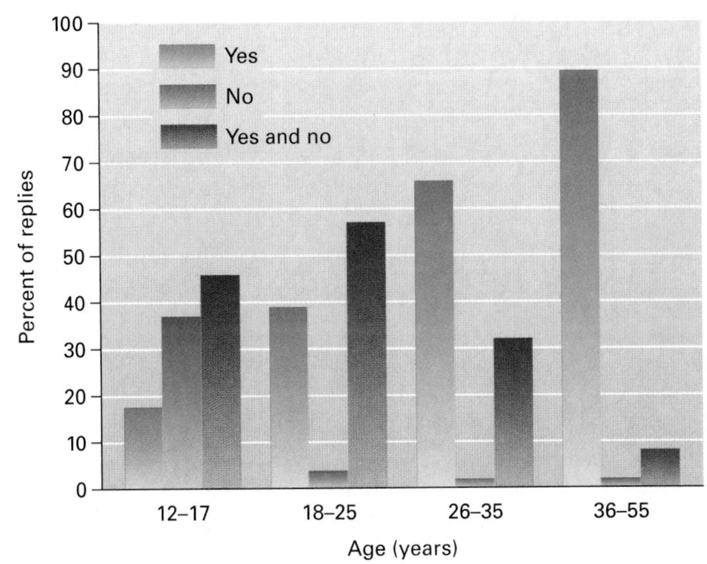


**FIGURE 1.7 Self-Perceptions of Adult Status** In one study, individuals were asked, "Do you feel that you have reached adult status?" and were given a choice of answering "yes," "no," or "in some respects yes, in some respects no" (Arnett, 2000). As indicated in the graph, the majority of the emerging adults (18 to 25) responded "in some respects yes, in some respects no."

*What characterizes emerging adulthood? Even when emerging adults have experienced a troubled childhood and adolescence, what are some factors that can help them become competent?*

obtain more education, and have a greater range of occupational and recreational opportunities" (Arnett, 2004, p. 23).

**Resilience** At the beginning of the chapter, you read about the captivating story of Michael Maddaus who got his life together as an emerging adult following a troubled childhood and adolescence. Michael Maddaus was resilient. What do we mean by the term *resilience?* **Resilience** refers to adapting positively and achieving successful outcomes in the face of significant risks and adverse circumstances (Borkowski & others, 2007; Masten, Obradovic, & Burt, 2006). In Project Competence, Ann Masten and her colleagues (Masten, Obradovic, & Burt, 2006) have examined the resilience of individuals from childhood through adulthood. They found that adults who experienced considerable adversity while growing up—but became competent young adults—were characterized by certain individual and contextual factors. Competence was assessed in such areas as achievement, conduct, and social relationships. In emerging adulthood (assessed at 17 to 23 years of age), individuals who became competent after experiencing difficulties while growing up were more intelligent, experienced higher parenting quality, and were less likely to have grown up in poverty or low-income circumstances than their counterparts who did not become competent as emerging adults.

A further analysis focused on individuals who were still showing maladaptive patterns in emerging adulthood but had gotten their lives together by the time they were in the late twenties and early thirties. The three characteristics shared by these "late-bloomers" were support by adults, being planful, and showing positive aspects of autonomy. In other longitudinal research (Clausen, 1991; Elder, 1999; Rutter, 2000; Werner & Smith, 1982), "military service, marriage and romantic relationships, higher education, religion affiliations, and work opportunities may provide turning-point opportunities for changing the life course during emerging adulthood" (Masten, Obradovic, & Burt, 2006, p. 179).

## Developmental Issues

**resilience** Adapting positively and achieving successful outcomes in the face of significant risks and adverse circumstances.

Is development due more to nature (heredity) or to nurture (environment)? Is it more continuous and smooth or discontinuous and stagelike? Is it due more to early experience or to later experience? These are three important issues raised in the study of adolescent development.

**Nature and Nurture** The **nature-nurture issue** involves the debate about whether development is primarily influenced by nature or nurture. *Nature* refers to an organism's biological inheritance, *nurture* to its environmental experiences. "Nature" proponents claim that the most important influence on development is biological inheritance. "Nurture" proponents claim that environmental experiences are the most important influence.

According to the nature advocates, just as a sunflower grows in an orderly way—unless flattened by an unfriendly environment—so does the human grow in an orderly way. The range of environments can be vast, but the nature approach argues that the genetic blueprint produces commonalities in growth and development. We walk before we talk, speak one word before two words, grow rapidly in infancy and less so in early childhood, experience a rush of sexual hormones in puberty, reach the peak of our physical strength in late adolescence and early adulthood, and then physically decline. The nature proponents acknowledge that extreme environments—those that are psychologically barren or hostile—can depress development. However, they believe that basic growth tendencies are genetically wired into humans.

By contrast, other psychologists emphasize the importance of nurture, or environmental experiences, in development. Experiences run the gamut from the individual's biological environment—nutrition, medical care, drugs, and physical accidents—to the social environment—family, peers, schools, community, media, and culture.

Some adolescent development researchers believe that, historically, too much emphasis has been placed on the biological changes of puberty as determinants of adolescent psychological development (Montemayor & Flannery, 1991). They recognize that biological change is an important dimension of the transition from childhood to adolescence, one that is found in all primate species and in all cultures throughout the world. However, they believe that social contexts (nurture) play important roles in adolescent psychological development as well, roles that until recently have not been given adequate attention (Powell, 2006; Selman & Dray, 2006).

**FIGURE 1.8 Continuity and Discontinuity in Development** Is human development like a seedling gradually growing into a giant oak? Or is it more like a caterpillar suddenly becoming a butterfly?

**Continuity and Discontinuity** Think for a moment about your development. Was your growth into the person you are today gradual, like the slow, cumulative growth of a seedling into a giant oak? Or did you experience sudden, distinct changes in your growth, like the remarkable change from a caterpillar into a butterfly (see Figure 1.8)? The **continuity-discontinuity issue** focuses on the extent to which development involves gradual, cumulative change (continuity) or distinct stages (discontinuity). For the most part, developmentalists who emphasize experience have described development as a gradual, continuous process; those who emphasize nature have described development as a series of distinct stages.

In terms of continuity, a child's first word, while seemingly an abrupt, discontinuous event, is actually the result of weeks and months of growth and practice. Similarly, puberty, while also seeming to be abrupt and discontinuous, is actually a gradual process that occurs over several years.

In terms of discontinuity, each person is described as passing through a sequence of stages in which change is qualitatively, rather than quantitatively, different. As the oak moves from seedling to giant tree, it becomes more oak—its development is continuous. As a caterpillar changes into a butterfly, it does not become more caterpillar; it becomes a different kind of organism—its development is discontinuous. For example, at some point a child moves from not being able to think abstractly about the world to being able to. This is a qualitative, discontinuous change in development, not a quantitative, continuous change.

**Early and Later Experience** Another important debate is the **early-later experience issue,** which focuses on the degree to which early experiences (especially

**nature-nurture issue** The issue involving the debate about whether development is primarily influenced by nature or nurture. Nature refers to an organism's biological inheritance, nurture to its environmental experiences.

**continuity-discontinuity issue** The issue regarding whether development involves gradual, cumulative change (continuity) or distinct stages (discontinuity).

**early-later experience issue** This issue focuses on the degree to which early experiences (especially early in childhood) or later experiences are the key determinants of development.

*To what extent is an adolescent's development due to earlier or later experiences?*

early in childhood) or later experiences are the key determinants of development (Caspi & Shiner, 2006; Laible & Thompson, 2007). That is, if infants or young children experience negative, stressful circumstances in their lives, can those experiences be overcome by later, more positive experiences in adolescence? Or are the early experiences so critical, possibly because they are the infant's first, prototypical experiences, that they cannot be overridden by a later, more enriched environment in childhood or adolescence?

The early-later experience issue has a long history, and developmentalists continue to debate it. Some believe that unless infants experience warm, nurturant caregiving in the first year or so of life, their development will never be optimal (Bowlby, 1989; Sroufe, 2007). Plato was sure that infants who were rocked frequently became better athletes. Nineteenth-century New England ministers told parents in Sunday sermons that the way they handled their infants would determine their children's future character. The emphasis on the importance of early experience rests on the belief that each life is an unbroken trail on which a psychological quality can be traced back to its origin.

The early-experience doctrine contrasts with the later-experience view that, rather than achieving statuelike permanence after change in infancy, our development continues to be like the ebb and flow of a river. The later-experience advocates argue that children and adolescents are malleable throughout development and that later sensitive caregiving is just as important as earlier sensitive caregiving. A number of life-span developmentalists, who focus on the entire life span rather than only on child development, stress that too little attention has been given to later experiences in development (Birren, 2007; Elder & Shanahan, 2006). They accept that early experiences are important contributors to development, but no more important than later experiences. Jerome Kagan (1992, 2000) points out that even children who show the qualities of an inhibited temperament, which is linked to heredity, have the capacity to change their behavior. In his research, almost one-third of a group of children who had an inhibited temperament at 2 years of age were not unusually shy or fearful when they were 4 years of age (Kagan & Snidman, 1991).

People in Western cultures, especially those steeped in the Freudian belief that the key experiences in development are children's relationships with their parents in the first five years of life, have tended to support the idea that early experiences are more important than later experiences (Chan, 1963). In contrast, the majority of people in the world do not share this belief. For example, people in many Asian countries believe that experiences occurring after about 6 to 7 years of age are more important aspects of development than earlier experiences are. This stance stems from the long-standing belief in Eastern cultures that children's reasoning skills begin to develop in important ways in the middle childhood years.

**Evaluating the Developmental Issues** As we consider further these three salient developmental issues—nature and nurture, continuity and discontinuity, and early and later experience—it is important to realize that most developmentalists recognize that it is unwise to take an extreme position on these issues. Development is not all nature or all nurture, not all continuity or discontinuity, and not all early experience or all later experience. Nature and nurture, continuity and discontinuity, and early and later experience all affect our development throughout the human life span. For example, in considering the nature-nurture issue, the key to development is the interaction of nature and nurture rather than either factor alone (Gottlieb, 2007). An individual's cognitive development, for instance, is the result of heredity-environment interaction, not heredity or environment alone. Much more about the role of heredity-environment interaction appears in Chapter 2.

Although most developmentalists do not take extreme positions on the developmental issues we have discussed, this consensus has not meant the absence of spirited debate about how strongly development is determined by these factors (Caspi & Shiner, 2006; Kagan & Fox, 2006; Rutter, 2007; Plomin, DeFries, & Fulker, 2007). Consider adolescents who, as children, experienced poverty, parental neglect, and poor schooling. Could enriched experiences in adolescence overcome the "deficits" they encountered earlier in development? The answers developmentalists give to such questions reflect their stance on the issues of nature and nurture, continuity and discontinuity, and early and later experiences. The answers also influence public policy about adolescents and how each of us lives throughout the human life span.

## REVIEW AND REFLECT ◆ LEARNING GOAL 3

### 3 Summarize the developmental processes, periods, transitions, and issues related to adolescence.

***Review***

- What are the key processes involved in adolescent development? What are the main childhood, adolescent, and adult periods of development?
- What is the transition from childhood to adolescence like? What is the transition from adolescence to adulthood like?
- What are three important developmental issues?

***Reflect***

- As you go through this course, ask yourself questions about how you experienced particular aspects of adolescence. Be curious. Ask your friends and classmates about their experiences in adolescence and compare them with yours. For example, ask them how they experienced the transition from childhood to adolescence. Also ask them how they experienced, or are experiencing, the transition from adolescence to adulthood.

# 4 The Science of Adolescent Development

Science and the Scientific Method | Theories of Adolescent Development | Research in Adolescent Development

How can we answer questions about the roles of nature and nurture, stability and change, and continuity and discontinuity in development? How can we determine, for example, whether an adolescent's achievement in school changes or stays the same from childhood through adolescence, or how can we find out whether positive experiences in adolescence can repair the harm done by neglectful or abusive parenting in childhood? To effectively answer such questions, we need to turn to science.

## Science and the Scientific Method

Some individuals have difficulty thinking of adolescent development as being a science in the same way that physics, chemistry, and biology are sciences. Can a discipline that studies pubertal change, parent-adolescent relationships, or adolescent thinking be equated with disciplines that investigate how gravity works and the molecular structure of compounds? The answer is yes, because science is not defined by what it investigates but by how it investigates. Whether you are studying photosynthesis, Saturn's moons, or adolescent development, it is the way you study the subject that matters.

In taking a scientific path to study adolescent development, it is important to follow the *scientific method,* which is essentially a four-step process: (1) conceptualize a process or problem to be studied, (2) collect research information (data), (3) analyze data, and (4) draw conclusions.

In step 1, when researchers are formulating a problem to study, they often draw on theories and develop hypotheses. A **theory** is an interrelated, coherent set of ideas that helps to explain phenomena and make predictions. It may suggest **hypotheses,** which are specific assertions and predictions that can be tested. For example, a theory on mentoring might state that sustained support and guidance from an adult makes a difference in the lives of children from impoverished backgrounds because the mentor gives the children opportunities to observe and imitate the behavior and strategies of the mentor.

Sigmund Freud, the architect of psychoanalytic theory.

**theory** An interrelated, coherent set of ideas that helps explain phenomena and make predictions.

**hypotheses** Specific assertions and predictions that can be tested.

**psychoanalytic theories** Describe development as primarily unconscious and heavily colored by emotion. Behavior is merely a surface characteristic, and the symbolic workings of the mind have to be analyzed to understand behavior. Early experiences with parents are emphasized.

## Theories of Adolescent Development

This section discusses key aspects of four theoretical orientations to development: psychoanalytic, cognitive, behavioral and social cognitive, and ecological. Each contributes an important piece to the adolescent development puzzle. Although the theories disagree about certain aspects of development, many of their ideas are complementary rather than contradictory. Together they let us see the total landscape of adolescent development in all its richness.

### Psychoanalytic Theories

**Psychoanalytic theories** describe development as primarily unconscious (beyond awareness) and heavily colored by emotion. Psychoanalytic theorists emphasize that behavior is merely a surface characteristic and that a true understanding of development requires analyzing the symbolic meanings of behavior and the deep inner workings of the mind. Psychoanalytic theorists also stress that early experiences with parents extensively shape development. These characteristics are highlighted in the main psychoanalytic theory, that of Sigmund Freud (1856–1939).

**Freud's Theory** As Freud listened to, probed, and analyzed his patients, he became convinced that their problems were the result of experiences early in life. He thought

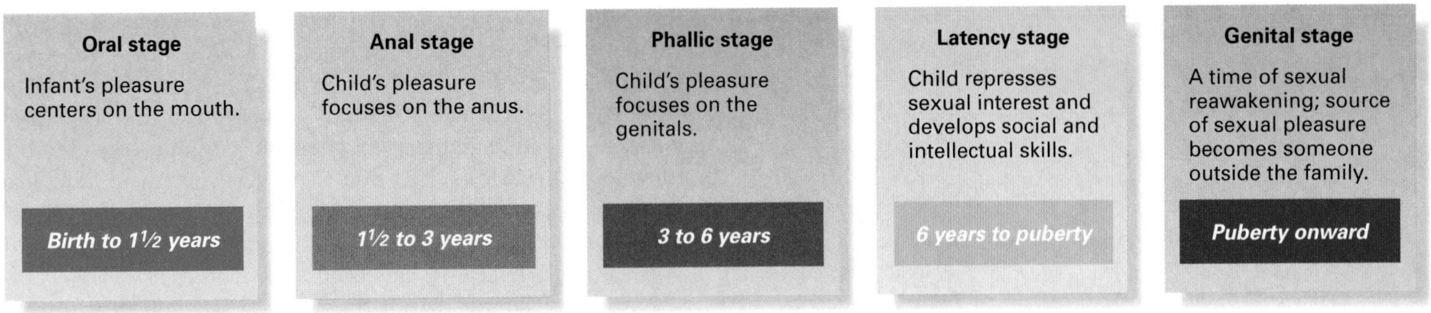

Oral stage
Infant's pleasure centers on the mouth.
Birth to 1½ years
Anal stage
Child's pleasure focuses on the anus.
1½ to 3 years
Phallic stage
Child's pleasure focuses on the genitals.
3 to 6 years
Latency stage
Child represses sexual interest and develops social and intellectual skills.
6 years to puberty
Genital stage
A time of sexual reawakening; source of sexual pleasure becomes someone outside the family.
Puberty onward


**FIGURE 1.9** **Freudian Stages**

that as children grow up, their focus of pleasure and sexual impulses shifts from the mouth to the anus and eventually to the genitals. As a result, according to Freud's theory, we go through five stages of psychosexual development: oral, anal, phallic, latency, and genital (see Figure 1.9). Our adult personality, Freud (1917) claimed, is determined by the way we resolve conflicts between sources of pleasure at each stage and the demands of reality.

Freud stressed that adolescents' lives are filled with tension and conflict. To reduce the tension, he thought adolescents bury their conflicts in their unconscious mind. Freud said that even trivial behaviors can become significant when the unconscious forces behind them are revealed. A twitch, a doodle, a joke, a smile—each might betray unconscious conflict. For example, 17-year-old Barbara, while kissing and hugging Tom, exclaims, "Oh, *Jeff,* I love you so much." Repelled, Tom explodes: "Why did you call me Jeff? I thought you didn't think about him anymore. We need to have a talk!" You probably can remember times when a Freudian slip revealed your own unconscious motives.

Freud (1917) divided personality into three structures: the id, the ego, and the superego. The *id* consists of instincts, which are an individual's reservoir of psychic energy. In Freud's view, the id is totally unconscious; it has no contact with reality. As children experience the demands and constraints of reality, a new structure of personality emerges—the *ego,* which deals with the demands of reality. The ego is called the "executive branch" of personality because it makes rational decisions.

The id and the ego have no morality—they do not take into account whether something is right or wrong. The *superego* is the moral branch of personality. The superego takes into account whether something is right or wrong. Think of the superego as what we often refer to as our "conscience." You probably are beginning to sense that both the id and the superego make life rough for the ego. Your ego might say, "I will have sex only occasionally and be sure to take the proper precautions because I don't want a child to interfere with the development of my career." However, your id is saying, "I want to be satisfied; sex is pleasurable." Your superego is at work, too: "I feel guilty about having sex."

Freud considered personality to be like an iceberg. Most of personality exists below our level of awareness, just as the massive part of an iceberg is beneath the water's surface. The ego resolves conflict between its reality demands, the id's wishes, and the superego's constraints through *defense mechanisms.* These are unconscious methods of distorting reality that the ego uses to protect itself from the anxiety produced by the conflicting demands of the three personality structures. When the ego senses that the id's demands may cause harm, anxiety develops, alerting the ego to resolve the conflict by means of defense mechanisms.

According to Freud, *repression* is the most powerful and pervasive defense mechanism. It pushes unacceptable id impulses out of awareness and back into the unconscious mind. Repression is the foundation on which all other defense mechanisms rest, since the goal of every defense mechanism is to repress, or push, threatening

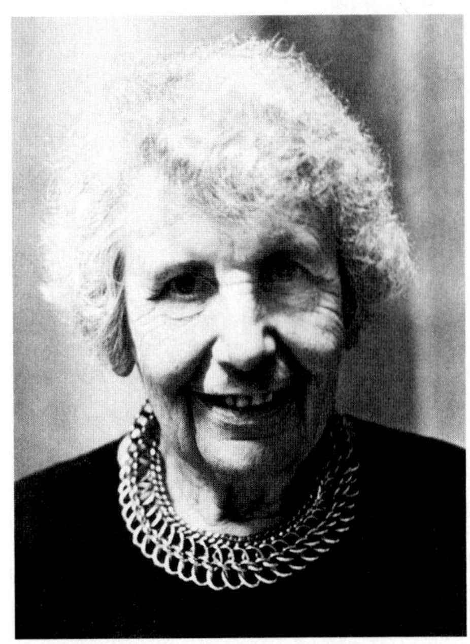

Anna Freud, Sigmund Freud's daughter. *How did her view differ from her father's?*

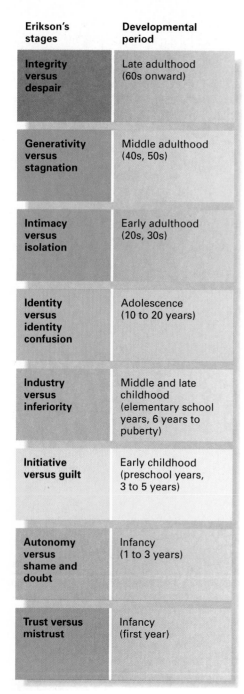

| Erikson's stages | Developmental period |
|---|---|
| Integrity versus despair | Late adulthood (60s onward) |
| Generativity versus stagnation | Middle adulthood (40s, 50s) |
| Intimacy versus isolation | Early adulthood (20s, 30s) |
| Identity versus identity confusion | Adolescence (10 to 20 years) |
| Industry versus inferiority | Middle and late childhood (elementary school years, 6 years to puberty) |
| Initiative versus guilt | Early childhood (preschool years, 3 to 5 years) |
| Autonomy versus shame and doubt | Infancy (1 to 3 years) |
| Trust versus mistrust | Infancy (first year) |

**FIGURE 1.10** Erikson's Eight Life-Span Stages

**Erikson's theory** Includes eight stages of human development. Each stage consists of a unique developmental task that confronts individuals with a crisis that must be faced.

impulses out of awareness. Freud thought that early childhood experiences, many of which he believed are sexually laden, are too threatening and stressful for people to deal with consciously, so they repress them.

However, Peter Blos (1989), a British psychoanalyst, and Anna Freud (1966), Sigmund Freud's daughter, argued that defense mechanisms provide considerable insight into adolescent development. Blos stated that regression during adolescence is actually not defensive at all, but rather an integral, normal, inevitable, and universal aspect of puberty. The nature of regression may vary from one adolescent to the next. It may involve compliance, and cleanliness, or it may involve a sudden return to the passiveness that characterized the adolescent's behavior during childhood.

Anna Freud (1966) developed the idea that defense mechanisms are the key to understanding adolescent adjustment. She believed that the problems of adolescence are not rooted in the id, or instinctual forces, but in the "love objects" in the adolescent's past. Attachment to these love objects, usually parents, is carried forward from the infant years and merely toned down or inhibited during the childhood years, she argued. During adolescence, these urges might be reawakened, or, worse, newly acquired urges might combine with them.

Bear in mind that defense mechanisms are unconscious; adolescents are not aware they are using them to protect their egos and reduce anxiety. When used temporarily and in moderation, defense mechanisms are not necessarily unhealthy. However, defense mechanisms should not be allowed to dominate an individual's behavior and prevent a person from facing reality.

Sigmund Freud's theory has been significantly revised by a number of other psychoanalytic theorists as well. Many contemporary psychoanalytic theorists stress that he overemphasized sexual instincts; they place more emphasis on cultural experiences as determinants of an individual's development. Unconscious thought remains a central theme, but most contemporary psychoanalysts argue that conscious thought plays a greater role than Freud envisioned. Next, we outline the ideas of an important revisionist of Freud's ideas—Erik Erikson.

**Erikson's Psychosocial Theory** Erik Erikson recognized Freud's contributions but believed that Freud misjudged some important dimensions of human development. For one thing, Erikson (1950, 1968) said we develop in *psychosocial* stages, rather than in *psychosexual* stages, as Freud maintained. According to Freud, the primary motivation for human behavior is sexual in nature; according to Erikson, it is social and reflects a desire to affiliate with other people. According to Freud, our basic personality is shaped in the first five years of life; according to Erikson, developmental change occurs throughout the life span. Thus, in terms of the early- versus later-experience issue described earlier in the chapter, Freud argued that early experience is far more important than later experiences, whereas Erikson emphasized the importance of both early and later experiences.

In **Erikson's theory,** eight stages of development unfold as we go through life (see Figure 1.10). At each stage, a unique developmental task confronts individuals with a crisis that must be resolved. According to Erikson, this crisis is not a catastrophe but a turning point marked by both increased vulnerability and enhanced potential. The more successfully an individual resolves the crises, the healthier development will be (Hopkins, 2000).

*Trust versus mistrust* is Erikson's first psychosocial stage, which is experienced in the first year of life. Trust in infancy sets the stage for a life long expectation that the world will be a good and pleasant place to live.

*Autonomy versus shame and doubt* is Erikson's second stage, occurring in late infancy and toddlerhood. After gaining trust, infants begin to discover that their behavior is their own, and they start to assert their independence.

*Initiative versus guilt,* Erikson's third stage of development, occurs during the preschool years. As preschool children encounter a widening social world, they face new challenges that require active, purposeful, responsible behavior. Feelings of guilt may arise, though, if the child is irresponsible and is made to feel too anxious.

*Industry versus inferiority* is Erikson's fourth developmental stage, occurring approximately in the elementary school years. Children now need to direct their energy toward mastering knowledge and intellectual skills. The negative outcome is that the child can develop a sense of inferiority—feeling incompetent and unproductive.

During the adolescent years, individuals face finding out who they are, what they are all about, and where they are going in life. This is Erikson's fifth developmental stage, *identity versus identity confusion.* If adolescents explore roles in a healthy manner and arrive at a positive path to follow in life, then they achieve a positive identity; if not, then identity confusion reigns.

*Intimacy versus isolation* is Erikson's sixth developmental stage, which individuals experience during the early adulthood years. At this time, individuals face the developmental task of forming intimate relationships. If young adults form healthy friendships and an intimate relationship with another, intimacy will be achieved; if not, isolation will result.

*Generativity versus stagnation,* Erikson's seventh developmental stage, occurs during middle adulthood. By *generativity* Erikson means primarily a concern for helping the younger generation to develop and lead useful lives. The feeling of having done nothing to help the next generation is stagnation.

*Integrity versus despair* is Erikson's eighth and final stage of development, which individuals experience in late adulthood. During this stage, a person reflects on the past. If the person's life review reveals a life well spent, integrity will be achieved; if not, the retrospective glances likely will yield doubt or gloom—the despair Erikson described.

Erik Erikson with his wife, Joan, an artist. Erikson generated one of the most important developmental theories of the twentieth century.

**Evaluating Psychoanalytic Theories** Contributions of psychoanalytic theories include an emphasis on a developmental framework, family relationships, and unconscious aspects of the mind. Criticisms include a lack of scientific support, too much emphasis on sexual underpinnings, and an image of people that is too negative.

**Cognitive Theories** Whereas psychoanalytic theories stress the importance of the unconscious, cognitive theories emphasize conscious thoughts. Three important cognitive theories are Piaget's cognitive developmental theory, Vygotsky's sociocultural cognitive theory, and information-processing theory.

**Piaget's Cognitive Developmental Theory** **Piaget's theory** states that individuals actively construct their understanding of the world and go through four stages of cognitive development. Two processes underlie this cognitive construction of the world: organization and adaptation. To make sense of our world, adolescents organize their experiences. For example, they separate important ideas from less important ideas, and connect one idea to another. In addition to organizing their observations and experiences, they *adapt,* adjusting to new environmental demands (Mooney, 2006).

Piaget (1954) also maintained that people go through four stages in understanding the world (see Figure 1.11). Each stage is age-related and consists of a distinct way of thinking, a *different* way of understanding the world. Thus, according to Piaget, cognition is *qualitatively* different in one stage compared with another. What are Piaget's four stages of cognitive development like?

The *sensorimotor stage,* which lasts from birth to about 2 years of age, is the first Piagetian stage. In this stage, infants construct an understanding of the world by coordinating sensory experiences (such as seeing and hearing) with physical, motoric actions—hence the term *sensorimotor.*

**Piaget's theory** States that children actively construct their understanding of the world and go through four stages of cognitive development.

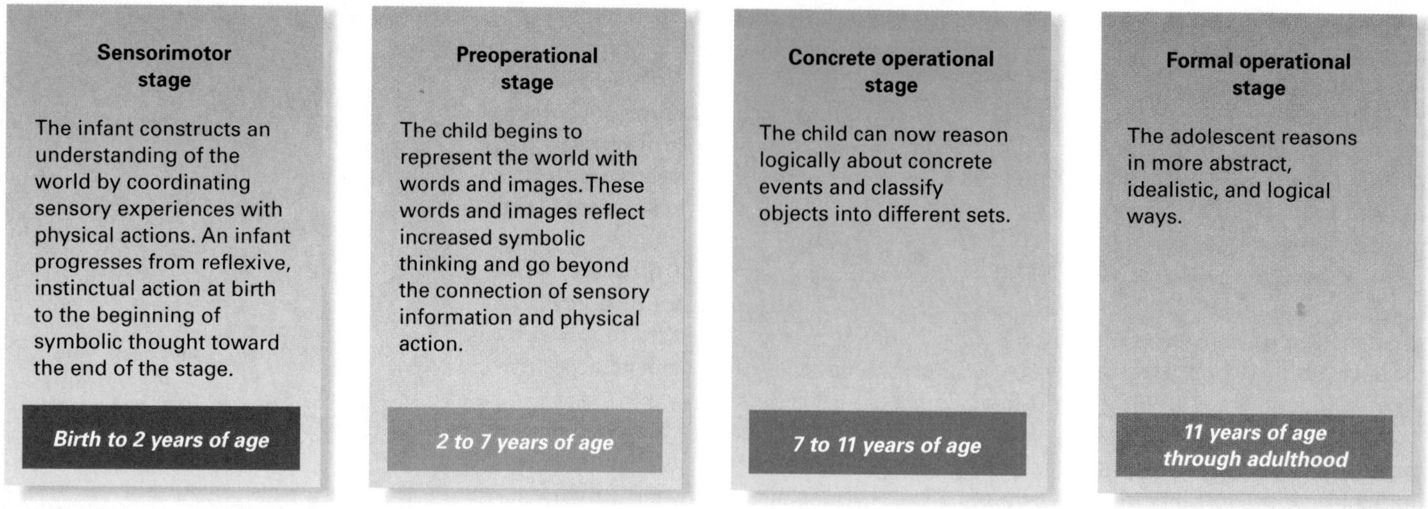

Sensorimotor stage
The infant constructs an understanding of the world by coordinating sensory experiences with physical actions. An infant progresses from reflexive, instinctual action at birth to the beginning of symbolic thought toward the end of the stage.
Birth to 2 years of age
Preoperational stage
The child begins to represent the world with words and images. These words and images reflect increased symbolic thinking and go beyond the connection of sensory information and physical action.
2 to 7 years of age
Concrete operational stage
The child can now reason logically about concrete events and classify objects into different sets.
7 to 11 years of age
Formal operational stage
The adolescent reasons in more abstract, idealistic, and logical ways.
11 years of age through adulthood


**FIGURE 1.11** **Piaget's Four Stages of Cognitive Development**

Jean Piaget, the famous Swiss developmental psychologist, changed the way we think about the development of children's minds. *What are some key ideas in Piaget's theory?*

The *preoperational stage,* which lasts from approximately 2 to 7 years of age, is Piaget's second stage. In this stage, children begin to go beyond simply connecting sensory information with physical action and represent the world with words, images, and drawings. However, according to Piaget, preschool children still lack the ability to perform what he calls *operations,* which are internalized mental actions that allow children to do mentally what they previously could only do physically. For example, if you imagine putting two sticks together to see whether they would be as long as another stick, without actually moving the sticks, you are performing a concrete operation.

The *concrete operational stage,* which lasts from approximately 7 to 11 years of age, is the third Piagetian stage. In this stage, children can perform operations that involve objects, and they can reason logically as long as reasoning can be applied to specific or concrete examples. For instance, concrete operational thinkers cannot imagine the steps necessary to complete an algebraic equation, which is too abstract for thinking at this stage of development.

The *formal operational stage,* which appears between the ages of 11 and 15 and continues through adulthood, is Piaget's fourth and final stage. In this stage, individuals move beyond concrete experiences and think in abstract and more logical terms. As part of thinking more abstractly, adolescents develop images of ideal circumstances. They might think about what an ideal parent is like and compare their parents to this ideal standard. They begin to entertain possibilities for the future and are fascinated with what they can be. In solving problems, they become more systematic, developing hypotheses about why something is happening the way it is and then testing these hypotheses. We examine Piaget's cognitive developmental theory further in Chapter 3.

**Vygotsky's Sociocultural Cognitive Theory** Like Piaget, the Russian developmentalist Lev Vygotsky (1896–1934) emphasized that individuals actively construct their knowledge. However, Vygotsky (1962) gave social interaction and culture far more important roles in cognitive development than Piaget did. **Vygotsky's theory** is a sociocultural cognitive theory that emphasizes how culture and social interaction guide cognitive development.

**Vygotsky's theory** A sociocultural cognitive theory that emphasizes how culture and social interaction guide cognitive development.

Vygotsky portrayed development as inseparable from social and cultural activities (Bodrova & Leong, 2007; Cole & Gajdamaschko, 2007). He stressed that cognitive development involves learning to use the inventions of society, such as language, mathematical systems, and memory strategies. Thus in one culture, individuals might learn to count with the help of a computer; in another, they might learn by using beads. According to Vygotsky, children's and adolescents' social interaction with more-skilled adults and peers is indispensable to their cognitive development (Alvarez & del Rio, 2007). Through this interaction, they learn to use the tools that will help them adapt and be successful in their culture (Hyson, Copple, & Jones, 2006). In Chapter 3, we examine ideas about learning and teaching that are based on Vygotsky's theory.

There is considerable interest today in Lev Vygotsky's sociocultural cognitive theory of child development.

**The Information-Processing Theory** **Information-processing theory** emphasizes that individuals manipulate information, monitor it, and strategize about it. Unlike Piaget's theory, but like Vygotsky's theory, information-processing theory does not describe development as stagelike. Instead, according to this theory, individuals develop a gradually increasing capacity for processing information, which allows them to acquire increasingly complex knowledge and skills (Munakata, 2006).

Robert Siegler (2006; Siegler & Alibali, 2005), a leading expert on children's information processing, states that thinking is information processing. In other words, when adolescents perceive, encode, represent, store, and retrieve information, they are thinking. Siegler emphasizes that an important aspect of development is learning good strategies for processing information. For example, becoming a better reader might involve learning to monitor the key themes of the material being read (Pressley & Hilden, 2006).

**Evaluating Cognitive Theories** Contributions of cognitive theories include a positive view of development and an emphasis on the active construction of understanding. Criticisms include skepticism about the pureness of Piaget's stages and too little attention to individual variations.

## *Through the Eyes of Adolescents*

### THE COBWEBS OF MEMORY

I think the point of having memories is to share them, especially with close friends or family. If you don't share them, they are just sitting inside your brain getting cobwebs. If you have a great memory of Christmas and no one to share it with, what's the point of memories?

*—Seventh-Grade Student*
*West Middle School*
*Ypsilanti, Michigan*

**information-processing theory** Emphasizes that individuals manipulate information, monitor it, and strategize about it. Central to this approach are the processes of memory and thinking.

Albert Bandura (*above*) and Walter Mischel are the architects of contemporary social cognitive theory.

**Behavioral and Social Cognitive Theories** *Behaviorism* essentially holds that we can study scientifically only what can be directly observed and measured. Out of the behavioral tradition grew the belief that development is observable behavior that can be learned through experience with the environment (Bugental & Grusec, 2006; Watson & Tharp, 2007). In terms of the continuity-discontinuity issue discussed earlier in this chapter, the behavioral and social cognitive theories emphasize continuity in development and argue that development does not occur in stage-like fashion. Let's explore two versions of behaviorism: Skinner's operant conditioning and Bandura's social cognitive theory.

**Skinner's Operant Conditioning** According to B. F. Skinner (1904–1990), through *operant conditioning* the consequences of a behavior produce changes in the probability of the behavior's occurrence. A behavior followed by a rewarding stimulus is more likely to recur, whereas a behavior followed by a punishing stimulus is less likely to recur. For example, when an adult smiles at an adolescent after the adolescent has done something, the adolescent is more likely to engage in the activity than if the adult gives the adolescent a nasty look.

In Skinner's (1938) view, such rewards and punishments shape development. For example, Skinner's approach argues that shy people learn to be shy as a result of experiences they have while growing up. It follows that modifications in an environment can help a shy adolescent become more socially oriented. Also, for Skinner the key aspect of development is behavior, not thoughts and feelings. He emphasized that development consists of the pattern of behavioral changes that are brought about by rewards and punishments.

**Bandura's Social Cognitive Theory** Some psychologists agree with the behaviorists' notion that development is learned and is influenced strongly by environmental interactions. However, unlike Skinner, they argue that cognition is also important in understanding development (Mischel, 2004). **Social cognitive theory** holds that behavior, environment, and cognition are the key factors in development.

American psychologist Albert Bandura (1925–) is the leading architect of social cognitive theory. Bandura (1986, 2001, 2004, 2006, 2007a, b) emphasizes that cognitive processes have important links with the environment and behavior. His early research program focused heavily on *observational learning* (also called *imitation,* or *modeling*), which is learning that occurs through observing what others do. For example, a young boy might observe his father yelling in anger and treating other people with hostility; with his peers, the young boy later acts very aggressively, showing the same characteristics as his father's behavior. Social cognitive theorists stress that people acquire a wide range of behaviors, thoughts, and feelings through observing others' behavior and that these observations form an important part of adolescent development.

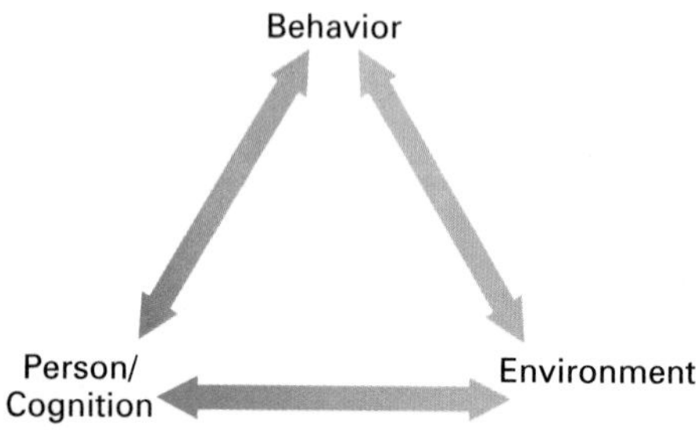


**FIGURE 1.12 Bandura's Social Cognitive Theory** Bandura's social cognitive theory emphasizes reciprocal influences of behavior, environment, and person/cognitive factors.

What is *cognitive* about observational learning in Bandura's view? He proposes that people cognitively represent the behavior of others and then sometimes adopt this behavior themselves.

Bandura's (2004, 2006, 2007a, b) most recent model of learning and development includes three elements: behavior, the person/cognition, and the environment. An individual's confidence that he or she can control his or her success is an example of a person factor; strategies are an example of a cognitive factor. As shown in Figure 1.12, behavior, person/cognitive, and environmental factors operate interactively.

**social cognitive theory** The view of psychologists who emphasize behavior, environment, and cognition as the key factors in development.

**Bronfenbrenner's ecological theory** Bronfenbrenner's ecological theory focuses on the influence of five environmental systems: microsystem, mesosystem, exosystem, macrosystem, and chronosystem.

**Evaluating Behavioral and Social Cognitive Theories** Contributions of the behavioral and social cognitive theories include an emphasis on scientific research and environmental determinants of behavior. Criticisms include too little emphasis on cognition in Skinner's views and giving inadequate attention to developmental changes.

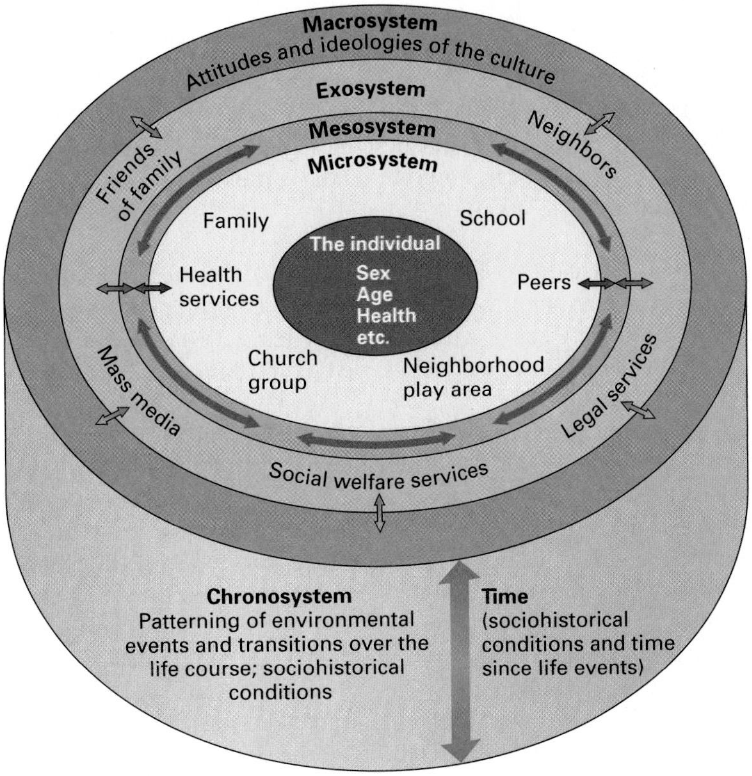


**FIGURE 1.13 Bronfenbrenner's Ecological Theory of Development** Bronfenbrenner's ecological contextual theory consists of five environmental systems: microsystem, mesosystem, exosystem, macrosystem, and chronosystem.

**Ecological Theory** One ecological theory that has important implications for understanding adolescent development was created by Urie Bronfenbrenner (1917–2005). **Bronfenbrenner's ecological theory** (1986, 2000, 2004; Bronfenbrenner & Morris, 1998, 2006) holds that development reflects the influence of five environmental systems: microsystem, mesosystem, exosystem, macrosystem, and chronosystem (see Figure 1.13).

The *microsystem* is the setting in which the adolescent lives. These contexts include the adolescent's family, peers, school, and neighborhood. It is in the microsystem that the most direct interactions with social agents take place—with parents, peers, and teachers, for example. The adolescent is not a passive recipient of experiences in these settings, but someone who helps to construct the settings.

The *mesosystem* involves relations between microsystems or connections between contexts. Examples are the relation of family experiences to school experiences, school experiences to church experiences, and family experiences to peer experiences. For example, adolescents whose parents have rejected them may have difficulty developing positive relations with teachers.

The *exosystem* consists of links between a social setting in which the adolescent does not have an active role and the individual's immediate context. For example, a husband's or an adolescent's experience at home may be influenced by a mother's experiences at work. The mother might receive a promotion that requires more travel, which might increase conflict with the husband and change patterns of interaction with the adolescent.

The *macrosystem* involves the culture in which adolescents live. *Culture* refers to the behavior patterns, beliefs, and all other products of a group of people that are passed on from generation to generation.

The *chronosystem* consists of the patterning of environmental events and transitions over the life course, as well as sociohistorical circumstances. For example, divorce is one transition. Researchers have found that the negative effects of divorce on children often peak in the first year after the divorce (Hetherington, 1993, 2006).

Urie Bronfenbrenner developed ecological theory, a perspective that is receiving increased attention. His theory emphasizes the importance of both micro and macro dimensions of the environment in which the child lives.

By two years after the divorce, family interaction is less chaotic and more stable. As an example of sociohistorical circumstances, consider how the opportunities for adolescent girls to pursue a career have increased during the last fifty years.

Bronfenbrenner (2004; Bronfenbrenner & Morris, 2006) has added biological influences to his theory and describes the newer version as a *bioecological* theory. Nonetheless, ecological, environmental contexts still predominate in Bronfenbrenner's theory (Ceci, 2000).

**Evaluating Ecological Theory** Contributions of the theory include a systematic examination of macro and micro dimensions of environmental systems, and attention to connections between environmental systems. Criticisms include giving inadequate attention to biological factors, as well as too little emphasis on cognitive factors.

### An Eclectic Theoretical Orientation

No single theory described in this chapter can explain entirely the rich complexity of adolescent development, but each has contributed to our understanding of development. Psychoanalytic theory best explains the unconscious mind. Erikson's theory best describes the changes that occur in adult development. Piaget's, Vygotsky's, and the information-processing views provide the most complete description of cognitive development. The behavioral and social cognitive and ecological theories have been the most adept at examining the environmental determinants of development.

In short, although theories are helpful guides, relying on a single theory to explain adolescent development is probably a mistake (Newman & Newman, 2007). This book instead takes an **eclectic theoretical orientation,** which does not follow any one theoretical approach but rather selects from each theory whatever is considered its best features. In this way, you can view the study of adolescent development as it actually exists—with different theorists making different assumptions, stressing different empirical problems, and using different strategies to discover information.

## Research in Adolescent Development

If they follow an eclectic orientation, how do scholars and researchers determine that one feature of a theory is somehow better than another? The scientific method discussed earlier provides the guide. Through scientific research, the features of theories can be tested and refined.

Generally, research in adolescent development is designed to test hypotheses, which in some cases, are derived from the theories just described. Through research, theories are modified to reflect new data and occasionally new theories arise. How are data about adolescent development collected? What types of research designs are used to study life-span development?

*Truth is arrived at by the painstaking process of eliminating the untrue.*

—Arthur Conan Doyle
*British Physician and Detective-Story Writer, 20th Century*

### Methods for Collecting Data

Whether we are interested in studying pubertal change, cognitive skills, or parent-adolescent conflict, we can choose from several ways of collecting data. Here we outline the measures most often used, beginning with observation.

**Observation** Scientific observation requires an important set of skills. For observations to be effective, they have to be systematic (McMillan, 2007; McMillan & Schumacher, 2006). We have to have some idea of what we are looking for. We have to know whom we are observing, when and where we will observe, how the observations will be made, and how they will be recorded.

Where should we make our observations? We have two choices: the laboratory and the everyday world.

When we observe scientifically, we often need to control certain factors that determine behavior but are not the focus of our inquiry (Rosnow & Rosenthal,

**eclectic theoretical orientation** An orientation that does not follow any one theoretical approach but rather selects from each theory whatever is considered the best in it.

*When conducting surveys or interviews with adolescents, what are some strategies that need to be exercised?*

2008). For this reason, some adolescent development research is conducted in a **laboratory,** a controlled setting with many of the complex factors of the "real world" removed. Laboratory research does have some drawbacks, however. First, it is almost impossible to conduct research without the participants' knowing they are being studied. Second, the laboratory setting is unnatural and therefore can cause the participants to behave unnaturally. Third, people who are willing to come to a university laboratory may not fairly represent groups from diverse cultural backgrounds. In addition, people who are unfamiliar with university settings, and with the idea of "helping science," may be intimidated by the laboratory setting.

Naturalistic observation provides insights that we sometimes cannot achieve in the laboratory (McBurney & White, 2007). **Naturalistic observation** means observing behavior in real-world settings, making no effort to manipulate or control the situation. Life-span researchers conduct naturalistic observations in neighborhoods, at schools, sporting events, work settings, and malls, and in other places adolescents frequent.

**Survey and Interview** Sometimes the best and quickest way to get information about adolescents is to ask them for it. One technique is to *interview* them directly. A related method is the *survey* (sometimes referred to as a questionnaire), which is especially useful when information from many people is needed. A standard set of questions is used to obtain people's self-reported attitudes or beliefs about a particular topic. In a good survey, the questions are clear and unbiased, allowing respondents to answer unambiguously (Nardi, 2006).

Surveys and interviews can be used to study a wide range of topics from religious beliefs to sexual habits to attitudes about gun control to beliefs about how to improve schools. Surveys and interviews today are conducted in person, over the telephone, and over the Internet.

One problem with surveys and interviews is the tendency of participants to answer questions in a way that they think is socially acceptable or desirable rather than telling what they truly think or feel (Graziano & Raulin, 2007 ). For example, on a survey or in an interview, some adolescents might say that they do not take drugs even though they do.

**Standardized Test** A **standardized test** has uniform procedures for administration and scoring. Many standardized tests allow a person's performance to be compared with the performance of other individuals; thus they provide information about

**laboratory** A controlled setting in which many of the complex factors of the "real world" are removed.

**naturalistic observation** Observing behavior in real-world settings.

**standardized test** A test with uniform procedures for administration and scoring. Many standardized tests allow a person's performance to be compared with the performance of other individuals.

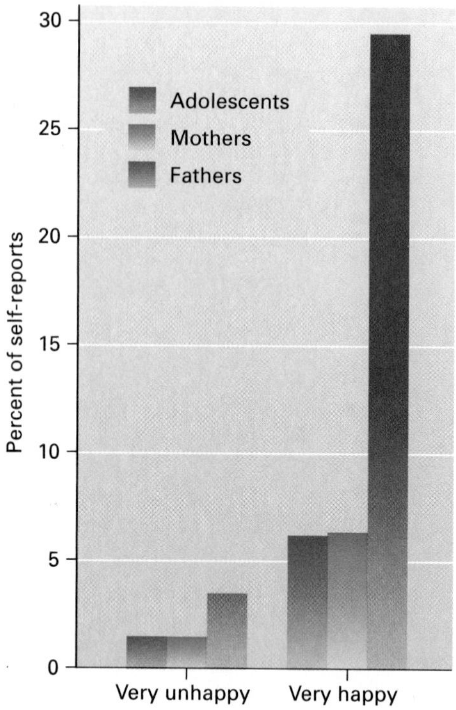


**FIGURE 1.14 Self-Reported Extremes of Emotion by Adolescents, Mothers, and Fathers Using the Experience Sampling Method** In the study by Reed Larson and Maryse Richards (1994), adolescents and their mothers and fathers were beeped at random times by researchers using the experience sampling method. The researchers found that adolescents were more likely to report more emotional extremes than their parents.

individual differences among people (Gregory, 2007; Gronlund, 2006). One example is the Stanford-Binet intelligence test, which is described in Chapter 3. Your score on the Stanford-Binet test tells you how your performance compares with that of thousands of other people who have taken the test.

One criticism of standardized tests is that they assume a person's behavior is consistent and stable, yet personality and intelligence—two primary targets of standardized testing—can vary with the situation. For example, an adolescent may perform poorly on a standardized intelligence test in an office setting but score much higher at home, where he or she is less anxious.

**Physiological Measures** Researchers are increasingly using physiological measures when they study adolescent development. One type of physiological measure involves an assessment of the hormones in an adolescent's bloodstream. As puberty unfolds, glandular secretions in the blood increase, raising the blood levels of hormone samples. To determine the nature of these hormonal changes, researchers take blood samples from willing adolescents (Dorn & others, 2006).

The body composition of adolescents also is a focus of physiological assessment. There is a special interest in the increase in fat content in the body during pubertal development. Until recently, little research had focused on the brain activity of adolescents. However, the development of neuroimaging techniques has led to a flurry of research studies (Dahl, 2006; Dorn & others, 2006; Nelson, Thomas, & de Haan, 2006). One technique that is being used in a number of them is *magnetic resonance imaging (MRI)*, in which radio waves are used to construct images of a person's brain tissue and biochemical activity (Galvan & others, 2006; Williams & others, 2006).

**Experience Sampling** In the **experience sampling method (ESM),** participants in a study are given electronic pagers. Then, researchers "beep" them at random times. When they are beeped, the participants report on various aspects of their immediate situation, including where they are, what they are doing, who they are with, and how they are feeling.

The ESM has been used in a number of studies to determine the settings in which adolescents are most likely to spend their time, the extent to which they spend time with parents and peers, and the nature of their emotions. Using this method, Reed Larson and Maryse Richards (1994) found that across the thousands of times they reported their feelings, adolescents experienced emotions that were more extreme and more fleeting than their parents. For example, adolescents were five times more likely than their parents to report being "very happy" when they were beeped, and three times more likely to feel "very unhappy" (see Figure 1.14).

**Case Study** A **case study** is an in-depth look at a single individual. Case studies are performed mainly by mental health professionals, when for practical or ethical reasons, the unique aspects of an individual's life cannot be duplicated and tested in other individuals (Fraenkel & Wallen, 2005). A case study provides information about one person's fears, hopes, fantasies, traumatic experiences, upbringing, family relationships, health, or anything else that helps the psychologist to understand the person's mind and behavior (Beins, 2004).

Consider the case study of Michael Rehbein, which illustrates the flexibility and resilience of the developing brain. At age 7, Michael began to experience uncontrollable seizures—as many as 400 a day. Doctors said that the only solution was to remove the left hemisphere of his brain where the seizures were occurring. Though Michael's recovery was slow, eventually his right hemisphere began to reorganize and take over functions that normally reside in the brain's left hemisphere, such as speech. The neuroimage in Figure 1.15 shows this reorganization of Michael's brain vividly. Although case histories provide dramatic, in-depth portrayals of people's lives, we must be cautious in generalizing from them. The subject of a case study

**experience sampling method (ESM)** Involves providing participants with electronic pagers and then beeping them at random times, at which point they are asked to report on various aspects of their lives.

**case study** An in-depth look at a single individual.

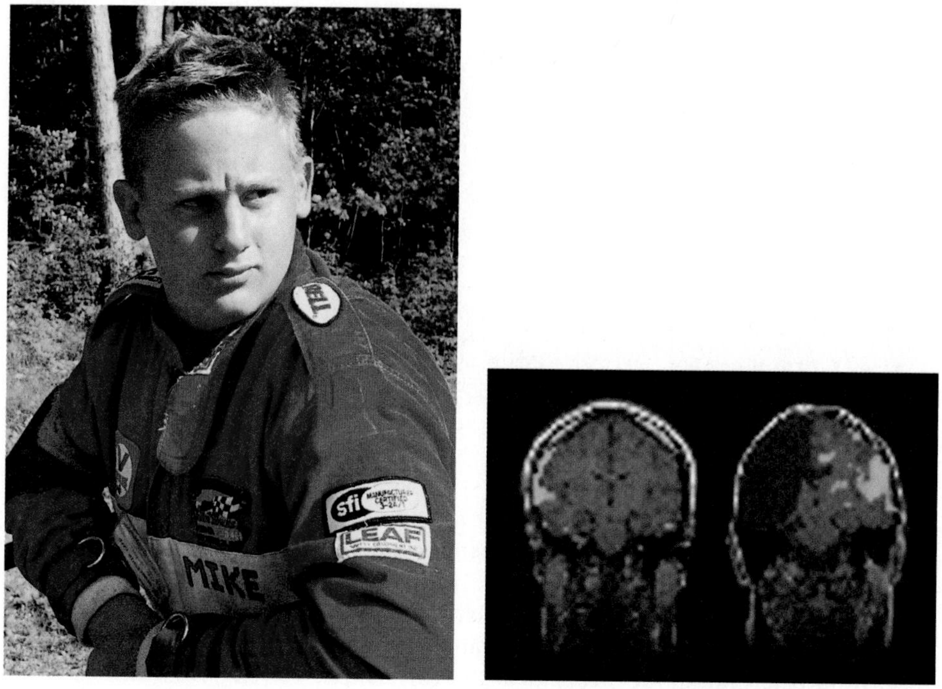


(a) (b)

**FIGURE 1.15 Plasticity in the Brain's Hemispheres** (*a*) Michael Rehbein at 14 years of age. (*b*) Michael's right hemisphere (*left*) has reorganized to take over the language functions normally carried out by corresponding areas in the left hemisphere of an intact brain (*right*). However, the right hemisphere is not as efficient as the left, and more areas of the brain are recruited to process speech.

is unique, with a genetic makeup and personal history that no one else shares. In addition, case studies involve judgments of unknown reliability. Psychologists who conduct a case study rarely check to see whether other psychologists agree with their observations.

### Research Designs

In conducting research on adolescent development, in addition to a method for collecting data, you also need a research design. There are three main types of research design: descriptive, correlational, and experimental.

#### Descriptive Research

All of the data-collection methods that we have discussed can be used in **descriptive research,** which aims to observe and record behavior. For example, a researcher might observe the extent to which adolescents are altruistic or aggressive toward each other. By itself, descriptive research cannot prove what causes some phenomena, but it can reveal important information about people's behavior.

#### Correlational Research

In contrast to descriptive research, correlational research goes beyond describing phenomena to provide information that will help us to predict how people will behave (Aron, Aron, & Coups, 2008). In **correlational research,** the goal is to describe the strength of the relation between two or more events or characteristics. The more strongly the two events are correlated (or related or associated), the more effectively we can predict one event from the other.

For example, to study if adolescents of permissive parents have less self-control than other adolescents, you would need to carefully record observations of parents' permissiveness and their children's self-control. The data could then be analyzed statistically to yield a numerical measure, called a **correlation coefficient,** a number based on a statistical analysis that is used to describe the degree of association between two variables. The correlation coefficient ranges from $+1.00$ to $-1.00$. A negative number means an inverse relation. For example, researchers often find a negative correlation between permissive parenting and adolescents' self-control. By contrast, they often find a positive correlation between parental monitoring of children and adolescents' self-control.

**descriptive research** Research that aims to observe and record behavior.

**correlational research** Research whose goal is to describe the strength of the relationship between two or more events or characteristics.

**correlation coefficient** A number based on a statistical analysis that is used to describe the degree of association between two variables.

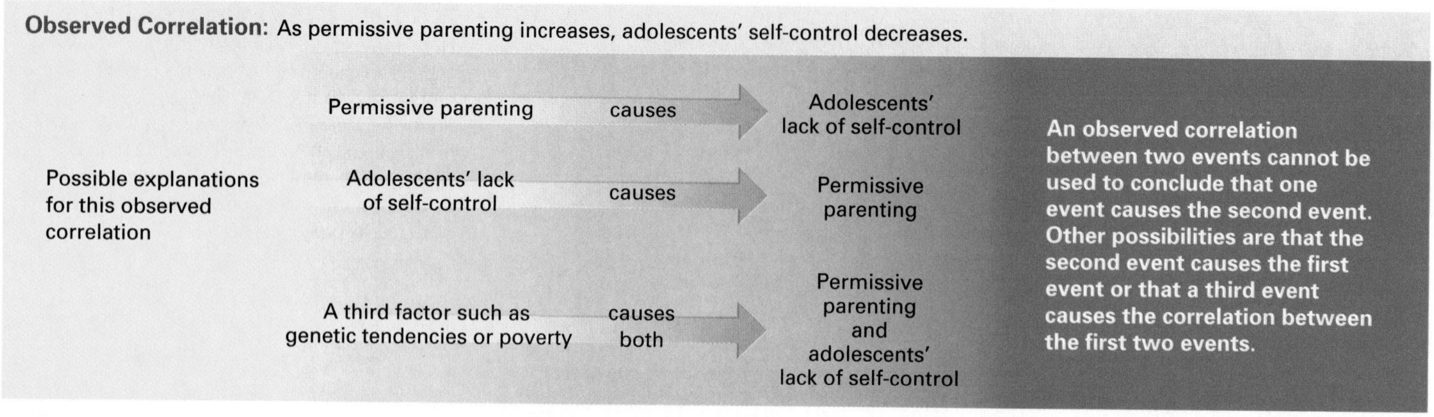


**FIGURE 1.16** **Possible Explanations of Correlational Data**

The higher the correlation coefficient (whether positive or negative), the stronger the association between the two variables. A correlation of 0 means that there is no association between the variables. A correlation of −.40 is stronger than a correlation of +.20 because we disregard whether the correlation is positive or negative in determining the strength of the correlation.

A caution is in order, however (Sprinthall, 2007). Correlation does not equal causation. The correlational finding just mentioned does not mean that permissive parenting necessarily causes low self-control in adolescents. It could mean that, but it also could mean that an adolescent's lack of self-control caused the parents to simply throw up their arms in despair and give up trying to control the adolescent. It also could mean that other factors, such as heredity or poverty, caused the correlation between permissive parenting and low self-control in adolescents. Figure 1.16 illustrates these possible interpretations of correlational data.

**Experimental Research** To study causality, researchers turn to **experimental research** (McBurney & White, 2007). An experiment is a carefully regulated procedure in which one or more factors believed to influence the behavior being studied are manipulated, while all other factors are held constant (Jackson, 2008). If the behavior under study changes when a factor is manipulated, we say that the manipulated factor has caused the behavior to change. In other words, the experiment has demonstrated cause and effect. The cause is the factor that was manipulated. The effect is the behavior that changed because of the manipulation. Nonexperimental research methods (descriptive and correlational research) cannot establish cause and effect because they do not involve manipulating factors in a controlled way.

All experiments involve at least one independent variable and one dependent variable. The **independent variable** is the factor that is manipulated. The term *independent* indicates that this variable can be manipulated independently of all other factors. For example, suppose we want to design an experiment to establish the effects of peer tutoring on adolescents' achievement. In this example, the amount and type of peer tutoring could be the independent variable.

The **dependent variable** is the factor that is measured; it can change as the independent variable is manipulated. The term *dependent* indicates that this variable depends on what happens as the independent variable is manipulated. In the peer tutoring study, adolescents' achievement would be the dependent variable. It might be assessed in a number of ways, perhaps by scores on a nationally standardized achievement test.

In an experiment, researchers manipulate the independent variable by giving different experiences to one or more experimental groups and one or more control groups. An *experimental group* is a group whose experience is manipulated. A

**experimental research** Research that involves an experiment, a carefully regulated procedure in which one or more of the factors believed to influence the behavior being studied are manipulated while all other factors are held constant.

**independent variable** The factor that is manipulated in experimental research.

**dependent variable** The factor that is measured in experimental research.

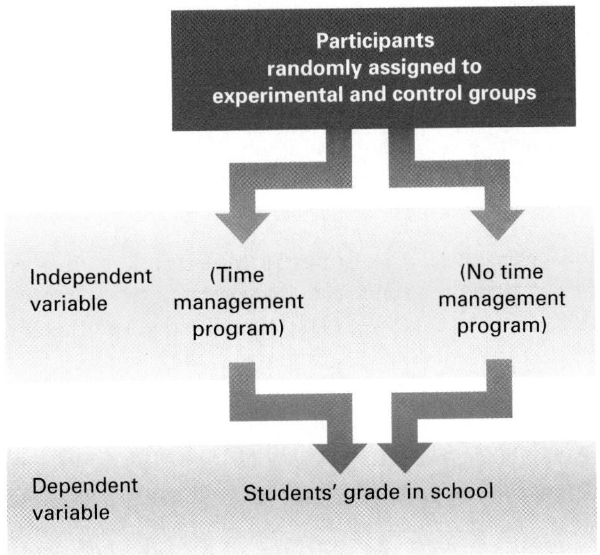


**FIGURE 1.17** Random Assignment and Experimental Design

*control group* is a group that is treated like the experimental group in every other way except for the manipulated factor. The control group serves as a baseline against which the effects on the manipulated group can be compared. In the peer tutoring study, we would need to have one group of adolescents that got peer tutoring (experimental group) and one that didn't (control group).

An important principle of experimental research is *random assignment*—assigning participants to experimental and control groups by chance (Martin, 2008). This practice reduces the likelihood that the results of the experiment will be affected by preexisting differences between the groups. In our study of peer tutoring, random assignment would greatly reduce the probability that the two groups differed in age, family background, initial achievement, intelligence, personality, or health.

To summarize, in our study of peer tutoring and adolescent achievement, we would assign participants randomly to two groups. One (the experimental group) would be given peer tutoring and the other (the control group) would not. The different experiences that the experimental and control groups receive would be the independent variable. After the peer tutoring had been completed, the adolescents would be given a nationally standardized achievement test (the dependent variable). Figure 1.17 applies the experimental research method to a different problem: whether a time management program can improve adolescents' grades.

### Time Span of Research

A special concern of developmentalists is the time span of a research investigation (Hartmann & Pelzel, 2005; Schaie, 2007). Studies that focus on the relation of age to some other variable are common. Researchers have two options: they can study different individuals of different ages and compare them; or they can study the same individuals as they age over time.

#### Cross-Sectional Research

**Cross-sectional research** involves studying people all at one time. For example, a researcher might study the self-esteem of 10-, 15-, and 20-year-olds. In a cross-sectional study, all participants' self-esteem would be assessed at one time.

The main advantage of a cross-sectional study is that researchers do not have to wait for the individuals to grow older. Despite its time efficiency, however, the cross-sectional approach has its drawbacks. It gives no information about how individuals change or about the stability of their characteristics. The increases and decreases of development—the hills and valleys of growth and development—can

**cross-sectional research** A research strategy in which individuals of different ages are compared at one time.

become obscured in the cross-sectional approach. For example, in a cross-sectional study of self-esteem, average increases and decreases might be revealed. But the study would not show how the life satisfaction of individual children waxed and waned over the years. It also would not tell us whether younger children who had high or low self-esteem as young adults continued to have high or low self-esteem, respectively, when they became older.

**Longitudinal Research** **Longitudinal research** involves studying the same individuals over a period of time, usually several years or more. In a longitudinal study of self-esteem, the researcher might examine the self-esteem of a group of 10-year-olds, then assess their self-esteem again when they are 15, and then again when they are 20.

Although longitudinal studies provide a wealth of information about such important issues as stability and change in development and the importance of early experience for later development, they are not without their problems (Raudenbush, 2001). They are expensive and time-consuming. The longer the study lasts, the more participants drop out—they move, get sick, lose interest, and so forth. Participants can bias the outcome of a study, because those who remain may be dissimilar to those who drop out. Those individuals who remain in a longitudinal study over a number of years may be more compulsive and conformity-oriented, for example, or they might have more stable lives.

**longitudinal research** A research strategy in which the same individuals are studied over a period of time, usually several years or more.

### Conducting Ethical Research

Ethics in research may affect you personally if you ever serve as a participant in a study. In that event, you need to know your rights as a participant and the responsibilities of researchers to assure that these rights are safeguarded.

If you ever become a researcher in life-span development yourself, you will need an even deeper understanding of ethics. Even if you carry out experimental projects in only psychology courses, you must consider the rights of the participants in those projects. A student might think, "I volunteer in a home for the mentally retarded several hours per week. I can use the residents of the home in my study to see if a particular treatment helps improve their memory for everyday tasks." But without proper permissions, the most well-meaning, kind, and considerate studies still violate the rights of the participants.

Today, proposed research at colleges and universities must pass the scrutiny of a research ethics committee before the research can be initiated. In addition, the American Psychological Association (APA) has developed ethics guidelines for its members. The code of ethics instructs psychologists to protect their participants from mental and physical harm. The participants' best interests need to be kept foremost in the researcher's mind (McBurney & White, 2007; Rosnow & Rosenthal, 2005). APA's guidelines address four important issues. First, *informed consent*—all participants must know what their research participation will involve and what risks might develop. Even after informed consent is given, participants must retain the right to withdraw from the study at any time and for any reason. Second, *confidentiality*—researchers are responsible for keeping all of the data they gather on individuals completely confidential and, when possible, completely anonymous. Third, *debriefing*—after the study has been completed, participants should be informed of its purpose and the methods that were used. In most cases, the experimenter also can inform participants in a general manner beforehand about the purpose of the research without leading participants to behave in a way they think that the experimenter is expecting. Fourth, *deception*—in some circumstances, telling the participants beforehand what the research study is about substantially alters the participants' behavior and invalidates the researcher's data. In all cases of deception, however, the psychologist must ensure that the deception will not harm the participants and that the participants will be told the complete nature of the study (debriefed) as soon as possible after the study is completed.

Look at the two photographs, one of all non-Latino Caucasian males, the other of a diverse group of females and males from different ethnic groups, including some White individuals. Consider a topic in psychology, such as parenting, love, or cultural values. *If you were conducting research on this topic, might the results of the study be different depending on whether the participants in your study were the individuals in the photograph on the left or those on the right?*

**Minimizing Bias** Studies of adolescent development are most useful when they are conducted without bias or prejudice toward any particular group of people. Of special concern is bias based on gender and bias based on culture or ethnicity.

**Gender Bias** Society continues to have a **gender bias,** a preconceived notion about the abilities of females and males that prevents individuals from pursuing their own interests and achieving their potential. But gender bias also has had a less obvious effect within the field of adolescent development. For example, too often researchers have drawn conclusions about females' attitudes and behaviors from research conducted with males as the only participants.

When gender differences are found, they sometimes are unduly magnified (Denmark & others, 1988; Hyde, 2005, 2007; Matline, 2008). For example, a researcher might report in a study that 74 percent of the boys had high achievement expectations versus only 67 percent of the girls and go on to talk about the differences in some detail. In reality, this might be a rather small difference. It also might disappear if the study were repeated, or the study might have methodological problems that don't allow such strong interpretations.

**Cultural and Ethnic Bias** At the same time as researchers have been struggling with gender bias, the realization that research needs to include more people from diverse ethnic groups has also been building (Graham, 1992, 2006). Historically, members of ethnic minority groups (African American, Latino, Asian American, and Native American) have been discounted from most research in the United States and simply thought of as variations from the norm or average. Because their scores don't always fit neatly into measures of central tendency (such as a mean score to reflect the average performance of a group of participants), minority individuals have been viewed as confounds or "noise" in data. Consequently, researchers have deliberately excluded them from the samples they have selected. Given the fact that individuals from diverse ethnic groups were excluded from research on adolescent development for so long, we might reasonably conclude that adolescents' real lives are perhaps more varied than research data have indicated in the past.

Researchers also have tended to overgeneralize about ethnic groups (Banks, 2008; Spring, 2007; Trimble, 1989). **Ethnic gloss** is using an ethnic label such as African American or Latino in a superficial way that portrays an ethnic group as being more homogeneous than it really is. For example, a researcher might describe a research sample like this: "The participants were 20 Latinos and 20 Anglo-Americans."

**gender bias** A preconceived notion about the abilities of females and males that prevents individuals from pursuing their own interests and achieving their potential.

**ethnic gloss** Using an ethnic label such as African American or Latino in a superficial way that portrays an ethnic group as being more homogeneous than it really is.

## Careers in ADOLESCENT DEVELOPMENT

**Pam Reid**

**Educational and Developmental Psychologist**

When she was a child, Pam Reid liked to play with chemistry sets. Pam majored in chemistry during college and wanted to become a doctor. However, when some of her friends signed up for a psychology class as an elective, she also decided to take the course. She was intrigued by learning about how people think, behave, and develop—so much so that she changed her major to psychology. Pam went on to obtain her Ph.D. in psychology (American Psychological Association, 2003, p. 16).

For a number of years, Pam was professor of education and psychology at the University of Michigan, where she also was a research scientist at the Institute for Research on Women and Gender. Her main focus has been on how children and adolescents develop social skills, with a special interest in the development of African American girls (Reid & Zalk, 2001). In 2004, Pam became provost and executive vice president at Roosevelt University in Chicago.

Pam Reid (*back row, center*) with graduate students she mentored at the University of Michigan.

A more complete description of the Latino group might be something like this: "The 20 Latino participants were Mexican Americans from low-income neighborhoods in the southwestern area of Los Angeles. Twelve were from homes in which Spanish is the dominant language spoken, 8 from homes in which English is the main language spoken. Ten were born in the United States, 10 in Mexico. Ten described themselves as Mexican American, 5 as Mexican, 3 as American, 2 as Chicano, and 1 as Latino." Ethnic gloss can cause researchers to obtain samples of ethnic groups that are not representative of the group's diversity, which can lead to overgeneralization and stereotyping.

Pam Reid is a leading researcher who studies gender and ethnic bias in development. To read about Pam's interests, see the *Careers in Adolescent Development* profile.

### REVIEW AND REFLECT ◆ LEARNING GOAL 4

**4 Characterize the science of adolescent development.**

***Review***

- What is the nature of the scientific study of adolescent development?
- What is meant by the concept of theory? What are four main theories of adolescent development?
- What are the main methods used to collect data on adolescent development? What are the main research designs? What are some concerns about potential bias in research on adolescents?

***Reflect***

- You have learned that correlation does not equal causation. Develop an example of two variables (two sets of observations) that are correlated but that you believe almost certainly have no causal relationship.

# REACH YOUR LEARNING GOALS

## 1 THE HISTORICAL PERSPECTIVE *Describe the historical perspective of adolescence.*

### Early History

Plato said that reasoning first develops in adolescence, and Aristotle argued that self-determination is the hallmark of maturity. In the Middle Ages, knowledge about adolescence moved a step backward: children were viewed as miniature adults. Rousseau provided a more enlightened view of adolescence, including an emphasis on different phases of development.

### The Twentieth and Twenty-First Centuries

Between 1890 and 1920, a cadre of psychologists, urban reformers, and others began to mold the concept of adolescence. G. Stanley Hall is the father of the scientific study of adolescence. In 1904, he proposed the storm-and-stress view of adolescence, which has strong biological foundations. In contrast to Hall's biological view, Margaret Mead argued for a sociocultural interpretation of adolescence. In the inventionist view, adolescence is a sociohistorical invention. Legislation was enacted early in the twentieth century that ensured the dependency of adolescents and delayed their entry into the workforce. From 1900 to 1930, there was a 600 percent increase in the number of high school graduates in the United States. Adolescents gained a more prominent place in society from 1920 to 1950. By 1950, every state had developed special laws for adolescents. Barriers prevented many ethnic minority individuals and females from entering the field of studying adolescent development in the early and middle part of the twentieth century. Leta Hollingworth was a pioneering female, and Kenneth and Mamie Clark and George Sanchez were pioneering ethnic minority individuals in studying adolescents. Two changes in adolescents in the twenty-first century involve technology and diversity.

### Stereotyping of Adolescents

Negative stereotyping of adolescents in any historical era has been common. Joseph Adelson described the concept of the "adolescent generalization gap," which states that generalizations are often based on a limited set of highly visible adolescents.

### A Positive View of Adolescence

For too long, adolescents have been viewed in negative ways. Research shows that a considerable majority of adolescents around the world have positive self-esteem. The majority of adolescents are not highly conflicted but rather are searching for an identity.

## 2 TODAY'S ADOLESCENTS IN THE UNITED STATES AND AROUND THE WORLD *Discuss today's U.S. adolescents and adolescents around the world.*

### Adolescents in the United States

Adolescents are heterogeneous. Although a majority of adolescents successfully make the transition from childhood to adulthood, too large a percentage do not and are not provided with adequate opportunities and support. Different portraits of adolescents emerge depending on the particular set of adolescents being described. Contexts, the settings in which development occurs, play important roles in adolescent development. These contexts include families, peers, schools, and culture. Social policy is a national government's course of action designed to influence the welfare of its citizens. The U.S. social policy on adolescents needs revision to provide more services for youth. Benson and his colleagues argue that U.S. youth social policy has focused too much on developmental deficits and not enough on strengths. Some experts argue that adolescents as an age group have been underserved by the government and that a generational inequity has evolved, with a much greater percentage of government support going to older adults.

**The Global Perspective**

There are both similarities and differences in adolescents across different countries. Much of what has been written and researched about adolescence comes from American and European scholars. With technological advances, a youth culture with similar characteristics may be emerging. However, there still are many variations in adolescents across cultures. In some countries, traditions are being continued in the socialization of adolescence, whereas in others, substantial changes in the experiences of adolescents are taking place. These traditions and changes involve health and well-being, gender, families, schools, and peers.

## 3 THE NATURE OF DEVELOPMENT *Summarize the developmental processes, periods, transitions, and issues related to adolescence.*

**Processes and Periods**

Development is the pattern of movement or change that occurs throughout the life span. Biological processes involve physical changes in the individual's body. Cognitive processes consist of changes in thinking and intelligence. Socioemotional processes focus on changes in relationships with people, in emotion, in personality, and in social contexts. Development is commonly divided into these periods: prenatal, infancy, early childhood, middle and late childhood, adolescence, early adulthood, middle adulthood, and late adulthood. Adolescence is the developmental period of transition between childhood and adulthood that involves biological, cognitive, and socioemotional changes. In most cultures, adolescence begins at approximately 10 to 13 years of age and ends at about 18 to 22 years of age. Developmentalists increasingly distinguish between early adolescence and late adolescence.

**Developmental Transitions**

Two important transitions in development are from childhood to adolescence and adolescence to adulthood. In the transition from childhood to adolescence, pubertal change is prominent, although cognitive and socioemotional changes occur as well. It sometimes has been said that adolescence begins in biology and ends in culture. The concept of emerging adulthood has been proposed to describe the transition from adolescence to adulthood. Five key characteristics of emerging adulthood are identity exploration (especially in love and work), instability, being self-focused, feeling in-between, and experiencing possibilities to transform one's life. Competent individuals in emerging adulthood who experienced difficulties while growing up are often characterized by support by adults, intelligence, and planfulness. Among the criteria for determining adulthood are self-responsibility, independent decision making, and economic independence.

**Developmental Issues**

Three important issues in development are (1) the nature-nurture issue (is development mainly due to heredity [nature] or environment [nurture]?), (2) the continuity-discontinuity issue (is development more gradual, cumulative [continuity] or more abrupt and sequential [discontinuity]?), and (3) the early-later experience issue (is development due more to early experiences, especially in infancy and early childhood, or to later [more recent and current] experiences?). Most developmentalists do not take extreme positions on these issues, although they are extensively debated.

## 4 The Science of Adolescent Development *Characterize the science of adolescent development.*

**Science and the Scientific Method**

To answer questions about adolescent development, researchers often turn to science. They usually follow the scientific method, which involves four main steps: (1) conceptualize a problem, (2) collect data, (3) analyze data, and (4) draw conclusions.

**Theories of Adolescent Development**

Theory is often involved in conceptualizing a problem. A theory is an interrelated, coherent set of ideas that helps to explain phenomena and to make predictions. Hypotheses are specific assertions and predictions, often derived from theory, that can be tested. According to psychoanalytic theories, development primarily depends on the unconscious mind and is heavily couched in emotion. Two main psychoanalytic theories were proposed by Freud and Erikson. Freud theorized that individuals go through five psychosexual stages. Erikson's theory emphasizes eight psychosocial stages of development Cognitive theories emphasize thinking, reasoning, language, and other cognitive processes. Three main cognitive theories are Piaget's, Vygotsky's, and information processing. The information-processing approach emphasizes that individuals manipulate information, monitor it, and strategize about it. Two main behavioral and social cognitive theories are Skinner's operant conditioning, and social cognitive theory. In Skinner's operant conditioning, the consequences of a behavior produce changes in the probability of the behavior's occurrence. In social cognitive theory, observational learning is a key aspect of life-span development. Bandura emphasizes reciprocal interactions among person/cognition, behavior, and environment. Ecological theory is Bronfenbrenner's environmental systems view of development. It proposes five environmental systems. An eclectic orientation does not follow any one theoretical approach but rather selects from each theory whatever is considered the best in it.

**Research in Adolescent Development**

The main methods for collecting data about life-span development are observation (in a laboratory or a naturalistic setting), survey (questionnaire) or interview, standardized test, physiological measures, experience sampling method, and case study. Three main research designs are descriptive, correlational, and experimental. Descriptive research aims to observe and record behavior. In correlational research, the goal is to describe the strength of the relationship between two or more events or characteristics. Experimental research involves conducting an experiment, which can determine cause and effect. To examine the effects of time and age, researchers can conduct cross-sectional or longitudinal studies. Researchers' ethical responsibilities include seeking participants' informed consent, ensuring confidentiality, debriefing them about the purpose and potential personal consequences of participating, and avoiding unnecessary deception of participants. Researchers need to guard against gender, cultural, and ethnic bias in research.

## KEY TERMS

storm-and-stress view 6
inventionist view 7
stereotype 8
adolescent generalization gap 9
contexts 11
social policy 11
generational inequity 13
development 15
biological processes 15
cognitive processes 16
socioemotional processes 16

prenatal period 16
infancy 16
early childhood 16
middle and late childhood adolescence 16
adolescence 16
early adolescence 17
late adolescence 17
early adulthood 17
middle adulthood 17
late adulthood 18
emerging adulthood 18
resilience 22
nature-nurture issue 23
continuity-discontinuity issue 23
early-later experience issue 23
theory 26
hypotheses 26
psychoanalytic theories 26
Erikson's theory 28
Piaget's theory 29
Vygotsky's theory 30
information-processing theory 31
social cognitive theory 32
Bronfenbrenner's ecological theory 33
eclectic theoretical orientation 34
laboratory 35
naturalistic observation 35
standardized test 35
experience sampling method (ESM) 36
case study 36
descriptive research 37
correlational research 37
correlation coeffecient 37
experimental research 38
independent variable 38
dependent variable 38
cross-sectional research 39
longitudinal research 40
gender bias 41
ethnic gloss 41

## KEY PEOPLE

G. Stanley Hall 6
Margaret Mead 6
Leta Hollingworth 8
Kenneth and Mamie Clark 8
George Sanchez 8
Daniel Offer 9
Marian Wright Edelman 12
Peter Benson 12
Bernice Neugarten 13
Brad Brown and Reed Larson 14
Jeffrey Arnett 19
Ann Masten 22
Sigmund Freud 26
Peter Blos 28
Anna Freud 28
Erik Erikson 28
Jean Piaget 29
Lev Vygotsky 30
Robert Siegler 31
B. F. Skinner 32
Albert Bandura 32
Urie Bronfenbrenner 33
Reed Larson and Maryse Richards 36

## RESOURCES FOR IMPROVING THE LIVES OF ADOLESCENTS

**Adolescence: Growing Up in America**
by Joy Dryfoos and Carol Barkin (2006)
New York: Oxford University Press

A follow-up to Dryfoos' (1990) earlier landmark book on adolescent problems. In *Adolescence: Growing Up in America*, the authors examine the problems adolescents are having today and the prevention and intervention strategies that work.

**Children's Defense Fund** **www.childrensdefense.org**
The Children's Defense Fund, headed by Marian Wright Edelman, exists to provide a strong and effective voice for children and adolescents who cannot vote, lobby, or speak for themselves.

**The Search Institute** **www.search-institute.org**
The Search Institute has available a large number of resources for improving the lives of adolescents. The brochures and books available address school improvement, adolescent literacy, parent education, program planning, and adolescent health—and include resource lists. A free quarterly newsletter is available.

**Handbook of Adolescent Psychology**
edited by Richard Lerner and Laurence Steinberg (2004, 2nd ed.)
New York: John Wiley

An outstanding collection of articles by leading researchers in the field of adolescent development. Includes chapters on social policy, health, volunteering, parent-adolescent relationships, peers, delinquency, sex, puberty, and many other topics.

**Emerging Adults in America**
edited by Jeffrey Arnett and Jennifer Tanner (2006)
Mahwah, NJ: Erlbaum

An excellent set of chapters that provide a contemporary look at major themes and issues in emerging adulthood.

# E-LEARNING TOOLS

To help you master the material in this chapter, visit the Online Learning Center for *Adolescence,* twelfth edition **(www.mhhe.com/santrocka12),** where you will find these additional resources:

## Taking It to the Net

1. About a century ago, G. S. Hall wrote that adolescence was an especially stressful period of time, a stereotype that continues today as evidenced in media representations of adolescence as well as in literary works. Adolescents often are portrayed as interested only in drugs, engaging in promiscuous and risky sex, and alcohol abusers. What is the evidence about the percentages of adolescents using drugs and alcohol and engaging in promiscuous sex?
2. As individuals delay finishing their education, beginning careers, achieving financial independence, and getting married, many people believe that, compared with other generations, youth today are not reaching adulthood until later in life. This transition period between adolescence and adulthood has been termed emergent adulthood. Do you think that emerging adulthood is a separate developmental period? Why or why not? Do you think this trend will continue or change? Why?
3. Child maltreatment (abuse and neglect) is a grave problem. It affects children and adolescents and has implications for how they will rear their own future children. Write an outline of how you might use Bronfenbrenner's theory to organize information about the factors underlying child maltreatment in a paper or class presentation.

## Self-Assessment

The Online Learning Center includes the following self-assessments for further exploration:

- Do I Have the Characteristics of an Emerging Adult?
- Models and Mentors in My Life
- Evaluating My Interest in a Career in Adolescent Development

## Health and Well-Being, Parenting, and Education

To practice your decision-making skills, complete the health and well-being, parenting, and education exercises on the Online Learning Center.

## Video Clips

The Online Learning Center includes the following videos for this chapter:

Relational Aggression

Impact of Media on Children

# Careers in Adolescent Development

Some of you may be quite sure about what you plan to make your life's work. Others may not have decided on a major yet and are uncertain about which career path you want to follow. Each of us wants to find a rewarding career and enjoy the work we do. The field of adolescent development offers an amazing breadth of career options that can provide extremely satisfying work.

If you decide to pursue a career in adolescent development, what career options are available to you? There are many. College and university professors teach courses in adolescent development, education, family development, and medicine. Middle school and high school teachers impart knowledge, understanding, and skills to adolescents. Counselors, clinical psychologists, and physicians help adolescents to cope more effectively with the unique challenges of adolescence. And various professionals work with families of adolescents to improve the adolescent's development.

By choosing one of these career options, you can guide youth in improving their lives, help others to understand them better, or even advance the state of knowledge in the field. You can have an enjoyable time while you are doing these things. Although an advanced degree is not absolutely necessary in some areas of adolescent development, you usually can expand your opportunities (and income) considerably by obtaining a graduate degree. Many careers in adolescent development pay reasonably well. For example, psychologists earn well above the median salary in the United States.

If you are considering a career in adolescent development, as you go through this term, try to spend some time with adolescents of different ages. Observe their behavior; talk with them about their lives. Think about whether you would like to work with youth in your life's work.

Another worthwhile activity is to talk with people who work with adolescents. For example, if you have some interest in becoming a school counselor, call a school, ask to speak with a counselor, and set up an appointment to discuss the counselor's career path and work. Be prepared with a list of questions to ask, and take notes if you wish.

Working in one or more jobs related to your career interests while you are in college can also benefit you. Many colleges and universities offer internships or work experiences for students who major in fields such as development. In some instances, these opportunities are for course credit or pay; in others, they are strictly on a volunteer basis. Take advantage of these opportunities. They can provide you with valuable experiences to help you decide if this is the right career area for you, and they can help you get into graduate school, if you decide you want to go.

In the following sections, we profile careers in three areas: education/research; clinical/counseling/medical; and families/relationships. These are not the only career options in the field of adolescent development, but they should provide you with an idea of the range of opportunities available and information about some of the main career avenues you might pursue. In profiling these careers, we address the amount of education required, the nature of the training, and a description of the work.

## EDUCATION/RESEARCH

Education and research offer a wide range of career opportunities to work with adolescents. These range from being a college professor to secondary school teacher to school psychologist.

**College/University Professor** Courses in adolescent development are taught in different programs and schools in college and universities, including psychology, education, child and family studies, social work, and medicine. They are taught at research universities that offer one or more master's or Ph.D. programs in development; at four-year colleges with no graduate programs; or at community colleges. The work college professors do includes teaching courses either at the undergraduate or graduate level (or both); conducting research in a specific area; advising students and/or directing their research; and serving on college or university committees. Some college instructors do not conduct research but instead focus mainly on teaching. Research is most likely to be part of the job description at universities with master's and Ph.D. programs.

A Ph.D. or master's degree almost always is required to teach in some area of adolescent development in a college or university. Obtaining a doctoral degree usually takes four to six years of graduate work. A master's degree requires approximately two years of graduate work. The training involves taking graduate courses, learning to conduct research, and attending and presenting papers at professional meetings. Many graduate students work as teaching or research assistants to professors, an apprenticeship relationship that helps them to develop their teaching and research skills.

If you are interested in becoming a college or university professor, you might want to make an appointment with your instructor to learn more about the profession and what his or her career/work is like.

**Researcher** In most instances, individuals who work in research positions will have either a master's degree or Ph.D. in some area of adolescent development. They might work at a university, perhaps in a research program; in government at agencies such as the National Institute of Mental Health; or in private industry. Those who have full-time research positions generate innovative research ideas, plan studies, and carry out research by collecting data, analyzing the data, and then interpreting it. Some spend much of their time in a laboratory; others work outside the lab in schools, hospitals, and other settings. Researchers usually attempt to publish their research in a scientific journal. They often work in collaboration with other researchers and may present their work at scientific meetings, where they learn about other research.

**Secondary School Teacher** Secondary school teachers teach one or more subjects, prepare the curriculum, give tests, assign grades, monitor students' progress, conduct parent-teacher conferences, and attend in-service workshops. At minimum, becoming a secondary school teacher requires an undergraduate degree. The training involves taking a wide range of courses, with a major or concentration in education, as well as completion of a supervised practice-teaching internship.

**Exceptional Children (Special Education) Teacher** Teachers of exceptional children concentrate their efforts on individual children who either have a disability or are gifted. Among the children they might work with are children with learning disabilities, ADHD (attention deficit hyperactivity disorder), mental retardation, or a physical disability such as cerebral palsy. Some of their work is done outside of the regular classroom, some of it in the regular classroom. The exceptional children teacher works closely with both the regular classroom teacher and parents to create the best educational program for each student. Becoming a teacher of exceptional children requires a minimum of an undergraduate degree. The training consists of taking a wide range of courses in education with a concentration of courses in educating children with disabilities or children who are gifted. Teachers of exceptional children often continue their education after obtaining their undergraduate degree, and many attain a master's degree in special education.

**Family and Consumer Science Educator** Family and consumer science educators may specialize in early childhood education or instruct middle and high school students about matters such as nutrition, interpersonal relationships, human sexuality, parenting, and human development. Hundreds of colleges and universities throughout the United States offer two- and four-year degree programs in family and consumer science. These programs usually include an internship requirement. Additional education courses may be needed to obtain a teaching certificate. Some family and consumer science educators go on to graduate school for further training, which provides preparation for jobs in college teaching or research.

**Educational Psychologist** Most educational psychologists teach in a college or university setting and conduct research on learning, motivation, classroom management, or assessment. These professors help to train students to enter the fields of educational psychology, school psychology, and teaching. Many educational psychologists have a doctorate in education, which requires four to six years of graduate work.

**School Psychologist** School psychologists focus on improving the psychological and intellectual well-being of elementary and secondary school students. They may work in a school district's centralized office or in one or more schools where they give psychological tests, interview students and their parents, consult with teachers, and provide counseling to students and their families. School psychologists usually have a master's or doctoral degree in school psychology. In graduate school, they take courses in counseling, assessment, learning, and other areas of education and psychology.

## CLINICAL/COUNSELING/MEDICAL

A wide variety of clinical, counseling, and medical professionals work with adolescents, from clinical psychologists to adolescent drug counselors and adolescent medicine specialists.

**Clinical Psychologist** Clinical psychologists seek to help people with their psychological problems. They work in a variety of settings, including colleges and universities, clinics, medical schools, and private practice. Most clinical psychologists conduct psychotherapy; some perform psychological assessment as well; and some do research.

Clinical psychologists must obtain either a Ph.D. that involves clinical and research training, or a Psy.D. degree, which involves only clinical training. This graduate training, which usually takes five to seven years, includes courses in clinical psychology and a one-year supervised internship in an accredited setting. In most cases, candidates for these degrees must pass a test to become licensed to practice and to call themselves clinical psychologists.

**Psychiatrist** Like clinical psychologists, psychiatrists might specialize in working with adolescents. They might work in medical schools, both as teachers and researchers, in medical clinics, and in private practice. Unlike psychologists, however, psychiatrists can administer psychiatric drugs to clients. Psychiatrists must first obtain a medical degree and then do a residency in psychiatry. Medical school takes approximately four years to complete and the psychiatric residency another three to four years.

**Psychiatric Nurse** Psychiatric nurses work closely with psychiatrists to improve adolescents' mental health. This career path requires two to five years of education in a certified nursing program. Psychiatric nursing students take courses in the biological sciences, nursing care, and psychology and receive supervised clinical training in a psychiatric setting. Designation as a clinical specialist in adolescent nursing requires a master's degree or higher in nursing.

**Counseling Psychologist** Counseling psychologists go through much the same training as clinical psychologists and work in the same settings. They may do psychotherapy, teach, or conduct research, but they normally do not treat individuals with severe mental disorders, such as schizophrenia. Counseling psychologists must have either a master's degree or a doctoral degree, as well as a license to practice their profession. One type of master's degree in counseling leads to the designation of licensed professional counselor.

**School Counselor** School counselors help students to identify their abilities and interests, and then guide them in developing academic plans and exploring career options. High school counselors advise students on choosing a major, meeting the admissions requirements for college, taking entrance exams, applying for financial aid, and obtaining vocational and technical training. School counselors may also help students to cope with adjustment problems, working with them individually, in small groups, or even in the classroom. They often consult with parents, teachers, and school administrators when trying to help students with their problems. School counselors usually have a master's degree in counseling.

**Career Counselor** Career counselors help individuals to identify their career options and guide them in applying for jobs. They may work in private industry or at a college or university, where they usually interview individuals to identify careers that fit their interests and abilities. Sometimes career counselors help individuals to create professional résumés, or they conduct mock interviews to help them prepare for a job interview. They may also create and promote job fairs or other recruiting events to help individuals obtain jobs.

**Social Worker** Social workers are often involved in helping people with their social or economic problems. They may investigate, evaluate, and attempt to rectify reported cases of abuse, neglect, endangerment, or domestic disputes. They can intervene in families if necessary and provide counseling and referral services to individuals and families. They often work for publicly funded agencies at the city, state, or national level, although increasingly they work in the private sector in areas such as drug rehabilitation and family counseling. In some cases, social workers specialize in certain types of work. For example, family-care social workers often work with families in which a child, adolescent, or older adult needs support services. Social workers must have at least an undergraduate degree from a school of social work, including course work in various areas of sociology and psychology. Some social workers also have a master's or doctoral degree.

**Drug Counselor** Drug counselors provide counseling to individuals with drug-abuse problems, either on an individual basis or in group therapy sessions. They may work in private practice, with a state or federal agency, for a company, or in a hospital setting. Some specialize in working with adolescents. At a minimum, drug counselors must have an associate degree or certificate. Many have an undergraduate degree in substance-abuse counseling, and some have master's and doctoral degrees. In most states, drug counselors must fulfill a certification procedure to obtain a license to practice.

**Health Psychologist** Health psychologists work with many different health-care professionals, including physicians, nurses, clinical psychologists, psychiatrists, and social workers, in an effort to improve the health of adolescents. They may conduct research, perform clinical assessments, or give treatment. Many health psychologists focus on prevention through research and clinical interventions designed to foster health and reduce the risk of disease. More than half of all health psychologists provide clinical services. Among the settings in which health psychologists work are primary care programs, inpatient medical units, and specialized care programs in areas such as women's health, drug treatment, and smoking cessation.

Health psychologists typically have a doctoral degree (Ph.D. or Psy.D.) in psychology. Some receive training in clinical psychology as part of their graduate work. Others have obtained their doctoral degree in some area other than health psychology and then pursue a postdoctoral degree in health psychology. A postdoctoral degree usually takes about two additional years of graduate study. Many doctoral programs in clinical, counseling, social, and experimental psychology have specialized tracks in health psychology.

**Adolescent Medicine Specialist** Adolescent medicine specialists evaluate the medical and behavioral problems that are common among adolescents, including growth disorders (such as delayed puberty), acne, eating disorders, substance abuse, depression, anxiety, sexually transmitted infections, contraception and pregnancy, and sexual identity concerns. They may work in private practice, in a medical clinic, in a hospital, or in a medical school. As a medical doctor, they can administer drugs and may counsel parents and adolescents on ways to improve the adolescent's health. Many adolescent medicine specialists on the faculty of medical schools also teach and conduct research on adolescents' health and diseases.

Adolescent medicine specialists must complete medical school and then obtain further training in their specialty, which usually involves at least three more years of schooling. They must become board certified in either pediatrics or internal medicine.

## FAMILIES/RELATIONSHIPS

Adolescents sometimes benefit from help that is provided to the entire family. One career that involves working with adolescents and their families is marriage and family therapy.

**Marriage and Family Therapist** Many individuals who have psychological problems benefit when psychotherapy is provided within the context of a marital or family relationship. Marriage and family therapists may provide marital therapy, couple therapy to those individuals who are not married, and family therapy to two or more members of a family.

Marriage and family therapists must have a master's or doctoral degree. Their training is similar to that of a clinical psychologist but with a focus on marital and family relationships. In most states, professionals must go through a licensing procedure to practice marital and family therapy.

## WEB SITE CONNECTIONS FOR CAREERS IN ADOLESCENT DEVELOPMENT

The Web site for this book offers more detailed information about the careers in adolescent development described in this Appendix. Go to the Web site links in the Career Appendix section, where you will find a description of the relevant Web sites. Then click on a title that interests you, and you will be linked directly to the Web site. Choose from the following Web site connections:

***Education/Research***

Careers in Psychology
Elementary and Secondary School Teaching
Exceptional Children Teachers
Educational Psychology
School Psychology

***Clinical/Counseling/Medical***

Clinical Psychology
Psychiatry
Counseling Psychology
School Counseling
Social Work
Drug Counseling
Health Psychology
Pediatrics
Adolescent Medicine

***Families/Relationships***

Marriage and Family Therapist

# 2 Puberty, Health, and Biological Foundations

*In youth, we clothe ourselves with rainbows and go brave as the zodiac.*

—Ralph Waldo Emerson
American Poet and Essayist, 19th Century

## CHAPTER OUTLINE

## LEARNING GOALS

### Puberty

Determinants of Puberty
Growth Spurt
Sexual Maturation
Secular Trends in Puberty
Psychological Dimensions of Puberty

**1** Discuss the determinants, characteristics, and psychological dimensions of puberty.

### Health

Adolescence: A Critical Juncture in Health
Emerging Adults' Health
Nutrition
Exercise and Sports
Sleep

**2** Summarize the nature of adolescents' and emerging adults' health.

### Evolution, Heredity, and Environment

The Evolutionary Perspective
The Genetic Process
Heredity-Environment Interaction

**3** Explain the contributions of evolution, heredity, and environment to adolescent development.

# *Images of Adolescent Development*

## Puberty's Mysteries and Curiosities

I am pretty confused. I wonder whether I am weird or normal. My body is starting to change, but I sure don't look like a lot of my friends. I still look like a kid for the most part. My best friend is only 13, but he looks like he is 16 or 17. I get nervous in the locker room during PE class because when I go to take a shower, I'm afraid somebody is going to make fun of me since I'm not as physically developed as some of the others.

—Robert, age 12

I don't like my breasts. They are too small, and they look funny. I'm afraid guys won't like me if they don't get bigger.

—Angie, age 13

I can't stand the way I look. I have zits all over my face. My hair is dull and stringy. It never stays in place. My nose is too big. My lips are too small. My legs are too short. I have four warts on my left hand, and people get grossed out by them. So do I. My body is a disaster!

—Ann, age 14

I'm short and I can't stand it. My father is 6 feet tall, and here I am only 5 feet 4. I'm 14 already. I look like a kid, and I get teased a lot, especially by other guys. I'm always the last one picked for sides in basketball because I'm so short. Girls don't seem to be interested in me either because most of them are taller than I am.

—Jim, age 14

The comments of these four adolescents in the midst of pubertal change underscore the dramatic upheaval in their bodies following the calm, consistent growth of middle and late childhood. Young adolescents develop an acute concern about their bodies.

## PREVIEW

***Puberty's changes are perplexing to adolescents. Although these changes bring forth doubts, fears, and anxieties, most adolescents eventually overcome them. We explore many aspects of pubertal change in this chapter from growth spurts and sexual maturation to the psychological aspects of puberty. We also examine other topics related to adolescent physical development, including health and nutrition, the role of evolution, and the interaction of heredity and the environment.***

## 1 PUBERTY

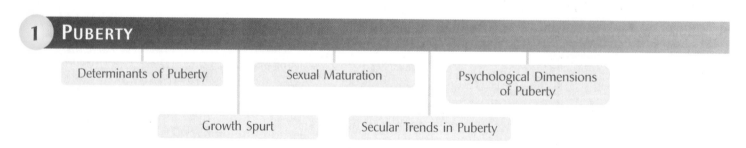

- Determinants of Puberty
- Growth Spurt
- Sexual Maturation
- Secular Trends in Puberty
- Psychological Dimensions of Puberty

**puberty** A period of rapid physical maturation involving hormonal and bodily changes that take place primarily in early adolescence.

Puberty can be distinguished from adolescence. For virtually everyone, puberty ends long before adolescence is exited. Puberty is often thought of as the most important marker for the beginning of adolescence. **Puberty** is a period of rapid physical maturation involving hormonal and bodily changes that take place primarily in early adolescence.

From *Penguin Dreams and Stranger Things* by Berkeley Breathed. Copyright © 1985 by The Washington Post Company. By permission of Little, Brown & Company. Copyright © 1985 by Barkeley Breathed. Reprinted by permission of International Creative Management, Inc.

## Determinants of Puberty

Although we do not know precisely what initiates puberty, a number of complex factors are involved. Puberty is accompanied by changes in the endocrine system, weight, body fat, and leptin, but we don't know if these are a cause or a consequence of puberty (Dorn & others, 2006). Also, there is increased interest in the role that birth weight, rapid weight gain in infancy, obesity, and sociocultural factors might play in pubertal onset and characteristics. As discussed next, heredity is an important factor in puberty.

**Heredity** Puberty is not an environmental accident. Programmed into the genes of every human being is the timing for the emergence of puberty (Hirschhorn, 2005; Roth & Ojeda, 2005). Puberty does not take place at 2 or 3 years of age and it does not occur in the twenties. In the future, molecular genetic studies may identify specific genes that are linked to the onset and progression of puberty. Nonetheless, as we see later in our discussion of puberty, which takes place between about 9 and 16 years of age for most individuals, environmental factors can also influence its onset and duration (vandenBerg & Boomsa, 2007).

**Hormones** Behind the first whisker in boys and the widening of hips in girls is a flood of **hormones,** powerful chemical substances secreted by the endocrine glands and carried throughout the body by the bloodstream. Two classes of hormones have significantly different concentrations in males and females: **androgens,** the main class of male sex hormones, and **estrogens,** the main class of female hormones. Note that although these hormones function more strongly in one sex or the other, they are produced by both males and females.

*Testosterone* is an androgen that plays an important role in male pubertal development. Throughout puberty, rising testosterone levels are associated with a number of physical changes in boys, including the development of external genitals, an increase in height, and voice changes (Campbell & Mbizo, 2006). Testosterone level in adolescent boys is also linked to sexual desire and activity (Cameron, 2004). *Estradiol* is an estrogen that plays an important role in female pubertal development. As estradiol levels rise, breast development, uterine development, and skeletal changes occur. The identity of hormones that contribute to sexual desire and activity in adolescent girls is less clear for girls than boys (Cameron, 2004). Both boys and girls experience an increase in both hormones during puberty. In one study, testosterone levels increased 18-fold in boys but only 2-fold in girls during puberty; estradiol levels increased 8-fold in girls but only 2-fold in boys during puberty (Nottelmann & others, 1987) (see Figure 2.1).

**hormones** Powerful chemicals secreted by the endocrine glands and carried through the body by the bloodstream.

**androgens** The main class of male sex hormones.

**estrogens** The main class of female sex hormones.

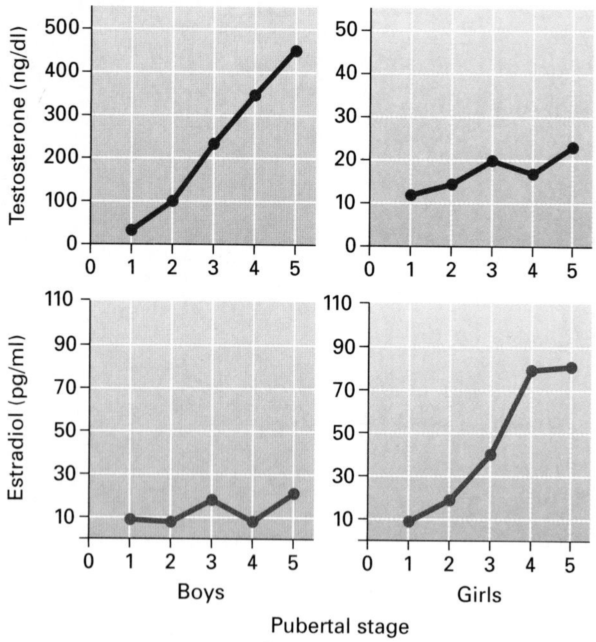
Testosterone (ng/dl)
500
400
300
200
100
0
50
40
30
20
10
0
0 1 2 3 4 5
0 1 2 3 4 5
Estradiol (pg/ml)
110
90
70
50
30
10
0 1 2 3 4 5
0 1 2 3 4 5
Boys
Girls
Pubertal stage

**FIGURE 2.1 Hormone Levels by Sex and Pubertal Stage for Testosterone and Estradiol** The five stages range from the early beginning of puberty (stage 1) to the most advanced stage of puberty (stage 5). Notice the significant increase in testosterone in boys and the significant increase in estradiol in girls.

**The Endocrine System** The endocrine system's role in puberty involves the interaction of the hypothalamus, the pituitary gland, and the gonads (sex glands) (see Figure 2.2). The *hypothalamus* is a structure in the higher portion of the brain that monitors eating, drinking, and sex. The *pituitary gland* is the endocrine gland that controls growth and regulates other glands. The *gonads* are the sex glands—the testes in males, the ovaries in females. How does the endocrine system work? The pituitary gland sends a signal via gonadotropins (hormones that stimulate sex glands) to the testes or ovaries to manufacture the hormone. Then, through interaction with the hypothalamus, the pituitary gland detects when the optimal level of hormones has been reached and maintains it with additional gonadotropin secretions (Clarkson & Herbison, 2006; Yoo & others, 2006).

Levels of sex hormones are regulated by two hormones secreted by the pituitary gland: *FSH* (*follicle-stimulating hormone*) and *LH* (*luteinizing hormone*). FSH stimulates follicle development in females and sperm production in males. LH regulates estrogen secretion and ovum development in females and testosterone production in males (Ojeda & others, 2006; Rapkin & others, 2006). In addition, the hypothalamus secretes a substance called *GnRH* (*gonadotropin-releasing hormone*) that is linked to pubertal timing (Hughes & Kumanan, 2006; Whitlock & others, 2006).

These hormones are regulated by a *negative feedback system*. If the level of sex hormones rises too high, the hypothalamus and pituitary gland reduce their stimulation of the gonads, decreasing the production

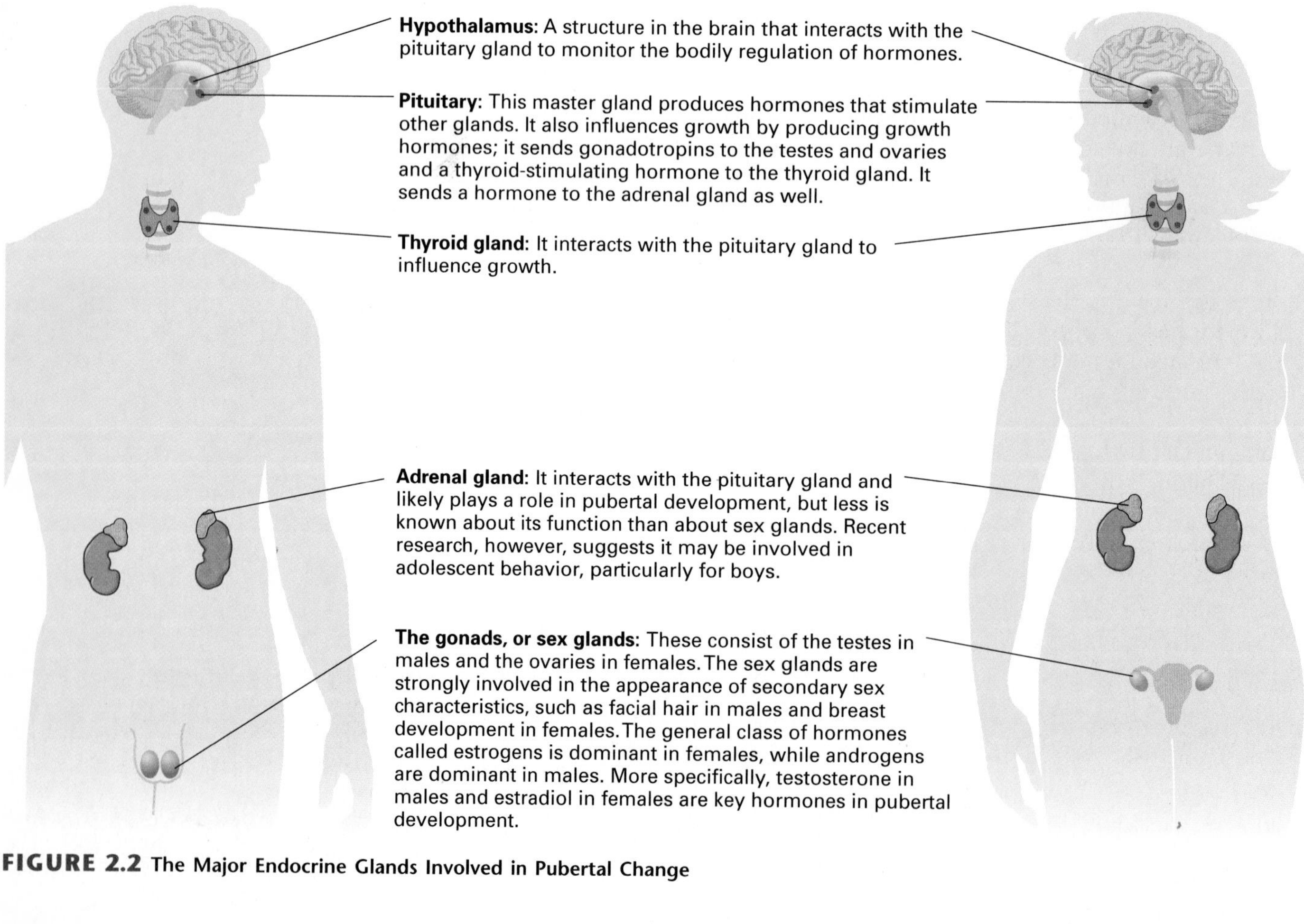
**Hypothalamus:** A structure in the brain that interacts with the pituitary gland to monitor the bodily regulation of hormones.
**Pituitary:** This master gland produces hormones that stimulate other glands. It also influences growth by producing growth hormones; it sends gonadotropins to the testes and ovaries and a thyroid-stimulating hormone to the thyroid gland. It sends a hormone to the adrenal gland as well.
**Thyroid gland:** It interacts with the pituitary gland to influence growth.
**Adrenal gland:** It interacts with the pituitary gland and likely plays a role in pubertal development, but less is known about its function than about sex glands. Recent research, however, suggests it may be involved in adolescent behavior, particularly for boys.
**The gonads, or sex glands:** These consist of the testes in males and the ovaries in females. The sex glands are strongly involved in the appearance of secondary sex characteristics, such as facial hair in males and breast development in females. The general class of hormones called estrogens is dominant in females, while androgens are dominant in males. More specifically, testosterone in males and estradiol in females are key hormones in pubertal development.

**FIGURE 2.2 The Major Endocrine Glands Involved in Pubertal Change**

of sex hormones. If the level of sex hormones falls too low, the hypothalamus and pituitary gland increase their production of the sex hormones.

Figure 2.3 shows how the feedback system works. In males, the pituitary gland's production of LH stimulates the testes to produce testosterone. When testosterone levels rise too high, the hypothalamus decreases its production of GnRH, which reduces the pituitary's production of LH. When the level of testosterone falls as a result, the hypothalamus produces more GnRH and the cycle starts again. The negative feedback system operates in a similar way in females, except that LH and GnRH regulate the ovaries and the production of estrogen.

This negative feedback system in the endocrine system can be compared to a thermostat and furnace. If a room becomes cold, the thermostat signals the furnace to turn on. The action of the furnace warms the air in the room, which eventually triggers the thermostat to turn off the furnace. The room temperature gradually begins to fall again until the thermostat once again signals the furnace to turn on, repeating the cycle. This type of system is called a *negative* feedback loop because a *rise* in temperature turns *off* the furnace, while a *decrease* in temperature turns *on* the furnace.

The level of sex hormones is low in childhood but increases in puberty. It is as if the thermostat is set at 50°F in childhood and now becomes set at 80°F in puberty. At the higher setting, the gonads have to produce more sex hormones, and that is what happens during puberty.

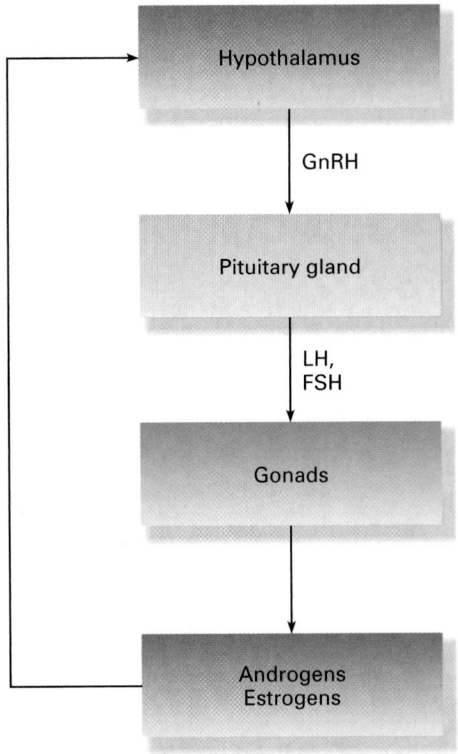


**FIGURE 2.3** **The Feedback System of Sex Hormones**

**Growth Hormones** We have seen that the pituitary gland releases gonadotropins that stimulate the testes and ovaries. In addition, through interaction with the hypothalamus, the pituitary gland also secretes hormones that lead to growth and skeletal maturation either directly or through interaction with the *thyroid gland,* located in the neck region (see Figure 2.2).

At the beginning of puberty, growth hormone is secreted at night. Later in puberty, it also is secreted during the day, although daytime levels are usually very low (Susman, Dorn, & Schiefelbein, 2003). Cortisol, a hormone that is secreted by the adrenal cortex, also influences growth as do testosterone and estrogen (Guercio & others, 2003).

**Adrenarche and Gonadarche** Two phases of puberty are linked with hormonal changes: adrenarche and gonadarche (Susman & Rogol, 2004). **Adrenarche** involves hormonal changes in the adrenal glands, located just above the kidneys. These changes occur surprisingly early, from about 6 to 9 years of age in girls and about one year later in boys, before what is generally considered the beginning of puberty (Dorn & others, 2006). During adrenarche and continuing through puberty, the adrenal glands secrete adrenal androgens, such as dehydroepiandrosterone (DHEA) (Blogowskal, Rzepka-Gorska, & Krzyzanowska-Swiniarska, 2005). Adrenarche is still not well understood (Dorn & others, 2006).

**Gonadarche,** which follows adrenarche by about two years, is the period most people think of as puberty (Archibald, Graber, & Brooks-Gunn, 2003). Gonadarche involves the maturation of primary sexual characteristics (ovaries in females, testes in males) and secondary sexual characteristics (pubic hair, breast, and genital development) (Dorn & others, 2006). "The hallmark of gonadarche is reactivation of the hypothalamic-pituitary-gonadal axis (HPG). . . . The initial activation of the HPG axis was during the fetal and neonatal period" (Dorn & others, 2006, p. 35).

In the United States, the gonadarche period begins at approximately 9 to 10 years of age in non-Latino White girls, and 8 to 9 years in African American girls (Herman-Giddens, Kaplowitz, & Wasserman, 2004). In boys, gonadarche begins at about 10 to 11 years of age. **Menarche,** the first menstrual period, occurs in mid to late gonadarche in girls. In boys, **spermarche,** a boy's first ejaculation of semen, occurs in early to mid gonadarche. Robert, Angie, Ann, and Jim, the adolescents we described in *Images of Adolescent Development,* are each in various phases of adrenarche and gonadarche.

**adrenarche** Puberty phase involving hormonal changes in the adrenal glands, located just above the kidneys. These changes occur from about 6 to 9 years of age in girls and about one year later in boys, before what is generally considered the beginning of puberty.

**gonadarche** Puberty phase involving the maturation of primary sexual characteristic (ovaries in females, testes in males) and secondary sexual characteristics (pubic hair, breast, and genital development). This period follows adrenarche by about two years and is what most people think of as puberty.

**menarche** A girl's first menstrual period.

**spermarche** A boy's first ejaculation of semen.

*What are some of the differences in the ways girls and boys experience pubertal growth?*

**Weight, Body Fat, and Leptin** Some researchers believe that a child must reach a critical body mass before puberty, especially *menarche*, emerges (Ackerman & others, 2006; Blogowskal, Rzepka-Gorska, & Krzyzanowska-Swiniarska, 2005). A number of studies have found that higher weight, especially obesity, is linked to earlier pubertal development (Dunger, Ahmed, & Ong, 2006). Some have even proposed that a body weight of 106 +/− 3 pounds triggers menarche and the end of the pubertal growth spurt (Friesch, 1984). However, this specific weight target is not well documented (Susman, 2001).

Other scientists have hypothesized that the onset of menarche is influenced by the percentage of body fat in relation to total body weight. For menarche to occur, they say that a minimum of 17 percent of a girl's body weight must be comprised of body fat. As with the weight target, this percentage has not been consistently verified. However, both anorexic adolescents whose weight drops dramatically and females who participate in certain sports (such as gymnastics and swimming) may not menstruate (Fujii & Demura, 2003). In boys, undernutrition may delay puberty (Susman, Dorn, and Schiefelbein, 2003).

The hormone *leptin* may signal the beginning and progression of puberty (Blogowskal, Rzepka-Gorska, & Krzyzanowska-Swiniarska, 2005). Leptin concentrations, which are higher in girls than in boys, are related to the amounts of fat in girls and androgen in boys (Cervero & others, 2006). Thus, a rise in leptin may indicate adequate fat stores for reproduction and the maintenance of pregnancy (Kelesidis & Mantzoros, 2006; Zeinoldini, Swarts, & Van de Heijning, 2006). Changes in leptin levels have not yet been studied in relation to adolescent behavior, however. Further, leptin is thought to be a necessary but not sufficient cause for puberty (Dorn, 2006).

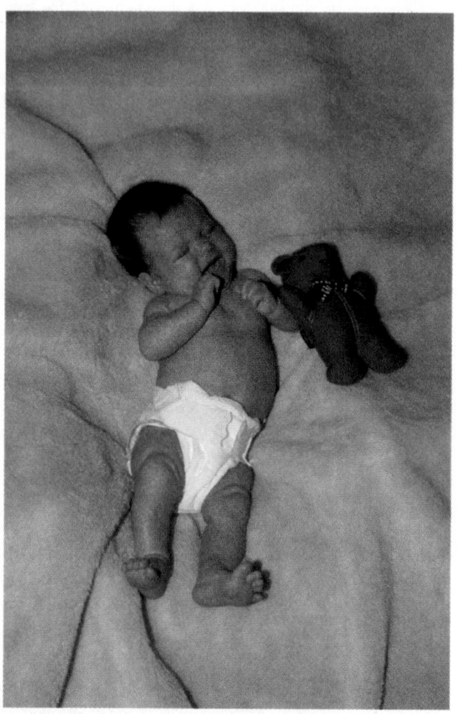

*How might birth weight and weight gain in infancy be linked to pubertal onset?*

**Weight at Birth and in Infancy** Might puberty's onset and characteristics be influenced by birth weight and weight gain during infancy? There is increasing research evidence for this link (van Weissenbruch & Delemarre-van de Waal, 2006). Low birth weight girls experience menarche approximately 5 to 10 months earlier than normal birth weight girls, and low birth weight boys are at risk for small testicular volume during adolescence (Ibanez & de Zegher, 2006). Researchers also have found that rapid weight gain in infancy is related to earlier pubertal onset (Dunger, Ahmed, & Ong, 2006).

**Sociocultural and Environmental Factors** Might sociocultural and environmental factors be linked to pubertal timing? Recent research indicates that cultural variations and early experiences may be related to earlier pubertal onset. Adolescents in developed countries and large urban areas reach puberty earlier than their counterparts in less developed countries and rural areas (Graham, 2005). Children who have been adopted from developing countries to developed countries often enter puberty earlier than their counterparts who continue to live in developing countries (Teilmann & others, 2002). African American females enter puberty earlier than non-Latino females, and African American males enter puberty earlier than non-Latino males (Biro & others, 2006; Herman-Giddens, 2006). Later in this chapter, we further examine variations in puberty in developed and developing countries.

Early experiences that are linked to earlier pubertal onset include father absence, low socioeconomic status, family conflict, and child maltreatment (Bogaert, 2005; Ellis, 2004; Maestripieri, & others, 2004; Romans & others, 2003). In many cases, puberty comes several months earlier in these situations. How can these links be explained? Researchers conclude that high rates of conflict and stress in these social contexts are the most likely explanation (Ellis, 2004).

There also has been interest in whether certain pollutants might influence the onset of puberty (Massart & others, 2006). Some studies have reported earlier menarche in girls exposed to polychlorinated biphenyls (PCBs), but other studies have not confirmed this link (Den Hond & Schoeters, 2006). PCBs are chemical compounds that no longer are manufactured in the United States but are still present in the environment; one source of PCBs are fish who live in contaminated water.

## Growth Spurt

Growth slows throughout childhood, so puberty brings forth the most rapid increases in growth since infancy. Figure 2.4 shows that the growth spurt associated with puberty occurs approximately two years earlier for girls than for boys. For girls, the mean beginning of the growth spurt is 9 years of age; for boys, it is 11 years of age. The peak of pubertal change occurs at 11½ years for girls and 13½ years for boys. During their growth spurt, girls increase in height about 3½ inches per year; boys, about 4 inches.

Boys and girls who are shorter or taller than their peers before adolescence are likely to remain so during adolescence. At the beginning of adolescence, girls tend to be as tall as or taller than boys of their age, but by the end of the middle school years most boys have caught up with them, or in many cases even surpassed them in height. Though height in elementary school is a good predictor of height later in adolescence, as much as 30 percent of an individual's height in late adolescence is unexplained by the child's height in elementary school.

The rate at which adolescents gain weight follows approximately the same developmental timetable as the rate at which they gain height. Marked weight gains coincide with the onset of puberty (Susman & Rogol, 2004). Fifty percent of adult body weight is gained during adolescence (Rogol, Roemmich, & Clark, 1998). At the peak of this weight gain, girls gain an average of 18 pounds in one year at roughly 12 years of age (approximately six months after their peak height increase). Boys' peak weight gain per year (20 pounds) occurs at about the same time as their peak increase in height, about 13 to 14 years of age. During early adolescence, girls tend to outweigh boys, but just as with height, by about 14 years of age, boys begin to surpass girls in weight.

In addition to increases in height and weight, puberty brings changes in hip and shoulder width. Girls experience a spurt in hip width, whereas boys undergo an increase in shoulder width. In girls, increased hip width is linked with an increase in estrogen. In boys, increased shoulder width is associated with an increase in testosterone (Susman & Rogol, 2004).

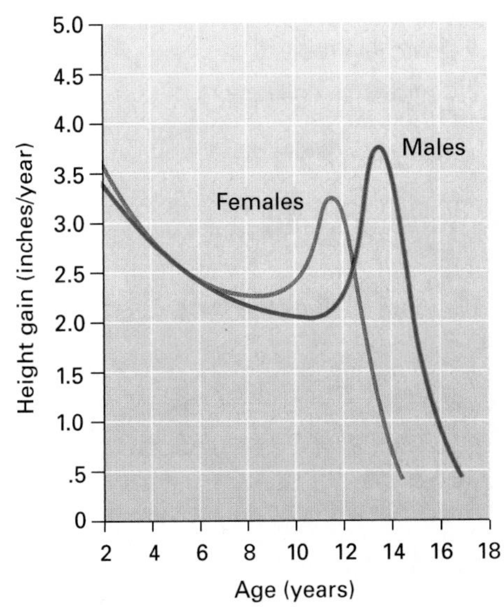


**FIGURE 2.4 Pubertal Growth Spurt** On the average, the peak of the growth spurt that characterizes pubertal changes occurs two years earlier for girls (11½) than for boys (13½).

**ZITS By Jerry Scott and Jim Borgman**

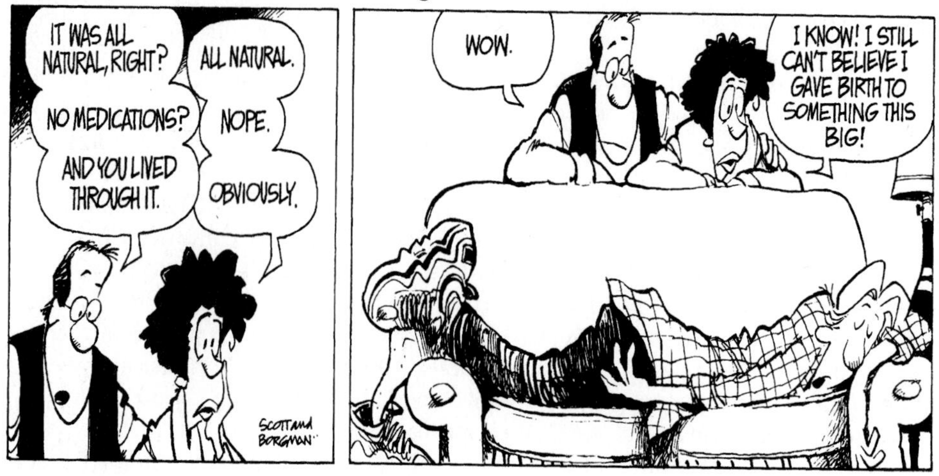




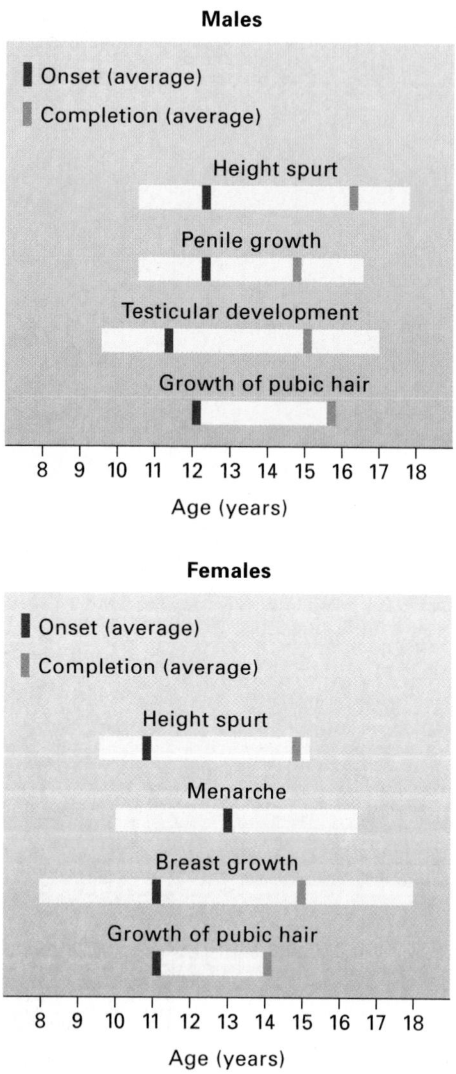


**FIGURE 2.5 Normal Range and Average Development of Sexual Characteristics in Males and Females** Adapted from "Growing Up" by J. M. Tanner. Copyright © 1973 by Scientific American, Inc. All rights reserved.

Finally, the later growth spurt of boys produces a greater leg length in boys than in girls. In many cases, boys' facial structure becomes more angular during puberty, whereas girls' facial structure becomes rounder and softer.

## Sexual Maturation

Think back to the onset of your puberty. Of the striking changes that were taking place in your body, what was the first that occurred? Researchers have found that male pubertal characteristics develop in this order: increased penis and testicle size; appearance of straight pubic hair; minor voice change; first ejaculation (spermarche—this usually occurs through masturbation or a wet dream); appearance of kinky pubic hair; onset of maximum growth; growth of hair in armpits; more detectable voice changes; and growth of facial hair. Three of the most noticeable signs of sexual maturation in boys are penis elongation, testes development, and growth of facial hair. The normal range and average age of development for these sexual characteristics, along with height spurt, are shown in Figure 2.5. Figure 2.6 illustrates the typical course of male sexual development during puberty. The five numbers in these figures reflect the five stages of secondary sexual characteristics known as the Tanner stages (Tanner, 1962).

What is the order of appearance of physical changes in females? First, either the breasts enlarge or pubic hair appears. Later, hair appears in the armpits. As these changes occur, the female grows in height, and her hips become wider than her shoulders. Her first menstruation (menarche) occurs rather late in the pubertal cycle. Initially, her menstrual cycles may be highly irregular and for the first several years, she might not ovulate every cycle. In some instances, a female does not become fertile until two years after her period begins. No voice changes occur that are comparable to those in pubertal males. By the end of puberty, the female's breasts have become more fully rounded. Two of the most noticeable aspects of female pubertal change are pubic hair and breast development. Figure 2.5 shows the normal range and average development for two of these female sexual characteristics. The figure also provides information about menarche and height gain. Figure 2.6 illustrates the typical course of female sexual development during puberty.

Note that there may be wide individual variations in the onset and progression of puberty. For boys, the pubertal sequence may begin as early as 10 years of age or as late as 13½. It may end as early as 13 years or as late as 17. The normal range is wide enough that given two boys of the same chronological age, one might complete the pubertal sequence before the other one has begun it. For girls, the normal age range for menarche is even wider, between 9 and 15 years of age.

**MALE SEXUAL DEVELOPMENT**

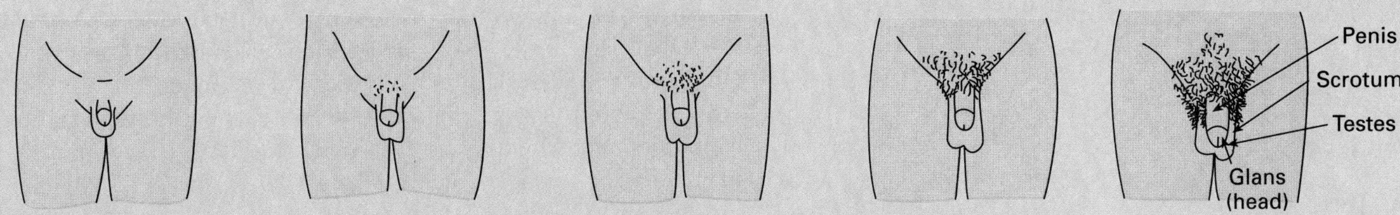


1.
No pubic hair. The testes, scrotum, and penis are about the same size and shape as those of a child.

2.
A little soft, long, lightly colored hair, mostly at the base of the penis. This hair may be straight or a little curly. The testes and scrotum have enlarged, and the skin of the scrotum has changed. The scrotum, the sack holding the testes, has lowered a bit. The penis has grown only a little.

3.
The hair is darker, coarser, and more curled. It has spread to thinly cover a somewhat larger area. The penis has grown mainly in length. The testes and scrotum have grown and dropped lower than in stage 2.

4.
The hair is now as dark, curly, and coarse as that of an adult male. However, the area that the hair covers is not as large as that of an adult male; it has not spread to the thighs. The penis has grown even larger and wider. The glans (the head of the penis) is bigger. The scrotum is darker and bigger because the testes have gotten bigger.

5.
The hair has spread to the thighs and is now like that of an adult male. The penis, scrotum, and testes are the size and shape of those of an adult male.

**FEMALE SEXUAL DEVELOPMENT**

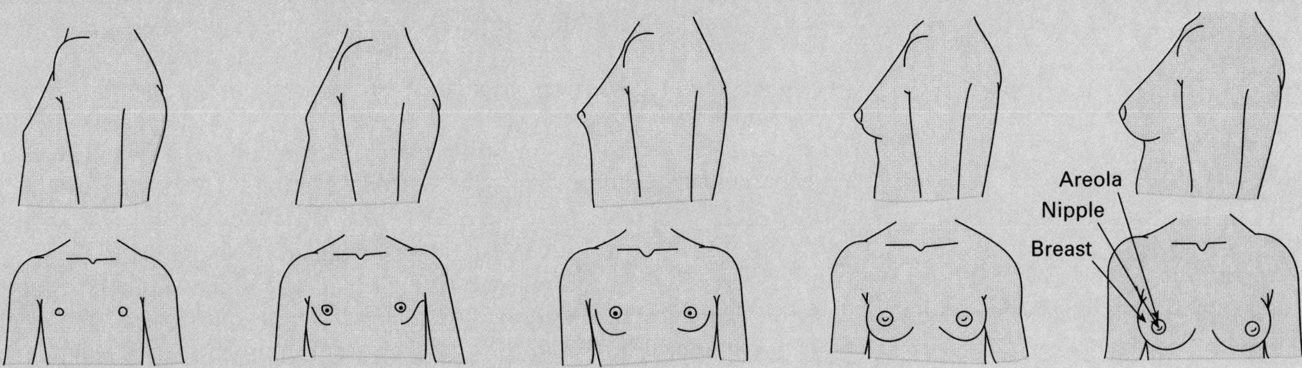


1.
The nipple is raised just a little. The rest of the breast is still flat.

2.
The breast bud stage. The nipple is raised more than in stage 1. The breast is a small mound, and the areola is larger than in stage 1.

3.
The areola and the breast are both larger than in stage 2. The areola does not stick out from the breast.

4.
The areola and the nipple make up a mound that sticks up above the shape of the breast. (Note: This may not happen at all for some girls; some develop from stage 3 to stage 5, with no stage 4.)

5.
The mature adult stage. The breasts are fully developed. Only the nipple sticks out. The areola has moved back to the general shape of the breast.

**FIGURE 2.6** The Five Pubertal Stages of Male and Female Sexual Development

## Secular Trends in Puberty

Imagine a toddler displaying all the features of puberty—a 3-year-old girl with fully developed breasts, or a boy just slightly older, with a deep male voice. That is what we would see by the year 2250 if the age at which puberty arrives continued to drop at the rate at which it occurred for much of the twentieth century. However, we are unlikely to ever see pubescent toddlers because of genetic limits on how early puberty can occur.

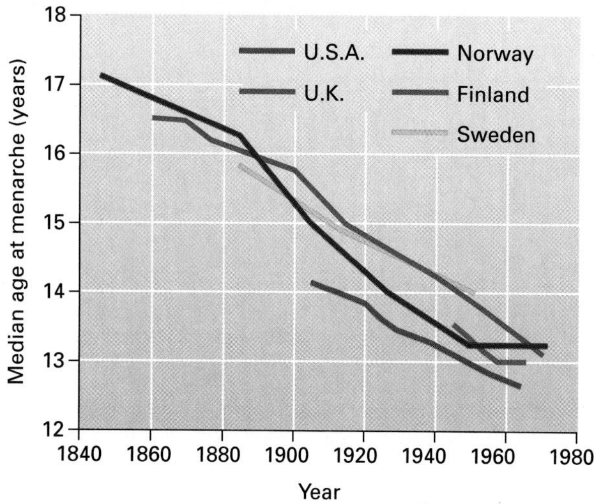


**FIGURE 2.7 Median Ages at Menarche in Selected Northern European Countries and the United States from 1845 to 1969** Notice the steep decline in the age at which girls experienced menarche in five different countries. Recently the age at which girls experience menarche has been leveling off.

The term **secular trends** refers to patterns of pubertal onset over historical time, especially across generations. For example, in Norway, menarche now occurs at just over 13 years of age, compared with 17 years of age in the 1840s (de Muinek Keizer-Schramm & Mul, 2001; Ong, Ahmed, & Dunger, 2006; Petersen, 1979). In the United States, where children mature physically up to a year earlier than in European countries, menarche now occurs at about 12½ years of age compared with over 14 years of age a century ago (see Figure 2.7). An increasing number of U.S. girls are beginning puberty at 8 and 9 years of age, with African American girls developing earlier than non-Latino white girls (Hermann-Giddens, 2006, 2007; Himes, 2006).

The earlier onset of puberty in the twentieth century was likely due to improved health and nutrition. An increase in obesity also is likely responsible (Biro, Khoury, & Morrison, 2006; Rudra & Williams, 2006).

So far, we have been concerned mainly with the physical dimensions of puberty. As we see next, the psychological dimensions of puberty are also important.

## Psychological Dimension of Puberty

A host of psychological changes accompanies an adolescent's pubertal development. Try to remember when you were entering puberty. Not only did you think of yourself differently, but your parents and peers also began treating you differently. Maybe you were proud of your changing body, even though it perplexed you. Perhaps your parents felt they could no longer sit in bed and watch television with you or even kiss you good night.

Far less research has been conducted on the psychosocial aspects of male pubertal transitions than on female pubertal transitions, possibly because of the difficulty in detecting when the male transitions occur. Wet dreams are one marker, yet there has been little research on the topic (Susman & others, 1995).

**secular trends** Patterns of the onset of puberty over historical time, especially across generations.

### Body Image

One psychological aspect of puberty is certain for both boys and girls: adolescents are preoccupied with their bodies (Nishina & others, 2006; Nollen & others, 2006). In puberty, adolescents develop individual images of their bodies. Perhaps you looked in the mirror on a daily—and sometimes even hourly—basis to see if you could detect anything different in your changing body. Preoccupation with one's body image is strong throughout adolescence, but it is especially acute during puberty.

**Gender Differences** Gender differences characterize adolescents' perceptions of their bodies. In general, girls are less happy with their bodies and have more negative body images than boys throughout puberty (Bearman & others, 2006; Brooks-Gunn & Paikoff, 1997). As pubertal change proceeds, girls often become more dissatisfied with their bodies, probably because their body fat increases. In contrast, boys become more satisfied as they move through puberty, probably because their muscle mass increases (Bearman & others, 2006). Here is a sampling of recent research on body image in adolescence:

- *Ethnicity.* Although there were more similarities than differences in body image across ethnic groups in early adolescence, in one study, African American girls were more dissatisfied with their body image than girls from other ethnic backgrounds (Nishina & others, 2006). In this study, higher levels of body dissatisfaction were linked to maladjustment in both girls and boys.

## *Through the Eyes of Adolescents*

### ATTRACTIVE BLOND FEMALES AND TALL MUSCULAR MALES

When columnist Bob Greene (1988) called Connections in Chicago, a chatline for teenagers, to find out what young adolescents were saying to each other, the first things the boys and girls asked–after first names–were physical descriptions. The idealism of the callers was apparent. Most of the girls described themselves as having long blond hair, being 5 feet 5 inches tall, and weighing 110 pounds. Most of the boys said that they had brown hair, lifted weights, were 6 feet tall, and weighed 170 pounds.

A meta-analysis (a statistical analysis that combines the results of many studies) found that during adolescence and college, non-Latino White females had more negative body images than African American females, but during adulthood there were no differences in their body images (Grabe & Hyde, 2006). The researchers concluded that in adolescence, girls are bombarded by media images of tall, thin, non-Latino White women. By the time they are in their late twenties, many of these women may be less likely to compare themselves with media images of tall, thin women. Another revealed that the more TV non-Latino White girls watch, the more their body images subsequently worsen. Watching TV with mainly non-Latino White casts was not linked to African American girls' body images, but when these girls watched TV shows with mainly African American casts, their body images improved (Schooler & others, 2004). Why? Possibly because a wider range of female body sizes and shapes are reflected in the cast of African American females on TV shows.

- *Appearance.* Adolescent males who evaluated their appearance more positively and who said appearance was very important to them were more likely to engage in risky sexy behavior, whereas adolescent females who evaluated their appearance more positively were less likely to engage in risky behavior (Gillen, Lefkowitz, & Shearer, 2006).
- *Developmental changes.* A longitudinal study of 428 boys and girls revealed that girls' body dissatisfaction increased, whereas boys' body dissatisfaction decreased as they went through early adolescence (Bearman & others, 2006). In this study, for both boys and girls, lack of parental support and dietary restraint preceded future increases in body satisfaction.
- *Mental health problems.* A study indicated that 12- to 17-year-old girls who were patients in psychiatric hospitals who had a negative body image were more depressed, anxiety-prone, and suicidal than same-aged patients who were less concerned about their body image (Dyl, Kittler, & Hunt, 2006).
- *Health.* A longitudinal study of more than 2,500 adolescents found that lower body satisfaction placed them at risk for poorer overall health (Neumark-Sztainer & others, 2006).
- *Perceived best and worst aspects of being a boy or a girl.* The negative aspects of puberty for girls appeared in a recent study that explored 400 middle school

Adolescents show a strong preoccupation with their changing bodies and develop images of what their bodies are like. *Why might adolescent males have more positive body images than adolescent females?*

boys' and girls' perceptions of the best and worst aspects of being a boy or a girl (Zittleman, 2006). In the views of the middle school students, at the top of the list of the worst things about being a girl was the biology of being female, which included such matters as childbirth, PMS, periods, and breast cancer. The middle school students said differential discipline (getting into trouble, being disciplined, and being blamed more than girls even when they were not at fault) is the worst thing about being a boy.

However, another aspect of physical development was at the top of the students' list of the best things about being a girl—appearance (which included choosing clothes, hair/styles, and beauty treatments). Students said the best thing about being a boy was playing sports.

Body Art, such as tattoos and body piercing, is increasing in adolescence and emerging adulthood. *Why do youth engage in such body modification?*

**Body Art** An increasing number of adolescents and college students are obtaining tattoos and getting parts of their body pierced (Armstrong, Caliendo, & Roberts, 2006; Beznos & Coates, 2007; Koch & others, 2005). Many of these youth engage in such body modification to be different, to stamp their identity as unique. In one study of adolescents, 60 percent of the students with tattoos had academic grades of As and Bs (Armstrong, 1995). In this study, the average age at which the adolescents got their first tattoo was 14 years of age. Some studies indicate that tattoos and body piercings are markers for risk taking in adolescence (Carroll & others, 2002; Deschesnes, Fines, & Demers, 2006; Roberts, & Ryan, 2004). A recent study revealed that having multiple body piercings is especially a marker for risk-taking behavior (Suris & others, 2007). However, other researchers argue that body art is increasingly used to express individuality and self-expression rather than rebellion (Armstrong & others, 2004).

A recent study of college students indicated that both students with body art and those without body art reported a positive image for body art (Armstrong & others, 2004). In this study, friends rather than parents provided the main support for body art. Students who had body art said that being unique was important to them.

**Hormones and Behavior** Are concentrations of hormones linked to adolescent behavior? Hormonal factors are thought to account for at least part of the increase in negative and variable emotions that characterize adolescents (Archibald, Graber, & Brooks-Gunn, 2003; Dorn, Williams, & Ryan, 2002). Researchers have found that in boys higher levels of androgens are associated with violence and acting-out problems (Van Goozen & others, 1998). There is also some indication that increased estrogen levels are linked to depression in adolescent girls (Angold, Costello, & Worthman, 1999). Further, high levels of adrenal androgens are associated with negative affect in girls (Susman & Rogol, 2004). One recent study found that early-maturing girls with high levels of adrenal androgens had higher emotional arousal and depressive affect than other girls (Graber, Brooks-Gunn, & Warren, 2006).

However, hormonal factors alone are not responsible for adolescent behavior (DeRose & Brooks-Gunn, 2006; DeRose, Wright, & Brooks-Gunn, 2006; Graber, Brooks-Gunn, & Warren, 2006). For example, one study found that social factors accounted for two to four times as much variance as hormonal factors in young adolescent girls' depression and anger (Brooks-Gunn & Warren, 1989). Another study found little direct connection between adolescent males' and females' testosterone levels and risk behavior or depression (Booth & others, 2003). In contrast, a link with risk behavior depended on the quality of parent-adolescent relations. When relationship quality decreased, testosterone-linked risk-taking behavior and symptoms of depression increased. And in a recent study, negative life events mediate links between hormones (estradiol and an adrenal hormone) and aggression in 10- to 14-year-old girls (Graber, Brooks-Gunn, & Warren, 2006). Thus, hormones do not function independently with hormonal activity being influenced by many environmental factors, including parent-adolescent relationships. Stress, eating patterns, sexual activity, and depression can also activate or suppress various aspects of the hormone system (Archibald, Graber, & Brooks-Gunn, 2003).

**Menarche and the Menstrual Cycle** In most historical accounts of adolescence, the onset of puberty and menarche have been treated as a "main event" (Erikson, 1968; Freud, 1917/1958; Hall, 1904). Basically, the idea is that pubertal changes and events such as menarche produce a different body that requires considerable change in one's self-conception, possibly resulting in an identity crisis. Only recently has empirical research been directed at understanding the female adolescent's adaptation to menarche and the menstrual cycle (Brooks-Gunn, Graber, & Paikoff, 1994; El-Khouri & Mellner, 2004; Yeung, So-kum Tang, & Lee, 2005).

One study of 639 girls revealed a wide range of reactions to menarche (Brooks-Gunn & Ruble, 1982). Most were quite mild: girls described their first period as a little upsetting, a little surprising, or a little exciting. In this study, 120 fifth- and sixth-grade girls were telephoned to obtain personal, detailed information about their experience with menarche. The most frequent theme of the responses was positive—namely, that menarche was an index of their maturity. Other positive reports indicated that the girls could now have children, were experiencing something that made them more like adult women, and now were more like their friends. The most frequently reported negatives were the hassle of having to carry around supplies and messiness. A minority of the girls reported physical discomfort, behavioral limitations, and emotional changes.

The researchers asked questions about the extent to which the girls communicated with others about their menarche; the extent to which they were prepared for it; and its relation to early or late maturation. Virtually all the girls told their mothers immediately, but most did not tell anyone else; only one in five informed a friend. After two or three periods, most girls had talked with their girlfriends about menstruation, however. Girls who were not prepared for menarche reported more negative feelings than those who were more prepared for it. In addition, girls who matured early had more negative reactions than average- or late-maturing girls. In sum, menarche may be disruptive at first, especially for unprepared and early-maturing girls, but it typically does not provoke the tumultuous, conflicting reactions described by some early theoreticians.

For many girls, menarche occurs on time, but for others it can come early or late. Next, we examine the effects of early and late maturation on both boys and girls.

**Early and Late Maturation** Some of you entered puberty early, others late; still others entered on time. When adolescents mature earlier or later than their peers, do they perceive themselves differently? In the Berkeley Longitudinal Study conducted in the middle of the twentieth century, early-maturing boys perceived themselves more positively and had more successful peer relations than their late-maturing counterparts (Jones, 1965). For early-maturing girls, the findings were similar but not as strong as for boys. When the late-maturing boys were studied in their thirties, however, they had developed a stronger sense of identity than the early-maturing boys (Peskin, 1967). Late-maturing boys may have had more time to explore a wide variety of options. They may have focused on how career development and achievement would serve them better in life than the emphasis on physical status by their early-maturing counterparts. However, another study indicated that early maturing boys were more successful and less likely to drink alcohol or smoke cigarettes than late-maturing boys 39 years later in middle adulthood (Taga, Markey, & Friedman, 2006).

Recent research confirms that at least during adolescence, it is advantageous to be an early-maturing rather than a late-maturing boy (Graber, Brooks-Gunn, & Warren, 2006; Petersen, 1987). Roberta Simmons and Dale Blyth (1987) studied more than 450 male and female adolescents for five years, beginning in the sixth grade and

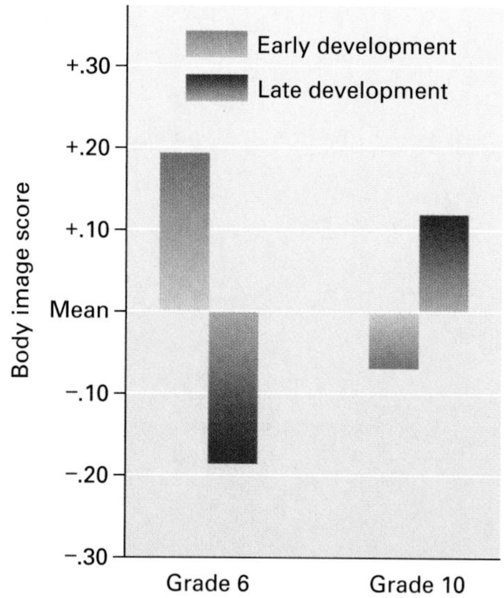


**FIGURE 2.8** **Early- and Late-Maturing Adolescent Girls' Perceptions of Body Image in Early and Late Adolescence**

continuing through the tenth grade, in Milwaukee, Wisconsin. They interviewed students and obtained their achievement test scores and grade point averages. The presence or absence of menstruation and the relative onset of menses were used to classify girls as early, middle, or late maturers. The peak of growth in height was used to classify boys in the same categories.

In the Milwaukee study, more mixed and complex findings emerged for girls (Simmons & Blyth, 1987). Early-maturing girls had more problems in school, were more independent, and were more popular with boys than late-maturing girls were. The time at which maturation was assessed also was a factor. In the sixth grade, early-maturing girls were more satisfied with their body image than late-maturing girls were, but by the tenth grade, late-maturing girls were more satisfied (see Figure 2.8). Why? Because by late adolescence, early-maturing girls are shorter and stockier, while late-maturing girls are taller and thinner. The late-maturing girls in late adolescence have body images that more closely approximate the current American ideal of feminine beauty—tall and thin.

In recent years, an increasing number of researchers have found that early maturation increases girls' vulnerability to a number of problems (Deardorff & others, 2007; Graber, 2007; Graber, Brooks-Gunn, & Warren, 2006; McCabe & Ricciardelli, 2003; Mendle, Turkheimer, & Emery, 2007; Waylen & Wolke, 2004). Early-maturing girls are more likely to smoke, drink, be depressed, have an eating disorder, request earlier independence from their parents, and have older friends; and their bodies are likely to elicit responses from males that lead to earlier dating and earlier sexual experiences. In one study, the early-maturing girls had lower educational and occupational attainment in adulthood (Stattin & Magnusson, 1990). In one study, early-maturing females had a higher incidence of mental disorders than late-maturing females (Graber & others, 2004). Apparently as a result of their social and cognitive immaturity, combined with early physical development, early-maturing girls are easily lured into problem behaviors, not recognizing the possible long-term effects of these on their development. To read further about early and late maturation, see the *Health and Well-Being* interlude.

# *Health and Well-Being*

## HEALTH-CARE CONSULTATION FOR EARLY AND LATE MATURERS

What can be done to identify early and late maturers who are at risk for health problems? Adolescents whose development is extremely early or late, such as a boy who has not had a growth spurt by age 16 or a girl who has not menstruated by age 15, are likely to come to the attention of a physician. Girls and boys who are early or late maturers, but are still well within the normal range, are less likely to be seen by a physician. Nonetheless, these boys and girls may have doubts and fears about being normal that they will not raise unless a physician, counselor, or other health-care provider does. A brief discussion of the usual sequence and timing of events, and the large individual variations in them, may be all that is required to reassure many adolescents who are maturing very early or late.

Health-care providers may want to discuss an adolescent's early or late development with parents as well. Information about peer pressures can be helpful, especially the peer pressures to date on early-maturing girls and engage in adultlike behavior. For girls and boys who are in the midst of puberty, the transition to middle school, junior high school, or high school may be more stressful (Wigfield & others, 2006).

If pubertal development is extremely late, a physician may recommend hormonal treatment. This approach may or may not be helpful (Carel, 2006; Richmond & Rogol, 2007; Spiliotis, 2006). In one study of extended pubertal delay in boys, hormonal treatment helped to increase height, dating interest, and peer relations in several boys but brought little or no improvement in other boys (Lewis, Money, & Bobrow, 1977).

In sum, most early- and late-maturing individuals manage to weather puberty's challenges and stresses. For those who do not, discussions with sensitive and knowledgeable health-care providers and parents can improve the adolescent's coping abilities.

**Are Puberty's Effects Exaggerated?** Some researchers have begun to question whether puberty's effects are as strong as was once believed. Have the effects of puberty been exaggerated? Puberty affects some adolescents more strongly than others, and some behaviors more strongly than others. Body image, interest in dating, and sexual behavior are quite clearly affected by pubertal change. In one study, early-maturing boys and girls reported more sexual activity and delinquency than late maturers (Flannery, Rowe, & Gulley, 1993). Yet, if we look at overall development and adjustment over the human life span, puberty and its variations have less dramatic effects than is commonly thought for most individuals. For some young adolescents, the path through puberty is stormy, but for most it is not. Each period of the human life span has its stresses and puberty is no different. Although it poses new challenges, the vast majority of adolescents weather the stresses effectively. Besides the biological influences on adolescent development, cognitive and social or environmental influences also shape who we become (Sarigiani & Petersen, 2000; Susman & Rogol, 2004). Singling out biological changes as the dominant influence during adolescence may not be wise.

Although extremely early and late maturation may be risk factors in development, we have seen that the overall effects of early or late maturation often are not great. Not all early maturers will date, smoke, and drink, and not all late maturers will have difficulty in peer relations. In some instances, the effects of an adolescent's grade in school are stronger than maturational timing (Petersen & Crockett, 1985). Because the adolescent's social world is organized by grade rather than physical development, this finding is not surprising. However, that does not mean that age of maturation has no influence on development. Rather, we need to evaluate puberty's effects within the larger framework of interacting biological, cognitive, and socioemotional contexts (Brooks-Gunn, 1992; Sarigiani & Petersen, 2000).

Anne Petersen has made numerous contributions to our understanding of puberty and adolescent development. To read about her work and career, see the *Careers in Adolescent Development* profile.

## Careers in ADOLESCENT DEVELOPMENT

### Anne Petersen
**Researcher and Administrator**

Anne Petersen has had a distinguished career as a researcher and administrator with a main focus on adolescent development. Anne obtained three degrees (B.A., M.A., and Ph.D.) from the University of Chicago in math and statistics. Her first job after she obtained her Ph.D. was as a research associate/professor involving statistical consultation, and it was on this job that she was introduced to the field of adolescent development, which became the focus of her subsequent work.

Anne moved from the University of Chicago to Pennsylvania State University, where she became a leading researcher in adolescent development. Her research included a focus on puberty and gender. Anne also has held numerous administrative positions. In the mid-1990s, Anne became deputy director of the National Science Foundation and from 1996 to 2006 was senior vice-president for programs at the W. K. Kellogg Foundation. In 2006, Anne Petersen became the deputy director of the Center for Advanced Study in the Behavioral Sciences at Stanford University and also assumed the position of professor of psychology at Stanford.

Anne says that what inspired her to enter the field of adolescent development and take her current position at the Kellogg Foundation was her desire to make a difference for people, especially youth. In her position at Kellogg, Anne is responsible for all programming and services provided by the foundation for adolescents. Her goal is to make a difference for youth in this country and around the world. She believes that too often adolescents have been neglected.

Anne Petersen, interacting with adolescents.

**REVIEW AND REFLECT ◆ LEARNING GOAL 1**

**1 Discuss the determinants, characteristics, and psychological dimensions of puberty.**

***Review***
- What are puberty's main determinants?
- What characterizes the growth spurt in puberty?
- How does sexual maturation develop in puberty?
- What are some secular trends in puberty?
- What are some important psychological dimensions of puberty?

***Reflect***
- Think back to when you entered puberty. How strong was your curiosity about the pubertal changes that were taking place? What misconceptions did you have about those changes?

## 2 HEALTH

- Adolescence: A Critical Juncture in Health
- Emerging Adults' Health
- Nutrition
- Exercise and Sports
- Sleep

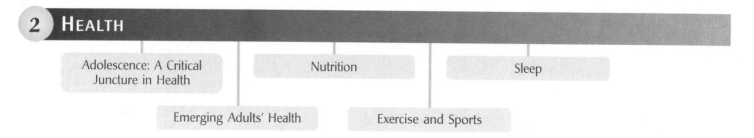

Why might adolescence be a critical juncture in health? What characterizes emerging adults' health? What are some concerns about adolescents' eating habits? How much do adolescents exercise, and what role do sports play in their lives? Do adolescents get enough sleep? These are among the questions we explore in this section.

### Adolescence: A Critical Juncture in Health

Adolescence is a critical juncture in the adoption of behaviors that are relevant to health (Neumark-Sztainer & others, 2006; Patton & Viner, 2007; Patton & others, 2006; Shribman, 2007). Many of the behaviors that are linked to poor health habits and early death in adults begin during adolescence. Conversely, the early formation of healthy behavior patterns, such as regular exercise and a preference for foods low in fat and cholesterol, not only has immediate health benefits but helps in adulthood to delay or prevent disability and mortality from heart disease, stroke, diabetes, and cancer (Anderson & others, 2006; Insel & Roth, 2008).

Unfortunately, even though the United States has become a health-conscious nation, many adolescents (and adults) still smoke, have poor nutritional habits, and spend too much of their lives as couch potatoes (Insel & Roth, 2006). Why is this so? In adolescence, many individuals reach a level of health, strength, and energy that they will never match during the remainder of their lives. They also have a sense of uniqueness and invulnerability that convinces them that they will never suffer from poor health, or if they do, they will quickly recover. Given this combination of physical strength and cognitive deception, it is not surprising that many adolescents develop poor health habits.

Many health experts conclude that improving adolescents' health involves far more than taking them to the doctor's office when they are sick. Increasingly, experts recognize that whether or not adolescents develop health problems depends primarily on their behavior (Foraker & others, 2005; Richer, 2006; Turbin & others, 2006). These experts' goals are to (1) reduce adolescents' *health-compromising behaviors*, such as drug abuse, violence, unprotected sexual intercourse, and dangerous driving; and (2) increase adolescents' *health-enhancing behaviors*, such as exercising, eating nutritiously, wearing seat belts, and getting adequate sleep.

A recent study found these activities, resources, and relationships to promote adolescents' health-enhancing behaviors (Youngblade & Curry, 2006): (1) participation in school-related organized activities, such as sports; (2) availability of positive community resources, such as boys and girls clubs, and volunteering; and (3) and secure attachment to parents. In this study, health-enchancing behavior was assessed by asking adolescents the extent to which they engaged in such behaviors as wearing a seat belt and engaging in physical activities in and out of school.

### Risk-Taking Behavior

One type of health-compromising behavior that increases in adolescence is risk taking (Baskin-Sommers & Sommers, 2006; Steinberg, 2007; Viner & others, 2006). For example, beginning in early adolescence, individuals

> *seek* experiences that create high intensity feelings. . . . Adolescents *like* intensity, excitement, and arousal. They are drawn to music videos that shock and bombard the senses. Teenagers flock to horror and slasher movies. They dominate queues waiting to ride the high-adrenaline rides at amusement parks. Adolescence is a time when sex, drugs, *very* loud music, and other high-stimulation experiences take on great appeal. It is a developmental period when an appetite for adventure, a predilection for risks, and a desire for novelty and thrills seem to reach naturally high levels. While these patterns of emotional changes are evident to some degree in most adolescents, it is important to acknowledge the wide range of individual differences during this period of development. (Dahl, 2004, p. 6)

Researchers also have found that the more resources there are in the community, such as youth activities and adults as role models, the less likely adolescents are to engage in risky behavior (Jessor, 1998). A recent study found that a higher level of what was labeled *social capital* (in this study, number of schools, number of churches/temples/synagogues, and number of high school diplomas) was linked with lower levels of adolescent risky behavior (in this study, gunshot wounds, pregnancy, alcohol and drug treatment, and sexually transmitted infections) (Youngblade & Curry, 2006). Another recent study revealed that "hanging out" with peers in unstructured

*What are some characteristics of adolescents' risk-taking behavior?*

contexts was linked with an increase in adolescents' risk-taking behavior (Youngblade & Curry, 2006). Also in this study, risk taking by siblings was related to the likelihood that an adolescent would engage in risk taking. Further, adolescents who had better grades were less likely to engage in risk taking than their counterparts with lower grades.

What can be done to help adolescents satisfy their motivation for risk taking without compromising their health? One strategy is to increase the social capital of a community as was recommended in the study just described (Youngblade & others, 2006). Also, as Laurence Steinberg (2004, p. 58) argues, another strategy is to limit

> opportunities for immature judgment to have harmful consequences. . . . Thus, strategies such as raising the price of cigarettes, more vigilantly enforcing laws governing the sale of alcohol, expanding access to mental health and contraceptive services, and raising the driving age would likely be more effective in limiting adolescent smoking, substance abuse, suicide, pregnancy, and automobile fatalities than strategies aimed at making adolescents wiser, less impulsive, and less short-sighted.

It also is important for parents, teachers, mentors, and other responsible adults to effectively monitor adolescents' behavior (Dahl, 2006). In many cases, adults decrease their monitoring of adolescents too early, leaving them to cope with tempting situations alone or with friends and peers (Masten, 2004). When adolescents are in tempting and dangerous situations with minimal adult supervision, their inclination to engage in risk-taking behavior combined with their lack of self-regulatory skills can make them vulnerable to a host of negative outcomes.

*What is the pattern of adolescent's use of health services?*

**Health Services** Though adolescents suffer from a greater number of acute health conditions than adults, they see private physicians less often than any other age group (Edelman, 1996). Adolescents also underutilize other health-care systems (Marcell & Halpern-Felsher, 2005). Health services are especially unlikely to meet the needs of younger adolescents, ethnic minority adolescents, and adolescents living in poverty.

In the National Longitudinal Study of Adolescent Health, more than 12,000 adolescents were interviewed about the extent to which they needed but did not receive health care (Ford, Bearman, & Moody, 1999). Approximately 19 percent of those interviewed reported forgoing health care in the preceding year. Among those who especially needed health care but did not seek it were adolescents who smoked cigarettes on a daily basis, drank alcohol frequently, and engaged in sexual intercourse.

Of special concern is the decrease in use of health services by older adolescent males (Wilson, Pritchard, & Revalee, 2005). A national study in the United States found that 16- to 20-year-old males have significantly less contact with health-care services than 11- to 15-year-old males (Marcell & others, 2002). In contrast, 16- to 20-year-old females have more contact with health-care services than younger females.

Among the chief barriers to better health care for adolescents are cost, poor organization and availability of health services, lack of confidentiality, and reluctance on the part of health-care providers to communicate with adolescents about sensitive health issues. Few health-care providers receive any special training in working with adolescents. Many say they feel unprepared to provide services such as contraceptive counseling or to evaluate what constitutes abnormal behavior in adolescents (Irwin, 1993). Health-care providers may transmit to their patients their discomfort in discussing topics such as sexuality and drugs, causing adolescents to avoid discussing sensitive issues with them (Marcell & Millstein, 2001). In one study, parents of urban adolescents reported that they want health-care providers to talk with their adolescents about sensitive health issues such as sexually transmitted infections, contraception, drug use, depression, nutrition, and stress (Cohall & others, 2004). However, the health-care providers rarely communicated with adolescents about these issues.

**Leading Causes of Death** Medical improvements have increased the life expectancy of today's adolescents and emerging adults compared with their counterparts in the early twentieth century. Still, life-threatening factors do exist in adolescents' and emerging adults' lives.

The three leading causes of death in adolescence and emerging adults are unintentional injuries, homicide, and suicide (National Center for Health Statistics, 2005). More than half of all deaths from 15 to 24 years of age are due to unintentional injuries, approximately three-fourths of them involving motor vehicles. Risky driving habits, such as speeding, tailgating, and driving under the influence of alcohol or other drugs, may be more important contributors to these accidents than lack of driving experience. In about 50 percent of motor vehicle fatalities involving adolescents, the driver has a blood alcohol level of 0.10 percent—twice the level needed to be designated as "under the influence" in some states. A high rate of intoxication is also found in adolescents who die as pedestrians, or while using recreational vehicles.

Homicide also is another leading cause of death in adolescence and emerging adults, especially among African American males, who are three times more likely to be killed by guns than by natural causes. Suicide is the third leading cause of death in adolescence and emerging adulthood. Since the 1950s, the adolescent and emerging adult suicide rate has tripled, although it has declined in recent years (Rueter & Kwon, 2005). We further discuss suicide in adolescence and emerging adulthood in Chapter 13, "Problems in Adolescence and Emerging Adulthood."

Emerging adults have more than twice the mortality rate of adolescents (Park & others, 2006) (see Figure 2.9). As indicated in Figure 2.9, males are mainly responsible for the higher mortality rate of emerging adults.

A makeshift memorial for Mehlville High School student Megan Landholt, stands on Lemay Ferry Road in South St. Louis County, MO, Friday, March 7, 2003. Car crashes resulting in eight teenage deaths in south S. Louis County in the past year and a half led police to hold a meeting at Oakville Senior High School Friday to talk about ways to reduce fatalities.

## Emerging Adults' Health

Although emerging adults have a higher death rate than adolescents, emerging adults have few chronic health problems, and they have fewer colds and respiratory problems than when they were children (Rimsza & Kirk, 2005). Most college students know what it takes to prevent illness and promote health. In one study, college students' ranking of health-protective activities—nutrition, sleep, exercise, watching one's weight, and so on—virtually matched that of licensed nurses (Turk, Rudy, & Salovey, 1984).

Although most college students know what it takes to prevent illness and promote health, they don't fare very well when it comes to applying this information to themselves (Lenz, 2004). In one study, college students reported that they probably would never have a heart attack or drinking problem, but that other college students would (Weinstein, 1984). The college students also said there was no relation between their risk of heart attack and how much they exercise, smoke, or eat meat or other high-cholesterol food such as eggs, even though they correctly recognized that factors such as family history influence risk. Many college students, it seems, have unrealistic, overly optimistic beliefs about their future health risks.

Few emerging adults stop to think about how their personal lifestyles will affect their health later in their adult lives (Sakamaki & others, 2005). As emerging adults, many of us develop a pattern of not eating breakfast, not eating regular meals, and relying on snacks as our main food source during the day, eating excessively to the point where we exceed the normal weight for our age, smoking moderately or excessively, drinking moderately or excessively, failing to exercise, and getting by with only a few hours of sleep at night (Cousineau, Goldstein, & Franco, 2005).

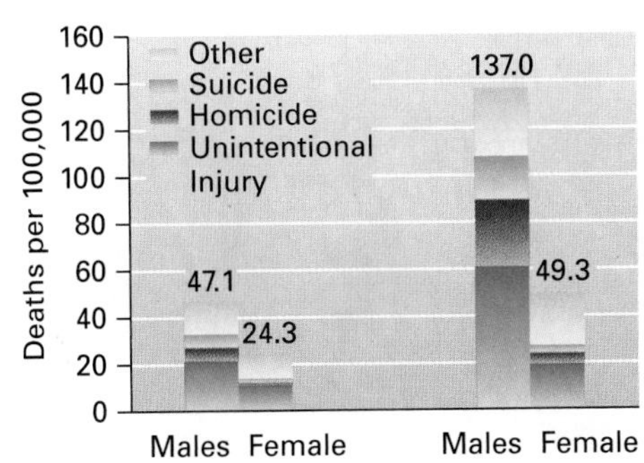


**FIGURE 2.9 Mortality Rates of U.S. Adolescents and Emerging Adults**

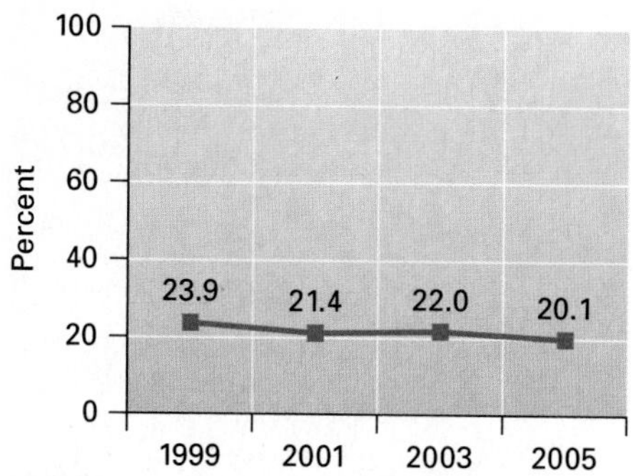

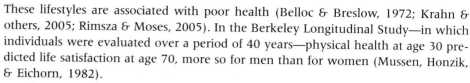

**FIGURE 2.10 Percentage of U.S. High School Students Who Ate Fruits and Vegetables Five or More Times a Day, 1999 to 2005**
*Note:* The slide shows the percentage of high school students over time who had eaten fruits and vegetables (100% fruit juice, fruit, green salad, potatoes–excluding french fries, fried potatoes, or potato chips–carrots, or other vegetables) five or more times per day during the seven days preceding the National Youth Risk Survey (2005).

These lifestyles are associated with poor health (Belloc & Breslow, 1972; Krahn & others, 2005; Rimsza & Moses, 2005). In the Berkeley Longitudinal Study—in which individuals were evaluated over a period of 40 years—physical health at age 30 predicted life satisfaction at age 70, more so for men than for women (Mussen, Honzik, & Eichorn, 1982).

There are some hidden dangers in the peaks of performance and health in early adulthood. Young adults can draw on physical resources for a great deal of pleasure, often bouncing back easily from physical stress and abuse. However, this can lead them to push their bodies too far. The negative effects of abusing one's body might not show up in emerging adulthood, but they probably will surface later in early adulthood or in middle adulthood (Csikszentmihalyi & Rathunde, 1998; Rathunde & Csikszentmihalyi, 2006).

## Nutrition

Nutrition is an important aspect of health-compromising and health-enhancing behaviors. The eating habits of many adolescents are health-compromising, and an increasing number of adolescents have an eating disorder (Casazza & Ciccazzo, 2006; Stevenson & others, 2007).

Concern is often expressed over adolescents' tendency to eat between meals. However, their choice of foods is much more important than the time or place of eating. Fresh vegetables and fruits as well as whole-grain products are needed to complement the foods adolescents commonly choose, which tend to be high in protein and energy value. U.S. adolescents are decreasing their intake of fruits and vegetables. The National Youth Risk Survey found that U.S. high school students decreased their intake of fruits and vegetables from 1999 through 2005 (MMWR, 2006) (see Figure 2.10).

A special concern in American culture is the amount of fat in our diet (Brom, 2006; Sizer & Whitney, 2006). Many of today's adolescents virtually live on fast-food meals, which contributes to the high fat levels in their diet (Ebbeling & others, 2004). One study found that from the late 1970s through the late 1990s, U.S. children, adolescents, and adults increasingly ate away from home and when they ate, they were more likely to consume salty snacks, soft drinks, and pizza (Nielssen, Siega-Riz, & Popkin, 2002).

We have much more to say about nutrition in Chapter 13, "Problems in Adolescence and Emerging Adulthood." There we examine three eating disorders: obesity, anorexia, and bulimia nervosa.

*What are some characteristics of adolescents' exercise patterns?*

## Exercise and Sports

Do American adolescents and emerging adults get enough exercise? How extensive is the role of sports in their lives? The answers to these questions have an impact on their health.

### Exercise

Researchers have found that individuals become less active as they reach and progress through adolescence (Hills, King, & Armstrong, 2007; Merrick & others, 2005; Pate & others, 2007). A recent study of more than 3,000 U.S. adolescents found that 34 percent were in the lowest fitness category (Carnethon, Gulati, & Greenland, 2005). Also, the National Youth Risk Survey revealed that in 2005 only 36 percent of adolescents had engaged in physical activity that made their heart and breathing rates difficult for at least 60 minutes a day on five or more of the seven days (currently recommended level of exercise) preceding the survey (MMWR, 2006). Boys attained this recommended level of exercise more than girls (44 percent versus 28 percent). Ten percent of the adolescents did not engage in even moderate exercise. A recent research study also revealed that physical fitness in adolescence was linked to physical fitness in adulthood (Mikkelsson & others, 2006). In this study, distance running in adolescence was most predictive for adult fitness in males, whereas sit-ups were the most predictive for females.

Researchers have found that exercise in adolescence has declined in recent years and that it also declines from early through late adolescence. In 1987, 31 percent of 12- to 17-year-olds said they exercised frequently, a figure that declined to only 18 percent in 2001 (American Sports Data, 2001). In a recent study, physical activity declined from 12 to 17 years of age (Duncan & others, 2007). In this study, having physically active friends was linked to higher physical activity levels for adolescents.

Ethnic differences in exercise participation rates are noteworthy, and they reflect the trend of decreasing exercise from early through late adolescence. A recent study found that Latino and African American 7- to 14-year-olds had lower aerobic fitness levels than their non-Latino White counterparts (Shaibi, Ball, & Goran, 2006). Also, as indicated in Figure 2.11, in the National Youth Risk Survey, non-Latino White boys exercised the most, African American girls the least (MMWR, 2006). Another study revealed that physical activity declined more in African American than non-Latino White girls as they went through adolescence (Kimm & Obarzanek, 2002).

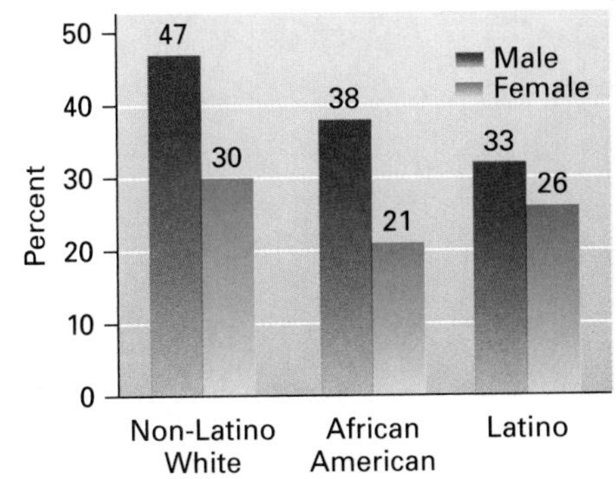


**FIGURE 2.11 Exercise Rates of U.S. High School Students: Gender and Ethnicity**
*Note:* Data are for high school students who were physically active doing any kind of physical activity that increased their heart rate and made them breathe hard some of the time for a total of at least 60 minutes per day on five or more of the seven days preceding the survey.

Low levels of exercise by adolescents not only appears in general exercise data but also in participation in physical education (PE) classes (Dwyer & others, 2006). Participation in PE classes was especially low for African American and Latino adolescents. Adolescents are less likely to take a PE class in high school than in middle school (MMWR, 2006). The percentage of high school students who take a daily physical education class decreased from 42 percent in 1991 to 33 percent in 2005 (MMWR, 2006).

Do U.S. adolescents exercise less than their counterparts in other countries? A comparison of adolescents in 28 countries found that U.S. adolescents exercised less and ate more junk food than adolescents in most of the other countries (World Health Organization, 2000). Just two-thirds of U.S. adolescents exercised at least twice a week compared with 80 percent or more of adolescents in Ireland, Austria, Germany, and the Slovak Republic. U.S. adolescents were more likely to eat fried food and less likely to eat fruits and vegetables than adolescents in most other countries studied. U.S. adolescents' eating choices were similar to those of adolescents in England.

Some health experts blame television for the poor physical condition of American adolescents. One study found that adolescents who watched little television were much more physically fit than those who watched heavily (Tucker, 1987). The more television adolescents watch, the more likely they are to be overweight. No one is sure whether their obesity results from spending their leisure time in front of a television set or from eating the junk food they see advertised on television. It may be that less physically fit youth simply find physical activity less reinforcing than watching television.

Some of the blame for the poor physical condition of U.S. children and adolescents falls on U.S. schools, many of which fail to provide physical education class on a daily basis (Buck & others, 2007). One extensive investigation of physical education classes at four different schools revealed how little vigorous exercise takes place in these classes (Parcel & others, 1987). Boys and girls moved through space only 50 percent of the time they were in the classes and moved continuously an average of only 2.2 minutes. More recent research confirms just how little adolescents exercise when they are in physical education classes (Cawley, Meyerhoefer, & Newhouse, 2006). In sum, not only does the adolescent's school week include inadequate physical education, but the majority of adolescents do not exercise vigorously even when they are in physical education. Furthermore, while much is made of the exercise revolution among adults, most children and adolescents report that

*What roles might schools play in improving the exercise habits of adolescents?*

their parents are poor role models when it comes to vigorous physical exercise (Feist & Brannon, 1989).

Does pushing children and adolescents to exercise more vigorously in school make a difference? In one study, sedentary adolescent females were assigned to one of two groups: (1) a special physical education class that met five times a week with about 40 minutes of activity (aerobic dance, basketball, swimming, or Tae Bo) a day for four of the five days and a lecture/discussion on the importance of physical activity and ways to become more physically active on the fifth day; or (2) a control group that did not take a physical education class (Jamner & others, 2004). After four months, the participants in the physical education class had improved their cardiovascular fitness and lifestyle activity (such as walking instead of taking the stairs and walking instead of driving short distances). Other research studies have found positive benefits for programs designed to improve the physical fitness of students (Timperio, Salmon, & Ball, 2004; Veugelers & Fitzgerald, 2005).

An exciting possibility is that physical exercise might act as a buffer against the stress adolescents experience and improve their mental health and life satisfaction (Dishman & others, 2006). Consider these studies that support this possibility:

- In one investigation of 364 girls in grades 7 through 11, the negative impact of stressful events on girls' health declined as their exercise levels rose (Brown & Siegel, 1988).
- In another investigation, adolescents who exercised regularly coped more effectively with stress and had more positive identities than adolescents who engaged in little exercise (Grimes & Mattimore, 1989).
- In another study, high school seniors who exercised frequently had higher grade point averages, used drugs less frequently, were less depressed, and got along better with their parents than those who rarely exercised (Field, Diego, & Sanders, 2001).
- And in a study of almost 5,000 adolescents, a low level of exercise and not participating on sports teams were linked with reduced life satisfaction (Valois & others, 2004).

In the fourth century B.C., Aristotle commented that the quality of life is determined by its activities. Today, we know that exercise is one of the principal activities that improves the quality of life, both in adolescence and adulthood (Asbury, Chandrruangphen, & Collins, 2006; Cleland & others, 2005).

## *Through the Eyes of Adolescents*

### IN PITIFUL SHAPE

A lot of kids in my class are in pitiful physical shape. They never exercise, except in gym class, and even then they hardly break a sweat. During lunch hour, I see some of the same loafers hanging out and smoking a bunch of cigarettes. Don't they know what they are doing to their bodies? All I can say is that I'm glad I'm not like them. I'm on the basketball team, and during the season, the coach runs us until we are exhausted. In the summer, I still play basketball and swim often. I don't know what I would do without exercise. I couldn't stand to be out of shape.

*—Brian, age 14*

**Sports** Sports play an important role in the lives of many adolescents (Beets & Pitetti, 2005; Stubbe, Boomsma, & De Geus, 2005). Some estimates indicate that as many as 40 to 70 percent of American youth participate in various organized sports (Ferguson, 1999).

Sports can have both positive and negative influences on adolescent development (Endresen & Olweus, 2005). Many sports activities can improve adolescents' physical health and well-being, self-confidence, motivation to excel, and ability to work with others (Cornock, Bowker, & Gadbois, 2001). Adolescents who spend considerable time in sports are less likely than others to engage in risk-taking behaviors, such as taking drugs. Three recent studies confirmed the positive benefits of organized sports for adolescents:

- Adolescents who participated in sports were less likely to engage in such risk-taking activities as truancy, cigarette smoking, sexual intercourse, and delinquency than non–sports participants (Nelson & Gordon-Larsen, 2006).

- Adolescents who participated in sports were 40 percent less likely to end up in a negative peer group and 40 percent less likely to be depressed than their counterparts who did not participate in sports; the sports participants also had a 26 percent greater likelihood of being in a positive peer group, a 25 percent greater probability of being in the high self-esteem group, and a 53 percent greater likelihood of being in the high connectedness to school group (Simpkins & others, 2006).
- Eleventh-grade students who participated in organized sports were more likely to be successful academically and less likely to take drugs than their counterparts who did not participate in organized sports (Fredricks & Eccles, 2006).

*What are some positive and negative aspects of sports participation in adolescence?*

The downside of the extensive participation in sports by American adolescents includes pressure by parents and coaches to win at all costs. Researchers have found that adolescents' participation in competitive sports is linked with competition anxiety and self-centeredness (Smith & Smoll, 1997). Furthermore, some adolescents spend so much time in sports that their academic skills suffer. Increasingly, adolescents are pushing their bodies beyond their capabilities, stretching the duration, intensity, and frequency of their training to the point that they cause overuse injuries (Brenner & the American Academy of Pediatrics Council on Sports Medicine and Fitness, 2007; DiFiori, 2006; Patel & Baker, 2006). Another problem that has surfaced is the use of performance-enhancing drugs, such as steroids, by adolescent athletes (Elliot & others, 2007; vandenBerg & others, 2007).

Some of the problems adolescents experience in sports involve their coaches. Many youth coaches create a performance-oriented motivational climate that is focused on winning, public recognition, and performance relative to others. But other coaches place more emphasis on mastery motivation that focuses adolescents' attention on the development of their skills and self-determined standards of success. Researchers have found that athletes who have a mastery focus are more likely than others to see the benefits of practice, to persist in the face of difficulty, and to show significant skill development over the course of a season (Roberts, Treasure, & Kavussanu, 1997).

A final topic involving sports that needs to be examined is the **female athlete triad,** which involves a combination of disordered eating (weight loss), amenorrhea (absent or irregular menstrual periods), and osteoporosis (thinning and weakening of bones) (Beals & Meyer, 2007; Stafford, 2005). Once menstrual periods have become somewhat regular in adolescent girls, not having a menstrual period for more than three or four months can reduce bone strength. Fatigue and stress fractures may develop. The female athlete triad often goes unnoticed (Birch, 2005). Recent research studies suggest that the incidence of the female athlete triad is low but that a significant number of female adolescents and college students have one of the characteristics of the disorder, such as disordered eating or osteoporosis (Beals & Hill, 2006; DiPietro & Stachenfeld, 2006; Nichols & others, 2006).

## Sleep

Might changing sleep patterns in adolescence contribute to adolescents' health-compromising behaviors? Recently there has been a surge of interest in adolescent sleep patterns (Carskadon, 2005, 2006; Carskadon, Mindell, & Drake, 2006; Chen, Wang, & Yeng, 2006; Dahl, 2006; Fuligni & Hardway, 2006; Yang & others, 2005).

The National Sleep Foundation (2006) conducted a U.S. survey of 1,602 caregivers and their 11- to 17-year-olds. Forty-five percent of the adolescents got inadequate sleep on school nights (less than eight hours). Older adolescents (ninth- to twelfth-graders) got markedly less sleep on school nights than younger adolescents (sixth- to eighth-graders)—62 percent of the older adolescents got inadequate sleep compared to 21 percent of the younger adolescents. Adolescents who got inadequate sleep (8 hours or less) on school nights were more likely to feel more tired or sleepy, more cranky and irritable, fall asleep in school, be in a depressed mood, and drink

**female athlete triad** A combination of disordered eating, amenorrhea, and osteoporosis that may develop in female adolescents and college students.

In Mary Carskadon's sleep laboratory at Brown University, an adolescent girl's brain activity is being monitored. Carskadon (2005) says that in the morning, sleep-deprived adolescents' "brains are telling them it's night time . . . and the rest of the world is saying it's time to go to school" (p. 19).

caffeinated beverages than their counterparts who got optimal sleep (nine or more hours). Another recent study of more than 600 13- to 18-year-old boys and girls found that 54 percent said they regularly got less than six to eight hours of sleep a night on school nights (Chen, Wang, & Jeng, 2006). In this study, getting less than 6 to 8 hours of sleep per night during adolescence was linked to lower levels of exercise, less effective stress management, and adopting an unhealthy diet. In another recent study of 750 14- to 15-year-olds, getting less sleep at night was linked to higher levels of anxiety, depression, and fatigue the next day (Fuligni & Hardway, 2006).

Many adolescents stay up later at night and sleep longer in the morning than they did when they were children, and this changing timetable has physiological underpinnings (Yang & others, 2005). These findings have implications for the hours during which adolescents learn most effectively in school (Carskadon, Mindell, & Drake, 2006; Hansen & others, 2005).

Mary Carskadon and her colleagues (2002, 2004, 2005, 2006; Carskadon, Acebo, & Jenni, 2004; Carskadon, Mindell, & Drake, 2006) have conducted a number of research studies on adolescent sleep patterns. They found that when given the opportunity adolescents will sleep an average of nine hours and 25 minutes a night. Most get considerably less than nine hours of sleep, especially during the week. This shortfall creates a sleep deficit, which adolescents often attempt to make up on the weekend. The researchers also found that older adolescents tend to be more sleepy during the day than younger adolescents. They theorized that this sleepiness was not due to academic work or social pressures. Rather, their research suggests that adolescents' biological clocks undergo a shift as they get older, delaying their period of wakefulness by about one hour. A delay in the nightly release of the sleep-inducing hormone melatonin, which is produced in the brain's pineal gland, seems to underlie this shift. Melatonin is secreted at about 9:30 p.m. in younger adolescents and approximately an hour later in older adolescents.

Carskadon has suggested that early school starting times may cause grogginess, inattention in class, and poor performance on tests. Based on her research, school officials in Edina, Minnesota, decided to start classes at 8:30 a.m. rather than the usual 7:25 a.m. Since then there have been fewer referrals for discipline problems, and the number of students who report being ill or depressed has decreased. The school system reports that test scores have improved for high school students, but not for middle school students. This finding supports Carskadon's suspicion that early start times are likely to be more stressful for older than for younger adolescents.

## REVIEW AND REFLECT ◆ LEARNING GOAL 2

### 2 Summarize the nature of adolescents' and emerging adults' health.

***Review***

- Why is adolescence a critical juncture in health? How extensive is risk taking in adolescence? How good are adolescents at using health services? What are the leading causes of death in adolescence?
- What characterizes emerging adults' health?
- What are some concerns about adolescents' eating habits?
- What roles do exercise and sports play in adolescents' lives?
- What are some concerns about adolescent sleep patterns?

***Reflect***

- What were your health habits like from the time you entered puberty to the time you completed high school? Describe your health-compromising and health-enhancing behaviors during this time. Since high school, have you reduced your health-compromising behaviors? Explain.

# 3 Evolution, Heredity, and Environment

The Evolutionary Perspective | The Genetic Process | Heredity-Environment Interaction

The size and complexity of the adolescent's brain emerged over the long course of evolution. Let's explore the evolutionary perspective on adolescent development and then examine how heredity and environment interact to influence adolescent development.

## The Evolutionary Perspective

In terms of evolutionary time, humans are relative newcomers to the earth. If we think of the broad expanse of time as a calendar year, then humans arrived on earth in the last moments of December (Sagan, 1977). As our earliest ancestors left the forest to feed on the savannahs, and finally to form hunting societies on the open plains, their minds and behaviors changed. How did this evolution come about?

### Natural Selection and Adaptive Behavior

*Natural selection* is the evolutionary process that favors those individuals of a species who are best adapted to survive and reproduce. To understand natural selection, let's return to the middle of the nineteenth century, when the British naturalist Charles Darwin was traveling the world, observing many different species of animals in their natural habitats. In his groundbreaking book, *On the Origin of Species* (1859), Darwin noted that most species reproduce at rates that would cause enormous increases in their population and yet populations remained nearly constant. He reasoned that an intense struggle for food, water, and resources must occur among the many young born in each generation, because many of them do not survive. Darwin believed that those who do survive to reproduce and pass on their genes to the next generation are probably superior to others in a number of ways. In other words, the survivors are better adapted to their world than the nonsurvivors (Johnson, 2008; Mader, 2007). Over the course of many generations, Darwin reasoned, organisms with the characteristics needed for survival would compose a larger and larger percentage of the population, producing a gradual modification of the species. If environmental conditions changed, however, other characteristics might be favored by natural selection, moving the evolutionary process in a different direction.

To understand the role of evolution in behavior, we need to understand the concept of adaptive behavior (Enger, 2007). In evolutionary conceptions of psychology, **adaptive behavior** is a modification of behavior that promotes an organism's survival in the natural habitat (Finn, 2006). All organisms must adapt to particular places, climates, food sources, and ways of life in order to survive. In humans, attachment ensures an infant's closeness to the caregiver for feeding and protection from danger. This behavioral characteristic promotes survival just as an eagle's claw, which facilitates predation, ensures the eagle's survival.

### Evolutionary Psychology

Although Darwin introduced the theory of evolution by natural selection in 1859, his ideas only recently have been used to explain behavior. The field of **evolutionary psychology** emphasizes the importance of adaptation, reproduction, and "survival of the fittest" in explaining behavior. Because evolution favors organisms that are best adapted to survive and reproduce in a particular environment, evolutionary psychology focuses on the conditions that allow individuals to survive or perish. In this view, the process of natural selection favors those behaviors that increase organisms' reproductive success and their ability to pass their genes on to the next generation (Freeman & Herron, 2007; Rose & Mueller, 2006).

**adaptive behavior** A modification of behavior that promotes an organism's survival in the natural habitat.

**evolutionary psychology** An approach that emphasizes the importance of adaptation, reproduction, and "survival of the fittest" in explaining behavior.

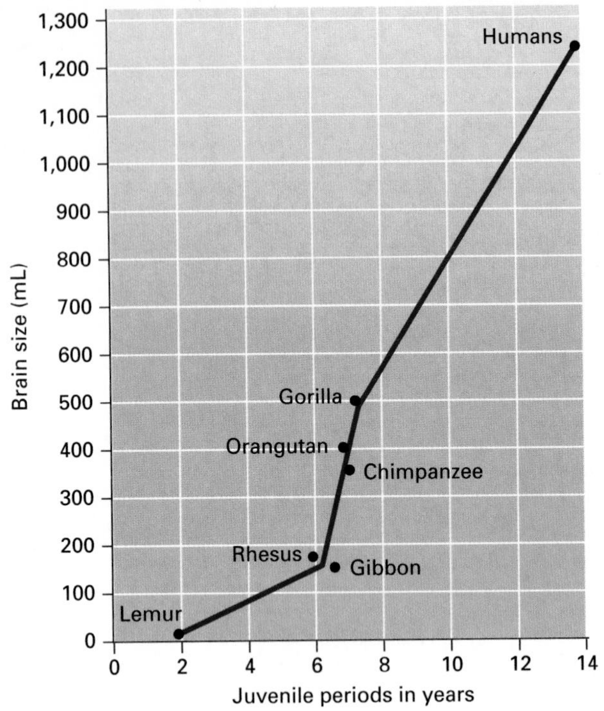


**FIGURE 2.12** **The Brain Sizes of Various Primates and Humans in Relation to the Length of the Juvenile Period**

David Buss' (1995, 1999, 2000, 2004, 2008; Larsen & Buss, 2005) ideas on evolutionary psychology have produced a wave of interest in how evolution can explain human behavior. Buss argues that just as evolution shapes our physical features, such as our body shape and height, it also influences our decision making, our aggressive behavior, our fears, and our mating patterns.

**Evolutionary Developmental Psychology** Recently, interest has grown in using the concepts of evolutionary psychology to understand human development (Bjorklund, 2006, 2007; Geary, 2006). Here are a few ideas proposed by evolutionary developmental psychologists (Bjorklund & Pellegrini, 2002, pp. 336–340):

- *An extended juvenile period evolved because humans require time to develop a large brain and learn the complexity of human social communities.* Humans take longer to become reproductively mature than any other mammal (see Figure 2.12). During this juvenile period, they develop a large brain and the experiences required for mastering the complexities of human society such as reading, writing, math skills, and communicating effectively with other humans.
- *Many evolved psychological mechanisms are domain-specific.* That is, the mechanisms apply only to a specific aspect of a person's makeup. According to evolutionary psychology, information processing is one example. In this view, the mind is not a general-purpose device that can be applied equally to a vast array of problems. Instead, as our ancestors dealt with certain recurring problems, specialized modules evolved that process information related to those problems, such as a module for physical knowledge, a module for mathematical knowledge, and a module for language. In Chapter 3, "The Brain and Cognitive Development," we examine the issue of whether intelligence is a general ability or consists of a number of specific intelligences.
- *Evolved mechanisms are not always adaptive in contemporary society.* Some behaviors that were adaptive for our prehistoric ancestors may not serve us well today. For example, the food-scarce environment of our ancestors likely led to humans' propensity to gorge when food is available and to crave high-calorie foods, a trait that that might lead to an epidemic of obesity when food is plentiful.

**Evaluating Evolutionary Psychology** Albert Bandura (1998), whose social cognitive theory was described in Chapter 1, has criticized the "biologizing" of psychology. Bandura acknowledges the influence of evolution on human adaptation and change. However, he rejects what he calls "one-sided evolutionism," in which social behavior is seen as the product of evolved biology. Bandura stresses that evolutionary pressures favored biological adaptations that encouraged the use of tools, allowing humans to manipulate, alter, and construct new environmental conditions. In time, humans' increasingly complex environmental innovations produced new pressures that favored the evolution of specialized brain systems to support consciousness, thought, and language.

In other words, evolution gave humans body structures and biological potentialities, not behavioral dictates. Having evolved our advanced biological capacities, we can use them to produce diverse cultures—aggressive or pacific, egalitarian or autocratic. As American scientist Stephen Jay Gould (1981) concluded, in most domains, human biology allows a broad range of cultural possibilities. The sheer pace of social change, Bandura (1998) notes, underscores the range of possibilities biology permits.

**chromosomes** Threadlike structures that contain deoxyribonucleic acid, or DNA.

**DNA** A complex molecule that contains genetic information.

**genes** The units of hereditary information, which are short segments composed of DNA.

## The Genetic Process

Every species has a mechanism for transmitting characteristics from one generation to the next. This mechanism is explained by the principles of genetics (Hartwell, 2008). Each of us carries a "genetic code" that we inherited from our parents, and it is a distinctly human code. Because it carries this human code, a fertilized human egg cannot grow into an egret, eagle, or elephant.

Each of us began life as a single cell weighing about one twenty-millionth of an ounce! This tiny piece of matter housed our entire genetic code—instructions that orchestrated growth from that single cell to a person made of trillions of cells, each containing a perfect replica of the original genetic code. That code is carried by our genes. What are they and what do they do?

### DNA and the Collaborative Gene

The nucleus of each human cell contains **chromosomes,** which are threadlike structures that contain the remarkable substance deoxyribonucleic acid, or DNA. **DNA** is a complex molecule that contains genetic information. It has a double helix shape, like a spiral staircase. **Genes,** the units of hereditary information, are short segments composed of DNA, as you can see in Figure 2.13. They direct cells to reproduce themselves and to assemble proteins. Proteins, in turn, serve as the building blocks of cells, as well as the regulators that direct the body's processes (Hartwell, 2008; Nester & others, 2007).

Each gene has its own function, and each gene has its own location, its own designated place on a particular chromosome. Today, there is a great deal of enthusiasm about efforts to discover the specific locations of genes that are linked to certain functions (Lewis, 2007; Weaver, 2008). An important step in this direction was accomplished when the Human Genome Project and the Celera Corporation completed a preliminary map of the human *genome*—the complete set of instructions for making a human organism (U.S. Department of Energy, 2001).

One of the big surprises of the Human Genome Project was a report indicating that humans have only about 30,000 genes (U.S. Department of Energy, 2001). More recently, the number of human genes has been revised further downward to the exacting figure of 21,774 (Ensembl Human, 2007). Scientists had thought that humans had as many as 100,000 or more genes. They had also believed that each gene programmed just one protein. In fact, humans appear to have far more proteins than they have genes, so there cannot be a one-to-one correspondence between them (Commoner, 2002; Moore, 2001). Each segment of DNA is not translated, in automation-like fashion, into one and only one protein. It does not act independently, as developmental psychologist David Moore (2001) emphasized by titling his book *The Dependent Gene.*

Rather than being an independent source of developmental information, DNA collaborates with other sources of information to specify our characteristics. The collaboration operates at many points. Small pieces of DNA are mixed, matched, and linked by the cellular machinery. That machinery is sensitive to its context—that is, it is influenced by what is going on around it. Whether a gene is turned "on," working to assemble proteins, is also a matter of collaboration. The activity of genes (*genetic expression*) is affected by their environment (Gottlieb, 2007). For example, hormones that circulate in the blood make their way into the cell where they can turn genes "on" and "off." And the flow of hormones can be affected by environmental conditions, such as light, day length, nutrition, and behavior. Numerous studies have shown that external events outside of the cell and the person, and internal events inside of the cell, can excite or inhibit gene expression (Gottlieb, Wahlsten, & Lickliter, 2006). For example, one recent study revealed that an increase in the concentration of stress hormones such as cortisol produced a five-fold increase in DNA damage (Flint & others, 2007).

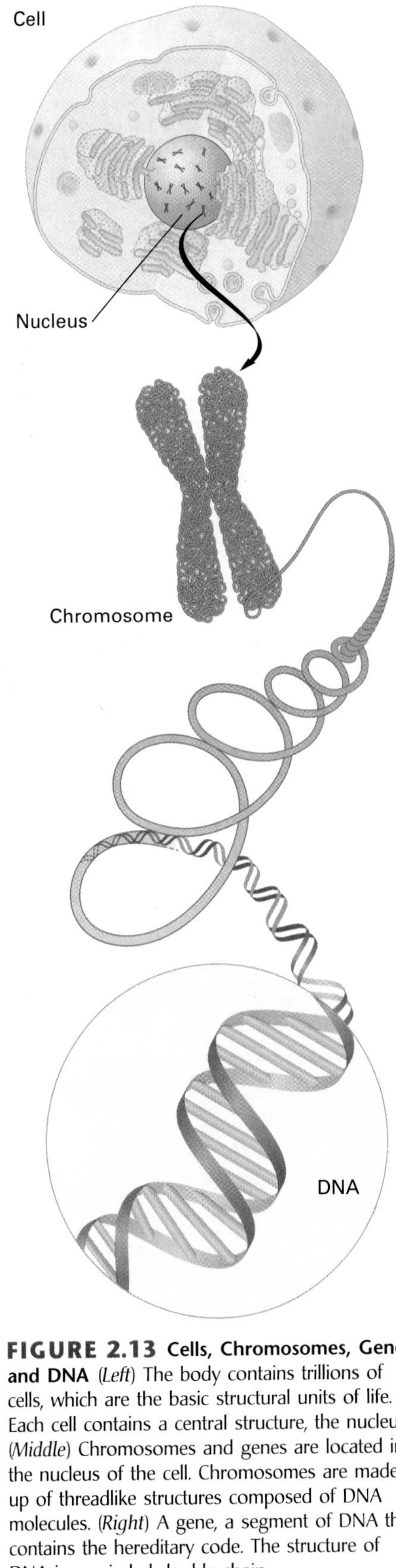


**FIGURE 2.13 Cells, Chromosomes, Genes, and DNA** (*Left*) The body contains trillions of cells, which are the basic structural units of life. Each cell contains a central structure, the nucleus. (*Middle*) Chromosomes and genes are located in the nucleus of the cell. Chromosomes are made up of threadlike structures composed of DNA molecules. (*Right*) A gene, a segment of DNA that contains the hereditary code. The structure of DNA is a spiraled double chain.

By permission of John L. Hart FLP, and Creators Syndicate, Inc.

In short, a single gene is rarely the source of a protein's genetic information, much less of an inherited trait (Gottlieb, 2007; Moore, 2001). Rather than being a group of independent genes, the human genome consists of many collaborative genes.

**Genotype and Phenotype** No one possesses all the characteristics that his or her genetic structure makes possible. A person's genetic heritage—the actual genetic material—is called a **genotype.** Not all of this genetic material is apparent in our observed and measurable characteristics. The way an individual's genotype is expressed in observed and measurable characteristics is called a **phenotype.** Phenotypes include physical traits, such as height, weight, eye color, and skin pigmentation, as well as psychological characteristics, such as intelligence, creativity, personality, and social tendencies.

For each genotype, a range of phenotypes can be expressed (Brooker & others, 2008; Talaro, 2008). Imagine that we could identify all the genes that would make an adolescent introverted or extraverted. Could we predict measured introversion or extraversion in a particular person from our knowledge of those genes? The answer is no, because even if our genetic model was adequate, introversion and extraversion are characteristics that are shaped by experience throughout life. For example, a parent might push an introverted child into social situations, encouraging the child to become more gregarious. Or the parent might support the child's preference for solitary play.

## Heredity-Environment Interaction

So far, we have described genes and how they work, and one theme is apparent: heredity and environment interact to produce development (Gottlieb, Wahlsten, & Lickliter, 2006; Kagan & Fox, 2006). Whether we are studying how genes produce proteins or their influence on how tall a person is, we end up discussing heredity-environment interactions. Is it possible, though, to untangle the influence of heredity from that of environment and discover the role of each in producing individual differences in development? When heredity and environment interact, how does heredity influence the environment, and vice versa?

**Behavior Genetics** **Behavior genetics** is the field that seeks to discover the influence of heredity and environment on individual differences in human traits and development (Plomin, DeFries, & Fulker, 2007; Gelhorn & others, 2006). If you think about all of the people you know, you have probably realized that people differ in terms of their level of introversion/extraversion. What behavior geneticists

**genotype** A person's genetic heritage; the actual genetic material.

**phenotype** The way an individual's genotype is expressed in observed and measurable characteristics.

**behavior genetics** The field that seeks to discover the influence of heredity and environment on individual differences in human traits and development.

try to do is to figure out what is responsible for those differences—that is, to what extent do people differ because of differences in genes, environment, or a combination of these?

To study the influence of heredity on behavior, behavior geneticists often use either twins or adoption situations. In the most common **twin study,** the behavioral similarity of identical twins is compared with the behavioral similarity of fraternal twins. *Identical twins* (called monozygotic twins) develop from a single fertilized egg that splits into two genetically identical replicas, each of which becomes a person. *Fraternal twins* (called dizygotic twins) develop from separate eggs and separate sperm, making them genetically no more similar than ordinary siblings. Although fraternal twins share the same womb, they are no more alike genetically than are nontwin brothers and sisters, and they may be of different sexes.

By comparing groups of identical and fraternal twins, behavior geneticists capitalize on the basic knowledge that identical twins are more similar genetically than are fraternal twins (Bishop & others, 2006; Whitfield & others, 2007). In one twin study, the extraversion and neuroticism (psychological instability) of 7,000 pairs of Finnish identical and fraternal twins were compared (Rose & others, 1988). On both of these personality traits, the identical twins were much more similar than the fraternal twins were, suggesting an important role for heredity in both traits. However, several issues complicate interpretation of twin studies (Derks, Dolan, & Boomsma, 2006). For example, perhaps the environments of identical twins are more similar than the environments of fraternal twins. Adults might stress the similarities of identical twins more than those of fraternal twins, and identical twins might perceive themselves as a "set" and play together more than fraternal twins do. If so, observed similarities in identical twins could be more strongly influenced by the environment than the results suggested.

*What is the nature of the twin study method?*

In an **adoption study,** investigators seek to discover whether the behavior and psychological characteristics of adopted children are more like those of their adoptive parents, who have provided a home environment, or more like those of their biological parents, who have contributed their heredity (Haugaard & Hazen, 2004; Loehlin, Horn, & Ernst, 2007). Another form of the adoption study involves comparing adoptive and biological siblings.

### Heredity-Environment Correlations

The difficulties that researchers encounter when they interpret the results of twin studies and adoption studies reflect the complexities of heredity-environment interaction. Some of these interactions are *heredity-environment correlations,* which means that individuals' genes influence the types of environments to which they are exposed. In a sense, individuals "inherit" environments that are related or linked to genetic propensities (Plomin & McGuffin, 2002). Behavior geneticist Sandra Scarr (1993) described three ways that heredity and environment are correlated (see Figure 2.14):

- **Passive genotype-environment correlations** occur because biological parents, who are genetically related to the child, provide a rearing environment for the child. For example, the parents might have a genetic predisposition to be intelligent and read skillfully. Because they read well and enjoy reading, they provide their children with books to read. The likely outcome is that their children, given their own inherited predispositions from their parents, will become skilled readers.
- **Evocative genotype-environment correlations** occur because an adolescent's genetically shaped characteristics elicit certain types of physical and social environments. For example, active, smiling children receive more social stimulation than passive, quiet children do. Cooperative, attentive adolescents evoke more pleasant and instructional responses from the adults around them than uncooperative, distractible adolescents do. Athletically inclined youth tend to elicit encouragement to engage in school sports. As a consequence,

**twin study** A study in which the behavioral similarity of identical twins is compared with the behavioral similarity of fraternal twins.

**adoption study** A study in which investigators seek to discover whether the behavior and psychological characteristics of adopted children are more like their adoptive parents, who have provided a home environment, or more like those of their biological parents, who have contributed their heredity. Another form of adoption study involves comparing adoptive and biological siblings.

**passive genotype-environment correlations** Correlations that occur because biological parents, who are genetically related to the child, provide a rearing environment for the child.

**evocative genotype-environment correlations** Correlations that occur because an adolescent's genetically shaped characteristics elicit certain types of physical and social environments.

| Heredity-Environment Correlation | Description | Examples |
|---|---|---|
| Passive | Children inherit genetic tendencies from their parents and parents also provide an environment that matches their own genetic tendencies. | Musically inclined parents usually have musically inclined children and they are likely to provide an environment rich in music for their children. |
| Evocative | The child's genetic tendencies elicit stimulation from the environment that supports a particular trait. Thus genes evoke environmental support. | A happy, outgoing child elicits smiles and friendly responses from others. |
| Active (niche-picking) | Children actively seek out "niches" in their environment that reflect their own interests and talents and are thus in accord with their genotype. | Libraries, sports fields, and a store with musical instruments are examples of environmental niches children might seek out if they have intellectual interests in books, talent in sports, or musical talents, respectively. |

**FIGURE 2.14** Exploring Heredity-Environment Correlations

these adolescents tend to be the ones who try out for sport teams and go on to participate in athletically oriented activities.

- **Active (niche-picking) genotype-environment correlations** occur when children seek out environments that they find compatible and stimulating. *Niche-picking* refers to finding a setting that is suited to one's abilities. Adolescents select from their surrounding environment some aspect that they respond to, learn about, or ignore. Their active selections of environments are related to their particular genotype. For example, attractive adolescents tend to seek out attractive peers. Adolescents who are musically inclined are likely to select musical environments in which they can successfully perform their skills.

Scarr concludes that the relative importance of the three genotype-environment correlations changes as children develop from infancy through adolescence. In infancy, much of the environment that children experience is provided by adults. Thus, passive genotype-environment correlations are more common in the lives of infants and young children than they are for older children and adolescents who can extend their experiences beyond the family's influence and create their environments to a greater degree.

Critics argue that the concept of heredity-environment correlation gives heredity too much influence in determining development (Gottlieb, 2004). Heredity-environment correlation stresses that heredity determines the types of environments children experience. Next, we examine a view that emphasizes the importance of the nonshared environment of siblings and their heredity as important influences on their development.

**Shared and Nonshared Environmental Experiences** Behavior geneticists emphasize that another way of analyzing the environment's role in heredity-environment interaction is to consider experiences that adolescents share in common with other adolescents living in the same home, as well as experiences that are not shared (Bricker & others, 2006; Young & others, 2006).

**Shared environmental experiences** are siblings' common experiences, such as their parents' personalities or intellectual orientation, the family's socioeconomic status, and the neighborhood in which they live. By contrast, **nonshared environmental experiences** are an adolescent's unique experiences, both within the family and outside the family; these are not shared with a sibling. Even experiences occurring within the family can be part of the "nonshared environment." For example, parents often interact differently with each sibling, and siblings interact differently with parents (Hetherington, Reiss, & Plomin, 1994; Reiss & others, 2000). Siblings

**active (niche-picking) genotype-environment correlations** Correlations that occur when children seek out environments that they find compatible and stimulating.

**shared environmental experiences** Siblings' common experiences such as their parents' personalities and intellectual orientation, the family's socioeconomic status, and the neighborhood in which they live.

**nonshared environmental experiences** The adolescent's own unique experiences, both within a family and outside the family, that are not shared by a sibling.

often have different peer groups, different friends, and different teachers at school.

Behavior geneticist Robert Plomin (1993) has found that common rearing, or shared environment, accounts for little of the variation in adolescents' personality or interests. In other words, even though two adolescents live under the same roof with the same parents, their personalities are often very different. Further, behavior geneticists argue that heredity influences the nonshared environments of siblings in the manner we described earlier in the concept of heredity-environment correlations (Plomin & others, 2001). For example, an adolescent who has inherited a genetic tendency to be athletic is likely to spend more time in environments related to sports, whereas an adolescent who has inherited a tendency to be musically inclined is more likely to spend time in environments related to music.

Tennis stars Venus and Serena Williams. *What might be some shared and nonshared environmental experiences they had while they were growing up that contributed to their tennis stardom?*

**The Epigenetic View** The heredity-environment correlation view emphasizes how heredity directs the kind of environmental experiences individuals have. However, earlier we described how DNA is collaborative, not determining an individual's traits in an independent matter, but rather in an interactive manner with the environment. In line with the concept of a collaborative gene, the **epigenetic view** emphasizes that development is the result of an ongoing, bidirectional interchange between heredity and the environment (Gottlieb, 2004, 2007; Gottlieb, Wahlsten, & Lickliter, 2006). Figure 2.15 compares the heredity-environment correlation and epigenetic views of development.

**Conclusions About Heredity-Environment Interaction** Heredity and environment operate together—or cooperate—to produce a person's intelligence, temperament, height, weight, ability to pitch a baseball, ability to read, and so on (Gottlieb, Wahlsten, & Lickliter, 2006). If an attractive, popular, intelligent girl is elected president of her senior class in high school, is her success due to heredity or to environment? Of course, the answer is both.

The relative contributions of heredity and environment are not additive. That is, we can't say that such-and-such a percentage of nature and such-and-such a percentage of experience make us who we are. Nor is it accurate to say that full genetic expression happens once, around conception or birth, after which we carry our genetic legacy into the world to see how far it takes us. Genes produce proteins throughout the life span, in many different environments. Or they don't produce these proteins, depending in part on how harsh or nourishing those environments are.

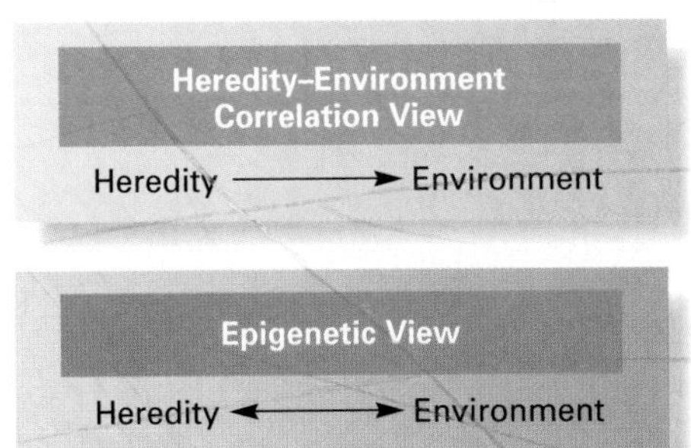


**FIGURE 2.15** **Comparison of the Heredity-Environment Correlation and Epigenetic Views**

The emerging view is that many complex behaviors likely have some *genetic loading* that gives people a propensity for a particular developmental trajectory (Maes & others, 2006; Plomin, DeFries, & Fulker, 2007). However, the actual development requires more: an environment. And that environment is complex, just like the mixture of genes we inherit (Grusec & Hastings, 2007; Maccoby, 2007). Environmental influences range from the things we lump together under "nurture" (such as parenting, family dynamics, schooling, and neighborhood quality) to biological encounters (such as viruses, birth complications, and even biological events in cells) (Greenough, 1997, 1999; Greenough & others, 2001).

Imagine for a moment that there is a cluster of genes somehow associated with youth violence (this example is hypothetical because we don't know of any such combination). The adolescent who carries this genetic mixture might experience a world of loving parents, regular nutritious meals, lots of books, and a series of masterful teachers. Or the adolescent's world might include parental neglect, a

**epigenetic view** Emphasizes that development is the result of an ongoing bidirectional interchange between heredity and environment.

*The interaction of heredity and environment is so extensive that to ask which is more important, nature or nurture, is like asking which is more important to a rectangle, height or width.*

—WILLIAM GREENOUGH
*Contemporary Psychologist, University of Illinois*

neighborhood in which gunshots and crime are everyday occurrences, and inadequate schooling. In which of these environments are the adolescent's genes likely to manufacture the biological underpinnings of criminality?

A controversy erupted when Judith Harris (1998) published *The Nurture Assumption.* In this provocative book, she argued that what parents do does not make a difference in their children's and adolescents' behavior. Yell at them. Hug them. Read to them. Ignore them. Harris says it won't influence how they turn out. She argues that genes and peers are far more important than parents in children's and adolescents' development.

Genes and peers do matter, but Harris' descriptions of peer influences do not take into account the complexity of peer contexts and developmental trajectories (Hartup, 1999). In addition, Harris is wrong in saying that parents don't matter. For example, in the early child years parents play an important role in selecting children's peers and indirectly influencing children's development (Baumrind, 1999). Many research studies document the importance of parents in children's and adolescents' development (Collins & Steinberg, 2006; Parke & Buriel, 2006). We discuss parents' important roles throughout this book.

## REVIEW AND REFLECT ◆ LEARNING GOAL 3

### 3 Explain the contributions of evolution, heredity, and environment to adolescent development.

***Review***

- What role has evolution played in adolescent development? How do the fields of evolutionary psychology and evolutionary developmental psychology describe evolution's contribution to understanding adolescence?
- What is the genetic process?
- What is the nature of heredity-environment interaction?

***Reflect***

- Someone tells you that she has analyzed her genetic background and environmental experiences and reached the conclusion that environment definitely has had little influence on her intelligence. What would you say to this person about her ability to make this self-diagnosis?

# Reach Your Learning Goals

## 1 Puberty *Discuss the determinants, characteristics, and psychological dimensions of puberty.*

**Determinants of Puberty**

Puberty is a period of rapid physical maturation involving hormonal and bodily changes that take place primarily in early adolescence. Puberty's determinants include heredity, hormones, and possibly weight, percentage of body fat, and leptin. Two classes of hormones that are involved in pubertal change and have significantly different concentrations in males and females are androgens and estrogens. The endocrine system's role in puberty involves the interaction of the hypothalamus, pituitary gland, and gonads. FSH and LH, which are secreted by the pituitary gland, are important aspects of this system. So is GnRH, which is produced by the hypothalamus. The sex hormone system is a negative feedback system. Growth hormone also contributes to pubertal change. Low birth weight and rapid weight gain in infancy are linked to earlier pubertal onset. Puberty has two phases: adrenarche and gonadarche. The culmination of gonadarche in boys is spermarche; in girls, it is menarche.

**Growth Spurt**

The onset of pubertal growth occurs on the average at 9 years of age for girls and 11 years for boys. The peak of pubertal change for girls is 11½ years; for boys it is 13½ years. Girls grow an average of 3½ inches per year during puberty; boys grow an average of 4 inches.

**Sexual Maturation**

Sexual maturation is a key feature of pubertal change. Individual variation in puberty is extensive and is considered to be normal within a wide age range.

**Secular Trends in Puberty**

Secular trends in puberty took place in the twentieth century with puberty coming earlier. Recently, there has been a slowdown in how early puberty occurs.

**Psychological Dimensions of Puberty**

Adolescents show heightened interest in their bodies and body images. Younger adolescents are more preoccupied with these images than older adolescents. Adolescent girls often have a more negative body image than adolescent boys. Adolescents and college students increasingly have tattoos and body piercings (body art). Some scholars conclude that body art is a sign of rebellion and is linked to risk taking, whereas others argue that increasingly body art is used to express uniqueness and self-expression rather than rebellion. Researchers have found connections between hormonal change during puberty and behavior, but environmental influences need to be taken into account. Menarche and the menstrual cycle produce a wide range of reactions in girls. Early maturation often favors boys, at least during early adolescence, but as adults, late-maturing boys have a more positive identity than early-maturing boys. Early-maturing girls are at risk for a number of developmental problems. Some scholars doubt that puberty's effects on development are as strong as once envisioned. Most early- and late-maturing adolescents weather the challenges of puberty successfully. For those who do not adapt well to pubertal changes, discussions with knowledgeable health-care providers and parents can improve the coping abilities of off-time adolescents. Puberty has important influences on development, but the significance of these influences needs to be considered in terms of the entire life span. Some scholars argue that too much emphasis has been given to the biological changes of puberty.

## 2 HEALTH *Summarize the nature of adolescents' and emerging adults' health.*

### Adolescence: A Critical Juncture in Health

Many of the behaviors that are linked to poor health habits and early death in adults begin during adolescence. Engaging in healthy behavior patterns in adolescence, such as regular exercise, helps to delay disease in adulthood. Important goals are to reduce adolescents' health-compromising behaviors and increase their health-enhancing behaviors. Risk-taking behavior increases during adolescence and combined with a delay in developing self-regulation makes adolescents vulnerable to a number of problems. Among the strategies for keeping this increased motivation for risk taking from compromising adolescents' health are to limit their opportunities for harm and monitor their behavior. Adolescents underutilize health services. The three leading causes of death in adolescence are (1) accidents, (2) homicide, and (3) suicide.

### Emerging Adults' Health

Although emerging adults have a higher death rate than adolescents, emerging adults have few chronic health problems. However, many emerging adults don't stop to think about how their personal lifestyles will affect their health later in their lives.

### Nutrition

Special nutrition concerns in adolescence are eating between meals, the amount of fat in adolescents' diets, and increased reliance on fast-food meals.

### Exercise and Sports

Recent research studies show that U.S. adolescents are getting less exercise today and are less likely to take a physical education class than their counterparts in the 1980s. African American girls especially have a low rate of exercise. A high rate of watching TV is associated with a low level of exercise. Special physical education programs in schools can improve students' physical fitness. Physical exercise in adolescence is linked with more effective coping with stress, better grades, lower depression, and higher life satisfaction. Sports play an important role in the lives of many adolescents. Sports can have positive (improve physical health and well-being, confidence, ability to work with others) or negative (intense pressure by parents and coaches to win at all costs, injuries) outcomes. Recently, the female athlete triad has become a concern.

### Sleep

Adolescents like to go to bed later and get up later than children do. This may be linked to developmental changes in the brain. A special concern is the extent to which these changes in sleep patterns in adolescents affect academic behavior and achievement.

## 3 Evolution, Heredity, and Environment *Explain the contributions of evolution, heredity, and environment to adolescent development.*

### The Evolutionary Perspective

Natural selection—the process that favors the individuals of a species that are best adapted to survive and reproduce—is a key aspect of the evolutionary perspective. Evolutionary psychology is the view that adaptation, reproduction, and "survival of the fittest" are important in explaining behavior. Evolutionary developmental psychology has promoted a number of ideas, including the view that an extended "juvenile" period is needed to develop a large brain and learn the complexity of human social communities. Critics argue that the evolutionary perspective does not give adequate attention to experience and humans as a culture-making species.

### The Genetic Process

The nucleus of each human cell contains chromosomes, which contain of DNA. Genes are short segments of DNA that direct cells to reproduce and manufacture proteins that maintain life. DNA does not act independently to produce a trait or behavior. Rather, it acts collaboratively. Genotype refers to the unique configuration of genes, whereas phenotype involves observed and measurable characteristics.

### Heredity-Environment Interaction

Behavior genetics is the field concerned with the degree and nature of behavior's hereditary basis. Methods used by behavior geneticists include twin studies and adoption studies. In Scarr's heredity-environment correlations view, heredity directs the types of environments that children experience. She describes three genotype-environment correlations: passive, evocative, and active (niche-picking). Scarr argues that the relative importance of these three genotype-environment correlations changes as children develop. Shared environmental experiences refer to siblings' common experiences, such as their parents' personalities and intellectual orientation, the family's socioeconomic status, and the neighborhood in which they live. Nonshared environmental experiences involve the adolescent's unique experiences, both within a family and outside a family, that are not shared with a sibling. Many behavior geneticists argue that differences in the development of siblings are due to nonshared environmental experiences (and heredity) rather than shared environmental experiences. The epigenetic view emphasizes that development is the result of an ongoing, bidirectional interchange between heredity and environment. Many complex behaviors have some genetic loading that gives people a propensity for a particular developmental trajectory. However, actual development also requires an environment, and that environment is complex. The interaction of heredity and environment is extensive. Much remains to be discovered about the specific ways that heredity and environment interact to influence development.

## KEY TERMS

puberty 54
hormones 55
androgens 55
estrogens 55
adrenarche 57
gonadarche 57
menarche 57
spermarche 57
secular trends 62
female athlete triad 75
adaptive behavior 77
evolutionary psychology 77
chromosomes 78
DNA 78
genes 78
genotype 80
phenotype 80
behavior genetics 80
twin study 81
adoption study 81
passive genotype-environment correlations 81
evocative genotype-environment correlations 81
active (niche-picking) genotype-environment correlations 82
shared environmental experiences 82
nonshared environmental experiences 82
epigenetic view 83

## KEY PEOPLE

Roberta Simmons and Dale Blyth 65
Mary Carskadon 76
David Buss 78
Albert Bandura 78
David Moore 79
Sandra Scarr 81
Robert Plomin 83

## RESOURCES FOR IMPROVING THE LIVES OF ADOLESCENTS

**The Society for Adolescent Medicine** **www.adolescenthealth.com**
This organization is a valuable source of information about competent physicians who specialize in treating adolescents. It maintains a list of recommended adolescent specialists across the United States. The society also publishes the *Journal of Adolescent Health,* which contains articles on a wide range of health-related and medical issues involving adolescents.

**Journal of School Health** **www.blackwellpublishing.com**
This journal publishes articles that pertain to the school-related aspects of children's and adolescents' health, including a number of health education programs.

# E-LEARNING TOOLS

To help you master the material in this chapter, visit the Online Learning Center for *Adolescence,* twelfth edition **(www.mhhe.com/santrocka12),** where you will find these additional resources:

## Taking It to the Net

1. A friend believes her younger sister is entering puberty much earlier than is "normal" and asks for your opinion. You tell your friend about the secular trend (puberty occurring at an earlier age across generations). Your friend asks what causes this. Which theory do you think best explains the secular trend and why?
2. Adolescents do not fall asleep until later than children, and most adolescents need more sleep than they are getting. There are significant negative consequences of sleep deprivation for adolescents. What can be done to solve this problem?
3. Research suggests that career choice is due to a variety of interacting factors. Your parents think you picked your current career plans just to spite them. You disagree. How can each of the three ways that heredity and environment interact (passive, evocative, and active) influence career choices of adolescents?

## Self-Assessment

The Online Learning Center includes the following self-assessments for further exploration:

- Is My Lifestyle Good for My Health?
- My Health Habits
- Do I Get Enough Sleep?

## Health and Well-Being, Parenting, and Education

To practice your decision-making skills, complete the health and well-being, parenting, and education exercises on the Online Learning Center.

## Video Clips

The Online Learning Center includes the following video for this chapter:

- Girls' Views on Body Image

# 3 The Brain and Cognitive Development

*The thoughts of youth are long, long thoughts.*

—Henry Wadsworth Longfellow
American Poet, 19th Century

## CHAPTER OUTLINE

## LEARNING GOALS

### The Brain

1 Describe the developmental changes in the brain during adolescence.

Neurons
Brain Structure, Cognition, and Emotion
Experience and Plasticity

### The Cognitive Developmental View

2 Discuss the cognitive developmental view of adolescence.

Piaget's Theory
Vygotsky's Theory

### The Information-Processing View

3 Characterize the information-processing view of adolescence.

Cognitive Resources
Mechanisms of Change
Attention and Memory
Executive Functioning

### The Psychometric/Intelligence View

4 Summarize the psychometric/intelligence view of adolescence.

Intelligence Tests
Multiple Intelligences
Heredity and Environment

### Social Cognition

5 Explain how social cognition is involved in adolescent development.

Adolescent Egocentrism
Perspective Taking
Social Cognition in the Remainder of the Text

# *Images of Adolescent Development*

## The Developing Thoughts of Adolescents

One of my most vivid memories of my oldest daughter, Tracy, is from when she was 12 years of age. I had accompanied her and her younger sister, Jennifer (10 at the time), to a tennis tournament. As we walked into a restaurant to have lunch, Tracy bolted for the restroom. Jennifer and I looked at each other, wondering what was wrong. Five minutes later, Tracy emerged, looking calmer. I asked what had happened. Her response: "This one hair was out of place and every person in here was looking at me!"

Consider another adolescent—Margaret. During a conversation with her girlfriend, 16-year-old Margaret says, "Did you hear about Catherine? She's pregnant. Do you think I would ever let that happen to me? Never."

Also think about 13-year-old Adam as he describes himself: "No one understands me, especially my parents. They have no idea of what I am feeling. They have never experienced the pain I'm going through."

Comments like Tracy's, Margaret's, and Adam's reflect the emergence of egocentric thought during adolescence. When we think about thinking, we usually consider it in terms of school subjects like math and English, or solving intellectual problems. But people's thoughts about social circumstances are also important. Later in the chapter, we further explore adolescents' social thoughts.

## PREVIEW

***When we think about adolescence, we often focus on the biological changes of puberty or socioemotional changes, such as the motivation for independence, relations with parents and peers, and problems such as drug abuse and delinquency. Further, when developmentalists have studied cognitive processes, their main focus has been on infants and young children, not adolescents. We see in this chapter, however, that adolescents also display some impressive cognitive changes and that increasingly researchers are finding that these changes are linked to the development of the brain. Indeed, to begin this chapter, we explore the explosion of interest in the changing adolescent brain and then study three different views of cognitive development: cognitive developmental, information processing, and psychometric. The chapter closes by examining social cognition, including the emergence of adolescent egocentrism.***

## 1 THE BRAIN

Neurons | Brain Structure, Cognition, and Emotion | Experience and Plasticity

Until recently, little research has been conducted on developmental changes in the brain during adolescence. Although research in this area is still in its infancy, an increasing number of studies are under way (Giedd & others, 2006; Lenroot & others, 2007; Whitford & others, 2007). Scientists now know that the adolescent's brain is different from the child's brain, and that in adolescence the brain is still growing (Kuhn & Franklin, 2006; Toga, Thompson, & Sowell, 2006).

## Neurons

**Neurons,** or nerve cells, are the nervous system's basic units. A neuron has three basic parts: the cell body, dendrites, and axon (see Figure 3.1). The *dendrite* is the receiving part of the neuron, and the *axon* carries information away from the cell body to other cells. Through a process called **myelination,** the axon portion of a neuron becomes covered and insulated with a layer of fat cells (called the myelin sheath) that increases the speed and efficiency of information processing in the nervous system (see Figure 3.2). Myelination continues to increase during adolescence (Giedd & others, 2006).

In addition to the encasement of axons through myelination, another important aspect of the brain's development is the dramatic increase in connections between neurons, a process that is called *synaptogenesis* (Stettler & others, 2006). **Synapses** are gaps between neurons, where connections between the axon and dendrites take place. Synaptogenesis begins in infancy and continues through adolescence.

Researchers have discovered that nearly twice as many synaptic connections are made than will ever be used (Huttenlocher & others, 1991; Huttenlocher & Dabholkar, 1997). The connections that are used are strengthened and survive, while the unused ones are replaced by other pathways or disappear. That is, in the language of neuroscience, these connections will be "pruned." Figure 3.3 vividly illustrates the dramatic growth and later pruning of synapses in the visual, auditory, and prefrontal cortex of the brain (Huttenlocher & Dabholkar, 1997). These areas are critical for higher-order cognitive functioning such as learning, memory, and reasoning.

As shown in Figure 3.3, the time course for synaptic "blooming and pruning" varies considerably by brain region. In the visual cortex, the peak of synaptic overproduction takes place at about the fourth postnatal month, followed by a gradual reduction until the middle to end of the preschool years (Huttenlocher & Dabholkar, 1997). In the auditory and prefrontal cortex, which are involved in hearing and language, synaptic production follows a similar although somewhat later course. In the prefrontal cortex (where higher-level thinking and self-regulation occur), the peak of overproduction takes place at about 1 year of age. Not until middle to late adolescence does this area reach its adult density of synapses.

What determines the timing and course of synaptic "blooming" and "pruning"? Both heredity and experience are thought to be influential (Greenough, 2000). For

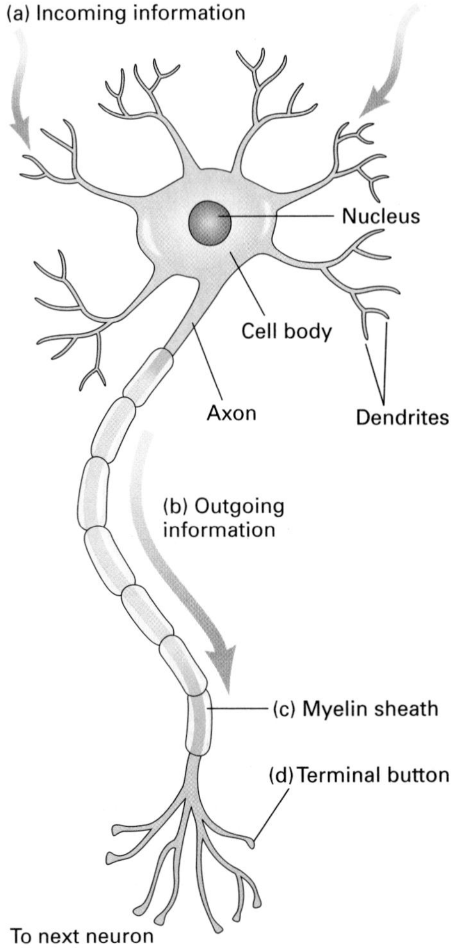


**FIGURE 3.1 The Neuron** *(a)* The dendrites of the cell body receive information from other neurons, muscles, or glands. *(b)* An axon transmits information away from the cell body. *(c)* A myelin sheath covers most axons and speeds information transmission. *(d)* As the axon ends, it branches out into terminal buttons.

**neurons** Nerve cells, which are the nervous system's basic units.

**myelination** The process by which the axon portion of the neuron becomes covered and insulated with a layer of fat cells, which increases the speed and efficiency of information processing in the nervous system.

**synapses** Gaps between neurons, where connections between the axon and dendrites occur.

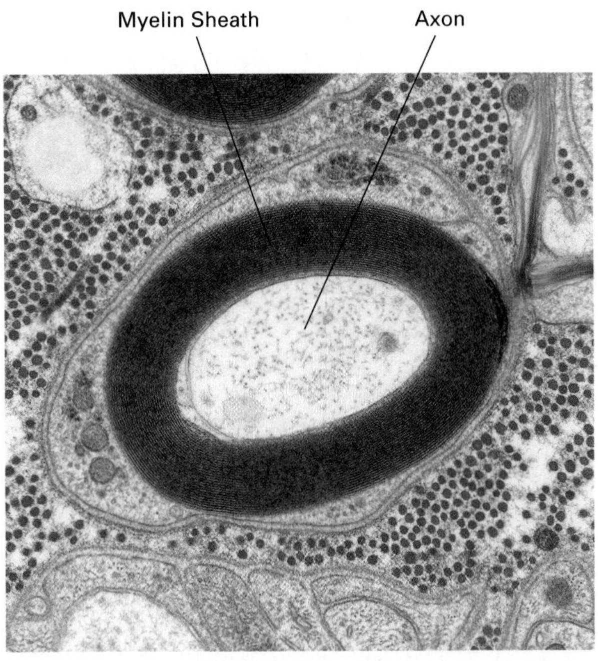


**FIGURE 3.2 A Myelinated Nerve Fiber** The myelin sheath, shown in brown, encases the axon (white). This image was produced by an electron microscope that magnified the nerve fiber 12,000 times. *What role does myelination play in the brain's development?*

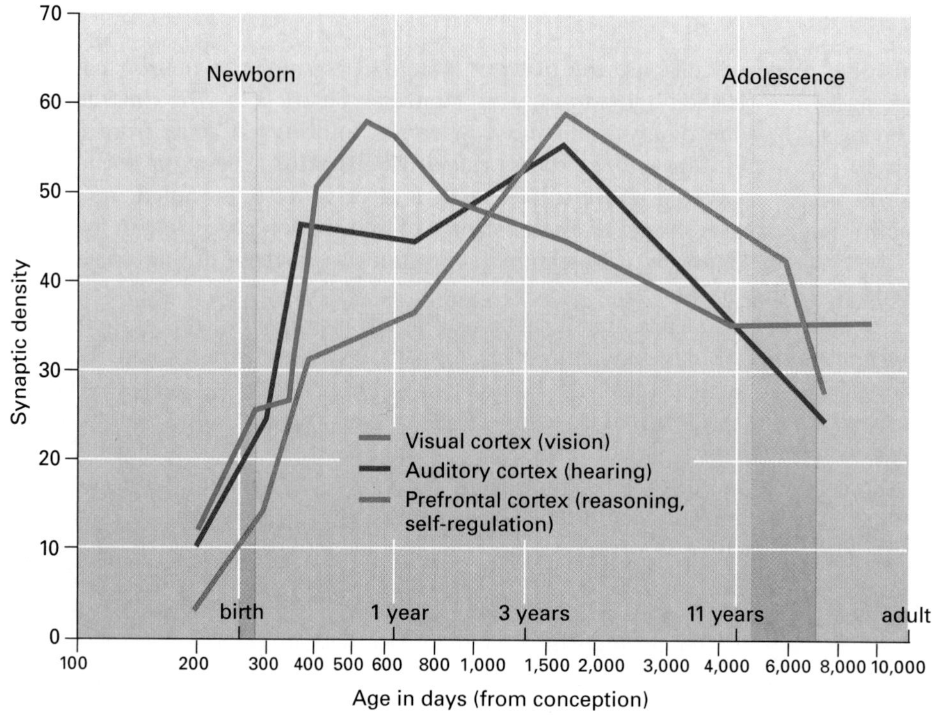


**FIGURE 3.3 Synaptic Density in the Human Brain from Infancy to Adulthood** The graph shows the dramatic increase and then pruning in synaptic density for three regions of the brain: visual cortex, auditory cortex, and prefrontal cortex. Synaptic density is believed to be an important indication of the extent of connectivity between neurons.

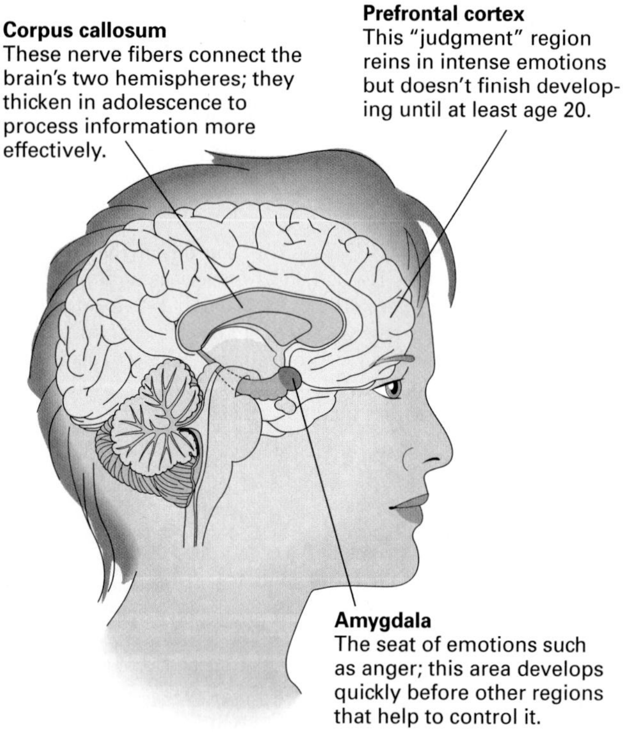

**Corpus callosum**
These nerve fibers connect the brain's two hemispheres; they thicken in adolescence to process information more effectively.
**Prefrontal cortex**
This "judgment" region reins in intense emotions but doesn't finish developing until at least age 20.
**Amygdala**
The seat of emotions such as anger; this area develops quickly before other regions that help to control it.


**FIGURE 3.4 The Prefrontal Cortex, Amygdala, and Corpus Callosum**

instance, the amount and quality of cognitive stimulation a child or adolescent experiences could speed up or delay the process.

With the onset of puberty, the levels of *neurotransmitters*—chemicals that carry information across the synaptic gap between one neuron and the next—change. For example, an increase in the neurotransmitter dopamine occurs in both the prefrontal cortex and the limbic system during adolescence (Lewis, 1997). Increases in dopamine have been linked to increased risk taking and the use of addictive drugs (Stansfield & Kirstein, 2006). Increases in dopamine may also be related to an increase in the onset of schizophrenia, one of the most debilitating mental disorders, during adolescence (Tseng & O'Donnell, 2007).

## Brain Structure, Cognition, and Emotion

Neurons do not simply float in the brain. Connected in precise ways, they form the various structures in the brain. Using functional magnetic resonance image (fMRI) brain scans, scientists have recently discovered that adolescents' brains undergo significant structural changes (Eshel & others, 2007; Keating, 2007; Toga, Thompson, & Sowell, 2006). An fMRI creates a magnetic field around a person's body and bombards the brain with radio waves. The result is a computerized image of the brain's tissues and biochemical activities (Tumeh & others, 2007).

**corpus collosum** A large bundle of axon fibers that connect the brain's left and right hemispheres.

**prefrontal cortex** The highest level of the brain's frontal lobes that is involved in reasoning, decision making, and self-control.

**amygdala** A portion of the brain's limbic system that is the seat of emotions such as anger.

Among the most important structural changes in the brain during adolescence are those involving the corpus collosum, the prefrontal cortex, and the amygdala. The **corpus callosum,** a large bundle of axon fibers that connects the brain's left and right hemispheres, thickens in adolescence, and this improves adolescents' ability to process information (Giedd, 2004). Advances in the development of the **prefrontal cortex**—the highest level of the frontal lobes that is involved in reasoning, decision making, and self-control—continue through the emerging adult years, approximately 18 to 25 years of age, or later. However, the **amygdala**—a part of the brain's limbic system that is the seat of emotions such as anger—matures much earlier than the prefrontal cortex (Spear, 2007; Steinberg, 2007; Yurgelun-Todd, 2007). Figure 3.4 shows the locations of the corpus callosum, prefrontal cortex, and amygdala.

Leading researcher Charles Nelson (2003; Nelson, Thomas, & de Haan, 2006) points out that although adolescents are capable of very strong emotions, their prefrontal cortex hasn't adequately developed to the point at which they can control these passions. It is as if the prefrontal cortex doesn't yet have the brakes to slow down the amygdala's emotional intensity. Or consider this interpretation of the development of emotion and cognition in adolescents: "early activation of strong 'turbo-charged' feelings with a relatively un-skilled set of 'driving skills' or cognitive abilities to modulate strong emotions and motivations" (Dahl, 2004, p. 18).

Are there implications of what we now know about the adolescent's brain for the legal system? For example, can the brain research we have just discussed be used to argue that because the adolescent's brain, especially the higher-level prefrontal cortex, is still developing, adolescents should not be given a death penalty? Some scientists argue that criminal behavior in adolescence should not be excused, but that adolescents should not be given the death penalty (Fassler, 2004). Other scientists, such as Jerome Kagan (2004), stress that whether adolescents should be given the death penalty is an ethical issue and that the brain research does not show that adolescents have a reduced blame for committing crimes. A similar stance is taken by some of the leading neuroscientists who study brain development in adolescence. Elizabeth Sowell (2004) says that scientists can't just do brain scans on adolescents and decide if they should be tried as adults. In 2005, the death penalty for adolescents (under the age of 18) was prohibited by the U.S. Supreme Court, but it still continues to be debated (Ash, 2006).

Lee Malvo was 17 years old when he and John Muhammad, an adult, went on a sniper spree in 2002, terrorizing the Washington, D.C., area and killing 10 people. A 2005 U.S. Supreme Court ruling stated that individuals who are 18 years of age and under, like Malvo, cannot be given the death penalty. *Are there implications for what scientists are learning about the adolescent's brain for legal decisions, such as the death penalty?*

## Experience and Plasticity

Scientists are especially interested in the extent to which environmental experiences influence the brain's development. They also want to know how much plasticity the brain retains as individuals progress through their childhood, adolescent, and adult years. Let's examine three questions involving the roles of experience and plasticity in the development of the brain in adolescence:

- *Can new brain cells be generated in adolescence?* Until close to the end of the twentieth century, scientists believed that the brain generated no new cells (neurons) after the early childhood years. However, researchers have recently discovered that people can generate new brain cells throughout their lives (Briones, 2006; Sun & Bartke, 2007). Furthermore, evidence now shows that exercise and enriched experiences can produce new brain cells (Mora, Segovia, & Del Arco, 2007; Pereira & others, 2007).
- *Can the adolescent's brain recover from injury?* In childhood and adolescence, the brain has a remarkable ability to repair itself (Kolb & Gibb, 2007; Sharp & others, 2006). In Chapter 1, you read about Michael Rehbein, whose left hemisphere was removed because of brain seizures. The plasticity of the human brain was apparent as his right hemisphere reorganized itself to take over functions, such as speech, that normally take place in the left hemisphere.

  Although the brain retains considerable plasticity in adolescence, the earlier a brain injury occurs, the more likelihood of a successful recovery (Yen & Wong, 2007). One study examined 68 children from 7 to 15 years of age and found that the later their brain injuries occurred, the less effective their performance was on a number of language and cognitive tasks (Slomine & others, 2002).
- *What do we know about applying information about brain development to adolescents' education?* Unfortunately, too often statements about the implications of brain science for secondary education are speculative and often far removed from what neuroscientists know about the brain (Bransford & others, 2006; Breur, 1999; Byrnes, 2007). We don't have to look any further than the hype about

"left-brained" individuals being more logical and "right-brained" individuals being more creative to see that links between neuroscience and brain education are incorrectly made (Sousa, 1995).

Another commonly promoted link between neuroscience and brain education is that most of the key changes in the brain occur prior to adolescence (Breur, 1999). However, the recent research on the plasticity of the adolescent's brain and the continuing development of the higher regions of the frontal cortex through adolescence support the view that education can considerably benefit adolescents (Byrnes, 2007; Lenroot & Giedd, 2007).

**REVIEW AND REFLECT ◆ LEARNING GOAL 1**

**1 Describe the developmental changes in the brain during adolescence.**

***Review***

- What are neurons? How do the brain's neurons change in adolescence?
- What changes involving brain structure, cognition, and emotion occur in adolescence?
- How much plasticity does the brain have in adolescence?

***Reflect***

- Find an article on brain-based education in a magazine or on the Internet. Use your critical-thinking skills to evaluate the article's credibility. Does the author present research evidence to support the link between neuroscience and the brain-based method being recommended? Explain.

## 2 The Cognitive Developmental View

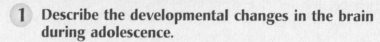

Piaget's Theory | Vygotsky's View

The development of the brain that we have just examined provides a biological foundation for the cognitive changes that characterize adolescence. Reflect for a moment about your thinking skills as a young adolescent. Were your thinking skills as good as they are now? Could you solve difficult abstract problems and reason logically about complex topics? Or did those skills improve in your high school years? Can you describe any ways in which your thinking skills are better now than they were in high school?

In Chapter 1, we briefly examined Jean Piaget's theory of cognitive development. Piaget was intrigued by the changes in thinking that take place through childhood and adolescence. In this section, we further explore his ideas about adolescent cognition, as well as the increasingly popular sociocultural cognitive theory of Lev Vygotsky.

### Piaget's Theory

We begin our coverage of Piaget's theory by describing the main processes he stressed are responsible for cognitive changes in development. Then we turn to his cognitive stages, giving special attention to concrete operational and formal operational thought.

**Cognitive Processes** Piaget's theory is the best-known, most widely discussed theory of adolescent cognitive development. According to his theory, adolescents are

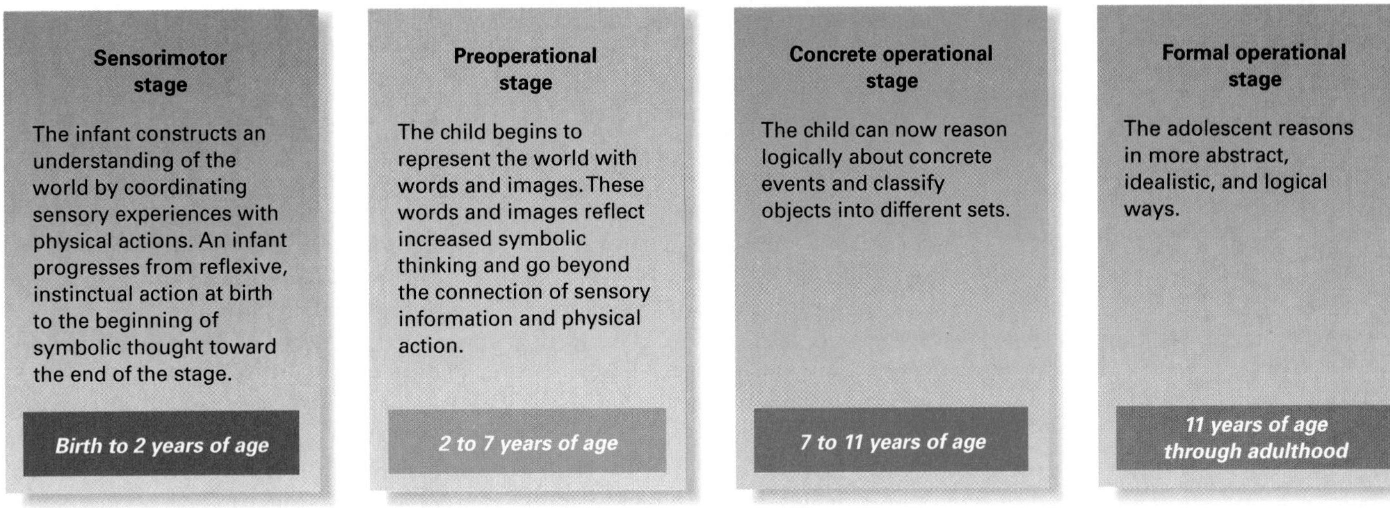

Sensorimotor stage
The infant constructs an understanding of the world by coordinating sensory experiences with physical actions. An infant progresses from reflexive, instinctual action at birth to the beginning of symbolic thought toward the end of the stage.
Birth to 2 years of age
Preoperational stage
The child begins to represent the world with words and images. These words and images reflect increased symbolic thinking and go beyond the connection of sensory information and physical action.
2 to 7 years of age
Concrete operational stage
The child can now reason logically about concrete events and classify objects into different sets.
7 to 11 years of age
Formal operational stage
The adolescent reasons in more abstract, idealistic, and logical ways.
11 years of age through adulthood


**FIGURE 3.5** Piaget's Four Stages of Cognitive Development

motivated to understand their world because doing so is biologically adaptive. Adolescents actively construct their own cognitive worlds; information doesn't just pour into their minds from the environment. To make sense out of the world, adolescents organize their experiences, separating important ideas from less important ones and connecting one idea to another. They also adapt their thinking to include new ideas, because the additional information furthers their understanding.

In actively constructing their world, adolescents use schemas. A **schema** is a mental concept or framework that is useful in organizing and interpreting information. Piaget was especially interested in how children and adolescents use schemas to organize and make sense out of their current experiences.

He found that children and adolescents use and adapt their schemas through two processes: assimilation and accommodation (Piaget, 1952). **Assimilation** is the incorporation of new information into existing knowledge. In assimilation, the schema does not change. **Accommodation** is the adjustment of a schema to new information. In accommodation, the schema changes.

Suppose, for example, that a 16-year-old girl wants to learn how to use a computer. Her parents buy her a computer for her birthday. Although she has never had the opportunity to use one, from her experience and observation, she realizes that she needs to press a switch to turn the computer on and insert a CD-ROM into a slot. These behaviors fit into an existing conceptual framework (assimilation). But as she strikes several keys, she makes some errors. Soon she realizes that she needs help in learning how to use the computer either from a friend or from a teacher. This adjustment in her approach shows her awareness of the need to alter her conceptual framework (accommodation).

**Equilibration,** another process Piaget identified, is a shift in thought from one state to another. At times adolescents experience cognitive conflict or a sense of disequilibrium in their attempt to understand the world. Eventually they resolve the conflict and reach a balance, or equilibrium, of thought. Piaget maintained that individuals move back and forth between states of cognitive equilibrium and disequilibrium. Consider Margaret's comment at the beginning of the chapter in *Images of Adolescent Development* that she will never get pregnant. Eventually Margaret will resolve these conflicts as her thought becomes more advanced. In the everyday world, adolescents constantly face such cognitive inconsistencies.

**Stages of Cognitive Development** Piaget theorized that individuals develop through four cognitive stages: sensorimotor, preoperational, concrete operational, and formal operational (see Figure 3.5). Each of these age-related stages consists of

**schema** A mental concept or framework that is useful in organizing and interpreting information.

**assimilation** The incorporation of new information into existing knowledge.

**accommodation** An adjustment of a schema to new information.

**equilibration** A mechanism in Piaget's theory that explains how individuals shift from one state of thought to the next. The shift occurs as they experience cognitive conflict or a disequilibrium in trying to understand the world. Eventually, the individual resolves the conflict and reaches a balance, or equilibrium, of thought.

*We are born capable of learning.*

—Jean-Jacques Rousseau
*Swiss-Born French Philosopher, 18th Century*

distinct ways of thinking. This *different* way of understanding the world is what makes one stage more advanced than another; simply knowing more information does not make an adolescent's thinking more advanced. Thus, in Piaget's theory, a person's cognition is *qualitatively* different in one stage compared with another.

**Sensorimotor and Preoperational Thought** The **sensorimotor stage,** which lasts from birth to about 2 years of age, is the first Piagetian stage. In this stage, infants construct an understanding of the world by coordinating sensory experiences (such as seeing and hearing) with physical, motoric actions—hence the term sensorimotor.

The **preoperational stage,** which lasts approximately from 2 to 7 years of age, is the second Piagetian stage. In this stage, children begin to represent the world with words, images, and drawings. Symbolic thought goes beyond simple connections of information and action.

**Concrete Operational Thought** The **concrete operational stage,** which lasts approximately from 7 to 11 years of age, is the third Piagetian stage. Logical reasoning replaces intuitive thought as long as the reasoning can be applied to specific or concrete examples. According to Piaget, concrete operational thought involves *operations*—mental actions that allow an individual to do mentally what was done before physically.

Piaget used the term *conservation* to refer to an individual's ability to recognize that the length, number, mass, quantity, area, weight, and volume of objects and substances do not change through transformations that alter their appearance. Concrete operational thinkers have conservation skills; preoperational thinkers don't.

Another characteristic of concrete operational thought is *classification,* or class inclusion reasoning. Children who engage in classification can systematically organize objects into hierarchies of classes and subclasses.

Although concrete operational thought is more advanced than preoperational thought, it has its limitations. Logical reasoning replaces intuitive thought as long as the principles can be applied to specific, *concrete* examples. For example, the concrete operational child cannot imagine the steps necessary to complete an algebraic equation, an abstract statement with no connection to the concrete world.

**Formal Operational Thought** The **formal operational stage** is Piaget's fourth and final stage of cognitive development. Piaget argued that this stage emerges at 11 to 15 years of age. Adolescents' developing power of thought opens up new cognitive and social horizons. What are the characteristics of formal operational thought, which Piaget noted develops in adolescence? Most significantly, formal operational thought is more abstract than concrete operational thought. Adolescents are no longer limited to actual, concrete experiences as anchors for thought. They can conjure up make-believe situations—events that are purely hypothetical possibilities or strictly abstract propositions—and try to reason logically about them.

The abstract quality of the adolescent's thought at the formal operational level is evident in the adolescent's verbal problem-solving ability. While the concrete operational thinker would need to see the concrete elements A, B, and C to be able to make the logical inference that if A = B and B = C, then A = C, the formal operational thinker can solve this problem merely through verbal representation.

Another indication of the abstract quality of adolescents' thought is their increased tendency to think about thought itself. As one adolescent commented, "I began thinking about why I was thinking what I was. Then I began thinking about why I was thinking about why I was thinking about what I was." If this statement sounds abstract, it is, and it characterizes the adolescent's enhanced focus on thought and its abstract qualities. Later in this chapter, we return to the topic of thinking about thinking, which is called *metacognition.*

Besides being abstract, formal operational thought is full of idealism and possibilities. While children frequently think in concrete ways about what is real and limited,

**sensorimotor stage** Piaget's first stage of development, lasting from birth to about 2 years of age. In this stage, infants construct an understanding of the world by coordinating sensory experiences with physical, motoric actions.

**preoperational stage** Piaget's second stage, which lasts approximately from 2 to 7 years of age. In this stage, children begin to represent their world with words, images, and drawings.

**concrete operational stage** Piaget's third stage, which lasts approximately from 7 to 11 years of age. In this stage, children can perform operations. Logical reasoning replaces intuitive thought as long as the reasoning can be applied to specific or concrete examples.

**formal operational stage** Piaget's fourth and final stage of cognitive development, which he argued emerges at 11 to 15 year of age. It is characterized by abstract, idealistic, and logical thought.

adolescents begin to engage in extended speculation about ideal characteristics—qualities they desire in themselves and others. Such thoughts often lead adolescents to compare themselves and others in regard to such ideal standards. And during adolescence, the thoughts of individuals are often fantasy flights into future possibilities. It is not unusual for the adolescent to become impatient with these newfound ideal standards and perplexed over which of many ideals to adopt. At the same time adolescents think more abstractly and idealistically, they also think more logically. Adolescents begin to reason more as a scientist does, devising ways to solve problems and test solutions systematically. Piaget gave this type of problem solving an imposing name, **hypothetical-deductive reasoning,** which means the ability to develop hypotheses, or best guesses, about how to solve problems, such as algebraic equations. Having developed a hypothesis, the formal operational thinker then systematically deduces, or concludes, the best path to follow in solving the problem. In contrast, children are more likely to solve problems by trial and error.

*"and give me good abstract-reasoning ability, interpersonal skills, cultural perspective, linguistic comprehension, and a high sociodynamic potential."*


One example of hypothetical-deductive reasoning involves a version of the familiar game "Twenty Questions." Individuals are shown a set of 42 color pictures displayed in a rectangular array of six rows of seven pictures each. They are asked to determine which picture the experimenter has in mind (that is, which is "correct") by asking questions to which the experimenter can answer only yes or no. The object of the game is to select the correct picture by asking as few questions as possible.

Adolescents who are deductive hypothesis testers will formulate a plan and test a series of hypotheses that considerably narrows the field of choices. The most effective plan is a "halving" strategy (Question: Is the picture in the right half of the array? Answer: No. Question: OK. Is it in the top half? And so on). An efficient halving strategy guarantees the answer to this problem in seven questions or less. In contrast, the concrete operational thinker might persist with questions that continue to test some of the same possibilities that previous questions could have eliminated. For example, after asking whether the correct picture is in row 1 and being told that it is not, the concrete operational thinker might later ask whether the picture is *x*, which is in row 1.

Thus, formal operational thinkers test their hypotheses with judiciously chosen questions and tests. Concrete operational thinkers, on the other hand, often fail to understand the relation between a hypothesis and a well-chosen test of it, stubbornly clinging to ideas that already have been discounted.

Piaget maintained that formal operational thought is the best description of how adolescents think. Formal operational thought is not a homogeneous stage of development, however. Not all adolescents are full-fledged formal operational thinkers. Instead, some developmentalists argue that formal operational thought consists of two subperiods (Broughton, 1983):

- *Early formal operational thought.* Adolescents' newfound ability to think in hypothetical ways produces unconstrained thoughts with unlimited possibilities. In this early period, flights of fantasy may submerge reality and the world is perceived too subjectively and idealistically. Assimilation is the dominant process in this subperiod.
- *Late formal operational thought.* As adolescents test their reasoning against experience, intellectual balance is restored. Through accommodation, adolescents begin to adjust to the upheaval they have experienced. Late formal thought may appear in the middle adolescent years.

In this view, assimilation characterizes early formal operational thought; accommodation characterizes late formal operational thought (Lapsley, 1990).

In his early writings, Piaget (1952) indicated that both the onset and consolidation of formal operational thought are completed during early adolescence, from about 11 to 15 years of age. Later, Piaget (1972) revised his view and concluded that formal operational thought is not completely achieved until later in adolescence, between approximately 15 and 20 years of age.

**hypothetical-deductive reasoning** Piaget's term for adolescents' ability, in the formal operational stage, to develop hypotheses, or best guesses, about ways to solve problems; they then systematically deduce, or conclude, the best path to follow in solving the problem.

Still, his theory does not adequately account for the individual differences that characterize the cognitive development of adolescents, which have been documented in a number of investigations (Kuhn & Franklin, 2006; Wigfield, Byrnes, & Eccles, 2006). Some young adolescents are formal operational thinkers; others are not. For instance, a review of formal operational thought investigations revealed that only about one out of every three eighth-grade students is a formal operational thinker (Strahan, 1983). Some investigators found that formal operational thought increased with age in adolescence; others did not. In fact, many college students and adults do not think in formal operational ways, either. Investigators have found that from 17 to 67 percent of college students think on the formal operational level (Elkind, 1961; Tomlinson-Keasey, 1972).

At the same time that many young adolescents are just beginning to think in a formal operational manner, others are at the point of consolidating their concrete operational thought, using it more consistently than they did in childhood. By late adolescence, many youth are beginning to consolidate their formal operational thought, using it more consistently. And there often is variation across the content areas of formal operational thought, just as there is in concrete operational thought in childhood. A 14-year-old adolescent might reason at the formal operational level when analyzing algebraic equations but not do so with verbal problem solving or when reasoning about interpersonal relations.

Adolescents are more likely to use formal operational thought in areas in which adolescents have the most experience and knowledge. Children and adolescents gradually build up elaborate knowledge through extensive experience and practice in various sports, games, hobbies, and school subjects, such as math, English, and science. The development of expertise in different domains may make possible high-level, developmentally mature-looking thought. In some instances, the sophisticated reasoning of formal operational thought might be responsible. In other instances, however, the thought might be largely due to the accumulation of knowledge that allows more automatic, memory-based processes to function. Some developmentalists wonder if the acquisition of knowledge could account for all cognitive growth. Most, however, argue that both cognitive changes in such areas as concrete and formal operational thought and the development of expertise through experience are at work in understanding the adolescent's cognitive world.

*Might adolescents' ability to reason hypothetically and to evaluate what is ideal versus what is real lead them to engage in demonstrations, such as this protest related to better ethnic relations? What other causes might be attractive to adolescents' newfound cognitive abilities of hypothetical-deductive reasoning and idealistic thinking?*

**Evaluating Piaget's Theory** What were Piaget's main contributions? Has his theory withstood the test of time? In this section, we examine both Piaget's contributions and criticisms of his work.

**Contributions** Piaget has been a giant in the field of developmental psychology. We owe to him the present field of cognitive development as well as a long list of masterful concepts of enduring power and fascination: assimilation, accommodation, conservation, and hypothetical-deductive reasoning, among others. We also owe to Piaget the current vision of children as active, constructive thinkers (Vidal, 2000).

Piaget was a genius when it came to observing children. His careful observations documented inventive new ways to discover how children act on and adapt to their world. Piaget showed us some important things to look for in cognitive development, such as the shift from preoperational to concrete operational thinking. He also pointed out that children need to make their experiences fit their schemas, or cognitive frameworks, yet can simultaneously adapt their schemas to experience. He also revealed that cognitive change is likely to occur if the context is structured to allow gradual movement to the next-higher level. We owe to Piaget the current belief that a concept does not emerge all of a sudden, full blown, but develops instead through a series of partial accomplishments that lead to an increasingly comprehensive understanding (Haith & Benson, 1998).

**Criticisms** Piaget's theory has not gone unchallenged (Wigfield, Byrnes, & Eccles, 2006; Keating, 2004; Kuhn & Franklin, 2006). Questions are raised about the timing and nature of his stage view of cognitive development, whether he failed to adequately study in detail key cognitive processes, and the effects of culture on cognitive development. Let's consider each of these criticisms in turn.

In terms of timing and stages, some cognitive abilities have been found to emerge earlier than Piaget had thought. For example, conservation of number (which Piaget said emerged at approximately 7 years of age in the concrete operational stage) has been demonstrated as early as age 3 (which instead is early in his preoperational stage). Other cognitive abilities often emerge later than Piaget indicated. Many adolescents still think in concrete operational ways or are just beginning to master formal operations. Even as adults, many individuals are not formal operational thinkers. Recent reviews conclude that the evidence does not support Piaget's view that prior to age 11 children don't engage in abstract thinking and that from 11 years on they do (Kuhn & Franklin, 2006; Wigfield, Byrnes, & Eccles, 2006). Thus, adolescents' cognitive development is not as stage-like as Piaget thought.

One group of cognitive developments, the **neo-Piagetians,** conclude that Piaget's theory does not adequately focus on attention, memory, and cognitive strategies that adolescents use to process information, and that Piaget's explanations of cognitive changes are too general. They especially believe that a more accurate vision of children's and adolescents' thinking requires more knowledge of the strategies they use, how fast and automatically they process information, the particular cognitive tasks involved in processing information, and the division of cognitive problems into smaller, more precise steps.

The leading proponent of the neo-Piagetian view has been Canadian developmental psychologist Robbie Case (1992, 2000). Case accepts Piaget's four stages of cognitive development but emphasizes that a more precise description of changes within each stage is needed. He notes that children's and adolescents' growing ability to process information efficiently is linked to their brain growth and memory development. In particular, Case cites the increasing ability to hold information in working memory (a workbench for memory similar to short-term memory) and manipulate it more effectively as critical to understanding cognitive development.

Finally, culture exerts stronger influence on development than Piaget envisioned. For example, the age at which individuals acquire conservation skills is associated to some extent with the degree to which their culture provides relevant educational

**neo-Piagetians** Theorists who argue that Piaget got some things right but that his theory needs considerable revision. In their revision, they give more emphasis to information processing that involves attention, memory, and strategies; they also seek to provide more precise explanations of cognitive changes.

*What are some ways that young adults might think differently than adolescents?*

practice (Cole, 2006). In many developing countries, educational opportunities are limited and formal operational thought is rare. You will read shortly about Lev Vygotsky's theory of cognitive development in which culture is given a more prominent role than in Piaget's theory.

### Cognitive Changes in Adulthood

As we indicated earlier, according to Piaget, adults and adolescents use the same type of reasoning. Adolescents and adults think in *qualitatively* the same way. Piaget did acknowledge that adults can be *quantitatively* more advanced in their knowledge. What are some ways that adults might be more advanced in their thinking than adolescents?

**Realistic and Pragmatic Thinking** Some developmentalists have proposed that as young adults move into the world of work, their way of thinking does change. One idea is that as they face the constraints of reality, which work promotes, their idealism decreases (Labouvie-Vief, 1986).

A related change in thinking was proposed by K. Warner Schaie (1977). He concluded that it is unlikely that adults go beyond the powerful methods of scientific thinking characteristic of the formal operational stage. However, Schaie argued that adults do progress beyond adolescents in their use of intellect. For example, in early adulthood individuals often switch from acquiring knowledge to applying knowledge as they pursue success in their work.

**Reflective and Relativistic Thinking** William Perry (1970, 1999) also described changes in cognition that take place in early adulthood. He said that adolescents often view the world in terms of polarities—right/wrong, we/they, or good/bad. As youth age into adulthood, they gradually move away from this type of absolutist thinking as they become aware of the diverse opinions and multiple perspectives of others. Thus, in Perry's view, the absolutist, dualistic thinking of adolescence gives way to the reflective, relativistic thinking of adulthood. Other developmentalists also concluded that reflective thinking is an important indicator of cognitive change in young adults (Fischer & Pruyne, 2003).

Expanding on Perry's view, Gisela Labouvie-Vief (2006) recently proposed that the increasing complexity of cultures in the past century has generated a greater need for more reflective, complex thinking that takes into account the changing nature of knowledge and challenges. She also emphasizes that the key aspects of cognitive development in emerging adulthood include deciding on a particular worldview, recognizing that the worldview is subjective, and understanding that diverse worldviews should be acknowledged. In her perspective, considerable individual variation characterizes the thinking of emerging adults with the highest level of thinking attained by only some. She argues that the level of education emerging adults achieve especially influences how likely they will maximize their cognitive potential.

**Is There a Fifth, Postformal Stage?** Some theorists have pieced together these descriptions of adult thinking and proposed that young adults move into a new qualitative stage of cognitive development, postformal thought (Sinnott, 2003). **Postformal thought** is

- *Reflective, relativistic, and contextual.* As young adults engage in solving problems, they might think deeply about many aspects of work, politics, relationships, and other areas of life (Kitchener, King, & DeLuca, 2006; Labouvie-Vief, 2006). They find that what might be the best solution to a problem at work (with a boss or co-worker) might not be the best solution at home (with a romantic partner). Thus, postformal thought holds that the correct answer to a problem requires reflective thinking and may vary from one situation to another.

**postformal thought** Thought that is reflective, relativistic, and contextual; provisional; realistic; and open to emotions and subjective.

- *Provisional.* Many young adults also become more skeptical about the truth and unwilling to accept an answer as final. Thus, they come to see the search for truth as an ongoing and perhaps never-ending process.
- *Realistic.* Young adults understand that thinking can't always be abstract. In many instances, it must be realistic and pragmatic.
- *Open to emotions and subjective.* Many young adults accept that emotion and subjective factors can influence thinking (Kitchener & King, 1981; Kramer, Kahlbaugh, & Goldston, 1992). For example, as young adults, they understand that a person thinks more clearly in a calm rather than an angry state.

How strong is the evidence for a fifth, postformal stage of cognitive development? Researchers have found that young adults are more likely to engage in this postformal thinking than adolescents are (Commons & Bresette, 2006; Commons & Richards, 2003). But critics argue that research has yet to document that postformal thought is a qualitatively more advanced stage than formal operational thought.

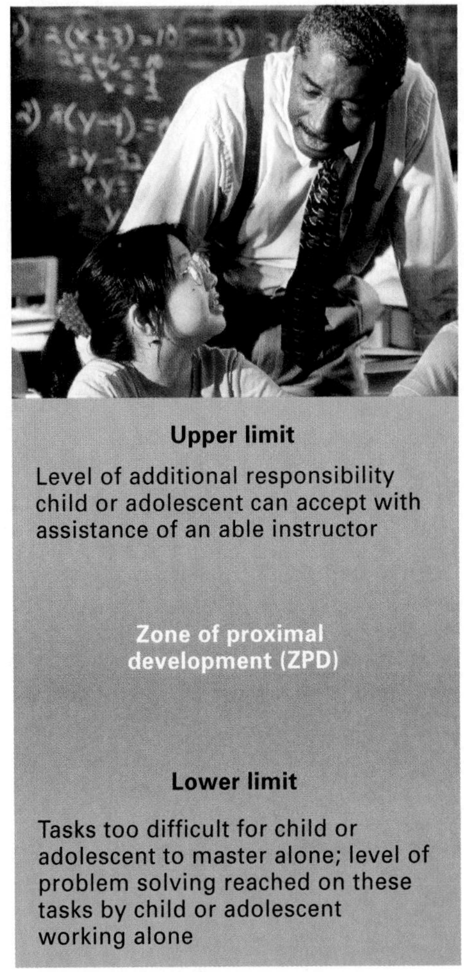

Upper limit
Level of additional responsibility child or adolescent can accept with assistance of an able instructor
Zone of proximal development (ZPD)
Lower limit
Tasks too difficult for child or adolescent to master alone; level of problem solving reached on these tasks by child or adolescent working alone


**FIGURE 3.6 Vygotsky's Zone of Proximal Development (ZPD)** Vygotsky's zone of proximal development has a lower limit and an upper limit. Tasks in the ZPD are too difficult for the child or adolescent to perform alone. They require assistance from an adult or a more-skilled youth. As children and adolescents experience the verbal instruction or demonstration, they organize the information in their existing mental structures so they can eventually perform the skill or task alone.

## Vygotksy's Theory

Lev Vygotsky's (1962) theory was introduced in Chapter 1, and it has stimulated considerable interest in the view that knowledge is *situated* and *collaborative* (Cole & Gajdamaschko, 2007; Daniels, Wertsch, & Cole, 2007). That is, knowledge is distributed among people and their environments, which include objects, artifacts, tools, books, and the communities in which people live. This distribution suggests that knowing can best be advanced through interaction with others in cooperative activities (Camilleri, 2005).

One of Vygotsky's most important concepts is the **zone of proximal development (ZPD),** which refers to the range of tasks that are too difficult for an individual to master alone, but that can be mastered with the guidance and assistance of adults or more-skilled peers. Thus, the lower level of the ZPD is the level of problem solving reached by an adolescent working independently. The upper limit is the level of thinking the adolescent can accept with the assistance of an able instructor (see Figure 3.6). Vygotsky's emphasis on the ZPD underscored his belief in the importance of social influences on cognitive development (Alvarez & del Rio, 2007).

In Vygotsky's approach, formal schooling is but one of the cultural agents that determine an adolescent's growth (Daniels, 2007). Parents, peers, the community, and the culture's technological orientation also influence adolescents' thinking (Rogoff & others, 2007). For example, parents' and peers' attitudes toward intellectual competence affect their motivation to acquire knowledge. So do the attitudes of teachers and other adults in the community.

Even though their theories were proposed at about the same time, most of the world learned about Vygotsky's theory later than they learned about Piaget's theory, so Vygotsky's theory has not yet been evaluated as thoroughly. Vygotsky's view of the importance of sociocultural influences on children's development fits with the current belief that it is important to evaluate the contextual factors in learning.

Although both theories are constructivist, Vygotsky's is a **social constructivist approach,** which emphasizes the social contexts of learning and the construction of knowledge through social interaction. In moving from Piaget to Vygotsky, the conceptual shift is from the individual to collaboration, social interaction, and sociocultural activity (Rogoff & others, 2007). The end point of cognitive development for Piaget is formal operational thought. For Vygotsky, the end point can differ depending on which skills are considered to be the most important in a particular culture. For Piaget, children construct knowledge by transforming, organizing, and reorganizing previous knowledge. For Vygotsky, children and adolescents construct knowledge through social interaction (Bodrova & Leong, 2007; Hyson, Copple, & Jones, 2006). The implication of Piaget's theory for teaching is that children need

**zone of proximal development (ZPD)** Vygotsky's concept that refers to the range of tasks that are too difficult for an individual to master alone, but that can be mastered with the guidance or assistance of adults or more-skilled peers.

**social constructivist approach** Emphasizes the social contexts of learning and the construction of knowledge through social interaction.

| | Vygotsky | Piaget |
|---|---|---|
| **Sociocultural context** | Strong emphasis | Little emphasis |
| **Constructivism** | Social constructivist | Cognitive constructivist |
| **Stages** | No general stages of development proposed | Strong emphasis on stages (sensorimotor, preoperational, concrete operational, and formal operational) |
| **Key processes** | Zone of proximal development, language, dialogue, tools of the culture | Schema, assimilation, accommodation, operations, conservation, classification, hypothetical-deductive reasoning |
| **Role of language** | A major role; language plays a powerful role in shaping thought | Language has a minimal role; cognition primarily directs language |
| **View on education** | Education plays a central role, helping children learn the tools of the culture. | Education merely refines the child's cognitive skills that have already emerged. |
| **Teaching implications** | Teacher is a facilitator and guide, not a director; establish many opportunities for children to learn with the teacher and more skilled peers | Also views teacher as a facilitator and guide, not a director; provide support for children to explore their world and discover knowledge |

**FIGURE 3.7** Comparison of Vygotsky's and Piaget's Theories

support to explore their world and discover knowledge. The main implication of Vygotsky's theory for teaching is that students need many opportunities to learn with the teacher and more-skilled peers (Daniels, 2007). In both Piaget's and Vygotsky's theories, teachers serve as facilitators and guides, rather than as directors and molders of learning. Figure 3.7 compares Vygotsky's and Piaget's theories.

Criticisms of Vygotsky's theory also have surfaced. Some critics say his emphasis on collaboration and guidance has potential pitfalls. Might facilitators be too helpful in some cases, as when a parent becomes too overbearing and controlling? Further, some adolescents might become lazy and expect help when they might have done something on their own.

### REVIEW AND REFLECT ◆ LEARNING GOAL 2

**2 Discuss the cognitive developmental view of adolescence.**

***Review***

- What is Piaget's view of adolescence?
- What is Vygotsky's view of adolescence?

***Reflect***

- Suppose an 8-year-old and a 16-year-old are watching a political convention on television. In terms of Piaget's stages of cognitive development, how would their perceptions of the proceedings be likely to differ? What would the 8-year-old "see" and comprehend? What would the 16-year-old "see" and comprehend? What Piagetian concepts would these differences in cognition reflect?

# 3 The Information-Processing View

Cognitive Resources | Attention and Memory | Mechanisms of Change | Executive Functioning

In Chapter 1, we briefly described the information-processing view. We saw that information processing includes how information gets into adolescents' minds, how it is stored, and how adolescents retrieve information to think about and solve problems.

Information processing is both a framework for thinking about adolescent development and a facet of that development. As a framework, the information-processing view includes certain ideas about how adolescents' minds work and how best to study those workings (Kuhn & Franklin, 2006; Munkata, 2006; Schraw, 2006; Siegler, 2006). As a facet of development, information processing changes as children make the transition from adolescence to adulthood (Keil, 2006; Kuhn & Franklin, 2006). Changes in attention and memory, for example, are essentially changes in the way individuals process information (Alexander, 2006). In our exploration of information processing, we discuss developmental changes in attention and memory, as well as a number of higher-order cognitive processes involved in executive functioning—but first let's examine some basic characteristics of the information-processing view.

## Cognitive Resources

Developmental changes in information processing are likely influenced by increases in both capacity and speed of processing (Frye, 2004). These two characteristics are often referred to as *cognitive resources,* which are proposed to have an important influence on memory and problem solving. During adolescence, "individuals increasingly develop the potential to manage and deploy their cognitive resources in consciously controlled and purposefully chosen ways" (Kuhn & Franklin, 2006).

Both biology and experience contribute to growth in cognitive resources. Think about how much faster you can process information in your native language than a second language. The changes in the brain we described earlier in this chapter provide a biological foundation for increased cognitive resources. Important biological developments occur both in brain structures, such as changes in the frontal lobes, and at the level of neurons, such as the blooming and pruning of connections between neurons (Giedd & others, 2006; Nelson, Thomas, & de Haan, 2006). Also, as we discussed earlier in this chapter, myelination (the process that covers the axon with a myelin sheath) increases the speed of electrical impulses in the brain. Myelination continues through childhood, adolescence, and emerging adulthood.

Most information-processing psychologists argue that an increase in capacity also improves processing of information (Case, 2000; Halford, 2004). For example, as adolescents' information-processing capacity increases, they likely can hold in mind several dimensions of a topic or problem simultaneously, whereas younger children are more prone to focus on only one dimension.

What is the role of processing speed? How fast adolescents process information often influences what they can do with that information. If an adolescent is trying to add up mentally the cost of items he is buying at the grocery store, the adolescent needs to be able to compute the sum before he has forgotten the price of the individual items. Adolescents' speed in processing information is linked with their competence in thinking (Bjorklund, 2005). For example, how fast adolescents can articulate a series of words affects how many words they can store and remember.

Generally, fast processing is linked with good performance on cognitive tasks. However, some compensation for slower processing speed can be achieved through effective strategies.

Researchers have devised a number of ways for assessing processing speed. For example, it can be assessed through a *reaction-time task* in which individuals are asked to push a button as soon as they see a stimulus such as a light. Or individuals might be asked to match letters or match numbers with symbols on a computer screen.

There is abundant evidence that the speed with which such tasks are completed improves dramatically across the childhood and adolescent years (Kail, 1988, 2000; Kail & Miller, 2006; Stigler, Nusbaum, & Chalip, 1988). Processing speed continues to improve in adolescence. Think how much faster you could process the answer to a simple arithmetic problem as an adolescent than as a child. In one study, 10-year-olds were approximately 1.8 times slower at processing information than young adults on such tasks as reaction time, letter matching, mental rotation, and abstract matching (Hale, 1990). Twelve-year-olds were approximately 1.5 times slower than young adults, but 15-year-olds processed information on the tasks as fast as the young adults.

## Mechanisms of Change

Robert Siegler (1998) described three main characteristics of the information-processing view. The first is an emphasis on thinking as information processing. When adolescents perceive, encode, represent, and store information from the world, Siegler says, they are engaging in thinking. Siegler argues that thinking is highly flexible, allowing individuals to adapt and adjust to many changes in their circumstances, task requirements, and goals (Siegler & Alibali, 2005). However, the human's remarkable thinking abilities do have some limitations. Individuals can attend to only a limited amount of information at one point in time, and they are constrained by how fast they can process it.

The second characteristic of the information-processing view is an emphasis on mechanisms of change. In this regard, Siegler states that four mechanisms—encoding, automaticity, strategy construction, and generalization—work together to create changes in children's and adolescents' cognitive skills.

*Encoding* is the process by which information gets into memory. A key to solving problems is encoding relevant information and ignoring what is irrelevant.

*Automaticity* refers to the ability to process information with little or no effort. With age and experience, information processing becomes increasingly automatic, allowing children and adolescents to detect connections among ideas and events that they otherwise would miss. An able 12-year-old zips through a list of multiplication problems with little conscious effort; a 16-year-old picks up the newspaper and quickly scans the entertainment section to learn the location and time of a movie. In both cases, information processing is more automatic and less effortful than it is for children.

Earlier in this chapter we described Robbie Case's neo-Piagetian view. Case's view emphasizes changes in the way adolescents process information differently than children do, including automaticity. In Case's (1992, 2000) view, adolescents have more cognitive resources available to them because of automaticity, increased information-processing capacity, and greater familiarity with a range of content knowledge. These advances in information processing reduce the load on the cognitive system, allowing the adolescent to hold in mind several dimensions of a topic or problem simultaneously. In contrast, children are more prone to focus on only one dimension of a topic.

### *Through the Eyes of Adolescents*

**WE THINK MORE THAN ADULTS THINK WE DO**

I don't think adults understand how much kids think today. We just don't take something at face value. We want to understand why things are the way they are and the reasons behind things. We want it to be a better world and we are thinking all of the time how to make it that way. When we get be adults, we will make the world better.

*–Jason, age 15*
*Dallas, Texas*

Let's examine the third and fourth change mechanisms proposed by Siegler: strategy construction and generalization. *Strategy construction* is the discovery of a new procedure for processing information. Siegler says to solve a problem, adolescents need to encode key information about it and then find a way to coordinate that information with relevant prior knowledge. To fully benefit from a newly constructed strategy, adolescents then need to *generalize* it, or apply it to other problems.

The third characteristic of the information-processing view is an emphasis on *self-modification.* Advocates of the contemporary version of the information-processing view argue, as does Piaget's theory, that adolescents play an active role in their development (Kuhn & Franklin, 2006). They use the knowledge and strategies they have learned to adapt their responses to new learning situations (Pressley & Harris, 2006; Pressley & Hilden, 2006). In this manner, adolescents construct more sophisticated responses from prior knowledge and strategies.

## Attention and Memory

Although the bulk of research on information processing has been conducted with children and adults, the information-processing view is still important in understanding adolescent cognition. Especially important in this view are the processes of attention and memory.

### Attention

*Pay attention* is a phrase children and adolescents hear all the time. Just what is attention? *Attention* is the concentration and focusing of mental effort. Attention is both selective and shifting. For example, when adolescents take a test, they must be able to focus their mental effort on certain stimuli (the test questions) while excluding other stimuli. This important aspect of attention is called *selectivity.* When selective attention fails adolescents, they have difficulty ignoring irrelevant information. For example, if a television set is blaring while an adolescent is studying, the adolescent might have difficulty concentrating.

Not only is attention selective; it is also *shiftable.* If a teacher asks students to pay attention to a certain question and they do so, their behavior indicates that they can shift the focus of their mental effort from one stimulus to another. If the telephone rings while the adolescent is studying, the adolescent may shift attention from studying to the telephone. An external stimulus is not necessary to cause a shift in attention, however. At any moment, adolescents can shift their attention from one topic to another, virtually at will. They might think about the last time they went to a play, then shift their thoughts to an upcoming music recital, and so on.

In one investigation, 12-year-olds were markedly better than 8-year-olds, and slightly worse than 20-year-olds, at allocating their attention between two tasks (Manis, Keating, & Morrison, 1980). Adolescents may have more resources available to them than children (through increased processing speed, capacity, and automaticity), or they may be more skilled at directing the resources.

### Memory

There are few moments when adolescents' lives are not steeped in memory. Memory is at work with each step adolescents take, each thought they think, and each word they utter. *Memory* is the retention of information over time. It is central to mental life and to information processing. To successfully learn and reason, adolescents need to hold on to information and retrieve it when necessary. Three important memory systems—short-term memory, working memory, and long-term memory—are involved in adolescents' learning.

**Short-Term Memory** *Short-term memory* is a limited-capacity memory system in which information is retained for as long as 30 seconds, unless the information is rehearsed, in which case it can be retained longer. A common way to assess short-term memory is to present a list of items to remember, which is often referred to as a memory span task. If you have taken an IQ test, you probably were asked to

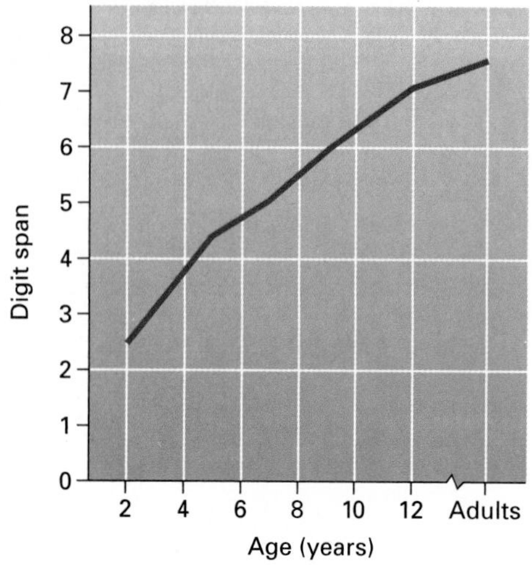


**FIGURE 3.8 Developmental Changes in Memory Span** In one study, memory span increased about 3 digits from 2 years of age to 5 digits at 7 years of age (Dempster, 1981). By 12 years of age, memory span had increased on average another 1½ digits.

remember a string of numbers or words. You simply hear a short list of stimuli—usually digits—presented at a rapid pace (one per second, for example). Then you are asked to repeat the digits back. Using the memory span task, researchers have found that short-term memory increases extensively in early childhood and continues to increase in older children and adolescents, but at a slower pace. For example, in one investigation, memory span increased by 1½ digits between the ages of 7 and 12 (Dempster, 1981) (see Figure 3.8). Keep in mind, though, memory span's individual differences, which is why IQ and various aptitude tests are used.

How might short-term memory be used in problem solving? In a series of experiments, Robert Sternberg and his colleagues (Sternberg, 1977; Sternberg & Nigro, 1980; Sternberg & Rifkin, 1979) attempted to answer this question by giving third-grade, sixth-grade, ninth-grade, and college students analogies to solve. The main differences occurred between the younger (third- and sixth-grade) and older (ninth-grade and college) students. The older students were more likely to complete the information processing required to solve the analogy task. The children, by contrast, often stopped their processing of information before they had considered all of the necessary steps required to solve the problems. Sternberg stressed that information processing was incomplete because the children's short-term memory was overloaded. Solving problems such as analogies requires individuals to make continued comparisons between newly encoded information and previously coded information. Sternberg argues that adolescents probably have more storage space in short-term memory, which results in fewer errors on problems like analogies.

In addition to more storage space, are there other reasons adolescents might perform better on memory span tasks and in solving analogies? Though many other factors could be involved, information-processing psychologists believe that changes in the speed and efficiency of information processing are important—especially the speed with which information is identified.

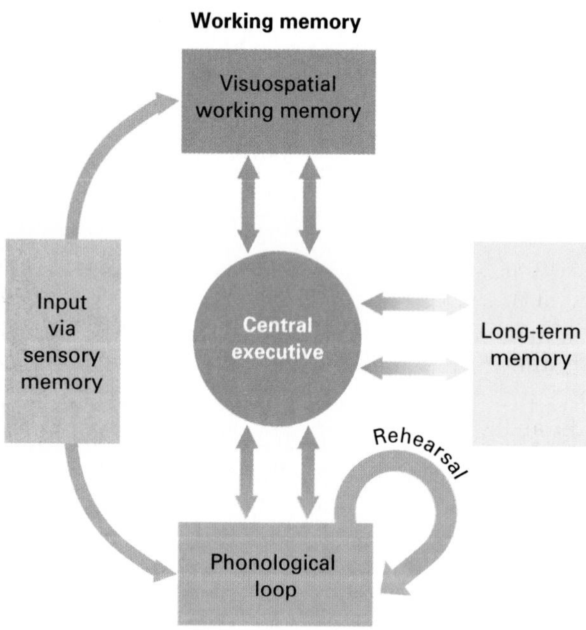


**FIGURE 3.9 Working Memory** In Baddeley's working memory model, working memory is like a mental workbench where a great deal of information processing is carried out. Working memory consists of three main components: the phonological loop and visuospatial working memory serve as assistants, helping the central executive do its work. Input from sensory memory goes to the phonological loop, where information about speech is stored and rehearsal takes place, and visuospatial working memory, where visual and spatial information, including imagery, is stored. Working memory is a limited-capacity system, and information is stored there for only a brief time. Working memory interacts with long-term memory, using information from long-term memory in its work and transmitting information to long-term memory for longer storage.

**Working Memory** Short-term memory is like a passive storehouse with shelves to store information until it is moved to long-term memory. *Working memory* is a kind of mental "workbench" where individuals manipulate and assemble information when they make decisions, solve problems, and comprehend written and spoken language (Baddeley, 2006, 2007a, b) (see Figure 3.9). Many psychologists prefer the term working memory over short-term memory to describe how memory works. Working memory is described as more active and powerful in modifying information than short-term memory (Swanson, 2005).

In one study, the performances of individuals from 6 to 57 years of age were examined on both verbal and visuospatial working memory tasks (Swanson, 1999). The two verbal tasks were auditory digit sequence (the ability to remember numerical information embedded in a short sentence, such as "Now suppose somebody wanted to go to the supermarket at 8651 Elm Street") and semantic association (the ability to organize words into abstract categories) (Swanson, 1999, p. 988). In the semantic association task, the participant was presented with a series of words (such as *shirt, saw, pants, hammer, shoes,* and *nails*) and then asked to remember how they go together. The two visuospatial tasks involved mapping/directions and a visual matrix. In the mapping/directions task, the participant was shown a street map indicating the route a bicycle (child/young adolescent) or car (adult) would take through a city. After briefly looking at the map, participants were asked to redraw the route on a blank map. In the visual matrix task, participants were asked to study a matrix showing a series of dots. After looking at the matrix for five seconds, they were asked to answer questions about the location of the dots.

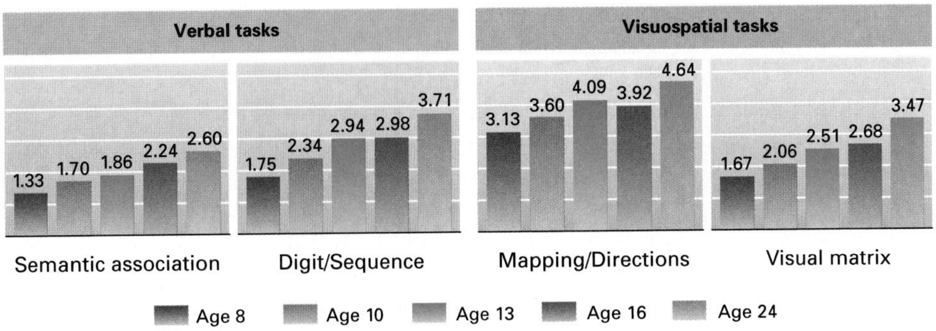


**FIGURE 3.10 Developmental Changes in Working Memory** *Note:* The scores shown here are the means for each age group and the age also represents a mean age. Higher scores reflect superior working memory performance.

As shown in Figure 3.10, working memory increased substantially from 8 through 24 years of age no matter what the task. Thus, the adolescent years are likely to be an important developmental period for improvement in working memory. Note that working memory continues to improve through the transition to adulthood and beyond.

**Long-Term Memory** *Long-term memory* is a relatively permanent memory system that holds huge amounts of information for a long period of time. Long-term memory increases substantially in the middle and late childhood years and likely continues to improve during adolescence, although this has not been well documented by researchers. If anything at all is known about long-term memory, it is that it depends on the learning activities engaged in, when learning and remembering information (Pressley & Hilden, 2006; Siegler, 2006). Most learning activities fit under the category of *strategies,* activities under the learner's conscious control. There are many such activities, but one of the most important is organization, the tendency to group or arrange items into categories. We have more to say about strategies shortly.

## Executive Functioning

Attention and memory are important dimensions of information processing, but other dimensions also are important. Once adolescents attend to information and retain it, they can use the information to engage in a number of higher-order cognitive activities, such as making decisions, reasoning, thinking critically, thinking creatively, and metacognition. These types of higher-order, complex cognitive processes are often called **executive functioning.** In his model of cognitive functioning described earlier in the chapter, Alan Baddeley (2000) recognized the importance of these higher-order cognitive processes and actually called this aspect of his model the *central executive.*

Executive functioning becomes increasingly strong during adolescence (Kuhn & Franklin, 2006). This executive functioning "assumes a role of monitoring and managing the deployment of cognitive resources as a function of task demands. As a result, cognitive development and learning itself become more effective. . . . Emergence and strengthening of this executive (functioning) is arguably the single most important and consequential intellectual development to occur in the second decade of life" (Kuhn & Franklin, 2006, p. 987). An example of how executive functioning increases in adolescence is its role in determining how attention will be allocated. We begin our examination of executive functioning by focusing on decision making.

### Decision Making

Adolescence is a time of increased decision making—which friends to choose, which person to date, whether to have sex, buy a car, go to college, and so on (Byrnes, 2005; Jacobs & Klaczynski, 2005; Klaczynski, 2005). How competent are adolescents at making decisions? In some reviews, older adolescents are described as more competent than younger adolescents, who in turn are more competent than children (Keating, 1990). Compared with children, young

**executive functioning** Higher-order, complex cognitive processes that include making decisions, reasoning, thinking critically, thinking creatively, and metacognition.

adolescents are more likely to generate different options, examine a situation from a variety of perspectives, anticipate the consequences of decisions, and consider the credibility of sources.

One study documents that older adolescents are better at decision making than younger adolescents are (Lewis, 1981). Eighth-, tenth-, and twelfth-grade students were presented with dilemmas involving the choice of a medical procedure. The oldest students were most likely to spontaneously mention a variety of risks, to recommend consultation with an outside specialist, and to anticipate future consequences. For example, when asked a question about whether to have cosmetic surgery, a twelfth-grader said that different aspects of the situation need to be examined along with its effects on the individual's future, especially relationships with other people. In contrast, an eighth-grader presented a more limited view, commenting on the surgery's effects on getting turned down for a date, the money involved, and being teased by peers.

In sum, older adolescents often make better decisions than younger adolescents, who in turn, make better decisions than children. The ability to regulate one's emotions during decision making, to remember prior decisions and their consequences, and to adapt subsequent decision making on the basis of those consequences appears to improve with age at least through the early adulthood years (Klaczynski, Byrnes, & Jacobs, 2001).

However, older adolescents' decision-making skills are far from perfect, as are adults' (Klaczynski, 2005). Indeed, some researchers have found that adolescents and adults do not differ in their decision-making skills (Quadrel, Fischoff, & Davis, 1993). Furthermore, adolescent decision making is linked to some personality traits. Adolescents who are impulsive and seek sensation are often not very effective decision makers, for example (Byrnes, 1998).

Being able to make competent decisions does not guarantee that one will make them in everyday life, where breadth of experience often comes into play (Jacobs & Klaczynski, 2005; Jacobs & Potenza, 1990; Keating, 1990, 2004, 2007). For example, driver-training courses improve adolescents' cognitive and motor skills to levels equal to, or sometimes superior to, those of adults. However, driver training has not been effective in reducing adolescents' high rate of traffic accidents (Potvin, Champagne, & Laberge-Nadeau, 1988). An important research agenda is to study the ways adolescents make decisions in practical situations (Fantino & Stolarz-Fantino, 2005).

Most people make better decisions when they are calm rather than emotionally aroused. That may especially be true for adolescents. Recall from our discussion of brain development earlier in the chapter that adolescents have a tendency to be emotionally intense. Thus, the same adolescent who makes a wise decision when calm may make an unwise decision when emotionally aroused (Dahl, 2004). In the heat of the moment, then, adolescents' emotions may especially overwhelm their decision-making ability.

*What are some of the decisions adolescents have to make? What characterizes their decision making?*

Adolescents need more opportunities to practice and discuss realistic decision making (Jones, Rasmussen, & Moffitt, 1997). Many real-world decisions on matters such as sex, drugs, and daredevil driving occur in an atmosphere of stress that includes time constraints and emotional involvement. One strategy for improving adolescent decision making in such circumstances is to provide more opportunities for them to engage in role-playing and group problem solving.

Another strategy is for parents to involve adolescents in appropriate decision-making activities. In one study of more than 900 young adolescents and a subsample of their parents, adolescents were more likely to participate in family decision making when they perceived themselves as in control of what happens to them and if they thought that their input would have some bearing on the outcome of the decision-making process (Liprie, 1993).

## Reasoning

*Reasoning* is logical thinking that uses induction and deduction to reach a conclusion. We begin by focusing on inductive reasoning.

### Inductive Reasoning

**Inductive reasoning** involves reasoning from the specific to the general. That is, it consists of drawing conclusions (forming concepts) about all members of a category based on observing only some of its members (Markman & Gentner, 2001). For example, when a student in English class reads only a few of Emily Dickinson's poems and is asked to draw conclusions from them about the general nature of Dickinson's poems, inductive reasoning is being requested. When a student is asked whether a concept in a math class applies to other contexts, such as business or science, again, inductive reasoning is being called for. Research on adolescent development is inductive as well when it studies a sample of participants in order to draw conclusions about the population from which the sample is drawn. It is also inductive in that scientists rarely take a single study as strong evidence to reach a conclusion about a topic, instead requiring a number of studies on the same topic to have more confidence in a conclusion.

Indeed, an important aspect of inductive reasoning is repeated observation so that information about similar experiences accumulates to the point that a repetitive pattern can be detected and a more accurate conclusion drawn about it. To study this aspect of inductive reasoning, researchers have examined whether inductive inferences are justified based on the evidence about a single instance of two co-occurring events (Kuhn, Katz, & Dean, 2004). Because the events occur together in time and space, one is often concluded to cause the other despite the likely presence of other factors that might be involved. For example, a parent might conclude, "Harry is a bad influence on my daughter; Sharon didn't drink before she met him." The boy might be the cause, but the event may have been a coincidence. Of course, if there is repeated evidence (for example, every girl Harry has ever gone out with develops a drinking problem), then the argument becomes more persuasive.

Consider also an adolescent who observes a black snake and concludes, "All snakes are black." The adolescent's cousin sends him an e-mail about a pet snake she recently bought, and the adolescent concludes that the snake must be black. However, the adolescent clearly has not observed all of the snakes in the world—actually only one in this case—so he has seen only a small sample of the world's snake population. Of course, he would be forced to change his mind if he saw a gray snake or a white snake. The process of inductive reasoning is never finally certain, only more or less probable. But induction can provide conclusive negative results—for example, seeing a yellow snake proves the assertion "All snakes are black" is false.

How good are adolescents at inductive reasoning? Adolescents are better at false inclusion about generalizing from a single event than children but not as good as young adults (Kuhn & Franklin, 2006).

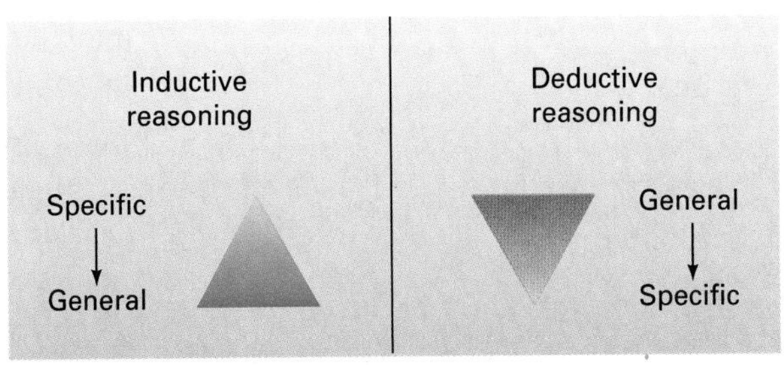


**FIGURE 3.11 Inductive and Deductive Reasoning** The pyramid on the left (right side up) represents inductive reasoning–going from specific to general. The pyramid or triangle on the right (upside down) represents deductive reasoning–going from general to specific.

### Deductive Reasoning

In contrast to inductive reasoning, **deductive reasoning** is reasoning from the general to the specific. Figure 3.11 provides a visual representation of the difference between inductive and deductive reasoning.

When you solve puzzles or riddles, you are engaging in deductive reasoning. When you learn about a general rule and then understand how it applies in some situations but not others, you are engaging in deductive reasoning (Kuhn & Franklin, 2006). When psychologists use theories and intuitions to make predictions,

**inductive reasoning** Reasoning from the specific to the general—that is, drawing conclusions about all members of a category based on observing only some of its members.

**deductive reasoning** Reasoning from the general to the specific.

then evaluate these predictions by making further observations, deductive reasoning is at work.

Deductive reasoning is always certain in the sense that if the initial rules or assumptions are true, then the conclusion will follow directly as a matter of logic. For example, if you know the general rule that dogs bark and cats meow (and if the rules are always true), you can deduce correctly whether your neighbor's strange-looking pet is a dog or a cat on the basis of the specific sound it makes. When psychologists develop a hypothesis from a theory, they are using a form of deductive reasoning because the hypothesis is a specific, logical extension of the general theory. If the theory is true, the hypothesis will turn out to be true as well.

Many aspects of deductive reasoning have been studied, including the occasions when knowledge and reasoning conflict. During adolescence, individuals are increasingly able to reason deductively even when the premises being reasoned about are false. Consider this deductive inference problem:

*All basketball players are motorcycle drivers.*
*All motorcycle drivers are women.*

Assuming that the above two statements are true, is the following statement true or false:

*All basketball players are women.*

Children rarely conclude that such conclusions are valid deductions from the premises. From early adolescence through early adulthood, individuals improve in their ability to make accurate conclusions when knowledge and reasoning conflict—that is, being able to "reason independently of the truth status of the premises" (Kuhn & Franklin, 2006).

**Critical Thinking** Making competent decisions and reasoning logically are closely related to critical thinking, currently a buzzword in education and psychology (Halpern, 2007; Mosely & others, 2006; Sternberg, Roediger, & Halpern, 2007; Van Gelder, 2005). **Critical thinking** is thinking reflectively and productively and evaluating evidence. In one study of fifth-, eighth-, and eleventh-graders, critical thinking increased with age, but still occurred only in 43 percent of eleventh-graders (Klaczynski & Narashimham, 1998). Many adolescents showed self-serving biases in their reasoning.

Adolescence is an important transitional period in the development of critical thinking (Keating, 1990). Among the cognitive changes that allow improved critical thinking during this period are the following:

- Increased speed, automaticity, and capacity of information processing, which frees cognitive resources for other purposes
- Greater breadth of content knowledge in a variety of domains
- Increased ability to construct new combinations of knowledge
- A greater range and more spontaneous use of strategies and procedures for obtaining and applying knowledge, such as planning, considering the alternatives, and cognitive monitoring

Although adolescence is an important period in the development of critical-thinking skills, if an individual has not developed a solid basis of fundamental skills (such as literacy and math skills) during childhood, critical-thinking skills are unlikely to mature in adolescence. For the subset of adolescents who lack such fundamental skills, potential gains in adolescent thinking are not likely.

Considerable interest has recently developed in teaching critical thinking in schools. Cognitive psychologist Robert J. Sternberg (1985) concludes that most school programs that teach critical thinking are flawed. He thinks that schools focus too much on formal reasoning tasks and not enough on the critical-thinking skills needed in everyday life. Among the critical-thinking skills that Sternberg notes adolescents need in everyday life are these: recognizing that problems exist, defining

**critical thinking** Thinking reflectively and productively and evaluating the evidence.

problems more clearly, handling problems with no single right answer or any clear criteria for the point at which the problem is solved (such as selecting a rewarding career), making decisions on issues of personal relevance (such as deciding to have a risky operation), obtaining information, thinking in groups, and developing long-term approaches to long-term problems.

One way to encourage students to think critically is to present them with controversial topics or articles that present both sides of an issue to discuss (Kuhn & Franklin, 2006). Some teachers shy away from having students engage in these types of critical-thinking debates or discussions because it is not "polite" or "nice" (Winn, 2004). However, critical thinking is promoted when students encounter conflicting accounts of arguments and debates, which can motivate them to delve more deeply into a topic and attempt to resolve an issue (Gong, 2005; Kuhn & Franklin, 2006; Van Gelder, 2005). In these circumstances, students often benefit when teachers refrain from stating their own views, allowing students to more freely explore different sides of issues and multiple perspectives on topics.

Getting students to think critically is not always an easy task (Case, 2005; Lauer, 2005). Many students come into a class with a history of passive learning, having been encouraged to recite the correct answer to a question, rather than put forth the intellectual effort to think in more complex ways. By using more assignments that require students to focus on an issue, a question, or a problem, rather than just reciting facts, teachers stimulate students' ability to think critically.

To read about the work of one secondary school teacher who encourages students to think critically, see the *Careers in Adolescent Development* profile.

## Careers in ADOLESCENT DEVELOPMENT

### Laura Bickford
**Secondary School Teacher**

Laura Bickford teaches English and journalism in grades 9 to 12, and she is chair of the English Department at Nordhoff High School in Ojai, California.

Laura especially believes it is important to encourage students to think. Indeed, she says that "the call to teach is the call to teach students how to think." She believes teachers need to show students the value in asking their own questions, in having discussions, and in engaging in stimulating intellectual conversations. Laura says that she also encourages students to engage in metacognitive strategies (knowing about knowing). For example, she asks students to comment on their learning after particular pieces of projects have been completed. She requires students to keep reading logs so they can observe their own thinking as it happens.

Laura Bickford, working with students writing papers.

**Creative Thinking** **Creativity** is the ability to think in novel ways and discover unique solutions to problems. Thus, intelligence, which we discuss shortly, and creativity are not the same thing. J. P. Guilford (1967) first made this distinction by contrasting **convergent thinking,** which produces one correct answer and is characteristic of the kind of thinking required on a conventional intelligence test, and **divergent thinking,** which produces many answers to the same question and is more characteristic of creativity. For example, a typical item on a conventional intelligence test is "How many quarters will you get in return for 60 dimes?" This question has only one correct answer. In contrast, the following questions have many possible answers: "What image comes to mind when you hear the phrase *sitting alone in a dark room*?" or "Can you think of some unique uses for a paper clip?"

Are intelligence and creativity related? Although most creative adolescents are quite intelligent, the reverse is not necessarily true (Lubart, 2003). Many highly intelligent adolescents are not very creative.

An important goal of education is to help adolescents become more creative (Csikszentmihalyi & Nakamura, 2006; Kaufman & Sternberg, 2006; Runco, 2006; Winner, 2006). Here are some good strategies for accomplishing this goal:

- *Have adolescents engage in brainstorming and come up with as many ideas as possible. Brainstorming* is a technique in which individuals are encouraged to come

**creativity** The ability to think in novel and unusual ways and discover unique solutions to problems.

**convergent thinking** A pattern of thinking in which individuals produce one correct answer; characteristic of the items on conventional intelligence tests; coined by Guilford.

**divergent thinking** A pattern of thinking in which individuals produce many answers to the same question; more characteristic of creativity than convergent thinking, coined by Guilford.

*"What do you mean 'What is it?' It's the spontaneous, unfettered expression of a young mind not yet bound by the restraints of narrative or pictorial representation."*
Sidney Harris. ScienceCartoonsPlus.com. Reprinted with permission.

up with creative ideas in a group, play off each other's ideas, and say practically whatever comes to mind. However, recognize that some adolescents are more creative when they work alone. Indeed, one review of research on brainstorming concluded that for many individuals, working alone can generate more ideas and better ideas than working in groups (Rickards & deCock, 2003). One reason for this is that in groups, some individuals contribute only a few ideas, whereas others do most of the creative thinking. Nonetheless, there may be benefits to brainstorming, such as team building, that support its use.

- *Introduce adolescents to environments that stimulate creativity.* Some settings nourish creativity; others depress it (Csikszentmihalyi & Nakamura 2006; Sternberg, Grigorenko, & Singer, 2004). People who encourage adolescents' creativity often rely on their natural curiosity. They provide exercises and activities that stimulate them to find insightful solutions to problems, rather than asking a lot of questions that require rote answers. Adults also encourage creativity by taking adolescents to locations where creativity is valued.
- *Don't overcontrol.* Teresa Amabile (1993) says that telling individuals exactly how to do things leaves them feeling that any originality is a mistake and any exploration is a waste of time. Letting adolescents select their interests and supporting their inclinations are less likely to destroy their natural curiosity than dictating which activities they should engage in.
- *Encourage internal motivation.* The excessive use of prizes such as gold stars or money can stifle creativity by undermining the intrinsic pleasure adolescents derive from creative activities. Creative adolesents' motivation is the satisfaction generated by the work itself. Competition for prizes and formal evaluations often undermine intrinsic motivation and creativity (Amabile & Hennessy, 1992).
- *Introduce adolescents to creative people.* Think about the identity of the most creative people in your community. Teachers can invite these people to their classrooms and ask them to describe what helps them become creative or to demonstrate their creative skills. A writer, poet, musician, scientist, and many others can bring their props and productions to the class, turning it into a theater for stimulating students' creativity.

An adolescent boy painting in the streets of the African nation of Zanzibar. *If you were going to work with adolescents to encourage their creativity, what strategies would you adopt?*

**Expertise** Recently, psychologists have shown an increased interest in experts and novices in a particular knowledge domain (Bransford & others, 2006; Ericsson & others, 2006; Keating, 2007). An expert is the opposite of a novice (someone who is just beginning to learn a content area). What is it, exactly, that experts do so well? They are better than novices at (National Research Council, 1999):

- Detecting features and meaningful patterns of information
- Accumulating more content knowledge and organizing it in a manner that shows an understanding of the topic
- Retrieving important aspects of knowledge with little effort.

In areas where children and adolescents are experts, their memory is often extremely good. In fact, it often exceeds that of adults who are novices in that content area. This was documented in a study of 10-year-old chess experts (Chi, 1978). These children were excellent chess players, but not especially brilliant in other ways. As with most 10-year-olds, their memory spans for digits were shorter than an adult's. However, when they were presented chessboards, they remembered the configurations far better than did the adults who were novices at chess (see Figure 3.12).

Experts' knowledge is organized around important ideas or concepts more than novices' knowledge is (National Research Council, 1999). This provides experts with a much deeper understanding of knowledge than novices. Experts in a particular area usually have far more elaborate networks of information about that area than novices do. The information they represent in memory has more nodes, more interconnections, and better hierarchical organization.

What determines whether or not someone becomes an expert? Can motivation and practice get someone to expert status? Or does expertise also require a great deal of talent?

One perspective is that a particular kind of practice—*deliberate practice*—is required to become an expert. Deliberate practice involves practice that is at an appropriate level of difficulty for the individual, provides corrective feedback, and allows opportunities for repetition (Ericsson, 1996; Ericsson & others, 2006). In one study of violinists at a music academy, the extent to which children engaged in deliberate practice distinguished novices and experts (Ericsson, Krampe, & Tesch-Römer, 1993). The top violinists averaged 7,500 hours of deliberate practice by age 18, the good violinists only 5,300 hours. Many individuals give up on becoming an expert because they won't put forth the effort it takes to engage in extensive deliberate practice over a number of years.

Such extensive practice requires considerable motivation. Students who are not motivated to practice long hours are unlikely to become experts in a particular area. Thus, a student who complains about all of the work, doesn't persevere, and doesn't extensively practice solving math problems over a number of years is not going to become an expert in math. However, talent is also usually required to become an expert (Bloom, 1985; Shiffrin, 1996; Sternberg & Ben-Zeev, 2001). Many individuals have attempted to become great musicians and athletes but have given up trying after only mediocre performances. Nonetheless, musicians such as Beethoven and athletes such as Tiger Woods would not have developed expertise in their fields without being highly motivated and engaging in extensive deliberate practice. Talent alone does not make an expert.

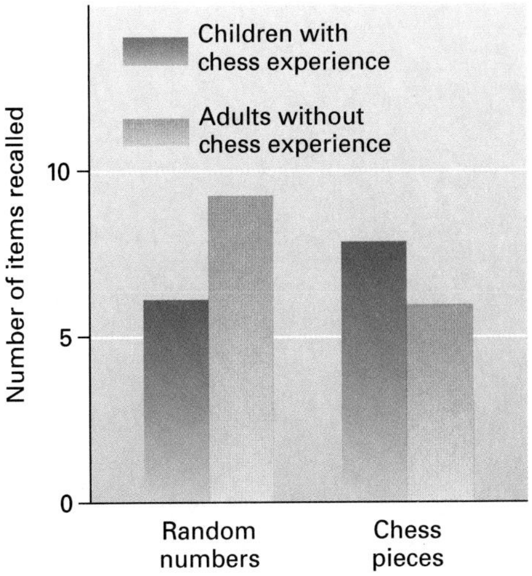


**FIGURE 3.12** **Memory for Numbers and Chess Pieces**

### Metacognition and Self-Regulatory Learning

We have discussed some important ways in which adolescents process information. In this section, we explore how they monitor their information processing and regulate their learning strategies.

**What Is Metacognition?** Earlier in this chapter in discussing Piaget's theory, we learned that adolescents increase their thinking about thinking. Cognitive psychologists call this kind of thought **metacognition**—that is, cognition about cognition, or "knowing about knowing" (Flavell, Miller, & Miller, 2002; Pressley & Hilden, 2006). Some experts on adolescents argue that the single most important advance in adolescent cognitive development is the ability to think about one's own thought (Kuhn & Franklin, 2006). Metacognition is increasingly recognized as a very important cognitive skill not only in adolescence but also in emerging adulthood, as reflected in recent research on the use of metacognition by college students (Maki & others, 2005; Nietfeld, Cao, & Osborne, 2005; Ross & others, 2006).

Metacognitive skills have been taught to students to help them solve math problems (Cardelle-Elawar, 1992). In each of 30 daily lessons involving verbal math problems, a teacher guided low-achieving students in learning to recognize when they did not know the meaning of a word, did not have all the necessary information to solve a problem, did not know how to subdivide a problem into specific steps, or did not know how to carry out a computation. After completing these lessons, the students who had received the metacognitive training had better math achievement and better attitudes toward math.

**metacognition** Cognition about cognition, or "knowing about knowing."

**Strategies and Self-Regulation** In the view of Michael Pressley (2003; Pressley & Harris, 2006; Pressley & Hilden, 2006), the key to education is helping students to learn a rich repertoire of strategies for solving problems. Good thinkers routinely use strategies and effective planning to solve problems. They also know when and where to use strategies (that is, they have metacognitive knowledge about strategies). An understanding of when and where to use strategies often results from the learner's monitoring of the learning situation. But Pressley thinks this skill can be taught. When students are given instruction about strategies that are new to them, they can often apply those strategies on their own.

Learning how to use strategies effectively usually takes time and requires guidance and support from the teacher (Block & Pressley, 2007; Gambrell, Morrow, & Pressley, 2007). With practice, students will execute strategies faster and more competently. "Practice" means using the effective strategy over and over again until it becomes automatic. To execute strategies effectively, learners must hold them in long-term memory, and extensive practice makes that retention possible.

Pressley and his colleagues (Pressley & Harris, 2006; Pressley & Hilden, 2006; Pressley & others, 2001, 2003, 2004) have spent considerable time in recent years observing strategy instruction by teachers and strategy use by students in elementary and secondary school classrooms. They conclude that strategy instruction is far less complete and intense than what students need in order to learn how to use strategies effectively. They argue that education needs to be restructured so that students are provided with more opportunities to become competent strategic learners.

**Self-Regulatory Learning** **Self-regulatory learning** is the self-generation and self-monitoring of one's thoughts, feelings, and behaviors in order to reach a goal. Those goals might be academic (improving reading comprehension, becoming a better organized writer, learning how to multiply, asking relevant questions) or they might be socioemotional (controlling one's anger, getting along better with peers). What are some of the characteristics of self-regulated learners? Self-regulatory learners (Winne, 1995, 1997; Winne & Perry, 2000) do the following:

- Set goals for extending their knowledge and sustaining their motivation.
- Are aware of their emotional makeup and follow strategies for managing their emotions.
- Periodically monitor their progress toward a goal.
- Fine-tune or revise their strategies based on the progress they have made.
- Evaluate obstacles that arise and make the necessary adaptations.

Researchers have found that most high-achieving students are self-regulatory learners (Schunk & Zimmerman, 2006). For example, compared with low-achieving students, high-achieving students set more specific learning goals, use more learning strategies, self-monitor their learning more, and evaluate their progress toward a goal more systematically (Schunk & Ertmer, 2000).

**Domain-Specific Thinking Skills** Our coverage of metacognition mainly emphasized the importance of some general cognitive skills, such as strategies and self-regulation, in becoming a better thinker. Indeed, researchers have found that metacognitive skills can be taught. For example, adolescents have been effectively taught to become aware of their thinking processes and engage in self-regulation of their learning (Pressley & Hilden, 2006; Schunk & Zimmerman, 2006).

However, it also is very important to teach domain-specific thinking skills to adolescents (Graham, 2006). In this regard, a recent review concluded that one of educational psychology's greatest accomplishments is the teaching of domain-specific thinking skills (Mayer & Wittrock, 2006). Thus, a rich tradition in quality education programs has been the teaching of thinking skills within specific subjects, such as writing, mathematics, science, and history. Researchers have found that "it is possible to analyze and teach the underlying cognitive processes required in tasks such as comprehending a passage, writing an essay, solving an arithmetic word problem, answering a scientific question, or explaining an historical event . . ." (Mayer & Wittrock, 2006).

**self-regulatory learning** The self-generation and self-monitoring of one's thoughts, feelings, and behaviors in order to reach a goal.

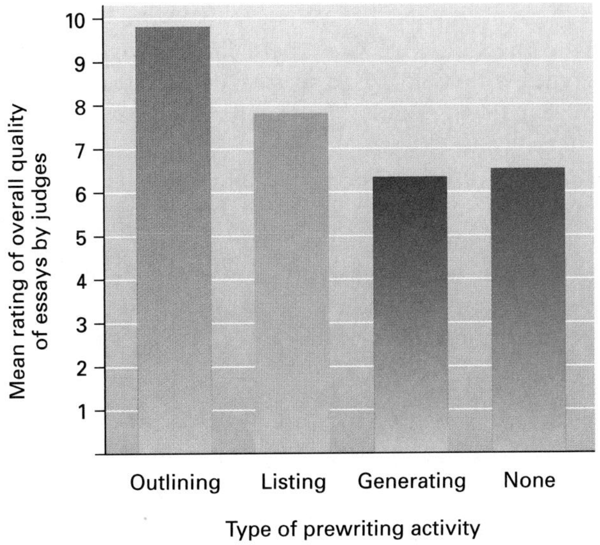


**FIGURE 3.13 The Relation of Prewriting Activities to Essay Quality** One study randomly assigned college students to one of four prewriting activity groups: (1) an outlining group produced an outline containing relevant ideas within a hierarchical structure; (2) a listing group generated a list of relevant ideas; (3) a generating group wrote down as many ideas as possible without evaluating or organizing them; and (4) a control group had no prewriting activity. Judges rated the quality of each essay on a 10-point scale from 1 (lowest quality) to 10 (highest quality) (Kellogg, 1994). Organization was the prewriting activity that was most positively related to judges' ratings. When students create an outline, they often use listing and generating strategies as part of the outlining process. Thus, an excellent teaching strategy is to require students to create an outline as a required prewriting activity.

Planning is an important general cognitive skill for adolescents and emerging adults to use, but they also benefit when they apply this and other cognitive skills to specific subjects. For example, one study examined how prewriting activities can affect the quality of college students' writing (Kellogg, 1994). As indicated in Figure 3.13 the planning activity of outlining was the prewriting activity that helped writers the most.

## REVIEW AND REFLECT ◆ LEARNING GOAL 3

### 3 Characterize the information-processing view of adolescence.

***Review***
- What characterizes the development of cognitive resources?
- What are the main mechanisms of change of the information-processing view?
- What developmental changes characterize attention and memory in adolescence?
- What is executive functioning? How can adolescent decision making be described? What characterizes reasoning and critical thinking in adolescence? What distinguishes experts from novices and how do individuals become experts? What is metacognition and how does it change developmentally? What is self-regulatory learning? How important is domain-specific thinking?

***Reflect***
- How might metacognition be involved in the improved study skills of adolescents and emerging adults?

## 4 THE PSYCHOMETRIC/INTELLIGENCE VIEW

Intelligence Tests | Multiple Intelligences | Heredity and Environment

The two views of adolescent cognition that we have discussed so far—cognitive developmental and information processing—do not emphasize individual variations in intelligence. The **psychometric/intelligence view** does emphasize the importance of individual differences in intelligence; many advocates of this view favor the use of intelligence tests. An increasing issue in the field of intelligence involves pinning down what the components of intelligence really are.

**psychometric/intelligence view** A view that emphasizes the importance of individual differences in intelligence; many advocates of this view also argue that intelligence should be assessed with intelligence tests.

Just what is meant by the concept of "intelligence"? Some experts describe intelligence as problem-solving skills. Others describe it as the ability to adapt to and learn from life's everyday experiences. Combining these ideas, we can arrive at a definition of **intelligence** as problem-solving skills and the ability to learn from and adapt to life's everyday experiences.

Interest in intelligence has often focused on individual differences and assessment. *Individual differences* are the stable, consistent ways in which people are different from each other. We can talk about individual differences in personality or any other domain, but it is in the domain of intelligence that the most attention has been directed at individual differences. For example, an intelligence test purports to inform us about whether an adolescent can reason better than others who have taken the test (Gregory, 2007).

## Intelligence Tests

Robert J. Sternberg recalls being terrified of taking IQ tests as a child. He literally froze, he says, when the time came to take such tests. Even as an adult, Sternberg is stung by humiliation when he recalls in the sixth grade being asked to take an IQ test with fifth-graders. Sternberg eventually overcame his anxieties about IQ tests. Not only did he begin to perform better on them, but at age 13 he devised his own IQ test and began using it to assess his classmates—that is, until the school principal found out and scolded him. Sternberg became so fascinated by intelligence that he made its study one of his lifelong pursuits. Later in this chapter, we discuss his theory of intelligence. To begin, though, let's step back in time to examine the first valid intelligence test.

**The Binet Tests** In 1904, the French Ministry of Education asked psychologist Alfred Binet to devise a method of identifying children who were unable to learn in school. School officials wanted to reduce crowding by placing students who did not benefit from regular classroom teaching in special schools. Binet and his student Theophile Simon developed an intelligence test to meet this request. The test is called the 1905 Scale. It consisted of 30 questions on topics ranging from the ability to touch one's ear to the ability to draw designs from memory and define abstract concepts.

Binet developed the concept of **mental age (MA),** an individual's level of mental development relative to others. Not much later, in 1912, William Stern created the concept of **intelligence quotient (IQ),** a person's mental age divided by chronological age (CA), multiplied by 100. That is: $IQ = MA/CA \times 100$. If mental age is the same as chronological age, then the person's IQ is 100. If mental age is above chronological age, then IQ is more than 100. If mental age is below chronological age, then IQ is less than 100.

The Binet test has been revised many times to incorporate advances in the understanding of intelligence and intelligence tests. These revisions are called the *Stanford-Binet tests* (Stanford University is where the revisions have been done). By administering the test to large numbers of people of different ages from different backgrounds, researchers have found that scores on the Stanford-Binet approximate a normal distribution (see Figure 3.14). A **normal distribution** is symmetrical, with a majority of the scores falling in the middle of the possible range of scores, and few scores appearing toward the extremes of the range.

**The Wechsler Scales** Another set of widely used tests is called the *Wechsler scales,* developed by David Wechsler. They include the Wechsler Preschool and Primary Scale of Intelligence—Third Edition (WPPSI-III) to test children 2 years 6 months to 7 years 3 months of age; the Wechsler Intelligence Scale for Children—Fourth Edition (WISC-IV) for children and adolescents 6 to 16 years of age; and the Wechsler Adult Intelligence Scale—Third Edition (WAIS-III) for adolescents and adults 16 to 89 years of age.

**intelligence** The ability to solve problems and to adapt to and learn from everyday experiences; not everyone agrees on what constitutes intelligence.

**mental age (MA)** An individual's level of mental development relative to others; a concept developed by Binet.

**intelligent quotient (IQ)** A person's tested mental age divided by chronological age, multiplied by 100.

**normal distribution** A symmetrical distribution of values or scores, with a majority of scores falling in the middle of the possible range of scores and few scores appearing toward the extremes of the range.

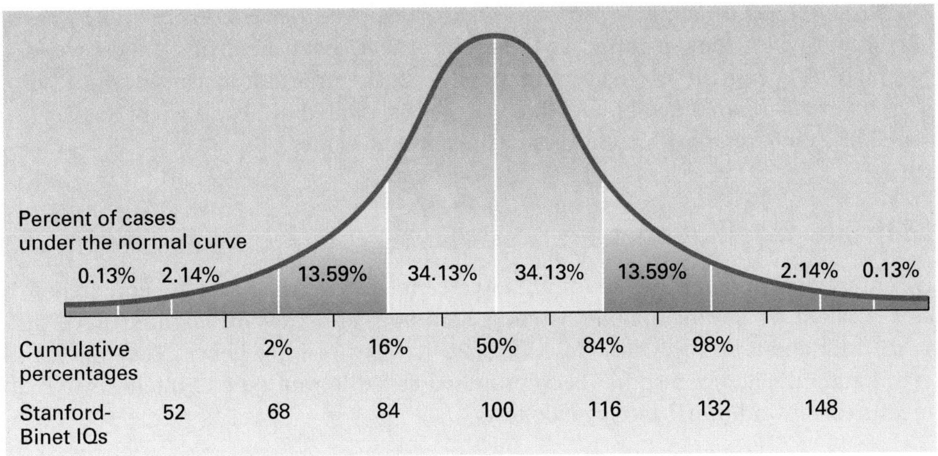


**FIGURE 3.14 The Normal Curve and Stanford-Binet IQ Scores** The distribution of IQ scores approximates a normal curve. Most of the population falls in the middle range of scores, between 84 and 116. Notice that extremely high and extremely low scores are rare. Only about 1 in 50 individuals has an IQ of more than 132 or less than 68.

Not only do the Wechsler scales provide an overall IQ, but they also yield a number of additional composite scores (for example, the Verbal Comprehension Index, the Working Memory Index, and the Processing Speed Index), allowing the examiner to quickly see patterns of strengths and weaknesses in different areas of the student's intelligence. Three of the Wechsler subscales are shown in Figure 3.15.

**Using Intelligence Tests** Psychological tests are tools. Like all tools, their effectiveness depends on the knowledge, skill, and integrity of the user. A hammer can be used to build a beautiful kitchen cabinet, or it can be used as a weapon of assault. Like a hammer, psychological tests can be used for positive purposes, or they can be badly abused. Here are some cautions about IQ that can help you avoid the pitfalls of using information about an adolescent's intelligence in negative ways:

- *Avoid stereotyping and expectations.* A special concern is that the scores on an IQ test easily can lead to stereotypes and expectations about adolescents. Sweeping generalizations are too often made on the basis of an IQ score. An IQ test should always be considered a measure of current performance. It is not a measure of fixed potential. Maturational changes and enriched environmental experiences can advance an adolescent's intelligence.

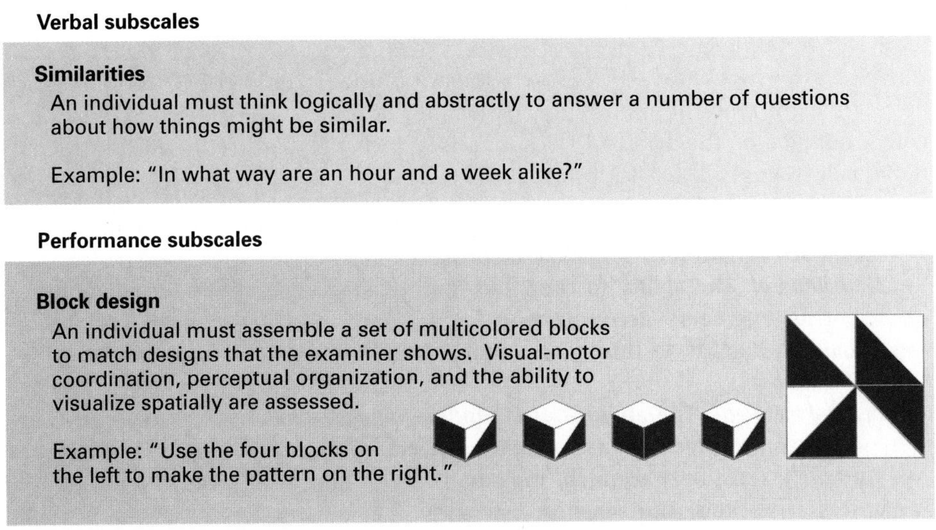

Verbal subscales
Similarities
An individual must think logically and abstractly to answer a number of questions about how things might be similar.
Example: "In what way are an hour and a week alike?"
Performance subscales
Block design
An individual must assemble a set of multicolored blocks to match designs that the examiner shows. Visual-motor coordination, perceptual organization, and the ability to visualize spatially are assessed.
Example: "Use the four blocks on the left to make the pattern on the right."


**FIGURE 3.15 Sample Subscales of the Wechsler Adult Intelligence Scale—Third Edition** Simulated items similar to those in the Wechsler Adult Intelligence Scale-Third Edition. Copyright © 1949, 1955, 1974 by The Psychological Corporation. Reproduced by permission. All rights reserved. "Wechsler Adult Intelligence Scale" and "WAIS-R" are trademarks of Harcourt Assessment, Inc., formerly known as The Psychological Corporation, registered in the United States of America and/or other jurisdictions.

*"You're wise, but you lack tree smarts."*


- *Know that IQ is not a sole indicator of competence.* Another concern about IQ tests occurs when they are used as the main or sole assessment of competence. A high IQ is not the ultimate human value. It is important to consider not only students' competence in such areas as verbal skills but also their practical skills, their relationship skills, and their moral values.

## Multiple Intelligences

Is it more appropriate to think of an adolescent's intelligence as a general ability or as a number of specific abilities? Robert Sternberg and Howard Gardner have proposed influential theories that describe specific types of intelligence. The concept of emotional intelligence also has been proposed as a different type of intelligence than measured by traditional intelligence tests.

**Sternberg's Triarchic Theory** Robert J. Sternberg (1986, 2003, 2006, 2007, 2008) developed the **triarchic theory of intelligence,** which states that intelligence comes in three forms: (1) *analytical intelligence,* which refers to the ability to analyze, judge, evaluate, compare, and contrast; (2) *creative intelligence,* which consists of the ability to create, design, invent, originate, and imagine; and (3) *practical intelligence,* which involves the ability to use, apply, implement, and put ideas into practice.

Sternberg (2002) says that children with different triarchic patterns "look different" in school. Students with high analytic ability tend to be favored in conventional schooling. They often do well under direct instruction, in which the teacher lectures and gives students objective tests. They often are considered to be "smart" students who get good grades, show up in high-level tracks, do well on traditional tests of intelligence and the SAT, and later get admitted to competitive colleges.

In contrast, children who are high in creative intelligence often are not on the top rung of their class. Many teachers have expectations about how assignments should be done, and creatively intelligent students may not conform to those expectations. Instead of giving conformist answers, they give unique answers, for which they might get reprimanded or marked down. No teacher wants to discourage creativity, but Sternberg notes that too often a teacher's desire to improve students' knowledge depresses creative thinking.

Like children high in creative intelligence, children who are practically intelligent often do not relate well to the demands of school. However, many of these children do well outside of the classroom's walls. They may have excellent social skills and good common sense. As adults, some become successful managers, entrepreneurs, or politicians, yet they have undistinguished school records.

*Which of Gardner's eight intelligences are adolescent girls using in this situation?*

**triarchic theory of intelligence** Sternberg's view that intelligence comes in three main forms: analytical, creative, and practical.

**Gardner's Eight Frames of Mind** Howard Gardner (1983, 1993, 2002) suggests there are eight types of intelligence, or "frames of mind." These are described here, with examples of the types of vocations in which they are reflected as strengths (Campbell, Campbell, & Dickinson, 2004):

- *Verbal.* The ability to think in words and use language to express meaning (occupations: authors, journalists, speakers)
- *Mathematical.* The ability to carry out mathematical operations (occupations: scientists, engineers, accountants)
- *Spatial.* The ability to think three-dimensionally (occupations: architects, artists, sailors)
- *Bodily-kinesthetic.* The ability to manipulate objects and be physically adept (occupations: surgeons, craftspeople, dancers, athletes)
- *Musical.* A sensitivity to pitch, melody, rhythm, and tone (occupations: composers, musicians, and sensitive listeners)

- *Interpersonal.* The ability to understand and effectively interact with others (occupations: successful teachers, mental health professionals)
- *Intrapersonal.* The ability to understand oneself. (occupations: theologians, psychologists)
- *Naturalist:* The ability to observe patterns in nature and understand natural and human-made systems (occupations: farmers, botanists, ecologists, landscapers)

According to Gardner, everyone has all of these intelligences but to varying degrees. As a result, we prefer to learn and process information in different ways. People learn best when they can apply their strong intelligences to the task.

Both Gardner's and Sternberg's theories include one or more categories related to social intelligence. In Gardner's theory, the categories are interpersonal intelligence and intrapersonal intelligence; in Sternberg's theory, practical intelligence. Another theory that emphasizes interpersonal, intrapersonal, and practical aspects of intelligence is called **emotional intelligence,** which has been popularized by Daniel Goleman (1995) in his book *Emotional Intelligence.* The concept of emotional intelligence was initially developed by Peter Salovey and John Mayer (1990), who define it as the ability to perceive and express emotion accurately and adaptively (such as taking the perspective of others), to understand emotion and emotional knowledge (such as understanding the roles that emotions play in friendship and marriage), to use feelings to facilitate thought (such as being in a positive mood, which is linked to creative thinking), and to manage emotions in oneself and others (such as being able to control one's anger).

| Sternberg | Gardner | Mayer/ Salovey/Goleman |
|---|---|---|
| Analytical | Verbal<br>Mathematical | |
| Creative | Spatial<br>Movement<br>Musical | |
| Practical | Interpersonal<br>Intrapersonal | Emotional |
| | Naturalistic | |

**FIGURE 3.16 Comparison of Sternberg's, Gardner's, and Mayer/Salovey/Goleman's Views**

**Do People Have One Intelligence or Many Intelligences?** Figure 3.16 provides a comparison of Sternberg's, Gardner's, and Mayer/Salovey/Goleman's views. Notice that Gardner includes a number of types of intelligence that are not addressed by the other views and that Sternberg is unique in emphasizing creative intelligence. These theories of multiple intelligence have much to offer (Sternberg, 2007, 2008). They have stimulated us to think more broadly about what makes up people's intelligence and competence. And they have motivated educators to develop programs that instruct students in different domains.

Theories of multiple intelligences also have many critics. Many argue that the research base to support these theories has not yet developed. In particular, some critics say that Gardner's classification seems arbitrary. For example, if musical skills represent a type of intelligence, why don't we also refer to chess intelligence, prizefighter intelligence, and so on?

A number of psychologists still support Spearman's concept of *g* (general intelligence). For example, one expert on intelligence, Nathan Brody (2000, 2007), argues that people who excel at one type of intellectual task are likely to excel in other intellectual tasks. Thus, individuals who do well at memorizing lists of digits are also likely to be good at solving verbal problems and spatial layout problems. This general intelligence includes abstract reasoning or thinking, the capacity to acquire knowledge, and problem-solving ability (Brody, 2000, 2007; Horn, 2007; Carroll, 1993).

Some experts who argue for the existence of general intelligence believe that individuals also have specific intellectual abilities (Brody, 2000, 2007). In one study, John Carroll (1993) conducted an extensive examination of intellectual abilities and concluded that all intellectual abilities are related to one another—which supports the concept of general intelligence—but that there are many specialized abilities as well. Some of these specialized abilities, such as spatial abilities and mechanical abilities, are not adequately reflected in the curriculum of most schools.

**emotional intelligence** The ability to perceive and express emotion accurately and adaptively, to understand emotion and emotional knowledge, to use feelings to facilitate thought, and to manage emotions in oneself and others.

## Heredity and Environment

An ongoing issue involving intelligence is the extent to which it is due to heredity or to environment. In Chapter 2, we indicated how difficult it is to tease apart these influences, but that has not kept psychologists from trying to untangle them.

**Heredity** How strong is the effect of heredity on intelligence? A committee of respected researchers convened by the American Psychological Association concluded that by late adolescence, research studies reveal a strong influence of heredity on intelligence (Neisser & others, 1996). However, most research on heredity and environment does not include environments that differ radically. Thus, it is not surprising that many studies of heredity, environment, and intelligence show environment to be a fairly weak influence on intelligence (Fraser, 1995).

One strategy for examining the role of heredity in intelligence is to compare the IQs of identical and fraternal twins, which we initially discussed in Chapter 2. Recall that identical twins have exactly the same genetic makeup but fraternal twins do not. If intelligence is genetically determined, say some investigators, identical twins' IQs should be more similar than the intelligence of fraternal twins. Researchers have found that the IQs of identical twins are more similar than those of fraternal twins, but in some studies, the difference is not very large (Grigorenko, 2000).

**Environment** One way to study the environment's influence on intelligence is to compare adolescents who have experienced different amounts of schooling. Schooling does influence intelligence, with the largest effects occurring when adolescents have been deprived of formal education for an extended period, which is linked to lower intelligence (Ceci & Gilstrap, 2000).

Another possible effect of education can be seen in rapidly increasing IQ test scores around the world (Daley & others, 2003; Flynn, 2006). IQ scores have been increasing so fast that a high percentage of people regarded as having average intelligence at the turn of the century would be considered below average in intelligence today (Howard, 2001) (see Figure 3.17). If a representative sample of people today took the Stanford-Binet test used in 1932, about one-fourth would be defined as having very superior intelligence, a label usually accorded to fewer than 3 percent of the population (Horton, 2001). Because the increase has taken place in a

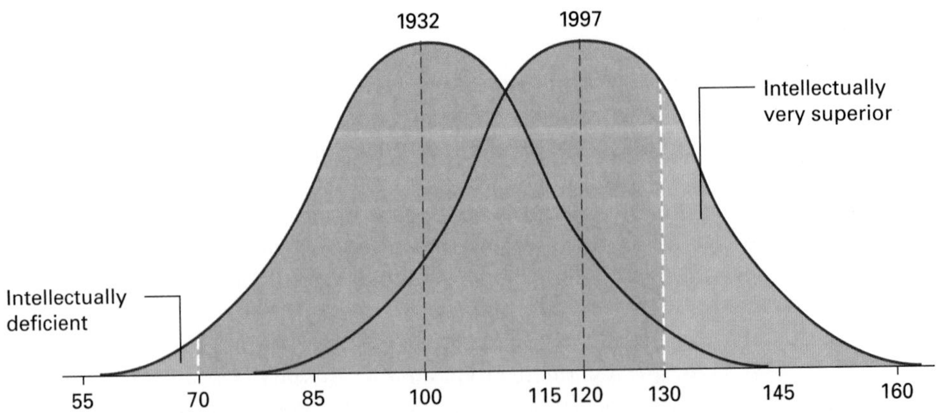


**FIGURE 3.17 The Increase in IQ Scores from 1932 to 1997** As measured by the Stanford-Binet intelligence test, American children seem to be getting smarter. Scores of a group tested in 1932 fell along a bell-shaped curve with half below 100 and half above. Studies show that if children took that same test today, half would score above 120 on the 1932 scale. Very few of them would score in the "intellectually deficient" end, on the left side, and about one-fourth would rank in the "very superior" range.

relatively short time, it can't be due to heredity, but rather may be due to increasing levels of education attained by a much greater percentage of the world's population or to other environmental factors such as the explosion of information to which people are exposed. The worldwide increase in intelligence test scores that has occurred over a short time frame has been called the *Flynn effect,* after the researcher who discovered it—James Flynn.

*How might stereotype threat affect African American children's scores on tests?*

Are there ethnic variations in intelligence? In the United States, adolescents from African American and Latino families score below children from White families on standardized intelligence tests. On the average, African American adolescents score 10 to 15 points lower on standardized intelligence tests than non-Latino White adolescents do (Brody, 2000; Lynn, 1996). These are *average scores,* however. About 15 to 25 percent of African American adolescents score higher than half of non-Latino White adolescents do, and many non-Latino Whites score lower than most African Americans. The reason is that the distribution of scores for African Americans and non-Latino Whites overlap.

As African Americans have gained social, economic, and educational opportunities, the gap between African Americans and Whites on standardized intelligence tests has begun to narrow (Ogbu & Stern, 2001; Onwuegbuzie & Daley, 2001). This gap especially narrows in college, where African American and White students often experience more similar environments than in the elementary and high school years (Myerson & others, 1998). Also, when children from disadvantaged African American families are adopted into more-advantaged middle-socioeconomic-status families, their scores on intelligence tests more closely resemble national averages for middle-socioeconomic-status children than for lower-socioeconomic-status children (Scarr & Weinberg, 1983).

One potential influence on intelligence test performance is *stereotype threat,* the anxiety that one's behavior might confirm a negative stereotype about one's group. For example, when African Americans take an intelligence test, they may experience anxiety about confirming the old stereotype that Blacks are "intellectually inferior." In one study, the verbal part of the GRE was given individually to African American and White students at Stanford University (Steele & Aronson, 1995). Half the students of each ethnic group were told that the researchers were interested in assessing their intellectual ability. The other half were told that the researchers were trying to develop a test and that it might not be reliable and valid (therefore, it would not mean anything in relation to their intellectual ability). The White students did equally well on the test in both conditions. However, the African American students did more poorly when they thought the test was assessing their intellectual ability; when they thought the test was just in the development stage and might not be reliable or valid, they performed as well as the White students.

Other studies have confirmed the existence of stereotype threat. African American students do more poorly on standardized tests if they believe they are being evaluated. If they believe the test doesn't count, they perform as well as White students (Aronson, 2002; Aronson, Fried, & Good, 2002; Aronson & others, 1999). However, some critics believe the extent to which stereotype threat explains the testing gap has been exaggerated (Ackerman & Lohman, 2006; Sackett, Hardison, & Cullen, 2004).

**Heredity and Environment Interaction** Today, most researchers agree that genetics and environment interact to influence intelligence (Gottlieb, Wahlsten, & Lickliter, 2006; Ramey, Ramey, & Lanzi, 2006; Sternberg & Grigorenko, 2004). For most people, this means that modifications in environment can change their IQ scores considerably. Although genetic endowment may always influence a person's intellectual ability, the environmental influences and opportunities we provide children and adults do make a difference (Ramey, Ramey, & Lanzi, 2006; Sternberg, 2006).

**REVIEW AND REFLECT ◆ LEARNING GOAL 4**

**4 Summarize the psychometric/intelligence view of adolescence.**

***Review***
- What is intelligence? What are the main individual tests of intelligence? What are some strategies in interpreting intelligence test scores?
- What theories of multiple intelligences have been developed? Do people have one intelligence or many intelligences?
- What roles do heredity and environment play in intelligence?

***Reflect***
- Apply Gardner's, Sternberg's, and Salovey, Mayer, and Goleman's categories of intelligence to yourself or someone you know well. Write a description of yourself or the person you know based on each of these views.

## 5 SOCIAL COGNITION

Adolescent Egocentrism | Perspective Taking | Social Cognition in the Remainder of the Text

**social cognition** The way individuals conceptualize and reason about their social worlds—the people they watch and interact with, their relationships with those people, the groups they participate in, and the way they reason about themselves and others.

**adolescent egocentrism** The heightened self-consciousness of adolescents, which is reflected in their belief that others are as interested in them as they themselves are, and in their sense of personal uniqueness and invulnerability.

**Social cognition** refers to the way individuals conceptualize and reason about their social worlds—the people they watch and interact with, their relationships with those people, the groups they participate in, and the way they reason about themselves and others. Our discussion will focus on egocentrism, perspective taking, and our coverage of social cognition in the remainder of the text.

### Adolescent Egocentrism

**Adolescent egocentrism** is the heightened self-consciousness of adolescents, which is reflected in their belief that others are as interested in them as they are themselves, and in their sense of personal uniqueness and invulnerability. David Elkind (1976) argues that adolescent egocentrism can be dissected into two types of social thinking—imaginary audience and personal fable.

The *imaginary audience* refers to the aspect of adolescent egocentrism that involves attention-getting behavior—the attempt to be noticed, visible, and "onstage." An adolescent boy might think that others are as aware of a few hairs that are out of place as he is. An adolescent girl walks into her classroom and thinks that all eyes are riveted on her complexion. Adolescents especially sense that they are onstage in early adolescence, believing they are the main actors and all others are the audience. You may recall the story of my daughter, Tracy, from *Images of Adolescent Development* at the beginning of the chapter. Tracy was exhibiting adolescent egocentrism when she perceived that every person in the restaurant was looking at her single, out of place hair.

*What is adolescent egocentrism?*

According to Elkind, the personal fable is the part of adolescent egocentrism that involves an adolescent's sense of personal uniqueness and invulnerability. Adolescents' sense of personal uniqueness makes them feel that no one can understand how they really feel. For example, an adolescent girl thinks that her mother cannot possibly sense the hurt she feels because her boyfriend has broken up with her. As part of their effort to retain a sense of personal uniqueness, adolescents might craft stories about themselves that are filled with fantasy, immersing themselves in a world that is far removed from reality. Personal fables frequently show up in adolescent diaries. To read about links between personal fables and adolescent adjustment, see the *Health and Well-Being* interlude.

## *Health and Well-Being*

### THE PERSONAL FABLE AND ADOLESCENT ADJUSTMENT

Some developmentalists conclude that the sense of uniqueness and invincibility that egocentrism generates is responsible for some of the seemingly reckless behavior of adolescents, including drag racing, drug use, suicide, and failure to use contraceptives during intercourse (Dolcini & others, 1989). For example, one study found that eleventh- and twelfth-grade females who were high in adolescent egocentrism were more likely to say they would not get pregnant from engaging in sex without contraception than were their counterparts who were low in adolescent egocentrism (Arnett, 1990).

A recent study of sixth- through twelfth-graders examined whether aspects of the personal fable were linked to various aspects of adolescent adjustment (Aalsma, Lapsley, & Flannery, 2006). A sense of invulnerability was linked to engaging in risky behaviors, such as smoking cigarettes, drinking alcohol, and delinquency, while a sense of personal uniqueness was related to depression and suicidal thoughts. A subsequent study confirmed the findings of the first with regards to the correlation between personal uniqueness, depression, and suicidal thoughts. (Goossens & others, 2002).

These findings indicate that personal uniqueness fables should be treated as a risk factor for psychological problems, especially depression and suicidal tendencies in girls (Aalsma, Lapsley, & Flannery, 2006). Treating invulnerability as a risk factor for adjustment problems is less certain because in the earlier study described (Aalsma, Lapsley, & Flannery, 2006), a sense of invulnerability was not only associated with risky behavior but also with some positive aspects of adjustment, such as coping and self-worth.

## Perspective Taking

Researchers have found that changes in *perspective taking,* the ability to assume another person's perspective and understand his or her thoughts and feelings, are likely involved in the development of adolescent egocentrism (Lapsley & Murphy, 1985). The link between perspective taking and adolescent egocentrism likely occurs because advances in perspective taking cause young adolescents to be acutely concerned about what others think.

Perspective taking can increase adolescents' self-understanding, and it also can improve their peer group status and the quality of their friendships (Selman & Adalbjarnardottir, 2000; Selman & Schultz, 1999). For example, in one investigation, the most popular children in the third and eighth grades had competent perspective-taking skills (Kurdek & Krile, 1982). Adolescents who are competent at perspective taking are better at understanding the needs of their companions so that they likely can communicate more effectively with them. Further, in one study, competence in social perspective coordination was an important influence on adolescent friendship formation following residential relocation (Vernberg & others, 1994).

*What characterizes perspective taking in adolescence?*

The relation between the self and another individual is complex. Most major developmental theorists believe that development changes in self-other relationships are characterized by movement from egocentrism to perspectivism, but the considerable overlap in the age range at which various levels of perspective taking emerge make generalizations about clear-cut stages difficult.

## Social Cognition in the Remainder of the Text

Interest in social cognition has blossomed, and the approach has infiltrated many aspects of the study of adolescent development. In the overview of the self and identity in Chapter 4, social cognition's role in understanding the self and identity is explored. In the evaluation of moral development in Chapter 7, considerable time is devoted to discussing Kohlberg's theory, which is a prominent aspect of the study of social cognition in adolescence. Further, in the discussion of families in Chapter 8, the emerging cognitive abilities of the adolescent are evaluated in concert with parent-adolescent conflict and parenting strategies. Also, in the description of peer relations in Chapter 9, the importance of social knowledge and social information processing in peer relations is highlighted.

**REVIEW AND REFLECT ◆ LEARNING GOAL 5**

**5 Explain how social cognition is involved in adolescent development.**

***Review***

- What characterizes adolescent egocentrism?
- How does perspective taking change during adolescence?
- How is social cognition related to other topics discussed in this text?

***Reflect***

- Does adolescent egocentrism ever disappear? Is it maladaptive in your late teens or early twenties to act as if all eyes are riveted on you, to have a strong desire to be noticed, visible, "onstage," and to feel that others are as interested in you as you are? How can you draw the line between self-interest that is adaptive, protective, and appropriate and self-interest that is maladaptive, selfish, and inappropriate? One good strategy is to consider the extent to which egocentrism overwhelms and dominates the person's life.

In this chapter, we have examined cognitive development in adolescence. In Chapter 4, we explore the development of the self and identity in adolescence. You will see that changes in cognitive development described in this chapter serve as foundations for some of the changes that take place in the self and identity during adolescence.

# Reach Your Learning Goals

## 1 The Brain *Describe the developmental changes in the brain during adolescence.*

**Neurons**

Neurons are the basic units of the nervous system and are made up of a cell body, dendrites, and an axon. Myelination is the process by which the axon portion of the neuron becomes covered and insulated with a layer of fat cells, which increases the speed and efficiency of information processing in the nervous system. Myelination continues to increase during adolescence. Synaptogenesis in the prefrontal cortex, where reasoning and self-regulation occur, also continues through adolescence.

**Brain Structure, Cognition, and Emotion**

The corpus callosum, a large bundle of axon fibers that connects the brain's left and right hemispheres, thickens in adolescence, and this improves the adolescent's ability to process information. The prefrontal cortex, the highest level of the frontal lobes that is involved in reasoning, decision making, and self-control, matures much later (continuing to develop in emerging adulthood) than the amygdala, the part of the limbic system that is the seat of emotions such as anger. The later development of the prefrontal cortex combined with the earlier maturity of the amygdala may explain the difficulty adolescents have in putting the brakes on their emotional intensity.

**Experience and Plasticity**

Experience plays an important role in development of the brain in childhood and adolescence. While early experiences are very important in the development of the brain, the brain retains considerable plasticity in adolescence. New brain cells may be generated during adolescence. The earlier brain injury occurs, the more successful recovery is likely to be.

## 2 The Cognitive Developmental View *Discuss the cognitive developmental view of adolescence.*

**Piaget's Theory**

Piaget's widely acclaimed theory stresses the concepts of adaptation, schemas, assimilation, accommodation, and equilibration. Piaget said that individuals develop through four cognitive stages: sensorimotor, preoperational, concrete operational, and formal operational. Formal operational thought, which Piaget emphasized appears from 11 to 15 years of age, is characterized by abstract, idealistic, and hypothetical-deductive thinking. Some experts argue that formal operational thought has two phases: early and late. Individual variation in adolescent cognition is extensive. Many young adolescents are still consolidating their concrete operational thought or are early formal operational thinkers rather than full-fledged ones. Although Piaget was not an educator, his ideas have been applied to education. In terms of Piaget's contributions, we owe to him the entire field of cognitive development and a masterful list of concepts. He also was a genius at observing children. Criticisms of Piaget's theory focus on estimates of competence, stages, training to reason at higher stages, and the role of culture and education. Neo-Piagetians have proposed some substantial changes in Piaget's theory. Some experts argue that the idealism of Piaget's formal operational stage declines in young adults, being replaced by more realistic, pragmatic thinking. Perry said that adolescents often engage in dualistic, absolutist thinking, whereas young adults are more likely to think reflectively and relativistically. Postformal thought is reflective, relativistic, and contextual; provisional; realistic; and open to emotions and subjective.

Vygotsky's Theory

Vygotsky's view stimulated considerable interest in the idea that knowledge is situated and collaborative. One of his important concepts is the zone of proximal development, which involves guidance by more-skilled peers and adults. Vygotsky argued that learning the skills of the culture is a key aspect of development. Piaget's and Vygotsky's views are both constructivist, although Vygotsky's view is a stronger social constructivist view than Piaget's. In both views, teachers should be facilitators, not directors, of learning. Criticisms of Vygotsky's view focus on facilitators possibly being too helpful and adolescents expecting others to do things for them.

## 3 THE INFORMATION-PROCESSING VIEW *Characterize the information-processing view of adolescence.*

Cognitive Resources

Capacity and speed of processing speed, often referred to as cognitive resources, increase across childhood and adolescence. Changes in the brain serve as biological foundations for developmental changes in cognitive resources. In terms of capacity, the increase is reflected in older children and adolescents being able to hold in mind several dimensions of a topic simultaneously. A reaction-time task has often been used to assess speed of processing. Processing speed continues to improve in adolescence.

Mechanisms of Change

Siegler states that the information-processing view emphasizes thinking, change mechanisms (encoding, automaticity, strategy construction, and generalization), and self-modification.

Attention and Memory

Adolescents typically have better attentional skills than children do. They also have better short-term memory, working memory, and long-term memory than children do.

Executive Functioning

Higher-order cognitive processes such as making decisions, reasoning, thinking critically, thinking creatively, and metacognition are often called executive functioning. It is increasingly thought that executive functioning becomes increasingly strong during adolescence. Adolescence is a time of increased decision making. Older adolescents make better decisions than younger adolescents, who in turn are better at this than children are. Being able to make competent decisions, however, does not mean they actually will be made in everyday life, where breadth of experience comes into play. Reasoning is logical thinking that uses induction and deduction to reach a conclusion. Inductive reasoning involves reasoning from the specific to the general, whereas deductive reasoning consists of reasoning from the general to the specific. Adolescents improve in their ability to reason inductively and deductively, and this ability often continues to increase in early adulthood. Critical thinking involves thinking reflectively and productively and evaluating the evidence. Adolescence is an important transitional period in critical thinking because of such cognitive changes as increased speed, automaticity, and capacity of information processing; more breadth of content knowledge; increased ability to construct new combinations of knowledge; and a greater range and spontaneous use of strategies. Thinking creatively is the ability to think in novel and unusual ways and discover unique solutions to problems. Guilford distinguished between convergent and divergent thinking. A number of strategies, including brainstorming, not overcontrolling, encouraging internal control, and introducing adolescents to creative people, can be used to stimulate creative thinking. An expert is the opposite of a novice (someone who is just beginning to learn a content area). Experts are better than novices at detecting features and meaningful patterns of information, accumulating more content knowledge and organizing it effectively, and retrieving important aspects of knowledge with little effort. Becoming an expert usually involves talent and deliberate practice and motivation. Metacognition is cognition about cognition, or knowing about knowing. In Pressley's view, the key to education is helping students learn a rich repertoire of strategies that results in solutions to problems. Self-regulatory learning is the self-generation and self-monitoring of one's thoughts, feelings, and behaviors in order to reach a goal. Most high-achieving students are self-regulatory learners. Adolescents' thinking skills benefit when they are taught general metacognitive skills and domain-specific thinking skills.

## 4 THE PSYCHOMETRIC/INTELLIGENCE VIEW *Summarize the psychometric/intelligence view of adolescence.*

### Intelligence Tests

Intelligence is the ability to solve problems and to adapt and learn from everyday experiences. A key aspect of intelligence focuses on its individual variations. Traditionally, intelligence has been measured by tests designed to compare people's performance on cognitive tasks. Alfred Binet developed the first intelligence test and created the concept of mental age. William Stern developed the concept of IQ for use with the Binet test. Revisions of the Binet test are called the Stanford-Binet. The test scores on the Stanford-Binet approximate a normal distribution. The Wechsler scales, created by David Wechsler, are the other main intelligence assessment tool. These tests provide an overall IQ and other composite scores, including the Working Memory Index and the Information Processing Speed Index. The single number provided by many IQ tests can lead to false expectations, and IQ test scores should be only one type of information used to evaluate an adolescent.

### Multiple Intelligences

Sternberg's triarchic theory states that there are three main types of intelligence: analytical, creative, and practical. Gardner has proposed that there are eight types of intelligence: verbal, mathematical, spatial, bodily-kinesthetic, musical, interpersonal, intrapersonal, skills, and naturalist. Emotional intelligence is the ability to perceive and express emotion accurately and adaptively, to understand emotion and emotional knowledge, to use feelings to facilitate thought, and to manage emotions in oneself and others. The multiple intelligences approaches have broadened the definition of intelligence and motivated educators to develop programs that instruct students in different domains. Critics maintain that the multiple intelligence theories have classifications that seem arbitrary and factors that really aren't part of intelligence, such as musical skills and creativity.

### Heredity and Environment

Many studies show that by late adolescence intelligence is strongly influenced by heredity, but many of these studies do not reflect environments that are radically different. A well-documented environmental influence on intelligence is schooling. Also, probably because of increased education, intelligence test scores have risen considerably around the world in recent decades—called the Flynn effect—and this supports the role of environment in intelligence. As the educational level of African Americans has increased, the gap in intelligence between African Americans and non-Latino Whites has decreased. Stereotype threat has been proposed as one reason African American intelligence test scores are lower than non-Latino Whites. In sum, intelligence is influenced by heredity and environment.

## 5 Social Cognition *Explain how social cognition is involved in adolescent development.*

**Adolescent Egocentrism**

Social cognition refers to how people conceptualize and reason about their social world, including the relation of the self to others. Adolescent egocentrism is adolescents' heightened self-consciousness, mirrored in their belief that others are as interested in them as they are. According to Elkind, adolescent egocentrism consists of an imaginary audience and a personal fable. Researchers have recently found that the personal fable (a sense of invulnerability and personal uniqueness) is linked to adjustment problems in adolescence.

**Perspective Taking**

Perspective taking is the ability to take another person's perspective and understand his or her thoughts and feelings. Adolescents are better at perspective taking than children are, but there is considerable overlap in the ages at which the higher states of perspective taking occur.

**Social Cognition in the Remainder of the Text**

We study social cognition throughout this text, especially in chapters on the self and identity, moral development, peers, and families.

## KEY TERMS

neurons 93
myelination 93
synapses 93
corpus callosum 94
prefrontal cortex 94
amygdala 94
schema 97
assimilation 97
accommodation 97
equilibration 97
sensorimotor stage 98
preoperational stage 98
concrete operational stage 98
formal operational stage 98
hypothetical-deductive reasoning 99
neo-Piagetians 101
postformal thought 102
zone of proximal development (ZPD) 103
social constructivist approach 103
executive functioning 109
inductive reasoning 111
deductive reasoning 111
critical thinking 112
creativity 113
convergent thinking 113
divergent thinking 113
metacognition 115
self-regulatory learning 116
psychometric/intelligence view 117
intelligence 118
mental age (MA) 118
intelligence quotient (IQ) 118
normal distribution 118
triarchic theory of intelligence 120
emotional intelligence 121
social cognition 124
adolescent egocentrism 124

## KEY PEOPLE

Charles Nelson 98
Jean Piaget 96
Robbie Case 101
K. Warner Schaie 102
Lev Vygotsky 103
Robert Siegler 106
Alan Baddeley 109
J. P. Guilford 113
Michael Pressley 115
Alfred Binet 118
William Stern 118
David Wechsler 118
Robert Sternberg 120
Howard Gardner 120
Peter Salovey and John Mayer 121
Daniel Goleman 121
Nathan Brody 121
David Elkind 124

## RESOURCES FOR IMPROVING THE LIVES OF ADOLESCENTS

**Children's Thinking**
by Robert Siegler and Martha Alibali (2005, 4th ed.)
Upper Saddle River, NJ: Prentice Hall

In-depth coverage of information processing by leading experts.

**The Second Decade: What Develops?**
by Deanna Kuhn and Sam Franklin
in W. Damon and R. Lerner (Eds.), *Handbook of Child Psychology* (2006, 6th ed.)
New York: Wiley

An up-to-date, in-depth examination of the important changes in executive functioning and other cognitive changes in adolescence.

**Teaching and Learning Through Multiple Intelligences**
by Linda Campbell, Bruce Campbell, and Dee Dickinson (2004, 3rd ed.)
Boston: Allyn & Bacon

Provides applications of Gardner's eight intelligences to classrooms.

## E-LEARNING TOOLS

To help you master the material in this chapter, visit the Online Learning Center for *Adolescence,* twelfth edition **(www.mhhe.com/santrocka12),** where you will find these additional resources:

### Taking It to the Net

1. Your psychology instructor notes that in surfing the Web one can find a large number of sites with IQ tests, including tests for emotional IQ, sports IQ, trivia IQ, social IQ, musical IQ, as well as tests for IQs in a variety of other areas. As an extra-credit assignment, the instructor challenges the class to write a two-page paper indicating whose theoretical stance about intelligence could encompass such IQ concepts and how it would do so. What stance would you pick and why? How does that stance encompass the above IQ concepts?
2. Suppose your roommate complains that there is just too much material to learn in her classes and that she has a lot of trouble getting all the information into memory. You recognize this as a metamemory problem. What means would you suggest your roommate use to improve getting information into memory?
3. Adolescent cognitive abilities, egocentrism, and perspective taking are likely linked. As cognitive abilities increase and egocentrism decreases, perspective taking is assumed to become more accurate. It is possible to target adolescent perspective taking directly? Should we intervene? If so, how? If not, why not?

### Self-Assessment

The Online Learning Center includes the following self-assessments for further exploration:

- Exploring Changes in My Thinking from Adolescence to Adulthood
- My Study Skills
- Examining My Creative Thinking
- Evaluating Myself on Gardner's Eight Types of Intelligence
- How Emotionally Intelligent Am I?

### Health and Well-Being, Parenting, and Education

To practice your decision-making skills, complete the health and well-being, parenting, and education exercises on the Online Learning Center.

### Video Clips

The Online Learning Center includes the following videos for this chapter:

- Mnemonic Strategies in Memory (Discovery Channel Video)
- Intelligence Testing
- The Adolescent Brain (Discovery Channel Video)

# 4 The Self, Identity, Emotions, and Personality

*"Who are you?" said the Caterpillar. Alice replied, rather shyly, "I—I hardly know, Sir, just at present—at least I know who I was when I got up this morning, but I must have changed several times since then."*

—Lewis Carroll
English Writer, 19th Century

## CHAPTER OUTLINE

### The Self

Self-Understanding
Self-Esteem and Self-Concept

### Identity

Erikson's Ideas on Identity
The Four Statuses of Identity
Developmental Changes in Identity
Identity and Social Contexts
Identity and Intimacy

### Emotional Development

The Emotions of Adolescence
Hormones, Experience, and Emotions
Emotional Competence

### Personality Development

Personality
Temperament

## LEARNING GOALS

1. Describe the development of the self in adolescence.
2. Explain the many facets of identity development.
3. Discuss the emotional development of adolescents.
4. Characterize the personality development of adolescents.

# Images of Adolescent Development

## A 15-Year-Old Girl's Self-Description

How do adolescents describe themselves? How would you have described yourself when you were 15 years old? What features would you have emphasized? The following is a self-portrait of one 15-year-old girl:

> "What am I like as a person? Complicated! I'm sensitive, friendly, outgoing, popular, and tolerant, though I can also be shy, self-conscious, and even obnoxious. Obnoxious! I'd like to be friendly and tolerant all of the time. That's the kind of person I want to be, and I'm disappointed when I'm not. I'm responsible, even studious now and then, but on the other hand, I'm a goof-off, too, because if you're too studious, you won't be popular. I don't usually do that well at school. I'm a pretty cheerful person, especially with my friends, where I can even get rowdy. At home I'm more likely to be anxious around my parents. They expect me to get all A's. It's not fair! I worry about how I probably should get better grades. But I'd be mortified in the eyes of my friends. So I'm usually pretty stressed-out at home, or sarcastic, since my parents are always on my case. But I really don't understand how I can switch so fast. I mean, how can I be cheerful one minute, anxious the next, and then be sarcastic? Which one is the real me? Sometimes, I feel phony, especially around boys. Say I think some guy might be interested in asking me out. I try to act different, like Madonna. I'll be flirtatious and fun-loving. And then everybody, I mean everybody else is looking at me like they think I'm totally weird. Then I get self-conscious and embarrassed and become radically introverted, and I don't know who I really am! Am I just trying to impress them or what? But I don't really care what they think anyway. I don't want to care, that is. I just want to know what my close friends think. I can be my true self with my close friends. I can't be my real self with my parents. They don't understand me. What do they know about what it's like to be a teenager? They still treat me like I'm still a kid. At least at school people treat you more like you're an adult. That gets confusing, though. I mean, which am I, a kid or an adult? It's scary, too, because I don't have any idea what I want to be when I grow up. I mean, I have lots of ideas. My friend Sheryl and I talk about whether we'll be flight attendants, or teachers, or nurses, veterinarians, maybe mothers, or actresses. I know I don't want to be a waitress or a secretary. But how do you decide all of this? I really don't know. I mean, I think about it a lot, but I can't resolve it. There are days when I wish I could just become immune to myself."
> (Harter, 1990a, pp. 352–353)

## PREVIEW

***This excerpt illustrates the increased self-understanding, identity exploration, and emotional changes that are among the hallmarks of adolescent development. Far more than children, adolescents seek to know who they are, what they are all about, and where they are going in life. In the first sections of this chapter, we explore the self and identity, which are often considered to be central aspects of personality development in adolescence. Next, we turn our attention to emotional development in adolescence and then conclude by examining the personality traits and temperament of adolescents.***

# 1 The Self

Self-Understanding

Self-Esteem and Self-Concept

Adolescents carry with them a sense of who they are and what makes them different from everyone else. Consider one adolescent male's self-description: "I am male, bright, an athlete, a political liberal, an extravert, and a compassionate individual." He takes comfort in his uniqueness: "No one else is quite like me. I am 5 feet 11 inches tall and weigh 160 pounds. I live in a suburb and plan to attend the state university. I want to be a sports journalist. I am an expert at building canoes. When I am not going to school and studying, I write short stories about sports figures, which I hope to publish someday." Real or imagined, an adolescent's developing sense of self and uniqueness is a motivating force in life. Our exploration of the self begins with information about adolescents' self-understanding and then turns to their self-esteem and self-concept.

## Self-Understanding

Though individuals become more introspective in adolescence and even more so in emerging adulthood, this self-understanding is not completely internal; rather, self-understanding is a social cognitive construction (Harter, 2006; McLean & Pratt, 2006). That is, adolescents' and emerging adults' developing cognitive capacities interact with their sociocultural experiences to influence their self-understanding. These are among the questions we examine in this section: What is self-understanding? What are some important dimensions of adolescents' and emerging adults' self-understanding?

### What Is Self-Understanding?

**Self-understanding** is the individual's cognitive representation of the self, the substance and content of self-conceptions. For example, a 12-year-old boy understands that he is a student, a football player, a family member, and a video game lover. A 14-year-old girl understands that she is a cheerleader, a student council member, a movie fan, and a rock music fan. An adolescent's self-understanding is based, in part, on the various roles and membership categories that define who adolescents are (Harter, 2006). Though self-understanding provides the rational underpinnings, it is not the whole of personal identity.

### Dimensions of Adolescents' and Emerging Adults' Self-Understanding

The development of self-understanding in adolescence is complex and involves a number of aspects of the self (Harter, 1998, 2006). Let's examine how the adolescent's self-understanding differs from the child's, then describe some changes in self-understanding during emerging adulthood.

**Abstraction and Idealism** Remember from our discussion of Piaget's theory of cognitive development in Chapters 1 and 3 that many adolescents begin to think in more *abstract* and *idealistic* ways. When asked to describe themselves, adolescents are more likely than children to use abstract and idealistic terms. Consider 14-year-old Laurie's abstract description of herself: "I am a human being. I am indecisive. I don't know who I am." Also consider her idealistic description of herself: "I am a naturally sensitive person who really cares about people's feelings. I think I'm pretty good-looking." Not all adolescents describe themselves in idealistic ways, but most adolescents distinguish between the real self and the ideal self.

**Differentiation** Over time, an adolescent's self-understanding becomes increasingly *differentiated* (Harter, 2006). Adolescents are more likely than children to note

**self-understanding** The individual's cognitive representation of the self; the substance and content of self-conceptions.

*What are some characteristics of self-understanding in adolescence?*

contextual or situational variations in describing themselves (Harter, Waters, & Whitesell, 1996). For example, a 15-year-old girl might describe herself by using one set of characteristics in connection with her family and another set of characteristics in connection with her peers and friends. Yet another set of characteristics might appear in her self-description of her romantic relationship. In sum, adolescents are more likely than children to understand that they possess several different selves, each one varying to some degree according to a particular role or context.

**The Fluctuating Self** Given the contradictory nature of the self in adolescence, it is not surprising that the self fluctuates across situations and across time (Harter, 1990a). The 15-year-old girl who was quoted at the beginning of this chapter remarked that she could not understand how she could switch from being cheerful one moment, to being anxious the next, and then sarcastic a short time later. One researcher has referred to the fluctuating adolescent's self as "the barometric self" (Rosenberg, 1979). In most cases, the self continues to be characterized by instability until late adolescence or even early adulthood, when a more unified theory of self is constructed. We have more to say about fluctuations in adolescents' emotions later in the chapter.

*The contemporary perspective on the self emphasizes the construction of multiple self-representations across different relational contexts.*

—Susan Harter
*Contemporary Psychologist, University of Denver*

**Contradictions Within the Self** As adolescents begin to differentiate their concept of the self into multiple roles in different relationship contexts, they sense potential contradictions between their differentiated selves. In one study, Susan Harter (1986) asked seventh-, ninth-, and eleventh-graders to describe themselves. She found that the number of contradictory self-descriptions they mentioned (moody *and* understanding, ugly *and* attractive, bored *and* inquisitive, caring *and* uncaring, introverted *and* fun-loving) increased dramatically between the seventh and ninth grades. Though the number of contradictory self-descriptions students mentioned declined in the eleventh grade, they still outnumbered those noted in the seventh grade. Adolescents develop the cognitive ability to detect these inconsistencies as they strive to construct a general theory of the self (Harter & Monsour, 1992).

**Real Versus Ideal, True Versus False Selves** Adolescents' emerging ability to construct ideal selves can be perplexing to them. While the capacity to recognize a discrepancy between the *real* and *ideal* selves represents a cognitive advance, the humanistic theorist Carl Rogers (1950) argued that a strong discrepancy between the real and ideal selves is a sign of maladjustment. Too great a discrepancy between one's actual self and one's ideal self—the person one wants to be—can produce a sense of failure and self-criticism and can even trigger depression.

Although some theorists consider a strong discrepancy between the ideal and real selves maladaptive, others argue that it need not always be, especially in adolescence. In one view, an important aspect of the ideal or imagined self is the **possible self:** what individuals might become, what they would like to become, and what they are afraid of becoming (Dunkel & Kerpelman, 2004; Markus & Nurius, 1986; Oyserman, Bybee, & Terry, 2006). Thus, adolescents' possible selves include both what they hope to be as well as what they dread they could become (Quinlan, Jaccard, & Blanton, 2006). In this view, the presence of both hoped-for and dreaded ideal selves is psychologically healthy, lending balance to an adolescent's perspective and motivation. That is, the attributes of the future positive self—getting into a good college, being admired, having a successful career—can direct an adolescent's positive actions, whereas the attributes of the future negative self—being unemployed, being lonely, not getting into a good college—can identify behaviors to be avoided.

**possible self** What individuals might become, what they would like to become, and what they are afraid of becoming.

Can adolescents distinguish between their *true* and *false* selves? In one research study, they could (Harter & Lee, 1989). Adolescents are most likely to show their false selves with classmates and in romantic or dating situations; they are least likely to show their false selves with close friends. Adolescents may display a false self to impress others or to try out new behaviors or roles. They may feel that others do not understand their true selves or that others force them to behave in false ways. Some adolescents report that they do not like their false-self behavior, but others say that it does not bother them. One study found that experienced authenticity of the self is highest among adolescents who say they receive support from their parents (Harter, Stocker, & Robinson, 1996).

**Social Comparison** Some developmentalists conclude that adolescents are more likely than children to use *social comparison* in evaluating themselves (Ruble & others, 1980). However, adolescents' willingness to *admit* that they engage in social comparison for this purpose declines during adolescence because they view social comparison as socially undesirable. That is, they think that acknowledging their social comparison motives will endanger their popularity. Relying on social comparison information can be confusing to adolescents because of the large number of reference groups available to them. Should adolescents compare themselves to classmates in general? To friends of their own gender? To popular adolescents, good-looking adolescents, athletic adolescents? Considering all of these social comparison groups simultaneously can be perplexing for adolescents.

**Self-Consciousness** Adolescents are more likely than children to be *self-conscious* about, and preoccupied with, their self-understanding (Harter, 2006). Although adolescents become more introspective, they do not always develop their self-understanding in social isolation. Adolescents turn to their friends for support and self-clarification, including their friends' opinions in their emerging self-definitions. As one researcher on self-development commented, adolescents' friends are often the main source of reflected self-appraisals, the social mirror into which adolescents anxiously stare (Rosenberg, 1979). A longitudinal study found that from 13 to 18 years of age adolescents' public self-consciousness (involving aspects of the self visible to others, such

*How does self-consciousness change as individuals go through adolescence?*

as appearance, actions, and speech) remained reasonably strong and stable from approximately 13 to 16 years of age and then declined slightly (Rankin & others, 2004). Girls revealed a greater public self-consciousness than boys. Private self-consciousness (involving aspects of the self hidden from view such as thoughts, emotions, and attitudes) increased from 13 to 18 years of age.

**Self-Protection** In adolescence, the sense of confusion and conflict that is stimulated by the efforts to understand oneself is accompanied by a need to *protect the self.* In an attempt to protect the self, adolescents are prone to deny their negative characteristics. For example, in Harter's investigation of self-understanding, adolescents were more likely than not to see positive self-descriptions such as *attractive, fun-loving, sensitive, affectionate,* and *inquisitive* as central, important aspects of the self, and to see negative self-descriptions such as *ugly, mediocre, depressed, selfish,* and *nervous* as peripheral, less important aspects of the self (Harter, 1986). This tendency is consistent with adolescents' tendency to describe the self in idealistic ways.

**The Unconscious Self** In adolescence, self-understanding involves greater recognition that the self includes *unconscious* as well as conscious components. This recognition is not likely to occur until late adolescence, however (Selman, 1980). That is, older adolescents are more likely than younger adolescents to believe that certain aspects of their mental experience are beyond their awareness or control.

**Not Quite Yet a Coherent, Integrated Self** Because of the proliferation of selves and unrealistic self-portraits during adolescence, the task of integrating these varying self-conceptions becomes problematic (Harter, 2006). Only later, usually in emerging adulthood, do individuals successfully *integrate* the many aspects of the self.

### Emerging Adulthood and Adulthood

In emerging adulthood, self-understanding becomes more *integrative,* with the disparate parts of the self pieced together more systematically. Emerging adults may detect inconsistencies in their earlier self-descriptions as they attempt to construct a general theory of self, an integrated sense of identity.

As we saw in Chapter 3, "The Brain and Cognitive Development," Gisela Labouvie-Vief (2006) concludes that considerable restructuring of the self can take place in emerging adulthood. She emphasizes that key aspects of self-development in emerging adulthood involve an increase in self-reflection and deciding on a particular worldview.

However, Labouvie-Vief (2006) argues that although emerging adults engage in more complex and critical thinking than when they were adolescents, many still have difficulty integrating their complex view of the world. She says this difficulty results from emerging adults still being easily influenced by their emotions, which can distort their thinking and cause them to be too self-serving and self-protective. In her research, it is not until 30 to 39 years of age that adults effectively develop a coherent, integrated worldview.

*How does self-understanding change in emerging adulthood?*

### Self-Understanding and Social Contexts

We have seen that the adolescent's self-understanding can vary across relationships and social roles. Researchers have found that adolescents' portraits of themselves can differ depending on whether they describe themselves when they are with their mother, father, close friend, romantic partner, or peer. They also can differ depending on whether they describe themselves in the role of student, athlete, or employee. Similarly, adolescents might create different selves depending on their ethnic and cultural background and experiences (Lalonde & Chandler, 2004).

The multiple selves of ethnically diverse youth reflect their experiences in navigating their multiple worlds of family, peers, school, and community (Cooper & others, 2002; Oyserman, Bybee, & Terry, 2006; Pizzolato, 2006). As U.S. youth from different ethnic backgrounds move from one culture to another, they can encounter barriers related to language, racism, gender, immigration, and poverty. In each of their different worlds, however, they also can find resources—in institutions, in other people, and in themselves. Youth who have difficultly moving between worlds can become alienated from their school, family, or peers. This in turn, can lead to other problems. However, youth who can navigate effectively between different worlds can develop bicultural or multicultural selves and become "culture brokers" for others.

Hazel Markus and her colleagues (Markus & Kitayama, 1994; Markus, Mullally, & Kitayama, 1999) stress that understanding how multiple selves emerge through participation in cultural practices is important. They argue that all selves are culture-specific, and emerge as individuals adapt to their cultural environments. In North American contexts, especially middle-socioeconomic-status (SES) contexts, the culture promotes and maintains individuality. When given the opportunity to describe themselves, North Americans often provide not only current portraits but notions of their future selves as well. They frequently show a need for multiple selves that are stable and consistent. In Japan, multiple selves are often described in terms of relatedness to others (Sedikides & Brewer, 2001). For many Japanese, self-improvement is also an important aspect of these multiple selves. Markus and her colleagues recognize that cultural groups are characterized by diversity but conclude that placing the dominant aspects of multiple selves in a culture is helpful (Markus & others, 2006; Snibbe & Markus, 2005).

Daphna Oyserman and her colleagues (2002, 2006) have created an intervention to promote the development of academically focused possible selves that increases adolescents' feelings of being connected and involved with school. In one study, the participants were low-income inner-city African American boys and girls in their last year of middle school (Oyserman, Terry, & Bybee, 2002). Slightly less than one-third of the adolescents received the intervention, while the others did not (control group). The intervention involved small groups of adolescents and took place weekly after school during a nine-week period, with each session lasting 90 minutes. The small-group facilitators were undergraduate students trained by the authors of the study. Intervention and nonintervention youth

*How are the multiple selves of a U.S. adolescent different than those of Japanese adolescents?*

were compared at the baseline and at year end (spring). The intervention, called School-to-Jobs, focused on such topics as the skills needed to be successful in school, creating time lines into the future, mapping out strategies for the coming year, solving everyday problems, and jobs and careers. By the end of the school year, the students who experienced the intervention "reported more bonding to school, concern about doing well in school, balanced possible selves, plausible strategies to attain these possible selves, better school attendance, and for boys, less trouble at school" (Oyserman, Terry, & Bybee, 2002, p. 313). More recently, improved academic outcomes for the intervention youth were documented two full years later (Oyserman & Fryberg, 2004).

At this point, we have discussed many aspects of self-understanding. Recall, however, that the self involves not only self-understanding but also self-esteem and self-concept. That is, adolescents not only try to define and describe the attributes of the self (self-understanding), they also evaluate those attributes (self-concept and self-esteem).

## Self-Esteem and Self-Concept

What are self-esteem and self-concept? How are they measured? Are some domains more salient to the adolescent's self-esteem than others? How do relationships with parents and peers influence adolescents' self-esteem? What are the consequences of low self-esteem in adolescents and emerging adults, and how can their self-esteem be raised?

### What Are Self-Esteem and Self-Concept?

**Self-esteem,** also referred to as *self-worth,* or *self-image,* is the global evaluative dimension of the self. For example, an adolescent or emerging adult might perceive that she is not merely a person, but a good person. Of course, not all adolescents and emerging adults have an overall positive image of themselves. An adolescent with low self-esteem may describe himself as a bad person. **Self-concept** refers to domain-specific evaluations of the self. Adolescents and emerging adults make self-evaluations in many domains—academic, athletic, physical appearance, and so on. For example an adolescent may have a negative academic self-concept because he is not doing well at school, but have a positive athletic self-concept because he is a star swimmer. In sum, self-esteem refers to global self-evaluations, self-concept to domain-specific evaluations.

Investigators have not always made a clear distinction between self-esteem and self-concept, sometimes using the terms interchangeably or not precisely defining them (Dusek & McIntyre, 2003; Harter, 2006). As you read the remaining discussion of self-esteem and self-concept, the distinction between self-esteem as global self-evaluation and self-concept as domain-specific self-evaluation should help you to keep the terms straight.

### Measuring Self-Esteem and Self-Concept

Measuring self-esteem and self-concept hasn't always been easy, especially in assessing adolescents (Dusek & McIntyre, 2003). For many years, such measures were designed primarily for children or for adults, with little attention paid to adolescents. Then, Susan Harter (1989) developed a separate measure for adolescents: the Self-Perception Profile for Adolescents. It assesses eight domains—scholastic competence, athletic competence, social acceptance, physical appearance, behavioral conduct, close friendship, romantic appeal, and job competence—plus global self-worth. The adolescent measure has three skill domains not present in the measure she developed for children: job competence, romantic appeal, and close friendship.

Some assessment experts argue that a combination of several methods should be used in measuring self-esteem. In addition to self-reporting, rating of an adolescent's self-esteem by others and observations of the adolescent's behavior in various settings could provide a more complete and more accurate self-esteem picture.

**self-esteem** The global evaluative dimension of the self; also referred to as self-worth, or self-image.

**self-concept** Domain-specific evaluations of the self.

**Positive indicators**

1. Gives others directives or commands
2. Uses voice quality appropriate for situation
3. Expresses opinions
4. Sits with others during social activities
5. Works cooperatively in a group
6. Faces others when speaking or being spoken to
7. Maintains eye contact during conversation
8. Initiates friendly contact with others
9. Maintains comfortable space between self and others
10. Has little hesitation in speech, speaks fluently

**Negative indicators**

1. Puts down others by teasing, name-calling, or gossiping
2. Uses gestures that are dramatic or out of context
3. Engages in inappropriate touching or avoids physical contact
4. Gives excuses for failures
5. Brags excessively about achievements, skills, appearance
6. Verbally puts self down; self-deprecation
7. Speaks too loudly, abruptly, or in a dogmatic tone

**FIGURE 4.1** Behavioral Indicators of Self–Esteem

Peers, teachers, parents, and even others who do not know the adolescent can be asked to rate the adolescent's self-esteem. Adolescents' facial expressions and the extent to which they congratulate or condemn themselves are also good indicators of how they view themselves. For example, adolescents who rarely smile or rarely act happy are revealing something about their self-esteem. One investigation that used behavioral observations in the assessment of self-esteem shows some of the positive as well as negative behaviors that can provide clues to the adolescent's self-esteem (see Figure 4.1) (Savin-Williams & Demo, 1983). By using a variety of methods (such as self-report and behavioral observations) and obtaining information from various sources (such as the adolescent, parents, friends, and teachers), investigators probably can construct a more accurate picture of the adolescent's self-esteem.

### Self-Esteem: Perception and Reality

Self-esteem reflects perceptions that do not always match reality (Baumeister & others, 2003). An adolescent's or emerging adult's self-esteem might indicate a perception about whether he or she is intelligent and attractive, for example, but that perception may not be accurate. Thus, high self-esteem may refer to accurate, justified perceptions of one's worth as a person and one's successes and accomplishments, but it can also indicate an arrogant, grandiose, unwarranted sense of superiority over others. In the same manner, low self-esteem may suggest either an accurate perception of one's shortcomings or a distorted, even pathological insecurity and inferiority.

### Does Self-Esteem Change During Adolescence and Emerging Adulthood?

Researchers have found that self-esteem often decreases when children make the transition from elementary school to middle or junior high school (Hawkins & Berndt, 1985; Simmons & Blyth, 1987; Twenge & Campbell, 2001). Indeed, during and just after many life transitions, individuals' self-esteem often decreases. This decrease in self-esteem may occur during the transition from middle or junior high school to high school, and from high school to college.

Self-esteem fluctuates across the life span. One cross-sectional study assessed the self-esteem of a very large, diverse sample of 326,641 individuals from 9 to 90 years of age (Robins & others, 2002). About two-thirds of the participants were from the United States. The individuals were asked to respond to the item, "I have high self-esteem" on a 5-point scale in which 5 stood for "strongly agree" and 1 stood for

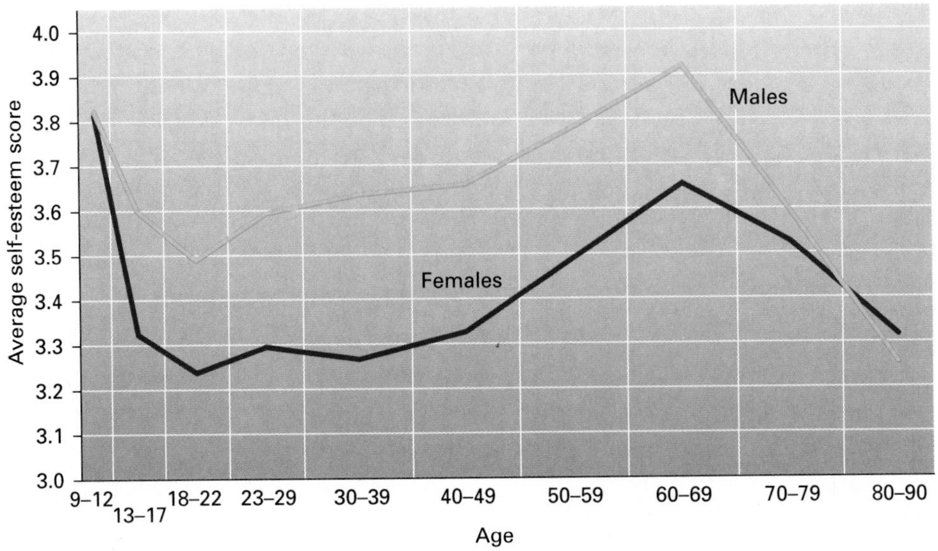


**FIGURE 4.2 Self-Esteem Across the Life Span** One large-scale study asked more than 300,000 individuals to rate the extent to which they have high self-esteem on a 5-point scale, 5 being "strongly agree" and 1 being "strongly disagree." Self-esteem dropped in adolescence and late adulthood. Self-esteem of females was lower than self-esteem of males through most of the life span.

"strongly disagree." Self-esteem decreased in adolescence, increased in the twenties, leveled off in the thirties, rose in the forties through the mid-sixties, and then dropped in the seventies and eighties (see Figure 4.2). At most ages, males reported higher self-esteem than females did. For example, one recent study found that female adolescents had lower self-esteem than male adolescents, and their lower self-esteem was associated with less healthy adjustment (Raty & others, 2005).

Another recent study also found that the gender gap (lower for females) in self-esteem decreased as individuals went through emerging adulthood from 18 to 25 years of age (Galambos, Barker, & Krahn, 2006). In this study, social support and marriage were linked with an increase in self-esteem, whereas unemployment was related to a decrease in self-esteem.

Some researchers argue that while there may be a decrease in self-esteem during adolescence, the drop is actually very slight and not nearly as pronounced as presented in the media (Harter, 2002; Hyde, 2005, 2007; Kling & others, 1999). Also note in Figure 4.2 that despite the drop in self-esteem among adolescent girls, their average score (3.3) was still slightly higher than the neutral point on the scale (3.0).

One explanation for the decline in the self-esteem among females during early adolescence focuses on girls' more negative body images during pubertal change compared with boys (Harter, 2006). Another explanation involves the greater interest young adolescent girls take in social relationships and society's failure to reward that interest.

Might adolescents' and emerging adults' self-esteem be influenced by cohort effects? (*Cohort effects* are effects that are due to a person's time of birth or generation but not to actual age.) An analysis of studies conducted from the 1960s into the 1990s found that the self-esteem of college students was higher in the 1990s than it was in the 1960s (Twenge & Campbell, 2001). The explanation given for this increase in self-esteem involves the self-esteem movement and the active encouragement of self-esteem in schools.

A current concern is that too many of today's college students grew up receiving empty praise and as a consequence have inflated self-esteem (Graham, 2005; Stipek, 2005). Too often they were given praise for performance that was mediocre or even poor. Now in college, they may have difficulty handling competition and criticism. The title of a book, *Dumbing Down Our Kids: Why American Children Feel Good About Themselves But Can't Read, Write, or Add* (Sykes, 1995), vividly captured the theme that many U.S. children's academic problems may stem at least in part from unmerited praise as part of an effort to prop up their self-esteem.

**Is Self-Esteem Linked to Success in School and Initiative?** School performance and self-esteem are only moderately correlated, and these correlations do not suggest that high self-esteem produces better school performance (Baumeister & others, 2003). Efforts to increase students' self-esteem have not always led to improved school performance (Davies & Brember, 1999; Hansford & Hattie, 1982). Adolescents with high self-esteem have greater initiative, but this can produce positive or negative outcomes (Baumeister & others, 2003). High-self-esteem adolescents are prone to both prosocial and antisocial actions.

| Domain | Harter's U.S. samples | Other countries |
|---|---|---|
| Physical Appearance | .65 | .62 |
| Scholastic Competence | .48 | .41 |
| Social Acceptance | .46 | .40 |
| Behavioral Conduct | .45 | .45 |
| Athletic Competence | .33 | .30 |

**FIGURE 4.3 Correlations Between Global Self-Esteem and Domains of Competence** *Note:* The correlations shown are the average correlations computed across a number of studies. The other countries in this evaluation were England, Ireland, Australia, Canada, Germany, Italy, Greece, the Netherlands, and Japan. Recall from Chapter 1 that correlation coefficients can range from −1.00 to +1.00. The correlations between physical appearance and global self-esteem (.65 and .62) are moderately high.

**Are Some Domains More Closely Linked to Self-Esteem Than Others?** In Chapter 2, we saw how preoccupied many adolescents are about their body image (Bearman & others, 2006). Physical appearance is an especially powerful contributor to self-esteem in adolescence (Harter, 2006). In Harter's research, for example, global self-esteem was correlated most strongly with physical appearance, a link that has been found in both the United States and other countries (Fox & others, 1994; Harter, 1999; Maeda, 1999) (see Figure 4.3). In another study, adolescents' concept of their physical attractiveness was the strongest predictor of their overall self-esteem (Lord & Eccles, 1994). This strong association between perceived appearance and general self-worth is not confined to adolescence, but holds across the life span, from early childhood through middle age (Harter, 1999).

**Social Contexts and Self-Esteem** Social contexts such as the family, peers, and schools contribute to the development of an adolescent's self-esteem (Dusek & McIntyre, 2003; Harter, 2006; Turnage, 2004). One study found that as family cohesiveness increased, adolescents' self-esteem increased over time (Baldwin & Hoffman, 2002). In this study, family cohesion was based on the amount of time the family spent together, the quality of their communication, and the extent to which the adolescent was involved in family decision making.

In another investigation of self-esteem and parent-child relationships, a measure of self-esteem was administered to boys, and the boys and their mothers were interviewed about family relationships (Coopersmith, 1967). Based on these assessments, the following parenting attributes were associated with boys' high self-esteem: expression of affection; concern about the boys' problems; harmony in the home; participation in joint family activities; availability to give competent, organized help when the boys needed it; setting clear and fair rules; abiding by the rules; and allowing the boys freedom within well-prescribed limits. Remember that because these findings are correlational, researchers cannot say that these parenting attributes *cause* children's high self-esteem. Expressing affection and allowing children freedom within well-prescribed limits probably do contribute to children's self-esteem, but researchers must still say that they are *related* to rather than *cause* children's self-esteem, based on the available research data.

Peer judgments gain increasing importance in adolescence. The correlation between peer approval and self-worth increases during adolescence (Harter, 1990a). However, support from the general peer group (classmates, peers in organizations) is more strongly related to self-worth than is support from close friends (Harter, 1999). Although peer approval is linked with self-worth, parental approval continues to be related to adolescents' self-worth through adolescence, and this correlation does not decline until emerging adulthood (Harter, 1999).

As we saw earlier, the transition from elementary school to middle or junior high school is associated with lowered self-esteem (Harter, 2006). Recall that self-esteem is higher in the last year of elementary school than in middle or junior high school, especially in the first year after the transition (Hawkins & Berndt, 1985; Simmons & Blyth, 1987). We have much more to say about the transition from elementary to middle or junior high school in Chapter 10, "Schools."

**Consequences of Low Self-Esteem** For most adolescents and emerging adults, the emotional discomfort of low self-esteem is only temporary, but for some, low self-esteem can develop into other problems. Low self-esteem has been implicated in depression, suicide, anorexia nervosa, delinquency, and other adjustment problems (Donnellan & others, 2005; Donnellan, Trzesniewski, & Robins, 2006; Flory & others, 2004). The seriousness of the problem depends not only on the nature of the adolescent's and emerging adult's low self-esteem, but on other conditions as well. When low self-esteem is compounded by difficult school transitions, a troubled family life, or other stressful events, an individual's problems can intensify.

Susan Harter (2006) recently described how self-esteem, coupled with other factors, might be involved in adolescent homicide and eating disorders. In one study, high narcissism, low empathy, and being sensitive to rejection combined with low-esteem, were linked to adolescents' violent thoughts (Harter & McCarley, 2004). In another study, adolescents who engaged in violent thinking showed fluctuating self-esteem, had more conduct problems, and had a history of humiliating events that threatened their egos (McCarley & Harter, 2004).

One study found that endorsing certain cultural values, such as thinking that being attractive will lead to higher self-esteem and make one more popular, is linked with more negative perceptions of one's appearance, lower self-esteem, and an increase in eating-disordered behavior (Kiang & Harter, 2004). This study was conducted with college students, but it is likely that many young adolescents as well are very much aware of the prevailing cultural standards of attractiveness, and when they can't meet these standards, their self-esteem is harmed. The coupling of not meeting cultural standards of attractiveness with low self-esteem may lead to depression and even life-threatening suicide ideation (Harter, 2006).

Does self-esteem in adolescence foreshadow adjustment and competence in adulthood? A New Zealand longitudinal study assessed self-esteem at 11, 13, and 15 years of age and adjustment and competence of the same individuals when they were 26 years old (Trzesniewski & others, 2006). The results revealed that adults characterized by poorer mental and physical health, worse economic prospects, and higher levels of criminal behavior were more likely to have low self-esteem in adolescence than their better-adjusted, more competent adult counterparts.

Given the potential consequences of low self-esteem, how can the low self-esteem of adolescents and emerging adults be increased? To explore this question, see the *Health and Well-Being* interlude.

## *Health and Well-Being*

### INCREASING ADOLESCENTS' SELF-ESTEEM

Four ways to improve adolescents' and emerging adults' self-esteem are to (1) identify the causes of low self-esteem and the domains of competence important to the self, (2) provide emotional support and social approval, (3) foster achievement, and (4) help adolescents to cope.

Identifying an adolescent's and emerging adult's sources of self-esteem—that is, the domains that are important to the self—is critical to improving self-esteem. Self-esteem theorist and researcher Susan Harter (1990a) points out that the self-esteem enhancement programs of the 1960s, in which self-esteem itself was the target and individuals were encouraged to simply feel good about themselves, were ineffective. Rather, Harter (1998) concludes that intervention must occur at the level of the *causes* of self-esteem if self-esteem is to improve significantly. Adolescents and emerging adults have the highest self-esteem when they perform competently in domains important to the self. Therefore, adolescents and emerging adults should be encouraged to identify and value their domains of competence. For example, some adolescents and emerging adults might have artistic strengths, others academic strengths, and yet others might excel in sports.

*What are some strategies for increasing self-esteem?*

Emotional support and social approval in the form of confirmation from others can also powerfully influence self-esteem (Harter, 1990a, b). Some youth with low self-esteem come from conflicted families or conditions in which they experienced abuse or neglect—situations in which support is unavailable. In some cases, alternative sources of support can be implemented, either informally through the encouragement of a teacher, a coach, or another significant adult, or more formally, through programs such as Big Brothers and Big Sisters. While peer approval becomes increasingly important during adolescence, both adult and peer support are important influences on the adolescent's self-esteem. In one study, both parental and peer support were related to the adolescent's general self-worth (Robinson, 1995).

Achievement can also improve adolescents' and emerging adults' self-esteem (Bednar, Wells, & Peterson, 1995). For example, the straightforward teaching of real skills to adolescents and emerging adults often results in increased achievement and, thus, in enhanced self-esteem. Adolescents and emerging adults develop higher self-esteem because they know what tasks are important for achieving goals, and they have experienced performing them or similar behaviors. The emphasis on the importance of achievement in improving self-esteem has much in common with Albert Bandura's (2000, 2002) social cognitive concept of *self-efficacy,* which refers to individuals' beliefs that they can master a situation and produce positive outcomes.

Self-esteem often increases when adolescents face a problem and try to cope with it rather than avoid it (Dyson & Renk, 2006; Nes & Segerstrom, 2006). Facing problems realistically, honestly, and nondefensively produces favorable self-evaluative thoughts, which lead to the self-generated approval that raises self-esteem.

## REVIEW AND REFLECT ◆ LEARNING GOAL 1

### 1 Describe the development of the self in adolescence.

***Review***

- What is self-understanding? What are the key dimensions of self-understanding in adolescence?
- What are self-esteem and self-concept? How can they be measured? Are some domains more salient than others to adolescents' self-esteem? How are social contexts linked with adolescents' self-esteem? What are the consequences of low self-esteem? How can adolescents' self-esteem be increased?

***Reflect***

- Think about what your future selves might be. What do you envision will make you the happiest about the future selves you aspire to become? What prospective selves hold negative possibilities?

## 2 Identity

Erikson's Ideas on Identity | The Four Statuses of Identity | Developmental Changes in Identity | Identity and Social Contexts | Identity and Intimacy

An important characteristic of self-understanding that was described earlier in this chapter was self-integration, or the piecing together of different aspects of the self. Self-integration is exemplified in the development of an identity. By far the most comprehensive and provocative theory of identity development is that of Erik Erikson. In fact, some experts on adolescence consider Erikson's ideas to be the single most influential theory of adolescent development. Erikson's theory was introduced in Chapter 1; we expand on that introduction, beginning with an analysis of his ideas on identity.

### Erikson's Ideas on Identity

Who am I? What am I all about? What am I going to do with my life? What is different about me? How can I make it on my own? These questions, not usually considered in childhood, surface as a common, virtually universal concern during adolescence. Adolescents clamor for solutions to questions of identity. Erik Erikson (1950, 1968) was the first to realize how central such questions are to understanding adolescent development. That today identity is believed to be a key concept in adolescent development results directly from Erikson's masterful thinking and analysis.

One of Erik Erikson's strategies for explaining the nature of identity development was to analyze the lives of famous individuals. One such individual was Mahatma Gandhi (*center*), the spiritual leader of India in the mid-twentieth century, about whom Erikson (1969) wrote in *Gandhi's Truth*.

**identity versus identity confusion** Erikson's fifth developmental stage, which occurs during adolescence. At this time, individuals are faced with deciding on who they are, what they are all about, and where they are going in life.

**psychosocial moratorium** Erikson's term for the gap between childhood security and adult autonomy that adolescents experience as part of their identity exploration.

**Revisiting Erikson's Views on Identity** **Identity versus identity confusion,** Erikson's fifth developmental stage, occurs during the adolescent years. At this time, adolescents are faced with deciding who they are, what they are all about, and where they are going in life. They confront many new roles, from vocational to romantic. As part of their identity exploration, adolescents experience a **psychosocial moratorium,** Erikson's term for the gap between childhood security and adult autonomy. In the course of exploring and searching their culture's identity files, they often experiment with different roles. Youth who successfully cope with these conflicting roles and identities emerge with a new sense of self that is both refreshing and acceptable. But adolescents who do not successfully resolve the identity crisis suffer what Erikson calls identity confusion. Either they withdraw, isolating themselves from peers and family, or they immerse themselves in the world of peers and lose their identity in the crowd.

Erikson's ideas about adolescent identity development reveal rich insights into adolescents' thoughts and feelings. Reading one or more of his original books is worthwhile. A good starting point is *Identity: Youth and Crisis* (1968). Other works that deal with identity development are *Young Man Luther* (1962) and *Gandhi's Truth* (1969), which won a Pulitzer Prize.

**Personality and Role Experimentation** Two core ingredients in Erikson's theory of identity development are personality and role experimentation. As we have seen, Erikson stressed that adolescents face an overwhelming number of choices and at some point during their youth enter a period of psychological moratorium (Hopkins, 2000). During this moratorium and before they reach a stable sense of self, they try out different roles and personalities. They might be argumentative one moment, cooperative the next. They might dress neatly one day and sloppily the next day. One week they might like a particular friend, the next week they might despise the friend. This personality experimentation is a deliberate effort on the part of adolescents to find their place in the world.

As adolescents gradually come to realize that they will soon be responsible for themselves and their lives, they search for what those lives are going to be. Many parents and other adults, accustomed to having children go along with what they say, may be bewildered or incensed by the wisecracks, rebelliousness, and rapid mood changes that accompany adolescence. But it is important for these adults to give adolescents the time and opportunity to explore different roles and personalities. In turn, most adolescents eventually discard undesirable roles.

There are literally hundreds of roles for adolescents to try out, and probably just as many ways to pursue each role. Erikson argued that by late adolescence, vocational roles become central to identity development, especially in a highly technological society like that of the United States. Youth who have been well trained to enter a workforce that offers the potential of reasonably high self-esteem will experience the least stress during this phase of identity development. Some youth may reject jobs offering good pay and traditionally high social status, choosing instead work that allows them to be more genuinely helpful to others, perhaps in the Peace Corps, a mental health clinic, or a school for children in a low-income neighborhood. Some youth may prefer unemployment to the prospect of work they feel they could not perform well or would make them feel useless. To Erikson, such choices reflect the desire to achieve a meaningful identity by being true to oneself, rather than by burying one's identity in the larger society.

Identity is a self-portrait that is composed of many pieces:

- The career and work path a person wants to follow (vocational/career identity)
- Whether a person is politically conservative, liberal, or middle of the road (political identity)
- A person's spiritual beliefs (religious identity)
- Whether a person is single, married, divorced, or cohabiting (relationship identity)
- The extent to which a person is motivated to achieve and is intellectual (achievement, intellectual identity)
- Whether a person is heterosexual, homosexual, or bisexual (sexual identity)
- Which part of the world or country a person is from and how intensely the person identifies with his or her cultural heritage (cultural/ethnic identity)
- The things a person likes to do, including sports, music, and hobbies (interest)
- An individual's personality characteristics (introverted or extraverted, anxious or calm, friendly or hostile, and so on) (personality)
- A person's body image (physical identity)

**Some Contemporary Thoughts on Identity** Contemporary views of identity development suggest that it is a lengthy process, in many instances more gradual and less cataclysmic than Erikson's term *crisis* implies (Baumeister, 1991). Today's theorists note that this extraordinarily complex process neither begins nor ends with adolescence (Cote, 2006; Kroger, 2007; Marcia & Carpendale, 2004). It begins in infancy with the appearance of attachment, the development of a sense of self, and the emergence of independence. It ends with a life review and integration in old age. What is important about identity development in adolescence—especially late adolescence—is that for the first time, physical, cognitive, and socioemotional development advance to the point at which the individual can sort through and synthesize childhood identities and identifications to construct a viable path toward adult maturity (Marcia & Carpendale, 2004). Resolution of the identity issue during adolescence does not mean that identity will be stable through the remainder of one's life. An individual who develops a healthy identity is flexible and adaptive, open to changes in society, in relationships, and in careers (Adams, Gulotta, & Montemayor,

1992). This openness assures numerous reorganizations of identity throughout the individual's life.

Just as researchers increasingly describe the adolescent's self-understanding in terms of multiple selves, there also is a trend in characterizing the adolescent's identity in terms of multiple identities (Brooks-Gunn & Graber, 1999). While adolescent identities are preceded by childhood identities, central questions such as "Who am I?" come up more frequently in the adolescent years. During adolescence, identities are characterized more strongly by the search for balance between the needs for autonomy and for connectedness.

Identity formation neither happens neatly, nor is it usually cataclysmic. At the bare minimum, it involves commitment to a vocational direction, an ideological stance, and a sexual orientation. Synthesizing the components of identity can be a long, drawn-out process, with many negations and affirmations of various roles. Identity development gets done in bits and pieces. Decisions are not made once and for all, but must be made again and again. While the decisions might seem trivial at the time—whom to date, whether or not to have intercourse, to break up, to take drugs; whether to go to college or get a job, to study or play, to be politically active or not—over the years, they begin to form the core of what an individual is all about.

## The Four Statuses of Identity

James Marcia (1980, 1994, 2002) stresses that Erikson's theory of identity development implies four identity statuses, or ways of resolving the identity crisis: identity diffusion, identity foreclosure, identity moratorium, and identity achievement. That is, Marcia uses the extent of an adolescent's crisis and commitment to classify individuals according to these four identity statuses. He defines the term **crisis** as a period of identity development during which the adolescent is choosing among meaningful alternatives. (Most researchers use the term *exploration.*) By **commitment,** he means a personal investment in what an individual is going to do.

Let's examine each of Marcia's four identity statuses:

- **Identity diffusion** is Marcia's term for the state adolescents are in when they have not yet experienced an identity crisis (that is, have not yet explored meaningful alternatives) and have not made any commitments. Not only are adolescents in this status undecided about occupational and ideological choices, they usually show little interest in such matters.
- **Identity foreclosure** is Marcia's term for the state adolescents are in when they have made a commitment but have not experienced an identity crisis. This status occurs most often when parents hand down commitments to their adolescents, usually in an authoritarian way. Thus, adolescents with this status have not had adequate opportunities to explore different approaches, ideologies, and vocations on their own.
- **Identity moratorium** is Marcia's term for the state of adolescents who are in the midst of an identity crisis, but who have not made a clear commitment to an identity.
- **Identity achievement** is Marcia's term for the status of adolescents who have undergone an identity crisis and made a commitment. Figure 4.4 summarizes Marcia's four statuses of identity development.

Let's explore some specific examples of Marcia's identity statuses. A 13-year-old adolescent has neither begun to explore her identity in a meaningful way nor made an identity commitment; she is *identity diffused.* An 18-year-old boy's parents want him to be a doctor, so he is planning on majoring in premedicine in college and has not adequately explored any other options; he is *identity foreclosed.* Nineteen-year-old Sasha is not quite sure what life path she wants to follow, but she recently went to the counseling center at her college to find out about different careers; she is in an

**crisis** A period of identity development during which the adolescent is choosing among meaningful alternatives.

**commitment** The part of identity development in which adolescents show a personal investment in what they are going to do.

**identity diffusion** Marcia's term for the state adolescents are in when they have not yet experienced an identity crisis or made any commitments.

**identity foreclosure** Marcia's term for the state adolescents are in when they have made a commitment but have not experienced an identity crisis.

**identity moratorium** Marcia's term for the state of adolescents who are in the midst of an identity crisis, but who have not made a clear commitment to an identity.

**identity achievement** Marcia's term for an adolescent who has undergone an identity crisis and made a commitment.

*identity moratorium.* Twenty-one-year-old Marcelo extensively explored a number of different career options in college, eventually got his degree in science education, and is looking forward to his first year of teaching high school; he is *identity achieved.* While these examples of identity statuses focus on careers, remember that the whole of identity has multiple dimensions.

| | | Has the person made a commitment? | |
|---|---|---|---|
| | | **Yes** | **No** |
| Has the person explored meaningful alternatives regarding some identity question? | **Yes** | Identity Achievement | Identity Moratorium |
| | **No** | Identity Foreclosure | Identity Diffusion |

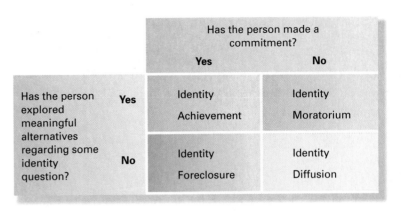

**FIGURE 4.4** **Marcia's Four Statuses of Identity**

Marcia's approach has been sharply criticized by some researchers who conclude that it distorts and overly simplifies Erikson's concepts of crisis and commitment (Bosma & Kunnen, 2001; Cote, 2006; Goossens, 2006; Kroger, 2005, 2007). Erikson emphasized that youth question the perceptions and expectations of their culture and the development of an autonomous position with regard to one's society. In Marcia's approach, these complex questions are reduced to whether a youth has thought about certain issues and considered the alternatives. Similarly, in Marcia's approach, Erikson's idea of commitment loses its meaning of investing oneself in certain lifelong projects and is interpreted simply as having made a firm decision. Other researchers still maintain that Marcia's approach is a valuable contribution to understanding identity (Berzonsky & Adams, 1999; Waterman, 1999).

Recently, some developmentalists have proposed an extension of Marcia's concepts of exploration and commitment (Bosma & Kunnen, 2001; Goossens, 2006). The revisionist theorizing stresses that effective identity development involves evaluating identity commitments on a continuing basis. Two concepts that have been devised to capture this ongoing identity examination are (1) *exploration in depth,* which involves "gathering information and talking to others about current commitments," and (2) *identification with commitment,* which consists of "the degree of security and certainty one experiences with regard to current commitments" (Luyckx, 2006, p. i).

For example, consider a first-year college student who makes a commitment to become a lawyer. Exploring this commitment in depth might include finding out as much as possible about what is involved in being a lawyer, such as educational requirements, the work conducted by lawyers in different areas, what types of college classes might be beneficial for this career, and so on. It might also include talking with several lawyers about their profession. As a result of this in-depth exploration, the college student may become more confident that being a lawyer is the career that best suits her, which reflects identification with commitment (Goossens, 2006). As she goes through the remainder of her college years, she will continue to evaluate the commitment she has made to becoming a lawyer and may change her commitment as she continues to gather new information and reflect on the life path she wants to take.

One way that researchers are examining identity changes in depth is to use a *narrative approach.* This involves asking individuals to tell their life stories and evaluate the extent to which their stories are meaningful and integrated (Kroger, 2007). The term *narrative identity* "refers to the stories people construct and tell about themselves to define who they are for themselves and others. Beginning in adolescence and young adulthood, our narrative identities are the stories we live by" (McAdams, Josselson, & Lieblich, 2006, p. 4).

A recent study used the narrative approach to examine the importance of turning points as important contributors to developing a meaningful identity in late adolescence and emerging adulthood (McLean & Pratt, 2006). In telling their life stories, turning points involving mortality events were more relevant to meaning-filled memories than achievement events. Combining this result with other research (McLean & Thorne, 2006), the researchers concluded that relationship, autonomy, and mortality events are likely to be especially important contributors

How does identity change in emerging adulthood?

to a meaningful identity in late adolescence and emerging adulthood. There also is increasing evidence that the effective management of difficult life events and circumstances contributes to the development of a meaningful identity in emerging adulthood (Pals, 2006).

## Developmental Changes in Identity

During early adolescence, most youth are primarily in the identity statuses of *diffusion, foreclosure,* or *moratorium.* According to Marcia (1987, 1996), at least three aspects of the young adolescent's development are important to identity formation. Young adolescents must be confident that they have parental support, must have an established sense of industry, and must be able to take a self-reflective stance toward the future.

A consensus is developing that the key changes in identity are more likely to take place in emerging adulthood or later than in adolescence (Arnett, 2006; Cote, 2006; Kroger, 2007; McLean & Pratt, 2006; Pals, 2006). For example, Alan Waterman (1985, 1989, 1992, 1999) has found that from the years preceding high school through the last few years of college, the number of individuals who are identity achieved increases, whereas the number who are identity diffused decreases. College upperclassmen are more likely to be identity achieved than college freshmen or high school students. Many young adolescents, on the other hand, are identity diffused. These developmental changes are especially true for vocational choice. In terms of religious beliefs and political ideology, fewer college students reach the identity-achieved status; a substantial number are characterized by foreclosure and diffusion. Thus, the timing of identity development may depend on the particular dimension involved (Harter, 1990a).

Recall from Chapter 1 that one of emerging adulthood's themes is not having many social commitments, which gives individuals considerable independence in developing a life path (Arnett, 2006). James Cote (2006) argues that because of this freedom, developing a positive identity in emerging adulthood requires considerable self-discipline and planning. Without this self-discipline and planning, emerging adults are likely to drift and not follow any particular direction. Cote also stresses that emerging adults who obtain a higher education are more likely to be on a positive identity path. Those who don't obtain a higher education, he says, tend to experience frequent job changes, not because they are searching for an identity but rather because they are just trying to eek out a living in a society that rewards higher education.

Researchers have shown that identity consolidation—the process of refining and enhancing the identity choices that are made in emerging adulthood—continues well into early adulthood and possibly the early part of middle adulthood (Kroger, 2007; Pals, 2006). One research study found that women and men continued to show identity development from 27 through 36 years of age with the main changes in the direction of greater commitment (Pulkkinen & Kokko, 2000). In this study, adults more often moved into achieved and foreclosed identities than into moratorium or diffused identities. Further, as individuals move from early to middle adulthood they become more certain about their identity. For example, a longitudinal study of Smith College women found that identity certainty increased from the thirties through the fifties (Stewart, Ostrove, & Helson, 2001; Zucker, Ostrove, & Stewart, 2002).

A common pattern of individuals who develop positive identities is called the "MAMA" cycle: *m*oratorium–*a*chievement–*m*oratorium–*a*chievement (Archer, 1989). Individuals may repeat this cycle throughout their lives as personal, family, and societal changes require them to explore new alternatives and develop new commitments (Francis, Fraser, & Marcia, 1989). More recently, Marcia (2002) has proposed that when adults' life circumstances are especially difficult and involve considerable disequilibrium, they may even recycle through the diffusion, foreclosure, moratorium, and achievement statuses. Indeed, Marcia (1996) stresses that the first identity an individual commits to is just that—it is not, and should not be expected to be, the final product.

*"Do you have any idea I am?"*


## Identity and Social Contexts

How might social contexts influence an adolescent's identity development? Do family relationships influence identity development? How are culture and ethnicity linked to identity development? Is the identity development of females and males different?

**Family Influences on Identity** Parents are influential figures in an adolescent's search for identity (Goossens, 2006). In studies that relate identity development to parenting style, democratic parents who encourage adolescents to participate in family decision making have been found to foster identity achievement. In contrast, autocratic parents, who control adolescents' behavior and do not give them an opportunity to express their opinions, encourage identity foreclosure and discourage identity exploration. A recent study focused on links between psychological control by parents and identity development in college students (Luyckx & others, 2006). Parents who were high in psychological control (intrusive, manipulative, and focused on their own needs) were less likely to have college-aged children who were in the process of making an identity commitment than parents who were low in psychological control. Permissive parents who provide little guidance and allow adolescents to make their own decisions promote identity diffusion. One study found that poor communication between mothers and adolescents and persistent conflicts with friends were linked to less positive identity development (Reis & Youniss, 2004).

*How might parents influence the adolescent's identity development?*

In addition to parenting style, researchers have examined the role of individuality and connectedness in the development of identity. Catherine Cooper and her colleagues (Carlson, Cooper, & Hsu, 1990; Cooper & Grotevant, 1989; Grotevant & Cooper, 1985, 1998) note that a family atmosphere promoting both individuality and connectedness is important to an adolescent's identity development. Cooper and her colleagues define these terms as follows:

- **Individuality** has two dimensions: self-assertion, or the ability to have and communicate a point of view; and separateness, or the use of communication patterns to express how one is different from others.
- **Connectedness** also has two dimensions: mutuality, or sensitivity to and respect for others' views; and permeability, or openness to others' views.

In general, Cooper's research findings reveal that identity formation is enhanced by family relationships that are both individuated, encouraging adolescents to develop their own point of view, and connected, providing a secure base from which to explore the social world. However, when connectedness is strong and individuation is weak, adolescents may move into identity foreclosure; when connectedness is weak, adolescents often reveal identity confusion (Archer & Waterman, 1994). Also, cultural conditions vary as to how individuality and connectedness are expressed.

**individuality** An important element in adolescent identity development. It consists of two dimensions: self-assertion, the ability to have and communicate a point of view; and separateness, the use of communication patterns to express how one is different from others.

**connectedness** An important element in adolescent identity development. It consists of two dimensions: mutuality, sensitivity to and respect for others' views; and permeability, openness to others' views.

Michelle Chin, age 16: "Parents do not understand that teenagers need to find out who they are, which means a lot of experimenting, a lot of mood swings, a lot of emotions and awkwardness. Like any teenager, I am facing an identity crisis. I am still trying to figure out whether I am a Chinese American or an American with Asian eyes."

For example, in many cultural traditions, daughters and sons may express their ideas to their fathers only indirectly through a third person rather than tell them directly (Cooper & others, 1993).

Stuart Hauser and his colleagues (Hauser & Bowlds, 1990; Hauser & others, 1984) have identified other family processes that promote adolescent identity development. Parents who engage in *enabling* behaviors (such as explaining, accepting, and giving empathy) facilitate the adolescent's identity development more than parents who engage in *constraining* behaviors (such as judging and devaluing). In sum, family interaction styles that give adolescents the right to question and to be different within a context of support and mutuality foster healthy patterns of identity development (Harter, 1990b).

**Cultural and Ethnic Identity** Erikson was especially sensitive to the role of culture in identity development. Throughout the world, he noted, ethnic minority groups have struggled to maintain their cultural identities while blending in with the dominant culture (Erikson, 1968). Erikson thought this struggle for an inclusive identity, or separate identity within the larger culture, has been the driving force in the founding of churches, empires, and revolutions throughout history.

For ethnic minority individuals, adolescence and emerging adulthood are often a special juncture in their development (Phinney, 2006; Phinney & Ong, 2007; Phinney & others, 2006; Umana-Taylor, Bhanot, & Shin, 2006). Although children are aware of some ethnic and cultural differences, individuals consciously confront their ethnicity for the first time in adolescence. Unlike children, adolescents and emerging adults have the ability to interpret ethnic and cultural information, to reflect on the past, and to speculate about the future. What is ethnic identity, and why is it a special part of identity development?

**Defining and Exploring Ethnic Identity** Jean Phinney (1996) defined **ethnic identity** as an enduring, basic aspect of the self that includes a sense of membership in an ethnic group, along with the attitudes and feelings related to that membership. Thus, for adolescents and emerging adults from ethnic minority groups, the process of identity formation has an added dimension: the choice between two or more sources of identification—their own ethnic group and the mainstream, or dominant culture (Bryant & LaFromboise, 2005; Phinney, 2006; Phinney & Ong, 2007; Phinney & others, 2006). Many adolescents resolve this choice by developing a **bicultural identity.** That is, they identify in some ways with their ethnic group and in other ways with the majority culture (Phinney, 2006; Phinney & Ong, 2007; Whitesell & others, 2006).

The indicators of identity change often differ for each succeeding generation (Phinney, 2003, 2006; Phinney & Ong, 2007). First-generation immigrants are likely to be secure in their identities and unlikely to change much; they may or may not develop a new identity. The degree to which they begin to feel "American" appears to be related to whether or not they learn English, develop social networks beyond their ethnic group, and become culturally competent in their new country. Second-generation immigrants are more likely to think of themselves as "American," possibly because citizenship is granted at birth. Their ethnic identity is likely to be linked to retention of their ethnic language and social networks. In the third and later generations, the issues become more complex. Historical, contextual, and political factors that are unrelated to acculturation may affect the extent to which members of this generation retain their ethnic identities. For non-European ethnic groups, racism and discrimination influence whether ethnic identity is retained.

Researchers have found that ethnic identity increases with age, and that higher levels of ethnic identity are linked to more positive attitudes, not only toward one's own ethnic group but also toward members of other ethnic groups (Kiang & others, 2006; Yip & others, 2006). Ethnic identity is also stronger among members of minority

**ethnic identity** An enduring, basic aspect of the self that includes a sense of membership in an ethnic group and the attitudes and feelings related to that membership.

**bicultural identity** Identity formation that occurs when adolescents identify in some ways with their ethnic group and in other ways with the majority culture.

groups than among members of mainstream groups. In one investigation, researchers found that ethnic identity exploration was higher among ethnic minority college students than among White non-Latino college students (Phinney & Alipuria, 1990). Minority students who had thought about and resolved issues involving their ethnicity had higher self-esteem than minority students who had not. In another investigation, the ethnic identity development of Asian American, African American, Latino, and White non-Latino tenth-grade students in Los Angeles was studied (Phinney, 1989). Adolescents in all three ethnic minority groups faced a need to deal with ethnicity in a predominantly White non-Latino culture. But in some instances, the adolescents from the three ethnic minority groups perceived different issues to be important in the resolution of their ethnic identity. For Asian American adolescents, pressures to achieve academically and concerns about quotas that make it difficult to get into good colleges were salient issues. Many African American adolescent females discussed their realization that White American standards of beauty (especially hair and skin color) did not apply to them; African American adolescent males were concerned with possible job discrimination and the need to distinguish themselves from a negative societal image of African American male adolescents. For Latino adolescents, prejudice was a recurrent theme, as was the conflict in values between their Latino cultural heritage and the majority culture.

*What characterizes ethnic identity development in adolescence?*

A recent study examined African Americans' ethnic identity in adolescence, emerging adulthood, and adulthood (Yip & others, 2006). Individuals who were identity achieved reported higher levels of racial centrality (extent to which being African American is central to a definition of oneself) and private regard (degree to which African Americans feel positive about their ethnic group) than their counterparts who were not identity achieved. Also, identity-diffused college students reported higher symptoms of depression than those who were identity achieved.

Researchers are also increasingly finding that a positive ethnic identity is related to positive outcomes for ethnic minority adolescents (Lee, 2005; Umana-Taylor, 2004, 2006; Yasui, Dorham, & Dishion, 2004). For example, one study revealed that ethnic identity was linked with higher school engagement and lower aggression (Van Buren & Graham, 2003). Another study indicated that a stronger ethnic identity was linked to higher self-esteem in African American, Latino, and Asian American youth (Bracey, Bamaca, & Umana-Taylor, 2004). And a recent study with ninth-grade students found that the strength of adolescents' ethnic identification was a better predictor of their academic success than the specific ethnic labels they used to describe themselves (Fuligni, Witkow, & Garcia, 2005). In this study, the ethnic groups most likely to incorporate more of their families' national origin and cultural background into their ethnic identifications were Mexican and Chinese immigrant adolescents.

*Many ethnic minority youth must bridge "multiple worlds" in constructing their identities.*

—Catherine Cooper
*Contemporary Developmental Psychologist, University of California-Santa Cruz*

**The Contexts of Ethnic Identity Development** The contexts in which ethnic minority youth live influence their identity development (Cuéllar, Siles, & Bracamontes, 2004; Newman, 2005). In the United States, many ethnic minority youth live in low-SES urban settings where support for developing a positive identity is lacking. Many of these youth live in pockets of poverty; are exposed to drugs, gangs, and criminal activities; and interact with youth and adults who have dropped out of school or are unemployed. In such settings, support organizations and programs for youth can make an important contribution to their identity development.

Shirley Heath and Milbrey McLaughlin (1993) studied 60 youth organizations that involved 24,000 adolescents over a period of five years. They found these organizations were especially good at building a sense of ethnic pride in inner-city youth. Heath and McLaughlin emphasize that many inner-city youth have too much time on their hands, too little to do, and too few places to go. Inner-city youth want to participate in organizations that nurture them and respond positively to their needs and interests. Organizations that perceive youth as fearful,

*How might certain experiences shorten or lengthen identity development for ethnic minority individuals in emerging adulthood?*

**intimacy versus isolation** Erikson's sixth developmental stage, which individuals experience during the early adulthood years. At this time, individuals face the developmental task of forming intimate relationships with others.

vulnerable, and lonely but also frame them as capable, worthy, and eager to have a healthy and productive life contribute in positive ways to the identity development of ethnic minority youth.

**Ethnic Identity in Emerging Adulthood** Jean Phinney (2006) recently described how ethnic identity may change in emerging adulthood, especially highlighting how certain experiences of ethnic minority individuals may shorten or lengthen emerging adulthood. For ethnic minority individuals who have to take on family responsibilities and do not go to college, identity formation may occur earlier. By contrast, especially for ethnic minority individuals who go to college, identity formation may take longer because of the complexity of exploring and understanding a bicultural identity. The cognitive challenges of higher education likely stimulate ethnic minority individuals to reflect on their identity and examine changes in the way they want to identify themselves. This increased reflection may focus on integrating parts of one's ethnic minority culture and the mainstream non-Latino White culture. For example, some emerging adults have to come to grips with resolving a conflict between family loyalty and interdependence emphasized in one's ethnic minority culture and the values of independence and self-assertion emphasized by the mainstream non-Latino White culture (Arnett, 2006). One recent study of Mexican American and Asian American college students found that they identified both with the American mainstream culture and their culture of origin (Devos, 2006).

### Gender and Identity

Erikson's (1968) classic presentation of identity development reflected the traditional division of labor between the sexes that was common at the time. Erikson wrote that males were mainly oriented toward career and ideological commitments, whereas females were mainly oriented toward marriage and childbearing. In the 1960s and 1970s, researchers found support for this assertion of gender differences in identity. For example, they found that vocational concerns were more central to male identity, whereas affiliative concerns were more central to female identity (LaVoie, 1976). In the last several decades, however, as females have developed stronger vocational interests, these gender differences have begun to disappear (Hyde, 2007; Madison & Foster-Clark, 1996; Sharp & others, 2007).

## Through the Eyes of Emerging Adults

### DEVELOPING AN IDENTITY BEFORE INTIMACY

"It wasn't until I found myself in an intimate relationship with my present partner that I realized that I hadn't had a really intimate relationship before. Although there were other people, nothing ever lasted and nothing was fulfilling or right. I feel this was because I had not yet discovered myself, I had not found my own identity. Before making the commitment to my present partner, though, I knew that I had found myself. I knew who I was and what I wanted to do with my life, where I wanted to go. I am now really happy to be the person I want to become."

—*20-Year-Old Female University Student*

(Source: Kroger, 2007, p. 97)

## Identity and Intimacy

Erikson (1968) argued that intimacy should develop after individuals are well on their way to establishing a stable and successful identity. **Intimacy versus isolation** is Erikson's sixth developmental stage, which individuals experience during early adulthood. At this time, individuals face the task of forming intimate relationships with others. Erikson describes intimacy as finding oneself, yet losing oneself in another. If young adults form healthy friendships and an intimate relationship with another individual, intimacy will be achieved; if not, isolation will result.

In one study of unmarried college students 18 to 23 years of age, a strong sense of self, expressed through identity achievement and an instrumental orientation, was an important factor in forming intimate connections, for both males and females (Madison & Foster-Clark, 1996). However, insecurity and a defensive posture in relationships were expressed differently in males' and females' relationships, with males displaying greater superficiality and females more dependency. A recent study also found that a higher level of intimacy was linked to a stronger identity for both male and female college students, although the intimacy scores of the college females were higher than for the males (Montgomery, 2005).

**REVIEW AND REFLECT ◆ LEARNING GOAL 2**

**2 Explain the many facets of identity development.**

***Review***
- What is Erikson's view of identity development?
- What are the four statuses of identity development?
- What developmental changes characterize identity?
- How do social contexts influence identity development?
- What is Erikson's view on identity and intimacy?

***Reflect***
- How would you describe your current identity? Which of Marcia's identity statuses best describes you?

## 3 Emotional Development

The Emotions of Adolescence | Hormones, Experience, and Emotions | Emotional Competence

Defining emotion is difficult because it is not easy to tell when an adolescent is in an emotional state. For our purposes, we will define **emotion** as feeling, or affect, that occurs when a person is in a state or an interaction that is important to the individual, especially to his or her well-being (Campos, Frankel, & Camras, 2007). Emotion is characterized by behavior that reflects (expresses) the pleasantness or unpleasantness of the state the individual is in, or the transactions he or she is experiencing (Barrett & others, 2007; Leary, 2007). Emotions also can be more specific and take the form of joy, fear, anger, and so on, depending on how a transaction affects the person (for example, is the transaction a threat, a frustration, a relief, something to be rejected, something unexpected, and so on). And emotions can vary in how intense they are (Denham, Bassett, & Wyatt, 2007). For example, an adolescent may show intense anger only in a particular situation.

How are emotions linked to the two main concepts we have discussed so far in this chapter—the self and identity? Emotion is closely connected to self-esteem. Negative emotions, such as sadness, are associated with low self-esteem, whereas positive emotions, such as joy, are linked to high self-esteem. Some psychologists argue that emotions are the "glue" that connects our life events (Haviland & others, 1994). The emotional experiences involved in events, such as emerging sexual experiences, dating and romantic encounters, and driving a car, contribute to the adolescent's developing identity (Rosenblum & Lewis, 2003).

Indeed, emotions are involved in many aspects of adolescence, from the hormonal fluctuations of puberty to the sadness of adolescent depression. In this section, we examine the extent to which adolescents' emotions are linked to both their hormones and their experience. We also explore what it means to be emotionally competent in adolescence. First, though, we need to survey the adolescent's emotional landscape.

### The Emotions of Adolescence

Adolescence has long been described as a time of emotional turmoil (Hall, 1904). In its extreme form, this view is too stereotypical because adolescents are not constantly

**emotion** Feeling, or affect, that occurs when a person is in a state or an interaction that is important to the individual, especially to his or her well-being.

*What characterizes adolescents' emotions?*

in a state of "storm and stress." Nonetheless, early adolescence is a time when emotional highs and lows occur more frequently (Rosenblum & Lewis, 2003). Young adolescents can be on top of the world one moment and down in the dumps the next. In many instances, the intensity of their emotions seems out of proportion to the events that elicit them (Steinberg & Levine, 1997). Young adolescents may sulk a lot, not knowing how to express their feelings adequately. With little or no provocation, they may blow up at their parents or siblings, projecting their unpleasant feelings onto another person.

As we saw in Chapter 1, Reed Larson and Maryse Richards (1994) found that adolescents reported more extreme emotions and more fleeting emotions than their parents. For example, adolescents were five times more likely than their parents to report being "very happy" and three times more likely to report being "very sad." These findings lend support to the perception that adolescents are moody and changeable (Rosenblum & Lewis, 2003). Researchers have also found that from the fifth through the ninth grades, both boys and girls experience a 50 percent decrease in the state of being "very happy" (Larson & Lampman-Petraitis, 1989). In this study, adolescents were more likely than preadolescents to report mildly negative mood states.

It is important for adults to recognize that moodiness is a *normal* aspect of early adolescence, and that most adolescents eventually emerge from these moody times and become competent adults. Nonetheless, for some adolescents, intensely negative emotions can reflect serious problems. For example, rates of depressed moods become more frequent in girls during adolescence (Nolen-Hoeksema, 2007). We have much more to say about depression in adolescence in Chapter 13, "Problems in Adolescence and Emerging Adulthood."

## Hormones, Experience, and Emotions

As we saw in Chapter 2, significant hormonal changes occur during puberty. The emotional fluctuations of early adolescence may be related to variability in hormone levels during this period. As adolescents move into adulthood, their moods become less extreme, perhaps due to their adaptation to hormone levels over time (Rosenblum & Lewis, 2003).

Researchers have discovered that pubertal change is associated with an increase in negative emotions (Archibald, Graber, & Brooks-Gunn, 2003; Dorn & others, 2006). However, most researchers conclude that such hormonal influences are small and are usually associated with other factors, such as stress, eating patterns, sexual activity, and social relationships (Susman, Dorn, & Schiefelbein, 2003; Susman & Rogol, 2004). Indeed, environmental experiences may contribute more to the emotions of adolescence than hormonal changes. Recall from Chapter 2 that in one study, social factors accounted for two to four times as much variance as hormonal factors in young adolescent girls' depression and anger (Brooks-Gunn & Warren, 1989).

Among the stressful experiences that might contribute to changes in emotion during adolescence are the transition to middle or junior high school and the onset of sexual experiences and romantic relationships. For many boys and girls, moving to the less protected, less personal, and more achievement-oriented context of middle school or junior high is stressful and can be expected to increase negative emotions. We explore this school transition further in Chapter 10. Moreover, the vulnerability and confusion involved in emerging sexual and romantic relationships can be expected to fuel emotional changes in adolescence. In one study, real and fantasized sexual/romantic relationships were responsible for more than one-third of ninth- to twelfth-graders' strong emotions (Wilson-Shockley, 1995). We examine sexuality and romantic relationships in greater detail in Chapters 6 and 9.

In sum, both hormonal changes and environmental experiences are involved in the changing emotions of adolescence. So is the young person's ability to manage his emotions (Saarni & others, 2006). In Chapter 3, we studied the concept of emotional intelligence. Now let's examine a closely related concept, emotional competence.

## Emotional Competence

In adolescence, individuals are more likely to become aware of their emotional cycles, such as feeling guilty about being angry. This new awareness may improve their ability to cope with their emotions. Adolescents also become more skillful at presenting their emotions to others. For example, they become aware of the importance of covering up their anger in social relationships. And they are more likely to understand the importance of being able to communicate their emotions constructively to improve the quality of a relationship (Saarni, 1999; Saarni & others, 2006).

Although the increased cognitive abilities and awareness of adolescents prepare them to cope more effectively with stress and emotional fluctuations, many adolescents do not effectively manage their emotions. As a result, they may become prone to depression, anger, and poor emotional regulation, which in turn can trigger problems such as academic difficulties, drug abuse, juvenile delinquency, or eating disorders. For example, one study illustrated the importance of emotion regulation and mood in academic success (Gumora & Arsenio, 2002). Even when their level of cognitive ability was controlled for, young adolescents who said they experienced more negative emotion regarding academic routines had lower grade point averages.

The emotional competencies that are important for adolescents to develop include the following (Saarni, 1999):

| Emotional Competence | Example |
|---|---|
| Being aware that the expression of emotions plays a major role in relationships | Knowing that expressing anger toward a friend on a regular basis can harm the friendship |
| Adaptively coping with negative emotions by using self-regulatory strategies that reduce the intensity and duration of such emotional states | Reducing anger by walking away from a negative situation and engaging in an activity that takes one's mind off it |
| Understanding that inner emotional states do not have to correspond to outer expressions. (As adolescents become more mature, they begin to understand how their emotionally expressive behavior may impact others, and take that understanding into account in the way they present themselves.) | Recognizing that one can feel angry yet manage one's emotional expression so that it appears more neutral |
| Being aware of one's emotional states without becoming overwhelmed by them | Differentiating between sadness and anxiousness, and focusing on coping rather than becoming overwhelmed by these feelings |
| Being able to discern others' emotions | Perceiving that another person is sad rather than afraid |

**REVIEW AND REFLECT ◆ LEARNING GOAL 3**

**3 Discuss the emotional development of adolescents.**

***Review***

- How would you characterize adolescents' emotions?
- How extensively are adolescents' emotions linked to their hormones and experiences?
- What does it take to be emotionally competent in adolescence?

***Reflect***

- How would you describe your emotions in early adolescence? Did you experience more extremes of emotion when you were in middle or junior high school than you do today? Have you learned how to control your emotions better now than you did in early adolescence? Explain.

# 4 PERSONALITY DEVELOPMENT

Personality | Temperament

So far in this chapter, we have discussed the development of the self, identity, and emotion in adolescence. How are these concepts linked with personality? In many views, the self is the central aspect of personality. During adolescence, through self-understanding, individuals develop an integrated sense of identity. In terms of personality traits, identity development can lead to both stability (the achievement of an identity) and change (the exploration of new identities and modification of personality traits) (Caspi & Shiner, 2006). The description of an individual's personality traits and temperament often involves emotions. For example, an adolescent may be described in terms of emotional stability/instability and positive/negative affectivity. How are such traits manifested in adolescence? Which traits are most important?

## Personality

The search for the core personality traits that characterize people has a long history (Caspi & Shiner, 2006; Mroczek, Spiro, & Griffin, 2006; Roberts & Wood, 2006). In recent years, researchers have focused on the **big five factors of personality:** openness to experience, conscientiousness, extraversion, agreeableness, and neuroticism (emotional stability) (see Figure 4.5). If you create an acronym from these trait names, you get the word OCEAN.

Much of the research on the big five factors has used adults as the participants in studies (Costa & McCrae, 1998; McCrae & Costa, 2003, 2006). However, an increasing number of studies involving the big five factors focus on adolescents (Branje, van Lieshout, & van Aken, 2004; McCrae, Costa, & Martin, 2005; Shiner, 2005). A recent study revealed that when adolescents scored higher on conscientiousness, they had higher-quality friendships and peer acceptance, and were less likely to experience peer victimization than their counterparts who scored lower on conscientiousness (Jenson-Campbell & Malcolm, 2007). In another study, adolescents who were characterized by openness, conscientiousness, and emotional stability were less likely to have a pattern of school absences (Lounsbury & others, 2004). In another study, the mothers of 12- to 13-year-old African American and non-Latino White boys rated the sons' personalities (John & others, 1994). The researchers found that the ratings reflected the big five factors, but that two additional factors described the boys: (1) irritability ("whines," "feelings are easily hurt") and (2) positive activity ("energetic," "physically active"). Researchers do not completely agree on the core

**big five factors of personality** Five core traits of personality: openness to experience, conscientiousness, extraversion, agreeableness, and neuroticism (emotional stability).

| Openness | Conscientiousness | Extraversion | Agreeableness | Neuroticism (emotional stability) |
|---|---|---|---|---|
| • Imaginative or practical | • Organized or disorganized | • Sociable or retiring | • Softhearted or ruthless | • Calm or anxious |
| • Interested in variety or routine | • Careful or careless | • Fun-loving or somber | • Trusting or suspicious | • Secure or insecure |
| • Independent or conforming | • Disciplined or impulsive | • Affectionate or reserved | • Helpful or uncooperative | • Self-satisfied or self-pitying |

**FIGURE 4.5 The Big Five Factors of Personality** Each of the broad supertraits encompasses more narrow traits and characteristics. Use the acronym OCEAN to remember the big five personality factors (*o*penness, *c*onscientiousness, and so on).

personality traits that typify adolescents (or children and adults for that matter). Two other traits that have appeared in some studies are excellent/ordinary and evil/decent (Almagor, Tellegen, & Waller, 1995).

How stable are personality traits in adolescence? Some researchers have found that personality is not as stable in adolescence as in adulthood (Roberts & Caspi, 2003). The greater degree of change in personality during adolescence may be linked to the exploration of new identities (Roberts & Caspi, 2003).

But while personality changes more in adolescence than during adulthood, it still shows some stability (Hair & Graziano, 2003; Shiner, 2005). In one longitudinal study, individuals' personalities were assessed at three points in their development: junior high school, senior high school, and 30 to 40 years of age (Block, 1993). There was both stability and change in the personality traits of the individuals over time. Some researchers have concluded that aggression, dominance, dependency, sociability, and shyness tend to remain stable from middle and late childhood through adolescence and adulthood (Caspi & Bem, 1990).

One longitudinal study examined stability and change in personality from 18 through 26 years of age (Roberts, Caspi, & Moffitt, 2001). Using the Multidimensional Personality Questionnaire (Tellegen, 1982), more stability than change was found. The personality changes that did occur from adolescence to adulthood reflected growth in the direction of greater maturity, with many adolescents becoming more controlled, socially more confident, and less angry as adults.

Many psychologists argue that it is better to view personality not only in terms of traits, but also in terms of contexts and situations (Mischel, 1968, 2004). They conclude that the trait approach ignores environmental factors and places too much emphasis on stability and lack of change. This criticism was first leveled by social cognitive theorist Walter Mischel (1968), who argued that personality varies according to the situation. Thus, adolescents might behave quite differently when they are in a library than when they are at a party.

Today, most psychologists are interactionists, believing that both traits and situations need to be taken into account in understanding personality (Block, 2002; Mischel, 2004; Roberts & Robins, 2004). Let's again consider the situations of being in a library or at a party and consider the preferences of two adolescents, Jane who is an introvert, and Sandra who is an extravert. Jane, the introvert, is more likely to enjoy being in the library, whereas Sandra, the extravert, is more likely to enjoy herself at the party.

## Temperament

Although the study of personality has focused mainly on adults, the study of temperament has been primarily confined to infants and children (Galambos & Costigan, 2003). However, both personality and temperament are important in understanding adolescent development. **Temperament** can be defined as an individual's behavioral style and characteristic way of responding. Many psychologists emphasize that temperament forms the foundation of personality (Galambos & Costigan, 2003). Through increasing capacities and interactions with the environment, temperament evolves or

**temperament** An individual's behavioral style and characteristic way of responding.

becomes elaborated across childhood and adolescence into a set of personality traits (Caspi & Shiner, 2006; Rothbart & Bates, 2006).

The close link between temperament and personality is supported by research that connects some of the big five personality factors to temperament categories (Caspi & Shiner, 2006). For example, the temperament category of positive emotionality is related to the personality trait of extraversion, negative emotionality maps onto neuroticism (emotional stability), and effortful control is linked to conscientiousness (Putnam, Sanson, & Rothbart, 2002).

**Temperament Categories** Just as with personality, researchers are interested in discovering what the key dimensions of temperament are (Rothbart & Bates, 2006). Psychiatrists Alexander Chess and Stella Thomas (Chess & Thomas, 1977; Thomas & Chess, 1991) followed a group of infants into adulthood and concluded that there are three basic types, or clusters, of temperament:

- An **easy child** is generally in a positive mood, quickly establishes regular routines, and adapts easily to new experiences.
- A **difficult child** reacts negatively to many situations and is slow to accept new experiences.
- A **slow-to-warm-up child** has a low activity level, is somewhat negative, and displays a low intensity of mood.

New classifications of temperament continue to be forged (Rothbart & Bates, 2006; Rothbart & Putnam, 2002; Wachs & Kohnstamm, 2001). In a review of temperament research, Mary Rothbart and John Bates (1998) concluded that the best framework for classifying temperament involves a revision of Chess and Thomas' categories of easy, difficult, and slow to warm up. The general classification of temperament now focuses more on the following:

- *Positive affect and approach.* This category is much like the personality trait of extraversion/introversion.
- *Negative affectivity.* This involves being easily distressed. Children with a temperament that involves negative affectivity may fret and cry often. Negative affectivity is closely related to the personality traits of introversion and neuroticism (emotional instability).
- *Effortful control (self-regulation).* This involves the ability to control one's emotions. Thus, adolescents who are high on effortful control show an ability to keep their arousal from getting too high and have strategies for soothing themselves. By contrast, adolescents who are low on effortful control often show an inability to control their arousal, and they become easily agitated and intensely emotional (Eisenberg & others, 2002).

**Developmental Connections and Contexts** How stable is temperament from childhood to adulthood? Do young adults show the same behavioral style and characteristic emotional responses that they did when they were infants or young children? For instance, activity level is an important dimension of temperament. Are children's activity levels linked to their personality in emerging and early adulthood? In one longitudinal study, children who were highly active at age 4 were likely to be very outgoing at age 23, which reflects continuity (Franz, 1996). Yet in other ways, temperament may change. From adolescence into early adulthood, most individuals show fewer emotional mood swings, become more responsible, and engage in less risk-taking behavior, reflecting discontinuity of temperament (Caspi, 1998).

Is temperament in childhood linked to adjustment in adolescence and adulthood? Here is what we know based on the few longitudinal studies that have been conducted on this topic (Caspi, 1998). A longitudinal study using Chess and Thomas' categories found a link between temperament assessed at 1 year of age and adjustment at 17 years of age (Guerin & others, 2003). Those with easier temperaments as infants showed more optimal development across behavioral and intellectual domains in late

**easy child** Generally is in a positive mood, quickly establishes regular routines, and adapts easily to new experiences.

**difficult child** Reacts negatively to many situations and is slow to accept new experiences.

**slow-to-warm-up child** Has a low activity level, is somewhat negative, and displays a low intensity of mood.

*What temperament categories have been used to describe adolescents?*

adolescence. The individuals with easier temperaments experienced a family environment that was more stimulating and cohesive and had more positive relationships with their parents during adolescence than their counterparts with more difficult temperaments. When the participants were characterized by a difficult temperament in combination with a family environment that was high in conflict, an increase in externalizing behavior problems (conduct problems, delinquency) occurred.

With regard to a link between temperament in childhood and adjustment in adulthood, in one longitudinal study, children who had an easy temperament at 3 to 5 years of age were likely to be well adjusted as young adults (Chess & Thomas, 1977). In contrast, many children who had a difficult temperament at 3 to 5 years of age were not well adjusted as young adults. Other researchers have found that boys who have a difficult temperament in childhood are less likely than others to continue their formal education as adults; girls with a difficult temperament in childhood are more likely to experience marital conflict as adults (Wachs, 2000).

In sum, across a number of longitudinal studies, an easy temperament in childhood is linked with more optimal development and adjustment in adolescence and adulthood. When the contexts in which individuals live are problematic, such as living in a family environment high in conflict, the long-term outcomes of having a difficult temperament are exacerbated.

Inhibition is another temperament characteristic that has been studied extensively (Kagan, 2002). Researchers have found that individuals with an inhibited temperament in childhood are less likely to be assertive or experience social support as adolescents and emerging adults, and more likely to delay entering a stable job track (Wachs, 2000).

Yet another aspect of temperament is emotionality and the ability to control one's emotions (Rothbart & Bates, 2006). In one longitudinal study, individuals who as 3-year-old children showed good control of their emotions and were resilient in the face of stress were likely to continue to handle their emotions effectively as adults (Block, 1993). In contrast, individuals who as 3-year-olds had low emotional control and were not very resilient were likely to show the same problems as young adults.

**Initial temperament trait: inhibition**

| | Child A | Child B |
|---|---|---|
| | **Intervening context** | |
| **Caregivers** | Caregivers (parents) who are sensitive and accepting, and let child set his or her own pace. | Caregivers who use inappropriate "low-level control" and attempt to force the child into new situations. |
| **Physical Environment** | Presence of "stimulus shelters" or "defensible spaces" that the children can retreat to when there is too much stimulation. | Child continually encounters noisy, chaotic environments that allow no escape from stimulation. |
| **Peers** | Peer groups with other inhibited children with common interests, so the child feels accepted. | Peer groups consist of athletic extraverts, so the child feels rejected. |
| **Schools** | School is "undermanned," so inhibited children are more likely to be tolerated and feel they can make a contribution. | School is "overmanned," so inhibited children are less likely to be tolerated and more likely to feel undervalued. |
| | **Personality outcomes** | |
| | As an adult, individual is closer to extraversion (outgoing, sociable) and is emotionally stable. | As an adult, individual is closer to introversion and has more emotional problems. |

**FIGURE 4.6 Temperament in Childhood, Personality in Adulthood, and Intervening Contexts** Varying experiences with caregivers, the physical environment, peers, and schools may modify links between temperament in childhood and personality in adulthood. The example given here is for inhibition.

In sum, these studies reveal some continuity between certain aspects of temperament in childhood and adjustment in early adulthood. Keep in mind, however, that these connections between childhood temperament and adult adjustment are based on only a small number of studies; more research is needed to verify the links. Indeed, Theodore Wachs (1994, 2000) has proposed ways that the links between childhood temperament and adult personality might vary, depending on the intervening contexts an individual experiences (see Figure 4.6).

The match between an individual's temperament and the environmental demands the individual must cope with, called **goodness of fit,** can be important to an adolescent's adjustment (Matheny & Phillips, 2001). In general, the temperament characteristics of effortful control, manageability, and agreeableness reduce the effects of adverse environments, whereas negative emotionality increases their effects (Rothbart & Bates, 2006).

**goodness of fit** The match between an individual's temperament style and the environmental demands the individual must cope with.

## REVIEW AND REFLECT ◆ LEARNING GOAL 4

### 4 Characterize the personality development of adolescents.

***Review***

- What are some key personality traits in adolescence? Is personality influenced by situations?
- What is temperament, and how is it linked to personality? What are some key temperament categories? What developmental connections and contexts characterize temperament?

***Reflect***

- Consider your own temperament. We described a number of different temperament categories. Which one best describes your temperament? Has your temperament changed as you have grown older, or is it about the same as when you were a child or an adolescent? If your temperament has changed, what factors contributed to the changes?

In this chapter, we examined many aspects of the self, identity, emotions, and personality. In our discussion of identity and emotion, we evaluated the role of gender. Chapter 5 is devoted exclusively to the topic of gender.

# REACH YOUR LEARNING GOALS

## 1 THE SELF *Describe the development of the self in adolescence.*

### Self-Understanding

Self-understanding is the adolescent's cognitive representation of the self, the substance and content of the adolescent's self-conceptions. Dimensions of the adolescent's self-understanding include abstract and idealistic; differentiated; contradictions within the self; real and ideal, true and false selves; social comparison; self-conscious; unconscious; and not yet being self-integrative. The increasing number of selves in adolescence can vary across relationships with people, social roles, and sociocultural contexts. In emerging adulthood, self-understanding become more integrative, reflective, more complex, and is characterized by deciding on a worldview. However, it is not until the thirties that a coherent and integrative worldview develops for many individuals.

### Self-Esteem and Self-Concept

Self-esteem is the global, evaluative dimension of the self, and also is referred to as self-worth, or self-image. Self-concept involves domain-specific self-evaluations. For too long, little attention was given to developing measures of self-esteem and self-concept specifically tailored to adolescents. Harter's Self-Perception Profile is one adolescent measure. Self-esteem reflects perceptions that do not always match reality. Thus, high self-esteem may be justified or it might reflect an arrogant, grandiose view of one's self that is not warranted. Controversy characterizes the extent to which self-esteem changes during adolescence and whether there are gender differences in self-esteem. Researchers have found that self-esteem often drops during and just after developmental transitions, such as going from elementary school to middle or junior high school. Some researchers have found that the self-esteem of girls declines in adolescence, especially during early adolescence, although other researchers argue that this decline has been exaggerated and actually is only modest in nature. Self-esteem is only moderately linked to school success. Adolescents with high self-esteem have greater initiative, but this can produce positive or negative outcomes. Perceived physical appearance is an especially strong contributor to global self-esteem. Peer acceptance also is linked to global self-esteem in adolescence. In Coopersmith's study, children's self-esteem was associated with such parenting practices as affection and allowing children freedom within well-prescribed limits. Peer and friendship relations also are linked with self-esteem. Self-esteem is higher in elementary school than in middle or junior high school. For most adolescents, low self-esteem results in only temporary emotional discomfort. However, for others, especially when low self-esteem persists, it is linked with depression, suicide, anorexia nervosa, and delinquency. Four ways to increase adolescents' self-esteem are to (1) identify the causes of low self-esteem and which domains of competence are important to the adolescent, (2) provide emotional support and social approval, (3) help the adolescent to achieve, and (4) improve the adolescent's coping skills.

## 2 IDENTITY *Explain the many facets of identity development.*

### Erikson's Ideas on Identity

Identity versus identity confusion is Erikson's fifth developmental stage, which individuals experience during adolescence. As adolescents are confronted with new roles, they enter a psychosocial moratorium. Personality and role experimentation are two key ingredients of Erikson's view. In technological societies like the United States, the vocational role is especially important. Identity development is extraordinarily complex and is done in bits and pieces.

**The Four Statuses of Identity**

Marcia proposed four identity statuses: diffused, foreclosed, moratorium, and achieved. A combination of crisis (exploration) and commitment yields one of the statuses. Some critics argue that Marcia's four identity statuses oversimplify identity development. Recently, emphasis has been given to expanding Marcia's concepts of exploration and commitment to focus more on in-depth exploration and ongoing evaluation of one's commitment.

**Developmental Changes in Identity**

Some experts argue that the main identity changes take place in late adolescence or youth, rather than in early adolescence. College upperclassmen are more likely to be identity achieved than are freshmen or high school students, although many college students are still wrestling with ideological commitments. Individuals often follow "*m*oratorium–*a*chievement–*m*oratorium–*a*chievement" cycles.

**Identity and Social Contexts**

Parents are important figures in adolescents' identity development. Researchers have found that democratic parenting, individuality, connectedness, and enabling behaviors are linked with positive aspects of identity. Erikson was especially sensitive to the role of culture in identity development, underscoring the fact that throughout the world ethnic minority groups have struggled to maintain their cultural identities while blending into majority culture. Adolescence is often a special juncture in the identity development of ethnic minority individuals because for the first time they consciously confront their ethnic identity. Many ethnic minority adolescents have a bicultural identity. Erikson noted that adolescent males have a stronger vocational identity, female adolescents a stronger social identity. However, researchers are finding that these gender differences are disappearing.

**Identity and Intimacy**

Intimacy versus isolation is Erikson's sixth stage of human development, which individuals experience during early adulthood. Erikson argued that an optimal sequence is to develop a positive identity before negotiating the intimacy versus isolation stage.

## 3 Emotional Development *Discuss the emotional development of adolescents.*

**The Emotions of Adolescence**

Emotion is feeling, or affect, that occurs when a person is in a state or an interaction that is important to the individual, especially to his or her well-being. Adolescents report more extreme and fleeting emotions than their parents, and as individuals go through early adolescence they are less likely to report being very happy. However, it is important to view moodiness as a normal aspect of early adolescence.

**Hormones, Experience, and Emotions**

Although pubertal change is associated with an increase in negative emotions, hormonal influences are often small, and environmental experiences may contribute more to the emotions of adolescence than hormonal changes.

**Emotional Competence**

Adolescents' increased cognitive abilities and awareness provide them with the opportunity to cope more effectively with stress and emotional fluctuations. However, the emotional burdens of adolescence can be overwhelming for some adolescents. Among the emotional competencies that are important for adolescents to develop are being aware that the expression of emotions plays a major role in relationships, adaptively coping with negative emotions by using self-regulatory strategies, understanding how emotionally expressive behavior influences others, being aware of one's emotional states without being overwhelmed by them, and being able to discern others' emotions.

## 4 PERSONALITY DEVELOPMENT *Characterize the personality development of adolescents.*

**Personality**

There has been a long history of interest in discovering the core traits of personality, and recently that search has focused on the big five factors of personality: openness to experience, conscientiousness, extraversion, agreeableness, and neuroticism (emotional stability). Much of the research on the big five factors has focused on adults, but an increasing number of these studies focus on adolescents. Researchers continue to debate what the core characteristics of personality are. Critics of the trait approach argue that it places too much emphasis on stability and not enough on change and situational influences. Today, many psychologists stress that personality is best described in terms of both traits and situational influences.

**Temperament**

Many psychologists emphasize that temperament forms the foundation for personality. Chess and Thomas described three basic types of temperament: easy child, difficult child, and slow-to-warm-up child. New classifications of temperament include positive affect and approach, negative affectivity, and effortful control (self-regulation). Connections between the temperament of individuals from childhood to adulthood have been found, although these links may vary according to the contexts of people's lives. Goodness of fit refers to the match between an individual's temperament and the environmental demands of individuals.

## KEY TERMS



## KEY PEOPLE

# RESOURCES FOR IMPROVING THE LIVES OF ADOLESCENTS

**The Development of Self-Representations in Childhood and Adolescence**
by Susan Harter
in W. Damon and R. Lerner (Eds.), *Handbook of Child Psychology* (2006, 6th ed.).
New York: Wiley

Leading self theorist and researcher, Susan Harter provides an in-depth analysis of how the self develops in childhood and adolescence.

**Emotional Development**
by Carolyn Saarni, Joseph Campos, Linda Camras, and David Witherspoon
in W. Damon and R. Lerner (Eds.), *Handbook of Child Psychology* (2006, 6th ed.)
New York: Wiley

Read about up-to-date research and views on how emotions develop in children and adolescents.

**Gandhi's Truth**
by Erik Erikson (1969)
New York: W.W. Norton

This Pulitzer Prize–winning book by Erik Erikson, who developed the concept of identity as a central aspect of adolescent development, analyzes the life of Mahatma Gandhi, the spiritual leader of India in the middle of the twentieth century.

**Identity Development: Adolescence Through Adulthood**
by Jane Kroger (2007, 2nd ed.)
Thousand Oaks, CA: Sage

Leading expert Jane Kroger provides a contemporary analysis of identity development research.

**Personality Development**
by Avshalom Caspi and Rebecca Shiner
in W. Damon and R. Lerner (Eds.), *Handbook of Child Psychology* (2006, 6th ed.)
New York: Wiley

Leading experts describe recent research on how personality develops.

# E-LEARNING TOOLS

To help you master the material in this chapter, visit the Online Learning Center for *Adolescence*, twelfth edition **(www.mhhe.com/santrocka12)**, where you will find these additional resources:

## Taking It to the Net

1. Your roommate returns from the computer lab and announces he took a self-esteem test on the Web and scored really high. Knowing something about test reliability and validity, you are really skeptical about such tests. What will you advise your roommate about the reliability and validity of online self-esteem tests?
2. Your sister returns home from her first few weeks at college and seems to be not as confident and self-assured as she was when she left. She complains about her friends at school tugging her in different directions, about feeling awkward in various social situations, and of having lost control of her attention and concentration. Do you think this might be due to her undergoing a change in identity, or is it something else? Why do you think that?
3. Developing emotional competence in adolescence is a crucial part of emotional development. It typically develops with age, but low levels of emotional competence can

leave adolescents vulnerable to a variety of negative experiences. Can emotional competence be taught? If so, how? If not, why not?

## Self-Assessment

The Online Learning Center includes the following self-assessments for further exploration:

- My Self-Esteem
- Exploring My Identity
- Am I Extraverted or Introverted?

## Health and Well-Being, Parenting, and Education

To practice your decision-making skills, complete the health and well-being, parenting, and education exercises on the Online Learning Center.

## Video Clips

The Online Learning Center includes the following videos for this chapter:

- Adolescent Self-Concept at Age 16
- Adolescent Self-Esteem
- Defining Ethnic Identity
- Ethnic and Racial Identity in Adolescence
- Talking About Ethnic Identity in Adolescence
- Adolescent Loneliness
- Adolescent and Parent Emotions

# 6 Sexuality

*If we listen to boys and girls at the very moment they seem most pimply, awkward, and disagreeable, we can penetrate a mystery most of us once felt heavily within us, and have not forgotten. This mystery is the very process of creation of man and woman.*

—Colin McInnes
Contemporary Scottish Author

## CHAPTER OUTLINE

## LEARNING GOALS

### Exploring Adolescent Sexuality

1 Discuss some basic ideas about the nature of adolescent sexuality.

A Normal Aspect of Adolescent Development
The Sexual Culture
Developing a Sexual Identity
Obtaining Research Information About Adolescent Sexuality

### Sexual Attitudes and Behavior

2 Summarize sexual attitudes and behavior in adolescence.

Heterosexual Attitudes and Behavior
Sexual Minority Attitudes and Behavior
Self-Stimulation
Contraceptive Use

### Adolescent Sexual Problems

3 Describe the main sexual problems that can emerge in adolescence.

Adolescent Pregnancy
Sexually Transmitted Infections
Forcible Sexual Behavior and Sexual Harassment

### Sexual Literacy and Sex Education

4 Characterize the sexual literacy of adolescents and sex education.

Sexual Literacy
Sources of Sex Information
Sex Education in Schools

# Images of Adolescent Development

## The Mysteries and Curiosities of Adolescent Sexuality

I guess when you give a girl a sexy kiss you're supposed to open your lips and put your tongue in her mouth. That doesn't seem very sexy to me. I can't imagine how a girl would like that. What if she has braces on her teeth and your tongue gets scratched? And how are you supposed to breathe? Sometimes I wish I had an older brother I could ask stuff like this.

—Frank, age 12

I can't believe I'm so much in love! I just met him last week, but I know this is the real thing. He is much more mature than the boys who have liked me before. He's a senior and has his own car. When he brought me home last night, we got so hot I thought we were going to have sex. I'm sure it will happen the next time we go out. It goes against everything I've been taught—but I can't see how it can be wrong when I'm so much in love and he makes me feel so fantastic!

—Amy, age 15

Ken and I went on a camping trip last weekend, and now I'm sure that I'm gay. For a long time I've known I've been attracted to other guys, like in the locker room at school it would sometimes be embarrassing. Ken and I are great friends, and lots of times we would mess around wrestling or whatever. I guessed that he felt the way I did. Now I know. Sooner or later, I'll have to come out, as they say, but I know that is going to cause a lot of tension with my parents and for me.

—Tom, age 15

I'm lucky because I have a good figure and I'm popular. I've had boyfriends since middle school, and I know how to take care of myself. It's fun when you're out with a guy and you can be intimate. The only thing is, Dan and I had sex a few weeks ago and I'm wondering if I'm pregnant. He used a contraceptive, but maybe it didn't work. Or maybe I'm just late. Anyway, if I have a baby, I could deal with it. My aunt wasn't married when she got pregnant with my cousin, and it turned out okay.

—Claire, age 16

About a month ago my mom's friend's daughter tested positive for HIV. Until then my mom and stepfather never talked about sex with me, but now they're taking turns lecturing me on the theme of "don't have sex until you're married." Give me a break! Nicole and I have been together for a year and a half. What do they think we do when we go out, play tiddlywinks? Besides, my real father never remarried and has girlfriends all the time. All my life I've been seeing movies and TV shows where unmarried people sleep together, and the worst that happens is maybe a broken heart. I don't know that woman's daughter, but she must have been mixed up with some pretty bad characters. Me, I always use a condom.

—Sean, age 17

## PREVIEW

***During adolescence and emerging adulthood, the lives of adolescents are wrapped in sexuality. Adolescence and emerging adulthood are time frames when individuals engage in sexual exploration and incorporate sexuality into their identity. In Chapter 2, we studied the biological basis of sexual maturation, including the timing of these changes and the hormones involved. This chapter focuses on the sexual experiences, attitudes, and behaviors of adolescents and emerging adults. We begin with an overview of sexuality in adolescence and emerging adulthood and then examine some problems involving sexual activity, such as adolescent pregnancy, sexually transmitted infections, and forcible sex. Next, we explore the ways in which adolescents learn about sex.***

# 1 Exploring Adolescent Sexuality

- A Normal Aspect of Adolescent Development
- Developing a Sexual Identity
- The Sexual Culture
- Obtaining Research Information About Adolescent Sexuality

Adolescents have an almost insatiable curiosity about the mysteries of sex. They wonder whether they are sexually attractive, how to behave sexually, and what the future holds for their sexual lives. Most adolescents eventually manage to develop a mature sexual identity, even though, as adults can attest, there are always times of vulnerability and confusion along life's sexual journey.

## A Normal Aspect of Adolescent Development

Much of what we hear about adolescent sexuality involves problems, such as adolescent pregnancy and sexually transmitted infections. Although these are significant concerns, it is important not to lose sight of the fact that sexuality is a normal part of adolescence (Diamond, 2006; Nichols & Good, 2004).

An important theme of adolescence that we have underscored in this book is that too often adolescents are negatively stereotyped (Benson & others, 2006). The themes of negative stereotyping and adolescent problems also apply to the topic of adolescent sexuality. Although we discuss a number of problems that can occur in the area of adolescent sexuality, we must keep in mind that the majority of adolescents have healthy sexual attitudes and engage in sexual behaviors that will not compromise their journey to adulthood (Crockett, Raffaelli, & Moilanen, 2003).

Every society pays some attention to adolescent sexuality (Feldman, 1999). In some societies, adults chaperone adolescent females to protect them from males; others promote very early marriage. Still other societies, such as the United States, allow some sexual experimentation, although there is a wide range of opinions about just how far this experimentation should be allowed to go.

Chapters 2, 3, 4, and 5 introduced topics that are a backdrop for understanding sexual attitudes and behavior in adolescence. In Chapter 2, we saw that an important aspect of pubertal change involves sexual maturation and a dramatic increase in androgens in males and estrogens in females. Puberty is coming earlier today than in previous generations, which can lead to early dating and early sexual activity.

In Chapter 3, we indicated that young adolescents tend to exhibit a form of egocentrism in which they perceive themselves as unique and invulnerable. This can lead them to take sexual risks. In emotional moments like those involved in sexual experimentation, adolescents' sexual urges can overwhelm their ability to make competent decisions.

In Chapter 4, we described sexual identity as one of the dimensions of personal identity (Russell & Truong, 2002). Intimacy with another is an important aspect of the dyadic nature of adolescent sexuality.

In Chapter 5, we examined the physical and biological differences between females and males. We also saw that according to the gender intensification hypothesis, pubertal changes can lead boys and girls to conform to traditional masculine and feminine behavior, respectively (Basow, 2006). Further, when college students are asked to rate the strength of their sex drive, men report higher levels of sexual desire than women. The adolescent developmental transition, then, may be seen as

*Sexual arousal emerges as a new phenomenon in adolescence and it is important to view sexuality as a normal aspect of adolescent development.*

—Shirley Feldman
*Contemporary Psychologist, Stanford University*

a bridge between the asexuality of childhood and the fully developed sexual identity of adulthood.

Chapters 8, 9, 10, and 12 also include discussions that are important for understanding adolescent sexuality. In Chapter 8, we learn that intense, prolonged conflict with parents is associated with adolescent sexual problems as is a lack of parental monitoring. Better relationships with parents are correlated with postponing sexual intercourse, less frequent intercourse, and fewer partners in adolescence (Miller, Benson, & Galbraith, 2001). Later in this chapter, we see that adolescents receive very little sex education from parents and that parents and adolescents rarely discuss sex.

In Chapter 9, we read about how same-sex siblings, peers, and friends often discuss sexuality (Caruthers & Ward, 2002). We also learn that early dating is associated with a number of adolescent problems and that romantic love is important (especially for girls) in adolescence (Marin & others, 2006).

In Chapter 10, we study how schools are playing an increasingly important role in adolescent sexuality. And as we see later in this chapter, most parents now recognize that sex education in schools is an important aspect of education.

In Chapter 12, we describe the vast cultural variations in sexuality. In some cultures sexuality is highly repressed; other cultures have far more liberal standards for sexuality.

As you can see, sexuality has ties to virtually all areas of adolescent development that we discuss in this book. Let's now explore the sexual culture American adolescents are exposed to.

## The Sexual Culture

It is important to put adolescent sexuality into the broader context of sexuality in the American culture (McCammon, Knox, & Schacht, 2007; Wiseman, Sunday, & Becker, 2005). Whereas 50 years ago sex was reserved for married couples, today adult sex is openly acknowledged among both married and single adults. Sex among unmarried teenagers is an extension of this general trend toward greater sexual permissiveness in the adult culture.

Sex is virtually everywhere in the American culture and is used to sell just about everything. *Is it surprising, then, that adolescents are so curious about sex and tempted to experiment with sex?*

A special concern is the way sex is portrayed in the media. Consider the following recent portrayal:

> The messages conveyed about sexuality (in the media) are not always ideal . . . and they are often limited, unrealistic, and stereotypical. Dominating is a recreational orientation to sexuality in which courtship is treated as a competition, a battle of the sexes, characterized by dishonesty, gay playing, and manipulation. . . . Also prominent are stereotypical sexual roles featuring women as sexual objects, whose value is based solely on their physical appearance, and men as sex-driven players looking to 'score' at all costs. . . . (Ward, Day, & Epstein, 2006, p. 57)

Sex is explicitly portrayed in movies, TV shows, videos, lyrics of popular music, MTV, and Internet Web sites (Collins, 2005; Comstock & Scharrer, 2006; Ward & Friedman, 2006; Ward, Hansbrough, & Walker, 2005). A study of 1,762 12- to 17-year-olds found that those who watched more sexually explicit TV shows were more likely than their counterparts who watched these shows less to initiate sexual intercourse in the next 12 months (Collins & others, 2004). Adolescents in the highest 10 percent of viewing sexually explicit TV shows were twice as likely to engage in sexual intercourse as those in the lowest 10 percent. The results held regardless of whether the exposure to explicit sex involved sexual behavior or just talk about sex. In another study, U.S. high school students who frequently viewed talk shows and "sexy" prime-time programs were more likely to endorse sexual stereotypes than their counterparts who viewed these shows infrequently (Ward & Friedman, 2006). Also in this study, more frequent viewing and stronger identification with popular TV characters were linked with greater levels of sexual experience in adolescents. We further explore media influences on adolescent sexuality in Chapter 12, "Culture."

## Developing a Sexual Identity

Mastering emerging sexual feelings and forming a sense of sexual identity is multifaceted (Brown & Brown, 2006; Carroll, 2007; Graber & Brooks-Gunn, 2002). This lengthy process involves learning to manage sexual feelings, such as sexual arousal and attraction, developing new forms of intimacy, and learning the skills to regulate sexual behavior to avoid undesirable consequences. Developing a sexual identity also involves more than just sexual behavior. Sexual identities emerge in the context of physical factors, social factors, and cultural factors, with most societies placing constraints on the sexual behavior of adolescents.

*We are born twice over; the first time for existence, the second for life; Once as human beings and later as men or as women.*

—JEAN-JACQUES ROUSSEAU
*Swiss-Born French Philosopher, 18th Century*

An adolescent's sexual identity involves an indication of sexual orientation (whether an individual has same-sex or other-sex attractions), and it also involves activities, interests, and styles of behavior. A study of 470 tenth- to twelfth-grade Australian youth found considerable variation in their sexual attitudes and practices (Buzwell & Rosenthal, 1996). Some were virgins and sexually naive. Some had high anxiety about sex and perceived their bodies as underdeveloped and unappealing, whereas others had low anxiety about sex and an interest in exploring sexual options. Yet others felt sexually attractive, were sexually experienced, and had confidence in their ability to manage sexual situations.

## Obtaining Research Information About Adolescent Sexuality

Assessing sexual attitudes and behavior is not always a straightforward affair. Consider how you would respond if someone asked you, "How often do you have intercourse?" or "How many different sexual partners have you had?" The people most likely to respond to sexual surveys are those with liberal sexual attitudes who engage in liberal sexual behaviors. Thus, research is limited by the reluctance of some individuals to answer questions about extremely personal matters candidly, and by researchers' inability to get any answer, candid or otherwise, from individuals who simply refuse to talk to strangers about sex (Halonen & Santrock, 1999). In addition, when asked about their sexual activity, individuals may respond truthfully or they may give socially desirable answers. For example, a ninth-grade boy might report that he has had sexual intercourse, even if he has not, because he is afraid someone will find out that he is sexually inexperienced.

Researchers have been developing methods to increase the validity of sexual self-report information. In one study, each adolescent spoke individually with a same-sex interviewer who asked questions of increasing sexual involvement until the respondent reported that he or she had not engaged in a behavior, at which point the interview was ended (Paikoff & others, 1997). This strategy might be preferable to a checklist, which can lead to over- or underreporting and embarrassment. Some researchers also have presented adolescents with audiotaped questions to reduce any embarrassment about reporting sexual behaviors to an interviewer.

**REVIEW AND REFLECT ◆ LEARNING GOAL 1**

**1 Discuss some basic ideas about the nature of adolescent sexuality.**

***Review***
- How can adolescence be explained as a normal aspect of adolescent development?
- What is the sexual culture of the United States like that adolescents are exposed to?
- What is involved in developing a sexual identity in adolescence?
- What are some difficulties in obtaining research information about adolescent sexuality?

***Reflect***
- What was your exposure to sex in the media during adolescence? Do you think it influenced your sexual behavior? If so, how?

# 2 SEXUAL ATTITUDES AND BEHAVIOR

- Heterosexual Attitudes and Behavior
- Sexual Minority Attitudes and Behavior
- Self-Stimulation
- Contraceptive Use

Let's now explore adolescents' sexual attitudes and behavior. First, we study heterosexual attitudes and behavior, and then sexual minority attitudes and behavior.

## Heterosexual Attitudes and Behavior

What is the progression of adolescent sexual behaviors, and how extensively did heterosexual attitudes and behaviors change in the twentieth century? What sexual scripts do adolescents follow? Are some adolescents more vulnerable than others to irresponsible sexual behavior? We examine each of these questions.

**Sequence and Change** In what sequence do adolescents engage in various sexual behaviors? In one study, 452 18- to 25-year-olds were asked about their own past sexual experiences (Feldman, Turner, & Araujo, 1999). The following progression of sexual behaviors occurred: kissing preceded petting, which preceded sexual intercourse and oral sex. However, in the twenty-first century, adolescents are increasingly engaging in oral sex earlier in the progression (National Center for Health Statistics, 2002).

Had you been a college student in 1940, you probably would have had a different attitude about many aspects of sexuality than you do today. A review of college students' sexual practices in the twentieth century reveals two important trends (Darling, Kallen, & VanDusen, 1984). First, the percentage of youth who said they had sexual intercourse increased dramatically. Second, the proportion of female college students who reported that they had sexual intercourse increased more rapidly than that of males, although the initial base for males was greater.

What is the current profile of sexual activity of adolescents? Based on a national survey of adolescents, sexual intercourse is uncommon in early adolescence but becomes more common in the high school and college years (see Figure 6.1) (Alan Guttmacher Institute, 1995, 1998; Centers for Disease Control and Prevention, 2000). These are some of the findings:

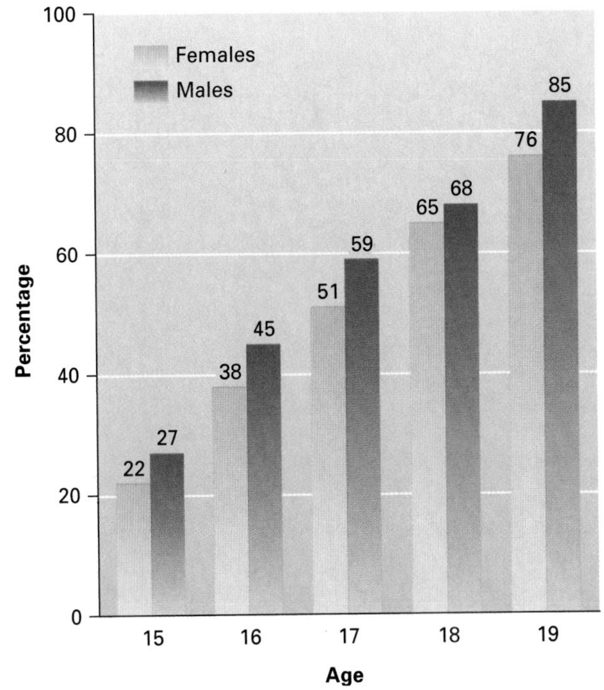


**FIGURE 6.1** **Percentage of Youth Who Say They Have Had Sexual Intercourse at Various Ages**

- Eight in ten girls and seven in ten boys are virgins at age 15.
- The probability that adolescents will have sexual intercourse increases steadily with age, but one in five individuals has not yet had sexual intercourse by age 19.
- Initial sexual intercourse occurs in the mid- to late-adolescent years for a majority of teenagers, about eight years before they marry; more than one-half of 17-year-olds have had sexual intercourse.

More recent data collected in 2005 in a national U.S. survey found similar developmental trends, with 63 percent of twelfth-graders reporting that they had experienced sexual intercourse compared with 34 percent of ninth-graders (MMWR, 2006).

Researchers are finding that adolescents are waiting until they are older to have sexual intercourse. For example, a national survey of U.S. ninth- to twelfth-graders revealed a linear decrease from 1991 (54.1 percent) to 2005 (46.8 percent) in the percentage who had ever had sexual intercourse and who were currently active (37.5 percent in 1991, 33.9 percent in 2005) (MMWR, 2006). Another study of more than 30,000 15- to 17-year-old girls found a decrease from 51 percent in 1991 to 43 percent in 2001 in ever having had sexual intercourse (Santelli & others, 2004a). The decrease for non-Latino White girls went from 47 to 41 percent and for African American girls from 75 to 54 percent. The percentage for Latino 15- to 17-year-old girls remained the same from 1991 to 2001: 45 percent.

*How is it that, in the human body, reproduction is the only function to be performed by an organ of which an individual carries only one half so that he has to spend an enormous amount of time and energy to find another half?*

—FRANÇOIS JACOB
*French Biologist, 20th Century*

Most studies find that adolescent males are more likely than adolescent females to say that they have had sexual intercourse and are sexually active (Feldman, Turner, & Araujo, 1999; MMWR, 2006). Adolescent males are also more likely than their female counterparts to describe sexual intercourse as an enjoyable experience. And African Americans are more likely to engage in sexual behaviors earlier than other ethnic groups, whereas Asian Americans are more likely to engage in them later (Feldman, Turner, & Araujo, 1999) (see Figure 6.2). In the recent national U.S. survey of ninth- to twelfth-graders, 67 percent of African Americans, 51 percent of Latinos, and 43 percent of non-Latino Whites said they had ever experienced sexual intercourse (MMWR, 2006). In this study, 16 percent of African Americans (compared with 7 percent of Latinos

| Sexual timetable | White | African American | Latino | Asian American |
|---|---|---|---|---|
| Kiss | 14.3 | 13.9 | 14.5 | 15.7 |
| French kiss | 15.0 | 14.0 | 15.3 | 16.2 |
| Touch breast | 15.6 | 14.5 | 15.5 | 16.9 |
| Touch penis | 16.1 | 15.0 | 16.2 | 17.8 |
| Touch vagina | 16.1 | 14.6 | 15.9 | 17.1 |
| Sexual intercourse | 16.9 | 15.5 | 16.5 | 18.0 |
| Oral sex | 17.1 | 16.9 | 17.1 | 18.3 |

**FIGURE 6.2** **Sexual Timetables of White, African American, Latino, and Asian American Adolescents** *Note:* These data were reported in 1999. In the twenty-first century, adolescents are reporting that they engage in oral sex earlier in the sexual timetable.

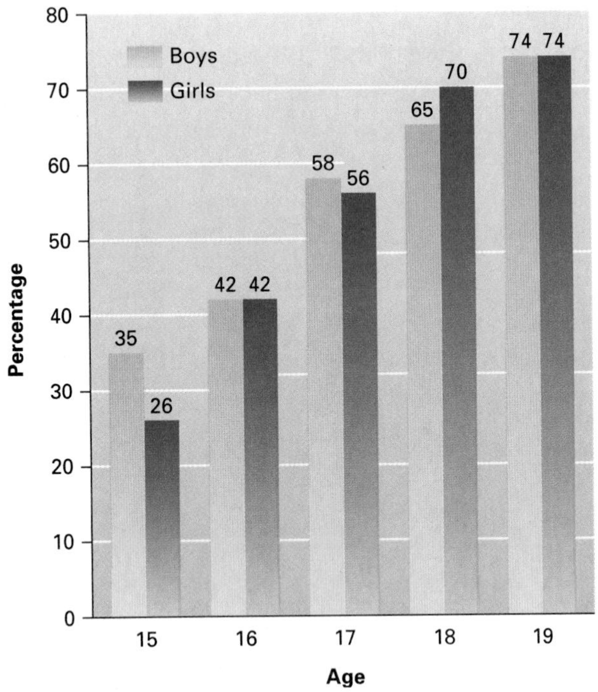


**FIGURE 6.3** **Percentage of U.S. 15- to 19-Year-Old Boys and Girls Who Report Engaging in Oral Sex**

*What are some trends in the sexual behavior of adolescents?*

and 4 percent of non-Latino Whites) said they had their first sexual experience before 13 years of age. It is important to keep in mind that in studies of adolescent sexuality, ethnic variations in sexual activity often disappear or are diminished when socioeconomic status is controlled for.

**Oral Sex** Recent research indicates that oral sex is now a common occurrence in U.S. adolescents (Bersamin & Walker, 2006). In a national survey, 55 percent of U.S. 15- to 19-year-old boys and 54 percent of girls said they had engaged in oral sex (National Center for Health Statistics, 2002). Figure 6.3 shows the developmental trends in oral sex from 15 to 19 years old for boys and girls. Noteworthy is that in this survey, a slightly higher percentage of 15- to 19-year-olds (55 percent of boys, 54 percent of girls) said they had engaged in oral sex than had engaged in sexual intercourse (49 percent of girls, 53 percent of boys). Also in the survey, more than 20 percent of the adolescents who had not had sexual intercourse had engaged in oral sex.

A recent study found that adolescents who engaged in oral sex were older, had engaged in heavy drinking in the past month, perceived their peers to be sexually active, and thought their friends would approve of their sexual activity more than adolescents who had not engaged in oral sex (Bersamin & Walker, 2006). Also in this study, adolescents who had participated in oral sex indicated they were less connected to their school and had a lower level of religiosity than their counterparts who had not engaged in oral sex. Similar findings were found for adolescents who had experienced sexual intercourse compared with those who had not.

What is especially worrisome about the increase in oral sex during adolescence is how casually many engage in the practice. It appears that for many adolescents oral sex is a recreational activity practiced outside of an intimate, caring relationship (Walsh & Bennett, 2004). One reason for the increase in oral sex during adolescence is the belief that oral sex is not really sex. Thus, according to this belief, those who engage in oral sex but not sexual intercourse consider themselves virgins. Another reason for the increase is the perception that oral sex is likely to be safer, and less likely to result in sexually transmitted infections than sexual intercourse. Thus, many adolescents appear to be unaware of the health risks linked to oral sex, and the possibility of contracting such infections.

**Early Maturation** Early maturation is also linked with early initiation of sexual activity. One study found that early maturation was related to early sexual activity in non-Latino White and Latino girls (Cavanaugh, 2004). In this study, these early-maturing girls had more older friends, although the nature of the older friendship varied by ethnic group. Non-Latino White early-maturing girls were more likely to have older friends who engaged in problem behavior than their late-maturing counterparts, whereas the Latino early-maturing girls were more likely to have older boys in their friendship circle than their late-maturing counterparts.

Though sexual intercourse can be a meaningful experience for older, mature adolescents, many adolescents are not emotionally prepared to handle sexual experiences, especially in early adolescence. In one study, early sexual activity was associated with adjustment problems (Bingham & Crockett, 1996).

**Cross-Cultural Comparisons** The timing of teenage sexual initiation varies widely by culture and gender, and in most instances is linked to the culture's values and customs. In one study, among females, the proportion having first intercourse by age 17 ranged from 72 percent in Mali to 47 percent in the United States, and 45 percent in Tanzania (Singh & others, 2000). The proportion of males who had their first intercourse by age 17 ranged from 76 percent in Jamaica to 64 percent in the United States and 63 percent in Brazil. Not all countries were represented in this study, and it is generally agreed that in some Asian countries, such as China and Japan, first intercourse occurs much later than in the United States.

Sexual activity patterns for 15- to 19-year-olds follow very different patterns for males and females in almost every geographic region of the world (Singh & others, 2000). In developing countries, the vast majority of sexually experienced males in this age group are unmarried, whereas two-thirds or more of the sexually experienced females at these ages are married. However, in the United States and in other developed nations such as the Netherlands, Sweden, and Australia, the overwhelming majority of 15- to 19-year-old females are unmarried.

## Through the Eyes of Adolescents

### STRUGGLING WITH A SEXUAL DECISION

Elizabeth is an adolescent girl who is reflecting on her struggle with whether to have sex with a guy she is in love with. She says it is not a question of whether she loves him or not. She does love him, but she still doesn't know if it is right or wrong to have sex with him. He wants her to have sex, but she knows her parents don't. With her friends, some say yes, others say no. So Elizabeth is confused. After a few days of contemplation, in a moment of honesty, she admits that she is not his special love. This finally tilts the answer to not having sex with him. She realizes that if the relationship falls through, she will look back and regret it if she does have sex. In the end, Elizabeth decides not to have sex with him.

Elizabeth's reflections reveal her struggle to understand what is right and what is wrong, whether to have sex or not. In her circumstance, the fact that in a moment of honesty she admitted that she was not his special love made a big difference in her decision.

**Sexual Scripts** As adolescents explore their sexual identities, they are guided by sexual scripts. A **sexual script** is a stereotyped pattern of role prescriptions for how individuals should behave sexually. By the time individuals reach adolescence, females and males have been socialized to follow different sexual scripts. Differences in female and male sexual scripting can cause problems and confusions for adolescents as they work out their sexual identities. Female adolescents learn to link sexual intercourse with love (Michael & others, 1994). They often rationalize their sexual behavior by telling themselves that they were swept away by the passion of the moment. A number of studies have found that adolescent females are more likely than their male counterparts to report being in love as the main reason they are sexually active (Hyde & DeLamater, 2006). Other reasons that females give for being sexually active include giving in to male pressure, gambling that sex is a way to get a boyfriend, curiosity, and sexual desire unrelated to loving and caring.

The majority of adolescent sexual experiences involve the male making sexual advances, and it is up to the female to set the limits on the male's sexual overtures (Goodchilds & Zellman, 1984). Adolescent boys experience considerable peer pressure to have sexual intercourse. As one adolescent remarked, "I feel a lot of pressure from my buddies to go for the score." I myself vividly remember the raunchy conversation that filled our basketball locker room when I was in junior high school. By the end of the ninth grade, I was sure that I was the only virgin left on the 15-member team, but I wasn't about to acknowledge that to my teammates.

In one study, adolescent boys reported they expect sex and put pressure on girls to have sex with them, but said that they do not force girls to have sex (Crump & others, 1996). And in a national survey, 12- to 18-year-olds said the following are "often a reason" teenagers have sex (Kaiser Family Foundation, 1996):

- A boy or girl is pressuring them (61 percent of girls, 23 percent of boys).
- They think they are ready (59 percent of boys, 51 percent of girls).
- They want to be loved (45 percent of girls, 28 percent of boys).
- They don't want people to tease them for being a virgin (43 percent of boys, 38 percent of girls).

Deborah Tolman (2002) interviewed a number of girls about their sexuality and was struck by how extensively a double standard still restricts girls from experiencing and talking about sexuality but allows boys more free rein on their sexuality. In movies, magazines, and music, girls are often depicted as the object of someone else's desire but rarely as someone who has acceptable sexual feelings of their own. Tolman says that girls face a difficult challenge related to their sexual selves: to be the perfect sexual object, they are supposed to be sexy but control their desire.

**sexual script** A stereotyped pattern of role prescriptions for how individuals should sexually behave. Females and males have been socialized to follow different sexual scripts.

## Through the Eyes of Emerging Adults

### CHRISTINE'S THOUGHTS ABOUT SEXUAL RELATIONSHIPS

As a college freshman, Christine tried to suppress the sexual feelings she had in her romantic relationship and later decided it was best to lose her virginity to a friend rather than a boyfriend:

> I think the first time you have sex should be with a friend, not necessarily with a boyfriend, because there's too many emotions involved. And with a friend, there's that closeness there but there's not those deep running feelings that could really (mess) you up if the relationship doesn't work out.

Christine also made these comments:

> I won't really enjoy (*sex*) until after college . . . because in college, everything's so helter-skelter. You don't know what you're going to do the next day or the day after that. And after college, you're probably going to get into a routine of going to work, coming back home, feeding your dog, feeding your boyfriend, you know? It's going to feel like you have more of a stable life with this person, and think that they're going to be more intimate. And with that, you're probably going to have better sex.

(*Source:* Gilmartin, 2006, pp. 444, 447)

A recent in-depth study that involved extensive, periodic interviews with 14 women in their freshman and sophomore years of college revealed that most of them desired emotional closeness and sexual intimacy but that opportunities to find this became more elusive in their sophomore than their freshman years (Gilmartin, 2006). Their sexual experiences changed from long-distance boyfriends or no boyfriends in the first year to break-ups and hook-ups (a catch-all term meaning anything from making out to engaging in sexual intercourse) in the second year.

Another recent study of 626 never-married, heterosexual college women found that those who frequently set personal goals had more conservative sexual attitudes, were more comfortable with their sexuality, and were more psychologically satisfied sexually than their female counterparts who infrequently set personal goals (Moore & Davidson, 2006). The college females who infrequently set personal goals were more likely to drink alcohol prior to sexual intercourse, become more intoxicated, and be less likely to ask new sexual partners if they had sexually transmitted infections. Thus, goal setting was linked to more responsible sexual decision making in these college women.

**Risk Factors, Youth Assets, and Sexual Problems** Most adolescents become sexually active at some point during adolescence, but many adolescents are at risk for sexual problems and other problems when they have sexual intercourse before 16 years of age (Buston, Williamson, & Hart, 2007). Adolescents who have sex before they are 16 years old are often ineffective users of contraceptives, which puts them at risk for adolescent pregnancy and sexually transmitted infections. One study found that use of alcohol and other drugs, as well as low academic achievement, were linked with the initiation of sexual intercourse in early adolescence (Santelli & others, 2004b).

In one longitudinal study, sexual involvement by girls in early adolescence was linked with lower self-esteem, more depression, more sexual activity, and lower grades in the high school years (Buhrmester, 2001). For boys, early sexual involvement was related to more substance abuse and sexual activity in the high school years. In another longitudinal study from 10 to 12 years of age to 25 years of age, early sexual intercourse and affiliation with deviant peers were linked to substance use disorders in emerging adulthood (Cornelius & others, 2007). Also, a recent study found that boys who had a girlfriend by the seventh grade were more likely than their male counterparts who did not have a girlfriend to be sexually active in the ninth grade (Marin & others, 2006).

Risk factors for sexual problems in adolescence include contextual factors such as socioeconomic status (SES), as well as family/parenting and peer factors (Aronowitz, Rennells, & Todd, 2006; Swenson & Prelow, 2005). The percentages of sexually active young adolescents may vary with location, being higher in low-income areas of inner cities (Silver & Bauman, 2006). In one review, living in a dangerous and/or a low-income neighborhood were at-risk factors for adolescent pregnancy (Miller, Benson, & Galbraith, 2001). Also in this review, these aspects of parenting were linked with reduced risk of adolescent pregnancy: parent/adolescent closeness or connectedness, parental supervision or regulation of adolescents' activities, and parental values against intercourse or unprotected intercourse in adolescence (Miller, Benson, & Galbraith, 2001). For example, a recent study indicated that low parental monitoring was linked with early initiation of sexual activity by adolescents, more sexual partners, and less likelihood of condom use (Wight, Williamson, & Henderson, 2006). Other researchers have found that an attachment style in which adolescents and parents avoid each other is associated with early sexual activity (Williams & Schmidt, 2003). A recent research review revealed that the amount of time adolescents reported being home alone with the opposite sex (or being home without a parent) and perceiving that peers have had sex were related to early initiation of sexual intercourse (Buhi & Goodson, 2007). Further, having older sexually active siblings or pregnant/parenting teenage sisters places adolescents at an elevated risk of adolescent pregnancy (Miller, Benson, & Galbraith, 2001).

Another important factor in sexual risk taking is *self-regulation*—the ability to control one's emotions and behavior (Lombardo, 2005). A recent longitudinal study found that weak self-regulation at 8 to 9 years of age and risk proneness (tendency to seek sensation and make poor decisions) at 12 to 13 years of age set the stage for sexual risk taking at 16 to 17 years of age (Crockett, Raffaelli, & Shen, 2006). Also, in this study, substance abuse and negative peer pressure tended to also reflect risk proneness and poor self-regulation along the developmental pathway to risky sexual behavior.

One study examined the potential protective influence of youth assets on sexual risk-taking behavior in adolescence (Vesely & others, 2004). In-home interviews were conducted with 1,253 inner-city African American adolescents (average age, 15 years) and their parents. Adolescents who had not yet had sexual intercourse were more likely than those who had to have positive nonparental adult role models and peer role models, be involved in religion, and have positive future aspirations.

**Further Exploration of Heterosexual Attitudes and Behavior in Emerging Adults** We already have covered some aspects of heterosexual attitudes and behavior in emerging adults. Here we provide further analysis and integration of information about patterns of heterosexual behavior in emerging adults.

At the beginning of emerging adulthood (age 18), surveys indicate that just more than half of individuals have experienced sexual intercourse, but by the end of emerging adulthood (age 25), most individuals have had sexual intercourse (Lefkowitz & Gillen, 2006). Also, the average age of marriage in the United States is currently 27 for males and 26 for females (Whitehead & Popenoe, 2006). Thus, emerging adulthood is a time frame during which most individuals are "both sexually active and unmarried" (Lefkowitz & Gillen, 2006, p. 235).

Patterns of heterosexual behavior for males and females in emerging adulthood include (Lefkowitz & Gillen, 2006) the following:

- Males have more casual sexual partners, and females report being more selective about their choice of a sexual partner.
- Approximately 60 percent of emerging adults have had sexual intercourse with only one individual in the past year, but compared with young adults in their late twenties and thirties, emerging adults are more likely to have had sexual intercourse with two or more individuals.
- Although emerging adults have sexual intercourse with more individuals than young adults, they have sex less frequently. Approximately 25 percent of emerging adults report having sexual intercourse only a couple of times a year or not at all (Michael & others, 1994).
- Casual sex is more common in emerging adulthood than in young adulthood. One study indicated that 30 percent of emerging adults said they had "hooked up" with someone and had sexual intercourse during college (Paul, McManus, & Hayes, 2000).

What are some predictors of risky heterosexual behavior in emerging adults, such as engaging in casual and unprotected sexual intercourse? Some research findings (Lefkowitz & Gillen, 2006) indicate that individuals who become sexually active in adolescence engage in more risky sexual behaviors in emerging adulthood than their counterparts who delay their sexual debuts until emerging adulthood (Capaldi & others, 2002). More religious emerging adults have had fewer sexual partners and engage in less risky sexual behaviors than their less religious counterparts (Lefkowitz, Boone, & Shearer, 2004). And when emerging adults drink alcohol, they are more likely to have casual sex and less likely to discuss possible risks (Cooper, 2002). A recent study also found that emerging adult women who engaged in casual sex were more likely to report having depressive symptoms than emerging adult men (Grello, Welsh, & Harper, 2006).

## Sexual Minority Attitudes and Behavior

The majority of sexual minority (same-sex) individuals experience their first same-sex attraction, sexual behavior, and self-labeling as a gay male or lesbian during adolescence (Savin-Williams, 2006, 2007; Savin-Williams & Cohen, 2007). However, some sexual minority individuals have these experiences for the first time in emerging adulthood. Also, while most gay males and lesbians have their first same-sex experience in adolescence, they often have their first extended same-sex relationship in emerging adulthood.

On the surface one might think that heterosexual behavior and sexual minority behavior are distinct patterns that can be easily defined. In fact, however, preference for a sexual partner of the same or other sex is not always a fixed decision, made once in life and adhered to forever. For example, it is not unusual for an individual, especially a male, to engage in same-sex experimentation in adolescence, but not engage in same-sex behavior as an adult. For others, the opposite progression applies.

Until the middle of the twentieth century, it was generally believed that people were either heterosexual or homosexual. However, there recently has been a move away from using the term "homosexual" because the term has negative historical connotations. Also, recent research indicates that the use of the term "homosexual" as a clear-cut sexual type is often oversimplified. For example, many individuals report having same-sex attractions and behavior than ever identify with being a **sexual minority**—someone who identifies with being lesbian, gay, or bisexual. The term **bisexual** refers to someone who is attracted to people of both sexes. Researchers have gravitated toward more descriptive and limited terms than "homosexual," preferring such terms as "individuals with same-sex attractions," or "individuals who have engaged in same-sex behavior."

National surveys reveal that 2.3 to 2.7 percent of U.S. individuals identify with being a gay male, and 1.1 to 1.3 percent identify with being a lesbian (Alan Guttmacher Institute, 1995; Michael & others, 1994).

**Factors Associated with Sexual Minority Behavior** Why do some people have same-sex attractions and identify with being a gay male or a lesbian? Speculation about this question has been extensive, but no firm answers are available. Heterosexual and sexual minority males and females have similar physiological responses during sexual arousal and seem to be aroused by the same types of tactile stimulation. In the 1970s, both the American Psychiatric Association and the American Psychological Association recognized that being attracted to someone of the same sex is not a form of mental illness and discontinued classification of this category as a disorder.

Researchers have explored the possible biological basis of sexual minority behavior (Quinsey, 2003; Swaab & others, 2002). In this regard, we evaluate hormone, brain, and twin studies regarding same-sex attraction. The results of hormone studies have been inconsistent. Indeed, if sexual minority males are given male sexual hormones (androgens), their sexual orientation does not change; their sexual desire merely increases. A very early critical period might influence sexual orientation. In the second to fifth months after conception, exposure of the fetus to hormone levels characteristic of females might cause the individual (female or male) to become attracted to males (Ellis & Ames, 1987). If this critical-period hypothesis turns out to be correct, it would explain why clinicians have found that sexual orientation is difficult, if not impossible, to modify (Meyer-Bahlburg & others, 1995).

**sexual minority** Someone who identifies with being lesbian, gay, or bisexual.

**bisexual** A person who is attracted to people of both sexes.

*Why are some individuals homosexual and others heterosexual? How do adolescents disclose their gay, lesbian, or bisexual identity to family members?*

With regard to anatomical structures, neuroscientist Simon LeVay (1991) found that a tiny area of the hypothalamus that governs sexual behavior is twice as large in heterosexual men as in sexual minority men. The area is about the same size in sexual minority men as in heterosexual women. Critics of LeVay's work point out that many of the sexual minority individuals in the study had AIDS, which could have altered their brains.

One study investigated sexual attraction in pairs of twins (Whitman, Diamond, & Martin, 1993). The researchers began with a group of sexual minority individuals, each of whom had a twin sibling, and investigated the sexual attraction of the siblings. Almost two-thirds of the siblings who were an identical twin of a sexual minority individual were attracted to individuals of the same sex. Less than one-third of the siblings who were a fraternal twin of a heterosexual individual were attracted to individuals of the same sex. The authors interpreted their results as supporting a biological interpretation of same-sex attraction since identical twins are more genetically similar than fraternal twins. However, not all of the identical twins had a same-sex orientation, so clearly environmental factors were involved.

Although research suggests there may be a genetic contribution to sexual attraction in some individuals, we are far from understanding the mechanisms involved (Diamond, 2004). Most experts believe that no one factor alone causes same-sex attraction and that the relative weight of each factor may vary from one individual to the next. An individual's sexual attraction is most likely determined by a combination of genetic, hormonal, cognitive, and environmental factors (Mustanski, Chivers, & Bailey, 2003). In effect, no one knows exactly what causes an individual to be attracted to individuals of the same sex. Having investigated and rejected a variety of hypotheses, scientists have a clearer picture of what does *not* cause same-sex attraction. For example, children raised by gay or lesbian parents or couples are no more likely to be homosexual than are children raised by heterosexual parents (Patterson, 2002; Patterson & Hastings, 2007). There also is no evidence to support the once popular theories that being a gay male is caused by a dominant mother or a weak father, or that being a lesbian is caused by girls' choosing male role models.

**Developmental Pathways** It is commonly perceived that most gay males and lesbians quietly struggle with same-sex attractions in childhood, do not engage in heterosexual dating, and gradually recognize that they are gay or lesbian in mid to late adolescence (Diamond, 2003; Savin-Williams, 2006, 2007; Savin-Williams & Diamond, 2004). Many youths do follow this developmental pathway, but others do not. For example, many youths have no recollection of same-sex attractions and experience a more abrupt sense of their same-sex attraction in late adolescence (Savin-Williams, 2001a). Researchers also have found that the majority of adolescents with same-sex attractions also experience some degree of other-sex attractions (Garofalo & others, 1999). And although some adolescents who are attracted to same-sex individuals fall in love with these individuals, others claim that their same-sex attractions are purely physical (Savin-Williams, 2001a, 2006; Savin-Williams & Ream, 2007).

In sum, sexual minority youth have diverse patterns of initial attraction, often have bisexual attractions, and may have physical or emotional attraction to same-sex individuals but do not always fall in love with them (Diamond, 2003; Savin-Williams, 2006, 2007). We have more to say about romantic development and dating in sexual minority youth in Chapter 9, "Peer and Romantic Relationships."

*In the last decade, an increasing number of youths have disclosed their gay, lesbian, or bisexual attraction to their parents.*

—Richard Savin-Williams
*Contemporary Psychologist, Cornell University*

**Gay Male or Lesbian Identity and Disclosure** Establishing a gay male or lesbian identity is often referred to as the coming-out process (Rosario & others, 2006). In one study of gay male adolescents, the majority of the gay adolescents said they felt different from other boys as children (Newman & Muzzonigro, 1993). The average age at having their first crush on another boy was 12.7 years, and the average age at realizing they were gay was 12.5 years. Most of the boys said they felt confused when they first became aware that they were gay. About half of the boys said they initially tried to deny their identity as a gay male.

Based on empirical research, these conclusions can be reached about adolescents who disclose their gay male or lesbian identity (Savin-Williams, 1998, 2001a, 2006):

- Parents are seldom the first person an adolescent tells about his or her same-sex attractions.
- Mothers are usually told before fathers, possibly because adolescents have more distant relationships with fathers.
- Mothers are more likely than fathers to know about their adolescent's (son's or daughter's) same-sex attractions.
- Approximately 50 to 60 percent of lesbian, gay, and bisexual adolescents have disclosed to at least one sibling, but siblings are still seldom the first person to whom a sexual minority youth discloses.
- The first person to whom adolescents may disclose their sexual minority identity is likely to be a friend.

**Peer Relations** Might the peer relations of sexual minority youth differ from those of heterosexual youth? A study of 15- to 23-year-olds found that younger sexual minority youth had smaller peer networks than their younger heterosexual counterparts (Diamond & Lucas, 2004). In this study, older sexual minority youth were more likely to have extremely close friends than older heterosexual youth. Regardless of their age, sexual minority youth showed excessive worry about losing friends and difficulties in romantic relationships.

**Discrimination and Bias** Having irrational negative feelings against individuals who have same-sex attractions is called **homophobia.** In its more extreme forms, homophobia can lead individuals to ridicule, physically assault, or even murder people they believe to have same-sex attractions. More typically, homophobia is associated with avoidance of same-sex individuals, faulty beliefs about sexual minority lifestyles (such as believing the falsehood that most child molesters have same-sex attractions), and subtle or overt discrimination in housing, employment, and other areas of life (Meyer, 2003).

One of the harmful aspects of the stigmatization of same-sex attraction is the self-devaluation engaged in by sexual minority individuals (Patterson, 2002; Savin-Williams, 2006, 2007; Savin Williams & Diamond, 2004). One common form of self-devaluation is called *passing,* the process of hiding one's real social identity.

**homophobia** Having irrational negative feelings against individuals who have same-sex attractions.

Passing strategies include giving out information that hides one's same-sex attraction. Passing behaviors include lying to others, saying, "I'm straight and attracted to opposite-sex individuals." Such defenses against self-recognition are heavily entrenched in our society. Without adequate support, and with fear of stigmatization, many gay male and lesbian youth retreat to the closet and then emerge at a safer time later, often in college. A special concern is the lack of support gay male and lesbian adolescents receive from parents, teachers, and counselors (Savin-Williams, 2001a, 2006, 2007; Savin-Williams & Cohen, 2007).

A recent large-scale study found similarities and differences in the lives of adolescents who are heterosexual, those who have same-sex attractions, and those who are bisexual (Busséri & others, 2006). Similarities across sexual orientations occurred for friendship quality, academic orientation, and perception of school climate. Bisexual adolescents reported the most negative results, including areas of their lives such as relationships with parents, psychological functioning, and victimization. Adolescents with same-sex attractions reported less positive experiences than exclusively heterosexual adolescents in relationships with parents, psychological functioning, and victimization. These results confirm findings in other studies that suggest that nonheterosexual adolescents face certain risks and challenges in their lives. However, the findings also indicate that adolescents with same-sex attractions have a number of positive aspects to their lives, including intrapersonal strengths (academic orientation), interpersonal resources (friendship quality), and environmental contexts (school climate) (Busseri & others, 2006).

Another concern is a possible link between suicide risk and sexual orientation (Morrison & L'Heureux, 2001; Rose & Rogers, 2000; Savin-Williams & Joyner, 2008). In one study of 12,000 adolescents, approximately 15 percent of gay male and lesbian youth said that they had attempted suicide compared with 7 percent of heterosexual youth (Russell & Joyner, 2001). However, a leading researcher on gay male and lesbian adolescents, Ritch Savin-Williams (2001b) argues that only slightly more sexual minority than heterosexual adolescents attempt suicide. In his view, many studies likely exaggerate the suicide rates for sexual minority adolescents because they surveyed only the most disturbed youth who were attending support groups or hanging out at shelters for sexual minority youth. One study found that although sexual minority youth had higher depression and anxiety, they did not differ from heterosexual youth in regard to perceived stress, self-esteem, or mastery (Diamond & Lucas, 2004).

## Self-Stimulation

Regardless of whether adolescents have a heterosexual or same-sex attraction, they must equally confront increasing feelings of sexual arousal. One way in which many youths who are not dating or who consciously choose not to engage in sexual intercourse or sexual explorations deal with these insistent feelings of sexual arousal is through masturbation, or self-stimulation.

As indicated earlier, a heterosexual continuum of kissing, petting, and intercourse or oral sex characterizes many adolescents' sexual experiences. Substantial numbers of adolescents, though, have sexual experience outside of this heterosexual continuum through masturbation or same-sex behavior. Most boys have an ejaculation for the first time at about 12 to 13 years of age. Masturbation, genital contact with a same-sex or other-sex partner, or a wet dream during sleep are common circumstances for ejaculation.

Masturbation is the most frequent sexual outlet for many adolescents (Gates & Sonenstein, 2000). Adolescents today do not feel as guilty about masturbation as they once did, although they still may feel embarrassed or defensive about it. In past eras, masturbation was denounced as causing everything from warts to insanity. Today, as few as 15 percent of adolescents attach any stigma to masturbation (Hyde & DeLamater, 2006).

In one study, the masturbation practices of female and male college students were studied (Leitenberg, Detzer, & Srebnik, 1993). Almost twice as many males as females said they had masturbated (81 percent versus 45 percent), and the males who masturbated did so three times more frequently during early adolescence and early adulthood than did the females who masturbated during the same age periods. No association was found between the quality of sexual adjustment in adulthood and a history of engaging in masturbation during preadolescence and/or early adolescence.

Much of the existing data on masturbation are difficult to interpret because they are based on self-reports in which many adolescents may not be responding accurately. Most experts on adolescent sexuality likely would agree that boys masturbate more than girls—but masturbation is more stigmatized behavior for girls, so they may actually masturbate more than they indicate in self-reports (Diamond, 2004).

## Contraceptive Use

Sexual activity, while a healthy behavior necessary for procreation, carries with it considerable risks if appropriate safeguards are not taken (Carroll, 2007; Davies & others, 2006; Feldman, 2006). Youth encounter two kinds of risks: unintended pregnancy and sexually transmitted infections. Both of these risks can be reduced significantly if contraception is used.

The good news is that adolescents are increasing their use of contraceptives. For example, a recent study examined trends in U.S. ninth- to twelfth-graders' contraceptive use from 1991 to 2003 (Anderson, Santelli, & Morrow, 2006). Approximately one-third of the adolescents reported being sexually active in the previous three months. The use of condoms by males increased from 46 percent in 1991 to 63 percent in 2003. The percentage of adolescents who used either withdrawal or no method steadily declined from 33 percent in 1991 to 19 percent in 2003.

Although adolescent contraceptive use is increasing, many sexually active adolescents still do not use contraceptives, or they use them inconsistently (Davies & others, 2006; Manlove & Terry-Humen, 2007; Singh & others, 2004). A recent national survey of U.S. 15- to 19-year-olds who have had sexual intercourse found that 47 percent of the boys said they always use a condom, but only 28 percent of the girls said they always use one (National Center for Health Statistics, 2004). Eleven percent of the boys and 18 percent of the girls said they never use a condom. A recent study of African American female adolescents living in low-income circumstances revealed that those who inconsistently used contraceptives were more likely to have a desire to become pregnant, have less frequent communication with their partners about contraceptive use, and have a greater number of life sexual partners than their counterparts who consistently used contraceptives (Davies & others, 2006). A longitudinal study revealed that adolescents who used condoms at first sexual intercourse were more likely to engage in subsequent protective behaviors, had fewer sexually transmitted infections, and did not have more sexual partners than their counterparts who failed to use condoms at first sexual intercourse (Shafii, Stovel, & Holmes, 2007).

Adolescents are increasing their use of contraceptives, although large numbers of sexually active adolescents still do not use contraceptives, especially at first intercourse.

Sexually active younger adolescents are less likely than older adolescents to take contraceptive precautions. Those who do are more likely to use a condom or withdrawal, whereas older adolescents are more likely to use the pill or a diaphragm. In one study, adolescent females reported changing their behavior in the direction of safer-sex practices more than did adolescent males (Rimberg & Lewis, 1994).

In thinking about contraceptive use in adolescence, it is important to consider the interpersonal context of adolescents' lives (Rimsza, 2003). For example, one reason adolescent girls have sex without condoms is that they don't want to risk losing their partners. In the eyes of the adolescent girl, then, the risk of pregnancy or sexually transmitted infection is not as threatening as the risk of losing a partner.

And a longitudinal study revealed that friends' intercourse without using condoms was linked to adolescents' subsequent engagement in intercourse without using condoms (Henry & others, 2007).

The issue of contraception is more difficult for adolescents than for adults because of differing patterns of sexual activity (Feldman, 1999). Whereas many adults, especially married adults, have sex on a regular and predictable schedule, and typically with one partner (or relatively few partners), adolescents' sexual activity often reflects a pattern of feast or famine, occurring unpredictably and intermittently (Creighton & Miller, 2003). Thus, some forms of contraception that are most effective and widely used by adults (such as the pill and IUD) are not as well suited for adolescents' patterns of sexual activity. Also, married couples often discuss and mutually agree on the form of contraception that they plan to use; such discussions are far less likely to occur among adolescent partners and unmarried young adults. This means that adolescents frequently resort to the use of condoms, which are not completely reliable. The good news, though, is that condoms (unlike the pill or IUD) help protect against sexually transmitted infections.

What factors are related to unsuccessful contraceptive use? Being from a low-SES family is one of the best predictors of adolescents' failure to use contraceptives (Nadeem, Romo, & Sigman, 2006). Younger adolescents are less likely to use contraceptives than older adolescents (Hofferth, 1990). Not being involved in a steady, committed dating relationship is also associated with a lack of contraceptive use (Chilman, 1979). Condom use is inhibited by concerns about embarrassment and reduced sexual pleasure. In addition, adolescents with poor coping skills, lack of a future orientation, high anxiety, poor social adjustment, and a negative attitude toward contraceptives are not as likely to use them.

Conversely, degree of personal concern about AIDS and the perception that a partner would appreciate condom use are associated with more consistent use of condoms by male adolescents (Pleck, Sonenstein, & Ku, 1991). Educational efforts that include information about AIDS and pregnancy prevention may promote more consistent use of condoms by adolescent males.

Although American adolescents' use of contraceptives has increased in the last two decades, adolescents in Canada, Great Britain, France, Sweden, and the Netherlands are still more likely to use contraceptives than are adolescents in the United States (Child Trends, 2000). U.S. adolescents are especially less likely to use effective contraceptives like the pill than their counterparts in other developed countries.

*Over the past 30 to 40 years dramatic changes have taken place in our society in adolescents' entry into sexuality, marriage, and parenting. Changes in links between sexual activity and marriage began to erode with increased options for contraception, changes in society's norms, and opening up of economic opportunities for women.*

—Jeanne Brooks-Gunn
*Contemporary Psychologist, Columbia University*

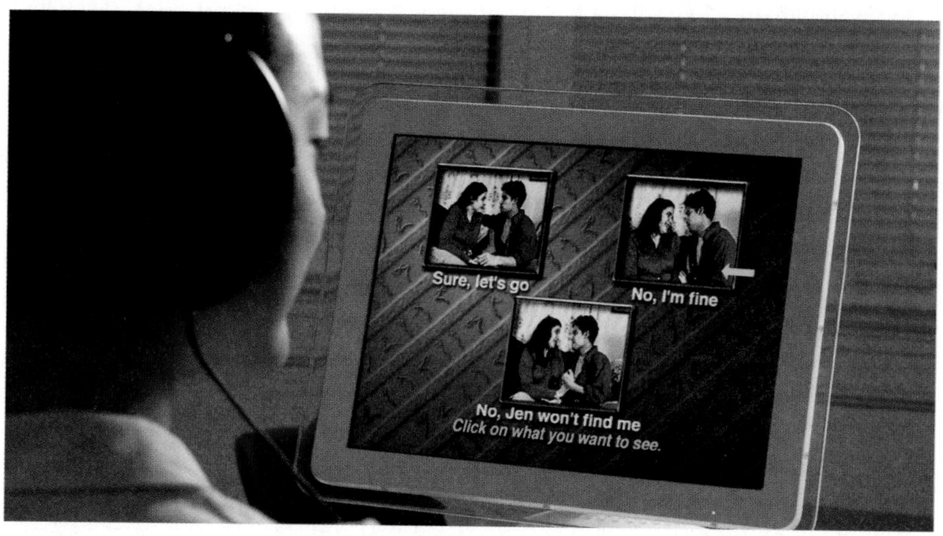


An adolescent participates in an interactive video session developed by Julie Downs and her colleagues at the Department of Social and Decision Making Sciences at Carnegie Mellon University. The videos help adolescents evaluate their responses and decisions in high-risk sexual contexts.

**REVIEW AND REFLECT ◆ LEARNING GOAL 2**

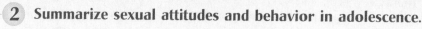

**2 Summarize sexual attitudes and behavior in adolescence.**

***Review***
- What are adolescent heterosexual attitudes and behaviors like?
- How would you characterize adolescent sexual minority behavior and attitudes?
- What is known about sexual self-stimulation in adolescence?
- How extensively do U.S. adolescents use contraceptives?

***Reflect***
- Think about your sexual experiences or lack of sexual experiences in adolescence. What would you change if you could relive your middle school and high school years?

# 3 Adolescent Sexual Problems

Adolescent Pregnancy | Sexually Transmitted Infections | Forcible Sexual Behavior and Sexual Harassment

Sexual problems in adolescence include adolescent pregnancy, sexually transmitted infections, and forcible sexual behavior and sexual harassment. Let's begin by exploring adolescent pregnancy and its prevalence in the United States and around the world.

## Adolescent Pregnancy

Angela is 15 years old. She reflects, "I'm three months pregnant. This could ruin my whole life. I've made all of these plans for the future, and now they are down the drain. I don't have anybody to talk with about my problem. I can't talk to my parents. There is no way they can understand." Pregnant adolescents were once virtually invisible and unmentionable, shuttled off to homes for unwed mothers where relinquishment of the baby for adoption was their only option, or subjected to unsafe and illegal abortions. But yesterday's secret has become today's dilemma. Our exploration of adolescent pregnancy focuses on its incidence and nature, its consequences, cognitive factors that may be involved, adolescents as parents, and ways in which adolescent pregnancy rates can be reduced.

**Incidence of Adolescent Pregnancy** Adolescent girls who become pregnant are from different ethnic groups and from different places, but their circumstances have the same stressfulness. To many adults, they represent a flaw in America's social fabric. Each year more than 200,000 females in the United States have a child before their eighteenth birthday. Like Angela, far too many become pregnant in their early or middle adolescent years. As one 17-year-old Los Angeles mother of a 1-year-old son said, "We are children having children."

**Cross-Cultural Comparisons** In cross-cultural comparisons, the United States continued to have one of the highest rates of adolescent pregnancy and childbearing in the developed world, despite a considerable decline in the 1990s (Alan Guttmacher Institute, 2003b; Centers for Disease Control and Prevention, 2003). U.S. adolescent pregnancy rates are similar to those of Russia and several Eastern European countries, such as Bulgaria; nearly twice those of Canada and England; and at least four times the rates in France, Sweden, Germany, and Japan (see Figure 6.4). While U.S. adolescents are no more sexually active than their counterparts in countries such as France and Sweden, their adolescent pregnancy rate is much higher.

Why are U.S. adolescent pregnancy rates so high? Three reasons based on cross-cultural studies are as follows (Boonstra, 2002, pp. 9–10):

- *"Childbearing regarded as adult activity."* European countries, as well as Canada, give a strong consensus that childbearing belongs in adulthood "when young people have completed their education, have become employed and independent from their parents and are living in stable relationships. . . . In the United States, this attitude is much less strong and much more variable across groups and areas of the country."
- *"Clear messages about sexual behavior.* While adults in other countries strongly encourage teens to wait until they have established themselves before having children, they are generally more accepting than American adults of teens having sex. In France and Sweden, in particular, teen sexual expression is seen as normal and positive, but there is also widespread expectation that sexual intercourse will take place within committed relationships. (In fact, relationships among U.S. teens tend to be more sporadic and of shorter duration.) Equally strong is the expectation that young people who are having sex will take actions to protect themselves and their partners from pregnancy and sexually transmitted infections," which is much stronger in Europe than in the United States. "In keeping with this view, . . . schools in Great Britain, France, Sweden, and most of Canada" have sex education programs that provide more comprehensive information about prevention than U.S. schools. In addition, these countries use the media more often in "government-sponsored campaigns for promoting responsible sexual behavior."
- *"Access to family planning services.* In countries that are more accepting of teenage sexual relationships, teenagers also have easier access to reproductive health services. In Canada, France, Great Britain, and Sweden, contraceptive services are integrated into other types of primary health care and are available free or at low cost for all teenagers. Generally, teens (in these countries) know where to obtain information and services and receive confidential and nonjudgmental care. . . . In the United States, where attitudes about teenage sexual relationships are more conflicted, teens have a harder time obtaining contraceptive services. Many do not have health insurance or cannot get birth control as part of their basic health care."

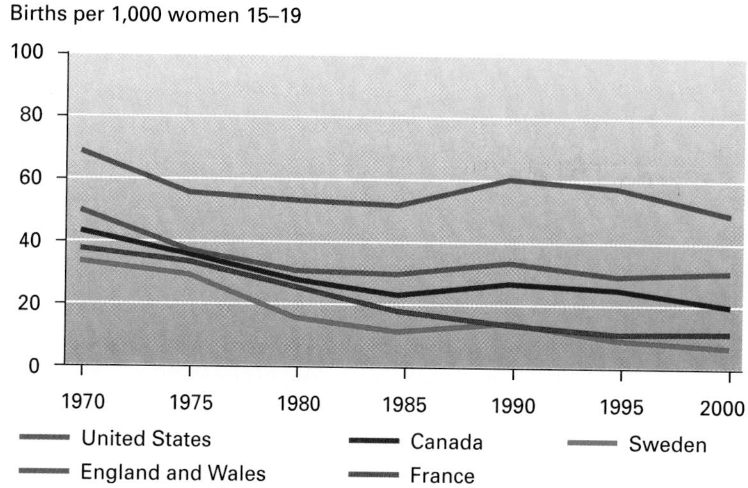

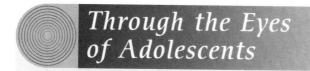

**FIGURE 6.4** **Cross-Cultural Comparisons of Adolescent Pregnancy Rates**

## *Through the Eyes of Adolescents*

### SIXTEEN-YEAR-OLD ALBERTO: WANTING A DIFFERENT KIND OF LIFE

Sixteen-year-old Alberto's maternal grandmother was a heroin addict who died of cancer at the age of 40. His father, who was only 17 when Alberto was born, had been in prison most of Alberto's life. His mother and stepfather are not married but have lived together for a dozen years and have four other children. Alberto's stepbrother dropped out of school when he was 17, fathered a child, and is now unemployed. But Alberto, who lives in the Bronx in New York City, has different plans for his own future. He wants to be a dentist, he said, "like the kind of woman who fixed his teeth at Bronx-Lebanon Hospital Center clinic when he was a child" (Bernstein, 2004, p. A22). And Alberto, along with his girlfriend, Jasmine, wants to remain a virgin until he is married.

Alberto with his girlfriend.

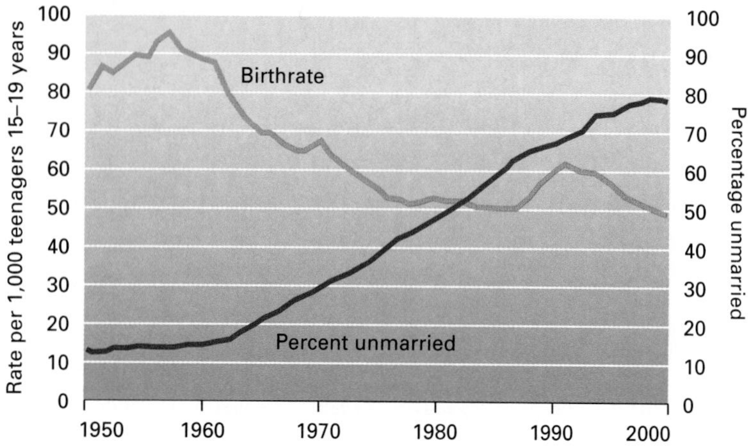


**FIGURE 6.5** Births to Married and Unmarried 15- to 19-Year-Old Girls from 1950 Through 2000

**Decreasing U.S. Adolescent Pregnancy Rates** Despite the negative comparisons of the United States with many other developed countries, there are encouraging trends in U.S. adolescent pregnancy rates. In 2004, births to adolescent girls fell to a record low (Child Trends, 2006). The rate of births to adolescent girls has dropped 30 percent since 1991. Reasons for these declines include increased contraceptive use and fear of sexually transmitted infections such as AIDS.

The greatest drop in the U.S. adolescent pregnancy rate in recent years has been for 15- to 17-year-old African American girls. Fear of sexually transmitted infections, especially AIDS; school/community health classes; and a greater hope for the future are the likely reasons for the recent decrease in U.S. adolescent pregnancy rates. Latino adolescents are more likely than African American and non-Latino White adolescents to become pregnant (Child Trends, 2006). Latino and African American adolescent girls who have a child are also more likely to have a second child than are non-Latino White adolescent girls.

Even though adolescent childbearing overall has declined steeply over the last half century, the proportion of adolescent births that are nonmarital has increased in equally dramatic fashion, from 13 percent in 1950 to 79 percent in 2000 (see Figure 6.5). Two factors are responsible for this trend. First, marriage in adolescence has now become quite rare (the average age of first marriage in the United States is now 25 for women and 27 for men). Second, pregnancy is no longer seen as a reason for marriage. In contrast to the days of the "shotgun marriage" (when youths were forced to marry if a girl became pregnant), very few adolescents who become pregnant now marry before their baby is born.

**Abortion** Impassioned debate characterizes abortion in the United States today, and this debate is likely to continue in the foreseeable future (Brown, 2006; Joyce, Kaestner, & Colman, 2006; Law, 2006). The experiences of U.S. adolescents who want to have an abortion vary by state and region. In 2003, 32 states restricted adolescents' access to abortion. Urban adolescents in New York or California, where parental consent is not required and public and private providers are available, have far greater access to abortion services than their counterparts in North Dakota or Mississippi, which require the consent of both parents, or who live in a rural area where there are no providers.

Abortion is easier to obtain in some countries, most notably the Scandinavian countries, than in the United States, where abortion and adolescent sexual activity are more stigmatized. In many developing countries, such as Nigeria, abortion is far more unsafe than in the United States (Murphy, 2003).

In the United States, 19 percent of abortions are performed on 15- to 19-year-old girls, whereas less than 1 percent are carried out with those less than 15 years of age (Alan Guttmacher Institute, 2003b). Adolescent girls are more likely than older women to delay having an abortion until after 15 weeks of pregnancy, when medical risks associated with abortion increase significantly (Alan Guttmacher Institute, 2003c).

Legislation mandating parental consent for an adolescent girl's abortion has been justified by several assumptions, including high risk of harm from abortion, adolescents' inability to make an adequately informed decision, and benefits of parental involvement. Research related to each of these assumptions was the focus of a review (Adler, Ozer, & Tschann, 2003).

Researchers have found that legal abortion in the United States itself carries few medical risks if performed in the first trimester of pregnancy, especially compared with the risks of childbearing, for adolescent girls (Centers for Disease Control and

Prevention, 1997). In terms of psychological risks, one study evaluated 360 adolescent girls over two years after they had been interviewed when seeking a pregnancy test (Zabin, Hirsch, & Emerson, 1989). Some had a negative test, some were pregnant and carried to term, and some were pregnant and had an abortion. The adolescent girls who had an abortion showed a drop in anxiety and an increase in self-esteem from the beginning of the study to two years later. Further, they appeared to be functioning as well as the girls who had a negative pregnancy test or who had carried until term. They also were more likely than the other two groups to be in school or to have graduated from high school and less likely to have a subsequent pregnancy. Other researchers have found that adolescents are not psychologically harmed by their abortion experience (Pope, Adler, & Tschann, 2001; Quinton, Major, & Richards, 2001).

A second rationale for restrictive abortion laws for adolescents is that they are not capable of making an adequately informed choice. As we saw in Chapter 3, some researchers have found that older adolescents are better at decision making than younger adolescents, whereas other researchers have discovered that adolescents and adults do not differ in their decision-making skills (Quadrel, Fischoff, & Davis, 1993). Several studies revealed that adolescents as young as 13 years of age do not differ from adults in their decision making about having an abortion (Ambuel & Rappaport, 1992; Lewis, 1980). These studies focus on the general quality of reasoning, an awareness of adolescents to understand the consequences of their decision, and the types of considerations expressed regarding the decision.

A third rationale for restrictive abortion laws is that parents need to be involved in their daughter's decision making and care. Thus, parental involvement laws seek to promote family communication and functioning. However, little research has been conducted about whether such laws actually do so.

Regardless of research outcomes, pro-life and pro-choice advocates are convinced of the rightness of their positions (Hyde & DeLamater, 2006). Their conflict has a foundation in religious beliefs, political convictions, and morality. This conflict has no easy solutions.

**Consequences of Adolescent Pregnancy** The consequences of America's high adolescent pregnancy rate are cause for great concern (Dryfoos & Barkin, 2006; Hock, 2007; McNulty & Burnette, 2004). Adolescent pregnancy creates health risks for both the baby and the mother. Infants born to adolescent mothers are more likely to have low birth weights—a prominent factor in infant mortality—as well as neurological problems and childhood illness (Malamitsi-Puchner & Boutsikou, 2006). Adolescent mothers often drop out of school. Although many adolescent mothers resume their education later in life, they generally do not catch up economically with women who postpone childbearing until their twenties. A longitudinal study revealed that these characteristics of adolescent mothers were related to their likelihood of having problems as emerging adults: a history of school problems, delinquency, hard substance use, and mental health problems (Oxford & others, 2006).

Though the consequences of America's high adolescent pregnancy rate are cause for great concern, it often is not pregnancy alone that leads to negative consequences for an adolescent mother and her offspring (Oxford & others, 2006). Adolescent mothers are more likely to come from low-SES backgrounds (Crosby & Holtgrave, 2006). Many adolescent mothers also were not good students before they became pregnant (Malamitsi-Puchner & Boutsikou, 2006). However, not every adolescent female who bears a child lives a life of poverty and low achievement. Thus, although adolescent pregnancy is a high-risk circumstance and adolescents who do not become pregnant generally fare better than those who do, some adolescent mothers do well in school and have positive outcomes (Ahn, 1994; Leadbeater & Way, 2000).

*What are some consequences of adolescent pregnancy?*

**Cognitive Factors in Adolescent Pregnancy** Cognitive changes have intriguing implications for adolescents' sex education (Lipsitz, 1980). With their developing idealism and ability to think in more abstract and hypothetical ways, young adolescents may become immersed in a mental world far removed from reality. They may see themselves as omnipotent and indestructible and believe that bad things cannot or will not happen to them, characteristics of adolescent egocentrism we discussed in Chapter 3. Consider the personal fable aspect of adolescent egocentrism reflected in this 14-year-old's words: "Hey, it won't happen to me."

Informing adolescents about contraceptives is not enough—what seems to predict whether or not they will use contraceptives is their acceptance of themselves and their sexuality. This acceptance requires not only emotional maturity but cognitive maturity.

Most discussions of adolescent pregnancy and its prevention assume that adolescents have the ability to anticipate consequences, to weigh the probable outcome of behavior, and to project into the future what will happen if they engage in certain acts, such as sexual intercourse. That is, prevention is based on the belief that adolescents have the cognitive ability to approach problem solving in a planned, organized, and analytical manner. However, while many adolescents 16 years of age and older have these capacities, it does not mean they use them, especially in emotionally charged situations, such as when they are sexually aroused or are being pressured by a partner.

Indeed, young adolescents (10 to 15 years of age) seem to experience sex in a depersonalized way that is filled with anxiety and denial. This depersonalized orientation toward sex is not likely to lead to preventive behavior. Middle adolescents (15 to 17 years of age) often romanticize sexuality. Late adolescents (18 to 19 years of age) are to some degree realistic and future oriented about sexual experiences, just as they are about careers and marriage.

**Adolescents as Parents** Children of adolescent parents face problems even before they are born. Only one of every five pregnant adolescent girls receives any prenatal care at all during the important first three months of pregnancy. Pregnant adolescents are more likely to have anemia and complications related to prematurity than are mothers aged 20 to 24. The problems of adolescent pregnancy double the normal risk of delivering a low birth weight baby (one that weighs under 5.5 pounds), a category that places that infant at risk for physical and mental deficits (Dryfoos, & Barkin, 2006). In some cases, infant problems may be due to poverty rather than the mother's age.

Infants who escape the medical hazards of having an adolescent mother might not escape the psychological and social perils (Brooks-Gunn & Chase-Lansdale, 1995; Luster & others, 1995). Adolescent mothers are less competent at child rearing and have less realistic expectations for their infants' development than do older mothers (Osofsky, 1990). Children born to adolescent mothers do not perform as well on intelligence tests and have more behavioral problems than children born to mothers in their twenties (Silver, 1988). One longitudinal study found that the children of women who had their first birth during their teens had lower achievement test scores and more behavioral problems than did children whose mothers had their first birth as adults (Hofferth & Reid, 2002).

These teenage mothers are involved in a program is Nebraska that is designed to help them care for their infants and keep them in school. *What are adolescents like as parents?*

So far, we have talked exclusively about adolescent mothers. Although some adolescent fathers are involved with their children, the majority are not. In one study, only one-fourth of adolescent mothers with a 3-year-old child said the father had a close relationship with them (Leadbeater, Way, & Raden, 1994).

Adolescent fathers have lower incomes, less education, and more children than do men who delay having children until their twenties. One reason for these difficulties is that the adolescent father often compounds the problem of becoming a parent at a young age by dropping out of school (Resnick, Wattenberg, & Brewer, 1992). As soon as he leaves school, the adolescent father moves directly into a low-paying job. Adolescent fathers are saying to themselves, "You need to be a good father. The least you can do is get a job and provide some support," but this short-term view ignores the importance of education as preparation for eventual success in a career.

Many young fathers have little idea of what a father is supposed to do. They may love their baby but not know how to behave. American society has given them few guidelines and few supports. Programs designed to help adolescent fathers are still relatively rare, but they are increasing. Terry, who is now 21, has a 17-month-old child and is himself the child of adolescent parents. After receiving support from the Teenage Pregnancy and Parenting Project in San Francisco, he is now a counselor there. He reports, "My father was a parent when he was an adolescent. So was my grandfather. I know it will stop with my son" (Stengel, 1985).

**Reducing Adolescent Pregnancy** Serious, extensive efforts are needed to help pregnant adolescents and young mothers enhance their educational and occupational opportunities. Adolescent mothers also need extensive help in obtaining competent child care and in planning for the future (Klaw & Saunders, 1994). John Conger (1988) offered the following four recommendations for reducing the high rate of adolescent pregnancy: (1) sex education and family planning, (2) access to contraceptive methods, (3) the life options approach, and (4) broad community involvement and support, each of which we consider in turn.

Age-appropriate family-life education benefits adolescents (Hulton, 2007; Weyman, 2003). One strategy that is used in some family-life education programs is the Baby Think It Over doll, a life-size computer-driven baby doll that engages in realistic responses and provides adolescents the opportunity to experience the responsibilities of being a parent. A recent study of primarily Latino ninth-grade students who took care of the Baby Think It Over doll found that the experience increased the age at which they said they wanted to have a child, produced a greater interest in career and educational planning, and raised their concerns about the possibility of how having a baby might interfere with those plans (de Anda, 2006). To read about the work of one individual who incorporates the Baby Think It Over simulated doll in her effort to educate adolescents about the reality of having a baby, see the *Careers in Adolescent Development* profile.

In addition to age-appropriate family-life and sex education, sexually active adolescents need access to contraceptive methods (Paukku & others, 2003; Santelli & others, 2006). These needs often can be handled through adolescent clinics that provide comprehensive, high-quality health services. In the 1980s when teen pregnancy rates were very high, four of the nation's oldest adolescent clinics, in St. Paul, Minnesota, managed to drop the overall annual rate of first-time pregnancies from 80 per 1,000 to 29 per 1,000 (Schorr,

## Careers in ADOLESCENT DEVELOPMENT

### Lynn Blankenship
**Family and Consumer Science Educator**

Lynn Blankenship is a family and consumer science educator. She has an undergraduate degree in this area from the University of Arizona. She has taught for more than 20 years, the last 14 at Tucson High Magnet School.

Lynn was awarded the Tucson Federation of Teachers Educator of the Year Award for 1999–2000 and the Arizona Association of Family and Consumer Science Teacher of the Year in 1999.

Lynn especially enjoys teaching life skills to adolescents. One of her favorite activities is having students care for an automated baby that imitates the needs of real babies. Lynn says that this program has a profound impact on students because the baby must be cared for around the clock for the duration of the assignment. Lynn also coordinates real-world work experiences and training for students in several child-care facilities in the Tucson area.

Lynn Blankenship, with students carrying their automated babies.

1989). These clinics offer everything from immunizations to sports physicals to treatment for sexually transmitted infections. Significantly, they also advise adolescents on contraception and dispense prescriptions for birth control (provided parents have agreed beforehand to allow their adolescents to visit the clinic). An important aspect of the clinics is the presence of individuals trained to understand the special needs and confusions of the adolescent age group.

Better sex education, family planning, and access to contraceptive methods alone will not remedy the adolescent pregnancy crisis, especially for high-risk adolescents. Adolescents have to become *motivated* to reduce their pregnancy risk. This motivation will come only when adolescents look to the future and see that they have an opportunity to become self-sufficient and successful. Adolescents need opportunities to improve their academic and career-related skills, job opportunities, life-planning consultation, and extensive mental health services.

Finally, for adolescent pregnancy prevention to ultimately succeed, we need broad community involvement and support (Duckett, 1997). This support is a major reason for the success of pregnancy prevention efforts in other developed nations where rates of adolescent pregnancy, abortion, and childbearing are much lower than in America despite similar levels of sexual activity. In the Netherlands, as well as other European countries such as Sweden, sex does not carry the mystery and conflict it does in American society. The Netherlands does not have a mandated sex education program, but adolescents can obtain contraceptive counseling at government-sponsored clinics for a small fee. The Dutch media also have played an important role in educating the public about sex through frequent broadcasts focused on birth control, abortion, and related matters. Perhaps as a result, Dutch adolescents are unlikely to have sex without contraception.

One strategy for reducing adolescent pregnancy, called the Teen Outreach Program (TOP), focuses on engaging adolescents in volunteer community service and stimulates discussions that help adolescents appreciate the lessons they learn through volunteerism (Dryfoos & Barkin, 2006). In one study, 695 adolescents in grades 9 to 12 were randomly assigned to either a Teen Outreach group or a control group (Allen & others, 1997). They were assessed at both program entry and at program exit nine months later. The rate of pregnancy was substantially lower for the Teen Outreach adolescents. These adolescents also had a lower rate of school failure and academic suspension.

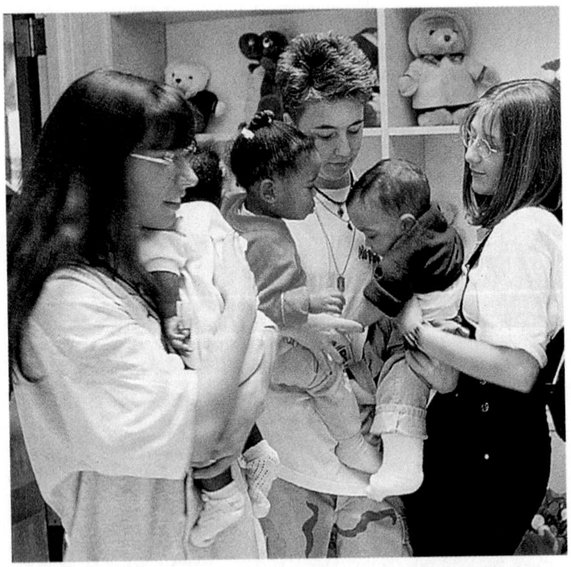

These are not adolescent mothers, but rather adolescents who are participating in the Teen Outreach Program (TOP), which engages adolescents in volunteer community service. These adolescent girls are serving as volunteers in a child-care center for crack babies. Researchers have found that such volunteer experiences can reduce the rate of adolescent pregnancy.

Girls, Inc., has four programs that are intended to increase adolescent girls' motivation to avoid pregnancy until they are mature enough to make responsible decisions about motherhood (Roth & others, 1998). Growing Together, a series of five two-hour workshops for mothers and adolescents, and Will Power/Won't Power, a series of six two-hour sessions that focus on assertiveness training, are for 12- to 14-year-old girls. For older adolescent girls, Taking Care of Business provides nine sessions that emphasize career planning as well as information about sexuality, reproduction, and contraception. Health Bridge coordinates health and education services—girls can participate in this program as one of their club activities. Research on girls' participation in these programs revealed a significant drop in their likelihood of getting pregnant, compared with girls who did not participate (Girls, Inc., 1991).

So far, we have discussed four ways to reduce adolescent pregnancy: sex education and family planning, access to contraceptive methods, life options, and broad community involvement and support. A fifth consideration, which is especially important for young adolescents, is abstinence. Abstinence is increasingly being included as a theme in sex education classes, which we discuss later in this chapter, criticisms of abstinence-only sex education programs have recently been made (Brindis, 2006; Santelli & others, 2006).

## Sexually Transmitted Infections

Tammy, age 15, just finished listening to an expert lecture in her health class. We overhear her talking to one of her girlfriends as she walks down the school corridor: "That was a disgusting lecture. I can't believe all the infections you can get by having sex. I think she was probably trying to scare us. She spent a lot of time talking about AIDS, which I have heard that normal people do not get. Right? I've heard that only homosexuals and drug addicts get AIDS. And I've also heard that gonorrhea and most other sexual infections can be cured, so what is the big deal if you get something like that?" Tammy's view of sexually transmitted infections—that they always happen to someone else, that they can be easily cured without any harm done, that they are too disgusting for a nice young person to hear about, let alone get—is common among adolescents. Tammy's view is wrong. Adolescents who are having sex run the risk of getting sexually transmitted infections.

**Sexually transmitted infections (STIs)** are infections that are contracted primarily through sexual contact. This contact is not limited to vaginal intercourse but includes oral-genital and anal-genital contact as well. STIs are an increasing health problem. In 2004, there were an estimated 19 million new STI cases, with slightly more than 9 million of these cases occurring in the 15- to 24-year-old age group (National Center for Chronic Disease Prevention and Health Promotion, 2005).

Among the main STIs adolescents can get are three STIs caused by viruses—AIDS (acquired immune deficiency syndrome), genital herpes, and genital warts—and three STIs caused by bacterial infections—gonorrhea, syphilis, and chlamydia.

### HIV and AIDS

No single STI has caused more deaths, had a greater impact on sexual behavior, or created more public fear in recent decades, than the HIV virus (Strong & others, 2008). We explore here its nature and incidence, how it is transmitted, and prevention.

**AIDS** is a sexually transmitted syndrome that is caused by a virus, the human immunodeficiency virus (HIV), which destroys the body's immune system. Following exposure to HIV, an individual is vulnerable to germs that a normal immune system could destroy.

Through December 2005, there were 41,149 cumulative cases of AIDS in 13- to 24-year-olds in the United States (Centers for Disease Control and Prevention, 2007). One estimate is that approximately 15,000 new HIV infections occur each year in the United States in the 15- to 24-year-old age group (Weinstock, Berman, & Cates, 2004).

Worldwide, the greatest concern about AIDS is in sub-Saharan Africa, where it has reached epidemic proportions (Alan Guttmacher Institute, 2005; UNICEF, 2006). Adolescent girls in many African countries are especially vulnerable to infection with the HIV virus by adult men. Approximately six times as many adolescent girls as boys have AIDS in these countries. In Kenya, 25 percent of the 15- to 19-year-old girls are HIV-positive, compared with only 4 percent of this age group of boys. In Botswana, more than 30 percent of the adolescent girls who are pregnant are infected with the HIV virus. In some sub-Saharan countries, less than 20 percent of women and 40 percent of 15- to 19-year-olds reported that they used a condom the last time they had sexual intercourse (Bankole & others, 2004).

AIDS also has resulted in a dramatic increase in the number of African children and adolescents who are orphaned and left to care for themselves because their parents acquired the disease. In 2006, there were 12 million children and adolescents who had become orphans because of the deaths of their parents due to AIDS (UNICEF, 2006). This figure is expected to increase to 16 million by 2010, which means that AIDS orphans could make up as many as 15 to 20 percent of the population of some sub-Saharan countries. As a result of the dramatic increase in AIDS orphans, more of these children and adolescents are being cared for by their

**sexually transmitted infections (STIs)** Infections that are contracted primarily through sexual contact. This contact is not limited to vaginal intercourse but includes oral-genital contact and anal-genital contact as well.

**AIDS** Acquired immune deficiency syndrome, a sexually transmitted syndrome caused by the HIV virus, which destroys the body's immune system.

A youth group presents a play in the local market place in Morogoro, Tanzania. The play is designed to educate the community about HIV and AIDS.

A 13-year-old boy pushes his friends around in his barrow during a break from his work as a barrow boy in a community in sub-Saharan Africa. He became the breadwinner in the family because both of his parents died of AIDS.

grandmothers or by no one, in which case all too often they turn to a lifestyle of crime or prostitution.

There continues to be great concern about AIDS in many parts of the world, not just sub-Saharan Africa (MMWR, 2006). In the United States, prevention is especially targeted at groups that show the highest incidence of AIDS. These include drug users, individuals with other STIs, young gay males, individuals living in low-income circumstances, Latinos, and African Americans (Centers for Disease Control and Prevention, 2006). Also, in recent years, there has been increased heterosexual transmission of the HIV virus in the United States.

There are some differences in AIDS cases in U.S. adolescents, compared with AIDS cases in U.S. adults:

- A higher percentage of adolescent AIDS cases are acquired by heterosexual transmission.
- A higher percentage of adolescents are asymptomatic individuals (but will become symptomatic in adulthood).
- A higher percentage of African American and Latino AIDS cases occur in adolescence.
- A special set of ethical and legal issues are involved in testing and informing partners and parents of adolescents.
- Adolescents have less access to contraceptives and are less likely to use them than are adults.

Experts say that the HIV virus can be transmitted only by sexual contact, the sharing of needles, or blood transfusion (which in recent years has been tightly monitored) (Kelly, 2000). Approximately 90 percent of AIDS cases in the United States continue to occur among men who have sex with other men and intravenous drug users. Penile-anal sex involves a higher risk of microscopic tearing and therefore blood-semen contact. A disproportionate increase among females who are heterosexual partners of bisexual males or of intravenous drug users has been recently noted (Centers for Disease Control and Prevention, 2006). This increase suggests that the risk of AIDS may be increasing among heterosexual individuals who have multiple sex partners. Figure 6.6 describes what's risky and what's not, regarding AIDS.

The HIV virus is not transmitted like colds or the flu, but by an exchange of infected blood, semen, or vaginal fluids. This usually occurs during sexual intercourse, in sharing drug needles, or to babies infected before or during birth.

**You won't get the HIV virus from:**

Everyday contact with individuals around you in school or the workplace, at parties, child-care centers, or stores

Swimming in a pool, even if someone in the pool has the AIDS virus

A mosquito bite, or from bedbugs, lice, flies, or other insects

Saliva, sweat, tears, urine, or feces

A kiss

Clothes, telephones, or toilet seats

Using a glass or eating utensils that someone else has used

Being on a bus, train, or crowded elevator with an individual who is infected with the virus or who has AIDS

**Blood donations and transfusions:**

You will not come into contact with the HIV virus by donating blood at a blood bank.

The risk of getting AIDS from a blood transfusion has been greatly reduced. Donors are screened for risk factors, and donated blood is tested for HIV antibodies.

**Risky behavior:**

Your chances of coming into contact with the virus increase if you:

Have more than one sex partner

Share drug needles and syringes

Engage in anal, vaginal, or oral sex without a condom

Perform vaginal or oral sex with someone who shoots drugs

Engage in sex with someone you don't know well or with someone who has several sex partners

Engage in unprotected sex (without a condom) with an infected individual

**Safe behavior:**

Not having sex

Having sex that does not involve fluid exchange (rubbing, holding, massage)

Sex with one mutually faithful, uninfected partner

Sex with proper protection

Not shooting drugs

Source: *America Responds to AIDS.* U.S. Government educational pamphlet, 1988.

**FIGURE 6.6** Understanding AIDS: What's Risky, What's Not

Merely asking a date about his or her sexual behavior, of course, does not guarantee protection from HIV or other STIs. For example, in one investigation, 655 college students were asked to answer questions about lying and sexual behavior (Cochran & Mays, 1990). Of the 422 respondents who said they were sexually active, 34 percent of the men and 10 percent of the women said they had lied so their partner would have sex with them. Much higher percentages—47 percent of the men and 60 percent of the women—said they had been lied to by a potential sexual partner. When asked what aspects of their past they would be most likely to lie about, more than 40 percent of the men and women said they would understate the number of their sexual partners. Twenty percent of the men, but only 4 percent of the women, said they would lie about their results from an HIV blood test.

Because it is possible, and even probable among high-risk groups, to have more than one STI at a time, efforts to prevent one infection help reduce the prevalence of other infections. Efforts to prevent AIDS can also help prevent adolescent pregnancy and other sexually related problems. Because of the high rate of sexually transmitted infections, it is crucial that both adolescents and adults understand these diseases (Johnston & others, 2003).

One study evaluated 37 AIDS prevention projects with children and adolescents (Janz & others, 1996). Small-group discussions, outreach to populations engaged in high-risk behaviors, and training of peers and volunteers were the activities rated the most effective. Small-group discussions, with an emphasis on open communication and repetition of messages, are excellent opportunities for adolescents to learn and share information about AIDS. The best outreach programs are culturally tailored and include incentives to participate. Outreach workers who are familiar and respected might be able to break through the barriers of fear and mistrust to ensure that appropriate messages are heard and heeded. For incentives to work, they also must be tailored for specific populations. School-age children might be attracted by academic credit or a stipend. For injection drug users, food, shelter, and a safe place to congregate might attract participants. For working women, child care and an opportunity to spend time with other adults might draw participants. The use of peer educators is often an effective strategy. As role models, peers can mirror healthy lifestyles for the target population as well as provide reinforcement and shape group norms in support of behavioral change. Peer educators often are effective at getting adolescents involved in AIDS prevention projects.

**Genital Herpes** **Genital herpes** is a sexually transmitted infection caused by a large family of viruses with many different strains, some of which produce other, non–sexually transmitted diseases such as cold sores, chicken pox, and mononucleosis. Three to five days after contact, itching and tingling can occur, followed by an eruption of painful sores and blisters. The attacks can last up to three weeks and can recur as frequently as every few weeks or as infrequently as every few years. It is direct contact with the sores that transmits the virus to a partner; the virus can also pass through non-latex condoms as well as contraceptive foams and creams. It is estimated that approximately 4.2 million of the 15- to 24-year-old age group in the United States have been infected with genital herpes (11 percent of the population in the age group) (Weinstock, Berman, & Cates, 2004). It also is estimated that more than 600,000 new genital herpes infections are appearing in the 15- to 24-year-old age group in the United States each year.

Although drugs such as acyclovir can alleviate symptoms, there is no known cure for herpes (Barton, 2005). Thus, individuals infected with herpes often experience severe emotional distress in addition to the considerable physical discomfort. They may feel conflicted or reluctant about sex, angry about the unpredictability of the infection, and fearful that they won't be able to cope with the pain of the next attack. For these reasons, many communities have established support groups for victims of herpes.

**Genital Warts** **Genital warts** are caused by the human papillomavirus (HPV), which is difficult to test for and does not always produce symptoms but is very contagious nonetheless. Genital warts usually appear as small, hard, painless bumps on the penis, in the vaginal area, or around the anus. More than 9 million individuals in the United States in the 15- to 24-year-old age group are estimated to have an HPV infection, making HPV the most commonly acquired STI in this age group (Weinstock, Berman, & Cates, 2004). Treatment involves the use of a topical drug, freezing, or surgery. Unfortunately genital warts may return despite treatment, and in some cases they are linked to cervical cancer and other genital cancers. Condoms afford some protection against HPV infection. In 2007, the Centers for Disease Control and Prevention recommended that all 11- and 12-year-old girls be given the vaccine Gardasil, which helps to fight off HPV and cervical cancer.

We now turn to three STIs—gonorrhea, syphilis, and chlamydia—caused by bacteria.

**Gonorrhea** **Gonorrhea** is an STI that is commonly called the "drip" or the "clap." It is caused by a bacterium called *Neisseria gonorrhoeae,* which thrives in the moist mucous membranes lining the mouth, throat, vagina, cervix, urethra, and anal tract. The bacterium is spread by contact between the infected moist membranes of one individual and the membranes of another. Although the incidence of gonorrhea has declined, it is estimated that more than 400,000 new cases appear each year in the 15- to 24-year-old age group (Weinstock, Berman, & Cates, 2004).

Early symptoms of gonorrhea are more likely to appear in males, who are likely to have a discharge from the penis and burning during urination. The early sign of

**genital herpes** A sexually transmitted infection caused by a large family of viruses of different strains. These strains produce other, non–sexually transmitted diseases such as chicken pox and mononucleosis.

**genital warts** Caused by the human papillomavirus, genital warts are very contagious and are the most common acquired STI in the United States in the 15- to 24-year-old age group.

**gonorrhea** This sexually transmitted infection is caused by a bacterium called *Neisseria gonorrhoeae,* which thrives in the moist mucous membranes lining the mouth, throat, vagina, cervix, urethra, and anal tract. This STI is commonly called the "drip" or the "clap."

gonorrhea in females, often undetectable, is a mild, sometimes irritating vaginal discharge. Complications of gonorrhea in males include prostate, bladder, and kidney problems, as well as sterility. In females, gonorrhea may lead to infertility due to the abdominal adhesions or pelvic inflammatory disease (PID) that it can cause (Crooks & Baur, 2008). Gonorrhea can be successfully treated in its early stages with penicillin or other antibiotics.

**Syphilis** **Syphilis** is an STI caused by the bacterium *Treponema pallidum,* a member of the spirochete family. The spirochete needs a warm, moist environment to survive, and it is transmitted by penile-vaginal, oral-genital, or anal contact. It can also be transmitted from a pregnant woman to her fetus after the fourth month of pregnancy; if she is treated before this time with penicillin, the syphilis will not be transmitted to the fetus. It is estimated that approximately 8,000 new cases of syphilis appear in the United States each year in the 15- to 24-year-old age group (Weinstock, Berman, & Cates, 2004).

If untreated, syphilis may progress through four phases: primary (chancre sores appear), secondary (general skin rash occurs), latent (can last for several years in which no overt symptoms are present), and tertiary (cardiovascular disease, blindness, paralysis, skin ulcers, liver damage, and mental problems may occur) (Crooks & Baur, 2008). In its early phases, syphilis can be effectively treated with penicillin.

**Chlamydia** **Chlamydia,** one of most common of all STIs, is named for *Chlamydia trachomatis,* an organism that spreads by sexual contact and infects the genital organs of both sexes. Although fewer individuals have heard of chlamydia than have heard of gonorrhea and syphilis, its incidence is much higher. About 4 million Americans are infected with chlamydia each year. About 10 percent of all college students have chlamydia. This STI is highly infectious; women run a 70 percent risk of contracting it in a single sexual encounter with an infected partner. The male risk is estimated at between 25 and 50 percent. The estimated annual incidence of chlamydia in the 15- to 24-year-old age group is 1 million individuals (Weinstock, Berman, & Cates, 2004).

Many females with chlamydia have few or no symptoms (McClure & others, 2006). When symptoms do appear, they include disrupted menstrual periods, pelvic pain, elevated temperature, nausea, vomiting, and headache. Possible symptoms of chlamydia in males are a discharge from the penis and burning during urination.

Because many females with chlamydia are asymptomatic, the infection often goes untreated and the chlamydia spreads to the upper reproductive tract, where it can cause pelvic inflammatory disease (PID). The resultant scarring of tissue in the fallopian tubes can result in infertility or in ectopic pregnancies (tubal pregnancies), or a pregnancy in which the fertilized egg is implanted outside the uterus. One-quarter of females who have PID become infertile; multiple cases of PID increase the rate of infertility to half. Some researchers suggest that chlamydia is the number one preventable cause of female infertility.

Although they can occur without sexual contact and are therefore not classified as STIs, urinary tract or bladder infections and vaginal yeast infections (also called *thrush*) are common in sexually active females, especially those who have an intense "honeymoon" lovemaking experience. Both of these infections clear up quickly with medication, but their symptoms (urinary urgency and burning in urinary tract infections; itching, irritation, and whitish vaginal discharge in yeast infections) may be frightening, especially to adolescents who may already have considerable anxiety about sex. We mention them because one of the non-STIs may be what brings an adolescent girl to a doctor, nurse practitioner, or family-planning clinic, providing an opportunity for her to receive sex education and contraception.

So far we have discussed these problems: adolescent pregnancy and sexually transmitted infections. Next, we explore these sexuality problems: forcible sexual behavior and sexual harassment.

**syphilis** A sexually transmitted infection caused by the bacterium *Treponema pallidum,* a spirochete.

**chlamydia** One of most common sexually transmitted infections, named for *Chlamydia trachomatis,* an organism that spreads by sexual contact and infects the genital organs of both sexes.

## Forcible Sexual Behavior and Sexual Harassment

Most people choose to engage in sexual intercourse or other sexual activities, but, unfortunately, some people force others to engage in sex. Too many adolescent girls and young women report that they believe they don't have adequate sexual rights (East & Adams, 2002). These include the right to not have sexual intercourse when they don't wish to, the right to tell a partner that he is being too rough, or the right to use any form of birth control during intercourse. One study found that almost 20 percent of 904 sexually active 14- to 26-year-old females believed that they never have the right to make decisions about contraception, to tell their partner that they don't want to have intercourse without birth control, that they want to make love differently or that their partner is being too rough, and to stop foreplay at any time, including at the point of intercourse (Rickert, Sanghvi, & Wiemann, 2002). In this study, poor grades in school and sexual inexperience were linked to a lack of sexual assertiveness in females.

**Forcible Sexual Behavior** **Rape** is forcible sexual intercourse with a person who does not give consent. Legal definitions of rape vary from state to state. In some states, for example, the law allows husbands to force their wives to have sex. Because of the difficulties involved in reporting rape, the actual incidence is not easily determined (Erlick Robinson, 2003; Nofziger & Stein, 2006). It appears that rape occurs most often in large cities, where it has been reported that 8 of every 10,000 women 12 years old and older are raped each year. Nearly 200,000 rapes are reported each year in the United States. We tend to assume that all rapists are men. In fact, while 95 percent of rapes are committed by men, 5% are committed by women.

Why is rape so pervasive in the American culture? Feminist writers assert that males are socialized to be sexually aggressive, to regard females as inferior beings, and to view their own pleasure as the most important objective. Researchers have found the following characteristics common among rapists: aggression enhances their sense of power or masculinity; they are angry at females generally; and they want to hurt their victims. For example, a recent study found that men who consistently engaged in sexually coercive behavior had hostile attitudes toward women and engaged in sexual harassment (Hall & others, 2006).

**rape** Forcible sexual intercourse with a person who does not give consent.

**date, or acquaintance, rape** Coercive sexual activity directed at someone whom the perpetrator knows.

A form of rape that went unacknowledged until recent decades is **date, or acquaintance, rape,** which is coercive sexual activity directed at someone whom the perpetrator knows. Acquaintance rape is an increasing problem in high schools and on college campuses (Caron, 2007; Christopher & Kisler, 2004; Olshen & others, 2007). A major study that focused on campus sexual assault involved a phone survey of 4,446 women attending two- or four-year colleges (Fisher, Cullen, & Turner, 2000). In this study, slightly less than 3 percent said that they either had experienced a rape or an attempted rape during the academic year. About one of ten college women said that they had experienced rape in their lifetime. Unwanted or uninvited sexual contacts were widespread, with more than one-third of the college women reporting such incidents. As shown in Figure 6.7, in this study, most women (about nine of ten) knew the person who sexually victimized them. Most of the women attempted to take protective actions against their assailants but were then reluctant to report the victimization to the police. Several factors were associated with sexual victimization: living on campus,

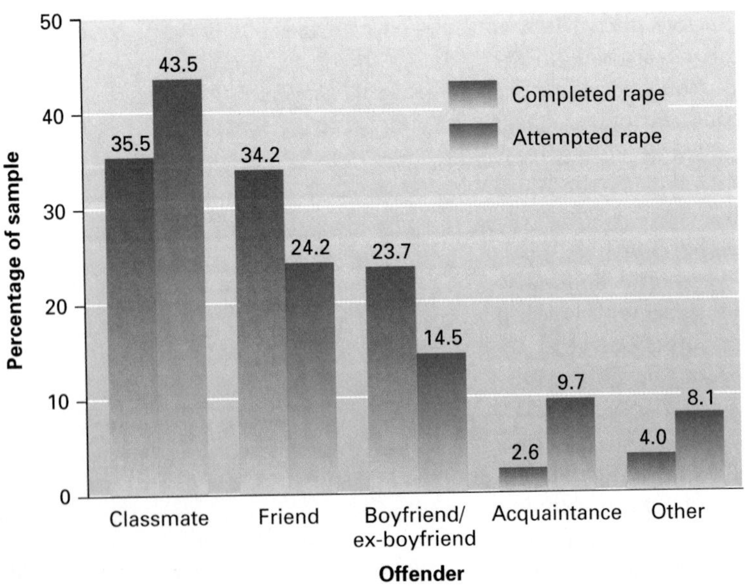


**FIGURE 6.7** **Completed Rape and Attempted Rape of College Women According to Victim-Offender Relationship**

being unmarried, getting drunk frequently, and having been sexually victimized on a prior occasion.

In another study, about two-thirds of the sexual victimization incidents were perpetrated by a romantic acquaintance (Flanagan, 1996). In yet another study, approximately 2,000 ninth- through twelfth-grade females were asked about the extent to which they had experienced physical and sexual violence (Silverman & others, 2001). About 20 percent of the girls said they had been physically or sexually abused by a dating partner. Further, the physical and sexual abuse was linked with substance use.

Rape is a traumatic experience for the victim and those close to her or him (Carroll, 2007; Ullman & others, 2006). The rape victim initially feels shock and numbness and often is acutely disorganized. Some women show their distress through words and tears, others show more internalized suffering. As victims strive to get their lives back to normal, they might experience depression, fear, and anxiety for months or years. Sexual dysfunctions, such as reduced sexual desire and the inability to reach orgasm, occur in 50 percent of rape victims. Many rape victims make lifestyle changes, moving to a new apartment or refusing to go out at night. About one-fifth of rape victims have made a suicide attempt—a rate eight times higher than that of women who have not been raped.

*What are some characteristics of acquaintance rape in adolescence and emerging adulthood?*

A girl's or woman's recovery depends on both her coping abilities and psychological adjustment prior to the assault (Macy, Nurius, & Norris, 2006). Social support from parents, partner, and others close to her are also important factors in recovery, as is the availability of professional counseling, sometimes obtained through a rape crisis center. Many rape victims become empowered by reporting their rape to the police and assisting in the prosecution of the rapist if caught. However, women who take a legal approach are especially encouraged to use supportive counselors to aid them throughout the legal ordeal. Each female must be allowed to make her own, individual decision about whether to report the rape or not.

Although most victims of rape are girls and women, rape of boys and men does occur. Men in prisons are especially vulnerable to rape, usually by heterosexuals who are using homosexual rape to establish their domination and power within the prison.

**Sexual Harassment** Girls and women encounter sexual harassment in many different forms—ranging from sexist remarks and covert physical contact (patting, brushing against bodies) to blatant propositions and sexual assaults (Duffy, Wareham, & Walsh, 2004; Sears & others, 2006). Literally millions of girls and women experience such sexual harassment each year in educational and work settings. In one study, 85 percent of eighth- to eleventh-grade girls reported that they were often sexually harassed (American Association of University Women, 1993). A surprisingly large percentage (75 percent) of boys also said they often were sexually harassed. Sexual comments, jokes, gestures, and looks were the most common forms of harassment. Students also reported other objectionable behavior, ranging from being the subject of sexual rumors to being forced to do something sexual.

A recent survey of 2,000 college women by the American Association of University Women (2006) revealed that 62 percent of them reported that they had experienced sexual harassment while attending college. Most of the college women said that the sexual harassment involved non-contact forms such as crude jokes, remarks, and gestures. However, almost one-third said that the sexual harassment was physical in nature. A recent study of almost 1,500 college women revealed that when they had been sexually harassed they reported an increase in psychological distress, greater physical illness, and an increase in disordered eating (Huerta & others, 2006).

The Office for Civil Rights in the U.S. Department of Education published a 40-page policy guide on sexual harassment. In this guide, a distinction is made between quid pro quo and hostile environment sexual harassment (Chmielewski, 1997):

- **Quid pro quo sexual harassment** occurs when a school employee threatens to base an educational decision (such as a grade) on a student's submission to unwelcome sexual conduct. For example, a teacher gives a student an A for allowing the teacher's sexual advances, or the teacher gives the student an F for resisting the teacher's approaches.
- **Hostile environment sexual harassment** occurs when students are subjected to unwelcome sexual conduct that is so severe, persistent, or pervasive that it limits the students' ability to benefit from their education. Such a hostile environment is usually created by a series of incidents, such as repeated sexual overtures.

Quid pro quo and hostile environment sexual harassment are illegal in the workplace as well as in educational settings, but potential victims are often not given access to a clear reporting and investigation mechanism where they can make a complaint.

Sexual harassment is a form of power and dominance of one person over another, which can result in harmful consequences for the victim. Sexual harassment can be especially damaging when the perpetrators are teachers, employers, and other adults who have considerable power and authority over students (Lee & others, 1995). As a society, we need to be less tolerant of sexual harassment (Shrier, 2003).

**quid pro quo sexual harassment** Sexual harassment in which a school employee threatens to base an educational decision (such as a grade) on a student's submission to unwelcome sexual conduct.

**hostile environment sexual harassment** Sexual harassment in which students are subjected to unwelcome sexual conduct that is so severe, persistent, or pervasive that it limits the students' ability to benefit from their education.

## REVIEW AND REFLECT ◆ LEARNING GOAL 3

### 3 Describe the main sexual problems that can emerge in adolescence.

***Review***
- How would you characterize adolescent pregnancy?
- What are the main sexually transmitted infections in adolescence?
- What is the nature of forcible sexual behavior and sexual harassment in adolescence?

***Reflect***
- Caroline contracted genital herpes from her boyfriend whom she had been dating for the past three years. After breaking off the relationship and spending some time on her own, she began dating Charles. Should Caroline tell Charles about her sexually transmitted infection? If so, how and when?

## 4 SEXUAL LITERACY AND SEX EDUCATION

Sexual Literacy | Sources of Sex Information | Sex Education in Schools

Given the high rate of STIs, a special concern is the knowledge that both adolescents and adults have about these infections and about other aspects of sexuality. How sexually literate are Americans? What are adolescents' sources of sex education? What is the role of schools in sex education?

## Sexual Literacy

According to June Reinisch (1990), director of the Kinsey Institute for Sex, Gender, and Reproduction, U.S. citizens know more about how their automobiles function than about how their bodies function sexually. American adolescents and adults are not sheltered from sexual messages; indeed, Reinisch says, adolescents too often are inundated with sexual messages, but not sexual facts. Sexual information is abundant, but much of it is misinformation. In some cases, even sex education teachers display sexual ignorance. One high school sex education teacher referred to erogenous zones as "erroneous zones," causing students to wonder if their sexually sensitive zones were in error!

Most adolescents do not know at what stage of the menstrual cycle females are most likely to get pregnant (Loewen & Leigh, 1986; Zelnik & Kantner, 1977). In one study, 12 percent of more than 8,000 students thought that birth control pills provide some protection against AIDS, and 23 percent believed they could tell by just looking at a potential sexual partner whether he or she was infected with HIV (Hechinger, 1992). In a national survey of more than 1,500 adolescents 12 to 18 years old, the respondents said that they have enough information to understand pregnancy but not enough about how to obtain and use birth control (Kaiser Family Foundation, 1996).

## Sources of Sex Information

Adolescents can get information about sex from many sources, including parents, siblings, schools, peers, magazines, television, and the Internet. A special concern is the accuracy of sexual information adolescents have access to on the Internet.

Many parents feel uncomfortable talking about sex with adolescents, and many adolescents feel uncomfortable about this as well (Lefkowitz & Stoppa, 2006). One study revealed that 94 percent of fathers and 76 percent of mothers had never discussed sexual desire with their daughters (Feldman & Rosenthal, 1999). Also, a recent study in China revealed that parent adolescent communication about sex was infrequent (Zhang & others, 2003).

Many adolescents say that they cannot talk freely with their parents about sexual matters, but those who can talk with their parents openly and freely about sex are less likely to be sexually active (Chia-Chen & Thompson, 2007). Contraceptive use by female adolescents also increases when adolescents report that they can communicate about sex with their parents (Fisher, 1987). Also, a recent study found that first semester college women who felt more comfortable talking openly about sex with their mothers were more likely to have positive beliefs about condoms and confidence in using them (Lefkowitz & Espinosa-Hernandez, 2006).

Adolescents are far more likely to have conversations about sex with their mothers than with their fathers (Kirkman, Rosenthal, & Feldman, 2002). This is true of both female and male adolescents, although female adolescents report having more frequent conversations about sex with their mothers than their male counterparts do (Feldman & Rosenthal, 1999, 2002; Lefkowitz & others, 1999). In one study that involved videotaped conversations about sexual matters between mothers and adolescents, adolescent girls were more responsive and enthusiastic than adolescent boys were (Lefkowitz & others, 1999).

## Sex Education in Schools

One survey found that 93 percent of Americans support the teaching of sex education in high schools, and 84 percent support its teaching in middle/junior high schools (SIECUS, 1999). The dramatic increase in HIV/AIDS and other STIs is the main reason that Americans have increasingly supported sex education in schools in recent years. This survey also found that more than eight of ten Americans think

The AIDS epidemic has led to an increased awareness of the importance of sex education in adolescence.

that adolescents should be given information to protect themselves from unwanted pregnancies and STIs, as well as about abstinence. And more than eight of ten Americans rejected the idea that providing such sex education encourages sexual activity.

The nature of sex education in schools is changing. In one study, trends in sex education in American public schools from 1988 through 1999 were examined (Darroch, Landry, & Singh, 2000). Among the results of the survey:

- Some topics—how HIV is transmitted, STIs, abstinence, how to resist peer pressure to have intercourse, and the correct way to use a condom—were taught in earlier grades in 1999 than in 1988.
- In 1999, 23 percent of secondary school sex education teachers taught abstinence as the only way of preventing pregnancy and STIs, compared with only 2 percent in 1988. Teachers surveyed in 1999 also were more likely than those in 1988 to cite abstinence as the most important message they wished to convey (41 percent versus 25 percent).
- Steep declines occurred between 1988 and 1999 in the percentage of teachers who supported teaching about birth control, abortion, and sexual orientation.

In sum, sex education in U.S. schools today is increasingly focused on abstinence and is less likely to present students with comprehensive teaching that includes information about birth control, abortion, and sexual orientation (Alan Guttmacher Institute, 2003a; Santelli & others, 2006).

In another study, 1,789 fifth- and sixth-grade U.S. teachers were asked about the nature of their sex education instruction in 1999 (Landry, Singh, & Darroch, 2000). The results included the following:

- Seventy-two percent said that sex education is taught in their schools at either the fifth grade, sixth grade, or both.
- More than 75 percent of teachers who include sex education in their instruction cover these topics: puberty, HIV and AIDS transmission, alcohol and drug use, and how to stick to a decision. However, many fifth- and sixth-grade teachers do not teach sex education at all. It was estimated that overall these topics are taught in about half of fifth- and sixth-grade classrooms.
- More than half of the teachers include the topic of abstinence in the sex education instruction.

To read further about sex education, see the *Health and Well-Being* interlude.

## *Health and Well-Being*

### TOWARD EFFECTIVE SEX EDUCATION

Currently, a major controversy in U.S. sex education is whether schools should have an abstinence-only program or a more comprehensive program that emphasizes contraceptive knowledge (Cabezon & others, 2005). Sex education is a politically charged issue, and the Bush administration has earmarked federal funds that are to be used for abstinence-only programs. The American Civil Liberties Union (ACLU) has especially been vocal in opposing abstinence-only programs and advocating more comprehensive sex education that includes contraceptive knowledge. A concern about some abstinence-only programs is that they have included inaccurate or stereotypical information, such as: a 43-day-old fetus is a thinking person; HIV can be spread through sweat and tears; and a man needs admiration and sexual fulfillment, whereas a woman needs financial support.

A recent research review of 83 studies around the world revealed that two-thirds of the programs significantly improved one or more sexual behaviors (Kirby, Laris, & Rolleri, 2007). The review also found that the programs did not hasten or increase sexual behavior and that some programs delayed sexual behavior and increased condom use. Another review of research concluded that some abstinence-only programs and some contraceptive-knowledge programs were effective in changing adolescents' sexual behavior (Bennett & Assefi, 2005). However, the positive outcomes were modest and most lasted only for a short time period. One criticism of the contraceptive-knowledge programs is that they increase adolescent sexual activity, but this research review revealed that is not the case. An important point to note about comparing sex education programs is that the variation in samples, interventions, and outcome measures makes conclusions about which programs are most effective difficult.

Critics of abstinence-only programs say that controversy arises when abstinence is the only option given to adolescents and when health information about other options is restricted or misrepresented (Santelli & others, 2006). They argue that the recent emphasis on abstinence-only education programs by the U.S. government undermines more comprehensive sex education programs (Brindis, 2006).

Sex education programs in schools might not by themselves prevent adolescent pregnancy and STIs. Researchers have found that sex education classes do improve adolescents' knowledge about human sexuality but do not always change their sexual behavior. When sex education programs are combined with contraceptive availability, the pregnancy rates of adolescents are more likely to drop (Wallis, 1985). This has led to the development of *school-linked* rather than school-based approaches to sex education and pregnancy prevention (Kirby & others, 1993). In one program pioneered by some Baltimore public schools in cooperation with Johns Hopkins University, family-planning clinics are located adjacent to the schools (Zabin, 1986). The clinics send a nurse and social worker into the schools, where they make formal presentations about the services available from the clinics and about sexuality. They also are available to the students several hours each day for counseling. The same health personnel also conduct after-school sessions at the clinics. These sessions involve further counseling, films, and family-planning information. The results have been very positive. Students who participated in the programs delayed their first intercourse longer than did students in a control group. After 28 months, the pregnancy rate had declined by 30 percent in the program schools, while it rose 60 percent in the control-group schools. This program demonstrates that a key dimension of pregnancy prevention is the link between information and support services (Kenney, 1987).

However, some critics charge that school-linked health clinics promote premarital sex and encourage abortion for pregnant adolescents. These critics believe that more effort should be devoted to promoting adolescents' abstention from sex. Supporters of the school-linked clinics argue that sexual activity in adolescence has become a normative behavior and, therefore, interventions should focus on teaching responsible sexual behavior and providing access to contraception (Dryfoos & Barkin, 2006). In one study, a school-wide program called Safer Choices, which discussed pregnancy prevention and condom use, was effective in increasing condom use and in decreasing the number of sex partners (Basen-Enquist & others, 2001). And in another study, students in high schools where condoms were available were more likely to receive condom use instruction and less likely to report lifetime or recent sexual intercourse than their counterparts in schools where condoms were not available (Blake & others, 2003). Sexually active adolescents in schools where condoms were available were twice as likely to use condoms, but less likely to use other contraceptive methods, in their most recent sexual encounter. In most cases, the condoms were available from the school nurse or from other school personnel, such as a gym teacher.

In the United States, the media entice adolescents with stories of romantic love and portrayals of sex. Parents encourage boy-girl contact but are often reluctant to discuss sex openly; are unwilling to make contraceptives, including condoms, available

*(continued on next page)*

In many countries, contraceptive knowledge is included in sex education. Here students in a sex education class in Beijing, China, learn about condoms.

to adolescents; and fail to offer alternatives other than abstinence (Crockett, Raffaelli, & Moilanen, 2003).

U.S. sex education typically has focused on the hazards of sex and the need to protect adolescent females from male predators (Fine, 1988). The contrast between the United States and other Western nations is remarkable. For example, the Swedish State Commission on Sex Education recommends that students gain knowledge to help them to experience sexual life as a source of happiness and fellowship with others. Swedish adolescents are sexually active at an earlier age than are American adolescents, and they are exposed to even more explicit sex on television. However, the Swedish National Board of Education has developed a curriculum to give every child, beginning at age 7, a thorough grounding in reproductive biology and, by the age of 10 or 12, information about various forms of contraception. Teachers handle the subject of sex whenever it becomes relevant, regardless of the subject they are teaching. The idea is to dedramatize and demystify sex so that familiarity will make students less vulnerable to unwanted pregnancy and STIs. Despite a relatively early onset of sexual activity, the adolescent pregnancy rate in Sweden is one of the lowest in the world.

**REVIEW AND REFLECT ◆ LEARNING GOAL 4**

### 4 Characterize the sexual literacy of adolescents and sex education.

***Review***
- How sexually literate are U.S. adolescents?
- What are adolescents' sources of sexual information?
- How would you describe sex education in schools?

***Reflect***
- Think about how you learned the "facts of life." Did most of your information come from well-informed sources? Were you able to talk freely and openly with your parents about what to expect sexually? Did you acquire some false beliefs through trial-and-error efforts? As you grew older, did you discover that some of what you thought you knew about sex was inaccurate? Think also about the sex education you received in school. How adequate was it? What do you wish the schools you attended would have done differently in regard to sex education?

# Reach Your Learning Goals

## 1 Exploring Adolescent Sexuality *Discuss some basic ideas about the nature of adolescent sexuality.*

**A Normal Aspect of Adolescent Development**

Too often the problems adolescents encounter with sexuality are emphasized rather than the fact that sexuality is a normal aspect of adolescent development. Adolescence is a bridge between the asexual child and the sexual adult. Adolescent sexuality is related to many other aspects of adolescent development, including physical development and puberty, cognitive development, the self and identity, gender, families, peers, schools, and culture.

**The Sexual Culture**

Increased permissiveness in adolescent sexuality is linked to increased permissiveness in the larger culture. Adolescent initiation of sexual intercourse is related to exposure to explicit sex on TV.

**Developing a Sexual Identity**

Developing a sexual identity is multifaceted. An adolescent's sexual identity involves an indication of sexual orientation, interests, and styles of behavior.

**Obtaining Research Information About Adolescent Sexuality**

Obtaining valid information about adolescent sexuality is not easy. Much of the data are based on interviews and questionnaires, which can involve untruthful or socially desirable responses.

## 2 Sexual Attitudes and Behavior *Summarize sexual attitudes and behavior in adolescence.*

**Heterosexual Attitudes and Behavior**

The progression of sexual behaviors is typically kissing, petting, sexual intercourse, and oral sex. The number of adolescents reporting having had sexual intercourse increased significantly in the twentieth century. The proportion of females engaging in intercourse increased more rapidly than for males. National data indicate that slightly more than half of all adolescents today have had sexual intercourse by age 17, although the percentage varies by sex, ethnicity, and context. Male, African American, and inner-city adolescents report the highest sexual activity. The percentage of 15- to 17-year-olds who have had sexual intercourse declined from 1991 to 2001. A common adolescent sexual script involves the male making sexual advances, and it is left up to the female to set limits on the male's sexual overtures. Adolescent females' sexual scripts link sex with love more than adolescent males' sexual scripts do. Risk factors for sexual problems include early sexual activity, having a number of sexual partners, not using contraception, engaging in other at-risk behaviors such as drinking and delinquency, living in a low-SES neighborhood, and ethnicity. Heterosexual behavior patterns change in emerging adulthood.

**Sexual Minority Attitudes and Behavior**

An individual's sexual attraction—whether heterosexual or sexual minority—is likely caused by a mix of genetic, hormonal, cognitive, and environmental factors. Terms such as "sexual minority individuals" (who identify with being a gay male, lesbian, or bisexual) and "same-sex attraction" are increasingly used, whereas the term "homosexual" is used less. Developmental pathways for sexual minority youth are often diverse, may involve bisexual attractions, and do not always involve falling in love with a same-sex individual. Recent research has focused on adolescents' disclosure of same-sex attractions and the struggle they often go through in doing this. The peer relations of sexual minority youth differ from those of heterosexual youth. Discrimination and bias against same-sex attraction produces considerable stress for adolescents with a same-sex attraction.

**Self-Stimulation**

Self-stimulation is part of the sexual activity of virtually all adolescents and one of their most frequent sexual outlets.

**Contraceptive Use**

Adolescents are increasing their use of contraceptives, but large numbers of sexually active adolescents still do not use them. Young adolescents and those from low-SES backgrounds are less likely to use contraceptives than their older, middle-SES counterparts.

## 3 Adolescent Sexual Problems *Describe the main sexual problems that can emerge in adolescence.*

**Adolescent Pregnancy**

The U.S. adolescent pregnancy rate is one of the highest in the Western world. Fortunately, the U.S. adolescent pregnancy rate has recently started to decline. A complex, impassioned issue involving an unintended pregnancy is the decision of whether to have an abortion. Adolescent pregnancy increases health risks for the mother and the offspring. Adolescent mothers are more likely to drop out of school and have lower-paying jobs than their adolescent counterparts who do not bear children. It is important to remember, though, that it often is not pregnancy alone that places adolescents at risk. Adolescent mothers often come from low-income families and were not doing well in school prior to their pregnancy. Cognitive factors, such as egocentric and immature thought, may be involved in adolescent pregnancy. The infants of adolescent parents are at risk both medically and psychologically. Adolescent parents are less effective in rearing their children than older parents are. Many adolescent fathers do not have a close relationship with their baby and the adolescent mother. Recommendations for reducing adolescent pregnancy include sex education and family planning, access to contraception, life options, community involvement and support, and abstinence. In one study, volunteer community service was linked with a lower incidence of adolescent pregnancy.

**Sexually Transmitted Infections**

Sexually transmitted infections (STIs) are contracted primarily through sexual contact with an infected partner. The contact is not limited to vaginal intercourse but includes oral-genital and anal-genital contact as well. AIDS (acquired immune deficiency syndrome) is caused by the HIV virus, which destroys the body's immune system. Currently, the rate of AIDS in U.S. adolescents is relatively low, but it has reached epidemic proportions in sub-Saharan Africa, especially in adolescent girls. AIDS can be transmitted through sexual contact, sharing needles, and blood transfusions. A number of projects are focusing on AIDS prevention. Genital herpes is caused by a family of viruses with different strains. Genital warts, caused by a virus, is the most common STI in the 15- to 24-year-old age group. Commonly called the "drip" or "clap," gonorrhea is another common STI. Syphilis is caused by the bacterium *Treponema pallidum,* a spirochete. Chlamydia is one of the most common STIs.

Forcible Sexual Behavior and Sexual Harassment

Some individuals force others to have sex with them. Rape is forcible sexual intercourse with a person who does not give consent. About 95 percent of rapes are committed by males. An increasing concern is date, or acquaintance, rape. Sexual harassment is a form of power of one person over another. Sexual harassment of adolescents is widespread. Two forms are quid pro quo and hostile environment sexual harassment.

## 4 SEXUAL LITERACY AND SEX EDUCATION *Characterize the sexual literacy of adolescents and sex education.*

Sexual Literacy

American adolescents and adults are not very knowledgeable about sex. Sex information is abundant, but too often it is misinformation.

Sources of Sex Information

Adolescents can get their information about sex from many sources, including parents, siblings, schools, peers, magazines, TV, and the Internet.

Sex Education in Schools

A majority of Americans support teaching sex education in schools, and this support has increased in concert with increases in STIs, especially AIDS. Some experts believe that school-linked sex education that ties in with community health centers is a promising strategy.

## KEY TERMS

sexual script 205
sexual minority 208
bisexual 208
homophobia 210
sexually transmitted infections (STIs) 221
AIDS 221
genital herpes 224
genital warts 224
gonorrhea 224
syphilis 225
chlamydia 225
rape 226
date, or acquaintance, rape 226
quid pro quo sexual harassment 228
hostile environment sexual harassment 228

## KEY PEOPLE

Deborah Tolman 205
Simon LeVay 209
Ritch Savin-Williams 211
June Reinisch 227

## RESOURCES FOR IMPROVING THE LIVES OF ADOLESCENTS

**AIDS Hotline**
National AIDS Information Clearinghouse
800–342–AIDS
800–344–SIDA (Spanish)
800–AIDS–TTY (Deaf)

The people answering the hotline will respond to any questions children, youth, or adults have about HIV infection or AIDS. Pamphlets and other materials on AIDS are available.

**Alan Guttmacher Institute** **www.guttmacher.org**
The Alan Guttmacher Institute is an especially good resource for information about adolescent sexuality. The Institute publishes a well-respected journal, *Perspectives on Sexual and Reproductive Health* (renamed in 2003, formerly *Family Planning Perspectives*), which includes articles on many dimensions of sexuality, such as adolescent pregnancy, statistics on sexual behavior and attitudes, and sexually transmitted infections.

**The New Gay Teenager**
by Ritch Savin-Williams (2006)
Cambridge, MA: Harvard University Press

Leading researcher on adolescent gay males and lesbians, Ritch Savin-Williams examines many aspects of their development and relationships.

**National Sexually Transmitted Diseases Hotline**
800–227–8922

This hotline provides information about a wide variety of sexually transmitted infections.

**Sex Information and Education Council of the United States (SIECUS)** **www.siecus.org**
This organization serves as an information clearinghouse about sex education. The group's objective is to promote the concept of human sexuality as an integration of physical, intellectual, emotional, and social dimensions.

## E-LEARNING TOOLS

To help you master the material in this chapter, visit the Online Learning Center for *Adolescence,* twelfth edition **(www.mhhe.com/santrockal2),** where you will find these additional resources:

### Taking It to the Net

1. Adolescence is a time when we not only are learning about sexuality but also are dealing with emerging sexuality and learning sexual scripts. Your instructor assigns a paper in which you are to evaluate the importance of sexual scripts in the change, or lack of change, of gender roles in dating. What information will you include? Write a brief outline of your paper.
2. While home for vacation you notice that your younger sister says that she wants to break up with her boyfriend but she fears he will hurt himself or someone else. She seems to feel guilty about wanting to break up because she seems to be the only person who loves and understands him. You begin to wonder if she might be in an abusive relationship. What are the signs of an abusive dating relationship?
3. Do you or any of your friends know a teenage father? How does he cope with being a father? What special needs might he have in becoming a responsible father? If you do not know a teenage father, speculate about how a young man might cope and what his needs might be.

## Self-Assessment

The Online Learning Center includes the following self-assessments for further exploration:

- My Knowledge of Sexual Myths and Realities
- How Much Do I Know About STIs?

## Health and Well-Being, Parenting, and Education

To practice your decision-making skills, complete the health and well-being, parenting, and education exercises on the Online Learning Center.

## Video Clips

The Online Learning Center includes the following videos for this chapter:

- Sex Among Teens at Age 15
- Sexual Activity in Adolescence
- Sexual Minority Youth
- Teen Pregnancy Prevention
- Coping as Teen Parents

# 8 Families

*It is not enough for parents to understand children. They must accord children the privilege of understanding them.*

—Milton Saperstein
American Author, 20th Century

## CHAPTER OUTLINE

## LEARNING GOALS

### 1 Family Processes

Discuss the nature of family processes in adolescence.

Reciprocal Socialization and the Family as a System
The Developmental Construction of Relationships
Maturation

### 2 Adolescents' and Emerging Adults' Relationships with Parents

Describe adolescents' and emerging adults' relationships with their parents.

Parents as Managers
Parenting Styles
Gender, Parenting, and Coparenting
Parent-Adolescent Conflict
Autonomy and Attachment
Emerging Adults' Relationships with Parents

### 3 Sibling Relationships

Characterize sibling relationships in adolescence.

Sibling Roles
Birth Order

### 4 The Changing Family in a Changing Society

Describe the changing family in a changing society.

Divorced Families
Stepfamilies
Working Parents
Adoption
Gay Male and Lesbian Parents
Culture and Ethnicity

### 5 Social Policy, Adolescents, and Families

Explain what is needed for improved social policy involving adolescents and their families.

# Images of Adolescent Development

## Variations in Adolescents' Perceptions of Parents

My mother and I depend on each other. However, if something separated us, I think I could still get along okay. I know that my mother continues to have an important influence on me. Sometimes she gets on my nerves, but I still basically like her, and respect her, a lot. We have our arguments, and I don't always get my way, but she is willing to listen to me.

—Amy, age 16

You go from a point at which your parents are responsible for you to a point at which you want a lot more independence. Finally, you are more independent, and you feel like you have to be more responsible for yourself; otherwise you are not going to do very well in this world. It's important for parents to still be there to support you, but at some point, you've got to look in the mirror and say, "I can do it myself."

—John, age 18

I don't get along very well with my parents. They try to dictate how I dress, who I date, how much I study, what I do on weekends, and how much time I spend talking on the phone. They are big intruders in my life. Why won't they let me make my own decisions? I'm mature enough to handle these things. When they jump down my throat at every little thing I do, it makes me mad and I say things to them I probably shouldn't. They just don't understand me very well.

—Ed, age 17

My father never seems to have any time to spend with me. He is gone a lot on business, and when he comes home, he is either too tired to do anything or plops down and watches TV and doesn't want to be bothered. He thinks I don't work hard enough and don't have values that were as solid as his generation. It is a very distant relationship. I actually spend more time talking to my mom than to him. I guess I should work a little harder in school than I do, but I still don't think he has the right to say such negative things to me. I like my mom a lot better because I think she is a much nicer person.

—Tom, age 14

We have our arguments and our differences, and there are moments when I get very angry with my parents, but most of the time they are like heated discussions. I have to say what I think because I don't think they are always right. Most of the time when there is an argument, we can discuss the problem and eventually find a course that we all can live with. Not every time, though, because there are some occasions when things just remain unresolved. Even when we have an unresolved conflict, I still would have to say that I get along pretty good with my parents.

—Ann, age 16

## PREVIEW

***Although parent-adolescent relationships can vary considerably, researchers are finding that for the most part, the relationships are both (1) very important aspects of development, and (2) more positive than once thought. This chapter examines families as a context for adolescent development. We begin by exploring family processes, then discuss parent-adolescent relationships, followed by relationships with siblings. Next, the substantial changes of families in a changing society are described. The chapter concludes by focusing on social policy recommendations for the well-being of adolescents and their families.***

## 1 FAMILY PROCESSES

Reciprocal Socialization and the Family as a System | The Developmental Construction of Relationships | Maturation

Researchers are especially interested in the family processes that adolescents experience. We begin our exploration of family processes by examining how family members interact with one another.

### Reciprocal Socialization and the Family as a System

For many years, socialization between parents and children/adolescents was considered to be a one-way process: children and adolescents were seen as the products of their parents' socialization techniques. As we see next, however, today parent-adolescent interaction is viewed as a reciprocal process.

**Reciprocal Socialization** **Reciprocal socialization** is the process by which children and adolescents socialize parents, just as parents socialize them (Bugental & Grusec, 2006; Grusec & Davidov, 2007; Kuczynski & Parkin, 2007; Maccoby, 2007). To get a better feel for how reciprocal socialization works, consider two situations: the first emphasizing the impact of growing up in a single-parent home (parental influences), the second presenting the dilemma of a talented teenage ice skater (adolescent influences). In the first situation, the speaker is 14-year-old Robert:

> I never have seen my father. He never married my mother, and she had to quit school to help support us. Maybe my mother and I are better off that he didn't marry her because he apparently didn't love her . . . but sometimes I get depressed about not having a father, especially when I see a lot of my friends with their fathers at ball games and such. My father still lives around here, but he has gotten married, and I guess he wants to forget about me and my mother. . . . A lot of times I wish my mother would get married and I could at least have a stepfather to talk with about things and do things with me.

In the second situation, the first speaker is 13-year-old Kathy:

> "Mother, my skating coach says that I have a lot of talent, but it is going to take a lot of lessons and travel to fully develop it." Her mother responds, "Kathy, I just don't know. We will have to talk with your father about it tonight when he gets home from work." That evening, Kathy's father tells his wife, "Look, to do that for Kathy, I will have to get a second job, or you will have to get a job. There is no way we can afford what she wants with what I make."

**Family as a System** As a social system, the family can be thought of as a constellation of subsystems defined in terms of generation, gender, and role. Divisions of labor among family members define particular subunits, and attachments define others. Each family member is a participant in several subsystems—some dyadic (involving two people), some polyadic (involving more than two people) (Minuchin, 2002). The father and adolescent represent one dyadic subsystem, the mother and father another; the mother-father-adolescent represent one polyadic subsystem, the mother and two siblings another.

An organizational scheme that highlights the reciprocal influences of family members and family subsystems is shown in Figure 8.1 (Belsky, 1981). As the arrows in the figure show, marital relations, parenting, and adolescent behavior can have both direct and indirect effects on each other. An example of a direct effect is the influence of the parent's behavior on the adolescent. An example of an indirect effect is how the relationship between the spouses mediates the way a parent acts toward the adolescent.

**reciprocal socialization** The process by which children and adolescents socialize parents, just as parents socialize them.

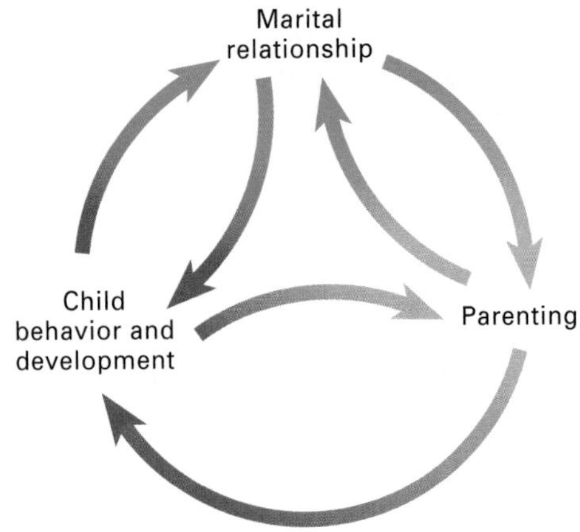


**FIGURE 8.1** **Interaction Between Adolescents and Their Parents: Direct and Indirect Effects**

For example, marital conflict might reduce the efficiency of parenting, in which case marital conflict would have an indirect effect on the adolescent's behavior.

Interaction between individuals in a family can change, depending on who is present (Maccoby, 2007). In one investigation, 44 adolescents were observed either separately with their mother and father (dyadic settings) or in the presence of both parents (triadic setting) (Gjerde, 1986). The presence of the father improved mother-son relationships, but the presence of the mother decreased the quality of father-son relations. This may have occurred because the father takes the strain off the mother by controlling the adolescent, or because the mother's presence reduces father-son interaction, which may not be high in many instances. Indeed, in one investigation, sons directed more negative behavior toward their mothers than toward their fathers in dyadic situations (Buhrmester & others, 1992). However, in a triadic context of adolescent-mother-father, fathers helped "rescue" mothers by attempting to control the sons' negative behavior. In one study that focused on adolescents in middle-socioeconomic-status African American families, both mothers' and fathers' communication was more positive in dyadic than triadic interactions (Smetana, Abernethy, & Harris, 2000).

**Marital Relationships and Parenting** As researchers have broadened their focus in families beyond just studying the parent-adolescent relationship, an increasingly studied aspect of the family system involves the link between marital relationships and parenting. The most consistent findings are that happily married parents are more sensitive, responsive, warm, and affectionate toward their children and adolescents (Grych, 2002). Researchers have also found that marital satisfaction is often related to good parenting. The marital relationship is an important support for parenting. When parents report more intimacy and better communication in their marriage, they are more affectionate to their children and adolescents (Grych, 2002). Thus, an important, if unintended, benefit of marriage enhancement programs is the improvement of parenting, and consequently healthier children and adolescents. Programs that focus on parenting skills might also benefit from including attention to the participants' marriages.

## The Developmental Construction of Relationships

**developmental construction views** Views sharing the belief that as individuals grow up, they acquire modes of relating to others. There are two main variations of this view. One emphasizes continuity and stability in relationships throughout the life span; the other emphasizes discontinuity and changes in relationships throughout the life span.

Developmentalists have shown an increased interest in understanding how we construct relationships as we grow up (Collins & Roisman, 2006; Collins & van Dulmen, 2006). Psychoanalytic theorists have always been interested in how this process works in families. However, the current explanations of how relationships are constructed is virtually stripped of Freud's psychosexual stage terminology and also is not always confined to the first five years of life, as has been the case in classical psychoanalytic theory. Today's **developmental construction views** share the belief that as individuals grow up, they acquire modes of relating to others. There are two main variations within this view, one of which emphasizes continuity and stability in relationships throughout the life span; the other emphasizes discontinuity and change in relationships throughout the life span.

**The Continuity View** The **continuity view** emphasizes the role that early parent-child relationships play in constructing a basic way of relating to people throughout the life span. These early parent-child relationships are carried forward to later points in development to influence all subsequent relationships (with peers, with friends, with teachers, and with romantic partners, for example) (Bowlby, 1989; Sroufe, 2002, 2007; Sroufe & others, 2005). In its extreme form, this view states that the basic components of social relationships are laid down and shaped by the security or insecurity of parent-infant attachment relationships in the first year or two of the infant's life. More about the importance of secure attachment in the adolescent's development appears later in the chapter when we discuss autonomy and attachment.

Close relationships with parents also are important in the adolescent's development because these relationships function as models or templates that are carried forward over time to influence the construction of new relationships. Clearly, close relationships do not repeat themselves in an endless fashion over the course of the child's and adolescent's development. And the quality of any relationship depends to some degree on the specific individual with whom the relationship is formed. However, the nature of earlier relationships that are developed over many years often can be detected in later relationships, both with those same individuals and in the formation of relationships with others at a later point in time. Thus, the nature of parent-adolescent relationships does not depend only on what happens in the relationship during adolescence. Relationships with parents over the long course of childhood are carried forward to influence, at least to some degree, the nature of parent-adolescent relationships. And the long course of parent-child relationships also could be expected to influence, again at least to some degree, the fabric of the adolescent's peer relationships, friendships, and dating relationships.

Alan Sroufe and his colleagues find evidence for continuity in their research (Sroufe, 2000, 2007; Sroufe, Egeland, & Carlson, 1999; Sroufe & others, 2005). Attachment history and early care were related to peer competence in adolescence, up to 15 years after the infant assessments. In interviews with adolescents, those who formed positive close relationships during camp retreats had been securely attached in infancy. Also, ratings of videotaped behavior revealed that those with secure attachment histories were more socially competent, which included having confidence in social situations and showing leadership skills. For most children and adolescents, there was a cascading effect in which early family relationships provided

**continuity view** A developmental view that emphasizes the role of early parent-child relationships in constructing a basic way of relating to people throughout the life span.

*To what extent is an adolescent's development likely to be influenced by early experiences with parents?*

the necessary support for effectively engaging in the peer world, which in turn provided the foundation for more extensive, complex peer relationships.

**The Discontinuity View** The **discontinuity view** emphasizes change and growth in relationships over time. As people grow up, they develop many different types of relationships (with parents, peers, teachers, and romantic partners, for example). Each of these relationships is structurally different. With each new type of relationship, individuals encounter new modes of relating (Furman & Wehner, 1997; Piaget, 1932; Sullivan, 1953). For example, Piaget (1932) argued that parent-child relationships are strikingly different from children's peer relationships. Parent-child relationships, he said, are more likely to consist of parents having unilateral authority over children. By contrast, peer relationships are more likely to consist of participants who relate to each other on a much more equal basis. In parent-child relationships, since parents have greater knowledge and authority, children often must learn how to conform to rules and regulations laid down by parents. In this view, we use the parental-child mode when relating to authority figures (such as with teachers and experts) and when we act as authority figures (by becoming parents, teachers, and experts).

In contrast, relationships with peers have a different structure and require a different mode of relating to others. This more egalitarian mode is later called upon in relationships with romantic partners, friends, and co-workers. Because two peers possess relatively equal knowledge and authority (their relationship is reciprocal and symmetrical), children learn a democratic mode of relating that is based on mutual influence. With peers, children learn to formulate and assert their own opinions, appreciate the perspective of peers, cooperatively negotiate solutions to disagreements, and evolve standards for conduct that are mutually acceptable. Because peer relationships are voluntary (rather than obligatory, as in the family), children and adolescents who fail to become skillful in the symmetrical, mutual, egalitarian, reciprocal mode of relating have difficulty being accepted by peers.

Although the discontinuity view does not deny that prior close relationships (such as with parents) are carried forward to influence later relationships, it does stress that each new type of relationship that children and adolescents encounter (such as with peers, with friends, and with romantic partners) requires the construction of different and even more sophisticated modes of relating to others. Further, in the change/growth version, each period of development uniquely contributes to the construction of relationship knowledge; development across the life span is not solely determined by a sensitive or critical period during infancy.

Evidence for the discontinuity view of relationships was found in the longitudinal study conducted by Andrew Collins and his colleagues (Collins, Hennighausen, & Sroufe, 1998). Quality of friendship interaction (based on observations of coordinated behavior, such as turn taking, sharing, eye contact, and touching, and their duration) in middle childhood was related to security with dating, and disclosure and intimacy with a dating partner, at age 16.

## Maturation

Nineteenth- and twentieth-century American author Mark Twain once remarked that when he was 14 his father was so ignorant he could hardly stand to have the man around him, but when Mark got to be 21, he was astonished at how much his father had learned in those seven years! Mark Twain's comments suggest that maturation is an important theme of parent-adolescent relationships. Adolescents change as they make the transition from childhood to adulthood, but their parents also change during their adult years (Grotevant, 1998).

**discontinuity view** A developmental view that emphasizes change and growth in relationships over time.

**Adolescent Changes** Among the changes in the adolescent that can influence parent-adolescent relationships are puberty, expanded logical reasoning, increased idealistic thought, violated expectations, changes in schooling, peers, friendships, dating, and movement toward independence. Several investigations have shown that conflict between parents and adolescents, especially between mothers and sons, is the most stressful during the apex of pubertal growth (Steinberg, 1988). Also, early-maturing adolescents experience more conflict with their parents than adolescents who mature late or on time (Collins & Steinberg, 2006).

In terms of cognitive changes, the adolescent can now reason in more logical ways with parents than in childhood. During childhood, parents may be able to get by with saying, "Okay. That is it. We do it my way or else," and the child conforms. But with increased cognitive skills, adolescents no longer are likely to accept such a statement as a reason for conforming to parental dictates. Adolescents want to know, often in fine detail, why they are being disciplined. Even when parents give what seem to be logical reasons for discipline, adolescents' cognitive sophistication may call attention to deficiencies in the reasoning.

In addition, the adolescent's increasing idealistic thought comes into play in parent-adolescent relationships. Parents are now evaluated vis-à-vis what an ideal parent is like. The very real interactions with parents, which inevitably involve some negative interchanges and flaws, are placed next to the adolescent's schema of an ideal parent. And, as part of their egocentrism, adolescents' concerns with how others view them are likely to produce overreactions to parents' comments. A mother may comment to her adolescent daughter that she needs a new blouse. The daughter might respond, "What's the matter? You don't think I have good taste? You think I look gross, don't you? Well, you are the one who is gross!" The same comment made to the daughter several years earlier in late childhood probably would have elicited a less intense response. One recent study revealed that Chinese American adolescents' perception of the wamth of an ideal parent exceeded their perception of their own parents' warmth more than non-Latino White American adolescents did, and this greater discrepancy was linked to less effective psychological adjustment in the Chinese American adolescents (Wu & Chao, 2005).

*Expectancy violations on the part of parents and adolescents are especially likely during the transition to adolescence.*

—W. Andrew Collins
*Contemporary Psychologist, University of Minnesota*

Another dimension of the adolescent's changing cognitive world related to parent-adolescent relations is the expectations parents and adolescents have for each other (Steinberg, 2006). Preadolescent children are often compliant and easy to manage. As they enter puberty, children begin to question or seek rationales for parental demands. Parents might perceive this behavior as resistant and oppositional because it departs from the child's previously compliant behavior. Parents often respond to the lack of compliance with increased pressure for compliance. In this situation, expectations that were stabilized during a period of relatively slow developmental change are lagging behind the behavior of the adolescent in the period of rapid pubertal change.

What dimensions of the adolescent's social world contribute to parent-adolescent relationships? Adolescence brings with it new definitions of socially appropriate behavior. In our society, these definitions are associated with changes in schooling. As they make the transition to middle or junior high school, adolescents are required to function in a more anonymous, larger environment with multiple and varying teachers. More work is required, and students must show more initiative and responsibility to adapt successfully. Adolescents spend more time with peers than when they were children, and they develop more sophisticated friendships than in childhood. Adolescents also begin to push more strongly for independence. In sum, parents are called on to adapt to the changing world of the adolescent's schooling, peer relations, and push for autonomy (Collins & Steinberg, 2006).

*What are some maturational changes in parents that might influence parent-adolescent relationships?*

**Parental Changes** Parental changes that contribute to parent-adolescent relationships involve marital satisfaction, economic burdens, career reevaluation and time perspective, and health and body concerns (Collins & Steinberg, 2006). For most parents, marital satisfaction increases after adolescents or emerging adults leave home (Fingerman, 2006; Fingerman & Lang, 2004). In addition, parents feel a greater economic burden when their children are in adolescence and emerging adulthood. During this time, parents may reevaluate their occupational achievement, deciding whether they have met their youthful aspirations of success. They may look to the

*The generations of living things pass in a short time, and like runners hand on the torch of life.*

—LUCRETIUS
*Roman Poet, 1st Century B.C.*

future and think about how much time they have remaining to accomplish their life goals. Many adolescents, meanwhile, look to the future with unbounded optimism, sensing that they have an unlimited amount of time to accomplish what they desire. Parents of adolescents may become preoccupied with concerns about their own health, body integrity, and sexual attractiveness (Aldwin, Spiro, & Park, 2006). Even when their body and sexual attractiveness are not deteriorating, many parents of adolescents perceive that they are. By contrast, many adolescents have reached or are beginning to reach the peak of their physical attractiveness, strength, and health. Although both adolescents and their parents show a heightened preoccupation with their bodies, adolescents' outcome probably is more positive.

The changes in adolescents' parents we have just described are typical of development in middle adulthood. Most adolescents' parents either are in middle adulthood or are rapidly approaching this period of life. However, in the last two decades, the timing of parenthood in the United States has undergone some dramatic shifts (Parke & Buriel, 2006; Popenoe & Whitehead, 2006). Parenthood is taking place earlier for some, and later for others, than in previous decades. First, the number of adolescent pregnancies in the United States increased considerably in the 1970s and 1980s. Although the adolescent pregnancy rate has decreased since then, the U.S. adolescent pregnancy rate remains one of the highest in the developed world. Second, the number of women who postpone childbearing until their thirties and early forties simultaneously increased (Popenoe & Whitehead, 2006). We discussed adolescents as parents in Chapter 6, "Sexuality." Here we focus on sociohistorical changes related to postponement of childbearing until the thirties or forties.

There are many contrasts between becoming a parent in adolescence and becoming a parent 15 to 30 years later. Delayed childbearing allows for considerable progress in occupational and educational domains. For both males and females, education usually has been completed, and career development is well established.

The marital relationship varies with the timing of parenthood onset. In one investigation, couples who began childbearing in their early twenties were compared with those who began in their early thirties (Walter, 1986). The late-starting couples had more egalitarian relationships, with men participating in child care and household tasks more often.

Is parent-child interaction different for families in which parents delay having children until their thirties or forties? Investigators have found that older fathers are warmer, communicate better, encourage more achievement, place fewer demands on their children, are more lax in enforcing rules, and show less rejection with their children than younger fathers. However, older fathers also are less likely to engage in physical play or sports with their children (MacDonald, 1987). These findings suggest that sociohistorical changes are resulting in different developmental trajectories for many families, trajectories that involve changes in the way marital partners and parents and adolescents interact.

## REVIEW AND REFLECT ◆ LEARNING GOAL 1

### 1 Discuss the nature of family processes in adolescence.

***Review***

- What is reciprocal socialization? How can the family be described as a system?
- How does the developmental construction of relationships take place?
- What roles do maturation of the adolescent and maturation of parents play in understanding parent-adolescent relationships?

***Reflect***

- What do you predict will be some major changes in the families of adolescents in the twenty-first century?

## 2 Adolescents' and Emerging Adults' Relationships with Parents

Parents as Managers

Gender, Parenting, and Coparenting

Autonomy and Attachment

Parenting Styles

Parent-Adolescent Conflict

Emerging Adults' Relationships with Parents

We have seen how the expectations of adolescents and their parents often seem violated as adolescents change dramatically during the course of puberty. Many parents see their child changing from a compliant being into someone who is noncompliant, oppositional, and resistant to parental standards. Parents often clamp down and put more pressure on the adolescent to conform to parental standards. Many parents often deal with the young adolescent as if they expect him or her to become a mature being within the next 10 to 15 minutes. But the transition from childhood to adulthood is a long journey with many hills and valleys. Adolescents are not going to conform to adult standards immediately. Parents who recognize that adolescents take a long time "to get it right" usually deal more competently and calmly with adolescent transgressions than do parents who demand immediate conformity to parental standards. Yet other parents, rather than placing heavy demands on their adolescents for compliance, do virtually the opposite, letting them do as they please in a very permissive manner.

As we discuss parent-adolescent relationships, we will discover that neither high-intensity demands for compliance nor an unwillingness to monitor and be involved in the adolescent's development is likely to be a wise parenting strategy. Further, we explore another misperception that parents of adolescents sometimes entertain. Parents may perceive that virtually all conflict with their adolescent is bad. We will discover that a moderate degree of conflict with parents in adolescence is not only inevitable but may also serve a positive developmental function. And to conclude our coverage of parenting, we explore relationships between emerging adults and their parents, including examination of strategies emerging adults and their parents can use to get along better.

### Parents as Managers

Parents can play important roles as managers of adolescents' opportunities, as monitors of adolescents' social relationships, and as social initiators and arrangers (Parke & Buriel, 2006). An important developmental task in adolescence is to develop the ability to make competent decisions in an increasingly independent manner (Mortimer & Larson, 2002). To help adolescents reach their full potential, an important parental role is to be an effective manager, one who finds information, makes contacts, helps structure choices, and provides guidance (Gauvain & Perez, 2007; Youniss & Ruth, 2002). Parents who fulfill this important managerial role help adolescents to avoid pitfalls and to work their way through a myriad of choices and decisions they face (Furstenberg & others, 1999; Mounts, 2007).

Parents can serve as regulators of opportunities for their adolescents' social contact with peers, friends, and adults. Mothers are more likely than fathers to have a managerial role in parenting. In adolescence, it could involve participating in a parent-teacher conference and subsequently managing the adolescent's homework activity.

Researchers have found that family-management practices are positively related to students' grades and self-responsibility, and negatively to school-related problems (Eccles, 2007; Simpkins & others, 2006; Taylor, 1996). One of the most important

## Through the Eyes of Adolescents

### NEEDING PARENTS AS GUIDES

Stacey Christensen, age 16: "I am lucky enough to have open communication with my parents. Whenever I am in need or just need to talk, my parents are there for me. My advice to parents is to let your teens grow at their own pace, be open with them so that you can be there for them. We need guidance; our parents need to help but not be too overwhelming."

Stacey Christensen

family-management practices in this regard is maintaining a structured and organized family environment, such as establishing routines for homework, chores, bedtime, and so on. One recent study focused on African American families, examining links between mothers' reports of family-management practices, including routine, and adolescents' school-related behavior (Taylor & Lopez, 2005). Family routine (well managed and organized) was positively related to adolescents' school achievement, paying attention in class, and attendance, and negatively linked to their school-related problems.

A key aspect of the managerial role of parenting is effective monitoring of the adolescent. This is especially important as children move into the adolescent years. Monitoring includes supervising adolescents' choice of social settings, activities, and friends, as well as academic efforts. A recent research review of family functioning in African American students' academic achievement found that when African American parents monitored their son's academic achievement by ensuring that homework was completed, restricted time spent on nonproductive distractions (such as video games and TV), and participated in a consistent, positive dialogue with teachers and school officials, their son's academic achievement benefited (Mandara, 2006). Also, as we see in Chapter 13, "Problems in Adolescence and Emerging Adulthood," a lack of adequate parental monitoring is the parental factor that is related to juvenile delinquency more than any other.

## Parenting Styles

Parents want their adolescents to grow into socially mature individuals, and they often feel a great deal of frustration in their role as parents. Psychologists have long searched for parenting ingredients that promote competent social development in adolescents. For example, in the 1930s, behaviorist John Watson urged parents not to be too affectionate with their children. Early research focused on a distinction between physical and psychological discipline, or between controlling and permissive parenting. More recently, there has been greater precision in unraveling the dimensions of competent parenting.

Especially widespread is the view of Diana Baumrind (1971, 1991), who notes that parents should be neither punitive nor aloof from their adolescents, but rather

should develop rules and be affectionate with them. She emphasizes four styles of parenting that are associated with different aspects of the adolescent's social behavior—authoritarian, authoritative, neglectful, and indulgent:

| | Accepting, responsive, child-centered | Rejecting, unresponsive, parent-centered |
| --- | --- | --- |
| Demanding, controlling | Authoritative reciprocal, high in bidirectional communication | Authoritarian, power assertive |
| Undemanding, low in control attempts | Indulgent | Neglectful, ignoring, indifferent, uninvolved |

**FIGURE 8.2** Fourfold Scheme of Parenting Styles

- **Authoritarian parenting** is a restrictive, punitive style in which the parent exhorts the adolescent to follow directions and to respect work and effort. The authoritarian parent places firm limits and controls on the adolescent and allows little verbal exchange. For example, an authoritarian parent might say, "You do it my way or else. There will be no discussion!" Authoritarian parenting is associated with adolescents' socially incompetent behavior. Adolescents of authoritarian parents often are anxious about social comparison, fail to initiate activity, and have poor communication skills.
- **Authoritative parenting** encourages adolescents to be independent but still places limits and controls on their actions. Extensive verbal give-and-take is allowed, and parents are warm and nurturant toward the adolescent. An authoritative father, for example, might put his arm around the adolescent in a comforting way and say, "You know you should not have done that. Let's talk about how you can handle the situation better next time." Authoritative parenting is associated with adolescents' socially competent behavior. The adolescents of authoritative parents are self-reliant and socially responsible.
- **Neglectful parenting** is a style in which the parent is very uninvolved in the adolescent's life. The neglectful parent cannot answer the question, "It is 10:00 p.m. Do you know where your adolescent is?" Neglectful parenting is associated with adolescents' socially incompetent behavior, especially a lack of self-control. Adolescents have a strong need for their parents to care about them; adolescents whose parents are neglectful develop the sense that other aspects of the parents' lives are more important than they are. Adolescents whose parents are neglectful are socially incompetent: they show poor self-control and do not handle independence well. Closely related to the concept of neglectful parenting is a lack of parental monitoring. In one study, parental monitoring of adolescents was linked with higher grades, lower sexual activity, and less depression in adolescents (Jacobson & Crockett, 2000).
- **Indulgent parenting** is a style in which parents are highly involved with their adolescents but place few demands or controls on them. Indulgent parents allow their adolescents to do what they want, and the result is that the adolescents never learn to control their own behavior and always expect to get their way. Some parents deliberately rear their adolescents in this way because they mistakenly believe that the combination of warm involvement with few restraints will produce a creative, confident adolescent. However, indulgent parenting is associated with adolescents' social incompetence, especially a lack of self-control.

In our discussion of parenting styles, we have talked about parents who vary along the dimensions of acceptance, responsiveness, demand, and control. As shown in Figure 8.2, the four parenting styles—authoritarian, authoritative, neglectful, and indulgent—can be described in terms of these dimensions (Maccoby & Martin, 1983).

In general, researchers have found authoritative parenting to be related to positive aspects of development (Steinberg & Silk, 2002). For example, one recent study of Israeli male adolescents revealed that authoritative parenting was related to better coping and adjustment even in an authoritarian context—basic training in the military—than authoritarian parenting (Mayseless, Scharf, & Sholt, 2003).

**authoritarian parenting** This is a restrictive, punitive style in which the parent exhorts the adolescent to follow the parent's directions and to respect work and effort. Firm limits and controls are placed on the adolescent, and little verbal exchange is allowed. This style is associated with adolescents' socially incompetent behavior.

**authoritative parenting** This style encourages adolescents to be independent but still places limits and controls on their actions. Extensive verbal give-and-take is allowed, and parents are warm and nurturant toward the adolescent. This style is associated with adolescents' socially competent behavior.

**neglectful parenting** A style in which the parent is very uninvolved in the adolescent's life. It is associated with adolescents' social incompetence, especially a lack of self-control.

**indulgent parenting** A style in which parents are highly involved with their adolescents but place few demands or controls on them. This is associated with adolescents' social incompetence, especially a lack of self-control.

Why is authoritative parenting likely to be the most effective style? These reasons have been given (Steinberg & Silk, 2002):

- Authoritative parents establish an appropriate balance between control and autonomy, giving adolescents opportunities to develop independence while providing the standards, limits, and guidance that children and adolescents need.
- Authoritative parents are more likely to engage adolescents in verbal give-and-take and allow adolescents to express their views. This type of family discussion is likely to help adolescents to understand social relationships and what is required for being a socially competent person.
- The warmth and parental involvement provided by authoritative parents make the adolescent more receptive to parental influence.

**Parenting Styles and Ethnicity** Do the benefits of authoritative parenting transcend the boundaries of ethnicity, socioeconomic status, and household composition? Although some exceptions have been found, evidence linking authoritative parenting with competence on the part of the adolescent occurs in research across a wide range of ethnic groups, social strata, cultures, and family structures (Steinberg, Blatt-Eisengart, & Cauffman, 2006; Steinberg & Silk, 2002). A recent study of more than 1,300 14- to 18-year-olds who had been adjudicated because of serious delinquent acts found that the juvenile offenders who had authoritative parents were more psychosocially mature and academically competent than those who had neglectful parents (Steinberg, Blatt-Eisengart, & Cauffman, 2006). The juvenile offenders whose parents were authoritarian or indulgent tended to score between the extremes of those whose parents were authoritative and neglectful, although those with authoritarian parents consistently functioned better than those with indulgent parents. Most of these youth came from poor, ethnic minority backgrounds.

Other research with ethnic groups suggests that some aspects of the authoritarian style may be associated with positive child outcomes (Parke & Buriel, 2006). Elements of the authoritarian style may take on different meanings and have different effects, depending on the context.

Aspects of traditional Asian child-rearing practices are often continued by Asian American families. In some cases, these practices have been described as authoritarian. However, Ruth Chao (2001, 2005, 2007) argues that the style of parenting used by many Asian American parents is best conceptualized as a type of training in which parents are concerned and involved in their children's lives rather than reflecting strict or authoritarian control. Thus, the parenting style Chao describes, training, is based on a type of parental control that is distinct from the more "domineering" control reflected in the authoritarian parenting style. The positive outcomes of the training parenting style in Asian American families occurs in the high academic achievement of Asian American children (Stevenson & Zusho, 2002).

*What parenting style do many Asian Americans practice?*

Latino child-rearing practices encourage the development of a self and identity that is embedded in the family and requires respect and obedience (Harwood & others, 2002). As in African American families, there is a high level of cross-generational and coresidence arrangements and assistance (Zinn & Wells, 2000).

Researchers have found that African American parents are more likely than non-Latino White parents to use physical punishment (Deater-Deckard & Dodge, 1997). However, the use of physical punishment is linked with more externalized child problems (such as acting out and high levels of aggression) in non-Latino White families but not in African American families. One explanation of this finding is the need for African American parents to enforce rules in the dangerous environments in which they are more likely to live (Harrison-Hale, McLoyd, & Smedley, 2004). In this context, requiring obedience to parental authority may be an adaptive strategy to keep children from engaging in antisocial behavior that can have serious consequences for the victim or the perpetrator.

**Further Thoughts on Parenting Styles** Several caveats about parenting styles are in order. First, the parenting styles do not capture the important themes of reciprocal socialization and synchrony (Collins & Steinberg, 2006). Keep in mind that adolescents socialize parents, just as parents socialize adolescents (Kuczyinski & Parkin, 2007). Second, many parents use a combination of techniques rather than a single technique, although one technique may be dominant. Although consistent parenting is usually recommended, the wise parent may sense the importance of being more permissive in certain situations, more authoritarian in others, and yet more authoritative in others. Also, some critics argue that the concept of parenting style is too broad and that more research needs to be conducted to "unpack" parenting styles by studying various components that comprise the styles (Maccoby, 2007; Vazsonyi, Hibbert, & Snider, 2003). For example, is parental monitoring more important than warmth in predicting adolescent outcomes?

## Gender, Parenting, and Coparenting

What is the mother's role in the family? The father's role? What is coparenting and how effective is it?

**The Mother's Role** What do you think of when you hear the word *motherhood?* If you are like most people, you associate motherhood with a number of positive qualities, such as being warm, selfless, dutiful, and tolerant (Matlin, 1993). And while most women expect that motherhood will be happy and fulfilling, the reality is that motherhood has been accorded relatively low prestige in our society. When stacked up against money, power, and achievement, motherhood unfortunately doesn't fare too well and mothers rarely receive the appreciation they warrant. When children and adolescents don't succeed or they develop problems, our society has had a tendency to attribute the lack of success or the development of problems to a single source—mothers. One of psychology's most important lessons is that behavior is multiply determined. So it is with adolescent development—when development goes awry, mothers are not the single cause of the problems, even though our society may stereotype them in this way.

The reality of motherhood today is that while fathers have increased their child-rearing responsibilities somewhat, the main responsibility for children and adolescents still falls on the mother's shoulders (Barnard & Solchany, 2002; Brooks & Bornstein, 1996). In one study, adolescents in both the ninth and twelfth grades said that their mothers were more involved in parenting than fathers (Sputa & Paulson, 1995).

In sum, the mother's role brings with it benefits as well as limitations. Although most women do not devote their entire lives to motherhood, for most mothers, it is one of the most meaningful experiences of their lives.

*It is clear that most American children suffer too . . . little father.*

—Gloria Steinem
*American Feminist and Author, 20th Century*

**The Father's Role** The father's role has undergone major changes (Parke & Buriel, 2006). During the colonial period in America, fathers were primarily responsible for moral teaching. Fathers provided guidance and values, especially through religion. With the Industrial Revolution, the father's role changed; he gained the responsibility as the breadwinner, a role that continued through the Great Depression. By the end of World War II, another role for fathers emerged, that of a gender-role model. Although being a breadwinner and a moral guardian continued to be important father roles, attention shifted to his role as a male, especially for sons. Then, in the 1970s, the current interest in the father as an active, nurturant, caregiving parent emerged. Rather than being responsible only for the discipline and control of older children and for providing the family's economic base, the father now is being evaluated in terms of his active, nurturant involvement with his children.

How actively are today's fathers involved with their children and adolescents? One longitudinal study of adolescents in fifth to twelfth grades found that fathers

*How can adolescents benefit when fathers spend time with them?*

spend only a small portion of their time with adolescents (Larson & others, 1996). Studies reveal that fathers spend from one-third to three-fourths as much time with children and adolescents as mothers do (Pleck, 1997; Yeung & others, 1999). In one study, fathers of more than 1,700 children up to 12 years old were spending an increasing amount of time with their children, compared with their counterparts in the early 1990s, but still less time than mothers were (Yeung & others, 1999). Though some fathers are exceptionally committed parents, others are virtual strangers to their adolescents, even though they reside in the same household (Day & Acock, 2004).

In sum, although U.S. fathers have increased the amount of time they spend with their children and adolescents, it is still less time than mothers spend (Parke & Buriel, 2006; Pleck & Masciadrelli, 2004). This gender difference in parenting involvement occurs not only for non-Latino White parents, but also for Latino and African American parents (Yeung & others, 2001). And researchers have found that fathers in many other countries—such as Australia, Great Britain, France, and Japan—also spend less time with their children than mothers do (Zuzanek, 2000).

Adolescents' social development can significantly benefit from interaction with a caring, accessible, and dependable father who fosters a sense of trust and confidence (Bronstein, 2006; Fabricius & Luecken, 2007; Jones, 2006). In one investigation, Frank Furstenberg and Kathleen Harris (1992) documented how nurturant fathering can overcome children's difficult life circumstances. In low-income African American families, children who reported close attachments and feelings of identification with their fathers during adolescence were twice as likely as young adults to have found a stable job or to have entered college and were 75 percent less likely to have become unwed parents, 80 percent less likely to have been in jail, and 50 percent less likely to have developed depression. Unfortunately, however, only 10 percent of the economically disadvantaged children they studied experienced a stable, close relationship with their father during childhood and adolescence. In two other studies, college females and males reported better personal and social adjustment when they had grown up in a home with a nurturant, involved father rather than a negligent or rejecting father (Fish & Biller, 1973; Reuter & Biller, 1973). And in another study, fathers characterized by positive affect had adolescents who were less likely to be depressed (Duckett & Richards, 1996).

**Coparenting: Partners in Parenting** A dramatic increase in research on coparenting has occurred in the last two decades (Maccoby, 2007; McHale, 2007; McHale & Sullivan, 2007). The organizing theme of this research is that poor coordination, active undermining and disparagement of the other parent, lack of cooperation and warmth, and disconnection by one parenting partner—either alone or in combination with overinvolvement by the other—are conditions that place children and adolescents at developmental risk (McHale, 2007; McHale & others, 2002). By contrast, parental solidarity, cooperation, and warmth show clear ties to children's and adolescents' prosocial behavior and competence in peer relations. When parents show cooperation, mutual respect, balanced communication, and attunement to each other's needs, this helps children and adolescents to develop positive attitudes toward both males and females (Tamis-LeMonda & Cabrera, 2002). It is much easier for working parents to cope with changing family circumstances when the mother and the father cooperate and equitably share child-rearing responsibilities. Mothers feel less stress and have more positive attitudes toward their husbands when the husband is a supportive partner.

A longitudinal study examined the influence of coparenting conflict on parental negativity and adolescent maladjustment (Feinberg, Kan, & Hetherington, 2007). In this study, parents reported that child-rearing issues were a central aspect of coparenting conflict and that coparenting conflict was linked to parents' negativity and adolescent adjustment three years later.

## Parent-Adolescent Conflict

Conflict with parents increases in early adolescence. *What is the nature of this conflict in a majority of American families?*

A common belief is that there is a huge gulf that separates parent and adolescents in the form of a so-called generation gap—that is, that during adolescence the values and attitudes of adolescents become increasingly distanced from those of their parents. For the most part, the generation gap is a stereotype. For example, most adolescents and their parents have similar beliefs about the value of hard work, achievement, and career aspirations (Gecas & Seff, 1990). They also often have similar religious and political beliefs. As you will see in our discussion of research on parent-adolescent conflict, a minority of adolescents (perhaps 20 to 25 percent) have a high degree of conflict with their parents, but for a substantial majority the conflict is moderate or low.

That said, the fact remains that early adolescence is a time when parent-adolescent conflict escalates beyond parent-child conflict (Allison & Schultz, 2004; Collins & Steinberg, 2006; Montemayor, 1982; Weng & Montemayor, 1997). This increase may be due to a number of factors already discussed involving the maturation of the adolescent and the maturation of parents: the biological changes of puberty, cognitive changes involving increased idealism and logical reasoning, social changes focused on independence and identity, violated expectations, and physical, cognitive, and social changes in parents associated with middle adulthood. In an analysis of a number of studies, it was concluded that parent-adolescent conflict decreases from early adolescence through late adolescence (Laursen, Coy, & Collins, 1998).

Although conflict with parents does increase in early adolescence, it does not reach the tumultuous proportions envisioned by G. Stanley Hall at the beginning of the twentieth century (Collins & Steinberg, 2006; Holmbeck, 1996; Steinberg & Silk, 2002). Rather, much of the conflict involves the everyday events of family life, such as keeping a bedroom clean, dressing neatly, getting home by a certain time, not talking on the phone forever, and so on. The conflicts rarely involve major dilemmas like drugs and delinquency. In a study of middle-socioeconomic-status African American families, parent-adolescent conflict was common but low in intensity and focused on everyday living issues such as the adolescent's room, chores, choice of activities, and homework (Smetana & Gaines, 1999). Nearly all conflicts were resolved by adolescents giving in to parents, but adolescent concession declined with age.

In one study of conflict in a number of social relationships, adolescents reported having more disagreements with their mother than with anyone else—followed in order by friends, romantic partners, siblings, fathers, other adults, and peers (Laursen, 1995). In another study of 64 high school sophomores, interviews were conducted in their homes on three randomly selected evenings during a three-week period (Montemayor, 1982). The adolescents were asked to tell about the events of the previous day, including any conflicts they had with their parents. Conflict was defined as "either you teased your parent or your parent teased you; you and your parent had a difference of opinion; one of you got mad at the other; you and your parent had a quarrel or an argument; or one of you hit the other." During a period of 192 days of tracking the 64 adolescents, an average of 68 arguments with parents was reported. This represents a rate of 0.35 arguments with parents per day or about one argument every three days. The average length of the arguments was 11 minutes. Most conflicts were with mothers, and the majority were between mothers and daughters.

Still, a high degree of conflict characterizes some parent-adolescent relationships. It has been estimated that in about 20 percent of families, parents and adolescents engage in prolonged, intense, repeated, unhealthy conflict (Montemayor, 1982). Although this figure represents a minority of adolescents, it indicates that 4 to 5 million American families encounter serious, highly stressful parent-adolescent

## Careers in ADOLESCENT DEVELOPMENT

**Martha Chan**
**Marriage and Family Therapist**

Martha Chan is a marriage and family therapist who works for Adolescent Counseling Services in Palo Alto, California. She has been the program director of Adolescent Counseling Services for more than a decade.

Among her activities, Martha counsels parents and adolescents about family issues, conducts workshops for parents at middle schools, and writes a monthly column that addresses such topics as "I'm a single mom; How do I talk with my son about sex?," "My daughter wants to dye her hair purple," and "My son is being bullied."

conflict. And this prolonged, intense conflict is associated with a number of adolescent problems—moving away from home, juvenile delinquency, school dropout rates, pregnancy and early marriage, membership in religious cults, and drug abuse (Brook & others, 1990). To read about the career of one individual who counsels families with high parent-adolescent conflict, see the *Careers in Adolescent Development* profile.

Although in some cases these problems may be caused by intense, prolonged parent-adolescent conflict, in others the problems might have originated before the onset of adolescence. Simply because children are physically much smaller than parents, parents might be able to suppress oppositional behavior. But by adolescence, increased size and strength—especially in boys—can result in an indifference to or confrontation with parental dictates. At the same time, some psychologists have argued that conflict is a normative part of adolescent development.

American psychologist Reed Larson (1999) spent six months in India studying middle-SES adolescents and their families. He observed that in India there seems to be little parent-adolescent conflict and that many families likely would be described as "authoritarian" in Baumrind's categorization. Larson also observed that in India adolescents do not go through a process of breaking away from their parents and that parents choose their youths' marital partners. Conflict between parents and adolescents in Japan has also been observed as lower than in the United States (Rothbaum & others, 2000).

## Autonomy and Attachment

It has been said that there are only two lasting bequests that we can leave our children—one is roots, the other wings. These words reflect the importance of attachment and autonomy in the adolescent's successful adaptation to the world. Historically, developmentalists have shown far more interest in autonomy than in attachment during the adolescent period. Recently, however, interest has heightened in attachment's role in healthy adolescent development. Adolescents and their parents live in a coordinated social world, one involving both autonomy and attachment. In keeping with the historical interest in these processes, we discuss autonomy first.

**Autonomy** The increased independence that typifies adolescence is interpreted as rebellion by some parents, but in many instances adolescents' push for autonomy has little to do with their feelings toward the parents. Psychologically healthy families adjust to adolescents' push for independence by treating the adolescents in more adult ways and including them more in family decision making. Psychologically unhealthy families often remain locked into power-oriented parent control, and parents move even more heavily toward an authoritarian posture in their relationships with their adolescents.

The adolescent's quest for autonomy and sense of responsibility creates puzzlement and conflict for many parents. Parents begin to see their teenagers slipping away from their grasp. As we have seen, the urge is to take stronger control as the adolescent seeks autonomy and personal responsibility. Heated, emotional exchanges might ensue, with either side calling names, making threats, and doing whatever seems necessary to gain control. Parents can become frustrated because they expected their teenager to heed their advice, to want to spend time with the family, and to grow up to do what is right. To be sure, they anticipated that their teenager would have some difficulty adjusting to the changes adolescence brings, but few parents are able to imagine and predict the strength of adolescents' determination to spend time with their peers and to show that it is they, not the parents, who are responsible for their success or failure.

**The Complexity of Adolescent Autonomy** Defining adolescent autonomy is more complex and elusive than it might at first seem (Collins & Steinberg, 2006; Rothbaum & Trommsdorff, 2007; Soenens & others, 2007). The term *autonomy* generally connotes self-direction and independence. But what does it really mean? Is it an internal personality trait that consistently characterizes the adolescent's immunity from parental influence? Is it the ability to make responsible decisions for oneself? Does autonomy imply consistent behavior in all areas of adolescent life, including school, finances, dating, and peer relations? What are the relative contributions of peers and other adults to the development of an adolescent's autonomy?

One aspect of autonomy that is especially important is **emotional autonomy,** the capacity to relinquish childlike dependencies on parents. In developing emotional autonomy, adolescents increasingly de-idealize their parents, perceive them as people rather than simply as parenting figures, and become less dependent on them for immediate emotional support.

**Gender and Culture** Gender differences characterize autonomy granting in adolescence, with boys usually being given more independence than girls. In one study, this gender difference was especially present in families with a traditional gender-role orientation (Bumpas, Crouter, & McHale, 2001).

Expectations about the appropriate timing of adolescent autonomy often vary across cultures, parents, and adolescents. For example, expectations for early autonomy on the part of adolescents are more prevalent in Whites, single parents, and adolescents themselves than they are in Asian Americans or Latinos, married parents, and parents themselves (Feldman & Rosenthal, 1999).

In one study, adolescents in the United States sought autonomy from parents earlier than adolescents in Japan (Rothbaum & others, 2000). Even Asian adolescents raised in the United States do not usually seek autonomy as early as their Anglo-American peers (Greenberger & Chu, 1996). Also in the transition to adulthood, Japanese are less likely to live outside the home than Americans (Hendry, 1999).

**emotional autonomy** The capacity to relinquish childlike dependence on parents.

**Developmental Transitions in Autonomy and Going Away to College** Many emerging adults experience a transition in the development of autonomy when they leave home and go away to college (Seiffge-Krenke, 2006; Silver & others, 2002). The transition from high school to college involves increased autonomy for most individuals. For some, homesickness sets in; for others, sampling the privileges of life without parents hovering around is marvelous. For the growing number of students whose families have been torn by separation and divorce, though, moving away can be especially painful. Adolescents in such families may find themselves in the roles of comforter, confidant, and even caretaker of their parents as well as their siblings. In the words of one college freshman, "I feel responsible for my parents. I guess I shouldn't, but I can't help it. It makes my separation from them, my desire to be free of others' problems, my motivation to pursue my own identity more difficult." For yet other students, the independence of being a college freshman is not always as stressful. According to 18-year-old Brian, "Becoming an adult is kind of hard. I'm having to learn to balance my own checkbook, make my own plane reservations, do my own laundry, and the hardest thing of all is waking up in the morning. I don't have my mother there banging on the door."

*How do relationships with parents change when individuals go to college?*

In one investigation, the psychological separation and adjustment of 130 college freshmen and 123 college upperclassmen were studied (Lapsley, Rice, & Shadid, 1989). As expected, freshmen showed more psychological dependency on their parents and poorer social and personal adjustment than upperclassmen. Female students also showed more psychological dependency on their parents than male students did. In one study, parent-child relationships were less satisfactory prior to the transition from high school to college (Silver, 1995). And in another study, students who went away to college reported feeling closer to their mother, less conflict with parents, and more decision-making control and autonomy than did college students who lived at home (Holmbeck, Durbin, & Kung, 1995).

**Adolescent Runaways** Why do adolescents run away from their homes? Generally, runaways are desperately unhappy at home. The reasons many of them leave seem legitimate by almost anyone's standards. When they run away, they usually do not leave a clue as to their whereabouts—they just disappear.

Many runaways are from families in which a parent or another adult beats them or sexually exploits them (Chen & others, 2004). Their lives may be in danger daily. Their parents may be drug addicts or alcoholics. In some cases, the family may be so impoverished that the parents are unable to feed and clothe their teenagers adequately. The parents may be so overburdened by their own emotional and/or material inadequacies that they fail to give their adolescents the attention and understanding they need. So teenagers hit the streets in search of the emotional and material rewards they are not getting at home.

But runaways are not all from our society's lower-SES tier. Teenage lovers, confronted by parental hostility toward their relationship, might decide to elope and make it on their own. Or the middle-SES teenager might decide that he has seen enough of his hypocritical parents—people who try to make him live by an unrealistically high set of moral standards, while they live by a loose, false set of ideals. Another teen might live with parents who constantly bicker. Any of these adolescents might decide that they would be happier away from home. In one study, homeless adolescents reported having experienced more parental maltreatment, been scolded more often, and felt less loved by their parents than did housed adolescents (Wolfe, Toro, & McCaskill, 1999).

This adolescent has run away from home. *What is it about family relationships that causes adolescents to run away from home? Are there ways society could better serve runaways?*

Running away often is a gradual process, as adolescents begin to spend less time at home and more time on the streets or with a peer group. The parents might be telling them that they really want to see them, to understand them; but runaways often feel that they are not understood at home and that the parents care much more about themselves.

Adolescent runaways are especially susceptible to drug abuse (Slesnick & Prestopnik, 2004). In one investigation, as part of the National Longitudinal Study of Youth Survey, runaway status at ages 14 to 15 was associated with drug abuse and alcohol problems four years later at ages 18 to 19 (Windle, 1989). Repeat runaways were more likely to be drug abusers than onetime runaways were. Both onetime and repeat runaways were more likely to be school dropouts when this was assessed four years later.

Some provision must be made for runaways' physical and psychological well-being. In recent years, nationwide hotlines and temporary shelters for runaways have been established. However, there are still too few of these shelters, and there is often a noted lack of professional psychological help for the runaways at such shelters.

**Conclusions** In sum, the ability to attain autonomy and gain control over one's behavior in adolescence is acquired through appropriate adult reactions to the adolescent's desire for control. An individual at the onset of adolescence does not have the knowledge to make appropriate or mature decisions in all areas of life. As the adolescent pushes for autonomy, the wise adult relinquishes control in those areas in which the adolescent can make reasonable decisions and continues to guide the adolescent in areas where the adolescent's knowledge is more limited. Gradually, adolescents acquire the ability to make mature decisions on their own (Collins & Steinberg, 2006; Harold, Colarossi, & Mercier, 2007). The discussion that follows reveals in greater detail how important it is to view the development of autonomy in relation to connectedness to parents.

### Attachment and Connectedness

Adolescents do not simply move away from parental influence into a decision-making world all their own. As they become more autonomous, it is psychologically healthy for them to be attached to their parents.

#### Secure and Insecure Attachment

Attachment theorists such as British psychiatrist John Bowlby (1989) and American developmental psychologist Mary Ainsworth (1979) argue that secure attachment in infancy is central to the development of social competence. In **secure attachment,** infants use the caregiver, usually the mother, as a secure base from which to explore the environment. Secure attachment is theorized to be an important foundation for psychological development later in childhood, adolescence, and adulthood. In **insecure attachment,** infants either avoid the caregiver or show considerable resistance or ambivalence toward the caregiver. Insecure attachment is theorized to be related to difficulties in relationships and problems in later development.

In the last decade, developmentalists have begun to explore the role of secure attachment and related concepts, such as connectedness to parents, in adolescence Allen, 2007; Allen, Kuperminc, & Moore, 2005; Collins & Steinberg, 2006; Furman, 2007; Zimmerman, 2007). They note that secure attachment to parents in adolescence can facilitate the adolescent's social competence and well-being, as reflected in such characteristics as self-esteem, emotional adjustment, and physical health (Egeland & Carlson, 2004; Hilburn-Cobb, 2004). In the research of Joseph Allen and his colleagues (Allen & others, 1994), securely attached adolescents have somewhat lower probabilities of engaging in problem behaviors. In one study, secure attachment to both the mother and the father was related positively to adolescents' peer and friendship relations (Lieberman, Doyle, & Markiewicz, 1999). A recent study by Allen and his colleagues (2007) revealed that secure attachment in early adolescence was linked to successful autonomy and good peer relations. The study also found that insecure attachment was related to an increase in externalized behavior and depression. And in another recent study, a secure attachment style in adolescence was linked to a higher capacity for intimacy and positive affect in peer relations (Mayseless & Scharf, 2007).

Many studies that assess secure and insecure attachment in adolescence use the Adult Attachment Interview (AAI) (George, Main, & Kaplan, 1984). This measure examines an individual's memories of significant attachment relationships. Based on the responses to questions on the AAI, individuals are classified as secure-autonomous (which corresponds to secure attachment in infancy) or as being in one of three insecure categories:

- **Dismissing/avoidant attachment** is an insecure category in which individuals deemphasize the importance of attachment. This category is associated with consistent experiences of rejection of attachment needs by caregivers. One possible outcome of dismissing/avoidant attachment is that parents and adolescents mutually distance themselves from each other, which lessens parents' influence. In one study, dismissing/avoidant attachment was related to violent and aggressive behavior on the part of the adolescent.
- **Preoccupied/ambivalent attachment** is an insecure category in which adolescents are hypertuned to attachment experiences. This is thought to

**secure attachment** In this attachment pattern, infants use their primary caregiver, usually the mother, as a secure base from which to explore the environment. Secure attachment is theorized to be an important foundation for psychological development later in childhood, adolescence, and adulthood.

**insecure attachment** In this attachment pattern, infants either avoid the caregiver or show considerable resistance or ambivalence toward the caregiver. This pattern is theorized to be related to difficulties in relationships and problems in later development.

**dismissing/avoidant attachment** An insecure attachment category in which individuals deemphasize the importance of attachment. This category is associated with consistent experiences of rejection of attachment needs by caregivers.

**preoccupied/ambivalent attachment** An insecure attachment category in which adolescents are hypertuned to attachment experiences. This is thought to mainly occur because parents are inconsistently available to the adolescents.

mainly occur because parents are inconsistently available to the adolescent. This can result in a high degree of attachment-seeking behavior, mixed with angry feelings. Conflict between parents and adolescents in this type of attachment classification can be too high for healthy development.

- **Unresolved/disorganized attachment** is an insecure category in which the adolescent has an unusually high level of fear and might be disoriented. This can result from such traumatic experiences as a parent's death or abuse by parents.

**Developmental Transformations** Transformations characterize adolescents' autonomy and connectedness with their families. In one study by Reed Larson and his colleagues (1996), 220 White middle-SES adolescents from 10 to 18 years of age carried beepers and, when beeped at random times, reported whom they were with, what they were doing, and how they were feeling. The amount of time adolescents spent with their families decreased from 35 percent for 10-year-olds to 14 percent for 18-year-olds, suggesting increased autonomy with age. However, increased family connectedness was evident with increased age, with more family conversation about interpersonal issues, especially for girls. As adolescents got older, they were more likely to perceive themselves as leading the interactions. Also, after a decrease in early adolescence, older teenagers reported more favorable affect with others during family interactions. In another study, African Americans who were approximately 18½ years old had a closer relationship with their mothers than their fathers (Smetana, Metzger, & Campione-Barr, 2004). However, when fathers were present on a consistent basis, they had more positive relationships with their children than when they were absent.

**Conclusions About Parent-Adolescent Conflict and Attachment in Adolescence** In sum, the old model of parent-adolescent relationships suggested that, as adolescents mature, they detach themselves from parents and move into a world of autonomy apart from parents. The old model also suggested that parent-adolescent conflict is intense and stressful throughout adolescence. The new model emphasizes that parents serve as important attachment figures, resources, and support systems as adolescents explore a wider, more complex social world. The new model also emphasizes that, in the majority of families, parent-adolescent conflict is moderate rather than severe and that everyday negotiations and minor disputes are normal, serving the positive developmental function of promoting independence and identity (see Figure 8.3).

**unresolved/disorganized attachment** An insecure category in which the adolescent has an unusually high level of fear and is disoriented. This can result from such traumatic experiences as a parent's death or abuse by parents.

**Attachment in Emerging Adults** Researchers are studying links between emerging adults' current attachment styles and many aspects of their lives (Feeney & Collins,

Old model
Autonomy, detachment from parents; parent and peer worlds are isolated
Intense, stressful conflict throughout adolescence; parent-adolescent relationships are filled with storm and stress on virtually a daily basis
New model
Attachment and autonomy; parents are important support systems and attachment figures; adolescent-parent and adolescent-peer worlds have some important connections
Moderate parent-adolescent conflict common and can serve a positive developmental function; conflict greater in early adolescence, especially during the apex of puberty


**FIGURE 8.3** Old and New Models of Parent-Adolescent Relationships

2007; Hazan, Gur-Yaish, & Campa, 2007; Shaver & Mikulincer, 2007). For example, securely attached emerging adults are more satisfied with their close relationships than insecurely attached emerging adults, and the relationships of securely attached emerging adults are more likely to be characterized by trust, commitment, and longevity (Feeney & Collins, 2007). Securely attached emerging adults also are more likely than insecurely attached emerging adults to provide support when they are distressed and more likely to give support when their partner is distressed (Rholes & Simpson, 2007). Also, one study found that emerging adults with avoidant and anxious attachment styles were more likely to be depressed than securely attached emerging adults (Hankin, Kassel, & Abela, 2005). Another study revealed that emerging adult women with anxious or avoidant attachment styles and emerging adult men with an avoidant attachment style were more likely to have unwanted but consensual sexual experiences than securely attached emerging adults (Gentzler & Kerns, 2004).

*What are some key dimensions of attachment in emerging adulthood, and how are they related to relationship patterns and well-being?*

A recent research review and conceptualization of attachment by leading experts Mario Mikulincer and Phillip Shaver (2007) concluded the following about the benefits of secure attachment. Individuals who are securely attached have a well-integrated sense of self-acceptance, self-esteem, and self-efficacy. They have the ability to control their emotions, are optimistic, and are resilient. Facing stress and adversity, they activate cognitive representations of security, are mindful of what is happening around them, and mobilize effective coping strategies.

Mikulincer and Shaver's (2007) review also concluded that attachment insecurity places couples at risk for relationship problems. For example, when an anxious individual is paired with an avoidant individual, the anxious partner's needs and demands frustrate the avoidant partner's preference for distance in the relationship; the avoidant partner's need for distance causes stress for the anxious partner's need for closeness. The result: both partners are unhappy in the relationship and the anxious-avoidant pairing can produce abuse or violence when a partner criticizes or tries to change the other's behavior. Researchers also have found that when both partners have an anxious attachment pattern, the pairing usually produces dissatisfaction with the marriage and can lead to a mutual attack and retreat in the relationship (Feeney & Collins, 2007). When both partners have an anxious attachment style, they feel misunderstood and rejected, excessively dwell on their own insecurities, and seek to control the other's behavior (Mikulincer & Shaver, 2007).

If you have an insecure attachment style, are you stuck with it and does it doom you to have problematic relationships? Attachment categories are somewhat stable in emerging adulthood, but emerging adults do have the capacity to change their attachment thinking and behavior. It also is important to note that although attachment insecurities are linked to relationship problems, attachment style makes only a moderate-size contribution to relationship functioning and that other factors contribute to relationship satisfaction and success (Mikulincer & Shaver, 2007).

## Emerging Adults' Relationships with Parents

For the most part, emerging adults' relationships with their parents improve when they leave home. They often grow closer psychologically to their parents and share more with them than they did before they left home (Arnett, 2004, 2007). However, challenges in the parent–emerging adult relationship involve the emerging adult's increasing autonomy by possessing adult status in many areas yet still depending on parents in some manner (Aquilino, 2006). Many emerging adults can make their own decisions about where to live, whether to stay in college, which lifestyle to adopt, whether to get married, and so on. At the same time, parents often provide support for their emerging adult children, even after they leave home. This might be accomplished through loans and monetary gifts for education, purchase of a car, and financial contribution to living arrangements, as well as emotional support.

In successful emerging adulthood, individuals separate from their parents family of origin without cutting off ties completely or fleeing to some substitute emotional refuge. Complete cutoffs from parents rarely solve emotional problems. Emerging adulthood is a time for young people to sort out emotionally what they will take along from the family of origin, what they will leave behind, and what they will create.

Many emerging adults no longer feel compelled to comply with parental expectations and wishes. They shift to learning to deal with their parents on an adult-to-adult basis, which requires a mutually respectful form of relating—in which, by the end of emerging adulthood, individuals can appreciate and accept their parents as they are.

In today's uncertain economic times, many emerging adults continue to live at home or return to live at home after several years of college, after graduating from college, or to save money after taking a full-time job (Furman, 2005). Emerging and young adults also may move back in with their parents after an unsuccessful career or a divorce. And some individuals don't leave home at all until their middle to late twenties because they cannot financially support themselves. Numerous labels have been applied to emerging and young adults who return to their parents' homes to live, including "boomerang kids," and "B2B" (or Back-to-Bedroom) (Furman, 2005).

As with most family living arrangements, there are both pluses and minuses when emerging adult children live at home or return to live at home. One of the most common complaints voiced by both emerging adults and their parents is a loss of privacy. Emerging adults complain that their parents restrict their independence, cramp their sex lives, reduce their rock music listening, and treat them as children rather than adults. Parents often complain that their quiet home has become noisy, that they stay up late worrying when their emerging adult children will come home, that meals are difficult to plan because of conflicting schedules, that their relationship as a married couple has been invaded, and that they have to shoulder too much responsibility for their emerging adult children. In sum, when emerging adults return home to live, a disequilibrium in family life is created, which requires considerable adaptation on the part of parents and their emerging adult children.

One recent longitudinal study examined the timing of leaving home on emerging adults' health (Seiffge-Krenke, 2006). Emerging adults were classified as on-time leavers (mean age: 21 for females, 23 for males), still residing with parents (21 to 25 years of age), late leavers (left later than the on-time leavers), and returners (returned home to live at some point from 21 to 25 years of age). Emerging adults who left home on time were more securely attached to parents and had been given more autonomy during adolescence than their counterparts who left home later or had returned to live in the family home. Emerging adults

with nonnormative (late, returned home, or remained home) patterns were perceived by parents to be less psychologically healthy than emerging adults who left home on time.

To read about strategies that emerging adults and their parents can use to get along better, see the *Health and Well-Being* interlude.

## Health and Well-Being

### STRATEGIES FOR EMERGING ADULTS AND THEIR PARENTS

When emerging adults ask to return home to live, parents and their emerging adult children should agree on the conditions and expectations beforehand. For example, they might discuss and agree on whether the emerging adults will pay rent, wash their own clothes, cook their own meals, do any household chores, pay their phone bills, come and go as they please, be sexually active or drink alcohol at home, and so on. If these conditions aren't negotiated at the beginning, conflict often results because the expectations of parents and young adult children will likely be violated. Parents need to treat emerging adult children more like adults than children and let go of much of their parenting role. Parents should not interact with emerging adult children as if they are dependent children who need to be closely monitored and protected but rather as young adults who are capable of responsible, mature behavior. Emerging adults have the right to choose how much they sleep and eat, how they dress, who they choose as friends and lovers, what career they pursue, and how they spend their money. However, if the emerging adult children act in ways that interfere with their parents' lifestyles, parents need to say so. The discussion should focus not on emerging adults' choices but on how their activities are unacceptable while living together in the same home.

Some parents don't let go of their emerging adult children when they should. They engage in "permaparenting," which can impede not only their emerging adult children's movement toward independence and responsibility but also their own postparenting lives. "Helicopter parents" is another label used for parents who hover too closely in their effort to ensure that their children succeed in college and adult life (Paul, 2003). Although well intentioned, this intrusiveness by parents can slow the process by which their children become responsible adults.

When they move back home, emerging adults need to think about how they will need to change their behavior to make the living arrangement work. Elina Furman (2005) provides some good recommendations in *Boomerang Nation: How to Survive Living with Your Parents . . . the Second Time Around.* She recommends that when emerging adults move back home, they should expect to make adjustments. And as recommended earlier, she urges emerging adults to sit down with their parents and negotiate the ground rules for living at home before they actually move back. Furman also recommends that emerging adults set a deadline for how long they will live at home and then stay focused on their goals (whether to save enough money to pay off their debts, save enough to start a business or buy their own home, finish graduate school, and so on). Too often emerging adults spend the money they save by moving home on such luxuries as spending binges, nights on the town, expensive clothes, and unnecessary travel, which only delay their ability to move out of their parents' home.

*What are some strategies that can benefit the relationship between emerging adults and their parents?*

**REVIEW AND REFLECT ◆ LEARNING GOAL 2**

**2 Describe adolescents' and emerging adults' relationships with their parents.**

***Review***

- How can parents be effective managers of adolescents?
- What are four important parenting styles, and how are they linked with adolescent development?
- What roles do mothers and fathers play in adolescent development? How effective is coparenting?
- How can parent-adolescent conflict be accurately described?
- What roles do autonomy and attachment play in the development of adolescents and emerging adults?
- What are some issues involved in relationships between emerging adults and their parents?

***Reflect***

- What are some ways that parents can reduce parent-adolescent conflict? Consider such things as curfews, choice of friends, keeping a room clean, respect for adults, and rules for dating.

So far in this chapter we have examined the nature of family processes and adolescent/emerging adult relationships with parents. In addition to adolescent/emerging adult relationships with parents, there is another aspect to the family worlds of most adolescents and emerging adults—sibling relationships—that we discuss next.

# 3 Sibling Relationships

Sibling Roles | Birth Order

Sandra describes to her mother what happened in a conflict with her sister:

> We had just come home from the ball game. I sat down in the chair next to the light so I could read. Sally [the sister] said, "Get up. I was sitting there first. I just got up for a second to get a drink." I told her I was not going to get up and that I didn't see her name on the chair. I got mad and started pushing her—her drink spilled all over her. Then she got really mad; she shoved me against the wall, hitting and clawing at me. I managed to grab a handful of hair. At this point, Sally comes into the room and begins to tell her side of the story. Sandra interrupts, "Mother, you always take her side."

Sound familiar? How much does conflict characterize sibling relations? As we examine the roles siblings play in social development, you will discover that conflict is a common dimension of sibling relationships but that siblings also play many other roles in social development.

## Sibling Roles

Approximately 80 percent of American adolescents have one or more siblings—that is, sisters and brothers (Dunn, 2007). As anyone who has had a sibling knows, the conflict experienced by Sally and Sandra in their relationship with each other is a common interaction style of siblings. However, conflict is only one of the many dimensions of sibling relations. Adolescent sibling relations include helping, sharing, teaching, fighting, and playing, and adolescent siblings can act as emotional supports, rivals, and communication partners (Pomery & others, 2006; Zukow-Goldring, 2002). One study found that adolescent siblings spent an average of 10 hours a week together, with an average of 12 percent of that time spent in constructive time (creative activities such as art, music, and hobbies; sports; religious activities; and games) and 25 percent in nonconstructive time (watching TV and hanging out) (Tucker, McHale, & Crouter, 2003). In Mexican American families, adolescent siblings spend even more time together—more than 17 hours a week (Updegraff & others, 2005).

About 80 percent of us have one or more siblings. *What are some characteristics of sibling relationships in adolescence?*

What do adolescent siblings talk about when they are together? A recent study revealed that siblings most often talked about extracurricular activities, media, and school (Tucker & Winzeler, 2007). Less than 10 percent of their time together, the focus of their discussion was friends, family, eating, and body image.

Judy Dunn (2007), a leading expert on sibling relationships, recently described three important characteristics of sibling relationships:

- *Emotional quality of the relationship.* Both intensive positive and negative emotions are often expressed by siblings toward each other. Many children and adolescents have mixed feelings toward their siblings.
- *Familiarity and intimacy of the relationship.* Siblings typically know each other very well, and this intimacy suggests that they can either provide support or tease and undermine each other, depending on the situation.
- *Variation in sibling relationships.* Some siblings describe their relationships more positively than others. Thus, there is considerable variation in sibling relationships. We've indicated that many siblings have mixed feelings about each other, but some adolescents mainly describe their sibling in warm, affectionate ways, whereas others primarily talk about how irritating and mean a sibling is.

Do parents usually favor one sibling over others, and if so does it make a difference in an adolescent's development? One recent study of 384 adolescent sibling pairs revealed that 65 percent of their mothers and 70 percent of their fathers showed favoritism toward one sibling (Shebloski, Conger, & Widaman, 2005). When favoritism of one sibling occurred, it was linked to lower self-esteem and sadness in the less-favored sibling.

In some instances, siblings can be stronger socializing influences on the adolescent than parents or peers are (Dunn, 2007; Teti, 2001). Someone close in age to the adolescent—such as a sibling—might be able to understand the adolescent's problems and communicate more effectively than parents can. In dealing with peers, coping with difficult teachers, and discussing taboo subjects (such as sex), siblings can be more influential in socializing adolescents than parents are. In one study, both younger and older adolescent siblings viewed older siblings as sources of support for social and scholastic activities (Tucker, McHale, & Crouter, 2001).

High sibling conflict can be detrimental to adolescent development, especially when combined with ineffective parenting (Smith & Ross, 2007). A longitudinal study revealed that a combination of ineffective parenting (poor problem-solving skills, weak supervision skills, parent-adolescent conflict) and sibling conflict (hitting, fighting, stealing, cheating) at 10 to 12 years of age was linked to antisocial behavior and poor peer relations from 12 to 16 years of age (Bank, Burraston, & Snyder, 2004). And another longitudinal study found that increased sibling conflict was linked to increased depression and increased sibling intimacy

## Through the Eyes of Adolescents

### DEALING WITH MY SISTER

Like a lot of brothers and sisters, my sister and I have our fights. Sometimes when I talk to her, it is like talking to a brick! Her favorite thing to do is storm off and slam the door when she gets mad at me. After a while, I cool off. When I calm down, I realize fighting with your sister is crazy. I go to my sister and apologize. It's a lot better to cool off and apologize than to keep on fighting and make things worse.

–Cynthia, age 11

was related to increased peer competence and, for girls, decreased depression (Kim & others, 2007).

What are sibling relationships like in emerging adulthood? Most siblings spend far less time with each other in emerging adulthood than they did in adolescence. Mixed feelings about siblings are still common in emerging adulthood. However, as siblings move out of their home and sibling contact becomes more optional, conflicted sibling relationships in adolescence often become less emotionally intense (Hetherington & Kelly, 2002).

## Birth Order

Birth order has been of special interest to sibling researchers, who want to identify the characteristics associated with being born into a particular slot in a family. Firstborns have been described as more adult oriented, helpful, conforming, anxious, and self-controlled, and less aggressive than their siblings. Parental demands and high standards established for firstborns may result in firstborns realizing higher academic and professional achievements than their siblings (Furman & Lanthier, 2002). For example, firstborns are overrepresented in *Who's Who* and among Rhodes scholars. However, some of the same pressures placed on firstborns for high achievement can be the reason firstborns also have more guilt, anxiety, difficulty in coping with stressful situations, and higher admission to guidance clinics.

Birth order also plays a role in siblings' relationships with each other (Vandell, Minnett, & Santrock, 1987). Older siblings invariably take on the dominant role in sibling interaction, and older siblings report feeling more resentful that parents give preferential treatment to younger siblings.

What are later-borns like? Characterizing later-borns is difficult because they can occupy so many different sibling positions. For example, a later-born might be the second-born male in a family of two siblings or a third-born female in a family of four siblings. In two-child families, the profile of the later-born child is related to the sex of his or her sibling. For example, a boy with an older sister is more likely to develop "feminine" interests than a boy with an older brother. Overall, later-borns usually enjoy better relations with peers than firstborns. Last-borns, who are often described as the "baby" in the family even after they have outgrown infancy, run the risk of becoming overly dependent. Middle-borns tend to be more diplomatic, often performing the role of negotiator in times of dispute (Sutton-Smith, 1982).

The popular conception of the only child is of a "spoiled brat" with such undesirable characteristics as dependency, lack of self-control, and self-centered behavior. But research presents a more positive portrayal of the only child, who often is achievement oriented and displays a desirable personality, especially in comparison to later-borns and children from large families (Thomas, Coffman, & Kipp, 1993).

So far our consideration of birth-order effects suggests that birth order might be a strong predictor of adolescent behavior. However, family researchers have found that birth order has often been overemphasized. The critics argue that, when all of the factors that influence adolescent behavior are considered, birth order itself shows limited ability to predict adolescent behavior. Consider just sibling relationships alone. They vary not only in birth order, but also in number of siblings, age of siblings, age spacing of siblings, and sex of siblings. In one study, male sibling pairs had a less positive relationship (less caring, less intimate, and lower conflict resolution) than male/female or female/female sibling pairs (Cole & Kerns, 2001). Consider also the temperament of siblings. Researchers have found that siblings' temperamental traits (such as "easy" and "difficult"), as well as differential treatment of siblings by parents, influence how siblings get along (Brody, Stoneman, & Burke, 1987). Siblings with "easy" temperaments who are treated in relatively equal ways by parents tend to get along with each other the best, whereas siblings with "difficult" temperaments, or siblings whose parents gave one sibling preferential treatment, get along the worst.

Beyond gender, temperament, and differential treatment of siblings by parents, think about some of the other important factors in adolescents' lives that influence their behavior beyond birth order. They include heredity, models of competency or incompetency that parents present to adolescents on a daily basis, peer influences, school influences, socioeconomic factors, sociohistorical factors, cultural variations, and so on. Although birth order itself may not be a good predictor of adolescent behavior, sibling relationships and interaction are important dimensions of family processes in adolescence (Dunn, 2005, 2007).

**REVIEW AND REFLECT ◆ LEARNING GOAL 3**

**3 Characterize sibling relationships in adolescence.**

***Review***

- What is the nature of sibling roles?
- How strongly is birth order linked to adolescent development?

***Reflect***

- If you grew up with a sibling, you likely showed some jealousy of your sibling and vice versa. How can parents help children reduce their jealousy toward a sibling?

## 4 THE CHANGING FAMILY IN A CHANGING SOCIETY

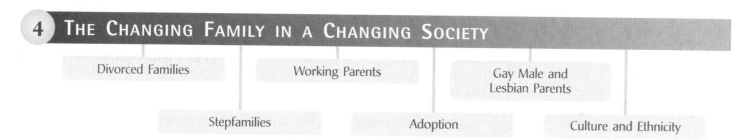

Divorced Families | Stepfamilies | Working Parents | Adoption | Gay Male and Lesbian Parents | Culture and Ethnicity

More U.S. adolescents are growing up in a variety of family structures than ever before in history. Many mothers spend the greater part of their day away from their children. More than one of every two mothers with a child under the age of 5, and more than two of every three with a child from 6 to 17 years of age, is in the labor force. The number of adolescents growing up in single-parent families is staggering (Fine & Harvey, 2006). The United States has the highest percentage of single-parent families, compared with virtually all other countries (see Figure 8.4). And, by age 18, approximately one-fourth of all American children will have lived a portion of their lives in a stepfamily.

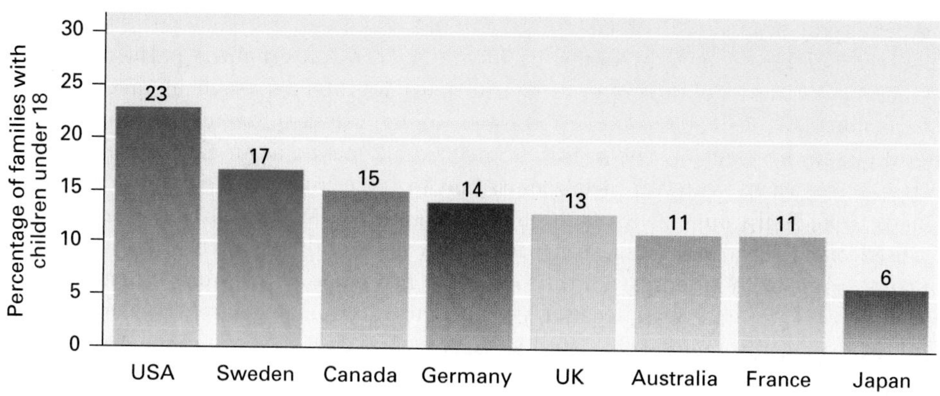


**FIGURE 8.4** **Single-Parent Families in Different Countries**

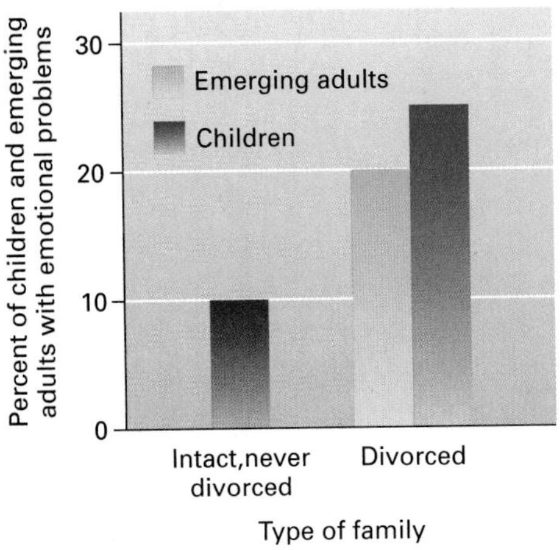


**FIGURE 8.5 Emotional Problems in Children and Emerging Adults from Divorced Families** In Hetherington's longitudinal study, 25 percent of children from divorced families had emotional problems, but that figure decreased to 20 percent in emerging adulthood. Ten percent of children and emerging adults from nondivorced families had emotional problems.

## Divorced Families

Divorce rates changed rather dramatically in the United States and many countries around the world in the late twentieth century (Amato & Irving, 2006). The U.S. divorce rate increased dramatically in the 1960s and 1970s but has declined since the 1980s. Many other countries around the world have also experienced significant changes in their divorce rate. For example, Japan has experienced an increase in its divorce rate in the 1990s and the first decade of the twenty-first century (Ministry of Health, Education, and Welfare, 2002). However, the divorce rate in the United States is still much higher than in Japan and higher than in most other countries as well. It is estimated that 40 percent of children born to married parents will experience their parents' divorce (Hetherington & Stanley-Hagan, 2002).

These are the questions that we now explore regarding the effects of divorce: Is the adjustment of adolescents and emerging adults better in intact, never-divorced families than in divorced families? Should parents stay together for the sake of their children and adolescents? How much do parenting skills matter in divorced families? What factors affect the adolescent's individual risk and vulnerability in a divorced family? What role does socioeconomic status play in the lives of adolescents in divorced families? (Hetherington, 2005, 2006; Hetherington and Kelly, 2002; Hetherington & Stanley-Hagan, 2002).

**Adolescents' Adjustment in Divorced Families** Most researchers agree that children, adolescents, and emerging adults from divorced families show poorer adjustment than their counterparts in nondivorced families (Amato, 2006; Clarke-Stewart 2006; Clarke-Stewart & Brentano, 2006; Hetherington, 2005, 2006; Hetherington & Stanley-Hagan, 2002; Kelly, 2007) (see Figure 8.5). In the longitudinal study conducted by E. Mavis Hetherington and her colleagues (Hetherington, 2005, 2006; Hetherington, Cox, & Cox, 1982; Hetherington and Kelly, 2002), 25 percent of children from divorced families had emotional problems, but that figure decreased to 20 percent in emerging adulthood. In this study, 10 percent of children and emerging adults from nondivorced families had emotional problems.

In the Hetherington study, the 20 percent of emerging adults from divorced families who continued to have emotional problems were characterized by impulsive, irresponsible, antisocial behavior, or were depressed. Toward the end of emerging adulthood, this troubled group was having problems at work and difficulties in romantic relationships. The 10 percent of emerging adults from nondivorced families who had emotional problems mainly came from homes where family conflict was high and authoritative parenting was rare. As in childhood, emerging adults who had gone from a highly conflicted intact family to a more harmonious divorced family context with a caring, competent parent had fewer emotional problems. In another longitudinal study, parental divorce in childhood and adolescence was linked to poor relationships with fathers, unstable romantic or marital relationships, and low levels of education in adulthood (Amato, 2006).

Those who have experienced multiple divorces are at greater risk. Adolescents and emerging adults in divorced families are more likely than adolescents from nondivorced families to have academic problems, to show externalized problems (such as acting out and delinquency) and internalized problems (such as anxiety and depression), to be less socially responsible, to have less-competent intimate relationships, to drop out of school, to become sexually active at an earlier age, to take drugs, to associate with antisocial peers, and to have lower self-esteem (Conger & Chao, 1996; Hetherington, 2005, 2006; Hetherington & Kelly, 2002). A recent study focused on children and adolescents who experienced the divorce of their parents at some point from kindergarten through the tenth grade (Lansford & others, 2006). Early parental divorce was negatively related to internalizing (anxiety, depression) and externalizing (aggression) problems, whereas later divorce was negatively related to grades. The researchers concluded that children who experience the divorce of their parents may benefit more from interventions that emphasize the prevention of internalizing/externalizing problems, and adolescents may benefit more from interventions that emphasize academic achievement.

Despite the emotional problems that some adolescents and emerging adults from divorced families have, the weight of the research evidence underscores that most adolescents and emerging adults competently cope with their parents' divorce and that a majority of adolescents and emerging adults in divorced families do not have significant adjustment problems (Ahrons, 2007; Barber & Demo, 2006). One study found that 20 years after their parents had divorced when they were children, approximately 80 percent of adults concluded that their parents' decision to divorce was a wise one (Ahrons, 2004).

*As marriage has become a more optional, less permanent institution in contemporary America, children and adolescents are encountering stresses and adaptive challenges associated with their parents' marital transitions.*

—E. Mavis Hetherington
*Contemporary Psychologist, University of Virginia*

**Should Parents Stay Together for the Sake of the Children and Adolescents?** Whether parents should stay in an unhappy or conflicted marriage for the sake of their children and adolescents is one of the most commonly asked questions about divorce (Hetherington, 2005, 2006). If the stresses and disruptions in family relationships associated with an unhappy, conflicted marriage that erode the well-being of the children and adolescents are reduced by the move to a divorced, single-parent family, divorce might be advantageous. However, if the diminished resources and increased risks associated with divorce also are accompanied by inept parenting and sustained or increased conflict, not only between the divorced couple but also between parents, children, and siblings, the best choice for the children would be for an unhappy marriage to be retained (Hetherington & Stanley-Hagan, 2002). These are "ifs," and it is difficult to determine how these will play out when parents either remain together in an acrimonious marriage or become divorced.

Note that marital conflict may have negative consequences for children and adolescents in the context of marriage or divorce (Buehler, Lange, & Franck, 2007; McDonald & Grych, 2006). A longitudinal study revealed that conflict in a nondivorced family was associated with emotional problems in children and adolescents (Amato, 2006).

**How Much Do Family Processes Matter in Divorced Families?** In divorced families, family processes matter a great deal (Clarke-Stewart & Brentano, 2006; Hetherington, 2005, 2006; Kelly, 2007; Walper & Beckh, 2006). When the divorced parents have a harmonious relationship and use authoritative parenting, the adjustment of adolescents is improved (Hetherington, 2005, 2006; Hetherington & Stanley-Hagan, 2002). However, two longitudinal studies revealed that conflict (especially when it is intense and prolonged) between divorced parents was linked to emotional problems, insecure social relationships, and antisocial behavior in adolescents (Hetherington, 2006; Walper & Beckh, 2006). A secure attachment also matters. One recent study found that experiencing a divorce in childhood was associated with insecure attachment in early adulthood (Brockmeyer, Treboux, & Crowell, 2005). Researchers have shown that a disequilibrium, including diminished parenting skills, occurs in the year following the divorce, but that by two years after the divorce restabilization has occurred and parenting skills have improved (Hetherington, 1989). About one-fourth to one-third of adolescents in divorced families, compared with 10 percent in nondivorced families, become disengaged from their families, spending as little time as possible at home and in interaction with family members (Hetherington & Kelly, 2002). This disengagement is higher for boys than for girls in divorced families. However, if there is a caring adult outside the home, such as a mentor, the disengagement can be a positive solution to a disrupted, conflicted family circumstance.

**What Factors Are Involved in the Adolescent's Individual Risk Vulnerability in a Divorced Family?** Among the factors involved in individual risk vulnerability are the adolescent's adjustment prior to the divorce, personality and temperament, developmental status, gender, and custody. Children and adolescents whose parents later divorce show poorer adjustment before the breakup (Amato & Booth, 1996).

## Through the Eyes of Emerging Adults

### COLLEGE STUDENTS REFLECT ON GROWING UP IN A DIVORCED FAMILY

"In my early adolescence, the lack of a consistent, everyday father figure in my life became a source of many problems. Because I felt deprived of a quality relationship with a man, I tried to satisfy this need by starting to date very young. I was desperate to please every boyfriend, and this often led to promiscuous behavior. I was anxious and seductive in my interactions with males. It seemed like no matter how hard I tried I could not make these relationships work. Just as with my dad—no matter how good I was, my father remained emotionally unavailable. I still feel a lot of anger that I did not deal with as a small child. As a young woman now, I am continuously struggling with these issues trying to get my life together.

It has always been painful knowing that I have a father who is alive and perfectly capable of acting like a parent, but who does not care about me. As a child, I was often depressed and acted out. As I grew older I had very low self-esteem. In junior high school, although I was successful, I felt like I belonged to the 'loser crowd.' . . . After I graduated from high school, I decided I still needed to fill the emptiness in my life by finding out at least a little bit about my father. I was seventeen when I found his number and called to see if he would be willing to talk. After a long hesitation, he agreed. We met and spent the day together. He has called me regularly ever since. Today I am better able to understand what I was feeling all those years. Now I am able to say without guilt that the absence of my father caused me much pain. I no longer feel abandoned, but many of the scars still remain. I still haven't been able to bring myself to call him 'Dad.'

There were two positive consequences of my parents' divorce for me: I discovered my own strength by living through this most difficult experience and surviving the loss of my father, and I developed this close bond with my mother from sharing the experience. She and I have become best friends.

Fortunately I had my friends, my teachers, my grandparents, and my brother to help me through the whole crazy-making time after my parents' divorce. The most important people were my brother and a teacher I had in the sixth and seventh grades. My brother was important because he was the only constant in my life; we shared every experience. My teacher was important because she took an interest in me and showed compassion. My grandparents offered consistent support. They gave my mother money for rent and food and paid for private schools for my brother and me; they were like second parents to us."



Personality and temperament also play a role in adolescent adjustment in divorced families. Adolescents who are socially mature and responsible, who show few behavioral problems, and who have an easy temperament are better able to cope with their parents' divorce. Children and adolescents with a difficult temperament often have problems coping with their parents' divorce (Hetherington & Stanley-Hagan, 2002).

Focusing on the developmental status of the child or adolescent involves taking into account the age of onset of the divorce and the time when the child's or adolescent's adjustment is assessed. In most studies, these factors are confounded with length of time since the divorce occurred. Some researchers have found that preschool children whose parents divorce are at greater risk for long-term problems than are older children (Zill, Morrison, & Coiro, 1993). The explanation for this focuses on their inability to realistically appraise the causes and consequences of divorce, their anxiety about the possibility of abandonment, their self-blame for the divorce, and their inability to use extrafamilial protective resources. However, problems in adjustment can emerge or increase during adolescence, even if the divorce occurred much earlier. As we indicated earlier, whether a divorce occurs earlier or later in children's or adolescents' development is linked to the type of problems the children and adolescents are likely to develop (Lansford & others, 2006).

In recent decades, an increasing number of children and adolescents have lived in father-custody and joint-custody families. What is their adjustment like, compared with the adjustment of children and adolescents in mother-custody families? Although there have been few thorough studies of the topic, a review of studies concluded that children benefit from joint custody because it facilitates ongoing positive involvement with both parents (Bauserman, 2003). Some studies have shown that boys adjust better in father-custody families and that girls adjust better in mother-custody families, but other studies have not. In one study, adolescents in father-custody families had higher rates of delinquency, believed to be due to less-competent monitoring by the fathers (Buchanan, Maccoby, & Dornsbusch, 1992).

Another factor involved in an adolescent's adjustment in a divorced family is relocation (Kelly & Lamb, 2003). One study found that when children and adolescents whose parents have divorced experience a move away of either of their parents, they show less effective adjustment (Braver, Ellman, & Fabricius, 2003).

**What Role Does Socioeconomic Status Play in the Lives of Adolescents in Divorced Families?** On average, custodial mothers' income decreases about 25 to 50 percent from their predivorce income, in comparison to a decrease of only 10 percent for custodial fathers (Emery, 1999). This income decrease for divorced mothers is typically accompanied by increased workloads, high rates of job instability, and residential moves to less desirable neighborhoods with inferior schools (Sayer, 2006).

## Stepfamilies

Not only are parents divorcing more, they are also getting remarried more (Ganong, Coleman, & Hans, 2006; Goldscheider & Sassler, 2006; Hetherington, 2006; Stewart, 2006). It takes time for couples to marry, have children, get divorced, and then remarry. Consequently, there are far more elementary and secondary schoolchildren than infant or preschool children in stepfamilies.

The number of remarriages involving children has grown steadily in recent years. As a result of their parents' successive marital transitions, about half of all children whose parents divorce will have a stepfather within four years of parental separation. Furthermore, divorces occur at a 10 percent higher rate in remarriages than in first marriages (Cherlin & Furstenberg, 1994).

*How does living in a stepfamily influence an adolescent's development?*

**Types of Stepfamilies** There are different types of stepfamilies. Some types are based on family structure, others on relationships. The stepfamily may have been preceded by a circumstance in which a spouse died. However, a large majority of stepfamilies are preceded by a divorce rather than a death.

Three common types of stepfamily structure are (1) stepfather, (2) stepmother, and (3) blended or complex. In stepfather families, the mother typically had custody of the children and became remarried, introducing a stepfather into her children's lives. In stepmother families, the father usually had custody and became remarried, introducing a stepmother into his children's lives. And in a blended or complex stepfamily, both parents bring children from previous marriages to live in the newly formed stepfamily.

Researchers have found that children's relationships with custodial parents (mother in stepfather families, father in stepmother families) are often better than with stepparents (Santrock, Sitterle, & Warshak, 1988). However, when adolescents have a positive relationship with their stepfather, it is related to fewer adolescent problems (Flouri, 2004; White & Gilbreth, 2001). Also, adolescents in simple stepfamilies (stepfather, stepmother) often show better adjustment than their counterparts in complex (blended) families (Anderson & others, 1999; Hetherington, 2006).

In addition to their structure (stepfather, stepmother, or blended), stepfamilies also develop certain patterns of relationships. In a study of 200 stepfamilies, James Bray and his colleagues (Bray, Berger, & Boethel, 1999; Bray & Kelly, 1998) found that over time stepfamilies often fall into three types based on their relationships: neotraditional, matriarchal, and romantic.

- *Neotraditional.* Both adults want a family and are able to successfully cope with the challenges of a new stepfamily. After three to five years, these families often look like intact, never-divorced families, with positive relationships often characterizing the stepfamily members.
- *Matriarchal.* In this type of stepfamily, the mother has custody and is accustomed to managing the family herself. The stepfather married her mainly because of his love for her, not because he wanted to be a father. She runs the family and the stepfather is kind of a bystander, often ignoring the children or occasionally engaging in some enjoyable activities with them. This type of stepfamily may function adequately except when the mother wants help and the stepfather doesn't want to give it. This type of stepfamily also may not function well if the husband decides to become very involved (which typically occurs after they have a baby of their own), and she feels that her turf has been invaded.
- *Romantic.* These adults married with very high, unrealistic expectations for their stepfamily. They try to create an instant, very happy family and can't understand why it doesn't happen immediately. This type of stepfamily is the one that is most likely to end in a divorce.

**Adjustment** As in divorced families, adolescents in stepfamilies have more adjustment problems than their counterparts in nondivorced families (Hetherington, 2006; Hetherington, Bridges, & Insabella, 1998; Hetherington & Kelly, 2002). The adjustment problems of adolescents in stepfamilies are much like those of adolescents in divorced families: academic problems, externalizing and internalizing problems, lower self-esteem, early sexual activity, delinquency, and so on (Hetherington, 2006). Adjustment for parents and children may take longer in stepfamilies (up to five years or more) than in divorced families, in which a restabilization is more likely to occur within two years (Anderson & others, 1999; Hetherington, 2006). One aspect of a stepfamily that makes adjustment difficult is **boundary ambiguity,** the uncertainty in stepfamilies about who is in or out of the family and who is performing or responsible for certain tasks in the family system.

There is an increase in adjustment problems of adolescents in newly remarried families (Hetherington, 2006; Hetherington & Clingempeel, 1992). In research conducted by Bray and his colleagues (Bray, Berger, & Boethel, 1999; Bray & Kelly, 1998), the formation of a stepfamily often meant that adolescents had to move, which involved changing schools and friends. It took time for the stepparent to get to know the stepchildren. The new spouses had to learn how to cope with the challenges of their relationship and parenting together. In Bray's view, the formation of a stepfamily was like merging two cultures.

Bray and his colleagues also found that it was not unusual for the following problems to develop early in the stepfamily's existence. When the stepparent tried to discipline the stepchild, this often did not work well. Most experts recommend that in the early period of a stepfamily the biological parent should be the parent doing any disciplining of the child that is needed. The stepparent-stepchild relationship develops

**boundary ambiguity** The uncertainty in stepfamilies about who is in or out of the family and who is performing or responsible for certain tasks in the family system.

best when the stepparent spends time with the stepchild in activities that the child enjoys.

A newly formed stepfamily sometimes has difficulty coping with changes that they cannot control. For example, the husband and wife may be looking forward to going away for a weekend without the children. At the last minute, the other biological parent calls and cancels taking the children. This is bound to cause some angry feelings. Unfortunately, both parents may take their frustration out on the children. Successful stepfamilies adjust to such unexpected circumstances and have backup plans (Coleman, Ganong, & Fine, 2004).

In Hetherington's (2006) most recent analysis, adolescents who had been in a simple stepfamily for a number of years were adjusting better than in the early years of the remarried family and were functioning well in comparison to adolescents in conflicted nondivorced families and adolescents in complex stepfamilies. More than 75 percent of the adolescents in long-established simple stepfamilies described their relationships with their stepparents as "close" or "very close." Hetherington (2006) concludes that in long-established simple stepfamilies adolescents seem to eventually benefit from the presence of a stepparent and the resources provided by the stepparent.

In terms of the age of the child, researchers have found that early adolescence is an especially difficult time for the formation of a stepfamily (Bray & Kelly, 1998; Hetherington & others, 1999). This may occur because the stepfamily circumstances exacerbate normal adolescent concerns about identity, sexuality, and autonomy. Now that we have considered the changing social worlds of adolescents when their parents divorce and remarry, we turn our attention to another aspect of the changing family worlds of adolescents—the situation when both parents work.

## Working Parents

Interest in the effects of parental work on the development of children and adolescents has increased in recent years. Our examination of parental work focuses on the following issues: the role of working parents in adolescents' development and the adjustment of latchkey adolescents.

**Working Parents** Most of the research on parental work has focused on young children. Until recently, little attention has been given to the role of parents' work in adolescence (Crosby & Sabattini, 2006; Crouter, 2006). Recent research indicates that what matters for adolescent development is the nature of parents' work rather than whether one parent works outside the home (Clarke-Stewart, 2006). Ann Crouter (2006) recently described how parents bring their experiences at work into their homes. She concluded that parents who have poor working conditions, such as long hours, overtime work, stressful work, and lack of autonomy at work, are likely to be more irritable home and engage in less effective parenting than their counterparts who have better work conditions in their jobs. The negative work conditions of parents are linked to more behavior problems and lower grades in their adolescents. One study found that when fathers worked more than 60 hours per week and perceived their work overload gave them too little time to do what they wanted, their relationship with their adolescents was more conflicted (Crouter & others, 2001).

*What are some strategies parents can adopt that benefit latchkey children and adolescents?*

**Self-Care/Latchkey Adolescents** Although the mother's working is not necessarily associated with negative outcomes for adolescents, a certain set of adolescents from working-mother families bears further scrutiny—those called latchkey adolescents. Latchkey adolescents typically do not see their parents from the time they leave for school in the morning until about 6:00 or 7:00 p.m. They are called "latchkey" children or adolescents because they carry a key to their home and let themselves into the home while their parents are still at work. Many latchkey adolescents are largely unsupervised for two to four hours a day during each school week, or for entire days, five days a week, during the summer months.

In one study of 819 10- to 14-year-olds, out-of-home care, whether supervised or unsupervised, was linked to delinquency, drug and alcohol use, and school problems (Coley, Morris, & Hernandez, 2004). In another study, researchers interviewed more than 1,500 latchkey children (Long & Long, 1983). They concluded that a slight majority of these children had had negative latchkey experiences. Some latchkey children may grow up too fast, hurried by the responsibilities placed on them. How do latchkey children handle the lack of limits and structure during the latchkey hours? Without limits and parental supervision, latchkey children find their way into trouble more easily, possibly stealing, vandalizing, or abusing a sibling. Ninety percent of the juvenile delinquents in Montgomery County, Maryland, are latchkey children. Joan Lipsitz (1983), in testifying before the Select Committee on Children, Youth, and Families, called the lack of adult supervision of children in the after-school hours a major problem. Lipsitz called it the "three-to-six o'clock problem" because it was during this time that the Center for Early Adolescence in North Carolina, when Lipsitz was director, experienced a peak of referrals for clinical help. And, in a 1987 national poll, teachers rated the latchkey children phenomenon the number one reason that children have problems in school (Harris, 1987).

Although latchkey adolescents can be vulnerable to problems, keep in mind that the experiences of latchkey adolescents vary enormously, just as do the experiences of all children with working mothers. Parents need to give special attention to the ways their latchkey adolescents' lives can be monitored effectively. Variations in latchkey experiences suggest that parental monitoring and authoritative parenting help the adolescent to cope more effectively with latchkey experiences, especially in resisting peer pressure (Galambos & Maggs, 1991; Steinberg, 1986). The degree to which latchkey adolescents are at developmental risk remains unsettled. A positive sign is that researchers are beginning to conduct more precise analyses of adolescents' latchkey experiences in an effort to determine which aspects of latchkey circumstances are the most detrimental and which aspects foster better adaptation. In one study that focused on the after-school hours, unsupervised peer contact, lack of neighborhood safety, and low monitoring were linked with externalizing problems (such as acting out and delinquency) in young adolescents (Pettit & others, 1999).

## Adoption

Adoption is the social and legal process by which a parent-child relationship is established between persons unrelated at birth. It is estimated that approximately 2½ percent of children and adolescents in the United States are adopted.

A number of changes began occurring in adoption practice in the last several decades of the twentieth century. These changes include the following (Brodzinsky & Pinderhughes, 2002, p. 281):

- A substantial decrease in the number of healthy, non-Latino White infants have become available for adoption. "With fewer healthy, European babies available for adoption in the United States, many prospective adoptive parents have explored other options." These options included transracial adoption (adopting a child of a different race) and adopting children from other countries. The number of intercountry adoptions is growing rapidly, and many of these are adoptions across racial lines.
- "Still other prospective adoptive parents began considering adopting foster children whose history and personal characteristics (such as older age at placement, minority [ethnic] status, exposure to neglect and/or abuse, chronic medical problems, and/or physical or mental health problems) were once thought to be barriers to adoption."

- Changes also have characterized adoptive parents. Until the last several decades of the twentieth century, most adoptive parents were of middle- or upper-socioeconomic-status background, "married, infertile, European American couples, usually in their 30s and 40s, and free of any form of disability. Adoption agencies routinely *screened out* couples who did not have these characteristics. Today, however, adoption agency policy and practice have moved in the direction of *screening in* as many different types of adoption applicants as possible. For example, public agencies (in the United States) now have no income requirement for adoptive parents and offer financial and medical subsidies for children with special needs, which in turn has supported the efforts of . . . low-income couples to adopt children, especially those . . . who otherwise might not find permanent homes." Many agencies now permit single adults, older adults, and gay and lesbian adults to adopt children (Rampage & others, 2003).

*What are some changes in adoption practice in recent decades in the United States?*

Researchers have found that adopted children and adolescents often show more psychological and school-related problems than nonadopted children (Brodzinsky & others, 1984; Brodzinsky, Lang, & Smith, 1995; Brodzinsky & Pinderhughes, 2002). For example, adopted adolescents are referred to psychological treatment two to five times as often as their nonadopted peers (Grotevant & McRoy, 1990).

In one study of 4,682 adopted adolescents and the same number of nonadopted adolescents, adoptees showed lower levels of adjustment (Sharma, McGue, & Benson, 1996). In another study, adopted adolescents had more school adjustment problems, were more likely to use illicit drugs, and were more likely to engage in delinquent behavior (Sharma, McGue, & Benson, 1998). However, adopted siblings were less withdrawn and engaged in more prosocial behavior (such as being altruistic, caring, and supportive of others) than nonadopted siblings. In one study of 1,587 adopted and 87,165 nonadopted adolescents, the adopted adolescents were at higher risk for all of the domains sampled, including school achievement and problems, substance abuse, psychological well-being, and physical health (Miller & others, 2000). In this study, the effects of adoption were more negative when the adoptive parents had low levels of education. Also, in this study, when a subsample consisting of the most negative problem profiles was examined, the differences between adopted and non-adopted adolescents even widened, with the adopted adolescents far more likely to have the most problems.

Research has documented that early adoption often has better outcomes for the child and adolescent than later adoption. In one study, the later adoption occurred, the more problems the adoptees had. Infant adoptees had the fewest adjustment difficulties; those adopted after they were 10 years of age had the most problems (Sharma, McGue, & Benson, 1996).

Although adoption is associated with increased academic and psychological difficulties, the changes in adoption practices over the last several decades that we mentioned earlier make it difficult to generalize about the average adopted adolescent or average adoptive family. Further, despite the overall group differences in adopted and nonadopted adolescents, the vast majority of adopted adolescents (including those adopted at older ages, transracially, and across national borders) adjust effectively, and their parents report considerable satisfaction in their adoption decision (Brodzinsky & Pinderhughes, 2002; Grotevant, 2006; Grotevant & others, 2006; Wrobel, Hendrickson, & Grotevant, 2006).

In addition, researchers have found that children whose biological parents could not or would not provide adequate care for them benefit from adoption. For example, there is consistent evidence that adopted children fare much better than children who reside in long-term foster care or in institutional-type environments (Brodzinsky & Pinderhughes, 2002).

Many of the keys to effectively parenting adopted adolescents are no different than those for effectively parenting biological adolescents: be supportive and caring, be involved and monitor the adolescent's behavior and whereabouts, be a good

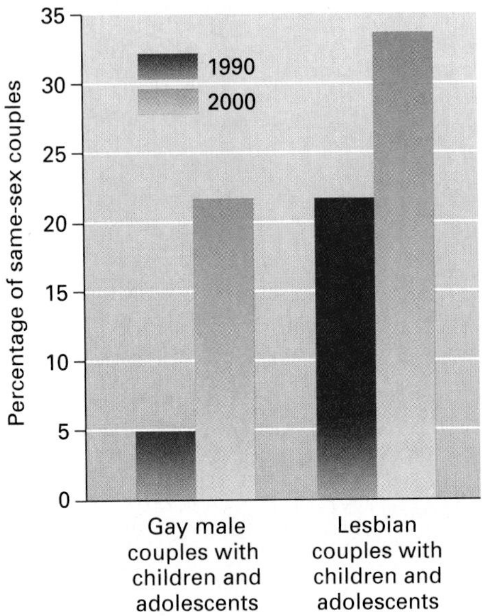


**FIGURE 8.6 Percentage of Gay Male and Lesbian Couples with Children and Adolescents: 1990 and 2000**

communicator, and help the adolescent to learn to develop self-control. However, parents of adopted adolescents face some unique circumstances. These include recognizing the differences involved in adoptive family life, providing child rearing that supports open communication about these differences, showing respect for the birth family, and supporting the adolescent's search for self and identity.

The emergence of more abstract and logical thinking in adolescence provides the foundation for adopted adolescents to reflect on their adoptive status in more complex ways. As pubertal change focuses adolescents' attention on their bodies, many adopted adolescents become preoccupied with the lack of physical resemblance between themselves and others in the family. The search for identity that characterizes adolescence may also give rise to extensive exploration of the fact that they are adopted and how this fits into their identity. Adoptive parents "need to be aware of these many complexities and provide teenagers with the support they need to cope with these adoption-related tasks" (Brodzinsky & Pinderhughes, 2002, p. 292).

## Gay Male and Lesbian Parents

Another aspect of the changing family in a changing society focuses on adolescents raised by gay male and lesbian parents (Patterson & Hastings, 2007). Increasingly, gay male and lesbian couples are creating families that include children and adolescents (Goldberg & Sayer, 2006) (see Figure 8.6). There may be more than 1 million gay male and lesbian parents in the United States today.

An important aspect of gay male and lesbian families with adolescents is the sexual identity of parents at the time of a child's birth or adoption (Patterson, 2002). The largest group of adolescents with gay male and lesbian parents are likely those who were born in the context of heterosexual relationships, with one or both parents only later identifying themselves as gay male or lesbian. Gay male and lesbian parents may be single or they may have same-gender partners. In addition, gay males and lesbians are increasingly choosing parenthood through donor insemination or adoption. Custodial arrangements also may vary.

Another issue focuses on custody arrangements for adolescents. Many gay fathers and lesbian mothers have lost custody of their adolescents to heterosexual spouses following divorce. For this reason, many gay male fathers and lesbian mothers are noncustodial parents.

Researchers have found few differences in children and adolescents growing up with gay fathers and lesbian mothers and in children and adolescents growing up with heterosexual parents (Patterson & Hastings, 2007). For example, adolescents growing up in gay male or lesbian families are just as popular with their peers, and there are no differences in the adjustment and mental health of adolescents living in these families when they are compared with adolescents in heterosexual families (Hyde & DeLamater, 2006). Also, the overwhelming majority of adolescents growing up in a gay male or lesbian family have a heterosexual orientation (Tasker & Golombok, 1997).

## Culture and Ethnicity

What are some variations in families across different cultures? How do families vary across different ethnic groups?

**Cross-Cultural Comparisons** Cultures vary on a number of issues involving families, such as what the father's role in the family should be, the extent to which support systems are available to families, and how children should be disciplined (Conner & White, 2006; Kagitcibasi, 2007; Rothbaum & Trommsdorff, 2007). Although there are cross-cultural variations in parenting, in one study of parenting behavior in 186 cultures around the world, the most common pattern was a warm and controlling style, one that was neither permissive nor restrictive (Rohner & Rohner, 1981). The investigators commented that the majority of cultures have discovered, over many centuries, a "truth" that only recently emerged in the Western world—namely, that children's and adolescents' healthy social development is most effectively promoted by love and at least some moderate parental control.

Nonetheless, in some countries, authoritarian parenting continues to be widely practiced (Rothbaum & Trommsdorff, 2007). In the Arab world, families today are still very authoritarian and dominated by the father's rule (Booth, 2002). In Arab countries, adolescents are taught strict codes of conduct and family loyalty.

Cultural change is coming to many families around the world (Berry, 2007; Berry & others, 2006; Bornstein & Cote, 2006). There are trends toward greater family mobility, migration to urban areas, family members working in distant cities or countries, smaller families, fewer extended-family households, and increases in the mothers' employment (Brown & Larson, 2002). These trends can change the resources that are available to adolescents. For example, many families have fewer extended family members nearby, resulting in a decrease in support and guidance for adolescents. Also, smaller families may produce more openness and communication between parents and adolescents. We have much more to say about culture and parenting in Chapter 12, "Culture."

**Ethnicity and Parenting** Ethnic minority families differ from non-Latino White American families in their size, structure and composition, reliance on kinship networks, and level of income and education (Gonzales & others, 2007; Hernandez, Denton, & McCartney, 2007). Large and extended families are more common among ethnic minority groups than among non-Latino White Americans. For example, more than 30 percent of Latino families consist of five or more individuals. African American and Latino children interact more with grandparents, aunts, uncles, cousins, and more distant relatives than do non-Latino White American children (McAdoo, 2006).

Ethnic minority adolescents are more likely to come from low-income families than non-Latino White American adolescents are (Magnuson & Duncan, 2002; McLoyd, Aikens, & Burton, 2006; Parke & Buriel, 2006). Single-parent families are more common among African Americans and Latinos than among non-Latino White Americans (Harris & Graham, 2007; McAdoo, 2006). In comparison with two-parent households, single-parent households often have more-limited resources of time, money, and energy. This shortage of resources can prompt parents to encourage autonomy among their adolescents prematurely. Ethnic minority parents, on average,

The family reunion of the Limon family in Austin, Texas. Mexican American children often grow up in families with a network of relatives that runs into scores of individuals.

A 14-year-old adolescent, his 6-year-old sister, and their grandmother. The African American cultural tradition of an extended family household has helped many African American parents cope with adverse social conditions.

are less well educated and engage in less joint decision making than non-Latino White American parents. Although impoverished families often raise competent youth, poor parents can have a diminished capacity for supportive and involved parenting (McLoyd, 1990).

Some aspects of home life can help to protect ethnic minority youth from social patterns of injustice. The community and family can filter out destructive racist messages, parents can provide alternate frames of reference than those presented by the majority, and parents can also provide competent role models and encouragement. And the extended-family system in many ethnic minority families provides an important buffer to stress (Gonzales & others, 2004, 2007).

A sense of family duty and obligation also varies across ethnic groups (Fuligni & Fuligni, 2007; Fuligni & Yoshikawa, 2004). Asian American and Latino families place a greater emphasis on family duty and obligation than do non-Latino White families (Harwood & Feng, 2006). In a study of 18- to 25-year-olds, Asian Americans said family interdependence was more important to them than did non-Latino Whites (Tseng, 2004). Researchers have found that Asian American and Latino adolescents believe that they should spend more time taking care of their siblings, helping around the house, assisting their parents at work, and being with their family than adolescents with a European heritage (Fuligni, Tseng, & Lamb, 1999).

Of course, individual families vary, and how ethnic minority families deal with stress depends on many factors (Fuligni & Yoshikawa, 2004; Hill & others, 2007). Whether the parents are native-born or immigrants, how long the family has been in this country, their socioeconomic status, and their national origin all make a difference (Kagitcibasi, 2006). The characteristics of the family's social context also influence its adaptation. What are the attitudes toward the family's ethnic group within its neighborhood or city? Can the family's children attend good schools? Are there community groups that welcome people from the family's ethnic group? Do members of the family's ethnic group form community groups of their own?

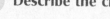

**REVIEW AND REFLECT ◆ LEARNING GOAL 4**

### 4 Describe the changing family in a changing society.

***Review***

- What are the effects of divorce on adolescents?
- How does growing up in a stepfamily influence adolescents' development?
- How do working parents influence adolescent development?
- How does being adopted affect adolescent development?
- What are the effects on adolescents of having gay male or lesbian parents?
- What roles do culture and ethnicity play in families with adolescents?

***Reflect***

- You have studied many aspects of families and adolescents in this chapter. Imagine that you have decided to write a book on adolescents and families. What would the title of the book be? What would be the main theme of the book?

## 5 Social Policy, Adolescents, and Families

We have seen in this chapter that parents play very important roles in adolescent development. Although adolescents are moving toward independence, they are still connected with their families, which are far more important to them than is commonly believed (Matjasko, Grunden, & Ernst, 2007). We know that competent adolescent development is most likely to happen when adolescents have parents who do the following:

- Show them warmth and respect.
- Demonstrate sustained interest in their lives.
- Recognize and adapt to their changing cognitive and socioemotional development.
- Communicate expectations for high standards of conduct and achievement.
- Display authoritative, constructive ways of dealing with problems and conflict.

Community programs such as this one in East Orange, New Jersey, can provide a monitored, structured context for adolescents to study in the after-school hours. *In addition to improving after-school options for adolescents, what are some other ways that U.S. social policy could be improved to support families with adolescents?*

However, compared with families with young children, families with adolescents have been neglected in community programs and public policies. The Carnegie Council on Adolescent Development (1995) identified some key opportunities for improving social policy regarding families with adolescents. As we near the end of the first decade of the twenty-first century, these recommendations they made in 1995 still need to be followed:

- School, cultural arts, religious and youth organizations, and health-care agencies should examine the extent to which they involve parents in activities with adolescents and should develop ways to engage parents and adolescents in activities they both enjoy.
- Professionals such as teachers, psychologists, nurses, physicians, youth specialists, and others who have contact with adolescents need not only to work with the individual adolescent but also to increase the time they spend interacting with the adolescent's family.
- Employers should extend to the parents of young adolescents the workplace policies now reserved only for the parents of young children. These policies include flexible work schedules, job sharing, telecommuting, and part-time work with benefits. This change in work/family policy would free parents to spend more time with their teenagers.
- Community institutions such as businesses, schools, and youth organizations should become more involved in providing after-school programs. After-school programs for elementary schoolchildren are increasing, but such programs for adolescents are rare. More high-quality, community-based programs for adolescents are needed in the after-school, weekend, and vacation time periods.

## REVIEW AND REFLECT ◆ LEARNING GOAL 5

### 5 Explain what is needed for improved social policy involving adolescents and their families.

***Review***

- What is needed for improved social policy regarding adolescents and their families?

***Reflect***

- If you were a U.S. senator, what would you seek to do to improve social policy involving the families of adolescents? What would be your number one priority?

# REACH YOUR LEARNING GOALS

## 1 FAMILY PROCESSES *Discuss the nature of family processes in adolescence.*

**Reciprocal Socialization and the Family as a System**

The concept of reciprocal socialization is that adolescents socialize parents just as parents socialize adolescents. The family is a system of interacting individuals with different subsystems—some dyadic, some polyadic.

**The Developmental Construction of Relationships**

The developmental construction views share the belief that as individuals develop they acquire modes of relating to others. There are two main variations within this view, one that emphasizes continuity and one that stresses discontinuity and change in relationships.

**Maturation**

Relationships are influenced by the maturation of the adolescent and the maturation of parents. Adolescent changes include puberty, expanded logical reasoning, increased idealistic and egocentric thought, violated expectations, changes in schooling, peers, friendships, dating, and movement toward independence. Changes in parents might include marital satisfaction, economic burdens, career reevaluation, time perspective, and health/body concerns.

## 2 ADOLESCENTS' AND EMERGING ADULTS' RELATIONSHIPS WITH PARENTS *Describe adolescents' and emerging adults' relationships with their parents.*

**Parents as Managers**

An increasing trend is to conceptualize parents as managers of adolescents' lives. This involves being a parent who finds information, makes contacts, helps structure choices, and provides guidance. Parents also can serve as regulators of their adolescents' social contacts with peers, friends, and adults.

**Parenting Styles**

Authoritarian, authoritative, neglectful, and indulgent are four main parenting styles. Authoritative parenting, which encourages independence but places limits and controls, is associated with socially competent adolescent behavior more than the other styles. Some ethnic variations in parenting have been found, such as the positive relation between training by Asian American parents and the achievement of their adolescents.

**Gender, Parenting, and Coparenting**

Most people associate motherhood with a number of positive images, but the reality is that motherhood is accorded a relatively low status in American society. Over time, the father's role in the development of children and adolescents has changed. Fathers are less involved in child rearing than mothers are, but fathers are increasing the time they spend with adolescents and children. Coparenting, father-mother cooperation, and mutual respect help the adolescent to develop positive attitudes toward males and females.

**Parent-Adolescent Conflict**

Conflict with parents does increase in early adolescence, but such conflict is usually moderate and can serve a positive developmental function of increasing independence and identity exploration. The generation gap is exaggerated, although in as many as 20 percent of families parent-adolescent conflict is too high and is linked with adolescent problems.

**Autonomy and Attachment**

Many parents have a difficult time handling the adolescent's push for autonomy. Autonomy is a complex concept with many referents. Developmental transitions in autonomy include the onset of early adolescence and the time when individuals leave home and go to college. A special concern about autonomy involves runaways. The wise parent relinquishes control in areas where the adolescent makes mature decisions and retains more control in areas where the adolescent makes immature decisions. Adolescents do not simply move away into a world isolated from parents. Attachment to parents in adolescence increases the probability that an adolescent will be socially competent and explore a widening social world in a healthy way. Increasingly, researchers classify attachment in adolescence into one secure category (secure-autonomous) and three insecure categories (dismissing/avoidant, preoccupied/ambivalent, and unresolved/disorganized). Increased interest in attachment during emerging adulthood is revealing that securely attached emerging adults have better social relationships than insecurely attached emerging adults.

**Emerging Adults' Relationships with Parents**

An increasing number of emerging adults are returning to live at home with their parents, often for economic reasons. Both emerging adults and their parents need to adapt when emerging adults return home to live.

## 3 Sibling Relationships *Characterize sibling relationships in adolescence.*

**Sibling Roles**

Sibling relationships often involve more conflict than relationships with other individuals. However, adolescents also share many positive moments with siblings through emotional support and social communication.

**Birth Order**

Birth order has been of special interest, and differences between firstborns and laterborns have been reported. The only child often is more socially competent than the stereotype "spoiled brat" suggests. An increasing number of family researchers believe that birth-order effects have been exaggerated and that other factors are more important in predicting the adolescent's behavior.

## 4 The Changing Family in a Changing Society *Describe the changing family in a changing society.*

**Divorced Families**

Adolescents in divorced families have more adjustment problems than their counterparts in nondivorced families, although the size of the effects is debated. Whether parents should stay together for the sake of the adolescent is difficult to determine, although conflict has a negative effect on the adolescent. Adolescents are better adjusted in divorced families when their parents have a harmonious relationship with each other and use authoritative parenting. Among other factors to be considered in adolescent adjustment are adjustment prior to the divorce, personality and temperament, and developmental status, gender, and custody. Income loss for divorced mothers is linked to a number of other stresses that can affect adolescent adjustment.

**Stepfamilies**

An increasing number of adolescents are growing up in stepfamilies. Stepfamilies involve different types of structure (stepfather, stepmother, blended) and relationships (neotraditional, matriarchal, and romantic). Adolescents in stepfamilies have more adjustment problems than children in nondivorced homes. Adjustment is especially difficult in the first several years of a stepfamily's existence and is difficult for young adolescents.

**Working Parents**

It is the nature of parents' work, not whether one parent works outside the home or not, that is linked to adolescents' development. Latchkey experiences do not have a uniformly negative effect on adolescents. Parental monitoring and structured activities in the after-school hours benefit latchkey adolescents.

**Adoption**

Although adopted adolescents have more problems than their nonadopted counterparts, the majority of adopted adolescents adapt effectively. When adoption occurs very early in development, the outcomes for the adolescent improve. Because of the dramatic changes that have occurred in adoption in recent decades, it is difficult to generalize about the average adopted adolescent or average adoptive family.

**Gay Male and Lesbian Parents**

There is considerable diversity among lesbian mothers, gay fathers, and their adolescents. Researchers have found few differences in adolescents growing up in gay male or lesbian families and adolescents growing up in heterosexual families.

**Culture and Ethnicity**

Authoritative parenting is the most common form of parenting around the world. Ethnic minority families differ from non-Latino White families in their size, structure, and composition, their reliance on kinship networks, and their levels of income and education.

## 5 Social Policy, Adolescents, and Families *Explain what is needed for improved social policy involving adolescents and their families.*

Families with adolescents have been neglected in social policy. A number of recommendations for improving social policy for families include the extent parents are involved in schools, youth organizations, and health-care agencies; the degree teachers and other professionals invite and encourage parents to be involved in schools and other settings that adolescents frequent; the extent to which policies are developed to allow employers to provide more flexible scheduling for parents; and greater funding by institutions such as businesses, schools, and youth organizations for high-quality programs for adolescents in after-school, weekend, and vacation time periods.

## KEY TERMS

reciprocal socialization 275
developmental construction views 276
continuity view 277
discontinuity view 278
authoritarian parenting 282
authoritative parenting 283
neglectful parenting 283
indulgent parenting 283
emotional autonomy 289
secure attachment 291
insecure attachment 291
dismissing/avoidant attachment 291
preoccupied/ambivalent attachment 291
unresolved/disorganized attachment 292
boundary ambiguity 304

## KEY PEOPLE

Andrew Collins 278
Diana Baumrind 282
John Bowlby and Mary Ainsworth 291
Joseph Allen 291
Judy Dunn 297
E. Mavis Hetherington 300
Ann Crouter 305

## RESOURCES FOR IMPROVING THE LIVES OF ADOLESCENTS

**Between Parent and Teenager**
by Haim Ginott (1988)
New York: Avon

Despite the fact that *Between Parent and Teenager* is well past its own adolescence (it was originally published in 1969), it continues to be one of the most widely read and recommended books for parents who want to communicate more effectively with their teenagers.

**Handbook of Socialization**
edited by Joan Grusec and Paul Hastings (2007)
New York: Guilford Press

An excellent collection of up-to-date reviews of research by leading experts on many topics in this chapter, including parenting, siblings, family diversity, autonomy and attachment, and culture.

**Big Brothers Big Sisters of America** **www.bbbsa.org**
Single mothers and single fathers who are having problems with a son or daughter might want to get a responsible adult to spend at least one afternoon every other week with the son or daughter.

**Divorce Lessons: Real Life Stories and What You Can Learn from Them**
by Alison Clarke-Stewart and Cornelia Brentano (2006)
Charleston, SC: BookSurge Publishing

An outstanding book that gives special attention to emerging adults' experiences and development while growing up in divorced families.

**Raising Black Children**
by James P. Comer and Alvin E. Poussaint (1992)
New York: Plume

This excellent book includes many wise suggestions for raising African American children.

**National Stepfamily Resource Center** **www.stepfamilies.info**
This organization serves as a clearinghouse of information, resources, and support for stepfamilies.

**You and Your Adolescent**
by Laurence Steinberg and Ann Levine (1997, 2nd ed.)
New York: Harper Perennial

*You and Your Adolescent* provides a broad, developmental overview of adolescence, with parental advice mixed in along the way.

## E-LEARNING TOOLS

To help you master the material in this chapter, visit the Online Learning Center for *Adolescence*, twelfth edition **(www.mhhe.com/santrocka12)**, where you will find these additional resources:

### Taking It to the Net

1. Parents are a valuable resource for adolescents who need to cope with extreme stress, such as that which often is felt when parents divorce, when the adolescent must deal with the death of a friend or family member, or when a disaster occurs. Develop a list of tips that parents can use to help their adolescents cope with extreme stress.
2. All parents must determine how to discipline their children. Discipline techniques used during childhood may have important implications for adolescent development and behavior. What would you advise parents about spanking their children? Does it have important consequences for later adolescent behavior?
3. Family members reciprocally socialize each other in a family system. How could a change in one person or in the interaction between two people affect adolescent development? Is it possible to use this to help adolescents?

### Self-Assessment

The Online Learning Center includes the following self-assessment for further exploration:

- How Much Did My Parents Monitor My Behavior During Adolescence?

### Health and Well-Being, Parenting, and Education

To practice your decision-making skills, complete the health and well-being, parenting, and education exercises on the Online Learning Center.

### Video Clips

The Online Learning Center includes the following videos for this chapter:

- Adolescent-Parent Conflict
- Relationship with Parents at Age 14
- Relationship with Parents at Age 16
- Sibling Differential Treatment
- Interview with Stay-at-Home Dad
- Interview with Adoptive Parents

# 9 Peer and Romantic Relationships

*A man's growth is seen in the successive choirs of his friends.*

—Ralph Waldo Emerson, 1841
American Poet and Essayist, 19th Century

## CHAPTER OUTLINE

## LEARNING GOALS

### Exploring Peer Relations and Friendship

Peer Relations
Friendship
Loneliness

1 Discuss the role of peer relations, friendship, and loneliness in adolescent development.

### Adolescent Groups

Group Function
Groups in Childhood and Adolescence
Cliques and Crowds
Youth Organizations

2 Summarize what takes place in adolescent groups.

### Gender and Culture

Gender
Socioeconomic Status and Ethnicity
Culture

3 Describe the roles of gender and culture in adolescent peer groups and friendships.

### Dating and Romantic Relationships

Functions of Dating
Types of Dating and Developmental Changes
Emotion, Adjustment, and Romantic Relationships
Romantic Love and Its Construction
Gender and Culture

4 Characterize adolescent dating and romantic relationships.

### Emerging Adult Lifestyles

Single Adults
Cohabiting Adults
Married Adults
Divorced Adults
Gay Male and Lesbian Adults

5 Explain the diversity of emerging adult lifestyles.

## *Images of Adolescent Development*

## Young Adolescent Girls' Friends and Relational Worlds

Lynn Brown and Carol Gilligan (1992) conducted in-depth interviews of one hundred 10- to 13-year-old girls who were making the transition to adolescence. They listened to what these girls were saying about how important friends were to them. The girls were very curious about the human world they lived in and kept track of what was happening to their peers and friends. The girls spoke about the pleasure they derived from the intimacy and fun of human connection, and about the potential for hurt in relationships. They especially highlighted the importance of clique formation in their lives.

One girl, Noura, said that she learned about what it feels like to be the person that everyone doesn't like and that it was very painful. A number of the girls talked about how many girls say nice and kind things to be polite but they often don't really mean them. They know the benefits of being perceived as the perfect, happy girl, at least on the surface. Suspecting that people prefer the "perfect girl," they experiment with their image and the happiness a change might bring. Cliques can provide emotional support for girls who are striving to be perfect but know they are not. One girl, Victoria, commented that some girls like her, who weren't very popular, nonetheless were accepted into a "club" with three other girls. She now felt that when she was sad or depressed she could count on the "club" for support. Though they were "leftovers" and did not get into the most popular cliques, these four girls said they knew they were liked.

Another girl, Judy, at age 13, spoke about her interest in romantic relationships. She said that although she and her girlfriends were only 13, they wanted to be romantic, and she talked about her lengthy private conversations with her girlfriends about boys.

## PREVIEW

***This chapter is about peers and romantic relationships. When you think back to your adolescent years, you may recall many of your most enjoyable moments as being spent with peers—on the telephone, in school activities, in the neighborhood, on dates, at dances, or just hanging out. Adolescents typically have a larger number of acquaintances than children do. Beginning in early adolescence, teenagers also typically prefer a smaller number of friendships that are more intense and intimate than those of children. Cliques and crowds take on more importance as adolescents "hang out" together. Dating and romantic relationships become part of most adolescents' and emerging adults' lives, and deciding on a particular lifestyle especially becomes important in emerging adulthood.***

## 1 Exploring Peer Relations and Friendship

Peer Relations | Friendship | Loneliness

Peers and friends play powerful roles in the lives of adolescents. Let's explore what these roles are.

## Peer Relations

What functions do peer groups serve? How are family and peer relations linked? How extensively do adolescents engage in conformity? What kinds of statuses do peers have? How do social cognition and emotions influence peer relations? What are some strategies for improving social skills?

### Peer Group Functions

Adolescents have strong needs to be liked and accepted by friends and the larger peer group, which can result in pleasurable feelings when accepted or extreme stress and anxiety when excluded and disparaged by peers. To many adolescents, how they are seen by peers is the most important aspect of their lives. Contrast Bob, who has no close friends, with Steve, who has three close buddies he pals around with all of the time. Sally was turned down by the group at school that she was working for six months to get into, in contrast to Sandra, who is a member of the group and who frequently is told by her peers how "super" her personality is.

Some friends of mine have a 13-year-old daughter. Last year, she had a number of girlfriends—she talked extensively with them on the phone and they frequently visited each other's homes. Then her family moved, which meant that she was transferred to a school with a lower socioeconomic mix of students than at her previous school. Many of the girls at the new school feel that my friend's daughter is "too good" for them, and because of this she is having difficulty making friends this year. One of her most frequent complaints is, "I don't have any friends. . . . None of the kids at school ever call me. And none of them ever ask me over to their houses. What can I do?"

**Peers** are individuals who are about the same age or maturity level. Same-age peer interaction serves a unique role in U.S. culture. Age grading would occur even if schools were not age graded, and adolescents were left alone to determine the composition of their own societies. After all, one can learn to be a good fighter only among age-mates: the bigger guys will kill you, and the little ones are no challenge. One of the most important functions of the peer group is to provide a source of information about the world outside the family. From the peer group, adolescents receive feedback about their abilities. Adolescents learn whether what they do is better than, as good as, or worse than what other adolescents do. Learning this at home is difficult because siblings are usually older or younger.

As you read about peers, also keep in mind that although peer experiences have important influences on adolescents' development, those influences vary according to the way peer experience is measured, the outcomes specified, and the developmental trajectories traversed (Hartup, 1999). "Peers" and "peer group" are global concepts. These can be beneficial concepts in understanding peer influences as long as their variations are considered. For example, the term *peers* is used to describe an acquaintance, members of a clique, neighborhood associates, friends, and participants in an activity group, such as a sports team. For example, one analysis of the peer groups describes these aspects of the youth culture: membership crowd, neighborhood crowd, reference crowd, church crowd, sports team, friendship group, and friend (Brown, 1999).

#### Developmental Changes in Peer Time

Boys and girls spend an increasing amount of time in peer interaction during middle and late childhood and adolescence. In one investigation, children interacted with peers 10 percent of their day at age 2, 20 percent at age 4, and more than 40 percent between the ages of 7 and 11 (Barker & Wright, 1951). In a typical school day, there were 299 episodes with peers per day. By adolescence, peer relations occupy large chunks of an individual's life. In one investigation, over the course of one weekend, young adolescent boys and girls spent more than twice as much time with peers as with parents (Condry, Simon, & Bronfenbrenner, 1968).

**peers** Individuals who are about the same age or maturity level.

What do adolescents do when they are with their peers? In one study, sixth-graders were asked what they do when they are with their friends (Medrich & others, 1982). Team sports accounted for 45 percent of boys' activities but only 26 percent of girls'. General play, going places, and socializing were common listings for both sexes. Most peer interactions occur outside the home (although close to home), occur more often in private than public places, and occur more between children of the same sex than of the opposite sex.

**Are Peers Necessary for Development?** Good peer relations might be necessary for normal social development in adolescence (Rubin, Bukowski, & Parker, 2006). Social isolation, or the inability to "plug in" to a social network, is linked with many different forms of problems and disorders, ranging from delinquency and problem drinking to depression (Bukowski & Adams, 2005; Connell & Dishion, 2006; Laird & others, 2005; La Greca & Harrison, 2005).

**Positive and Negative Peer Relations** Peer influences can be both positive and negative (Bergeron & Schneider, 2005; Ladd, 2005; Rubin, Bukowski, & Parker, 2006). Both Jean Piaget (1932) and Harry Stack Sullivan (1953) were influential theorists who stressed that it is through peer interaction that children and adolescents learn the symmetrical reciprocity mode of relationships discussed in Chapter 8. Adolescents explore the principles of fairness and justice by working through disagreements with peers. They also learn to be keen observers of peers' interests and perspectives in order to smoothly integrate themselves into ongoing peer activities. In addition, Sullivan argued that adolescents learn to be skilled and sensitive partners in intimate relationships by forging close friendships with selected peers. These intimacy skills are carried forward to help form the foundation of later dating and marital relationships, according to Sullivan.

In contrast, some theorists have emphasized the negative influences of peers on adolescents' development. Being rejected or overlooked by peers leads some adolescents to feel lonely or hostile. Further, such rejection and neglect by peers are related to an individual's subsequent mental health and criminal problems (Bukowski, Brendgen, & Vitaro, 2007; Dodge, Coie, & Lynam, 2006). Some theorists have also described the adolescent peer culture as a corrupt influence that undermines parental values and control. Further, peer relations are linked to adolescents' patterns

Peer relations in adolescence and emerging adulthood can be positive or negative. *What are some of the positive and negative aspects of peer relations?*

of drug use, delinquency, and depression. Consider the results of these three recent studies:

- Time spent hanging out with antisocial peers in adolescence was a stronger predictor of substance abuse than time spent with parents (Nation & Heflinger, 2006).
- Higher levels of antisocial peer involvement in early adolescence (13 to 16 years of age) were linked with higher rates of delinquent behavior in late adolescence (17 to 18 years of age) (Laird & others, 2005)
- Deviant peer affiliation was related to adolescents' depressive symptoms (Connell & Dishion, 2006)

**Family-Peer Linkages** Some researchers have found that parents and adolescents perceive that parents have little authority over adolescents' choices in some areas but more authority of choices in other areas. For example, Judith Smetana's research has revealed that both parents and adolescents view peer relations as an arena in which parents have little authority to dictate adolescents' choices, in contrast to moral, religious, and educational arenas in which parents are perceived as having more authority (Smetana, 2002; Smetana & Turiel, 2003).

Adolescents do show a strong motivation to be with their peers and become independent. However, it is incorrect to assume that movement toward peer involvement and autonomy are unrelated to parent-adolescent relationships. Researchers have provided persuasive evidence that adolescents live in a connected world with parents and peers, not a disconnected one (Dodge & others, 2006; Tilton-Weaver & Leighter, 2002).

What are some of the ways the worlds of parents and peers are connected? Parents' choices of neighborhoods, churches, schools, and their own friends influence the pool from which their adolescents select possible friends (Cooper & Ayers-Lopez, 1985). For example, parents can choose to live in a neighborhood with playgrounds, parks, and youth organizations or in a neighborhood where houses are far apart, few adolescents live, and youth organizations are not well developed.

Parents can model or coach their adolescents in ways of relating to peers. In one study, parents acknowledged that they recommended specific strategies to their adolescents to help them develop more positive peer relations (Rubin & Solman, 1984). For example, parents discussed with their adolescents ways that disputes could be mediated and how to become less shy. They also encouraged them to be tolerant and to resist peer pressure. And in one study, young adolescents talked more frequently about peer-related problems with their mothers than with their fathers (Gauze, 1994).

The important role that parents play in adolescents' lives was documented in a recent longitudinal study (Goldstein, Davis-Kean, & Eccles, 2005). Young adolescents' perceptions of autonomy and warmth in relationships with parents in the seventh grade were linked with the adolescents' participation in risky peer contexts (such as going along with a peer to engage in problem behavior) in the eighth grade, which in turn was related to the adolescents' engagement in problem behavior (such as delinquency or drug use) in the eleventh grade. In terms of autonomy, young adolescents who perceived that they had a high degree of freedom over their daily activities (such as how late they could stay out and whether they could date) engaged in considerable unsupervised interactions with peers, which in turn was related to problem behaviors in the eleventh grade. Also, young adolescents who perceived that their parents were too intrusive tended to frequently interact with peers who engaged in problem behaviors, which in turn was related to problem behaviors in the eleventh grade. Thus, it is important for parents to develop a delicate balance between not permitting too much freedom with peers and being too intrusive in their young adolescents' lives. Also in this study, young adolescents who indicated they had less positive relationships with their parents tended to have an

*What are some links between parent-adolescent and adolescent-peer relations?*

extreme peer orientation, which in turn was linked to engaging in problem behaviors in the eleventh grade.

In addition, as we discussed in Chapter 8, an increasing number of researchers have found that secure attachment to parents is related to the adolescent's positive peer relations (Allen & others, 2007; Collins & Roisman, 2006). In one study, adolescents who were securely attached to parents were also securely attached to their peers; adolescents who were insecurely attached to their parents were likewise insecurely attached to their peers (Armsden & Greenberg, 1984). And in another study, older adolescents who had an ambivalent attachment history with their parents reported less satisfaction in their relationship with their best friend than did their securely attached counterparts (Fisher, 1990).

However, whereas adolescent-parent attachments are correlated with adolescent outcomes, the correlations are moderate, indicating that the success or failure of parent-adolescent attachments does not necessarily guarantee success or failure in peer relationships. Clearly, secure attachment with parents can be an asset for the adolescent, fostering the trust to engage in close relationships with others and lay down the foundation for close relationship skills. But a significant minority of adolescents from strong, supportive families, nonetheless, struggle in peer relations for a variety of reasons, such as being physically unattractive, maturing late, and experiencing cultural and SES discrepancies. On the other hand, some adolescents from troubled families find a positive, fresh start with peer relations that can compensate for their problematic family backgrounds.

**Peer Conformity** Conformity comes in many forms and affects many aspects of adolescents' lives. Do adolescents take up jogging because everyone else is doing it? Do adolescents let their hair grow long one year and cut it short the next because of fashion? Do adolescents take cocaine if pressured by others, or do they resist the pressure? **Conformity** occurs when individuals adopt the attitudes or behavior of others because of real or imagined pressure from them. The pressure to conform to peers becomes very strong during the adolescent years.

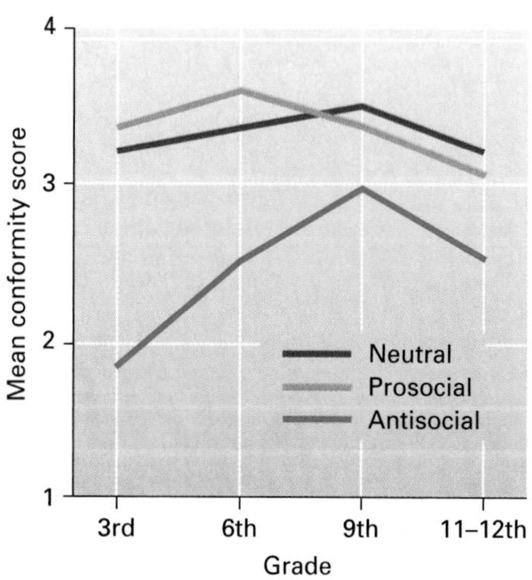


**FIGURE 9.1 Developmental Changes in Conformity to Peer Standards** The conformity scale ranged from 1 to 7, with higher scores indicating greater conformity.

Conformity to peer pressure in adolescence can be positive or negative. Teenagers engage in all sorts of negative conformity behavior—using seedy language, stealing, vandalizing, and making fun of parents and teachers. However, a great deal of peer conformity is not negative and consists of the desire to be involved in the peer world, such as dressing like friends and wanting to spend huge chunks of time with members of a clique. Such circumstances may involve prosocial activities as well, as when adolescents involved in clubs raise money for worthy causes.

In a study focused on negative, neutral, and positive aspects of peer conformity, Thomas Berndt (1979) studied 273 third-grade through twelfth-grade students. Hypothetical dilemmas that were presented to the students required the students to make choices about conformity with friends on prosocial and antisocial behavior and about conformity with parents on neutral and prosocial behaviors. For example, one prosocial item questioned whether students relied on their parents' advice in such situations as deciding about helping at the library or instructing another child to swim. An antisocial question asked a boy what he would do if one of his peers wanted him to help steal some candy. A neutral question asked a girl if she would follow peer suggestions to engage in an activity she wasn't interested in, such as going to a movie she did not want to see.

Some interesting developmental patterns were found in this investigation (see Figure 9.1). In the third grade, parent and peer influences often directly contradicted each other. Since parent conformity is much greater for third-grade children, children of this age are probably still closely tied to and dependent on their parents. However, by the sixth grade, parent and peer influences were found to be no longer in direct opposition. Peer conformity had increased, but parent and peer influences were operating in different situations—parents had more impact in some situations, while peers had more clout in others.

**conformity** This occurs when individuals adopt the attitudes or behaviors of others because of real or imagined pressure from them.

By the ninth grade, parent and peer influences were once again in strong opposition to each other, probably because the conformity of adolescents to the social behavior of peers is much stronger at this grade level than at any other. At this time, adolescent adoption of antisocial standards endorsed by the peer group inevitably leads to conflict between adolescents and parents. Researchers have also found that the adolescent's attempt to gain independence meets with more parental opposition around the ninth grade than at any other time (Douvan & Adelson, 1966).

A stereotypical view of parent-child relationships suggests that parent-peer opposition continues through high school into the college-age years. But Berndt (1979) found that adolescent conformity to antisocial, peer-endorsed behavior decreases in the late high school years, and agreement between parents and peers begins to increase in some areas. In addition, by the eleventh and twelfth grades, students show signs of developing a decision-making style more independent of peer and parental influence.

Most adolescents conform to the mainstream standards of their peers. However, the rebellious or anticonformist adolescent reacts counter to the mainstream peer group's expectations, deliberately moving away from the actions or beliefs this group advocates.

In sum, peer pressure is a pervasive theme of adolescents' lives. Its power can be observed in almost every dimension of adolescents' behavior—their choice of dress, music, language, values, leisure activities, and so on. Parents, teachers, and other adults can help adolescents to deal with peer pressure (Clasen & Brown, 1987). Adolescents need many opportunities to talk with both peers and adults about their social worlds and the pressures involved. The developmental changes of adolescence often bring forth a sense of insecurity. Young adolescents may be especially vulnerable because of this insecurity and the many developmental changes taking place in their lives. To counter this stress, young adolescents need to experience opportunities for success, both in and out of school, that increase their sense of being in control. Adolescents can learn that their social world is reciprocally controlled. Others might try to control them, but they can exert personal control over their actions and influence others in turn. Next, in our discussion of peer popularity, neglect, and rejection, we discuss further the powerful role that peer relations play in adolescent development.

**Peer Statuses** The term **sociometric status** is used to describe the extent to which children and adolescents are liked or disliked by their peer group (Cillessen & Mayeux, 2004; Jiang & Cillessen, 2005). Sociometric status is typically assessed by asking children to rate how much they like or dislike each of their classmates. Or it may be assessed by asking children and adolescents to nominate the peers they like the most and those they like the least. Developmentalists have distinguished five types of peer statuses (Wentzel & Asher, 1995):

- **Popular children** are frequently nominated as a best friend and are rarely disliked by their peers.
- **Average children** receive an average number of both positive and negative nominations from their peers.
- **Neglected children** are infrequently nominated as a best friend but are not disliked by their peers.
- **Rejected children** are infrequently nominated as someone's best friend and are actively disliked by their peers.
- **Controversial children** are frequently nominated both as someone's best friend and as being disliked.

Popular children have a number of social skills that contribute to their being well liked. Researchers have found that popular children give out reinforcements, listen carefully, maintain open lines of communication with peers, are happy, control their negative emotions, act like themselves, show enthusiasm and concern for others, and are self-confident without being conceited (Hartup, 1983; Rubin, Bukowski, & Parker, 1998).

One recent longitudinal study found that adolescents who were popular with their peers were characterized by higher levels of ego development, secure attachment, and

**sociometric status** The extent to which children and adolescents are liked or disliked by their peer group.

**popular children** Children who are frequently nominated as a best friend and are rarely disliked by their peers.

**average children** Children who receive an average number of both positive and negative nominations from their peers.

**neglected children** Children who are infrequently nominated as a best friend but are not disliked by their peers.

**rejected children** Children who are infrequently nominated as a best friend and are actively disliked by their peers.

**controversial children** Children who are frequently nominated both as a best friend and as being disliked.

*What are some peer statuses that characterize adolescents?*

more positive interactions with mothers and best friends than adolescents who were less popular with their peers (Allen & others, 2005). Interestingly, though, adolescents who increased behaviors that received peer group approval, such as minor levels of delinquency and alcohol use, and decreased behaviors that were less likely to be well received by peers, such as being hostile toward peers, improved their peer popularity over time.

Neglected children engage in low rates of interaction with their peers and are often described as shy by peers. Rejected children often have more serious adjustment problems than those who are neglected (Bukowski, Brendgen, & Vitaro, 2007; Coie, 2004; Dodge, Coie, & Lynam, 2006; Dodge, Dishion, & Lansford, 2007; Rubin, Bukowski, & Parker, 2006). For example, one study found that in kindergarten, rejected children were less likely to engage in classroom participation, express a desire to avoid school, and are more likely to report being lonely (Buhs & Ladd, 2001). In another study, 112 fifth-grade boys were evaluated over a period of seven years until the end of high school (Kupersmidt & Coie, 1990). The best predictor of whether rejected children would engage in delinquent behavior or drop out of school later during adolescence was aggression toward peers in elementary school. Another study found that when third-grade boys were highly aggressive and rejected by their peers, they showed markedly higher levels of delinquency as adolescents and young adults (Miller-Johnson, Coie, & Malone, 2003).

An analysis by John Coie (2004, pp. 252–253) provided three reasons why aggressive peer-rejected boys have problems in social relationships:

- First, the rejected, aggressive boys are more impulsive and have problems sustaining attention. As a result, they are more likely to be disruptive of ongoing activities in the classroom and in focused group play.
- Second, rejected, aggressive boys are more emotionally reactive. They are aroused to anger more easily and probably have more difficulty calming down once aroused. Because of this they are more prone to become angry at peers and attack them verbally and physically. . . .
- Third, rejected children have fewer social skills in making friends and maintaining positive relationships with peers.

Not all rejected children are aggressive (Haselager & others, 2002; Hymel, McDougall, & Renshaw, 2004). Although aggression and its related characteristics of impulsiveness and disruptiveness underlie rejection about half the time, approximately 10 to 20 percent of rejected children are shy. In a later section, Strategies for Improving Social Skills, we discuss ways to improve the social skills of rejected and neglected children and adolescents.

A final comment about peer statuses in adolescence is in order (Wentzel, 2004). Much of the peer status research involves samples from middle and late childhood, and in some cases early adolescence, but not late adolescence. One reason for this is that to assess peer status a fairly well-defined group of classmates who know each other well and interact on a regular basis is needed. In contrast to elementary school and middle school, where students stay with the same group most of the day (more for elementary school than middle school), it is very difficult to assess peer status in high school contexts, where students are in contact with large numbers of peers and are not likely to know all of their classmates.

### Social Cognition and Emotion

The social cognitive skills and social knowledge of adolescents are important aspects of successful peer relations. So is the ability to manage and regulate one's emotions.

**Social Cognition** A distinction can be made between knowledge and process in cognition. In studying cognitive aspects of peer relations, this distinction can be made.

Learning about the social knowledge adolescents bring with them to peer relations is important, as is studying how adolescents process information during peer interaction.

As children move into adolescence, they acquire more social knowledge, and there is considerable individual variation in how much one adolescent knows about what it takes to make friends, to get peers to like him or her, and so forth. For example, does the adolescent know that giving out reinforcements will increase the likelihood that she will be popular? That is, does Mary consciously know that, by telling Barbara such things as "I really like that sweater you have on today" and "Gosh, you sure are popular with the guys," she will enhance the likelihood Barbara will want her to be her friend? Does the adolescent know that, when others perceive that he is similar to them, he will be liked better by the others? Does the adolescent know that friendship involves sharing intimate conversations and that a friendship likely is improved when the adolescent shares private, confidential information with another adolescent? To what extent does the adolescent know that comforting and listening skills will improve friendship relations? To what extent does the adolescent know what it takes to become a leader? Think back to your adolescent years. How sophisticated were you in knowing about such social matters? Were you aware of the role of nice statements and perceived similarity in determining popularity and friendship? While you may not have been aware of these factors, those of you who were popular and maintained close friendships likely were competent at using these strategies.

From a social cognitive perspective, children and adolescents may have difficulty in peer relations because they lack appropriate social cognitive skills (Dodge, Coie, & Lynam, 2006; Gifford-Smith & Rabiner, 2004). One investigation explored the possibility that social cognitive skill deficits characterize children who have peer-related difficulties (Asarnow & Callan, 1985). Boys with and without peer adjustment difficulties were identified, and then a number of social cognitive processes or skills were assessed. These included the boys' ability to generate alternative solutions to hypothetical problems, to evaluate these solutions in terms of their effectiveness, and to describe self-statements. It was found that boys without peer adjustment problems generated more alternative solutions, proposed more assertive and mature solutions, gave less intense aggressive solutions, showed more adaptive planning, and evaluated physically aggressive responses less positively than the boys with peer adjustment problems. For example, as shown in Figure 9.2, negative-peer-status sixth-grade boys were not as likely to generate alternative solutions and were much less likely to adaptively plan ahead than their positive-peer-status counterparts.

Now let's examine how social information processing might be involved in peer relations. For example, consider the situation when a peer accidentally trips and knocks a boy's soft drink out of his hand. The boy misinterprets the encounter as hostile, which leads him to retaliate aggressively against the peer. Through repeated encounters of this kind, peers come to perceive the boy as having a habit of acting

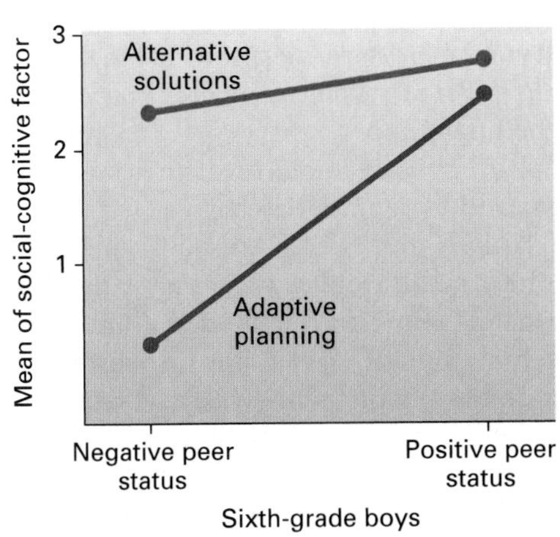

**FIGURE 9.2 Generation of Alternative Solutions and Adaptive Planning by Negative- and Positive-Peer-Status Boys** Notice that negative-peer-status boys were less likely to generate alternative solutions and plan ahead than were positive-peer-status counterparts.

inappropriately. Kenneth Dodge (1993) argues that adolescents go through five steps in processing information about their social world: decoding of social cues, interpretation, response search, selecting an optimal response, and enactment. Dodge has found that aggressive boys are more likely to perceive another child's actions as hostile when the peer's intention is ambiguous. And when aggressive boys search for cues to determine a peer's intention, they respond more rapidly, less efficiently, and less reflectively than nonaggressive children. These are among the social cognitive factors believed to be involved in adolescents' conflicts with one another.

**Emotion** Not only does cognition play an important role in peer relations, so does emotion. For example, the ability to regulate emotion is linked to successful peer relations (Eisenberg, Fabes, & Spinrad, 2006; Underwood, 2003). Moody and emotionally negative individuals experience greater rejection by peers, whereas emotionally positive individuals are more popular (Saarni & others, 2006). Adolescents who have effective self-regulatory skills can modulate their emotional expressiveness in contexts that evoke intense emotions, as when a peer says something negative. In one study, rejected children were more likely than popular children to use negative gestures in a provoking situation (Underwood & Hurley, 1997).

A recent study focused on the emotional aspects of social information processing in aggressive boys (Orobio de Castro & others, 2005). Highly aggressive boys and a control group of less-aggressive boys listened to vignettes involving provocations involving peers. The highly aggressive boys expressed less guilt, attributed more hostile intent, and generated less adaptive emotion-regulation strategies than the comparison group of boys.

### Strategies for Improving Social Skills

A number of strategies have been proposed for improving social skills that can lead to better peer relations (Ladd, 2005; Rubin, Bukowski, & Parker, 2006). **Conglomerate strategies,** also referred to as coaching, involve the use of a combination of techniques, rather than a single approach, to improve adolescents' social skills. A conglomerate strategy might consist of demonstration or modeling of appropriate social skills, discussion, and reasoning about the social skills, as well as the use of reinforcement for their enactment in actual social situations.

In one study using a conglomerate strategy, middle school adolescents were instructed in ways to improve their self-control, stress management, and social problem solving (Weissberg & Caplan, 1989). For example, as problem situations arose, teachers modeled and students practiced six sequential steps: (1) stop, calm down, and think before you act; (2) go over the problem and state how you feel; (3) set a positive goal; (4) think of lots of solutions; (5) plan ahead for the consequences; (6) go ahead and try the best plan. The 240 adolescents who participated in the program improved their ability to devise cooperative solutions to problem situations, and their teachers reported that the students showed improved social relations in the classroom following the program. In another study, boys and girls in a low-income area of New Jersey were given instruction in social decision making, self-control, and group awareness (Clabby & Elias, 1988). When compared with boys and girls who did not receive the training, the program participants were more sensitive to the feelings of others, more mindful of the consequences of their actions, and better able to analyze problem situations and act appropriately.

More specifically, how can neglected children and adolescents be trained to interact more effectively with their peers? The goal of training programs with neglected children and adolescents is often to help them attract attention from their peers in positive ways and to hold their attention by asking questions, by listening in a warm and friendly way, and by saying things about themselves that relate to the peers' interests. They also are taught to enter groups more effectively.

The goal of training programs with rejected children and adolescents is often to help them listen to peers and "hear what they say" instead of trying to dominate

**conglomerate strategies** The use of a combination of techniques, rather than a single approach, to improve adolescents' social skills; also called coaching.

peer interactions. Rejected children and adolescents are trained to join peers without trying to change what is taking place in the peer group.

One issue that has been raised about improving the peer relations of rejected children and adolescents is whether the focus should be on improving their prosocial skills (better empathy, careful listening, improved communication skills, and so on) or on reducing their aggressive, disruptive behavior and improving their self-control (Coie & Koeppl, 1990). In one study, socially rejected young adolescents were coached on the importance of showing behaviors that would improve their chance of being liked by others (Murphy & Schneider, 1994). The intervention was successful in improving the friendships of the socially rejected youth.

One recent social-skills intervention program was successful in increasing social acceptance and self-esteem and decreasing depression and anxiety in peer-rejected children (DeRosier & Marcus, 2005). Students participated in the program once a week (50 to 60 minutes) for eight weeks. The program included instruction in how to manage emotions, how to improve prosocial skills, how to become better communicators, and how to compromise and negotiate.

Despite the positive outcomes of some programs that attempt to improve the social skills of adolescents, researchers have often found it difficult to improve the social skills of adolescents who are actively disliked and rejected. Many of these adolescents are rejected because they are aggressive or impulsive and lack the self-control to keep these behaviors in check. Still, some intervention programs have been successful in reducing the aggressive and impulsive behaviors of these adolescents (Ladd, Buhs, & Troop, 2004).

Social-skills training programs have generally been more successful with children 10 years of age or younger than with adolescents (Malik & Furman, 1993). Peer reputations become more fixed as cliques and peer groups become more salient in adolescence. Once an adolescent gains a negative reputation among peers as being "mean," "weird," or a "loner," the peer group's attitude is often slow to change, even after the adolescent's problem behavior has been corrected. Thus, researchers have found that skills interventions may need to be supplemented by efforts to change the minds of peers. One such intervention strategy involves cooperative group training (Slavin, Hurley, & Chamberlain, 2003). In this approach, children or adolescents work toward a common goal that holds promise for changing reputations. Most cooperative group programs have been conducted in academic settings, but other contexts might be used. For example, participation in cooperative games and sports increases sharing and feelings of happiness. And some video games require cooperative efforts by the players.

**FIGURE 9.3** **The Functions of Friendship**

## Friendship

Earlier we indicated that peers are individuals who are about the same age or maturity level. **Friends** are a subset of peers who engage in mutual companionship, support, and intimacy. Thus, relationships with friends are much closer and more involved than is the case with the peer group. Some adolescents have several close friends, others one, and yet others none.

**friends** A subset of peers who engage in mutual companionship, support, and intimacy.

### Its Importance

The functions that adolescents' friendships serve can be categorized in six ways (Gottman & Parker, 1987) (see Figure 9.3):

1. *Companionship.* Friendship provides adolescents with a familiar partner, someone who is willing to spend time with them and join in collaborative activities.
2. *Stimulation.* Friendship provides adolescents with interesting information, excitement, and amusement.
3. *Physical support.* Friendship provides resources and assistance.
4. *Ego support.* Friendship provides the expectation of support, encouragement, and feedback that helps adolescents to maintain an impression of themselves as competent, attractive, and worthwhile individuals.

5. *Social comparison.* Friendship provides information about where adolescents stand vis-á-vis others and whether adolescents are doing okay.
6. *Intimacy/affection.* Friendship provides adolescents with a warm, close, trusting relationship with another individual, a relationship that involves self-disclosure.

The importance of friendship was underscored in a two-year longitudinal study (Wentzel, Barry, & Caldwell, 2004). Sixth-grade students who did not have a friend engaged in less prosocial behavior (cooperation, sharing, helping others), had lower grades, and were more emotionally distressed (depression, low well-being) than their counterparts who had one or more friends. Two years later, in the eighth grade, the students who did not have a friend in the sixth grade were still more emotionally distressed. In a recent study, spending time with friends was consistently associated with positive affect in ninth-grade European Americans, Mexican Americans, and Chinese Americans (Witkow & others, 2005).

However, the quality of friendship varies (Cillessen & others, 2005). Some friendships are deeply intimate and long-lasting, others more shallow and short-lived. Some friendships run smoothly, others can be conflicted. One study focused on conflict with parents and friends (Adams & Laursen, 2001). Parent-adolescent conflicts were more likely to be characterized by a combination of daily hassle topics, neutral or angry affect afterward, power-assertive outcomes, and win-lose outcomes. Friend conflicts were more likely to involve a combination of relationship topics, friendly affect afterward, disengaged resolutions, and equal or no outcomes. Another study revealed that adolescent girls and adolescents with low self-worth reported having the most friendship jealousy—that is, being jealous of a close friend's relationship with other peers (Parker & others, 2004).

Not only does the quality of friendships have important influences on adolescents, but the friend's character, interests, and attitudes also matter (Brown, 2004). For example, researchers have found that delinquent adolescents often have delinquent friends, and they reinforce each other's delinquent behavior (Dishion, Andrews, & Crosby, 1995). Other research has indicated that nonsmoking adolescents who become friends with smoking adolescents are more likely to start smoking themselves (Urberg, 1992). Also, a recent study of more than 2,400 adolescents over 9 to 18 months revealed that adolescents whose friends were sexually experienced were more likely to initiate sexual intercourse than those whose friends were sexually inexperienced (Sieving & others, 2006). By the same token, having friends who are into school, sports, or religion is likely to have a positive influence on the adolescent.

**Sullivan's Ideas on Changes in Friendship in Early Adolescence** Harry Stack Sullivan (1953) is the most influential theorist to discuss the importance of adolescent friendships. He argued that there is a dramatic increase in the psychological importance and intimacy of close friends during early adolescence. In contrast to other psychoanalytic theorists' narrow emphasis on the importance of parent-child relationships, Sullivan contended that friends also play important roles in shaping children's and adolescents' well-being and development. In terms of well-being, he argued that all people have a number of basic social needs, including the need for tenderness (secure attachment), playful companionship, social acceptance, intimacy, and sexual relations. Whether or not these needs are fulfilled largely determines our emotional well-being. For example, if the need for playful companionship goes unmet, then we become bored and depressed; if the need for social acceptance is not met, we suffer a lowered sense of self-worth. Developmentally, friends become increasingly depended on to satisfy these needs during adolescence, and thus the ups and downs of experiences with friends increasingly shape adolescents' state of well-being. In particular, Sullivan noted that the need for intimacy intensifies during early adolescence, motivating teenagers to seek out close friends. He felt that, if adolescents failed to forge such close friendships, they would experience painful feelings of loneliness coupled with a reduced sense of self-worth.

Although Sullivan formulated his ideas more than half a century ago, more recent research findings support many of Sullivan's ideas (Buhrmester, 2005). For example, adolescents report more often disclosing intimate and personal information to their friends than do younger children (Buhrmester & Furman, 1987) (see Figure 9.4). Adolescents also say they depend more on friends than parents to satisfy needs for companionship, reassurance of worth, and intimacy (Furman & Buhrmester, 1992). In one study, researchers conducted daily interviews with 13- to 16-year-old adolescents over a five-day period to find out how much time they spent engaged in meaningful interactions with friends and parents (Buhrmester & Carbery, 1992). Adolescents spent an average of 103 minutes per day in meaningful interactions with friends, compared with just 28 minutes per day with parents. In addition, the quality of friendship is more strongly linked to feelings of well-being during adolescence than during childhood. Teenagers with superficial friendships, or no close friendships at all, report feeling lonelier and more depressed, and they have a lower sense of self-esteem than teenagers with intimate friendships (Buhrmester, 1990; Yin, Buhrmester, & Hibbard, 1996). And in another study, friendship in early adolescence was a significant predictor of self-worth in early adulthood (Bagwell, Newcomb, & Bukowski, 1994).

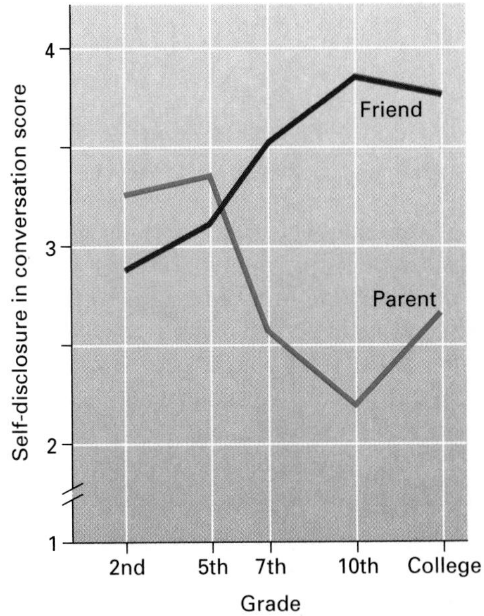


**FIGURE 9.4 Developmental Changes in Self-Disclosing Conversations** Self-disclosing conversations with friends increased dramatically in adolescence while declining in an equally dramatic fashion with parents. However, self-disclosing conversations with parents began to pick up somewhat during the college years. The measure of self-disclosure involved a 5-point rating scale completed by the children and youth, with a higher score representing greater self-disclosure. The data shown represent the means for each age group.

The increased closeness and importance of friendship challenges adolescents to master ever-more sophisticated social competencies (Buhrmester, 2005). Viewed from the developmental constructionist perspective described in Chapter 8, adolescent friendship represents a new mode of relating to others that is best described as a *symmetrical intimate mode*. During childhood, being a good friend involves being a good playmate: children must know how to play cooperatively and must be skilled at smoothly entering ongoing games on the playground. By contrast, the greater intimacy of adolescent friendships demands that teenagers learn a number of close relationship competencies, including knowing how to self-disclose appropriately, being able to provide emotional support to friends, and managing disagreements in ways that do not undermine the intimacy of the friendship. These competencies require more sophisticated skills in perspective taking, empathy, and social problem solving than were involved in childhood playmate competencies.

In addition to the role they play in the socialization of social competence, friendship relationships are often important sources of support (Burhmester, 2005; Collins & Steinberg, 2006). Sullivan described how adolescent friends support one another's sense of personal worth. When close friends disclose their mutual insecurities and fears about themselves, they discover that they are not "abnormal" and that they have nothing to be ashamed of. Friends also act as important confidants who help adolescents work through upsetting problems (such as difficulties with parents or the breakup of romance) by providing both emotional support and informational advice. Friends can also protect "at-risk" adolescents from victimization by peers. In addition, friends can become active partners in building a sense of identity. During countless hours of conversation, friends act as sounding boards as teenagers explore issues ranging from future plans to stances on religious and moral issues.

Willard Hartup (1996), who has studied peer relations across four decades, concluded that children and adolescents use friends as cognitive and social resources on a regular basis. Hartup also commented that normative transitions, such as moving from elementary to middle school, are negotiated more competently by children who have friends than by those who don't. The quality of friendship is also important to consider. Supportive friendships between socially skilled individuals are developmentally advantageous, whereas coercive and conflict-ridden friendships are not. Friendship and its developmental significance can vary from one adolescent to another. Adolescents' characteristics, such as temperament ("easy" versus "difficult," for example), likely influence the nature of friendships.

**Friendship in Emerging Adulthood** Many aspects of friendship are the same in adolescence as in emerging adulthood. One difference between close relationships

## Through the Eyes of Adolescents

### WE DEFINED EACH OTHER WITH ADJECTIVES

"I was funky. Dana was sophisticated. Liz was crazy. We walked to school together, went for bike rides, cut school, got stoned, talked on the phone, smoked cigarettes, slept over, discussed boys and sex, went to church together, and got angry at each other. We defined each other with adjectives and each other's presence. As high school friends, we simultaneously resisted and anticipated adulthood and womanhood. . . .

"What was possible when I was 15 and 16? We still had to tell our parents where we were going! We wanted to do excitedly forbidden activities like going out to dance clubs and drinking whiskey sours. Liz, Dana, and I wanted to do these forbidden things in order to feel: to have intense emotional and sensual experiences that removed us from the suburban sameness we shared with each other and everyone else we knew. We were tired of the repetitive experiences that our town, our siblings, our parents, and our school offered to us. . . .

"The friendship between Dana, Liz, and myself was born out of another emotional need: the need for trust. The three of us had reached a point in our lives when we realized how unstable relationships can be, and we all craved safety and acceptance. Friendships all around us were often uncertain. We wanted and needed to be able to like and trust each other."

(*Source:* Garrod & others, 1992, pp. 199–200)

in adolescence and emerging adulthood was found in a recent longitudinal study (Collins & van Dulmen, 2006). Close relationships—between friends, family members, and romantic partners—were more integrated and similar than in adolescence. Also in this study, the number of friendships declined from the end of adolescence through emerging adulthood.

Another research study indicated that best friendships often decline in satisfaction and commitment in the first year of college (Oswald & Clark, 2003). In this study, maintaining communication with high school friends and keeping the same best friends across the transition to college lessened the decline.

### Intimacy and Similarity

Two important characteristics of friendship are intimacy and similarity.

**Intimacy** In the context of friendship, *intimacy* has been defined in different ways. For example, it has been defined broadly to include everything in a relationship that makes the relationship seem close or intense. In most research studies, though, **intimacy in friendship** is defined narrowly as self-disclosure, or sharing of private thoughts. Private or personal knowledge about a friend also has been used as an index of intimacy (Selman, 1980; Sullivan, 1953).

The most consistent finding in the last two decades of research on adolescent friendships is that intimacy is an important feature of friendship (Berndt & Perry, 1990; Bukowski, Newcomb, & Hoza, 1987). When young adolescents are asked what they want from a friend, or how they can tell if someone is their best friend, they frequently say that a best friend will share problems with them, understand them, and listen when they talk about their own thoughts or feelings. When young children talk about their friendships, comments about intimate self-disclosure or mutual understanding are rare. In one investigation, friendship intimacy was more prominent in 13- to 16-year-olds than in 10- to 13-year-olds (Buhrmester, 1990).

**Similarity** Another predominant characteristic of friendship is that, throughout the childhood and adolescent years, friends are generally similar—in terms of age, sex, ethnicity, and many other factors. Friends often have similar attitudes toward school, similar educational aspirations, and closely aligned achievement orientations. Friends enjoy the same music, wear the same style of clothes, and prefer the same leisure activities (Berndt, 1982). If friends have different attitudes about school, one of them may want to play basketball or go shopping rather than do homework. If one friend insists on completing homework while the other insists on playing basketball, the conflict may weaken the friendship and the two may drift apart.

### Mixed-Age Friendships

Although most adolescents develop friendships with individuals who are close to their own age, some adolescents become best friends with younger or older individuals. A common fear, especially among parents, is that adolescents who have older friends will be encouraged to engage in delinquent behavior or early sexual behavior. Researchers have found that adolescents who interact with older youths do engage in these behaviors more frequently, but it is not known whether the older youths guide younger adolescents toward deviant behavior or whether the younger adolescents were already prone to deviant behavior before they developed the friendship with the older youths (Billy, Rodgers, & Udry, 1984).

**intimacy in friendship** In most research studies, this is defined narrowly as self-disclosure, or sharing of private thoughts.

In a longitudinal study of eighth-grade girls, early-maturing girls developed friendships with girls who were chronologically older but biologically similar to them (Magnusson, 1988). Because of their associations with older friends, the early-maturing girls were more likely than their peers to engage in a number of deviant behaviors, such as being truant from school, getting drunk, and stealing. Also, as adults (26 years of age), the early-maturing girls were more likely to have had a child and were less likely to be vocationally and educationally oriented than their later-maturing counterparts. Thus, parents do seem to have reason to be concerned when their adolescents become close friends with individuals who are considerably older than they are.

Loneliness can develop when individuals go through life transitions. *What are some strategies for reducing loneliness?*

## Loneliness

In some cases individuals who don't have friends are vulnerable to loneliness, and loneliness can set in when individuals leave a close relationship. Each of us has times in our lives when we feel lonely, but for some individuals loneliness is a chronic condition. More than just an unwelcome social situation, chronic loneliness is linked with impaired physical and mental health (Cacioppo & Hawkley, 2003; Karnick, 2005; Pressman & others, 2005).

It is important to distinguish loneliness from the desire for solitude. Some individuals value solitary time. How do you determine if you are lonely? Scales of loneliness ask you to respond to items like "I don't feel in tune with the people around me" and "I can find companionship when I want it." If you consistently respond that you never or rarely feel in tune with people around you and rarely or never can find companionship when you want it, you are likely to fall into the category of people who are described as moderately or intensely lonely (Russell, 1996).

Loneliness is often interwoven with the passage through life transitions, such as a move to a different part of the country, a divorce, or the death of a close friend or family member (Valeri, 2003). Another situation that often creates loneliness is the first year of college, especially if students leave the familiar world of their hometown and family to enter college. As one student commented:

> My first year here at the university has been pretty lonely. I wasn't lonely at all in high school. I lived in a fairly small town—I knew everybody and everyone knew me. I was a member of several clubs and played on the basketball team. It's not that way at the university. It is a big place, and I've felt like a stranger on so many occasions. I'm starting to get used to my life here, and the last few months I've been making myself meet people and get to know them, but it has not been easy.

As this comment illustrates, freshmen rarely bring their popularity and social standing from high school into the college environment. There may be a dozen high school basketball stars, National Merit scholars, and former student council presidents in a single dormitory wing. Especially if students attend college away from home, they face the task of forming completely new social relationships.

One study found that two weeks after the school year began, 75 percent of 354 college freshmen felt lonely at least part of the time (Cutrona, 1982). More than 40 percent said their loneliness was moderate to severe. Students who were the most optimistic and had the highest self-esteem were more likely to overcome their loneliness by the end of their freshman year. Loneliness is not reserved for college freshmen, though. Upperclassmen are often lonely as well.

In one study of more than 2,600 undergraduates, lonely individuals were less likely to actively cope with stress than individuals who were able to make friends (Cacioppo & others, 2000). Also in this study, lonely college students had higher levels of stress-related hormones and poorer sleep patterns than students who had positive relationships with others.

To read about some strategies for reducing loneliness and making friends, see the *Health and Well-Being* interlude.

## Health and Well-Being

### STRATEGIES FOR REDUCING LONELINESS

If you are lonely, how can you become better connected with others? Here are some positive strategies:

- *Participate in activities that you can do with others.* Join organizations or volunteer your time for a cause you believe in. You likely will get to know others whose views are similar to yours. Going to just one social gathering can help you develop social contacts. When you go, introduce yourself to others and start a conversation. Another strategy is to sit next to new people in your classes or find someone to study with.
- *Engage in positive behaviors when you meet new people.* You will improve your chances of developing enduring relationships if, when you meet new people, you are nice, considerate, honest, trustworthy, and cooperative. Have a positive attitude, be supportive of the other person, and make positive comments about him or her.
- *See a counselor or read a book on loneliness.* If you can't get rid of your loneliness on your own, you might want to contact the counseling services at your college. The counselor can talk with you about strategies for reducing your loneliness. You also might want to read a good book on loneliness such as *Intimate Connections* by David Burns (1985).

**REVIEW AND REFLECT ◆ LEARNING GOAL 1**

**1 Discuss the roles of peer relations, friendship, and loneliness in adolescent development.**

***Review***
- What roles do peers play in adolescent development?
- How does friendship contribute to adolescent development?
- How would you distinguish between loneliness and the desire to be alone?

***Reflect***
- How much time did you spend in adolescence with friends, and what activities did you engage in? What were your friends like? Were they similar to you or different? Has the nature of your friendships changed since adolescence? Explain.

## 2 ADOLESCENT GROUPS

Group Function

Groups in Childhood and Adolescence

Cliques and Crowds

Youth Organizations

During your adolescent years, you probably were a member of both formal and informal groups. Examples of formal groups include the basketball team or drill team, the Girl Scouts or Boy Scouts, the student council, and so on. A more informal group could be a group of peers, such as a clique. Our study of adolescent groups focuses on the functions of groups and how groups are formed, differences between children groups and adolescent groups, cliques and crowds, and youth organizations.

## Group Function

Why does an adolescent join a study group? A church? An athletic team? A clique? Groups satisfy adolescents' personal needs, reward them, provide information, raise their self-esteem, and give them an identity. Adolescents might join a group because they think that group membership will be enjoyable and exciting and satisfy their need for affiliation and companionship. They might join a group because they will have the opportunity to receive rewards, either material or psychological. For example, an adolescent may reap prestige and recognition from membership on the school's student council. Groups also are an important source of information. As adolescents participate in a study group, they learn effective study strategies and valuable information about how to take tests. The groups in which adolescents are members—their family, their school, a club, a team—often make them feel good, raise their self-esteem, and provide them with an identity.

Any group to which adolescents belong has two things in common with all other groups: norms and roles. **Norms** are rules that apply to all members of a group. An honor society, for example, might require all members to have a 3.5 grade point average. A school might require its male students to keep their hair cut so that it does not touch their shirt. A football team might require its members to work on weight lifting in the off-season. **Roles** are certain positions in a group that are governed by rules and expectations. Roles define how adolescents should behave in those positions. In a family, parents have certain roles, siblings have other roles, and grandparents have still other roles. On a basketball team, many different roles must be filled: center, forward, guard, rebounder, defensive specialist, and so on.

## Groups in Childhood and Adolescence

Childhood groups differ from adolescent groups in several important ways. The members of childhood groups often are friends or neighborhood acquaintances, and the groups usually are not as formalized as many adolescent groups. During the adolescent years, groups tend to include a broader array of members; in other words, adolescents other than friends or neighborhood acquaintances often are members of adolescent groups. Try to recall the student council, honor society, art club, football team or another organized group at your junior high school. If you were a member of any of these organizations, you probably remember that they were made up of many individuals you had not met before and that they were a more heterogeneous group than your childhood peer groups. Rules and regulations were probably well defined, and captains or leaders were formally elected or appointed in the adolescent groups.

A well-known observational study by Dexter Dunphy (1963) indicates that opposite-sex participation in social groups increases during adolescence. In late childhood, boys and girls tend to form small, same-sex groups. As they move into the early adolescent years, the same-sex groups begin to interact with each other. Gradually, the leaders and high-status members form further groups based on mixed-sex relationships. Eventually, the newly created mixed-sex groups replace the same-sex groups. The mixed-sex groups also interact with each other in large crowd activities, too—at dances and athletic events, for example. In late adolescence, the crowd begins to dissolve as couples develop more serious relationships and make long-range plans that may include engagement and marriage. A summary of Dunphy's ideas is presented in Figure 9.5.

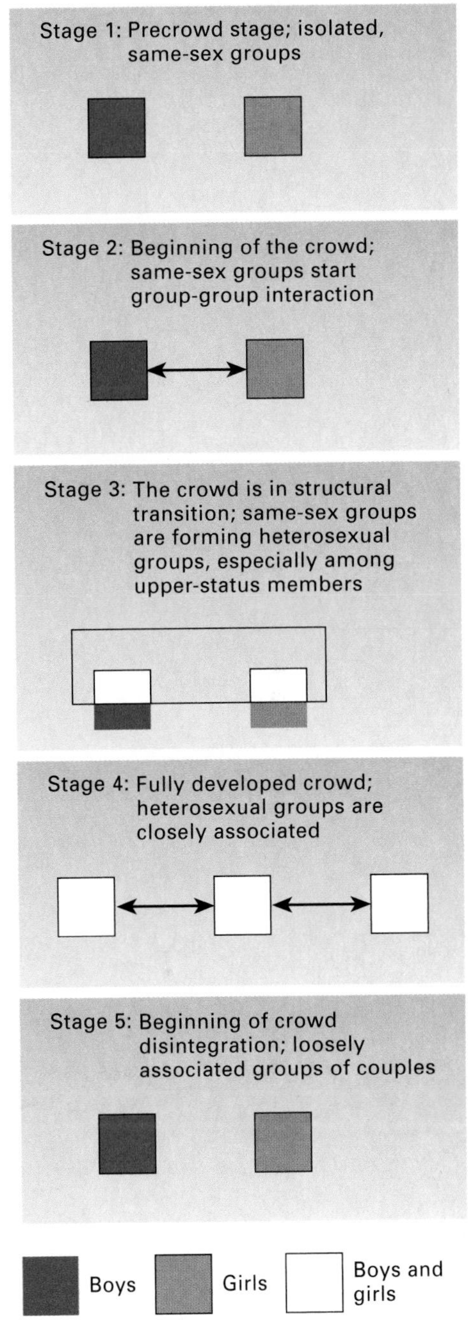


**FIGURE 9.5** **Dunphy's Progression of Peer Group Relations in Adolescence**

**norms** Rules that apply to all members of a group.

**roles** Certain positions in a group that are governed by rules and expectations. Roles define how adolescents should behave in those positions.

## Cliques and Crowds

In our discussion of Dunphy's work, the importance of heterosexual relationships in the evolution of adolescent crowds was noted. Let's now examine adolescent cliques and crowds in greater detail.

### Cliques

**Cliques** are small groups that range from two to about twelve individuals and average about five to six individuals. These clique members are usually of the same sex and are similar in age.

Cliques can form because adolescents engage in similar activities, such as being in a club together or on a sports team. Some cliques also form purely because of friendship. Several adolescents may form a clique because they have spent time with each other and enjoy each other's company. Not necessarily friends before forming the clique, they often develop a friendship if they stay in the clique.

What do adolescents do in cliques? They share ideas, hang out together, and often develop an in-group identity in which they believe their clique is better than other cliques. Recall that Noura, one of the girls in the *Images of Adolescent Development* at the beginning of the chapter, discussed her feelings about being rejected by a clique.

### Crowds

**Crowds** are a larger group structure than cliques. Adolescents are usually members of a crowd based on reputation and may or may not spend much time with other crowd members (Brown, 2003, 2004). Crowds are less personal than cliques. Many crowds are defined by the activities adolescents engage in (such as "jocks" who are good at sports or "druggies" who take drugs), although some crowds are defined more by the nature of their interaction (Delsing & others, 2007; Verkooijen, de Vries, & Nielsen, 2007). For example, in Dexter Dunphy's developmental sequence that was described earlier in the chapter, the crowds are interaction-based, not reputation-based. Reputation-based crowds often appear for the first time in early adolescence and usually become less prominent in late adolescence (Collins & Steinberg, 2006).

In one study, Bradford Brown and Jane Lohr (1987) examined the self-esteem of 221 seventh- through twelfth-graders. The adolescents were either associated with one of the five major school crowds or were relatively unknown by classmates and not associated with any school crowd. Crowds included the following: jocks (athletically oriented), populars (well-known students who lead social activities), normals (middle-of-the-road students who make up the masses), druggies/toughs (known for illicit drug use or other delinquent activities), and nobodies (low in social skills or intellectual abilities). The self-esteem of the jocks and the populars was highest, that of the nobodies was lowest. But one group of adolescents not in a crowd had self-esteem equivalent to the jocks and the populars. This group was the independents, who indicated that crowd membership was not important to them. Keep in mind that these data are correlational—self-esteem could increase an adolescent's probability of becoming a crowd member just as clique membership could increase the adolescent's self-esteem.

One of the main factors that distinguishes crowds is group norms regarding school orientation (Brown, 2003, 2004; Brown & Theobald, 1998). In one study of adolescents in nine midwestern and West Coast high schools, grade point differences of almost two full letter grades were found between the highest achievers ("brains") and lowest achievers ("druggies") (Brown & others, 1993). The norms of particular crowds can place adolescents on a trajectory for school failure. Members of deviantly oriented crowds are more likely to drop out of school early (Cairns & Cairns, 1994).

**cliques** Small groups that range from two to about twelve individuals and average about five to six individuals. Members are usually of the same sex and are similar in age; cliques can form because of similar interests, such as sports, and also can form purely from friendship.

**crowds** A larger group structure than cliques. Adolescents are usually members of a crowd based on reputation and may or may not spend much time together.

## Youth Organizations

Youth organizations can have an important influence on the adolescent's development (Brown, 2004; Mahoney, Larson, & Eccles, 2004; Pearce & Larson, 2006). More than 400 national youth organizations currently operate in the United States (Erickson, 1996). The organizations include career groups, such as Junior Achievement;

groups aimed at building character, such as Girl Scouts and Boy Scouts; political groups, such as Young Republicans and Young Democrats; and ethnic groups, such as Indian Youth of America (Price & others, 1990). They serve approximately 30 million young people each year. The largest youth organization is 4-H, with nearly 5 million participants. Among the smallest organizations are ASPIRA, a Latino youth organization that provides intensive educational enrichment programs for about 13,000 adolescents each year, and WAVE, a dropout-prevention program that serves about 8,000 adolescents each year.

Adolescents who join such groups are more likely to participate in community activities in adulthood and have higher self-esteem, are better educated, and come from families with higher incomes than their counterparts who do not participate in youth groups (Erickson, 1982). Participation in youth groups can help adolescents practice the interpersonal and organizational skills that are important for success in adult roles.

The Search Institute (1995) conducted a study that sheds light on both the potential for and barriers to participation in youth programs. The study focused on Minneapolis, which faces many of the same challenges regarding youth as other major U.S. cities. The after-school hours and summer vacations are important time slots during which adolescents could form positive relationships with adults and peers. Yet this study found that more than 50 percent of the youth said they don't participate in any type of after-school youth program in a typical week. More than 40 percent reported no participation in youth programs during the summer months.

About 350 youth programs were identified in Minneapolis, about one program for every 87 adolescents. However, about one-half of the youth and their parents agreed that there were not enough youth programs. Parents with the lowest incomes were the least satisfied with program availability.

Some of the reasons given by middle school adolescents for not participating in youth programs were a lack of interest in available activities, a lack of transportation, and lack of awareness about what is available. Here are several adolescents' comments about why they don't participate in youth programs:

"Some things I don't like, like sports stuff because I'm not good at it."
"Nobody is going to take a bus across town just to get to a program."
"I have enough time but my parents don't. I need them to take me there."

Parents see similar barriers, especially transportation and costs. Adolescents express an interest in activities that would foster their peer relations. They want more informal programs or places where their time is not highly structured—places where they can drop by, hang out, and spontaneously choose what they want to do. However, many adolescents also reported having an interest in participating more in structured activities such as taking lessons, playing sports, dances, youth-led programs, and youth service.

According to Reed Larson (2000; Larson, Hansen, & Walker, 2004), structured voluntary youth activities are especially well suited for the development of initiative. One study of structured youth activities that led to increased initiative involved adolescents in low-income areas who began participating in art and drama groups, sports teams, Boys and Girls Clubs, YMCA gang intervention programs, and other community organizations (Heath, 1999; Heath & McLaughlin, 1993). When the adolescents first joined these organizations, they seemed bored. Within three to four weeks, though, they reported greater confidence in their ability to affect their world and adjusted their behavior in pursuit of a goal.

In sum, youth activities and organizations provide excellent developmental contexts in which to provide adolescents opportunities to develop many positive qualities (Flanagan, 2004). Participation in these contexts can help to increase achievement and decrease delinquency (Dworkin & others, 2001; Larson, 2000).

These adolescents are participating in Girls Club and Boys Club activities. *What effects do youth organizations have on adolescents?*

**REVIEW AND REFLECT ◆ LEARNING GOAL 2**

**2 Summarize what takes place in adolescent groups.**

***Review***

- What functions do adolescent groups serve?
- How are childhood groups different from adolescent groups?
- What are cliques and crowds? What roles do they play in adolescent development?
- How can youth organizations be characterized?

***Reflect***

- What do you think would have been the ideal youth organization to support your needs when you were an adolescent?

## 3 GENDER AND CULTURE

Gender | Socioeconomic Status and Ethnicity | Culture

The social worlds of adolescent peer groups and friendships are linked to gender and culture. In Chapter 5, we indicated that during the elementary school years children spend a large majority of their free time with children of their own sex. Preadolescents spend an hour or less a week interacting with the other sex (Furman & Shaeffer, 2003). With puberty, though, more time is spent in heterosexual peer groups, which was reflected in Dunphy's developmental view that we just described. And by the twelfth grade, boys spend an average of five hours a week with the other sex, girls ten hours a week (Furman, 2002). Nonetheless, there are some significant differences between adolescent peer groups made up of males and those made up of females.

### Gender

There is increasing evidence that gender plays an important role in the peer group and friendships (Underwood, 2004). The evidence related to the peer group focuses on group size and interaction in same-sex groups (Maccoby, 2002):

- *Group size.* From about 5 years of age forward, boys are more likely than girls to associate in larger clusters. Boys are more likely to participate in organized games and sports than girls are.
- *Interaction in same-sex groups.* Boys are more often likely than girls to engage in competition, conflict, ego displays, and risk taking and to seek dominance. By contrast, girls are more likely to engage in "collaborative discourse," in which they talk and act in a more reciprocal manner.

Are the friendships of adolescent girls more intimate than the friendships of adolescent boys? When asked to describe their best friends, girls refer to intimate conversations and faithfulness more than boys do (Collins & Steinberg, 2006; Ruble, Martin, & Berenbaum, 2006). For example, girls are more likely to describe their best friend as "sensitive just like me" or "trustworthy just like me" (Duck, 1975). When conflict is present, girls place a higher priority on relationship goals such as being patient until the relationship improves, whereas boys are more likely to seek control over a friend (Ruble, Martin, & Berenbaum, 2006). Girls' friendships in adolescence are more likely to focus on intimacy, and boys' friendships tend to emphasize power and excitement (Rose, 2002; Ruble, Martin, & Berenbaum, 2006). Boys may discourage one another from openly disclosing their problems because self-disclosure is not masculine (Maccoby, 1996). Boys make themselves vulnerable to being called "wimps" if they can't handle their own problems and insecurities. These gender differences are generally assumed to reflect a greater orientation toward interpersonal relationships among girls than boys.

*What are some gender differences in peer relations and friendships in adolescence?*

## Socioeconomic Status and Ethnicity

In many schools, peer groups are strongly segregated according to socioeconomic status and ethnicity. In schools with large numbers of middle- and lower-SES students, middle-SES students often assume the leadership roles in formal organizations, such as student council, the honor society, fraternity-sorority groups, and so on. Athletic teams are one type of adolescent group in which African American adolescents and adolescents from low-income families have been able to gain parity or even surpass adolescents from middle- and upper-SES families in achieving status.

For many ethnic minority youth, especially immigrants, peers from their own ethnic group provide a crucial sense of brotherhood or sisterhood within the majority culture. Peer groups may form to oppose those of the majority group and to provide adaptive supports that reduce feelings of isolation.

## Culture

So far, we have considered adolescents' peer relations in regard to gender, socioeconomic status, and ethnicity. Are there also some foreign cultures in which the peer group plays a different role than in the United States?

In some countries, adults restrict adolescents' access to peers. For example, in many areas of rural India and in Arab countries, opportunities for peer relations in adolescence are severely restricted, especially for girls (Brown & Larson, 2002). If girls attend school in these regions of the world, it is usually in sex-segregated schools. In these countries, interaction with the other sex or opportunities for romantic relationships are restricted (Booth, 2002).

In Chapter 8, we indicated that Japanese adolescents seek autonomy from their parents later and have less conflict with them than American adolescents do. In a cross-cultural analysis, the peer group was more important to U.S. adolescents than to Japanese adolescents (Rothbaum & others, 2000). Japanese adolescents spend less time outside the home, have less recreational leisure time, and engage in fewer extracurricular activities with peers than U.S. adolescents do (White, 1993). Also, U.S. adolescents are more likely to put pressure on their peers to resist parental influence than Japanese adolescents are (Rothbaum & others, 2000).

A trend, though, is that in societies in which adolescents' access to peers has been restricted, adolescents are engaging in more peer interaction during school and in shared leisure activities, especially in middle-SES contexts (Brown & Larson, 2002). For example, in Southeast Asia and some Arab regions, adolescents are starting to rely more on peers for advice and share interests with them (Booth, 2002; Santa Maria, 2002).

In many countries and regions, though, peers play more prominent roles in adolescents' lives (Brown & Larson, 2002). For example, in sub-Saharan Africa, the peer group is a pervasive aspect of adolescents' lives (Nsamenang, 2002); similar results have been observed throughout Europe and North America (Arnett, 2002).

In some cultures, children are placed in peer groups for much greater lengths of time at an earlier age than they are in the United States. For example, in the Murian culture of eastern India, both male and female children live in a dormitory from the age of 6 until they get married (Barnouw, 1975). The dormitory is a religious haven where members are devoted to work and spiritual harmony. Children work for their parents, and the parents arrange the children's marriages. The children continue to live in the dormitory through adolescence, until they marry.

In some cultural settings, peers even assume responsibilities usually assumed by parents. For example, street youth in South America rely on networks of peers to help them negotiate survival in urban environments (Welti, 2002).

**REVIEW AND REFLECT ◆ LEARNING GOAL 3**

**3 Describe the roles of gender and culture in adolescent peer groups and friendships.**

***Review***
- What role does gender play in adolescent peer groups and friendships?
- How are socioeconomic status and ethnicity linked to adolescent peer relations?
- How is culture involved in adolescent peer relations?

***Reflect***
- Do you think the peer group has too strong of an influence on adolescents in the United States? Explain.

## 4 Dating and Romantic Relationships

- Functions of Dating
- Types of Dating and Developmental Changes
- Emotion, Adjustment, and Romantic Relationships
- Romantic Love and Its Construction
- Gender and Culture

Though many adolescent boys and girls have social interchanges through formal and informal peer groups, it is through dating that more serious contacts between the sexes occur (Furman & Simon, 2006). Young male adolescents spend many agonizing moments worrying about whether they should call a certain girl and ask her out: "Will she turn me down?" "What if she says yes, what do I say next?" "How am I going to get her to the dance? I don't want my mother to take us!" "I want to kiss her, but what if she pushes me away?" "How can I get to be alone with her?" And, on the other side of the coin, young adolescent girls wonder: "What if no one asks me to the dance?" "What do I do if he tries to kiss me?" Or, "I really don't want to go out with him. Maybe I should wait two more days before I give him an answer and see if Bill will call me."

### Functions of Dating

Dating is a relatively recent phenomenon. It wasn't until the 1920s that dating as we know it became a reality, and even then, its primary role was to select and win a mate. Prior to this period, mate selection was the sole purpose of dating, and "dates" were carefully monitored by parents, who completely controlled the nature of any heterosexual companionship. Often, parents bargained with each other about the merits of their adolescents as potential marriage partners and even chose mates for their children. In recent times, of course, adolescents have gained much more control over the dating process and whom they go out with. Furthermore, dating has evolved into something more than just courtship for marriage.

Dating today can serve at least eight functions (Paul & White, 1990):

1. Dating can be a form of recreation. Adolescents who date seem to have fun and see dating as a source of enjoyment and recreation.
2. Dating is a source of status and achievement. Part of the social comparison process in adolescence involves evaluating the status of the people one dates: are they the best looking, the most popular, and so forth?
3. Dating is part of the socialization process in adolescence: it helps the adolescent to learn how to get along with others and assists in learning manners and sociable behavior.
4. Dating involves learning about intimacy and serves as an opportunity to establish a unique, meaningful relationship with a person of the opposite sex.
5. Dating can be a context for sexual experimentation and exploration.
6. Dating can provide companionship through interaction and shared activities in an opposite-sex relationship.
7. Dating experiences contribute to identity formation and development; dating helps adolescents to clarify their identity and to separate from their families of origin.
8. Dating can be a means of mate sorting and selection, thereby retaining its original courtship function.

## Types of Dating and Developmental Changes

A number of dating variations and developmental changes characterize dating and romantic relationships. First, we examine heterosexual romantic relationships and then turn to romantic relationships in sexual minority youth (gay male and lesbian adolescents).

In the first half of the twentieth century, dating served mainly as a courtship for marriage.

Today the functions of dating include courtship but also many others. *What are some of these other functions of dating?*

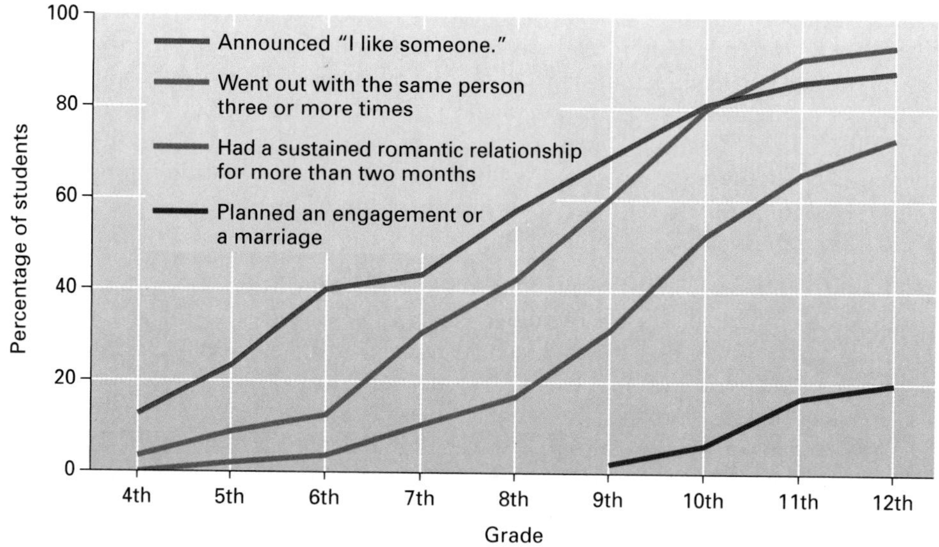


**FIGURE 9.6 Age of Onset of Romantic Activity** In this study, announcing that "I like someone" occurred earliest, followed by going out with the same person three or more times, having a sustained romantic relationship for over two months, and finally planning an engagement or marriage (which characterized only a very small percentage of participants by the twelfth grade) (Buhrmester, 2001).

**Heterosexual Romantic Relationships** One recent study of 14- to 19-year-olds found that adolescents who were not involved in a romantic relationship had more social anxiety than their counterparts who were dating or romantically involved (La Greca & Harrison, 2005). In another study, announcing that "I like someone" occurred by the sixth grade for about 40 percent of the individuals sampled (Buhrmester, 2001) (see Figure 9.6). However, it was not until the tenth grade that 50 percent of the adolescents had a sustained romantic relationship that lasted two months or longer. By their senior year, 25 percent still had not engaged in this type of sustained romantic relationship. Also, in this study, girls' early romantic involvement was linked with lower grades, less active participation in class discussion, and school-related problems. A rather large portion of adolescents in a steady dating relationship said that their steady relationship had persisted 11 months or longer: 20 percent of adolescents 14 or younger, 35 percent of 15- to 16-year-olds, and almost 60 percent of 17- and 18-year-olds (Carver, Joyner, & Udry, 2003).

In their early romantic relationships, many adolescents are not motivated to fulfill attachment or even sexual needs. Rather, early romantic relationships serve as a context for adolescents to explore how attractive they are, how to interact romantically, and how all of this looks to the peer group. Only after adolescents acquire some basic competencies in interacting with romantic partners does the fulfillment of attachment and sexual needs become a central function of these relationships (Furman & Wehner, 1998).

*What are some developmental changes in dating during adolescence?*

Adolescents often find comfort in numbers in their early exploration of romantic relationships (Connolly & others, 2004). They may begin hanging out together in heterosexual groups. Sometimes they just hang out at someone's house or get organized enough to ask an adult to drive them to a mall or a movie. A special concern in early dating and "going with" someone is the associated risk for adolescent pregnancy and problems at home and school.

One study had fifth- to eighth-grade adolescents carry electronic pagers for one week and complete self-report forms in response to signals sent to them at random times (Richards & others, 1998). Four years later, the participants underwent the same procedure. Time with, and thoughts about, the opposite sex occupied more of the adolescents' week in high school than in fifth and sixth grade. Fifth- and sixth-grade girls spent approximately one hour a week in the presence of a boy, and their male counterparts spent even less time in the presence of a girl. Although more time was spent thinking about an individual of the opposite sex, it still added up to less than two hours a week for girls, and less than one hour per week for boys, in fifth and sixth grades. By eleventh and twelfth grades, girls were spending about ten hours a week with a boy, boys about half that time with a girl. Frequency of thoughts had increased as well. The high school girls spent about eight hours a week thinking about a boy, the high school boys about five or six hours thinking about a girl.

In sum, during early adolescence, individuals spent more time thinking about the opposite sex than they actually spent with them. In seventh and eighth grades, they spent four to six hours thinking about them but only about one hour actually with them. By eleventh and twelfth grades, this had shifted to more time spent in their actual presence than thinking about them.

**Romantic Relationships in Sexual Minority Youth** Most research on romantic relationships in adolescence has focused on heterosexual relationships. Recently, researchers have begun to study romantic relationships in gay male, lesbian, and bisexual youth (Diamond & Savin-Williams, 2003; Savin-Williams & Diamond, 2004; Savin-Williams, 2006).

The average age of the initial same-sex activity for females ranges from 14 to 18 years of age and for males from 13 to 15 (Savin-Williams & Diamond, 2004). The most common initial same-sex partner is a close friend. More lesbian adolescent girls have sexual encounters with boys before same-sex activity, whereas gay adolescent boys are more likely to show the opposite sequence (Savin-Williams, 2006, 2007; Savin-Williams & Diamond, 2004).

Most sexual minority youth have same-sex sexual experience, but relatively few have same-sex romantic relationships because of limited opportunities and the social disapproval such relationships may generate from families or heterosexual peers (Diamond, 2003; Savin-Williams, 2006, 2007). The importance of romance to sexual minority youth was underscored in a study that found that they rated the breakup of a current romance as their second most stressful problem, second only to disclosure of their sexual orientation to their parents (D'Augelli, 1991).

The romantic possibilities of sexual minority youth are complex (Savin-Williams, 2006, 2007; Savin-Williams & Diamond, 2004). To adequately address the relational interests of sexual minority youth, we can't generalize from heterosexual youth and simply switch the labels. Instead, the full range of variation in sexual minority youths' sexual desires and romantic relationships for same- and other-sex partners needs to be considered.

## Emotion, Adjustment, and Romantic Relationships

Romantic emotions can envelop adolescents' and emerging adults' lives (Barber & Eccles, 2003). In some cases, these emotions are positive, in others negative. A concern is that in some cases the negative emotions are too intense and prolonged, and can lead to adjustment problems.

**Emotions in Romantic Relationships** A 14-year-old reports being in love and unable to think about anything else. A 15-year-old is distressed that "everyone else has a boyfriend but me." As we just saw, adolescents spend a lot of time thinking about romantic involvement. Some of this thought can involve positive emotions of compassion and joy, but it also can include negative emotions such as worry, disappointment, and jealousy. And the breakup of a romantic relationship can result in depression or other problems (Little & others, 2006; Sbarra, 2006).

Romantic relationships often are involved in an adolescent's emotional experiences. In one study of ninth- to twelfth-graders, girls gave real and fantasized heterosexual relationships as the explanation for more than one-third of their strong emotions, and boys gave this reason for 25 percent of their strong emotions (Wilson-Shockley, 1995). Strong emotions were attached far less to school (13 percent), family (9 percent), and same-sex peer relations (8 percent). The majority of the emotions were reported as positive, but a substantial minority (42 percent), were reported as negative, including feelings of anxiety, anger, jealousy, and depression.

*How is emotion involved in adolescent romantic relationships?*

Adolescents who have a boyfriend or girlfriend reported wider daily emotional swings than their counterparts who did not (Richards & Larson, 1990). In a period of three days, one eleventh-grade girl went from feeling "happy because I'm with Dan" to upset, because they had a "huge fight" and "he won't listen to me and keeps hanging up on me" to feeling "suicidal because of the fight" to feeling "happy because everything between me and Dan is fine."

**Dating and Adjustment** Researchers have linked dating and romantic relationships with various measures of how well adjusted adolescents are (Barber, 2006; Fisher, 2006). Not surprisingly, one study of tenth-grade adolescents found that those who dated were more likely than those who did not date to be accepted by their peers and to be perceived as more physically attractive (Furman, Ho, & Low, 2005). Another recent study of 14- to 19-year-olds found that adolescents who were not involved in a romantic relationship had more social anxiety than their counterparts who were dating or romantically involved (La Greca & Harrison, 2005). But tenth-grade adolescents who dated also had more externalized problems such as delinquency and engaged in substance use (as well as genital sexual behavior) more than their counterparts who did not date (Furman, Ho, & Low, 2005).

Dating and romantic relationships at an unusually early age have been linked with several problems (Smetana, Campione-Barr, & Metzger, 2006). Early dating and "going with" someone is associated with adolescent pregnancy and problems at home and school (Florsheim, 2003). In one study (Buhrmester, 2001), girls' early romantic involvement was linked with lower grades, less active participation in class discussion, and school-related problems. In a recent study, having a boyfriend or a girlfriend (especially an older one) in middle school was linked with early sexual activity (Marin & others, 2006).

**Dissolution of a Romantic Relationship** When things don't go well in a romantic relationship, adolescents and emerging adults need to consider dissolving the relationship. In particular, falling out of love may be wise if you are obsessed with a person who repeatedly betrays your trust; if you are involved with someone who is draining you emotionally or financially; or if you are desperately in love with someone who does not return your feelings.

Being in love when love is not returned can lead to depression, obsessive thoughts, sexual dysfunction, inability to work effectively, difficulty in making new friends, and self-condemnation. Thinking clearly in such relationships is often difficult, because they are so colored by arousing emotions.

Some individuals get taken advantage of in relationships. For example, without either person realizing it, a relationship can evolve in a way that creates dominant and submissive roles. Detecting this pattern is an important step toward learning either to reconstruct the relationship or to end it if the problems cannot be worked out.

Studies of romantic breakups have mainly focused on their negative aspects (Kato, 2005; Kurdek, 1997). Few studies have examined the possibility that a romantic breakup might lead to positive changes (Sbarra & Ferrer, 2006). One study of college students assessed the personal growth that can follow the breakup of a romantic relationship (Tashiro & Frazier, 2003). The participants were 92 undergraduate students who had experienced a relationship breakup in the past nine months. They were asked to describe "what positive changes, if any, have happened as a result of your breakup that might serve to improve your future romantic relationships" (p. 118). Self-reported positive growth was common following the romantic breakups. The most commonly reported types of growth were feeling stronger emotionally and being more self-confident, being more independent, and developing new friendships. Women reported more positive growth than did men.

## Romantic Love and Its Construction

**Romantic love** is also called passionate love or eros; it has strong sexual and infatuation components, and it often predominates in the early part of a love relationship. Romantic love characterizes most adolescent love, and romantic love is also extremely important among college students. In one investigation, unmarried college males and females were asked to identify their closest relationship (Berscheid, Snyder, & Omoto, 1989). More than half named a romantic partner, rather than a parent, sibling, or friend.

*Love is a canvas furnished by nature and embroidered by imagination.*

–Voltaire
*French Philosopher, 18th Century*

Another type of love is **affectionate love,** also called companionate love, which occurs when individuals desire to have another person near and have a deep, caring affection for that person. There is a strong belief that affectionate love is more characteristic of adult love than adolescent love and that the early stages of love have more romantic ingredients than the later stages (Berscheid & Reis, 1998).

Similarity, physical attractiveness, and sexuality are important ingredients of dating relationships, but to fully understand dating relationships in adolescence, we need to know how experiences with family members and peers contribute to the way adolescents construct their dating relationships. In Chapter 8, we discussed the developmental construction view of relationships. Recall that in this view, as individuals grow up, they acquire modes of relating to others. There are two main variations within this view, the continuity version and the discontinuity version.

In the continuity version of the developmental construction view, relationships with parents are carried forward to influence the construction of other relationships, such as dating (Collins & van Dulmen, 2006; Dalton, Frick-Horbury, & Kitzman, 2006). Thus, adolescents' relationships with opposite-sex parents, as well as same-sex parents, contribute to adolescents' dating. For example, the adolescent male whose mother has been nurturant but not smothering probably feels that relationships with females will be rewarding. By contrast, the adolescent male whose mother has been cold and unloving toward him likely feels that relationships with females will be unrewarding.

In Chapter 8, "Families," we saw that attachment history and early child care were precursors to forming positive couple relationships in adolescence (Sroufe & others, 2005). For example, infants who had an anxious attachment with their caregiver in infancy were less likely to develop positive couple relationships in adolescence than were their securely attached counterparts. It might be that adolescents with a history of secure attachment are better able to control their emotions and more comfortable self-disclosing in romantic relationships.

Wyndol Furman and Elizabeth Wehner (1998) discussed how specific insecure attachment styles might be related to adolescents' romantic relationships. Adolescents with a secure attachment to parents are likely to approach romantic relationships expecting closeness, warmth, and intimacy. Thus, they are likely to feel comfortable developing close, intimate romantic relationships. Adolescents with a dismissing/avoidant attachment to parents are likely to expect romantic partners to be unresponsive and unavailable. Thus, they might tend to behave in ways that distance themselves from romantic relationships. Adolescents with a preoccupied/ambivalent attachment to parents are likely to be disappointed and frustrated with intimacy and closeness in romantic relationships.

Adolescents' observations of their parents' marital relationship also contribute to their own construction of dating relationships. Consider an adolescent girl from a divorced family who grew up watching her parents fight on many occasions. Her dating relationships may take one of two turns: she may immerse herself in dating relationships to insulate herself from the stress she has experienced, or she may become aloof and untrusting with males and not wish to become involved heavily in dating relationships. Even when she does become involved in dating, she may find it difficult to develop a trusting relationship with males because she has seen promises broken by her parents.

**romantic love** Also called passionate love or eros, this love has strong sexual and infatuation components, and it often predominates in the early part of a love relationship.

**affectionate love** Also called companionate love, this love occurs when an individual desires to have another person near and has a deep, caring affection for that person.

Mavis Hetherington (1972, 1977) found that divorce was associated with a stronger heterosexual orientation of adolescent daughters than was the death of a parent or living in an intact family. Further, the daughters of divorced parents had a more negative opinion of males than did the girls from other family structures. And girls from divorced and widowed families were more likely to marry images of their fathers than were girls from intact families. Hetherington believes that females from intact families likely have had a greater opportunity to work through relationships with their fathers and therefore are more psychologically free to date and marry someone different from their fathers. Parents are also likely to be more involved or interested in their daughters' dating patterns and relationships than their sons'. For example, in one investigation, college females were much more likely than their male counterparts to say that their parents tried to influence whom they dated during adolescence (Knox & Wilson, 1981). They also indicated that it was not unusual for their parents to try to interfere with their dating choices and relationships.

So far we have been discussing the continuity version of the developmental construction view. In contrast, the discontinuity version emphasizes change and growth in a relationship over time. Peer relations and friendships provide the opportunity to learn modes of relating that are carried over into romantic relationships (Furman & Wehner, 1998; Sullivan, 1953). Remember that in Chapter 8, "Families," we described longitudinal research in which friendship in middle childhood was linked with security in dating, as well as intimacy in dating, at age 16 (Collins, Henninghausen, & Sroufe, 1998; Collins & van Dulmen, 2006). Other researchers also have found links between adolescents' friendships and romantic relationships (Furman, 2002).

Harry Stack Sullivan (1953) theorized that it is through intimate friendships that adolescents learn a mature form of love he referred to as "collaboration." Sullivan felt that it was this collaborative orientation, coupled with sensitivity to the needs of the friend, that forms the basis of satisfying dating and marital relationships. He also pointed out that dating and romantic relationships give rise to new interpersonal issues that youths had not encountered in prior relationships with parents and friends. Not only must teenagers learn tactics for asking partners for dates (and gracefully turning down requests), but they must also learn to integrate sexual desires with psychological intimacy desires. These tactics and integration are not easy tasks, and it is not unusual for them to give rise to powerful feelings of frustration, guilt, and insecurity.

In addition to past relationships with parents and friends influencing an adolescent's dating relationships, family members and peers can directly influence dating experiences (Niederjohn, Welsh, & Scheussler, 2000). For example, sibling relationships can serve as important resources for dating. In one study, adolescents said that they got more support for dating from siblings than from their mothers (O'Brien, 1990). In late adolescence, siblings were viewed as more important advisers and confidants than mothers when concerns about dating were involved. Adolescents sometimes use siblings to their advantage when dealing with parents. In one study, younger siblings pointed to how their older siblings were given dating privileges that they had been denied (Place, 1975). In this investigation, an adolescent would sometimes side with a sibling when the sibling was having an argument with parents in the hope that the sibling would reciprocate when the adolescent needed dating privileges the parents were denying.

Research by Jennifer Connolly and her colleagues (Connolly, Furman, & Konarski, 2000; Connolly & others, 2004; Connolly & Stevens, 1999) documents the role of peers in the emergence of romantic involvement in adolescence. In one study, adolescents who were part of mixed-sex peer groups moved more readily into romantic relationships than their counterparts whose mixed-sex peer groups were more limited (Connolly, Furman, & Konarski, 2000). And a more recent study also found that young adolescents increase their participation in mixed-gender peer groups (Connolly & others, 2004). This participation was "not explicitly focused on dating but rather brought boys and girls together in settings in which heterosocial interaction might occur but is not obligatory. . . . We speculate that mixed-gender groups are important because they are easily available to young adolescents who can take part at their own comfort level" (p. 201).

*What characterizes dating scripts in adolescence?*

## Gender and Culture

Dating and romantic relationships may vary according to gender and culture. Think back to your middle school/junior high and high school years and consider how gender likely influenced your romantic relationships.

**Gender** Do male and female adolescents bring different motivations to the dating experience? Candice Feiring (1996) found that they did. Fifteen-year-old girls were more likely to describe romance in terms of interpersonal qualities, boys in terms of physical attraction. For young adolescents, the affiliative qualities of companionship, intimacy, and support were frequently mentioned as positive dimensions of romantic relationships, but love and security were not. Also, the young adolescents described physical attraction more in terms of being cute, pretty, or handsome than in terms of sexuality (such as being a good kisser). Possibly, however, the failure to discuss sexual interests was due to the adolescents' discomfort in talking about such personal feelings with an unfamiliar adult.

**Dating scripts** are the cognitive models that adolescents and adults use to guide and evaluate dating interactions. In one study, first dates were highly scripted along gender lines (Rose & Frieze, 1993). Males followed a proactive dating script, females a reactive one. The male's script involved initiating the date (asking for and planning it), controlling the public domain (driving and opening doors), and initiating sexual interaction (making physical contact, making out, and kissing). The female's script focused on the private domain (concern about appearance, enjoying the date), participating in the structure of the date provided by the male (being picked up, having doors opened), and responding to his sexual gestures. These gender differences give males more power in the initial stage of a relationship.

**Ethnicity and Culture** The sociocultural context exerts a powerful influence on adolescent dating patterns and on mate selection (Booth, 2002; Stevenson & Zusho, 2002). Values and religious beliefs of people in various cultures often dictate the age at which dating begins, how much freedom in dating is allowed, the extent to which dates are chaperoned by parents or other adults, and the respective roles of males and females in dating. In the Arab world, Asian countries, and South America, adults are typically highly restrictive of adolescent girls' romantic relationships.

*What are some ethnic variations in dating during adolescence?*

Immigrants to the United States have brought these restrictive standards with them. For example, in the United States, Latino and Asian American families typically have more conservative standards regarding adolescent dating than the Anglo-American culture. Especially when an immigrant adolescent wants to date outside of his or her ethnic group, dating can be a source of cultural conflict for families who come from cultures in which dating begins at a late age, little freedom in dating is allowed, dates are chaperoned, and adolescent girls' dating is especially restricted.

In one study, Latino young adults living in the midwestern region of the United States reflected on their socialization for dating and sexuality (Raffaelli & Ontai, 2001). Because most of their parents viewed U.S.-style dating as a violation of traditional courtship styles, strict boundaries were imposed on youths' romantic involvements. As a result, many of the Latinos described their adolescent dating experiences as filled with tension and conflict. The average age at which the girls began dating was 15.7 years, with early dating experiences usually occurring without parental knowledge or permission. Over half of the girls engaged in "sneak dating."

**dating scripts** The cognitive models that adolescents and adults use to guide and evaluate dating interactions.

## REVIEW AND REFLECT ◆ LEARNING GOAL 4

### 4 Characterize adolescent dating and romantic relationships.

***Review***

- What functions does dating serve?
- What are some different types of dating? How does dating change developmentally during adolescence?
- How are romantic relationships linked to emotion and adjustment?
- What is romantic love, and how is it constructed?
- How are gender and culture involved in dating and romantic relationships?

***Reflect***

- Think back to your middle school/junior high and high school years. How much time did you spend thinking about dating? If you dated, what were your dating experiences like? What would you do over again the same way? What would you do differently?
- What characteristics did you seek in the people you wanted to date? Were you too idealistic?
- What advice would you give today's adolescents about dating and romantic relationships?

# 5 EMERGING ADULT LIFESTYLES

Single Adults | Married Adults | Gay Male and Lesbian Adults | Cohabiting Adults | Divorced Adults

Emerging adulthood is not only a time when changes often take place in romantic relationships; it also is a time characterized by residential and lifestyle changes. In 2000, approximately one-half of U.S. 18- to 24-year-olds were living with their parents or other relatives, whereas about one-fourth of the 18- to 24-year-olds had formed their own households and another one-fourth were living with nonrelatives, such as roommates or an unmarried partner (Jekielek & Brown, 2005). Among the questions that many emerging adults pose to themselves as they consider their lifestyle options are: Should I get married? If so, when? If I wait too long, will I get left out? Should I stay single or is it too lonely a life? Do I want to have children?

A striking social change in recent decades is the decreased stigma attached to individuals who do not maintain what were long considered conventional families. Emerging adults today choose many lifestyles and form many types of families (Benokratis, 2008). They live alone, cohabit, marry, divorce, or live with someone of the same sex. Let's explore each of these lifestyles.

## Single Adults

There has been a dramatic rise in the percentage of single adults. In 2000, 25 percent of U.S. adults lived alone (National Center for Health Statistics, 2002). This is more than three times the percentage in 1970 (8 percent). The majority of emerging adults are single. In 2000, 79 percent of U.S. 18- to 24-year-olds had never married (Jekielek & Brown, 2005). In the 18- to 20-year-old group, 89 percent had never married, and in the 21- to 24-year-old group, 71 percent had never married.

Even when singles enjoy their lifestyles and are highly competent individuals, they often are stereotyped (DePaulo & Morris, 2005; Schwartz & Scott, 2007). Stereotypes associated with being single range from the "swinging single" to the "desperately lonely, suicidal" single. Of course, most single adults are somewhere between these extremes. Among the difficulties some single adults experience are forming intimate relationships with other adults, confronting loneliness, and finding a niche in a society that is marriage oriented.

Advantages of being single include having time to make decisions about one's life course, time to develop personal resources to meet goals, freedom to make autonomous decisions and pursue one's own schedule and interests, opportunities to explore new places and try out new things, and privacy. One woman who never married commented, "I enjoy knowing that I can satisfy my own whims without someone else's interferences. If I want to wash my hair at two o'clock in the morning, no one complains. I can eat when I'm hungry and watch my favorite television shows without contradictions from anyone. I enjoy these freedoms."

## Cohabiting Adults

**Cohabitation** refers to living together in a sexual relationship without being married. Cohabitation has undergone considerable changes in recent years (Casper & Bianchi, 2007; Popenoe & Whitehead, 2006; Cherlin, 2007) (see Figure 9.7). The percentage of U.S. couples who cohabit before marriage has increased from approximately 11 percent in 1970 to more than 50 percent in 2005 (Popenoe & Whitehead, 2006). Cohabiting rates are even higher in some countries—in Sweden, cohabitation before marriage is virtually universal (Hoem, 1995).

Many couples view their cohabitation not as a precursor to marriage but as an ongoing lifestyle. These couples do not want the official aspects of marriage. In the United States, cohabiting arrangements tend to be short-lived, with one-third lasting less than a year (Hyde & DeLamater, 2006). Less than one out of ten lasts five years. Of course, it is easier to dissolve a cohabitation relationship than to divorce.

Do cohabiting relationships differ from marriage in other ways? Relationships between cohabiting men and women tend to be more equal than those between husbands and wives (Wineberg, 1994).

Although cohabitation offers some advantages, it also can produce some problems (Seltzer, 2004; Popenoe & Whitehead, 2006; Trask & Koivur, 2007). Researchers have found a higher rate of domestic violence among cohabiting couples than in married couples (Kenney & McLanahan, 2006). Also, disapproval by parents and other family members can place emotional strain on the cohabiting couple. Some cohabiting couples have difficulty owning property jointly. Legal rights on the dissolution of the relationship are less certain than in a divorce.

Does cohabiting help or harm the chances that a couple will have a stable and happy marriage? Some researchers have found no differences in marital quality between individuals who earlier cohabited and those who did not (Newcomb & Bentler, 1980; Watson & DeMeo, 1987). Other researchers have found lower rates of marital satisfaction in couples who lived together before getting married (Booth & Johnson, 1988; Whitehead & Popenoe, 2003). In one study, after ten years of marriage, 40 percent of couples who lived together before marriage had divorced, whereas 31 percent of those who had not cohabited first had divorced (Centers for Disease Control and Prevention, 2002).

What might explain the finding that cohabiting is linked with divorce more than not cohabiting? The most frequently given explanation is that the less traditional lifestyle of cohabitation may attract less conventional individuals who are not great believers in marriage in the first place (Whitehead & Popenoe, 2003). An alternative explanation is that the experience of cohabiting changes people's attitudes and habits in ways that increase their likelihood of divorce (Solot & Miller, 2002).

What are adolescents' plans to cohabit and to marry? A recent study of more than 1,200 seventh- to twelfth-graders revealed that 55 percent said they are at least

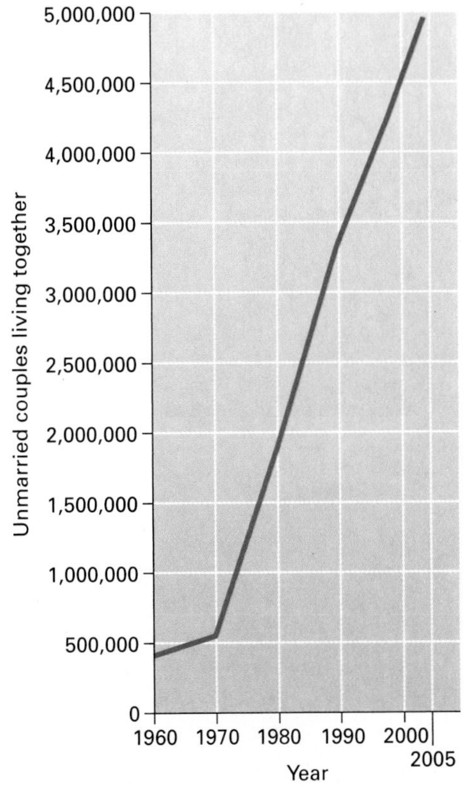


**FIGURE 9.7 The Increase in Cohabitation in the United States** Since 1970, there has been a dramatic increase in the number of unmarried adults living together in the United States.

*What are some differences in cohabiting relationships and marriages?*

**cohabitation** Living together in a sexual relationship without being married.

(a)

(b)

(*a*) In Scandinavian countries, cohabitation is popular; only a small percentage of 20- to 24-year-olds are married. (*b*) Japanese young adults live at home longer with their parents before marrying than young adults in most countries.

somewhat likely to cohabit at some point in the future (Manning, Longmore, & Giordano, 2007). The study revealed stronger expectations for marriage than cohabitation, with 76 percent saying they definitely or probably will get married in the future.

## Married Adults

Until about 1930, stable marriage was widely accepted as the endpoint of adult development. In the last 60 years, however, personal fulfillment both inside and outside marriage has emerged as a goal that competes with marital stability.

**Marital Trends** In recent years, marriage rates in the United States have declined. More adults are remaining single longer today, and the average duration of a marriage in the United States is currently just over nine years. In 2005, the U.S. average age for a first marriage climbed to just over 27 years for men and 25 years for women, higher than at any point in history (U.S. Census Bureau, 2005). In addition, the increase in cohabitation and a slight decline in the percentage of divorced individuals who remarry contribute to the decline in marriage rates in the United States (Popenoe & Whitehead, 2006).

What percentage of U.S. emerging adults are married? In 2000, 18.5 percent of U.S. 18- to 24-year-olds were married (Jekielek & Brown, 2005). In the 18- to 20-year-old group, 10 percent were married, and in the 21- to 24-year-old group, 25 percent were married. Ethnic variations in marriage occur in emerging adulthood. In 2000, 31 percent of Latino, 18 percent of Asian American, and 12 percent of African American 18- to 24-year-olds were married, whereas 22 percent of non-Latino Whites in this age range were married (Jekielek & Brown, 2005).

Is there a best age to get married? Marriages in adolescence are more likely to end in divorce than marriages in adulthood (Furstenberg, 2007). One survey revealed that getting married in the United States between 23 and 27 years of age resulted in a lower likelihood of becoming divorced (Glenn, 2005). However, overall, researchers have not been able to pin down a specific age or age span of several years in adulthood for getting married that is most likely to result in a successful marriage (Furstenberg, 2007).

International comparisons of marriage also reveal that individuals in Scandinavian countries marry later than Americans, whereas their counterparts in Eastern Europe marry earlier (Bianchi & Spain, 1986). In Denmark, for example, almost 80 percent of the women and 90 percent of the men aged 20 to 24 have never been married. In Hungary, less than 40 percent of the women and 70 percent of the men the same age have never been married. In Scandinavian countries, cohabitation is popular among young adults; however, most Scandinavians eventually marry (Popenoe & Whitehead, 2006). In Sweden, on average women delay marriage until they are 31, men until they are 33. Some countries, such as Hungary, encourage early marriage and childbearing to offset declines in the population. Like Scandinavian countries, Japan has a high proportion of unmarried young people. However, rather than cohabiting as the Scandinavians do, unmarried Japanese young adults live at home longer with their parents before marrying.

**Premarital Education** Premarital education occurs in a group and focuses on relationship advice (Busby & others, 2007; Duncan, Holman, & Yang, 2007). Might premarital education improve the quality of a marriage and possibly reduce the chances that the marriage will end in a divorce? Researchers have found that it can (Carroll & Doherty, 2003). For example, a recent survey of more than 3,000 adults revealed that premarital education was linked to a higher level of marital satisfaction and commitment to a spouse, a lower level of destructive marital conflict, and a 31 percent lower likelihood of divorce (Stanley & others, 2006). The premarital education programs in the study ranged from several hours to 20 hours with a median of 8 hours. It is recommended that premarital education begin approximately six months to a year before the wedding.

To improve their relationships, some couples seek counseling. To read about the work of couples counselor Susan Orenstein, see the *Careers in Adolescent Development* profile.

## Careers in ADOLESCENT DEVELOPMENT

### Susan Orenstein
**Couples Counselor**

Susan Orenstein provides counseling to emerging adults and young adults in Cary, North Carolina. She specializes in premarital and couple counseling to help couples increase their intimacy and mutual appreciation, and also works with couples to resolve long-standing conflicts, reduce destructive patterns of communication, and restore trust in the relationship. In addition to working privately with couples, she conducts workshops on relationships and gives numerous talks at colleges, businesses, and organizations.

Dr. Orenstein obtained an undergraduate degree in psychology from Brown University, a master's degree in counseling from Georgia Tech University, and a doctorate in counseling psychology from Temple University. Some couples therapists have advanced degrees in clinical psychology or marriage and family therapy rather than counseling, and some practice with a master's degree. After earning a master's or doctoral degree in an appropriate program, before practicing couples therapy, individuals are required to do an internship and pass a state licensing examination.

At most colleges, the counseling or health center has a counselor or therapist who works with couples to improve their relationship.

## Divorced Adults

Divorce has become epidemic in the United States (Fine & Harvey, 2006). The number of divorced adults rose from 2 percent of the adult population in 1950 to 3 percent in 1970 to 10 percent in 2002. The divorce rate was increasing annually by 10 percent, but has been declining since the 1980s (Amato & Irving, 2006; Hernandez, 2007).

Although divorce has increased for all socioeconomic groups, those in disadvantaged groups have a higher incidence of divorce. Youthful marriage, low educational level, low income, not having a religious affiliation, having parents who are divorced, and having a baby before marriage are associated with increases in divorce (Popenoe & Whitehead, 2006; Rodrigues, Hall, & Fincham, 2006).

If a divorce is going to occur, it usually takes place early in a marriage; most occur in the fifth to tenth year of marriage (National Center for Health Statistics, 2000) (see Figure 9.8). This timing may reflect an effort by partners in troubled marriages to stay in the marriage and try to work things out. If after several years these efforts don't improve the relationship, they may then seek a divorce.

Even those adults who initiated their divorce experience challenges after a marriage dissolves (Amato & Irving, 2006; Hetherington & Kelly, 2002). Both divorced women and divorced men complain of loneliness, diminished self-esteem, anxiety about the unknowns in their lives, and difficulty in forming satisfactory new intimate relationships. Separated and divorced women and men have higher rates of psychiatric disorders, depression, alcoholism, and psychosomatic problems, such as sleep disorders, than do married adults (Eng & others, 2005).

Psychologically, one of the most common characteristics of divorced adults is difficulty in trusting someone else in a romantic relationship. Following a divorce, though, people's lives can take diverse turns (Tashiro, Frazier, & Berman, 2006). For example, in one research study, 20 percent of the divorced group "grew more competent, well-adjusted, and self-fulfilled" following their divorce (Hetherington & Kelly, 2002, p. 98). They were competent in multiple areas of life, showed a remarkable ability to bounce back from stressful circumstance, and to create something meaningful out of problems.

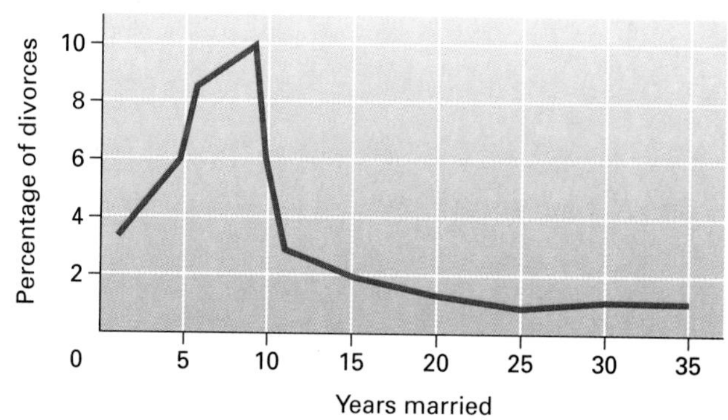


**FIGURE 9.8 The Divorce Rate in Relation to Number of Years Married** Shown here is the percentage of divorces as a function of how long couples have been married. Notice that most divorces occur in the early years of marriage, peaking in the fifth to tenth years of marriage.

## Gay Male and Lesbian Adults

The legal and social context of marriage creates barriers to breaking up that do not usually exist for same-sex partners (Stiers, 2007;

*What characterizes the relationships of lesbian and gay male emerging adults?*

Weston, 2007). But in other ways, researchers have found that gay male and lesbian relationships are similar—in their satisfactions, loves, joys, and conflicts—to heterosexual relationships (Hyde & DeLamater, 2006; Kurdek, 2006; Oswald & Clausell, 2005; Peplau & Fingerhut, 2007). For example, like heterosexual couples, gay male and lesbian couples need to find the balance of romantic love, affection, autonomy, and equality that is acceptable to both partners (Kurdek, 2003). In one study, gay male and lesbian couples listed their areas of conflict in order of frequency: finances, driving style, affection and sex, being overly critical, and household tasks (Kurdek, 1995). The components of this list are likely to be familiar to heterosexual couples.

Lesbian couples especially place a high priority on equality in their relationships (Kurdek, 2007; Peplau & Fingerhut, 2007). Indeed, some researchers have found that gay male and lesbian couples are more flexible in their gender roles than heterosexual individuals are (Marecek, Finn, & Cardell, 1988).

There are a number of misconceptions about gay male and lesbian couples (Kurdek, 2006). Contrary to stereotypes, one partner is masculine and the other feminine in only a small percentage of gay male and lesbian couples. Only a small segment of the gay male population has a large number of sexual partners, and this is uncommon among lesbians. Furthermore, researchers have found that gay males and lesbians prefer long-term, committed relationships (Peplau & Beals, 2004). About half of committed gay male couples do have an open relationship that allows the possibility of sex (but not affectionate love) outside of the relationship. Lesbian couples usually do not have this open relationship.

**REVIEW AND REFLECT ◆ LEARNING GOAL 5**

### 5 Explain the diversity of emerging adult lifestyles.

***Review***
- What characterizes single adults?
- What are the lives of cohabiting adults like?
- What are some key aspects of the lives of married adults?
- How does divorce affect adults?
- What characterizes the lifestyles of gay male and lesbian adults?

***Reflect***
- Which type of lifestyle are you living today? What do you think are its advantages and disadvantages for you? If you could have a different lifestyle, which one would it be? Why?

# REACH YOUR LEARNING GOALS

## 1 EXPLORING PEER RELATIONS AND FRIENDSHIP *Discuss the role of peer relations, friendship, and loneliness in adolescent development.*

### Peer Relations

Peers are individuals who are about the same age or maturity level. Peers provide a means of social comparison and a source of information beyond the family. Good peer relations may be necessary for normal social development. The inability to "plug in" to a social network is associated with a number of problems. Peer relations can be negative or positive. Piaget and Sullivan each stressed that peer relations provide the context for learning the symmetrical reciprocity mode of relationships. Healthy family relations usually promote healthy peer relations. Conformity to antisocial peer standards peaks around the ninth grade. Popular children are frequently nominated as a best friend and are rarely disliked by their peers. Average children receive an average number of both positive and negative nominations from their peers. Neglected children are infrequently nominated as a best friend but are not disliked by their peers. Rejected children are infrequently nominated as a best friend and are disliked by their peers. Controversial children are frequently nominated both as a best friend and as being disliked by peers. Social knowledge and social information-processing skills are associated with improved peer relations. Self-regulation of emotion is associated with positive peer relations. Conglomerate strategies, also referred to as coaching, involve the use of a combination of techniques, rather than a single strategy, to improve adolescents' social skills.

### Friendship

Friends are a subset of peers who engage in mutual companionship, support, and intimacy. The functions of friendship include companionship, stimulation, physical support, ego support, social comparison, and intimacy/affection. Sullivan argued that the psychological importance and intimacy of close friends increases dramatically in adolescence. Research supports this view. Some changes in friendship in emerging adulthood occur. Intimacy and similarity are two of the most important characteristics of friendships. Children and adolescents who become close friends with older individuals engage in more deviant behaviors than their counterparts with same-age friends. Early-maturing girls are more likely than late-maturing girls to have older friends, which can contribute to problem behaviors.

### Loneliness

Chronic loneliness is linked with impaired physical and mental health. Loneliness often emerges when people make life transitions, so it is not surprising that loneliness is common among college freshmen. Moderately or intensely lonely individuals never or rarely feel in tune with others and rarely or never find companionship when wanted, whereas other individuals may value solitary time.

## 2 ADOLESCENT GROUPS *Summarize what takes place in adolescent groups.*

### Group Function

Groups satisfy adolescents' personal needs, reward them, provide information, can raise their self-esteem, and contribute to their identity. Norms are the rules that apply to all members of a group. Roles are rules and expectations that govern certain positions in the group.

### Groups in Childhood and Adolescence

Childhood groups are less formal, less heterogeneous, and less mixed-sex than adolescent groups. Dunphy's study found that adolescent group development proceeds through five stages.

**Cliques and Crowds**

Cliques are small groups that range from two to about twelve individuals and average about five to six individuals. Clique members are similar in age, usually of the same sex, and often participate in similar activities, sharing ideas, hanging out, and developing an in-group identity. Crowds are a larger group structure than cliques and are less personal. Adolescents are members of crowds usually based on reputation and may or may not spend much time together. Many crowds are defined by adolescents' activities, such as jocks, druggies, populars, and independents.

**Youth Organizations**

Youth organizations can have important influences on adolescent development. More than 400 national youth organizations currently exist in the United States. Boys and Girls Clubs are examples of youth organizations designed to increase membership in youth organizations in low-income neighborhoods. Participation in youth organizations may increase achievement and decrease delinquency. Youth activities and organizations also may provide opportunities for adolescents to develop initiative.

## 3 Gender and Culture *Describe the roles of gender and culture in adolescent peer groups and friendships.*

**Gender**

The social world of adolescent peer groups varies according to gender, socioeconomic status, ethnicity, and culture. In terms of gender, boys are more likely to associate in larger clusters and organized games than girls are. Boys also are more likely than girls to engage in competition, conflict, ego displays, and risk taking and to seek dominance. By contrast, girls are more likely to engage in collaborative discourse. Girls engage in more intimacy in their friendships than boys do.

**Socioeconomic Status and Ethnicity**

In many cases, peer groups are segregated according to socioeconomic status. In some cases, ethnic minority adolescents rely on peers more than non-Latino White adolescents in the United States do.

**Culture**

In some countries, such as rural India, Arab countries, and Japan, adults restrict access to the peer group. In North America and Europe, the peer group is a pervasive aspect of adolescents' lives.

## 4 Dating and Romantic Relationships *Characterize adolescent dating and romantic relationships.*

**Functions of Dating**

Dating can be a form of recreation, a source of social status and achievement, an aspect of socialization, a context for learning about intimacy and sexual experimentation, a source of companionship, and a means of mate sorting.

**Types of Dating and Developmental Changes**

Younger adolescents often begin to hang out together in mixed-sex groups. A special concern is early dating, which is associated with a number of problems. In early adolescence, individuals spend more time thinking about the opposite sex than actually being with them, but this tends to reverse in the high school years. Most sexual minority youth have same-sex sexual experience, but relatively few have same-sex romantic relationships. Many sexual minority youth date other-sex peers, which can help them to clarify their sexual orientation or disguise it from others.

**Emotion, Adjustment, and Romantic Relationships**

The emotions of romantic relationships can envelop adolescents' lives. Sometimes these emotions are positive, sometimes negative, and can change very quickly. Adolescents who date have more problems, such as substance abuse, than those who do not date, but they also have more acceptance with peers.

**Romantic Love and Its Construction**

Romantic love, also called passionate love, involves sexuality and infatuation more than affectionate love. Romantic love is especially prominent among adolescents and traditional-aged college students. Affectionate love is more common in middle and late adulthood, characterizing love that endures over time. The developmental construction view emphasizes how relationships with parents, siblings, and peers influence how adolescents construct their romantic relationships. Connolly's research revealed the importance of peers and friends in adolescent romantic relationships.

**Gender and Culture**

Girls tend to view dating as an interpersonal experience, boys view dating more in terms of physical attraction. Culture can exert a powerful influence on dating. Many adolescents from immigrant families face conflicts with their parents about dating.

## 5 EMERGING ADULT LIFESTYLES *Explain the diversity of emerging adult lifestyles.*

**Single Adults**

Being single has become an increasingly prominent lifestyle. Myths and stereotypes about singles abound, ranging from "swinging single" to "desperately lonely, suicidal single." There are advantages and disadvantages to being single, autonomy being one of the advantages. Intimacy, loneliness, and finding a positive identity in a marriage-oriented society are concerns of single adults.

**Cohabiting Adults**

Cohabitation is an increasing lifestyle for many adults. Cohabitation offers some advantages as well as problems. Cohabitation does not lead to greater marital happiness but rather to no differences or differences suggesting that cohabitation is not good for a marriage.

**Married Adults**

Even though adults are remaining single longer and the divorce rate is high, Americans still show a strong predilection for marriage. The age at which individuals marry, expectations about what the marriage will be like, and the developmental course of marriage vary not only over time within a culture, but also across cultures. Premarital education is associated with positive relationship outcomes.

**Divorced Adults**

The U.S. divorce rate increased dramatically in the twentieth century but began to decline in the 1980s. Divorce is complex and emotional. In the first year following divorce, a disequilibrium in the divorced adult's behavior occurs, but by several years after the divorce, more stability has been achieved. The divorced displaced homemaker may encounter excessive stress. Men do not go through a divorce unscathed either.

**Gay Male and Lesbian Adults**

One of the most striking findings about gay and lesbian couples is how similar they are to heterosexual couples. There are many misconceptions about gay male and lesbian adults.

## KEY TERMS

peers 319
conformity 322
sociometric status 323
popular children 323
average children 323
neglected children 323
rejected children 323
controversial children 323
conglomerate strategies 326
friends 327
intimacy in friendship 330
norms 333
roles 333
cliques 334
crowds 334
romantic love 343
affectionate love 343
dating scripts 345
cohabitation 347

## KEY PEOPLE

Thomas Berndt 322
Kenneth Dodge 326
Harry Stack Sullivan 328
Willard Hartup 329
Dexter Dunphy 333
Bradford Brown 334
Reed Larson 335
Wyndol Furman 343
Jennifer Connolly 344
Candice Feiring 345

## RESOURCES FOR IMPROVING THE LIVES OF ADOLESCENTS

**Adolescent Relationships with Peers**
by Bradford Brown
in R. Lerner and L. Steinberg (Eds.),
*Handbook of Adolescent Psychology* (2004)
New York: Wiley

A leading researcher provides a number of ideas about the current state of knowledge in the field of adolescent peer relations and describes some key areas where more research is needed.

**Adolescent Romantic Relations and Sexual Behavior**
by Paul Florsheim (2003)
Mahwah, NJ: Erlbaum

A number of experts address the much-neglected topic of romantic relationships in adolescence.

**Just Friends**
by Lillian Rubin (1985)
New York: HarperCollins

*Just Friends* explores the nature of friendship and intimacy.

## E-LEARNING TOOLS

To help you master the material in this chapter, visit the Online Learning Center for *Adolescence,* twelfth edition **(www.mhhe.com/santrocka12),** where you will find these additional resources:

### Taking It to the Net

1. Media portrayals of adolescents' peer interactions often involve negative instances of peer pressure, including drinking and smoking, delinquency, and drug use. What would you and your friends say to a reporter from the campus newspaper to illustrate the positive side of peer pressure and influence?
2. Having stressed the importance of adolescence as a period of transition from childhood to adult forms of behavior, your adolescent psychology instructor assigns as a paper topic the emergence of romantic relationships. How would you describe adolescence as a transition from immature to adult forms of romantic relationships?

3. Adolescent groups provide a number of functions in adolescent development. How do cliques and crowds influence adolescent identity development?

## Self-Assessment

The Online Learning Center includes the following self-assessment for further exploration:

- The Characteristics I Desire in a Potential Mate

## Health and Well-Being, Parenting, and Education

To practice your decision-making skills, complete the health and well-being, parenting, and education exercises on the Online Learning Center.

## Video Clips

The Online Learning Center includes the following videos for this chapter:

- Views on Family and Peers at Age 15
- Talking About Cliques at Age 15
- 15-year-old Girls' Relationships with Boys
- Friendship in Adolescence at Age 15
- What Is Love?
- Children's Social Networks

# 13 Problems in Adolescence and Emerging Adulthood

*They cannot scare me with their empty spaces. Between stars—on stars where no human race is. I have it in me so much nearer home. To scare myself with my own desert places.*

—ROBERT FROST
American Poet, 20th Century

## CHAPTER OUTLINE

### 1 EXPLORING ADOLESCENT AND EMERGING ADULT PROBLEMS

The Biopsychosocial Approach
The Developmental Psychopathology Approach
Characteristics of Adolescent and Emerging Adult Problems
Stress and Coping
Resilience

**Learning Goal 1:** Discuss the nature of problems in adolescence and emerging adulthood.

### 2 PROBLEMS AND DISORDERS

Drug Use
Juvenile Delinquency
Depression and Suicide
Eating Disorders

**Learning Goal 2:** Describe some main problems that characterize adolescents and emerging adults.

### 3 INTERRELATION OF PROBLEMS AND PREVENTION/INTERVENTION

Adolescents with Multiple Problems
Prevention and Intervention

**Learning Goal 3:** Summarize the interrelation of problems and ways to prevent or intervene in problems.

## *Images of Adolescent Development*

## The Adolescent Problems of Annie and Arnie

Annie, a 15-year-old cheerleader, was tall, blond, and attractive. No one who sold liquor to her questioned her age. She got her money from baby-sitting and what her mother gave her to buy lunch. Annie was kicked off the cheerleading squad for missing practice so often, but that didn't stop her drinking. Soon she and several of her peers were drinking almost every day. Sometimes they skipped school and went to the woods to drink. Annie's whole life began to revolve around her drinking. After a while, her parents began to detect Annie's problem. But their attempts to get her to stop drinking by punishing her were unsuccessful. It went on for two years, and, during the last summer, anytime she saw anybody, she was drunk. Not long ago, Annie started dating a boy she really liked and who refused to put up with her drinking. She agreed to go to Alcoholics Anonymous and has just successfully completed treatment. She has stopped drinking for four consecutive months now, and her goal is continued abstinence.

Arnie is 13 years old. He has a history of committing thefts and physical assaults. The first theft occurred when Arnie was 8—he stole a cassette player from an electronics store. The first physical assault took place a year later, when he shoved his 7-year-old brother up against the wall, bloodied his face, and then threatened to kill him with a butcher knife. Recently, the thefts and physical assaults have increased. In just the past week, he stole a television set, struck his mother repeatedly and threatened to kill her, broke some neighborhood streetlights, and threatened youths with a wrench and a hammer. Arnie's father left home when Arnie was 3 years old. Until the father left, his parents argued extensively, and his father often beat up his mother. Arnie's mother indicates that, when Arnie was younger, she was able to control him, but in the last several years she has lost that control. Arnie's volatility and dangerous behavior have resulted in the recommendation that he be placed in a group home with other juvenile delinquents.

## PREVIEW

***At various points in this book, we have described adolescent and emerging adult problems. For example, we discussed sexual problems in Chapter 6, "Sexuality"; explored school-related problems in Chapter 10, "Schools"; and examined achievement-related problems in Chapter 11, "Achievement, Work, and Careers." We devote this chapter exclusively to adolescent and emerging adult problems, covering different approaches to understanding these problems, some main problems we have not yet discussed, and ways to prevent and intervene in problems.***

# 1 Exploring Adolescent and Emerging Adult Problems

- The Biopsychosocial Approach
- The Developmental Psychopathology Approach
- Characteristics of Adolescent and Emerging Adult Problems
- Stress and Coping
- Resilience

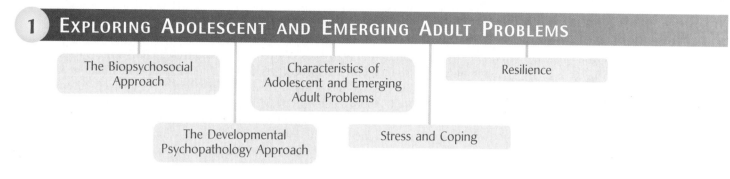

What causes adolescents like Annie and Arnie to have problems? What are some characteristics of the problems adolescents and emerging adults develop? How are stress and coping involved these problems? What characterizes resilient adolescents?

## The Biopsychosocial Approach

The **biopsychosocial approach** emphasizes that biological, psychological, and social factors interact to produce the problems that adolescents, emerging adults, and people of other ages develop. Thus, if an adolescent or emerging adult engages in substance abuse it may be due to a combination of biological (heredity or brain processes), psychological (emotional turmoil or relationship difficulties), and social (poverty) factors. Let's further explore each of these factors.

**Biological Factors** In the biological approach, adolescent and emerging adult problems are believed to be caused by a malfunctioning of the body. Scientists who adopt a biological approach usually focus on the brain and genetic factors as causes of adolescent and emerging adult problems (Lemery & Doelger, 2005). In the biological approach, drug therapy is frequently used to treat problems. For example, if an adolescent or emerging adult is depressed, an antidepressant drug might be prescribed.

**Psychological Factors** Among the psychological factors that have been proposed as causing adolescent and emerging adult problems are distorted thoughts, emotional turmoil, inappropriate learning, and troubled relationships. Two of the theoretical perspectives that we discussed in Chapter 1 address why adolescents and emerging adults might develop problems. Recall that psychoanalytic theorists attribute problems to stressful early experiences with parents and that behavioral and social cognitive theorists see adolescent and emerging adult problems as a consequence of social experiences with others.

Family and peer influences are especially believed to be important contributors to adolescent and emerging adult problems (Bukowski, Brendgen, & Vitaro, 2007; Cavell & others, 2007). For example, when we discuss substance abuse as well as juvenile delinquency, you will see that relationships with parents and peers are linked with these problems.

**Social Factors** The psychological problems that adolescents and emerging adults develop appear in most cultures. However, the frequency and intensity of the problems vary across cultures, with the variations being linked to social, economic, technological, and religious aspects of the cultures (Hammond, 2005; Shiraev & Levy, 2007).

Social factors that influence the development of adolescent and emerging adult problems include socioeconomic status (SES) and neighborhood quality (Conger & Dogan, 2007; McLoyd, Aikens, & Burton, 2006). For example, poverty is a factor in the occurrence of delinquency. In one recent study, low SES was linked to the presence of disruptive behavior problems in 9- to 12-year-old boys (Barry & others, 2005).

**biopsychosocial approach** Emphasizes that problems develop through an interaction of biological, psychological, and social factors.

## The Developmental Psychopathology Approach

*The term "developmental pathways" is central to discussions of developmental psychopathology as a way of conceptualizing the relations between early and later adaption.*

—Byron Egeland
*Contemporary Psychologist, University of Minnesota*

The field of **developmental psychopathology** focuses on describing and exploring the developmental pathways of problems. Many researchers in this field seek to establish links between early precursors of a problem (such as risk factors and early experiences) and outcomes (such as delinquency or depression) (Cicchetti, 2006; Cicchetti & Toth, 2006; Egeland & Carlson, 2004; Sroufe & others, 2005; Masten, Obradović, & Burt, 2006). A developmental pathway describes continuities and transformations in factors that influence outcomes (Chang & Gjerde, 2000). For example, Arnie's story in *Images of Adolescent Development* indicated a possible link between early negative parenting experiences, including his father's abuse of his mother, and Arnie's delinquency in adolescence.

Adolescent and emerging adult problems can be categorized as internalizing or externalizing:

- **Internalizing problems** occur when individuals turn their problems inward. Examples of internalizing problems include anxiety and depression.
- **Externalizing problems** occur when problems are turned outward. An example of an externalizing problem is juvenile delinquency.

Links have been established between patterns of problems in childhood and outcomes in emerging adulthood. In one study, males with internalizing patterns (such as anxiety and depression) in the elementary school years were likely to have similar forms of problems at age 21, but they did not have an increased risk of externalizing problems as young adults (Quinton, Rutter, & Gulliver, 1990). Similarly, the presence of an externalizing pattern (such as aggression or antisocial behavior) in childhood elevated the risk for antisocial problems at age 21. For females in the same study, early internalizing and externalizing patterns both predicted internalizing problems at age 21.

Alan Sroufe and his colleagues (Sroufe, 2007; Sroufe & others, 2005) have found that anxiety problems in adolescence are linked with insecure resistant attachment in infancy (sometimes the infant clings to the caregiver, at other times pushes away from closeness), and that conduct problems in adolescence are related to avoidant attachment in infancy (the infant avoids the caregiver). Sroufe concludes that a combination of early supportive care (attachment security) and early peer competence helps to buffer adolescents from developing problems. In another developmental psychopathology study, Ann Masten (2001; Masten & Reed, 2002) followed 205 children for ten years from childhood into adolescence. She found that good intellectual functioning and parenting served protective roles in keeping adolescents from engaging in antisocial behaviors. Later in this chapter, we further explore such factors in our discussion of resilient adolescents and emerging adults.

John Schulenberg and Nicole Zarrett (2006) recently described mental health, well-being, and problems during emerging adulthood and their continuity/discontinuity with adolescence. In general, for the population, well-being tends to increase during emerging adulthood and some problems, such as theft and property damage, decrease. However, some mental health disorders, such as major depression, increase for some individuals during emerging adulthood. Overall, though, there is continuity between the presence of mental health problems in adolescence and in emerging adulthood. As we describe various problems later in the chapter, such as drugs, delinquency, and depression, we will revisit the continuity and discontinuity of these problems from adolescence through emerging adulthood.

**developmental psychopathology** The area of psychology that focuses on describing and exploring the developmental pathways of problems.

**internalizing problems** Occur when individuals turn problems inward. Examples include anxiety and depression.

**externalizing problems** Occur when individuals turn problems outward. An example is juvenile delinquency.

## Characteristics of Adolescent and Emerging Adult Problems

The spectrum of adolescent and emerging adult problems is wide. The problems vary in their severity and in how common they are for females and males, and for different socioeconomic groups. Some problems are short-lived; others can persist over many years. One 13-year-old might show a pattern of acting-out behavior that is disruptive to his classroom. As a 14-year-old, he might be assertive and aggressive, but no longer disruptive. Another 13-year-old might show a similar pattern of acting-out behavior. At age 16, she might still be a disruptive influence in the classroom and have been arrested for numerous juvenile offenses.

Some problems are more likely to appear at one developmental level than at another. For example, fears are more common in early childhood, many school-related problems surface for the first time in middle and late childhood, and drug-related problems become more common in adolescence (Achenbach & Edelbrock, 1981). In one study, depression, truancy, and drug abuse were more common among older adolescents, whereas arguing, fighting, and being too loud were more common among younger adolescents (Edelbrock, 1989).

In a large-scale investigation by Thomas Achenbach and Craig Edelbrock (1981), adolescents from a lower-SES background were more likely to have problems than those from a middle-SES background. Most of the problems reported for adolescents from a lower-SES background were undercontrolled, externalizing behaviors—destroying others' belongings and fighting, for example. These behaviors also were more characteristic of boys than girls. The problems of middle-SES adolescents and girls were more likely to be overcontrolled and internalizing—anxiety or depression, for example. In one study, Latino adolescent boys who had good relationships with their mothers were less likely to have externalizing problems than their counterparts with poor mother-son relationships (Loukas & Prelow, 2004).

The behavioral problems most likely to cause adolescents to be referred to a clinic for mental health treatment were feelings of unhappiness, sadness, or depression, and poor school performance (see Figure 13.1). Difficulties in school achievement, whether secondary to other kinds of problems or primary problems in themselves, account for many referrals of adolescents.

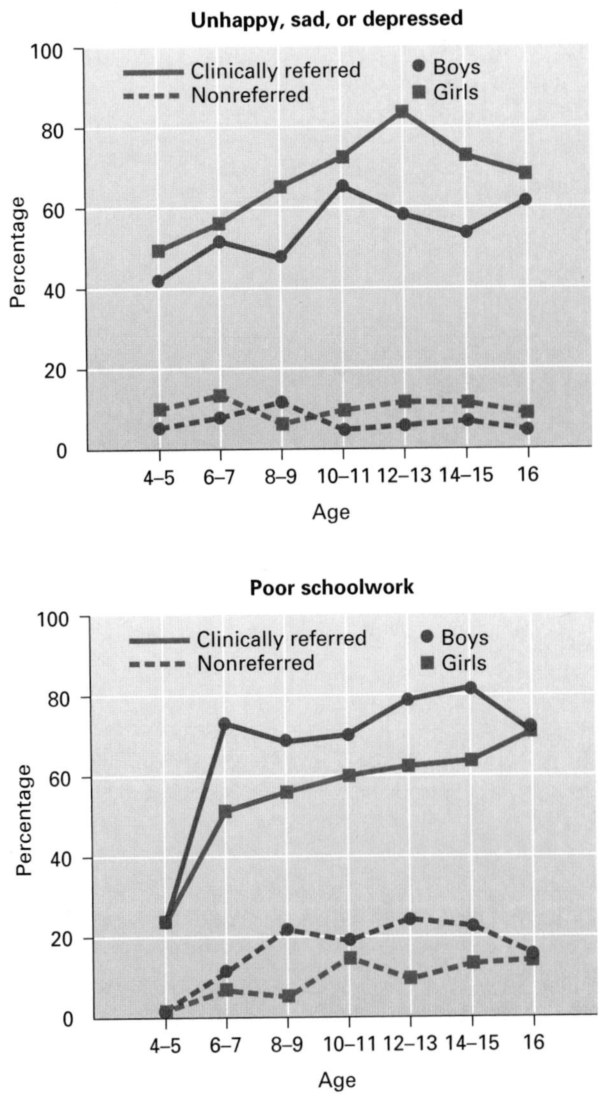


**FIGURE 13.1 The Two Items Most Likely to Differentiate Clinically Referred and Nonreferred Children and Adolescents**

In another investigation, Achenbach and his colleagues (1991) compared the problems and competencies of 2,600 children and adolescents 4 to 16 years old assessed at intake into mental health services with those of 2,600 demographically matched nonreferred children and adolescents. Lower-SES children and adolescents had more problems and fewer competencies than did their higher-SES counterparts. Children and adolescents had more problems when they had fewer related adults in their homes, had biological parents who were unmarried in their homes, had parents who were separated or divorced, lived in families who received public assistance, and lived in households in which family members had received mental health services. Children and adolescents who had more externalized problems came from families in which parents were unmarried, separated, or divorced, as well as from families receiving public assistance.

Many studies have shown that factors such as poverty, ineffective parenting, and mental disorders in parents *predict* adolescent problems (Pianta, 2005). Predictors of problems are called *risk factors*. Risk factor means that there is an elevated probability of a problem outcome in groups of people who have that factor. Children with many risk factors are said to have a "high risk" for problems in childhood and adolescence, but not every one of these children will develop problems.

Some researchers think primarily in terms of risk factors when they study adolescent problems, whereas others argue that conceptualizing problems in terms of risk factors creates a perception that is too negative. Instead, they highlight the developmental assets of youth. For example, Peter Benson (2006; Benson & others, 2006), Director of the Search Institute in Minneapolis, has prescribed 40 developmental assets that adolescents need to achieve positive outcomes in their lives. Half of these assets are external, half internal. The 20 *external* assets include support (such as family and neighborhood), empowerment (such as adults in the community valuing youth, and youth being given useful community roles), boundaries and expectations (such as the family setting clear rules and consequences, and monitoring the adolescent's whereabouts, as well as positive peer influence), and constructive use of time (such as engaging in creative activities three or more times a week and participating three or more hours a week in organized youth programs). The 20 *internal* assets include commitment to learning (such as motivation to achieve in school and doing at least one hour of homework on school days), positive values (such as helping others and demonstrating integrity), social competencies (such as knowing how to plan and make decisions and having interpersonal competencies like empathy and friendship skills), and positive identity (such as having a sense of control over life and high self-esteem). In research conducted by the Search Institute, adolescents with more assets reported engaging in fewer risk-taking behaviors, such as alcohol and tobacco use, sexual intercourse, and violence. For example, in one survey of more than 12,000 ninth- to twelfth-graders, 53 percent of the students with 0 to 10 assets reported using alcohol three or more times in the past month or getting drunk more than once in the past two weeks, compared with only 16 percent of the students with 21 to 30 assets or 4 percent of the students with 31 to 40 assets.

## Stress and Coping

Seventeen-year-old Alan comments, "I never thought it would be so hard to grow up. I feel pressure all of the time. My parents put tremendous pressure on me. I wish someone could help me cope better with all of these pressures." Let's explore the nature of stress in individuals like Alan and ways they can cope effectively with the stress.

### Stress

Although G. Stanley Hall (1904) and others overdramatized the extent of storm and stress in adolescence, many adolescents and emerging adults today experience stressful circumstances that can affect their development. Just what is stress? **Stress** is the response of individuals to *stressors,* which are circumstances and events that threaten them and tax their coping abilities.

A car accident, a low grade on a test, a lost wallet, a conflict with a friend—all these might be stressors in your life. Some stressors are *acute;* in other words, they are sudden events or stimuli such as being cut by falling glass. Other stressors are *chronic,* or long-lasting, such as being malnourished or HIV-positive. These are physical stressors, but there are emotional and psychosocial stressors, such as the death of a loved one or being discriminated against.

Stress may come from many different sources for adolescents and emerging adults. Among the sources are life events, daily hassles, and sociocultural factors.

#### Life Events and Daily Hassles

Think about your own life. What events have created the most stress for you? Were they big problems or clusters, like the breakup of a long-standing relationship, the death of someone you loved, your parents' divorce, or a personal injury? Or were they the everyday circumstances of your life, such as not having enough time to study, arguing with your girlfriend or boyfriend, not getting enough credit for work you did at your job?

Some health psychologists have studied the effects of individual significant life events. People who have had major life changes (loss of a close relative, the divorce of parents) have a higher incidence of cardiovascular disease and early death than

**stress** The response of individuals to *stressors,* which are circumstances and events that threaten and tax their coping abilities.

those who do not (Taylor, 2006). Other psychologists have evaluated the effects of *clusters* of life events and their possible influence on mental and physical health (Wilburn & Smith, 2005). One recent study found that adolescents who engaged in suicide ideation were more likely to have experienced negative life events in the past year than adolescents who did not engage in suicide ideation (Liu & Tein, 2005).

Researchers have found that when several stressors are simultaneously experienced, the effects may be compounded (Rutter & Garmezy, 1983). For example, one study found that people who felt besieged by two chronic life stressors were four times more likely to eventually need psychological services than those who had to cope with only one chronic stressor (Rutter, 1979). When people experience clusters of stressful life events, chances are they will become ill (Maddi, 1996).

However, the ability to predict illness from life events alone is modest. Total scores of life-events scales are frequently ineffective at predicting future health problems. A life-events checklist tells us nothing about a person's physiological makeup, constitutional strengths and weaknesses, ability to cope with stressful circumstances, support systems, or the nature of the social relationships involved. For some adolescents, the divorce of their parents, for example, might be less stressful than living in a family where their parents' marriage is filled with day-to-day tension. And the changes related to positive events, such as reconciling with a partner and gaining a new family member, are not as difficult to cope with as the changes that result from negative events.

Because of these limitations, some health psychologists believe information about daily hassles and daily uplifts provide better clues to the effects of stressors than life events (D'Angelo & Wierzbicki, 2003). Enduring a boring and tense job and living in poverty do not show up on scales of major life events. Yet the everyday tension involved in these living conditions creates a highly stressful life and, in some cases, psychological disorder or illness.

What are the biggest hassles for college students? One study showed that the most frequent daily hassles of college students were wasting time, being lonely, and worrying about meeting high achievement standards (Kanner & others, 1981). In fact, the fear of failing in our success-oriented world often plays a role in college students' depression. College students also found that the small things in life—having fun, laughing, going to movies, getting along well with friends, and completing a task—were their main sources of daily uplifts.

Critics of the daily-hassles approach argue that it suffers from some of the same weaknesses as life-events scales (Dohrenwend & Shrout, 1985). For example, knowing about a person's daily irritations and problems tells us nothing about her or his perceptions of stressors, physiological resilience to stress, or coping ability or strategies. Further, the daily-hassles and daily-uplifts scale has not been consistently related to objective measures of health and illness.

## *Through the Eyes of Adolescents*

### ALL STRESSED OUT

"Some of my friends are so messed up. My friend Abby is depressed all the time. She secretly told me that she thinks about killing herself. I want to tell someone, but she made me promise not to. I don't know what to do. I'm pretty sure my other friend Alexandra has an eating disorder. She's constantly talking about how many calories something has, and all she eats is lettuce! I try to be there for them, but I've got so much of my own stuff to deal with. I feel anxious and depressed all of the time. I don't know what to do."

*—Lauren*

(*Source:* Zager & Rubenstein, 2002, p. 141)

**Sociocultural Factors** Sociocultural factors help to determine which stressors individuals are likely to encounter, whether they are likely to perceive events as stressful or not, and how they believe stressors should be confronted (Berry, 2007; Berry & others, 2006). As examples of sociocultural factors involved in stress, let's examine gender, conflict between cultures, and poverty.

Do males and females respond to stressors in the same way? Recently, Shelley Taylor and her colleagues (2000; Taylor, 2004, 2006) proposed that females are less

*What characterizes the acculturative stress of immigrant adolescents in the United States?*

likely to respond to stressful and threatening situations with a fight-or-flight response than males are. They argue that females are likelier to "tend and befriend." That is, females often respond to stressful situations by protecting themselves and others through nurturing behaviors (the *tend* part of the model) and forming alliances with a larger social group, especially one populated by other women (the *befriend* part of the model).

Is there evidence for this model? Taylor (2002) cites the following. Although females do show the same immediate hormonal and sympathetic nervous system response to acute stress that males do, other factors can intervene and make the fight-or-flight response less likely in females. In terms of the fight response, male aggression is regulated by androgen hormones, such as testosterone, and is linked to sympathetic nervous system reactivity and hostility. In contrast, female aggression appears to be more cerebral in nature, moderated more by social circumstances, learning, culture, and the situation.

**Acculturative stress** refers to the negative consequences that result from contact between two distinctive cultural groups. Many individuals who have immigrated to the United States have experienced acculturative stress (Berry, 2007; Berry & others, 2006).

South Florida middle school teacher Daniel Arnoux (1998) learned firsthand about acculturative stress when he called out a student's name in his class and asked her if she was Haitian. She was so embarrassed by his question that she slid under her seat and disappeared from his view. Later she told him, "You are not supposed to say you are Haitian around here!" That is when Arnoux realized how stressful school could be for many immigrant students, some of whom were beaten and harassed for being Haitian. He began developing lessons to help students gain empathy and tolerance for individuals from different ethnic and cultural backgrounds.

Poverty can cause considerable stress for individuals and families (Compas, 2004; Fairbrother & others, 2005; McLoyd, Aikens, & Burton, 2006). One expert on coping in youth, Bruce Compas (2004, p. 279), calls poverty "the single most important social problem facing young people in the United States." As we saw in Chapter 12, chronic conditions such as inadequate housing, dangerous neighborhoods, burdensome responsibilities, and economic uncertainties are potent stressors in the lives of the poor. Adolescents are more likely to experience threatening and uncontrollable life events if they live in low-income contexts than if they live in more economically robust contexts (Conger & Dogan, 2007).

### Coping

Not every adolescent and emerging adult responds the same way to stress. Some youth throw in the towel when the slightest thing goes wrong in their lives. Others are motivated to work hard to find solutions to personal problems, and some successfully adjust to even extremely taxing circumstances. A stressful circumstance can be rendered considerably less stressful if you know how to cope with it (Corbin & others, 2006; Greenberg, 2006).

**What Is Coping?** **Coping** involves managing taxing circumstances, expending effort to solve life's problems, and seeking to master or reduce stress. What makes the difference between effective and ineffective efforts to cope?

Characteristics of the individual provide part of the answer. Success in coping has been linked with several characteristics, including a sense of personal control, positive emotions, and personal resources (Folkman & Moskowitz, 2004). Success in coping, however, also depends on the strategies used and on the

**acculturative stress** The negative consequences that result from contact between two distinctive cultural groups.

**coping** Involves managing taxing circumstances, expending effort to solve life's problems, and seeking to master or reduce stress.

context (Frydenberg, 2008). People have many ways of coping—some more successful than others.

*How can problem-focused and emotion-focused coping be distinguished?*

**Problem-Focused and Emotion-Focused Coping** One way of classifying coping strategies has been especially influential among psychologists who study coping: problem-focused coping and emotion-focused coping, which was proposed by Richard Lazarus (1993, 2000).

**Problem-focused coping** is Lazarus' term for the strategy of squarely facing one's troubles and trying to solve them. For example, if you are having trouble with a class, you might go to the study skills center at your college or university and enter a training program to learn how to study more effectively. Having done so, you have faced your problem and attempted to do something about it. A review of 39 research studies documented that problem-focused coping was associated with positive change following trauma and adversity (Linley & Joseph, 2004).

**Emotion-focused coping** is Lazarus' term for responding to stress in an emotional manner, especially by using defensive mechanisms. Emotion-focused coping includes avoiding a problem, rationalizing what has happened, denying it is occurring, laughing it off, or calling on our religious faith for support. If you use emotion-focused coping, you might avoid going to a class that you find difficult. You might say the class doesn't matter, deny that you are having a problem, laugh and joke about it with your friends, or pray that you will do better. This is not necessarily a good way to face a problem. For example, in one study, depressed individuals tried to avoid facing problems more than individuals who were not depressed (Ebata & Moos, 1989). In one study of inner-city youth, emotion-focused coping was linked to an increased risk for developing problems (Tolan & others, 2004).

Sometimes emotion-focused coping is adaptive. For example, denial is a protective mechanism for dealing with the flood of feelings that comes when the reality of death or dying becomes too great. Denial can protect against the destructive impact of shock by postponing the time when you have to deal with stress. In other circumstances, however, emotion-focused coping is maladaptive. Denying that the person you were dating doesn't love you anymore when that person has become engaged to someone else keeps you from getting on with your life.

Many individuals successfully use both problem-focused and emotion-focused coping to deal with a stressful circumstance (Pincus & Friedman, 2004). For example, in one study, individuals said they used both problem-focused and emotion-focused coping strategies in 98 percent of the stressful encounters they face (Folkman & Lazarus, 1980). Over the long term, though, problem-focused coping usually works better than emotion-focused coping (Heppner & Lee, 2001).

**Thinking Positively** Thinking positively and avoiding negative thoughts is a good strategy when trying to handle stress in just about any circumstance (Aronowitz, 2005). Why? A positive mood improves our ability to process information efficiently and enhances self-esteem. In most cases, an optimistic attitude is superior to a pessimistic one. It gives us a sense that we are controlling our environment, much like what Albert Bandura (2001, 2004, 2006, 2007a, b) talks about when he describes the importance of self-efficacy in coping.

**Support** Support from others is an important aspect of being able to cope with stress (Wang & Yeh, 2005). Close, positive attachments to others—such as family members, friends, or a mentor—consistently show up as buffers to stress in adolescents' and emerging adults' lives (Mikulincer & Shaver, 2007). In one study, adolescents coped more effectively with stress when they had a close affective relationship with their mothers (Wagner, Cohen, & Brook, 1991). In another study, peers were the

**problem-focused coping** Lazarus' term for the strategy of squarely facing one's troubles and trying to solve them.

**emotion-focused coping** Lazarus' term for responding to stress in an emotional manner, especially by using defense mechanisms.

## Careers in ADOLESCENT DEVELOPMENT

**Luis Vargas**
**Child Clinical Psychologist**

Luis Vargas is Director of the Clinical Child Psychology Internship Program and a professor in the Department of Psychiatry at the University of New Mexico Health Sciences Center. He also is Director of Psychology at the University of New Mexico Children's Psychiatric Hospital.

Dr. Vargas obtained an undergraduate degree in psychology from St. Edwards University in Texas, a master's degree in psychology from Trinity University in Texas, and a Ph.D. in clinical psychology from the University of Nebraska–Lincoln.

His main interests are cultural issues and the assessment and treatment of children, adolescents, and families. He is motivated to find better ways to provide culturally responsive mental health services. One of his special interests is the treatment of Latino youth for delinquency and substance abuse.

Luis Vargas (*left*) conducting a child therapy session with an adolescent girl.

most likely source of support for adolescents, followed by mothers (O'Brien, 1990). In this study, peers provided more support than siblings did in all categories and more than both parents in all areas except financial support, future/career planning, and personal values. Siblings provided more support for dating than mothers did.

Individuals who provide support can recommend specific actions and plans to help an adolescent or emerging adult under stress cope more effectively. For example, a mentor or counselor might notice that an adolescent is overloaded with schoolwork and this is causing considerable stress. The mentor or counselor might suggest ways for the adolescent or emerging adult to manage time better or delegate tasks more efficiently. Friends and family members can reassure the adolescent or emerging adult under stress that he or she is a valuable person who is loved by others. Knowing that others care allows adolescents and emerging adults to cope with stress with greater assurance.

**Contexts and Coping** Coping is not a stand-alone process; it is influenced by the demands and resources of the environment. Strategies for coping need to be evaluated in the specific context in which they occur (Folkman & Moskowitz, 2004; Meyers & Miller, 2004). For example, a particular strategy may be effective in one situation but not another, depending on the extent to which the situation is controllable. Thus, it is adaptive to engage in problem-focused coping before an exam and in mental disengagement while waiting for the results. The contextual approach to coping points to the importance of *coping flexibility,* the ability to modify coping strategies to match the demands of the situation (Lester, Smart, & Baum, 1994).

To read about one individual who helps adolescents cope with stress, see the *Careers in Adolescent Development* interlude. And to read further about coping strategies, see the *Health and Well-Being* interlude, where we summarize and elaborate on some of the strategies already discussed and include several others.

## Health and Well-Being

### COPING STRATEGIES IN ADOLESCENCE AND EMERGING ADULTHOOD

Here are some effective coping strategies that can benefit adolescents and emerging adults:

- ***Think positively and optimistically.*** Thinking positively and avoiding negative thoughts is a good strategy when trying to handle stress in just about any circumstance. Why? A positive mood improves the ability to process information efficiently and enhances self-esteem. In most cases, an optimistic attitude is superior to a pessimistic one. It provides a sense of controlling the environment, much like what Albert Bandura (2001, 2004, 2006, 2007a, b) talks about when he describes the importance of self-efficacy in coping.

- ***Increase self-control.*** Developing better self-control is an effective coping strategy. Coping successfully with a problem usually takes time—weeks, months, even years in some cases. Many adolescents and emerging adults who engage in problematic behavior have difficulty maintaining a plan for coping because their problematic behavior provides immediate gratification (such as eating, smoking, drinking, going to a party instead of studying for an exam, and so on). To maintain a self-control program over time, it is important to be able to forego immediate satisfaction (Mischel, 2004).
- ***Seek social support.*** Researchers consistently have found that social support helps adolescents and emerging adults cope with stress (Arnold, 2004; Janisse & others, 2004). For example, depressed adolescents and emerging adults usually have fewer and less supportive relationships with family members, friends, and co-workers than their counterparts who are not depressed (Nolen-Hoeksema, 2007).
- ***See a counselor or therapist.*** If adolescents and emerging adults are not able to cope with the problem(s) they are encountering, it is very important for them to seek professional help from a counselor or therapist. Most colleges have a counseling service that provides unbiased, professional advice to students.
- ***Use multiple coping strategies.*** Adolescents and emerging adults who face stressful circumstances have many strategies from which to choose (Cheng & Cheung, 2005). Often it is wise to choose more than one because a single strategy may not work in a particular context (Huang & others, 2005). For example, an adolescent or emerging adult who has experienced a stressful life event or a cluster of such life events (such as the death of a parent or the breakup of a romantic relationship) might see a mental health professional, seek social support, exercise regularly, reduce drinking, and practice relaxation. When used alone, no one of these strategies might be adequate, but their combined effect may allow the adolescent or emerging adult to cope successfully with stress.

## Resilience

Even when adolescents and emerging adults are faced with adverse conditions, such as poverty, are there characteristics that help buffer and make them resilient to developmental outcomes? As we saw in Chapter 1, some adolescents and emerging adults do triumph over life's adversities. Ann Masten (2001, 2006; Masten & Coatsworth, 1998; Masten & Obradović, 2007; Masten, Obradović, & Burt, 2006; Masten & Reed, 2002) analyzed the research literature on resilience and concluded that a number of individual factors (such as good intellectual functioning), family factors (close relationship to a caring parent figure), and extrafamilial factors (bonds to prosocial adults outside the family) characterize resilient adolescents (see Figure 13.2).

Masten and her colleagues (2006) recently described resilience in emerging adulthood. They concluded that being resilient in adolescence is linked to continuing to be resilient in emerging adulthood, but that resilience can develop in emerging adulthood. They also indicated that during emerging adulthood some individuals become motivated to improve their lives and develop an improved ability to plan and make more effective decisions that place their life on a more positive developmental course. In some instances, a particular person may influence an emerging adult in very positive ways, as was the case in Michael Maddaus' life, which we described at the beginning

| Source | Characteristic |
|---|---|
| Individual | Good intellectual functioning<br>Appealing, sociable, easygoing disposition<br>Self-confidence, high self-esteem<br>Talents<br>Faith |
| Family | Close relationship to caring parent figure<br>Authoritative parenting: warmth, structure, high expectations<br>Socioeconomic advantages<br>Connections to extended supportive family networks |
| Extrafamilial context | Bonds to caring adults outside the family<br>Connections to positive organizations<br>Attending effective schools |

**FIGURE 13.2 Characteristics of Resilient Children and Adolescents**

of Chapter 1. You might recall that after a childhood and adolescence filled with stress, conflict, disappointment, and problems, his connection with a very competent mentor in emerging adulthood helped him to turn his life around, and he went on to become a successful surgeon. According to Masten and her colleagues (2006), a romantic relationship or the birth of a child may stimulate change and lead an emerging adult to develop a stronger commitment to a positive future.

**REVIEW AND REFLECT ◆ LEARNING GOAL 1**

**1 Discuss the nature of problems in adolescence and emerging adulthood.**

***Review***

- How can the biopsychosocial approach be characterized?
- What is the developmental psychopathology approach like?
- What are some general characteristics of adolescent and emerging adult problems?
- What is the nature of stress and coping in adolescence and emerging adulthood?
- How can the resilience of some adolescents and emerging adults be explained?

***Reflect***

- Why do you think adolescent and emerging adult males are more likely to develop externalizing problems and adolescent and emerging adult females internalizing problems?

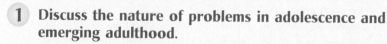

## 2 Problems and Disorders

Drug Use | Juvenile Delinquency | Depression and Suicide | Eating Disorders

What are some of the major problems and disorders in adolescence and emerging adulthood? They include drugs and alcohol abuse, juvenile delinquency, school-related problems, high-risk sexual behavior, depression and suicide, and eating disorders. We discussed school-related and sexual problems in earlier chapters. Here we examine the other problems, beginning with drugs.

### Drug Use

Why do adolescents and emerging adults use drugs? How pervasive is adolescent and emerging adult drug use in the United States? What are the nature and effects of various drugs taken by adolescents and emerging adults? What factors contribute to adolescent and emerging adult drug use? Let's now explore these questions.

**Why Do Adolescents and Emerging Adults Take Drugs?** Since the beginning of history, humans have searched for substances that would sustain and protect them and also act on the nervous system to produce pleasurable sensations. Individuals are attracted to drugs because drugs help them to adapt to an ever-changing environment. Smoking, drinking, and taking drugs reduce tension and frustration, relieve boredom and fatigue, and in some cases help adolescents to escape the harsh realities of their world. Drugs provide pleasure by giving inner peace, joy, relaxation, kaleidoscopic perceptions, surges of exhilaration, or prolonged heightened sensation. They may help some adolescents to get along better in their world. For example, amphetamines might help the adolescent to stay awake to study for an exam. Drugs also satisfy adolescents' curiosity—some adolescents take drugs because they are intrigued by sensational accounts of drugs in the media, whereas others may listen to a popular song and wonder if the drugs described can provide them with unique, profound experiences. Drugs are also taken for social reasons, allowing adolescents to feel more comfortable and to enjoy the company of others (Ksir, Hart, & Ray, 2006).

But the use of drugs for personal gratification and temporary adaptation carries a very high price tag: drug dependence, personal and social disorganization, and a predisposition to serious and sometimes fatal diseases (Hales, 2006; Kinney, 2006). Thus, what is intended as adaptive behavior is maladaptive in the long run. For example, prolonged cigarette smoking, in which the active drug is nicotine, is one of the most serious yet preventable health problems. Smoking has been described by some experts as "suicide in slow motion."

As adolescents and emerging adults continue to take a drug, their bodies develop **tolerance,** which means that a greater amount of the drug is needed to produce the same effect. The first time someone takes 2 milligrams of Valium, for example, the drug will make them feel very relaxed. But after taking the pill every day for six months, the same person might need 10 milligrams to achieve the same calming effect.

**Physical dependence** is the physical need for a drug that is accompanied by unpleasant withdrawal symptoms when the drug is discontinued. **Psychological dependence** is the strong desire and craving to repeat the use of a drug because of various emotional reasons, such as a feeling of well-being and reduction of stress. Both physical and psychological dependence mean that the drug is playing a powerful role in the adolescent's and emerging adult's life.

**Trends in Overall Drug Use** The 1960s and 1970s were a time of marked increases in the use of illicit drugs. During the social and political unrest of those years, many youth turned to marijuana, stimulants, and hallucinogens. Increases in adolescent and emerging adult alcohol consumption during this period also were noted (Robinson & Greene, 1988). More precise data about drug use by adolescents and emerging adults have been collected in recent years. Each year since 1975, Lloyd Johnston and his colleagues, working at the Institute of Social Research at the University of Michigan, have carefully monitored the drug use of America's high school seniors in a wide range of public and private high schools. Since 1991, they also have surveyed drug use by eighth- and tenth-graders, and from time to time assess drug use in emerging adults and continuing into the middle adulthood years. The University of Michigan study is called the Monitoring the Future Study. In 2006, the study surveyed 50,000 secondary school students (Johnston & others, 2007).

The use of drugs among U.S. secondary school students declined in the 1980s but began to increase in the early 1990s (Johnston & others, 2007). In the late 1990s and early part of the twenty-first century, the proportion of secondary school students reporting the use of any illicit drug has been declining. The overall decline in the use of illicit drugs by adolescents during this time frame is approximately one-third for eighth-graders, one-fourth for tenth-graders, and one-eighth for twelfth-graders. Figure 13.3 shows the overall trends in drug use by U.S. high school seniors since 1975 and by U.S. eighth- and tenth-graders since 1991. The most notable declines in drug use by U.S. adolescents in the twenty-first century have occurred for marijuana, LSD, cocaine, Ecstasy, steroids, and cigarettes.

Nonetheless, even with the recent decline in use, the United States still has one of the highest rates of adolescent drug use of any industrialized nation. As shown in

**tolerance** The condition in which a greater amount of a drug is needed to produce the same effect as a smaller amount produced in the past.

**physical dependence** Physical need for a drug that is accompanied by unpleasant withdrawal symptoms when the drug is discontinued.

**psychological dependence** Strong desire and craving to repeat the use of a drug for various emotional reasons, such as a feeling of well-being and reduction of distress.

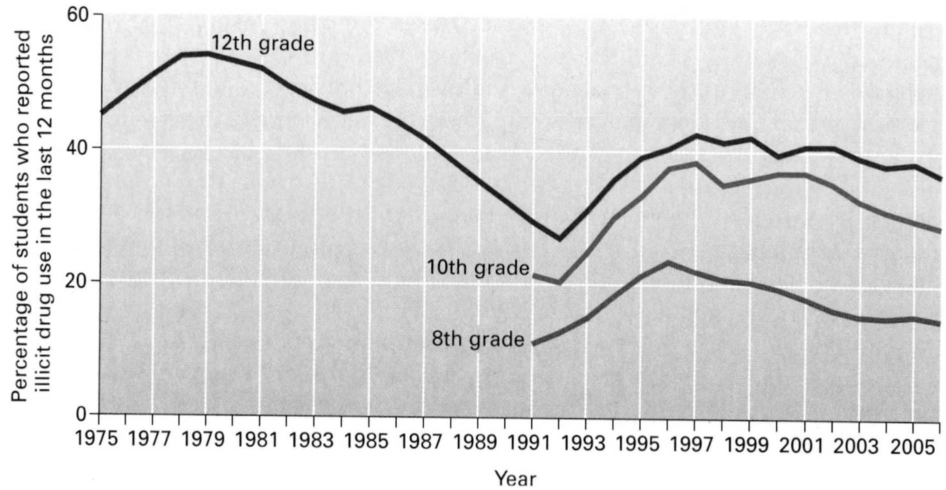


**FIGURE 13.3 Trends in Drug Use by U.S. Eighth-, Tenth-, and Twelfth-Grade Students** This graph shows the percentage of U.S. eighth-, tenth-, and twelfth-grade students who reported having taken an illicit drug in the last 12 months from 1991 to 2006 for eighth- and tenth-graders, and from 1975 to 2006 for twelfth-graders (Johnston & others, 2007).

Figure 13.4, a higher percentage of U.S. adolescents have used an illicit drug than adolescents in most European countries (Hibell & others, 2004). In most instances, the illicit drug used by adolescents in these countries was marijuana. Moreover, the University of Michigan survey likely underestimates the percentage of adolescents who take drugs because it does not include high school dropouts, who have a higher rate of drug use than do students who are still in school. Johnston and his colleagues (2005) note that "generational forgetting" contributed to the rise of adolescent drug use in the 1990s, with adolescents' beliefs about the dangers of drugs eroding considerably. The recent downturn in drug use by U.S. adolescents has been attributed to such factors as an increase in the perceived dangers of drug use and the tragedy of the terrorist attacks of September 11, 2001, having a sobering effect on youth (Johnston & others, 2007).

Although drug use in adolescence is high in the United States, it increases further in emerging adulthood (Park & others, 2006). In one national survey, approximately 20 percent of U.S. 18- to 25-year-olds reported recent illicit drug use compared with 11 percent of adolescents (Substance Abuse and Mental Health Services Administration, 2005).

Let's now consider separately a number of drugs that are abused by some adolescents and emerging adults.

**FIGURE 13.4 Percentage of European and U.S. Adolescents Who Reported Using an Illicit Drug at Any Point in Their Lifetime** *Note:* The numbers in the parentheses are for all adolescents; data were collected in 2003.

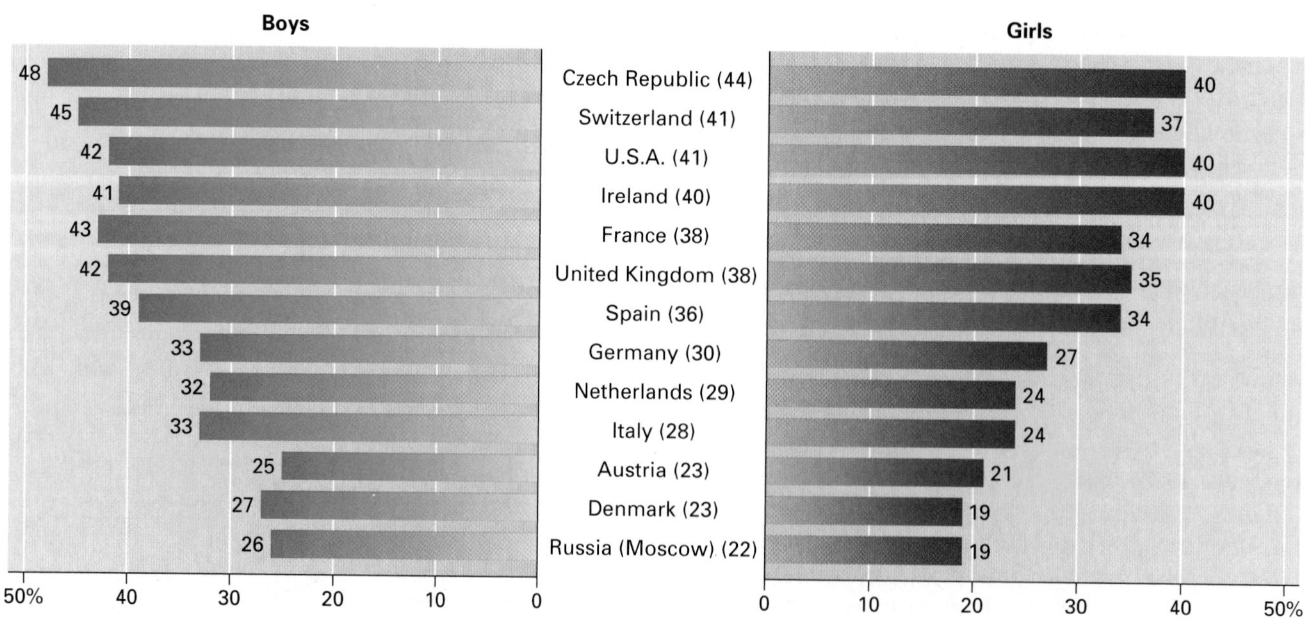

**Alcohol** To learn more about the role of alcohol in adolescents' and emerging adults' lives, we examine how alcohol influences behavior and brain activity, the use and abuse of alcohol by adolescents and emerging adults, and risk factors in alcohol abuse.

**Effects of Alcohol on Adolescents' and Emerging Adults' Behavior and Brain Activity** Alcohol is an extremely potent drug. It acts on the body as a depressant and slows down the brain's activities. If used in sufficient quantities, it will damage or even kill biological tissues, including muscle and brain cells. The mental and behavioral effects of alcohol include reduced inhibition and impaired judgment. Initially, adolescents feel more talkative and more confident when they use alcohol. However, skilled performances, such as driving, become impaired, and as more alcohol is ingested, intellectual functioning, behavioral control, and judgment become less efficient. Eventually, the drinker becomes drowsy and falls asleep. With extreme intoxication, the drinker may lapse into a coma. Each of these behavioral effects varies according to how the adolescent's body metabolizes alcohol, the individual's body weight, the amount of alcohol ingested, and whether previous drinking has led to tolerance.

Alcohol is the drug most widely used by U.S. adolescents and emerging adults. Alcoholism is the third-leading killer in the United States. Each year, approximately 25,000 individuals are killed, and 1.5 million injured, by drunk drivers. In 65 percent of the aggressive male acts against females, the offender has been under the influence of alcohol (Goodman & others, 1986). In numerous instances of drunk driving and assaults on females, the offenders have been adolescents and emerging adults. More than 13 million individuals are classified as alcoholics, many of whom established their drinking habits during adolescence.

**Alcohol Use in Adolescence and Emerging Adulthood** Sizable drops at all three grade levels in the percentage of U.S. students who say that they drank alcohol in the past 30 days have recently occurred (Johnston & others, 2007). The 30-day prevalence of alcohol use by eighth-graders fell from a 1996 high of 26 percent to 17 percent in 2006. From 2000 to 2006, 30-day prevalence among tenth-graders fell from 41 to 34 percent. Monthly prevalence among high school seniors was 72 percent in 1980 but declined to 45 percent in 2006. Binge drinking (defined in the University of Michigan surveys as having five or more drinks in a row in the last two weeks) by high school seniors fell from 41 percent in 1980 to 30 percent in 2006. Binge drinking by eighth- and tenth-graders has dropped in recent years. A consistent sex difference occurs in binge drinking, with males engaging in this more than females. In 2005, 33 percent of male high school seniors said they had been drunk in the last two weeks, compared with 23 percent of their female counterparts.

Do U.S. adolescents drink alcohol more than their counterparts in other countries? In a comparison of U.S. and European 15- to 16-year olds, frequent drinking was more prevalent in Europe than the United States, being especially pronounced in western European countries such as Denmark (Hibell & others, 2004) (see Figure 13.5).

The transition from high school to college may be a critical transition in alcohol abuse (Schulenberg & others, 2001). The large majority of older adolescents and youth who drink recognize that drinking is common among people their age and is largely acceptable, even expected by their peers. They also may perceive some social and coping benefits from alcohol use and even occasional heavy drinking.

In 2005, approximately 40 percent of U.S. college students reported that they drink heavily, a rate that is unchanged since 1993 (Johnston & others, 2006). The effects of heavy drinking take their toll on them. In a national survey of drinking patterns on 140 campuses, almost half of the binge drinkers reported problems that included missing classes, physical injuries, trouble with police, and having unprotected sex (Wechsler & others, 1994). Also in this study, binge-drinking college students were 11 times more likely to drive after drinking, and twice as likely to have unprotected sex, than college students who did not binge drink. In another study, first-year college students who met the criteria of alcohol dependence were more

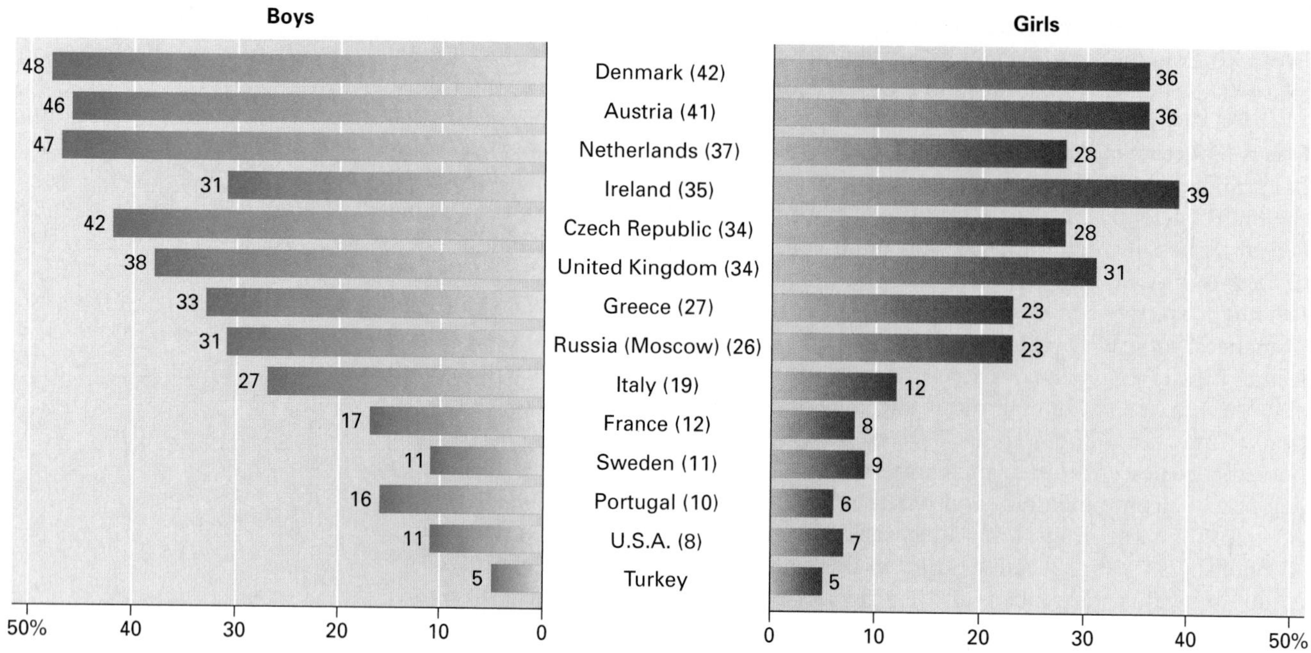


**FIGURE 13.5 Percentage of European and U.S. 15- to 16-Year-Olds Who Reported Drinking Alcoholic Beverages 20 Times or More During the Last 12 Months**
*Note:* The numbers in the parentheses are for all adolescents; data were collected in 2003.

*What kinds of problems are associated with binge drinking in college?*

likely to have failing grades than their counterparts who did not meet the criteria (Aertgeerts & Buntinx, 2002).

In one research program, more than 40,000 full-time U.S. college students were asked about their drinking habits in 1993, 1997, 1999, and 2001 (Wechsler & others, 2002). Binge-drinking rates (men who drank five or more drinks in a row and women who drank four or more drinks at least once in the two weeks prior to the questionnaire) remained remarkably consistent—at about 44 percent—over the eight years. Further, almost 75 percent of underage students living in fraternities or sororities were binge drinkers, and 70 percent of traditional-age college students who lived away from home were binge drinkers. The lowest rate of binge drinking—25 percent—occurred for students living at home with their parents. Another recent study found "that higher rates of substance use among U.S. college students who join fraternities or sororities predate their college attendance, and that membership in a sorority or a fraternity is associated with considerably greater than average increases in heavy episodic drinking and annual marijuana use in college" (McCabe & others, 2005, p. 512).

A special concern is the increase in binge drinking by females during emerging adulthood (Young & others, 2005). One study found a 125 percent increase in binge drinking at all-women colleges from 1993 through 2001 (Wechsler & others, 2002).

**Risk Factors in Alcohol Abuse** Among the risk factors in adolescents' and emerging adults' abuse of alcohol are heredity, family influences, peer relations, and certain personality and motivational characteristics. There is evidence of a genetic predisposition to alcoholism, although it is important to remember that both genetic and environmental factors are involved (Jang, 2005).

Adolescents' and emerging adults' alcohol use is related to parent and peer relations. Adolescents who drink heavily often come from unhappy homes in which there is a great deal of tension, have parents who give them little nurturance, are insecurely attached to their parents, have parents who use poor family-management practices (low monitoring, unclear expectations, few rewards for positive behavior), and have parents who sanction alcohol use (Barnes, Farrell, & Banerjee, 1995; Peterson & others, 1994).

The peer group is especially important in adolescent and emerging adult alcohol abuse. In one study, exposure to peer use and misuse of alcohol, along with susceptibility to peer pressure, were strong predictors of adolescent alcohol abuse (Dielman, Shope, & Butchart, 1990). Whether adolescents have older, same-age, or younger peers as friends is also related to alcohol and drug abuse in adolescence. In one study, adolescents who took drugs were more likely to have older friends than were their counterparts who did not take drugs (Blyth, Durant, & Moosbrugger, 1985).

In another study, the Friendly PEERsuasion program reduced the incidence of drinking among girls who already drank and delayed the onset of drinking among girls who had not drunk previously (Girls, Inc., 1991). This program also improved the girls' resistance skills; the participants indicated that they were less likely than nonparticipants to stay in a drinking situation. The PEERsuasion program consists of 14 one-hour sessions that include enjoyable, interactive activities targeted at avoiding drug use. Adolescents are taught healthy ways to manage stress, detect media and peer pressure to use drugs, and practice skills for making responsible decisions about drug use. Then the girls serve as peer leaders to plan and implement substance-abuse prevention activities for 6- to 10-year-olds.

*What are some factors that contribute to whether adolescents drink heavily?*

In one study of more than 3,000 eleventh-grade students, peer pressure was strongly related to alcohol use (Borden, Donnermeyer, & Scheer, 2001). Also in this study, participation in school-based and non-school-based activities was related to lower incidence of drug use and getting drunk less in the past year.

In another study, three types of tenth-grade adolescent drinkers were found: (1) those involved in problem behaviors at high rates; (2) highly anxious adolescents who report that they have performance anxiety; and (3) popular, well-functioning adolescents (these included crowds such as "jocks" and "brains") (Barber, Eccles, & Stone, 2001). Later, as they were making the transition to adulthood, the "jocks" and "criminals" showed the highest rates of being in substance-abuse rehabilitation programs. Thus, associating with certain crowds in adolescence is linked with drinking behavior in adolescence and alcohol problems in the transition to adulthood.

A strong family support system is clearly an important preventive strategy in reducing alcohol abuse by adolescents (Waldron, Brody, & Slesnick, 2001). Are there others? Would raising the minimum drinking age have an effect? In one investigation, raising the minimum drinking age did lower the frequency of automobile crashes involving adolescents, but raising the drinking age alone did not reduce alcohol abuse (Wagenaar, 1983). Another effort to reduce alcohol abuse involved a school-based program in which adolescents discussed alcohol-related issues with peers (Wodarski & Hoffman, 1984). At a one-year follow-up, students in the intervention schools reported less alcohol abuse and had discouraged each other's drinking more often than had students in other schools who had not been involved in the peer discussion of alcohol-related issues. Efforts to help the adolescent with a drinking problem vary enormously. Therapy may include working with other family members, peer group discussion sessions, and specific behavioral techniques. Unfortunately, there has been little interest in identifying different types of adolescent alcohol abusers and then attempting to match treatment programs to the particular problems of the adolescent drinker. Most efforts simply assume that adolescents with drinking problems are a homogeneous group, and they do not take into account the varying developmental patterns and social histories of different adolescents. Some adolescents with drinking problems may be helped more through family therapy, others through peer counseling, and yet others through intensive behavioral strategies, depending on the type of drinking problem and the social agents who have the most influence on the adolescent (Maguin, Zucker, & Fitzgerald, 1995).

In one study, binge-drinking trajectories from early adolescence to emerging adulthood were studied (Chassin, Pitts, & Prost, 2001). Individuals who were binge drinkers at 18 to 23 years of age often began drinking early and heavily, had parents who had alcohol problems, associated with peers who drank heavily, took other drugs, and engaged in antisocial behavior. These risk factors for binge drinking in emerging adulthood were assessed when the individuals were 13 years of age.

A recent research review examined the motives and personality traits that are linked to drinking in adolescence and emerging adulthood (Kuntsche & others, 2006). A developmental trend indicated the presence of general, undifferentiated motives in early adolescence to more gender-specific drinking motives in late adolescence and emerging adulthood. In particular, extraverted, sensation-seeking males were more likely to drink for self-enhancement motives, whereas neurotic, anxious females were more likely to drink for social coping motives.

It is not just alcohol use by U.S. adolescents that is a major concern. There also is concern about adolescent use of other drugs. Next, we examine adolescent use of a number of other drugs, beginning with hallucinogens.

**Hallucinogens** **Hallucinogens,** also called psychedelic (mind-altering) drugs, are drugs that modify an individual's perceptual experiences and produce hallucinations. First, we discuss LSD, which has powerful hallucinogenic properties, and then marijuana, a milder hallucinogen.

**LSD** *LSD (lysergic acid diethylamide)* is a hallucinogen that, even in low doses, produces striking perceptual changes. Objects glow and change shape. Colors become kaleidoscopic. Fabulous images unfold as users close their eyes. Sometimes the images are pleasurable, sometimes unpleasant or frightening. In one drug "trip," an LSD user might experience a cascade of beautiful colors and wonderful scenes; in another drug trip, the images might be frightening and grotesque. LSD's effects on the body may include dizziness, nausea, and tremors. Emotional and cognitive effects may include rapid mood swings or impaired attention and memory.

LSD's popularity in the 1960s and 1970s was followed by a reduction in use by the mid-1970s as its unpredictable effects become publicized. However, adolescents' use of LSD increased in the 1990s (Johnston & others, 2007). In 1985, 1.8 percent of U.S. high school seniors reported LSD use in the last 30 days; in 1994, this increased to 4.0 percent. However, LSD use had declined to 2.3 percent in 2001 and dropped further by 2006 to 0.6 percent (Johnston & others, 2007).

**Marijuana** *Marijuana,* a milder hallucinogen than LSD, comes from the hemp plant *Cannabis sativa,* which originated in Central Asia but is now grown in most parts of the world. Marijuana is made of the hemp plant's dry leaves; its dried resin is known as hashish. The active ingredient in marijuana is THC, which stands for the chemical delta-9-tetrahydrocannabinol. Because marijuana is metabolized slowly, its effects may be present over the course of several days.

The physical effects of marijuana include increases in pulse rate and blood pressure, reddening of the eyes, coughing, and dryness of the mouth. Psychological effects include a mixture of excitatory, depressive, and hallucinatory characteristics, making the drug difficult to classify. The drug can produce spontaneous and unrelated ideas, distort perceptions of time and place, and increase sensitivity to sounds and colors. An individual who is "high" on marijuana may become very talkative or may cease talking. Because marijuana also can impair attention and memory, smoking marijuana is not conducive to optimal school performance. When marijuana is used daily in heavy amounts, it also can impair the human reproductive system and may be involved in some birth defects.

Marijuana use by adolescents decreased in the 1980s. For example, in 1979, 37 percent of high school seniors said they had used marijuana in the last month, but in 1992 that figure had dropped to 14 percent. Figure 13.6 shows the increase in marijuana use by eighth-, tenth-, and twelfth-graders in the United States in the early 1990s and the leveling off and slight decline in use in recent years (Johnston & others, 2007). In one analysis, the increased use of marijuana in the early 1990s was not related to such factors as religious commitment or grades but was linked with increased approval of using the drug and decreased perception that the drug is harmful (Johnston, O'Malley, & Bachman, 1999).

**hallucinogens** Also called psychedelic (mind-altering) drugs, these drugs alter an individual's perceptual experiences and produce hallucinations.

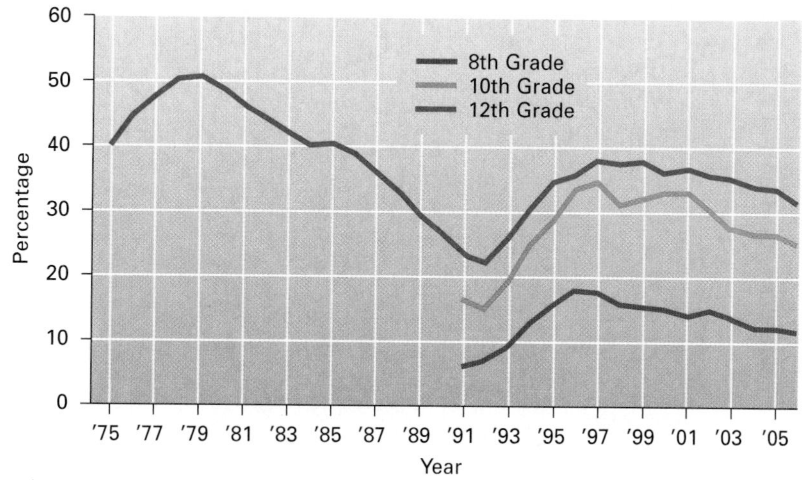


**FIGURE 13.6 Trends in Marijuana Use by U.S. Eighth-, Tenth-, and Twelfth-Graders: Use in the Past Year** Note the increase in marijuana use in the last half of the 1970s, the decreased use in the 1980s, the increased use in the 1990s, and the leveling off and slight decline in recent years (Johnston & others, 2007).

**Stimulants** **Stimulants** are drugs that increase the activity of the central nervous system. The most widely used stimulants are caffeine, nicotine, amphetamines, and cocaine. Stimulants increase heart rate, breathing, and temperature but decrease appetite. They increase energy, decrease feelings of fatigue, and lift mood and self-confidence. After the effects wear off, though, the user often becomes tired, irritable, and depressed and may experience headaches. Stimulants can be physically addictive.

**Cigarette Smoking** Cigarette smoking (in which the active drug is nicotine) is one of the most serious yet preventable health problems (Mathers & others, 2006). A recent world survey indicated that approximately 20 percent of adolescents in more than 130 countries use a tobacco product (Centers for Disease Control and Prevention, 2006). In the United States, smoking is likely to begin in grades seven through nine, although sizable portions of youth are still establishing regular smoking habits during high school and college. Since the national surveys by Johnston and others began in 1975, cigarettes have been the substance most frequently used on a daily basis by high school seniors (Johnston & others, 2007).

The peer group especially plays an important role in smoking (Picotte & others, 2006). In one study, the risk of current smoking was linked with peer networks in which at least half of the members smoked, one or two best friends smoked, and smoking was common in the school (Alexander & others, 2001).

Engaging in risk-taking behavior is also linked to cigarette smoking in adolescence. A longitudinal study compared adolescent smokers in 1991 and 2003 (Camenga, Klein, & Roy, 2006). Adolescent smokers in 2003 were more likely to engage in risk-taking behavior involving sex, drinking alcohol, and using a vehicle (not using a seat belt or bicycle helmet).

Cigarette smoking is decreasing among adolescents (see Figure 13.7). Cigarette smoking peaked in 1996 and 1997 and has declined since then. In the national survey by the Institute of Social Research, the percentage of U.S. adolescents who are current cigarette smokers has continued to decline in the early twenty-first century (Johnston & others, 2007). Following peak use in 1996, smoking rates for U.S. eighth-graders have fallen by 50 percent. In 2006, the percentage of adolescents who said they smoked cigarettes in the last 30 days were 21.6 percent (twelfth grade), 14.5 percent (tenth grade), and 8.7 percent (eighth grade).

There are a number of explanations for the decline in cigarette use by U.S. youth. These include increasing prices, less tobacco advertising reaching adolescents, more antismoking advertisements, and an increase in negative publicity about the tobacco industry (Myers & MacPherson, 2004). Since the mid-1990s an increasing percentage of adolescents have reported that they perceive cigarette smoking as dangerous, that they disapprove of it, that they are less accepting of being around smokers, and that they prefer to date nonsmokers (Johnston & others, 2007).

**stimulants** Drugs that increase the activity of the central nervous system.

**FIGURE 13.7** Trends in Cigarette Smoking by U.S. Secondary School Students

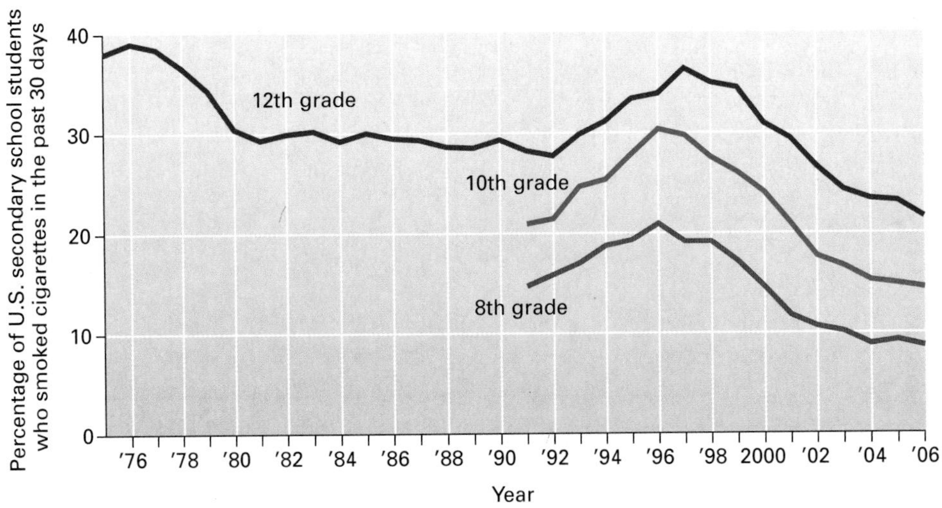


Do individuals smoke cigarettes more in emerging adulthood than adolescence? According to the 2003 National Survey on Drug Use and Health (NSCUH), 18- to 25-year-olds reported a smoking rate in the past month that was more than three times the rate of 12- to 17-year-olds (Substance Abuse and Mental Health Administration Services, 2005). The smoking rate of emerging adults in this survey was also 1.6 times the rate of individuals who were 26 years and older. Thus, cigarette smoking peaks during emerging adulthood (Park & others, 2006).

The devastating effects of early smoking were brought home in a research study that found that smoking in the adolescent years causes permanent genetic changes in the lungs and forever increases the risk of lung cancer, even if the smoker quits (Wiencke & others, 1999). The damage was much less likely among smokers in the study who started in their twenties. One of the remarkable findings in the study was that the early age of onset of smoking was more important in predicting genetic damage than how heavily the individuals smoked.

*"I'll tell you one thing. As soon as I'm thirteen I'm gonna stop!"*
Wayne Stayskal © Tribune Media Services, Inc. All Rights Reserved. Reprinted with permission.

In two studies, cigarette smoking in adolescence was linked with emotional problems. In the first study, more than 15,000 adolescents were tracked for one year to assess the possible link between cigarette smoking and depression (Goodman & Capitman, 2000). Those who began smoking during the one-year duration of the study were four times more likely to become depressed at the end of that year. In the second study, more than 600 adolescents (average age 16) were followed into their early adulthood years (average age 22) to discover possible connections between cigarette smoking in adolescence and the prevalence of mental disorders in early adulthood (Johnson & others, 2000). Those who smoked heavily as adolescents were far more likely to have anxiety disorders as adults.

Despite various campaigns to encourage stores to require identification for tobacco purchase, cigarettes are readily available to these underage youth. Of the eighth-graders, most of whom are 13 to 14 years of age, three-fourths said that they can get cigarettes fairly easily if they want them. By the tenth grade, more than 90 percent say they can buy cigarettes easily.

In another study, smoking initiation rates increased rapidly after 10 years of age and peaked at 13 to 14 years of age (Escobedo & others, 1993). Students who began smoking at 12 years of age or younger were more likely to be regular and heavy smokers than were students who began at older ages. Students who had participated in interscholastic sports were less likely to be regular and heavy smokers than were their counterparts who were not sports participants. In another study, adolescents whose parents smoked were more likely to be smokers themselves than were adolescents whose parents did not smoke (Kandel & Wu, 1995). Maternal smoking was more strongly related to smoking by young adolescents (especially girls) than paternal smoking was.

There is controversy about whether school-based programs are effective in reducing adolescent smoking. One recent review of school-based smoking prevention programs revealed little or no long-term effectiveness to age 18 or the twelfth grade (Wiehe & others, 2005). However, several other reviews concluded that a number of school-based programs have been documented to be effective in reducing adolescent smoking (Skara & Sussman, 2003; Sussman & others, 2005; Tobler & others, 2000). The need for effective intervention has prompted investigators to focus on those factors that place young adolescents at high risk for future smoking, especially social pressures from peers, family members, and the media (Copeland, Heim, & Rome, 2001; Kulig & others, 2001).

*What are some factors that contribute to adolescents' decision to smoke cigarettes?*

A number of researchers have developed strategies for interrupting behavioral patterns that lead to smoking (Bruess & Richardson, 1992; Perry, Kelder, & Komro, 1993). In one investigation, high school students were recruited to help seventh-grade students resist peer pressure to smoke (McAlister & others, 1980). The high school students encouraged the younger adolescents to resist the influence of high-powered ads suggesting that liberated women smoke by saying, "She is not really liberated if she is hooked on tobacco." The students also engaged in role-playing exercises called "chicken." In these situations, the high school students called the younger adolescents "chicken" for not trying a cigarette. The seventh-graders practiced resistance to the peer pressure by saying, "I'd be a real chicken if I smoked just to impress you." Following several sessions, the students in the smoking prevention group were 50 percent less likely to begin smoking compared with a group of seventh-grade students in a neighboring junior high school, even though the parents of both groups of students had the same smoking rate.

One comprehensive health approach that includes an attempt to curb cigarette smoking by adolescents was developed by clinical psychologist Cheryl Perry and her colleagues (1988). Three programs were developed based on peer group norms, healthy role models, and social skills training. Elected peer leaders were trained as instructors. In seventh grade, adolescents were offered "Keep It Clean," a six-session course emphasizing the negative effects of smoking. In eighth grade, students were involved in "Health Olympics," an approach that included exchanging greeting cards on smoking and health with peers in other countries. In ninth grade, students participated in "Shifting Gears," which included six sessions focused on social skills. In the social skills program, students critiqued media messages and created their own positive health videotapes. At the same time as the school intervention, a community-wide smoking cessation program as well as a diet and health awareness campaign were initiated. After five years, students who were involved in the smoking and health program were much less likely to smoke cigarettes, use marijuana, or drink alcohol than their counterparts who were not involved in the program.

**Cocaine** *Cocaine* is a stimulant that comes from the coca plant, native to Bolivia and Peru. For many years, Bolivians and Peruvians chewed on the plant to increase their stamina. Today, cocaine is either heated and the fumes inhaled or it is injected in the form of crystals or powder. The effect is a rush of euphoric feelings, which eventually wear off, followed by depressive feelings, lethargy, insomnia, and irritability. Cocaine can have a number of seriously damaging effects on the body, including heart attacks, strokes, and brain seizures.

How many adolescents use cocaine? Use of cocaine in the last 30 days by high school seniors dropped from a peak of 6.7 percent in 1985 to 2.5 percent in 2006 (Johnston & others, 2007). From 2000 to 2006, the percentage of U.S. students reporting that they use cocaine has slightly increased.

A growing percentage of high school students are reaching the conclusion that cocaine use entails considerable unpredictable risk. Still, the percentage of adolescents who have used cocaine is precariously high. About 1 of every 13 high school seniors has tried cocaine at least once.

A troublesome chapter in the cocaine story began in the 1980s with the advent of crack cocaine—an inexpensive, purified, smokable form of the drug. Because crack is snorted and enters the lungs, it delivers a stronger, quicker "rush" than regular cocaine. Crack use is especially heavy among non-college-bound youth in urban settings.

**Amphetamines** *Amphetamines,* often called "pep pills" and "uppers," are widely prescribed stimulants, sometimes appearing in the form of diet pills. Amphetamine use among high school seniors has decreased significantly. Use of amphetamines in the last 30 days by high school seniors declined from 10.7 percent in 1982 to 3.7 percent in 2005 (Johnston & others, 2007). However, use of over-the-counter stay-awake pills, which usually contain caffeine as their active ingredient, sharply increased. Although use of over-the-counter diet pills has decreased in recent years, fully 40 percent of today's females have tried using diet pills by the time they graduate from high school.

**Ecstasy** *Ecstasy,* the street name for the synthetic drug MDMA, has stimulant and hallucinogenic effects. Its chemical structure is similar to methamphetamines. It usually comes in a pill form. Tolerance builds up rapidly, so users may take three or four pills at a time. Ecstasy produces euphoric feelings and heightened sensations (especially touch and sight). The drug is popular at raves, all-night parties where youth dance with light sticks and other visual enhancements. Users often become hyperactive and sleepless. Ecstasy use can lead to dangerous increases in blood pressure, as well as a stroke or a heart attack. Repeated Ecstasy use may damage the areas of the brain that involve learning and memory, regulation of mood, sexual response, sleep, and pain sensitivity.

Ecstasy use by U.S. adolescents began in the 1980s and then peaked in 2000 to 2001. Ecstasy use declined from 2002 to 2005 but increased slightly in 2006 (Johnston & others, 2007). Thirty-day prevalence of use in 2006 by eighth-, tenth-, and twelfth-graders was 0.7, 1.2, and 1.3 percent (down from 1.8, 2.6, and 2.8 percent in 2001). The downturn in reported use of Ecstasy in 2002 coincides with adolescents' increasing knowledge that Ecstasy use can be dangerous (Johnston & others, 2007).

### Depressants

**Depressants** are drugs that slow down the central nervous system, bodily functions, and behavior. Medically, depressants have been used to reduce anxiety and to induce sleep. Among the most widely used depressants are alcohol, which we discussed earlier; barbiturates; and tranquilizers. Though used less frequently than other depressants, the opiates are especially dangerous.

*Barbiturates,* such as Nembutal and Seconal, are depressant drugs that induce sleep or reduce anxiety. *Tranquilizers,* such as Valium and Xanax, are depressant drugs that reduce anxiety and induce relaxation. They can produce symptoms of withdrawal when an individual stops taking them. Since the initial surveys, begun in 1975, of drug use by high school seniors, use of depressants has decreased. For example, use of barbiturates by high school seniors at least every 30 days in 1975 was 4.7 percent; in 2006, it was 3.0 percent (Johnston & others, 2007). Over the same time period, tranquilizer use also decreased, from 4.1 percent to 2.7 percent, for 30-day prevalence.

*Opiates,* which consist of opium and its derivatives, depress the activity of the central nervous system. They are commonly known as narcotics. Many drugs have been produced from the opium poppy, among them morphine and heroin (which is converted to morphine when it enters the brain). For several hours after taking an opiate, an individual feels euphoria, pain relief, and an increased appetite for food and sex; however, the opiates are among the most physically addictive drugs.

**depressants** Drugs that slow down the central nervous system, bodily functions, and behavior.

The body soon craves more heroin and experiences very painful withdrawal unless more is taken.

The rates of heroin use among adolescents are quite low, but they rose significantly for grades 8, 10, and 12 in the 1990s (Johnston & others, 2007). In 2006, 0.4 percent of high school seniors said they had used heroin in the last 30 days. A positive note occurred in the University of Michigan's recent surveys—more students perceived heroin as dangerous than in surveys conducted in the early to mid-1990s. Perceived dangerousness is usually a precursor to a drop in a drug's use.

An alarming trend has recently emerged in adolescents' use of prescription painkillers. A 2004 survey revealed that 18 percent of U.S. adolescents had used Vicodin at some point in their lifetime, whereas 10 percent had used OxyContin (Partnership for a Drug-Free America, 2005). These drugs fall into the general class of drugs called narcotics, and they are highly addictive. In this recent national survey, 9 percent of adolescents also said they had abused cough medications to intentionally get high. The University of Michigan began including OxyContin in its survey in 2002. For twelfth-graders, 4 percent reported using OxyContin on an annual basis in 2002, a figure that peaked in 2005 at 5.5 percent, then declined to 4.3 percent in 2006. A significant increase in OxyContin on an annual basis was reported in 2006 by eighth- and tenth-graders (1.8 percent in 2005 to 2.6 percent in 2006 for eighth-graders and 3.2 to 3.8 percent for tenth-graders) (Johnston & others, 2007).

Eighteen-year-old Paul Michaud (*above*) began taking OxyContin in high school. Michaud says, "I was hooked." Now he is in drug treatment.

In the Partnership for a Drug Free America (2005) survey, almost one-half of the adolescents said that using prescription medications to get high was much safer than using street drugs. About one-third of the adolescents erroneously believed that prescription painkillers are not addictive. The adolescents cited the medicine cabinets of their parents or of friends' parents as the main source for their prescription painkillers.

A recent analysis of data from the National Survey on Drug Use and Health revealed that abuse of prescription painkillers by U.S. adolescents may become an epidemic (Sung & others, 2005). In this survey, adolescents especially at risk for abusing prescription painkillers were likely to already be using illicit drugs, came from low-socioeconomic-status families, had detached parents, or had friends who used drugs.

At this point, we have discussed a number of depressants, stimulants, and hallucinogens. Their medical uses, short-term effects, overdose symptoms, health risks, physical addiction risk, and psychological dependence risk are summarized in Figure 13.8.

### Anabolic Steroids

**Anabolic steroids** are drugs derived from the male sex hormone, testosterone. They promote muscle growth and increase lean body mass. Anabolic steroids have medical uses, but they increasingly have been abused by some athletes and others who hope to improve their sports performance and physical attractiveness. Nonmedical uses of these drugs carry a number of physical and psychological health risks (National Clearinghouse for Alcohol and Drug Information, 1999).

Both males and females who take large doses of anabolic steroids usually experience changes in sexual characteristics. In males, this can involve a shrinking of the testicles, reduced sperm count, impotence, premature baldness, enlargement of the prostate gland, breast enlargement, and difficulty or pain in urinating. In females, their use can trigger severe acne on the face and body, a weakening of tendons (which can result in rupturing or tearing), reduction in HDL (the "good" cholesterol), and high blood pressure. Psychological effects in both males and females can involve irritability, uncontrollable bursts of anger, severe mood swings (which can lead to depression when individuals stop using the steroids), impaired judgment stemming from feelings of invincibility, and paranoid jealousy.

In the University of Michigan study, in 2006, 0.5 percent of eighth-graders, 0.6 percent of tenth-graders, and 1.1 percent of twelfth-graders said they had used anabolic steroids in the past 30 days (Johnston & others, 2007). The rate of steroid

**anabolic steroids** Drugs derived from the male sex hormone, testosterone. They promote muscle growth and lean body mass.

| Drug classification | Medical uses | Short-term effects | Overdose | Health risks | Risk of physical/ psychological dependence |
|---|---|---|---|---|---|
| **Depressants** | | | | | |
| Alcohol | Pain relief | Relaxation, depressed brain activity, slowed behavior, reduced inhibitions | Disorientation, loss of consciousness, even death at high blood-alcohol levels | Accidents, brain damage, liver disease, heart disease, ulcers, birth defects | Physical: moderate; psychological: moderate |
| Barbiturates | Sleeping pill | Relaxation, sleep | Breathing difficulty, coma, possible death | Accidents, coma, possible death | Physical and psychological moderate to high |
| Tranquilizers | Anxiety reduction | Relaxation, slowed behavior | Breathing difficulty, coma, possible death | Accidents, coma, possible death | Physical: low to moderate; psychological: moderate to high |
| Opiates (narcotics) | Pain relief | Euphoric feelings, drowsiness, nausea | Convulsions, coma, possible death | Accidents, infectious diseases such as AIDS (when the drug is injected) | Physical: high; psychological: moderate to high |
| **Stimulants** | | | | | |
| Amphetamines | Weight control | Increased alertness, excitability; decreased fatigue, irritability | Extreme irritability, feelings of persecution, convulsions | Insomnia, hypertension, malnutrition, possible death | Physical: possible; psychological: moderate to high |
| Cocaine | Local anesthetic | Increased alertness, excitability, euphoric feelings; decreased fatigue, irritability | Extreme irritability, feelings of persecution, convulsions, cardiac arrest, possible death | Insomnia, hypertension, malnutrition, possible death | Physical: possible; psychological: moderate (oral) to very high (injected or smoked) |
| **Hallucinogens** | | | | | |
| LSD | None | Strong hallucinations, distorted time perception | Severe mental disturbance, loss of contact with reality | Accidents | Physical: none; psychological: low |

**FIGURE 13.8 Psychoactive Drugs: Depressants, Stimulants, and Hallucinogens**

use by twelfth-graders is a decline from 2004 (1.6 percent). In one study conducted in Sweden, use of anabolic steroids by high school students was linked with strength training, tobacco use, heavy alcohol consumption, and truancy (Kindlundh & others, 1999).

**Inhalants** *Inhalants* are ordinary household products that are inhaled or sniffed by children and adolescents to get high. Examples of inhalants include model airplane glue, nail polish remover, and cleaning fluids. Short-term, inhalants can cause intoxicating effects that last for several minutes or even several hours if the inhalants are taken repeatedly. Initially, users feel slightly stimulated and then with successive inhalations, they may feel less inhibited. Eventually they can lose consciousness. Long-term use of inhalants can lead to heart failure and even death.

In the University of Michigan national survey, inhalant use by U.S. adolescents has decreased in the twenty-first century (Johnston & others, 2007). Use in the last 30 days by twelfth-graders decreased from 22.4 percent in 2000 to 18.3 percent in 2006.

**Factors in Adolescent and Emerging Adult Drug Abuse** Earlier, we discussed the factors that place adolescents and emerging adults at risk for alcohol abuse. Researchers also have examined the factors that are related to drug use in adolescence and emerging adulthood, especially the roles of development, parents, peers, and schools.

Most adolescents become drug users at some point in their development, whether their use is limited to alcohol, caffeine, and cigarettes, or extended to marijuana, cocaine, and hard drugs. A special concern involves adolescents who begin to use drugs early in adolescence or even in childhood. A recent study revealed that individuals who began drinking alcohol before 14 years of age were more likely to become alcohol dependent than their counterparts who began drinking alcohol at 21 years of age or older (Hingson, Heeren, & Winter, 2006). A longitudinal study of individuals from 8 to 42 years of age also found that early onset of drinking was linked to increased risk of heavy drinking in middle age (Pitkänen, Lyrra, & Pulkkinen, 2005). A longitudinal study conducted by Kenneth Dodge and his colleagues (2006) examined the joint contributions of parents and peers to early substance use. The sequence of factors that were related to whether an adolescent would take drugs by 12 years of age was:

1. Being born into a high-risk family (especially a poor, single, or teenage mother)
2. Experiencing an increase in harsh parenting in childhood
3. Having conduct problems in school and getting rejected by peers in childhood
4. Experiencing increased conflict with parents in early adolescence
5. Having low parental monitoring by parents
6. Hanging out with deviant peers in early adolescence and increased substance use

There also is a concern about adolescents who use drugs as a way of coping with stress, which can interfere with the development of competent coping skills and responsible decision making. Researchers have found that drug use in childhood or early adolescence has more detrimental long-term effects on the development of responsible, competent behavior than drug use that occurs in late adolescence (Newcomb & Bentler, 1989). When they use drugs to cope with stress, young adolescents often enter adult roles of marriage and work prematurely without adequate socioemotional growth and experience greater failure in adult roles.

Fortunately, by the time individuals reach their mid-twenties, many have reduced their use of alcohol and drugs. That is the conclusion reached by Jerald Bachman and his colleagues (2002) in a longitudinal analysis of more than 38,000 individuals (see Figure 13.9). They were evaluated from the time they were high

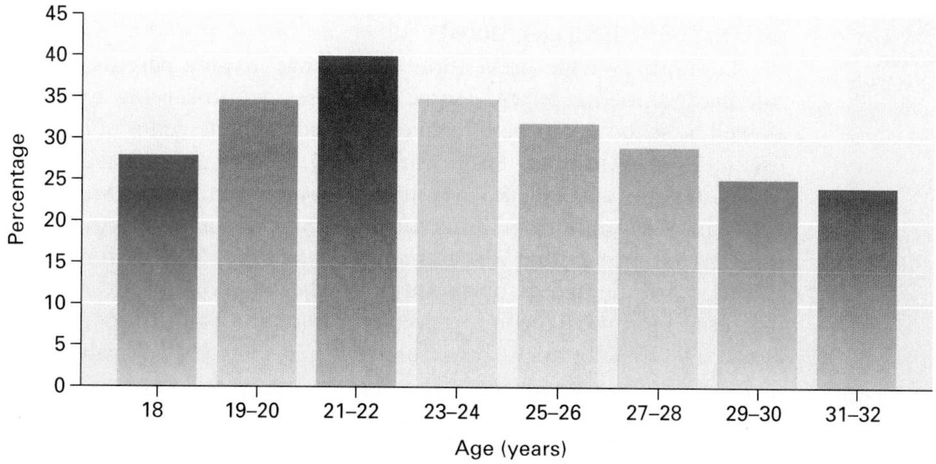


**FIGURE 13.9 Binge Drinking in the Transition from Adolescence to Adulthood** This figure shows the percentage of individuals from age 18 through 32 who said they had engaged in binge drinking (having five or more drinks on any one occasion) during the past two weeks. Notice the decline in binge drinking in the mid-twenties.

school seniors through their twenties. Some of the main findings in the study were as follows:

- College students drink more than youths who end their education after high school.
- Those who don't go to college smoke more.
- Singles use marijuana more than married individuals.
- Drinking is heaviest among singles and divorced individuals. Becoming engaged, married, or even remarried quickly brings down alcohol use. Thus, living arrangements and marital status are key factors in alcohol and drug use rates during the twenties.
- Individuals who considered religion to be very important in their lives and who frequently attended religious services were less likely to take drugs than their less religious counterparts.

Parents and peers play important roles in preventing adolescent drug abuse (Eitle, 2005; Engels & others, 2005). One study revealed that parental control and monitoring were linked with lower drug use by adolescents (Fletcher, Steinberg, & Williams-Wheeler, 2004). In another study, low parental involvement, peer pressure, and associating with problem-behaving friends were linked with higher use of drugs by adolescents (Simons-Morton & others, 2001). Also, in a national survey, parents who were more involved in setting limits (such as where adolescents went after school and what they were exposed to on TV and the Internet) were more likely to have adolescents who did not use drugs (National Center for Addiction and Substance Abuse, 2001). Further, one longitudinal study linked the early onset of substance abuse with early childhood predictors (Kaplow & others, 2002). Risk factors at kindergarten for substance use at 10 to 12 years of age included being male, having a parent who abused substances, a low level of verbal reasoning by parents, and low social-problem-solving skills.

In one study of more than 4,000 sixth- through eighth-grade students, parent involvement, parent expectations for not abusing drugs, and adolescents' positive regard for their parents were related to less smoking and drinking by the young adolescents (Simons-Morton & others, 2001). Also in this study, direct peer pressure and associating with problem-behaving friends were linked with drinking and smoking. In another study, heavy drug use by peers was linked with initial drug use by adolescents (Simons, Walker-Barnes, & Mason, 2001). A recent study of more than 5,000 middle school students revealed that having friends in their school's social network and having fewer friends who use substances were related to a lower level of substance use (Ennett & others, 2006). Another recent study investigated a number of factors that might be linked to adolescent substance use and found that interacting with antisocial peers and engaging in delinquency were the best predictors of binge drinking and marijuana use (Nation & Heflinger, 2006).

*What are ways that parents have been found to influence whether their adolescents take drugs?*

Community-wide prevention efforts that involve parents, peers, role models, media, police, courts, businesses, youth-serving agencies, as well as schools, can be effective in reducing adolescents' substance use (Jenson, Anthony, & Howard, 2005; Schensul, Nastasi, & de Moura Castro, 2005). The basic philosophy of community-wide programs is that a number of different programs have to be in place. The Midwestern Prevention Program, developed by Mary Ann Pentz (1994), implemented a community-wide health-promotion campaign that used local media, community education, and parent programs in concert with a substance-abuse curriculum in the schools. Evaluations of the program after 18 months and after four years revealed significantly lower rates of alcohol and marijuana use by adolescents in the program than by their counterparts in other areas of the city where the program was not in operation.

## Juvenile Delinquency

Thirteen-year-old Arnie, in the section that opened this chapter, is a juvenile delinquent with a history of thefts and physical assaults. What is a juvenile delinquent? What are the antecedents of delinquency? What types of interventions have been used to prevent or reduce delinquency?

*What is juvenile delinquency? What distinctions are made between index and status offenses?*

**What Is Juvenile Delinquency?** The term **juvenile delinquency** refers to a broad range of behaviors, from socially unacceptable behavior (such as acting out in school) to status offenses (such as running away) to criminal acts (such as burglary). For legal purposes, a distinction is made between index offenses and status offenses:

- **Index offenses** are criminal acts, whether they are committed by juveniles or adults. They include such acts as robbery, aggravated assault, rape, and homicide.
- **Status offenses,** such as running away, truancy, underage drinking, sexual promiscuity, and uncontrollability, are less serious acts. They are performed by youth under a specified age, which classifies them as juvenile offenses. One study found that status offenses increased through adolescence (Bongers & others, 2004).

States often differ in the age used to classify an individual as a juvenile or an adult. Approximately three-fourths of the states have established age 18 as a maximum for defining juveniles. Two states use age 19 as the cutoff, seven states use age 17, and four states use age 16. Thus, running away from home at age 17 may be an offense in some states but not others.

One issue in juvenile justice is whether an adolescent who commits a crime should be tried as an adult (Cassell & Bernstein, 2001; Redding, 2005). One study found that trying adolescent offenders as adults increased rather than reduced their crime rate (Myers, 1999). The study evaluated more than 500 violent youths in Pennsylvania, which has adopted a "get tough" policy. Although these 500 offenders had been given harsher punishment than a comparison group retained in juvenile court, they were more likely to be rearrested—and rearrested more quickly—for new offenses once they were returned to the community. This suggests that the price of short-term public safety attained by prosecuting juveniles as adults might increase long-term criminal offenses.

Some psychologists have proposed that individuals 12 and under should not be evaluated under adult criminal laws and that those 17 and older should be (Steinberg & Cauffman, 1999, 2001). They also recommended that individuals 13 to 16 years of age be given some type of individualized assessment in terms of whether to be tried in a juvenile court or an adult criminal court. This framework argues strongly against court placement based solely on the nature of an offense and takes into account the offender's developmental maturity. The Society for Adolescent Medicine has argued that the death penalty should not be used with adolescents (Morreale, 2004).

In addition to the legal classifications of index offenses and status offenses, many of the behaviors considered delinquent are included in widely used classifications of abnormal behavior (Cavell & others, 2007). **Conduct disorder** is the psychiatric diagnostic category used when multiple behaviors occur over a six-month period. These behaviors include truancy, running away, fire setting, cruelty to animals, breaking and entering, excessive fighting, and others (Pajer & others, 2007). When three or more of these behaviors co-occur before the age of 15 and the child or adolescent is considered unmanageable or out of control, the clinical diagnosis is conduct disorder.

In sum, most children or adolescents at one time or another act out or do things that are destructive or troublesome for themselves or others. If these behaviors occur often in childhood or early adolescence, psychiatrists diagnose them as conduct

**juvenile delinquency** A broad range of behaviors, including socially unacceptable behavior, status offenses, and criminal acts.

**index offenses** Whether they are committed by juveniles or adults, these are criminal acts, such as robbery, rape, and homicide.

**status offenses** Performed by youth under a specified age, these are juvenile offenses that are not as serious as index offenses. These offenses may include such acts as underage drinking, truancy, and sexual promiscuity.

**conduct disorder** The psychiatric diagnostic category for the occurrence of multiple delinquent activities over a six-month period. These behaviors include truancy, running away, fire setting, cruelty to animals, breaking and entering, and excessive fighting.

disorders. If these behaviors result in illegal acts by juveniles, society labels them as *delinquents.*

How many adolescents are arrested each year for committing juvenile delinquency offenses? In 1997, law enforcement agencies made an estimated 2.8 million arrests of individuals under the age of 18 in the United States (Office of Juvenile Justice and Prevention, 1998). This represents about 10 percent of adolescents 10 to 18 years of age in the United States. Note that this figure reflects only adolescents who have been arrested and does not include those who committed offenses but were not apprehended.

U.S. government statistics reveal that eight of ten cases of juvenile delinquency involve males (Snyder & Sickmund, 1999). Although males are still far more likely to engage in juvenile delinquency, there has been a greater percentage increase in female than male juvenile delinquents in the last two decades (Quinsey & others, 2004). Rates for male and female delinquents' property offenses are higher than rates for other offenses such as assault, drug offenses, and public order offenses.

As adolescents become emerging adults, do their rates of delinquency and crime change? Recent analyses indicate that theft, property damage, and physical aggression decrease from 18 to 26 years of age (Schulenberg & Zarrett, 2006). The peak for property damage is 16 to 18 years of age for males, 15 to 17 years of age for females. However, the peak for violence is 18 to 19 years of age for males and 19 to 21 years of age for females (Farrington, 2004).

A distinction is made between early-onset—before age 11—and late-onset—after 11—antisocial behavior. Early-onset antisocial behavior is associated with more negative developmental outcomes than late-onset antisocial behavior (Schulenberg & Zarrett, 2006). Early-onset antisocial behavior is more likely to persist into emerging adulthood and is associated with more mental health and relationship problems (Roisman, Aguilar, & Egeland, 2004; Stouthamer-Loeber & others, 2004).

**Antecedents of Juvenile Delinquency** Predictors of delinquency include conflict with authority, minor covert acts that are followed by property damage and other more serious acts, minor aggression followed by fighting and violence, identity (negative identity), self-control (low degree), cognitive distortions (egocentric bias), age (early initiation), sex (male), expectations for education (low expectations, little commitment), school achievement (low achievement in early grades), peer influence (heavy influence, low resistance), socioeconomic status (low), parental role (lack of monitoring, low support, and ineffective discipline), siblings (having an older sibling who is a delinquent), and neighborhood quality (urban, high crime, high mobility). A summary of these antecedents of delinquency is presented in Figure 13.10. In the Pittsburgh Youth Study, a longitudinal study focused on more than 1,500 inner-city boys, three developmental pathways to delinquency were identified (Loeber & Farrington, 2001; Loeber & others, 1998; Stouthamer-Loeber & others, 2002):

- *Authority conflict.* Youth on this pathway showed stubbornness prior to age 12, then moved on to defiance and avoidance of authority.
- *Covert.* This pathway included minor covert acts, such as lying, followed by property damage and moderately serious delinquency, then serious delinquency.
- *Overt.* This pathway included minor aggression followed by fighting and violence.

Another study examined the developmental trajectories of childhood disruptive behaviors and adolescent delinquency (Broidy & others, 2003). For boys, early problem behavior involving aggression was linked with delinquency in adolescence. However, no connection between early aggression problems and later delinquency was found for girls.

Let's look in more detail at several other factors that are related to delinquency. Erik Erikson (1968) notes that adolescents whose development has restricted their access to acceptable social roles or made them feel that they cannot measure up to

| Antecedent | Association with delinquency | Description |
|---|---|---|
| Authority conflict | High degree | Youth show stubbornness prior to age 12, then become defiant of authority. |
| Covert acts | Frequent | Minor covert acts, such as lying, are followed by property damage and moderately serious delinquency, then serious delinquency. |
| Overt acts of aggression | Frequent | Minor aggression is followed by fighting and violence. |
| Identity | Negative identity | Erikson argues that delinquency occurs because the adolescent fails to resolve a role identity. |
| Cognitive distortions | High degree | The thinking of delinquents is frequently characterized by a variety of cognitive distortions (such as egocentric bias, externalizing of blame, and mislabeling) that contribute to inappropriate behavior and lack of self-control. |
| Self-control | Low degree | Some children and adolescents fail to acquire the essential controls that others have acquired during the process of growing up. |
| Age | Early initiation | Early appearance of antisocial behavior is associated with serious offenses later in adolescence. However, not every child who acts out becomes a delinquent. |
| Sex | Male | Boys engage in more antisocial behavior than girls do, although girls are more likely to run away. Boys engage in more violent acts. |
| Expectations for education and school grades | Low expectations and low grades | Adolescents who become delinquents often have low educational expectations and low grades. Their verbal abilities are often weak. |
| Parental influences | Monitoring (low), support (low), discipline (ineffective) | Delinquents often come from families in which parents rarely monitor their adolescents, provide them with little support, and ineffectively discipline them. |
| Sibling relations | Older delinquent sibling | Individuals with an older delinquent sibling are more likely to become delinquent. |
| Peer influences | Heavy influence, low resistance | Having delinquent peers greatly increases the risk of becoming delinquent. |
| Socioeconomic status | Low | Serious offenses are committed more frequently by low-socioeconomic-status males. |
| Neighborhood quality | Urban, high crime, high mobility | Communities often breed crime. Living in a high-crime area, which also is characterized by poverty and dense living conditions, increases the probability that a child will become a delinquent. These communities often have grossly inadequate schools. |

**FIGURE 13.10** **The Antecedents of Juvenile Delinquency**

the demands placed on them may choose a negative identity. Adolescents with a negative identity may find support for their delinquent image among peers, reinforcing the negative identity. For Erikson, delinquency is an attempt to establish an identity, although it is a negative identity.

Family support systems are also associated with delinquency (Cavell & others, 2007; Dodge, Coie, & Lynam, 2006; Feinberg & others, 2007). Parents of delinquents are less skilled in discouraging antisocial behavior and in encouraging skilled behavior than are parents of nondelinquents. Parental monitoring of adolescents is especially important in determining whether an adolescent becomes a delinquent (Patterson, DeBaryshe, & Ramsey, 1989). One longitudinal study found that the less parents knew about their adolescents' whereabouts, activities, and peers, the more likely they were to engage in delinquent behavior (Laird & others, 2003). Family discord and inconsistent and inappropriate discipline are also associated with delinquency (Capaldi & Shortt, 2003). One study revealed that father absence, assessed when youth were 14 to 17 years of age, was linked with a higher risk of incarceration in males, assessed at 15 to 30 years of age (Harper & McLanahan, 2004). An increasing number of studies have found that siblings can have a strong influence on delinquency (Bank, Burraston, & Snyder, 2004; Conger & Reuter, 1996). In one study, high levels of hostile sibling relationships and older sibling delinquency were linked with younger sibling delinquency in both brother pairs and sister pairs (Slomkowski & others, 2001).

Peer relations also play an important role in delinquency (Bukowski, Brendgen, & Vitaro, 2007; Dodge, Coie, & Lynam, 2006; Dodge & Sherrill, 2006). Having delinquent peers increases the risk of becoming delinquent for example, two recent studies found that the link between associating with delinquent; peers and engaging in delinquency held for both boys and girls (Heinze, Toro, & Urberg, 2004; Laird & others, 2005).

Although delinquency is less exclusively a lower-SES phenomenon than it was in the past, some characteristics of lower-SES culture can promote delinquency. The norms of many low-SES peer groups and gangs are antisocial, or counterproductive, to the goals and norms of society at large. Getting into and staying out of trouble are prominent features of life for some adolescents in low-income neighborhoods. Adolescents from low-income backgrounds may sense that they can gain attention and status by performing antisocial actions. Being "tough" and "masculine" are high-status traits for low-SES boys, and these traits are often measured by the adolescent's success in performing and getting away with delinquent acts.

The nature of a community can contribute to delinquency (Farrington, 2004; Kroneman, Loeber, & Hipwell, 2004). A community with a high crime rate allows adolescents to observe many models who engage in criminal activities and might be rewarded for their criminal accomplishments (Richards & others, 2004). Such communities often are characterized by poverty, unemployment, and feelings of alienation. The quality of schools, funding for education, and organized neighborhood activities are other community factors that might be related to delinquency. Are there caring adults in the schools and neighborhood who can convince adolescents with delinquent tendencies that education is the best route to success? When family support becomes inadequate, then such community supports take on added importance in preventing delinquency.

A current special concern in low-income areas is escalating gang violence.

**Violence and Youth** An increasing concern is the high rate of adolescent violence (Jackson, Bass, & Sharpe, 2005; Taylor & others, 2005). Special concerns in adolescent violence are gangs and school violence.

**Gangs** It is estimated that there are more than 750,000 gang members in more than 24,000 gangs in the United States (Egley, 2002). Most gang members are 12 to 26 years of age, with an average age of 17 to 18 years of age. Gang members are more likely to be male than female, with estimates of female gang members ranging from 10 to 40 percent. Gangs are often composed of adolescents from low-income and ethnic minority backgrounds (Decker & Curry, 2000). However, it is estimated that approximately one-fourth of U.S. gang members are made up of non-Latino Whites.

Gangs often engage in violent and criminal activities and use these activities as an indication of gang identity and loyalty (Lauber, Marshall, & Meyers, 2005). Among the risk factors that increase the likelihood an adolescent will become a gang member are disorganized neighborhoods characterized by economic hardship, having other family members involved in a gang, drug use, lack of family support, and peer pressure from gang members to join their gang (Lauber, Marshall, & Meyers, 2005; Thomas, 2005). Also, a recent study found that peer rejection, doing poorly in school, and engaging in antisocial behavior were linked with whether middle students were gang members (Dishion, Nelson, & Yasui, 2005).

**School Violence and Shootings** Although school violence is an issue of national concern in the United States (Molina, Dulmus, & Sowers, 2005; Robinson & Clay, 2005), a 2005 national survey revealed a decline in violence-related behaviors in schools. The national survey indicated that from 1991 to 2005 physical fighting declined from 16 percent to 13.6 percent. Weapon carrying in schools declined from 12 percent of students to 6.5 percent. However, being injured in a fist fight remained stable, and not going to school because of safety concerns increased from 4.4 percent of students in 1993 to 6 percent of students in 2005. Violence figures for some subgroups of adolescents increased. For example, being threatened or injured with a weapon on school property increased for ninth-grade students and for African American students.

In the late 1990s, a series of school shootings gained national attention. In April 1999, two Columbine High School (in Littleton, Colorado) students, Eric Harris (age 18) and Dylan Klebold (age 17), shot and killed 12 students and a teacher, wounded 23 others, and then killed themselves. In May 1998, slightly built Kip Kinkel strode into a cafeteria at Thurston High School in Springfield, Oregon, and opened fire on his fellow students, murdering two and injuring many others. Later that day, police went to Kip's home and found his parents lying dead on the floor, also victims of Kip's violence. In 2001, 15-year-old Charles Andrew "Andy" Williams fired shots at Santana High School in Santee, California, that killed 2 classmates and injured 13 others. According to students at the school, Andy was a victim of bullying at the school and had joked the previous weekend of his violent plans, but no one took him seriously after he later said he was just kidding.

Is there any way that psychologists can predict whether a youth will turn violent? It's a complex task, but they have pieced together some clues (Cowley, 1998). The violent youth are overwhelmingly male, and many are driven by feelings of powerlessness. Violence seems to infuse these youth with a sense of power (Fritzon & Brun, 2005). Suburban and small-town shooting sprees attract attention, but youth violence is far greater in poverty-infested areas of inner cities. Urban poverty fosters powerlessness and the rage that goes with it. Living in poverty is frustrating, and many inner-city neighborhoods provide almost daily opportunities to observe violence. Many urban youth who live in poverty also lack adequate parental involvement and supervision.

James Garbarino (1999, 2001) says there is a lot of ignoring that goes on in these kinds of situations. Parents often don't want to acknowledge what might be a very upsetting reality. Harris and Klebold were members of the Trenchcoat Mafia clique of Columbine outcasts. The two even had made a video for a school video class the previous fall that depicted them walking down the halls at the school and shooting other students. Allegations were made that a year earlier the Sheriff's Department had been given information that Harris had bragged openly on the Internet that he and Klebold had built four bombs. Kip Kinkel had an obsession with guns and explosives, a history of abusing animals, and a nasty temper when crossed. When police examined his room, they found two pipe bombs, three larger bombs, and bomb-making recipes that Kip had downloaded from the Internet. Clearly, some signs were present in these students' lives to suggest some serious problems, but it is still very difficult to predict whether youth like these will actually act on their anger and sense of powerlessness to commit murder.

Garbarino (1999, 2001) has interviewed a number of youth killers. He concludes that nobody really knows precisely why a tiny minority of youth kill but that it might be a lack of a spiritual center. In the youth killers he interviewed, Garbarino often found a spiritual or emotional emptiness in which the youth sought meaning in the dark side of life.

Andrew "Andy" Williams, escorted by police after being arrested for killing 2 classmates and injuring 13 others at Santana High School. *What factors might contribute to youth murders?*

## Careers in ADOLESCENT DEVELOPMENT

### Rodney Hammond
**Health Psychologist**

Rodney Hammond described his college experiences, "When I started as an undergraduate at the University of Illinois, Champaign–Urbana, I hadn't decided on my major. But to help finance my education, I took a part-time job in a child development research program sponsored by the psychology department. There, I observed inner-city children in settings designed to enhance their learning. I saw first-hand the contribution psychology can make, and I knew I wanted to be a psychologist" (American Psychological Association, 2003, p. 26).

Rodney Hammond went on to obtain a doctorate in school and community college with a focus on children's development. For a number of years, he trained clinical psychologists at Wright State University in Ohio and directed a program to reduce violence in ethnic minority youth. There, he and his associates taught at-risk youth how to use social skills to effectively manage conflict and to recognize situations that could lead to violence. Today, Rodney is Director of Violence Prevention at the Centers for Disease Control and Prevention in Atlanta. Rodney says that if you are interested in people and problem solving, psychology is a wonderful way to put these together.

Rodney Hammond talking with an adolescent about strategies for coping with stress and avoiding risk-taking behaviors.

The following factors often are present in at-risk youths and seem to propel them toward violent acts (Walker, 1998): early involvement with drugs and alcohol; easy access to weapons, especially handguns; association with antisocial, deviant peer groups; and pervasive exposure to violence in the media.

Many at-risk youths are also easily provoked to rage, reacting aggressively to real or imagined slights and acting on them, sometimes with tragic consequences (Knox & Roberts, 2005). They might misjudge the motives and intentions of others toward them because of the hostility and agitation they carry (Coie & Dodge, 1998; Dodge, Coie, & Lynam, 2006). Consequently, they frequently engage in hostile confrontations with peers and teachers. It is not unusual to find the anger-prone youth issuing threats of bodily harm to others.

In one study based on data collected in the National Longitudinal Study of Adolescent Health, secure attachment to parents, living in an intact family, and attending church services with parents were linked with lower incidences of engaging in violent behavior in seventh- through twelfth-graders (Franke, 2000).

These are some of the Oregon Social Learning Center's recommendations for reducing youth violence (Walker, 1998):

- *Recommit to raising adolescents safely and effectively.* This includes engaging in parenting practices that have been shown to produce healthy, well-adjusted adolescents. Such practices include consistent, fair discipline that is not harsh or severely punitive, careful monitoring and supervision, positive family-management techniques, involvement in the adolescent's daily life, daily debriefings about the adolescent's experiences, and teaching problem-solving strategies.
- *Make prevention a reality.* Too often lip service is given to prevention strategies without investing in them at the necessary levels to make them effective.
- *Give more support to schools, which are struggling to educate a population that includes many at-risk adolescents.*
- *Forge effective partnerships among families, schools, social service systems, churches, and other agencies to create the socializing experiences that will provide all youth with the opportunity to develop in positive ways.*

To read about the work of one individual who has a commitment to reducing violent behavior in adolescence, see the *Careers in Adolescent Development* profile.

## Depression and Suicide

As mentioned earlier in the chapter, one of the most frequent characteristics of adolescents referred for psychological treatment is sadness or depression, especially among girls. In this section, we discuss the nature of adolescent depression and adolescent suicide.

**Depression** An adolescent who says "I'm depressed" or "I'm so down" may be describing a mood that lasts only a few hours or a much longer lasting mental disorder. In **major depressive disorder,** an individual experiences a major depressive episode and depressed characteristics, such as lethargy and hopelessness, for at least two weeks or longer and daily functioning becomes impaired. According to the *Diagnostic and Statistical Manual of Mental Disorders—Fourth Edition (DSM-IV)* classification of mental disorders (American Psychiatric Association, 1994), nine symptoms define a major depressive episode, and to be classified as having major depressive disorder, at least five of these must be present during a two-week period:

1. Depressed mood most of the day
2. Reduced interest or pleasure in all or most activities
3. Significant weight loss or gain, or significant decrease or increase in appetite
4. Trouble sleeping or sleeping too much
5. Psychomotor agitation or retardation
6. Fatigue or loss of energy
7. Feeling worthless or guilty in an excessive or inappropriate manner
8. Problems in thinking, concentrating, or making decisions
9. Recurrent thoughts of death and suicide

In adolescence, pervasive depressive symptoms might be manifested in such ways as tending to dress in black clothes, writing poetry with morbid themes, or a preoccupation with music that has depressive themes. Sleep problems can appear as all-night television watching, difficulty in getting up for school, or sleeping during the day. Lack of interest in usually pleasurable activities may show up as withdrawal from friends or staying alone in the bedroom most of the time. A lack of motivation and energy level can show up in missed classes. Boredom might be a result of feeling depressed. Adolescent depression also can occur in conjunction with conduct disorder, substance abuse, or an eating disorder.

How serious a problem is depression in adolescence? Surveys have found that approximately one-third of adolescents who go to a mental health clinic suffer from depression (Fleming, Boyle, & Offord, 1993). Depression is more common in the adolescent years than the elementary school years (Compas & Grant, 1993). By about age 15, adolescent females have a rate of depression that is twice that of adolescent males. Some of the reasons for this sex difference that have been proposed are these:

- Females tend to ruminate in their depressed mood and amplify it.
- Females' self-images, especially their body images, are more negative than males'.
- Females face more discrimination than males do.
- Hormonal changes alter vulnerability to depression in adolescence, especially among girls.

Depression is more likely to occur in adolescence than in childhood and more likely to characterize female adolescents than male adolescents. *Why might female adolescents be more likely to develop depression than adolescent males?*

Mental health professionals note that depression often goes undiagnosed in adolescence. Why is this so? According to conventional wisdom, normal adolescents often show mood swings, ruminate in introspective ways, express boredom with life, and indicate a sense of hopelessness. Thus, parents, teachers, and other observers may see these behaviors as simply transitory and not reflecting a mental disorder but rather normal adolescent behaviors and thoughts.

Follow-up studies of depressed adolescents indicate that the symptoms of depression experienced in adolescence predict similar problems in adulthood (Garber & others, 1988; Lewinsohn & others, 2006). This means that adolescent depression needs to be taken seriously. It does not just automatically go away. Rather, adolescents who are diagnosed as having depression are more likely to experience the problem on a continuing basis in adulthood than are adolescents not diagnosed as having depression. In one longitudinal study, transient problems in adolescence were related to situation-specific factors (such as negative peer events), whereas

**major depressive disorder** The diagnosis when an individual experiences a major depressive episode and depressed characteristics, such as lethargy and depression, for two weeks or longer and daily functioning becomes impaired.

chronic problems were defined by individual characteristics, such as internalizing behaviors (Brooks-Gunn & Graber, 1995).

Does the incidence of depression change from adolescence to emerging adulthood? Researchers have found a linear increase in major depressive disorder from 15 years of age to 22 years of age (Kessler & Walters, 1998). However, an early onset of a mood disorder, such as major depressive disorder in adolescence, is linked with more negative outcomes than late onset of a mood disorder (Schulenberg & Zarrett, 2006). For example, the early onset is associated with further recurrences of depression and with an increased risk of being diagnosed with an anxiety disorder, substance abuse, eating disorder, suicide attempt, and unemployment at a future point in development (Graber, 2004; Johnson & others, 2002).

Other family factors are involved in adolescent depression (Graber, 2004; Seroczynski, Jacquez, & Cole, 2003). A recent study revealed that parent-adolescent conflict and low parental support were linked to adolescent depression (Sheeber & others, 2007). Further, having a depressed parent is a risk factor for depression in childhood and adolescence (Windle & Dumenci, 1998). Parents who are emotionally unavailable, immersed in marital conflict, or who have economic problems may set the stage for the emergence of depression in their adolescent children (Sheeber, Hops, & Davis, 2001).

Poor peer relationships also are associated with adolescent depression (Kistner, 2006). Not having a close relationship with a best friend, having less contact with friends, and peer rejection increase depressive tendencies in adolescents (Vernberg, 1990). Problems in adolescent romantic relationships can also trigger depression (Davila & Steinberg, 2006).

The experience of difficult changes or challenges is associated with depressive symptoms in adolescence (Compas, 2004). Parental divorce increases depressive symptoms in adolescents. Also, when adolescents go through puberty at the same time as they move from elementary school to middle or junior high school, they report being depressed more than do adolescents who go through puberty after the school transition (Petersen, Sarigiani, & Kennedy, 1991).

Depression has been treated with drug therapy and psychotherapy techniques (Sanders & Wills, 2005). Antidepressant drugs reduce the symptoms of depression in about 60 to 70 percent of cases, often taking about two to four weeks to improve mood. Cognitive therapy also has been effective in treating depression (Hollon, 2006).

**Suicide** Depression is linked to an increase in suicidal ideation and suicide attempts in adolescence (Werth, 2004). One study found that the psychological factors of being overly self-critical and having a sense of hopelessness were also related to suicide ideation and behavior (Cox, Enns, & Clara, 2004).

Suicide behavior is rare in childhood but escalates in adolescence and then increases further in emerging adulthood (Judge & Billick, 2004; Park & others, 2006). Suicide is the third leading cause of death in 10- to 19-year-olds today in the United States (National Center for Health Statistics, 2002). After increasing to high levels in the 1990s, suicide rates in adolescents have declined in recent years (Gould & others, 2003). In 2004, 4,214 U.S. individuals from 15 to 24 years of age committed suicide (Minino, Heron, & Smith, 2006). Emerging adults have triple the rate of suicide as adolescents (Park & others, 2006).

A suicide threat should always be taken seriously. Far more adolescents contemplate or attempt it unsuccessfully than actually commit it (Mazza, 2005). In a national study, in 2005, 17 percent of U.S. high school students said that they had seriously considered or attempted suicide in the last 12 months (Eaton & others, 2006). As shown in Figure 13.11, this percentage has declined since 1991. In

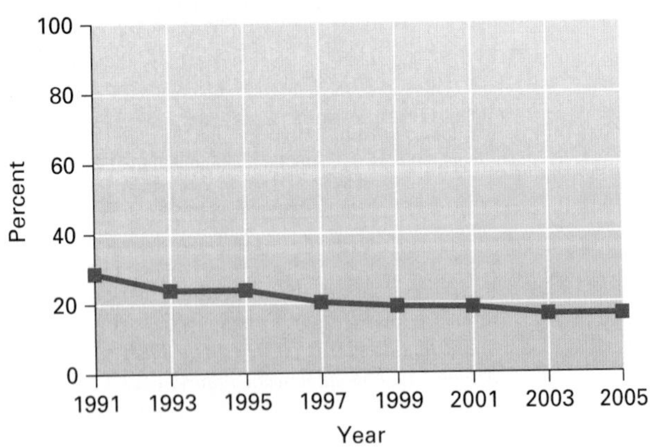


**FIGURE 13.11 Percentage of U.S. Ninth- to Twelfth-Grade Students Who Seriously Considered Attempting Suicide in the Previous 12 Months from 1991 to 2005** *Source:* Centers for Disease Control and Prevention (2006, June 8) *National Youth Risk Behavior Survey 1991–2005: Trends in the prevalence of suicide ideation and attempts.* Atlanta: Centers for Disease Control and Prevention.

the national survey, in 2005, 2.3 percent reported a suicide attempt that resulted in an injury, poisoning, or drug overdose that had been treated by a doctor. Females were more likely to attempt suicide than males, but males were more likely to succeed in committing suicide. In emerging adulthood, males are six times as likely to commit suicide as females (National Center for Injury Prevention and Control, 2006). Males use more lethal means, such as guns, in their suicide attempts, whereas adolescent females are more likely to cut their wrists or take an overdose of sleeping pills—methods less likely to result in death. A recent study of adolescents indicated that suicide ideation peaked at age 15 (Rueter & Kwon, 2005). In this study, adolescents who thought about committing suicide often had parents who had engaged in suicide ideation. Another recent study also revealed that suicidal behavior in their families placed adolescents at risk for engaging in suicidal ideation and attempts themselves (Cerel & Roberts, 2005). A recent study revealed that for both male and female adolescents, alcohol use was associated with an increase in suicidal ideation and suicide attempts (Swahn & Bossarte, 2007).

A recent concern related to adolescent suicide is a possible link between the use of antidepressants and suicidal thoughts. In 2004, the Federal Drug Administration issued a report based on its review of a number of research studies; the report concluded that 2 to 3 percent of adolescents taking antidepressants experience an increase in suicidal thoughts. It is estimated that antidepressants are prescribed for approximately one million U.S. children and adolescents. However, some researchers question the link between adolescents' antidepressant use and suicidal behavior (Kaizar & others, 2006; Valuck & others, 2004).

Some researchers argue that sexual minority adolescents may be vulnerable to suicide. For example, in one study of 12,000 adolescents, approximately 15 percent of gay male and lesbian youth said that they had attempted suicide compared with 7 percent of heterosexual youth (Russell & Joyner, 2001). However, in another study, gay male and lesbian adolescents were only slightly more likely than heterosexual adolescents to attempt suicide (Savin-Williams, 2001). According to a leading researcher on sexual minority youth, Ritch Savin-Williams (2001), the earlier studies likely exaggerated the suicide rates for gay adolescents because they only surveyed the most disturbed youth who were attending support groups or hanging out at shelters for gay youth.

Both early and later experiences may be involved in suicide attempts. The adolescent might have a long-standing history of family instability and unhappiness. Lack of affection and emotional support, high control, and pressure for achievement by parents during childhood are likely to show up as factors in suicide attempts. One recent review of research found a link that adolescents who had been physically or sexually abused were more likely to have suicidal thoughts than adolescents who had not experienced such abuse (Evans, Hawton, & Rodham, 2005). The adolescent might also lack supportive friendships. Recent and current stressful circumstances, such as getting poor grades in school and experiencing the breakup of a romantic relationship, may trigger suicide attempts (Antai-Otong, 2003).

Genetic factors are also associated with suicide. The closer a person's genetic relationship to someone who has committed suicide, the more likely that person is to also commit suicide (Baud, 2005; Marusic, 2005).

What is the psychological profile of the suicidal adolescent? Suicidal adolescents often have depressive symptoms (Sinclair & others, 2005). Although not all depressed adolescents are suicidal, depression is the most frequently cited factor associated with adolescent suicide (Pelkonen & Marttunen, 2003; Werth, 2004). One study also found that the psychological factors of being overly self-critical and having a sense of hopelessness were also related to suicide ideation and behavior (Cox, Enns, & Clara, 2004). Low self-esteem is also associated with adolescent suicide (Harter & Whitesell, 2001). A recent study also revealed that overweight middle school students were more likely to think about, plan, and attempt suicide than their counterparts who were not overweight (Whetstone, Morrisey, & Cummings, 2007).

| What to do | What not to do |
|---|---|
| 1. Ask direct, straightforward questions in a calm manner: "Are you thinking about hurting yourself?" | 1. Do not ignore the warning signs. |
| 2. Assess the seriousness of the suicidal intent by asking questions about feelings, important relationships, who else the person has talked with, and the amount of thought given to the means to be used. If a gun, pills, a rope, or other means have been obtained and a precise plan developed, clearly the situation is dangerous. Stay with the person until help arrives. | 2. Do not refuse to talk about suicide if a person approaches you about it. |
| 3. Be a good listener and be very supportive without being falsely reassuring. | 3. Do not react with humor, disapproval, or repulsion. |
| 4. Try to persuade the person to obtain professional help and assist him or her in getting this help. | 4. Do not give false reassurances by saying such things as "Everything is going to be OK." Also do not give out simple answers or platitudes, such as "You have everything to be thankful for." |
| | 5. Do not abandon the individual after the crisis has passed or after professional help has commenced. |

**FIGURE 13.12** What to Do and What Not to Do When You Suspect Someone Is Likely to Attempt Suicide

In some instances, suicides in adolescence occur in clusters. That is, when one adolescent commits suicide, other adolescents who find out about this also commit suicide. Such "copycat" suicides raise the issue of whether or not suicides should be reported in the media; a news report might plant the idea of committing suicide in other adolescents' minds.

Figure 13.12 provides valuable information about what to do and what not to do when you suspect someone is likely to commit suicide.

## Eating Disorders

Eating disorders have become increasingly common among adolescents (Kirsch & others, 2007; Stice & others, 2007). Here are some research findings involving adolescent eating disorders:

- *Body image.* Girls who felt negatively about their bodies in early adolescence were more likely to develop eating disorders, two years later, than their counterparts who did not feel negatively about their bodies (Attie & Brooks-Gunn, 1989). Another study revealed adolescent girls with an eating disorder rated their physical appearance lower and the importance of physical appearance higher than their adolescent female counterparts who did not have an eating disorder (Kirsch & others, 2007).
- *Parenting.* Adolescents who reported observing more healthy eating patterns and exercise by their parents had more healthy eating patterns and exercised more themselves (Pakpreo & others, 2005). Negative parent-adolescent relationships were linked with increased dieting by girls over a one-year period (Archibald, Graber, & Brooks-Gunn, 1999).
- *Sexual activity.* Girls who were both sexually active with their boyfriends and in pubertal transition were the most likely to be dieting or engaging in disordered eating patterns (Cauffman, 1994).
- *Role models and the media.* Girls who were highly motivated to look like same-sex figures in the media were more likely than their peers to become very concerned about their weight (Field & others, 2001). Watching commercials with idealized thin female images increased adolescent girls' dissatisfaction with their bodies (Hargreaves & Tiggemann, 2004). A recent study of adolescent girls revealed that frequently reading magazine articles about dieting and weight loss was linked with unhealthy weight-control behaviors such as fasting, skipping meals, and smoking more cigarettes five years later (van den Berg & others, 2007).

Let's now examine different types of eating problems in adolescence, beginning with overweight and obesity.

**Overweight and Obesity** The Centers for Disease Control and Prevention (2007) has a category of obesity for adults but does not have an obesity category for children and adolescents because of the stigma the label *obesity* may bring. Rather they have categories for being overweight or at risk for being overweight in childhood and adolescence. These categories are determined by *body mass index (BMI)*, which is computed by a formula that takes into account height and weight. Only children and adolescents at or above the 95th percentile of BMI are included in the overweight category, and those at or above the 85th percentile are included in the at risk for overweight category.

The percentage of overweight adolescents has been increasing. Being overweight increased from 11 to 17 percent for U.S. 12- to 19-year-olds from the early 1990s through 2004 (Eaton & others, 2006). This represents a significant increase in obesity over past years. Other research indicates increases in being overweight during adolescence in European countries (Irwin, 2004; Lissau & others, 2004).

Being overweight as a child is a strong predictor for being overweight as an adolescent. One recent study computed the BMI of more than 1,000 children at seven different times from 2 to 12 years of age (Nader & others, 2006). Eighty percent of the children who were at risk for overweight at 3 years of age were also at risk for overweight or were overweight at 12 years of age.

An increase in being overweight has also occurred in emerging adulthood (Park & others, 2006). The average BMI of U.S. 20- to 29-year-old males increased from 24.3 in the early 1960s to 26.6 in 2002 and in the same time frame the average BMI of 20- to 29-year-old females increased from 22.2 to 26.6. Approximately 17 percent of emerging adults are estimated to be obese (Brown, Moore, & Bzostek, 2005).

Are there ethnic variations in being overweight during adolescence in the United States? A survey by the National Center for Health Statistics (2002) found that African American girls and Latino boys have especially high risks of being overweight during adolescence (see Figure 13.13). Another study of 2,379 girls from 9 to 19 years of age found that the prevalence of being overweight was considerably higher for African American girls than non-Latino White girls (Kimm & others, 2002). One study revealed that the higher obesity rate for African American females is linked with a diet higher in calories and fat, as well as sedentary behavior (Sanchez-Johnsen & others, 2004).

U.S. children and adolescents are more likely to be overweight or obese than their counterparts in most other countries. One recent comparison of 34 countries found that the United States had the second highest rate of child obesity (Janssen & others, 2005). In another study, U.S. children and adolescents (6 to 18 years of age) were four times more likely to be classified as obese than their counterparts in China and almost three times as likely to be classified as obese than their counterparts in Russia (Wang, 2000).

One study examined the extent to which adolescents in the United States, China, Brazil, and Russia have been overweight in the last two to three decades (Wang, Monteiro, & Popkin 2002). In the last two to three decades, adolescent overweight increased 7.7 percent in China, 13.9 percent in Brazil, and 25.6 percent in the United States.

Eating patterns established in childhood and adolescence are highly associated with obesity in adulthood. For example, 80 percent of obese adolescents become obese adults.

In one U.S. study, adolescents who had an overweight mother or father were more likely to be overweight than their counterparts without an overweight parent (Dowda & others, 2001). Also in this study, adolescent girls who watched four or more hours of television per day were more likely to be overweight than those who watched less than four hours a day. Adolescent boys who participated in team sports

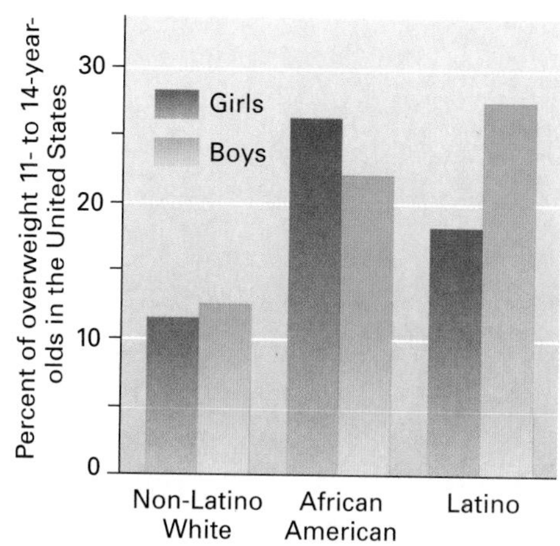


**FIGURE 13.13 Percentage of Overweight U.S. Adolescent Boys and Girls in Different Ethnic Groups**

and exercise programs were less likely to be overweight than those who did not participate in these programs. And in a recent study, watching two or more hours of television a day was linked to being overweight for both adolescent boys and girls (Fleming-Moran & Thiagarajah, 2005).

Both heredity and environmental factors are involved in obesity (Stunkard, 2000). Some individuals inherit a tendency to be overweight. Only 10 percent of children who do not have obese parents become obese themselves, whereas 40 percent of children who become obese have one obese parent, and 70 percent of children who become obese have two obese parents. Identical twins, even when they are reared apart, have similar weights.

Strong evidence of the environment's role in obesity is the doubling of the rate of obesity in the United States since 1900, as well as the significant increase in adolescent obesity since the 1960s, which was described earlier. This dramatic increase in obesity likely is due to greater availability of food (especially food high in fat), energy-saving devices, and declining physical activity. American adolescents also are more obese than European adolescents and adolescents in many other parts of the world.

A longitudinal study of more than 6,000 participants examined the relation of family environment and adolescent behavior in the seventh to twelfth grades to their risk of obesity six years later in emerging adulthood (Crossman, Sullivan, & Benin, 2006). Parental obesity and being overweight in adolescence were linked to being obese in emerging adulthood for both males and females. Parents' higher educational level, a stronger perception that parents care about them, and higher self-esteem reduced female adolescents' risk for obesity in emerging adulthood, whereas participating in sedentary activities increased their obesity risk. For male adolescents, perceiving that their parents were trying to control their diets was linked to being obese in emerging adulthood.

Being overweight or obese has negative effects on adolescent health, both in terms of biological development and socioemotional development (Dietz, 2004; Ruxton, 2004). In terms of biological development, being overweight in adolescence is linked with high blood pressure, hip problems, pulmonary problems, and type II (adult-onset) diabetes (Botero & Wolfsdorf, 2005; Cara & Chaiken, 2006). Researchers have found that U.S. adolescents' blood pressure has increased in the twenty-first century, and this is linked with the increase in being overweight in adolescence (Daniels, 2005; Muntner & others, 2004). In terms of socioemotional development, adolescents who are overweight are more likely than their normal weight counterparts to have lower self-esteem, be depressed, and have more problems in relationships with peers (Irwin, 2004; Schwimmer, Burwinkle, & Varni, 2003). A recent study of 8- to 16-year-olds revealed that obese girls were more dissatisfied with their bodies than were obese boys (Lundstedt & others, 2006).

What types of interventions have been successful in reducing overweight in adolescents? One research review indicated that clinical approaches that focus on the individual adolescent and include a combination of caloric restriction, exercise (walking or biking to school, participating in a regular exercise program), reduction of sedentary activity (watching TV, playing video games), and behavioral therapy (such as keeping weight-loss diaries and rewards for meeting goals) have been moderately effective in helping overweight adolescents lose weight (Fowler-Brown & Kahwati, 2004). In general, school-based approaches (such as instituting a school-wide program to improve eating habits) have been less effective than the clinically based individual approaches (Lytle & others, 2004). A recent research review concluded that school-based approaches for reducing adolescents' weight have modest results, with TV watching the easiest behavior to change, followed by physical activity and then nutrition (Sharma, 2006).

A concern is that as schools are under increasing pressure to spend more time on academic topics, health-oriented programs are likely to be shortchanged (Paxson & others, 2006). When this is an impediment, one possibility is to include

These overweight adolescent girls are attending a weight-management camp. *What are some factors that contribute to whether adolescents become overweight?*

obesity prevention in after-school programs, which conflict less with schools' academic mandates (Story, Kaphingst, & French, 2006). Another promising strategy is to provide students with healthier foods to eat at school. In 2005, several states began enacting laws that require more healthy foods and less nonhealthy foods be sold in vending machines at schools (Story, Kaphingst, & French, 2006). In one intervention, reducing soft drink consumption at schools was linked with a subsequent reduction in the number of 7- to 11-year-old children who were overweight or obese (James & others, 2004). Schools also can play an important role by implementing programs that increase the amount of time children exercise (Datar & Sturm, 2004; Paxson & others, 2006).

### Anorexia Nervosa and Bulimia Nervosa

Two eating disorders that may appear in adolescence and emerging adulthood are anorexia nervosa and bulimia nervosa.

#### Anorexia Nervosa

**Anorexia nervosa** is an eating disorder that involves the relentless pursuit of thinness through starvation. Anorexia nervosa is a serious disorder that can lead to death. Three main characteristics of anorexia nervosa are:

- Weighing less than 85 percent of what is considered normal for age and height.
- Having an intense fear of gaining weight. The fear does not decrease with weight loss.
- Having a distorted image of body shape (Rigaud & others, 2007). Even when they are extremely thin, anorexics see themselves as too fat. They never

**anorexia nervosa** An eating disorder that involves the relentless pursuit of thinness through starvation.

Anorexia nervosa has become an increasing problem for adolescent girls and young adult women. *What are some possible causes of anorexia nervosa?*

think they are thin enough, especially in the abdomen, buttocks, and thighs. They usually weigh themselves frequently, often take their body measurements, and gaze critically at themselves in mirrors (Seidenfeld, Sosin, & Rickert, 2004).

Anorexia nervosa typically begins in the early to middle teenage years, often following an episode of dieting and some type of life stress (Lee & others, 2005). It is about ten times more likely to characterize females than males. Although most U.S. adolescent girls have been on a diet at some point, slightly less than 1 percent ever develop anorexia nervosa (Walters & Kendler, 1994). When anorexia nervosa does occur in males, the symptoms and other characteristics (such as a distorted body image and family conflict) are usually similar to those reported by females who have the disorder (Araceli & others, 2005; Olivardia & others, 1995).

Most anorexics are non-Latino White adolescents or young adult females from well-educated, middle- and upper-income families that are competitive and high-achieving (Schmidt, 2003). They set high standards, become stressed about not being able to reach the standards, and are intensely concerned about how others perceive them (Striegel-Moore, Silberstein, & Rodin, 1993). Unable to meet these high expectations, they turn to something they can control: their weight. Problems in family functioning are increasingly being found to be linked to the appearance of anorexia nervosa in adolescent girls (Benninghoven & others, 2007), and a recent research review indicated that family therapy is often the most effective treatment of adolescent girls with anorexia nervosa (Bulik & others, 2007).

The fashion image in U.S. culture contributes to the incidence of anorexia nervosa. The media portray thin as beautiful in their choice of fashion models, who many adolescent girls strive to emulate (Wiseman, Sunday, & Becker, 2005). And many adolescent girls who strive to be thin hang out together. A recent study of adolescent girls revealed that friends often share similar body image and eating problems (Hutchinson & Rapee, 2007). In this study, an individual girl's dieting and extreme weight-loss behavior could be predicted from her friends' dieting and extreme weight-loss behavior. In addition, social-networking Web sites, such as MySpace and Facebook, connect thousands of anorexics who are able to share pro-ana (pro-anorexic) information on how to deprive their bodies and become unhealthily thin.

**Bulimia Nervosa** Although anorexics control their eating by restricting it, most bulimics cannot (Mitchell & Mazzeo, 2004). **Bulimia nervosa** is an eating disorder in which the individual consistently follows a binge-and-purge eating pattern. The bulimic goes on an eating binge and then purges by self-inducing vomiting or using a laxative. Although some people binge and purge occasionally and some experiment with it, a person is considered to have a serious bulimic disorder only if the episodes occur at least twice a week for three months.

As with anorexics, most bulimics are preoccupied with food, have a strong fear of becoming overweight, and are depressed or anxious (Ramacciotti & others, 2005; Speranza & others, 2005). A recent study revealed that bulimics overvalued their body weight and shape, and this overvaluation was linked to higher depression and lower self-esteem (Hrabosky & others, 2007). Unlike anorexics, people who binge and purge typically fall within a normal weight range, which makes bulimia more difficult to detect (Orbanic, 2001).

Bulimia nervosa typically begins in late adolescence or early adulthood. About 90 percent of the cases are women. Approximately 1 to 2 percent of women are estimated to develop bulimia nervosa (Gotesdam & Agras, 1995). Many women who develop bulimia nervosa were somewhat overweight before the onset of the disorder, and the binge eating often began during an episode of dieting. One study of adolescent girls found that increased dieting, pressure to be thin, exaggerated importance of appearance, body dissatisfaction, depression symptoms, low self-esteem, and

**bulimia nervosa** An eating disorder in which the individual consistently follows a binge-and-purge eating pattern.

low social support predicted binge eating two years later (Stice, Presnell, & Spangler, 2002). As with anorexia nervosa, about 70 percent of individuals who develop bulimia nervosa eventually recover from the disorder (Agras & others, 2004; Keel & others, 1999).

**REVIEW AND REFLECT ◆ LEARNING GOAL 2**

**2 Describe some main problems that characterize adolescents and emerging adults.**

***Review***

- Why do adolescents and emerging adults take drugs? What are some trends in adolescent drug use? What are some characteristics of the use of alcohol, hallucinogens, stimulants, depressants, and anabolic steroids by adolescents? What are the main factors that are related to adolescent and emerging adult drug use?
- What is juvenile delinquency? What are the antecedents of juvenile delinquency? What characterizes violence in youth?
- What characterizes adolescent and emerging adult depression? How common is suicide in adolescence and emerging adulthood? What are some possible causes of suicide in adolescence and emerging adulthood?
- What are the main eating disorders in adolescence and emerging adulthood? What are some of their characteristics?

***Reflect***

- Imagine that you have just been appointed to head the U.S. President's Commission on Adolescent Drug Abuse. What would be the first program you would try to put in place? What would its components be?

# 3 Interrelation of Problems and Prevention/Intervention

Adolescents with Multiple Problems | Prevention and Intervention

What characterizes at-risk adolescents? What are the best strategies for preventing or intervening in adolescent problems?

## Adolescents with Multiple Problems

The four problems that affect the most adolescents are (1) drug abuse, (2) juvenile delinquency, (3) sexual problems, and (4) school-related problems (Dryfoos, 1990; Dryfoos & Barkin, 2006). The adolescents most at risk have more than one of these problems. Researchers are increasingly finding that problem behaviors in adolescence are interrelated (Nation & Heflinger, 2006; Mason, Hitchings, & Spoth, 2007; Thompson, Ho, & Kingree, 2007). For example, heavy substance abuse is related to early sexual activity, lower grades, dropping out of school, and delinquency. Early initiation of sexual activity is associated with the use of cigarettes and alcohol, use of marijuana and other illicit drugs, lower grades, dropping out of school, and delinquency. Delinquency is related to early sexual activity, early pregnancy, substance abuse, and dropping out of school. As many as 10 percent of the adolescent population in the United States have serious multiple-problem behaviors (adolescents who have dropped out of school, or are behind in their grade level, are users of heavy drugs, regularly use cigarettes and marijuana, and are sexually active but do not use contraception). Many, but not all, of these very high-risk youth "do it all." In 1990, it was estimated that another 15 percent of adolescents participate in many of these same behaviors but with slightly lower frequency and less deleterious consequences (Dryfoos, 1990). These high-risk youth often engage in two- or three-problem behaviors (Dryfoos, 1990). Recently, it was estimated that in 2005 the figure for high-risk youth had increased to 20 percent of all U.S. adolescents (Dryfoos & Barkin, 2006).

## Prevention and Intervention

In addition to understanding that many adolescents engage in multiple-problem behaviors, it also is important to develop programs that reduce adolescent problems (Weissberg, Kumpfer, & Seligman, 2003). We described a number of prevention and intervention strategies for specific adolescent problems, such as drug abuse and juvenile delinquency, earlier in the chapter. Here we focus on some general strategies for preventing and intervening in adolescent problems. In a review of the programs that have been successful in preventing or reducing adolescent problems, adolescent researcher Joy Dryfoos (1990, 1997; Dryfoos & Barkin, 2006) described the common components of these successful programs. The common components include these:

1. *Intensive individualized attention.* In successful programs, high-risk youth are attached to a responsible adult who gives the youth attention and deals with the child's specific needs (Glidden-Tracey, 2005; Nation & others, 2003). This theme occurred in a number of different programs. In a successful substance-abuse program, a student assistance counselor was available full-time for individual counseling and referral for treatment. Successful programs often require highly trained personnel, and they extend over a long period (Dryfoos & Barkin, 2006).
2. *Community-wide, multiagency collaborative approaches.* The basic philosophy of community-wide programs is that a number of different programs and services have to be in place. In one successful substance-abuse program, a community-wide health promotion campaign was implemented that used local media and community education in concert with a substance-abuse curriculum in the schools. Community programs that include policy changes and media campaigns are more effective when they are coordinated with family, peer, and school components (Wandersman & Florin, 2003).
3. *Early identification and intervention.* Reaching children and their families before children develop problems, or at the beginning of their problems, is a successful strategy (Aber & others, 2006; Pianta, 2005).

Here are three prevention programs/research studies that merit attention:

- *High Scope.* One preschool program serves as an excellent model for the prevention of delinquency, pregnancy, substance abuse, and dropping out of school. Operated by the High Scope Foundation in Ypsilanti, Michigan, the Perry Preschool has had a long-term positive impact on its students. This enrichment program, directed by David Weikart, services disadvantaged African American children. They attend a high-quality two-year preschool program and receive weekly home visits from program personnel. Based on official police records, by age 19 individuals who had attended the Perry Preschool program were less likely to have been arrested and reported fewer adult offenses than a control group. The Perry Preschool students also were less likely to drop out of school, and teachers rated their social behavior as more competent than that of a control group who did not receive the enriched preschool experience.

- *Fast Track.* Another program that seeks to intervene in the lives of children who show early conduct problems is called Fast Track (Dodge, 2001; Dodge & the Conduct Problems Prevention Research Group, 2007; Lochman & the Conduct Problems Prevention Research Group, 2007; Milan, Pinderhughes, & the Conduct Problems Prevention Research Group, 2006). High-risk children who showed conduct problems at home and at kindergarten were identified. Then, during the elementary school years, the at-risk children and their families were given support and training in parenting, problem-solving and coping skills, peer relations, classroom atmosphere and curriculum, academic achievement, and home-school relations. Ten project interventionists worked with the children, their families, and schools to increase the protective factors and decrease the risk factors in these areas. Thus far, results show that the intervention effectively improved parenting practices and children's problem-solving and coping skills, peer relations, reading achievement, and problem behavior at home and school during the elementary school years compared with a control group of high-risk children who did not experience the intervention. However, more recent analysis of the Fast Track participants indicated that long-term outcomes were positive only for the highest-risk group of children (Dodge & the Conduct Problems Prevention Research Group, 2007). The intervention reduced their likelihood of developing conduct disorder by one-half (41 percent to 21 percent).
- *National Longitudinal Study on Adolescent Health.* This study is based on interviews with 12,118 adolescents and has implications for the prevention of adolescent problems (Allen & MacMillan, 2006; Cubbin & others, 2005; Resnick & others, 1997). Perceived adolescent connectedness to a parent and to a teacher were the main factors that were linked with preventing these adolescent problems: emotional distress, suicidal thoughts and behavior, violence, use of cigarettes, use of alcohol, use of marijuana, and early sexual intercourse. This study also provides support for the first component of successful prevention/intervention programs described under the preceding number 1. That is, intensive individualized attention is especially important when coming from important people in the adolescent's life such as parents and teachers (Greenberg & others, 2003; Kumpfer & Alvarado, 2003).

**REVIEW AND REFLECT ◆ LEARNING GOAL 3**

## 3 Summarize the interrelation of problems and ways to prevent or intervene in problems

***Review***
- How are adolescent problems interrelated?
- What are the three main ways to prevent or intervene in adolescent problems?

***Reflect***
- Why might risk taking in adolescence have more serious consequences than in the past?

# REACH YOUR LEARNING GOALS

## 1 EXPLORING ADOLESCENT AND EMERGING ADULT PROBLEMS *Discuss the nature of problems in adolescence and emerging adulthood.*

**The Biopsychosocial Approach**

Biological, psychological, and social factors have been proposed as causes of problems that adolescents, emerging adults, and others can develop. In the biopsychosocial approach, all three factors—biological, psychological, and social—are emphasized.

**The Developmental Psychopathology Approach**

In the developmental psychopathology approach, the emphasis is on describing and exploring developmental pathways of problems. One way of classifying adolescent and emerging adult problems is as internalizing or externalizing.

**Characteristics of Adolescent and Emerging Adult Problems**

The spectrum of adolescent and emerging adult problems is wide, varying in severity, developmental level, sex, and socioeconomic status. Middle-SES adolescents and females have more internalizing problems; low-SES adolescents and males have more externalizing problems. Adolescents who have a number of external and internal assets have fewer problems than their counter-parts with few external and internal assets. Well-being tends to increase during emerging adulthood, and problems such as theft decrease, but some mental health disorders increase for some emerging adults.

**Stress and Coping**

Stress is the response of individuals to stressors, which are circumstances and events that threaten them and tax their coping abilities. Sources of stress include life events, daily hassles, and sociocultural factors (such as gender, acculturative stress, and poverty). Coping involves managing taxing circumstances, expending effort to solve life's problems, and seeking to master or reduce stress. Successful coping has been linked to personal control, positive emotions, personal resources, and the strategies used. One way of classifying coping strategies focuses on problem-focused coping and emotion-focused coping. In most situations, problem-focused coping is recommended over emotion-focused coping. Among the strategies for coping effectively are thinking positively and having support from others. Coping is influenced by the demands and resources of the environment, and individuals who face stressful circumstances often benefit from using more than one strategy.

**Resilience**

Three sets of characteristics are reflected in the lives of adolescents and emerging adults who show resilience in the face of adversity and disadvantage: (1) individual factors—such as good intellectual functioning; (2) family factors—such as a close relationship with a caring parent figure; and (3) extrafamilial factors—bonds to prosocial adults outside the family. Resilience in adolescence often continues into emerging adulthood, but resilience can develop in emerging adulthood.

## 2 PROBLEMS AND DISORDERS *Describe some main problems that characterize adolescents and emerging adults.*

### Drug Use

Drugs have been used since the beginning of human existence for pleasure, utility, curiosity, and social reasons. Understanding drugs requires an understanding of physical dependence and psychological dependence. The 1960s and 1970s were a time of marked increase in the use of illicit drugs. Drug use began to decline in the 1980s but increased again in the 1990s. Since the late-1990s, there has been a decline in the overall use of illicit drugs by U.S. adolescents. Still, the United States has the highest adolescent drug-use rate of any industrialized nation. Alcohol is a depressant and is the drug most widely used by adolescents and emerging adults. Alcohol abuse is a major problem, although its use by secondary school students has begun to decline. There is an increase in alcohol use and binge drinking during emerging adulthood. Binge drinking by college students is very high. Use of alcohol and drugs typically declines by the mid-twenties. Risk factors for alcohol use include heredity and negative family and peer influences. Other drugs that can be harmful to adolescents include hallucinogens (LSD and marijuana—their use increased in the 1990s), stimulants (such as nicotine, cocaine, and amphetamines), and depressants (such as barbiturates, tranquilizers, and alcohol). A special concern is cigarette use by adolescents, although the good news is that it has been declining in recent years. An alarming trend has recently occurred in the increased use of prescription painkillers by adolescents. Adolescents' use of inhalants has decreased in recent years. Drug use in childhood and early adolescence has more negative long-term effects than when it first occurs in late adolescence. Parents and peers can provide important supportive roles in preventing adolescent drug use. Community-wide prevention efforts, early intervention, teacher training, social skills training, and other strategies can be used in school-based efforts to reduce adolescent drug use.

### Juvenile Delinquency

Juvenile delinquency consists of a broad range of behaviors, from socially undesirable behavior to status offenses. For legal purposes, a distinction is made between index and status offenses. Conduct disorder is a psychiatric diagnostic category used to describe multiple delinquent-type behaviors occurring over a six-month period. Predictors of juvenile delinquency include authority conflict, minor covert acts such as lying, overt acts of aggression, a negative identity, cognitive distortions, low self-control, early initiation of delinquency, being a male, low expectations for education and school grades, low parental monitoring, low parental support and ineffective discipline, having an older delinquent sibling, heavy peer influence and low resistance to peers, low socioeconomic status, and living in a high-crime, urban area. The high rate of violence among youth is an increasing concern. Two areas that are targets for reduction are gang involvement and school violence. A number of strategies have been proposed for reducing youth violence, including conflict resolution training.

**Depression and Suicide**

Adolescents have a higher rate of depression than children do. Female adolescents are far more likely to develop depression than adolescent males are. Adolescents who develop depression are more likely than nondepressed adolescents to have depression as adults. There is a linear increase in major depressive disorder in emerging adulthood. Treatment of depression has involved both drug therapy and psychotherapy. Emerging adults have triple the rate of suicide as adolescents. The U.S. adolescent suicide rates increased in the 1990s, but have fallen in recent years. Both proximal and distal factors likely are involved in suicide.

**Eating Disorders**

Eating disorders have become increasing problems in adolescence and emerging adulthood. The percentage of adolescents who are overweight has increased in recent in years in the United States, China, Brazil, and European countries. Being obese in adolescence is linked with being obese as an adult. An increase in obesity has also occurred in emerging adulthood. Both heredity and environmental factors are involved in obesity. Being overweight in adolescence has negative effects on physical health and socioemotional development. Clinical approaches that focus on the individual adolescent and involve a combination of caloric restriction, exercise, reduction of sedentary behavior, and behavioral therapy have been moderately effective in helping overweight adolescents lose weight. Anorexia nervosa is an eating disorder that involves the relentless pursuit of thinness through starvation. Bulimia nervosa is an eating disorder in which the individual consistently follows a binge-and-purge eating pattern.

## 3 Interrelation of Problems and Prevention/Intervention *Summarize the interrelation of problems and ways to prevent or intervene in problems.*

**Adolescents with Multiple Problems**

The four problems that affect the most adolescents are (1) drug abuse, (2) juvenile delinquency, (3) sexual problems, and (4) school-related problems. Researchers are finding that adolescents who are the most at risk often have more than one problem and that the highest-risk adolescents often have all four of these problems.

**Prevention and Intervention**

In Dryfoos' analysis, these were the common components of successful prevention/intervention programs: (1) extensive individual attention, (2) community-wide intervention, and (3) early identification and intervention.

## KEY TERMS



## KEY PEOPLE



## RESOURCES FOR IMPROVING THE LIVES OF ADOLESCENTS

**Adolescence**
by Joy Dryfoos and Carol Barkin (2006)
New York: Oxford University Press

An outstanding book on adolescent problems and the programs and strategies that can successfully prevent and intervene in these problems.

**Developmental Psychopathology**
edited by Dante Cicchetti and Donald Cohen (2006)
New York: Wiley

This up-to-date three-volume set provides extensive information about many aspects of developmental psychopathology.

**Lost Boys**
by James Garbarino (1999)
New York: Free Press

This book explores why some youth are violent and kill.

**National Adolescent Suicide Hotline**
800–621–4000

This hotline can be used 24 hours a day by teenagers contemplating suicide, as well as by their parents.

**National Clearinghouse for Alcohol Information** **www.health.org**

This clearinghouse provides information about a wide variety of issues related to drinking problems, including adolescent drinking.

**Reducing Adolescent Risk**
edited by Daniel Romer (2003)
Thousand Oaks, CA: Sage

A number of experts analyze ways to reduce adolescent risk in a number of problem areas.

# E-LEARNING TOOLS

To help you master the material in this chapter, visit the Online Learning Center for *Adolescence*, twelfth edition **(www.mhhe.com/santrocka12),** where you will find these additional resources:

## Taking It to the Net

1. Depression is one example of a mood disorder. How common are mood disorders in adolescents? What are other examples of mood disorders, and how do the symptoms differ from "normal" behavior?
2. Juvenile delinquency is a grave problem in this country. Part of solving this problem is understanding what leads adolescents to engage in delinquent behavior. Which approach to understanding adolescent problems (biopsychosocial or developmental psychopathology) do you think best explains juvenile delinquency? Why?
3. Many people are concerned about adolescents in our current culture. What social policy would you create to prevent or intervene with adolescents with problems? Why?

## Self-Assessment

The Online Learning Center includes the following self-assessment for further exploration:

- Stressful Events in My Life
- My Coping Strategies
- Am I Depressed?

## Health and Well-Being, Parenting, and Education

To practice your decision-making skills, complete the health and well-being, parenting, and education exercises on the Online Learning Center.

## Video Clips

The Online Learning Center includes the following videos for this chapter:

- Talking About Drugs at Age 14
- Talking About Drugs at Age 15
- Substance Use Among Young Adults: Expert Interview

# GLOSSARY

## A

**accommodation** An adjustment to new information. 97

**acculturation** Cultural change that results from continuous, firsthand contact between two distinctive cultural groups. 434

**acculturative stress** The negative consequences that result from contact between two distinctive cultural groups. 470

**active (niche-picking) genotype-environment correlations** Correlations that occur when children seek out environments that they find compatible and stimulating. 82

**adaptive behavior** A modification of behavior that promotes an organism's survival in the natural habitat. 77

**adolescence** The developmental period of transition from childhood to adulthood; it involves biological, cognitive, and socioemotional changes. 16

**adolescent egocentrism** The heightened self-consciousness of adolescents, which is reflected in their belief that others are as interested in them as they themselves are, and in their sense of personal uniqueness and invulnerability. 124

**adolescent generalization gap** Adelson's concept of generalizations about adolescents based on information about a limited, highly visible group of adolescents. 9

**adolescents who are gifted** Adolescents who have above-average intelligence (usually defined as an IQ of 130 or higher) and/or superior talent in some domain, such as art, music, or mathematics. 385

**adoption study** A study in which investigators seek to discover whether the behavior and psychological characteristics of adopted children are more like their adoptive parents, who have provided a home environment, or more like those of their biological parents, who have contributed their heredity. Another form of adoption study involves comparing adoptive and biological siblings. 81

**adrenarche** Puberty phase involving hormonal changes in the adrenal glands, located just above the kidneys. These changes occur from about 6 to 9 years of age in girls and about one year later in boys, before what is generally considered the beginning of puberty. 57

**affectionate love** Also called companionate love, this love occurs when an individual desires to have another person near and has a deep, caring affection for that person. 343

**AIDS** Acquired immune deficiency syndrome, a sexually transmitted syndrome caused by the HIV virus, which destroys the body's immune system. 221

**alternation model** This model assumes that it is possible for an individual to know and understand two different cultures. It also assumes that individuals can alter their behavior to fit a particular social context. 434

**altruism** Unselfish interest in helping another person. 250

**amygdala** A portion of the brain's limbic system that is the seat of emotions such as anger. 94

**anabolic steroids** Drugs derived from the male sex hormone, testosterone. They promote muscle growth and lean body mass. 485

**androgens** The main class of male sex hormones. 55

**androgyny** The presence of a high degree of feminine and masculine characteristics in the same individual. 189

**anorexia nervosa** An eating disorder that involves the relentless pursuit of thinness through starvation. 501

**anxiety** A vague, highly unpleasant feeling of fear and apprehension. 404

**assimilation** Occurs when individuals relinguish their cultural identity and move into the larger society. 433

**assimilation** The incorporation of new information into existing knowledge. 97

**attention deficit hyperactivity disorder (ADHD)** A disability in which children and adolescents show one or more of the following characteristics over a period of time: inattention, hyperactivity, and impulsivity. 383

**authoritarian parenting** This is a restrictive, punitive style in which the parent exhorts the adolescent to follow the parent's directions and to respect work and effort. Firm limits and controls are placed on the adolescent, and little verbal exchange is allowed. This style is associated with adolescents' socially incompetent behavior. 282

**authoritative parenting** This style encourages adolescents to be independent but still places limits and controls on their actions. Extensive verbal give-and-take is allowed, and parents are warm and nurturant toward the adolescent. This style is associated with adolescents' socially competent behavior. 283

**authoritative strategy of classroom management** This teaching strategy encourages students to be independent thinkers and doers but still involves effective monitoring. Authoritative teachers engage students in considerable verbal give-and-take and show a caring attitude toward them. However, they still declare limits when necessary. 369

**average children** Children who receive an average number of both positive and negative nominations from their peers. 323

## B

**behavior genetics** The field that seeks to discover the influence of heredity and environment on individual differences in human traits and development. 80

**bicultural identity** Identity formation that occurs when adolescents identify in some ways with their ethnic group and in other ways with the majority culture. 152

**big five factors of personality** Five core traits of personality: openness to experience, conscientiousness, extraversion, agreeableness, and neuroticism (emotional stability). 158

**biological processes** Physical changes in an individual's body. 15

**biopsychosocial approach** Emphasizes that problems develop through an interaction of biological, psychological, and social factors. 465

**bisexual** A person who is attracted to people of both sexes. 208

**boundary ambiguity** The uncertainty in stepfamilies about who is in or out of the family and who is performing or responsible for certain tasks in the family system. 304

**Bronfenbrenner's ecological theory** Bronfenbrenner's ecological theory focuses on the influence of five environmental systems: microsystem, mesosystem, exosystem, macrosystem, and chronosystem. 33

**bulimia nervosa** An eating disorder in which the individual consistently follows a binge-and-purge eating pattern. 502

## C

**care perspective** The moral perspective of Carol Gilligan, which views people in terms of their connectedness with others and emphasizes interpersonal communication, relationships with others, and concern for others. 247

**career self-concept theory** Super's theory that an individual's self-concepts play a central role in his or her career choices and that in adolescence individuals first construct their career self-concept. 414

**case study** An in-depth look at a single individual. 36

**character education** A direct moral education approach that involves teaching students a basic moral literacy to prevent them from engaging in immoral behavior or doing harm to themselves or others. 257

**chlamydia** One of most common sexually transmitted infections, named for *Chlamydia trachomatis*, an organism that spreads by sexual contact and infects the genital organs of both sexes. 225

**chromosomes** Threadlike structures that contain deoxyribonucleic acid, or DNA. 78

**cliques** Small groups that range from two to about twelve individuals and average about five to six individuals. Members are usually of the same sex and are similar in age; cliques can form because of similar interests, such as sports, and also can form purely from friendship. 334

**cognitive constructivist approaches** Approaches that emphasize the adolescent's active, cognitive construction of knowledge and understanding; an example is Piaget's theory. 359

**cognitive developmental theory of gender** In this view, children's gender-typing occurs after they have developed a concept of gender. Once they begin to consistently conceive of themselves as male or female, children often organize their world on the basis of gender. 176

**cognitive moral education** An approach based on the belief that students should learn to value things like democracy and justice as their moral reasoning develops; Kohlberg's theory has been the basis for many of the cognitive moral education approaches. 258

**cognitive processes** Changes in an individual's thinking and intelligence. 16

**cohabitation** Living together in a sexual relationship without being married. 347

**commitment** The part of identity development in which adolescents show a personal investment in what they are going to do. 148

**concrete operational stage** Piaget's third stage, which lasts approximately from 7 to 11 years of age. In this stage, children can perform operations. Logical reasoning replaces intuitive thought as long as the reasoning can be applied to specific or concrete examples. 98

**conduct disorder** The psychiatric diagnostic category for the occurrence of multiple delinquent activities over a six-month period. These behaviors include truancy, running away, fire setting, cruelty to animals, breaking and entering, and excessive fighting. 489

**conformity** This occurs when individuals adopt the attitudes or behaviors of others because of real or imagined pressure from them. 322

**conglomerate strategies** The use of a combination of techniques, rather than a single approach, to improve adolescents' social skills; also called coaching. 326

**connectedness** An important element in adolescent identity development. It consists of two dimensions: mutuality, sensitivity to and respect for others' views; and permeability, openness to others' views. 151

**conscience** The component of the superego that involves behaviors disapproved of by parents. 251

**contexts** The settings in which development occurs. These settings are influenced by historical, economic, social, and cultural factors. 11

**continuity view** A developmental view that emphasizes the role of early parent-child relationships in constructing a basic way of relating to people throughout the life span. 277

**continuity-discontinuity issue** The issue regarding whether development involves gradual, cumulative change (continuity) or distinct stages (discontinuity). 23

**controversial children** Children who are frequently nominated both as a best friend and as being disliked. 323

**conventional reasoning** The second, or intermediate, level in Kohlberg's theory of moral development. Internalization is intermediate. Individuals abide by certain standards (internal), but they are the standards of others (external), such as parents or the laws of society. 242

**convergent thinking** A pattern of thinking in which individuals prodsuce one correct answer; characteristic of the items on conventional intelligence tests; coined by Guilford. 113

**coping** Involves managing taxing circumstances, expending effort to solve life's problems, and seeking to master or reduce stress. 470

**corpus collosum** A large bundle of axon fibers that connect the brain's left and right hemispheres. 94

**correlation coefficient** A number based on a statistical analysis that is used to describe the degree of association between two variables. 37

**correlational research** Research whose goal is to describe the strength of the relationship between two or more events or characteristics. 37

**creativity** The ability to think in novel and unusual ways and discover unique solutions to problems. 113

**crisis** A period of identity development during which the adolescent is choosing among meaningful alternatives. 148

**critical thinking** Thinking reflectively and productively and evaluating the evidence. 112

**cross-cultural studies** Studies that compare a culture with one or more other cultures. Such studies provide information about the degree to which development in adolescents and emerging adults is similar, or universal, across cultures or about the degree to which it is culture-specific. 431

**cross-sectional research** A research strategy in which individuals of different ages are compared at one time. 39

**crowds** A larger group structure than cliques. Adolescents are usually members of a crowd based on reputation and may or may not spend much time together. 334

**cults** Groups that have been defined in various ways, ranging from "dangerous institutions that cause severe emotional harm" to "marginal and deviant groups" to "fringe, often new, religious movements." 266

**culture** The behavior, patterns, beliefs, and all other products of a particular groups of people that are passed on from generation to generation. 429

## D

**date, or acquaintance, rape** Coercive sexual activity directed at someone whom the perpetrator knows. 226

**dating scripts** The cognitive models that adolescents and adults use to guide and evaluate dating interactions. 345

**deductive reasoning** Reasoning from the general to the specific. 111

**dependent variable** The factor that is measured in experimental research. 38

**depressants** Drugs that slow down the central nervous system, bodily functions, and behavior. 484

**descriptive research** Research that aims to observe and record behavior. 37

**development** The pattern of change that begins at conception and continues through the life span. Most development involves growth, although it also includes decay (as in death and dying). 15

**developmental career choice theory** Ginzberg's theory that children and adolescents go through three career choice stages: fantasy, tentative, and realistic. 414

**developmental construction views** Views sharing the belief that as individuals grow up, they acquire modes of relating to others. There are two main variations of this view. One emphasizes continuity and stability in relationships throughout the life span; the other emphasizes discontinuity and changes in relationships throughout the life span. 276

**developmental psychopathology** The area of psychology that focuses on describing and exploring the developmental pathways of problems. 466

**difficult child** Reacts negatively to many situations and is slow to accept new experiences. 160

**direct instruction approach** A teacher-centered approach characterized by teacher direction and control, mastery of academic skills, high expectations for students, and maximum time spent on learning tasks. 359

**discontinuity view** A developmental view that emphasizes change and growth in relationships over time. 278

**dismissing/avoidant attachment** An insecure attachment category in which individuals deemphasize the importance of attachment. This category is associated with consistent experiences of rejection of attachment needs by caregivers. 291

**divergent thinking** A pattern of thinking in which individuals produce many answers to the same question; more characteristic of creativity than convergent thinking; coined by Guilford. 113

**DNA** A complex molecule that contains genetic information. 78

## E

**early adolescence** The developmental period that corresponds roughly to the middle school or junior high school years and includes most pubertal change. 17

**early adulthood** The developmental period beginning in the late teens or early twenties and lasting through the thirties. 17

**early childhood** The developmental period extending from the end of infancy to about 5 or 6 years of age; sometimes called the preschool years. 16

**early-later experience issue** This issue focuses on the degree to which early experiences (especially early in childhood) or later experiences are the key determinants of development. 23

**easy child** Generally is in a positive mood, quickly establishes regular routines, and adapts easily to new experiences. 160

**eclectic theoretical orientation** An orientation that does not follow any one theoretical approach but rather selects from each theory whatever is considered the best in it. 34

**ego ideal** The component of the superego that involves ideal standards approved by parents. 251

**emerging adulthood** The developmental period occurring from approximately 18 to 25 years of age, this transitional period between adolescence and adulthood is characterized by experimentation and exploration. 18

**emotion** Feeling, or affect, that occurs when a person is in a state or an interaction that is important to the individual, especially to his or her well-being. 154

**emotional autonomy** The capacity to relinquish childlike dependence on parents. 289

**emotional intelligence** The ability to perceive and express emotion accurately and adaptively, to understand emotion and emotional knowledge, to use feelings to facilitate thought, and to manage emotions in oneself and others. 121

**emotion-focused coping** Lazarus' term for responding to stress in an emotional manner, especially by using defense mechanisms 471

**empathy** Reacting to another's feelings with an emotional response that is similar to the other's feelings. 252

**epigenetic view** Emphasizes that development is the result of an ongoing bidirectional interchange between heredity and environment. 83

**equilibration** A mechanism in Piaget's theory that explains how individuals shift from one state of thought to the next. The shift occurs as they experience cognitive conflict or a disequilibrium in trying to understand the world. Eventually, the individual resolves the conflict and reaches a balance, or equilibrium, of thought. 97

**Erikson's theory** Includes eight stages of human development. Each stage consists of a unique developmental task that confronts individuals with a crisis that must be faced. 28

**estrogens** The main class of female sex hormones. 55

**ethnic gloss** Using an ethnic label such as African American or Latino in a superficial way that portrays an ethnic group as being more homogeneous than it really is. 41

**ethnic identity** An enduring, basic aspect of the self that includes a sense of membership in an ethnic group and the attitudes and feelings related to that membership. 152

**ethnicity** A dimension of culture based on cultural heritage, nationality characteristics, race, religion, and language. 429

**ethnocentrism** A tendency to favor one's own group over other groups. 430

**evocative genotype-environment correlations** Correlations that occur because an adolescent's genetically shaped characteristics elicit certain types of physical and social environments. 81

**evolutionary psychology** An approach that emphasizes the importance of adaptation, reproduction, and "survival of the fittest" in explaining behavior. 77

**executive functioning** Higher-order, complex cognitive processes that include making decisions, reasoning, thinking critically, thinking creatively, and metacognition. 109

**experience sampling method (ESM)** Involves providing participants with electronic pagers and then beeping them at random times, at which point they are asked to report on various aspects of their lives. 36

**experimental research** Research that involves an experiment, a carefully regulated procedure in which one or more of the factors believed to influence the behavior being studied are manipulated while all other factors are held constant. 38

**externalizing problems** Occur when individuals turn problems outward. An example is juvenile delinquency. 466

**extrinsic motivation** External motivational factors such as rewards and punishments. 395

## F

**female athlete triad** A combination of disordered eating, amenorrhea, and osteoporosis that may develop in female adolescents and college students. 75

**feminization of poverty** The fact that far more women than men live in poverty. Women's low income, divorce, and the resolution of divorce cases by the judicial system, which leaves women with less money than they and their children need to adequately function, are the likely causes. 439

**flow** Csikszentmihalyi's concept of optimal life experiences, which he believes occur most often when people develop a sense of mastery and are absorbed in a state of concentration when they're engaged in an activity. 396

**forgiveness** This is an aspect of prosocial behavior that occurs when an injured person releases the injurer from possible behavioral retaliation. 251

**formal operational stage** Piaget's fourth and final stage of cognitive development, which he argued emerges at 11 to 15 years of age. It is characterized by abstract, idealistic, and logical thought. 98

**friends** A subset of peers who engage in mutual companionship, support, and intimacy. 327

## G

**gender** The characteristics of people as males and females. 170

**gender bias** A preconceived notion about the abilities of females and males that prevents individuals from pursuing their own interests and achieving their potential. 41

**gender intensification hypothesis** States that psychological and behavioral differences between boys and girls become greater during early adolescence because of increased socialization pressure to conform to traditional masculine and feminine gender roles. 188

**gender role** A set of expectations that prescribes how females and males should think, act, and feel. 170

**gender-role transcendence** The belief that, when an individual's competence is at issue, it should be conceptualized on a person basis rather than on the basis of masculinity, femininity, or androgyny. 187

**gender schema** A cognitive structure that organizes the world in terms of male and female. 176

**gender schema theory** According to this theory, gender-typing emerges as individuals gradually develop gender schemas of what is gender-appropriate and gender-inappropriate in their culture. 176

**gender stereotypes** Broad categories that reflect our impressions and beliefs about females and males. 177

**gender-typing** The process by which children acquire the thoughts, feelings, and behaviors considered gender-appropriate in a particular culture. 172

**generational inequity** The unfair treatment of younger members of an aging society in which older adults pile up advantages by receiving inequitably large allocations of resources, such as Social Security and Medicare. 13

**genes** The units of hereditary information, which are short segments composed of DNA. 78

**genital herpes** A sexually transmitted infection caused by a large family of viruses of different strains. These strains produce other, non–sexually transmitted diseases such as chicken pox and mononucleosis. 224

**genital warts** Caused by the human papillomavirus, genital warts are very contagious and are the most common acquired STI in the United States in the 15- to 24-year old age group. 224

**genotype** A person's genetic heritage; the actual genetic material. 80

**gonadarche** Puberty phase involving the maturation of primary sexual characteristics (ovaries in females, testes in males) and secondary sexual characteristics (pubic hair, breast, and genital development). This period follows adrenarche by about two years and is what most people think of as puberty. 57

**gonorrhea** This sexually transmitted infection is caused by a bacterium called *Neisseria gonorrhoeae,* which thrives in the moist mucous membranes lining the mouth, throat, vagina, cervix, urethra, and anal tract. This STI is commonly called the "drip" or the "clap." 224

**goodness of fit** The match between an individual's temperament style and the environmental demands the individual must cope with. 162

## H

**hallucinogens** Also called psychedelic (mind-altering) drugs, these drugs alter an individual's perceptual experiences and produce hallucinations. 480

**helpless orientation** An outlook in which individuals seem trapped when experiencing difficulty and they focus on their personal inadequacies; they attribute their difficulty to a lack of ability. This orientation undermines performance. 398

**hidden curriculum** The pervasive moral atmosphere that characterizes every schools. 257

**homophobia** Having irrational negative feelings against individuals who have same-sex attractions. 210

**hormones** Powerful chemicals secreted by the endocrine glands and carried through the body by the bloodstream. 55

**hostile environment sexual harassment** Sexual harassment in which students are subjected to unwelcome sexual conduct that is so severe, persistent, or pervasive that it limits the students' ability to benefit from their education. 228

**hypotheses** Specific assertions and predictions that can be tested. 26

**hypothetical-deductive reasoning** Piaget's term for adolescents' ability, in the formal operational stage, to develop hypotheses, or best guesses, about ways to solve problems; they then systematically deduce, or conclude, the best path to follow in solving the problem. 99

## I

**identity achievement** Marcia's term for an adolescent who has undergone an identity crisis and made a commitment. 148

**identity diffusion** Marcia's term for the state adolescents are in when they have not yet experienced an identity crisis or made any commitments. 148

**identity foreclosure** Marcia's term for the state adolescents are in when they have made a commitment but have not experienced an identity crisis. 148

**identity moratorium** Marcia's term for the state of adolescents who are in the midst of an identity crisis, but who have not made a clear commitment to an identity. 148

**identity versus identity confusion** Erikson's fifth developmental stage, which occurs during adolescence. At this time, individuals are faced with deciding on who they are, what they are all about, and where they are going in life. 146

**inclusion** Educating a child or adolescent with special education needs full-time the regular classroom. 385

**independent variable** The factor that is manipulated in experimental research. 38

**index offenses** Whether they are committed by juveniles or adults, these are criminal acts, such as robbery, rape, and homicide. 489

**individuality** An important element in adolescent identity development. It consists of two dimensions: self-assertion, the ability to have and communicate a point of view; and separateness, the use of communication patterns to express how one is different from others. 151

**Individuals with Disabilities Education Act (IDEA)** This spells out broad mandates for services to all children and adolescents with disabilities. These include evaluation and eligibility determination, appropriate education and an individualized education plan (IEP), and education in the least restrictive environment. 384

**induction** A discipline technique in which a parent uses reason and explanation of the consequences for others of the adolescents's actions. 255

**inductive reasoning** Reasoning from the specific to the general—that is, drawing conclusions about all members of a category based on observing only some of its members. 111

**indulgent parenting** A style in which parents are highly involved with their adolescents but place few demands or controls on them. This is associated with adolescents' social incompetence, especially a lack of self-control. 283

**infancy** The developmental period that extends from birth to 18 or 24 months of age. 16

**information-processing theory** Emphasizes that individuals manipulate information, monitor it, and strategize about it. Central to this approach are the processes of memory and thinking. 31

**insecure attachment** In this attachment pattern, infants either avoid the caregiver or show considerable resistance or ambivalence toward the caregiver. This pattern is theorized to be related to difficulties in relationships and problems in later development. 291

**intelligence** The ability to solve problems and to adapt to and learn from everyday experiences; not everyone agrees on what constitutes intelligence. 118

**intelligent quotient (IQ)** A person's tested mental age divided by chronological age, multiplied by 100. 118

**internalization** The developmental change from behavior that is externally controlled to behavior that is controlled by internal standards and principles. 241

**internalizing problems** Occur when individuals turn problems inward. Examples include anxiety and depression. 466

**Internet** The core of computer-mediated communication. The Internet system is worldwide and connects thousands of computer networks, providing an incredible array of information adolescents can access. 453

**intimacy in friendship** In most research studies, this is defined narrowly as self-disclosure, or sharing of private thoughts. 330

**intimacy versus isolation** Erikson's sixth developmental stage, which individuals experience during the early adulthood years. At this time, individuals face the developmental task of forming intimate relationships with others. 154

**intrinsic motivation** Internal motivational factors such as self-determination, curiosity, challenge, and effort. 395

**inventionist view** The view that adolescence is a sociohistorical creation. Especially important in this view are the sociohistorical circumstances at the beginning of the twentieth century, a time when legislation was enacted that ensured the dependency of youth and made their move into the economic sphere more manageable. 7

## J

**jigsaw classroom** A strategy in which students from different cultural backgrounds are placed in a cooperative group in which, together, they have to construct different parts of a project to reach a common goal. 377

**justice perspective** A moral perspective that focuses on the rights of the individual; individuals independently make moral decisions. 247

**juvenile delinquency** A broad range of behaviors, including socially unacceptable behavior, status offenses, and criminal acts. 489

## L

**laboratory** A controlled setting in which many of the complex factors of the "real world" are removed. 35

**late adolescence** Approximately the latter half of the second decade of life. Career interests, dating, and identity exploration are often more pronounced in late adolescence than in early adolescence. 17

**late adulthood** The developmental period that lasts from about 60 to 70 years of age until death. 18

**learning disability** Individuals with a learning disability are of normal intelligence or above, have difficulties in at least one academic area and usually several, and their difficulties cannot be attributed to any other diagnosed problem or disorder, such as mental retardation. 382

**least restrictive environment** A setting that is as similar as possible to the one in which the children or adolescents without a disability are educated; under the IDEA, the child or adolescent with a disability must be educated in this setting. 385

**longitudinal research** A research strategy in which the same individuals are studied over a period of time, usually several years or more. 40

**love withdrawal** A discipline technique in which a parent removes attention or love from the adolescent. 255

## M

**major depressive disorder** The diagnosis when an individual experiences a major depressive episode and depressed characteristics, such as lethargy and depression, for two weeks or longer and daily functioning becomes impaired. 495

**mastery orientation** An outlook in which individuals focus on the task rather than on their ability; they concentrate on learning strategies and the process of achievement instead of the outcome. 398

**menarche** A girl's first menstrual period. 57

**mental age (MA)** An individual's level of mental development relative to others; a concept developed by Binet. 118

**mentors** Individuals who are usually older and more experienced and are motivated to improve the competence and character of a younger person. 402

**metacognition** Cognition about cognition, or "knowing about knowing." 115

**middle adulthood** The developmental period that is entered at about 35 to 45 years of age and exited at about 55 to 65 years of age. 17

**middle and late childhood** The developmental period extending from about 6 to about 10 or 11 years of age; sometimes called the elementary school years. 16

**mindset** The cognitive view, either fixed or growth, that individuals develop for themselves. 398

**moral development** Thoughts, feelings, and behaviors regarding standards of right and wrong. 240

**moral exemplars** People who have lived exemplary lives. 253

**moral identity** An aspect of personality that is present when individuals have moral notions and commitments that are central to their lives. 253

**multicultural model** This model promotes a pluralistic approach to understanding two or more cultures. It argues that people can maintain their distinctive identities while working with others from different cultures to meet common national or economic needs. 434

**myelination** The process by which the axon portion of the neuron becomes covered and insulated with a layer of fat cells, which increases the speed and efficiency of information processing in the nervous system. 93

## N

**naturalistic observation** Observing behavior in real-world settings. 35

**nature-nurture issue** The issue involving the debate about whether development is primarily influenced by nature or nurture. Nature refers to an organism's biological inheritance, nurture to its environmental experiences. 23

**neglected children** Children who are infrequently nominated as a best friend but are not disliked by their peers. 323

**neglectful parenting** A style in which the parent is very uninvolved in the adolescent's life. It is associated with adolescents' social incompetence, especially a lack of self-control. 283

**neo-Piagetians** Theorists who argue that Piaget got some things right but that his theory needs considerable revision. In their revision, they give more emphasis to information processing that involves attention, memory, and strategies; they also seek to provide more precise explanations of cognitive changes. 101

**neurons** Nerve cells, which are the nervous system's basic units 93

**non-shared environmental experiences** The adolescent's own unique experiences, both within a family and outside the family, that are not shared by sibling. 82

**normal distribution** A symmetrical distribution of values or scores, with a majority of scores falling in the middle of the possible range of scores and few scores appearing toward the extremes of the range. 118

**norms** Rules that apply to all members of a group. 333

## P

**passive genotype-environment correlations** Correlations that occur because biological parents, who are genetically related to the child, provide a rearing environment for the child. 81

**peers** Individuals who are about the same age or maturity level. 319

**performance orientation** An outlook in which individuals are focused on winning rather than achievement outcome. For performance-oriented students, winning is what results in happiness. 398

**permissive strategy of classroom management** This strategy offers students considerable autonomy but provides them with little support for developing learning skills or managing their behavior. 370

**personality type theory** Holland's theory that an effort should be made to match an individual's career choice with his or her personality. 415

**phenotype** The way an individual's genotype is expressed in observed and measurable characteristics. 80

**physical dependence** Physical need for a drug that is accompanied by unpleasant withdrawal symptoms when the drug is discontinued. 475

**Piaget's theory** States that children actively construct their understanding of the world and go through four stages of cognitive development. 29

**popular children** Children who are frequently nominated as a best friend and are rarely disliked by their peers. 323

**possible self** What individuals might become, what they would like to become, and what they are afraid of becoming. 136

**postconventional reasoning** The highest level in Kohlberg's theory of moral development. Morality is completely internalized and not based on the standards of others. 243

**postformal thought** Thought that is reflective, relativistic, and contextual; provisional; realistic; and open to emotions and subjective. 102

**power assertion** A discipline technique in which a parent attempts to gain control over the adolescent or the adolescent's resources. 255

**preconventional reasoning** The lowest level in Kohlberg's theory of moral development. The individual shows no internalization of moral values—moral reasoning is controlled by external rewards and punishment. 242

**prefrontal cortex** The highest level of the brain's frontal lobes that is involved in reasoning, decision making, and self-control. 94

**prejudice** An unjustified negative attitude toward an individual because of the individual's membership in a group. 445

**prenatal period** The time from conception to birth. 16

**preoccupied/ambivalent attachment** An insecure attachment category in which adolescents are hypertuned to attachment experiences. This is thought to mainly occur because parents are inconsistently available to the adolescents. 291

**preoperational stage** Piaget's second stage, which lasts approximately from 2 to 7 years of age. In this stage, children begin to represent their world with words, images, and drawings. 98

**problem-focused coping** Lazarus' term for the strategy of squarely facing one's troubles and trying to solve them. 471

**psychoanalytic theories** Describe development as primarily unconscious and heavily colored by emotion. Behavior is merely a surface characteristic, and the symbolic workings of the mind have to be analyzed to understand behavior. Early experiences with parents are emphasized. 26

**psychological dependence** Strong desire and craving to repeat the use of a drug for various emotional reasons, such as a feeling of well-being and reduction of distress. 475

**psychometric/intelligence view** A view that emphasizes the importance of individual differences in intelligence; many advocates of this view also argue that intelligence should be assessed with intelligence tests. 117

**psychosocial moratorium** Erikson's term for the gap between childhood security and adult autonomy that adolescents experience as part of their identity exploration. 146

**puberty** A period of rapid physical maturation involving hormonal and bodily changes that take place primarily in early adolescence. 54

**Public Law 94-142** The Education for All Handicapped Children Act, which requires all students with disabilities to be given a free, appropriate public education. 384

## Q

**quid pro quo sexual harassment** Sexual harassment in which a school employee threatens to base an educational decision (such as a grade) on a student's submission to unwelcome sexual conduct. 228

## R

**rape** Forcible sexual intercourse with a person who does not give consent. 226

**rapport talk** The language of conversation, establishing connections, and negotiating relationships. 181

**reciprocal socialization** The process by which children and adolescents socialize parents, just as parents socialize them. 275

**rejected children** Children who are infrequently nominated as a best friend and are actively disliked by their peers. 323

**report talk** Talk that gives information; public speaking is an example. 181

**resilience** Adapting positively and achieving successful outcomes in the face of significant risks and adverse circumstances. 22

**rites of passage** Ceremonies or rituals that mark an individual's transition from one status to another, such as the entry into adulthood. 434

**roles** Certain positions in a group that are governed by rules and expectations. Roles define how adolescents should behave in those positions. 333

**romantic love** Also called passionate love or eros, this love has strong sexual and infatuation components, and it often predominates in the early part of a love relationship. 343

## S

**schema** A mental concept or framework that is useful in organizing and interpreting information. 97

**secular trends** Patterns of the onset of puberty over historical time, especially across generations. 62

**secure attachment** In this attachment pattern, infants use their primary caregiver, usually the mother, as a secure base from which to explore the environment. Secure attachment is theorized to be an important foundation for psychological development later in childhood, adolescence, and adulthood. 291

**self-concept** Domain-specific evaluations of the self. 140

**self-efficacy** The belief that one can master a situation and produce positive outcomes. 399

**self-esteem** The global evaluative dimension of the self; also referred to as self-worth or self-image. 140

**self-handicapping** Use of failure avoidance strategies such as not trying in school or putting off studying until the last minute so that circumstances, rather than a lack of trying, will be seen as the cause of low-level performance. 405

**self-regulatory learning** The self-generation and self-monitoring of one's thoughts, feelings, and behaviors in order to reach a goal. 116

**self-understanding** The individual's cognitive representation of the self; the substance and content of self-conceptions. 135

**sensorimotor stage** Piaget's first stage of development, lasting from birth to about 2 years of age. In this stage, infants construct an understanding of the world by coordinating sensory experiences with physical, motoric actions. 98

**service learning** A form of education that promotes social responsibility and service to the community. 258

**sexism** Prejudice and discrimination against an individual because of her or his sex. 178

**sexual minority** Someone who identifies with being lesbian, gay, or bisexual. 208

**sexual script** A stereotyped pattern of role prescriptions for how individuals should sexually behave. Females and males have been socialized to follow different sexual scripts. 205

**sexually transmitted infections (STIs)** Infections that are contracted primarily through sexual contact. This contact is not limited to vaginal intercourse but includes oral-genital contact and anal-genital contact as well. 221

**shared environmental experiences** Siblings' common experiences such as their parents' personalities and intellectual orientation, the family's socioeconomic status, and the neighborhood in which they live. 82

**slow-to-warm-up child** Has a low activity level, is somewhat negative, and displays a low intensity of mood. 160

**social cognition** The way individuals conceptualize and reason about their social worlds—the people they watch and interact with, their relationships with those people, the groups they participate in, and the way they reason about themselves and others. 124

**social cognitive theory** The view of psychologists who emphasize behavior, environment, and cognition as the key factors in development. 32

**social cognitive theory of gender** This view emphasizes that children's and adolescents' gender development is influenced by observation and imitation of gender behavior, and by rewards and punishments they experience for gender-appropriate and gender-inappropriate behavior. 173

**social cognitive theory of moral development** The theory that distinguishes between moral competence (the ability to produce moral behaviors) and moral performance (enacting those behaviors in specific situations). 249

**social constructivist approach** Emphasizes the social contexts of learning and the construction of knowledge through social interaction. 103

**social constructivist approaches** Approaches that focus on collaboration with others to produce knowledge and understanding; an example is Vygotsky's theory. 359

**social conventional reasoning** Thoughts about social consensus and convention, as opposed to moral reasoning that stresses ethical issues. 248

**social policy** A national government's course of action designed to influence the welfare of its citizens. 11

**social role theory** States that gender differences result from the contrasting roles of females and males, with females having less power and status and control fewer resources than males. 172

**socioeconomic status (SES)** A grouping of people with similar occupational, educational, and economic characteristics. 429

**socioemotional processes** Changes in an individual's personality, emotions, relationships with other people, and social contexts. 16

**sociometric status** The extent to which children and adolescents are liked or disliked by their peer group. 323

**spermarche** A boy's first ejaculation of semen. 57

**standardized test** A test with uniform procedures for administration and scoring. Many standardized tests allow a person's performance to be compared with the performance of other individuals. 35

**status offenses** Performed by youth under a specified age, these are juvenile offenses that are not as serious as index offenses. These offenses may include such acts as underage drinking, truancy, and sexual promiscuity. 489

**stereotype** A generalization that reflects our impressions and beliefs about a broad group of people. All stereotypes refer to an image of what the typical member of a particular group is like. 8

**stimulants** Drugs that increase the activity of the central nervous system. 481

**storm-and-stress view** G. Stanley Hall's concept that adolescence is a turbulent time charged with conflict and mood swings. 6

**stress** The response of individuals to *stressors,* which are circumstances and events that threaten and tax their coping abilities. 468

**synapses** Gaps between neurons, where connections between the axon and dendrites occur. 93

**syphilis** A sexually transmitted infection caused by the bacterium *Treponema pallidum,* a spirochete. 225

## T

**temperament** An individual's behavioral style and characteristic way of responding. 159

**theory** An interrelated, coherent set of ideas that helps explain phenomena and make predictions. 26

**tolerance** The condition in which a greater amount of a drug is needed to produce the same effect as a smaller amount produced in the past. 475

**top-dog phenomenon** The circumstance of moving from the top position (in elementary school, the oldest, biggest, and most powerful students) to the lowest position (in middle or junior high school, the youngest, smallest, and least powerful). 363

**triarchic theory of intelligence** Sternberg's view that intelligence comes in three main forms: analytical, creative, and practical. 120

**twin study** A study in which the behavioral similarity of identical twins is compared with the behavioral similarity of fraternal twins. 81

## U

**unresolved/disorganized attachment** An insecure category in which the adolescent has an unusually high level of fear and is disoriented. This can result from such traumatic experiences as a parent's death or abuse by parents. 292

## V

**values clarification** An educational approach that focuses on helping people clarify what is important to them, what is worth working for, and what purpose their lives are to serve. Students are encouraged to define their own values and understand others' values. 257

**values** Beliefs and attitudes about the way things should be. 260

**Vygotsky's theory** A sociocultural cognitive theory that emphasizes how culture and social interaction guide cognitive development. 30

## Z

**zone of proximal development (ZPD)** Vygotsky's concept that refers to the range of tasks that are too difficult for an individual to master alone, but that can be mastered with the guidance or assistance of adults or more-skilled peers. 103

# REFERENCES


## A

**Aalsma, M. C., Lapsley, D. K., & Flannery, D. J.** (2006). Personal fables, narcissism, and adolescent adjustment. *Psychology in the Schools, 43,* 481–491.

**Aber, J. L., Bishop-Josef, S. J., Jones, S. M., McLern, T., & Phillips, D. A.** (2006). *Child development and social policy.* Washington, DC: American Psychological Association.

**Acebo, C., & Carskadon, M. A.** (2002). Influence of irregular sleep patterns on waking behavior. In M. A. Carskadon (Ed.), *Adolescent sleep patterns.* New York: Cambridge University Press.

**Achenbach, T. M., & Edelbrock, C. S.** (1981). Behavioral problems and competencies reported by parents of normal and disturbed children aged four through sixteen. *Monographs of the Society for Research in Child Development, 46* (1, Serial No. 188).

**Achenbach, T. M., Howell, C. T., Quay, H. C., & Conners, C. K.** (1991). National survey of problems and competencies among four- to sixteen-year-olds. *Monographs for the Society for Research in Child Development, 56* (3, Serial No. 225).

**Ackerman, A., Thornton, J. C., Wang, J., Pierson, R. N., & Horlick, M.** (2006). Sex differences in the effect of puberty on the relationship between fat mass and bone mass in 926 healthy subjects, 6 to 18 years old. *Obesity, 14,* 819–825.

**Ackerman, P. L., & Lohman, D. F.** (2006). Individual differences in cognitive function. In P. A. Alexander & P. H. Winne (Eds.), *Handbook of educational psychology* (2nd ed.). Mahwah, NJ: Erlbaum.

**Adams, G. R., Gulotta, T. P., & Montemayor, R.** (Eds.). (1992). *Adolescent identity formation.* Newbury Park, CA: Sage.

**Adams, R., & Laursen, B.** (2001). The organization and dynamics of adolescent conflict with parents and friends. *Journal of Marriage and the Family, 63,* 97–110.

**Adelson, J.** (1979, January). Adolescence and the generalization gap. *Psychology Today,* pp. 33–37.

**Adler, N. E., Ozer, E. J., & Tschann, J.** (2003). Abortion among adolescents. *American Psychologist, 58,* 211–217.

**Aertgeerts, B., & Buntinx, F.** (2002). The relation between alcohol abuse or dependence and academic performance in first-year college students. *Journal of Adolescent Health, 31,* 223–225.

**Agras, W. S. & others.** (2004). Report of the National Institutes of Health workshop on overcoming barriers to treatment research in anorexia nervosa. *International Journal of Eating Disorders, 35,* 509–521.

**Ahn, N.** (1994). Teenage childbearing and high school completion: Accounting for individual heterogencity. *Family Planning Perspectives, 26,* 17–21.

**Ahrons, C. R.** (2004). *We're still family.* New York: HarperCollins.

**Ahrons, C. R.** (2007). Family ties after divorce: Long-term implications for children. *Family Process, 46,* 53–65.

**Ainsworth, M.D.S.** (1979). Infant-mother attachment. *American Psychologist, 34,* 932–937.

**Alan Guttmacher Institute.** (1995). *National survey of the American male's sexual habits.* New York: Author.

**Alan Guttmacher Institute.** (1998). *Teen sex and pregnancy.* New York: Author.

**Alan Guttmacher Institute.** (2003a). *Sex education: Needs, programs, and policies.* New York: Author.

**Alan Guttmacher Institute.** (2003b). *U.S. teenage pregnancy statistics.* New York: Author.

**Alan Guttmacher Institute.** (2003c). *An overview of abortion in the United States.* New York: Author.

**Alan Guttmacher Institute.** (2005). Adolescents in Uganda: Sexual and reproductive health. *Research in Brief, No. 2,* 1–4.

**Aldridge, J., & Goldman, R.** (2007). *Current issues and trends in education* (2nd ed.). Boston: Allyn & Bacon.

**Aldwin, C. M., Spiro, A., & Park, C. L.** (2006). Health, behavior, and optimal aging. In J. E. Birren & K. W. Schaie (Eds.), *Handbook of the psychology of aging.* San Diego: Academic Press.

**Alexander, C., Piazza, M., Mekos, D., & Valente, T.** (2001). Peers, schools, and cigarette smoking. *Journal of Adolescent Health, 29,* 22–30.

**Alexander, P. A.** (2006). *Psychology in learning and instruction.* Upper Saddle River, NJ: Prentice Hall.

**Allen, G., & MacMillan, R.** (2006). *Depression, suicidal behavior, and strain: Extending strain theory.* Paper presented at the meeting of the American Sociological Association, Montreal.

**Allen, J. P.** (2007, March). *A transformational perspective on the attachment system in adolescence.* Paper presented at the meeting of the Society for Research in Child Development, Boston.

**Allen, J. P., Hauser, S. T., Eickholt, C., Bell, K., & O'Connor, T.** (1994). Autonomy and relatedness in family interactions as predictors of expressions of negative adolescent effect. *Journal of Research on Adolescence, 4,* 535–552.

**Allen, J. P., Kuperminc, G. P., Moore, C.** (2005, April). *Stability and predictors of change in attachment security across adolescence.* Paper presented at the Biennial Meetings of the Society for Research on Child Development, Atlanta.

**Allen, J. P., Mc Elhaney, K. B., Land, D. J., Kuperminc, G. P., Moore, C. W., O'Beirne-Kelly, H., Kilmer, S. L.** (2003). A secure base in adolesence: Markers of attachment security in the mother-adolescent relationship. *Child Development, 74,* 294–307.

**Allen, J. P., Philliber, S., Herring, S., & Kuperminc, G. P.** (1997). Preventing teen pregnancy and academic failure: Experimental evaluation of a developmentally-based approach. *Child Development, 68,* 729–742.

**Allen, J. P., Porter, M. R., McFarland, F. C., Marsh, P., & McElhaney, K. B.** (2005). The two faces of adolescents' success with peers: Adolescent popularity, social adaptation, and deviant behavior. *Child Development, 76,* 1–14.

**Allen, J. P., Porter, M. R., McFarland, F. C., McElhaney, K. B., & Marsh, P.** (2007). The relation of attachment security to adolescents' paternal and peer relationships, depression, and externalizing behavior. *Child Development, 78,* 1222–1239.

**Allison, B. N., Schultz, J. B.** (2004). Parent-adolescent conflict in early adolescence. *Adolescence, 39,* 101–119.

**Almagor, M., Tellegen, A., & Waller, N. G.** (1995). The big seven model: A cross-cultural replication and further exploration of the basic dimensions of natural language trait descriptors.

**Alsaker, F. D. & Flammer, A.** (1999). *The Adolescent experience: European and American adolescents in the 1990s.* Mahwah, NJ: Erlbaum.

**Alvarez, A., & del Rio, P.** (2007). Inside and outside the zone of proximal development: An eco-functional reading of Vygotsky. In H. Daniels, J. Wertsch, & M. Cole (Eds.), *The Cambridge companion to Vygotsky.* New York: Cambridge University Press.

**Amabile, T. M.**(1993). Commentary in D. Goleman, P. Kafman, & M. Ray (Eds.), *The creative spirit.* New York: Plume.

**Amabile, T. M., & Hennessey, B. A.** (1992). The motivation for creativity in children. In A. K. Boggiano & T. S. Pittman (Eds.), *Achievement and motivation.* New York: Cambridge University Press.

**Amato, P. R.** (2006). Marital discord, divorce, and children's well-being: Results from a 20-year longitudinal study of two generations. In A. Clarke-Stewart & J. Dunn (Eds.), *Families count.* New York: Cambridge University Press.

**Amato, P. R., & Booth, A.** (1996). A prospective study of divorce and parent-child relationships. *Journal of Marriage and the Family, 58,* 356–365.

**Amato, P. R., & Irving, S.** (2006). Historical trends in divorce and dissolution. In M. A. Fine & J. H. Harvey (Eds.), *Handbook of divorce and relationship dissolution.* Mahwah, NJ: Erlbaum.

**Ambuel, B., & Rappaport, J.** (1992). Developmental trends in adolescents' psychological and legal competence to consent to abortion. *Law and Human Behavior, 16,* 129–154.

**American Association of University Women.** (1992). *How schools shortchange girls: A study of major findings on girls and education.* Washington, DC: Author.

**American Association of University Women.** (1993). *Hostile hallways.* Washington, DC: Author.

**American Association of University Women** (2006). *Drawing the line: Sexual harassment on campus.* Washington, DC: Author.

**American Psychiatric Association.** (1994). *Diagnostic and statistical manual of mental disorders* (4th ed.). Washington, DC: Author.

**American Psychological Association.** (2003). *Psychology: Scientific problem solvers.* Washington, DC: Author.

**American Sports Data.** (2001). *Superstudy of sports participation.* Hartsdale, NY: Author.

**Anderman, E. M., & Wolters, C. A.** (2006). Goals, values, and affect: Influences on student motivation. In P. A. Alexander & P. H. Winne (Eds.), *Handbook of educational psychology* (2nd ed.). Mahwah, NJ: Erlbaum.

**Anderson, C. A., & Bushman, B. J.** (2001). Effects of violent video games on aggressive behavior, aggressive cognition, aggressive affect, physiological arousal, and prosocial behavior: A meta-analytic review of the scientific literature. *Psychological Science, 12,* 353–359.

**Anderson, C. A., & Dill, K. E.** (2000). Video games and aggressive thoughts, feelings, and behavior in the laboratory and in life. *Journal of Personality and Social Psychology, 78,* 772–790.

**Anderson, C. A., Gentile, D. A., & Buckley, K. E.** (2007). *Violent video game effects on children and adolescents.* New York: Oxford University Press.

**Anderson, D. R., Huston, A. C., Schmitt, K., Linebarger, D. L., & Wright, J. C.** (2001). Early childhood viewing and adolescent behavior: The recontact study. *Monographs of the Society for Research in Child Development, 66* (1), Serial No. 264.

**Anderson, E., Greene, S. M., Hetherington, E. M., & Clingempeel, W. G.** (1999). The dynamics of parental remarriage. In E. M. Hetherington (Ed.), *Coping with divorce, single parenting, and remarriage.* Mahwah, NJ: Erlbaum.

**Anderson, J. E., Santelli, J. S., & Morrow, B.** (2006). Trends in adolescent contraceptive use, unprotected and poorly protected sex, 1991–2003. *Journal of Adolescent Health, 38,* 734–739.

**Anderson, L. B., Harro, M., Sardinha, L. B., Froberg, K., Ekelund, U., Brage, S., & Anderssen, S. A.** (2006). Physical activity and clustered cardiovascular risk in children: A cross-sectional study (The European Youth Heart Study). *Lancet, 368,* 299–304.

**Anderson, R. E.** (2002). Youth and information technology. In J. T. Mortimer & R. W. Larson (Eds.), *The changing adolescent experience.* New York: Cambridge University Press.

**Angold, A., Costello, E. J., & Worthman, C. M.** (1999). Puberty and depression: The roles of age, pubertal status and pubertal timing. *Psychological Medicine, 28,* 51–61.

**Antal-Otong, D.** (2003). Suicide: Life span considerations. *Nursing Clinics of North America, 38,* 137–150.

**Aquilino, W. S.** (2006). Family relationships and support systems in emerging adulthood. In J. J. Arnett & J. L. Tanner (Eds.), *Emerging adults in America.* Washington, DC: American Psychological Association.

**Araceli, G., Castro, J., Cesena, J., & Toro, J.** (2005). Anorexia nervosa in male adolescents: Body image, eating attitudes, and psychological traits. *Journal of Adolescent Health, 36,* 221–226.

**Archer, S. L.** (1989). The status of identity: Reflections on the need for intervention. *Journal of Adolescence, 12,* 345–359.

**Archer, S. L., & Waterman, A. S.** (1994). Adolescent identity development: Contextual perspectives. In C. B. Fisher & R. M. Lerner (Eds.), *Applied developmental psychology.* New York: McGraw-Hill.

**Archibald, A. B., Graber, J. A., & Brooks-Gunn, J.** (1999). Associations among parent-adolescent relationships, pubertal growth, dieting, and body image in young adolescent girls: A short-term longitudinal study. *Journal of Research on Adolescence, 9,* 395–415.

**Archibald, A. B., Graber, J. A., & Brooks-Gunn, J.** (2003). Pubertal processes and physical growth in adolescence. In G. R. Adams & M. Berzonsky (Eds.), *Handbook on adolescence.* Malden, MA: Blackwell.

**Armsden, G., & Greenberg, M. T.** (1984). *The inventory of parent and peer attachment.* Unpublished manuscript, University of Washington.

**Armstrong, M. L.** (1995) Adolescent tattoos: Educating and pontificating. *Pediatric Nursing, 21* (6), 561–564.

**Armstrong, M. L., Caliendo, C., & Roberts, A. E.** (2006). Genital piercings: What is known and what people with genital piercings tell us. *Urologic Nursing, 26,* 173–180.

**Armstrong, M. L., Roberts, A. E., Owen, D. C., & Koch, J. R.** (2004). Contemporary college students and body piercing. *Journal of Adolescent Health, 35,* 58–61.

**Carnegie Council on Adolescent Development.** (1989). *Turning points: Preparing American youth for the twenty-first century.* New York: Carnegie Foundation.

**Arnett, J. J.** (1990). Contraceptive use, sensation seeking, and adolescent egocentrism. *Journal of Youth and Adolescence, 19,* 171–180.

**Arnett, J. J.** (1995, March). *Are college students adults?* Paper presented at the meeting of the Society for Research in Child Development, Indianapolis.

**Arnett, J. J.** (2000). Emerging adulthood. *American Psychologist, 55,* 469–480.

**Arnett, J. J.** (2002). Adolescents in Western countries in the 21st century: Vast opportunities—for all? In B. B. Brown, R. W. Larson, & T. S. Saraswathi (Eds.), *The world's youth.* New York: Cambridge University Press.

**Arnett, J. J.** (2004). *Emerging adulthood.* New York: Oxford University Press.

**Arnett, J. J.** (2006). Emerging adulthood: Understanding the new way of coming of age. In J. J. Arnett & J. L. Tanner (Eds.), *Emerging adults in America.* Washington, DC: American Psychological Association.

**Arnett, J. J.** (2006). The psychology of emerging adulthood: What is known, and what remains to be known. In J. J. Arnett & J. L. Tanner (Eds.), *Emerging adults in America.* Washington, DC: American Psychological Association.

**Arnett, J. J.** (2007). Socialization in emerging adulthood. In J. E. Grusec & P. D. Hastings (Eds.), *Handbook of socialization.* New York: Guilford.

**Arnett, J. J., & Tanner, J. L.** (Eds.). (2006). *Emerging adults in America.* Washington, DC: American Psychological Association.

**Arnold, E. M.** (2004). Factors that influence consideration of hastening death among people with life-threatening illnesses. *Health and Social Work, 29,* 17–26.

**Arnoux, D.** (1998, September). Description of teaching experiences prepared for John Santrock's text, *Educational psychology* (New York: McGraw-Hill).

**Aron, A., Aron, E., & Coups, E.** (2008). *Statistics for the behavioral and social sciences.* Upper Saddle River, NJ: Prentice Hall.

**Aronowitz, T.** (2005). The role of "envisioning the future" in the development of resilience among at-risk youth. *Public Health Nursing, 22,* 200–208.

**Aronowitz, T., Rennels, R. E., & Todd, E.** (2006). Ecological influences of sexuality on early adolescent African American females. *Journal of Community Mental Health, 23,* 113–122.

**Aronson, E.** (1986, August). *Teaching students things they think they know all about: The case of prejudice and desegregation.* Paper presented at the meeting of the American Psychological Association, Washington, DC.

**Aronson, J. M.**(2002). Stereotype threat; Contending and coping with unnerving expectations. In J. Aronson (Ed.), *Improving academic achievement: Impact of psychological factors on education.* San Diego: Academic Press.

**Aronson, J. M., Fried, C. B., & Good. C.** (2002). Reducing the effects of stereotypes threat on African American college students by shaping theories of intelligence. *Journal of Experimental Social Psychology, 38,* 113–125.

**Aronson, J. M., Lustina, M. J., Good, C., Keough, K., Steele, C. M., & Brown, J.** (1999). When white men can't do math: Necessary and sufficient factors in stereotype threat. *Journal of Experimental Social Psychology, 35,* 29–46.

**Asarnow, J. R., & Callan, J. W.** (1985). Boys with peer adjustment problems: Social cognitive processes. *Journal of Consulting and Clinical Psychology, 53,* 80–87.

**Asbury, E. A., Chandrruangphen, P., & Collins, P.** (2006). The importance of continued exercise participation in quality of life and psychological well-being in previously inactive postmenopausal women: A pilot study. *Menopause, 13,* 561–567.

**Ash, P.** (2006). Adolescents in adult court: Does the punishment fit the criminal? *The Journal of the American Academy of Psychiatry and the Law, 34,* 145–149.

**Atkinson, J. W.** (1957). Motivational determinants of risk-taking behavior. *Psychological Review, 64,* 359–372.

**Attie, I., & Brooks-Gunn, J.** (1989). Development of eating problems in adolescent girls: A longitudinal study. *Developmental Psychology, 25,* 70–79.

# B

**Bachman, J. G., O'Malley, P. M., Schulenberg, J., Johnston, L. D., Bryant, A. L., & Merline, A. C.** (2002). *The decline of substance abuse in young adulthood.* Mahwah. NJ: Erlbaum.

**Bachman, J. G., & Schulenberg, J.** (1993). How part-time work intensity relates to drug use, problem behavior, time use, and satisfaction among high school seniors: Are these consequences or just correlates? *Developmental Psychology, 29,* 220–235.

**Bacon, M. K., Child, I. L., & Barry, H.** (1963). A cross-cultural study of correlates of crime. *Journal of Abnormal and Social Psychology, 66,* 291–300.

**Baddeley, A.** (2000). Short-term and working memory. In E. Tulving & F. L. M. Craik (Eds.), *The Oxford handbook of memory.* New York: Oxford University Press.

**Baddeley, A. D.** (2006) Working memory: An overview. In S. Pickering (Ed.), *Working memory and education.* New York: Academic Press.

**Baddeley, A. D.** (2007a). *Working memory, thought and action.* New York: Oxford University Press.

**Baddeley, A. D.** (2007b) Working memory: Multiple models, multiple mechanisms. In H. L. Roediger, Y. Dudai, & S. M. Fitzpatrick (Eds.), *Science of memory: Concepts.* New York: Oxford University Press.

**Bagwell, C. L., Newcomb, A. F., & Bukowski, W. M.** (1994, February). *Early adolescent friendship as a predictor of adult adjustment: A twelve-year follow-up investigation.* Paper presented at the biennial meeting of the Society for Research on Adolescence, San Diego.

**Baillargeon, R. H., Zoccolillo, M., Keenna, K., Cote, S., Perusse, D., Wu, H-X., Boivin, M., & Tremblay, R. E.** (2007). Gender differences in physical aggression: A prospective population-based survey of children before and after two years of age. *Developmental Psychology, 43,* 13–26.

**Baird, A. A., Gruber, S. A., Cohen, B. M., Renshaw, R. J., & Yurgelun-Todd, D. A.** (1999). FMRI of the amygdala in children and adolescents. *American Academy of Child and Adolescent Psychiatry, 38,* 195–199.

**Baldwin, S., & Hoffman, J. P.** (2002). The dynamics of self-esteem: A growth curve analysis. *Journal of Youth and Adolescence, 31,* 101–113.

**Baltes, P. B., Lindenberger, U., & Staudinger, U.** (2006). Life span theory in developmental psychology. In W. Damon & R. Lerner (Eds.), *Handbook of child psychology* (6th ed.), New York: Wiley.

**Bandura, A.** (1986). *Social foundations of thought and action: A social cognitive theory.* Englewood Cliffs, NJ: Prentice Hall.

**Bandura, A.** (1991). Social cognitive theory of moral thought and action. In W. M. Kurtines & J. Gewirtz (Eds.), *Handbook of moral behavior and development* (Vol. 1). Hillsdale, NJ: Erlbaum.

**Bandura, A.** (1997). *Self-efficacy.* New York: W. H. Freeman.

**Bandura, A.** (1998, August). *Swimming against the mainstream: Accentuating the positive aspects of humanity.* Paper presented at the meeting of the American Psychological Association, San Francisco.

**Bandura, A.** (1999). Moral disengagement in the perpetuation of inhumanities. *Personality and Social Psychology Review, 3,* 193–209.

**Bandura, A.** (2000). Self-efficacy. In A. Kazdin (Ed.), *Encyclopedia of psychology.* Washington, DC & New York: American Psychological Association and Oxford University Press.

**Bandura, A.** (2001). Social cognitive theory. *Annual Review of Psychology* (Vol. 52). Palo Alto, CA: Annual Reviews.

**Bandura, A.** (2002). Selective moral disengagement in the exercise of moral agency. *Journal of Moral Education, 31,* 101–119.

**Bandura, A.** (2002). Social cognitive theory. *Annual Review of Psychology* (Vol. 52). Palo Alto, CA: Annual Reviews.

**Bandura, A.** (2004). *Toward a psychology of human agency.* Paper presented at the meeting of the American Psychological Society, Chicago.

**Bandura, A.** (2006). Going global with social cognitive theory: From prospect to paydirt. In S. I. Donaldson, D. E. Berger, & K. Pezdek, (Eds.), *The rise of applied psychology: New frontiers and rewarding careers.* Mahwah, NJ: Erlbaum.

**Bandura, A.** (2007a). Self-efficacy in health functioning. In S. Ayers & others (Eds.), *Cambridge handbook of psychology, health, and medicine.* New York: Cambridge University Press.

**Bandura, A.** (2007b). Social cognitive theory. In S. Donsbach (Ed.), *International encyclopedia of communication.* Thousand Oaks, CA: Sage.

**Bank, L., Burraston, B., & Snyder, J.** (2004). Sibling conflict and ineffective parenting as predictors of adolescent boys' antisocial behavior and peer difficulties: Additive and interactive effects. *Journal of Research on Adolescence, 14,* 99–125.

**Bankole, A., Singh, S., Woog, V., & Wulf, D.** (2004). *Risk and protection: Youth and HIV/AIDS in sub-Saharan Africa.* New York: Alan Guttmacher Institute.

**Banks, J. A.** (2002). *Introduction to multicultural education.* Boston: Allyn & Bacon.

**Banks, J. A.** (2006). *Cultural diversity and education* (5th ed.). Boston: Allyn & Bacon.

**Banks, J. A.** (2008), *Introduction to multicultural education* (4th ed.). Boston: Allyn & Bacon.

**Barbaresi, W. J., Katusic, S. K., Colligan, R. C., Weaver, A. L., Leibson, C. L., & Jacobsen, S. J.** (2006). Long-term stimulant medication treatment of attention-deficit/hyperactivity disorder: Results from a population-based study. *Journal of Developmental and Behavioral Pediatrics, 27,* 1–10.

**Barber, B. L.** (2006). To have loved and lost . . . Adolescent romantic relationships and rejection. In A. C. Crouter & A. Booth (Eds.), *Romance and sex in adolescence and emerging adulthood.* Mahwah, NJ: Erlbaum.

**Barber, B. L., & Demo, D.** (2006). The kids are alright (at least most of them): Links to divorce and dissolution. In M. A. Fine & J. H. Harvey (Eds.), *Handbook of divorce and relationship dissolution.* Mahwah, NJ: Erlbaum.

**Barber, B. L., & Eccles, J.** (2003). The joy of romance: Healthy adolescent relationships as an educational agenda. In P. Florsheim (Ed.), *Adolescent romantic relations and sexual behavior.* Mahwah, NJ: Erlbaum.

**Barber, B. L., Eccles, J. S., & Stone, M. R.** (2001, April). *Whatever happened to the jock, the brain, and the princess? Young adult pathways linked to adolescent activity involvement and identity.* Paper presented at the meeting of the Society for Research in Child Development, Minneapolis.

**Barker, R., & Wright, H. F.** (1951). *One boy's day.* New York: Harper.

**Barnard, K. E., & Solchany, J. E.** (2002). Mothering. In M. H. Bornstein (Ed.), *Handbook of parenting* (2nd ed.). Mahwah, NJ: Erlbaum.

**Barnes, G. M., Farrell, M. P., & Banerjee, S.** (1995). Family influences on alcohol abuse and other problem behaviors among Black and White Americans. In G. M. Boyd, J. Howard, & R. A. Zucker (Eds.), *Alcohol problems among adolescents.* Hillsdale, NJ: Erlbaum.

**Barnouw, V.** (1975). *An introduction to anthropology: Vol. 2 Ethnology.* Homewood, IL: Dorsey Press.

**Barrett, L. F., Mesquita, B., Ochsner, K. N., & Gross, J. J.** (2007). The experience of emotion. *Annual Review of Psychology* (Vol. 58). Palo Alto, CA: Annual Reviews.

**Barry, T. D., Dunlap, S. T., Cotton, S. J., Lochman, J. E., & Wells, K. C.** (2005). The influence of maternal stress and distress on disruptive behavior problems in boys. *Journal of the American Academy of Child and Adolescent Psychiatry, 44,* 265–273.

**Bartko, T. W., & Eccles, J. S.** (2003). Adolescent participation in structured and unstructured activities: A person-oriented analysis. *Journal of Youth and Adolescence, 32,* 233–241.

**Barton, S. E.** (2005). Reducing the transmission of genital herpes. *British Medical Journal, 330,* 157–158.

**Basen-Enquist, K., Coyle K. K., Parcel, G. S., Kirby, D., Banspach, S. W., Carvajal, S. C., & Baumler, E.** (2001). Schoolwide effects of a multicomponent HIV, STD, and pregnancy prevention program for high school students. *Health Education and Behavior, 28,* 166–185.

**Baskins-Sommers, A., & Sommers, I.** (2006). The co-occurrence of substance use and high-risk behaviors. *Journal of Adolescent Health, 38,* 609–611.

**Basow, S. A.** (2006). Gender role and gender identity development. In J. Worell & C. D. Good- heart (Eds.), *Handbook of girls' and women's psychological health.* New York: Oxford University Press.

**Baud, P.** (2005). Personality traits as intermediary phenotypes in suicidal behavior: Genetic issues. *American Journal of Medical Genetics, 133c,* 34–42.

**Baumeister, R. F.** (1991). Identity crisis. In R. M. Lerner, A. C. Petersen, & J. Brooks-Gunn (Eds.), *Encyclopedia of adolescence* (Vol. 1). New York: Garland.

**Baumeister, R. F., Campbell, J. D., Krueger, J. I., & Vohs, K. D.** (2003). Does high self-esteem cause better performance, interpersonal success, happiness, or healthier lifestyles? *Psychological Science in the Public Interest, 4* (1), 1–44.

**Baumrind, D.** (1971). Current patterns of parental authority. *Developmental Psychology Monographs, 4* (1, Pt. 2).

**Baumrind, D.** (1991). Effective parenting during the early adolescent transition. In P. A. Cowan & E. M. Hetherington (Eds.), *Advances in family research* (Vol. 2). Hillsdale, NJ: Erlbaum.

**Baumrind, D.** (1999, November). Unpublished review of J. W. Santrock's *Child development,* 9th ed. (New York: McGraw-Hill).

**Bauserman, R.** (2003). Child adjustment in joint-custody versus sole-custody arrangements: A meta-analytic review. *Journal of Family Psychology, 16,* 19–102.

**Beal, C. R.** (1994). *Boys and girls: The development of gender roles.* New York: McGraw-Hill.

**Beals, K. A., & Hill, A. K.** (2006). The prevalence of disordered eating, menstrual dysfunction, and low bone mineral density among U.S. college athletes. *International Journal of Sport Nutrition and Exercise Metabolism, 16,* 1–23.

**Beals, K. A., & Meyer, N. L.** (2007). Female athlete triad update. *Clinical Sports Medicine, 26,* 69–89.

**Bearman, S. K., Presnell, K., Martinez, E., & Stice, E.** (2006). The skinny on body dissatisfaction: A longitudinal study of adolescent girls and boys. *Journal of Youth and Adolescence, 35,* 217–229.

**Bednar, R. L., Wells, M. G., & Peterson, S. R.** (1995). *Self-esteem* (2nd ed.). Washington, DC: American Psychological Association.

**Beets, M. W., & Pitetti, K. H.** (2005). Contribution of physical education and sport to health-related fitness in high school students. *Journal of School Health, 75,* 25–30.

**Beins, B.** (2004). *Research methods.* Boston: Allyn & Bacon.

**Belloc, N. B., & Breslow, L.** (1972). Relationships of physical health status and health practices. *Preventive Medicine, 1,* 409–421.

**Belsky, J.** (1981). Early human experience: A family perspective. *Developmental Psychology, 17,* 3–23.

**Belson, W.** (1978). *Television violence and the adolescent boy.* London: Saxon House.

**Bender, W. N.** (2008). *Learning disabilities* (6th ed.). Boston: Allyn & Bacon.

**Bennett, S. E., & Assefi, N. P.** (2005). School-based teenage pregnancy prevention programs: A systematic review of randomized controlled trials. *Journal of Adolescent Health, 36,* 72–81.

**Bennett, W.** (1993). *The book of virtues.* New York: Simon & Schuster.

**Benninghoven, D., Tetsch, N., Kunzendorf, S., & Jantschek, G.** (2007). Body image in patients with eating disorders and their mothers, and the role of family functioning. *Comprehensive Psychiatry, 48,* 118–123.

**Benokratis, N.** (2008). *Marriages and families* (6th ed.). Upper Saddle River, NJ: Prentice Hall.

**Benson, P. L.** (2006). *All kids are our kids.* San Francisco: Jossey-Bass.

**Benson, P. L.** (2006). The science of child and adolescent spiritual development: Definitional, theoretical, and field-building challenges. In E. C. Roehlkepartain, P. E. King, & L. M. Wagener (Eds.), *The handbook of spiritual development in childhood and adolescence.* Thousand Oaks, CA: Sage.

**Benson, P. L., Mannes, M., Pittman, K., & Ferber, T.** (2004). Youth development, developmental assets, and Public policy. In R. Lerner & L. Steinberg (Eds.), *Handbook of adolescent psychology* (2nd ed.). New York: Wiley.

**Benson, P. L., Scales, P. C., Hamilton, S. F., & Sesma, A.** (2006). Positive youth development. In W. Damon & R. Lerner (Eds.), *Handbook of child psychology* (6th ed.). New York: Wiley.

**Benveniste, L., Carnoy, M., & Rothstein, R.** (2003). *All else equal.* New York: Routledge-Farmer.

**Beran, T. N., & Tutty, L.** (2002). *An evaluation of the Bully Proofing Your School, School Program,* Unpublished manuscript, Calgary: RESOLVE, Alberta, CAN.

**Bergeron, N., & Schneider, B. H.** (2005). Explaining cross-national differences in peer-directed aggression: A quantitative analysis. *Agressive Behavior, 31,* 116–137.

**Bergman, R.** (2004). Identity as motivation: Toward a theory of the moral self. In D. K. Lapsley & D. Narvaez (Eds.), *Moral development, self, and identity.* Mahwah, NJ: Erlbaum.

**Berkowitz, M. W., & Bier, M. C.** (2004). Research-based character education. *Annals of the American Academy of Political and Social Science, 591,* 72–85.

**Berkowitz, M. W., & Gibbs, J. C.** (1983). Measuring the developmental features of moral discussion. *Merrill-Palmer Quarterly, 29,* 399–410.

**Berkowitz, M. W., Sherblom, S., Bier, M., & Battistich, V.** (2006). Educating for positive youth development. In M. Killen & J. Smetana (Eds.), *Handbook of moral development.* Mahwah, NJ: Erlbaum.

**Bem, S. L.** (1977). On the utility of alternative procedures for assessing psychological androgyny. *Journal of Consulting and Clinical Psychology, 45,* 196–205.

**Berndt, T. J.** (1979). Developmental changes in conformity to peers and parents. *Developmental Psychology, 15,* 608–616.

**Berndt, T. J.** (1982). The features and effects of friendship in early adolescence. *Child Development, 53,* 1447–1460.

**Berndt, T. J., & Keefe, K.** (1996). Friends' influence on school adjustment: A motivational analysis. In J. Juvonen & K. Wentzel (Eds.), *Social motivation: Understanding children's school adjustment* (pp. 248–278). New York: Cambridge.

**Berndt, T. J., & Perry, T. B.** (1990). Distinctive features and effects of early adolescent friendships. In R. Montemayor (Ed.), *Advances in adolescent research.* Greenwich, CT: JAI Press.

**Berninger, V. W.** (2006). Learning disabilities. In W. Damon & R. Lerner (Eds.), *Handbook of child psychology* (6th ed.). New York: Wiley.

**Bernstein, N.** (2004, March). Behind fall in pregnancy, a new teenage culture of restraint. *New York Times,* pp. A1, A22.

**Berry, J. W.** (1990). Psychology of acculturation: Understanding individuals moving between cultures. In R. W. Brislin (Ed.), *Applied cross-cultural psychology.* Thousand Oaks, CA: Sage.

**Berry, J. W.** (2003). Conceptual approaches to acculturation. In K. M. Chun, P. B. Organista, & G. Marin (Eds.), *Acculturation.* Washington, DC: American Psychological Association.

**Berry, J. W.** (2007). Acculturation. In J. E. Grusec & P. D. Hastings (Eds.), *Handbook of socialization.* New York: Guilford.

**Berry, J. W., Phinney, J. S., Sam, D. L., & Vedder, P.** (Eds.) (2006). *Immigrant youth in cultural transition.* Mahwah, NJ: Erlbaum.

**Bersamin, M. M., & Walker, S.** (2006). Correlates of oral sex and vaginal intercourse in early and middle adolescence. *Journal of Research on Adolescence, 16,* 59–68.

**Berscheid, E., & Reis, H. T.** (1998). Attraction and close relationships. In D. T. Gilbert, S. T. Fiske, & G. Lindzey (Eds.), *The handbook of social psychology* (4th ed.). New York: McGraw-Hill.

**Berscheid, E., Snyder, M., & Omoto, A. M.** (1989). Issues in studying close relationships. In C. Hendrick (Ed.), *Close relationships.* Newbury Park, CA: Sage.

**Berzonsky, M. D., & Adams, G. R.** (1999). Reevaluating the identity status paradigm: Still useful after 35 years. *Developmental Review, 19,* 557–590.

**Best, D.** (2001). Cross-cultural gender roles. In J. Worell (Ed.), *Encyclopedia of women and gender.* San Diego: Academic Press.

**Betz, N. E.** (2004). Contributions of self-efficacy theory to career counseling: A personal perspective. *Career Development Quarterly, 52,* 340–353.

**Betz, N. E.** (2006). Women's career development. In J. Worell & C. D. Goodheart (Eds.), *Handbook of girls' and women's psychological health.* New York: Oxford University Press.

**Beznos, G. W., & Coates, V.** (2007, March). *Piercing and tattooing in adolescence: Psychological aspects.* Workshop at the meeting of the Society for Adolescent Medicine, Denver.

**Bianchi, S. M., & Spain, D.** (1986). *American women in transition.* New York: Russell Sage Foundation.

**Billy, J. O. G., Rodgers, J. L., & Udry, J. R.** (1984). Adolescent sexual behavior and friendship choice. *Social Forces, 62,* 653–678.

**Bingham, C. R., & Crockett, L. J.** (1996). Longitudinal adjustment patterns of boys and girls experiencing early, middle, and late sexual intercourse. *Developmental Psychology, 32,* 647–658.

**Birch, K.** (2005). Female athlete triad. *British Medical Journal, 330,* 244–246.

**Biro, F. M., Huang, G., Crawford, P. B., Lucky, A. W., Striegel-Moore, R., Barton, B. A., & Daniels, S.** (2006). Pubertal correlates in black and white girls. *Journal of Pediatrics, 148,* 234–240.

**Biro, F. M., Khoury, P., & Morrison, J. A.** (2006). Influence of obesity on timing of puberty. *International Journal of Andrology, 29,* 272–277.

**Birren, J. E.** (Ed.). (2007). *Encyclopedia of gerontology* (2nd ed.). San Diego: Academic Press.

**Bishop, D. V., Laws, G., Adams, C., & Norbury, C. F.** (2006). High heritability of speech and language impairments in 6-year-old twins demonstrated using parent and teacher report. *Behavior Genetics, 36,* 173–184.

**Bitter, G. G., & Legacy, J. M.** (2006). *Using technology in the classroom* (Brief version). Boston: Allyn & Bacon.

**Bitter, G. G., & Legacy, J. M.** (2008). *Using technology in the classroom* (7th ed.). Boston: Allyn & Bacon.

**Bjorklund, D.** (2005). *Children's thinking* (4th ed.). Belmont, CA: Wadsworth.

**Bjorklund, D. F.** (2006). Mother knows best: Epigenetic inheritance, maternal effects, and the evolution of human intelligence. *Developmental Review, 26,* 213–242.

**Bjorklund, D. F.** (2007). *Why youth is not wasted on the young.* Malden, MA: Blackwell.

**Bjorklund, D. F., & Pellegrini, A. D.** (2002). *The origins of human nature.* Washington, DC: American Psychological Association.

**Blake, S. M., Ledsky, R., Goodenow, C., Sawyer, R., Lohrmann, D., & Windsor, R.** (2003). Condom availability programs in Massachusetts high schools: Relationships with condom use and sexual behavior. *American Journal of Public Health, 93,* 955–962.

**Blakemore, J. E. O., Berenbaum, S. A., & Liben, L. S.** (2005). *Gender development.* Mahwah, NJ: Erlbaum.

**Blash, R., & Unger, D. G.** (1992, March). *Cultural factors and the self-esteem and aspirations of African-American adolescent males.* Paper presented at the meeting of the Society for Research on Adolescence, Washington, DC.

**Blasi, A.** (1995). Moral understanding and the moral personality: The process of moral integration. In W. Kurtines & J. L. Gewirtz (Eds.), *Moral development: An introduction.* Boston: Allyn & Bacon.

**Blasi, A.** (2005). Moral character: A psychological approach. In D. K. Lapsley & F. C. Power (Eds.) *Character psychology and character education.* Notre Dame, IN: University of Notre Dame Press.

**Blatchford, P., & Mortimore, P.** (1994). The issue of class size for young children in school: What can we learn from research? *Oxford Review of Education, 20* (4), 411–428.

**Block, C. C., & Pressley, M.** (2007). Best practices in teaching comprehension. In L. B. Gambrell, L. M. Morrow, & M. Pressley (Eds.), *Best practices in literacy instruction.* New York: Guilford.

**Block, J.** (1993). Studying personality the long way. In D. C. Funder, R. D. Peake, C. Tomlinson-Keasey, & K. Widaman (Eds.), *Studying lives through time.* Washington, DC: American Psychological Association.

**Block, J.** (2002). *Personality as an affect processing system.* Mahwah, NJ: Erlbaum.

**Block, J. H., & Block, J.** (1980). The role of ego-control and ego-resiliency in the organization of bahavior. In W. A. Collins (Ed.), *Minnesota symposium on child psychology* (Vol. 13). Minneapolis: University of Minnesota Press.

**Blogowskal, A., Rzepka-Gorska, I., & Krzyzanowska-Swiniarska, B.** (2005). Body composition, dehydroepiandrosterone sulfate and leptin concentrations in girls approaching menarche. *Journal of Pediatric Endocrinology and Metabolism, 18,* 975–893.

**Bloom, B.** (1985). *Developing talent in young people.* New York: Ballantine.

**Bloom, B., & Dey, A. N.** (2006). Summary health statistics for U.S. children: National Health Interview Survey, 2004. *Vital Health Statistics, 227,* 1–85.

**Blos, P.** (1989). The inner world of the adolescent. In A. H. Esman (Ed.), *International annals of adolescent psychiatry* (Vol. 1). Chicago: University of Chicago Press.

**Blum, R., & Nelson-Mmari, K.** (2004). Adolescent health from an international perspective. In R. Lerner & L. Steinberg (Eds.), *Handbook of adolescent psychology.* New York: Wiley.

**Blumenfeld, P. C., Kempler, T. M., & Krajcik, J. S.** (2006). Motivation and cognitive engagement in learning environments. In R. K. Sawyer (Ed.), *The Cambridge handbook of the learning sciences.* New York: Cambridge University Press.

**Blumenfeld, P. C., Marx, R. W., & Harris, C. J.** (2006). Learning environments. In W. Damon & R. Lerner (Eds.), *Handbook of child psychology* (6th ed.). New York: Wiley.

**Blumenfeld, P., Modell, J., Bartko, T., Secada, J., Fredricks, J., Friedel, J., & Paris, A.** (2005). School engagement of inner city students during middle childhood. In C. R. Cooper, C. T. G. Coll, W. T. Bartko, H. M. Davis, & C. Chatman (Eds.), *Developmental pathways through middle childhood.* Mahwah, NJ: Erlbaum.

**Blyth, D. A., Durant, D., & Moosbrugger, L.** (1985, April). *Perceived intimacy in the social relationships of drug- and nondrug-using adolescents.* Paper presented at the meeting of the Society for Research in Child Development, Toronto.

**Bo, I.** (1994). The sociocultural environment as a source of support. In F. Nestmann & K. Hurrelmann (Eds.), *Social networks and social support in childhood and adolescence.* New York: Walter de Gruyter.

**Bodrova, E., & Leong, D. J.** (2007). *Tools of the mind: The Vygotskian approach to early childhood education* (2nd ed). Upper Saddle River, NJ: Merrill/Prentice Hall.

**Boekaerts, M.** (2006). Self-regulation and effort investment. In W. Damon & R. Lerner (Eds.), *Handbook of child psychology* (6th ed.). New York: Wiley.

**Bogaert, A. F.** (2005). Age at puberty and father absence in a national probability sample. *Journal of Adolescence, 28,* 541–546.

**Bongers, I. L., Koot, H. M., van der Ende, J., & Verhulst, F. C.** (2004). Developmental trajectories of externalizing behaviors in childhood and adolescence. *Child Development, 75,* 1523–1537.

**Booher-Jennings, J.** (2006). Rationing education in an era of accountability. *Phi Delta Kappan, 87,* 756–761.

**Boonstra, H.** (2002, February). Teen pregnancy: Trends and lessons learned. *The Guttmacher Report on Public Policy,* pp. 7–10.

**Booth, A., & Johnson, D.** (1988). Premarital cohabitation and marital success. *Journal of Family Issues, 9,* 255–272.

**Booth, A., Johnson, D. R., Granger, D. A., Crouter, A. C., & McHale, S.** (2003). Testosterone and child and adolescent adjustment: The moderating role of parent-child relationships. *Developmental Psychology, 39,* 85–98.

**Booth, M.** (2002). Arab adolescents facing the future: Enduring ideals and pressures to change. In B. B. Brown, R. W. Larson, & T. S. Saraswathi (Eds.), *The world's youth.* New York: Cambridge University Press.

**Borden, L. M., Donnermeyer, J. F., & Scheer, S. D.** (2001). The influence of extracurricular activities and peer influence on substance use. *Adolescent and Family Health, 2,* 12–19.

**Borkowski, J. G., Farris, J. R., Whitman, T. L., Carothers, S. S., Weed, K., & Keogh, D. A.** (Eds.). (2007). *Risk and resilience.* Mahwah, NJ: Erlbaum.

**Bornstein, M. H., & Cote L. R.** (2006). *Acculturation and parent-child relationships: Measurement and development.* Mahwah, NJ: Erlbaum.

**Bosma, H. A., & Kunnen, E. S.** (Eds.). (2001). *Identity and emotion.* New York: Cambridge University Press.

**Botero, D., & Wolfsdorf, J. I.** (2005). Diabetes mellitus in children and adolescents. *Archives of Medical Research, 36,* 281–290.

**Bowlby, J.** (1989). *Secure attachment.* New York: Basic Books.

**Bowlby, J.** (1989). *Secure attachment.* New York: Basic Books.

**Boyes, M. C., Giordano, R., & Galperyn, K.** (1993, March). *Moral orientation and interpretive contexts of moral deliberation.* Paper presented at the biennial meeting of the Society for Research in Child Development, New Orleans.

**Brabek, M. M., & Brabek, K. M.** (2006). Women and relationships. In J. Worell & C. D. Goodheart (Eds.), *Handbook of girls' and women's psychological health.* New York: Oxford University Press.

**Bracey, J. R., Bamaca, M. Y., & Umaña-Taylor, A. J.** (2004). Examining ethnic identity among biracial and monoracial adolescents. *Journal of Youth and Adolescence, 33,* 123–132.

**Bradley, R. H., Corwyn, R. F., McAdoo, H., & Coll, C.** (2001). The home environments of children in the United States: Part I. Variations by age, ethnicity, and poverty status. *Child Development, 72,* 1844–1867.

**Branje, S. J. T., van Lieshout, C. F. M., & van Aken, M. A. G.** (2004). Relations between big five personality characteristics and perceived support in adolescents' families. *Journal of Personality and Social Psychology, 86,* 615–628.

**Bransford, J. & others.** (2006). Learning theories in education. In P. A. Alexander & P. H. Winne (Eds.), *Handbook of educational psychology* (2nd ed.). Mahwah, NJ: Erlbaum.

**Bransford, J., Stevens, R., Schwartz, D., Meltzoff, A., Pea, R., Roschelle, J., Vye, N., Kuhl, P., Bell, P., Barron, B., Reeves, B., & Sabelli, N.** (2006). Learning theories and education: Toward a decade of synergy. In P. A. Alexander & P. H. Winne (Eds.), *Handbook of educational psychology* (2nd ed.). Mahwah, NJ: Erlbaum.

**Braver, S. L., Ellman, I. M., & Fabricius, W. V.** (2003). Relocation of children after divorce and children's best interests: New evidence and legal considerations. *Journal of Family Psychology, 17,* 206–219.

**Bray, J. H., Berger, S. H., & Boethel, C. L.** (1999). Marriage to remarriage and beyond. In E. M. Hetherington (Ed.), *Coping with divorce, single parenting, and remarriage.* Mahwah, NJ: Erlbaum.

**Bray, J. H., & Kelly, J.** (1998). *Stepfamilies.* New York: Broadway.

**Brenner, J. S., & the American Academy of Pediatrics Council on Sport Medicine and Fitness.** (2006). Overuse Injuries, Overtraining, and Burnout in Child and Adolescent Athletes. *Pediatrics, 119,* 1242–1245.

**Breur, J. T.** (1999). In search of . . . brain-based education. *Phi Delta Kappan, 80,* 648–655.

**Brewer, M.** (2007). The social psychology of intergroup relations: Social categorization, in group bias, and outgroup prejudice. In A. W. Kruglanski & E. T. Higgins (Eds.), *Social psychology: Handbook of basic principles* (2nd ed.). New York: Guilford.

**Brewer, M. B., & Campbell, D. T.** (1976). *Ethnocentrism and intergroup attitudes.* New York: Wiley.

**Bricker, J. B. & others.** (2006). Genetic and environmental influences on age of sexual initiation in the Colorado Adoption Project. *Behavior Genetics, 36,* 820–832.

**Briggs, T. W.** (1999, October 14). Honorees find keys to unlocking kids' minds. Retrieved July 22, 2004, from www.usatoday.com/education/1999

**Briggs, T. W.** (2005, October 13). *USA Today's* 2005 all-USA teacher team. *USA Today,* p. 6D.

**Brindis, C. D.** (2006). A public health success: Understanding policy changes related to teen sexual activity and pregnancy. *Annual Review of Public Health, 27,* 277–295.

**Briones, T. L.** (2006). Environment, physical activity, and neurogenesis: Implications for prevention and treatment of Alzheimer's disease. *Current Alzheimer Research, 3,* 49–54.

**Brislin, R.** (1993). *Understanding culture's influence on behavior.* Fort Worth, TX: Harcourt Brace.

**Brislin, R. W.** (2000). Cross-cultural training. In A. Kazdin (Ed.), *Encyclopedia of psychology.* Washington, DC & New York: American Psychological Association and Oxford University Press.

**Brockmeyer, S., Treboux, D., & Crowell, J. A.** (2005, April). *Parental divorce and adult children's attachment status and marital relationships.* Paper presented at the meeting of the Society for Research in Child Development, Atlanta.

**Broderick, R.** (2003, July/August). A surgeon's saga. *Minnesota: The Magazine of the University of Minnesota Alumni Association,* 26–31.

**Brody, G. H., Ge, X., Conger, R. D., Gibbons, F., Murry, V., Gerrard, M., & Simons, R.** (2001). The influence of neighborhood disadvantage, collective socialization, and parenting on African American children's affiliation with deviant peers. *Child Development, 72,* 1231–1246.

**Brody, G. H., & Schaffer, D. R. (1982).** Contributions of parents and peers to children's moral socialization. *Developmental Review, 2,* 31–75.

**Brody, G. H., Stoneman, Z., & Burke, M.** (1987). Child temperaments, maternal differential behavior and sibling relationships. *Developmental Psychology, 23,* 354–362.

**Brody, N.** (2000). Intelligence. In A. Kazdin (Ed.), *Encyclopedia of psychology.* Washington, DC & New York: American Psychological Association and Oxford University Press.

**Brody, N.** (2007). Does education influencce intelligence? In P. C. Kyllonen, R. D. Roberts, & L. Stankov (Eds.), *Extending intelligence.* Mahwah, NJ: Erlbaum.

**Brodzinsky, D. M., Lang, R., & Smith, D. W.** (1995). Parenting adopted children. In M. H. Bornstein (Ed.), *Handbook of parenting* (Vol. 3). Hillsdale, NJ: Erlbaum.

**Brodzinsky, D. M., & Pinderhughes, E.** (2002). Parenting and child development in adoptive families. In M. H. Bornstein (Ed.), *Handbook of parenting* (Vol. 1). Mahwah, NJ: Erlbaum.

**Brodzinsky, D. M., Schechter, D. E., Braff, A. M., & Singer, L. M.** (1984). Psychological and academic adjustment in adopted children. *Journal of Consulting and Clinical Psychology, 52,* 582–590.

**Broidy, L. M., Nagin, D. S., Tremblay, R. E., Bates, J. E., Dodge, K. A., Fergusson, D., Horwood, J. L., Loeber, R., Laird, R., Lynam, D. R., Moffitt, T. E., Pettit, G. S., & Vitaro, F.** (2003). Developmental trajectories of childhood disruptive behaviors and adolescent delinquency: A six-site, cross-national study. *Developmental Psychology, 39,* 222–245.

**Brom, B.** (2005). *Nutrition Now* (4th ed.). Belmont CA: Wadsworth.

**Bronfenbrenner, U.** (1986). Ecology of the family as a context for human development: Research perspectives. *Developmental Psychology, 22,* 723–742.

**Bronfenbrenner, U.** (2000). Ecological theory. In A. Kazdin (Ed.), *Encyclopedia of psychology.* Washington, DC & New York: American Psychological Association and Oxford University Press.

**Bronfenbrenner, U.** (2004). Making human beings human. Thousand Oaks, CA: Sage.

**Bronfenbrenner, U., & Morris, P.** (1998). The ecology of developmental processes. In W. Damon (Ed.), *Handbook of child psychology* (5th ed., Vol. 1). New York: Wiley.

**Bronfenbrenner, U., & Morris, P. A.** (2006). The ecology of developmental processes. In W. Damon & R. Lerner (Eds.), *Handbook of child psychology* (6th ed.). New York: Wiley.

**Bronstein, P.** (2006). The family environment: Where gender role socialization begins. In J. Worell & C. D. Goodheart (Eds.), *Handbook of girls' and women's psychological health.* New York: Oxford University Press.

**Brook, J. S., Brook, D. W., Gordon, A. S., Whiteman, M., & Cohen, P.** (1990). The psychological etiology of adolescent drug use: A family interactional approach. *Genetic Psychology Monographs, 116,* no. 2.

**Brook, J. S., Whiteman, M., Balka, E. B., Win, P. T., & Gursen, M. D.** (1998). Drug use among Puerto Ricans: Ethnic identity as a protective factor. *Hispanic Journal of Behavioral Sciences, 20,* 241–254.

**Brooker, R. J., Widmaier, E. P., Graham, L., & Stiling, P.** (2008). *Biology.* New York: McGraw-Hill.

**Brooks, T., & Bornstein, P.** (1996, March). *Cross-cultural comparison of mothers' and fathers' behaviors toward girls and boys.* Paper presented at the Society for Research on Adolescence, Boston.

**Brooks-Gunn, J.** (1992, March). *Revisiting theories of "storm and stress": The role of biology.* Paper presented at the meeting of the Society for Research on Adolescence, Washington, DC.

**Brooks-Gunn, J., & Chase-Lansdale, P. L.** (1995). Adolescent parenthood. In M. H. Bornstein (Ed.), *Children and parenting* (Vol. 3). Hillsdale, NJ: Erlbaum.

**Brooks-Gunn, J., & Graber, J. A.** (1995, March). *Depressive affect versus positive adjustment: Patterns of resilience in adolescent girls.* Paper presented at the meeting of the Society for Research in Child Development, Indianapolis.

**Brooks-Gunn, J., & Graber, J. A.** (1999). *What's sex got to do with it? The development of health and sexual identities during adolescence.* Unpublished manuscript, Department of Psychology, Columbia University, New York City.

**Brooks-Gunn, J., Graber, J. A, & Paikoff, R. L.** (1994). Studying links between hormones and negative affect: Models and measures. *Journal of Research on Adolescence, 4,* 469–486.

**Brooks-Gunn, J., & Paikoff, R. L.** (1993). "Sex is a gamble, kissing is a game": Adolescent sexuality and health promotion. In S. G. Millstein, A. C. Petersen, & E. O. Nightingale (Eds.), *Promoting the health of adolescents.* New York: Oxford University Press.

**Brooks-Gunn, J., & Paikoff, R. L.** (1997). Sexuality and developmental transitions during adolescence. In J. Schulenberg, J. Maggs, & K. Hurrelmann (Eds.), *Health risks and developmental transitions during adolescence.* New York: Cambridge University Press.

**Brooks-Gunn, J., & Ruble, D. N.** (1982). The development of menstrual-related beliefs and behaviors during early adolescence. *Child Development, 53,* 1567–1577.

**Brooks-Gunn, J., & Warren, M. P.** (1989). The psychological significance of secondary sexual characteristics in 9- to 11-year-old girls. *Child Development, 59,* 161–169.

**Brophy, J.** (2004). *Motivating students to learn* (2nd ed.). Mahwah, NJ: Erlbaum.

**Broughton, J.** (1983). The cognitive developmental theory of adolescent self and identity. In B. Lee & G. Noam (Eds.), *Developmental approaches to self.* New York: Plenum.

**Brown, B., Moore, K., & Bzostek, S.** (2005). A portrait of well-being in early adulthood: A report to the William and Flora Hewlett Foundation. Retrieved November 15, 2005, from Publications/portraitOfWellBeing.htm

**Brown, B.** (Ed.). (2007). *Key indicators of child and youth well-being.* Mahwah, NJ: Erlbaum.

**Brown, B. B.** (1999). Measuring the peer environment of American adolescents. In S. L. Friedman & T. D. Wachs (Eds.), *Measuring environment across the life span.* Washington, DC: American Psychological Association.

**Brown, B. B.** (2003). Crowds, cliques, and friendships. In G. Adams & M. Berzonsky (Eds.), *Blackwell handbook of adolescence.* Malden, MA: Blackwell.

**Brown, B. B.** (2004). Adolescents' relationships with peers. In R. Lerner & L. Steinberg (Eds.). *Handbook of adolescent psychology* (2nd ed.). New York: Wiley.

**Brown, B. B., & Larson, R. W.** (2002). The kaleidoscope of adolescence: Experiences of the world's youth at the beginning of the 21st century. In B. B. Brown, R. W. Larson, & T. S. Saraswathi (Eds.), *The world's youth.* New York: Cambridge University Press.

**Brown, B. B., Lambron, S. L., Mounts, N. S., & Steinberg, L.** (1993). Parenting practices and peer group affiliation in adolescence. *Child Development, 64,* 467–482.

**Brown, B. B., & Lohr, M. J.** (1987). Peer-group affiliation and adolescent self-esteem: An integration of ego-identity and symbolic interaction theories. *Journal of Personality and Social Psychology, 52,* 47–55.

**Brown, B. B., Mory, M. S., & Kinney, D.** (1994). Casting adolescent crowds in a relational perspective: Caricature, channel, and context. In R. Montemayor, G. R. Adams, & T. P. Gullotta (Eds.), *Personal relationships during adolescence.* Newbury Park, CA: Saga.

**Brown, B. B., & Theobald, W.** (1998). Learning contexts beyond the classroom: Extracurricular activities, community organizations, and peer groups. In K. Borman & B. Schneider (Eds.), *The adolescent years.* Chicago: University of Chicago Press.

**Brown, J. D., Halpern, C. T., & L'Engle, K. L.** (2005). Mass media as a sexual super peer for early maturing girls. *Journal of Adolescent Health, 36,* 420–427.

**Brown, J. D., & Siegel, J. D.** (1988). Exercise as a buffer of life stress: A prospective study of adolescent health. *Health Psychology, 7,* 341–353.

**Brown, L. M., & Gilligan, C.** (1992). *Meeting at the crossroads: Women's and girls' development.* Cambridge, MA: Harvard University Press.

**Brown, R. T.** (2006). Pregnancy and abortion in adolescents. *Pediatric Endocrinology Review, 3 Suppl 1,* 167–169.

**Brown, R. T., & Brown, J. D.** (2006). Adolescent sexuality. *Primary Care, 33,* 373–390.

**Bronstein, P.** (2006). The family environment: where gender role socialization begins In J. Worell & C. D. Goodheart (eds.), *Handbook of girls' and women's psychological health.* New York: Oxford University Press.

**Bruess, C. E., & Richardson, G. E.** (1992). *Decisions for health* (3rd ed.). Dubuque, IA: Brown & Benchmark.

**Brunstein Klomek, A., Marrocco, F., Kleinman, M., Schonfeld, I. S., & Gould, M. S.** (2007). Bullying, depression, and suicidality in adolescents. *Journal of the American Academy of Child and Adolescent Psychiatry, 46,* 40–49.

**Bryant, A., & LaFromboise, T. D.** (2005). The racial identity and cultural orientation of Lumbee American Indian high school students. *Cultural Diversity and Ethnic Minority Psychology, 11,* 82–89.

**Bryant, B. K., Zvonkovic, A. M., & Reynolds, P.** (2006). Parenting in relation to child and adolescent vocational development. *Journal of Vocational Behavior, 69,* 149–175.

**Bryant, D. P., Smith, D. D., & Bryant, B. R.** (2008). *Teaching students with special needs in inclusive classrooms.* Boston: Allyn & Bacon.

**Bryant, J., & Rockwell, S. C.** (1994). Effects of massive exposure to sexually oriented prime-time television programming on adolescents' moral judgment. In D. Zillman, J. Bryant, & A. C. Huston (Eds.), Media, children, and the family: Social scientific, psychodynamic, and clinical perspectives. Hillsdale, NJ: Erlbaum.

**Buchanan, C. M., Maccoby, E. E., & Dornbusch, S.** (1992). Adolescents and their families after divorce: Three residential arrangements compared. *Journal of Research on Adolescence, 2,* 261–291.

**Buchanan, C. M., Williams, A., Halfond, R., & Snyder, J. C.** (2006, March). *The impact of mentoring on developmental assets in Latino youth.* Paper presented at the meeting of the Society for Research on Adolescence, San Francisco.

**Buck, M., Lund, J. L., Harrison, J. M., & Blakemore-Cook, C.** (2007). *Instructional strategies for school physical education* (6th ed.). New York: McGraw-Hill.

**Buehler, C., Lange, G., & Franck, K. L.** (2007). Adolescents' cognitive and emotional responses to marital hostility. *Child Development, 78,* 775–789.

**Bugental, D. B., & Goodnow, J. J.** (2006). Socialization processes. In W. Damon & R. Lerner (Eds.), *Handbook of child psychology* (6th ed.). New York: Wiley.

**Buhi, E. R., & Goodson, P.** (2007). Predictors of adolescent sexual behavior and intention: A theory-guided systematic review. *Journal of Adolescent Health, 40,* 4–21.

**Buhrmester, D.** (1990). Friendship, interpersonal competence, and adjustment in preadolescence and adolescence. *Child Development, 61,* 1101–1111.

**Buhrmester, D.** (2001, April). *Does age at which romantic involvement start matter?* Paper presented at the meeting of the Society for Research in Child Development, Minneapolis.

**Buhrmester, D.** (2005, April). *The antecedents of adolescents' competence in close relationships: A six-year-study.* Paper presented at the meeting of the Society for Research in Child Development, Atlanta.

**Buhrmester, D., Camparo, L., Christensen, A., Gonzalez, L. S., & Hinshaw, S. P.** (1992). Mothers and fathers interacting in dyads and triads with normal and hyperactive sons. *Developmental Psychology, 28,* 500–509.

**Buhrmester, D., & Carbery, J.** (1992, March). *Daily patterns of self-disclosure and adolescent adjustment.* Paper presented at the biennial meeting of the Society for Research on Adolescence, Washington, DC.

**Buhrmester, D., & Furman, W.** (1987). The development of companionship and intimacy. *Child Development, 58,* 1101–1113.

**Buhs, E. S., & Ladd, G. W.** (2001). Peer rejection as an antecedent of young children's school adjustment: An examination of mediating processes. *Developmental Psychology, 37,* 550–560.

**Bukowski, W. M., & Adams, R.** (2005). Peer relationships and psychopathology. *Journal of Clinical Child and Adolescent Psychology, 34,* 3–10.

**Bukowski, W. M., Brendgen, M., & Vitaro, F.** (2007). Peers and socialization: Effects on externalizing and internalizing problems. In J. E. Grusec & P. D. Hastings (eds.), *Handbook of socialization.* New York: Guilford.

**Bukowski, W. M., Newcomb, A. F., & Hoza, B.** (1987). Friendship conceptions among early adolescents: A longitudinal study of stability and change. *Journal of Early Adolescence, 7,* 143–152.

**Bulik, C. M., Berkman, N. D., Brownley, K. A., Sedway, J. A., & Lohr, K. N.** (2007). Anorexia nervosa treatment: A systematic review of randomized controlled trials. *Internationl Journal of Eating Disorders.*

**Bumpas, M. F., Crouter, A. C. & McHale, S. M.** (2001). Parental autonomy granting during adolescence: Gender differences in context. *Developmental Psychology, 37,* 163–173.

**Burchinal, M. R., Peisner-Feinberg, E., Pianta, R., & Howes, C.** (2002). Development of academic skills from preschool through second grade: Family and classroom predictors of developmental trajectories. *Journal of School Psychology, 40* (5), 415–436.

**Burke, R., & Vinnicombe, S.** (2005). Advancing women's careers. *Career Development International, 10,* 165–167.

**Burns. D.** (1985). *Intimate connections.* New York: Morrow.

**Bursuck, W. D., & Damer, M.** (2007). *Reading instruction for students who are at risk or have disabilities.* Boston: Allyn & Bacon.

**Burton, R. V.** (1984). A paradox in theories and research in moral development. In W. M. Kurtines & J. L. Gewirtz (Eds.), *Morality, moral behavior, and moral development.* New York: Wiley.

**Busby, D. M., Ivey, D. C., Harris, S. M., & Ates, C.** (2007). Self-directed, therapist-directed, and assessment-based interventions for premarital couples. *Family Relations, 56,* 279–290.

**Buss, D. M.** (1995). Psychological sex differences: Origins through sexual selection. *American Psychologist, 50,* 164–168.

**Buss, D. M.** (1999). *Evolutionary psychology: The new science of the mind.* Boston: Allyn & Bacon.

**Buss, D. M.** (2000). Evolutionary psychology. In A. Kazdin (Ed.), *Encyclopedia of psychology.* Washington, DC & New York: American Psychological Association and Oxford University Press.

**Buss, D. M.** (2001). Human nature and culture: an evolutionary psychology perspective. *Journal of Personality, 69,* 955–978.

**Buss, D. M.** (2004). *Evolutionary psychology* (2nd ed.). Boston: Allyn & Bacon.

**Buss, D. M.** (2007). Foreward. In G. Geher & G. Miller (Eds.), *Mating intelligence.* Mahwah, NJ: Erlbaum.

**Buss, D. M.** (2008). *Evolutionary psychology* (3rd ed.). Boston: Allyn & Bacon.

**Buss, D. M., & Schmitt, D. P.** (1993). Sexual strategies theory: An evolutionary perspective on human mating. *Psychological Review, 100,* 204–232.

**Busseri, M. A., Willoughby, T., Chalmers, H., & Bogaert, A. R.** (2006). Same-sex attraction and successful adolescent development. *Journal of Youth and Adolescence, 35,* 563–575.

**Bussey, K., & Bandura A.** (1999). Social cognitive theory of gender development and differentiation. *Psychological Review, 106,* 676–713.

**Buston, K., Williamson, L., & Hart, G.** (2007). Young women under 16 years of age with experience of sexual intercourse: Who becomes pregnant. *Journal of Epidemiological and Community Health, 61,* 221–225.

**Buzwell, S., & Rosenthal, D.** (1996). Constructing a sexual self: Adolescents' sexual self-perceptions and sexual risk-taking. *Journal of Research on Adolescence, 6,* 489–513.

**Byars-Winston, A. M., & Fouad, N. A.** (2006). Metacognition and multicultural competence: Expanding the culturally appropriate career counseling model. *Career Development Quarterly, 54,* 187–201.

**Byrnes, J. P.** (1998). *The nature and development of decision making.* Mahwah, NJ: Erlbaum.

**Byrnes, J. P.** (2005). The development of regulated decision making. In J. E. Jacobs & P. A., Klaczynski (Eds.), *The development of judgement and decision making in children and adolescents.* Mahwah, NJ: Erlbaum.

**Byrnes, J. P.** (2007). Some ways in which neuroscientific research can be relevant to education. In D. Coch, K. W. Fischer, & G. Dawson (Eds.), *Human behavior, learning, and the developing brain.* New York: Guilford.

**Cabezon, C., Vigil, P., Rojas, I., Leiva, M. E., Riquelme, R., Aranda, W., & García, C.** (2005). Adolescent pregnancy prevention: An abstinence-centered randomized controlled intervention in a Chilean public high school. *Journal of Adolescent Health, 36,* 64–69.

**Cacioppo, J. T., Ernst, J. M., Burleson, M. H., McClintock, M. K., Malarkey, W. B., Hawkley, L. C., Kowalewski, R. B., Paulsen, A., Hobson, J. A., Hugdahl, K., Spiegel, D., Bernston, G. G.** (2000). Lonely traits and concomitant physiological processes: The MacArthur Social Neuroscience Studies. *International Journal of Psychophysiology, 35,* 143–154.

**Cacioppo, J. T., & Hawkley, L. C.** (2003). Social isolation and health, with an Emphasis on Underlying Mechanisms. *Perspectives on Biology and Medicine, 46 Suppl 3,* 539–552.

## C

**Cairnes, R. B., & Cairns, B. D.** (1994). *Lifelines and risks: Pathways of youth in our time.* New York: Cambridge University Press.

**Calabrese, R. L., & Schumer, H.** (1986). The effects of service activities on adolescent alienation. *Adolescence, 21,* 675–687.

**Call, K. A. Riedel, A., Hein, K., McLoyd, V., Kipke, M., & Petersen, P.** (2002). Adolescent health and well-being in the 21st century: A global perspective. *Journal of Research on Adolescence, 12,* 69–98.

**Calvert, S.** (1999). *Children's journeys through the information age.* New York: McGraw-Hill.

**Camenga, D. R., Klein, J. D., & Roy, J.** (2006). The changing risk profile of the American adolescent smoker: Implications for prevention programs and tobacco interventions. *Journal of Adolescent Health, 39,* 120e1–120e10.

**Cameron, J. L.** (2004). Interrelationships between hormones, behavior, and affect during adolescence: Understanding hormonal, physical, and brain changes occurring in association with pubertal activation of the reproductive axis. Introduction to Part III. *Annals of the New York Academy of Sciences, 1021,* 110–123.

**Cameron, J., Cowan, L., Holmes, B., Hurst, P., & McLean, M.** (Eds.). (1983). *International handbook of educational systems.* New York: Wiley.

**Camilleri, B.** (2005). Dynamic assessment and intervention: Improving children's narrative abilities. *International Journal of Language and Communication Disorders, 40,* 240–242.

**Campbell, B., & Mbizo, M.** (2006). Reproductive maturation, somatic growth, and testosterone among Zimbabwe boys. *Annals of Human Biology, 33,* 17–25.

**Campbell, C. Y.** (1988, August 24). Group raps depiction of teenagers. *Boston Globe,* p. 44.

**Campbell, L., Campbell, B., & Dickinson, D.** (2004). *Teaching and learning through multiple intelligences* (3rd ed.). Boston: Allyn & Bacon.

**Campos, J., Frankel, C., & Camras, L.** (2004). On the nature of emotion regulation. *Child Development, 75,* 377–394.

**Capaldi, D. M., & Shortt, J. W.** (2003). Understanding conduct problems in adolescence from a lifespan perspective. In G. R. Adams & M. D. Berzonsky (Eds.), *Blackwell handbook of adolescence.* Malden, MA: Blackwell.

**Capaldi, D. M., Stoolmiller, M., Clark, S., & Owen, L. D.** (2002). Heterosexual risk behaviors in at-risk young men from early adolescence to young adulthood: Prevalence, prediction, and association with STD contraction. *Developmental Psychology, 38,* 394–406.

**Caplan, P. J., & Caplan, J. B.** (1999). *Thinking critically about research on sex and gender* (2nd ed.). New York: Longman.

**Cara, J. F., & Chaiken, R. L.** (2006). Type 2 diabetes and the metabolic syndrome in children and adolescents. *Current Diabetes Reports, 6,* 241–250.

**Cardelle-Elawar, M.** (1992). Effect of teaching metacognitive skills to students with low mathematics ability. *Teaching and Teacher Education, 8,* 109–121.

**Carel, J. C.** (2006). Management of short stature with GnRH agonist and co-treatment with growth hormone: A controversial issue. *Molecular and Cellular Endocrinology,* 226–233, 254–255.

**Carlo, G.** (2006). Care-based altruistically based morality. In M. Killen & J. Smetana (Eds.), *Handbook of moral development.* Mahwah, NJ: Erlbaum.

**Carlson, C., Cooper, C., & Hsu, J.** (1990, March). *Predicting school achievement in early adolescence: The role of family process.* Paper presented at the meeting of the Society for Research in Adolescence, Atlanta.

**Carlson, D. S., Kaacmar, K. M., Wayne, J. H., & Grzywacz, J. G.** (2006). Measuring the positive side the work-family interface: Development and validation of a work-family enrichment scale. *Journal of Vocational Behavior, 68,* 131–164.

**Carnagey, N. L., Anderson, C. A., & Bushman, B. J.** (2007, in press). The effect of video game violence on physiological desensitization to real-life violence. *Journal of Experimental Social Psychology, 43,* 489–496.

**Carnegie Council on Adolescent Development.** (1995). *Great transitions.* New York: Carnegie Foundation.

**Carnethon, M. R., Gulati, M., & Greenland, P.** (2005). Prevalence of cardiovascular disease correlates of low cardiorespiratory fitness in adolescents and adults. *Journal of the American Medical Association, 294,* 2981–2988.

**Caron, S.** (2007). *Sex matters for college students* (2nd ed.).Upper Saddle River, NJ: Prentice Hall.

**Carroll, J.** (1993). *Human cognitive abilities.* Cambridge: Cambridge University Press.

**Carroll, J. L.** (2007). *Sexuality now* (2nd ed.). Belmont, CA: Wadsworth.

**Carroll, J. S., & Doherty, W. J.** (2003). Evaluating the effectiveness of premarital prevention programs: A meta-analytic review of outcome research. *Family Relations, 52,* 105–118.

**Carroll, S. T., Riffenburgh, R. H., Robert, T. A. Myhre, E. H.** (2002). Tattoos and body piercings as indicators of adolescent risk-taking behaviors. *Pediatrics, 109* (6), 1021–1027.

**Carskadon, M.** (2006, March). *Too little, too late: Sleep bioregulatory processes across adolescence.* Paper presented at the meeting of the Society for Research on Adolescence, San Francisco.

**Carskadon, M. A.** (Ed.). (2002). *Adolescent sleep patterns.* New York: Cambridge University Press.

**Carskadon, M. A.** (2004). Sleep difficulties in young people. *Archives of Pediatric and Adolescent Medicine, 158,* 597–598.

**Carskadon, M. A.** (2005). Sleep and circadian rhythms in children and adolescents: Relevance for athletic performance of young people. *Clinical Sports Medicine, 24,* 319–328.

**Carskadon, M. A., Acebo, C., & Jenni, O. G.** (2004). Regulation of adolescent sleep: Implications for behavior. *Annals of the New York Academy of Sciences, 102,* 276–291.

**Carskadon, M. A., Mindell, J., & Drake, C.** (2006, September). *Contemporary sleep patterns in the USA: Results of the 2006 National Sleep Foundation Poll.* Paper presented at the European Sleep Research Society, Innsbruck, Austria.

**Caruthers, A. S., & Ward, L. M.** (2002, April). *Mixed messages: The divergent nature of sexual communication received from parents, peers, and the media.* Paper presented at the meeting of the Society for Research on Adolescence, New Orleans.

**Carver, K., Joyner, K., & Udry, J. R.** (2003). National estimates of romantic relationships. In P. Florsheim (Ed.), *Adolescent romantic relations and sexual behavior.* Mahwah, NJ: Erlbaum.

**Casazza, K., & Ciccazzo, M.** (2006). Improving the dietary patterns of adolescents using a computer-based approach. *Journal of School Health, 76,* 43–46.

**Case, R.** (Ed.). (1992). *The mind's staircase: Exploring the conceptual underpinnings of children's thought and knowledge.* Hillsdale, NJ: Erlbaum.

**Case, R.** (2000). Conceptual development. In M. Bennett (Ed.), *Developmental psychology.* Philadelphia: Psychology Press.

**Case, R.** (2005). Bring critical thinking to the main stage. *Education Canada. 45,* 45–48.

**Casper, L. M., & Bianchi, S. M.** (2007). Cohabitation. In A. S. Skolnick & J. H. Skolnick (Eds.), *Family in transition* (14th ed.). Boston: Allyn & Bacon.

**Caspi, A.** (1998). Personality development across the life course. In W. Damon (Series Ed.) & N. Eisenberg (Ed.), Handbook of child psychology: Vol. 3. *Social, emotional, and personality development* (5th ed., pp. 311–388). New York: Wiley.

**Caspi, A., & Bem, D. J.** (1990). Personality continuity and change across the life course. In L. Pervin (Ed.), *Handbook of personality.* New York: Guilford.

**Caspi, A., & Shiner, R.** (2006). Personality development. In W. Damon & R. Lerner (Eds.), *Handbook of child psychology* (6th ed.). New York: Wiley.

**Cassell, E., & Bernstein, D. A.** (2001). *Criminal behavior.* Boston: Allyn & Bacon.

**Cassell, J., Huffaker, J., Tversky, D., & Ferriman, K.** (2006). The language of online leadership: Gender and youth engagement on the Internet. *Developmental Psychology, 42,* 436–449.

**Castellano, J. A., & Diaz, E. (Eds.)** (2002). *Reaching new horizons: Gifted and talented education for culturally and linguistically diverse students.* Boston: Allyn & Bacon.

**Cauffman, B. E.** (1994, February). *The effects of puberty, dating, and sexual involvement on dieting and disordered eating in young adolescent girls.* Paper presented at the meeting of the Society for Research on Adolescence, San Diego.

**Cavanaugh, S. E.** (2004). The sexual debut of girls in adolescence: The intersection of race, pubertal timing, and friendship group characteristics. *Journal of Research on Adolescence, 14,* 285–312.

**Cavell, T. A., Hymel, S., Malcolm, K. T., & Seay, A.** (2007). Socialization and interventions for antisocial youth. In J. E. Grusec & P. D. Hastings (Eds.), *Handbook of socialization.* New York: Guilford.

**Cawley, J., Newhouse, D., & Meyerhoefer, C.** (2006). Not your father's PE: Obesity, exercise, and the role of schools. *Education Next, 4,* 60–66.

**Ceci, S. J.** (2000). Bronfenbrenner, Urie. In A. Kazdin (Ed.), *Encyclopedia of psychology.* Washington, DC & New York: American Psychological Association and Oxford University Press.

**Ceci, S. J., & Gilstrap, L. L.** (2000). Determinants of intelligence: Schooling and intelligence. In A. Kazdin (Ed.), *Encyclopedia of Psychology.* Washington, DC & New York: American Psychological Association and Oxford University Press.

**Centers for Disease Control and Prevention.** (2003). Births: Final data for 2002. *National Vital Statistics Reports, 52,* No. 10, 1–5.

**Centers for Disease Control and Prevention.** (1997, August 8). Abortion surveillance—United States, 1993 and 1994. *MMWR, 46* (No. SS-4), 37–98.

**Centers for Disease Control and Prevention.** (2000). Youth risk behavior surveillance—United States, 1999, *MMWR, 49* (No. SS-5).

**Centers for Disease Control and Prevention.** (2002). *Cohabitation,* Atlanta, GA: Author.

**Centers for Disease Control and Prevention.** (2006). Use of cigarettes and other tobacco products among students aged 13–15 years—worldwide, 1999–2005. *MMWR 55,* 553–556.

**Centers for Disease Control and Prevention.** (2006). *Sexually transmitted diseases.* Atlanta: Author.

**Centers for Disease Control and Prevention.** (2007). *Obesity and overweight.* Retrieved January 6, 2007, from www.cdc.qov/az.do

**Centers for Disease Control and Prevention** *(2007). AIDS.* Atlanta: Author.

**Cerel, J., & Roberts, T. A.** (2005). Suicidal behavior in the family and adolescent risk behavior. *Journal of Adolescent Health, 36,* e8–e14.

**Cervero, A., Dominquez, F., Horcajadas, J. A., Quiinonero, A., Pellicer, A., & Simon, C.** (2006). The role of leptin in reproduction. *Current Opinions in Obstetrics and Gynecology, 18,* 297–303.

**Chaffee, S. H., & Yang, S. M.** (1990). Communication and political socialization. In O. Ichilov (Ed.), *Political socialization, citizen education, and democracy.* New York: Columbia University Press.

**Chan, W. S.** (1963). *A source book in Chinese philosophy.* Princeton, NJ: Princeton Books.

**Chang, R., & Gjerde, P. F.** (2000, April). *Pathways toward and away from depression in young adult females: Person-centered analysis of longitudinal data.* Paper presented at the meeting of the Society for Research on Adolescence, Chicago.

**Chao, R.** (2001). Extending research on the consequences of parenting style for Chinese Americans and European Americans. *Child Development, 72,* 1832–1843.

**Chao, R. K.** (2005, April). *The importance of Guan in describing control of immigrant Chinese.* Paper presented at the meeting of the Society for Research in Child Development, Atlanta.

**Chao, R. K.** (2007, March). *Research with Asian Americans: Looking back and moving forward.* Paper presented at the meeting of the Society for Research in Child Development, Boston.

**Chassin, L., Pitts, S. C., & Prost, J.** (2001, April). *Binge drinking trajectories from adolescence to emerging adulthood in a high risk sample: Predictors and substance abuse outcomes.* Paper presented at the meeting of the Society for Research in Child Development, Minneapolis.

**Chaves, A. P., Diemer, M. A., Blustein, D. L., Gallagher, L. A., DeVoy, J. E., Casares, M. T., & Perry, J. C.** (2004). Conceptions of work: The view from urban youth. *Journal of Counseling Psychology, 51,* 257–286.

**Chavous, T., Branch, L., Cogburn, C., Griffin, T., Maddox, J., & Sellers, R. M.** (2007, in press). Achievement motivation among African American college students at predominantly White institutions: Risk and protective processes related to group identity and contextual experiences. In F. Salili & R. Hoosain (Eds.), *Culture, motivation and learning: A multicultural, perspective.* Charlotte, NC: Publishing.

**Chen, C., & Stevenson, H. W.** (1989). Homework: A cross-cultural examination. *Child Development, 60,* 551–561.

**Chen, M. Y., Wang, E. K., & Yeng, Y. J.** (2006). Adequate sleep among adolescents is positively associated with health status and health-related behaviors. *BMC Public Health, 6,* 59.

**Chen, X., Tyler, K. A., Whitbeck, L. B., & Hoyt, D. R.** (2004). Early sexual abuse, street adversity, and drug use among female homeless and runaway adolescents in the Midwest. *Journal of Drug Issues, 34,* 1–20.

**Cheng, C., & Cheung, M. W.** (2005). Cognitive processes underlying coping flexibility: differentiation and integration. *Journal of Personality, 73,* 859–886.

**Cherlin, A. J.** (2007). The deinstitutionalization of marriage. In S. J. Ferguson (ed.), *Shifting the center: Understanding contemporary families* (3rd ed.). New York: McGraw-Hill.

**Cherlin, A. J., & Furstenberg, F. F.** (1994). Stepfamilies in the United States: A reconsideration. In J. Blake & J. Hagen (Eds.), *Annual review of sociology.* Palo Alto, CA: Annual Reviews.

**Chess, S., & Thomas, A.** (1977). Temperamental individuality from childhood to adolescence. *Journal of Child Psychiatry, 16,* 218–226.

**Chi, M. T. H.** (1978). Knowledge structures and memory development. In R. S. Siegler (Ed.), *Children's thinking: What develops?* Hillsdale, NJ: Erlbaum.

**Chia-Chen, C. A., & Thompson, E. A.** (2007). Preventing adolescent risky sexual behavior: Parents matter! *Journal for Specialists in Pediatric Nursing, 12,* 119–122.

**Child Trends.** (2000). Trends in sexual activity and contraceptive use among teens. *Child trends research brief.* Washington, DC: Author.

**Child Trends.** (2006). Fast facts at a glance. Washington, DC: Author

**Children's Defense Fund.** (2007). Children's welfare and mental health. Retrieved April 24, 2007, www.childrensdefense.org.

**Chilman, C.** (1979). *Adolescent sexuality in a changing American society: Social and psychological perspectives.* Washington, DC: Public Health Service, National Institute of Mental Health.

**Chira, S.** (1993, June 23). What do teachers want most? Help from parents. *New York Times,* p. 17.

**Chiu, C., & Hong, Y.** (2007). Cultural processes: Basic principles. In A. W. Kruglanski & E. T. Higgins (Eds.), *Social psychology: Handbook of basic principles* (2nd ed.). New York: Guilford.

**Chmielewski, C.** (1997, September). Sexual harassment meet Title IX. *NEA Today, 16* (2), 24–25.

**Choi, N.** (2004). Sex role group differences in specific, academic, and general self-efficacy. *Journal of Psychology, 138,* 149–159.

**Christenson, S. L., & Thurlow, M. L.** (2004). School dropouts: Prevention considerations, interventions, and challenges. *Current Directions in Psychological Science, 13,* 36–39.

**Christopher, F. S., & Kisler, T. S.** (2004). Sexual aggression in romantic relationships. In J. H. Harvey, A. Wenzel, & S. Sprecher (Eds.), *The handbook of sexuality in close relationships.* Mahwah, NJ: Erlbaum.

**Cialdini, R., & Rhoads, K.** (1999). *Cults: Questions and answers.* Retrieved from the World Wide Web: http://www.influenceatwork.com/cult.html.

**Cicchetti, D.** (2006). Intervention and policy implications of research on neurobiological functioning in maltreated children. In L. Aber & others (Eds.), *Child development and social policy.* Washington, DC: American Psychological Association.

**Cicchetti, D., & Toth, S. L.** (2006). A developmental psychopathology perspective on preventive interventions with high risk children and families. In W. Damon & R. Lerner (Eds.), *Handbook of child psychology* (6th ed.). New York: Wiley.

**Cillessen, A. H. N., Lu Jiang, X., West, T. V., & Laszkowski, D. K.** (2005). Predictors of dyadic friendship quality in adolescence. *International Journal of Behavioral Development, 29,* 165–172.

**Cillessen, A. H. N., & Mayeux, L.** (2004). Sociometric status and peer group behavior: Previous findings and current directions. In J. B. Kupersmidt & K. A. Dodge (Eds.), *Children's peer relations: From development to intervention.* Washington, DC: American Psychological Association.

**Clabby, J. G., & Elias, M. J.** (1988). Improving social problem-solving and awareness. *William T. Grant Foundation Annual Report,* p. 18.

**Clark, K. B., & Clark, M. P.** (1939). The development of the self and the emergence of racial identification in Negro preschool children. *Journal of Social Psychology, 10,* 591–599.

**Clark, M. S., Powell, M. C., Ovellette, R., & Milberg, S.** (1987). Recipient's mood, relationship type, and helping. *Journal of Personality and Social Psychology, 43,* 94–103.

**Clark, R. D., & Hatfield, E.** (1989). Gender differences in receptivity to sexual offers, *Journal of Psychology and Human Sexuality, 2,* 39–55.

**Clarke-Stewart, A.** (2006). What have we learned: Proof that families matter, policies for families and children, prospects for future research. In A. Clarke-Stewart & J. Dunn (Eds.), *Families count.* New York: Cambridge University Press.

**Clarke-Stewart, A., & Brentano, C.** (2006). *Divorce: Causes and consequences.* New Haven, CT: Yale University Press.

**Clarkson, J., & Herbison, A. E.** (2006). Development of GABA and glutamate signaling at the GnRH neuron in relation to puberty. *Molecular and Cellular Endocrinology 254–255,* 32–38.

**Clasen, D. R., & Brown, B. B.** (1987). Understanding peer pressure in the middle school. *Middle School Journal, 19,* 21–23.

**Clausen, J. S.** (1991). Adolescent competence and the shaping of the life course. *American Journal of Sociology, 96,* 805–842.

**Clifford, B. R., Gunter, B., & McAleer, J. L.** (1995). *Television and children.* Hillsdale, NJ: Erlbaum.

**CNN and the National Science Foundation.** (1997). *Poll on technology and education.* Washington, DC: National Science Foundation.

**Cochran, S. D., & Mays, V. M.** (1990). Sex, lies, and HIV. *New England Journal of Medicine, 322* (11), 774–775.

**Cohall, A. T., Cohall, R., Ellis, J. A., Vaughan, R. D., Northridge, M. E., Watkins-Bryant, G., & Butcher, J.** (2004). More than heights and weights: What parents of urban adolescents want from health care providers. *Journal of Adolescent Health, 34,* 258–261.

**Cohen, P., Kasen, S., Chen, H., Hartmark, C., & Gordon, K.** (2003). Variations in patterns of developmental transitions in the emerging adulthood period. *Developmental Psychology, 39,* 657–669.

**Cohn, A., & Canter, A.** (2003). *Bullying: Facts for schools and parents.* Washington, DC: National Association of School Psychologists Center.

**Coie, J. D.** (2004). The impact of negative social experiences on the development of antisocial behavior. In J. B. Kupersmidt & K. A. Dodge (Eds.), *Children's peer relations: From development to intervention.* Washington, DC: American Psychological Association.

**Coie, J. D., & Dodge, K. A.** (1998). Aggression and antisocial behavior. In N. Eisenberg (Ed.), *Handbook of child psychology* (5th ed., Vol. 3). New York: Wiley.

**Coie, J. D., & Koeppl, G. K.** (1990). Adapting intervention to the problems of aggressive and disruptive rejected children. In S. R. Asher & J. D. Coie (Eds.), *Peer rejection in childhood.* New York: Cambridge University Press.

**Colby, A., Kohlberg, L., Gibbs, J., & Lieberman, M.** (1983). A longitudinal study of moral judgment. *Monographs of the Society for Research in Child Development, 48* (21, Serial No. 201).

**Cole, A. K., & Kerns, K. A.** (2001). Perceptions of sibling qualities and activities of early adolescents. *Journal of Early Adolescence, 21,* 204–226.

**Cole, M.** (2006) Culture and cognitive development in phylogenetic, historical, and ontogenetic perspective. In W. Damon & R. Lerner (Eds.), *Handbook of child psychology* (6th ed.). New York: Wiley.

**Cole, M., & Gajdamaschko, N.** (2007). Vygotsky and culture. In H. Daniels, J. Wertsch, & M. Cole (Eds.), *The Cambridge companion to Vygotsky.* New York: Cambridge University Press.

**Coleman, M. C., & Webber, J.** (2002). *Emotional and behavioral disorders* (4th ed.). Boston: Allyn & Bacon.

**Coleman, M., Ganong, L., & Fine, M.** (2004). Communication in stepfamilies. In A. L. Vangelisti (Ed.), *Handbook of family communication.* Mahwah, NJ: Erlbaum.

**Coley, R.** (2001). *Differences in the gender gap: Comparisons across/racial/ethnic groups in the United States.* Princeton, NJ: Educational Testing Service.

**Coley, R. L., Morris, J. E., & Hernandez, D.** (2004). Out-of-school care and problem behavior trajectories among low-income adolescents: Individual, family, and neighborhood characteristics as added risks. *Child development, 75,* 948-965.

**College Board Commission on Precollege Guidance and Counseling.** (1986). *Keeping the options open.* New York: College Entrance Examination Board.

**Collins, M.** (1996, Winter). The job outlook for '96 grads. *Journal of Career Planning,* pp. 51–54.

**Collins, R. L.** (2005). Sex on television and its impact on American youth: Background and results from the RAND Television and Adolescent Sexuality Study. *Child and Adolescent Psychiatric Clinics of North America, 14,* 371–385.

**Collins, R. L., Elliott, M. N., Berry, S. H., Kanocouse, D. E., Kunkel, D., Hunter, S. B., & Miu, A.** (2004). Watching sex on television predicts adolescent initiation of sexual behavior. *Pediatrics, 114,* e280–e289.

**Collins, W. A., Hennighausen, K. H., & Sroufe, L. A.** (1998, June). *Developmental precursors of intimacy in romantic relationships: A longitudinal analysis.* Paper presented at the International Conference on Personal Relationships, Saratoga Springs, NY.

**Collins, W. A., & Roisman, G. I.** (2006). The influence of family and peer relationships in the development of competence during adolescence. In A. Clarke-Stewart & J. Dunn (Eds.), *Families count.* New York: Cambridge University Press.

**Collins, W. A., & Steinberg, L.** (2006). Adolescent development in interpersonal context. In W. Damon & R. Lerner (Eds.), *Handbook of child psychology* (6th ed.). New York: Wiley.

**Collins, W. A., & van Dulmen, M.** (2006). Friendship and romance in emerging adulthood. In J. J. Arnett & J. L. Tanner (Eds.), *Emerging adults in America.* Washington, DC: American Psychological Association.

**Collins, W. A., & van Dulmen, M.** (2006). The significance of middle childhood peer competence for work and relationships in early adulthood. In A. C. Huston & M. N. Ripke (Eds.), *Developmental contexts in middle childhood.* New York: Cambridge University Press.

**Coltrane, S. L., Parke, R. D., Schofield, T. J., Tsuha, S. J., Chavez, M., & Lio, S.** (2007). Mexican American families and poverty. In D. R. Crane & T. B. Heaton (Eds.), *Handbook of families and poverty.* Thousand Oaks, CA: Sage.

**Comer, J. P.** (1988). Educating poor minority children. *Scientific American, 259,* 42–48.

**Comer, J. P.** (1993). *African-American parents and child development: An agenda for school success.* Paper presented at the biennial meeting of the Society for Research on Child Development, New Orleans.

**Comer, J. P.** (2004). *Leave no child behind.* New Haven, CT: Yale University Press.

**Comer, J. P.** (2005). Child and adolescent development: The critical missing focus in school reform. *Phi Delta Kappan, 86,* 757–763.

**Comer, J. P.** (2006). Child development: The under-weighted aspect of intelligence. In P. C. Kyllonen, R. D. Roberts, & L. Stankov (Eds.), *Extending intelligence.* Mahwah, NJ: Erlbaum.

**Commoner, B.** (2002). Unraveling the DNA myth: The spurious foundation of genetic engineering. *Harper's, 304,* 39–47.

**Commons, M. L., & Bresette, L. M.** (2006). Illuminating major creative scientific innovators with postformal stages. In C. Hoare (Ed.), *Handbook of adult development and learning.* New York: Oxford University Press.

**Commons, M. L., & Richards, F. A.** (2003). Four postformal stages. In J. Demick & C. Andreoletti (Eds.), *Handbook of adult development.* New York: Kluwer.

**Compas, B. E.** (2004). Processes of risk and resilience during adolescence: Linking contexts and individuals. In R. Lerner & L. Steinberg (Eds.), *Handbook of adolescent psychology.* New York: Wiley.

**Compas, B. E.** (2004). Processes of risk and resillience during adolescence: Linking context and individuals. In R. Lerner & L. Steinberg (Eds.), *Handbook of adolescent psychology.* New York: Wiley.

**Compas, B. E., & Grant, K. E.** (1993, March). *Stress and adolescent depressive symptoms: Underlying mechanisms and processes.* Paper presented at the biennial meeting of the Society for Research in Child Development, New Orleans.

**Comstock, G., & Scharrer, E.** (2006). Media and popular culture. In W. Damon & R. Lerner (Eds.), *Handbook of child psychology* (6th ed.). New York: Wiley.

**Condry, J. C., Simon, M. L., & Bronfenbrener, U.** (1968). *Characteristics of peer- and adult-oriented children.* Unpublished manuscript, Cornell University, Ithaca, NY.

**Conger, J. J.** (1981). Freedom and commitment: Families, youth, and social change. *American Psychologist, 36,* 1475–1484.

**Conger, J. J.** (1988). Hostages to the future: Youth, values, and the public interest. *American Psychologist, 43,* 291–300.

**Conger, R. D., & Chao, W.** (1996). Adolescent depressed mood. In R. L. Simons (Ed.), *Understanding differences between divorced and intact families: Stress, interaction, and child outcome.* Thousand Oaks, CA: Sage.

**Conger, R. D., & Dogan, S. J.** (2007). Social class and socialization in families. In J. E. Grusec & P. D. Hastings (Eds.), *Handbook of socialization.* New York: Guilford.

**Conger, R. D., & Reuter, M.** (1996). Siblings, parents, and peers: A longitudinal study of social influences in adolescent risk for alcohol use and abuse. In G. H. Brody (Ed.), *Sibling relationships: Their causes and consequences.* Norwood, NJ: Ablex.

**Connell, A. M., & Dishion, T. J.** (2006). The contribution of peers to monthly variation in adolescent depressed mood: A short-term longitudinal study with time-varying predictors. *Developmental Psychopathology, 18,* 139–154.

**Conner, M. E., & White, J. L.** (Eds.). (2006). *Black fathers.* Mahwah, NJ: Erlbaum.

**Connolly, J. A., Furman, W., & Konarski, R.** (2000). The role of peers in the emergence of heterosexual romantic relationships in adolescence. *Child Development, 71,* 1395–1408.

**Connolly, J. A., Goldberg, A., Pepler, D., & Craig, W.** (2004). Mixed-gender groups, dating, and romantic relationships in early adolescence. *Journal of Research on Adolescence, 14,* 185–207.

**Connolly, J. A., & Stevens, V.** (1999, April). *Best friends, cliques, and young adolescents' romantic involvement.* Paper presented at the meeting of the Society for Research in Child Development, Albuquerque.

**Connors, J.** (2007). Casualities of reform. *Phi Delta Kappan, 88,* 518–522.

**Conrad, D., & Hedin, D.** (1982). The impact of experiential education on adolescent development. In D. Conrad & D. Hedin (Eds.), *Child and Youth Services,* special issue *Youth participation and experiential education, 4,* 57–76.

**Cook, T. D., Hunt, H. D., & Murphy, R. F.** (2001, April). *Comer's school development program in Chicago: A theory-based evaluation.* Paper presented at the meeting of the Society for Research in Child Development, Minneapolis.

**Cooper, C. R., & Ayers-Lopez, S.** (1985). Family and peer systems in early adolescence: New models of the role of relationships in development. *Journal of Early Adolescence, 5,* 9–22.

**Cooper, C. R., Baker, H., Polichar, D., & Welsh, M.** (1993). Values and communication of Chinese, European, Filipino, Mexican, and Vietnamese American adolescents with their families and friends. *New Directions in Child Development,* 73–89.

**Cooper, C. R., Cooper, R. G., Azmitia, M., & Chavira, G.** (2001). *Bridging multiple worlds: How African American and Latino youth in academic outreach programs navigate math pathways to college.* Unpublished manuscript, University of California at Santa Cruz.

**Cooper, C. R., Cooper, R. G., Azmitia, M., Chavira, G., & Gullatt, Y.** (2002). Bridging multiple worlds: How African American and Latino youth in academic outreach programs navigate math pathways to college. *Applied Developmental Science, 6,* 73–87.

**Cooper, C. R., & Grotevant, H. D.** (1989, April). *Individuality and connectedness in the family and adolescents' self and relational competence.* Paper presented at the meeting of the Society for Research in Child Development, Kansas City.

**Cooper, M. L.** (2002). Alcohol use and risky sexual behavior among college students and youth: Evaluating the evidence. *Journal of Studies on Alcohol, 14,* 101–107.

**Coopersmith, S.** (1967). *The antecedents of self-esteem.* San Francisco: W.H. Freeman.

**Copeland, H. L., Heim, A., & Rome E. S.** (2001, March). *Developing a relevant and effective* *smoking program.* Paper presented at the meeting of the Society for Adolescent Medicine, San Diego.

**Corbin, C. B., Welk, G. J., Corbin, W. R., & Welk, K. A.** (2006). *Concepts of fitness and wellness* (6th ed.). New York: McGraw-Hill.

**Cornelius, J. R., Clark, D. B., Reynolds, M., Kirisci, L., & Tarter, R.** (2007). Early age of first sexual intercourse and affiliation with deviant peers predict development of SUD: A prospective longitudinal study. *Addictive Behavior, 32,* 850–859.

**Cornock, B., Bowker, A., & Gadbois, S.** (2001, April). *Sports participating and self-esteem: Examining the goodness of fit.* Paper presented at the meeting of the Society for Research in Child Development, Minneapolis.

**Costa, P. T., & McCrae, R. R.** (1998). Personality assessment. In H. S. Friedman (Ed.), *Encyclopedia of mental health* (Vol. 3). San Diego: Academic Press.

**Cote, J. E.** (2006). Emerging adulthood as an institutionalized moratorium: Risks and benefits to identity formation. In J. J. Arnett & J. L. Tanner (Eds.), *Emerging adults in America.* Washington, DC: American Psychological Association.

**Cotton, S., Zebracki, M. A., Rosenthal, S. L., Tsevat, J., & Drotar, D.** (2006). Religion/spirituality and adolescent health outcomes: a review. *Journal of Adolescent Health, 38,* 472–480.

**Covey, S. R.** (1989) *The seven habits of highly effective people.* New York: Simon & Schuster.

**Covington, M. V.** (2002). Patterns of adaptive learning study: Where do we go from here? In C. Midgley (Ed.), *Goals, goal structures, and patterns of adaptive learning.* Mahwah, NJ: Erlbaum.

**Covington, M. V., & Teel, K. T.** (1996) *Overcoming student failure.* Washington, DC: American Psychological Association.

**Cowley, G.** (1998, April 6). Why children turn violent. *Newsweek,* 24–25.

**Cox, B. J., Enns, M. W., & Calara, I. P.** (2004). Psychological dimensions associated with suicidal ideation and attempts in the National Comorbidity Study. *Suicide and Life-Threatening Behavior, 34,* 209–219.

**Creighton, S., & Miller, R.** (2003). Unprotected sexual intercourse in teenagers—causes and consequences. *Journal of Research on Social Health, 123,* 7–18.

**Crick, N. R.** (2005, April). *Gender and psychopathology.* Paper presented at the meeting of the Society for Research in Child Development. Atlanta.

**Crick, N. R., Ostrov, J. M., & Werner, N. E.** (2006, in press). A longitudinal study of relational aggression, physical aggression, and children's social-psychological adjustment. *Journal of Abnormal Child Psychology.*

**Crockett, L. J., Raffaelli, M., & Shen, Y.-L.** (2006). Linking self-regulation and risk proneness to risky sexual behavior: Pathways through peer pressure and early substance use. *Journal of Research on Adolescence, 16,* 503–525.

**Crockett, L. J., Raffaelli, M., & Moilanen, K.** (2003). Adolescent sexuality: Behavior and meaning. In G. Adams & M. Berzonsky (Eds.), *Blackwell handbook of adolescence.* Malden, MA: Blackwell.

**Crooks, R., & Baur, K.** (2005). *Our sexuality* (9th ed.). Belmont, CA: Wadsworth.

**Crooks, R. L., & Baur, K.** (2008). *Our sexuality* (10th ed.). Belmont, CA: Wadsworth.

**Crosby, F. J., & Sabattini, L.** (2006). Family and work balance. In J. Worell & C. D. Goodheart (Eds.), *Handbook of girls' and women's psychological health.* New York: Oxford University Press.

**Crosby, R. A., & Holtgrave, D. R.** (2006). The protective value of social capital against teen pregnancy: A state-level analysis. *Journal of Adolescent Health, 38,* 556–559.

**Crossman, A., Sullivan, A., & Benin, M.** (2006). The family environment American adolescents' risk of obesity as young adults. *Social Science Medicine, 63,* 2255–2267.

**Crouter, A. C.** (2006). Mothers and fathers at work. In A. Clarke-Stewart & J. Dunn (Eds.), *Families count.* New York: Cambridge University Press.

**Crouter, A. C., Bumpus, M. F., Head, M. R., & McHale, S. M.** (2001). Implications of overwork and overload for the quality of men's family relationships. *Journal of Marriage and Family, 63,* 404–416.

**Crouter, A. C., Manke, B. A, & McHale, S. M.** (1995). The family context of gender intensification in early adolescence. *Child Development, 66,* 317–329.

**Crump, A. D., Haynie, D., Aarons, S., & Adair, E.** (1996, March). *African American teenagers' norms, expectations, and motivations regarding sex, contraception, and pregnancy.* Paper presented at the meeting of the Society for Research on Adolescence, Boston.

**Csikszentmihalyi, M.** (1990). *Flow.* New York: HarperCollins.

**Csikszentmihalyi, M.** (1993). *The evolving self.* New York: Harper & Row.

**Csikszentmihalyi, M., & Csikszentmihalyi, I. S.** (Eds.), (2006). *A life worth living.* New York: Oxford University Press.

**Csikzsentmihalyi, M., & Nakamura, J.** (2006). Creativity through the life span from an evolutionary systems perspective. In C. Hoare (Ed.), *Handbook of adult development and learning.* New York: Oxford University Press.

**Csikszentmihalyi, M., & Rathunde, K.** (1998). The development of the person: An experiential perspective on the ontogenesis of psychological complexity. In W. Damon (Ed.), *Handbook of child psychology* (5th ed., Vol. 1). New York: Wiley.

**Csikszentmihalyi, M., & Schneider, B.** (2000). *Becoming adult.* New York: Basic Books.

**Cuellar, I., Siles, R. I., & Bracamontes, E.** (2004). Acculturation: A psychological construct of continued relevance for Chicana/o psychology. In R. J. Velasquez, B. W. McNeil, & L. M. Arellano (Eds.), *The handbook of Chicano psychology and mental health.* Mahwah, NJ: Erlbaum.

**Cubbin, C., Santelli, J., Brindis, C. D., & Braverman, P.** (2005). Neighborhood context and sexual behaviors among adolescents: Findings from the National Longitudinal Study of Adolescent Health. *Perspectives on Sexual and Reproductive Health, 37,* 125–134.

**Cushner, K. H.** (2006). *Human diversity in action* (3rd ed.). New York: McGraw-Hill.

**Cushner, K. H., McClelland, A., & Safford, P.** (2003). *Human diversity in education* (3rd ed.). Boston: Allyn & Bacon.

**Cutrona, C. E.** (1982). Transition to college: Loneliness and the process of social adjustment. In L. A. Peplau & D. Perlman (Eds.), *Loneliness.* New York: Wiley.

# D

**D'Angelo, B., & Wierzbicki, M.** (2003). Relations of daily hassles with both anxious and depressed mood in students. *Psychological Reports, 92,* 416–418.

**D'Augelli, A. R.** (1991). Gay men in college: Identity processes and adaptations. *Journal of College Student Development, 32,* 140–146.

**Dahl, R. E.** (2004). Adolescent brain development: A period of vulnerabilities and opportunities. *Annals of the New York Acadeiny of Sciences, 1021,* 1–22.

**Dahl, R. E.** (2006). *Adolescent brain development: Exploring the frontiers of imaging and genetics.* Paper presented at the meeting of the Society for Research on Adolescence, San Francisco.

**Dahl, R. E.** (2006). Sleeplessness and aggression in youth. *Journal of Adolescent Health, 38,* 641–642.

**Daley, T. C., Whaley, S. E., Sigman, M. D., Espinosa, M. P., & Neumann, C.** (2003). IQ on the rise: The Flynn effect in rural Kenyan children. *Psychological Science, 14,* 215–219.

**Dalton, W. T., Frick-Horbury, D., & Kitzmann, K. M.** (2006). Young adults' retrospective reports of parenting by mothers and fathers: Associations with current relationship quality. *Journal of General Psychology, 133,* 5–18.

**Damon, W.** (1988). *The moral child.* New York: Free Press.

**Damon, W.** (1995). *Greater expectations.* New York: Free Press.

**Daniels, H.** (2007). Pedagogy. In H. Daniels, J. Wertsch, & M. Cole (Eds.), *The Cambridge companion to Vygotsky.* New York: Cambridge University Press.

**Daniels, H., Wertsch, J., & Cole, M.** (Eds.). (2007). *The Cambridge companion to Vygotsky.* New York: Cambridge University Press.

**Daniels, S. R.** (2005). What is the best method to identify cardiovascular risk related to obesity? *Journal of Pediatrics, 146,* A3.

**Dao, T. K., Kerbs, J. J., Rollin, S. A., Potts, I., Gutierrez, R., Choi, K., Creason, A. H., Wolf, A., & Prevatt, F.** (2006). The association of bullying dynamics and psychological distress. *Journal of Adolescent Health, 39,* 277–282.

**Darling, C. A., Kallen, D. J., & VanDusen, J. E.** (1984). Sex in transition, 1900–1984. *Journal of Youth and Adolescence, 13,* 385–399.

**Darling, N.** (2005). Mentoring adolescents. In D. L. Dubois & M. J. Karcher (Eds.), *Handbook of youth mentoring.* Thousand Oaks, CA: Sage.

**Darling-Hammond, L., & Bransford, J.** (Eds.). (2005). *Preparing teachers for a changing world.* San Francisco: Jossey-Bass.

**Darroch, J. E., Landry, D. J., & Singh, S.** (2000). Changing emphases in sexuality education in U.S. public secondary schools, 1988–1999. *Family Planning Perspectives, 32,* 204–211, 265.

**Darwin, C.** (1859). *On the origin of species.* London: John Murray.

**Datar, A., & Sturm, R.** (2004). Physical education in elementary school and body mass index: Evidence from the early childhood longitudinal study. *American Journal of Public Health, 94,* 1501–1506.

**Davidson, J.** (2000). Giftedness. In A. Kazdin (Ed.), *Encyclopedia of psychology.* Washington, DC & New York: American Psychological Association and Oxford University Press.

**Davies, J., & Brember, I.** (1999). Reading and mathematics attainments and self-esteem in years 2 and 6—an eight-year cross sectional study. *Educational Studies, 25,* 145–157.

**Davies, S. L., DeClemente, R. J., Wingood, G. M., Person, S. D., Dix, E. S., Harrington, K., Crosby, R. A., & Oh, K.** (2006). Predictors of inconsistent contraceptive use among adolescent girls: Findings from a prospective study. *Journal of Adolescent Health, 39,* 43–49.

**Davila, J., & Steinberg, S. J.** (2006). Depression and romantic dysfunction during adolescence. In **T. E. Joiner, J. S. Brown, & J. Kistner** (Eds.), *The interpersonal, cognitive, and social nature of depression.* Mahwah, NJ: Erlbaum.

**Davis, A. E., Hyatt, G., & Arrasmith, D.** (1998, February). "I Have a Dream" program. *Class One Evaluation Report,* Portland, OR: Northwest Regional Educational Laboratory.

**Davis, G. A., & Rimm, S. B.** (2004). *Education of the gifted and talented* (5th ed.). Boston: Allyn & Bacon.

**Davis, S. S., & Davis, D. A.** (1989). *Adolescence in a Moroccan town.* New Brunswick, NJ: Rutgers University Press.

**Day, A. L., & Chamberlin, T. C.** (2006). Committing to your work, spouse, and children: Implications for work-family conflict. *Journal of Vocational Behavior, 68,* 116–130.

**Day, R. D., & Acock, A.** (2004). Youth ratings of family processes and father role performance of resident and nonresident fathers. In R. D. Day & M. E. Lamb (Eds.), *Conceptuzalizing and measuring father involvement.* Mahwah, NJ: Erlbuam.

**Day, S., Markiewitcz, D., Doyle, A. B., & Ducharme, J.** (2001, April). *Attachment to mother, father, and best friend as predictors to the quality of adolescent romantic relationships.* Paper presented at the meeting of the Society for Research in Child Development, Minneapolis.

**de Anda, D.** (2005). Baby Think It Over: Evaluation of an infant simulation intervention for adolescent pregnancy prevention. *Health and Social Work, 31,* 26–35.

**de Muinck Keizer-Schrama, S. M., & Mul, D.** (2001). Trends in pubertal development in Europe. *Human Reproduction Update, 7,* 287–291.

**Deardorff, J., Hayward, C., Wilson, K. A., Bryson, S., Hammer, L. D., & Agras, S.** (2007). *Journal of Adolescent Health, 41,* 102–104.

**Deater-Deckard K. Dodge K.** (1997). Externalizing behavior problems and discipline revisited: Non-linear effects and variation by culture, context and gender. *Psychological Inquiry, 8,* 161–75.

**deCharms, R.** (1984). Motivation enhancement in educational settings. In R. Ames & C. Ames (Eds.), *Research on motivation in education* (Vol. 1). Orlando: Academic Press.

**Deci, E. L., Koestner, R., & Ryan, R. M.** (2001). Extrinsic rewards and intrinsic motivation in education: Reconsidered once again. *Review of Educational Research, 71,* 1–28.

**Deci, E., & Ryan, R.** (1994). Promoting self-determined education. *Scandinavian Journal of Educational Research, 38,* 3–14.

**Decker, S. H., & Curry, D. G.** (2000). Addressing key features of gang membership: Measuring the involvement of gang members. *Journal of Criminal Justice, 28,* 473–482.

**DeGarmo, D. S., & Martinez, C. R.** (2006). A culturally informed model of academic well-being for Latino youth: The importance of discriminatory experiences and social support. *Family Relations, 55,* 267–278.

**Delsing, M. J., ter Bogt, T. F., Engels, R. C., & Meeus, W. H.** (2007). Adolescents' peer crowd identification in the Netherlands: Structure and associations with problem behavior. *Journal of Research on Adolescence, 17,* 467–480.

**DeMirjyn, M.** (2006, April). *Surviving the system: Narratives of Chicana/Latina undergraduates.* Paper presented at the meeting of the American Educational Research Association, San Francisco.

**Dempster, F. N.** (1981). Memory span: Sources of individual and developmental differences. *Psychological Bulletin, 89,* 63–100.

**Den Hond, E., & Schoeters, G.** (2006). Endocrine disrupters and human puberty *International Journal of Andrology, 29,* 264–271.

**Denham, S. A., Bassett, H. H., & Wyatt, T.** (2007). The socialization of emotional competence. In J. E. Grusec & P. D. Hastings (Eds.), *Handbook of Socialization.* New York: Guilford.

**Denmark, F. L., Rabinowitz, V. C., & Sechzer, J. A.** (2005). *Engendering psychology: Women and gender revisited* (2nd ed.). Boston: Allyn & Bacon.

**Denmark, F. L., Russo, N. F., Frieze, I. H., & Sechzer, J.** (1988). Guidelines for avoiding sexism in psychological research: A report of the ad hoc committee on nonsexist research. *American Psychologist, 43,* 582–585.

**DePaulo, B. M., & Morris, W. L.** (2005). Singles in society and science. *Psychological Inquiry, 16,* 57–83.

**Derks, E. M., Dolan, C. V., & Boomsma, D. I.** (2006). A test of the equal environment assumption (EEA) in multivariate twin studies. *Twin Research and Human Genetics,* 9, 403–411.

**DeRose, L. M., & Brooks-Gunn, J.** (2006). Transition into adolescence: The role of pubertal processes. In L. Butler & C. S. Tamis-LeMonda (Eds.), *Child psychology: A handbook of contemporary issues.* New York: Psychology Press.

**DeRose, L. M., Wright, A. J., & Brooks-Gunn, J.** (2006). Does puberty account for the differential in depression? In C. L. M. Keyes & S. H. Goodman (Eds.), *Women and depression: A handbook for social, behavioral, and biomedical sciences.* New York: Cambridge University Press.

**DeRosier, M. E., & Marcus, S. R.** (2005). Building friendships and combating bullying: Effectiveness of S. S. GRIN at one-year follow-up. *Journal of Clinical Child and Adolescent Psychology, 34,* 140–150.

**Deschesnes, M., Fines, P., & Demers, S.** (2006). Are tattooing and body piercing indicators of risk-taking behaviors among high school students? *Journal of Adolescence, 29,* 379–393.

**Devos, T.** (2006). Implicit bicultural identity among Mexican American and Asian American college students. *Cultural Diversity and Ethnic Minority Psychology, 12,* 381–402.

**Dewey, J.** (1933). *How we think.* Lexington, MA: D. C. Heath.

**DeZolt, D. M. & Hull, S. H.** (2001). Classroom and school climate. In J. Worell (Ed.), *Encyclopedia of women and gender.* San Diego: Academic Press.

**Diamond, L.** (2003). Love matters: Romantic relations among sexual minority youth. In P. Florsheim (Ed.), *Adolescent romantic relations and sexual behavior.* Mahwah, NJ: Erlbaum.

**Diamond, L.** (2004). Unpublished review of J. W. Santrock's *Adolescence,* 11th ed. (New York: McGraw-Hill).

**Diamond, L. M.** (2006). Introduction: In search of good sexual-developmental pathways for adolescent girls. *New Directions in Child and Adolescent Development, 112,* 1–8.

**Diamond, L. M., & Lucas, S.** (2004). Sexual-minority and heterosexual youths' peer relationships: Experiences, expectations, and implications for well-being. *Journal of Research on Adolescence, 14,* 313–340.

**Diamond, L. M., & Savin-Williams, R. C.** (2003). The intimate relationships of sexual-minority youths. In G. Adams & M. Berzonsky (Eds.), *Blackwell handbook of adolescence.* Malden, MA: Blackwell.

**Diaz, C. F., Pelletier, C. M., & Provenzo, E. F.** (2006). *Touch the future . . . teach!* Boston: Allyn & Bacon.

**Dickerscheid, J. D., Schwarz, P. M., Noir S., & El-Taliawy, T.** (1988). Gender concept development of preschool-aged children in the United States and Egypt. *Sex Roles, 18,* 669–677.

**Dielman, T. E., Shope, J. T., & Butchart, A. T.** (1990, March). *Peer, family, and intrapersonal predictors of adolescent alcohol use and misuse.* Paper presented at the meeting of the Society for Research in Adolescence, Atlanta.

**Diemer, M. A., Kauffman, A., Koenig, N., Trahan, E., & Hsieh, C. A.** (2006). Challenging racism, sexism, and social injustice: Support for urban adolescents' critical consciousness development. *Cultural Diversity and Ethnic Minority Psychology, 12,* 444–460.

**Dietz, W. H.** (2004). Overweight in children and adolescents. *New England Journal of Medicine, 350,* 855–857.

**DiFiori, J. P.** (2006). Overuse injury and the youth athlete: The case of chronic wrist pain in gymnasts. *Current Sports Medicine Reports, 5,* 165–167.

**Dindia, K.** (2006). Men are from North Dakota, women are from South Dakota. In K. Dindia & D. J. Canary (Eds.), *Sex differences and similarities in communication.* Mahwah, NJ: Erlbaum.

**DiPietro, L., & Stachenfeld, N. S.** (2006). The female athlete triad myth. *Medical Science and Sports Exercise, 38,* 795.

**Dishion, T. J., Andrews, D. W., & Crosby, L.** (1995). Antisocial boys and their friends in early adolescence: Relationship characteristics, quality, and interactional process. *Child Development, 66,* 139–151.

**Dishion, T. J., Nelson, S. E., & Yasui, M.** (2005). Predicting early adolescent gang involvement from middle school adaptation. *Journal of Clinical Child and Adolescent Psychology, 34,* 62–73.

**Dishman, R. K., Hales, D. P., Pfeiffer, K. A., Felton, G. A., Saunders, R., Ward, D. S., Dowda, M., & Pate, R. R.** (2006). Physical self-concept and self-esteem mediate cross-sectional relations of physical activity and sport participation with depression symptoms among adolescent girls. *Health Psychology, 25,* 396–407.

**Dodge, K. A.** (1993). Social cognitive mechanisms in the development of conduct disorder and depression. *Annual Review of Psychology, 44,* 559–584.

**Dodge, K. A.** (2001). The science of youth violence prevention: Progressing from developmental psychopathology to efficacy to effectiveness in public policy. *American Journal of Preventive Medicine, 20,* 63–70.

**Dodge, K. A., Coie, J. D., & Lynam, D. R.** (2006). Aggression and antisocial behavior in youth. In W. Damon & R. Lerner (Eds.), *Handbook of child psychology* (6th ed.). New York: Wiley.

**Dodge, K. A., Dishion, T. J., & Lansford, J. E.** (Eds.). (2007). *Deviant peer influences in programs for youth.* New York: Guilford.

**Dodge, K. A., Malone, P. S., Lansford, J. E. Miller-Johnson, S., Pettit, G. S., Bates, J. E.** (2006). Toward a dynamic developmental model of the role of parents and peers in early onset substance abuse. In A. Clarke-Stewart & J. Dunn (Eds.), *Families count.* New York: Cambridge University Press.

**Dodge, K. A., & Sherrill, M. R.** (2006). Deviant peer group effects in youth mental health interventions. In K. A. Dodge, T. J. Dishion, & J. E. Lansford (Eds.), *Deviant peer influences in programs for youth: Problems and solutions.* New York: Guilford.

**Dodge, K. A., & the Conduct Problems Prevention Research Group.** (2007, March). *The impact of Fast Track on adolescent conduct disorder.* Paper presented at the meeting of the Society for Research in Child Development, Boston.

**Dohrenwend, B. S., & Shrout, P. E.** (1985). "Hassles" in the conceptualization and measurement of life event stress variables. *American Psychologist, 40,* 780–785.

**Dolcini, M. M., Coh, L. D., Adler, N. E., Millstein, S. G., Irwin, C. E., Kegeles, S. M., & Stone, G. C.** (1989). Adolescent egocentrism and feelings of invulnerability: Are they related? *Journal of Early Adolescence, 9,* 409–418.

**Donnellan, M. B., Trzesniewski, K. H., Robins, R. W.** (2006). Personality and self-esteem development in adolescence. In D. K. Mroczek & T. D. Little (Eds.), *Handbook of Personality Development. Mahwah,* NJ: Erlbaum.

**Donnellan, M. B., Trzesniewski, K. H., Robins, R. W., Mobbit, T. E. & Caspi, A.** (2005). Low self-esteem is related to aggression, antisocial behavior, and delinquency. *Psychological Science, 16,* 328–335.

**Donnerstein, E.** (2002). The Internet. In V. C. Strasburger, & B. J. Wilson, *Children, adolescents, and the media.* Newbury Park, CA: Sage.

**Dorn, L. D.** (2006). Unpublished review of J. W. Santrock's *Adolescence,* 12th ed. (New York: McGraw-Hill).

**Dorn, L. D., Dahl, R. E., Woodward, H. R., & Biro, F.** (2006). Defining the boundaries of early adolescence: A user's guide to assessing pubertal status and pubertal timing in research with adolescents. *Applied Developmental Science, 10,* 30–56.

**Dorn, L. D., Williamson, D. E., & Ryan, N. D.** (2002, April). *Maturational hormone differences in adolescents with depression and risk for depression.* Paper presented at the meeting of the Society for Research on Adolescence, New Orleans.

**Doucet, F., & Hamon, R. R.** (2007). A nation of diversity: Demographics of the United States of America and their implications for diverse families. In B. S. Trask & R. R. Hamon (Eds.), *Cultural diversity and families.* Thousand Oaks, CA: Sage.

**Douvan, E., & Adelson, J.** (1966). *The adolescent experience.* New York: Wiley.

**Dowda, M., Ainsworth, B. E., Addy, C. L., Saunders, R., & Riner, W.** (2001). Environmental influences, physical activity, and weight status in 8- to 16-year-olds. *Archives of Pediatric and Adolescent Medicine, 155,* 711–717.

**Dowling, E. M., Gestsdottir, S., Anderson, P. M., Eye, A. V., Almerigi, J., & Lerner, R. M.** (2004). Strutural relations among spirituality, religiosity, and thriving in adolescence. *Applied Developmental Science, 8,* 7–16.

**Dryfoos, J. G.** (1990). *Adolescents at risk: Prevalence and prevention.* New York: Oxford University Press.

**Dryfoos, J. G.** (1997). The prevalence of problem behaviors: Implications for programs. In R. P. Weissberg, T. P. Gullotta, R. L. Hampton, B. A. Ryan, & G. R. Adams (Eds.), *Healthy children 2010: Enhancing children's wellness.* Thousand Oaks, CA: Sage.

**Dryfoos, J. G., & Barkin, C.** (2006). *Adolescence: Growing up in America today.* New York: Oxford University Press.

**Dubois, D. L., & Karcher, M. J. (Eds.).** (2005). *Handbook of youth mentoring.* Thousand Oaks, CA: Sage.

**Dubow, E. F., Huesmann, L. R., & Greenwood, D.** (2007). Media and youth socialization. In J. E. Grusec & P. D. Hastings (Eds.), *Handbook of socialization.* New York: Guilford.

**Duck, S. W.** (1975). Personality similarity and friendship choices by adolescents. *European Journal of Social Psychology, 5,* 351–365.

**Duckett, E., & Richards, M. H.** (1996, March). *Fathers' time in child care and the father-child relationship.* Paper presented at the meeting of the Society for Research on Adolescence, Boston.

**Duckett, R. H.** (1997, July). *Strengthening families/building communities.* Paper presented at the conference on Working with America's Youth, Pittsburgh.

**Duffy, J., Wareham, S., & Walsh, M.** (2004). Psychological consequences for high school students of having been sexually harassed. *Sex Roles, 50,* 811–821.

**Duncan, G. J., Brooks-Gunn, J., & Klebanov, P. K.** (1994). Economic deprivation and early childhood development. *Child Development, 65,* 296–318.

**Duncan, G. J., & Magnuson, K.** (2006). Costs and Benefits from early investments to promote human capital and positive behavior. In N. Watt, K., Ayoub, R. Bradley, J. Puma, and W. LeBoeuf (Eds.), *The crisis in youth mental health: Critical issues and effective programs.* Westport, CT: Praeger.

**Duncan, G. J., & Magnuson, K.** (2007, in press). Can society profit from investing in early education programs? In A. Tarlov (Ed.), *Nurturing the national treasure: Childhood education and development before kindergarten.* New York: Palgrave Macmillan.

**Duncan, S. C., Duncan, T. E., Strycker, L. A., & Chaumeton, N. R.** (2007). A cohort-sequential latent growth model of physical activity from 12 to 17 years. *Annals of Behavioral Medicine, 33,* 80–89.

**Duncan, S. F. Holman, T. B., & Yang, C.** (2007). Factors associated with involvement in marriage preparation programs. *Family Relations, 56,* 270–278.

**Dunger, D. B., Ahmed, M. L., & Ong, K. K.** (2006). Early and late weight gains and the timing of puberty. *Molecular and Cellular Endocrinology 254–255,* 140–145.

**Dunkel, C., & Kerpelman, J.** (Eds.). (2004). Possible selves: Theory, research and application. Hungtington, NY: Nova.

**Dunn, J.** (2005). Commentary: Siblings in their families. *Journal of Family Psychology, 19,* 654–657.

**Dunn, J.** (2007). Siblings and socialization. In J. E. Grusec & P. D. Hastings (Eds.), *Handbook of socialization.* New York: Guilford.

**Dunphy, D. C.** (1963). The social structure of urban adolescent peer groups. *Society, 26,* 230–246.

**Durik, A. M., Hyde, J. S., Marks, A. C., Roy, A. L., Anaya, D., & Schultz, G.** (2006, in press). Ethnicity and gender stereotypes of emotion. *Sex Roles.*

**Dusek, J. B., & McIntyre, J. G.** (2003). Self-concept and self-esteem development. In G. Adams & M. Berzonsky (Eds.), *Blackwell handbook of adolescence.* Malden, MA: Blackwell.

**Dweck, C. S.** (2006). *Mindset.* New York: Random House.

**Dworkin, J., Larson, R., Hansen, D., Jones, J., & Midle, T.** (2001, April). *Adolescents' accounts of their growth experiences in youth activities.* Paper presented at the meeting of the Society for Research in Child Development, Minneapolis.

**Dwyer, J. J. M., Allison, K. R., LeMoine, K. N., Adlaf, E. M., Goodman, J., Faulkner, E. J., & Lysy, D. C.** (2006). A provincial study of opportunities for school-based physical activity in secondary schools. *Journal of Adolescent Health, 39,* 80–86.

**Dyl, J., Kittler, J., Phillips, K. A., & Hunt, J. I.** (2006). Body dysmorphic disorder and other clinically significant body image concerns in adolescent psychiatric inptients: Prevalence and clinical characteristics. *Child Psychiatry and Human Development, 36,* 369–382.

**Dyson, R., & Renk, K.** (2006). Freshman adaptation to university life: Depressive symptoms, stress, and coping. *Journal of Clinical Psychology, 62,* 1231–1244.

## E

**Eagly, A. H.** (2000). Gender roles. In A. Kazdin (Ed.), *Encyclopedia of psychology.* Washington, DC & New York: American Psychological Association and Oxford University Press.

**Eagly, A. H.** (2001). Social role theory of sex differences and similarities. In J. Worell (Ed.), *Encyclopedia of women and gender.* San Diego: Academic Press.

**Eagly, A. H., & Crowley, M.** (1986). Gender and helping behavior: A meta-analytic review of the social psychological literature. *Psychological Bulletin, 100,* 283–308.

**Eagly, A. H., & Koenig, A. M.** (2006). Social role theory of sex differences and similarities: Implications for prosocial behavior. In K. Dindia & D. J. Canary (Eds.), *Sex differences and similarities in communication.* Mahwah, NJ: Erlbaum.

**Eagly A. H., & Steffen V. J.** (1986). Gender and aggressive behavior: A meta-analytic review of the social psychological literature. *Psychological Bulletin, 100,* 309–330.

**East, P., & Adams, J.** (2002). Sexual assertiveness and adolescents' sexual rights. *Perspectives on Sexual and Reproductive Health, 34,* 198–202.

**Eaton, D. K. & others.** (2006, June 9). Youth risk behavior survillance—United States, 2005. *MMWR, 55,* 1–108.

**Ebata, A. T., & Moos, R. H.** (1989, April). *Coping and adjustment in four groups of adolescents.* Paper presented at the biennial meeting of the Society for Research in Child Development, Kansas City.

**Ebbeling, C. B., Sinclair, K. B., Pereira, M. A., Garcia-Lago, E., Feldman, H. A., & Ludwig, D. S.** (2004). Compensation for energy intake from fast food among overweight and lean adolescents. *Journal of the American Medical Association, 291,* 2828–2833.

**Eccles, J. S.** (1987). Gender roles and achievement patterns: An expectancy value perspective. In J. M. Reinisch, L. A. Rosenblum, & S. A. Sanders (Eds.), *Masculinity/femininity.* New York: Oxford University Press.

**Eccles, J. S.** (1987). Gender roles and women's achievement-related decisions. *Psychology of Women Quarterly, 11,* 135–172.

**Eccles, J. S.** (1993). School and family effects on the ontogeny of children's interests, self-perceptions, and activity choice. In J. Jacobs (Ed.) *Nebraska Symposium on Motivation, 1992: Developmental perspectives on motivation.* Lincoln: University of Nebraska Press.

**Eccles, J. S.** (2004). Schools, academic motivation and stage-environment fit. In R. Lerner & L. Steinberg (Eds.), *Handbook of adolescent psychology.* New York: Wiley.

**Eccles, J. S.** (2007). Families, schools and developing achievement-related motivations and engagement. In J. E. Grusec & P. D. Hastings (Eds.), *Handbook of socialization.* New York: Guilford.

**Eccles, J. S.** (2007). Families, schools, and developing achievement-related motivations and engagements. In J. E. Grusec & P. D. Hastings (Eds.), *Handbook of socialization.* New York: Guilford.

**Eccles, J. S., Brown, B., & Templeton, J.** (2007). A developmental framework for selecting indictors of well-being during the adolescent and young adult years. In B. Brown (Ed.), *Key indicators of child and youth well-being.* Mahwah, NJ: Erlbaum.

**Eccles J. S., & Gootman, J. A.** (Eds.). (2002). *Community programs to promote youth development.* Washington, DC: National Academies Press.

**Eccles, J. S., & Harold, R. D.** (1993). Parent-school involvement during the adolescent years. In R. Takanishi (Ed.), *Adolescence in the 1990s.* New York: Columbia University Press.

**Eccles, J. S., Wigfield, A., & Schiefele, U.** (1998). Motivation to succeed. In W. Damon (Ed.), *Handbook of child psychology* (5th ed., Vol. 3). New York: Wiley.

**Edelbrock, C. S.** (1989, April). *Self-reported internalizing and externalizing problems in a community sample of adolescents.* Paper presented at the meeting of the Society for Research in Child Development, Kansas City.

**Edelman, M. W.** (1996). *The state of America's children.* Washington, DC: Children's Defense Fund.

**Edelman, M. W.** (1997, April). *Children, families, and social policy.* Paper presented at the meeting of the Society for Research in Child Development, Washington, DC.

**Edwards, R., & Hamilton, M. A.** (2004). You need to understand my gender role: An empirical test of Tannen's model of gender and communication. *Sex Roles, 50,* 491–504.

**Egeland, B., & Carlson, B.** (2004). Attachment and psychopathology. In L. Atkinson & S. Goldberg (Eds.), *Attachment issues in psychopathology and intervention.* Mahwah, NJ: Erlbaum.

**Egley, A.** (2002). *National youth gang survey trends from 1996 to 2000.* Washington, DC: U.S. Department of Justice, Office of Justice Programs, Office of Juvenile Justice and Delinquency Prevention.

**Eisenberg, N., Fabes, R. A.** (1998). Prosocial development. In N. Eisenberg (Ed.), *Handbook of child psychology* (5th ed., Vol. 3). New York: Wiley.

**Eisenberg, N., Fabes, R. A., Guthrie, I. K., & Reiser, M.** (2002). The role of emotionality and regulation in children's social competence and adjustment. In L. Pulkkinen & A. Caspi (Eds.), *Paths to successful development.* New York: Cambridge University Press.

**Eisenberg, N., Fabes, R. A., & Spinrad, T. L.** (2006). Prosocial development. In W. Damon & R. Lerner (Eds.), *Handbook of child psychology* (6th ed.). New York: Wiley:

**Eisenberg, N., Martin, C. L., & Fabes, R. A.** (1996). Gender development and gender effects. In D. C. Berliner & R. C. Calfee (Eds.), *Handbook of educational psychology.* New York: Macmillan.

**Eisenberg, N., & Morris, A.** (2004). Moral cognitions and prosocial responding in adolescence. In R. Lerner & L. Steinberg (Eds.), *Handbook of adolescent psychology.* New York: Wiley.

**Eisenberg, N., Spinrad, T., & Sadovsky, A.** (2006). Empathy-related responding in children. In M. Killen & J. Smetana (Eds.), *Handbook of moral development.* Mahwah, NJ: Erlbaum.

**Eisenberg, N., Spinard, T. L., & Smith, C. L.** (2004). Emotion-related regulation: Its conceptualization, relations to social functioning, and socialization. In P. Philippot & R. S. Feldman (Eds.), *The regulation of emotion.* Mahwah, NJ: Erlbaum.

**Eisenberg, N., & Valiente, C.** (2002). Parenting and children's prosocial and moral development. In M. H. Bornstein (Ed.), *Handbook of parenting* (2nd ed.). Mahwah, NJ: Erlbaum.

**Eisenberg, N., Zhou, Q., & Koller, S.** (2001). Brazilian adolescents' prosocial moral judgment and behavior: Relations to sympathy, perspective taking, gender-role orientation, and demographic characteristics. *Child Development, 72,* 518–534.

**Eisenhower Corporation.** (2007). Quantum Opportunities program. Retrieved on August 7, 2007, from www.eisenhowerfoundation.org/qop.php

**Eitle, D.** (2005). The moderating effects of peer substance abuse on the family structure-adolescent substance use association: Quantity versus quality of parenting. *Addictive Behaviors, 30,* 963–980.

**Elder, G. H.** (1975). Adolescence in the life cycle. In S. E. Dragastin & G. H. Elder (Eds.), *Adolescence in the life cycle: Psychological change and social context.* New York: Wiley.

**Elder, G. H.** (1999). *Children of the Great Depression: Social change in life experience.* Boulder, CO: Westview Press.

**Elder, G. H., & Shanahan, M. J.** (2006). The life course and human development. In W. Damon & R. Lerner (Eds.), *Handbook of child psychology* (6th ed.). New York: Wiley.

**El-Khouri, B. M., & Mellner, C.** (2004). Symptom development and timing of menarche: A longitudinal study. *International Journal of Methods in Psychiatric Research, 13,* 40–53.

**Elkind, D.** (1961). Quantity conceptions in junior and senior high school students. *Child Development, 32,* 531–560.

**Elkind, D.** (1976). *Child development and education: A Piagetian perspective.* New York: Oxford University Press.

**Elliot, A. J., & Thrash, T. M.** (2001). Achievement goals and the hierarchical model of achievement motivation. *Educational Psychology Review, 13,* 139–156.

**Elliot, D. L., Cheong, J., Moe, E., & Goldberg, L.** (2007). Cross-sectional study of female athletes reporting anabolic steroid use. *Archives of Pediatric and Adolescent Medicine, 161,* 572–577.

**Ellis, B. J.** (2004). Timing of pubertal maturation in girls: An integrated life history approach. *Psychological Bulletin, 130,* 920–958.

**Ellis, L., & Ames, M. A.** (1987). Neurohormonal functioning and sexual orientation: A theory of homosexuality-heterosexuality. *Psychological Bulletin, 101,* 233–258.

**Emery, R. E.** (1999). *Renegotiating family relationships* (2nd ed.). New York: Guilford-Press.

**Emery, R. E., & Laumann-Billings, L.** (1998). An overview of the nature, causes, and consequences of abusive family relationships. *American Psychologist, 53,* 121–135.

**Emmer, E. T., Evertson, C. M., & Worsham, M. E.** (2006). *Classroom management for middle and high school teachers* (7th ed.). Boston: Allyn & Bacon.

**Endresen, I. M., & Olweus, D.** (2005). Participation in power sports and antisocial involvement in preadolescent and adolescent boys. *Journal of Child Psychology and Psychiatry, 46,* 468–478.

**Eng, P. M., Kawachi, I., Fitzmaurice, G., & Rimm, E. B.** (2005). Effects of marital transitions on changes in dietary and other health behaviors in U.S. male health professionals. *Journal of Epidemiology and Community Health, 59,* 56–62.

**Engels, R. C., Vermulst, A. A., Dubas, J. S., Bot, S. M., & Gerris, J.** (2005). Long-term effects of family functioning and child characteristics on problem drinking in young adulthood. *European Addiction Research, 11,* 32–37.

**Enger, E.** (2007). *Concepts in biology* (12th ed.). New York: McGraw-Hill.

**Englund, M. M., Luckner, A. E., & Whaley, G.** (2003, April). The importance of early parenting for children's long-term educational attainment. Paper presented at the meeting of the Society for Research in Child Development, Tampa.

**Ennett, S. T., Bauman, K. E., Hussong, A., Faris, R., Foshee, V. A., & Cai, L.** (2006). The peer context of adolescent substance use: Findings from social network analysis. *Journal of Research on Adolescence, 16,* 159–186.

**Enright, R. D., Levy, V. M., Harris, D., & Lapsley, D. K.** (1987). Do economic conditions influence how theorists view adolescents? *Journal of Youth and Adolescence, 16,* 541–559.

**Enright, R. D., Santos, M. J. D., & Al-Mabuk, R.** (1989). The adolescent as forgiver. *Journal of Adolescence, 12,* 95–110.

**Ensembl Human.** (2007). *Explore the human genome.* Retrieved April 28, 2007, from www.ensembl.org/Homo_sapiens/index.html

**Epstein, J. A., Botvin, G. J., & Diaz, T.** (1998). Linguistic acculturation and gender effects on smoking among Hispanic youth. *Preventive Medicine, 27,* 538–589.

**Epstein, J. L.** (2001). *School, family, and community partnerships.* Boulder, CO: Westview Press.

**Epstein, J. L.** (2005). Results of the Partnership Schools—CSR model for student achievement over three years. *Elementary School Journal, 106,* 151–170.

**Epstein, J. L.** (2007a). Family and community involvement. In K. Borman, S. Cahill, & B. Cotner (eds.), *American high school: an encyclopedia.* Westport, CT: Greenwood.

**Epstein, J. L.** (2007b). Homework. In K. Borman, S. Chaill, & B. Cotner (Eds.), *American high school: an encyclopedia.* Westport, CT: Greenwood.

**Epstein, J. L., & Sheldon, S. B.** (2006). Moving forward: Ideas for research on school, family, and community partnerships. In C. F. Conrad & R. Serlin (Eds.), *Sage handbook for research in education.* Thousand Oaks, CA: Sage.

**Ercikan, K.** (2006). Developments in assessment of student learning. In P. A. Alexander & P. H. Winne (Eds.), *Handbook of educational psychology* (2nd ed.). Mahwah, NJ: Erlbaum.

**Erickson, J. B.** (1982). *A profile of community youth organization members, 1980.* Boys Town, NE: Boys Town Center for the Study of Youth Development.

**Erickson, J. B.** (1996). *Directory of American youth organizations* (2nd rev. ed.). Boys Town, NE: Boys Town Communication and Public Services Division.

**Ericson, N.** (2001, June). *Addressing the problem of juvenile bullying.* Washington, DC: Office of Juvenile Justice and Delinquency Prevention, Office of Justice Programs, U.S. Department of Justice.

**Ericsson, K. A.** (Ed.). (1996). *The road to excellence.* Mahwah, NJ: Erlbaum.

**Ericsson, K. A., Charness, N., Feltovich, P. J., & Hoffman, R. R.** (2006). *The Cambridge handbook of expertise and expert performance.* New York: Cambridge University Press.

**Ericsson, K. A., Krampe, R. T., & Tesch-Römer, C.** (1993). The role of deliberate practice in the acquisition of expert performance. *Psychological Review, 100,* 363–406.

**Erikson, E. H.** (1950). *Childhood and society.* New York: W. W. Norton.

**Erikson, E. H.** (1962). *Young man Luther.* New York: W. W. Norton.

**Erikson, E. H.** (1968). *Identity: Youth and crisis.* New York: W. W. Norton.

**Erikson, E. H.** (1969). *Gandhi's truth.* New York: W. W. Norton.

**Erikson, E. H.** (1970). Reflections on the dissent of contemporary youth. *International Journal of Psychoanalysis, 51,* 11–22.

**Erlick Robinson, G.** (2003). Violence against women in North America. *Archives of Women's Mental Health, 6,* 185–191.

**Escobedo, L. G., Marcus, S. E., Holtzman, D., & Giovino, G. A.** (1993). Sports participation, age at smoking initiation, and risk of smoking among U.S. high school students. *Journal of the American Medical Association, 269,* 1391–1395.

**Eshel, N., Nelson, E. E., Blair, R. J., Pine, D. S., & Ernst, M.** (2007). Neural substrates of choice selection in adults and adolescents: Development of the ventrolateral prefrontal and anterior cingulated cortices. *Neuropsychologia, 45,* 1270–1279.

**Espelage, D. L., Swearer, S. M.** (Eds.). (2003). Bullying in American schools. Mahwah, NJ: Erlbaum.

**Estell, D. B., Farmer, T. W., & Carins, B. D.** (2007). Bullies and victims in rural African American youth: Behavioral characteristics and social network placement. *Aggressive Behavior, 33,* 145–159.

**Evans, B. J., & Whitfield, J. R.** (Eds.). (1988). *Black males in the United States: An annotated bibliography from 1967 to 1987.* Washington, DC: American Psychological Association.

**Evans, E., Hawton, K., & Rodham, K.** (2005). Suicidal phenomena and abuse in adolescents: A review of epidemiological studies. *Child Abuse and Neglect, 29,* 45–58.

**Evans, G. W.** (2004). The environment of childhood poverty. *American Psychologist, 59,* 77–92.

**Evertson, C. M., Emmer, E. T., & Worsham, M. E.** (2006). *Classroom management for elementary teachers* (7th ed.). Boston: Allyn & Bacon.

**Evertson, C. M., & Weinstein, C. S.** (2006). Classroom management as a field of inquiry. In C. M. Evertson & C. S. Weinstein (Eds.), *Handbook of classroom management.* Mahwah, NJ: Erlbaum.

## F

**Fabricius, W. V., & Luecken, L. J.** (2007). Postdivorce living arrangements, parent conflict, and long-term physical health correlates for children of divorce. *Journal of Family Psychology, 21,* 195–205.

**Fairbrother, G., Kenney, G., Hanson, K., & Dubay, L.** (2005). How do stressful family environments relate to reported access and use of health care by low-income children? *Medical Care Research Review, 62,* 205–230.

**Fajardo, G., Wakefield, W. D., Godinez, M., & Simental, J. F.** (2003, April). *Latino and African American adolescents' experiences with discrimination.* Paper presented at the meeting of the Society for Research in Child Development, Tampa.

**Fan, X., & Chen, M.** (2001). Parental involvement and students' academic achievement: A meta-analysis. *Educational Psychology Review, 13* (1), 1–22.

**Fantino, E., & Stolarz-Fantino, S.** (2005). Decision-making: Context matters. *Behavioural Processes, 69,* 165–171.

**Faraone, S. V., Biederman, J., & Mick, E.** (2006). The age-dependent decline of attention deficit hyperactivity disorder: A meta-analysis of follow-up studies. *Psychological Medicine, 36,* 159–165.

**Farrington, D. P.** (2004). Conduct disorder, aggresion, and delinquency. In R. M. Lerner & L. Steinberg (Eds.), *Handbook of adolescent psychology* (2nd ed.). New York: Wiley.

**Fasick, F. A.** (1994). On the "invention" of adolescence. *Journal of Early Adolescence, 14,* 6–23.

**Fassler, D.** (2004, May 8). Commentary in teen brains on trial, *Science News Online,* p. 1.

**Feather, N. T.** (1966). Effects of prior success and failure on expectations of success and subsequent performance. *Journal of Personality and Social Psychology, 3,* 287–298.

**Federal Drug Administration.** (2004 March 22). *FDA issues public health advisory on cautions for use of antidepressants in adults and children.* Washington, DC: U.S. Food and Drug Administration.

**Feeney, B. C., & Collins, N. L.** (2007). Interpersonal safe haven and secure base caregiving processes in adulthood. In W. S. Rholes & J. A. Simpson (Eds.), *Adult attachment.* New York: Guilford.

**Fehring, R. J., Cheever, K. H., German, K., & Philpot, C.** (1998). Religiosity and sexual activity among older adolescents. *Journal of Religion and Health, 37,* 229–239.

**Feinberg, M. E., Button, T. M., Neiderhiser, J. M., Reiss, D., & Hetherington, E. M.** (2007). Parenting and antisocial behavior and depression: Evidence of genotype parenting environment interaction. *Archives of General Psychiatry, 64,* 457–465.

**Feinberg, M. E., Kan, M. L., & Hetherington, E. M.** (2007). The longitudinal influence of coparenting conflict on parental negativity and adolescent maladjustment. *Journal of Marriage and the Family, 69,* 687–702.

**Feiring, C.** (1996). Concepts of romance in 15-year-old adolescents. *Journal of Research on Adolescence, 6,* 181–200.

**Feist, J., & Brannon, L.** (1989). *An introduction to behavior and health.* Belmont, CA: Wadsworth.

**Fekkes, M., Pijpers, F. I., Verlove-Vanhorick, S. P.** (2004). Bullying behavior and associations with psychosomatic complaints and depression in victims. *Journal of Pediatrics, 144,* 17–22.

**Fekkes, M., Pijpers, F. I., & Verlove-Vanhorick, S. P.** (2006). Effects of antibullying school program on bullying and health complaints. *Archives of Pediatric and Adolescent Medicine, 160,* 638–644.

**Feldman, D. C., & Whitcomb, K. M.** (2005). The effects of framing vocational choices on young adults' sets of career options. *Career Development International, 10,* 7–25.

**Feldman, E.** (2006). Contraceptive care for the adolescent. *Primary Care, 33,* 405–431.

**Feldman, S. S.** (1999). Unpublished review of J. W. Santrock's *Adolescence,* 8th ed. (New York: McGraw-Hill).

**Feldman, S. S., & Elliott, G. R.** (1990). Progress and promise of research on normal adolescent development. In S. S. Feldman & G. Elliott (Eds.), *At the threshold: The developing adolescent.* Cambridge, MA: Harvard University Press.

**Feldman, S. S., & Rosenthal, D. A.** (1999). *Factors influencing parents' and adolescents' evaluations of parents as sex communicators.* Unpublished manuscript, Stanford Center on Adolescence, Stanford University.

**Feldman, S. S., & Rosenthal, D. A.** (Eds.) (2002). *Talking sexually: Parent-adolescent communication.* San Francisco: Jossey-Bass.

**Feldman, S. S., Turner, R., & Araujo, K.** (1999). Interpersonal context as an influence on sexual timetables of youths: Gender and ethnic effects. *Journal of Research on Adolescence, 9,* 25–52.

**Fenzel, L. M., Blyth, D. A., & Simmons, R. G.** (1991). School transitions, secondary. In R. M. Lerner, A. C. Petersen, & J. Brooks-Gunn (Eds.), *Encyclopedia of adolescence* (Vol. 2). New York: Garland.

**Ferguson, A.** (1999, July 12). Inside the crazy culture of kids' sports. *Time,* pp. 52–60.

**Ferrando-Lucas, M. T.** (2006). Attention deficit hyperactivity disorder: Its aetiological factors and endophenotypes. *Revista de Neurologia* (Spanish), *42* (Suppl.), S9–S11.

**Field, A. E. Camargo, C. A., Taylor, C. B., Berkey, C. S., Roberts, S. B., & Colditz, G. A.** (2001). Peer, parent, and media influences on the development of weight concerns and frequent dieting among preadolescent and adolescent girls and boys. *Pediatrics, 107,* 54–60.

**Field, T., Diego, M., & Sanders, C. E.** (2001). Exercise is positively related to adolescents' relationships and academics. *Adolescence, 36,* 105–110.

**Fine, M.** (1988). Sexuality, schooling, and adolescent females: The missing discourse of desire. *Harvard Educational Review, 58* (1), 29–53.

**Fine, M. A., & Harvey, J. H.** (2006). Divorce and relationship dissolution in the 21st century. In M. A. Fine & J. H. Harvey (Eds.), *Handbook of divorce and relationship dissolution.* Mahwah, NJ: Erlbaum.

**Fingerman, K. L.** (2006). Social relations. In J. E. Birren & K. W. Schaie (Eds.), *Handbook of the psychology of aging* (6th ed.). San Diego: Academic Press.

**Fingerman, K. L., & Lang, F. R.** (2004). Coming together: A perspective on relationships across the life span. In F. R. Lang & K. L. Fingerman (Eds.), *Growing together.* New York: Cambridge University Press.

**Finn, J. D.** (2002). Class size reduction in grades K–3. In A. Moinar (Ed.), *School reform proposals: The research evidence.* Greenwich, CT: Information Age Publishing.

**Fisch, S. M.** (2004). *Children's learning from educational television.* Mahwah, NJ: Erlbaum.

**Fischer, K. W., & Pruyne, E.** (2003). Reflective thinking in adulthood: Emergence, development, and variation. In J. Demick & C. Andreoletti (Eds.), *Handbook of adult development.* New York: Kluwer.

**Fish, K. D., & Biller, H. B.** (1973). Perceived childhood paternal relationships and college females' personal adjustment. *Adolescence, 8,* 415–420.

**Fisher, B. S., Cullen, F. T. S, Turner, M. G.** (2000). *The sexual victimization of college women.* Washington, DC: National Institute of Justice.

**Fisher, D.** (1990, March). *Effects of attachment on adolescents' friendships.* Paper presented at the meeting of the Society for Research in Adolescence, Atlanta.

**Fisher, H. E.** (2006). Broken hearts: The nature and risks of romantic rejection. In A. C. Crouter & A. Booth (Eds.), *Romance and sex in adolescence and emerging adulthood.* Mahwah, NJ: Erlbaum.

**Fisher, T. D.** (1987). Family communication and the sexual behavior and attitudes of college students. *Journal of Youth and Adolescence, 16,* 481–495.

**Flanagan, A. S.** (1996, March). *Romantic behavior of sexually victimized and nonvictimized women.* Paper presented at the meeting of the Society for Research on Adolescence, Boston.

**Flanagan, C. A.** (2002, April). *Inclusion and reciprocity: Developmental sources of social trust and civic hope.*Paper presented at the meeting of the Society for Research on Adolescence, New Orleans.

**Flanagan, C. A.** (2004). Volunteerism, leadership, political socialization, and civic engagement. In R. Lerner & L. Steinberg (Eds.), *Handbook of adolescent psychology* (2nd ed.). New York: Wiley.

**Flanagan, C. A., & Faison, N.** (2001). Youth civic development: Implications for social policy and programs. *SRCD Social Policy Report, XV, (No. 1),* 1–14.

**Flanagan, C. A., Gill, S., & Gallay, L.** (1998, November). *Intergroup understanding, social justice, and the "social contract" in diverse communities of youth.* Project report prepared for the workshop on research to improve intergroup relations among youth, Forum on Adolescence, National Research Council, Washington, DC.

**Flannery, D. J., Rowe, D. C., & Gulley, B. L.** (1993). Impact of pubertal status, timing, and age on adolescent sexual experience and deliquency. *Journal of Adolescent Research, 8,* 21–40.

**Flavell, J. H., Miller, P. H., & Miller, S. A.** (2002). *Cognitive development* (4th ed.). Upper Saddle River, NJ: Prentice Hall.

**Fleming, J. E., Boyle, M., & Offord, D. R.** (1993). The outcome of adolescent depression in the Ontario child health study follow-up. *Journal of the American Academy of Child and Adolescent Psychiatry, 32,* 28–29.

**Fleming-Moran, M., & Thiagarajah, K.** (2005). Behavioral interventions and the role of television in the growing epidemic of adolescent obesity—data from the 2001 Youth Risk Behavioral Survey. *Methods of Information in Medicine, 44,* 303–309.

**Fletcher, A. C., Steinberg, L., & Williams-Wheeler, M.** (2004). Parental influences on adolescent problem behavior: Revisiting Stattin and Kerr. *Child Development, 75,* 781–796.

**Fletcher, J. M., Lyon, G. R., Fuchs, L. S., & Barnes, M. A.** (2007). *Learning disabilities.* New York: Guilford.

**Flinn, M. V.** (2006). Evolution and ontogeny of stress response to social challenges in the human child. *Developmental Review, 26,* 138–174.

**Flint, M. S., Baum, A., Chambers, W. H., & Jenkins, F. J.** (2007, in press). Induction of DNA damage, alteration of DNA repair, and transcriptional activation by stress hormones. *Psychoneuroendocrinology.*

**Florsheim, P.** (Ed.). (2003). *Adolescent romantic relations and sexual behavior.* Mahwah, NJ: Erlbaum.

**Flory, K. & others.** (2004). Early adolescent through young adult alcohol and marijuana use trajectories: Early predictors, young adult outcomes, and predictive utility. *Development and Psychopathology, 16,* 193–213.

**Flouri, E.** (2004). Correlates of parents' involvement with their adolescent children in restructured and biological two-parent families: Role of child characteristics. *International Journal of Behavioral Development, 28,* 148–156.

**Flye, D.** (2004). Unpublished review of J. W. Santrock's *Child development,* 11th ed. (New York: McGraw-Hill).

**Flynn, J. R.** (2007). The history of the American mind in the 20th century: A scenario to explain gains over time and a case for the irrelevance of *g*. In P. C. Kyllonen, R. D. Roberts, & L. Stankov (Eds.), *Extending intelligence,* Mahwah, NJ: Erlbaum.

**Folkman, S., & Lazarus, R. S.** (1980). An analysis of coping in a middle-aged community sample. *Journal of Health and Social Behavior, 21,* 219–239.

**Folkman, S., & Moskowitz, J. T.** (2004). Coping: Pitfalls and promises. *Annual Review of Psychology* (Vol. 55). Palo Alto, CA: Annual Reviews.

**Fone, K. C., & Nutt, D. J.** (2005). Stimulants: Use and abuse in the treatment of attention deficit hyperactivity disorder. *Current Opinions in Pharmacology, 5,* 87–93.

**Foraker, R. E., Patten, C. A., Lopez, K. N., Croghan, I. T., & Thomas, J. L.** (2005). Beliefs and attitudes regarding smoking among young adult Latinos: A pilot study. *Preventive Medicine, 41,* 126–133.

**Forcier, R. C., & Descy, D. E.** (2008). *The computer as an educational tool* (5th ed.). Upper Saddle River, NJ: Prentice Hall.

**Ford, C. A., Bearman, P. S., & Moody, J.** (1999). Foregone health care among adolescents. *Journal of the American Medical Association, 282* (23), 2227–2234.

**Fouad, N. A.** (1995). Career behavior of Hispanics: Assessment and career intervention. In F. T. L. Leong (Ed.), *Career development and vocational behavior of racial and ethnic minorities.* Hillsdale, NJ: Erlbaum.

**Fowler, J. W.** (1981). *Stages of faith: The psychology of human development and the quest for faith.* New York: HarperCollins.

**Fowler, J. W.** (1996). *Faithful change.* Nashville, TN: Abingdon Press.

**Fowler, J. W., & Dell, M. L.** (2006). Stages of faith from infancy through adolescence: Reflections on three decades of faith development theory. In E. C. Roehlkepartain, P. E. King, & L. M. Wegener (Eds.), *The handbook of spiritual development in childhood and adolescence.* Thousand Oaks, CA: Sage.

**Fowler-Brown, A., & Kahwati, L. C.** (2004). Prevention and treatment of overweight in children and adolescents. *American Family Physician, 69,* 2591–2598.

**Fox, K., Page, A., Armstrong, N., & Kirby, B.** (1994). Dietary restraint and self-esteem in early adolescence. *Personality and Individual Differences, 17,* 87–96.

**Fraenkel, J. R., & Wallen, N. E.** (2005). *How to design and evaluate research in education* (6th ed.). New York: McGraw-Hill.

**Francis, J., Fraser, G., & Marcia, J. E.** (1989). *Cognitive and experimental factors in moratorium-achievement (MAMA) cycles.* Unpublished manuscript, Department of Psychology, Simon Fraser University, Burnaby, British Columbia.

**Franke, T. M.** (2000, winter). The role of attachment as a protective factor in adolescent violent behavior. *Adolescent and Family Health, 1,* 29–39.

**Franz, C. E.** (1996). The implications of preschool tempo and motoric activity level for personality decades later. Reported in Caspi, A. (1998). Personality development across the life course. In W. Damon (Ed.), *Handbook of child psychology* (Vol 3). New York: Wiley.

**Fraser, S.** (Ed.). (1995). *The bell curve wars: Race, intelligence, and the future of America.* New York: Basic Books.

**Frederikse, M., Lu, A., Aylward, E., Barta, P., Sharma, T., & Pearlson, G.** (2000). Sex differences in inferior lobule volume in schizophrenia. *American Journal of Psychiatry, 157,* 422–427.

**Fredricks, J. A., & Eccles, J. S.** (2006). Extracurricular involvement and adolescent adjustment: Impact of duration, number of activities, and breadth of participation. *Applied Developmental Science, 10,* 132–146.

**Fredricks, J. A., & Eccles, J. S.** (2006). Is extracurricular participation associated with benefical outcomes? Concurrent and longitudinal relations. *Developmental Psychology, 42,* 698–713.

**Freeman, D.** (1983). *Margaret Mead and Samoa.* Cambridge, MA: Harvard University Press.

**Freeman, S., & Herron, J. C.** (2007). *Evolutionary analysis* (4th ed.). Upper Saddle River, NJ: Prentice Hall.

**Freud, A.** (1966). Instinctual anxiety during puberty. In *The writings of Anna Freud: The ego and the mechanisms of defense.* New York: International Universities Press.

**Freud, S.** (1917/1958). *A general introduction to psychoanalysis.* New York: Washington Square Press.

**Frey, K. S., Hirschstein, M. K., Snell, J. L., Edstrom, L. V. S., & Broderick, C. J.** (2005). Reducing playground bullying and supporting beliefs: An experimental trial of the Steps to Respect program. *Developmental Psychology, 41,* 479–790.

**Friesch, R. E.** (1984). Body fat, puberty and fertility, *Biological Review, 59,* 161–188.

**Frings, L., Wagner, K., Unterrainer, J., Spreer, J., Halsband, U., & Schulze-Bonhage, A.** (2006). Gender-related differences in lateralization of hippocampal activation and cognitive strategy. *Neuroreport, 17,* 417–421.

**Fritzon, K., & Brun, A.** (2005). Beyond Columbine: A faceted model of school-associated homicide. *Psychology, Crime, and Law, 11,* 53–61.

**Frost, J., & McKelvie, S.** (2004). Self-esteem and body satisfaction in male and female elementary school, high school, and university students. *Sex Roles, 51,* 45–54.

**Frydenberg, E.** (2008). *Adolescent coping.* London: Routledge.

**Fujii, K., & Demura, S.** (2003). Relationship between change in BMI with age and delayed menarche in female athletes. *Journal of Physiological Anthropology and Applied Human Scince, 22,* 97–104.

**Fuligni, A. J., & Fuligni, A. S.** (2007). Immigrant families and the educational achievement of their children. In J. E. Lansford, K. Deater-Deckard, & M. H. Bornstein (Eds.), *Immigrant families in contemporary society.* New York: Guilford.

**Fuligni, A. J., & Hardway, C.** (2004). Preparing diverse adolescents for the transition to adulthood. *Future of Children, 14,* 99–119.

**Fuligni, A. J., & Hardway, C.** (2006). Daily variation in adolescents' sleep, activities, and psychological well-being. *Journal of Research on Adolescence, 16,* 353–378.

**Fuligni, A. J., & Stevenson, H. W.** (1995). Time use and mathematics achievement among American, Chinese, and Japanese high school students. *Child Development, 66,* 830–842.

**Fuligni, A. J., Tseng, V., & Lamb. M.** (1999). Attitudes toward family obligations among American adolescents from Asian, Latin American, and European backgrounds. *Child Development, 70,* 1030–1044.

**Fuligni, A. J., Witkow, M.** (2004). The postsecondary educational progress of youth from immigrant families. *Journal of Research on Adolescence, 14,* 159–183.

**Fuligni, A. J., Witkow, M., & Garcia, C.** (2005, April). *Ethnic identity and the academic adjustment of adolescents from Mexican, Chinese, and European backgrounds.* Paper presented at the meeting of the Society for Research in Child Development, Atlanta.

**Fuligni, A. J., & Yoshikawa, H.** (2004). Investments in children among immigrant families. In A. Kalil & T. DeLeire (Eds.), *Family investments in children's potential.* Mahwah, NJ: Erlbaum.

**Fuligni, A. J., & Yoshikawa, H.** (2003). Socioeconomic resources, poverty, and child development among immigrant families. In M. H. Bornstein & R. H. Bradley (Eds.). *Socioeconomic status, parenting, and child development.* Mahwah, NJ: Erlbaum.

**Furman, E.** (2005). *Boomerang nation.* New York: Fireside.

**Furman, W. C.** (2002). The emerging field of adolescent romantic relationships. *Current Directions in Psychological Science, 11,* 177–180.

**Furman, W. C.** (2007, March). *The conceptualization of attachment in adolescents' relationships.* Paper presented at the meeting of the Society for Research in Child Development, Boston.

**Furman, W. C., & Buhrmester, D.** (1992). Age and sex differences in perceptions of networks of personal relationships. *Child Development, 63,* 103–115.

**Furman, W. C., Ho, M., & Low, S.** (2005, April). *Adolescent dating experiences and adjustment.* Paper presented at the meeting of the Society for Research in Child Development, Atlanta.

**Furman, W. C., & Lanthier, R.** (2002). Parenting siblings. In M. Bornstein (Ed.), Handbook of *parenting* (2nd ed., Vol. 1). Mahwah, NJ: Erlbaum.

**Furman, W. C., & Shaeffer, L.** (2003). The role of romantic relationships in adolescence. In P. Florsheim (Ed.), *Adolescent romantic relations and sexual behavior.* Mahwah, NJ.

**Furman, W. C., & Simon, V. A.** (2006). Actor and partner effects of adolescents' romantic working models and styles on interactions with romantic partners. *Child Development, 77,* 588–604.

**Furman, W. C., & Wehner, E. A.** (1997). Adolescent romantic relationships: A developmental perspective. In S. Shulman & W. A. Collins (Eds.), *New directions for child development:Adolescent romantic relationships.* San Francisco: Jossey-Bass.

**Furstenberg, F. F.** (2007). The future of marriage. In A. S. Skolnick & J. H. Skolnick (Eds.), *Family in transition* (14th ed.). Boston: Allyn & Bacon.

**Furstenburg, F. F., Cook, T. D., Eccles, J., Elder, G. H., Jr., & Sameroff, A.** (1999). *Managing to make it: Urban families and adolescent success.* Chicago: University of Chicago Press.

**Furstenberg, F. F., & Harris, K. Y.** (1992). When fathers matter/where fathers matter. In R. Lerman and T. Ooms (Eds.), *Young unwed fathers.* Philadelphia: Temple University Press.

**Fussell, E., & Furstenberg, F. F.** (2005). The transition to adulthood during the twentieth century. In R. A. Settersten, F. F. Furstenberg, &

R. G. Rumbaut (Eds.), *On the frontier of adulthood: Theories, research, and social policy.* Chicago: University of Chicago Press.

**Fussell, E., & Greene, M. E.** (2002). Demographic trends affecting youth around the world. In B. B. Brown, R. W. Larson, & T. S. Saraswathi (Eds.), *The world's youth.* New York: Cambridge University Press.

# G

**Galambos, N. L.** (2004). Gender and gender-role development in adolescence. In R. Lerner & L. Steinberg (Eds.), *Handbook of adolescence.* New York: Wiley.

**Galambos, N. L., Barker, E. T., & Krahn, H. J.** (2006). Depression, self-esteem, and anger in emerging adulthood: Seven-year trajectories. *Developmental Psychology, 42,* 350–365.

**Galambos, N. L., & Costigan, C. L.** (2003). Emotional and personality development in adolescence. In I. B. Weiner (Ed.), *Handbook of psychology* (Vol. 6). New York: Wiley.

**Galambos, N. L., & Maggs, J. L.** (1991). Out-of-school care of young adolescents and self-reported behavior. *Developmental Psychology, 27,* 644–655.

**Galambos, N. L., Petersen, A. C., Richards, M., & Gitleson, J. B.** (1985). The Attitudes toward Women Scale for Adolescents (AWSA): A study of reliability and validity. *Sex Roles, 13,* 343–356.

**Galanter, M.** (1999). *Cults.* New York: Oxford University Press.

**Galanter, M.** (2000). Cults. In A. Kazdin (Ed.), *Encyclopedia of psychology.* Washington, DC & New York: American Psychological Association and Oxford University Press.

**Galliano, G.** (2003). *Gender: Crossing boundaries.* Belmont, CA: Wadsworth.

**Gallup, G. W., & Bezilla, R.** (1992). *The religious life of young Americans.* Princeton, NJ: Gallup Institute.

**Galvan, A., Hare, T. A., Parra, C. E., Penn, J., Voss, H., Gloer, G., & Casey, B. J.** (2006) Earlier development of the accumbens relative to orbitofrontal cortex might underlie risk-taking behavior in adolescents. *Journal of Neuroscience, 26,* 6885–6892.

**Gambrell, L. B., Morrow, L. M., & Pressley, M.** (Eds.). (2007). *Best practices in literary instruction.* New York: Guilford.

**Ganahl, D. J., Prinsen, T. J., & Netzley, S. B.** (2003). A content analysis of prime time commercials: A contextual framework of gender representation. *Sex Roles, 49,* 545–551.

**Ganong, L., Coleman, M., & Hans, J.** (2006). Divorce as prelude to stepfamily living and the consequences of re-divorce. In M. A. Fine & J. H. Harvey (Eds.), *Handbook of divorce and relationship dissolution.* Mahwah, NJ: Erlbaum.

**Garbarino, J.** (1999). *Lost boys: Why our sons turn violent and how we can save them.* New York: Free Press.

**Garbarino, J.** (2001). Violent children. *Archives of Pediatrics and Adolescent Medicine, 155,* 1–2.

**Garber, J., Kriss, M. R., Koch, M., & Lindholm, L.** (1998). Recurrent depression in adolescents: A follow-up study. *Journal of the American Academy of Child and Adolescent Psychiatry, 27,* 49–54.

**Gardner, H.** (1983). *Frames of mind.* New York: Basic Books.

**Gardner, H.** (1993). *Multiple intelligences.* New York: Basic Books.

**Gardner, H.** (2002). The pursuit of excellence through education. In M. Ferrari (Ed.), *Learning from extraordinary minds.* Mahwah, NJ: Erlbaum.

**Garofalo, R., Wolf, R. C., Wissow, L. S., Woods, E. R., & Goodman, E.** (1999). Sexual orientation and risk of suicide attempts among a representative sample of youth. *Archives of Pediatrics and Adolescent Medicine, 153,* 487–493.

**Garrett, P., Ng'andu, N., & Ferron, J.** (1994). Poverty experiences of young children and the quality of their home environments. *Child Development, 65,* 331–345.

**Garrod, A., Smulyan, L., Powers, S. I., & Kilkenny, R.** (1992). *Adolescent portraits.* Boston: Allyn & Bacon.

**Gates, G. J., & Sonenstein, F. L.** (2000). Heterosexual genital activity among adolescent males: 1988 and 1995. *Family Planning Perspectives, 32,* 295–297, 304.

**Gates, J. L.** (2001, April). *Women's career choices in math and science-related fields.* Paper presented at the meeting of the Society for Research in Child Development, Minneapolis.

**Gautheir, A. H., & Furstenberg, F. F.** (2005). Historical trends in the patterns of time use among young adults in developed countries. In R. A. Settersten, F. F. Furstenberg, & R. G. Rumbaut (Eds.), *On the frontier of adulthood: Theories, research, and social policy.* Chicago: University of Chicago Press.

**Gauvain, M., & Perez, S. M.** (2007). The socialization of cognition. In J. E. Grusec & P. D. Hastings (Eds.), *Handbook of socialization.* New York: Guilford.

**Gauze, C. M.** (1994, February). *Talking to Mom about friendship: What do mothers know?* Paper presented at the meeting of the Society for Research on Adolescence, San Diego.

**Geary, D. C.** (2006). Evolutionary developmental psychology: Current status and future directions. *Developmental Review, 26,* 113–119.

**Gecas, V., & Seff, M.** (1990). Families and adolescents: A review of the 1980s. *Journal of Marriage and the Family, 52,* 941–958.

**Geher, G., & Miller, G.** (Eds.). (2007). *Mating intelligence.* Mahwah, NJ: Erlbaum.

**Gelhorn, H., Stallings, M., Young, S., Corley, R., Rhee, S. H., Christian, H., & Hewitt, J.** (2006). Common and specific genetic influences on aggressive and nonaggressive conduct disorder domains. *Journal of the American Academy of Child and Adolescent Psychiatry, 45,* 570–577.

**Gentzler, A. L., & Kerns, K. A.** (2004). Associations between insecure attachment and sexual experiences. *Personal Relationships, 2,* 249–266.

**George, C., Main, M., & Kaplan, N.** (1984). *Attachment-interview with adults.* Unpublished manuscript, University of California, Berkeley.

**Germeijs, V., & De Boeck, P.** (2003). Career indecision: Three factors from decision theory. *Journal of Vocational Behavior, 62,* 11–25.

**Germeijs, V., & Verschueren, K.** (2006). High school students' career decision-making process: A longitudinal study of one choice. *Journal of Vocational Behavior, 68,* 189–204.

**Giannantonio, C. M., & Hurley-Hansen, A. E.** (2006). Applying image norms across Super's career development stages. *Career Development Quarterly, 54,* 318–330.

**Gibbons, J. L.** (2000). Gender development in cross-cultural perspective. In T. Eckes & H. M. Trautner (Eds.), *The developmental social psychology of gender.* Mahwah, NJ: Erlbaum.

**Gibbs, J. C.** (2003). Moral development and reality: Beyond the theories of Kohlberg and Hoffman. Thousand Oaks, CA: Sage.

**Gibbs, J. T.** (1989). Black American adolescents. In J. T. Gibbs & L. N. Huang (Eds.), *Children of color.* San Francisco: Jossey-Bass.

**Gibbs, J. T., & Huang, L. N.** (1989). A conceptual framework for assessing and treating minority youth. In J. T. Gibbs & L. N. Huang (Eds.), *Children of color.* San Francisco: Jossey-Bass.

**Giedd, J. N.** (2004). Structural magnetic resonance imaging of the adolescent brain. *Annals of the New York Academy of Sciences, 1021,* 77–85.

**Giedd, J. N. & others.** (2006). Puberty-related influences on brain development. *Molecular and Cellular, Endocrinology, 25,* 154–162.

**Gifford-Smith, M. E., & Rabiner, D. L.** (2004). The relation between social information processing and children's adjustment. In J. B. Kupersmidt & K. A. Dodge (Eds.), *Children's peer relations: From development to intervention.* Washington, DC: American Psychological Association.

**Gillen, M. M., Lefkowitz, E. S., & Shearer, C. L.** (2006). Does body image play a role in risky sexual behavior and attitudes? *Journal of Youth and Adolesnce, 35,* 230–242.

**Gilliam, F. D., & Bales, S. N.** (2001). Strategic frame analysis: Reframing America's youth. *Social Policy Report, Society for Research in Child Development, XV* (3), 1–14

**Gilligan, C.** (1982). *In a different voice.* Cambridge, MA: Harvard University Press.

**Gilligan, C.** (1992, May). *Joining the resistance: Girls' development in adolescence.* Paper presented at the symposium on development and vulnerability in close relationships, Montreal, Quebec.

**Gilligan, C.** (1996). The centrality of relationships in psychological development: A puzzle, some evidence, and a theory. In G. G. Noam & K. W. Fischer (Eds.), *Development and vulnerability in close relationships.* Hillside, NJ: Erlbaum.

**Gilligan, C., Brown, L. M., & Rogers, A. G.** (1990). Psyche embedded: A place for body, relationships, and culture in personality theory. In A. I. Rabin, R. A. Zuker, R. A. Emmons, & S. Frank (Eds.), *Studying persons and lives.* New York: Springer.

**Gilligan, C., Spencer, R., Weinberg, M. K., & Bertsch, T.** (2003). On the listening guide: A voice-centered relational model. In P.M. Carnic & J. E. Rhodes (Eds.), *Qualitative research in psychology.* Washington, DC: American Psychological Association.

**Gilmartin, S. K.** (2006). Changes in college women's attitudes toward sexual intimacy. *Journal of Research on Adolescence, 16,* 429–454.

**Ginorio, A. B., & Huston, M.** (2001). *Sil Se Puede! Yes, we can: Latinas in school.* Washington, DC: AAUW.

**Ginzberg, E.** (1972). Toward a theory of occupational choice: A restatement. *Vocational Guidance Quarterly, 20,* 169–176.

**Ginzberg, E., Ginzberg, S. W., Axelrad, S., & Herman, J. L.** (1951). *Occupational choice.* New York: Columbia University.

**Girls, Inc.** (1991). *It's my party: Girls choose to be substance free.* Indianapolis: Author.

**Girls, Inc.** (1991). *Truth, trusting, and technology: New research on preventing adolescent pregnancy.* Indianapolis: Author.

**Gjerde, P. F.** (1986). The interpersonal structure of family interaction settings: Parent-adolescents relations in dyads and triads. *Developmental Psychology, 22,* 297–304.

**Gladstone, G. L., Parker, G. B., & Malhi, G. S.** (2006). Do bullied children become anxious and depressed adults? A cross-sectional investigation of the correlates of bullying and anxious depression. *Journal of Nervous and Mental Disorders, 194,* 201–208.

**Glenn, N. D.** (2005). *Fatherhood in America.* Report to the National Fatherhood Initiative, Washington, DC.

**Glidden-Tracey, C.** (2005). *Counseling and therapy with clients who abuse alcohol or other drugs.* Mahwah, NJ: Erlbaum.

**Goldberg, A. E., & Sayer, A.** (2006). Lesbian couples' relationship quality across the transition to parenthood. *Journal of Marriage and the Family, 68,* 87–100.

**Goldman, R.** (1964). *Religious thinking from childhood to adolescence.* London: Routledge & Kegan Paul.

**Goldman-Rakic, P.** (1996). *Bridging the gap.* Presentation at the workshop sponsored by the Education Commission of the States and the Charles A. Dana Foundation, Denver.

**Goldscheider, F., & Goldscheider, C.** (1999). *The changing transition to adulthood: Leaving and returning home.* Thousand Oaks, CA: Sage.

**Goldscheider, F., & Sassler, S.** (2006). Creating stepfamilies: Integrating children into the study of union formation. *Journal of Marriage and the Family, 68,* 275–291.

**Goldstein, J. M., Seidman, L. J., Horton, N. J., Makris, N., Kennedy, D. N., Caviness, V. S., Faraone, S. V., & Tsuang, M. T.** (2001). Normal sexual dimorphism of the adult human brain assessed by in vivo magnetic resonance imaging. *Cerebral Cortex, 11,* 490–497.

**Goldstein, S. E., Davis-Kean, P. E., & Eccles, J. S.** (2005). Parents, peers, and problem behavior: A longitudinal investigation of the impact of relationship perceptions and characteristics on the development of adolescent problem behavior. *Developmental Psychology, 41,* 401–413.

**Goleman, D.** (1995). *Emotional intelligence.* New York: Basic Books.

**Gong, R.** (2005). The essence of critical thinking. *Journal of Developmental Education, 28,* 40–42.

**Gonzales, N. A., Deardorff, J., Formoso, D., Barr, A., & Barrera, M.** (2006). Family mediators of the relation between acculturation and adolescent mental health. *Family Relations, 55,* 318–330.

**Gonzales, N. A., Dumka, L. E., Mauricio, A. M., & German, M.** (2007). Building bridges: Strategies to promote academic and psychological resilience for adolescents of Mexican origin. In J. E. Lansford, K. Deater Deckard, & M. H. Bornstein (Eds.), *Immigrant families in contemporary society.* New York: Guilford.

**Gonzales, N. A., Knight, G. P., Birman, D., & Sirolli, A. A.** (2004). Acculturation and enculturation among Latino youths. In K. L. Maton, C. J. Schellenbach, B. J. Leadbetter, & A. L. Solarz (Eds.), *Investing in children, families, and communities.* Washington, DC: American Psychological Association.

**Gonzales, P., Buzman, J. C., Partelow, L., Pahlke, E., Jocelyn, L., Kastberg, D., & Williams, T.** (2004). *Highlights from the Tends in International Mathematics and Science Study (TIMSS) 2003* (NCES 2005-005). Washington, DC: U.S. Department of Education, National Center for Education Statistics.

**Goodchilds, J. D., & Zellman, G. L.** (1984). Sexual signaling and sexual aggression in adolescent relationships. In N. M. Malamuth & E. D. Donnerstein (Eds.), *Pornography and sexual aggression.* New York: Academic Press.

**Goodman, E., & Capitman, J.** (2000). Depressive symptoms and cigarette smoking among teens. *Pediatrics, 106,* 748–755.

**Goodman, R. A., Mercy, J. A., Loya, F., Rosenberg, M. L., Smith, J. C., Allen, N. H., Vargas, L., & Kolts, R.** (1986). Alcohol use and interpersonal violence: Alcohol detected in homicide victims. *American Journal of Public Health, 76,* 144–149.

**Goossens, L.** (2006, March). *Parenting, identity, and adjustment in adolescence.* Paper presented at the meeting of the Society for Research on Adolescence, San Francisco.

**Goossens. L., Beyers. W., Emmen. M., & van Aken, M. A. G.** (2002). The imaginary audience and personal fable: Factor analyses and concurrent validity of the "new look measures." *Journal of Research on Adolescence, 12,* 193–215.

**Gore, P. A., & Metz, A. J.** (2005). Career assessment. In S. W. Lee (Ed.), *Handbook of child psychology.* Thousand Oaks, CA: Sage.

**Gorski, P.** (2005). *Multicultural education and the Internet* (2nd ed.). New York: McGraw-Hill.

**Gotesdam, K. G., & Agras, W. S.** (1995). General population-based epidemiological survey of eating disorders in Norway. *International Journal of Eating Disorders, 18,* 119–126.

**Gottlieb, G.** (2004). Normally occurring environmental and behavioral influences on gene activity. In C. G. Coll, E. L. Bearer, & R. M. Lerner, (Eds.), *Nature and nurture.* Mahwah, NJ: Erlbaum.

**Gottlieb, G.** (2007). Probabalistic epigenesis. *Developmental Science, 10,* 1–11.

**Gottlieb, G., Wahlsten, D., & Lickliter, R.** (2006). The significance of biology for human development: A developmental psychobiological systems view. In W. Damon & R. Lerner (Eds.), *Handbook of child psychology* (6th ed.). New York: Wiley.

**Gottman, J. M., & Parker, J. G.** (Eds.). (1987). *Conversations of friends.* New York: Cambridge University Press.

**Gould, M. S., Greenberg, T., Velting, D. M., & Shaffer, D.** (2003). Youth suicide risk and preventive interventions: A review of the past 10 years. *Journal of the American Academy of Child and Adolescent Psychiatry, 42,* 386–405.

**Gould, S. J.** (1981). *The mismeasure of man.* New York: W. W. Norton.

**Grabe, S., & Hyde, J. S.** (2006). Ethnicity and body dissatisfaction among women in the United States: A meta-analysis. *Psychological Bulletin, 132,* 622–640.

**Graber, J. A.** (2004). Internalizing problems during adolescence. In R. Lerner & L. Steinberg (Eds.), *Handbook of adolescent psychology.* New York: Wiley.

**Graber, J. A.** (2007, in press). *Pubertal and neuroendocrine development and risk for depressive disorders.* In N. B. Allen & L. Sheeber (Eds.), *Adolescent emotional development and the emergence of depressive disorders.* New York: Cambridge University Press.

**Graber, J. A., & Brooks-Gunn, J.** (2002). Adolescent girls' sexual development. In G. M. Wingood & R. J. DiClemente (Eds.), *Handbook of women's sexual and reproductive health.* New York: Kluwer Academic/Plenum Publishers.

**Graber, J. A., Brooks-Gunn, J., & Warren, M. P.** (2006). Pubertal effects on adjustment in girls: Moving from demonstrating effects to identifying pathways. *Journal of Youth and Adolescence, 35,* 391–401.

**Graber, J. A., Seeley, J. R., Brooks-Gunn, J., & Lewinsohn, P. M.** (2004). Is pubertal timing associated with psychopathology in young adulthood? *Journal of the American Academy of Child and Adolescent Psychiatry, 43,* 718–726.

**Graham, E. A.** (2005). Economic, racial, and cultural influences on the growth and maturation of children. *Pediatrics in Review, 26,* 290–294.

**Graham, J.** (2006). Strategy instruction and the teaching of writing: A meta-analysis. In C. A. MacArthur, S. Graham, & J. Fitzgerald (Eds.), *Handbook of writing research.* Mahwah, NJ: Erlbaum.

**Graham, J. H., & Beller, A. H.** (2002). Nonresident fathers and their children: Child support and visitation from an economic perspective. In C. S. Tamis-LeMonda & N. Cabrera (Eds.), *The handbook of father involvement.* Mahwah, NJ: Erlbaum.

**Graham, S.** (1986, August). *Can attribution theory tell us something about motivation in blacks?* Paper presented at the meeting of the American Psychological Association, Washington, DC.

**Graham, S.** (1990). Motivation in Afro-Americans. In G. L. Berry & J. K. Asamen (Eds.), *Black students: Psychosocial issues and academic achievement.* Newbury Park, CA: Sage.

**Graham, S.** (1992). Most of the subjects were white and middle class. *American Psychologist, 47,* 629–637.

**Graham, S.** (2005, February 16). Commentary in *USA Today,* p. 2D.

**Graham, S.** (Ed.). (2006). Our children too: A history of the first 25 years of the Society for Research in Child Development. *Monographs of the Society for Research in Child Development* (Vol. 71, No. 1), 1–227.

**Graham, S. & Taylor, A. Z.** (2001). Ethnicity, gender, and the development of achievement values. In A. Wigfield & J. S. Eccles (Eds.), *Development of achievement motivation.* San Diego: Academic Press.

**Granqvist, P., & Dickie, J. R.** (2006). Attachment and spiritual development in childhood and adolescence. In E. C. Roehlkepartain, P. E. King, & L. M. Wegener (Eds.), *The handbook of spiritual development in childhood and adolescence.* Thousand Oaks, CA: Sage.

**Gray, J.** (1992). *Men are from Mars, women are from Venus.* New York: HarperCollins.

**Graziano, A. M., & Raulin, M. L.** (2007). *Research methods* (6th ed.). Boston: Allyn & Bacon.

**Greder, K. A., & Allen, W. D.** (2007). Parenting in color: Culturally diverse perspectives on parenting. In B. S. Trask & R. R. Hamon (Eds.), *Cultural diversity and families.* Thousand Oaks, CA: Sage.

**Greenberg, B. S., Stanley, C., Siemicki, M., Heeter, C., Soderman, A., & Linsangan, R.** (1986). *Sex content on soaps and prime-time television series most viewed by adolescents.* Project CAST Report/ns/2. East Lansing: Michigan State Department of Telecommunication.

**Greenberg, J. S.** (2006). *Comprehensive stress management* (9th ed.). New York: McGraw-Hill.

**Greenberg, M. T., Weissberg. R. P., O'Brien, M. U., Zins, J. E., Fredericks, L., Resnik, H., & Elias, M. J.** (2003). Enhancing school-based prevention and youth development through coordinated social, emotional, and academic learning. *American Psychologist, 58,* 466–474.

**Greenberger, E., & Chu, C.** (1996). Perceived family relationships and depressed mood in early adolescence: A comparison of European and Asian Americans. *Developmental Psychology, 32,* 707–716.

**Greenberger, E., & Steinberg, L.** (1981). *Project for the study of adolescent work: Final report.* Report prepared for the National Institute of Education, U.S. Department of Education, Washington, DC.

**Greenberger, E., & Steinberg, L.** (1986). *When teenagers work: The psychological social costs of adolescent employment.* New York: Basic Books.

**Greene, B.** (1988, May). The children's hour. *Esquire,* pp. 47–49.

**Greene, J. P., & Forster, G.** (2003). *Public high school graduation and college readiness rates in the United States.* New York: The Manhattan Institute.

**Greenfield, P. M., & Subrahmanyam, K.** (2003). Online discourse in a teen chat room: New codes and new modes of coherence in a visual medium. *Journal of Applied Developmental Psychology, 24,* 713–738.

**Greenfield, P., & Yan, Z.** (2006). Children, adolescents, and the Internet: A new field of inquiry in developmental psychology. *Developmental Psychology, 42,* 391–394.

**Greenough, W. T.** (1997, April 21). Commentary in article, "Politics of biology." *U.S. News & World Report,* p. 79.

**Greenough, W. T.** (1999, April). *Experience, brain development, and links to mental retardation.* Paper presented at the meeting of the Society for Research in Child Development, Albuquerque.

**Greenough, W. T.** (2000). Brain development. In A. Kazdin (Ed.), *Encyclopedia of psychology.* Washington, DC & New York: American Psychological Association and Oxford University Press.

**Greenough, W. T., Klintsova, A. Y., Irvan, S. A., Galvez, R., Bates, K. E., & Weiler, I. J.** (2001). Synaptic regulation of protein synthesis and the fragile X protein. *Proceedings of the National Academy of Science USA, 98,* 7101–7106.

**Gregory, R. J.** (2007). *Psychological testing* (5th ed.). Boston: Allyn & Bacon.

**Grello, C. M., Welsh, D. P., & Harper, M. S.** (2006). No strings attached: The nature of casual sex in college students. *The Journal of Sex Research, 43,* 255–267.

**Greydanus, D. E., Pratt, H. D., & Patel, D. R.** (2007). Attention deficit hyperactivity disorder across the lifespan: The child, adolescent, and adult. *Disease-A-Month, 53,* 70–131.

**Grigorenko, E.** (2000). Heritability and intelligence. In R. J. Sternberg (Ed.), *Handbook of intelligence.* New York: Cambridge University Press.

**Grimes, B., & Mattimore, K.** (1989, April). *The effects of stress and exercise on identity formation in adolescence.* Paper presented at the biennial meeting of the Society for Research in Child Development, Kansas City.

**Gronlund, N. W.** (2006). *Assessment of student achievement* (8th ed.). Boston: Allyn & Bacon.

**Gross, E. F.** (2004). Adolescent Internet use: What we expect. What teens report. *Journal of Applied Developmental Psychology, 24,* 633–649.

**Grossman, J. B., & Rhodes, J. E.** (2002). The test of time: Predictors and effects of duration in youth mentoring relationships. *American Journal of Community Psychology, 30* (2), 199–219.

**Grotevant, H. D.** (1996). Unpublished review of J. W. Santrock's *Adolescence,* 7th ed. (Dubuque, IA: Brown & Benchmark).

**Grotevant, H. D.** (1998). Adolescent development in family contexts. In W. Damon (Ed.), *Handbook of child psychology* (5th ed., Vol. 3). New York: Wiley.

**Grotevant, H. D.** (2006, March). *Adoption and adolescents.* Paper presented at the meeting of the Society for Research on Adolescence, San Francisco.

**Grotevant, H. D., & Cooper, C. R.** (1985). Patterns of interaction in family relationships and the development of identity exploration in adolescence. *Child Development, 56,* 415–428.

**Grotevant, H. D., & Cooper, C. R.** (1998). Individuality and connectedness in adolescent development: Review and prospects for research on identity, relationships, and context. In E. Skoe & A. von der Lippe (Eds.), *Personality development in adolescence: A cross-national and life-span perspective.* London: Routledge.

**Grotevant, H. D., & Durrett, M. E.** (1980). Occupational knowledge and career development in adolescence. *Journal of Vocational Behavior, 17,* 171–182.

**Grotevant, H. D., & McRoy, R. G.** (1990). Adopted adolescents in residential treatment: The role of the family. In D. M. Brodzinsky & M. D. Schechter (Eds.), *The psychology of adoption.* New York: Oxford University Press.

**Grotevant, H. D., van Dulmen, M. H., Dunbar, N., Nelson-Christinedaughter, J., Christensen, M., Fanx, X., & Miller, B. C.** (2006). Antisocial behavior of adoptees and nonadoptees: Prediction from early history and adolescent relationships. *Journal of Research on Adolescence, 16,* 105–131.

**Grusec, J. E.** (2006). The development of moral behavior and conscience from a socialization perspective. In M. Killen & J. Smetana (Eds.), *Handbook of moral development.* Mahwah, NJ: Erlbaum.

**Grusec, J. E., & Davidov, M.** (2007). Socialization in the family: The roles of parents. In J. E. Grusec & P. D. Hastings (Eds.), *Handbook of socialization.* New York: Guilford.

**Grusec, J. E., Goodnow, J. J., & Kuczynski, L.** (2000). New directions in analyses of parenting contributions to children's acquisition of values. *Child Development, 71,* 205–211.

**Grusec, J. E., & Hastings, P. D.** (Eds.) (2007). *Handbook of socialization.* New York: Guilford.

**Grych, J. H.** (2002). Marital relationships and parenting. In M. H. Bornstein (Ed.), *Handbook of parenting* (2nd ed.). Mahwah, NJ: Erlbaum.

**Guercio, G., Rivarola, M. A., Charler, E., Maceiras, M., & Belgorosky, A.** (2003). Relationship between the growth hormone/insulin-like growth factor-I axis, insulin sensitivity, and adrenal androgens in normal prepubertal and pubertal girls. *Journal of Clinical Endocrinology and Metabolism, 88,* 1389–1393.

**Guerin, D. W., Gottfried, A. W., Oliver, P. H. & Thomas, C. W.** (2003). Temperament: Infancy through adolescence. New York: Kluwer.

**Guilford, J. P.** (1967). *The structure of intellect.* New York: McGraw-Hill.

**Gumora, G., & Arsenio, W.** (2002). Emotionality, emotion regulation, and school performance in middle school children. *Journal of School Psychology, 40,* 395–413.

**Gupta, A., Thornton, J. W., & Huston, A. C.** (2007). Working families should not be poor—the New Hope project. In D. R. Crane & T. B. Heaton (Eds.), *Handbook of families and poverty.* Thousand Oaks, CA: Sage.

**Gur, R. C., Mozley, L. H., Mozley, P. D., Resnick, S. M., Karp, J. S., Alavi, A., Arnold, S. E., & Gur, R. E.** (1995). Sex differences in regional cerebral glucose metabolism during a resting state. *Science,* 267, 528–531.

**Gushue, G. V., Clarke, C. P., Pantzer, K. M., & Scanlan, K. R. L.** (2006). Self-efficacy, perceptions of barriers, vocational identity, and the career exploration behavior of Latino/a high school students. *Career Development Quarterly, 54,* 307–317.

**Guttentag, M., & Bray, H.** (1976). *Undoing sex stereotypes: Research and resources for educators.* New York: McGraw-Hill.


## H


**Hafferth, S. L., Reid, L.** (2002). Early child bearing and children's achievement and behavior over time. *Perspectives on Sexual and Reproductive Health, 34,* 444–449.

**Hair, E. C., & Graziano, W. G.** (2003). Self-esteem, personality, and achievement in high school: A prospective longitudinal study in Texas. *Journal of Personality, 71,* 971–994.

**Hale, S.** (1990). A global developmental trend in cognitive processing speed. *Child Development, 61,* 653–663.

**Hales, D.** (2006). *An invitation to health* (4th ed., Brief). Belmont CA: Wadsworth.

**Halford, G. S.** (2004). Information-processing models of coqnitive development. In V. Goswami (Ed.), *Blackwell handbook of childhood coqnitive development.* Malden, MA: Blackwell.

**Hall, G. C., DeGarmo, D. S., Eap, S., Teten, A. L., & Sue, S.** (2006). Initiation, desistance, and persistence of men's sexual coercion. *Journal of Consulting and Clinical Psychology, 74,* 732–742.

**Hall, G. S.** (1904). *Adolescence* (Vols. 1 & 2). Englewood Cliffs, NJ: Prentice Hall.

**Hallahan, D. P., & Kauffman, J. M.** (2006). *Exceptional learners* (10th ed.). Boston: Allyn & Bacon.

**Hallfors, D. D., Waller, M. W., Ford, C. A., Halpern, C. T., Brodish, P. H., & Iritani, B.** (2004). Adolescent depression and suicide risk: Association with sex and drug behavior. *American Journal of Preventive Medicine, 27,* 224–231.

**Halonen, J. A., & Santrock, J. W.** (1999). *Psychology: Contexts and applications* (3rd ed.). New York: McGraw-Hill.

**Halpern, D.** (2001). Sex difference research: Cognitive abilities. In J. Worell (Ed.), *Encyclopedia of Women and Gender.* San Diego: Academic Press.

**Halpern, D. F.** (2006). Girls and academic success: Changing patterns of academic achievement. In J. Worell & C. D. Goodheart (Eds.), *Handbook of girls' and women's psychological health.* New York: Oxford University Press.

**Halpern, D. F.** (2007). The nature and nurture of critical thinking. In R. J. Sternberg, H. Roediger, & D. F. Halpern (Eds.), *Critical thinking in psychology.* New York: Cambridge University Press.

**Halverson, S.** (2004). Teaching ethics: The role of the classroom teacher. *Childhood Education, 80,* 157–158.

**Hamburg, D. A.** (1997). Meeting the essential requirements for healthy adolescent development in a transforming world. In R. Takanishi & D. Hamburg (Eds.), *Preparing adolescents for the 21st century.* New York: Cambridge University Press.

**Hamilton, S. F., & Hamilton, M. A.** (2004). Contexts for mentoring: Adolescent-adult relationships in workplaces and communities. In R. Lerner & L. Steinberg (Eds.), *Handbook of adolescent psychology* (2nd ed.). New York: Wiley.

**Hamilton, S. F., & Hamilton, M. A.** (2006). School, work, and emerging adulthood. In J. J. Arnett & J. L. Tanner (Eds.), *Emerging adults in America.* Washington, DC: American Psychological Associaton.

**Hamm, J. V., Brown, B. B., & Heck, D. J.** (2005). Bridging the ethnic divide: Student and school characteristics in African American, Asian-descent, Latino, and White adolescents' cross-ethnic friend nominations. *Journal of Research on Adolescence, 15,* 21–46.

**Hammond, L. S.** (2005). *Culture, psychotherapy, and counseling.* Thousand Oaks, CA: Sage.

**Hankin, B. L., Kassel, J. D., & Abela, J. R.** (2005). Adult attachment dimensions and specificity of emotional distress symptoms: Prospective investigations of cognitive risk and interpersonal stress generation as mediating mechanisms. *Personality and Social Psychology Bulletin, 31,* 136–151.

**Hansen, M., Janssen, I., Schiff, A., Zee, P. C., & Dubocovich, M. L.** (2005). The impact of school daily schedule on adolescent sleep. *Pediatrics, 115,* 1555–1561.

**Hansford, B. C., & Hattie, J. A.** (1982). The relationship between self and achievement/performance measures. *Review of Educational Research, 52,* 123–142.

**Hardman, M. L., Drew, C. J., & Egan, M. W.** (2006). *Human exceptionality* (8th ed. Update). Boston: Allyn & Bacon.

**Hare, B. R., & Castenell, L. A.** (1985). No place to run, no place to hide: Comparative status and future prospects of Black boys. In M. B. Spencer, G. K. Brookins, & W. R. Allen (Eds.), *Beginnings: The social and affective development of Black children.* Hillsdale, NJ: Erlbaum.

**Hargreaves, D. A., & Tiggemann, M.** (2004). Idealized body images and adolescent body image: "Comparing" boys and girls. *Body Image, 1,* 351–361.

**Hargrove, B. K., Creagh, M. G., & Burgess, B. L.** (2003). Family interaction patterns as predictors of vocational identity and career decision-making self-efficacy. *Journal of Vocational Behavior, 61,* 185–201.

**Harold, R. D., Colarossi, L. G., & Mercier, L. R.** (2007). *Smooth sailing or troubled waters? Stories of family transitions through adolescence and their implications for practice and policy.* Mahwah, NJ: Erlbaum.

**Harper, C. C., & McLanahan, S. S.** (2004). Father absence and youth incarceration. *Journal of Research on Adolescence, 14,* 369–397.

**Harris, J. B.** (1998). *The nurture assumption: Why children turn out the way they do: Parents matter less than you think and peers matter more.* New York: Free Press.

**Harris, L.** (1987, September 3). The latchkey child phenomenon. *Dallas Morning News,* pp. IA, 10A.

**Harris, P. L.** (2006). Social coqnition. In W. Damon, R. Lerner (Eds.), *Handbook of child psychology* (6th ed.). New York: Wiley.

**Harris, Y. R., & Graham, J. A.** (2007). *The African American child.* New York: Springer.

**Harrison-Hale, A. O., McLoyd, V. C., & Smedley, B.** (2004). Racial and ethnic status: Risk and protective processes among African-American families. In K. L. Maton, C. J. Schellenbach, B. J. Leadbetter, & A. L. Solarz (Eds.), *Investing in children, families, and communities.* Washington, DC: American Psychological Association.

**Hart, D., Atkins, R., & Donnelly, T. M.** (2006). Community service and moral development. In M. Killen & J. Smetana (Eds.), *Handbook of moral development.* Mahwah, NJ: Erlbaum.

**Hart, D., Atkins, R., Markey, P., & Youniss, J.** (2004). Youth bulges in communities: The effects of age structure on adolescent civic knowledge and civic participation. *Psychological Science, 15,* 591–597.

**Harter, S.** (1986). Processes underlying the construction, maintenance, and enhancement of the self-concept of children. In J. Suls & A. Greenwald (Eds.), *Psychological perspective on the self* (Vol. 3). Hillsdale, NJ: Erlbaum.

**Harter, S.** (1989). *Self-perception profile for adolescents.* Denver: University of Denver, Department of Psychology.

**Harter, S.** (1990a). Self and identity development. In S. S. Feldman & G. R. Elliott (Eds.), *At the threshold: The developing adolescent.* Cambridge, MA: Harvard University Press.

**Harter, S.** (1990b). Processes underlying adolescent self-concept formation. In R. Montemayor, G. R. Adams, & T. P. Gullotta (Eds.), *From childhood to adolescence: A transitional period?* Newbury Park, CA: Sage.

**Harter, S.** (1998). The development of self-representations. In W. Damon (Ed.), *Handbook of child psychology* (5th ed., Vol. 3). New York: Wiley.

**Harter, S.** (1999). *The construction of the self.* New York: Guilford.

**Harter, S.** (2002). Unpublished review of J. W. Santrock's *Child development,* 10th ed. (New York: McGraw-Hill).

**Harter, S.** (2006). The development of self-representations in childhood and adolescence. In W. Damon & R. Lerner (Eds.), *Handbook of child psychology* (6th ed.). New York: Wiley.

**Harter, S., & Lee, L.** (1989). *Manifestations of true and false selves in adolescence.* Paper presented at the meeting of the Society for Research in Child Development, Kansas City.

**Harter, S., & McCarley, K. E.** (2004, April). Is there a dark side to high self-esteem leading to adolescent violence? Paper presented at the meeting of the American Psychological Association, Honolulu.

**Harter, S., & Monsour, A.** (1992). Developmental analysis of conflict caused by opposing attributes in the adolescent self-portrait. *Developmental Psychology, 28,* 251–260.

**Harter, S., Stocker, C., & Robinson, N. S.** (1996). The perceived directionality of the link between approval and self-worth: The liabilities of a looking-glass self-orientation among young adolescents. *Journal of Research on Adolescence, 6,* 285–308.

**Harter, S., Waters, P., & Whitesell, N.** (1996, March). *False self behavior and lack of voice among adolescent males and females.* Paper presented at the meeting of the Society for Research on Adolescence, Boston.

**Harter, S., & Whitesell, N.** (2001, April). *What we have learned from Columbine: The impact of self-esteem on suicidal and violent ideation among adolescents.* Paper presented at the meeting of the Society for Research in Child Development, Minneapolis.

**Hartmann, D. P., & Pelzel, K. E.** (2005). Design, measurement, and analysis in developmental research. In M. H. Bornstein & M. E. Lamb (Eds.), *Developmental psychology* (5th ed.). Mahwah, NJ: Erlbaum.

**Hartshorne, H., & May, M. S.** (1928–1930). *Moral studies in the nature of character: Studies in deceit* (Vol. 1); *Studies in self-control* (Vol. 2). *Studies in the organization of character* (Vol. 3). New York: Macmillan.

**Hartung, P. J., Porfeli, E. J., & Vondracek, F. W.** (2005). Child vocational development: A review and reconsideration. *Journal of Vocational Development, 66,* 385–419.

**Hartup, W. W.** (1983). The peer system. In P. H. Mussen (Ed.), *Handbook of child psychology* (4th ed., Vol. 4). New York: Wiley.

**Hartup, W. W.** (1996). The company they keep: Friendships and their developmental significance. *Child Development, 67,* 1–13.

**Hartup, W. W.** (1999, April). *Peer relations and the growth of the individual child.* Paper presented at the meeting of the Society for Research in Child Development, Albuquerque.

**Hartwell, L.** (2008). *Genetics* (3rd ed.). New York: McGraw-Hill.

**Harwood, R., Leyendecker, B., Carlson, V., Asencio, M., & Miller, A.** (2002). Parenting among Latino families in the U.S. In M. H. Bornstein (Ed.), *Handbook of parenting* (2nd ed.). Mahwah, NJ: Erlbaum.

**Harwood, R. L., & Feng, X.** (2006). Studying acculturation among Latinos in the United States. In M. H. Bornstein & L. R. Cote (Eds.), *Acculturation and parent-child relationships.* Mahwah, NJ: Erlbaum.

**Haselager, G. J. T. Cillessen, A. H. N., Van Lieshout, C. F. M., Riksen-Walraven, J. M. A. & Hartup, W. W.** (2002). Heterogeneity among peer-rejected boys across middle childhood: Developmental pathways of social behavior. *Developmental Psychology, 38,* 446–456.

**Hastings, P. D., Utendale, W. T., & Sullivan, C.** (2007). The socialization of prosocial development. In J. E. Grusec & P. D. Hastings (Eds.), *Handbook of socialization.* New York: Guilford.

**Hattery, A. J., & Smith, E.** (2007). *African American families.* Thousand Oaks, CA: Sage.

**Haugaard, J. J., & Hazan, C.** (2004). Adoption as a natural experiment. *Developmental Psychopathology, 15,* 909–926.

**Hauser, S. T., & Bowlds, M. K.** (1990). Stress, coping, and adaptation. In S. S. Feldman &

G. R. Elliott (Eds.), *At the threshold: The developing adolescent.* Cambridge, MA: Harvard University Press.

**Hauser, S. T., Powers, S. I., Noam, G. G., Jacobson, A. M., Weisse, B., & Follansbee, D. J.** (1984). Familial contexts of adolescent ego development. *Child Development, 55,* 195–213.

**Haviland, J. M., Davidson, R. B., Ruetsch, C., & Gebelt, J. L.** (1994). The place of emotion in identity. *Journal of Research on Adolescence, 4,* 503–518.

**Hawkins, J. A., & Berndt, T. J.** (1985, April). *Adjustment following the transition to junior high school.* Paper presented at the biennial meeting of the Society for Research in Child Development, Toronto.

**Haynie, D. L., Nansel, T., Eitel, P., Crump, A. D., Saylor, K., Yu, K., & Simons-Morton, B.** (2001). Bullies, victims, and bully/victims: Distinct groups of at-risk youth. *Journal of Early Adolescence, 21,* 29–49.

**Hazan, C., Gur-Yaish, N., & Campa, M.** (2007). What does it mean to be attached? In W. S. Rholes & J. A. Simpson (Eds.), *Adult attachment.* New York: Guilford.

**Heath, S. B.** (1999). Dimensions of language development: Lessons from older children. In A. S. Masten (Ed.), *Cultural processes in child development: The Minnesota symposium on child psychology* (Vol. 29). Mahwah NJ: Erlbaum.

**Heath, S. B., & McLaughlin, M. W.** (Eds.). (1993). *Identity and inner-city youth: Beyond ethnicity and gender.* New York: Teachers College Press.

**Hechinger, J.** (1992). *Fateful Choices.* New York: Hill & Wang.

**Heinze, H. J., Toro, P. A., & Urberg, K. A.** (2004). Antisocial behavior and affiliation with deviant peers. *Journal of Clinical Child and Adolescent Psychology,* 33, 336–346.

**Helson, R., Elliot, T., & Leigh, J.** (1989). Adolescent antecedents of women's work patterns. In D. Stern & D. Eichorn (Eds.), *Adolescence and work.* Hillsdale, NJ: Erlbaum.

**Hemmings, A.** (2004). *Coming of age in U.S. high schools.* Mahwah, NJ: Erlbaum.

**Henderson, V. L., & Dweck, C. S.** (1990). Motivation and achievement. In S. S. Feldman & G. R. Elliott (Eds.), *At the threshold: The developing adolescent.* Cambridge, MA: Harvard University Press.

**Hendry, J.** (1999). *Social anthropology.* New York: Macmillan.

**Henry, D. B., Schoeny, M. E., Deptula, D. P., & Slavick, J. T.** (2007). Peer selection and socialization effects on adolescent intercourse without a condom and attitudes about the costs of sex. *Child Development, 78,* 825–838.

**Heppner, M. J., & Heppner, P. P.** (2003). Identifying process variables in career counseling: A research agenda. *Journal of Vocational Behavior, 62,* 429–452.

**Heppner, P., & Lee, D.** (2001). Problem-solving appraisal and psychological adjustment. In C. R. Snyder & S. J. Lopez (Eds.), *Handbook of positive psychology.* New York: Oxford University Press.

**Herman-Giddens, M. E.** (2006). Recent data on pubertal milestones in United States children: The secular trend toward earlier development. *International Journal of Andrology, 29,* 241–246.

**Herman-Giddens, M. E.** (2007). The decline in the age of menarche in the United States: Should we be concerned? *Journal of Adolescent Health, 40,* 201–203.

**Herman-Giddens, M. E., Kaplowitz, P. B., & Wasserman, R.** (2004). Navigating the recent articles on girls' puberty in *Pediatrics:* What do we know and where do we go from here? *Pediatrics, 113,* 911–917.

**Hernandez, D. J.** (2007). Changes in the demographics of families over the course of American history. In A. S. Skolnick & J. H. Skolnick (Eds.), *Family in transition* (14th ed.). Boston: Allyn & Bacon.

**Hernandez, D. J., Denton, N. A., & McCartney, S. E.** (2007). Family circumstances of children in immigrant families. In J. E. Lansford, K. Deater-Deckard, & M. H. Bornstein (eds.), *Immigrant families in contemporary society.* New York: Guilford.

**Hess, L., Lonky, E., & Roodin, P. A.** (1985, April). *The relationship of moral reasoning and ego strength to cheating behavior.* Paper presented at the meeting of the Society for Research in Child Development, Toronto.

**Hetherington, E. M.** (1972). Effects of father-absence on personality development in adolescent daughters. *Developmental Psychology, 7,* 313–326.

**Hetherington, E. M.** (1977). *My heart belongs to daddy: A study of the remarriages of daughters of divorces and widows.* Unpublished manuscript, University of Virginia.

**Hetherington, E. M.** (1989). Coping with family transitions: Winners, losers, and survivors. *Child Development, 60,* 1–14.

**Hetherington, E. M.** (1993). An overview of the Virginia Longitudinal Study of Divorce and Remarriage with a focus on early adolescence. *Journal of Family Psychology, 7,* 39–56.

**Hetherington, E. M.** (2005). Divorce and the adjustment of children. *Pediatrics in Review, 26,* 163–169.

**Hetherington, E. M.** (2006). The influence of conflict, marital problem solving, and parenting on children's adjustment in nondivorced, divorced, and remarried families. In A. Clarke-Stewart & J. Dunn (eds.), *Families count.* New York: Cambridge University Press.

**Hetherington, E. M., Bridges, M., & Insabella, G. M.** (1998). What matters? What does not? Five perspectives on the association between marital transitions and children's adjustment. *American Psychologist, 53,* 167–184.

**Hetherington, E. M., & Clingempeel, W. G.** (1992). Coping with marital transitions: A family systems perspective. *Monographs of the Society for Research in Child Development, 57* (2–3, Serial No. 227).

**Hetherington, E. M., Cox, M., & Cox, R.** (1982). Effects of divorce on parents and children. In M. E. Lamb (Ed.), *Nontraditional families: Parenting and child development.* Hillsdale, NJ: Erlbaum.

**Hetherington, E. M., Henderson, S. H., Reiss, D., & others.** (1999). Adolescent siblings in stepfamilies: Family functioning and adolescent adjustment. *Monographs of the Society for Research in Child Development, 64* (No. 4).

**Hetherington, E. M., & Kelly, J.** (2002). *For better or for worse: Divorce reconsidered.* New York: Norton.

**Hetherington, E. M., Reiss, D., & Plomin, R.** (Eds.). (1994). *Separate social worlds of siblings: The impact of nonshared environment on development.* Hillsdale, NJ: Erlbaum.

**Hetherington, E. M., & Stanley-Hagan, M.** (2002). Parenting in divorced and remarried families. In M. Bornstein (Ed.), *Handbook of parenting* (2nd ed.). Mahwah, NJ: Erlbaum.

**Heward, W. L.** (2006). *Exceptional children* (8th ed.). Upper Saddle River, NJ: Prentice Hall.

**Hibell, B., Andersson, B., Bjarnasson, T., & others** (2004), *The ESPAD report 2003: Alcohol and other drug use among students in 35 European countries.* The Swedish Council for Information on Alcohol and Other Drugs (CAN) and Council of Europe Pompidou Group.

**Higgins, A., Power, C., & Kohlberg, L.** (1983, April). *Moral atmosphere and moral judgment.* Paper presented at the biennial meeting of the Society for Research in Child Development, Detroit.

**Hilburn-Cobb, C.** (2004). Adolescent psychopathology in terms of multiple behavior systems. In L. Atkinson & S. Goldberg (Eds.), *Attachment issues in psychopathology and intervention.* Mahwah, NJ: Erlbaum.

**Hill, J. P., & Lynch, M. E.** (1983). The intensification of gender-related role expectations during early adolescence. In J. Brooks-Gunn & A. C. Petersen (Eds.), *Girls at puberty: Biological and psychological perspectives.* New York: Plenum.

**Hill, N. E., Bromell, L., Tyson, D. F., & Flint, R.** (2007). Developmental commentary: Ecological perspectives on parental influences during adolescence. *Journal of Clinical Child and Adolescent Psychology, 36,* 367–377.

**Hills, A. P., King, N. A., & Armstrong, T. P.** (2007). The contribution of physical activity and sedentary behaviors to the growth and development of children and adolescents: Implications for overweight and obesity. *Sports Medicine, 37,* 533–545.

**Himes, J. H.** (2006). Examining the evidence for secular changes in the timing of puberty in U.S. children in light of increases in the prevalence of obesity. *Molecular and Cellular Endocrinology, 254–255,* 13–21.

**Hingson, R. W., Heeren, T., & Winter, M. R.** (2006). Age at drinking onset and alcohol dependence: Age at onset, duration, and severity. *Archives of Pediatric and Adolescent Medicine, 160,* 739–746.

**Hirsch, B. J., & Rapkin, B. D.** (1987). The transition to junior high school: A longitudinal study of self-esteem, psychological symptomatology, school life, and social support. *Child Development, 58,* 1235–1243.

**Hirschhorn, J. N.** (2005). Genetic and genomic approaches to studying stature and pubertal timing. *Pediatric Endocrinology Review, 2* (Suppl. 3), 351–354.

**Hock, R. R.** (2007). *Human sexuality.* Upper Saddle River, NJ: Prentice Hall.

**Hoem, B.** (1995). Sweden. In. H. P. Blossfeld (Ed.), *The new role of women: Family formation in modern societies.* Boulder, CO: Westview Press.

**Hofer, A., Seidentopf, C. M., Ischebeck, A., Rettenbacher, M. A., Verius, M., Felber, S., & Fleischhacker, W.** (2006). Gender differences in regional cerebral activity during the perception of emotion: A functional MRI study. Neuroimage, 32, 854–862.

**Hoff, E., Laursen, B., & Tardif, T.** (2002). Socioeconomic status and parenting. In M. H. Bornstein (Ed.), *Handbook of parenting* (2nd ed.). Mahwah, NJ: Erlbaum.

**Hofferth, S. L.** (1990). Trends in adolescent sexual activity, contraception, and pregnancy in the United States. In J. Bancroft & J. M. Reinisch (Eds.), *Adolescence and puberty.* New York: Oxford University Press.

**Hoffman, M. L.** (1970). Moral development. In P. H. Mussen (Ed.), *Manual of child psychology* (3rd ed., Vol. 2). New York: Wiley.

**Hoffman, M. L.** (1988). Moral development. In M. H. Bornstein & E. Lamb (Eds.), *Developmental psychology: An advanced textbook* (2nd ed.). Hillsdale, NJ: Erlbaum.

**Holland, J. L.** (1973). *Making vocational choices: A theory of careers.* Englewood Cliffs, NJ: Prentice Hall.

**Holland, J. L.** (1987). Current status of Holland's theory of careers: Another perspective. *Career Development Quarterly, 36,* 24–30.

**Hollingworth, L. S.** (1914). *Functional periodicity: An experimental study of the mental and motor abilities of women during menstruation.* New York: Columbia University, Teachers College.

**Hollingworth, L. S.** (1916). Sex differences in mental tests. *Psychological Bulletin 13,* 377–383.

**Hollon, S. D.** (2006). Cognitive therapy in the treatment and prevention of depression. In T. E. Joiner, J. S. Brown, & J. Kistner (Eds.), *The interpersonal, cognitive, and social nature of depression* Mahwah, NJ: Erlbaum.

**Holmbeck, G. N.** (1996). A model of family relational transformations during the transition to adolescence: Parent-adolescent conflict and adaptation. In J. A. Graber, J. Brooks-Gunn, & A. C. Petersen (Eds.), *Transitions in adolescence.* Mahwah, NJ: Erlbaum.

**Holmbeck, G. N., Durbin, D., & Kung, E.** (1995, March). *Attachment, autonomy, and adjustment before and after leaving home: Sullivan and Sullivan revisited.* Paper presented at the meeting of the Society for Research in Child Development, Indianapolis.

**Holmes, L. D.** (1987). *Quest for the real Samoa: The Mead-Freeman controversy and beyond.* South Hadley, MA: Bergin & Garvey.

**Holtzmann, W.** (1982). Cross-cultural comparisons of personality development in Mexico and the United States. In D. Wagner & H. W. Stevenson (Eds.), *Cultural perspectives on child development.* San Francisco: W. H. Freeman.

**Hopkins, J. R.** (2000). Erikson, E. H. (2000). In A. Kazdin (Ed.), *Encyclopedia of psychology.* Washington, DC & New York: American Psychological Association and Oxford University Press.

**Hopkins, J. R.** (2000). Erikson, E. H. In A. Kazdin (Ed.), *Encyclopedia of psychology.* Washington, DC & New York: American Psychological Association and Oxford University Press.

**Horn, J.** (2007). Spearman, *g*, expertise, and the nature of human cognitive capacity. In P. C. Kyllonen, R. D. Roberts, & L. Stankov (Eds.), *Extending intelligence.* Mahwah, NJ: Erlbaum.

**Horn, L., & Nevill, S.** (2006). *Profile of undergraduates in U.S. postsecondary education institutions: 2003–04: With a special analysis of community college students* (NCES 2006-184). Washington, DC: U.S. Department of Education, National Center for Education Statistics.

**Horowitz, F. D., Darling-Hammond, L., Bransford, J., Comer, J., Rosebrock, K., Austin, K., & Rust, F.** (2005). Educating teachers for developmentally appropriate practice. In N. Darling-Hammond & J. Bransford (Eds.), *Preparing teachers in a changing world.* San Francisco: Jossey-Bass.

**Horton, D. M.** (2001). The disappearing bell curve. *Journal of Secondary Gifted Education, 12,* 185–188.

**Houston, P. D.** (2005, February). NCLB: Dreams and nightmares. *Phi Delta Kappan,* 469–470.

**Howard, R. W.** (2001). Searching the real world for signs of rising population intelligence. *Personality and Individual Differences, 30,* 1039–1058.

**Hrabosky, J. I., Masheb, R. M., White, M. A., & Grilo, C. M.** (2007). Overvaluation of shape and weight in binge eating disorder. *Journal of Consulting and Clinical Psychology, 75,* 175–180.

**Huang, C. Y., Sousa, V. D., Tu, S. Y., & Hwang, M. Y.** (2005). Depressive symptoms and learned resourcefulness among Taiwanese female adolescents. *Archives of Psychiatric Nursing, 19,* 133–140.

**Huang, L. N.** (1989). Southeast Asian refugee children and adolescents. In J. T. Gibbs & L. N. Huang (Eds.), *Children of color.* San Francisco: Jossey-Bass.

**Huang, L. N., and Ying, Y.** (1989). Chinese American children and adolescents. In J. T. Gibbs and L. N. Huang, (Eds.), *Children of color.* San Francisco: Jossey-Bass.

**Huebner, A. M., & Garrod, A. C.** (1993). Moral reasoning among Tibetan monks: A study of Buddhist adolescents and young adults in Nepal. *Journal of Cross-Cultural Psychology, 24,* 167–185.

**Huerta, M., Cortina, L. M., Pang, J. S., Torges, C. M., & Magley, V. J.** (2006). Sex and power in the academy: Modeling sexual harassment in the lives of college women. *Personality and Social Psychology Bulletin, 32,* 616–628.

**Huesmann, L. R.** (1986). Psychological processes promoting the relation between exposure to media violence and aggressive behavior by the viewer. *Journal of Social Issues, 42,* 125–139.

**Huesmann, L. R., Dubow, E. F., Eron, L. D., & Boxer, P.** (2006). Middle childhood family-contextual and personal factors as predictors of adult outcomes. In A. C. Huston & M. K. Ripke (Eds.), *Developmental contexts in middle childhood.* Mahwah, NJ: Erlbaum.

**Huesmann, L. R., Moise-Titus, J., Podolski, C., & Eron, L. D.** (2003). Longitudinal relations between children's exposure to TV violence and their aggressive and violent behavior in young adulthood: 1977–1992. *Developmental Psychology, 39,* 201–221.

**Hughes, I. A., & Kumanan, M.** (2006). A wider perspective on puberty. *Molecular and Cellular Endocrinology, 254–255,* 1–7.

**Hulton, L. J.** (2007). An evaluation of a school-based teenage pregnancy prevention program using a logic model framework. *Journal of School Nursing, 23,* 104–110.

**Huston, A. C., Epps, S. R., Shim, M. K, Duncan, G. J., Crosby, D. A., & Ripke, M. N.** (2006). Effects of a family poverty intervention program last from middle childhood to adolescence. In A. C. Huston & M. N. Ripke (Eds.), *Developmental contexts in middle childhood.* Mahwah, NJ: Erlbaum.

**Huston, A. C., & Ripke, M. N.** (2006). Experiences in middle childhood and children's development: A summary and integration of research.

In A. C. Huston & M. N. Ripke (Eds.), *Developmental contexts in middle childhood.* New York: Cambridge University Press.

**Huston, A. C., Siegle, J., & Bremer, M.** (1983, April). *Family environment television use by preschool children.* Paper presented at the biennial meeting of the Society for Reserch in Child Development, Detroit.

**Hutchinson, D. M., & Rapee, R. M.** (2007, in press). Do friends share similar body image and eating problems? The role of social networks and peer influences in early adolescence. *Behavior Research and Therapy.*

**Huttenlocher, J., Haight, W., Bruk, A., Seltzer, M., & Lyons, T.** (1991). Early vocabulary growth: Relation to language input and gender. *Developmental Psychology, 27,* 236–248.

**Huttenlocher, P. R., & Dabholkar, A. S.** (1997). Regional differences in synaptogenesis in human cerebral cortex. *Journal of Comparative Neurology, 37* (2), 167–178.

**Hyde, J. S.** (1993). Meta-analysis and the psychology of women. In F. L. Denmark & M. A. Paludi (Eds.), *Handbook on the psychology of women.* Westport, CT: Greenwood.

**Hyde, J. S.** (2005). The gender similarities hypothesis. *American Psychologist, 60* (6), 581–592.

**Hyde, J. S.** (2007). *Half the human experience* (7th ed.). Boston: Houghton Mifflin.

**Hyde, J. S., & DeLamater, J. D.** (2006). *Understanding human sexuality* (9th ed.). New York: McGraw-Hill.

**Hyman, I., Kay, B., Tabori, A., Weber, M., Mahon, M., & Cohen, I.** (2006). Bullying: Theory, research, and interventions. In C. M. Evertson & C. S. Weinstein (Eds.), *Handbook of classroom management.* Mahwah, NJ: Erlbaum.

**Hymel, S., McDougall, P., & Renshaw, P.** (2002). Peer acceptance/rejection. In P. K. Smith & C. H. Hart (Eds.), *Blackwell handbook of childhood social development.* Malden, MA: Blackwell.

**Hyson, M., Copple, C., & Jones, J.** (2006). Early childhood development and education. In W. Damon & R. Lerner (Eds.), *Handbook of child psychology* (6th ed.). New York: Wiley.

## I

**"I Have a Dream" Foundation.** (2006). *About us.* Retrieved November 16, 2006, www.ihad.org

**Ianni, F. A. J., & Orr, M. T.** (1996). Dropping out. In J. A. Graber, J. Brooks-Gunn, & A. C. Petersen (Eds.), *Transitions in adolescence.* Mahwah, NJ: Erlbaum.

**Ibanez, L., & de Zegher, F.** (2006). Puberty after prenatal growth restraint. *Hormone Research, 65* (Suppl. 3), 112–115.

**Indiana University High School Survey of Student Engagement.** (2004). Bloomington, IN: School of Education, University of Indiana.

**Insel, P. M., & Roth, W. T.** (2006). *Core concepts in health* (10th ed.). New York: McGraw-Hill.

**Insel, P. M., & Roth, W. T.** (2008). *Core concepts in health update* (10th ed.). New York: McGraw-Hill.

**International Society for Technology in Education.** (2000). *National educational technology standards for students: Connecting curriculum and technology.* Eugene, OR: Author.

**International Society for Technology in Education.** (2001). *National educational technology standards for teachers—preparing teachers to use technology.* Eugene, OR: Author.

**Irwin, C. E.** (1993). The adolescent, health, and society: From the perspective of the physician. In S. G. Millstein, A. C. Petersen, & E. O. Nightingale (Eds.), *Promoting the health of adolescents.* New York: Oxford University Press.

**Irwin, C. E.** (2004). Eating and physical activity during adolescence: Does it make a difference in adult health status? *Journal of Adolescent Health, 34,* 459–460.

**ISTE.** (2007). *National educational technology standards for students* (2nd ed.). Eugene, OR: Author.

## J

**Jackson, A., & Davis, G.** (2000). *Turning points 2000.* New York: Teachers College Press.

**Jackson, L. A., Eye, A., Biocca, F. A., Barbatsis, G., Zhao, G., & Fitzgerald, H. E.** (2006). Does home Internet use influence the academic performance of low-income children? *Developmental Psychology, 42,* 429–435.

**Jackson, M. S., Bass, L., & Sharpe, E. G.** (2005). Working with youth street gangs and their families: Utilizing a nurturing model for social work practice. *Journal of Gang Research, 12,* 1–18.

**Jackson, N., & Butterfield, E.** (1996). A conception of giftedness designed to promote research. In R. J. Steinberg & J. E. Davidson (Eds.), *Conceptions of giftedness.* New York: Cambridge University Press.

**Jackson, S. L.** (2008). *Research methods.* Belmont, CA: Wadsworth.

**Jacobs, J. E., & Klaczynski, P.** (Eds.) (2005). *The development of judgment and decision making in children and adolescents.* Mahwah, NJ: Erlbaum.

**Jacobs, J. E., & Potenza, M.** (1990, March). *The use of decision-making strategies in late adolescence.* Paper presented at the meeting of the Society for Research in Adolescence, Atlanta.

**Jacobson, K. C., & Crockett, L. J.** (2000). Parental monitoring and adolescent adjustment: An ecological perspective. *Journal of Research on Adolescence, 10,* 65–97.

**Jaffe, S., & Hyde, J. S.** (2000). Gender differences in moral orientation: A meta-analysis. *Psychological Bulletin, 126,* 703–726.

**James, J., Thomas, P., Cavan, D., & Kerr, D.** (2004). Preventing childhood obesity by reducing consumption of carbonated drinks: Cluster randomized trial. *British Medical Journal, 328,* 1237.

**Jamner, M. S., Spruit-Meitz, D., Bassin, S., & Cooper, D. M.** (2004). A controlled evaluation of a school-based intervention to promote physical activity among sedentary adolescent females: Project FAB. *Journal of Adolescent Health 34,* 279–289.

**Jang, K. L.** (2005). *Genetics of psychopathology.* Mahwah, NJ: Erlbaum.

**Janisse, H. C., Nedd, D., Escamilla, S., & Nies, M. A.** (2004). Physical activity, social support, and family structure as determinants of mood among European-American and African-American women. *Women and Health, 39,* 101–116.

**Janssen, I., Katzmarzyk, P. T., Boyce, W. F., Vereecken, C., Mulvihill, C., Roberts, C., Currie, C., & Pickett.** (2005). Comparison of overweight and obesity prevalence in school-aged youth from 34 countries and their relationships with physical activity and dietary patterns. *Obesity Research, 6,* 123–132.

**Janz, N. K., Zimmerman, M. A., Wren, P. A., Israel, B. A., Freudenberg, N., & Carter, R. J.** (1996). Evaluation of 37 AIDS prevention projects: Successful approaches and barriers to program effectiveness. *Health Education Quarterly, 23,* 80–97.

**Jarrett, R. L.** (1995). Growing up poor: The family experiences of socially mobile youth in low-income African-American neighborhoods. *Journal of Adolescent Research, 10,* 111–135.

**Jayson, S.** (2006, June 29). The "millennials" come of age. *USA Today,* pp. 1–2D.

**Jekielek, S., & Brown, B.** (2005). *The transition to adulthood: Characteristics of young adult ages 18 to 24 in America.* Washington, DC: Child Trends and the Annie E. Casey Foundation.

**Jenkins, A. M., Albee, G. W., Paster, V. S., Sue, S., Baker, D. B., Comas-Diaz, L., Puente, A., Suinn, R. M., Caldwell-Colbert, A. T., Williams, V. M., & Root, M. P. P.** (2003). Ethnic minorities. In I. B. Weiner (Ed.), *Handbook of psychology.* New York: Wiley.

**Jenson, J. M., Anthony, E. K., & Howard, M. O.** (2005). Policies and programs for adolescent substance abuse. In J. M. Jenson & M. W. Fraser (Eds.), *Social policy for children and families.* Thousand Oaks, CA: Sage.

**Jenson-Campbell, L. A., & Malcolm, K. T.** (2007). The importance of conscientiousness in adolescent interpersonal relationships. *Personality and Social Psychology Bulletin, 33,* 368–373.

**Jessor, R.** (Ed.). (1998). *New perspectives on adolescent risk behavior.* Cambridge: Cambridge University Press.

**Jeynes, W. H.** (2003). A meta-analysis: The effects of parental involvement on minority children's academic achievement. *Education and Urban Society, 35,* 202–218.

**Jhally, S.** (1990). *Dreamworlds: Desire/sex/power in rock video* (Video). Amherst: University of Massachusetts at Amherst, Department of Communications.

**Jiang, X. L., & Cillessen, A. H. N.** (2005). Stability of continuous measures of sociometric status: A meta-analysis. *Developmental Review, 25,* 1–25.

**Jodl, K. M., Michael, A., Malanchuk, O., Eccles, J. S., & Sameroff, A.** (2001). Parents' roles in shaping early adolescents' occupational aspirations. *Child Development, 72,* 1247–1265.

**John, O. P., Caspi, A., Robins, R. W., Moffitt, T. E., & Stouthamer-Loeber, M.** (1994). The "little five": Exploring the nomological network of the five-factor model of personality in adolescent boys. *Child Development, 65,* 160–178.

**Johnson, G. B.** (2008). *The living world* (5th ed.). New York: McGraw-Hill.

**Johnson, J. G., Cohen, P., Kotler, L., Kasen, S., & Brook, J.** (2002). Psychiatric disorders associated with risk for development of eating disorders in during adolescence and early adulthood. *Journal of Consulting and Clinical Psychology, 70,* 1119–1128.

**Johnson, J. G., Cohen, P., Pine, D. S., Klein, D. F., Kasen, S., & Brook, J. S.** (2000). Association between cigarette smoking and anxiety disorders during adolescence and adulthood. *Journal of the American Medical Association, 284,* 348–351.

**Johnson, M. K., Beebe, T., Mortimer, J. T., & Snyder, M.** (1998). Volunteerism in adolescence: A process perspective. *Journal of Research on Adolescence, 8,* 309–332.

**Johnson, V. K.** (2002). *Managing the transition to college: The role of families' and adolescents' coping strategies.* Paper presented at the meeting of the Society for Research on Adolescence, New Orleans.

**Johnston, B. T., Carey, M. P., Marsh, K. L., Levin, K. D., & Scott-Sheldon, L. A.** (2003). Intervention to reduce sexual risk for the human immunodeficiency virus in adolescents, 1985–2000: A research synthesis. *Archives of Pediatric and Adolescent Medicine, 157,* 381–388.

**Johnston, L. D., O'Malley, P. M., & Bachman, J. G.** (1999, December 17). *Drug trends in the United States are mixed.* (Press Release). Ann Arbor, MI: Institute of Social Research, University of Michigan.

**Johnston, L. D., O'Malley, P. M., Bachman, J. G.** (2004). *Monitoring the Future national survey results on drug use, 1975–2003: Volume II, College students and adults ages 19–45* (NIH Publication No. 04-5508). Bethesda, MD: National Institute on Drug Abuse.

**Johnston, L. D., O'Malley, P. M., Bachman, J. G., & Schulenberg, J. E.** (2005). *Monitoring the Future national results on adolescent drug use: Overview of key findings, 2004* (NIH Publication No. 05–5726). Bethesda, MD: National Institute on Drug Abuse.

**Johnston, L. D., O'Malley, P. M., Bachman, J. G., & Schulenberg, J. E.** (2006). *Monitoring the Future national survey results on drug use, 1975–2005. Volume II: College students and adults ages 19–45* (NIH Publication No. 06–5884). Bethesda, MD: National Institute on Drug Abuse.

**Johnston, L. D., O'Malley, P. M., Bachman, J. G., & Schulenberg, J. E.** (2007). *Monitoring the Future national results on adolescent drug use: Overview of key findings, 2006.* Bethesda, MD: National Institute on Drug Abuse.

**Jonassen, D. H., Howland, J., Marra, R. M., & Crismond, D.** (2008). *Meaningful learning with technology* (3rd ed.). Upper Saddle River, NJ: Prentice Hall.

**Jones, B. F., Rasmussen, C. M., & Moffit, M. C.** (1997). *Real-life problem solving,* Washington, DC: American Psychological Association.

**Jones, C. L.** (2006). Fatherhood training: The Concordia Project. In M. E. Connor & J. L. White (Eds.), *Black fathers.* Mahwah, NJ: Erlbaum.

**Jones, J. M.** (1994). The African American: A duality dilemma? In W. J. Lonner & R. Malpass (Eds.), *Psychology and culture.* Needham Heights, MA: Allyn & Bacon.

**Jones, J. M.** (2005, October 7). *Gallup Poll: Most Americans approve of interracial dating.* Princeton, NJ: Gallup.

**Jones, M. C.** (1965). Psychological correlates of somatic development. *Child Development, 36,* 899–911.

*Journal, 191,* 52–54.

**Joyce, T., Kaestner, R., & Colman, S.** (2006). Changes in abortion and births and the Texas parental notification law. *New England Journal of Medicine, 354,* 1031–1038.

**Judge, B., & Billick, S. B.** (2004). Suicidality in adolescence: Review and legal considerations. *Behavioral Science and the Law, 22,* 627.

**Judge, S.** (2005, April). *Impact of computer technology on the academic achievements of young African American children.* Paper presented at the meeting of the Society for Research in Child Development, Atlanta.

**Jussim, L., & Eccles, J. S.** (1993). Teacher expectations II: Construction and reflection of student achievement. *Journal of Personality and Social Psychology, 63,* 947–961.

## K

**Kafai, Y. B.** (2006). Constructivism. In R. K. Sawyer (Ed.), *The Cambridge handbook of the learning sciences.* New York: Cambridge University Press.

**Kagan, J.** (1992). Yesterday's premises, tomorrow's promises. *Developmental Psychology, 28,* 990–997.

**Kagan, J.** (2000). Temperament. In A. Kazdin (Ed.), *Encyclopedia of psychology.* Washington, DC & New York: American Psychological Association and Oxford University Press.

**Kagan, J.** (2002). Behavioral inhibition as a temperamental category. In R. J. Davidson, K. R. Scherer, & H. H. Goldsmith (Eds.), *Handbook of affective sciences.* New York: Oxford University Press.

**Kagan, J.** (2004, May 8). Commentary in teen brains on trial, *Science News Online,* p. 2.

**Kagan, J., & Fox, N. A.** (2006). Biology, culture, and temperamental biases. In W. Damon & R. Lerner (Eds.), *Handbook of child psychology* (6th ed.). New York: Wiley.

**Kagan, J., & Snidman, N.** (1991). Infant predictors of inhibited and uninhibited behavioral profiles. *Psychological Science, 2,* 40–44.

**Kagan, S., & Madsen, M. C.** (1972). Experimental analysis of cooperation and competition of Anglo-American and Mexican children. *Developmental Psychology, 6,* 49–59.

**Kagitcibasi, C.** (2006). An overview of acculturation and parent-child relationships. In M. H. Bornstein & L. R. Cote (Eds.), *Acculturation and parent-child relationships.* Mahwah, NJ: Erlbaum.

**Kagitcibasi, C.** (2007). *Family, self, and human development across cultures.* Mahwah, NJ: Erlbaum.

**Kail, R.** (1988). Reply to Stigler, Nusbaum, and Chalip. *Child Development, 59,* 1154–1157.

**Kail, R.** (2000). Speed of information processing: Developmental change and links to intelligence. *Journal of School Psychology, 38,* 51–62.

**Kail, R. V., & Miller, C. A.** (2006). Developmental change in processing speed: Domain specificity and stability during childhood and adolescence. *Journal of Cognition and Development, 7,* 119–137.

**Kaiser Family Foundation.** (1996). *Kaiser Family Foundation survey of 1,500 teenagers ages 12–18.* San Francisco: Kaiser Foundation.

**Kaiser Family Foundation.** (2002). *Teens say sex on TV influences behavior of peers.* Menlo Park, CA: Henry J. Kaiser Family Foundation.

**Kaiser Family Foundation.** (2005). *Sex on TV4.* San Francisco: Author.

**Kaizar, E. E., Greenhouse, J. B., Seltman, H., & Kelleher, K.** (2006). Do antidepressants cause suicidality in children? A Bayesian meta-analysis. *Clinical Trials, 3,* 73–98.

**Kandel, D. B., & Wu, P.** (1995). The contributions of mothers and fathers to the intergenerational transmission of cigarette smoking. *Journal of Research on Adolescence, 5,* 225–252.

**Kanner, A. D., Coyne, J. C., Schaeter, C., & Lazarus, R. S.** (1981). Comparisons of two modes of stress measurement: Daily hassles and uplifts versus major life events. *Journal of Behavioral Medicine, 4,* 1–39.

**Kaplan, M. J., Middleton, T., Urdan, C., & Midgley, C.** (2002). Achievement goals and goal structures. In C. Midgley (Ed.), *Goals, goal structures, and patterns of adaptive learning.* Mahwah, NJ: Erlbaum.

**Kaplow, J. B., Curran, P. J., Dodge, K. A., & The Conduct Problems Prevention Research Group.** (2002). Child, parent, and peer predictors of early-onset substance use: A multisite longitudinal study. *Journal of Abnormal Child Psychology, 30,* 199–226.

**Karcher, M. J.** (2005). Cross-age peer mentoring. In D. L. Dubois & M. J. Karcher (Eds.), *Handbook of youth mentoring.* Thousand Oaks, CA: Sage.

**Karcher, M. J., Nakkula, M. J., & Harris, J.** (2005). Developmental mentoring match characteristics: Correspondence between mentors' and mentees' assessments of relationship quality. *Journal of Primary Prevention, 26,* 93–110.

**Karcher, M. J., Roy-Carlson, L., Allen, C., & Gil-Hernandez, D.** (2005). Mentoring. In S. W. Lee (Ed.), *Encyclopedia of school psychology.* Thousand Oaks, CA: Sage.

**Karnick, P. M.** (2005). Feeling lonely: Theoretical perspectives. *Nursing Science Quarterly, 18,* 7–12.

**Karniol, R., Gabay, R., Ochion, Y., & Harari, Y.** (1998). Is gender or gender-role orientation a better predictor of empathy in adolescence? *Sex Roles, 39,* 45–59.

**Kato, T.** (2005). The relationship between coping with stress due to romantic break-ups and mental health. *Japanese Journal of Social Psychology, 20,* 171–180.

**Kauffman, J. M., & Hallahan, D. P.** (2005). *Special education.* Boston: Allyn & Bacon.

**Kauffman, J. M., McGee, K. J., & Brigham, M.** (2004). Enabling or disabling? Observations on changes in special education. *Phi Delta Kappan, 85,* 613–620.

**Kauffman, J. M., Mostert, M. P., Trent, S. C., & Pullen, P. L.** (2006). *Managing classroom behavior* (4th ed.). Boston: Allyn & Bacon.

**Kaufman, J. C., Sternberg, R. J.** (Eds.). (2006). *International handbook of creativity.* New York: Cambridge University Press.

**Kavale, K. A., Holdnack, J. A., & Mostert, M. P.** (2005). Responsivenes to intervention and the identification of specific learning disability: A critique and alternative proposal. *Learning Disability Quarterly, 28,* 2–16.

**Keating, D. P.** (1990). Adolescent thinking. In S. S. Feldman & G. R. Elliott (Eds.), *At the threshold: The developing adolescent.* Cambridge, MA: Harvard University Press.

**Keating, D. P.** (2004). Cognitive and brain development. In R. Lerner & L. Steinberg (Eds.), *Handbook of adolescence* (2nd ed.). New York: Wiley.

**Keating, D. P.** (2007). Understanding adolescent development: Implications for driving safety. *Journal of Safety Research, 38,* 147–157.

**Keel, P. K., Mitchell, J. E., Miller, K. B., Davis, T. L., & Crowe, S. J.** (1999). Long-term outcome of bulimia nervosa. *Archives of Genernal Psychiatry 56,* 63–69.

**Keil, F.** (2006). Cognitive science and cognitive development. In W. Damon & R. Lerner (Eds.), *Handbook of child psychology* (6th ed.). New York: Wiley.

**Kelesidis, T., & Mantzoros, C. S.** (2006). The emerging role of leptin in humans. *Pediatric Endocrinology Review, 3,* 239–248.

**Kellogg, R. T.** (1994). *The psychology of writing.* New York: Oxford University Press.

**Kelly, J.** (2000). Sexually transmitted diseases. In A. Kazdin (Ed.), *Encyclopedia of psychology.* Washington, DC & New York: American Psychological Association and Oxford University Press.

**Kelly, J. B.** (2007). Children's living arrangements following separation and divorce: Insights from empirical and clinical research. *Family Process, 46,* 35–52.

**Kelly, J. B., & Lamb, M. E.** (2003). Developmental issues in relocation cases involving young children: When, whether, and how? *Journal of Family Psychology, 17,* 193–205.

**Kenney, A. M.** (1987, June). Teen pregnancy: An issue for schools. *Phi Delta Kappan,* pp. 728–736.

**Kenney, C. T., & McLanahan, S. S.** (2006). Why are cohabiting relationships more violent than marriages? *Demography, 43,* 127–140.

**Kenney-Benson, G. A., Pomerantz, E. M., Ryan, A. M., & Patrick, H. (**2006). Sex differences in math performance: The role of children's approach to schoolwork. *Developmental Psychology, 42,* 11–26.

**Kessler, R. C., & Walters, E. E.** (1998). Epidemiology of *DSM-III-R* major major depression and minor depression among adolescents and young adults in the National Comorbidity Survey. *Depression and Anxiety, 7,* 3–14.

**Kiang, L., & Harter, S.** (2004). Sociolcultural values or appearance and attachment processes: An integrated model of eating disorder symptomatology. University of Denver. Unpublished manuscript, Department of Psychology.

**Kiang, L., Yip, T., Gonzales-Backen, M., Witkow, M., & Fuligni, A. J.** (2006). Ethnic identity and the daily psychological well-being of adolescents from Mexican and Chinese bakgrounds. *Child Development, 77,* 1338–1350.

**Kiete, M.** (2001). Gender stereotypes. In J. Worell (Ed.), *Encyclopedia of women and gender.* San Diego: Academic Press.

**Kim, J.-Y., McHale, S. M., Crouter, A. C., & Osgood, D. W.** (2007). Longitudinal linkages between sibling relationships and adjustment from middle childhood through adolescence. *Developmental Psychology, 43,* 960–973.

**Kimm, S. Y., Barton, B. A., Obarzanek, E., McMahon, R. P., Kronsberg, S. S., Waclawiw, M. A., Morrison. J. A., Schreiber, G. G., Sabry, Z. I., & Daniels, S. R.** (2002). Obesity development during adolescence in a biracial cohort: The NHLBI Growth and Health Study. *Pediatrics,* 110, e54.

**Kimm, S. Y., & Obarzanek, E.** (2002). Childhood obesity: A new pandemic of the new millennium. *Pediatrics, 110,* 1003–1007.

**Kimura, D.** (2000). *Sex and cognition.* Cambridge, MA: MIT Press.

**Kindlundh, A. M. S., Isacson, D. G. L., Berlund, L., & Nyberg, F.** (1999). Factors associated with adolescence use of doping agents: Anabolic androgenic steroids. *Addiction, 94,* 543–553.

**King, P. E., & Benson, P. L.** (2006). Spiritual development and adolescent well-being and thriving. In E. C. Roehlkepartain, P. E. King, L. Wagner, & P. L. Benson (Eds.), *Handbook of spiritual development in childhood and adolescence.* Thousand Oaks, CA: Sage.

**Kinney, J.** (2006). *Loosening the grip: A handbook of alcohol information* (8th ed.). New York: McGraw-Hill.

**Kirby, D. B., Laris, B. A., & Rolleri, L. A.** (2007). Sex and HIV education programs: Their impact on sexual behavior of young people throughout the world. *Journal of Adolescent Health, 40,* 206–217.

**Kirby, D., Resnick, M. D., Downes, B., Kocher, T., Gunderson, P., Pothoff, S., Zelterman, D., & Blum, R. W.** (1993). The effects of school-based health clinics in St. Paul on school-wide birthrates. *Family Planning Perspectives, 25,* 12–16.

**Kirchmeyer, C.** (2006). The different effects of family on objective career success across gender: A test of alternative explanations. *Journal of Vocational Behavior, 68,* 323–346.

**Kirkman, M., Rosenthal, D. A., & Feldman, S. S.** (2002). Talking to a tiger: Fathers reveal their difficulties in communicating sexually with adolescents. In S. S. Feldman & D. A. Rosenthal (Eds.), *Talking sexually: Parent-adolescent communication.* San Francisco: Jossey-Bass.

**Kirsch, G., McVey, G., Tweed, S., & Katzman, D. K.** (2007). Psychosocial profiles of young adolescent females seeking treatment for an eating disorder. *Journal of Adolescent Health, 40,* 351–356.

**Kitayama, S., & Cohen, D.** (Eds.), (2007). *Handbook of cultural psychology.* New York: Guilford.

**Kitchener, K. S., & King, P. M.** (1981). Reflective judgment: Concepts of justification and their relationship to age and education. *Journal of Applied Developmental Psychology, 2,* 89–111.

**Kitchener, K. S., King, P. M., & DeLuca, S.** (2006). The development of reflective judgment in adulthood. In C. Hoare (Ed.), *Handbook of adult development and learning.* New York: Oxford University Press.

**Klaczynski, P.** (2005). Metacognition and cognitive varibility: A two-process model of decision making and its development. In J. Jacobs & P. Klaczynski (Eds.), *The development of decision making: Cognitive, sociocultural, and legal perspectives.* Mahwah, NJ: Erlbaum.

**Klaczynski, P. A., Byrnes, J. P., & Jacobs, J. E.** (2001). Introduction to the special issue: The development of decision making. *Applied Developmental Psychology, 22,* 225–236.

**Klaczynski, P. A., & Narashimham, G.** (1998). Development of scientific reasoning biases: Cognitive versus ego-protective explanations. *Developmental Psychology, 34,* 175–187.

**Klaw, E., & Saunders, N.** (1994). *An ecological model of career planning in pregnant African American teens.* Paper presented at the biennial meeting of the Society for Research on Adolescence, San Diego.

**Kling, K. C., Hyde, J. S., Showers, C., & Buswell, B.** (1999). Gender differences in self-esteem: A meta-analysis. *Psychological Bulletin, 125,* 470–500.

**Knox, D., & Wilson, K.** (1981). Dating behaviors of university students. *Family Relations, 30,* 255–258.

**Knox, K. S., & Roberts, A. R.** (2005). Crisis intervention and crisis team models in schools. *Children and Schools, 27,* 93–100.

**Koch, J. R., Roberts, A. E., Armstrong, M. R., Owen, D. C.** (2005). College students, tattoos, and sexual activity. *Psychological Reports, 97,* 887–890.

**Kohlberg, L.** (1958). *The development of modes of moral thinking and choice in the years 10 to 16.* Unpublished doctoral dissertation, University of Chicago.

**Kohlberg, L.** (1966). A cognitive-developmental analysis of children's sex-role concepts and attitudes. In E. E. Maccoby (Ed.), *The development of sex differences.* Palo Alto, CA: Stanford University Press.

**Kohlberg, L.** (1969). Stage and sequence: The cognitive-developmental approach to socialization. In D. A. Goslin (Ed.), *Handbook of socialization theory and research.* Chicago: Rand McNally.

**Kohlberg, L.** (1976). Moral stages and moralization: The cognitive-developmental approach. In T. Lickona (Ed.), *Moral development and behavior.* New York: Holt, Rinehart & Winston.

**Kohlberg, L.** (1986). A current statement on some theoretical issues. In S. Modgil & C. Modgil (Eds.), *Lawrence Kohlberg.* Philadelphia: Falmer.

**Kohlberg, L., & Candee, D.** (1979). *Relationships between moral judgment and moral action.* Unpublished manuscript, Harvard University.

**Kohn, M. L.** (1977). *Class and conformity: A study in values* (2nd ed.). Chicago: University of Chicago Press.

**Kolb, B., & Gibb, R.** (2007). Brain plasticity and recovery from early cortical injury. *Developmental Psychobiology, 49,* 107–118.

**Koppelman, K., & Goodhart, L.** (2008). *Understanding human differences* (2nd ed.). Boston: Allyn & Bacon.

**Kornblum, J.** (2006, March 9). How to monitor the kids? *USA Today, 1D,* p.1.

**Kottak, C. P.** (2002). *Cultural anthropology* (9th ed.). New York: McGraw-Hill.

**Kottak, C. P., & Kozaitis, K. A.** (2008). *On being different: Diversity and multiculturalism in the United States* (3rd ed.). New York: McGraw-Hill.

**Kozol, J.** (1991). *Savage inequalities.* New York: Crown.

**Kozol, J.** (2005). *The shame of the nation.* New York: Crown.

**Krahn, D. D., Kurth, C. L., Gomberg, E., & Drewnowski, A.** (2005). Pathological dieting and alcohol use in college women—a continuum of behaviors. *Eating Behavior, 6,* 43–52.

**Kralovec, E.** (2003). *Schools that do too much.* Boston: Beacon Press.

**Kramer, D., Kahlbaugh, P. E., & Goldston, R. B.** (1992). A measure of paradigm beliefs about the social world. *Journal of Gerontology: Psychological Sciences, 47,* P180–P189.

**Kroger, J.** (2005). Erikson on development in adulthood: New insights from the unpublished papers. *Identity: An International Journal of Theory and Research, 5,* 91–94.

**Kroger, J.** (2007). Identity development: Adolescence Through adulthood (2nd ed.). Thousand Oaks, CA: Sage.

**Kroneman, L., Loeber, R., & Hipwell, A. E.** (2004). Is neighborhood context differently related to externalizing problems and delinquency for girls compared with boys? *Clinical Child and Family Psychology Review, 7,* 109–122.

**Kruglanski, A. W., & Higgins, E. T.** (Eds.). *Social psychology* (2nd ed.). New York: Guilford.

**Ksir, C. J., Hart, C. L., & Ray, O. S.** (2006). *Drugs, society, and human behavior* (11th ed.). New York: McGraw-Hill.

**Kuczynski, L., & Parkin, C. M.** (2007). Agency and bidirectionality in socialization. In J. E. Grusec & P. D. Hastings (Eds.), *Handbook of socialization.* New York: Guilford.

**Kuhn, D., Katz, J., & Dean, D.** (2004). Developing reason. *Thinking and Reasoning, 10* (2), 197–219.

**Kuhn, D., & Franklin, S.** (2006). The second decade: What develops (and how)? In W. Damon & R. Lerner (Eds.), *Handbook of child psychology* (6th ed.). New York: Wiley.

**Kulig, J. W., Mandel, L., Ruthazer, R., & Stone, D.** (2001, March). *School-based substance use prevention for female students.* Paper presented at the meeting of the Society for Adolescent Medicine, San Diego.

**Kumpfer, K. L., & Alvarado, R.** (2003). Family-strengthening approaches for the prevention of youth problem behaviors. *American Psychologist, 58,* 457–465.

**Kuntsche, E., Knibbe, R., Gmel, G., & Engels, R.** (2006). Who drinks and why? A review of socio-demographic, personality, and contextual issues behind drinking motives in young people. *Addictive Behaviors, 31,* 1844–1857.

**Kupersmidt, J. B., & Coie, J. D.** (1990). Preadolescent peer status, aggression, and school adjustmentas predictors of externalizing problems in adolescence. *Child Development, 61,* 1350–1363.

**Kurdek, L. A.** (1997). Adjustment to relationship dissolution in gay, lesbian, and heterosexual partners. *Personal Relationships, 4,* 145–161.

**Kurdek, L. A.** (2006). Differences between partners from heterosexual, gay, and lesbian cohabiting couples. *Journal of Marriage and the Family, 68,* 509–528.

**Kurdek, L. A.** (2007). The allocation of household labor between partners in gay and lesbian couples. *Journal of Family Issues, 28,* 132–148.

**Kurdek, L. A., & Krile, D.** (1982). A developmental analysis of the relation between peer acceptance and both interpersonal understanding and perceived social self-competence. *Child Development, 53,* 1485–1491.


## L


**La Greca, A. M., & Harrison, H. M.** (2005). Adolescent peer relations, friendships, and romantic relationships: Do they predict social anxiety and depression? *Journal of Clinical Child and Adolescent Psychology, 34,* 49–61.

**Labouvie-Vief, G.** (1986, August). *Modes of knowing and life-span cognition.* Paper presented at the meeting of the American Psychological Association, Washington, DC.

**Labouvie-Vief, G.** (2006). Emerging structures of adult thought. In J. J. Arnett & J. L. Tanner (Eds.), *Emerging adults in America.* Washington, DC: American Psychological Association.

**Ladd, G. W.** (2005). *Peer relationships and social competence of children and adolescents.* New Haven, CT: Yale University Press.

**Ladd, G. W., Buhs, E., & Troop, W.** (2004). School adjustment and social skills training. In P. K. Smith & C. H. Hart (Eds.), *Blackwell handbook of childhood social development.* Malden, MA: Blackwell.

**LaFromboise, T., Coleman, H. L. K., & Gerton, J.** (1993). Psychological impact of biculturalism: Evidence and theory. *Psychological Bulletin, 114,* 393–412.

**Laible, D., & Thompson, R. A.** (2007). Early socialization: A relationship perspective. In J. E. Grusec & P. D. Hastings (Eds.), *Handbook of socialization.* New York: Guilford.

**Laird, R. D., Pettit, G. S., Bates, J. E., & Dodge, K. A.** (2003). Parents' monitoring-relevant knowledge and adolescents' delinquent behavior: Evidence of correlated developmental changes and reciprocal influences. *Child Development, 74,* 752–768.

**Laird, R. D., Pettit, G. S., Dodge, K. A., & Bates, J. E.** (2005). Peer relationship antecedents of delinquent behavior in late adolescence: Is there evidence of demographic group differences in developmental processes? *Developmental Psychopathology, 17,* 127–144.

**Lalonde, C., & Chandler, M.** (2004). Culture, selves, and time. In C. Lightfoot, C. Lalonde, & M. Chandler (Eds.), *Changing conceptions of psychological life.* Mahwah, NJ: Erlbaum.

**Landry, D. J., Singh, S., & Darroch, J. E.** (2000). Sexuality education in fifth and sixth grades in U.S. public schools, 1999. *Family Planning Perspectives, 32,* 212–219.

**Lansford, J. E., Malone, P. S., Castellino, D. R., Dodge, K. A., Pettit, G. S., & Bates, J. E.** (2006). Trajectories of internalizing, externalizing, and grades for children who have and have not experienced their parents' divorce or separation. *Journal of Family Psychology, 20,* 292–301.

**Lapierre, C.** (2005). Goal-attainment scaling. In S. W. Lee (Ed.), *Encyclopedia of school psychology.* Thousand Oaks, CA: Sage.

**Lapsley, D. K.** (1990). Continuity and discontinuity in adolescent social cognitive development. In R. Montemayor, G. Adams, & T. Gulotta (Eds.), *From childhood to adolescence: A transitional period?* Newbury Park, CA: Sage.

**Lapsley, D. K.** (1996). *Moral psychology.* Boulder, CO: Westview Press.

**Lapsley, D. K.** (2005). Moral stage theory. In M. Killen & J. Smetana (Eds.), *Handbook of moral development.* Mahwah, NJ: Erlbaum.

**Lapsley, D. K., Enright, R. D., & Serlin, R. C.** (1985). Toward a theoretical perspective on the legislation of adolescence. *Journal of Early Adolescence, 5,* 441–466.

**Lapsley, D. K., & Murphy, M. N.** (1985). Another look at the theoretical assumptions of adolescent egocentrism. *Developmental Review, 5,* 201–217.

**Lapsley, D. K., & Narvaez, D.** (Eds.). (2004). *Moral development, self, and identity.* Mahwah, NJ: Erlbaum.

**Lapsley, D. K., & Narvaez, D.** (2006). Character education. In W. Damon & R. Lerner (Eds.), *Handbook of child psychology* (6th ed.). New York: Wiley.

**Lapsley, D. K., Rice, K. G., & Shadid, G. E.** (1989). Psychological separation and adjustment to college. *Journal of Counseling Psychology, 36,* 286–294.

**Lara, L. E.** (2006, April). *Young Latinas and their relation to the new technologies.* Paper presented at the meeting of the American Educational Research Association, San Francisco.

**Larose, S., & Tarabulsy, G. M.** (2005). Academically at-risk students. In D. L. Dubois & M. J. Karcher (Eds.), *Handbook of youth mentoring.* Thousand Oaks, CA: Sage.

**Larsen, R. J., & Buss, D. M.** (2005). *Personality psychology: Domains of knowledge about human nature* (2nd ed.). New York: McGraw-Hill.

**Larson, R. W.** (1999, September). Unpublished review of J. W. Santrock's *Adolescence,* 8th ed. (New York: McGraw-Hill).

**Larson, R. W.** (2000). Toward a psychology of positive youth development. *American Psychologist, 55,* 170–183.

**Larson, R. W.** (2001). How U.S. children and adolescents spend time: What it does (and doesn't) tell us about their development. *Current Directions in Psychological Science, 10,* 160–164.

**Larson, R. W.** (2007). Development of the capacity for teamwork in youth development. In R. K. Silbereisen & R. M. Lerner (eds.), *Approaches to positive youth development.* Thousand Oaks, CA: Sage.

**Larson, R. W., Hansen, D., & Walker, K.** (2004). Everybody's gotta give: Adolescents' development of initiative within a youth program. In J. L. Mahoney, R. W. Larson, & J. S. Eccles (Eds.), *Organized activities as contexts of development.* Mahwah, NJ: Erlbaum.

**Larson, R. W., & Lampman-Petraitis, C.** (1989). Daily emotional states as reported by children and adolescents. *Child Development, 60,* 1250–1260.

**Larson, R. W., & Richards, M. H.** (1994). Divergent realities. New York: Basic Books.

**Larson, R. W., Richards, M. H., Moneta, G., Holmbeck, G., & Duckett, E.** (1996). Changes in adolescents' daily interactions with their families from 10 to 18: Disengagement and transformation. *Developmental Psychology, 32,* 744–754.

**Larson, R. W., & Seepersad, S.** (2003). Adolescents' leisure time in the U.S.: Partying, sports, and the American Experiment. In S. Verma & R. W. Larson (Eds.), *Examining Adolescent Leisure Time Across Cultures: Developmental Opportunities and Risks: New Directions for Child and Adolescent Development,* no. 99. San Francisco: Jossey-Bass.

**Larson, R. W., & Sheeber, L.** (2007, in press). The daily emotional experience of adolescence. In N. Allen & L. Sheeber (Eds.), *Adolescent emotional development and the emergence of depressive disorders.* New York: Cambridge University Press.

**Larson, R. W., & Verma, S.** (1999). How children and adolescents spend time across the world: Work, play, and developmental opportunities. *Psychological Bulletin, 125,* 701–736.

**Larson, R. W., & Wilson, S.** (2004). Adolescence across place and time: Globalization and the changing pathways to adulthood. In R. Lerner & L. Steinberg (Eds.), *Handbook of adolescent psychology.* New York: Wiley.

**Lauber, M. O., Marshall, M. L., & Meyers, J.** (2005). Gangs. In S. W. Lee (Ed.), *Encyclopedia of school psychology.* Thousand Oaks, CA: Sage.

**Lauer, T.** (2005). Teaching critical-thinking skills using course content material. *Journal of College Science Teaching, 34,* 37.

**Laursen, B.** (1995). Conflict and social interaction in adolescent relationships. *Journal of Research on Adolescence, 5,* 55–70.

**Laursen, B., Coy, K. C., & Collins, W. A.** (1998). Reconsidering changes in parent-child conflict across adolescence: A meta-analysis. *Child Development, 69,* 817–832.

**LaVoie, J.** (1976). Ego identity formation in middle adolescence. *Journal of Youth and Adolescence, 5,* 371–385.

**Law, N.** (2006). Abortion: Supreme Court avoids disturbing abortion precedents by ruling on grounds of Remedy—Ayotte v. Planned Parenthood of New England. *Journal of Law and Medical Ethics, 34,* 469–471.

**Lazarus, R. S.** (1993). From psychological stress to the emotions: A history of a changing outlook. *Annual Review of Psychology, 44,* 1–21.

**Lazarus, R. S.** (2000). Toward better research on stress and coping. *American Psychologist, 55* (6), 665–673.

**Le Vay, S.** (1994). *The sexual brain.* Cambridge, MA: MIT Press.

**Leadbeater, B. J., & Way, N.** (2000). *Growing up fast.* Mahwah, NJ: Erlbaum.

**Leadbeater, B. J., Way, N., & Raden, A.** (1994, February). *Barriers to involvement of* *father of the children of adolescent mothers.* Paper presented at the meeting of the Society for Research on Adolescence, San Diego.

**Leaper, C., Carson, M., Baker, C., Holliday, H., & Myers, S. B.** (1995). Self-disclosure and listener verbal support in same-gender and cross-gender friends' conversations. *Sex Roles, 33,* 387–404.

**Leaper, C., & Friedman, C. K.** (2007). The socialization of gender. In J. E. Grusec & P. D. Hastings (Eds.), *Handbook of socialization.* New York: Guilford.

**Leaper, C., & Smith, T. E.** (2004). A meta-analytic review of gender variations in children's talk: Talkativeness, affiliative speech, and assertive speech. *Developmental Psychology, 40,* 993–1027.

**Learner-Centered Principles Work Group.** (1997). *Learner-centered psychological principles: A framework for school reform and redesign.* Washington, DC: American Psychological Association.

**Leary, M. R.** (2007). Motivational and emotional aspects of the self. *Annual Reviews of Psychology* (Vol. 58). Palo Alto, CA: Annual Reviews.

**Lee, H. Y., Lee, E. L., Pathy, P., & Chan, Y. H.** (2005). Anorexia nervosa in Singapore: An eight-year retrospective study. *Singapore Medical Journal, 46,* 275–281.

**Lee, R. M.** (2005). Resilience against discrimination: Ethnic identity and other-group orientation as protective factors for Korean Americans. *Journal of Counseling Psychology, 52,* 36–44.

**Lee, V. E., Croninger, R. G., Linn, E., & Chen, X.** (1995, March). *The culture of sexual harassment in secondary schools.* Paper presented at the meeting of the Society for Research in Child Development, Indianapolis.

**Lefkowitz, E. S., Afifi, T. L., Sigman, M., & Au, T. K.** (1999, April). He said, she said: *Gender differences in mother-adolescent conversations about sexuality.* Paper presented at the meeting of the Society for Research in Child Development, Albuquerque.

**Lefkowitz, E. S., Boone, T. L., & Shearer, T. L.** (2004). Communication with best friends about sex-related topics during emerging adulthood. *Journal of Youth and Adolescence, 33,* 339–351.

**Lefkowitz, E. S., & Espinosa-Hernandez, G.** (2006). Sex-related communication with mothers and close friends during the transition to university. Unpublished manuscript, Department of Human Development and Family Studies, University Park, PA.

**Lefkowitz, E. S., & Gillen, M. M.** (2006). "Sex is just a normal part of life": Sexuality in emerging adulthood. In J. J. Arnett & J. L. Tanner (Eds.), *Emerging adults in America.* Washington, DC: American Psychological Association.

**Lefkowitz, E. S., & Stoppa, T. M.** (2006). Positive sexual communication and socialization in the parent-adolescent context. *New Directions in Child and Adolescent Development, 112,* 39–55.

**Lehr, C. A., Hanson, A., Sinclair, M. F., & Christenson, S. L.** (2003). Moving beyond dropout prevention towards school completion. *School Psychology Review, 32,* 342–364.

**Leitenberg, H., Detzer, M. J., & Srebnik, D.** (1993). Gender differences in masturbation and the relation of masturbation experience in preadolescence and/or early adolescence to sexual behavior and adjustment in young adulthood. *Archives of Sexual Behavior, 22,* 87–98.

**Lemery, K. S., & Doelger, L.** (2005). Genetic vulnerabilities to the development of psychopathology. In B. J. Hankin & J. R. Z. Abela (Eds.), *Development of psychopathology.* Thousand Oaks, CA: Sage.

**Lenroot, R. K., & Giedd, J. N.** (2007). The structural development of the human brain measured longitudinally. In D. Coch, K. W. Fischer, & G. Dawson (Eds.), *Human behavior, learning, and the developing brain.* New York: Guilford.

**Lenroot, R. K. & others.** (2007). Sexual dimorphism of brain development trajectories during childhood and adolescence. *Neuroimage, 36,* 1065–1073.

**Lent, R. W., Brown, S. D., Nota, L., & Soresi, S.** (2003). Testing social cognitive interest and choice hypotheses across Holland types in Italian high school students. *Journal of Vocational Behavior, 62,* 101–118.

**Lenz, B. K.** (2004). Tobacco, depression, and lifestyle choices in the pivotal early college years. *Journal of American College Health, 52,* 213–219.

**Leong, F. T. L.** (1995). Introduction and overview. In F. T. L. Leong (Ed.), *Career development and vocational behavior in racial and ethnic minorities.* Hillsdale, NJ: Erlbaum.

**Leong, F. T. L.** (2000). Cultural pluralism. In A. Kazdin (Ed.), *Encyclopedia of psychology.* Washington, DC & New York: American Psychological Association and Oxford University Press.

**Lepper, M. R., Corpus, J. H., & Iyengar, S. S.** (2005). Intrinsic and extrinsic orientations in the classroom: Age differences and academic correlates. *Journal of Educational Psychology, 97,* 184–196.

**Lerner, R. M., Alberts, A. E., Anderson, P. M., & Dowling, E. M.** (2006). On making humans human: Spirituality and the promotion of positive youth development. In E. C. Roehlkepartain, P. E. King, & L. M. Wagener (Eds.), *The handbook of spiritual development in childhood and adolescence.* Thousand Oaks, CA: Sage.

**Lester, N., Smart, L., & Baum, A.** (1994). Measuring coping flexibility. *Psychology and Health, 9* (6), 409–424.

**Levant, R. F.** (1999, August). *Boys in crisis.* Paper presented at the meeting of the American Psychological Association, Boston.

**Levant, R. F.** (2001). Men and masculinity. In J. Worell (Ed.), *Encyclopedia of women and gender.* San Diego: Academic Press.

**LeVay, S.** (1991). A difference in hypothalamic structure between heterosexual and homosexual men. *Science, 253,* 1034–1037.

**Leventhal, T., Graber, J. A., & Brooks-Gunn, J.** (2001). *Adolescent transitions into young adulthood.* Unpublished manuscript, Center for Children and Families, Columbia University, New York.

**Lever-Duffy, J., & McDonald, J. B.** (2008). *Teaching and learning with technology* (3rd ed.). Boston: Allyn & Bacon.

**Lewinsohn, P. M., Rohde, P., Seeley, J. R., Kline, D. N., & Gotlib, L. H.** (2006). The psychosocial consequences of adolescent major depressive disorder on young adults. In T. E. Joiner, J. S. Brown, & J. Kistner (Eds.), *The interpersonal, cognitive, and social nature of depression.* Mahwah, NJ: Erlbaum.

**Lewis, A. C.** (2006). Clean up the test mess. *Phi Delta Kappan, 87,* 643–644.

**Lewis, A. C.** (2007). Looking beyond NCLB. *Phi Delta Kappan, 88,* 483–484.

**Lewis, C. C.** (1980). A comparison of minors' and adults' pregnancy decisions. *American Journal of Orthopsychiatry, 50,* 446–453.

**Lewis, C. G.** (1981). How adolescents approach decisions: Changes over grades seven to twelve and policy implications. *Child Development, 52,* 538–554.

**Lewis, D. A.** (1997). Development of the prefrontal cortex during adolescence: Insights into vulnerable neural circuits in schizophrenia. *Neuropsychopharmacology, 16,* 385–398.

**Lewis, R.** (2007). *Human genetics* (7th ed.). New York: McGraw-Hill.

**Lewis, V. G., Money, J., & Bobrow, N. A.** (1977). Idiopathic pubertal delay beyond the age fifteen: Psychologic study of 12 boys. *Adolescence, 12,* 1–11.

**Liben, L. S.** (1995). Psychology meets geography: Exploring the gender gap on the national geography bee. *Psychological Science Agenda, 8,* 8–9.

**Lieberman, M., Doyle, A., & Markiewicz, D.** (1999). Developmental patterns in security of attachment to mother and father in late childhood and early adolescence: Associations with peer relations. *Child Development, 70,* 202–213.

**Liederman, J., Kantrowitz, L., & Flannery, K.** (2005). Male vulnerability to reading disability is not likely to be a myth: A call for new data. *Journal of Learning Disabilities, 38,* 109–129.

**Limber, S. P.** (2004). Implementation of the Olweus Bullying Prevention Program in American schools: Lessons learned from the field. In D. L. Espelage & S. M. Swearer (Eds.), *Bullying in American schools.* Mahwah, NJ: Erlbaum.

**Linley, P. A., & Joseph, S.** (2004). Positive change following trauma and adversity: A review. *Journal of Traumatic Stress, 17,* 11–21.

**Lippman, L. A., & Keith, J. D.** (2006). The demographics of spirituality among youth: International perspectives. In E. Roehlkepartain, P. E. King, L. Wagener, & P. L. Benson (Eds.), *The handbook of spirituality in childhood and adolescence.* Thousand Oaks, CA: Sage.

**Liprie, M. L.** (1993). Adolescents' contributions to family decision making. In B. H. Settles, R. S. Hanks, & M. B. Sussman (Eds.), *American families and the future: Analyses of possible destinies.* New York: Haworth Press.

**Lipsitz, J.** (1980, March). *Sexual development in young adolescents.* Invited speech given at the American Association of Sex Educators, Counselors, and Therapists, New York City.

**Lipsitz, J.** (1983, October). *Making it the hard way: Adolescents in the 1980s.* Testimony presented at the Crisis Intervention Task Force, House Select Committee on Children, Youth, and Families, Washington, DC.

**Lipsitz, J.** (1984). *Successful schools for young adolescents.* New Brunswick, NJ: Transaction Books.

**Lissau, I., Overpeck, M. D., Ruan, W. J., Due, P., Holstein, B. E., & Hediger, M. L.** (2004). Body mass index and overweight in adolescents in 13 European countries, Israel, and the United States. *Archives of Pediatrics and Adolescent Medicine, 158,* 27–33.

**Little, K., Widman, L., Welsh, D. P., & Darling, N.** (2006, March). *Predictors of romantic relationship trajectories: Break-up and recovery.* Paper presented at the meeting of the Society for Research on Adolescence, San Francisco.

**Liu, X., & Tein, J. Y.** (2005). Life events, psychopathology, and suicidal behavior in Chinese adolescents. *Journal of Affective Disorders, 86,* 195–203.

**Lochman, J., & the Conduct Problems Prevention Research Group.** (2007, March). *Fast Track intervention outcomes in the middle school years.* Paper presented at the meeting of the Society for Research in Child Development, Boston.

**Loeber, R., & Farrington, D. P.** (Eds.). (2001). *Child delinquents: Development, intervention and service needs.* Thousand Oaks, CA: Sage.

**Loeber, R., DeLamatre, M., Keenan, K., & Zhang, Q.** (1998). A prospective replication of developmental pathways in disruptive and delinquent behavior. In R. Cairns, L. Bergman, & J. Kagan (Eds.), *Methods and models for studying the individual.* Thousand Oaks, CA: Sage.

**Loehlin, J. C., Horn, J. M., & Ernst, J. L.** (2007). Genetic and environmental influences on adult life outcomes: Evidence from the Texas adoption project. *Behavior Genetics, 37,* 463–476.

**Loewen, I. R., & Leigh, G. K.** (1986). *Timing of transition to sexual intercourse: A multivariate analysis of white adolescent females ages 15–17.* Paper presented at the meeting of the Society for the Scientific Study of Sex, St. Louis.

**Lombardo, S.** (2005, April). *Sexually active and abstinent adolescents: Correlates of decision making.* Paper presented the meeting of the Society for Research in Child Development, Atlanta.

**Long, T., & Long, L.** (1983). *Latchkey children.* New York: Penguin.

**Lord, S. E., & Eccles, J. S.** (1994, February). *James revisited: The relationship of domain self-concepts and values to Black and White adolescents' self-esteem.* Paper presented at the meeting of the Society for Research on Adolescence, San Diego.

**Loukas, A., & Prelow, H. M.** (2004). Externalizing and internalizing problems in low-income Latino early adolescents: Risk, resource, and protective factors. *Journal of Early Adolescence, 24,* 250–273.

**Lounsbury, J. W., Steel, R. P., Loveland, J. M., & Gibson, L. W.** (2004). An investigation of personality traits in relation to adolescent school absenteeism. *Journal of Youth and Adolescence, 33,* 457–466.

**Lubart, T. I.** (2003). In search of creati*** intelligence. In R. J. Sternberg, J. Lautrey. & T. I. Lubert (Eds.), Models of intelligence: International perspectives.

**Lundstedt, G., Edlund, B., Engström, I., Thurfjell, B., & Marcus, C.** (2006). Eating disorder traits in obese children and adolescents. *Eating and Weight Disorders, 11,* 45–50.

**Luria, A., & Herzog, E.** (1985, April). *Gender segregation across and within settings.* Paper presented at the biennial meeting of the Society for Research in Child Development, Toronto.

**Luster, T. J., Perlstadt, J., McKinney, M. H., & Sims, K. E.** (1995, March). *Factors related to the quality of the home environment adolescents provide for their infants.* Paper presented at the meeting of the Society for Research in Child Development, Indianapolis.

**Luyckx, K.** (2006). *Identity formation in emerging adulthood: Developmental trajectories, antecedents, and consequences.* Doctoral Disseration, Katholieke Universiteit Leuven, Leuven, Belgium.

**Luyckx, L., Soenens, B., Vansteenkiste, L., Goossens, L., & Berzonsky, M. D.** (2006) Parent psychological control and dimensions of identity formation in emerging adulthood. *Journal of Family Psychology, 42,* 305–318.

**Lynch, M. E.** (1991). Gender intensification. In R. M. Lerner, A. C. Petersen, & J. Brooks-Gunn (Eds.), *Encyclopedia of adolescence* (Vol. 1). New York: Garland.

**Lynn, R.** (1996). Racial and ethnic differences in intelligence in the U.S. on the Differential Ability Scale. *Personality and Individual Differences, 26,* 271–273.

**Lyon, G. R.** (1996). Learning disabilities. In *Special education for students with disabilities.* Los Altos, CA: Packard Foundation.

**Lytle, L. A., Murray, D. M., Perry, C. L., Story, M., Birnbaum, A. S., Kubik, M. Y., & Varnell, S.** (2004). School-based approaches to affect adolescents' diets: Results from the TEENS study. *Health Education and Behavior, 31,* 270–287.

## M

**Miltenberger, R. G.** (2008). *Behavior modification* (3rd ed.). Belmont, CA: Wadsworth.

**Ma, X.** (2002). Bullying in middle school: Individual and school characteristics of victims and offenders. *School Effectiveness and School Improvement, 13,* 63–89.

**Maclean, A. M., Walker, L. J., & Matsuba, M. K.** (2004). Transcendence and the moral self: Identity, integration, religion, and moral life. *Journal for the Scientific Study of Religion, 43,* 429–437.

**Maccoby, E. E.** (1987, November). Interview with Elizabeth Hall: All in the family. *Psychology Today,* pp. 54–60.

**Maccoby, E. E.** (1996). Peer conflict and intrafamily conflict: Are there conceptual bridges? *Merrill-Palmer Quarterly, 42,* 165–176.

**Maccoby, E. E.** (1998). *The two sexes.* Cambridge, MA: Harvard University Press.

**Maccoby, E. E.** (2002). Gender and group process: A developmental perspective. *Current Directions in Psychological Science, 11,* 54–57.

**Maccoby, E. E.** (2007). Historical overview of socialization theory and research. In J. E. Grusec & P. D. Hastings (Eds.), *Handbook of socialization.* New York: Guilford.

**Maccoby, E. E., & Jacklin, C. N.** (1974). *The psychology of sex differences.* Palo Alto, CA: Stanford University Press.

**Maccoby, E. E., & Martin, J. A.** (1983). Socialization in the context of the family. In E. M. Hetherington (Ed.), *Handbook of child psychology: Vol. 4. Socialization, personality, and social development.* New York: Wiley.

**MacDonald, K.** (1987). Parent-child physical play with rejected, neglected, and popular boys. *Developmental Psychology, 23,* 705–711.

**MacGeorge, E. L.** (2004). The myth of gender cultures: Similarities outweigh differences in men's and women's provisions of and responses to supportive communication. *Sex Roles, 50,* 143–175.

**Macy, R. J., Nurius, P. S., & Norris, J.** (2006). Responding in their best interests: Contextualizing women's coping with acquaintance sexual aggression. *Violence Against Women, 12,* 478–500.

**Maddi, S.** (1996). *Personality theories* (6th ed.). Pacific Grove, CA: Brooks/Cole.

**Mader, S. S.** (2007). *Biology* (9th ed.). New York: McGraw-Hill.

**Madison, B. E., & Foster-Clark, F. S.** (1996, March). *Pathways to identity and intimacy: Effects of gender and personality.* Paper presented at the meeting of the Society for Research on Adolescence, Boston.

**Maeda, K.** (1999) *The Self-Perception Profile for Children administered to a Japanese sample.* Unpublished data, Ibaraki Prefectural University of Health Sciences, Ibaraki, Japan.

**Mael, F. A.** (1998). Single-sex and coeducational schooling: Relationships to socioemotional and academic development. *Review of Educational Research, 68* (2), 101–129.

**Maes, H. H., Neale, M. C., Kendler, K. S., Martin, N. G., Heath, A. C., & Eaves, L. J.** (2006). Genetic and cultural transmission of smoking initiation: An extended twin kinship model. *Behavior Genetics, 19,* 795–808.

**Maestripieri, D., Roney, J. R., DeBias, N., Durante, K. M., & Spaepen, G. M.** (2004). Father absence, menarche, and interest in infants among adolescent girls. *Developmental Science, 7,* 560–566.

**Magnuson, K. A., & Duncan, G. J.** (2002). Parents in poverty. In M. H. Bornstein (Ed.), *Handbook of parenting* (2nd ed., Vol. 4). Mahwah, NJ: Erlbaum.

**Magnuson, K., Duncan, G. J., & Kalil, A.** (2006). The contribution of middle childhood contexts to adolescent achievement and behavior. In A. C. Huston & M. N. Ripke (Eds.), *Developmental contexts in middle childhood.* New York: Cambridge University Press.

**Magnusson, D.** (1988). *Individual development from an interactional perspective: A longitudinal study.* Hillsdale, NJ: Erlbaum.

**Maguin, E., Zucker, R. A., & Fitzgerald, H. E.** (1995) The path to alcohol problems through conduct problems: a family-based approach to very early intervention with risk. In G. M. Boyd, J. Howard, & R. A. Zucker (Eds.) *Alcohol problems among adolescents.* Hillsdale, NJ: Erlbaum.

**Mahoney, J. L., Larson, R. W., & Eccles, J. S.** (Eds.). (2004). *Organized activities as contexts of development.* Mahwah, NJ: Erlbaum.

**Majhanovich, S.** (1998, April). *Unscrambling the semantics of Canadian multiculturalism.* Paper presented at the meeting of the American Educational Research Association, San Diego.

**Maki, R. H., Shields, M., Wheeler, A. E., & Zacchilli, T. L.** (2005). Individual differences in absolute and relative metacomprehension accuracy. *Journal of Educational Psychology, 97,* 723–731.

**Malamitsi-Puchner, A., & Boutsikou, T.** (2006). Adolescent pregnancy and perinatal outcome. *Pediatric Endocrinology Review, 3* (Suppl. 1), 170–171.

**Male, M.** (2003). *Technology for inclusion* (3rd ed.). Boston: Allyn & Bacon.

**Malik, N. M., & Furman, W.** (1993). Practitioner review: Problems in children's peer relations: What can the clinician do? *Journal of Child Psychology and Psychiatry, 34,* 1303–1326.

**Mandara, J.** (2006). The impact of family functioning on African American males' academic achievement: A review and clarification of the empirical literature. *Teachers College Record, 108,* 206–233.

**Manis, F. R., Keating, D. P., & Morrison, F. J.** (1980). Developmental differences in the allocation of processing capacity. *Journal of Experimental Child Psychology, 29,* 156–169.

**Manlove, J., & Terry-Humen, E.** (2007). Contraceptive use patterns within females' first sexual relationships: The role of relationships, partners, and methods. *Journal of Sexual Research, 44,* 3–16.

**Manning, W. D., Longmore, M. A., & Giordano, P. C.** (2007). The changing institution of marriage: Adolescents' expectations to cohabit and to marry. *Journal of Marriage and the Family, 69,* 559–575.

**Marcell, A. V., & Halpern-Felsher, B. L.** (2005). Adolescents' health beliefs are critical in their intentions to seek physician care. *Preventive Medicine, 41,* 118–125.

**Marcell, A. V., Klein, J. D., Fischer, I., Allan, M. J., & Kokotailo, P. K.** (2002). Male adolescent use of health care services: Where are the boys? *Journal of Adolescent Health Care, 30,* 35–43.

**Marcell, A. V., & Millstein, S. G.** (2001, March). *Quality of adolescent preventive services: The role of physician attitudes and self-efficacy.* Paper presented at the meeting of the Society for Adolescent Medicine, San Diego.

**Marcia, J.** (1987). The identity status approach to the study of ego identity development. In T. Honess & K. Yardley (Eds.), *Self and identity: Perspectives across the lifespan.* London: Routledge & Kegan Paul.

**Marcia, J. E.** (1980). Ego identity development. In J. Adelson (Ed.), *Handbook of adolescent psychology.* New York: Wiley.

**Marcia, J. E.** (1994). The empirical study of ego identity. In H. A. Bosma, T. L. G. Graafsma, H. D. Grotevant, & D. J. De Levita (Eds.), *Identity and development.* Newbury Park, CA: Sage.

**Marcia, J. E.** (1996). Unpublished review of J. W. Santrock's *Adolescence,* 7th ed. (Dubuque, IA: Brown & Benchmark).

**Marcia, J. E.** (2002). Identity and psychosocial development in adulthood. *Identity: An International Journal of Theory and Research, 2,* 7–28.

**Marcia, J. E., & Carpendale, J.** (2004). Identity: Does thinking make it so? In C. Lightfoot, C. Lalonde, & M. Chandler (Eds.), *Changing -conceptions of psychological life.* Mahwah, NJ: Erlbaum.

**Marecek, J., Finn, S. E., & Cardell, M.** (1988). Gender roles in the relationships of lesbians and gay men. In J. P. De Cecco (Ed.), *Relationships.* New York: Harrington Park Press.

**Marin, B. V., Kirby, D. B., Hudes, E. S., Coyle, K. K., & Gomez, C. A.** (2006). Boyfriends, girlfriends, and teenagers' risk of sexual involvement. *Perspectives on Sexual and Reproductive Health, 38,* 76–83.

**Markman, A., & Gentner, D.** (2001). Learning and reasoning. *Annual Review of Psychology* (Vol. 51). Palo Alto, CA: Annual Reviews.

**Markus, H. R., & Kitayama, S.** (1994). The cultural construction of self and emotion: Implications for social behavior. In S. Kitayama & H. R. Markus (Eds.), *Emotion and culture.* Washington, DC: American Psychological Association.

**Markus, H. R., Mullally, P. R., & Kitayama, S.** (1999). *Selfways: Diversity in modes of cultural participation.* Unpublished manuscript, Department of Psychology, University of Michigan.

**Markus, H. R., & Nurius, P.** (1986). Possible selves. *American Psychologist, 41,* 954–969.

**Markus, H. R., Uchida, Y., Omoregie, H., Townsend, S. S., & Kitayama, S.** (2006). Going for the gold: Models of agency in Japanese and American contexts. *Psychological Science, 17,* 103–112.

**Marsh, H. W.** (1991). Employment during high school: Character building or a subversion of academic goals? *Sociology of Education, 64,* 172–189.

**Martin, C. L., & Dinella, L.** (2001). Gender development: Gender schema theory. In J. Worell (Ed.), *Encyclopedia of women and gender.* San Diego: Academic Press.

**Martin, C. L., & Halverson, C. F.** (1981). A Schematic Processing model of sex typing and stereo typing in children. *Child Development, 52,* 1119–1134.

**Martin, C. L., Ruble, D. N., & Szkrybalo, J.** (2002). Cognitive Theories of early gender development. *Psychological Bulletin, 128,* 903–933.

**Martin, D. W.** (2008). *Doing psychology experiments* (7th ed.). Belmont, CA: Wadsworth.

**Martin, E. W., Martin, R., & Terman, D. L.** (1996). The legislative and litigation history of special education. *Future of Children, 6* (1), 25–53.

**Martinez, A.** (2006). In the fast lane: Boosting your career through cooperative education and internships. *Careers and Colleges, 26,* 8–10.

**Marusic, A.** (2005). History and geography of suicide: Could genetic risk factors account for the variation in suicide rates? *American Journal of Medical Genetics, 133C,* 43–47.

**Mason, W. A., Hitchings, J. E., & Spoth, R. L.** (2007). Emergence of delinquency and depressed mood throughout adolescence as predictors of late adolescent problem substance use. *Psychology of Addictive Behaviors, 21,* 13–24.

**Massart, F., Parrino, R., Seppia, P., Federico, G., & Saggese, G.** (2006). How do environmental estrogen disruptors induce precocious puberty? *Minerva Pediatrica, 58,* 247–254.

**Masten, A. S.** (2001). Ordinary magic: Resilience processes in development. *American Psychologist, 56,* 227–238.

**Masten, A. S.** (2004). Regulatory processes, risk and resilience in adolescent development. *Annals of the New York Academy of Sciences, 1021,* 310–319.

**Masten, A. S.** (2006). Developmental psychopathology: Pathways to the future. *International Journal of Behavioral Development, 31,* 46–53.

**Masten, A. S., & Coatsworth, J. D.** (1998). The development of competence in favorable and unfavorable environments: Lessons from research on successful children. *American Psychologist, 53,* 205–220.

**Masten, A. S., & Obradovic, J.** (2007). Competence and resilience in development. In B. M. Lester, A. S. Masten, & B. McEwen (Eds.), Resilience in children. New York: Annals of the New York Academy of Sciences.

**Masten, A. S., Obradovic, J., & Burt, K. B.** (2006). Resilience in emerging adulthood: Developmental perspectives on continuity and transformation. In J. J. Arnett & J. L. Tanner (Eds.), *Emerging adults in America.* Washington, DC: American Psychological Association.

**Masten, A. S., & Reed, M. G.** (2002). Resilience in development. In C. R. Snyder & S. J. Lopez (Eds.), *The handbook of positive psychology.* Oxford University Press.

**Mastropieri, M. A., & Scruggs, T. E.** (2007). *Inclusive classroom* (3rd ed.). Upper Saddle River, NJ: Prentice Hall.

**Matheny, A. P., & Phillips, K.** (2001). Temperament and context: Correlates of home environment with temperament continuity and change. In T. D. Wachs & G. A. Kohnstamm (Eds.), *Temperament in context.* Mahwah, NJ: Erlbaum.

**Mathers, M., Toumbourou, J. W., Catalano, R. F., Williams, J., & Patton, G. C.** (2006). Consequences of youth tobacco use: A review of prospective behavioral studies. *Addiction, 101,* 948–958.

**Matjasko, J. L., Gruden, L. N., & Ernst, J. L.** (2007). Structural and dynamic process family risk factors: Consequences for holistic adolescent functioning. *Journal of Marriage and the Family, 69,* 654—674.

**Matlin, M. W.** (1993). *The psychology of women* (2nd ed.). San Diego: Harcourt Brace Jovanovich.

**Matlin, M. W.** (2008). *The psychology of women* (6th ed.). Belmont, CA: Wadsworth.

**Matsuba, M. K., & Walker, L. J.** (2004). Extraordinary moral commitment: Young adults involved in social organizations. *Journal of Personality, 72,* 413–436.

**Matsumoto, D., & Juang, L.** (2008). *Culture and psychology.* Belmont, CA: Wadsworth.

**Mayer, R. E., & Wittrock, M. C.** (2006). Problem solving. In P. A. Alexander & P. H. Winne (Eds.), *Handbook of educational psychology* (2nd ed.). Mahwah, NJ: Erlbaum.

**Mayseless, O., Scharf, M., & Sholt, M.** (2003). From authoritative parenting practices to an authoritarian context: Exploring person-environment fit. *Journal of Research on Adolescence, 13,* 427–456.

**Mayseless, O., & Scharf, M.** (2007). Adolescents' attachment representations and their capacity for intimacy in close relationships. *Journal of Research on Adolescence, 17,* 23–50.

**Mazza, J. J.** (2005). Suicide. In S. W. Lee (Ed.), *Encyclopedia of schoool psychology.* Thousand Oaks CA: Sage.

**McAdams, D. P., Josselson, R., & Lieblich, A.** (Eds.). (2006). *Identity and story: Creating self in narrative.* Washington, DC: American Psychological. Association Press.

**McAdoo, H. P.** (2007). *Black families.* Thousand Oaks, CA: Sage.

**McAlister, A., Perry, C., Killen, J., Slinkard, L. A., & Maccoby, N.** (1980). Pilot study of smoking, alcohol, and drug abuse prevention. *American Journal of Public Health, 70,* 719–721.

**McBurney, D. H., & White, T. L.** (2007). *Research methods* (7th ed.). Belmont, CA: Wadsworth.

**McCabe, M. P., & Ricciardelli, L. A.** (2003). Sociocultural influences on body image and body changes among adolescent boys and girls. *Journal of Social Psychology, 143,* 5–26.

**McCabe, S. E., Schulenberg, J. E. Johnston, L. D., O'Malley, P. M., Bachman, J. G., & Kloska, D. D.** (2005). Selection and socialization effects of fraternities and sororities on U.S. college student substance use: A multi-cohort national longitudinal study. *Addiction, 100,* 512–524.

**McCammon, S., Knox, D., & Schacht, C.** (2007). *Choices in sexuality* (3rd ed.). Belmont, CA: Thompson.

**McCarley, K. E. & Harter, S.** (2004, April). The current controversy over high self-esteem. Paper presented at the meeting of the Society for Research on Adolescence, Baltimore.

**McClure, J. B., Scholes, D., Grothaus, L., Fishman, P., Reid, R., Lindenbaum, J., & Thompson, R. S.** (2006). Chlamydia screening in at-risk adolescent females: An evaluation of screening practices and modifiable screening correlates. *Journal of Adolescent Health, 38,* 726–733.

**McCrae, R. R., & Costa, P. T.** (2003). *Personality in adulthood* (2nd ed.). New York: Guilford.

**McCrae, R. R., & Costa, P. T.** (2006). Cross-cultural perspectives on adult personality trait development. In D. K. Mroczek & T. D. Little (Eds.), *Handbook of personality development.* Mahwah, NJ: Erlbaum.

**McCrae, R. R., Costa, P. T., & Martin, T. A.** (2005). The NEO-PI-3: A more readable revised NEO Personality Inventory. *Journal of Personality Assessment, 84,* 261–270.

**McDonald, R., & Grych, J. H.** (2006). Young children's appraisals of interparental conflict: Measurement and links with adjustment problems. *Journal of Family Psychology, 20,* 88–99.

**McHale, J.** (2007). *Charting the bumpy road of coparenthood.* Washington: Zero to Three Press.

**McHale, J. & Sullivan, M.** (2007, in press). Family systems. In M. Hersen & A. Gross (Eds.), *Handbook of clinical psychology,* Volume II: Children and adolescents. New York: Wiley.

**McHale, J., Khazan, I. Erera, P., Rotman, T., DeCourcey, W., & McConnell, M.** (2002). Coparenting in diverse family systems. In M. H. Bornstein (Ed.), *Handbook of parenting* (2nd ed., Vol. 3). Mahwah, NJ: Erlbaum.

**McHale, S. M., Updegraff, K. A., Helms-Erikson, H., & Crouter, A. C.** (2001). Sibling influences on gender development in middle childhood and early adolescence: A longitudinal study. *Developmental Psychology, 37,* 115–125.

**McLean, K. C., & Pratt, M. W.** (2006). Life's little (and big) lessons: Identity statuses and meaning-making in the turning point narratives of emerging adults. *Developmental Psychology, 42,* 714–722.

**McLean, K. C., & Thorne, A.** (2006). Identity light: Entertainment stories as vehicle for self-development. In D. P. McAdams, R. Josselson, & A. Lieblich (Eds.), *Identity and story.* Washington, DC: American Psychological Association.

**McLoyd, V. C.** (1990). The impact of economic hardship on Black families and children: Psychological distress, parenting, and socioemotional development. *Child Development, 61,* 311–346.

**McLoyd, V. C.** (1998). Children in poverty. In I. E. Siegel & K. A. Renninger (Eds.), *Handbook of child psychology* (5th ed., Vol. 4). New York: Wiley.

**McLoyd, V. C., Aikens, N. L., & Burton, L. M.** (2006). Childhood poverty, policy, and practice. In W. Damon & R. Lerner (Eds.), *Handbook of child psychology* (6th ed.). New York: Wiley.

**McMillan, J.** (2007). *Classroom assessment* (4th ed.). Boston: Allyn & Bacon.

**McMillan, J. H.** (2007). *Educational research* (5th ed.). Boston: Allyn & Bacon.

**McMillan, J. H., & Schumacher, S.** (2006). Research in education: Evidence-based inquiry (6th ed.). Boston: Allyn & Bacon.

**McNergney, R. F., & McNergney, J. M.** (2007). *Education* (5th ed.). Boston: Allyn & Bacon.

**McNulty, R. D., & Burnette, M. M.** (2004). *Exploring human sexuality* (2nd ed.). Boston: Allyn & Bacon.

**Mead, M.** (1928). *Coming of age in Samoa.* New York: Morrow.

**Medrich, E. A., Rosen, J., Rubin, V., & Buckley, S.** (1982). *The serious business of growing up.* Berkeley: University of California Press.

**Meece, J. L., & Scantlebury, K.** (2006). Gender and schooling: Progress and persistent barriers. In J. Worell & C. D. Goodheart (Eds.), *Handbook of girls' and women's psychological health.* New York: Oxford University Press.

**Meichenbaum, D., & Butler, L.** (1980). Toward a conceptual model of the treatment of test anxiety: Implications for research and treatment. In I. G. Sarason (Ed.), *Test anxiety.* Mahwah, NJ: Erlbaum.

**Mendle, J., Turkheimer, E., & Emery, R. E.** (2007). Detrimental psychological outcomes associated with early pubertal timing in adolescent girls. *Developmental Review, 27,* 151–171.

**Merrick, J., Morad, M., Halperin, I., & Kandel, I.** (2005). Physical fitness and adolescence. *International Journal of Adolescent Medicine, 17,* 89–91.

**Messinger, J. C.** (1971). Sex and repression in an Irish folk community. In D. S. Marshal & R. C. Suggs (Eds.), *Human sexual behavior: Variations in the ethnographic spectrum.* New York: Basic Books.

**Metz, E. C., & Youniss, J.** (2005). Longitudinal gains in civic development through school-based required service. *Political Psychology, 26,* 413–437.

**Metz, I.** (2005). Advancing the careers of women with children. *International Career Development International, 10,* 228–245.

**Meyer, I. H.** (2003). Prejudice, social stress, and mental health in gay, lesbian, and bisexual populations: Conceptual issues and research evidence. *Psychological Bulletin, 129,* 674–697.

**Meyer-Bahlburg, H. F., Ehrhardt, A. A., Rosen, L. R., Gruen, R. S., Veridiano, N. P., Vann, F. H., & Neuwalder, H. F.** (1995). Prenatal estrogens and the development of homosexual orientation. *Developmental Psychology, 31,* 12–21.

**Meyers, S. A., & Miller, C.** (2004). Direct, mediated, moderated, and cumulative relations between neighborhood characteristics and adolescent outcomes. *Adolescence, 39,* 121–144.

**Michael, R. T., Gagnon, J. H., Laumann, E. O., & Kolata, G.** (1994). *Sex in America.* Boston: Little, Brown.

**Mikkelsson, L., Kaprio, J., Kautiainen, H., Kujala, U., Mikkelsson, M., & Nupponen, H.** (2006). School fitness tests as predictors of adult health-related fitness. *American Journal of Human Biology, 18,* 342–349.

**Mikulincer, M., & Shaver, P. R.** (2007). *Attachment in adulthood.* New York: Guilford.

**Milan, S., Pinderhughes, E. E., & The Conduct Problems Prevention Research Group.** (2006). Family instability and child maladjustment trajectories during elementary school. *Journal of Abnormal Child Psychology, 34,* 43–56.

**Millar, R., & Shevlin, M.** (2003). Predicting career information-seeking behavior of school pupils using the theory of planned behavior. *Journal of Vocational Behavior, 62,* 26–42.

**Miller, B. C., Benson, B., & Galbraith, K. A.** (2001). Family relationships and adolescent pregnancy risk: A research synthesis. *Developmental Review, 21,* 1–38.

**Miller, B. C., Fan, X., Christensen, M., Grotevant, H. D., & van Dulmen, M.** (2000). Comparisons of adopted and nonadopted adolescents in a large, nationally representative sample. *Child Development, 71,* 1458–1473.

**Miller, J.** (2006). Insights into moral development from cultural psychology. In M. Killen & J. G. Smetana (Eds.), *Handbook of moral development.* Mahwah, NJ: Erlbaum.

**Miller, J.** (2007). Cultural psychology of moral development. In S. Kitayama & D. Cohen (Eds.), *Handbook of cultural psychology.* New York: Guilford.

**Miller, L., Gur, M.** (2002). Religiousness and sexual responsibility in adolescent girls. *Journal of Adolescent Health, 81,* 401–406.

**Miller-Johnson, S., Coie, J., & Malone, P. S.** (2003, April). *Do aggression and peer rejection in childhood predict early adult outcomes?* Paper to be presented at the biennial meeting of the Society for Research in Child Development, Tampa, FL.

**Minino, A. M., Heron, M. P., & Smith, B. L.** (2006, June 28). Deaths: Preliminary data for 2004. *National Vital Statistics Report, 54,* 1–49.

**Ministry of Health, Education, and Welfare.** (2002). *Divorce trends in Japan.* Tokyo: Author.

**Minuchin, P.** (2002). Looking toward the horizon: Present and future in the study of family systems. In J. P. McHale & W. S. Grolnick (Eds.), *Retrospect and prospect in the study of families.* Mahwah, NJ: Erlbaum.

**Minuchin, P. P., & Shapiro, E. K.** (1983). The school as a context for social development. In P. H. Mussen (Ed.), *Handbook of child psychology* (4th ed., Vol. 4). New York: Wiley.

**Mischel, W.** (1968). *Personality and assessment.* New York: Wiley.

**Mischel, W.** (2004). Toward an integrative science of the person. *Annual Review of Psychology* (Vol. 55). Palo Alto, CA: Annual Reviews.

**Mischel, W., & Mischel, H.** (1975, April). *A cognitive social-learning analysis of moral development.* Paper presented at the meeting of the Society for Research in Child Development, Denver.

**Mitchell, K. S., & Mazzeo, S. E.** (2004). Binge eating and psychological distress in ethnically diverse college men and women. *Eating Behavior, 5,* 157–169.

**Mitchell, M. L., & Jolley, J. M.** (2007). *Research design explained* (6th ed.). Belmont, CA: Wadsworth.

**MMWR.** (2006, June 9). *Youth risk behavior surveillance—United States 2005* (Vol. 255). Atlanta: Centers for Disease Control and Prevention.

**MMWR.** (2006, August 11). The global HIV/AIDS pandemic, 2006. *MMWR, 55,* 841–844.

**Molina, L. A., Dulmus, C. N., & Sowers, K. M.** (2005). Secondary prevention for youth violence: A review of selected school-based programs. *Brief Treatment and Crisis Intervention, 5,* 1–3.

**Montemayor, R.** (1982). The relationship between parent-adolescent conflict and the amount of time adolescents spend with parents, peers, and alone. *Child Development, 53,* 1512–1519.

**Montemayor, R., & Flannery, D. J.** (1991). Parent-adolescent relations in middle and late adolescence. In R. M. Lerner, A. C. Petersen, & J. Brooks-Gunn (Eds.), *Encyclopedia of adolescence* (Vol. 2). New York: Garland.

**Montgomery, M.** (2005). Psychosocial intimacy and identity: From early adolescence to emerging adulthood. *Journal of Adolescent Research, 20,* 346–374.

**Mooney, C. G.** (2006). *Theories of childhood.* Upper Saddle River, NJ: Prentice Hall.

**Moore, D.** (1998, Fall). Gleanings: Focus on workbased learning. *Center Work Newletter* (NCRVE, University of California, Berkeley), pp. 1–4.

**Moore, D.** (2001). *The dependent gene.* New York: W. H. Freeman.

**Moore, N. B., & Davidson, J. K.** (2006). College women and personal goals: Cognitive dimensions that differentiate risk-reduction sexual decisions. *Journal of Youth and Adolescence, 35,* 577–589.

**Mora, F., Segovia, G., & Del Arco, A.** (2007, in press). Aging, plasticity, and environmental enrichment: Structural changes and neurotransmitter dynamics in several areas of the brain. *Brain Research Review.*

**Morreale, M. C.** (2004). Executing juvenile offenders: A fundamental failure of society. *Journal of Adolescent Health, 35,* 341.

**Morris, P., & Kalil, A.** (2006). Out of school time use during middle childhood in a low-income sample: Do combinations of activities affect achievement and behavior? In A. Huston & M. Ripke (Eds.), *Middle childhood: Contexts of development.* New York: Cambridge University Press.

**Morrison, G.** (2006). *Teaching in America* (4th ed.). Boston: Allyn & Bacon.

**Morrison, L. L., & L'Heureux, J.** (2001). Suicide and gay/lesbian/bisexual youth: Implications for clinicians. *Journal of Adolescence, 24,* 39–50.

**Mortimer, J. T., Finch, M., Ryu, S., Shanahan, M., & Call, K.** (1996). The effects of work intensity on adolescent mental health, achievement, and behavioral adjustment: New evidence from a prospective study. *Child Development, 67,* 1243–1261.

**Mortimer, J. T., Finch, M., Shanahan, M., & Ryu, S.** (1992). Work experience, mental health, and behavioral adjustment in adolescence. *Journal of Research on Adolescence, 2,* 24–57.

**Mortimer, J. T., Harley, C., & Johnson, M. K.** (1998, February). *Adolescent work quality and the transition to adulthood.* Paper presented at the meeting of the Society for Research on Adolescence, San Diego, CA.

**Mortimer, J. T., & Larson, R. W.** (2002). Macrostructural trends and the reshaping of adolescence. In J. T. Mortimer & R. W. Larson (Eds.), *The changing adolescent experience.* New York: Cambridge University Press.

**Mortimer, J., & Lorence, J.** (1979). Work experience and occupational value socialization: A longitudinal study. *American Journal of Sociology, 84,* 1361–1385.

**Mosely, D., Baumfield, V., Elliott, J., Higgins, S., Miller, J., Newton, D. P., & Gregson, M.** (2006). *Frameworks for thinking.* New York: Cambridge University Press.

**Mounts, N. S.** (2007). Adolescents' and their mothers' perceptions of parental management of peer relationships. *Journal of Research on Adolescence, 17,* 169–178.

**Mrocek, D., Spiro, A., & Griffin, P. W.** (2006). Personality and aging. In J. E. Birren & K. W. Schaie (Eds.), *Handbook of the psychology of aging* (6th ed.). San Diego: Academic Press.

**Mullis, I. V. S., Martin, M. O., Beaton, A. E., Gonzales, E. J., Kelly, D. L., & Smith, T. A.** (1998). *Mathematics and science and achievement in the final year of secondary school.* Chestnut Hill, MA: Boston College, TIMSS International Study Center.

**Munakata, Y.** (2006). Information processing approaches to development. In W. Damon & R. Lerner (Eds.), *Handbook of child psychology* (6th ed.). New York: Wiley.

**Muntner, P., He, J., Cutler, J. A., Wildman, R. P., & Whelton, P. K.** (2004). Trends in blood pressure among children and adolescents. *Journal of the American Medical Association, 29,* 2107–2113.

**Murnane, R. J., & Levy, F.** (1996). *Teaching the new basic skills.* New York: Free Press.

**Murphy, E. M.** (2003). Being born female is dangerous for your health. *American Psychologist, 58,* 205–210.

**Murphy, K., & Schneider, B.** (1994). Coaching socially rejected early adolescents regarding behaviors used by peers to infer liking: A dyadspecific intervention. *Journal of Early Adolescence, 14,* 83–95.

**Mussen, P. H., Honzik, M., & Eichorn, D.** (1982). Early adult antecedents of life satisfaction at age 70. *Journal of Gerontology, 37,* 316–322.

**Mustanski, B. S., Chivers, M. L., & Bailey, J. M.** (2003). A critical review of recent biological research on human sexual orientation. *Annual Review of Sex Research, 13,* 89–140.

**Myers, D. L.** (1999). *Excluding violent youths from juvenile court: The effectiveness of legislative waiver.* Doctoral dissertation, University of Maryland, College Park.

**Myers, D., Baer, W., & Choi, S.** (1996). The changing problem of overcrowded housing. *Journal of the American Planning Association, 62,* 66–84.

**Myers, M. G., & MacPherson, L.** (2004). Smoking cessation efforts among substance abusing adolescents. *Drug and Alcohol Dependency, 73,* 209–213.

**Myerson, J., Rank M. R., Raines, F. Q., & Schnitzler, M. A.** (1998). Race and general cognitive ability: The myth of diminishing returns in education. *Psychological Science, 9,* 139–142.

## N

**Nadeem, E., Romo, L. F., & Sigman, M.** (2006). Knowledge about condoms among low-income pregnant Latina adolescents in relation to explicit maternal discussion of contraceptives. *Journal of Adolescent Health, 39,* 119, e9–e15.

**Nader, P., O'Brien, M., Houts, R., Bradley, R., Belsky, J., Crosnoe, R., Friedman, S., Mei, Z., & Susman, E. J.** (2006). Identifying risk for obesity in early childhood. *Pediatrics, 118,* e594–e601.

**Nagata, P. K.** (1989). Japanese American children and adolescents. In J. T. Gibbs & L. N. Huang (Eds.), *Children of color.* San Francisco: Jossey-Bass.

**Nansel, T. R., Overpeck, M., Pilla, R., Ruan, W., Simons-Morton, B., & Scheidt, P.** (2001). Bullying behaviors among U. S. youth. *Journal of the American Medical Association, 285,* 2094–2100.

**Nardi, P. M.** (2006). *Doing survey research* (2nd ed.). Boston: Allyn & Bacon.

**Narvaez, D.** (2006). Integrative moral education. In M. Killen & J. Smetana (Eds.), *Handbook of moral development.* Mahwah, NJ: Erlbaum.

**Narvaez, D., Endicott, L., Bock, T., & Lies, J.** (2004). Minnesota's Community Voices and Character Education Project. *Journal of Research in Character Education, 2,* 89–112.

**Nation, M., & Heflinger, C. A.** (2006). Risk factors for serious alcohol and drug use: The role of psychosocial variables in predicting the frequency of substance abuse among adolescents. *American Journal of Alcohol Abuse, 32,* 415–433.

**Nation, M., Crusto, C., Wandersman, A., Kumpfer, K. L., Seybolt, D., Morrissey-Kane, E., & Davino, K.** (2003). What works in prevention: Principles of effective prevention programs. *American Psychologist, 58,* 449–456.

**National Assessment of Educational Progress.** (1976). *Adult work skills and knowledge* (Report No. 35-COD-01). Denver: National Assessment of Educational Progress.

**National Assessment of Educational Progress.** (2005). *2005 assessment results.* Washington, DC: National Center for Education Statistics.

**National Center for Addiction and Substance Abuse.** (2001). *2000 teen survey.* New York: Author.

**National Center for Chronic Disease Prevention and Health Promotion** (2005). *Healthy youth!* Atlanta: Centers for Disease Control and Prevention.

**National Center for Education Statistics.** (1997). *School-family linkages* [Unpublished manuscript]. Washington, DC: U.S. Department of Education.

**National Center for Education Statistics.** (1998). *Postsecondary financing strategies: How undergraduates combine work, borrowing, and attendance.* Washington, DC: U.S. Office of Education.

**National Center for Education Statistics.** (2002). *Contexts of postsecondary education: Learning opportunities.* Washington, DC: U.S. Office of Education.

**National Center for Education Statistics.** (2003). *Digest of Education Statistics, Table 52.* Washington, DC: Author.

**National Center for Education Statistics.** (2005). *Dropout rates in the United States: 2003.* Washington, DC: U.S. Department of Education.

**National Center for Education Statistics.** (2005). *Internet access in U.S. public schools.* Washington, DC: U.S. Department of Education.

**National Center for Education Statistics.** (2005). *School dropouts.* Washington DC: U.S. Department of Education.

**National Center for Education Statistics** (2007). *High school dropout rates.* Washington, DC: U.S. Department of Education.

**National Center for Health Statistics.** (2000). *Health United States, 1999.* Atlanta: Centers for Disease Control and Prevention.

**National Center for Health Statistics.** (2002, September 16.) Death statistics. *National Vital Statistics Report, 50,* pp. 13, 194.

**National Center for Health Statistics.** (2002). *Sexual behavior and selected health measures: Men and women 15–44 years of age, United States, 2002,* PHS 2003–1250. Atlanta: Centers for Disease Control and Prevention.

**National Center for Health Statistics.** (2004). *Health United States, 2004.* Atlanta: Center for Disease Control and Prevention.

**National Center for Health Statistics.** (2002). *America's families and living arrangements.* Atlanta: Centers for Disease Control and Prevention.

**National Center for Health Statistics.** (2002). Prevalence of overweight among children and adolescents: United States 1999–2000 (Table 71). *Health United States, 2002.* Atlanta, GA: Centers for Disease Control and Prevention.

**National Center for Health Statistics.** (2005). *Health United States, 2005.* Bethesda, MD: U.S. Department of Health and Human Services.

**National Clearinghouse for Alcohol and Drug Information.** (1999). *Physical and psychological effects of anabolic steroids.* Washington, DC: Substance Abuse and Mental Health Services Administration.

**National Commission on the High School Senior Year.** (2001). *Youth at the crossroads: Facing high school and beyond.* Washington, DC: The Education Trust.

**National Reasearch Council.** (1999). *How people learn.* Washington, DC: National Academic Press.

**National Research Council.** (2004). *Engaging schools: Fostering high school students' motivation to learn.* Washington, DC: National Academies Press.

**National Sleep Foundation.** (2006). *2006 Sleep in America poll.* Washington, DC: Author.

Natonal Center for Injury Prevention and Control. Fatal Injury Reports online database. Retrieved March 16, 2006, from www.ede.gov/ncipe/wisqars/

**Nelson, C. A.** (2003). Neural development and lifelong plasticity. In R. M. Lerner, F. Jacobs, & D. Wertlieb (Eds.), *Handbook of applied developmental science* (Vol. 1). Thousand Oaks, CA: Sage.

**Nelson, C. A., Thomas, K. M., & de Haan, M.** (2006). Neural bases of cognitive development. In W. Damon, R. Lerner, D. Kuhn, & R. Siegler (Eds.), *Handbook of child psychology* (6th ed., Vol. 2). New York: Wiley.

**Nelson, L. J., Badger, S., & Wu, B.** (2004). The influence of culture in emerging adulthood: Perspectives of Chinese college students. *International Journal of Behavioral Development, 28,* 26–36.

**Nelson, M. C., & Gordon-Larsen, P.** (2006). Physical activity and sedentary behavior patterns are associated with selected adolescent health risk behaviors. *Pediatrics, 117,* 1281–1290.

**Neisser, U., Boodoo, G., Bouchard, T. J., Boykin, A. W., Brody, N., Ceci, S. J., Halpern, D. E., Loehlin, J. C., Perloff, R. J., Sternberg, R., & Urbina, S.** (1996). Intelligence: Knowns and unkowns. *American Psychologist, 51,* 77–101.

**Nes, L. S., & Segerstrom, S. C.** (2006). Dispositional optimism and coping: A meta-analytic review. *Personality and Social Psychology Review, 10,* 235–251.

**Nester, E. W., Anderson, D. G., Roberts, C. E., & Nester, M. T.** (2007). *Microbiology* (5th ed.). New York: McGraw-Hill.

**Neugarten, B. L.** (1988, August). *Policy issues for an aging society.* Paper presented at the meeting of the American Psychological Association, Atlanta.

**Neumark-Sztainer, D., Levine, M. P., Paxton, S. J., Smolak, L., Piran, N., & Wertheim, E. H.** (2006). Prevention of body dissatisfaction and disordered eating: What next? *Eating Disorders, 14,* 265–285.

**Neumark-Sztainer, D., Paxton, S. J., Hannan, P. J., Haines, J., & Story, M.** (2006). Does body satisfaction matter? Five-year longitudinal associations between body satisfaction and health behaviors in adolescent females and males. *Journal of Adolescent Health, 39,* 244–251.

**Newby, T. J., Stepich, D. A., Lehman, J. D., & Russell, J. D.** (2000). *Instructional technology for teaching and learning* (2nd ed.). Upper Saddle River, NJ: Prentice Hall.

**Newcomb, M., & Bentler, P. M.** (1980). Assessment of personality and demographic aspects of cohabitation and marital success. *Journal of Personality Development, 4,* 11–24.

**Newcomb, M. D., & Bentler, P. M.** (1989). Substance use and abuse among children and teenagers. *American Psychologist, 44,* 242–248.

**Newman, B. M., & Newman, P. R.** (2007). *Theories of human development.* Mahwah, NJ: Erlbaum.

**Newman, B. S., & Muzzonigro, P. G.** (1993). The effects of traditional family values on the coming out process of gay male adolescents. *Adolescence, 28,* 213–226.

**Newman, D. L.** (2005). Ego development and ethnic identity formation in rural American Indian adolescents. *Child Development, 76,* 734–746.

**Nichols, J. F., Rauh, M. J., Lawson, M. J., Ji, M., & Barkai, H. S.** (2006). Prevalence of female athlete triad syndrome among high school athletes. *Archives of Pediatric and Adolescent Medicine, 160,* 137–142.

**Nichols, S., & Good, T. L.** (2004). *America's teenagers—myths and realities.* Mahwah, NJ: Erlbaum.

**Niederjohn, D. M., Welsh, D. P., & Scheussler, M.** (2000, April). *Adolescent romantic relationships: Developmental influences of parents and peers.* Paper presented at the meeting of the Society for Research on Adolescence, Chicago.

**Nielssen, S. J., Siega-Riz, A. M., & Popkin, B. M.** (2002). Trends in energy intake in U.S. between 1977 and 1996: Similar shifts seen across age groups. *Obesity Research, 10,* 370–378.

**Nietfeld, J. L., Cao, L., & Osborne, J. W.** (2005). Metacognitive monitoring accuracy and student performance in the postsecondary classroom. *The Journal of Experimental Education, 74,* 7–28.

**Nieto, S., & Bode, P.** (2007). *Affirming diversity* (5th ed.). Boston: Allyn & Bacon.

**Nishina, A., Ammon, N., Bellmore, A., & Graham, S.** (2006). Body dissatisfaction and physical developoment among ethnic minority adolescents. *Journal of Youth and Adolescence, 35,* 179–191.

**Nofziger, S., & Stein, R. E.** (2006). To tell or not to tell: Lifestyle impacts on whether adolescents tell about violent victimization. *Violence and Victims, 21,* 371–382.

**Nolen-Hoeksema, S.** (2007). *Abnormal psychology* (4th ed.), New York: McGraw-Hill.

**Nollen, N., Kaur H., Pulvers, K., Choi, W., Fitzgibbon, M., Li, C., Nazir, N., & Ahluwalia, J. S.** (2006). Correlates of ideal body size among Black and White adolescents. *Journal of Youth ad Adolescence, 35,* 276–284.

**Nottelmann, E. D., Susman, E. J., Blue, J. H., Inoff-Germain, G., Dorn, L. D., Loriaux, D. L., Cutler, G. B., & Chrousos, G. P.** (1987). Gonadal and adrenal hormone correlates of adjustment in early adolescence. In R. M. Lerner & T. T. Foch (Eds.), *Biological-psychological interactions in early adolescence.* Hillsdale, NJ: Erlbaum.

**Nsamenang, A. B.** (2002). Adolescence in sub-Saharan Africa: An image constructed from Africa's triple inheritance. In B. Brown, R. W. Larson, & T. S. Saraswathi (Eds.), *The world's youth.* New York: Cambridge University Press.

**Nucci, L.** (2006). Education for moral development. In M. Killen & J. Smetana (Eds.), *Handbook of moral development.* Mahwah, NJ: Erlbaum.

# O

**O'Brien, R. W.** (1990, March). *The use of family members and peers as resources during adolescence.* Paper presented at the meeting of the Society for Research in Adolescence, Atlanta.

**O'Keefe, E.** (2006). Time management—getting it done. *Careers and Colleges, 26,* 12.

**Oakes, J., & Lipton, M.** (2007). Teaching to change the world (3rd ed.). New York: McGraw-Hill.

**Occupational Outlook Handbook.** (2006–2007). Washington, DC: U.S. Department of Labor.

**Offer, D., Ostrov, E., Howard, K. I., & Atkinson, R.** (1988). *The teenage world: Adolescents' self-image in ten countries.* New York: Plenum.

**Office of Juvenile Justice and Prevention.** (1998). *Arrests in the United States under age 18: 1997.* Washington, DC: Author.

**Ogbu, J. U.** (1989, April). *Academic socialization of black children: An inoculation against future failure?* Paper presented at the meeting of the Society for Research in Child Development, Kansas City.

**Ogbu, J. U., & Stern, P.** (2001). Caste status and intellectual development. In R. J. Sternberg & E. L. Grigorenko (Eds.), *Environmental effects on cognitive abilities.* Mahwah, NJ: Erlbaum.

**Ojeda, S. R., Roth, C., Mungenast, A., Heger, S., Mastronardi, C., Parent, A. S., Lomniczi, A., & Jung, H.** (2006). Neuroendocrine mechanisms controlling female puberty: New approaches, new concepts. *International Journal of Andrology, 29,* 256–263.

**Okagaki, L.** (2006). Ethnicity, learning. In P. A. Alexander & P. H. Winne (Eds.), *Handbook of educational psychology* (2nd ed.). Mahwah, NJ: Erlbaum.

**Olivardia, R., Pope, H. G., Mangweth, B., & Hudson, J. I.** (1995). Eating disorders in college men. *American Journal of Psychiatry, 152,* 1279–1284.

**Olshen, E., McVeigh, K. H., Wunsch-Hitzig, R. A., & Rickert, V. I.** (2007). Dating violence, sexual assault, and suicide attempts among urban teenagers. *Archives of Pediatric and Adolescent Medicine, 161,* 539–546.

**Olszewski-Kubilius, P.** (2003). Gifted education programs and procedures. In I. B. Weiner (Ed.), *Handbook of psychology* (Vol. 7). New York: Wiley.

**Olweus, D.** (1980). Bullying among school boys. In R. Barnen (Ed.), *Children and violence.* Stockholm: Academic Literature.

**Olweus, D.** (1994). Bullying at school: Basic facts and effects of a school based intervention program. *Journal of Child Psychology and Psychiatry, 33* (7), 1171–1190.

**Olweus, D.** (1999). *Bullying at school.* Cambridge, MA: Blackwell.

**Olweus, D.** (2003). Prevalence estimation of school bullying with the Olweus bully/victim questionnaire. *Aggressive Behavior, 29* (3), 239–269.

**Oman, D., & Thoresen, C. E.** (2006). Religion, spirituality, and children's physical health. In E. C. Roehlkepartain, P. E. King, & L. M. Wagener (Eds.), *The handbook of spiritual development in childhood and adolescence.* Thousand Oaks, CA: Sage.

**Ong, K. K., Ahmed, M. L., & Dunger, D. B.** (2006). Lesson from large population studies on timing and tempo of puberty (secular trends and relation to body size): The European trend. *Molecular and Cellular Endocrinology, 254–255,* 8–12.

**Onwuegbuze, A. J., & Daley, C. E.** (2001). Racial differences in IQ revisited: A synthesis of nearly a century of research. *Journal of Black Psychology, 27,* 209–220.

**Orbanic, S.** (2001). Understanding bulimia. *American Journal of Nursing, 101,* 35–41.

**Orobio de Castro, B., Merk, W., Koops, W., Veerman, J. W., & Bosch, J. D.** (2005). Emotions in social information processing and their relations with reactive and proactive aggression in referred aggressive boys. *Journal of Clinical Child and Adolescent Psychology, 34,* 105–116.

**Oser, F., & Gmünder, P.** (1991). *Religious judgment: A developmental perspective.* Birmingham, AL: Religious Education Press.

**Oser, F., Scarlett, W. G., & Bucher, A.** (2006). Religious and spiritual development through the lifespan. In W. Damon & R. Lerner (Eds.), *Handbook of child psychology* (6th ed.). New York: Wiley.

**Osgood, D. W., Ruth, G., Eccles, J. S., Jacobs, J. E., & Barber, B. L.** (2005). Six paths to adulthood: Fast starters, parents without careers, educated partners, educated singles, working singles, and slow starters. In R. A. Settersten, F. F. Furstenberg, & R. G. Rumbaut (Eds.), *On the frontier of adulthood: Theories, research, and social policy.* Chicago: University of Chicago Press.

**Osipow, S. H., & Littlejohn, E. M.** (1995). Toward a multicultural theory of career development: Prospects and dilemmas. In F. T. L. Leong (Ed.), *Career development and vocational behavior of racial and ethnic minorities.* Hillsdale, NJ: Erlbaum.

**Osofsky, J. D.** (1990, Winter). Risk and protective factors for teenage mothers and their infants. *SRCD Newsletter,* pp. 1–2.

**Oswald, D. L., & Clark, E. M.** (2003). Best friends forever? High school best friendships and the transition to college. *Personal Relationships, 10,* 187–196.

**Oswald, R. F., & Clausell, E.** (2005). Same-sex relationships and their dissolution. In M. A. Fine & J. H. Harvey (Eds.), *Handbook of divorce and relationship dissolution.* Mahwah, NJ: Erlbaum.

**Owens, T., Stryker, S., & Goodman, N. (Eds.),** (2001). *Extending self-esteem theory and research.* New York: Cambridge University Press.

**Oxford, M. L., Gilchrist, L. D., Gillmore, M. R., & Lohr, M. J.** (2006). Predicting variation in the life course of adolescent mothers as they enter adulthood. *Journal of Adolescent Health, 39,* 20–36.

**Oyserman, D., Bybee, D., & Terry, K.** (2006). Possible selves and academic outcomes: How and when possible selves impel action. *Journal of Personality and Social Psychology, 91,* 188–204.

**Oyserman, D., & Fryberg, S.** (2004). The possible selves of diverse adolescents: Content and function across gender, race, and national origin. In C. Dunkel & J. Kerpelman (Eds.), *Possible selves: Theory, research, and application.* Huntington, NY: Nova.

**Oyserman, D., Terry, K., & Bybee, D.** (2002). A possible selves intervention to enhance school involvement. Journal of Adolescence, *25,* 313–326.

# P

**Padilla-Walker, L., & Thompson, R. A.** (2005). Combating conflicting messages of values: A closer look at parental strategies. *Social Development, 14,* 305–323.

**Pagan, J. L., Rose, R. J., Viken, R. J., Pulkkinen, L., Kaprio, J., & Dick, D. M.** (2006). Genetic and environmental influences on stages of alcohol use across adolescence and into young adulthood. *Behavior Genetics, 36,* 483–497.

**Paikoff, R. L., Parfenoff, S. H., Williams, S. A., McCormick, A., Greenwood, G. L., & Holmbeck, G. N.** (1997). Parenting, parent-child relationships, and sexual possibility situations among urban African American preadolescents: Preliminary findings and implications for HIV prevention. *Journal of Family Psychology, 11,* 11–22.

**Pajer, K. A., Kazmi, A., Gardner, W. P., & Wang, K.** (2007). Female conduct disorder: Health status in young adulthood. *Journal of Adolescent Health, 84,* e1–e7.

**Pakpreo, P., Ryan, S., Auinger, P., & Aten, M.** (2005). The association between parental lifestyle behaviors and adolescent knowledge, attitudes, intentions, and nutritional and physical activity behaviors. *Journal of Adolescent Health, 34,* 129–130.

**Pals, J. L.** (2006). Constructing the "springboard effect": Causal connections, selfmaking, and growth within the life story. In D. P. McAdams, R. Josselson, & A. Lieblich (Eds.), *Identity and story.* Washington, DC: American Psychological Association.

**Paludi, M. A.** (2002). *The psychology of women* (2nd ed.). Upper Saddle River, NJ: Prentice Hall.

**Papini, D., & Sebby, R.** (1988). Variations in conflictual family issues by adolescent pubertal status, gender, and family member. *Journal of Early Adolescence, 8,* 1–15.

**Parcel, G. S., Simons-Morton, G. G., O'Hara, N. M., Baranowski, T., Kolbe, L. J., & Bee,**

D. E. (1987). School promotion of healthful diet and exercise behavior: An integration of organizational change and social learning theory interventions. *Journal of School Health, 57,* 150–156.

**Park, M. J., Mulye, T. P., Adams, S. H., Brindis, C. D., & Irwin, C. E.** (2006). The health status of young adults in the United States. *Journal of Adolescent Health, 39,* 305–317.

**Parke, R. D., & Buriel, R.** (2006). Socialization in the family: Ethnic and ecological perspectives. In W. Damon & R. Lerner (Eds.), *Handbook of child psychology* (6th ed.). New York: Wiley.

**Parker, J. G., Walker, A. R., Low, C. M., & Gamm, B. K.** (2004). Friendship jealousy in young adolescents: Individual differences and links to sex, self-esteem, aggression, and social adjustment. *Developmental Psychology, 41,* 235–250.

**Partnership for a Drug-Free America.** (2005). *Partnership Attitude Tracking Study.* New York: Author.

**Pate, R. R., Dowda, M., O'Neil, J. R., & Ward, D. S.** (2007). Change in physical activity participation among girls from 8th to 12th grade. *Journal of Physical Activity and Health, 4,* 3–16.

**Patel, D. R., & Baker, R. J.** (2006). Musculoskeletal injuries in sports. *Primary Care, 33,* 545–579.

**Patterson, C. J.** (2002). Lesbian and gay parenthood. In M. H. Bornstein (Ed.), *Handbook of parenting* (2nd ed., Vol. 3). Mahwah, NJ: Erlbaum.

**Patterson, C. J., & Hastings, P. D.** (2007). Socialization in the context of family diversity. In J. E. Grusec & P. D. Hastings (Eds.), *Handbook of socialization.* New York: Guilford.

**Patterson, G. R., DeBaryshe, B. D., & Ramsey, E.** (1989). A developmental perspective on antisocial behavior. *American Psychologist, 44,* 329–335.

**Patton, G. C., Coffey, C., Carlin, J. B., Sawyer, S. M., & Wakefield, M.** (2006). Teen smokers reach their mid twenties. *Journal of Adolescent Health, 39,* 214–220.

**Patton, G. C., & Viner, R.** (2007). Pubertal transitions in health. *Lancet, 369,* 1130–1139.

**Paukku, M., Quan, J., Darney, P., & Raine, T.** (2003). Adolescents' contraceptive use and pregnancy history: Is there a pattern? *Obstetrics and Gynecology, 101,* 534–538.

**Paul, E. L., McManus, B., & Hayes, A.** (2000). "Hookups": Characteristics and correlates of college students' spontaneous and anonymous sexual experiences. *The Journal of Sexual Research, 37,* 76–88.

**Paul, E. L., & White, K. M.** (1990). The development of intimate relationships in late adolescence. *Adolescence, 25,* 375–400.

**Paul, P.** (2003, September/October). The Perma-Parent trap. *Psychology Today, 36* (5), 40–53.

**Paulsen, A. M., & Betz, N. E.** (2004). Basic confidence predictors of career decision-making self-efficacy. *Career Development Quarterly, 52,* 354–362.

**Paxson, C., Donahue, E., Orleans, C. T., & Grisso, J. A.** (2006) Introducing the issue. *The Future of Children, 16,* 3–17.

**Peak, L.** (1996). *Pursuing excellence: A study of U.S. eighth-grade mathematics and science teaching, learning, curriculum, and achievement in international context.* Washington, DC: U.S. Department of Education, National Center for Educational Statistics.

**Pearce, N., & Larson, R. W.** (2006). How teens become engaged in youth development programs: The process of motivational change in a civic activism organization. *Applied Developmental Science, 10,* 121–131.

**Pelkonen, M., & Marttunen, M.** (2003). Child and adolescent suicide: Epidemiology, risk factors, and approaches to prevention. *Pediatric Drug, 5,* 243–265.

**Pentz, M. A.** (1994). Primary prevention of adolescent drug abuse. In C. Fisher & R. Lerner (Eds.), *Applied developmental psychology.* New York: McGraw-Hill.

**Peplau, L. A., & Beals, K. P.** (2004). Family lives of lesbians and gay men. In A. L. Vangelisti (Ed.), *Handbook of family communication.* Mahwah, NJ: Erlbaum.

**Peplau, L. A., & Fingerhut, A. W.** (2007). The close relationships of lesbians and gay men. *Annual Review of Psychology* (Vol. 58). Palo Alto, CA: Annual Reviews.

**Pereira, A. C. & others.** (2007). An in vivo correlate of exercise-induced neurogenesis in the adult dentate gyrus. *Proceedings of the National Academy of Sciences USA, 104,* 5638–5643.

**Perry, C. L., Hearn, M., Murray, D., & Klepp, K.** (1998). *The etiology and prevention of adolescent alcohol and drug abuse.* Unpublished manuscript, University of Minnesota.

**Perry, C. L. Kelder, S. H., & Komro, K. A.** (1993). The social world of adolescents: Families, peers, schools, and the community. In S. G. Millstein, A. C. Petersen, & E. O. Nightingale (Eds.), *Promoting the health of adolescents.* New York: Oxford University Press.

**Perry, W. G.** (1970). *Forms of intellectual and ethical development in the college years.* New York: Holt, Rinehart & Winston.

**Perry, W. G.** (1999). *Forms of ethical and intellectual development in the college years: A scheme.* San Francisco. Jossey-Bass.

**Peskin, H.** (1967). Pubertal onset and ego functioning. *Journal of Abnormal Psychology, 72,* 1–15.

**Peskin, M. F., Tortolero, S. R., Markham, C. M., Addy, R. C., & Baumler, E. R.** (2007). Bullying and victimization an internalizing symptoms among low-income Black and Hispanic students. *Journal of Adolescent Health, 40,* 372–375.

**Petersen, A. C.** (1979, January). Can puberty come any faster? *Psychology Today,* pp. 45–56.

**Petersen, A. C.** (1987, September). Those gangly years. *Psychology Today,* pp. 28–34.

**Petersen, A. C.** (2006). Conducting policy-relevant developmental psychopathology research. *International Journal of Behavioral Development, 30,* 39–46.

**Petersen, A. C., & Crockett, L.** (1985). Pubertal timing and grade effects on adjustment. *Journal of Youth and Adolescence, 14,* 191–206.

**Petersen, A. C., Sarigiani, P. A., & Kennedy, R. E.** (1991). Coping with adolescence. In M. E. Colte & S. Gore (Eds.), *Adolescent stress: Causes and consequences.* New York: Aldine de Gruyter.

**Peterson, P. L., Hawkins, J. D., Abbott, R. D., & Catalano, R. F.** (1994). Disentangling the effects of parent alcohol norms on current drinking by Black and White adolescents. *Journal of Research on Adolescence, 4,* 203–228.

**Pettit, G. S., Bates, J. E., Dodge, K. A., & Meece, D. W.** (1999). The impact of after-school peer contact on early adolescent externalizing problems is moderated by parental monitoring, perceived neighborhood safety, and prior adjustment. *Child Development, 70,* 768–778.

**Phinney, J. S.** (1989). Stages of ethnic identity development in minority group adolescents. *Journal of Early Adolescence, 9,* 34–49.

**Phinney, J. S.** (1996). When we talk about American ethnic groups, what do we mean? *American Psychologist, 51,* 918–927.

**Phinney, J. S.** (2003). Ethnic identity and acculturation. In K. M. Chun, P. B. Organista, & G. Marin (Eds.), Acculturation, Washington, DC: American Psychological Association.

**Phinney, J. S.** (2006). Ethic identity exploration in emerging adulthood. In J. J. Arnett & J. L. Tanner (Eds.), *Emerging adults in America.* Washington, DC: American Psychological Association.

**Phinney, J. S., & Alipuria, L. L.** (1990). Ethnic identity in college students from four ethnic groups. *Journal of Adolescence, 13,* 171–183.

**Phinney, J. S., Berry, J. W., Vedder, K., & Liebkind, K.** (2006). The acculturation experience: Attitudes, identities, and behaviors of immigrant youth. In J. W. Berry, J. S. Phinney, D. L. Sam, & P. Vedder (Eds.), *Immigrant youth in cultural transition.* Mahwah, NJ: Erlbaum.

**Phinney, J. S., Ferguson, D. L., & Tate, J. D.** (1997). Intergroup attitudes among ethnic minority adolescents: A causal model. *Child Development, 68,* 955–969.

**Phinney, J. S., Madden, T., & Ong. A.** (2000). Cultural values and intergenerational discrepancies in immigrant and non-immigrant families. *Child Development, 71,* 528–539.

**Phinney, J. S., & Ong, A. D.** (2007). Conceptualization and measurement of ethnic identity: Current status and future directions. *Journal of Counseling Psychology, 54,* 271–281.

**Piaget, J.** (1932). *The moral judgment of the child.* New York: Harcourt Brace Jovanovich.

**Piaget, J.** (1952). *The origins of intelligence in children.* New York: International Universities Press.

**Piaget, J.** (1954). *The construction of reality in the child.* New York: Basic Books.

**Piaget, J.** (1972). Intellectual evolution from adolescence to adulthood. *Human Development, 15,* 1–12.

**Pianta, R. C.** (2005). Prevention. In H. W. Lee (Ed.), *Encyclopedia of school psychology.* Thousand Oaks, CA: Sage.

**Picotte, D. M., Strong, D. R., Abrantes, A. M., Tarnoff, G., Ramsey, S. E., Kazura, A. N., & Brown, R. A.** (2006). Family and peer influences on tobacco use among adolescents with psychiatric disorders. *Journal of Nervous and Mental Disorders, 194,* 518–253.

**Piko, B. F., & Fitzpatrick, K. M.** (2004). Substance use, religiosity, and other protective factors among Hungarian adolescents. *Addictive Behavior, 29,* 1095–1107.

**Pincus, D. B., & Friedman, A. G.** (2004). Improving children's coping with everyday stress: Transporting treatment interventions to the school setting. *Clinical Child and Family Psychology Reivew, 7,* 223–240.

**Pintrich, P. R.** (2003). Motivation for classroom learning. In I. B. Weiner (Ed.), *Handbook of psychology* (Vol. 7). New York: Wiley.

**Piron, N., & Ross, E.** (2006). From girlhood to womanhood: Multiple transitions in context. In J. Worell & C. D. Goodheart (Eds.), *Handbook of girls' and women's psychological health.* New York: Oxford University Press.

**Pitkänen, T., Lyyra, A. L., & Pulkkinen, L.** (2005). Age of onset of drinking and the use of alcohol in adulthood: A follow-up study from age 8–42 for females and males. *Addiction, 100,* 652–661.

**Pizzolato, J. E.** (2006). Achieving college student possible selves: Navigating the space between commitment and achievement of long-term identity goals. *Cultural Diversity and Ethnic Minority Psychology, 12,* 57–69.

**Place, D. M.** (1975). The dating experience for adolescent girls. *Adolescence, 38,* 157–173.

**Pleck, J. H.** (1983). The theory of male sex role identity: Its rise and fall, 1936–present. In M. Levin (Ed.), *In the shadow of the past: Psychology portrays the sexes.* New York: Columbia University Press.

**Pleck, J. H.** (1995). The gender-role strain paradigm. In R. F. Levant & W. S. Pollack (Eds.), *A new psychology of men.* New York: Basic Books.

**Pleck, J. H., Sonenstein, F., & Ku, L.** (1991). Adolescent males' condom use: Relationships between perceived cost benefits and consistency. *Journal of Marriage and the Family, 53,* 733–745.

**Pliszka, S. R.** (2007). Pharmacologic treatment of attention deficit hyperactivity disorder: Efficacy, safety, and mechanisms of action. *Neuropsychology Review, 17,* 61–72.

**Plog, A., Epstein, L., & Porter, W.** (2004, April). *Implementation fidelity: Lessons learned from the Bully-Proofing Your School Program.* Paper presented at the meeting of the National School Psychologists Association, Dallas, TX.

**Plomin, R.** (1993, March). *Human behavioral genetics and development: An overview and update.* Paper presented at the biennial meeting of the Society for Research in Child Development, New Orleans.

**Plomin, R., & McGuffin, P.** (2002). Psychopathology in the postgenomic era. *Annual Review of Psychology, 52.* Palo Alto, CA: Annual Reviews.

**Plomin, R., DeFries, J. C., & Fulker, D. W.** (2007). *Nature and nurture during infancy and childhood.* Mahwah, NJ: Erlbaum.

**Plomin, R., DeFries, J. C., McClearn, G. E., & McGuffin, P.** (2001). *Behavioral genetics* (4th ed.). New York: Worth.

**Polce-Lynch, M., Myers, B. J., Kliewer, W., & Kilmartin, C.** (2001). Adolescent self-esteem and gender: Exploring relations to sexual harassment, body image, media influence and emotional expression. *Journal of Youth and Adolescence, 30,* 225–244.

**Poll Finds Racial Tension Decreasing.** (1990, June 29). *Asian Week,* p. 4.

**Pollack, W.** (1999). *Real boys.* New York: Henry Holt.

**Pomery, E. A., Gibbons, F. X., Gerrard, M., & Cleveland, M. J.** (2006). Families and risk: Prospective analyses of familial and social influences on adolescent substance abuse. *Journal of Family Psychology, 19,* 560–570.

**Pope, L. M., Adler, N. E., & Tschann, J. M.** (2001). Post-abortion psychological adjustment: Are minors at increased risk? *Journal of Adolescent Health, 29,* 2–11.

**Popenoe, D., & Whitehead, B.** (2006). *The state of our unions 2006.* New Brunswick, NJ: The National Marriage Project, Rutgers University.

**Potvin, L, Champagne, F., & Laberge-Nadeau, C.** (1988). Mandatory driver training and road safety: The Quebec experience. *American Journal of Public Health, 78,* 1206–1212.

**Powell, D. R.** (2006). Families and early childhood interventions. In W. Damon & R. Lerner (Eds.), *Handbook of child psychology* (6th ed.). New York: Wiley.

**Pressley, M.** (2003). Psychology of literacy and literacy instruction. In I. B. Weiner (Ed.), *Handbook of psychology* (Vol. 7). New York: Wiley.

**Pressley, M., Allington, R., Wharton-McDonald, R., Block, C. C., & Morrow, L. M.** (2001). *Learning to read: Lessons from exemplary first grades.* New York: Guilford.

**Pressley, M., Dolezal, S. E., Raphael, L. M., Welsh, L. M., Bogner, K., & Roehrig, A. D.** (2003). *Motivating primary-grades teachers:* New York: Guilford.

**Pressley, M., & Harris, K. R.** (2006). Cognitive strategies instruction: From basic research to classroom instruction. In P. A. Alexander & P. H. Wine (Eds.), *Handbook of educational psychology* (2nd ed.). Mahwah, NJ: Erlbaum.

**Pressley, M., & Hilden, K.** (2006). Cognitive strategies. In W. Damon & R. Lerner (Eds.), *Handbook of child psychology* (6th ed.). New York: Wiley.

**Pressley, M., Raphael, L., Gallagher, D., & DiBella, J.** (2004). Providence-St. Mel School: How a school that works for African-American students works. *Journal of Educational Psychology, 96,* 216–235.

**Pressman, S. D., Cohen, S., Miller, G. E., Barkin, A., Rabin, B. S., & Treanor, J. J.** (2005). Loneliness, social network size, and immune response to influenza vaccination in college freshmen. *Health Psychology, 24,* 297–306.

**Price, R. H., Cioci, M., Penner, W., & Trautlein, B.** (1990). *School and community support systems that enhance adolescent health and education.* Washington, DC: Carnegie Council on Adolescent Development.

**Pryor, J. H., Hurtado, S., Saenz, V. B., Lindholm, J. A., Korn, W. S., & Mahoney, K. M.** (2005). *The American freshman: National norms for fall 2005.* Los Angeles: Higher Education Research Institute, UCLA.

**Pulkkinen, L., & Kokko, K.** (2000). Identity development in adulthood: A longitudinal study. *Journal of Research in Personality, 34,* 445–470.

**Putnam, S. P., Sanson, A. V., & Rothbart, M. K.** (2002). Child temperament and parenting. In M. Bornstein (Ed.), *Handbook of parenting* (2nd ed.). Mahwah, NJ: Erlbaum.


# Q


**Quadrel, M. J., Fischhoff, B., & Davis, W.** (1993). Adolescent (in)vulnerability. *American Psychologist, 48,* 102–116.

**Quimby, J. L., & O'Brien, K. M.** (2004). Predictors of student and career decision-making self-efficacy among nontraditional college women. *Career Development Quarterly, 52,* 323–339.

**Quinlan, S. L., Jaccard, J., & Blanton, H.** (2006). A decision theoretic and prototype conceptualization of possible selves: Implications for the prediction of risk behavior. *Journal of Personality, 74,* 599–630.

**Quinsey, V. L.** (2003). The etiology of anomalous sexual preferences in men. *Annals of the New York Academy of Science, 989,* 105–117.

**Quinsey, V. L., Skilling, T. A., Lalumière, M. L., & Craig, W. M.**, (2004). *Juvenile delinquency.* Washington, DC: American Psychological Association.

**Quinton, D., Rutter, M., & Gulliver, L.** (1990). Continuities in psychiatric disorders from childhood to adulthood in the children of psychiatric patients. In L. Robins & M. Rutter (Eds.), *Straight and devious pathways from childhood to adulthood.* New York: Cambridge University Press.

**Quinton, W., Major, B., & Richards, C.** (2001). Adolescents and adjustment to abortion: Are minors at greater risk? *Psychology, Public Policy, and Law, 7,* 491–514.


# R


**Raffaelli, M., & Ontai, L.** (2001). "She's sixteen years old and there's boys calling over to the house": An exploratory study of sexual socialization in Latino families. *Culture, Health, and Sexuality, 3,* 295–310.

**Raffaelli, M., & Ontai, L. L.** (2004). Gender socialization in Latino/a families: Results from two retrospective studies. *Sex Roles, 50,* 287–299.

**Rainey, R.** (1965). The effects of directed vs. non-directed laboratory work on high school chemistry achievement. *Journal of Research in Science Teaching, 3,* 286–292.

**Ramacciotti, C. E., Coli, E., Paoli, R., Gabriellini, G., Schulte, F., Castrogiovanni, S., Dell'Osso, L., & Garfinkel, P. E.** (2005). The relationship between binge eating disorder and non-purging bulimia nervosa. *Eating and Weight Disorders, 10,* 8–12.

**Ramey, C. T., Ramey, S. L., & Lanzi, R. G.** (2006). Children's health and education. In W. Damon & R. Lerner (Eds.), *Handbook of child psychology* (6th ed.). New York: Wiley.

**Rampage, C., Eovaldi, M., Ma, C., & Weigel-Foy, C.** (2003). Adoptive familes. In P. Walsh (Ed.), *Normal family processes: growing diversity and complexity.* New York: Guilford (3rd ed.).

**Rankin, J. L., Lane, D. J., Gibbons, F. X., & Gerrard, M.** (2004). Adolescents' self-consciousness: Longitudinal age changes and gender differences in two cohorts. *Journal of Research on Adolescence, 14,* 1–21.

**Rapkin, A. J. Tsao, J. C., Turk, N., Anderson, M., & Zeltzer, L. K.** (2006). Relationships among self-rated Tanner staging, hormones, and psychological factors in healthy female adolescent. *Journal of Pediatric and Adolescent Gynecology 19,* 181–187.

**Raskin, P. M.** (1985). Identity in vocational development. In A. S. Waterman (Ed.), *Identity in adolescence.* San Francisco: Jossey-Bass.

**Ratey, J.** (2006, March 27). Commentary in L. Szabo, "ADHD treatment is getting a workout." *USA Today,* p. 6D.

**Rathunde, K., & Csikszentmihalyi, M.** (2006). The developing person: An experiential perspective. In W. Damon & R. Lerner (Eds.), *Handbook of child psychology* (6th ed.). New York: Wiley.

**Raty, L. K., Larsson, G., Soderfeldt, B. A., & Larsson, B. M.** (2005). Psychosocial aspects of health in adolescence: The influence of gender and general self-concept. *Journal of Adolescent Health, 36,* 530.

**Raudenbush, S.** (2001). Longitudinal data analysis. *Annual Review of Psychology* (Vol. 52). Palo Alto, CA: Annual Reviews.

**Raymond, E. B.** (2004). *Learners with mild disabilities* (2nd ed.). Boston: Allyn & Bacon.

**Ream, G. L., Savin-Williams, R.** (2003). Religious development in adolescence. In G. Adams M. Berzonsky (Eds.), *Blackwell Handbook of Adolescence.* Malden, MA: Blackwell.

**Rebollo, M. A., & Montiel, S.** (2006). Attention and the executive functions. *Revista de Neurologia* (Spanish), *42,* (Suppl.), S3–S7.

**Redding, R. E.** (2005). Adult punishment for juvenile defenders: Does it reduce crime? In N. E. Dowd, D. G. Singer, R. F. Wilson (Eds.), *Handbook of children, culture, and violence.* Thousand Oaks, CA: Sage.

**Reed, V. A.** (2005). *Introduction to children with language disorders* (2nd ed.). Boston: Allyn & Bacon.

**Reeve, J.** (2006). Extrinsic rewards and inner motivation. In C. M. Evertson & C. S. Weinstein (Eds.), *Handbook of classroom management.* Mahwah, NJ: Erlbaum.

**Reeves, G., & Schweitzer, J.** (2004). Pharmacological management of attention deficit hyperactivity disorder. *Expert Opinions in Pharmacotherapy, 5,* 1313–1320.

**Regnerus, M. D.** (2001). *Making the Grade: The Influence of Religion upon the Academic Performance in Youth in Disadvantaged Communities.* Report 01–04, Center for Research on Religion and Urban Civil Society, University of Pennsylvania.

**Regnerus, M. D., Smith, C., & Smith, B.** (2004). Social context in the development of religiosity. *Applied Developmental Science, 8,* 27–38.

**Reid, P. T., & Zalk, S. R.** (2001). Academic environments: Gender and ethnicity in U.S. higher education. In J. Worell (Ed.), *Encyclopedia of women and gender.* San Diego: Academic Press.

**Reinders, H., & Youniss, J.** (2006). School-based required community service and civic development in adolescents. *Applied Developmental Science, 10,* 2–12.

**Reinisch, J. M.** (1990). *The Kinsey Institute new report on sex: What you must know to be sexually literate.* New York: St. Martin's Press.

**Reis, O., & Youniss, J.** (2004). Patterns of identity change and development in relationships with mothers and friends. *Journal of Adolescent Research, 19,* 31–44.

**Reis, S., D., Neiderhiser, J. M., Hetherington, E. M., & Plomin, R.** (2000). *The relationship code.* Cambridge, MA: Harvard University Press.

**Resnick, M. D., Bearman, P. S., Blum, R. W., Auman, K. E., Harris, K. M., Jones, J., Tabor, J., Beuhring, T., Sieving, R. E., Shew, M., Ireland, M., Bearinger, L. H., & Udry, J. R.** (1997). Protecting adolescents from harm: Findings from the National Longitudinal Study on Adolescent Health. *Journal of the American Medical Association, 278,* 823–832.

**Resnick, M. D., Wattenberg, E., & Brewer, R.** (1992, March). *Paternity avowal/disavowal among partners of low income mothers.* Paper presented at the meeting of the Society for Research on Adolescence, Washington, DC.

**Rest, J. R.** (1986). *Moral development: Advances in theory and research.* New York: Praeger.

**Rest, J. R.** (1995). *Concerns for the social-psychological development of youth and educational strategies: Report for the Kauffman Foundation.* Minneapolis: University of Minnesota, Department of Educational Psychology.

**Reuter, M. W., & Biller, H. B.** (1973). Perceived paternal nurturance-availability and personality adjustment among college males. *Journal of Consulting and Clinical Psychology, 40,* 339–342.

**Revelle, S. P.** (2004). High standards + high-stakes = high achievement in Massachusetts. *Phi Delta Kappan, 85,* 591–597.

**Rew, L., & Wong, Y. J.** (2006). A systematic review of associations among religiosity/spirituality and adolescent health attitudes and behaviors. *Journal of Adolescent Health, 38,* 433–442.

**Reynolds, C. R., Livingston, R., & Willson, V.** (2006). *Measurement and assessment in education.* Boston: Allyn & Bacon.

**Rhodes, J. E.** (2005). A model of youth mentoring. In D. L. Dubois & M. J. Karcher (Eds.), *Handbook of youth mentoring.* Thousand Oaks, CA: Sage.

**Rhodes, J. E., Grossman, J. B., & Resch, N. L.** (2000). Agents of change: Pathways through which mentoring relationships influence adolescents' academic adjustment. *Child Development, 71,* 1662–1671.

**Rholes, W. S., & Simpson, J. A.** (2007). Introduction: New directions and emerging issues in adult attachment. In W. S. Rholes & J. A. Simpson (Eds.), *Adult attachment.* New York: Guilford.

**Richards, M. H., Crowe, P. A., Larson, R., & Swarr, A.** (1998). Developmental patterns and gender differences in the experience of peer companionship during adolescence. *Child Development, 69,* 154–163.

**Richards, M. H., & Larson, R.** (1990, July). *Romantic relations in early adolescence.* Paper presented at the Fifth International Conference on Personal Relations, Oxford University, England.

**Richards, M. H., Larson, R., Miller, B. V., Luo, Z., Sims, B., Parrella, D. P., & McCauley, C.** (2004). Risky and protective contexts and exposure to violence in urban African American young adolescents. *Journal of Clinical Child and Adolescent Psychology, 33,* 138–148.

**Richards, M. H., Suleiman, L, Sims, B., & Sedeno, A.** (1994, February). *Experiences of ethnically diverse young adolescents growing up in poverty.* Paper presented at the meeting of the Society for Research on Adolescence, San Diego.

**Richmond, E. J., & Rogol, A. D.** (2007). Male pubertal development and the role of androgen therapy. *Nature General Practice: Endocrinology and Metabolism, 3,* 338–344.

**Richmond, L. J.** (2004). When spirituality goes awry: Students in cults. *Professional School Counseling, 7,* 367–375.

**Richter, L. M.** (2006). Studying adolescence. *Science, 312,* 1902–1905.

**Rickards, T., & deCock, C.** (2003). Understanding organizatinal creativity: Toward a paradigmatic approach. In M. A. Runco (Ed.), *Creativity research handbook.* Cresskill, NJ: Hampton Press.

**Rickert, V. I., Sanghavi, R., Wiemann, C. M.** (2002). Is lack of sexual assertiveness among adolescent women a cause for concern? *Perspectives on Sexual and Reproductive Health, 34,* 162–173.

**Rideout, V., Roberts, D. F., & Foehr, U. G.** (2005). *Generation M: Media in the lives of 8–18 year-olds.* San Francisco: Kaiser Family Foundation.

**Rigaud, D., Verges, B., Colas-Linhart, N., Petiet, A., Moukkaddem, M., Van Wymelbeke, V., & Brondel, L.** (2007, in press). Hormonal and psychological factors linked to the increased thermic effect of food in malnourished fasting anorexia nervosa. *Journal of Clinical Endocrinology and Metabolism.*

**Rigby, K.** (2004). Bullying in childhood. In P. K. Smith & C. H. Hart (Eds.), *Blackwell handbook of childhood social development.* Malden, MA: Blackwell.

**Rimberg, H. M., & Lewis, R. J.** (1994). Older adolescents and AIDS: Correlates of self-reported safer sex practices. *Journal of Research on Adolescence, 4,* 453–464.

**Rimsza, M. E.** (2003). Counseling the adolescent about contraception. *Pediatric Review, 24,* 162–170.

**Rimsza, M. E., & Kirk, G. M.** (2005). Common medical problems of the college student. *Pediatric Clinics of North America, 52,* 9–24.

**Rimsza, M. E., & Moses, K. S.** (2005). Substance abuse on the college campus. *Pediatric Clinics of North America, 52,* 307–319.

**Roberts, B. W., & Caspi, A.** (2003). The cumulative model of personality development. In R. M. Staudinger & U. Lindenberger (Eds.), Understanding human development. Dordrecht: Kluwer.

**Roberts, B. W., Caspi, A., & Moffitt, T. E.** (2001). The kids are alright: Growth and stability in personality development from adolescence to adulthood. *Journal of Personality and Social Psychology, 81,* 670–683.

**Roberts, B. W., & Robins, R. W.** (2004). Person-environment fit and its implications for personality development: A longitudinal study. *Journal of Personality, 72,* 89–110.

**Roberts, B. W., & Wood, D.** (2006). Personality development in the context of the neo-socioanalytic model of personality. In D. Mroczek & T. Little (Eds.), *Handbook of personality.* Mahwah, NJ: Erlbaum.

**Roberts, D. F.** (1993). Adolescents and the mass media: From "Leave It to Beaver" to "Beverly Hills 90210." In R. Takanishi (Ed.), *Adolescence in the 1990s.* New York: Teachers College Press.

**Roberts, D. F., & Foehr, U. G.** (2003). *Kids and media in America: Patterns of use at the millennium.* New York: Cambridge University Press.

**Roberts, D. F., Foehr, U. G., Rideout, V. J., & Brodie, M.** (1999). *Kids and media at the new millennium: A Kaiser Family Foundation Report.* Menlo Park, CA: Henry J. Kaiser Family Foundation.

**Roberts, D. F., Henriksen, L., & Foehr U. G.** (2004). Adolescents and the media. In R. Lerner & L. Steinberg (Eds.), *Handbook of adolescent psychology* (2nd ed.), New York: Wiley.

**Roberts, G. C., Treasure, D. C., & Kavussanu, M.** (1997). Motivation in physical activity contexts: An achievement goal perspective. *Advances in Motivation and Achievement, 10,* 413–447.

**Roberts, T. A., Ryan, S. A.** (2004). Body piercing, and high-risk behavior in adolescents. *Journal of Adolescent Health, 34* (3), 224–229.

**Roberts, W. B.** (2006). *Bullying from both sides.* Thousand Oaks, CA: Sage.

**Robins, R. W., Trzesniewski, K. H., Tracey, J. L., Potter, J., & Gosling, S. D.** (2002). Age differences in self-esteem from age 9 to 90. *Psychology and Aging, 17,* 423–434.

**Robinson, D. P., & Greene, J. W.** (1988). The adolescent alcohol and drug problem: A practical approach, *pediatric Nursing, 14,* 305–310.

**Robinson, J. H., & Clay, D. L.** (2005). Potential school violence: Relationship between teacher anxiety and warning-sign identification. *Psychogy in the Schools, 42,* 623–635.

**Robinson, N. S.** (1995). Evaluating the nature of perceived support and its relation to perceived self-worth in adolescents. *Journal of Research on Adolescence, 5,* 253–280.

**Rodrigues, A. E., Hall, J. H., & Fincham, F. D.** (2006). What predicts divorce and relationship dissolution. In M. A. Fine & J. H. Harvey (Eds.), *Handbook of divorce and relationship dissolution.* Mahwah, NJ: Erlbaum.

**Rodriguez-Galindo, C. A.** (2006, April). *What's left behind: Home and school understandings of literacy.* Paper presented at the meeting of the American Educational Research Association, San Francisco.

**Roe, A.** (1956). *The psychology of occupations.* New York: Wiley.

**Roehlkepartain, E. C., King, P. E., & Wagener, L. M.** (Eds.). (2006). *The handbook of spiritual development in childhood and adolescence.* Thousand Oaks, CA: Sage.

**Roeser, R. W., Peck, S. C., & Nasir, N. S.** (2006). Self and identity processes in school motivation, learning, and achievement. In P. A. Alexander & P. H. Winne (Eds.), *Handbook of educational psychology* (2nd ed.). Mahwah, NJ: Erlbaum.

**Rog, E., Hunsberger, B., & Alisat, S.** (2002, April). *Bridging the gap between high-school and college through a social support intervention: A long-term evaluation.* Paper presented at the meeting of the Society for Research on Adolescence, New Orleans.

**Rogers, C. R.** (1950). The significance of the self regarding attitudes and perceptions. In M. L. Reymart (Ed.), *Feelings and emotions.* New York: McGraw-Hill.

**Rogoff, B., Moore, L., Najafi, B., Dexter, A., Correa-Chávez, M., & Solís, J.** (2007). Children's development of cultural repertoires through participation in everyday routines and practices. In J. E. Grusec & P. D. Hastings (Eds.), *Handbook of socialization.* New York: Guilford.

**Rogol, A. D., Roemmich, J. N., & Clark, P. A.** (1998, September). *Growth at Puberty.* Paper presented at a workshop, Physical Development, Health Futures of Youth II: Pathways to Adolescent Health, Maternal and Child Health Bureau, Annapolis, MD.

**Rohner, R. P., & Rohner, E. C.** (1981). Parental acceptance-rejection and parental control: Cross-cultural codes. *Ethnology, 20,* 245–260.

**Roisman, G. I., Aguillar, B., & Egeland, B.** (2004). Antisocial behavior in the transition to adulthood: The independent and interactive roles of developmental history and emerging developmental tasks. *Development and Psychopatology, 16,* 857–872.

**Romans, S. E., Martin, J. M., Gendall, K., & Herbison, G. P.** (2003). Age of menarche: The role of some psychosocial factors. *Psychological Medicine, 33,* 933–939.

**Rosario, M., Scrimshaw, E. W., Hunter, J., & Braun, L.** (2006). Sexual identity development among lesbian, gay, and bisexual youths: Consistency and change over time. *The Journal of Sex Research, 43,* 46–58.

**Rose, A. J.** (2002). Co-rumination in the friendships of girls and boys. *Child Development, 73,* 1830–1843.

**Rose, H. A., & Rodgers, K. B.** (2000, April). Suicide ideation in adolescents who are confused about sexual orientation: A risk and resiliency approach. Paper presented at the meeting of the Society for Research in Adolescence, Chicago.

**Rose, M. R., & Mueller, L. D.** (2006). *Evolution and ecology of the organism.* Upper Saddle River, NJ: Prentice Hall.

**Rose, R. J., Koskenvuo, M., Kaprio, J., Sarna, S., & Langinvainio, H.** (1988). Shared genes, shared experiences and similarity of personality: Data from 14,288 adult Finnish co-twins. *Journal of Personality and Social Psychology, 54,* 161–171.

**Rose, S., & Frieze, I. R.** (1993). Young singles' contemporary dating scripts. *Sex Roles, 28,* 499–509.

**Rosenberg, M.** (1979). *Conceiving the self.* New York: Basic Books.

**Rosenberg, M. S., Westling, D. L., & McLeskey, J.** (2008). *Special education for today's teachers.* Upper Saddle River, NJ: Prentice Hall.

**Rosenblum, G. D., & Lewis, M.** (2003). Emotional development in adolescence. In G. Adams & M. Berzonsky (Eds.), *Blackwell handbook of adolescence.* Malden, MA: Blackwell.

**Rosner, B. A., & Rierdan, J.** (1994, February). *Adolescent girls' self-esteem: Variations in developmental trajectories.* Paper presented at the meeting of the Society for Research on Adolescence, San Diego.

**Rosnow, R. L., & Rosenthal, R.** (2005). *Beginning behavioral research* (5th ed.). Upper Saddle River, NJ: Prentice-Hall.

**Ross, M., Green, S, Salisbury-Glennon, J., & Tollefson, N.** (2006). An investigation into metacognitive self-regulation. *Innovative Higher Education, 30,* 361–375.

**Roth, C. L., & Ojeda, S. R.** (2005). Genes involved in the neuroendocrine control of normal puberty and abnormal puberty of central origin. *Pediatric Endocrinology Review, 3,* 67–76.

**Roth, J., Brooks-Gunn, J., Murray, L., & Foster, W.** (1998). Promoting healthy adolescents: Synthesis of youth development program evaluations. *Journal of Research on Adolescence, 8,* 423–459.

**Rothbart, M. K., & Bates, J. E.** (1998). Temperament. In W. Damon (Ed.). *Handbook of child psychology* (5th ed., Vol. 3). New York: Wiley.

**Rothbart, M. K., & Bates, J. E.** (2006). Temperament. In W. Damon & R. Lerner (Eds.), *Handbook of child psychology* (6th ed.). New York: Wiley.

**Rothbart, M. K., & Putnam, S. P.** (2002). Temperament and socialization. In L. Pulkkinen & A. Caspi (Eds.), *Paths to successful development.* New York: Cambridge University Press.

**Rothbaum, F., & Trommsdorff, G.** (2007). Do roots and wings complement or oppose one another?: The socialization of relatedness and autonomy in cultural context. In J. E. Grusec & P. D. Hastings (Eds.), *Handbook of socialization.* New York: Guilford.

**Rothbaum, F., Poll, M., Azuma, H., Miyake, K., & Weisz, J.** (2000). The development of close relationships in Japan and the United States: Paths of symbiotic harmony and generative tension. *Child Development, 71,* 1121–1142.

**Rowe, R., Maughan, B., Worthman, C. M., Costello, E. J., & Angold, A.** (2004). Testosterone, antisocial behavior, and social dominance in boys: Pubertal developoment and biosocial interaction. *Biological Psychiatry, 55,* 546–552.

**Rubin, K. H., Bukowski, W., & Parker, J. G.** (1998). Peer interactions, relationships, and groups. In N. Eisenberg (Ed.), *Handbook of child psychology* (5th ed., Vol. 3). New York: Wiley.

**Rubin, K. H., Bukowski, W., & Parker, J. G.** (2006). Peer interactions, relationships, and groups. In W. Damon & R. Lerner (Eds.), *Handbook of child psychology* (6th ed.). New York: Wiley.

**Rubin, Z., & Sloman, J.** (1984). How parents influence their children's friendships. In M. Lewis (Ed.), *Beyond the dyad.* New York: Plenum.

**Ruble, D. N.** (2000). Gender constancy. In A. Kazdin (Ed.), Encyclopedia of psychology. Washington, DC & New York: American Psychological Association and Oxford University Press.

**Ruble, D. N., Boggiano, A. K., Feldman, N. S., & Loebl, J. H.** (1980). Developmental analysis of the role of social comparison in self evaluation. *Developmental Psychology, 16,* 105–115.

**Ruble, D. N., Martin, C. L., & Berenbaum, S.** (2006). Gender development. In W. Damon & R. Lerner (Eds.), *Handbook of child psychology* (6th ed.). New York: Wiley.

**Rudra, C. L., & Williams, M. A.** (2005). BMI as a modifying factor in the relations between age at menarche, menstrual cyclke characteristics, and risk of preeclampsia. *Gynecological Endocrinology, 21,* 200–205.

**Rueter, M. A., & Kwon, H. K.** (2005). Developmental trends in adolescent suicide ideation. *Journal of Research on Adolescence, 15,* 205–222.

**Rumberger, R. W.** (1983). Dropping out of high school: The influence of race, sex, and family background. *American Educational Research Journal, 20,* 199–220.

**Runco, M. A. (Ed.).** (2006). *Creativity research handbook.* Cresskill, NJ: Hampton Press.

**Russell, D. W.** (1996). UCLA Loneliness Scale (Version 3): Reliability, validity and factor structure. *Journal of Personality, Assessment, 66,* 20–43.

**Russell, S. T. & Joyner, K.** (2001). Adolescent sexual orientation and suicide risks: Evidence from a national study. *American Journal of Public Health, 91,* 1276–1281.

**Russell, S. T., & Truong, N. L.** (2002, April). *Adolescent sexual orientation, family relationships, and emotional health.* Paper presented at the meeting of the Society for Research on Adolescence, New Orleans.

**Rutter, M.** (1979). Protective factors in children's response to stress and disadvantage. In M. W. Kent & J. E. Rolf (Eds.), *Primary prevention in psychopathology* (Vol. 3). Hanover, NH: University of New Hamphire Press.

**Rutter, M.** (2000). Resilience reconsidered: Conceptual reconsiderations, empirical findings, and policy implications. In J. P. Shonkoff & S. J. Meisels (Eds.), *Handbook of early intervention.* New York: Cambridge University Press.

**Rutter, M.** (2007). Gene-environment interplay and developmental psychopathology. In A. S. Masten (Ed.), *Multilevel dynamics in developmental psychology.* Mahwah, NJ: Erlbaum.

**Rutter, M. Maughan, B., Mortimore, P., & Ouston, J.** (1979). *Fifteen thousand hours: Secondary schools and their effects on children.* Cambridge, MA: Harvard University Press.

**Rutter, M., & Garmezy, N.** (1983). Developmental psychopathology. In P. H. Mussen (Ed.), *Handbook of child psychology* (4th ed., Vol. 4). New York: Wiley.

**Ruxton, C.** (2004). Obesity in children. *Nursing Standards, 18,* 47–52.

**Ryan, M. K.** (2003). Gender differences in ways of knowing: The context dependence of the Attitudes Toward Thinking and Learning Survey. *Sex Roles, 49,* 11–12.

**Ryu, S., & Mortimer, J. T.** (1996). The "occupational linkage hypothesis" applied to occupational value formation in adolescence. In J. T. Mortimer & M. D. Finch (Eds.), Adolescents, work, and family: An intergenerational developmental analysis. *Understanding Families* (Vol. 6). Thousand Oaks, CA: Sage Publications.

## S

**Saarni, C.** (1999). *The development of emotional competence.* New York: Guilford.

**Saarni, C., Campos, J. J., Camras, L., & Witherington, D.** (2006). Emotional development. In W. Damon & R. Lerner (Eds.), *Handbook of child psychology* (6th ed.). New York: Wiley.

**Sackett, P. R., Hardison, C. M., & Cullen, M. J.** (2004). On interpreting stereotype threat as accounting for African-American White differences in cognitive tests. *American Psychologist, 59,* 7–13.

**Sadker, M. P. & Sadker, D. M.** (2005). *Teachers, schools, and society* (7th ed.). New York: McGraw-Hill.

**Saettler, P.** (2005). *The evolution of American educational technology* (3rd ed.). Mahwah, NJ: Erlbaum.

**Sagan, C.** (1977). *The dragons of Eden.* New York: Random House.

**Sakamaki, R., Toyama, K., Amamoto, R., Liu, C. J., & Shinfuku, N.** (2005). Nutritional knowledge, food habits, and health attitude of Chinese university students—a cross-sectional study. *Nutrition Journal, 9,* 4.

**Saliba, J. A.** (1996). *Understanding new religious movements.* Grand Rapids, MI: William B. Eerdmans.

**Salovy, P., & Mayer, J. D.** (1990). Emotional intelligence. *Imagination, Cognition, and Personality, 9,* 185–211.

**Sanchez-Johnsen, L. A., Fitzgibbon, M. L., Martinovich, A., Stolley, M. R., Dyer, A. R., & Van Horn, L.** (2004). Ethnic differences in correlates of obesity between Latin-American and Black women. *Obesity Research, 12,* 652–660.

**Sanders, D., & Wills, F.** (2005). *Cognitive therapy.* Thousand Oaks, CA: Sage.

**Santa Maria, M.** (2002). Youth in Southeast Asia: Living within the continuity of tradition and the turbulence of change. In B. B. Brown, R. W. Larson, & T. S. Saraswathi (Eds.), *The world's youth.* New York: Cambridge University Press.

**Santelli, J. S., Abma, V., Ventura, S., Lindberg, L., Morrow, B., Anderson, J. E., Lyss, S., & Hamilton, B. E.** (2004a). Can changes in sexual behavior among high school students explain the decline in teen pregnancy rates in the 1990s? *Journal of Adolescent Health, 35,* 80–90.

**Santelli, J. S., Kaiser, J., Hirsch, L., Radosh, A., Simkin, L., & Middlestadt, S.** (2004b). Initiation of intercourse among middle school adolescents: The influence of social factors. *Journal of Adolescent Health, 34,* 200–208.

**Santelli, J., Ott, M. A., Lyon, M., Rogers, J., Summers, D., & Schleifer, R.** (2006). Abstinence and abstinence-only education: A review of U.S. policies and programs. *Journal of Adolescent Health, 38,* 72–81.

**Santrock, J. W.** (2008). *Educational psychology* (3rd ed.). New York: McGraw-Hill.

**Santrock, J. W., Sitterle, K. A., & Warshak, R. A.** (1988). Parent-child relationships in stepfather families. In P. Bronstein & C. P. Cowan (Eds.), *Fatherhood today: Men's changing roles in the family.* New York: Wiley.

**Saraswathi, T. S.** (2006, April). *Globalization and its consequences for adolescent development in the majority world.* Paper presented at the meeting of the Society for Research on Adolescence, San Francisco.

**Sarigiani, P. A., & Petersen, A. C.** (2000). Adolescence: Puberty and biological maturation. In A. Kazdin (Ed.), *Encyclopedia of psychology.* Washington, DC & New York: American Psychological Association and Oxford University Press.

**Savin-Williams, R. C.** (1998). *"... And then I became gay": Young men's stories.* New York: Routledge.

**Savin-Williams, R. C.** (2001). A critique of research on sexual minority youths. *Journal of Adolescence, 24,* 5–13.

**Savin-Williams, R. C.** (2001). *Mom, dad, I'm gay.* Washington, DC: American Psychological Association.

**Savin-Williams, R. C.** (2006). *The new gay teenager.* Cambridge, MA: Harvard University Press.

**Savin-Williams, R. C.** (2007). Girl-on-girl sexuality. In B. J. R. Leadbetter & N. Way (eds.), *Urban girls revisited: building strengths.* New York: New York University Press.

**Savin-Williams, R. C., & Cohen, K. M.** (2007). Development of same-sex attracted youth. In H. Meyer & M. E. Northridge (eds.), *The health of sexual minorities.* New York: Springer.

**Savin-Williams, R. C., & Demo, D. H.** (1983). Conceiving or misconceiving the self: Issues in adolescent self-esteem. *Journal of Early Adolescence, 3,* 121–140.

**Savin-Williams, R. C., & Diamond, L.** (2004). Sex. In R. Lerner & L. Steinberg (Eds.), *Handbook of adolescent psychology* (2nd ed.). New York: Wiley.

**Savin-Williams, R. C., & Joyner, K.** (2008). *Sexual identity and suicide attempts: Research and clinical implications of differentiating sexual subgroups.* Unpublished manuscript, Department of Human Development, Cornell University.

**Savin-Williams, R. C., & Ream, G. L.** (2007). Prevalence of stability of sexual orientation components during adolescence and young adulthood. *Archieves of Sexual Behavior, 36,* 385–394.

**Sax, L. J., & Bryant, A. N.** (2006). The impact of college on sex-atypical career choices of men and women. *Journal of Vocational Behavior, 68,* 52–63.

**Sax, L. J., Hurtado, S., Lindholm, J. A., Astin, A. W., Korn, W. S., & Mahoney, K. M.** (2004). *The American freshman: National norms for fall 2004.* Los Angeles: Higher Education Research Institute, UCLA.

**Sayer, L. C.** (2006). Economic aspects of divorce and relationship dissolution. In M. A. Fine & J. H. Harvey (Eds.), *Handbook of divorce and relationship dissolution.* Mahwah, NJ: Erlbaum.

**Sbarra, D. A.** (2006). Predicting the onset of emotional recovery following nonmarital relationship dissolution: Survival analysis of sadness and anger. *Personality and Social Psychology Bulletin, 32,* 298–312.

**Sbarra, D. A., & Ferrer, E.** (2006). The structure and process of emotional experience following nonmarital relationship dissolution: Dynamic factor analysis of love, anger, and sadness. *Emotion, 6,* 224–238.

**Scarlett, W. G.** (2006). Toward a developmental analysis of religious and spiritual development. In E. C. Roehlkepartain, P. E. King, & L. M. Wagener (Eds.). (2006). *The handbook of spiritual development in childhood and adolescence.* Thousand Oaks, CA: Sage.

**Scarr, S.** (1993). Biological and cultural diversity: The legacy of Darwin for development. *Child Development, 64,* 1333–1353.

**Scarr, S., & Weinberg, R. A.** (1983). The Minnesota adoption studies: Genetic differences and malleability. *Child Development, 54,* 182–259.

**Schaie, K. W.** (1977). Toward a stage theory of adult cognitive development. *Aging and Human Development, 8,* 129–138.

**Schaie, K. W.** (2000). Review of J. W. Santrock's *Life-span development,* 8th ed. (New York: McGraw-Hill).

**Schaie, K. W.** (2007). Generational differences: The age-cohort period model. In J. E. Birren (Ed.), *Encyclopedia of gerontology* (2nd ed.). Oxford: Elsevier.

**Scheer, S. D.** (1996, March). *Adolescent to adult transitions: Social status and cognitive factors.* Paper presented at the meeting of the Society for Research on Adolescence, Boston.

**Scheer, S. D., & Unger, D. G.** (1994, February). *Adolescents becoming adults: Attributes for adulthood.* Paper presented at the meeting of the Society for Research on Adolescence, San Diego.

**Schlegel, A.** (2000). The global spread of adolescent culture. In L. J. Crockett & R. K. Silbereisen (Eds.), *Negotiating adolescence in times of social change.* New York: Cambridge University Press.

**Schensul, J. J., Nastasi, B. K., & de Moura Castro, H.** (2005). Substance abuse. In S. W. Lee (Ed.), *Encyclopedia of school psychology.* Thousand Oaks, CA: Sage.

**Schiefele, U.** (1996). Topic interest, text representation, and quality of experience. *Contemporary Educational Psychology, 21,* 3–18.

**Schiff, J. L., & Truglio, R. T.** (1995, March). *In search of the ideal family: The use of television family portryals during early adolescence.* Paper presented at the meeting of the Society for Research in Child Development, Indianapolis.

**Schmidt, M. E., Marks, J. L., & Derrico, L.** (2004). What a difference mentoring makes: Service learning and engagement for college students. *Mentoring and Tutoring Partnership in Learning, 12,* 205–217.

**Schmidt, U.** (2003). Aetiology of eating disorders in the 21st century: New answers to old questions. *European Child and Adolescent Psychiatry, 12, Supplkon. 1,* 1130–1137.

**Schneider, B., & Stevenson, D.** (1999). *The ambitious generation.* New Haven, CT: Yale University.

**Schooler, D., Ward, L. M., Merriwether, A., & Caruthers, A.** (2004). Who's that girl: Television's role in the body image development of young White and Black women. *Psychological of Women Quarterly, 28,* 38–47.

**Schoon, I., Parsons, S., & Sacker, A.** (2004). Socioeconomic adversity, educational resilience, and subsequent levels of adult adaptation. *Journal of Adolescent Research, 19,* 383–404.

**Schorr, L. B.** (1989, April). *Within our reach: Breaking the cycle of disadvantage.* Paper presented at the biennial meeting of the Society for Research in Child Development, Kansas City.

**Schraw, G.** (2006). Knowledge: Structures and processes. In P. A. Alexander & P. H. Winne (Eds.), *Handbook of educational psychology* (2nd ed.). Mawah, NJ: Erlbaum.

**Schulenberg, J. E.** (2006). Understanding the multiple contexts of adolescent risky behavior and positive development: Advances and future directions. *Applied Developmental Science, 10,* 107–113.

**Schulenberg, J. E., Maggs, J. L., Steinman, K. J., & Zucker, R. A.** (2001). Development matters: Taking the long view on substance abuse etiology and intervention during adolescence. In P. M. Monti, S. M. Colby, & T. A. O'Leary (Eds.), *Adolescents, alcohol, and substance abuse.* New York: Guilford.

**Schulenberg, J. E., & Zarett, N. R.** (2006). Mental health during emerging adulthood: Continuity and discontinuity in courses, causes, and functions. In J. J. Arnett & J. L. Tanner (Eds.), *Emerging adults in America.* Washington, DC: American Psychological Association.

**Schunk, D. H.** (1991). Self-efficacy and cognitive skill learning. In C. Ames & R. Ames (Eds.), *Research on motivation and education* (Vol. 3). Orlando, Academic Press.

**Schunk, D. H.** (2001). Social cognitive theory and self-regulated learning. In B. J. Zimmerman & D. H. Schunk (Eds.), *Self-regulated learning and academic achievement* (2nd ed.). Mahwah, NJ: Erlbaum.

**Schunk, D. H.** (2004). *Learning theories* (4th ed.). Upper Saddle River, NJ: Prentice Hall.

**Schunk, D. H.,** (2008). *Learning theories* (5th ed.). Upper Saddle River, NJ: Prentice Hall.

**Schunk, D. H., & Ertmer, P. A.** (2000). Self-regulation and academic learning: Self-efficacy enhancing interventions. In M. Boekaerts, P. R. Pintrich, & M. Zeidner (Eds.), *Handbook of self-regulation.* San Diego: Academic Press.

**Schunk, D. H., Pintrich, P. R., & Meece, J.** (2008). *Motivation in education* (3rd ed.). Upper Saddle River, NJ: Prentice Hall.

**Schunk, D. H., & Zimmerman, B. J.** (2003). Self-regulation and learning. In I. B. Weiner (Ed.), *Handbook of psychology* (Vol. 7). New York: Wiley.

**Schunk, D. H., & Zimmerman, B. J.** (2006). Competence and control beliefs: Distinguishing the means and ends. In P. A. Alexander & P. H. Winne (Eds.), *Handbook of educational psychology* (2nd ed.). Mahwah, NJ: Erlbaum.

**Schwartz, M. A., & Scott, B.** (2007). *Marriages and families* (5th ed.). Upper Saddle River, NJ: Prentice Hall.

**Schwimmer, J. B., Burwinkle, T. M., & Varni, J. W.** (2003). Health-related quality of life of severely obese children and adolescents. *Journal of the American Medical Association, 289,* 1813–1819.

**Scott-Jones, D.** (1995, March). *Incorporating ethnicity and socioeconomic status in research with children.* Paper presented at the meeting of the Society for Research in Child Development, Indianapolis.

**Scrimsher, S., & Tudge, J.** (2003). The teaching/learning relationship in the first years of school: Some revolutionary implications of Vygotsky's theory. *Early Education and Development, 14,* 293–312.

**Search Institute.** (1995). *Barriers to participation in youth programs.* Unpublished manuscript, the Search Institute, Minneapolis.

**Sears, H. A., Byers, E. S., Whelan, J. J., & Saint-Pierre, M.** (2006). "If it hurts you, then it is not a joke": Adolescents' ideas about girls' and boys' use and experience of abusive behavior in dating relationships. *Journal of Interpersonal Violence, 21,* 1191–1207.

**Sedikdes, C., & Brewer, M. B.** (Eds.). (2001). *Individual self, relational self, and collective self.* Philadelphia: Psychology Press.

**Seidenfeld, M. E., Sosin, E., & Rickert, V. I.** (2004). Nutrition and eating disorders in adolescents. *Mt. Sinai Journal of Medicine, 71,* 155–161.

**Seiffge-Krenke, I.** (2006). Leaving home or still in the nest?: Parent-child relationships and psychological health as predictors of different leaving home patterns. *Developmental Psychology, 42,* 864–876.

**Seligman, M. E. P., & Csikszentmihalyi, M.** (2000). Positive psychology. *American Psychologist, 55,* 5–14.

**Sellers, R. M., Copeland-Linder, N., Martin, P. P., & Lewis, R. L.** (2006). Racial identity matters: The relationship between racial discrimination and psychological functioning in African American adolescents. *Journal of Research on Adolescence, 16,* 187–216.

**Selman, R. L. & Dray, A. J.** (2006). Risk and prevention. In W. Damon & R. Lerner (Eds.), *Handbook of child psychology* (6th ed.). New York: Wiley.

**Selman, R. L.** (1980). *The growth of interpersonal understanding.* New York: Academic Press.

**Selman, R. L., & Adalbjarnardottir, S.** (2000). Developmental method to analyze the personal meaning adolescents make of risk and relationship: The case of "drinking." *Applied Developmental Science, 4,* 47–65.

**Selman, R. L., & Schultz, L. H.** (1999, August). *The GSID approach to developmental evaluation of conflict resolution and violence prevention programs.* Paper presented at the meeting of the American Psychological Association, Boston.

**Seltzer, J.** (2004). Cohabitation and family change. In M. Coleman & L. Ganong (Eds.), *Handbook of contemporary families.* Thousand Oaks. CA: Sage.

**Semaj, L. T.** (1985). Afrikanity, cognition, and extended self-identity. In M. B. Spencer, G. K. Brookins, & W. R. Allen (Eds.), *Beginnings: The social and affective development of Black children.* Hillsdale, NJ: Erlbaum.

**Seroczynski, A. D., Jacquez, F. M., & Cole, D.** (2003). Depression and suicide in adolescence. In G. Adams & M. Berzonsky (Eds.), *Blackwell handbook of adolescence.* Malden, MA: Blackwell.

**Serow, R. C., Ciechalski, J., & Daye, C.** (1990). Students as volunteers. *Urban Education, 25,* 157–168.

**Settersten, R. A., Furstenberg, F. F., & Rumbaut, R. G.** (Eds.). (2005). *On the frontier of adulthood: Theory, research, and public policy.* Chicago: University of Chicago Press.

**Settler, D. D., Yamahachi, H., Li, W., Denk, W., & Gilbert, C. D.** (2006). Axons and synaptic boutons are highly dynamic in adult visual cortex. *Neuron, 49,* 877–887.

**Shade, S. C., Kelly, C., & Oberg, M.** (1997). *Creating culturally responsive schools.* Washington, DC: American Psychological Association.

**Shafii, T., Stovel, K., & Holmes, K.** (2007). Association between condom use at sexual debut and subsequent sexual trajectories: A longitudinal study using biomarkers. *American Journal of Public Health, 97,* 1090–1095.

**Shaibi, G. Q., Ball, G. D., & Goran, M. I.** (2006). Aerobic fitness among Caucasian, African American, and Latino youth. *Ethnicity and Disease, 16,* 120–125.

**Sharma, A. R., McGue, M. K., & Benson, P. L.** (1996). The emotional and behavioral adjustment of adopted adolescents: Part I: Age at adoption. *Children and Youth Services Review, 18,* 101–114.

**Sharma, A. R., McGue, M. K., & Benson, P. L.** (1998). The psychological adjustment of United States adopted adolescents and their nonadopted siblings. *Child Development, 69,* 791–802.

**Sharma, M.** (2006). School-based interventions for childhood and adolescent obesity. *Obesity Review, 7,* 261–269.

**Sharp, E. H., Coatsworth, J. D., Darling, N., Cumsille, P., & Ranieri, S.** (2007). Gender differences in the self-defining activities and identity experiences of adolescents and emerging adults. *Journal of Adolescence, 30,* 251–269.

**Sharp, N. L., Bye, R. A., Llewellyn, G. M., & Cusick, A.** (2006). Fitting back in: Adolescents returning to school after severe acquired brain injury. *Disability and Rehabilitation, 28,* 767–778.

**Shaver, P. R., & Mikulincer, M.** (2007). Attachment theory and research. In A. W. Shaywitz, B. A., Lyon, G. R., & Shaywitz, S. E. (2006). The role of functional magnetic resonance imaging in understanding reading and dyslexia. *Developmental Neuropsychology, 30,* 613–632.

**Shebloski, B., Conger, K. J., & Widaman, K. F.** (2005). Reciprocal links among differential parenting, perceived partiality, and self worth: A three-wave longitudinal study. *Journal of Family Psychology, 19,* 633–642.

**Sheeber, L. B., Davis, B., Leve, C., Hops, H., & Tildesley, E.** (2007). Adolescents' relationships with their mothers and fathers: Associations with depressive disorder and subdiagnostic symptomatology. *Journal of Abnormal Psychology, 116,* 144–154.

**Sheeber, L., Hops, H., & Davis, B.** (2001). Family processes in adolescent depression. *Clinical Child and Family Psychology Review, 4,* 19–32.

**Shields, S. A.** (1991). Gender in the psychology of emotion: A selective research review. In K. T. Strongman (Ed.), *International review of studies on emotion.* New York: Wiley.

**Shiffrin, R. M.** (1996). Laboratory experimentation on the genesis of expertise. In K. A. Ericsson (Ed.), *The road to excellence.* Mahwah, NJ: Erlbaum.

**Shifren, K., Furnham. A., & Bauserman, R. L.** (2003). Emerging adulthood in American and British samples: Individuals' personality and health risk behaviours. *Journal of Adult Development, 10,* 75–88.

**Shin, N.** (2004). Exploring pathways from television viewing to academic achievement in school age children. *Journal of Genetic Psychology, 165,* 367–381.

**Shiner, R. L.** (2005). A developmental perspective on personality disorders: Lessons from research on normal personality in childhood and adolescence. *Journal of Personality Disorders, 19,* 202–210.

**Shiraev, E., & Levy, D.** (2007). *Cross-cultural psychology* (3rd ed.). Boston: Allyn & Bacon.

**Shribman, S.** (2007). Adolescence: An opportunity not to be missed. *Lancet, 369,* 1788–1799.

**Shrier, D. K.** (2003). Psychosocial aspects of women's lives: Work, family, and life cycle issues. *Psychiatric Clinics of North America, 26,* 741–757.

**Shulman, S., Laursen, B., Kalman, Z., & Karpovsky, S.** (1997). Adolescent intimacy revisited. *Journal of Youth and Adolescence, 26,* 597–617.

**Shweder, R. A.** (1991). *Thinking through cultures: Expeditions in cultural psychology.* Cambridge, MA: Harvard University Press.

**Shweder, R., Goodnow, J., Hatano, G., Le Vine, R. A., Markus, H., & Miller, P.** (2006). The cultural psychology of development. In W. Damon & R. Lerner (Eds.), *Handbook of child psychology* (6th ed.). New York: Wiley.

**SIECUS.** (1999). *Public support for sexuality education.* Washington, DC: Author.

**Siegel, L. S., & Wiener, J.** (1993, Spring). Canadian special education policies: Children with learning disabilities in a bilingual and multicultural society. *Social Policy Report, Society for Research in Child Development, 7,* 1–16.

**Siegler, R. S.** (1998). Children's thinking (3rd ed.). Upper Saddle River, NJ: Erlbaum.

**Siegler, R. S.** (2006). Microgenetic analysis of learning. In W. Damon & R. Lerner (Eds.), *Handbook of child psychology* (6th ed.). New York: Wiley.

**Siegler, R. S., & Alibali, M. W.** (2005). Children's thinking (4th ed.). Upper Saddle River, NJ: Prentice Hall.

**Sieving, R. E., Eisenberg, M. E., Pettingell, S., & Skay, C.** (2006). Friends' influence on adolescents first sexual intercourse. *Perspectives on Sexual and Reproductive Health, 38,* 13–19.

**Silva, C.** (2005, October 31). When teen dynamo talks, city listens. *Boston Globe,* pp. B1, B4.

**Silver, E. J., and Bauman, L. J.** (2006). The association of sexual experience with attitudes, beliefs, and risk behaviors of inner-city adolescents. *Journal of Research on Adolescence, 16,* 29–45.

**Silver, M. E., Levin, M. J., Santos, J., & Perdue, L.** (2002, April). *Changes in family relationships as adolescents become young adults.* Paper presented at the meeting of the Society for Research on Adolescence, New Orleans.

**Silver, S.** (1988, August). *Behavior problems of children born into early-childbearing families.* Paper presented at the meeting of the American Psychological Association, Atlanta.

**Silver, S.** (1995, March). *Late adolescent-parent relations and the high school to college transition.* Paper presented at the meeting of the Society for Research in Child Development, Indianapolis.

**Silverman, J. G., Raj, A., Mucci, L. A., & Hathaway, J. E.** (2001). Dating violence against adolescent girls and associated substance use, unhealthy weight control, sexual risk behavior, pregnancy, and suicidality. *Journal of the American Medical Association, 386,* 572–579.

**Simmons, R. G., & Blyth, D. A.** (1987). *Moving into adolescence.* Hawthorne, NY: Aldine.

**Simons, J. M., Finlay, B., & Yang, A.** (1991). *The adolescent and young adult fact book.* Washington, DC: Children's Defense Fund.

**Simons, J. S., Walker-Barnes, C., & Mason, C. A.** (2001, April). *Predicting increases in adolescent drug use: A longitudinal investigation.* Paper presented at the meeting of the Society for Research in Child Development, Minneapolis.

**Simons-Morton, B., Haynie, D. L., Crump, A. D., Eitel, P., & Saylor, K. E.** (2001). Peer and parent influences on smoking and drinking among early adolescents. *Health Education & Behavior, 28,* 95–107.

**Simpkins, S. D., Fredricks, J. A., Davis-Kean, P. E. & Eccles, J. S.** (2006). Healthy mind, healthy habits: The influence of activity involvement in middle childhood. In A. C. Huston & M. N. Ripke (Eds.), *Middle childhood: Contexts of development.* New York: Cambridge University Press.

**Simpkins, S. D., Fredricks, J. A., Davis-Kean, P. E., & Eccles, J. S.** (2006). Healthy mind, healthy habits: The influence of activity involvement in middle childhood. In A. C. Huston & M. N. Ripke (Eds.), *Developmental contexts in middle childhood.* Mahwah, NJ: Erlbaum.

**Simpson, R. L.** (1962). Parental influence, anticipatory socialization, and social mobility. *American Sociological Review, 27,* 517–522.

**Sinclair, J. M., Harriss, L., Baldwin, D. S., & King, E. A.** (2005). Suicide in depressive disorders: A retrospective case-control study of 127 suicides. *Journal of Affective Studies, 87,* 107–113.

**Singh, S., Darroch, J. E., Vlassof, M., & Nadeau, J.** (2004). *Adding it up: The benefits of investing in sexual and reproductive health care.* New York: The Alan Guttmacher Institutes.

**Singh, S., Wulf, D., Samara, R., & Cuca, Y. P.** (2000). Gender differences in the timing of first intercourse: Data from 14 countries. *International Family Planning Perspectives, 26,* 21–28, 43.

**Sinha, J. W., Cnaan, R. A., & Gelles, R. J.** (2007). Adolescent risk behaviors and religion: Findings from a national study. *Journal of Adolescence, 30,* 231–249.

**Sinnott, J. D.** (2003). Postformal thought and adult development: Living in balance. In J. Demick & C. Andreoletti (Eds.), *Handbook of adult development.* New York: Kluwer.

**Sizer, F., & Whitney, E.** (2006). *Nutrition* (10th ed.). Belmont, CA: Wadsworth.

**Skara, S. N., & Sussman, S.** (2003). A review of 25 long-term tobacco and other drug use prevention program evaluations. *Preventive Medicine, 37,* 451–474.

**Skinner, B. F.** (1938). *The behavior of organisms: An experimental analysis.* New York: Appelton-Century-Crofts.

**Skoe, E. E. A., Cumberland, A., Eisenberg, N., Hansen, K., & Perry, J.** (2002). The influences of sex and gender-role identity on moral cognition and prosocial personality traits. *Sex Roles, 46,* 295–309.

**Skoe, E. E., Pratt, M. W., Matthews, M. & Curror, S. E.** (1996). The ethic of care: Stability over time, gender differences and correlates in mid to late adulthood. *Psychology and Aging, 11,* 280–202.

**Skorikov, V., & Vondracek, F. W.** (1998). Vocational identity development: Its relationship to other identity domains and to overall identity development. *Journal of Career Assessment, 6* (1), 13–35.

**Slavin, R. E., Hurley, E. A., & Chamberlain, A.** (2003). Cooperative learning and achievement theory and research. In I. B. Weiner (Ed.), *Handbook of psychology* (Vol. VII). New York: Wiley.

**Slesnick, N., & Prestopnik, J. L.** (2004). Perceptions of the family environment and youth behaviors: Alcohol-abusing runaway adolescents and their primary caretakers. *Family Journal, 12,* 243–253.

**Slomine, B. S., Gerring, J. P., Grados, M. A., Vasa, R., Brady, K. D., Christensen, J. R., & Denckla, M. B.** (2002). Performance on measures of executive function following pediatric traumatic brain injury. *Brain Injury, 16,* 759–772.

**Slomkowski, C., Rende, R., Conger, K. J., Simons, R. L., & Conger, R. D.** (2001). Sisters, brothers, and delinquency: Social influence during early and middle adolescence. *Child Development, 72,* 271–283.

**Smaldino, S. E., Lowther, D. L., & Russell, J. D.** (2008). *Instructional technology and media for learning* (9th ed.). Upper Saddle River, NJ: Prentice Hall.

**Smalls, C., White, R., Chavous, T., & Sellers, R.** (2007 in press). Racial ideological beliefs and racial discrimination experiences as predictors of academic engagement among African American adolescents. In *Journal of Black Psychology.*

**Smetana, J. G.** (2002). Culture, autonomy, and personal jurisdiction in adolescent-parent relationships. In H. W. Rease & R. Kail (Eds.), *Advances in child development and behavior* (Vol. 29). New York: Academic Press.

**Smetana, J. G.** (2006). Social domain theory. In M. Killen & J. G. Smetana (2005). *Handbook of moral development.* Mahwah, NJ: Erlbaum.

**Smetana, J. G., Abernethy, A., & Harris, A.** (2000). Adolescent-parent interactions in middle-class African-American families: Longitudinal change and contextual variations. *Journal of Family Psychology, 14,* 458–474.

**Smetana, J. G., Campione-Barr, N., & Metzger, A.** (2006). Adolescent development in interpersonal and societal contexts. *Annual Review of Psychology, (Vol. 57).* Palo Alto, CA: Annual Reviews.

**Smetana, J. G., & Gaines, C.** (1999). Adolescent-parent conflict in middle-class African-American families. *Child Development, 70,* 1447–1463.

**Smetana, J. G., Metzger, A., & Campione-Barr, N.** (2004). African American late adolescents' relationships with parents: Developmental transitions and longitudinal patterns. *Child Development, 75,* 932–947.

**Smetana, J. G., & Turiel, E.** (2003). Moral development during adolescence. In G. Adams & M. Berzonsky (Eds.), *Blackwell handbook of adolescence.* Malden, MA: Blackwell.

**Smith, B.** (2007). *The psychology of sex and gender.* Boston: Allyn & Bacon.

**Smith, D. D.** (2007). *Introduction to special education* (6th ed.). Boston: Allyn & Bacon.

**Smith, J., & Ross, H.** (2007). Training parents to mediate sibling disputes affects children's negotiation and conflict understanding. *Child Development, 78,* 790—805.

**Smith, R. E., & Smoll, F. L.** (1997). Coaching the coaches: Youth sports as a scientific and applied behavioral setting. *Current Directions in Psychological Science, 6,* 16–21.

**Smith, T. E. C., Polloway, E. A., Patton, J. R., & Dowdy, C. A.** (2008). *Teaching students with special needs in inclusive settings* (5th ed.). Boston: Allyn & Bacon.

**Snarey, J.** (1987, June). A question of morality. *Psychology Today,* pp. 6–8.

**Snibbe, A. C., & Markus, H. R.** (2005). You can't always get what you want: Educational attainment, agency, and choice. *Journal of Personality and Social Psychology, 88,* 703–720.

**Snyder, C. R., & Lopez, S. J.** (2006). *Positive psychology.* Thousand Oaks, CA: Sage.

**Snyder, H. N., & Sickmund, M.** (1999, October). *Juvenile offenders and victims, 1999 national report.* Washington, DC: National Center for Juvenile Justice.

**Soenens B., Vansteenkiste, M., Lens, W., Luyckx, K., Goossens, L., Beyers, W., & Ryan, R. M.** (2007). Conceptualizing parental autonomy support: Adolescent perceptions of independence versus promotion of volitional functioning. *Developmental Psychology,* 43, 633–646.

**Solomon, D., Battistich, V., Watson, M., Schaps, E., & Lewis, C.** (2000). A six-district study of educational change: Direct and mediated effects of the Child Development Project. *Social Psychology of Education, 4,* 3–51.

**Solomon, D., Watson, M., Delucchi, K., Schaps, E., & Battistich, V.** (1988). Enhancing children's prosocial behavior in the classroom. *American Educational Research Journal, 25,* 527–554.

**Solomon, D., Watson, Schapes, E., Battistich, V., & Solomon, J.** (1990). Cooperative learning as part of a comprehensive program designed to promote prosocial development. In S. Sharan (Ed.), *Cooperative learning: Theory and research.* New York: Praeger.

**Solot, D., & Miller, M.** (2002). *Unmarried to each other.* New York: Marlowe.

**Sommer, B. B.** (1978). *Puberty and adolescence.* New York: Oxford University Press.

**Sousa, D. A.** (1995). *How the brain learns: A classroom teacher's guide.* Reston, VA: National Association of Secondary School Principals.

**Sowell, E.** (2004, July). Commentary in M. Beckman, "Crime, culpability, and the adolescent brain." *Science Magazine, 305,* p. 599.

**Spear, L. P.** (2007). Brain development and adolescent behavior. In D. Coch, K. W. Fischer, & G. Dawson (Eds.), *Human behavior, learning, and the developing brain.* New York: Guilford.

**Spence, J. T., & Helmreich, R.** (1978). *Masculinity and femininity: Their psychological dimensions.* Austin: University of Texas Press.

**Spencer, M. B.** (2000). Ethnocentrism. In A. Kazdin (Ed.), *Encyclopedia of psychology.* Washington, DC & New York: American Psychological Association and Oxford University Press.

**Spencer, M. B.** (2006). Phenomenology and ecological systems theory: Development of diverse groups. In W. Damon: R. Lerner (Eds.), *Handbook of child psychology* (6th ed.), New York: Wiley.

**Spencer, M. B., & Dornbusch, S. M.** (1990). Challenges in studying minority youth. In S. S. Feldman & G. R. Elliott (Eds.), *At the threshold: The developing adolescent.* Cambridge, MA: Harvard University Press.

**Speranza, M., Corcos, M., Loas, G., Stephan, P., Guilbaud, O., Perez-Diaz, F., Venisse, J. L., Bizouard, P., Halfon, O., Flament, M., & Jeammet, P.** (2005). Depressive personality dimensions and alexithymia in eating disorders. *Psychiatry Research, 135,* 153–163.

**Spiliotis, B. E.** (2006). Growth and long-term hormonal therapy. *Pediatric Endocrinology Review, 3,* (Suppl. 1), 192–194.

**Spokane, A. R.** (2000). Career choice. In A. Kazdin (Ed.), *Encyclopedia of psychology.* Washington, DC & New York: American Psychological Association and Oxford University Press.

**Spokane, A. R., Fouad, N. A., & Swanson, J. L.** (2003). Culture-centered career interventions. *Journal of Vocational Behavior, 62,* 453–458.

**Spring, J.** (2007). *Deculturalization and the struggle for equality* (5th ed.). New York: McGraw-Hill.

**Spring, J.** (2008). *American education* (13th ed.). New York: McGraw-Hill.

**Sprinthall, R. C.** (2007). *Basic statistical analysis* (8th ed.). Boston: Allyn & Bacon.

**Sputa, C. L., & Paulson, S. E.** (1995, March). *A longitudinal study of changes in parenting across adolescence.* Paper presented at the meeting of the Society for Research in Child Development, Indianapolis.

**Srabstein, J. C., McCarter, R. J., Shao, C., & Huang, Z. J.** (2006). Morbidities associated with bullying behaviors in adolescents: School based study of American adolescents. *International Journal of Adolescent Medicine and Health, 18,* 587–596.

**Sroufe, L. A.** (2002). From infant attachment to promotion of adolescent autonomy. In I. G. Borkowski, S. L. Ramey, M. Bristol-Power (Eds.), *Parenting and the child's world.* Mahwah, NJ: Erlbaum.

**Sroufe, L. A.** (2007). Commentary: The place of development in developmental psychology. In A. Masten (Ed.), *Multilevel dynamics in developmental psychology.* Mahwah, NJ: Erlbaum.

**Sroufe, L. A., Egeland, B., & Carlson, E. A.** (1999). One social world: The integrated development of parent-child and peer relationships. In W. A. Collins & B. Laursen (Eds.), *Minnesota symposium on child psychology* (Vol. 31). Mahwah, NJ: Erlbaum.

**Sroufe, L. A., Egeland, B., Carlson, E. A., & Collins, W. A.** (2005). *The development of the person.* New York: Oxford.

**St. Pierre, R., Layzer, J., & Barnes, H.** (1996). *Regenerating two-generation programs.* Cambridge, MA: Abt Associates.

**Stafford, D. E.** (2005). Altered hypothalamic-pituitary-ovarian axis function in young female athletes: Implications and recommendations for management. *Treatment in Endocrinology, 4,* 147–154.

**Stake, J. E.** (2000). When situations call for instrumentality and expressiveness: Resource appraisal, copying strategy choice, and adjustment. *Sex Roles, 42,* 865–885.

**Stanley, S. M., Amato, P. R., Johnson, C. A., & Markman, H. J.** (2006). Premarital education, marital quality, and marital stability: Findings from a large, household survey. *Journal of Family Psychology, 20,* 117–126.

**Stansfield, K. H., & Kirstein, C. L.** (2006). Effects of novelty on behavior in the adolescent and adult rat. *Developmental Psychobiology, 48,* 273.

**Stattin, H., & Magnusson, D.** (1990). *Pubertal maturation in female development: Paths through life* (Vol. 2). Hillsdale, NJ: Erlbaum.

**Steele, C. M., & Aronson, J.** (1995). Stereotype threat and the intellectual test performance of African-Americans. *Journal of Personality and Social Psychology, 69,* 797–811.

**Steen, T. A., Kachorek, L. V., & Peterson, C.** (2003). Character strengths among youth. *Journal of Youth and Adolescence, 32,* 5–16.

**Steer, C. R.** (2005). Managing attention deficit hyperactivity disorder: Unmet needs and future directions. *Archives of Disease in Childhood, 90* (Suppl.), S19–S25.

**Stein, D. J., Fan, J., Fossella, J., & Russell, V. A.** (2007). Inattention and hyperactivity-impulsivity: Psychobiological and evolutionary underpinnings. *CNS Spectrum, 12,* 190–196.

**Steinberg, L. D.** (1986). Latchkey children and susceptibility to peer pressure: An ecological analysis. *Developmental Psychology, 22,* 433–439.

**Steinberg, L. D.** (1988). Reciprocal relation between parent-child distance and pubertal maturation. *Developmental Psychology, 24,* 122–128.

**Steinberg, L. D.** (2004). Risk taking in adolescence: What changes, and why? *Annals of the New York Academy of Sciences, 1021,* 51–58.

**Steinberg, L. D.** (2007). Risk taking in adolescence. *Current Directions in Psychological Science, 16,* 55–59.

**Steinberg, L., Blatt-Eisengart, I., & Cauffman, E.** (2006). Patterns of competence and adjustment among adolescents from authoritative, authoritarian, indulgent, and neglectful homes: A replication in a sample of serious juvenile delinquents. *Journal of Research on Adolescence, 16,* 47–58.

**Steinberg, L. D., & Cauffman, E.** (1999). A developmental perspective on jurisdictional boundary. In J. Fagan & F. Zimring (Eds.), *A developmental perspective on jurisdictional boundary.* Chicago: Univrsity of Chicago Press.

**Steinberg, L. D., & Cauffman, E.** (2001). Adolescents as adults in court. *SRCD Social Policy Report, 15* (4), 1–13.

**Steinberg, L. D., Fegley, S., & Dornbusch, S. M.** (1993). Negative impact of part-time work on adolescent adjustment: Evidence from a longitudinal study. *Developmental Psychology, 29,* 171–180.

**Steinberg, L. D., & Levine, A.** (1997). You and your adolescent (2nd ed.). New York: Harper Perennial.

**Steinberg, L. D., & Silk, J. S.** (2002). Parenting adolescents. In M. Bornstein (Ed.), *Handbook of parenting* (2nd ed., Vol. 1). Mahwah, NJ: Erlbaum.

**Steinman, K. J., & Zimmerman, M. A.** (2004). Religious activity and risk behavior among African American adolescents: Concurrent and development effects. *American Journal of Community Psychology, 33,* 151–161.

**Stengel, R.** (1985, December 9). The missing-father myth. *Time,* p. 90.

**Sternberg, R. J.** (1977). *Intelligence, information processing, and analogical reasoning: The componential analysis of human abilities. Hillsdale, NJ: Erlbaum.*

**Sternberg, R. J.** (1985, December). Teaching critical thinking, Part 2: Possible solutions. *Phi Delta Kappan,* pp. 277–280.

**Sternberg, R. J.** (1986). *Intelligence applied.* Fort Worth: Harcourt Brace.

**Sternberg, R. J.** (2002). Intelligence: The triarchic theory of intelligence. In J. W. Gutherie (Ed.), *Encyclopedia of education* (2nd ed.). New York: Macmillan.

**Sternberg, R. J.** (2003). Contemporary theories of intelligence. In I. B. Weiner (Ed.), *Handbook of psychology* (Vol. 3). New York: Wiley.

**Sternberg, R. J.** (2006). *Cognitive psychology* (4th ed.). Belmont, CA: Wadsworth.

**Sternberg, R. J.** (2007). g, g's, or Jeez: Which is the best model for developing abilities, competence, and expertise? In P. C. Kyllonen, R. D. Roberts, & L. Stankov (Eds.), *Extending intelligence.* Mahwah, NJ: Erlbaum.

**Sternberg, R. J.** (2008, in press). The triarchic theory of successful intelligence. In N. Salkind (Ed.), *Encyclopedia of educational psychology.* Thousand Oaks, CA: Sage.

**Sternberg, R. J., & Ben-Zeev, T.** (2001). *Complex cognition.* New York: Oxford University Press.

**Sternberg, R. J., & Grigorenko, E. L.** (Eds.). (2004). *Culture and competence.* Washington, DC: American Psychological Association.

**Sternberg, R. J., Grigorenko, E. L., & Singer, J. L.** (Eds.). (2004). *Creativity: From potential to realization.* Washington, DC: American Psychological Association.

**Sternberg, R. J., & Nigro, C.** (1980). Developmental patterns in the solution of verbal analogies. *Child Development, 51, 27–38.*

**Sternberg, R. J., & Rifkin, B.** (1979). The development of analogical reasoning processes. *Journal of Experimental Child Psychology, 27,* 195–232.

**Sternberg, R. J., Roediger, H., & Halpern D. F.** (Eds.), (2007). *Critical thinking in psychology.* New York: Cambridge University Press.

**Stern, D., & Hallinan, M. T.** (1997, Winter). The high schools, they are achangin. *Center Work Newsletter* (NCRVE, University of California, Berkeley), 1–6.

**Stetsenko, A.** (2002). Adolescents in Russia: Surviving the turmoil and creating a brighter future. In B. B. Brown, R. W. Larson, & T. S. Saraswathi (Eds.), *The world's youth.* New York: Cambridge University Press.

**Steur, F. B., Applefield, J. M., & Smith, R.** (1971). Televised aggression and the interpersonal aggression of preschool children. *Journal of Experimental Child Psychology, 11,* 442–447.

**Stevenson, C., Doherty, G., Barnett, J., Muldoon, O. T., & Trew, K.** (2007). Adolescents' views of food and eating: Identifying barriers to healthy eating. *Journal of Adolescence, 30,* 417–434.

**Stevenson, H. W.** (1992, December). Learning from Asian schools. *Scientific American,* pp. 6, 70–76.

**Stevenson, H. W.** (1995). Mathematics achievement of American students: First in the world by the year 2000? In C. A. Nelson (Ed.), *Basic and applied perspectives on learning, cognition, and development.* Minneapolis: University of Minnesota Press.

**Stevenson, H. W., Hofer, B. K., & Randel, B.** (2000). Middle childhood: Education and schooling. In W. Damon (Ed.), *Encyclopedia of psychology.* Washington, DC & New York: American Psychological Association and Oxford University Press.

**Stevenson, H. W., Lee, S., & Stigler, J. W.** (1986). Mathematics achievement of Chinese, Japanese, and American children. *Science, 231,* 693–699.

**Stevenson, H. W., & Zusho, A.** (2002). Adolescence in China and Japan: Adapting to a changing environment. In B. B. Brown, R. W. Larson, & T. S. Saraswathi (Eds.), *The world's youth.* New York: Cambridge University Press.

**Stewart, A. J., Ostrove, J. M., & Helson, R.** (2001). Middle aging in women: Patterns of personality change from the 30s to the 50s. *Journal of Adult Development, 8,* 23–37.

**Stewart, S. D.** (2006). *Brave new stepfamilies.* Thousand Oaks, CA: Sage.

**Stice, E., Presnell, K., Gau, J., & Shaw, H.** (2007). Testing mediators of intervention effects in randomized controlled trials: An evaluation of two eating disorder programs. *Journal of Consulting and Clinical Psychology, 75,* 20–32.

**Stice, E., Presnell, K., & Spangler, D.** (2002). Risk factors for binge eating onset in adolescent girls: A 2-year prospective investigation. *Health Psychology, 21,* 131–138.

**Stiers, G. A.** (2007). From this day forward: Commitment, marriage, and the family in lesbian and gay relationships. In S. J. Ferguson (Ed.), *Shifting the center: Understanding contemporary families* (3rd ed.). New York: McGraw-Hill.

**Stigler, J. W., Nusbaum, H. C., & Chalip, L.** (1988). Developmental changes in speed of processing: Central limiting mechanism or skill transfer. *Child Development, 59,* 1144–1153.

**Stipek, D.** (2005, February 16). Commentary in *USA Today,* p. 1D.

**Stipek, D. J.** (2002). *Motivation to learn* (4th ed.). Boston: Allyn & Bacon.

**Story, M., Kaphingst, K. M., & French, S.** (2006). The role of schools in obesity prevention. *Future of Children, 16,* 109–142.

**Stouthamer-Loeber, M. Wei, E., Loeber, R., & Masten, A.** (2004). Desistance from persistent serious delinquency in the transition to adulthood. *Development and Psychopathology, 16,* 897–918.

**Stouthamer-Loeber, M., Loeber, R., Wei, E., Farrington, D. P., & Wikstrom, P.H.** (2002). Risk and promotive effects in the explanation of persistent serious delinquency in boys. *Journal of Consulting and Clinical Psychology, 70,* 111–123.

**Strahan, D. B.** (1983). The emergence of formal operations in adolescence. *Transcendence, 11,* 7–14.

**Strasburger, V. C., & Donnerstein, E.** (1999). Children, adolescents, and the media: Issues and solutions. *Pediatrics, 103,* 129–137.

**Streib, H.** (1999). Off-road religion? A narrative approach to fundamentalist and occult orientations of adolescents. *Journal of Adolescence, 22,* 255–267.

**Striegel-Moore, R. H., Silberstein, L. R., & Rodin, J.** (1993). The social self in bulimia nervosa: Public self-consciousness, social anxiety, and perceived fraudulence. *Journal of Abnormal Psychology, 102,* 297–303.

**Strong, B., Yarber, W., Sayad, B., & DeVault, C.** (2008) *Human sexuality* (8th ed.). New York: McGraw-Hill.

**Stubbe, J. H., Boomsma, D. I., & De Geus, E. J.** (2005). Sports participation during adolescence: A shift from environmental to genetic factors. *Medical Science and Sports Exercise, 37,* 563–570.

**Stunkard, A. J.** (2000). Obesity. In A. Kazdin (Ed.), *Encyclopedia of psychology.* Washington, DC & New York: American Psychological Association and Oxford University Press.

**Suarez-Orozco, C.** (2002). Afterwards: Understanding and serving the children of immigrants. *Harvard Educational Review, 71,* 579–589.

**Suárez-Orozco, C.** (2007, March). *Immigrant family educational advantages and challenges.* Paper presented at the meeting of the Society for Research in Child Development, Boston.

**Suárez-Orozco, C., & Qin, D. B.** (2006). Gendered perspectives in psychology: Immigrant origin youth. *International Migration Review, 40,* 165–198.

**Subrahmanyam, K., Smahel, D., & Greenfield, P.** (2006). Connecting developmental constructions on the Internet: Identity presentation and sexual exploration in online chat rooms. *Developmental Psychology, 42,* 395–406.

**Substance Abuse and Mental Health Services Administration.** (2005). Substance use tables [online database] Retrieved on November 15, 2005 from www.icpsr.umich.edu/

**Sue, S.** (1990, August). *Ethnicity and culture in psychological research and practice.* Paper presented at the meeting of the American Psychological Association, Boston.

**Sue, S., & Morishima, J. K.** (1982). *The mental health of Asian Americans: Contemporary issues in identifying and treating mental problems.* San Francisco: Jossey-Bass.

**Sullivan, H. S.** (1953). *The interpersonal theory of psychiatry.* New York: W. W. Norton.

**Sullivan, K., & Sullivan, A.** (1980). Adolescent-parent separation. *Developmental Psychology, 16,* 93–99.

**Sun, L. Y., & Bartke, A.** (2007). Adult neurogenesis in the hippocampus of long-lived mice during aging. *Journal of Gerontology A: Biological Sciences and Medical Sciences, 62,* 117–125.

**Sung, H. E., Richter, L., Vaughan, R., Johnson, P. B., & Thom, B.** (2005). Nonmedical use of prescription opiods among teenagers in the United States: Trends and correlates. *Journal of Adolescent Health, 37,* 44–51.

**Super, D. E.** (1967). *The psychology of careers.* New York: Harper & Row.

**Super, D. E.** (1976). *Career education and the meanings of work.* Washington, DC: U.S. Office of Education.

**Suris, J. C., Jeannin, A., Chossis, I., & Michaud, P. A.** (2007). Piercing among adolescents: Body art as a risk marker: A population-based study. *Journal of Family Practice, 56,* 126–130.

**Susman, E. J.** (2001). Review of Santrock's *Adolescence,* 9th ed. (New York: McGraw-Hill).

**Susman, E. J., Dorn, L. D., & Schiefelbein, V. L.** (2003). Puberty, sexuality, and health. In R. M. Lerner, M. A. Easterbrooks, & J. Mistry (Eds.), *Comprehensive handbook of psychology: Development psychology* (Vol. 6). New York: Wiley.

**Susman, E. J., Murowchick, E., Worrall, B. K., & Murray, D. A.** (1995, March). *Emotionality, adrenal hormones, and context interactions during puberty and pregnancy.* Paper presented at the meeting of the Scoeity for Research in Child Development, Indianapolis.

**Susman, E. J., & Rogol, A.** (2004). Puberty and psychological development. In R. Lerner & L. Steinberg (Eds.), *Handbook of adolescence* (2nd ed.). New York: Wiley.

**Sussman, S., Unger, J., Rohrbach, L. A., & Johnson, C. A.** (2005). School-based smoking prevention research. *Journal of Adolescent Health, 37,* 4–8.

**Sutton-Smith, B.** (1982). Birth order and sibling status effects. In M. E. Lamb & B. Sutton-Smith (Eds.), *Sibling relationships: Their nature and significance across the life span.* Hillsdale, NJ: Erlbaum.

**Swaab, D. F., Chung, W. C. Kruijver, F. P., Hofman, M. A., & Ishunina, T. A.** (2002). Sexual differentiation of human hypothalamus. *Advances in Experimental Medicine and Biology, 511,* 75–100.

**Swaab, D. F., Chung, W. C., Kruijver, F. P., Hofman, M. A., & Ishunina, T. A.** (2001). Structural and functional sex differences in the human hypothalamus. *Hormones and Behavior, 40,* 93–98.

**Swahn, M. H., & Bossarte, R. M.** (2007). Gender, early alcohol use, and suicide ideation and attempts: Findings from the 2005 Youth Risk Behavior Survey. *Journal of Adolescent Health, 41,* 175–181.

**Swanson, H. L.** (1999). What develops in working memory? A life-span perspective. *Developmental Psychology, 35,* 986–1000

**Swanson, H. L.** (2005). Memory. In S. W. Lee (Ed.), *Encyclopedia of school psychology.* Thousand Oaks, CA: Sage.

**Swenson, R. R., & Prelow, H. M.** (2005, April). *Predictors of early sexual initiation among low income, urban minority youth.* Paper presented at the meeting of the Society for Research in Child Development, Atlanta.

**Swim, J. K., Aikin, K. J., Hall, W. S., & Hunter, B. A.** (1995). Sexism and racism: Old-fashioned and modern prejudices. *Journal of Personality and Social Psycholoy, 67,* 199–214.

**Swim, J. K., Mallett, R., & Stangor, C.** (2004). Understanding subtle sexism: Detection and use of sexist language. *Sex Roles, 51,* 117–128.

**Sykes, C. J.** (1995). *Dumbing down our kids: Why American children feel good about themselves but can't read, write, or add.* New York: St. Martin's Press.

## T

**Talaro, K. P.** (2008). *Foundations of microbiology* (6th ed.). New York: McGraw-Hill.

**Tamis-LeMonda, C. S., & Cabrera, N.** (Eds.) (2002). *The handbook of father involvement.* Mahwah, NJ: Erlbaum.

**Tannen, D.** (1990). *You just don't understand!* New York: Ballantine.

**Tanner, J. M.** (1962). *Gowth at adolescence* (2nd ed.). Oxford, OK: Blackwell.

**Tarpley, T.** (2001). Children, the Internet, and other new technologies. In D. Singer & J. Singer (Eds.), *Handbook of children and the media.* Thousand Oaks, CA: Sage.

**Tashiro, T., & Frazier, P.** (2003). "I'll never be in a relationhip like that again": Personal growth following romantic relationship breakups. *Personal Relationships, 10,* 113–128.

**Tashiro, T., Frazier, P., & Berman, M.** (2006). Stress-related growth following divorce and relationship dissolution. In M. A. Fine & J. H. Harvey (Eds.) *Handbook of divorce and relationship dissolution.* Mahwah, NJ: Erlbaum.

**Tasker, F. L., & Golombok, S.** (1997). *Growing up in a lesbian family: Effects on child development.* New York: Guilford.

**Tassell-Baska, J., & Stambaugh, T.** (2006). *Comprehensive curriculum for gifted learners* (3rd ed.). Boston: Allyn & Bacon.

**Tavris, C., & Wade, C.** (1984). *The longest war: Sex differences in perspective* (2nd ed.). Fort Worth: Harcourt Brace.

**Taylor, C. S., Smith, P. R., Taylor, V. A., von Eye, A., Lerner, R. M., Balsano, A. B., Anderson, P. M., Banik, R., & Almerigi, J. B.** (2005). Individual and ecological assets and thriving among African American adolescent male gang and community-based organization members: A report from wave 3 of the "Overcoming the Odds" Study. *Journal of Early Adolescence, 25,* 72–93.

**Taylor, J. H., & Walker, L. J.** (1997). Moral climate and the development of moral reasoning: The effects of dyadic discussions between young offenders. *Journal of Moral Education, 26,* 21–43.

**Taylor, R. D.** (1996). Kinship support, family management, and adolescent adjustment and competence in African American families. *Developmental Psychology, 32,* 687–695.

**Taylor, R. D., & Lopez, E. I.** (2005). Family management practice, school achievement, and problem behavior in African American adolescents: Mediating processes. *Applied Developmental Psychology, 26,* 39–49.

**Taylor, S. E.** (2002). *The tending instinct.* New York: Times Books.

**Taylor, S. E.** (2004). Commentary in "Taylor takes on 'fight-or-flight.'" *American Psychological Society, 17,* 21.

**Taylor, S. E.** (2006). *Health psychology* (6th ed.). New York: McGraw-Hill.

**Taylor, S. E., Klein, L. S., Lewis, B. P., Gruenewald, T. L., Gurung, R. A., & Updegraff, J. A.** (2000). Biobehavioral responses in females: Tend-and-befriend, not fight-or-flight. *Psychological Review, 107,* 411–429.

**Teenage Research Unlimited.** (2004, November 10). *Diversity in word and deed: Most teens claim multicultural friends.* Northbrook, IL: Author.

**Teilmann, G., Juul, A., Skakkebaek, N. E., & Toppari, J.** (2002). Putative effects of endocrine disruptors on pubertal developoment in the human. *Best Practices in Research and Clinical Endocrinology and Metabolism, 16,* 105–121.

**Tellegen, A.** (1982). *Brief manual of the Multidimensional Personality Questionnaire.* Unpublished manuscript, University of Minnesota.

**Templeton, J. L., & Eccles, J. S.** (2006). The relation between spiritual development and identity processes. In E. Roehlkepartain, P. E. King, L. Wagener, & P. L. Benson (Eds.), *The handbook of spirituality in childhood and adolescence.* Thousand Oaks, CA: Sage.

**Ter Bogt, T., Raaijmakers, Q., & van Wel, F.** (2005). Socialization and development of the work ethic among adolescents and young adults. *Journal of Vocational Behavior, 66,* 420–437.

**Teti, D. M.** (2001). Retrospect and prospect in the study of sibling relationships. In J. P. McHale & W. S. Grolnick (Eds.), *Retrospect and prospect in the psychological study of families.* Mahwah, NJ: Erlbaum.

**Thoma, S. J.** (2006). Research on the Defining Issues Test. In M. Killen & J. Smetana (Eds.), *Handbook of moral development.* Mahwah, NJ: Erlbaum.

**Thomas, A., & Chess, S.** (1991). Temperament in adolescence and its functional significance. In R. M. Lerner, A. C. Petersen, & J. Brooks-Gunn (Eds.), *Encyclopedia of adolescence* (Vol. 2). New York: Garland.

**Thomas, C. R.** (2005). Serious delinquency and gang membership. *Psychiatric Times, 22* (4), 18–22.

**Thomas, C. W., Coffman, J. K., & Kipp, K. L.** (1993, March). *Are only children different from children with siblings? A longitudinal study of behavioral and social functioning.* Paper presented at the biennial meeting of the Society for Research in Child Development, New Orleans.

**Thompson, M. P., Ho, C. H., & Kingree, J. B.** (2007). Prospective associations between delinquency and suicidal behaviors in a nationally representative sample. *Journal of Adolescent Health, 40,* 232–237.

**Thompson, R. A., Meyer, S., & McGinley, M.** (2006). Understanding values in relationships: The development of conscience. In M. Killen & J. Smetana (Eds.), *Handbook of moral development.* Mahwah, NJ: Erlbaum.

**Thorsen, C.** (2006). *Tech tactics* (2nd ed.). Boston: Allyn & Bacon.

**Tilton-Weaver, L., & Leighter, S.** (2002, April). *Peer management behavior: Linkages to parents' beliefs about adolescents and adolescents' friends.* Paper presented at the meeting of the Society for Research on Adolescence, New Orleans.

**Timimi, S., & Taylor, E.** (2004). ADHD is best understood as a cultural construct. *British Journal of Psychiatry, 184,* 8–9.

**Timperio, A. Salmon, J., & Ball, K.** (2004). Evidence-based strategies to promote physical activity among children, adolescents, and young adults: Review and update. *Journal for Science and Medicine in Sport, 7* (Suppl. 1), 20–29.

**Tobler, N. S. & others.** (2000). School-based adolescent drug prevention programs: 1998 meta-analysis. *Journal of Primary Prevention, 20,* 275–336.

**Toga, A. W., Thompson, P. M., & Sowell, E. R.** (2006). *Trends in Neuroscience, 29,* 148–159.

**Tolan, P. H., Gorman-Smith, D., Henry, D., Chung, K., & Hunt, M.** (2004). The relation of patterns of coping of inner-city youth to psychopathology symptoms. *Journal of Research on Adolescence, 12,* 423–449.

**Tolman, D.** (2002). *Dilemmas of desire: Teenage girls talk about sexuality.* Cambridge, MA: Harvard University Press.

**Tomlinson-Keasey, C.** (1972). Formal operations in females from 11 to 54 years of age. *Development Psychology, 6,* 364.

**Torney-Purta, J.** (1993, August). *Cross-cultural examination of stages of faith development.* Paper presented at the meeting of the American Psychological Association, Toronto.

**Tracey, T. J. G., Robbins, S. B., & Hofsess, C. D.** (2005). Stability and change in interests: A longitudinal study of adolescents from grades 8 through 12. *Journal of Vocational Behavior, 66,* 1–25.

**Trask, B. S., & Koivur, M.** (2007). Trends in marriage and cohabitation. In B. S. Trask & R. R. Hamon (Eds.), *Cultural diversity and families.* Thousand Oaks, CA: Sage.

**Triandis, H. C.** (2007). Culture and psychology: A history of their relationship. In S. Kitayama & D. Cohen (Eds.), *Handbook of cultural psychology.* New York: Guilford.

**Trimble, J. E.** (1989, August). *The enculturation of contemporary psychology.* Paper presented at the meeting of the American Psychological Association, New Orleans.

**Trulear, H. D.** (2000). Faith-based institutions and high-risk youth: First report to the field. Philadelphia, PA: Public/Private Ventures.

**Trzesniewski, K. H., Donnellan, M. B., Moffitt, T. E., Robins, R. W., Poulton, R., & Caspi, A.** (2006). Low self-esteem during adolescence predicts poor health, criminal behavior, and limited economic prospects during adulthood. *Developmental Psychology, 42,* 381–390.

**Tsal, Y., Shalev, L., & Mevorach, C.** (2005). The diversity of attention deficits in ADHD. *Journal of Learning Disabilities, 38,* 142–157.

**Tseng, K. Y., & O'Donnell, P.** (2007). Dopamine modulation of prefrontal cortical interneurons: Changes during adolescence. *Cerebral Cortex, 17,* 1235–1240.

**Tseng, V.** (2004). Family interdependence and academic adjustment in college: Youth from immigrant and U.S. born families. *Child Development, 75,* 966-983.

**Tucha, O., Prell, S., Mecklinger, L., Bormann-Kischkel, C., Kubber, S., Linder, M., Walitza, S., & Lange, K. W.** (2006). Effects of methylphenidate on multiple components of attention in children with attention deficit hyperactivity disorder. *Psychopharmacology 185,* 315–326.

**Tucker, C. J., & Winzeler, A.** (2007). Adolescent siblings' daily discussions: Connections to perceived academic, athletic, and peer competence. academic, athletic, and peer competency. *Journal of Research on Adolescence, 17,* 145–152.

**Tucker, C. J., McHale, S. M., & Crouter, A. C.** (2001). Conditions of sibling support in adolescence. *Journal of Family Psychology, 15,* 254–271.

**Tucker, C. J., McHale, S. M., & Crouter, A. C.** (2003). Conflict resolution: Links with adolescents' family relationships and individual well-being. *Journal of Family Issues, 24,* 715–726.

**Tucker, L. A.** (1987). Television, teenagers, and health. *Journal of Youth and Adolescence, 16,* 415–425.

**Tumeh, P. C., Alavi, A., Houseni, M., Greenfield, A., Chryssikos, T., Newberg, A., Torigian, D. A., & Moonis, G.** (2007). Structural and functional imaging correlates for age-related changes in the brain. *Seminars in Nuclear Medicine, 37,* 69–87.

**Turbin, M. S., Jessor, R., Costa, F. M., Dong, Q., Zhang, H., & Wang, C.** (2006). Protective and risk factors in health-enhancing behavior among adolescents in China and the United States: Does social context matter? *Health Psychology, 25,* 445–454.

**Turiel, E.** (2006). The development of morality. In W. Damon & R. Lerner (Eds.) *Handbook of child psychology* (6th ed.). New York: Wiley.

**Turk, D. C., Rudy, T. E., & Salovey, P.** (1984). Health protection: Attitudes and behaviors of LPN's teachers, and college students. *Health Psychology, 3,* 189–210.

**Turnage, B. F.** (2004). African American mother-daughter relationships mediating daughters' self-esteem. *Child and Adolescent Social Work Journal, 21,* 155–173.

**Turnbull, A., Turnbull, H. R., & Tompkins, J. R.** (2007). *Exceptional lives* (5th ed.). Upper Saddle River, NJ: Prentice-Hall.

**Twenge, J. M., & Campbell, W. K.** (2001). Age and birth cohort differences in self-esteem: A cross-temporal meta-analysis. *Personality and Social Psychology Bulletin, 5,* 321–344.

## U

**U.S. Census Bureau.** (2005). *People.* Washington, DC: Author.

**U.S. Department of Education.** (1996). *International comparisons of education.* Washington, DC: Author.

**U.S. Department of Education.** (1996). *Number and disabilities of children and youth served under IDEA.* Washington, DC: Office of Special Education Programs, Data Analysis System.

**U.S. Census Bureau.** (2006). *Annual Social and Economic Supplement to the Current Population Survey.* Washington, DC: Author.

**U.S. Department of Energy.** (2001). *The human genome project.* Washington, DC: Author.

**Udry, J. R.** (1990). Hormonal and social determinants of adolescents sexual initiation. In J. Bancroft & J. M. Reinisch (Eds.), *Adolescence and puberty.* New York: Oxford University Press.

**Uhart, M., Chong, R. Y., Oswald, L., Lin, P. I., & Wand, G. S.** (2006). Gender differences in hypothalamic-pituitary-adrenal (HPA) axis reactivity. *Psychoneuroendocrinology, 31,* 642–652.

**Ullman, S. E., Filipas, H. H., Townsend, S. M., & Starzynski, L. L.** (2006). The role of victim-offender relationship in women's sexual assault experiences. *Journal of Interpersonal Violence, 21,* 798–819.

**Ulloa, E. C., & Herrera, M.** (2006). Strategies for multicultural student success: What about grad school? *Career Development Quarterly, 54,* 361–366.

**Umaña-Taylor, A. J.** (2004). Ethnic identity and self-esteem: Examining the role of social contexts. *Journal of Adolescence, 27,* 139–146.

**Umaña-Taylor, A. J.** (2006, March). *Ethnic identity, acculturation, and enculturation: Considerations in methodology and theory.* Paper presented at the meeting of the Society for Research on Adolescence, San Francisco.

**Umaña-Taylor, A. J., Bhanot, R., & Shin, N.** (2006). Ethnic identity formation in adolescence: The critical role of families. *Journal of Family Issues, 27,* 390–414.

**Underwood, M.** (2003). Social aggression among girls. New York: Guilford.

**Underwood, M. K.** (2004). Gender and peer relations. In J. B. Kupersmidt & K. A. Dodge (Eds.), *Children's peer relations.* Washington, DC: American Pschological Association.

**Underwood, M. K., & Hurley, J. C.** (1997, April). *Children's responses to angry provocation as a function of peer status and aggression.* Paper presented at the meeting of the Society for Research in Child Development, Washington, DC.

**UNICEF.** (2003). *State of the world's children, 2003.* Geneva: Author.

**UNICEF.** (2006). *The state of the world's children, 2006.* Geneva: Author.

**UNICEF.** (2007). *The state of the world's children,2007.* Geneva: Author.

**University of Buffalo Counseling Services.** (2003). *Procrastination.* Buffalo, NY: Author.

**University of Illinois Counseling Center.** (1984). *Overcoming procrastination.* Urbana-Champaign, IL: Department of Student Affairs.

**Updegraff, K. A., McHale, S., Whiteman, S. D., Thayer, S. M., & Delgado, M. Y.** (2005). Adolescent sibling relationships in Mexican American families: Exploring the role of familism. *Journal of Family Psychology, 19,* 512–522.

**Urberg, K.** (1992). Locus of peer influence: Social crowd and best friend. *Journal of Youth and Adolescence, 21,* 439–450.

**Urdan, T., & Midgley, C.** (2001). Academic self-handicapping: What we know, what more is there to learn. *Educational Psychology Review, 13,* 115–138.

**USA Today.** (2001, October 10). All-USA first teacher team. Retrieved November 20, 2004, from www.usatoday/com/news/education2001

# V

**Valeri, S. M.** (2003). Social factors: Isolation and loneliness versus social activity. In A. Spirito & J. C. Overholser (Eds.), *Evaluating and treating adolescent suicide attempters.* San Diego: Academic Press.

**Valois, R. F., Zullig, K. J., Huebner, E. S., & Drane, J. W.** (2004). Physical activity behaviors and perceived life satisfaction among public high school students. *Journal of School Health, 74,* 59–65.

**Valuck, R. J., Lily, A. M., Sills, M. R., Giese, A. A., & Allen, R. R.** (2004). Antidepressant treatment and risk of suicide attmept by adolescents with major depressive disorder: A propensity-adjusted retrospective cohort study. *CNS Drugs Review, 18,* 119–1132.

**Van Buren, E., & Graham, S.** (2003). *Redefining ethnic identity: Its relationship to positive and negative school adjustment outcomes for minority youth.* Paper presented at the meeting of the Society for Research in Child Development, Tampa.

**van den Berg, P., Neumark-Sztainer, D., Hannan, P. J., & Haines, J.** (2007). Is dieting advice from magazines helpful or harmful? Five-year associations with weight-control behaviors and psychological outcomes in adolescents. *Pediatrics, 119,* e30–e37.

**van den Berg, S. M., & Boomsa, D. I.** (2007, in press). The familial clustering of age at menarche in extended twin studies. *Behavior Genetics.*

**Van Gelder, T.** (2005). Teaching critical thinking. *College Teaching, 53,* 41–46.

**Van Goozen, S. H. M., Matthys, W., Cohen-Kettenis, P. T., Thijssen, J. H. H., & van Engeland, H.** (1998). Adrenal androgens and aggression in conduct disorder prepubertal boys and normal control. *Biological Psychiatry, 43,* 156–158.

**van Weissenbruch, M. M., & Delemarre-van de Waal, H. A.** (2006). Early influences on the tempo of puberty. *Hormone Research, 65* (Suppl. 3), S105–S111.

**Vandell, D. L., Minnett, A., & Santrock, J. W.** (1987). Age differences in sibling relationships during middle childhood, *Applied Developmental Psychology, 8,* 247–257.

**vandenBerg, P., Neumark-Sztainer, D., Cafri, G., & Wall, M.** (2007). Steroid use among adolescents: Longitudinal findings from Project EAT. *Pediatrics, 119,* 476–486.

**Vazsonyi, A. T., Hibbert, J. R., & Snider, J. B.** (2003). Exotic enterprise no more? Adolescent reports of family and parenting processes from youth in four countries. *Journal of Research on Adolescence, 13,* 129–160.

**Verkooijen, K. T., de Vries, N. K., & Nielsen, G. A.** (2007). Youth crowds and substance use: The impact of perceived group norm and multiple group identification. *Psychology of Addictive Behaviors, 21,* 55–61.

**Verma, S., & Saraswathi, T. S.** (2002). Adolescence in India: Street urchins or silicon valley millionaires? In B. B. Brown, R. W. Larson, & T. S. Saraswathi (Eds.), *The world's youth.* New York: Cambridge University Pres.

**Vernberg, E. M.** (1990). Psychological adjustment and experience with peers during early adolescence: Reciprocal, incidental, or unidirectional relationships? *Journal of Abnormal Child Psychology, 18,* 187–198.

**Vernberg, E. M., Ewell, K. K., Beery, S. H., & Abwender, D. A.** (1994). Sophistication of adolescents' interpersonal negotiation strategies and friendship formation after relocation: A naturally occurring experiment. *Journal of Research on Adolescence, 4,* 5–19.

**Vesely, S. K., Wyatt, V. H., Oman, R. F., Aspy, C. B., Kegler, M. C., Rodine, S., Marshall, L., & McLeroy, K. R.** (2004). The potential protective effects of youth assets from adolescent sexual risk behaviors. *Journal of Adolescent Health, 34,* 356–365.

**Veugelers, P. J., & Fitzgerald, A. L.** (2005). Effectiveness of school programs in preventing obesity: A multilevel comparison. *American Journal of Public Health, 95,* 432–435.

**Vidal, F.** (2000). Piaget, Jean. In A. Kazdin (Ed.), *Encyclopedia of psychology.* Washington, DC., New York: American Psychological Association and Oxford University Press.

**Viner, R. M., Haines, M. M., Head, J. A., Bhui, K., Taylor, S., Stansfeld, S. A., Hillier, S., & Booy, R.** (2006). Variations in associations of health risk behaviors among ethnic minority early adolescents. *Journal of Adolescent Health, 38,* 55.

**Vondracek, F. W.** (1991). Vocational development and choice in adolescence. In R. M. Lerner, A. C. Petersen, & J. Brooks-Gunn (Eds.), *Encyclopedia of adolescence* (Vol. 2). New York: Garland.

**Vondracek, F. W., & Porfeli, E. J.** (2003). The world of work and careers. In G. Adams & M. Berzonsky (Eds.), *Blackwell handbook of adolescence.* Malden, MA: Blackwell.

**Vreeman, R. C., & Carroll, A. E.** (2007). A systematic review of school-based interventions to prevent bullying. *Archives of Pediatric and Adolescent Medicine, 161,* 78–88.

**Vygotsky, L. S.** (1962). *Thought and language.* Cambridge, MA: MIT Press.

# W

**Wachs, T. D.** (1994). Fit, context and the transition between temperament and personality. In C. Halverson, G. Kohnstamm, & R. Martin (Eds.), *The developing structure of personality from infancy to adulthood.* Hillsdale, NJ: Erlbaum.

**Wachs, T. D.** (2000). *Necessary but not sufficient.* Washington, DC: American Psychological Association.

**Wachs, T. D., & Kohnstamm, G. A.** (Eds.). (2001). *Temperament in context.* Mahwah, NJ: Erlbaum.

**Wagenaar, A. C.** (1983) *Alcohol, young drivers, and traffic accidents.* Lexington, MA: D. C. Heath.

**Wagner, B. M., Cohen, P., & Brook, J. S.** (1991, March). *Parent-adolescent relationships as moderators of the effects of stressful live events during adolescence.* Paper presented at the meeting of the Society for Research in Adolescence, Atlanta.

**Wainryb, C.** (2006). Culture and morality. In M. Killen & J. G. Smetana (Eds.), *Handbook of moral development.* Mahwah, NJ: Erlbaum.

**Waldron, H. B., Brody, J. L., & Slesnick, N.** (2001). Integrative behavioral and family therapy for adolescent substance abuse. In P. M. Monti, S. M. Colby, & T. A. O'Leary (Eds.), *Adolescents, alcohol, and substance abuse.* New York: Guilford.

**Walker, H.** (1998, May 31). Youth violence: Society's problem. *Eugene Register Guard,* p. 1C.

**Walker, L. J.** (2002). Moral Exemplarity. In W. Damon (Ed.), *Bringing in a new era of character education.* Stanford, CA: Hoover Press.

**Walker, L. J.** (2006). Gender and moral development. In M. Killen & J. Smetana (Eds.), *Handbook of moral development.* Mahwah, NJ: Erlbaum.

**Walker, L. J., de Vries, B., & Trevethan, S. D.** (1987). Moral stages and moral orientation in real-life and hypothetical dilemmas. *Child Development, 58,* 842–858.

**Walker, L. J., & Hennig, K. H.** (2004). Differing conceptions of moral exemplars: Just, brave, and caring. *Journal of Personality and Social Psychology, 86,* 629–647.

**Walker, L. J., Hennig, K. H., & Krettenauer, R.** (2000). Parent and peer contexts for children's moral reasoning development. *Child Development, 71,* 1033–1048.

**Walker, L. J., & Pitts, R. C.** (1998). Naturalistic conceptions of moral maturity. *Developmental Psychology, 34,* 403–419.

**Walker, L. J., Pitts, R. C., Hennig, K. H., & Matsuba, M. K.** (1995). Reasoning about morality and real-life moral problems. In M. Killen & D. Hart (Eds.), *Morality in everyday life.* New York: Cambridge University Press.

**Walker, L. J., & Reimer, K. S.** (2006). The relationship between moral and spiritual development. In E. C. Roehlkepartain, P. E. King, & L. M. Wagener (Eds.), *The handbook of spiritual development in childhood and adolescence.* Thousand Oaks, CA: Sage.

**Walker, L. J., & Taylor, J. H.** (1991). Family interaction and the development of moral reasoning. *Child Development, 62,* 264–283.

**Wallace-Broscious, A., Serafica, F. C., & Osipow, S. H.** (1994). Adolescent career development: Relationships to self-concept and identity status. *Journal of Research on Adolescence, 4,* 127–150.

**Waller, B.** (2006). Math interest and choice intentions of non-traditional African-American college students. *Journal of Vocational Behavior, 68,* 538–547.

**Wallis, C.** (1985, December 9). Children having children. *Time,* pp. 78–88.

**Walper, S., & Beckh, K.** (2006). Adolescents' development in high-conflict and separated families: Evidence from a German longitudinal study. In A. Clarke-Stewart & J. Dunn (Eds.), *Families count.* New York: Cambridge University Press.

**Walsh, D., & Bennett, N.** (2004). *WHY do they act that way?: A survival guide to the adolescent brain for you and your teen.* New York: Free Press.

**Walter, C. A.** (1986). *The timing of motherhood.* Lexington, MA: D. C. Heath.

**Walters, E., & Kendler, K. S.** (1994). Anorexia nervosa and anorexia-like symptoms in a population based twin sample. *American Journal of Psychiatry, 152,* 62–71.

**Wandersman, A., & Florin, P.** (2003). Community interventions and effective prevention. *American Psychologist, 58,* 441–448.

**Wang, H. F., & Yeh, M. C.** (2005). Stress, coping, and psychological health of vocational high school nursing students associated with a competitive entrance exam. *Journal of Nursing Research, 13,* 106–116.

**Wang, J. Q.** (2000, November). *A comparison of two international standards to assess child and adolescent obesity in three populations.* Paper presented at the meeting of American Public Health Association, Boston.

**Wang, Y., Monteiro, C., & Popkin, B. M.** (2002). Trends in obesity and underweight in older children and adolescents in the United States, Brazil, China, and Russia. *American Journal of Clinical Nutrituion, 75,* 971–977.

**Ward, L. M.** (1995). Talking about sex: Common themes about sexuality in the prime-time television programs children and adolescents view most. *Journal of Youth and Adolescence, 24,* 595–615.

**Ward, L. M.** (2002). Does television exposure affect emerging adults' attitudes and assumptions about sexual relationships? Correlational and experimental confirmation. *Journal of Youth and Adolescence, 31,* 1–15.

**Ward, L. M.** (2003). Understanding the role of entertainment media in the sexual socialization of American youth: A review of empirical research. *Developmental Review, 23,* 347–388.

**Ward, L. M., Day, K. M., & Epstein, M.** (2006). Uncommonly good: Exploring how mass media may be a positive influence on young women's sexual health and development. *New Directions for Child and Adolescent Development, 112,* 57–70.

**Ward, L. M., & Friedman, K.** (2006). Using TV as a guide: Associations between television viewing and adolescents' sexual attitudes and behavior. *Journal of Research on Adolescence, 16,* 133–156.

**Ward, L. M., Gorvine, B., & Cytron, A.** (2002). Would that really happen? Adolescents' perceptions of sexual relationships according to prime-time television. In J. D. Brown, J. R. Steele, & K. Walsh-Childers (Eds.), *Sexual teens, sexual media.* Mahwah, NJ: Erlbaum.

**Ward, L. M., Hansbrough, E., & Walker, E.** (2005). Contributions of music video exposure to Black adolescents' gender and sexual schemas. *Journal of Adolescent Research, 20,* 143–166.

**Wark, G. R., & Krebs, D. L.** (1996). Gender and dilemma differences in real-life moral judgment. *Developmental Psychology, 32,* 220–230.

**Wark, G. R., & Krebs, D. L.** (2000). The construction of moral dilemmas in everyday life. *Journal of Moral Education, 29,* 5–21

**Warrington, M., & Younger, M.** (2003). "We decided to give it a twirl": Single-sex teaching in English comprehensive school. *Gender and Education, 15,* 339–350.

**Waterman, A. S.** (1985). Identity in the context of adolescent psychology. In A. S. Waterman (Ed.), *Identity in adolescence: Processes and contents.* San Francisco: Jossey-Bass.

**Waterman, A. S.** (1989). Curricula interventions for identity change: Substantive and ethical considerations. *Journal of Adolescence, 12,* 389–400.

**Waterman, A. S.** (1992). Identity as an aspect of optimal psychological functioning. In G. R. Adams, T. P. Gullotta, & R. Montemayor (Eds.), *Adolescent identity formation.* Newbury Park, CA: Sage.

**Waterman, A. S.** (1999). Identity, the identity statuses, and identity status development: A contemporary statement. *Developmental Review, 19,* 591–621.

**Watkins, N., Larson, R., & Sullivan, P.** (2007, in press). Learning to bridge difference: Community youth programs as contexts for developing multicultural competencies. *American Behavioral Scientist.*

**Watson, D. L., & Tharp, R. G.** (2007). *Self-directed behavior* (9th ed.). Belmont, CA: Wadsworth.

**Watson, R., & DeMeo, P.** (1987). Premarital cohabitation vs. traditional courtship and subsequent marital adjustment: A replication and follow-up. *Family Relations, 36,* 193–197.

**Waylen, A., & Wolke, D.** (2004). Sex 'n' rock 'n' roll: The meaning and consequences of pubertal timing. *European Journal of Endocrinology, 151* (Suppl. 3), U151–U159.

**Weaver, R. F.** (2008). *Molecular biology* (4th ed.). New York: McGraw-Hill.

**Wechsler, H., Davenport, A., Dowdall, G., Moeykens, B., & Castillo, S.** (1994). Health and behavioral consequences of binge drinking in college. *Journal of the American Medical Association, 272,* 1672–1677.

**Wechsler, H., Lee, J. E., Kuo, M., Seibring, M., Nelson, T. F., & Lee, H.** (2002) Trends in college binge drinking during a period of increased prevention efforts: Findings from 4 Harvard School of Public Health college alcohol study surveys: 1993–2001. *Journal of American College Health, 50,* 203–217.

**Weinstein, C. S.** (2007). *Middle and secondary management: Lessons from research and practice* (3rd ed). New York: McGraw-Hill.

**Weinstein, N. D.** (1984). Reducing unrealistic optimism about illness susceptibility. *Health Psychology, 3,* 431–457.

**Weinstock, H., Berman, S., & Cates, W.** (2004). Sexually transmitted diseases among American youth: Incidence and prevalence estimates, 2000. *Perspectives on Sexual and Reproductive Health, 36,* 6–10.

**Weissberg, R. P., & Caplan, M.** (1989, April). *A followup study of a school-based social competence program for young adolescents.* Paper presented at the meeting of the Society for Research in Child Development, Kansas City.

**Weissberg, R. P., Kumpfer, K. L., & Seligman, M. E. P.** (2003). Prevention that works for children and youth. *American Psychologist, 58,* 425–432.

**Weisz, A. N., & Black, B. M.** (2002). Gender and moral reasoning: African American youth respond to dating dilemmas. *Journal of Human Behavior in the Social Environment, 5,* 35–52.

**Welti, C.** (2002). Adolescents in Latin America: Facing the future with skepticism. In B. B. Brown, R. W. Larson, & T. S. Saraswathi (Eds.), *The world's youth.* New York: Cambridge University Press.

**Weng, A., & Montemayor, R.** (1997, April). *Conflict between mothers and adolescents.* Paper presented at the meeting of the Society for Research in Child Development, Washington, DC.

**Wentzel, K. R.** (2002). Are effective teachers like good parents? Teaching styles and student adjustment in early adolescence. *Child Development, 73,* 287–301.

**Wentzel, K. R.** (2003). School adjustment. In I. B. Weiner (Ed.), *Handbook of* psychology (Vol. 7). New York: Wiley.

**Wentzel, K. R.** (2004). Unpublished review of J. W. Santrock's *Adolescence,* 11th ed. (New York: McGraw-Hill).

**Wentzel, K. R.** (2006). A social motivational perspective for classroom management. In C. M. Evertson & C. S. Weinstein (Eds.), *Handbook of classroom management.* Mahwah, NJ: Erlbaum.

**Wentzel, K. R., & Asher, S. R.** (1995). The academic lives of neglected, rejected, popular, and controversial children. *Child Development, 66,* 754–763.

**Wentzel, K. R., Barry, C. M., & Caldwell, K. A.** (2004). Friendships in middle school: Influences on motivation and school adjustment. *Journal of Educational Psychology, 96,* 195–203.

**Wentzel, K. R., & Caldwell, K.** (1997). Close friend and group influence on adolescent cigarette smoking and alcohol use. *Child Development, 31,* 540–547.

**Werner, E., & Smith, R. S.** (1982). *Overcoming the odds: High risk children from birth to adulthood.* Ithaca, NY: Cornell University Press.

**Werth, J. L.** (2004). The relationships among clinical depression, suicide, and other actions that may hasten death. *Behavioral Science and the Law, 22,* 627.

**Weston, K.** (2007). Exiles from kinship. In S. J. Ferguson (Ed.), *Shifting the center: Understanding contemporary families* (3rd ed.). New York: McGraw-Hill.

**Weyandt, L. L.** (2006). *An ADHD primer.* Mahwah NJ: Erlbaum.

**Weyman, A.** (2003). Promoting sexual health to young people. *Journal of Research on Social Health, 123,* 6–7.

**Whetstone, L. M., Morrissey, S. L., & Cummings, D. M.** (2007). Children at risk: The association between perceived weight status and suicidal thoughts and attempts in middle school youth. *Journal of School Health, 77,* 59–66.

**White, F. A., & Matawie, K. M.** (2004). Parental morality and family processes as predictors of morality. *Journal of Child and Family Studies, 13,* 219–233.

**White, L., & Gilbreth, J. G.** (2001). When children have two fathers: Effects of relationships with stepfathers and noncustodial fathers on adolescent outcomes. *Journal of Marriage and the Family, 63,* 155–167.

**White, M.** (1993). *The material child: Coming of age in Japan and America.* New York: Free Press.

**Whitehead, B. D., & Popenoe, D.** (2003). *The state of our unions: 2003.* New Brunswick, NJ: Rutgers University.

**Whitesell, N. R., Mitchell, C. M., Kaufman, C. E. Spicer, P., & the Voices of Indian Teens Project Team.** (2006). Developmental trajectories of personal and collective self-concept among American Indian adolescents. *Child Development, 77,* 1487–1503.

**Whitfield, K. E., King, G., Moller, S., Edwards, C. L., Nelson, T., & Vandenbergh, D.** (2007). Concordance rates for smoking among African-American twins. *Journal of the American Medical Association, 99,* 213–217.

**Whitford, T. J., Rennie, C. J., Grieve, S. M., Clark, C. R., Gordon, E., & Williams, L. M.** (2007). Brain maturation in adolescence: Concurrent changes in neuroanatomy and neurophysiology. *Human Brain Mapping, 28* (3), 228–237.

**Whiting, B. B.** (1989, April). *Culture and interpersonal behaviour.* Paper presented at the meeting of the Society for Research in Child Development, Kansas City.

**Whitlock, J. L., Powers, J. L. & Eckenrode, J.** (2006). The virtual cutting edge: The Internet and adolescent self-injury. *Developmental Psychology, 42,* 407–417.

**Whitlock, K. E., Illing, N., Brideau, N. J., Smith, K. M., & Twomey, S.** (2006). Development of GnRH cells: Setting the stage for puberty. *Molecular and Cellular Endocrinology, 254–255,* 39–50.

**Whitman, F. L., Diamond, M., & Martin, J.** (1993). Homosexual orientation in twins: A report on 61 pairs and three triplet sets. *Archives of Sexual Behavior, 22,* 187–206.

**Wiehe, S. E., Garrison, M. M., Christakis, D. A., Ebel, B. E., & Rivara, F. P.** (2005). A systematic review of school-based smoking prevention trials with long-term follow-up. *Journal of Adolescent Health, 36,* 162–169.

**Wiencke, J. K., Thurston, S. W., Kelsey, K. T., Varkonyi, A., Wain, J. C., Mark, E. J., & Christiani, D. C.** (1999). Early age at smoking initiation and tobacco carcinogen DNA damage in the lung. *Journal of the National Cancer Institute, 91,* 614–619.

**Wigfield, A., Byrnes, J. P., & Eccles, J. S.** (2006). Development during early and middle adolescence. In P. A. Alexander & P. H. Winne (Eds.), *Handbook of educational psychology* (2nd ed.). Mahwah, NJ: Erlbaum.

**Wigfield, A., & Eccles, J. S.** (1989). Test anxiety in elementary and secondary school students. *Journal of Educational Psychology, 24,* 159–183.

**Wigfield, A., & Eccles, J. S.** (Eds.). (2002). *Development of achievement motivation.* San Diego: Academic Press.

**Wigfield, A., Eccles, J. S., Schiefele, U., Roeser, R., & Davis-Kean, P.** (2006). Development of achievement motivation. In W. Damon & R. Lerner (Eds.), *Handbook of child psychology* (6th ed.). New York: Wiley.

**Wight, D., Williamson, L., & Henderson, M.** (2006). Parental influences on young people's sexual behavior: A longitudinal analysis. *Journal of Adolescence, 29,* 473–494.

**Wilburn, V. R., & Smith, D. E.** (2005). Stress, self-esteem, and suicidal ideation in late adolescents. *Adolescence, 40,* 33–45.

**William T. Grant Foundation Commission on Work, Family, and Citizenship.** (1988, February). *The forgotten half: Noncollege-bound youth in America.* New York: William T. Grant Foundation.

**Williams, C., & Bybee, J.** (1994). What do children feel guilty about? Developmental and gender differences. *Developmental Psychology, 30,* 617–623.

**Williams, D. D., Yanchar, S. C., Jensen, L. C., & Lewis, C.** (2003). Character education in a public high school: A multi-year inquiry into unified studies. *Journal of Moral Education, 32,* 3–33.

**Williams, F., & Schmidt, M.** (2003, April). *Parent and peer relationships predicting early adolescent sexual behavior.* Paper presented at the meeting of the Society for Research in Child Development, Tampa.

**Williams, J. E., & Best, D. L.** (1982). *Measuring sex stereotypes: A thirty-nation study.* Newbury Park, CA: Sage.

**Williams, J. E., & Best, D. L.** (1989). *Sex and psyche: Self-concept viewed cross-culturally.* Newbury Park, CA: Sage.

**Williams, L. M., Brown, K. J., Palmer, D., Liddell, B. J., Kemp, A. H., Olivieri, G., Peduto, A., & Gordon, E.** (2006). The mellow years?: Neural basis of improving emotional stability over age. *Journal of Neuroscience, 26,* 6422–6430.

**Williams, T. M., & Cox, R.** (1995, March). *Informative versus other children's TV programs: Portrayals of ethnic diversity, gender, and aggression.* Paper presented at the meeting of the Society for Research in Child Development, Indianapolis.

**Wills, T. A., Yaeger, A. M., & Sandy, J. M.** (2003). Buffering effect of religiosity for adolescent substance use. *Psychology of Addictive Behaviors, 17,* 24–31.

**Wilson, G. S., Pritchard, M. E., & Revalee, B.** (2005). Individual differences in adolescent health symptoms: The effects of gender and coping. *Journal of Adolescence, 28,* 369–379.

**Wilson-Shockley, S.** (1995). *Gender differences in adolescent depression: The contribution of negative affect.* M.S. thesis, University of Illinois at Urbana-Champaign.

**Windle, M.** (1989). Substance use and abuse among adolescent runaways: A four-year follow-up study. *Journal of Youth and Adolescence, 18,* 331–341.

**Windle, M., & Dumenci, L.** (1998). An investigation of maternal and adolescent depressed mood using a latent trait-state model. *Journal of Research on Adolescence, 8,* 461–484.

**Wineberg, H.** (1994). Marital reconciliation in the United States: Which couples are successful? *Journal of Marriage and the Family, 56,* 80–88.

**Winerman, L.** (2005, January). Leading the way. *Monitor on Psychology, 36* (1), 64–67.

**Winn, I. J.** (2004). The high cost of uncritical teaching. *Phi Delta Kappan, 85,* 496–497.

**Winne, P. H.** (1995). Inherent details in self-regulated learning. *Educational Psychologist, 30,* 173–187.

**Winne, P. H.** (1997). Experimenting to bootstrap self-regulated learning. *Journal of Educational Psychology, 89,* 397–410.

**Winne, P. H., & Perry, N. E.** (2000). Measuring self-regulated learning. In M. Boekaerts, P. R. Pintrich, & M. Zeidner (Eds.), *Handbook of self-regulation.* San Diego: Academic Press.

**Winner, E.** (1996). *Gifted children: Myths and realities.* New York: Basic Books.

**Winner, E.** (2006). Development in the arts. In W. Damon & R. Lerner (Eds.), *Handbook of child psychology* (6th ed.). New York: Wiley.

**Wiseman, C. V., Sunday, S. R., & Becker, A. E.** (2005) Impact of the media on adolescent body image. *Child and Adolescent Psychiatry Clinics of North America, 14,* 453–471.

**Witkow, M., Flook, L., Hardway, C., & Fuligni, A. J.** (2005, April). *Balancing daily time with friends and family during adolescence: Consequences for well-being.* Paper presented at the meeting of the Society for Research in Child Development, Atlanta.

**Wodarski, J. S., & Hoffman, S. D.** (1984) Alcohol education for adolescents. *Social Work in Education, 6,* 69–92.

**Wolak, J., Mitchell, K., & Finkelhor, D.** (2007). Unwanted and wanted exposure to online pornography in a national sample of youth Internet users. *Pediatrics, 119,* 247–257.

**Wolfe, J. B., & Betz, N. E.** (2005). The relationship of attachment variables to career decision-making self-efficacy and fear of commitment. *Career Development Quarterly, 52,* 363–369.

**Wolfe, S. M., Toro, P. A., & McCaskill, P. A.** (1999). A comparison of homeless and matched housed adolescents on family environment variables. *Journal of Research on Adolescence, 9,* 53–66.

**Wong, B. P.** (2007). Immigration, globalization, and the Chinese American family. In J. E. Lansford, K. Deater-Deckard, & M. H. Bornstein (Eds.), *Immigrant families in contemporary society.* New York: Guilford.

**Wood, W., & Eagly, A. H.** (2007). Social structural origins of sex differences in human mating. In S. W. Gangestad & J. A. Simpson (Eds.), *The evolution of mind.* New York: Guilford.

**Woodard. E.** (2000). *Media in the Home 2000: The Fifth Annual Survey of Parents and Children Philadelpha:* The Annenberg Public Policy Center.

**Woodhill, B. M., & Samuels, C. A.** (2004). Desirable and undesirable androgyny: A prescription for the twenty-first century. *Journal of Gender Studies, 13,* 15–28.

**Woodrich, D. L.** (1994). *Attention-deficit hyperactivity disorder: What every parent should know.* Baltimore: Paul H. Brookes.

**World Health Organization.** (2000). *The world health report.* Geneva: Author.

**World Health Organization.** (2002). *The world health report 2002.* Geneva, Author.

**Wrobel, G. M., Hendrickson, Z., & Grotevant, H. D.** (2006). Adoption. In G. G. Bear & K. Minke (Eds.). *Children's needs III: Development, problems, and alternatives.* Washington, DC: National Association of School Psychologists.

**Wu, C. X., & Chao, R. K.** (2005). Intergenerational cultural conflicts for Chinese American youth with immigrant parents: Norms of parental warmth and the consequences. *International Journal of Behavioral Development, 29,* 516–523.

## Y

**Yang, C. K., Kim, J. K., Patel, S. R., & Lee, J. H.** (2005). Age-related changes in sleep/wake patterns among Korean teenagers. *Pediatrics, 115* (Suppl. 1), S250–S256.

**Yasui, M., Dorham, C. L., & Dishion, T. J.** (2004). Ethnic identity and psychological adjustment: A validity analysis for European American and African American adolescents. *Journal of Adolescent Research, 19,* 807–825.

**Yates, M.** (1995, March). *Community service and political-moral discussions among Black urban adolescents.* Paper presented at the meeting of the Society for Research in Child Development, Indianapolis.

**Yen, H. L., & Wong, J. T.** (2007). Rehabilitation for traumatic brain injury to children and adolescents. *Annals of the Academy of Medicine Singapore, 36,* 62–66.

**Yeung, D. Y., So-kum Tang, C., & Lee, A.** (2005). Psychosocial and cultural factors in influencing expectations of menarche. *Journal of Adolescent Research, 20,* 118–135.

**Yeung, W. J., Sandberg, J. F., Davis-Kean P. E., & Hofferth, S. L.** (2001). Children's time-use with fathers in intact families. *Journal of Marriage and the Family, 63* (1), 136–154.

**Yeung, W. J., Sandberg, J. F., Davis-Kearn, P. E., & Hofferth, S. L.** (1999, April). *Children's time with fathers in intact families.* Paper presented at the meeting of the Society for Research in Child Development, Albuquerque.

**Yin, Y., Buhrmester, D., & Hibbard, D.** (1996, March). *Are there developmental changes in the influence of relationships with parents and friends on adjustment during early adolescence?* Paper presented at the meeting of the Society for Research on Adolescence, Boston.

**Yip, T., Seaton, E. K., & Sellers, R. M.** (2006). African American racial identity across the lifespan: Identity status, identity content, and depressive symptoms. *Child Development, 77,* 1504–1517.

**Yoo, H. J., Choi, K. M., Ryu, O. H., Suh, S. I., Kim, N. H., Baik, S. H., & Choi, D. S.** (2006). Delayed puberty due to pituitary stalk dysgenesis and ectopic neurohypophysis. *Korean Journal of Internal Medicine, 21,* 68–72.

**Young, A. M., Morales, M., McCabe, S. E., Boyd, C. J., & Darcy, H.** (2005). Drinking like a guy: Frequent binge drinking among undergraduate women. *Substance Use and Misuse, 40,* 241–267.

**Young, E. L., Boye, A. E., & Nelson, D. A.** (2006). Relational aggression: Understanding, identifying and responding in schools. *Psychology in the Schools, 43,* 297–312.

**Young, R. A.** (1994). Helping adolescents with career development: The active role of parents. *Career Development Quarterly, 42,* 195–203.

**Young, S. E., Rhee, S. H., Stallings, M. C., Corley, R. P., & Hewitt, J. K.** (2006). Genetic and environmental vulnerabilities underlying substance use and problem use: General or specific? *Behavior Genetics, 36,* 603–615.

**Youngblade, L. M., & Curry, L. A.** (2006). The people they know: Links between interpersonal contexts and adolescent risky and health-promoting behavior. *Developmental Science, 10,* 96–106.

**Youngblade, L. M., & Theokas, C.** (2006). The multiple contexts of youth development: Implications for theory, research, and practice. *Applied Developmental Science, 10,* 58–60.

**Youniss, J., McLellan, J. A., & Yates, M.** (1999). Religion, community service, and identity in American youth. *Journal of Adolescence, 22,* 243–253.

**Youniss, J., & Ruth, A. J.** (2002). Approaching policy for adolescent development in the 21st century. In J. T. Mortimer & R. W. Larson (Eds.), *The changing adolescent experience.* New York: Cambridge University Press.

**Yurgelun-Todd, D.** (2007). Emotional and cognitive changes during adolescence. *Current Opinion in Neurobiology, 17,* 251–257.

**Yussen, S. R.** (1977). Characteristics of moral dilemmas written by adolescents. *Developmental Psychology, 13,* 162–163.

## Z

**Zabin, L. S.** (1986, May/June). Evaluation of a pregnancy prevention program for urban teenagers. *Family Planning Perspectives,* p. 119.

**Zabin, L. S., Hirsch, M. B., & Emerson, M. R.** (1989). When urban adolescents choose abortion: Effects on education, psychological status and subsequent pregnancy. *Family Planning Perspectives, 21,* 248–255.

**Zager, K., & Rubenstein, A.** (2002). *The inside story on teen girls.* Washington, DC: American Psychological Association.

**Zakriski, A. L., Wheeler, E., Burda, J., & Shields, A.** (2005). Justifiable psychopharmacology or overzealous prescription? *Child and Adolescent Mental Health, 10,* 16–22.

**Zarate, M. E., Bhimji, F., & Reese, L.** (2005). Ethnic identity and academic achievement among Latino/a adolescents. *Journal of Latinos and Education, 4,* 95–104.

**Zeinoldini, S., Swarts, J. J., & Van de Heijning, B. J.** (20060. Chronic leptin infusion advances, and immunoneutralization of leptin postpones puberty onset in normally fed and feed restricted female rats. *Peptides, 27,* 1652–1658.

**Zelnik, M., & Kantner, J. F.** (1977). Sexual and contraceptive experiences of young unmarried women in the United States, 1976 and 1971. *Family Planning Perspectives, 9,* 55–71.

**Zentall, S. S.** (2006). *ADHD and education.* Upper Saddle River, NJ: Prentice Hall.

**Zhang, L., Li, X., Shah, I. H., Baldwin, W., & Stanton, B.** (2007). Parent-adolescent sex communication in China. *European Journal of Contraceptive and Reproductive Health Care, 12,* 138–147.

**Zill, N., Morrison, D. R., & Coiro, M. J.** (1993). Long-term effects of parental divorce on parent-child relationships, adjustment, and achievement in young adulthood. *Journal of Family Psychology, 7,* 91–103.

**Zimbardo, P.** (1997, May). What messages are behind today's cults? *APA Monitor,* p. 14.

**Zimmerman, B. J., Bonner, S., & Kovach, R.** (1996). *Developing self-regulated learners.* Washington, DC: American Psychological Association.

**Zimmerman, P.** (2007, March). *Attachment in adolescence.* Paper presented at the meeting of the Society for Research in Child Development, Boston.

**Zimmerman, R. S., Khoury, E., Vega, W. A., Gil, A. G., & Warheit, G. J.** (1995). Teacher and student perceptions of behavior problems among a sample of African American, Hispanic, and non-Hispanic White students. *American Journal of Community Psychology, 23,* 181–197.

**Zinn, M. B., Wells, B.** (2000). Diversity within Latino families: New lessons for family social science.

**Zittleman, K.** (2006, April). *Being a girl and being a boy: The voices of middle schoolers.* Paper presented at the meeting of the American Educational Research Association, San Francisco.

**Zucker, A. N., Ostrove, J. M., & Stewart, A. J.** (2002). College educated women's personality development in adulthood: Perceptions and age differneces. *Psychology and Aging, 17,* 236–244.

**Zukow-Goldring, P.** (2002). Sibling caregiving. In M. H. Bornstein (Ed.), *Handbook of parenting* (Vol. 3). Mahwah, NJ: Erlbaum.

**Zuzanek, J.** (2000). *The effects of time use and time pressure on child parent relationships.* Waterloo, Ontario: Otium.

# CREDITS

## Photo Credits

### Chapter 1

**Opener:** © John Henley/CORBIS; **p. 4 (top & middle):** © AP/Wide World Photos; **p. 4 (bottom):** © Michael Maddaus, University of Minnesota, Division of Thoracic & Foregut Surgery; **p. 6 (top):** © Archives of the History of American Psychology, University of Akron, Akron, Ohio; **p. 6 (bottom):** Courtesy of the Institute for Intercultural Studies, Inc., New York; **p. 8:** © Archives of the History of American Psychology, University of Akron, Ohio; **p. 9:** © PhotoDisc website; **p. 13:** Courtesy of Peter Benson, Search Institute; **p. 14 (top):** © AFP/Getty; **p. 14** (middle): © Dain Gair Photographic/Index Stock; **p.14 (bottom):** © AP/Wide World Photos; 1.4 **(left to right):** Prenatal: Courtesy of Landrum Shettles; Infancy: John Santrock; Early childhood: © Joe Sohm/Chromosohm Media/The Image Works; Middle childhood: © CORBIS website; Adolescence: © James L. Shaffer; Early adulthood: © Vol. 155/CORBIS; Middle adulthood: © CORBIS website; Late adulthood: © CORBIS website; **p. 19 (left):** © Bill Aron/Photo Edit; **p. 19 (right):** © Myrleen Ferguson/Photo Edit; **p. 19 (bottom):** © Andrew Council; **p. 22:** © Chuck Savage/The Stock Market/Corbis; **p. 24 (left)** © Stockbyte/Getty RF; **p. 24 (right):** © Photodisc/Getty RF; **p. 26:** © Bettmann/CORBIS; **p. 27:** © Barton Silverman/NYT Pictures/Redux Pictures; **p. 29:** © Sarah Putnam/Index Stock Imagery; **p. 30:** © Yves Debraine/Black Star/ Stock Photo; **p. 31:** © A.R. Lauria/Dr. Michael Cole, Laboratory of Human Cognition; **p. 32:** © Nita Winter; **p. 34:** Courtesy of Cornell University, Dept. of Human Development and Family Services; **p. 35:** © Michael Newman/ Photo Edit; **p. 37 (top):** © David Grubin Productions, Inc. Reprinted by permission; **p. 37 (bottom):** Image courtesy of Dana Boatman, Ph.D., Department of Neurology, Johns Hopkins University. Reprinted with permission from *The Secret Life of the Brain* © 2001 by the National Academy of Sciences. Courtesy of the National Academies Press, Washington, D.C.; **p. 41 (left):** © Syndicated Features Limited/The Image Works; **p. 41 (right):** © Thomas Craig/Index Stock; **p. 42:** Courtesy of Pamela Trotman Reid

### Chapter 2

**Opener:** © Mug Shots/The Stock Market/Corbis; **p. 58 (top):** © David Young-Wolff/Photo Edit; **p. 58 (bottom):** © Buddy Mays/CORBIS; **p. 63:** © Jon Feingersh/The Stock Market/CORBIS; **p. 64:** © CORBIS RF; **p. 67:** Courtesy of Anne Petersen, W.K. Kellogg Foundation; **p. 69:** © Photodisc Green/PunchStock; **p. 70:** © Spencer Grant/ Photo Edit; **p. 71:** © Kyle Ericson/AP Wide World Photos; **p. 72:** © Tom Stewart/ CORBIS; **p. 73:** © Richard T. Nowitz/CORBIS; **p. 75:** © Duomo/CORBIS; **p. 76:** © Jim Lo Scalzo; **p. 81:** © Tony Freeman/Photo Edit; **p. 83:** © Duomo/Corbis

### Chapter 3

**Opener:** © Vol. RFCD697/CORBIS; **3.2:** © Steve Gschmeissner/ Photo Researchers; **p. 95:** © Davis Turner-Pool/Getty Images; **p. 100:** © David Young-Wolff/Photo Edit; **p. 102:** © Johnny Le Fortune/zefa/CORBIS; **3.6:** © Cleve Bryant/ Photo Edit; **3.7 (left):** © A.R. Lauria/Dr. Michael Cole, Laboratory of Human Cognition; **3.7 (right):** © Bettmann/CORBIS; **p. 110:** © Big Cheese Photo/SuperStock RF; **p. 113:** Courtesy of Laura Bickford; **p. 114:** © Gideon Mendel/ Corbis; **p. 120:** © Tom Stewart/Corbis; **p. 123:** © Will & Deni McIntyre/CORBIS; **p. 124:** Stewart Cohen/Stone/Getty Images; **p. 125:** © Richard Hutchings/Corbis

### Chapter 4

**Opener:** © Dominic Rouse/The Image Bank/Getty Images; **p. 136:** © A. Huber/U. Starke/zefa/Corbis; **p. 137 (left):** © M. Regine/The Image Bank/Getty Images; **p. 137 (right):** © Randy Faris/CORBIS; **p. 138:** © M.L. Harris/Ionica/Getty; **p. 139 (left):** © Tim Pannell/Corbis RF; **p. 139 (right):** © Charles Gupton/Getty; **p. 145:** © Anthony Redpath/Corbis; **p.146:** © Bettmann/CORBIS; **p. 150:** © John Henley/Corbis; **p. 151:** © Mike Watson Images/Corbis RF; **p. 152:** © USA Today Library, photo by Robert Deutsch; **p. 153:** © ThinkStock/SuperStock; **p. 154:** © Charles Gupton/ Corbis; **p. 156:** © C. Devan/zefa/Corbis; **p. 161:** © M.M.Productions/Corbis RF

### Chapter 5

**Opener:** © Jack Hollingsworth/CORBIS; **p. 173 (left):** © Charles Gullung/zefa/Corbis; **p. 173 (right):** © Dylan Ellis/Corbis RF; **p. 174:** © LWA-Dann Tardif/CORBIS; **p. 175:** © David Young-Wolff/Photo Edit; **p. 181:** © Ariel Skelley/ Blend Images/CORBIS RF; **p. 183:** © Reuters NewMedia Inc./CORBIS; **p. 186:** Courtesy Cynthia de las Fuentes, Our Lady of the Lakes University, San Antonio, Texas; **p. 187:** © Image100/Corbis RF; **p. 188:** © Tony Freeman/Photo Edit; **p. 189:** © Keith Carter Photography

### Chapter 6

**Opener:** © Gabriela Medina/SuperStock; **p. 200:** © Joel Gordon 1995; **p. 204:** © Lawrence Migdale/Stock Boston; **p. 209:** © Marilyn Humphries; **p. 212:** © Bernard Gotfryd/Woodfin Camp & Associates; **p. 213:** © Michael Ray; **p. 215:** © Suzanne DeChillo/The New York Times/Redux Pictures; **p. 217:** © Dana Fineman; **p. 218:** © Karen Kasmauski/Corbis; **p. 219:** Courtesy of Lynn Blankinship; **p. 220:** © 1998 Frank Fournier; **p. 222 (left):** © Wendy Stone/Corbis; **p. 222 (right):** © Louise Gubb/Corbis SABA; **p. 227:** © Creasource/Corbis; **p. 230:** © James D. Wilson/Woodfin Camp & Associates; **p. 232:** © Li Ge/China Feature/ Corbis Sygma

### Chapter 7

**Opener:** © David Young-Wolff/Photo Edit; **p. 240:** © Matthew J. Lee, The Boston Globe; **p. 245 (top):** © Photodisc/Getty RF; **p. 245 (bottom):** © Reuters/New Media, Inc./CORBIS; **p. 247:** © Raghu-Rai/Magnum Photos; **p. 248:** © Tim Pannell/Corbis; **p. 250:** © Tom Prettyman/Photo Edit; **p. 252:** © ThinkStock/CORBIS RF; **p. 254 (top):** © Bettmann/Corbis; **p. 254 (bottom):** © Alain Nogues/Corbis Sygma; **p. 256:** © Comstock Select/CORBIS RF; **p. 258:** © Tony Freeman/Photo Edit; **p. 259:** © Ronald Cortes; **7.6:** © Penney Tweedie/Stone/Getty Images; **p. 262:** Courtesy of Connie Flanagan; **p. 263 (top):** © SuperStock; **p. 263 (bottom):** © Bob Daemmrich/The Image Works; **p. 266:** ©Paul Chesley/Stone/Getty Images; **p. 267:** © SuperStock

### Chapter 8

**Opener:** © Paul Barton/CORBIS; **p. 276:** © Michael Newman/Photo Edit; **p. 277 (left & right):** © David Young-Wolff/Photo Edit; **p. 279:** © Jack Hollingsworth/CORBIS RF; **p. 282:** © Pat Vasquez-Cunningham 1999; **8.2:** © Peter Correz/Stone/Getty Images; **p. 284:** © Pure Stock/Getty RF; **p. 286:** © Andersen Ross/Blend Images/CORBIS RF; **p. 287:** © Jeffry W. Myers/ Stock Boston; **p. 289:** © Tom Stewart/CORBIS; **p. 290:** © Bill Aron/Photo Edit; **8.3:** © Spencer Grant/Photo Edit; **p. 293:** © CORBIS RF; **p. 295:** © David Young-Wolff/Photo Edit; **p. 297:** © James G. White Photography; **p. 303:** © Michael Newman/Photo Edit; **p. 305:** © Getty Images RF; **p. 307:** © Kathy Heister/Index Stock; **p. 309 (left):** © Bob Daemmrich/The Image Works; **p. 309 (right):** © Erika Stone/Peter Arnold, Inc.; **p. 311:** © Tim Farrell/Star Ledger/Corbis

### Chapter 9

**Opener:** © George Disario/The Stock Market/ CORBIS/; **p. 320 (left):** © Tom Grill/CORBIS RF; **p. 320 (right):** © Creasource/Corbis; **p. 321 (top):** © Mary Kate Denny/Photo Edit; **p. 321 (bottom):** © Michael Newman/Photo Edit; **p. 322:** © Michael Siluk/The Image Works; **p. 324:** © Images100/CORBIS RF; **9.2:** © Tony Freeman/Photo Edit; **9.3:** © CORBIS RF; **p. 331:** © CORBIS RF; **p. 335:** Courtesy of Boys and Girls Clubs of America; **p. 337 (top):** © Kevin Dodge/Corbis; **p. 337 (bottom):** © Michael A. Keller/zefa/Corbis; **p. 339 (left):** © Photo by Bob Barrett/FPG/Hulton Archive/Getty Images;

**p. 339 (right):** © PhotoDisc/Getty RF; **p. 340:** © Tessa Codrington/Stone/Getty Images; **p. 342:** © David De Lossy/The Image Bank/Getty Images; **p. 345 (top):** © Mike Watson/CORBIS RF; **p. 345 (bottom):** © Tom & Dee Ann McCarthy/CORBIS; **p. 347:** © Reed Kaestner/CORBIS RF; **p. 348 (top):** © Explorer/J.P. Nacivet/Photo Researchers; **p. 348 (bottom):** © David Hanover/Stone/Getty Images; **p. 350:** © Jack Hollingsworth/CORBIS RF

### Chapter 10

**Opener:** © CORBIS RF; **p. 358 (tl):** © Andrew Itkoff; **p. 358 (bl):** © Dale Sparks; **p. 358 (tr):** © Patty Wood; **p. 358 (br):** © Michael A. Schwarz Photography, Inc.; **p. 361:** © Jose Luis Pelaez/Corbis; **p. 363:** © Big Cheese Photo/SuperStock RF; **p. 365:** © Paul S. Howell; **p. 366 (top):** © Ed Kashi/Corbis; **p. 366 (bottom):** Courtesy of I Have a Dream—Houston, Houston, TX; **p. 367 (top):** © Patsy Davidson/The Image Works; **p. 367 (bottom):** © PhotoDisc/Getty Images RF; **p. 368:** © Wally McNamee/Corbis; **p. 370:** © Gill Ross/CORBIS; **p. 372:** © Vol. 71 Photodisc/Getty RF; **p. 374:** © Photodisc/Getty RF; **p. 375 (left):** © ThinkStock/Superstock RF; **p. 375 (right):** © Comstock select/CORBIS RF; **p. 376:** © Joan Marcus; **p. 377:** © ImageSource/CORBIS RF; **p. 379:** © John S. Abbott; **p. 380:** © Fujifots/The Image Works; **p. 382:** © AP/Wide World Photos; **p. 384:** © David Young-Wolff/Photo Edit; **p. 385:** The Dallas Morning News/Milton Hinnant; **p. 386:** Courtesy of Sterling C. Jones, Jr.; **p. 387:** © Koichi Kamoshida/Newsmakers/Getty Images

### Chapter 11

**Opener:** © Gabe Palmer/Corbis; **p. 399:** © AP/Wide World Photos; **p. 400:** © Michael Tweed/AP/Wide World Photos; **p. 403:** © Irwin Thompson/The Dallas Morning News; **p. 406:** Courtesy Sandra Graham; **p. 407:** © Robert A. Isaacs/Photo Researchers; **p. 409:** © Dennis MacDonald/Photo Edit; **p. 412:** © Jose Luis Perez/Corbis; **p. 417:** Courtesy of Grace Leaf; **p. 419:** © Bill Stanton; **p. 420:** Courtesy of Armando Ronquillo

### Chapter 12

**Opener:** © Mug Shots/The Stock Market/CORBIS/; **p. 430:** © Jay Dickman; **p. 434:** © Alison Wright/Corbis; **p. 435 (left):** © Daniel Lanie; **p. 435 (right):** © Bill Gillette/Stock Boston; **p. 440 (top):** Courtesy Eisenhower Foundation, Washington, D.C.; **p. 440 (bottom):** Courtesy of El Puente; **p. 443:** Courtesy of Carola Suárez-Orozco and photographer Kris Snibble/Harvard News Office, © President and Fellows of Harvard College; **p. 444:** Courtesy of Margaret Beale Spencer; **p. 445:** © USA Today Library, photo by H. Darr Beiser; **p. 451:** © Bob Daemmrich/The Image Works; **p. 455:** © L. Clarke/Corbis

### Chapter 13

**Opener:** © David Young-Wolff/Stone/Getty Images; **p. 470:** © Stephanie Maze/Corbis; **p. 471:** © Gary Houlder/CORBIS; **p. 472:** Courtesy of Luis Vargas; **p. 478:** © Joe Raedle/Newsmakers/Getty Images; **p. 479:** © Daniel Allan/Taxi/Getty; **p. 483:** © Penny Tweedie/Stone/Getty; **p. 485:** © Josh Reynolds; **p. 488:** © Charles Gullung/zefa/Corbis; **p. 489:** © Chuck Savage/Corbis; **p. 492:** © Mark Richards/Photo Edit; **p. 493:** © Charlie Neuman/SDUT/Zuma; **p. 494:** Courtesy of Dr. Rodney Hammond, Director, Division of Violence Prevention, Centers for Disease Control and Prevention; **p. 495:** © Jim Smith/Photo Researchers; **p. 501:** © Karen Kasmausk/Corbis; **p. 502:** © Tony Freeman/Photo Edit

## Text and Line Art Credits

### Chapter 1

**Figure 1.1:** After data presented by the U.S. Census Bureau (2002). *National Population Projections I. Summary Files.* Washington, DC: U.S. Census Bureau. **Figure 1.2:** After data presented by the U.S. Census Bureau (2002). *National Population Projections I. Summary Files.* Washington DC: U.S. Census Bureau. **Figure 1.3:** John W. Santrock, *Life-Span Development*, 9th ed., Figure 1.5, **p. 19.** Copyright © 2004 by The McGraw-Hill Companies, Inc. Reprinted with permission. **Figure 1.4:** John W. Santrock, *Life-Span Development*, 9th ed., line art from Figure 1.6, **p. 21.** Copyright © 2004 by The McGraw-Hill Companies, Inc. Reprinted with permission. **Figure 1.5:** Schulenberg, J. E., & Zarrett, N. R. (2006). Mental health during emerging adulthood: Continuity and discontinuity in courses, causes, and consequences. In J. J. Arnett & J. L. Tanner (Eds.), *Emerging adults in America: Coming of age in the 21st century.* Washington, DC: American Psychological Association, Figure 6.1, **p. 136.** Copyright © 2006 by the American Psychological Association. Adapted with permission. The use of APA information does not imply endorsement by the APA. Source of data: Monitoring the Future study, Institute for Social Research, University of Michigan. **Figure 1.6:** Schulenberg, J. E., & Zarrett, N. R. (2006). Mental health during emerging adulthood: Continuity and discontinuity in courses, causes, and consequences. In J. J. Arnett & J. L. Tanner (Eds.), *Emerging adults in America: Coming of age in the 21st century.* Washington, DC: American Psychological Association, Figure 6.4, **p. 139.** Copyright © 2006 by the American Psychological Association. Adapted with permission. The use of APA information does not imply endorsement by the APA. Source of data: Monitoring the Future study, Institute for Social Research, University of Michigan. **Figure 1.7:** Arnett, J. (2002). Emerging adulthood: A theory of development from the late teens through the twenties. *American Psychologist* 55(5), 469–480 (Figure 2). Copyright © 2000 by the American Psychological Association. Reproduced with permission. The use of APA information does not imply endorsement by the APA. **Figure 1.9:** John W. Santrock, *Life-Span Development*, 9th ed., Figure 2.1, **p. 45.** Copyright © 2004 by The McGraw-Hill Companies, Inc. Reprinted with permission. **Figure 1.11:** John W. Santrock, *Psychology*, 7th ed., Figure 4.7. Copyright © 2003 by The McGraw-Hill Companies, Inc. Reprinted with permission. **Figure 1.12:** John W. Santrock, *Psychology*, 7th ed., Figure 12.6. Copyright © 2003 by The McGraw-Hill Companies, Inc. Reprinted with permission. **Figure 1.13:** Claire B. Kopp and Joanne B. Krakow, eds., *The Child: Development in a Social Context*, p. 648. Copyright © 1982 by Addison-Wesley Publishing Company, Inc. Reprinted by permission of Pearson Education, Inc., Glenview, IL. **Figure 1.16:** John W. Santrock, *Psychology*, 7th ed., Figure 2.4. Copyright © 2003 by The McGraw-Hill Companies, Inc. Reprinted with permission. **Figure 1.17:** John W. Santrock, *Psychology*, 7th ed., Figure 2.5. Copyright © 2003 by The McGraw-Hill Companies, Inc. Reprinted with permission.

### Chapter 2

**Figure 2.2:** John W. Santrock, *Children*, Figure 15.2, p. 445. Copyright © by The McGraw-Hill Companies, Inc. Reprinted with permission. **Figure 2.4:** J. M. Tanner, R. H. Whitehouse, and M. Takaishi, "Standards from Birth to Maturity for Height, Weight, Height Velocity, and Weight Velocity: British Children 1965," *Archives of Diseases in Childhood*, 1966, f. 41, pp. 613–633. Copyright © 1966. Reprinted with permission from the BMJ Publishing Group. **Figure 2.6:** John W. Santrock, *Children*, Figure 15.5, **p. 447.** Copyright © by The McGraw-Hill Companies, Inc. Reprinted with permission. **Figure 2.7:** From A. F. Roche, "Secular Trends in Stature, Weight and Maturation," *Monographs of the Society for Research in Child Development*, n. 179. © Society for Research in Child Development. Reprinted with permission of the Society for Research in Child Development. **Figure 2.8:** R. G. Simmons, D. A. Blyth, and K. L. McKinney, "The Social and Psychological Effects of Puberty on White Females." In J. Brooks-Gunn and A. C. Petersen, eds., *Girls at Puberty: Biological, Psychological, and Social Perspectives*, Figure 3 (p. 249). © 1983 Plenum Press, New York. With kind permission from Springer Science and Business Media. **Figure 2.9:** Adapted from Figure 1 from Park, M. J. et al. (2006). The health status of young adults in the United States. *Journal of Adolescent Health*, 39(3): 305–317. Copyright © 2006 Society for Adolescent Medicine. Reprinted by permission of Elsevier Ltd. **Figure 2.10:** After data presented by *MMWR: Morbidity and Mortality Weekly Report*, Vol. 55, No. SS-5 (June 9, 2006). U.S. Department of Health and Human Services. **Figure 2.11:** After Table 52 from *MMWR: Morbidity and Mortality Weekly Report*, Vol. 55, No. SS-5 (June 9, 2006). U.S. Department of Health and Human Services. **Figure 2.12:** From John T. Bonner, *The Evolution of Culture in Animals.* © 1980 Princeton University Press. Reprinted by permission of Princeton University Press. **Figure 2.13:** John W. Santrock, *A Topical Approach to Life-Span Development*, 3rd ed., Figure 2.3. Copyright © 2007 by The McGraw-Hill Companies, Inc. Reprinted with permission. **Figure 2.14:** John W. Santrock,

*Children*, 7th ed., Figure 3.14. Copyright © 2003 by The McGraw-Hill Companies, Inc. Reprinted with permission.

## Chapter 3

**Figure 3.1:** John W. Santrock, *Child Development*, 10th ed., Figure 5.1, **p. 131.** Copyright © 2004 by The McGraw-Hill Companies, Inc. Reprinted with permission. **Figure 3.3:** P. R. Huttenlocher and A. S. Dabholkar, "Regional Differences in the Synaptogenesis in the Human Cerebral Cortex," *Journal of Comparative Neurology*, Vol. 387, No. 2 (1997), Figure 2, p. 170. © 1997 Wiley-Liss, Inc. Reprinted with permission of Wiley-Liss, Inc., a subsidiary of John Wiley & Sons, Inc. **Figure 3.7:** John W. Santrock, *Life-Span Development*, 9th ed., text from figure 8.11, p. 248. Copyright © 2004 by The McGraw-Hill Companies, Inc. Reprinted with permission. **Figure 3.8:** After data from Dempster, F. N. (1981). Memory span: Sources of individual and developmental differences. *Psychological Bulletin*, 89: 63–100. **Figure 3.9:** John W. Santrock, *Psychology*, 7th ed., Figure 8.8, p. 314. Copyright © 2003 by The McGraw-Hill Companies, Inc. Reprinted with permission. **Figure 3.10:** John W. Santrock, *Educational Psychology*, 3rd ed., Figure 8.6, p. 275. Copyright © 2008 by The McGraw-Hill Companies, Inc. Reprinted with permission. **Figure 3.11:** John W. Santrock, *Child Development*, 10th ed., Figure 10.8, p. 254. Copyright © 2004 by The McGraw-Hill Companies, Inc. Reprinted with permission. **Figure 3.12:** John W. Santrock, *Child Development*, 10th ed., Figure 8.10, p. 254. Copyright © 2004 by The McGraw-Hill Companies, Inc. Reprinted with permission. **Figure 3.13:** John W. Santrock, *Educational Psychology*, 3rd ed., Figure 11.4, p. 377. Copyright © 2008 by The McGraw-Hill Companies, Inc. Reprinted with permission. **Figure 3.14:** John W. Santrock, *Children*, 5th ed., Figure 10.1. Copyright © 1997 by The McGraw-Hill Companies, Inc. Reprinted with permission. **Figure 3.16:** John W. Santrock, *Psychology*, 7th ed., Figure 10.5, **p. 405.** Copyright © 2003 by The McGraw-Hill Companies, Inc. Reprinted with permission. **Figure 3.17:** From "The Increase in IQ Scores from 1932–1997" by Dr. Ulric Neisser. Reprinted with permission.

## Chapter 4

PP. 134 From "Self and Identity Development" by Susan Harter. In S. S. Feldman and G. R. Elliott (eds.), *At the Threshold: The Developing Adolescent*. Cambridge, MA: Harvard University Press, 1990, pp. 352–353. Used with permission of Dr. Susan Harter. **Figure 4.2:** Robins, R. W., Trzesniewski, K. H., Tracy, J. L, Gosling, S. D., & Potter, J. (2002). Global self-esteem across the life span. *Psychology and Aging* 17(3), 423–434 (Figure 1). Copyright © 2002 by the American Psychological Association. Adapted with permission. The use of APA information does not imply endorsement by the APA. **Figure 4.3:** S. Harter (1999). *The Construction of Self*, Table 6.1. New York: The Guilford Press. Reprinted with permission. **Figure 4.4:** John W. Santrock, *Educational Psychology*, 2nd ed., Figure 3.7. Copyright © 2004 by The McGraw-Hill Companies, Inc. Reprinted with permission. **Figure 4.5:** John W. Santrock, *Psychology*, 7th ed., Figure 12.11, p. 499. Copyright © 2003 by The McGraw-Hill Companies, Inc. Reprinted with permission.

## Chapter 5

**P. 170** From Zager, K., & Rubenstein, A. (2002). *The Inside Story on Teen Girls*. Washington, DC: American Psychological Association, pp. 21–22. Copyright © 2002 by the American Psychological Association. Reproduced with permission. **Figure 5.2:** John W. Santrock, *A Topical Approach to Life-Span Development*, 3rd ed., Figure 12.4. Copyright © 2007 by The McGraw-Hill Companies, Inc. Reprinted with permission. **Figure 5.4:** John W. Santrock, *A Topical Approach to Life-Span Development*, 3rd ed., Figure 12.5. Copyright © 2007 by The McGraw-Hill Companies, Inc. Reprinted with permission. **Figure 5.5:** From Pryor, J. H., Hurtado, S., Saenz, V. B., Lindholm, J. A., Korn, W. S., & Mahoney, K. M. (2005). *The American freshman: National norms for fall 2005*. Los Angeles: Higher Education Research Institute, UCLA. Used with permission.

## Chapter 6

**Figure 6.3:** After data presented by the National Center for Health Statistics (2002). *Sexual behavior and selected health measures: Men and women 15–44 years of age, United States 2002*. PH2003-1250. Atlanta: Centers for Disease Control and Prevention. **P. 206** From pp. 444 and 447 from Gilmartin, S. K. (2006). Changes in college women's attitudes toward sexual intimacy. *Journal of Research on Adolescence*, 16(3): 429–454. **Figure 6.4:** Darroch, J. E. et al., Teenage sexual and reproductive behavior in developed countries: Can more progress be made? *Occasional Report*, New York: The Alan Guttmacher Institute, 2001, No. 3, p. 14. Reprinted by permission of Guttmacher Institute. **P. 215** Boonstra, H., Teen pregnancy: Trends and lessons learned, *The Guttmacher Report on Public Policy*, 2002, 5(1), 9–10. Reprinted by permission of Guttmacher Institute. **Figure 6.5:** National Center for Health Statistics. Births to Teenagers in the United States, 1940–2000. *National Vital Statistics Report*, Vol. 49, No. 10. **Figure 6.7:** B. S. Fisher, F. T. Cullen, and M. G. Turner. (2000). *The Sexual Victimization of College Women*. Washington, DC: National Institute of Justice, Exhibit 8, p. 19.

## Chapter 7

**Figure 7.1:** From Selman, R. S. (1976). Social-cognitive understanding. In Thomas Lickona (Ed.) *Moral Development and Behavior*. Reprinted with permission of Thomas Lickona. **Figure 7.2:** From Kohlberg, L. (1969). Stage and sequence: The cognitive-developmental approach to socialization. In D. A. Goslin (Ed.), *Handbook of Socialization Theory and Research*. Chicago: Rand McNally. Reprinted with permission of David Goslin. **Figure 7.3:** From Colby, A. et al. (1983). *A Longitudinal Study of Moral Judgment*. Monographs for the Society for Research in Child Development, Serial #201. © Society for Research in Child Development. Reprinted with permission of the Society for Research in Child Development. **Figure 7.4:** Yussen, S. R. (1977). Characteristics of moral dilemmas written by adolescents. *Developmental Psychology* 13(2), 162–163 (Table 1). Copyright © 1977 by the American Psychological Association. Adapted with permission. The use of APA information does not imply endorsement by the APA. **Figure 7.5:** Narvaez, D. (2006). Integrative ethical education. In M. Killen & J. Smetana (Eds.), *Handbook of Moral Development*, Table 26.1, p. 717. Copyright 2006 by Lawrence Erlbaum Associates Inc. – Books [T]. Reproduced with permission of Lawrence Erlbaum Associates Inc. – Books [T] in the format Textbook via Copyright Clearance Center. **Figure 7.6 (art):** From Pryor, J. H., Hurtado, S., Saenz, V. B., Lindholm, J. A., Korn, W. S., & Mahoney, K. M. (2005). *The American freshman: National norms for fall 2005*. Los Angeles: Higher Education Research Institute, UCLA.

## Chapter 8

**Figure 8.1:** Belsky, J. (1981). Early human experience: A family perspective. *Developmental Psychology* 17(1), 3–23 (Figure 1). Copyright © 1981 by the American Psychological Association. Reproduced with permission. The use of APA information does not imply endorsement by the APA. **Figure 8.4:** John W. Santrock, *Children*, Figure 11.5, p. 306. Copyright © by The McGraw-Hill Companies, Inc. Reprinted with permission. **Figure 8.5:** John W. Santrock, *Child Development*, 10th ed., Figure 15.6, p. 495. Copyright © 2004 by The McGraw-Hill Companies, Inc. Reprinted with permission. PP. 306–307 from Brodzinsky, D. M., & Pinderhughes, E. (2002). Parenting and child development in adoptive families. In M. H. Bornstein (ed.), *Handbook of Parenting*, 2nd ed., Vol. 1: Children and Parenting, p. 281. Copyright 2002 by Lawrence Erlbaum Associates Inc. – Books [T]. Reproduced with permission of Lawrence Erlbaum Associates Inc. – Books [T] in the format Textbook via Copyright Clearance Center. **Figure 8.6:** John W. Santrock, *Life-Span Development*, 10th ed., Figure 15.10, p. 492. Copyright © 2006 by The McGraw-Hill Companies, Inc. Reprinted with permission.

## Chapter 9

**Figure 9.4:** John W. Santrock, *Child Development*, 11th ed., Figure 16.4, p. 513. Copyright © 2007 by The McGraw-Hill Companies, Inc. Reprinted with permission. **P. 330** Garrod, A., Smulyan, L., Powers, S. L., & Kilkenny, R. (1992). *Adolescent Portraits*. Boston: Allyn & Bacon, pp. 199–200. Figure 9.5: From Dunphy, D. C. (1963). The social structure of urban adolescent peer groups. *Sociometry*, 26. **Figure 9.6:** From "Romantic Development: Does Age at Which Romantic Involvement Starts Matter?" by Duane Buhrmester, April 2001. Paper presented at the meeting of the Society for Research in Child Development, Minneapolis, MN. Reprinted with permission of the author. **Figure 9.7:** John W. Santrock, *Life-Span Development*, 11th ed.,

Figure 15.4, p. 508. Copyright © 2008 by The McGraw-Hill Companies, Inc. Reprinted with permission.

### Chapter 10

**Figure 10.2:** John W. Santrock, *Life-Span Development*, 11th ed., Figure 12.10, p. 413. Copyright © 2008 by The McGraw-Hill Companies, Inc. Reprinted with permission. **Figure 10.3:** From Nansel T. R. et al. (2001, April 25). Bullying behaviors among U.S. youth. *Journal of the American Medical Association* 285(16): 2094–2100. **Figure 10.4:** John W. Santrock, *Life-Span Development*, 11th ed., Figure 10.3, p. 320. Copyright © 2008 by The McGraw-Hill Companies, Inc. Reprinted with permission.

### Chapter 11

**Figure 11.3:** From S. Covey, 1989. *The 7 Habits of Highly Effective People*. Simon & Schuster. Source: Franklin Covey Co. Reprinted with permission. **Figure 11.4:** Janet A. Simons, Seth Kalichman, and John W. Santrock, *Human Adjustment*, 1st ed., Figure 10.2, p. 296. Copyright © 1994 by The McGraw-Hill Companies, Inc. Reprinted with permission. **Figure 11.5:** Gonzales, P. et al. (2004). *Highlights from The Trends in International Mathematics and Science Study (TIMMS) 2003*. NCES 2005-005. Washington, DC: National Center for Education Statistics, U.S. Department of Education, adapted from Table 13, p. 19. **Figure 11.8:** Reproduced by special permission of the publisher, Psychological Assessment Resources, Inc., 16204 North Florida Avenue, Lutz, FL 33549 from *Making Vocational Choices*, third edition. Copyright 1973, 1985, 1992, 1997 by PAR, Inc. All rights reserved.

### Chapter 12

**Figure 12.1:** Larson, R. W., & Verma, S. (1999). How children and adolescents spend time across the world: Work, play, and developmental opportunities. *Psychological Bulletin* 125(6), 701–736 (Table 6). Copyright © 1999 by the American Psychological Association. Reproduced with permission. The use of APA information does not imply endorsement by the APA. **Figure 12.3:** After Table 1 from Sellers, R. M. et al. (2006). Racial identity matters: The relationship between racial discrimination and psychological functioning in African American adolescents. *Journal of Research on Adolescence* 16(2): 187–216. Reprinted by permission of Blackwell Publishing Ltd. **Figure 12.4:** Compiled from data in Rideout, V., Roberts, D. F., & Foehr, U. G. (2005). *Generation M: Media in the Lives of 8-18 Year-olds—Report.* Executive Summary (#7250), pp. 7, 8. The Henry J. Kaiser Family Foundation, March 2005. This information was reprinted with permission from the Henry J. Kaiser Family Foundation. The Kaiser Family Foundation, based in Menlo Park, California, is a nonprofit, private operating foundation focusing on the major health care issues facing the nation and is not associated with Kaiser Permanente or Kaiser Industries. **Figure 12.5:** From Rideout, V., Roberts, D. F., & Foehr, U. G. (2005). *Generation M: Media in the Lives of 8-18 Year-olds—Report.* Executive Summary (#7250), p. 16. The Henry J. Kaiser Family Foundation, March 2005. This information was reprinted with permission from the Henry J. Kaiser Family Foundation. The Kaiser Family Foundation, based in Menlo Park, California, is a nonprofit, private operating foundation focusing on the major health care issues facing the nation and is not associated with Kaiser Permanente or Kaiser Industries. **Figure 12.6:** John W. Santrock, *Child Development*, 10th ed., Figure 18.7, p. 598. Copyright © 2004 by The McGraw-Hill Companies, Inc. Reprinted with permission.

### Chapter 13

**P. 463** Excerpt from "Desert Places" from *The Poetry of Robert Frost* edited by Edward Connery Lathem. Copyright © 1947, 1969 by Henry Holt and Company. Copyright © 1975 by Leslie Frost Ballantine. Reprinted by permission of Henry Holt and Company, LLC. **Figure 13.1:** From Achenbach, T. M., & Edelbrock, C. S. (1981). *Behavioral Problems and Competencies Reported by Parents of Normal and Disturbed Children Aged Four through Sixteen*. Monographs of the Society for Research in Child Development, 46 (1, Serial No. 188). © Society for Research in Child Development. Reprinted with permission of the Society for Research in Child Development. **P. 469** From Zager, K., & Rubenstein, A. (2002). *The Inside Story on Teen Girls*. Washington, DC: American Psychological Association, **p. 141.** Copyright © 2002 by the American Psychological Association. Reproduced with permission. **Figure 13.2:** Masten, A. S., & Coatsworth, J. D. (1998). The development of competence in favorable and unfavorable environments: Lessons from research on successful children. *American Psychologist* 53(2), 205–220 (Table 2). Copyright © 1998 by the American Psychological Association. Reproduced with permission. The use of APA information does not imply endorsement by the APA. **Figure 13.3:** From Johnston, L. D., O'Malley, P. M., Bachman, J. G., & Schulenberg, J. E. (2007). *Monitoring the Future national results on adolescent drug use: Overview of key findings, 2006.* (NIH Publication No. 07-6202). Bethesda, MD: National Institute on Drug Abuse. **Figure 13.4:** Adapted from Figure 50b from Hibell, B., Andersson, B., Bjarnason, T., et al. (2004). *The ESPAD Report 2003: Alcohol and Other Drug Use among Students in 35 European Countries*. Stockholm, Sweden: The Swedish Council for Information on Alcohol and Other Drugs, p. 164. Used with permission. **Figure 13.5:** Adapted from Figure 33b from Hibell, B., Andersson, B., Bjarnason, T., et al. (2004). *The ESPAD Report 2003: Alcohol and Other Drug Use among Students in 35 European Countries.* Stockholm, Sweden: The Swedish Council for Information on Alcohol and Other Drugs, p. 136. Used with permission. **Figure 13.6:** From Johnston, L. D., O'Malley, P. M., Bachman, J. G., & Schulenberg, J. E. (2007). *Monitoring the Future national results on adolescent drug use: Overview of key findings, 2006.* (NIH Publication No. 07-6202). Bethesda, MD: National Institute on Drug Abuse. **Figure 13.7:** From Johnston, L. D., O'Malley, P. M., Bachman, J. G., & Schulenberg, J. E. (2007). *Monitoring the Future national results on adolescent drug use: Overview of key findings, 2006.* (NIH Publication No. 07-6202). Bethesda, MD: National Institute on Drug Abuse. **Figure 13.11:** Centers for Disease Control and Prevention. (2006, June 8). *National Youth Risk Behavior Survey 1991–2005: Trends in the Prevalence of Suicide Ideation and Attempts*. Atlanta: GA: Centers for Disease Control and Prevention. **Figure 13.13:** From H. Selye, *The Stress of Life*. Copyright © 1976 by The McGraw-Hill Companies, Inc. Reprinted with permission.

# NAME INDEX

## A



## B

# C

# D

# E



# F

# G

## H

## I



## J



## K

## L



## M

# N

# S

# Y



# Z

# SUBJECT INDEX

## A



## B

## G



## H



## I

# R



# S

## T



## U



## V



## W



## Y



## Z